Mirrors & Windows

Connecting with Literature

"The whole purpose of education
is to turn mirrors into windows."

— Sydney J. Harris

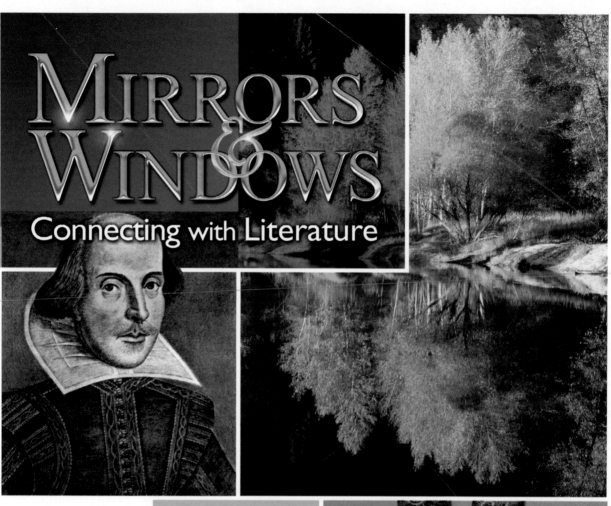

MIRRORS & WINDOWS
Connecting with Literature

British Tradition

EMC
Publishing

ST. PAUL • LOS ANGELES • INDIANAPOLIS

Staff Credits

Senior Editor: Brenda Owens
Editor: Susan Freese
Associate Editors: Stephanie Djock, Keri Henkel Stifter
Assistant Editors: Carley Bomstad, Brendan Curran, Julie Nelson
Editorial Assistants: Lindsay Ryan, Erin Saladin
Teacher's Edition Editors: Sheila Anderson, Stephanie Djock, Cheryl Drivdahl, Nancy Papsin
Permissions Coordinator: Valerie Murphy
Proofreader: Carol Rogers
Photo Researchers: Brendan Curran, Julie Nelson
Marketing Managers: Bruce Ayscue, Laurie Skiba
Production Editor: Bob Dreas
Cover Designer: Leslie Anderson
Page Layout Designers: Matthias Frasch, Jack Ross
Production Specialist: Petrina Nyhan
Production Services: Shepherd, Inc.

Literary Acknowledgments: Literary Acknowledgments appear following the Glossary of Vocabulary Words. We have made every effort to trace the ownership of all copyrighted material and to secure permission from copyright holders. In the event of any question arising as to the use of any material, we will be pleased to make the necessary corrections in future printings. Thanks are due to the authors, publishers, and agents for permission to use the materials indicated.

Art and Photo Credits: Art and Photo Credits appear following the Literary Acknowledgments.

ISBN 978-0-82193-217-9 (Student Edition Text)
ISBN 978-0-82193-219-3 (Annotated Teacher's Edition Text)

© 2009, 2011 by EMC Publishing, LLC
875 Montreal Way
St. Paul, MN 55102
E-mail: educate@emcp.com
Web site: www.emcp.com

Printed in the United States of America

17 16 15 14 13 12 11 10   3 4 5 6 7 8 9 10

17 16 15 14 13 12 11 10   2 3 4 5 6 7 8 9 10 (ATE)

Consultants, Reviewers, and Focus Group Participants

Jean Martorana
Reading Specialist/English Teacher
Desert Vista High School
Phoenix, Arizona

Tracy Pulido
Language Arts Instructor
West Valley High School
Fairbanks, Alaska

Cindy Johnston
English Teacher
Argus High School
Ceres, California

Susan Stoehr
Language Arts Instructor
Aragon High School
San Mateo, California

John Owens
Reading Specialist
St. Vrain Valley Schools
Longmont, Colorado

Fred Smith
Language Arts Instructor
St. Bernard High School
Uncasville, Connecticut

Penny Austin-Richardson
English Department Chair
Seaford Senior High School
Seaford, Delaware

Cecilia Lewis
Language Arts Instructor
Mariner High School
Cape Coral, Florida

Jane Feber
Teacher
Mandarin Middle School
Jacksonville, Florida

Dorothy Fletcher
Language Arts Instructor
Wolfson Senior High School
Jacksonville, Florida

Tamara Doehring
English/Reading Teacher
Melbourne High School
Melbourne, Florida

Patti Magee
English Instructor
Timber Creek High School
Orlando, Florida

Margaret J. Graham
Language Arts/Reading Teacher
Elizabeth Cobb Middle School
Tallahassee, Florida

Elizabeth Steinman
English Instructor
Vero Beach High School
Vero Beach, Florida

Wanda Bagwell
Language Arts Department Chair
Commerce High School
Commerce, Georgia

Betty Deriso
Language Department Chairperson
Crisp County High School
Cordele, Georgia

Dr. Peggy Leland
English Instructor
Chestatee High School
Gainsville, Georgia

Matthew Boedy
Language Arts Instructor
Harlem High School
Harlem, Georgia

Patty Bradshaw
English Department Chair
Harlem High School
Harlem, Georgia

Dawn Faulkner
English Department Chair
Rome High School
Rome, Georgia

Carolyn C. Coleman
AKS Continuous Improvement
   Director
Gwinnett County Public Schools
Suwanee, Georgia

Elisabeth Blumer Thompson
Language Arts Instructor
Swainsboro High School
Swainsboro, Georgia

Toi Walker
English Instructor
Northeast Tifton County High
   School
Tifton, Georgia

Jeanette Rogers
English Instructor
Potlatch Jr.-Sr. High School
Potlatch, Idaho

Gail Taylor
Language Arts Instructor
Rigby High School
Rigby, Idaho

Carey Robin
Language Arts Instructor
St. Francis College Prep
Brookfield, Illinois

Patricia Meyer
English Department Chair
Glenbard East High School
Lombard, Illinois

Liz Rebmann
Language Arts Instructor
Morton High School
Morton, Illinois

Helen Gallagher
English Department Chair
Main East High School
Park Ridge, Illinois

Rosemary Ryan
Dean of Students
Schaumburg High School
Schaumburg, Illinois

Donna Cracraft
English Department Co-Chair/IB
   Coordinator
Pike High School
Indianapolis, Indiana

Consultants, Reviewers, and Focus Group Participants (cont.)

K. C. Salter
Language Arts Instructor
Knightstown High School
Knightstown, Indiana

Lisa Broxterman
Language Arts Instructor
Axtell High School
Axtell, Kansas

Shirley Wells
Language Arts Instructor
Derby High School
Derby, Kansas

Karen Ann Stous
Speech & Drama Teacher
Holton High School
Holton, Kansas

Martha-Jean Rockey
Language Arts Instructor
Troy High School
Troy, Kansas

Shelia Penick
Language Arts Instructor
Yates Center High School
Yates Center, Kansas

John Ermilio
English Teacher
St. Johns High School
Shrewsbury, Massachusetts

James York
English Teacher
Waverly High School
Lansing, Michigan

Mary Spychalla
Gifted Education Coordinator
Valley Middle School
Apple Valley, Minnesota

Shari K. Carlson
Advanced ILA Teacher
Coon Rapids Middle School
Coon Rapids, Minnesota

Rebecca Benz
English Instructor
St. Thomas Academy
Mendota Heights, Minnesota

Michael F. Graves
Professor Emeritus
University of Minnesota
330A Peik Hall
Minneapolis, Minnesota

Kathleen Nelson
English Instructor
New Ulm High School
New Ulm, Minnesota

Adonna Gaspar
Language Arts Teacher
Cooper High School
Robbinsdale, Minnesota

Sara L. Nystuen
English Department Chair; AP
 Instructor
Concordia Academy
Roseville, Minnesota

Tom Backen
English Teacher
Benilde-St. Margaret's School
St. Louis Park, Minnesota

Daniel Sylvester
Jr. High English & American
 Experience Teacher
Benilde-St. Margaret's School
St. Louis Park, Minnesota

Jean Borax
Literacy Coach
Harding High School
St. Paul, Minnesota

Erik Brandt
English Teacher
Harding High School
St. Paul, Minnesota

Kevin Brennan
High School English Teacher
Cretin-Derham Hall
St. Paul, Minnesota

Anna Newcombe
English Instructor
Harding High School
St. Paul, Minnesota

Rosemary Ruffenach
Language Arts Teacher, Consultant,
 and Writer
St. Paul, Minnesota

Nancy Papsin
English Teacher/Educational
 Consultant
White Bear Lake, Minnesota

Shannon Umfleet
Communication Arts Instructor
Northwest High School
Cedar Hill, Missouri

Ken Girard
Language Arts Instructor
Bishop LeBlond High School
St. Joseph, Missouri

Jessica Gall
Language Arts Instructor
Fremont High School
Fremont, Nebraska

Michael Davis
Language Arts Instructor
Millard West High School
Omaha, Nebraska

Lisa Larnerd
English Teacher
Basic High School
Henderson, Nevada

Jo Paulson
Title I Reading Teacher
Camino Real Middle School
Las Cruces, New Mexico

Stacy Biss
Language Arts Instructor
Hackensack High School
Hackensack, New Jersey

J. M. Winchock
Reading Specialist, Adult Literacy
 Instructor
Hillsborough High School
Hillsborough, New Jersey

Consultants, Reviewers, and Focus Group Participants (cont.)

Matthew Cahn
Department of English & Related
 Arts Supervisor
River Dell High School
Oradell, New Jersey

Jean Mullooly
Language Arts Instructor
Holy Angels High School
Trenton, New Jersey

Fenice Boyd
Assistant Professor, Learning and
 Instruction
State University of New York at
 Buffalo
Buffalo, New York

Michael Fedorchuk
Assistant Principal
Auburn High School
Auburn, New York

Robert Balch
English Instructor
Beacon High School
Beacon, New York

Rene A. Roberge
Secondary English/AP English
 Instructor
Hudson Falls High School
Hudson Falls, New York

Melissa Hedt
Literacy Coach
Asheville Middle School
Asheville, North Carolina

Jane Shoaf
Educational Consultant
Durham, North Carolina

Kimberly Tufts
Department Chair for ELA
Cranberry Middle School
Elk Park, North Carolina

Cheryl Gackle
English Instructor
Kulm High School
Kulm, North Dakota

Barbara Stroh
English Department Chair
Aurora High School
Aurora, Ohio

Mary Jo Bish
Language Arts Instructor
Lake Middle School
Millbury, Ohio

Judy Ellsesser-Painter
Language Arts Instructor
South Webster High School
South Webster, Ohio

Adele Dahlin
English Department Chair
Central Catholic High School
Toledo, Ohio

Joshua Singer
English Instructor
Central Catholic High School
Toledo, Ohio

Debbie Orendorf
Language Arts Instructor
Berlin Brothers Valley High School
Berlin, Pennsylvania

Dona Italiano
English Teacher/Language Arts
 Coordinator
Souderton Area High School
Souderton, Pennsylvania

Tina Parlier
Secondary English Instructor
Elizabethton High School
Elizabethton, Tennessee

Wayne Luellen
English Instructor
Houston High School
Germantown, Tennessee

Ed Farrell
Senior Consultant
Emeritus Professor of English
 Education
University of Texas at Austin
Austin, Texas

Terry Ross
Secondary Language Arts
 Supervisor
Austin Independent School District
Austin, Texas

Angelia Greiner
English Department Chair
Big Sandy High School
Big Sandy, Texas

Sharon Kremer
Educational Consultant
Denton, Texas

E. J. Brletich
Supervisor of English/Language
 Arts
Spotsylvania City School
Fredericksburg, Virginia

Jeffrey Golub
Educational Consultant
Bothell, Washington

Clifford Aziz
Language Arts Instructor
Washington High School
Tacoma, Washington

Becky Palmer
Reading Teacher
Madison Middle School
Appleton, Wisconsin

Mary Hoppe
English Teacher
Bonduel High School
Bonduel, Wisconsin

Lou Wappel
English, Humanities & Guidance
 Instructor
St. Lawrence Seminary High School
Mount Calvary, Wisconsin

Gregory R. Keir
Language Arts Instructor
East Elementary School
New Richmond, Wisconsin

CONTENTS IN BRIEF

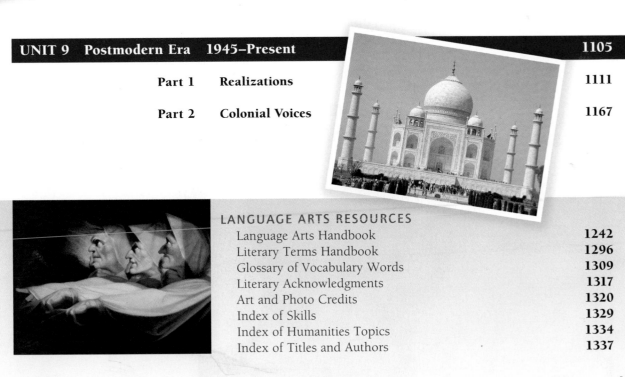

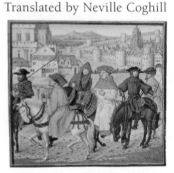

Part 2 Mind, Body, and Spirit   281

Author Focus   294

Independent Reading

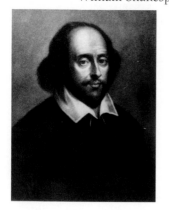

Language Arts Resources

LANGUAGE ARTS WORKSHOPS

Grammar & Style

Vocabulary & Spelling

Speaking & Listening

Writing

Test Practice

Reading Skills

Writing Skills

Revising and Editing Skills

"The whole purpose of education
is to turn mirrors into windows."

— Sydney J. Harris

Think about when you were young and about to start school for the first time. When you stood in front of the mirror, your view was focused on your own reflection and limited by your own experience. Then the windows of learning began to open your mind to new ideas and new experiences, broadening both your awareness and your curiosity.

As you discovered reading, you learned to connect with what you read and to examine your own ideas and experiences. And the more you read, the more you learned to connect with the ideas and experiences of other people from other times and other places. Great literature provides *mirrors* that help you reflect on your own world and *windows* that lead you into new worlds. This metaphor for the reading experience expresses the power of words to engage and transform you.

EMC's literature program, *Mirrors & Windows: Connecting with Literature,* provides opportunities for you to explore new worlds full of people, cultures, and perspectives different from your own. This book contains stories, essays, plays, and poems by outstanding authors from around the globe. Reading these selections will expand your appreciation of literature and your world view. Studying them will help you examine universal themes such as honesty, integrity, and justice and common emotions such as fear, pride, and belonging. You may already have thought about some of these ideas and feelings yourself.

As you read the selections in this book, try to see yourself in the characters, stories, and themes. Also try to see yourself as a citizen of the world—a world from which you have much to learn and to which you have much to offer.

Bayeux Tapestry [detail], c. 1077.
Bayeux Tapestry Museum, Bayeux, Normandy, France.

Anglo-Saxon Period

Unit 1

"You each have something divine
in your soul, namely Reason
and Memory and a discerning
will to make choices in life."

—ALFRED THE GREAT,
KING OF WEST SAXONS

449–1066

Anglo-Saxon Period 449–1066

3000 BCE   500 CE

BRITISH LITERATURE BRITISH LITERATURE BRITISH LITERATURE BRITISH LIT

c. 50 BCE
Julius Caesar writes *The Conquest of Gaul*, which provides modern historians with valuable information about ancient Briton tribes

c. 90 CE
Roman historian Tacitus transcribes the geography and ethnography of ancient Briton in *The Life and Character of Julius Agricola*

c. 303 CE
Lactantius writes *The Divine Institutions*

c. 400 CE
Orosius writes *The History of the World*

524 CE
Boethius writes *Consolation of Philosophy*

c. 540 CE
St. Gildas the Wise criticizes the British government in *Of the Ruin of Britain*

c. 590 CE
Gregory the Great writes *The Pastoral Care,* a manual of priestly duties

c. 660 CE
The poet Cædmon composes *Cædmon's Hymn*

BRITISH HISTORY BRITISH HISTORY BRITISH HISTORY BRITISH HISTORY BRIT

c. 3000 BCE
The first part of Stonehenge is built

c. 600 BCE
Britons arrive on the continent

55 BCE
Julius Caesar invades Britain

61 CE
Queen Boadicea leads the Britons in a revolt against Roman rule

410 CE
The last Roman legions leave Britain

450 CE
The Anglo-Saxons invade England

495 CE
The Britons defeat the Anglo-Saxons at the Battle of Mount Badon

597 CE
Pope Gregory the Great sends Augustine of Canterbury to convert King Ethelbert of Kent to Christianity

c. 600 CE
The Christianization of Anglo-Saxon England begins

616 CE
King Ethelbert dies

627 CE
King Edwin of Northumbria is baptized

655 CE
Penda of Mercia, the last pagan Anglo-Saxon king, dies at the Battle of Winwaed

698 CE
Anglo-Saxon missionaries establish Echternach, the first Christian monastery in mainland Europe

WORLD HISTORY WORLD HISTORY WORLD HISTORY WORLD HISTORY WORLD

c. 2205 BCE
The Xia Dynasty begins in China

1324 BCE
King Tutankhamen of Egypt dies

510 BCE
The Romans establish the Roman Republic

323 BCE
Alexander the Great dies at age thirty-three after conquering most of the world known to him

c. 150 CE
Coastal East Africans start trading with Romans and Arabs

312 CE
Roman Emperor Constantine converts to Christianity, marking an end to the religion's fringe status

ALEXANDER THE GREAT

c. 500 CE
The Mexican city of Teotihuacan becomes a center of culture and commerce

552 CE
Baekje missionaries from the Korean peninsula introduce Buddhism to Japan

554 CE
The bubonic plague strikes Constantinople and spreads throughout the Byzantine Empire

600 CE
Arabs invade northern Africa, spreading Islam throughout the Sahara

632 CE
Muhammad, the founder of Islam, dies in the city of Medina

Note: Eras are designated as BCE ("before the common era"; formerly BC) and CE ("of the common era"; formerly AD).

c. 700
Beowulf is written

725
St. Bede attempts to explain astronomy in *On the Reckoning of Time*

731
St. Bede writes *Ecclesiastical History of the English People*

c. 800
King Alfred writes *Lays of Boethius*

c. 800
An unknown Mercian author compiles *The Martyrology*

c. 890
A Christian scribe in Wessex compiles the *Anglo-Saxon Chronicles,* one of the oldest histories of Great Britain

KING ALFRED

c. 900
Bald's *Leechbook* provides medical remedies for common ailments

937
The Battle of Brunanburh takes place, inspiring an epic poem

c. 955
Aelfric of Eynsham, one of the greatest prose writers of the period, is born

c. 975
The Exeter Book is written

c. 1000
Aelfric of Eynsham writes *Judith*

c. 1000
Wulfstan II, Archbishop of York, preaches *Sermo Lupi ad Anglos* (Sermon of the Wolf to the English)

793
The Vikings invade England and raid northwestern India

829
Egbert of Wessex becomes the first Saxon overlord of England

866
The Vikings capture York, renaming it *Jórvík*

878
King Alfred the Great repels a major Viking attack at Edington

899
King Alfred the Great dies

1016
Danish King Canute claims the English throne

1042
The Saxons regain temporary control when Edward the Confessor becomes king

1055
Westminster Abbey is completed

1057
Malcolm III of Scotland deposes the usurper Macbeth

1066
The Normans invade and conquer England

c. 700
The Maya city of Tikal replaces Teotihuacan as the largest city in Mesoamerica

740
The Moors, Muslims from North Africa, invade Spain, ruling it until 1492

800
Pope Leo III crowns Charlemagne ruler of the Western Roman Empire

850
Norse settlers establish colonies in Iceland

885
St. Cyril develops the Cyrillic alphabet, providing the foundation for many modern Eastern European languages

c. 900
The Toltec civilization begins in Mexico

932
The Chinese are the first to use gunpowder in battle

c. 1000
Leif Ericsson reaches North America, naming it *Vinland*

c. 1050
The Ghana Empire, founded in West Africa in the fourth century CE, reaches its height of power

1054
The Christian church separates into Western Catholicism and Eastern Orthodoxy

1057
King Anawrahta unites Myanmar in southeast Asia

> # *"For the barbarous conquerors spread the conflagration from the eastern to the western sea, without any opposition."*
>
> —SAINT BEDE THE VENERABLE

Ancient Britain

In ancient times, the British Isles were inhabited first by Stone Age cultures, the Cro-Magnon and then the Neolithic peoples, reminders of whom can be still seen in long barrow tombs and in Stonehenge. Near the dawning of the Bronze Age, Britain was cut off from the European continent by the melt at the end of the Ice Age. The Beaker people, named for their distinctive wine beakers, were the next to arrive. They completed Stonehenge, lived in huts rather than caves, farmed the land, and perfected the making of bronze from copper and tin.

The Iron Age followed, from 750 BCE until the arrival of the Romans some seven hundred years later.

An excavated bog corpse.

Two different groups of Celtic (kel´ tik *or* sel´ tik) peoples arrived from the European continent between 200 and 100 BCE: the Gaels, who settled in Ireland and Northern Scotland and whose language survives in Scots and Irish Gaelic, and the Britons, who settled in England, southern Scotland, and Wales and whose language survives as Welsh and Breton.

The Iron Age in Britain was characterized by tribal societies that were divided into classes and ruled by elected chieftains. Clans of hunters and farmers lived in massive hill forts and frequently warred with each other. In battle, warriors painted their bodies blue with a substance known as *woad* and fought from light-weight, mobile chariots.

The religion of the Britons was based on reverence for nature. Their priests, the Druids, composed hymns and poems, compiled historical records, served as judges, and conducted religious ceremonies in oak groves and sites such as Stonehenge. Iron Age Britons produced haunting myths, made precise astronomical observations, and created intricate artifacts. Remains of a few Iron Age people have been found completely preserved in peat bogs.

Roman Britain

To gain political support and then seize power, Roman General Gaius Julius Caesar sought a military victory. When he discovered that British warriors were helping Gallic tribes fight his legions in western Europe, he led a force across the English Channel in 54 BCE. After defeating the Britons, he returned to the continent without establishing a settlement. The next year, he

returned, again defeating the Britons and leaving the region. Not until 43 CE, under the reign of Emperor Claudius, did the Romans reconquer Britain and establish colonies such as Londonium (London) that later became great cities. Despite attempts by local clans to resist domination, by 84 CE, the Romans held England, Wales, and most of Scotland but not Ireland.

After the conquest, the Romans took over Britonic towns, linked them with straight-running roads, and built military fortifications such as Hadrian's Wall. No aqueducts (canals) have been discovered in Britain, as they have in other regions conquered by the Romans. However, the Romans did build extensive public baths, such as those in the city of Bath, which stand to this day. Exactly when Christianity was brought to Britain is uncertain, but it spread quickly after the Roman emperors converted to the faith in the fourth century.

Angles and Saxons Arrive

By the beginning of the fifth century, Roman Britain was facing challenges on several fronts. The northern clans were raiding the nation's borderlands, and the Saxons were attacking the coast. Meanwhile, Rome itself was facing invasion by Germanic tribes and needed its legions back home.

The withdrawal of Roman forces left Britain vulnerable to fierce invaders from the continent, who crossed the North Sea during the next hundred years. The Angles and the Saxons, both Germanic tribes, first raided the eastern coast of Britain. They eventually established outposts and finally conquered much of the country. From the name of one of these tribes come the modern words *England* (*Angle-lond*) and *English* (*Angle-isc*).

Anglo-Saxon society was organized into a class of warriors called *earls* or *thanes,* a class of freemen called *churls,* and a class of slaves called *thralls.* The king depended for protection on his earls and for guidance on a council of elders, the *Witenagemot* or *witan.* Anglo-Saxon justice was simple and crude, and blood feuds, invasions, and desire for land or treasure led to frequent warfare. Legends told of ancient Germanic heroes and kings, including the epic *Beowulf.*

The Anglo-Saxons were not much interested in Christianity, but the Irish church was determined to spread its faith and sent out monks to convert the tribal kingdoms. It was at the monasteries of the Celtic church, such as Kells and Lindisfarne, that illuminated manuscripts of literary texts were painstakingly created by hand, thus preserving the written heritage of the West. At this time, a monk known as Bede the Venerable wrote the first history of England, the *Ecclesiastical History of the English People.*

The Roman church grew increasingly suspicious of the customs of the Celtic church. In 664 CE, the Romans sent their representatives to force a showdown at Whitby Abbey. There, the English representatives rejected Celtic religious traditions and chose to follow those of Europe.

Alfred the Great

In the eighth and ninth centuries, Anglo-Saxon Britain was invaded by the Norsemen, also called the *Danes* or *Vikings.* Arriving from Scandinavia in longboats, they plundered monasteries and burned cities and towns from their base on the Isle of Man. Several Celtic and Saxon kings battled the Norse as they consolidated

NOTABLE NUMBERS

- **4,720** Legionnaires (ordinary soldiers) in a legion of the Roman army; there were about thirty legions in all

- **73** Length in miles of Hadrian's Wall, which runs straight across Britain and remains a symbol of Roman power

- **680** Pages in the ninth-century Celtic illuminated manuscript known as the *Book of Kells,* created over thirty-four years with only two pages lacking color

- **30,000** Lines of Anglo-Saxon verse still in existence

- **700** Ships that transported William the Conqueror's troops, animals, and supplies across the English Channel prior to the Battle of Hastings

> *"I desire to leave to the men that come after me
> a remembrance of me in good works."*
>
> —ALFRED THE GREAT

their own power. In Scotland, it was Kenneth MacAlpin, an Irish Scotti, who destroyed the rival Picts, fought the Vikings, and then allied with them to drive the Angles out of Scotland. The Welsh also developed a distinctive identity during this period, uniting first to fight the Vikings and then turning on the Saxons before finally working with them to secure their territory.

By the 870s, the Norse had settled a large area in northern and eastern England known as *Danelaw*, since it followed the law of the Danes. The only kingdom left unconquered was Wessex in southwestern England. Its king, Alfred, escaped when the Vikings invaded; he then raised an army and routed the Vikings at Edington in 878 CE. Soon, all of southern and central England had come under Alfred's command, earning him the title of *Bretwalda*, or "King of Britain."

During Alfred's reign, the Norse in England converted to Christianity, and many Danish and Old Norse words, such as *law* and *husband*, entered the English

Whitby Abbey.

language. A fine scholar, Alfred brought in Irish monks to create a school for future leaders at Glastonbury. He also drew up legal codes, sponsored the translation of many great works into the Anglo-Saxon language (since most people no longer spoke Latin), and commissioned the *Anglo-Saxon Chronicles*, one of the first histories of Britain.

Because of Alfred's many and varied achievements, history would refer him as "the Great," the only British monarch in history to be granted that designation. Alfred the Great was followed by two strong kings, his son and grandson, and during their combined sixty-eight-year reign (871–939), Britain was free from Viking raids.

The End of the Anglo-Saxon Era

In Ireland, Brian Boru, King of Munster, arose to become high king. When the Norse in Dublin rebelled and recruited outside Viking help, Boru's forces crushed their forces at Clontarf. Boru was killed by a fleeing Viking, however, and civil war broke out among the Irish clans. The Scots also were fighting among themselves for the crown. After a long series of murders, Macbeth (about whom Shakespeare would write a play) ended up ruling successfully for eighteen years before being killed in 1057 at the Battle of Dunsinane.

Meanwhile, in England, the Danes again had invaded and then set up King Canute, who reformed laws and oversaw twenty years of peace. The crown briefly passed back into Saxon control when Edward from the House of Wessex (known as "the Confessor" because of his religious devotion) became king in 1042. After he died, a dispute arose over succession. It was settled in 1066, when a Norman duke, William the Conqueror, crossed the English Channel, defeated the English king Harold at the Battle of Hastings, and brought the Anglo-Saxon Era to a close.

Language Change

One of the most remarkable characteristics of language is its ability to change over time, adding words to label new ideas and objects and dropping words that have become irrelevant or fallen into disuse. Across the years, these changes accumulate and an entirely new language emerges. Languages that do not evolve die, taking with them the history and literature of entire peoples.

The development of the English language generally is divided into three periods: Old English (450 to 1100), Middle English (1100 to 1400; see Unit 2), and Modern English (1400 to 1600; see Unit 3). Each period was defined by events ranging from exploration and military conquests to cultural and political transformations. The effects produced in the language included changes in vocabulary, spelling, pronunciation, and grammar, altering both the spoken and written forms.

To get a sense of how much English has evolved, look at the samples of Old English on pages 15 and 25–26. A thousand years ago, this is what the English language looked like in print. While most of the letters are recognizable, they are combined in unfamiliar ways (particularly the vowels). It follows that these combinations of letters produce unfamiliar sounds when spoken.

Given this extent of change, it is impossible today to read Old English without special training. However, it still is possible to identify many words. For example, the sentence *We sungeon monige songas* is quite similar to *We sang many songs.* In comparing the two, you likely can match up old and new forms of the same words. Compare and contrast the following words from Old English and Modern English, noting the similarities and differences between them:

Old English	Modern English
folc	folk
mynd	mind
seon	see
sittan	sit
weorc	work

Language Families

English belongs to the *Indo-European* family of languages, which also includes French, Spanish, German, and most of the other European languages (see the chart on the next page). These languages developed from a long-dead language known as *Proto-Indo-European,* which probably was spoken by a people called the *Kurgans* who lived in southern Russia around 4000 BCE. From there, the language spread east and west to India and to Europe, slowly developing into many different but related languages.

The common ancestry of these languages can be seen by comparing the similar words they contain. Consider the following examples of the Modern English word *father:*

Latin	pater
French	père
Spanish	padre
Italian	padre
German	vater

All these words probably came from the common Proto-Indo-European word *pater.*

The study of word origins, called *etymology,* involves examining both printed works and cultural history to identify how language changes across time. Specifically, etymologists trace the use of a given word as far back as possible, determining from what language the word derived and when and in what form the word entered the English vocabulary. Dates of origin before 1700, when printed materials became widely distributed, must be considered approximate. Many words likely were used for centuries in conversation before they were recorded in printed works.

The Emergence of English

The Anglo-Saxons who invaded England in the fifth century spoke several West Germanic dialects, which today are known collectively as *Old English* or *Anglo-Saxon.* Modern English, as a descendant of Old English, therefore is related to modern Danish, German, Norwegian, Icelandic, and Dutch (see the lower part of the chart on page 8).

Early Borrowings from Other Languages

As noted earlier, Old English was spoken in Britain from roughly 450 CE to 1100 CE. During that time, English borrowed words from the native people's Celtic language and from the Latin and Danish spoken by the Roman and Viking invaders.

Borrowings from Latin included many words for trade, public works, religious figures, and institutions, such as *abbot* and *port*. The Latin *moneta*, meaning "mint," became the English word *money*. The Latin

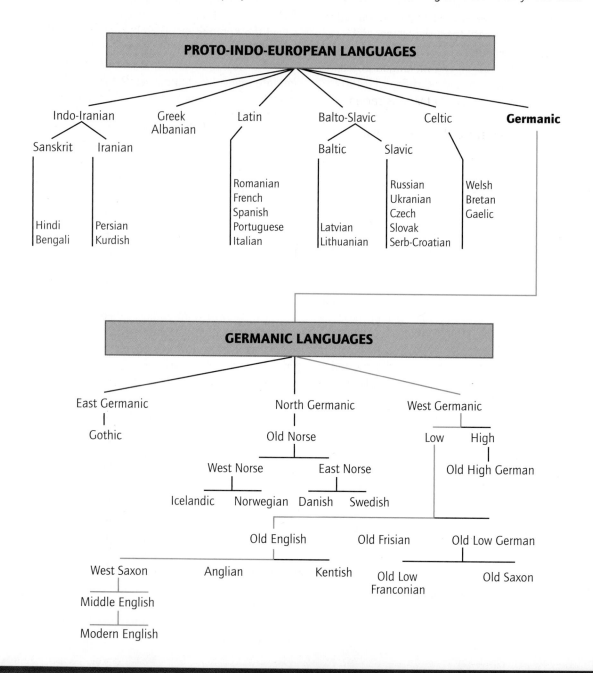

dies malus, meaning "bad day," became the English word *dismal.* Early borrowings from Scandinavian languages, such as Danish, include *outlaw, knife, husband, fellow, take, egg,* and *sky.*

The Written Language

In its earliest stages, English was written in an ancient Germanic script known as *Runic* or *Futhark,* which is believed to have been created around 100 BCE. The oldest surviving examples date from around 200 CE and include inscriptions on stones, tools, and weapons—all hard surfaces into which text was carved.

The original Futhark alphabet consisted of twenty-four letters, six vowels and eighteen consonants (see chart below), and text could be written either left to right or right to left. Nine characters were added to the alphabet after the Anglo-Saxons brought Futhark to England in the fifth century CE. The alphabet evolved primarily to accommodate new vowel sounds in Old English, the language spoken by the Anglo-Saxons.

The Futhark writing system continued to thrive until around the ninth century CE, when it started to be replaced with the Latin alphabet introduced by the Romans in the first century CE. By the end of the Old English period in 1066, the use of Futhark had been discontinued. Refer to a history of language, such as *The Cambridge History of the English Language,* for more information on the development of the English language.

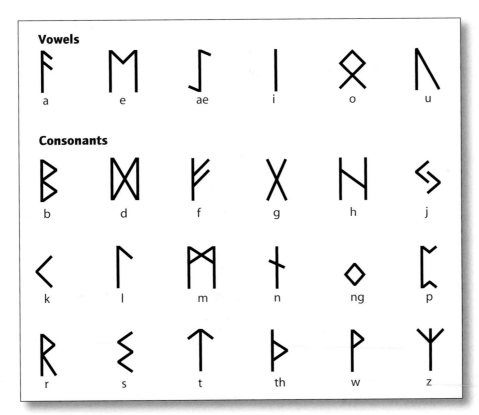

Original Futhark alphabet.

The Conversion of King Edwin

The Story of Cædmon

from Ecclesiastical History of the English People

Historical Nonfiction by Saint Bede the Venerable

Build Background

Literary Context The *Historia Ecclesiastica Gentis Anglorum,* or ***Ecclesiastical History of the English People,*** is Saint Bede's five-book Latin history of Christianity in England. The history covers the period from Julius Caesar's invasion of Britain (55–54 BCE) to Bede's own time. (The history was finished around 731 CE.) King Alfred the Great considered the book important enough to have it translated into Old English, the language of the common people.

 "The Conversion of King Edwin" comes from Book II of Bede's history and relates how Christian missionaries converted the Anglo-Saxon kings. The selection shows the dramatic contrast between the Anglo-Saxons' grim view of the afterlife and the positive alternative offered by the missionaries.

 "The Story of Cædmon," which appears in Book IV of Bede's *Ecclesiastical History,* provides rare biographical information about an early Anglo-Saxon poet. Little is known of Cædmon, other than the miraculous story that Bede recounts. Indeed, "The Story of Cædmon" is an excellent example of an early *miracle tale,* a genre often associated with the lives and works of saints.

Reader's Context Think about a time someone tried to persuade you to change your mind. How much thought did you give to this other point of view? Were you persuaded to change your mind?

Meet the Author

Saint Bede the Venerable (672– or 673–735 CE) was born in Jarrow, in the kingdom of Northumbria, which is in the northeastern part of modern-day England. Bede entered the monastery at age seven. At nineteen, he was ordained a deacon, and at thirty, he was ordained a priest.

 Like other monastics of his time, Bede wrote in Latin. He traveled very little, but his fame spread throughout Europe due to his writings on subjects as varied as history, poetry, grammar, mathematics, science, the scriptures, and the lives of the saints. Bede's histories make fascinating reading, not only for the light they shed on the distant Anglo-Saxon past but also for their engaging accounts of miraculous and legendary events. Bede was canonized (made a saint by the Roman Catholic Church) in 1899, eleven hundred years after his death.

Analyze Literature

Allegory and Caesura

An **allegory** is a work in which each element symbolizes, or represents, something else.

A **caesura** is a major pause in a line of poetry. A typical Old English verse is composed of lines that have four strong stresses, or beats. In the middle of the line is a pause, or caesura.

Set Purpose

Allegory and caesura are both characteristic of Anglo-Saxon literature. As you read "The Conversion of King Edwin," look for an example of allegory and list the symbolic elements it mentions. In reading "Cædmon's Hymn," recite aloud the sample lines of Old English and listen for the pattern in each line of two strong stresses, a pause, and two strong stresses.

Preview Vocabulary

ecclesiastical, 11
precept, 12
temporal, 12
adversity, 12
diligently, 13
efficacious, 13
agency, 14
secular, 14
literal, 15

The Conversion of King Edwin

from Ecclesiastical History of the English People

by Saint Bede the Venerable

The Last Chapter, 1906. James Doyle Penrose.
(See detail on page 10.)

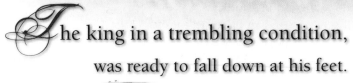

The king in a trembling condition,

was ready to fall down at his feet.

At this time the nation of the Northumbrians, that is, the nation of the Angles that live on the north side of the river Humber, with their king, Edwin, received the faith through the preaching of Paulinus.[1]

1. **Paulinus.** Pope Gregory I sent Paulinus as a missionary to Northumbria in 601 CE.

> **ec • cle • si • as • ti • cal** (i klē′ sē as′ ti k'l) *adj.,* having to do with the church

Bede's Legacy

In writing his histories, Bede followed the practice of dating events from the birth of Christ, using a notation similar to the abbreviations used today: AD (from the Latin *Anno Domini,* meaning "the year of our Lord") and CE ("of the common era"). The popularity and importance of Bede's writings helped to spread the practice of this method of dating history throughout Europe during the following centuries. Likewise, Bede's histories identified the era before Christ's birth with a different nomenclature, which was an early version of the abbreviation BC used today. The use of BC (now commonly designated as BCE, or "before the common era") did not become popular until several hundred years later. Nonetheless, Bede's

histories still represent an important link in the chain of establishing our modern method of dating historical events.

In addition to his linguistic contributions, Bede also was an avid astronomer and became one of the earliest people to suggest that the world was spherical. In addition, he wrote extensively about the moon's influence on tidal patterns and correlated different lunar phases with the European calendar. Bede's scientific writings caused a stir within the church when his recalculation of the origin of the world differed from the church's accepted date. Bishop Wilfred accused St. Bede of aiding the devil's work by contradicting the church's official stance.

This Edwin, as a reward of his receiving the faith, and as an earnest of his share in the heavenly kingdom, received an increase of that which he enjoyed on earth, for he reduced under his dominion all the borders of Britain that were provinces either of the aforesaid nation, or of the Britons, a thing which no British king had ever done before. . . .

For some time he delayed to receive the word of God at the preaching of Paulinus, and used to sit several hours alone, and seriously to ponder with himself what he was to do, and what religion he was to follow. Then the man of God came to him, laid his right hand on his head, and asked whether he knew that sign.[2] The king in a trembling condition, was ready to fall down at his feet, but he raised him up, and in a familiar manner said to him, "Behold, by the help of God you have escaped the hands of the enemies whom you feared. Behold you have of His gift obtained the kingdom which

Then the man of God came to him, laid his right hand on his head, and asked whether he knew that sign.

you desired. Take heed not to delay that which you promised to perform; embrace the faith, and keep the <u>precepts</u> of Him who, delivering you from <u>temporal</u> <u>adversity</u>, has raised you to

---

2. **that sign.** The laying on of hands is a ceremony for transmitting spiritual grace to the recipient, as in the ordination of a clergy.

pre • cept (prē´ sept) *n.,* commandment or direction meant as a rule of action or conduct
tem • po • ral (tem´ pər 'l) *adj.,* lasting only for a time, limited; of this world, not spiritual
ad • ver • si • ty (ad vʉr´ sə tē) *n.,* misfortune, trouble

the honor of a temporal kingdom; and if, from this time forward, you shall be obedient to His will, which through me He signifies to you, He will not only deliver you from the everlasting torments of the wicked, but also make you partaker[3] with Him of His eternal kingdom in Heaven."

The king, hearing these words, answered, that he was both willing and bound to receive the faith which he taught; but that he would confer about it with his principal friends and counselors, to the end that if they also were of his opinion, they might all together be cleansed in Christ the Fountain of Life. Paulinus consenting, the king did as he said; for, holding a council with the wise men,[4] he asked of every one in particular what he thought of the new doctrine, and the new worship that was preached. To which the chief of his own priests, Coifi, immediately answered, "O king, consider what this is which is now preached to us; for I verily declare to you, that the religion which we have hitherto professed has, as far as I can learn, no virtue in it. For none of your people has applied himself more <u>diligently</u> to the worship of our gods than I; and yet there are many who receive greater favors from you, and are more preferred than I, and are more prosperous in all their undertakings. Now if the gods were good for any thing, they would rather forward me, who have been more careful to serve them. It remains, therefore, that if upon examination you find those new doctrines, which are now preached to us, better and more <u>efficacious</u>, we immediately receive them without any delay."

Another of the king's chief men, approving of his words and exhortations, presently added: "The present life of man, O king, seems to me, in comparison to that time which is unknown to us, like to the swift flight of a sparrow through the room wherein you sit at supper in winter, with your commanders and ministers, and a good fire in the midst, whilst the storms of rain and snow prevail abroad; the sparrow, flying in at one door, and immediately out at another, whilst he is within, is safe from the wintry storm; but after a short

So this life of a man appears for a short space, but of what went before, or what is to follow, we are utterly ignorant.

space of fair weather, he immediately vanishes out of your sight, into the dark winter from which he had emerged. So this life of man appears for a short space, but of what went before, or what is to follow, we are utterly ignorant. If, therefore, this new doctrine contains something more certain, it seems justly to deserve to be followed." The other elders and king's counselors, by Divine inspiration, spoke to the same effect. ❖

---

3. **partaker.** One who takes part or shares in something
4. **wise men.** Anglo-Saxon *Witenagemot*, or council of elders

> **dil • i • gent • ly** (di´ lə jənt lē) *adv.*, with great care and attention
> **ef • fi • ca • cious** (e fə kā´ shəs) *adj.*, effective, producing the desired result

MIRRORS & WINDOWS — King Edwin delayed converting to Christianity for some time and asked his counselors for advice on the matter. What type of leader would you prefer: one who asks for guidance or one who makes decisions independently?

The Story of Cædmon

from Ecclesiastical History
of the English People

by Saint Bede the Venerable

Inspiration of Cædmon, c. 1900. Lexden L. Pocock.
Cheltenham Art Gallery and Museum, England.

It often happened that his songs kindled a contempt for this world
and a longing for the life of Heaven in the hearts of many men.

Heavenly grace had especially singled out a certain one of the brothers in the monastery ruled by this abbess,[1] for he used to compose devout and religious songs. Whatever he learned of holy Scripture with the aid of interpreters, he quickly turned into the sweetest and most moving poetry in his own language, that is to say English. It often happened that his songs kindled a contempt for this world and a longing for the life of Heaven in the hearts of many men. Indeed, after him others among the English people tried to compose religious poetry, but no one could equal him because he was not taught the art of song by men or by human <u>agency</u> but received this gift through heavenly grace. Therefore, he was never able to compose any vain and idle songs but only such as dealt with religion and were proper for his religious tongue to utter. As a matter of fact, he had lived in the <u>secular</u> estate until he

---

1. **abbess.** Hild, or Hilda, founded the Monastery of Whitby, a religious community that included both men and women. An abbess is the head of such a community, which is called an *abbey.*

> **agen • cy** (ā´ jən[t] sē) *n.,* force or power
> **sec • u • lar** (se´ kyə lər) *adj.,* of the world; not sacred or religious

Cædmon's Hymn

(handwritten note: "not right format")

Nu sculon herigean
Now we must praise

heofonrices Weard
heaven-kingdom's Guardian,

Meotodes meahte
the Measurer's might

and his modgepanc
and his mind-plans,

weorc Wuldor-Fæder
the work of the Glory-Father,

swa he wundra gehwæs
when he of all wonders,

ece Drihten
eternal Lord,

or onstealde
the beginning established.

He ærest sceop
He first created

ielda bearnum
for men's sons

heofon to hrofe
heaven as a roof,

halig Scyppend
holy Creator;

ða middángeard
then middle-earth

moncynnes Weard
mankind's Guardian,

ece Drihten
eternal Lord,

æfter teode
afterward made—

firum foldan
for men earth,

Frea ælmihtig
Master almighty.

was well advanced in age without learning any songs. Therefore, at feasts, when it was decided to have a good time by taking turns singing, whenever he would see the harp[2] getting close to his place, he got up in the middle of the meal and went home.

> It is impossible to make a literal translation, no matter how well-written, of poetry into another language without losing some of the beauty and dignity.

Once when he left the feast like this, he went to the cattle shed, which he had been assigned the duty of guarding that night. And after he had stretched himself out and gone to sleep, he dreamed that someone was standing at his side and greeted him, calling out his name. "Cædmon," he said, "sing me something."

And he replied, "I don't know how to sing; that is why I left the feast to come here—because I cannot sing."

"All the same," said the one who was speaking to him, "you have to sing for me."

"What must I sing?" he said.

And he said, "Sing about the Creation."

At this, Cædmon immediately began to sing verses in praise of God the Creator, which he had never heard before and of which the sense is this:

This is the general sense but not the exact order of the words[3] that he sang in his sleep; for it is impossible to make a <u>literal</u> transla-

---

2. **singing . . . harp.** In Anglo-Saxon times, poetry was performed aloud to the accompaniment of a harp.
3. **the general sense . . . words.** Bede is referring to his Latin version of the poem, not printed here.

---

lit • er • al (li′ tər əl) *adj.,* word for word; true to the actual or original meaning

It was evident to all of them that he had been granted the heavenly grace of God.

abbess and ordered to tell his dream and to recite his song to an audience of the most learned men so that they might judge what the nature of that vision was and where it came from. It was evident to all of them that he had been granted the heavenly grace of God. Then they expounded some bit of sacred story or teaching to him, and instructed him to turn it into poetry if he could. He agreed and went away. And when he came back the next morning, he gave back what had been commissioned to him in the finest verse.

Therefore, the abbess, who cherished the grace of God in this man, instructed him to give up secular life and to take monastic vows. And when she and all those subject to her had received him into the community of brothers, she gave orders that he be taught the whole sequence of sacred history. He remembered everything that he was able to learn by listening, and turning it over in his mind like a clean beast[6] that chews the cud, he converted it into sweetest song, which sounded so delightful that he made his teachers, in their turn, his listeners. ❖

tion, no matter how well-written, of poetry into another language without losing some of the beauty and dignity. When he woke up, he remembered everything that he had sung in his sleep, and to this he soon added, in the same poetic measure,[4] more verses praising God.

The next morning he went to the reeve,[5] who was his foreman, and told him about the gift he had received. He was taken to the

---

4. **measure.** As used here, the word means "rhythm" or "poetic form."
5. **reeve.** Person who oversees farms
6. **clean beast.** In the Old Testament and in ancient Hebrew law, *clean beasts* are those such as cattle that have cloven hooves and regurgitate and chew again plants they have eaten.

If you could wake up tomorrow with one extraordinary new talent, such as musical ability, what would you want it to be? How would having this talent change your life?

Refer to Text ▶ ▶ ▶ ▶ ▶	**Reason with Text**	
1a. Who is Paulinus?	**1b.** Think about Paulinus's speech to King Edwin. Describe Paulinus's goal.	**Understand** Find meaning
2a. Who urges Cædmon to compose his first song, and what does this person say the song should be about?	**2b.** How might Bede explain the "someone" who appears and urges Cædmon to sing? How does the way in which Cædmon gains his poetic ability make him an unequaled poet, according to Bede?	**Apply** Use information
3a. State the opinion of King Edwin's chief priest Coifi about the current religion.	**3b.** Compare and contrast the details presented about the old Germanic religion with those presented about Christianity.	**Analyze** Take things apart
4a. What evidence does Coifi offer to support his opinion of the current religion?	**4b.** Evaluate Coifi's argument. Determine whether he chose the best approach for his audience, the king.	**Evaluate** Make judgments
5a. What is the subject of Cædmon's first hymn? To whom or what does Cædmon give many names in this hymn?	**5b.** Explain why this subject is fitting for a religious poet's first hymn.	**Create** Bring ideas together

Analyze Literature

Allegory and Caesura

The last paragraph of "The Conversion of King Edwin" contains an allegory comparing human life to the flight of a sparrow. What elements did you identify in the allegory, and what does each element represent in the human world?

Where does the caesura fall in the first and second lines of Old English in "Cædmon's Hymn"? When reading the modern translation of the lines, what is the effect of the caesura?

Extend the Text

Writing Options

Creative Writing Imagine that Cædmon has come to King Edwin's court to perform his poetry. Write a one-page dialogue between King Edwin and Cædmon in which they discuss their experiences with religious transformation. Compare your dialogue with the dialogues of your classmates.

Descriptive Writing A sixth-grade student has asked you to explain how to accomplish a certain goal. Write a one-paragraph allegory in which you use symbols to create a simplified description of reaching this goal.

Collaborative Learning

Identify Tone The emotional attitude that a literary work implies toward the reader or the subject is called the *tone*. A work might be playful or serious, sarcastic or sincere, and so on. In a small group, discuss words and phrases from "The Story of Cædmon" that suggest Bede's attitude toward the poet. What one word best describes his attitude, or tone?

Critical Literacy

Conduct an Interview Suppose you have traveled back in time to interview King Edwin. Prepare a set of questions you would like to ask him. Then with a partner, take turns role-playing the interviewer and King Edwin. As the interviewer, ask the questions you prepared. As King Edwin, use what you learned about him from Bede's account, as well as your own imagination, to respond.

 Go to **www.mirrorsandwindows.com** for more.

1. Which of the following best states the main advantage of Christianity, as presented in "The Conversion of King Edwin"?
   A. "Behold, by the help of God you have escaped the hands of the enemies whom you feared."
   B. "Then the man of God came to him, laid his right hand on his head, and asked whether he knew that sign."
   C. "'Behold you have of His gift obtained the kingdom which you desired.'"
   D. "'He will not only deliver you from the everlasting torments of the wicked, but also make you partaker with Him of His eternal kingdom in Heaven.'"
   E. "They might together all be cleansed in Christ the Fountain of Life"

2. In "The Conversion of King Edwin," Bede writes, "The religion which we have hitherto professed has / as far as I can learn, no virtue in it." What do these lines mean?
   A. Our old religion has nothing to recommend it.
   B. A person doesn't have to be virtuous to be a Christian.
   C. I have learned that what we once believed is all a lie.
   D. What the missionary Paulinus says does not make sense.
   E. Although we have claimed to be religious, we have not acted that way.

3. How is "the swift flight of a sparrow" similar to the life of humans?
   A. It is fast.
   B. It is just and fair.
   C. It is short and uncertain.
   D. It rarely gets noticed because it occurs at such a high level.
   E. It rarely gets noticed because it is plain and ordinary.

4. For what purpose or purposes did Bede write "The Conversion of King Edwin"?
   A. to inform
   B. to persuade
   C. to reflect
   D. to inform and persuade
   E. to inform, persuade, and reflect

5. Which of the following words from "Cædmon's Hymn" is not another name for God?
   A. Nu
   B. Weard
   C. Meotodes
   D. Wuldor-Fæder
   E. Frea

6. Determine what these various names for God have in common. What quality do they all describe God as having?
   A. He is loving.
   B. He is forgiving.
   C. He is all knowing.
   D. He is the creator of everything.
   E. He is a powerful protector of humans.

7. Which of the following quotations from "The Story of Cædmon" does not indicate that this is a miracle tale, which tells the story of a saint's life?
   A. "the gift he [Cædmon] had received"
   B. "he [Cædmon] had been granted the heavenly grace of God."
   C. "he [Cædmon] gave back what had been commissioned to him in the finest verse"
   D. "who cherished the grace of God in this man [Cædmon]"
   E. "instructed him [Cædmon] to give up secular life and to take monastic vows"

8. In "The Story of Cædmon," Bede writes, "He remembered everything that he was able to learn by listening, and turning it over in his mind like a clean beast that chews the cud." This is an example of
   A. a caesura.
   B. a simile.
   C. a metaphor.
   D. verbal irony.
   E. foreshadowing.

9. **Constructed Response:** Compare and contrast the two religions referred to in "The Conversion of King Edwin." Then explain why King Edwin agrees to convert.

10. **Constructed Response:** Based on the information presented in these two selections, discuss what issues were central in people's lives during the Anglo-Saxon Period. Use details from both "The Conversion of King Edwin" and "The Story of Cædmon" to support your response.

Understand the Concept

When you write a sentence, be sure that the subject and the verb agree. If the subject is **singular** (referring to one person or thing), then the verb also must be singular. If the subject is **plural** (two or more), then the verb also must be plural. (The **subject** tells who or what the sentence is about; the **verb** indicates what the subject is or does.)

To check for agreement in your sentences, first identify the subject and the verb:

EXAMPLES

Cædmon sings a hymn to the abbess.

Edwin is a king who converts to Christianity.

In the first example, *Cædmon* is the subject of the sentence because that is who the sentence is about. *Sings* is the verb because it tells what Cædmon, the subject, does. In the second example, *Edwin* is the subject, or who the sentence is about, and *is* is the verb, telling who Edwin is.

In every sentence, the verb must agree with its subject in number. In other words, if the subject of a sentence is in the plural form, then the verb also must be in the plural form:

EXAMPLES

Singular	**Plural**
The boat is broken.	The boats are broken.
He walks the countryside.	They walk the countryside.

A subject that contains two or more parts is called a **compound subject.** If the parts of a compound subject are joined by *and,* the verb must be plural. If the items are joined by *or* or *nor,* the verb must agree with the subject closer to it, whether singular or plural.

EXAMPLES

"The Story of Cædmon" and "The Conversion of King Edwin" are interesting works to study. [Plural noun and verb]

Neither "The Story of Cædmon" nor "The Conversion of King Edwin" is covered on today's quiz. [Singular noun and verb]

Neither "The Story of Cædmon" nor other Anglo-Saxon works are covered on today's quiz. [Plural noun and verb]

Collective nouns, such as *family, committee,* and *class,* name groups. In their singular forms, they can be either singular or plural, depending on how the group acts. When the group acts together as one unit, it is considered singular. When the group comprises individuals acting independently, it is considered plural.

EXAMPLES

The class is studying Anglo-Saxon literature. [Singular]

The class *are* choosing their own topics for their final term papers. [Plural]

Apply the Skill

Identify Noun Types

In each sentence, identify whether the noun is singular, plural, compound, or collective.

1. Neither the abbess nor the monks sing as well as Cædmon.
2. Cædmon's teachers listen to many of his poems.
3. The abbess is pleased with Cædmon's hymns.
4. Edwin's council of advisors recommends that he convert to Christianity.
5. Paulinus urges King Edwin to convert.

Fix Subject-Verb Agreement

Find and correct the errors in subject-verb agreement in the following passage.

"The Story of Cædmon" are recorded in Bede's *Ecclesiastical History of the English People.* This story is about an ordinary man who begins to speak poetry about the creation of the world. At the nearby abbey, the abbess and the monks are so impressed by Cædmon's poetry that the abbess instruct him to join the monastery. A group of teachers give Cædmon many religious texts and ask him to convert them into poetry. Neither Cædmon's teachers nor the abbess are able to match the poetry he creates.

Use Correct Subject-Verb Agreement in Your Writing

Write a paragraph explaining the roles of the various people and groups in "The Conversion of King Edwin" and "The Story of Cædmon." Review your writing to make sure the subject and verb agree in each sentence.

Poetry Defined

Poetry is a major genre of literature and includes dramatic, narrative, and lyric forms. It features imaginative language that is carefully chosen and arranged to communicate experiences, thoughts, and emotions.

Poetry differs from **prose** in that it compresses meaning into fewer words and often uses meter, rhyme, and imagery. A poem usually is arranged in lines and stanzas, as opposed to sentences and paragraphs, and it can be more free in the ordering of words and use of punctuation. Although conventional poetry adheres strictly to meter and rhyme, British poetry from the mid-eighteenth century on has a more liberated quality, using the rhythms and cadences of spoken language.

Some literary historians believe that poetry found its original voice in song, and it clearly has roots in religious scripture. The Classical culture of ancient Greece produced *The Iliad* and *The Odyssey,* **epic poems** that tell tales of gods and heroes, while Anglo-Saxon epics mixed pagan and religious elements. Works such as these are **narrative poems,** which tell stories. Like many other narrative poems, epics have intricate plots and wide casts of characters. Other examples of narrative poems are Geoffrey Chaucer's *The Canterbury Tales* (Unit 2) and Samuel Taylor Coleridge's "The Rime of the Ancient Mariner" (Unit 6).

Lyric poetry, which flowered in Europe with the courtly love tradition, also dates back to the Classical Period. A **lyric poem** is a highly musical type of poetry that expresses the emotions of a speaker. In form, the lyric usually relies on a regular metrical pattern or a combination of patterns. Lyric poems often are contrasted with narrative poems because they do not have storytelling as their main purpose. Among the greatest lyric poems in Western civilization are the **sonnets** of Shakespeare, Petrarch, and John Donne (see Unit 3). Some modern poets also write sonnets, finding a unique beauty and formal balance in the sonnet structure. The **themes** of lyric poetry are as varied as love and loss, war and peace, religion and nature. Some lyric poetry is **elegiac,** mourning the dead in the manner of Thomas Gray's "Elegy Written in a Country Churchyard" (Unit 5).

A **dramatic poem** relies heavily on dramatic elements such as **monologue** (speech by a single charac-

ter) and **dialogue** (conversation involving two or more characters). Unlike lyric or narrative poems, dramatic poems are told from the point of view of a speaker who is not the poet. Dramatic poems tell stories, reveal the character of the speaker, or present an argument. Andrew Marvell's "To His Coy Mistress" (Unit 5) and Robert Browning's "My Last Duchess" (Unit 7) are examples of dramatic poems.

A **concrete poem**, or **shape poem**, is a poem whose words are arranged on the page to reflect its content. "Easter Wings," by George Herbert (Unit 3), is an example. Concrete poetry originated in Greece in the third century BCE. Some ancient poems were, like Herbert's, shaped like wings; others were shaped like altars or axes. The shape poem was revived in Brazil in the 1950s and continues to attract poets who consider visual elements to be intrinsic parts of a poem's artistry.

"Poetry is a mirror which makes beautiful that which is distorted."

—PERCY BYSSHE SHELLEY,
NINETEENTH-CENTURY BRITISH POET

Elements of Poetry

Form and Structure

Form refers to the organization of the parts of a poem. You can look at poetic form broadly, asking What type of poem is this? Is it a lyrical ode, a sonnet, an elegy, or perhaps an example of free verse? Next, you can analyze the poem's structure, noting how the author has arranged lines on a page. Some poems have a continuous form, as does the sonnet. Most, however, are divided into stanzas, which are similar to the paragraphs of prose. A **stanza,** or group of lines in a poem, varies in average length from two to eight lines.

Examining a stanza, you will notice the presence or absence of a **rhyme scheme,** which is the pattern of **end rhymes,** or rhyming words at the ends of lines of verse. The rhyme scheme of a poem is designated by letters (such as *abab*), with matching letters signifying matching sounds. Even poems without exact end rhyme may include **slant rhyme,** in which the rhyming sounds are similar but not identical, or **internal rhyme,** in which words rhyme within lines. In Anglo-Saxon poetry, you will notice strongly accented lines,

alliteration, and the **caesura,** a pause between the two halves of a line.

Also look for the pattern of ideas and images that hold the poem together. For example, in *Sir Gawain and the Green Knight* (Unit 2), a poem in alliterative unrhymed verse, the pattern of threes helps to organize the episodic narrative: three times Gawain crosses himself, three times he sets out on the hunt.

Meter and Rhythm

As you read poetry, you also will notice the presence or absence of a fixed **meter,** or a regular rhythmic pattern. The meter of a poem creates its **rhythm,** the pattern of beats, or stresses, in a line of verse. Rhythm can be regular or irregular. The metrical pattern is determined by the number of stresses in each line. Stressed and unstressed syllables are divided into rhythmical units called **feet.**

Figurative Language

Figurative language is writing or speech meant to be understood imaginatively instead of literally. Poets use figurative language to help readers see things in new ways. Types of figurative language, or *figures of speech,* include **hyperbole, metaphor, personification, simile,** and **understatement.**

In "She Walks in Beauty" (Unit 6), George Gordon, Lord Byron, compares a woman to a beautiful night: "She walks in beauty, like the night / Of cloudless climes and starry skies." Use of the word *like* indicates a simile. Andrew Marvell's "To His Coy Mistress" (Unit 5) is constructed around a central metaphor: "Time's wingéd chariot." The speaker tries to beguile his beloved by making her see that youth and life are fleeting. John Donne uses personification when he addresses Death in Holy Sonnet 10: "Death, be not proud" (Unit 3).

Sound Devices

Poets use a variety of *sound devices* to create and enhance meaning. **Repetition** is the intentional reuse of a sound, word, phrase, or sentence to emphasize ideas or create a musical effect. Many lyric poems have a **refrain,** which is a repeated line or group of lines. **Alliteration** is the repetition of initial consonant sounds, as in "cloudless climes and starry skies" and "Then shall the fall further the flight in me" from George Herbert's "Easter Wings" (Unit 3). **Assonance** is the repetition of vowel sounds in stressed syllables that end with different consonant sounds. An example is the repetition in Edmund Spenser's Sonnet 75 (Unit 3) of the long *a* sound: "One *day* I wrote her *name* upon the strand."

HOW TO READ

Poetry

Read the poem aloud. Many of the elements of poetry—including rhythm, meter, and sound devices—are best realized by reading a poem aloud. Doing so will let you hear and feel how the language is used, which is key both to understanding and appreciating poetry.

Visualize. Because poems often contain sensory details, they lend themselves well to visualization. Create images in your mind, using your senses to see, hear, smell, feel, and taste the poem.

Make inferences. Unlike other types of writing, poetry does not allow much room for explanation. To understand a poem, make inferences, or put together the clues given in the poem with your own prior knowledge.

Ask questions. As you read a poem, write down the words and phrases you do not understand. Also jot down questions you may have about imagery, form, rhyme, and other elements. Discuss your questions with your classmates and teacher.

Compare and contrast. The possibilities for comparing and contrasting poems are wide and varied. Doing so can help you better understand poetic forms, figurative language, themes, historical context, and authors and also identify what you like and dislike in poetry.

The Epic Defined

An **epic** is a long narrative poem that portrays the heroic acts of legendary figures and mythical gods. Grand in style, length, and scope, an epic provides a portrait of an entire culture, of the legends, beliefs, values, laws, arts, and ways of life of a people.

The Anglo-Saxon epic *Beowulf* and the Sumerian epic *Gilgamesh* are about heroes based partially on historical figures. The original sources were altered in the retellings. In the case of *Gilgamesh,* parts of which were first recorded around 2000 BCE on stone tablets in *cuneiform* (wedge-shaped characters), the language of the oral storytellers included Sumerian, Akkadian (related to Hebrew), and Hittite (an Indo-European language). Each culture contributed something of its worldview to the epic poem that has survived.

The heroes of both these epics are faced with slaying a demonic figure of monstrous power. The warrior-king Gilgamesh, aided by his foil, Enkidu, goes to the great cedar forest to cut down the trees. Humbaba, guardian of the forest, turns back the trespassers, and a mighty struggle ensues. In *Beowulf,* the embodiment of evil is Grendel, offspring of the murderous Cain. The biblical reference may, in fact, have been added centuries after the original Scandinavian verses were composed. The anonymous author of the poem we know today would have recast the epic in Christian terms. Thus, Grendel's death has religious as well as mythological significance.

Elements of the Epic

Figurative Language

Common to Anglo-Saxon literature is a figurative device called a **kenning,** in which a new word or noun phrase is coined to describe an object in an original manner. For example, in *Beowulf,* the kennings *hell-serf* and *herdsman of evil* are applied to the monster Grendel.

Also notice the use of **metaphors** and **similes** to create comparisons in these poems. In "The Head of Humbaba," from *Gilgamesh,* the monster Humbaba's "sobs and desperate appeals" to the warrior hero are compared to "The way the sea contorts under a violent squall," creating a vivid metaphor. The nighttime stars are described using this simile: "The stars against the midnight sky / Were sparkling like mica in a riverbed." Another simile about stars can be found in *Grendel:* "Stars . . . like jewels scattered in a dead king's grave."

Alliteration and Hyperbole

The repetition of initial consonant sounds, or **alliteration,** is a device frequently used in epic verse—for instance, "hell-forged hands" (Canto 2, *Beowulf*) and "strangled sobs" (*Gilgamesh*). The epic also is rich in **hyperbole,** deliberate exaggerations made for effect: "[Humbaba's] single stroke could cut a cedar down" (*Gilgamesh*), while Grendel "made his home in a hell" (*Beowulf*).

Theme

The major themes of an epic are rooted in the culture that produces it. In pre-Christian *Gilgamesh,* there are strong traces of mythology. Gilgamesh, who ruled in Sumer sometime around 2700 BCE, is mythologized as a superhuman being, two-thirds god and one-third mortal. Enkidu, the being who becomes his ally, is part animal and part human. When the two join forces, they prevail over evil—a strong theme of the work. Other themes include the quest for wisdom, the inevitability of suffering, and the value of life.

Beowulf, which tells the story of a hero who saves a kingdom through a symbol-laden struggle against evil, pits a pagan demon against a Christian thane (knight). Another theme is that of honor and loyalty to a lord. Beowulf defends King Hrothgar and his court and is duly rewarded with wealth and status. The religious themes that later were imposed on the work do not obscure the guiding beliefs of an older culture. Secular (nonreligious) ties, such as those that bind the noble to the king and court, are particularly important.

See page 21 for guidelines on how to read poetry.

from **Beowulf**

Heroic Epic, Anonymous, Verse Translation by Burton Raffel

Interlinear Translation of Prologue by Robin Lamb

Build Background

Historical Context Widely acknowledged as the masterpiece of Anglo-Saxon literature, ***Beowulf*** was composed in Northumbria or West Mercia, kingdoms in the northern part of present-day Great Britain, by an unknown singer of tales. Such singers were known as *gleemen* or *scops*. The poem probably dates from the early 700s, but it tells a story that is much older. The poem's characters are not Anglo-Saxon but rather related Germanic people—Geats and Danes from Scandinavia. The hero of the poem, Beowulf, may be based on a historical figure, but there is no independent record of his existence. (See page 24 for a chart depicting tribes and geneologies in *Beowulf*.)

Literary Context No one knows precisely when *Beowulf* was first written down. The poem survives in a West Saxon manuscript created in the late 900s by a monastic copyist, or scribe, who added to the original pre-Christian poem many references to stories from the Old Testament. The single existing manuscript contains many errors introduced by the scribe. Nonetheless, the poem is fairly complete and remains the finest surviving example of the ancient epic.

The poem consists of a prologue and forty-three sections, known as *cantos*. The first three-fourths of the poem tells the story of Beowulf's heroic exploits as a young man, while the final portion tells of Beowulf as an aged king of the Geats. The parts of the poem presented here are perhaps the most famous parts of the epic. They deal with Beowulf's heroic confrontation with a monster named Grendel, his subsequent battle with Grendel's vengeful mother, and finally, as an aged king, his fatal battle with a dragon.

The excerpts from *Beowulf* that follow begin with the Prologue reprinted in Old English with a word-for-word translation by Robin Lamb. Studying this Prologue will give you a sense of the sound of the original. The remaining excerpts are given in a verse translation by Burton Raffel. The portions of the text not given in verse translation have been summarized; those summaries appear in italic type.

Reader's Context What are the qualities of a modern hero? Has the definition of *hero* changed since the era in which *Beowulf* was written?

Analyze Literature

Alliteration and Motif
Alliteration is the repetition of initial consonant sounds.

A **motif** is any element that recurs in one or more works of literature or art.

Set Purpose

Good translators strive to preserve the original sounds of the literature they translate. In reading *Beowulf,* which was translated from Old English into Modern English, identify examples of alliteration. Read these lines aloud to hear the sounds of the language. Also identify examples of motifs, and note the famous literary works in which they appear.

Preview Vocabulary

tribute, 26
spoils, 27
brood, 28
purge, 31
relish, 32
bolt, 33
infamous, 33
cower, 34
hoary, 43
lament, 49

Tribes and Genealogies in *Beowulf*

A. Tribes mentioned in *Beowulf*

1. **The Danes** (Also called Gar-Danes, Ring-Danes, Spear-Danes, and Scyldings)
2. **The Geats** (Also called Sea-Geats, War-Geats, and Weather-Geats)
3. **The Swedes**
4. **The Frisians** (or Jutes)
5. **The Heatho-Bards** (or Battle-Bards)

B. Genealogy and Descendents of the Danish King Hrothgar

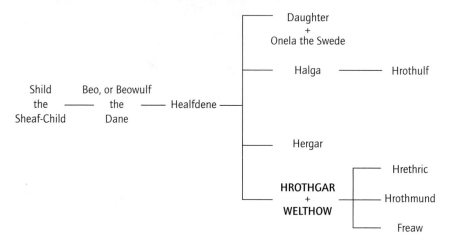

C. Genealogy of Beowulf of the Geats

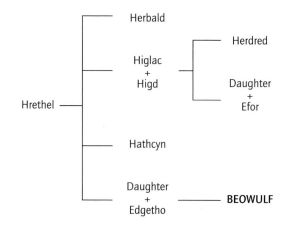

Kin Ælla's Messengers Before Ragnar Lodbroke's Sons, 1857. J. A. Malmström.
Norrköping Art Museum, Sweden. (See detail on page 23.)

FROM

BEOWULF

Verse Translation by Burton Raffel
Interlinear Translation of Prologue by Robin Lamb

Prologue (lines 1–11), in Old English, with an interlinear translation[1]

Hwaet we Gar-Dena
Yes, we of the Gar-Danes

Oft Scyld Scefing
Often Scyld the Sheaf-child

Þeod-cyninga,
The great kings'

Monegum mægÞum,
From many tribes,

Hu ða æÞelingas
How those princes

egsode eorlas
Inspired earls with fear,

---

1. To be read across, left to right

feasceaft funden:
Found helpless.

sceaÞena Þreatum
from bands of robbers,

Weox under wolcnum,
Flourished under the clouds,

meodo-setla ofteah:
their mead-benches dragged away,

OðÞœt him æghwylc
Until him every one

śyððan ærest weárð
after he first was

Ofer hron-rade
Over the whale-road

he Þæs frofre gebad,
He thence looked for comfort,

Gomban gyldan:
[and] tribute pay.

weorÞmyntum Þah,
in dignities prospered,

in gear-dagum,
in days of old,

Þara ymb-sittendra
of those sitting around

Þrym gefrunon:
renown have heard of,

hyran scolde,
must obey,

ellen fremendon.
bravery displayed.

Þæt wæs god cyning.
That was a good king!

Prologue (lines 1–11), in verse translation

> Hear me! We've heard of Danish heroes,
> Ancient kings and the glory they cut
> For themselves, swinging mighty swords!
> How Shild[1] made slaves of soldiers from every
> 5 Land, crowds of captives he'd beaten
> Into terror; he'd traveled to Denmark alone,
> An abandoned child, but changed his own fate,
> Lived to be rich and much honored. He ruled
> Lands on all sides: wherever the sea
> 10 Would take them his soldiers sailed, returned
> With <u>tribute</u> and obedience. There was a brave King!

> . . .

> *Shild has a son and dies. He is laid to rest on a ship loaded with*
> *treasures and weapons, and the ship is then set adrift on the sea.*

---

1. **Shild.** Shild's name can be translated literally as "Shild the Sheaf-Child." The name comes from a legend that he was found as a baby floating in a basket of reeds (as Moses was in the Old Testament). This legend is what the poet refers to when he calls Shild "an abandoned child."

trib • ute (tri´ byüt) *n.,* regular payment of money or goods made by one ruler or nation to another as acknowledgment of servitude, for protection from invasion, and so on

The Bayeux Tapestry

The Bayeux Tapestry, shown in part in the Unit 1 opener (see page 1), is a 230-foot embroidered cloth that provides a visual narrative of the Norman invasion of England in 1066. No one knows who commissioned the tapestry or when it was sewn, but scholars believe that its creator probably was William the Conqueror's half brother and that it likely was constructed in the late 1070s.

The Bayeux Tapestry is an invaluable resource. It provides historians with important visual evidence about ancient technology, battle tactics, and cultural practices during an era from which little information has survived. Even so, the tapestry does not perfectly recreate the Battle of Hastings. Since it was designed by the victors, the tapestry cannot be considered an impartial record. For example, Halley's Comet makes an appearance in the tapestry as an omen from God predicting a Norman victory. The tapestry's designer also took a somewhat sadistic pleasure in recounting the gruesome Anglo-Saxon death scenes.

Other details in the Bayeux Tapestry have completely bewildered modern scholars. Soldiers are shown fighting with their bare hands within its battle scenes, but other sources indicate that protective hand gear was indispensable during medieval war. One scene depicts a priest slapping a woman across the face, but there is no explanation relating this event to the Norman Conquest.

In fact, unexplainable details are associated with every primary source (original texts and other material) from the Middle Ages. The discrepancies about the content of the Bayeux Tapestry do not diminish its historical significance or importance to modern-day medieval scholars.

Critical Viewing The Bayeux Tapestry is an elaborate record of the Norman invasion. What does its creation suggest about the Normans and their conquest of England? What might a tapestry created by the English look like in terms of the images portrayed?

Canto 1

Shild's son rules; Shild's grandson rules; and then finally Shild's great-grandson attains the throne.

    Then Hrothgar, taking the throne, led
The Danes to such glory that comrades and kinsmen
Swore by his sword, and young men swelled
15 His armies, and he thought of greatness and resolved
To build a hall that would hold his mighty
Band and reach higher toward Heaven than anything
That had ever been known to the sons of men.
And in that hall he'd divided the <u>spoils</u>
20 Of their victories, to old and young what they'd earned
In battle, but leaving the common pastures
Untouched, and taking no lives. The work
Was ordered, the timbers tied and shaped

---

spoils (spoi´ 'lz) *n.,* arms, money, or goods taken from a defeated foe

By the hosts that Hrothgar ruled. It was quickly
25 Ready, that most beautiful of dwellings, built
As he'd wanted, and then he whose word was obeyed
All over the earth named it Herot.
His boast come true he commanded a banquet,
Opened out his treasure-full hands.
30 That towering place, gabled and huge,
Stood waiting for time to pass, for war
To begin, for flames to leap as high
As the feud that would light them, and for Herot to burn.
   A powerful monster, living down
35 In the darkness, growled in pain, impatient
As day after day the music rang
Loud in that hall,[2] the harp's rejoicing
Call and the poet's clear songs, sung
Of the ancient beginnings of us all, recalling
40 The Almighty making the earth, shaping
These beautiful plains marked off by oceans,
Then proudly setting the sun and moon
To glow across the land and light it;
The corners of the earth were made lovely with trees
45 And leaves, made quick with life, with each
Of the nations who now move on its face. And then
As now warriors sang of their pleasure:
So Hrothgar's men lived happy in his hall
Till the monster stirred, that demon, that fiend,
50 Grendel, who haunted the moors,[3] the wild
Marshes, and made his home in a hell
Not hell but earth. He was spawned in that slime,
Conceived by a pair of those monsters born
Of Cain,[4] murderous creatures banished
55 By God, punished forever for the crime
Of Abel's death. The Almighty drove
Those demons out, and their exile was bitter,
Shut away from men; they split
In a thousand forms of evil—spirits
60 And fiends, goblins, monsters, giants,
A <u>brood</u> forever opposing the Lord's
Will, and again and again defeated.

---

2. **hall.** Herot
3. **moors.** Tracts of open, rolling wasteland, usually covered with heather and often marshy
4. **Of Cain.** The Christian copyist has made Grendel a descendant of Cain, the oldest son of
   Adam and Eve. According to Genesis 4, Cain killed his brother, Abel, and so was made an
   outcast, despised by others.

brood (brüd) *n.,* offspring or a family of offspring of animals

Canto 2

*Grendel terrorizes Herot. Hrothgar and his councilors seek a plan
to rid themselves of Grendel, but to no avail.*

Then, when darkness had dropped, Grendel
Went up to Herot, wondering what the warriors
65   Would do in that hall when their drinking was done.
He found them sprawled in sleep, suspecting
Nothing, their dreams undisturbed. The monster's
Thoughts were as quick as his greed or his claws:
He slipped through the door and there in the silence
70   Snatched up thirty men, smashed them
Unknowing in their beds and ran out with their bodies,
The blood dripping behind him, back
To his lair, delighted with his night's slaughter.
    At daybreak, with the sun's first light, they saw
75   How well he had worked, and in that gray morning
Broke their long feast with tears and laments
For the dead. Hrothgar, their lord, sat joyless
In Herot, a mighty prince mourning
The fate of his lost friends and companions,
80   Knowing by its tracks that some demon had torn
His followers apart. He wept, fearing
The beginning might not be the end. And that night
Grendel came again, so set
On murder that no crime could ever be enough,
85   No savage assault quench his lust
For evil. Then each warrior tried
To escape him, searched for rest in different

Beds, as far from Herot as they could find,
Seeing how Grendel hunted when they slept.
90 Distance was safety; the only survivors
Were those who fled him. Hate had triumphed.
    So Grendel ruled, fought with the righteous,
One against many, and won; so Herot
Stood empty, and stayed deserted for years,
95 Twelve winters of grief for Hrothgar, king
Of the Danes, sorrow heaped at his door
By hell-forged hands.

Cantos 3–5

*Beowulf, the hero of this epic, hears of Grendel's deeds and vows
revenge. He has a ship built to carry him and his followers to
Hrothgar's aid. After a sea-journey, Beowulf and his men are challenged by one of Hrothgar's men who overlooks the coast. Beowulf
asks to be taken to see Hrothgar, king of the Danes. On being told
of this, Hrothgar remembers having known Beowulf as a child. He
asks that Beowulf be brought to him, and then Wulfgar, a servant of
Hrothgar, shows Beowulf in.*

Canto 6

. . . Then Wulfgar went to the door and addressed
The waiting seafarers with soldier's words:
100   "My lord, the great king of the Danes,[5] commands me
To tell you that he knows of your noble birth
And that having come to him from over the open
Sea you have come bravely and are welcome.
Now go to him as you are, in your armor and helmets,
105 But leave your battle-shields here, and your spears,
Let them lie waiting for the promises your words
May make."
                    Beowulf arose, with his men
Around him, ordering a few to remain
110 With their weapons, leading the others quickly
Along under Herot's steep roof into Hrothgar's
Presence. Standing on that prince's own hearth,
Helmeted, the silvery metal of his mail shirt
Gleaming with a smith's high art, he greeted
115 The Danes' great lord:

---

5. **the great king of the Danes.** Hrothgar

"Hail, Hrothgar!
Higlac[6] is my cousin and my king; the days
Of my youth have been filled with glory. Now Grendel's
Name has echoed in our land: sailors
120 Have brought us stories of Herot, the best
Of all mead-halls, deserted and useless when the moon
Hangs in skies the sun had lit,
Light and life fleeing together.
My people have said, the wisest, most knowing
125 And best of them, that my duty was to go to the Danes'
Great king. They have seen my strength for themselves,
Have watched me rise from the darkness of war,
Dripping with my enemies' blood. I drove
Five great giants into chains, chased
130 All of that race from the earth. I swam
In the blackness of night, hunting monsters
Out of the ocean, and killing them one
By one; death was my errand and the fate
They had earned. Now Grendel and I are called
135 Together, and I've come. Grant me, then,
Lord and protector of this noble place,
A single request! I have come so far,
O shelterer of warriors and your people's loved friend,
That this one favor you should not refuse me—
140 That I, alone and with the help of my men,
May <u>purge</u> all evil from this hall. I have heard,
Too, that the monster's scorn of men
Is so great that he needs no weapons and fears none.
Nor will I. My lord Higlac
145 Might think less of me if I let my sword
Go where my feet were afraid to, if I hid
Behind some broad linden[7] shield: my hands
Alone shall fight for me, struggle for life
Against the monster. God must decide
150 Who will be given to death's cold grip."

Beowulf plans to confront Grendel in the hall. He asks Hrothgar
to return his armor to Beowulf's king, Higlac, if he dies in the
confrontation.

---

6. **Higlac.** Higlac, King of the Geats, was Beowulf's feudal lord and uncle. The term *cousin* refers generally to any relative.
7. **linden.** Type of wood known for its strength

> **purge** (pʉrj) *v.*, cleanse or rid of impurities and other undesirable elements

Cantos 7–10

One of Hrothgar's thanes, or pledged warriors, named Unferth challenges Beowulf, doubting that he can best Grendel. Beowulf answers the challenge by telling a story about a mighty feat he performed as a boy, a swimming match against a man named Brecca. Beowulf tells how he encountered sea monsters while swimming and was dragged to the sea floor by one of them. He managed to escape and killed nine of the sea monsters. Beowulf then points out that no such brave tales are told about Unferth and accuses him of murdering his own brothers. Hrothgar is pleased by the tales and Beowulf's boldness of spirit. Hrothgar's wife then serves mead to the guests and thanks God for Beowulf's assistance. Hrothgar and his men retire for the night, leaving Beowulf and his men to face Grendel in the hall.

Canto 11

    Out from the marsh, from the foot of misty
Hills and bogs, bearing God's hatred,
Grendel came, hoping to kill
Anyone he could trap on this trip to high Herot.
155 He moved quickly through the cloudy night,
Up from his swampland, sliding silently
Toward that gold-shining hall. He had visited Hrothgar's
Home before, knew the way—
But never, before nor after that night,
160 Found Herot defended so firmly, his reception
So harsh. He journeyed, forever joyless,
Straight to the door, then snapped it open,
Tore its iron fasteners with a touch
And rushed angrily over the threshold.
165 He strode quickly across the inlaid
Floor, snarling and fierce: his eyes
Gleamed in the darkness, burned with a gruesome
Light. Then he stopped, seeing the hall
Crowded with sleeping warriors, stuffed
170 With rows of young soldiers resting together.
And his heart laughed, he <u>relished</u> the sight,
Intended to tear the life from those bodies
By morning; the monster's mind was hot
With the thought of food and the feasting his belly
175 Would soon know. But fate, that night, intended
Grendel to gnaw the broken bones

---

rel • ish (rel´ ish) *v.*, enjoy; like

Of his last human supper. Human
Eyes were watching his evil steps,
Waiting to see his swift hard claws.
180 Grendel snatched at the first Geat[8]
He came to, ripped him apart, cut
His body to bits with powerful jaws,
Drank the blood from his veins and <u>bolted</u>
Him down, hands and feet; death
185 And Grendel's great teeth came together,
Snapping life shut. Then he stepped to another
Still body, clutched at Beowulf with his claws,
Grasped at a strong-hearted wakeful sleeper
—And was instantly seized himself, claws
190 Bent back as Beowulf leaned up on one arm.
    That shepherd of evil, guardian of crime,
Knew at once that nowhere on earth
Had he met a man whose hands were harder;
His mind was flooded with fear—but nothing
195 Could take his talons and himself from that tight
Hard grip. Grendel's one thought was to run
From Beowulf, flee back to his marsh and hide there:
This was a different Herot than the hall he had emptied.
But Higlac's follower[9] remembered his final
200 Boast and, standing erect, stopped
The monster's flight, fastened those claws
In his fists till they cracked, clutched Grendel
Closer. The <u>infamous</u> killer fought
For his freedom, wanting no flesh but retreat,
205 Desiring nothing but escape; his claws
Had been caught, he was trapped. That trip to Herot
Was a miserable journey for the writhing monster!
    The high hall rang, its roof boards swayed,
And Danes shook with terror. Down
210 The aisles the battle swept, angry
And wild. Herot trembled, wonderfully
Built to withstand the blows, the struggling
Great bodies beating at its beautiful walls;
Shaped and fastened with iron, inside
215 And out, artfully worked, the building
Stood firm. Its benches rattled, fell

---

8. **Geat.** Beowulf's people, who are ruled by Higlac, are known as the Geats.
9. **Higlac's follower.** Beowulf

bolt (bōlt) *v.*, swallow (food) hurriedly; gulp down
in • fa • mous (in´ fə məs) *adj.*, having a bad reputation; notorious

To the floor, gold-covered boards grating
As Grendel and Beowulf battled across them.
Hrothgar's wise men had fashioned Herot

220 To stand forever; only fire,
They had planned, could shatter what such skill had put
Together, swallow in hot flames such splendor
Of ivory and iron and wood. Suddenly
The sounds changed, the Danes started

225 In new terror, <u>cowering</u> in their beds as the terrible
Screams of the Almighty's enemy sang
In the darkness, the horrible shrieks of pain
And defeat, the tears torn out of Grendel's
Taut throat, hell's captive caught in the arms

230 Of him who of all the men on earth
Was the strongest.

Canto 12

That mighty protector of men
Meant to hold the monster till its life
Leaped out, knowing the fiend was no use

235 To anyone in Denmark. All of Beowulf's
Band had jumped from their beds, ancestral
Swords raised and ready, determined
To protect their prince if they could. Their courage
Was great but all wasted: they could hack at Grendel

240 From every side, trying to open
A path for his evil soul, but their points
Could not hurt him, the sharpest and hardest iron
Could not scratch at his skin, for that sin-stained demon
Had bewitched all men's weapons, laid spells

245 That blunted every mortal man's blade.
And yet his time had come, his days
Were over, his death near; down
To hell he would go, swept groaning and helpless
To the waiting hands of still worse fiends.

250 Now he discovered—once the afflictor
Of men, tormentor of their days—what it meant
To feud with Almighty God: Grendel
Saw that his strength was deserting him, his claws
Bound fast, Higlac's brave follower tearing at

255 His hands. The monster's hatred rose higher,
But his power had gone. He twisted in pain,

---

cow • er (kou´ ər) *v.*, shrink and tremble, as from fear or cold

And the bleeding sinews deep in his shoulder
Snapped, muscle and bone split
And broke. The battle was over, Beowulf
260 Had been granted new glory: Grendel escaped,
But wounded as he was could flee to his den,
His miserable hole at the bottom of the marsh,
Only to die, to wait for the end
Of all his days. And after that bloody
265 Combat the Danes laughed with delight.
He who had come to them from across the sea,
Bold and strong-minded, had driven affliction
Off, purged Herot clean. He was happy,
Now, with that night's fierce work; the Danes
270 Had been served as he'd boasted he'd serve them; Beowulf,
A prince of the Geats, had killed Grendel,
Ended the grief, the sorrow, the suffering
Forced on Hrothgar's helpless people
By a bloodthirsty fiend. No Dane doubted
275 The victory, for the proof, hanging high
From the rafters where Beowulf had hung it, was the monster's
Arm, claw and shoulder and all.

Canto 13

And then, in the morning, crowds surrounded
Herot, warriors coming to that hall
280 From faraway lands, princes and leaders
Of men hurrying to behold the monster's
Great staggering tracks. They gaped with no sense
Of sorrow, felt no regret for his suffering,
Went tracing his bloody footprints, his beaten
285 And lonely flight, to the edge of the lake
Where he'd dragged his corpselike way, doomed
And already weary of his vanishing life.
The water was bloody, steaming and boiling
In horrible pounding waves, heat
290 Sucked from his magic veins; but the swirling
Surf had covered his death, hidden
Deep in murky darkness his miserable
End, as hell opened to receive him.
Then old and young rejoiced, turned back
295 From that happy pilgrimage, mounted their hard-hooved
Horses, high-spirited stallions, and rode them
Slowly toward Herot again, retelling
Beowulf's bravery as they jogged along.
And over and over they swore that nowhere

300   On earth or under the spreading sky
        Or between the seas, neither south nor north,
        Was there a warrior worthier to rule over men. . . .

Cantos 14–18

People gather from far and wide to praise Beowulf's mighty deed. Hrothgar promises to treat Beowulf, thereafter, as his own son, then commands that Herot be cleaned and decorated with golden tapestries in preparation for a feast. Beowulf's victory is rewarded by gifts of armor, horses, and weapons.

Beowulf's warriors receive gifts from Hrothgar, and the man whom Grendel killed is honored. The entertainment continues.

The scop finishes his song. Then Queen Welthow gives Beowulf presents—a corselet, rings, and a collar. After the feast, Hrothgar's thanes lie down to sleep in the hall, their armor beside them.

Canto 19

    . . . And now it was known that a monster had died
    But a monster still lived, and meant revenge.
305   She'd brooded on her loss, misery had brewed
    In her heart, that female horror, Grendel's
    Mother, living in the murky cold lake
    Assigned her since Cain had killed his only
    Brother, slain his father's son
310   With an angry sword. God drove him off,
    Outlawed him to the dry and barren desert,
    And branded him with a murderer's mark. And he bore
    A race of fiends accursed like their father;
    So Grendel was drawn to Herot, an outcast
315   Come to meet the man who awaited him.
    He'd snatched at Beowulf's arm, but that prince
    Remembered God's grace and the strength He'd given him
    And relied on the Lord for all the help,
    The comfort and support he would need. He killed
320   The monster, as God had meant him to do,
    Tore the fiend apart and forced him
    To run as rapidly as he could toward death's
    Cold waiting hands. His mother's sad heart,
    And her greed, drove her from her den on the dangerous
325   Pathway of revenge.[10]. . .

---

10. **Pathway of revenge.** Germanic custom required that the kin of a slain person avenge the death.

*Seeking vengeance, Grendel's mother kills Hrothgar's closest friend
and advisor and takes the severed arm of her son back to the fen.
Because Beowulf is not present, she is able to do as she wishes.
Hrothgar summons Beowulf for help.*

Cantos 20–21

*Hrothgar tells Beowulf of the loss of his trusted friend Aeschere,
and of the murderous mother of Grendel:*

"I've heard that my people, peasants working
In the fields, have seen a pair of such fiends
Wandering in the moors and marshes, giant
Monsters living in those desert lands.
330 And they've said to my wise men that, as well as they could see,
One of the devils was a female creature.
The other, they say, walked through the wilderness
Like a man—but mightier than any man.
They were frightened, and they fled, hoping to find help
335 In Herot. They named the huge one Grendel:
If he had a father no one knew him,
Or whether there'd been others before these two,
Hidden evil before hidden evil.
They live in secret places, windy
340 Cliffs, wolf-dens where water pours
From the rocks, then runs underground, where mist
Steams like black clouds, and the groves of trees
Growing out over their lake are all covered

With frozen spray, and wind down snakelike
345 Roots that reach as far as the water
And help keep it dark. At night that lake
Burns like a torch. No one knows its bottom,
No wisdom reaches such depths. A deer,
Hunted through the woods by packs of hounds,
350 A stag with great horns, though driven through the forest
From faraway places, prefers to die
On those shores, refuses to save its life
In that water. It isn't far, nor is it
A pleasant spot! When the wind stirs
355 And storms, waves splash toward the sky,
As dark as the air, as black as the rain
That the heavens weep. Our only help,
Again, lies with you. Grendel's mother
Is hidden in her terrible home, in a place
360 You've not seen. Seek it, if you dare! Save us,
Once more, and again twisted gold,
Heaped-up ancient treasure, will reward you
For the battle you win!"

. . .

Beowulf agrees to fight Grendel's maker, "this lady monster," and to avenge the death of Aeschere. Hrothgar and his men lead Beowulf to the water under which is Grendel's mother's cave. The water is filled with sea serpents and boils with blood. Beowulf dons a helmet and mail shirt, and borrows from one of Hrothgar's men the sword named Hrunting.

Canto 22

. . . As his words ended
365 He leaped into the lake, would not wait for anyone's
Answer; the heaving water covered him
Over. For hours he sank through the waves;
At last he saw the mud of the bottom.[11]
And all at once the greedy she-wolf
370 Who'd ruled those waters for half a hundred
Years discovered him, saw that a creature
From above had come to explore the bottom
Of her wet world. She welcomed him in her claws,
Clutched at him savagely but could not harm him,
375 Tried to work her fingers through the tight
Ring-woven mail on his breast, but tore

---

11. **For hours . . . bottom.** Such impossible feats are a common element, or *motif*, in folklore.

Anglo-Saxon Conventions

The epic *Beowulf* reveals several interesting conventions of Anglo-Saxon culture. For instance, during this time, a Germanic king would gather around him a group of loyal followers, known as *earls* or *thanes,* who shared his house and fought in his battles. The king earned his followers' loyalty through generosity, as demonstrated by holding feasts and dispensing gifts such as gold and silver, armor, and weapons.

Another Anglo-Saxon convention explains the ongoing warfare between Germanic tribes. According to Germanic law, the death of a family member, even if accidental, had to be paid for by the person responsible for the death. This payment was known as a *wergild,* which meant literally "man-price." If a payment was not made, the family

would avenge their member's death in battle to uphold the family's honor. Given this practice, blood feuds and battles were common among Germanic tribes.

Although these excerpts from *Beowulf* deal with three of the hero's brave exploits, the complete epic contains many references to the harshness of life and the fickleness of *Wyrd,* or fate. Anglo-Saxons viewed the world with pessimism, believing that everyone eventually would meet his or her doom. The most one could hope for was to do great deeds and live on after death through a gleeman's song.

    And scratched in vain. Then she carried him, armor
    And sword and all, to her home; he struggled
    To free his weapon, and failed. The fight
380 Brought other monsters swimming to see
    Her catch, a host of sea beasts who beat at
    His mail shirt, stabbing with tusks and teeth
    As they followed along. Then he realized, suddenly,
    That she'd brought him into someone's battle-hall,
385 And there the water's heat could not hurt him,
    Nor anything in the lake attack him through
    The building's high-arching roof. A brilliant
    Light burned all around him, the lake
    Itself like a fiery flame.
390   Then he saw
    The mighty water witch,[12] and swung his sword,
    His ring-marked blade, straight at her head;
    The iron sang its fierce song,
    Sang Beowulf's strength. But her guest
395 Discovered that no sword could slice her evil
    Skin, that Hrunting could not hurt her, was useless
    Now when he needed it. They wrestled, she ripped
    And tore and clawed at him, bit holes in his helmet,
    And that too failed him; for the first time in years
400 Of being worn to war it would earn no glory;

---

12. **mighty water witch.** Grendel's mother

It was the last time anyone would wear it. But Beowulf
Longed only for fame, leaped back
Into battle. He tossed his sword aside,
Angry; the steel-edged blade lay where
405 He'd dropped it. If weapons were useless he'd use
His hands, the strength in his fingers. So fame
Comes to the men who mean to win it
And care about nothing else! He raised
His arms and seized her by the shoulder; anger
410 Doubled his strength, he threw her to the floor.
She fell, Grendel's fierce mother, and the Geats'
Proud prince was ready to leap on her. But she rose
At once and repaid him with her clutching claws,
Wildly tearing at him. He was weary, that best
415 And strongest of soldiers; his feet stumbled
And in an instant she had him down, held helpless.
Squatting with her weight on his stomach, she drew
A dagger, brown with dried blood, and prepared
To avenge her only son. But he was stretched
420 On his back, and her stabbing blade was blunted
By the woven mail shirt he wore on his chest.
The hammered links held; the point
Could not touch him. He'd have traveled to the bottom of the earth,
Edgetho's son,[13] and died there, if that shining
425 Woven metal had not helped—and Holy
God, who sent him victory, gave judgment
For truth and right, Ruler of the Heavens,
Once Beowulf was back on his feet and fighting.

Canto 23

Then he saw, hanging on the wall, a heavy
430 Sword, hammered by giants,[14] strong
And blessed with their magic, the best of all weapons
But so massive that no ordinary man could lift
Its carved and decorated length. He drew it
From its scabbard,[15] broke the chain on its hilt,
435 And then, savage, now, angry
And desperate, lifted it high over his head
And struck with all the strength he had left,
Caught her in the neck and cut it through,
Broke bones and all. Her body fell

---

13. **Edgetho's son.** Beowulf
14. **giants.** *Beowulf* contains many references to giants. Some echo Genesis 6:3: "In those days
   there were giants on the earth."
15. **scabbard.** Sheath for a sword

440 To the floor, lifeless, the sword was wet
With her blood, and Beowulf rejoiced at the sight.
    The brilliant light shone, suddenly,
As though burning in that hall, and as bright as Heaven's
Own candle,[16] lit in the sky. He looked
445 At her home, then following along the wall
Went walking, his hands tight on the sword,
His heart still angry. He was hunting another
Dead monster, and took his weapons with him
For final revenge against Grendel's vicious
450 Attacks, his nighttime raids, over
And over, coming to Herot when Hrothgar's
Men slept, killing them in their beds,
Eating some on the spot, fifteen
Or more, and running to his loathsome moor
455 With another such sickening meal waiting
In his pouch. But Beowulf repaid him for those visits,
Found him lying dead in his corner,
Armless, exactly as that fierce fighter
Had sent him out from Herot, then struck off
460 His head with a single swift blow. The body
Jerked for the last time, then lay still.

*The men waiting on the shore see the water
turn red and fear for Beowulf.*

*After the blade of Beowulf's sword melts,
Beowulf swims to shore with the jeweled
hilt and Grendel's head. He is greeted
with much rejoicing. Beowulf presents
Grendel's head to Hrothgar.*

Cantos 24–30

*Beowulf tells Hrothgar of his adven-
ture and gives the king the hilt of Grendel's
mother's sword, which is decorated with ancient
runic[17] letters describing the war of the giants before
Noah's flood. Beowulf returns the sword Hrunting to Hun-
ferth. Graciously, he says nothing about how the sword had
failed him. Then Beowulf and his men set sail for the land of the
Geats, their home.*

*Once home, Beowulf recounts his adventures and the gifts that
he received in the land of the Danes.*

---

16. **Heaven's / Own candle.** The sun
17. **runic.** Ancient Germanic alphabet

Canto 31

. . . Afterwards, in the time when Higlac was dead
And Herdred, his son, who'd ruled the Geats
After his father, had followed him into darkness—
465 Killed in battle with the Swedes, who smashed
His shield, cut through the soldiers surrounding
Their king—then, when Higd's one son
Was gone, Beowulf ruled in Geatland,
Took the throne he'd refused, once,
470 And held it long and well. He was old
With years and wisdom, fifty winters
A king, when a dragon awoke from its darkness
And dreams and brought terror to his people. The beast
Had slept in a huge stone tower, with a hidden
475 Path beneath; a man stumbled on
The entrance, went in, discovered the ancient
Treasure, the pagan jewels and gold
The dragon had been guarding, and dazzled and greedy
Stole a gem-studded cup, and fled.
480 But now the dragon hid nothing, neither
The theft nor itself; it swept through the darkness,
And all Geatland knew its anger.

Cantos 32–34

*Furious at the theft of the cup, the dragon begins attacking the
countryside and setting fire to buildings by night. Having made up his
mind to fight the dragon, Beowulf and some companions go to view the
monster in his lair. Sitting some distance from the dragon, the companions listen to Beowulf tell of other battles and of other warriors slain.*

Canto 35

. . . And Beowulf uttered his final boast:
   "I've never known fear; as a youth I fought
485 In endless battles. I am old, now,
But I will fight again, seek fame still,
If the dragon hiding in his tower dares
To face me."
            Then he said farewell to his followers,
490 Each in his turn, for the last time:
   "I'd use no sword, no weapon, if this beast
Could be killed without it, crushed to death

Like Grendel, gripped in my hands and torn
Limb from limb. But his breath will be burning
495 Hot, poison will pour from his tongue.
I feel no shame, with shield and sword
And armor, against this monster: when he comes to me
I mean to stand, not run from his shooting
Flames, stand till fate decides
500 Which of us wins. My heart is firm,
My hands calm: I need no hot
Words. Wait for me close by, my friends.
We shall see, soon, who will survive
This bloody battle, stand when the fighting
505 Is done. No one else could do
What I mean to, here, no man but me
Could hope to defeat this monster. No one
Could try. And this dragon's treasure, his gold
And everything hidden in that tower, will be mine
510 Or war will sweep me to a bitter death!"
        Then Beowulf rose, still brave, still strong,
And with his shield at his side, and a mail shirt on his breast,
Strode calmly, confidently, toward the tower, under
The rocky cliffs: no coward could have walked there!
515 And then he who'd endured dozens of desperate
Battles, who'd stood boldly while swords and shields
Clashed, the best of kings, saw
Huge stone arches and felt the heat
Of the dragon's breath, flooding down
520 Through the hidden entrance, too hot for anyone
To stand, a streaming current of fire
And smoke that blocked all passage. And the Geats'
Lord and leader, angry, lowered
His sword and roared out a battle cry,
525 A call so loud and clear that it reached through
The <u>hoary</u> rock, hung in the dragon's
Ear. The beast rose, angry,
Knowing a man had come—and then nothing
But war could have followed. Its breath came first,
530 A steaming cloud pouring from the stone,
Then the earth itself shook. Beowulf
Swung his shield into place, held it
In front of him, facing the entrance. The dragon
Coiled and uncoiled, its heart urging it
535 Into battle. Beowulf's ancient sword

hoary (hôr´ ē) *adj.,* gray or white with age; extremely old

Was waiting, unsheathed, his sharp and gleaming
Blade. The beast came closer; both of them
Were ready, each set on slaughter. The Geats'
Great prince stood firm, unmoving, prepared
540 Behind his high shield, waiting in his shining
Armor. The monster came quickly toward him,
Pouring out fire and smoke, hurrying
To its fate. Flames beat at the iron
Shield, and for a time it held, protected
545 Beowulf as he'd planned; then it began to melt,
And for the first time in his life that famous prince
Fought with fate against him, with glory
Denied him. He knew it, but he raised his sword
And struck at the dragon's scaly hide.
550 The ancient blade broke, bit into
The monster's skin, drew blood, but cracked
And failed him before it went deep enough, helped him
Less than he needed. The dragon leaped
With pain, thrashed and beat at him, spouting
555 Murderous flames, spreading them everywhere.
And the Geats' ring-giver did not boast of glorious
Victories in other wars: his weapon
Had failed him, deserted him, now when he needed it
Most, that excellent sword. Edgetho's
560 Famous son[18] stared at death,
Unwilling to leave this world, to exchange it
For a dwelling in some distant place—a journey
Into darkness that all men must make, as death
Ends their few brief hours on earth.
565　　Quickly, the dragon came at him, encouraged
As Beowulf fell back; its breath flared,
And he suffered, wrapped around in swirling
Flames—a king, before, but now
A beaten warrior. None of his comrades
570 Came to him, helped him, his brave and noble
Followers; they ran for their lives, fled
Deep in a wood. And only one of them
Remained, stood there, miserable, remembering,
As a good man must, what kinship should mean.

Canto 36

575　　His name was Wiglaf, he was Wexstan's son
And a good soldier; his family had been Swedish,

---

18. **Edgetho's / Famous son.** Beowulf

Once. Watching Beowulf, he could see
How his king was suffering, burning. Remembering
Everything his lord and cousin had given him,
580 Armor and gold and the great estates
Wexstan's family enjoyed, Wiglaf's
Mind was made up; he raised his yellow
Shield and drew his sword . . .
    Then he ran to his king, crying encouragement
585 As he drove through the dragon's deadly fumes:
   "Beloved Beowulf, remember how you boasted,
Once, that nothing in the world would ever
Destroy your fame: fight to keep it,
Now, be strong and brave, my noble
590 King, protecting life and fame
Together. My sword will fight at your side!"
    The dragon heard him, the man-hating monster,
And was angry; shining with surging flames
It came for him, anxious to return his visit.
595 Waves of fire swept at his shield
And the edge began to burn. His mail shirt
Could not help him, but before his hands dropped
The blazing wood Wiglaf jumped
Behind Beowulf's shield; his own was burned
600 To ashes. Then the famous old hero, remembering
Days of glory, lifted what was left
Of Nagling, his ancient sword, and swung it
With all his strength, smashed the gray
Blade into the beast's head. But then Nagling
605 Broke to pieces, as iron always

Had in Beowulf's hands. His arms
Were too strong, the hardest blade could not help him,
The most wonderfully worked. He carried them to war
But fate had decreed that the Geats' great king
610 Would be no better for any weapon.
　　Then the monster charged again, vomiting
Fire, wild with pain, rushed out
Fierce and dreadful, its fear forgotten.
Watching for its chance it drove its tusks
615 Into Beowulf's neck; he staggered, the blood
Came flooding forth, fell like rain.

Canto 37

　　And then when Beowulf needed him most
Wiglaf showed his courage, his strength
And skill, and the boldness he was born with. Ignoring
620 The dragon's head, he helped his lord
By striking lower down. The sword
Sank in; his hand was burned, but the shining
Blade had done its work, the dragon's
Belching flames began to flicker
625 And die away. And Beowulf drew
His battle-sharp dagger: the blood-stained old king
Still knew what he was doing. Quickly, he cut
The beast in half, slit it apart.
It fell, their courage had killed it, two noble
630 Cousins had joined in the dragon's death.
Yet what they did all men must do
When the time comes! But the triumph was the last
Beowulf would ever earn, the end
Of greatness and life together. The wound
635 In his neck began to swell and grow;
He could feel something stirring, burning
In his veins, a stinging venom, and knew
The beast's fangs had left it. He fumbled
Along the wall, found a slab
640 Of stone, and dropped down; above him he saw
Huge stone arches and heavy posts,
Holding up the roof of that giant hall.
Then Wiglaf's gentle hands bathed
The blood-stained prince, his glorious lord,
645 Weary of war, and loosened his helmet.
　　Beowulf spoke, in spite of the swollen,
Livid wound, knowing he'd unwound

His string of days on earth, seen
As much as God would grant him; all worldly
650 Pleasure was gone, as life would go,
Soon:
      "I'd leave my armor to my son,
Now, if God had given me an heir,
A child born of my body, his life
655 Created from mine. I've worn this crown
For fifty winters: no neighboring people
Have tried to threaten the Geats, sent soldiers
Against us or talked of terror. My days
Have gone by as fate willed, waiting
660 For its word to be spoken, ruling as well
As I knew how, swearing no unholy oaths,
Seeking no lying wars. I can leave
This life happy; I can die, here,
Knowing the Lord of all life has never
665 Watched me wash my sword in blood
Born of my own family. Beloved
Wiglaf, go, quickly, find
The dragon's treasure: we've taken its life,
But its gold is ours, too. Hurry,
670 Bring me ancient silver, precious
Jewels, shining armor and gems,
Before I die. Death will be softer,
Leaving life and this people I've ruled
So long, if I look at this last of all prizes."

Canto 38

675 . . . Then Wiglaf went back, anxious
To return while Beowulf was alive, to bring him
Treasure they'd won together. He ran,
Hoping his wounded king, weak
And dying, had not left the world too soon.
680 Then he brought their treasure to Beowulf, and found
His famous king bloody, gasping
For breath. But Wiglaf sprinkled water
Over his lord, until the words
Deep in his breast broke through and were heard.
685 Beholding the treasure he spoke, haltingly:
    "For this, this gold, these jewels, I thank
Our Father in heaven, Ruler of the Earth—
For all of this, that His grace has given me,
Allowed me to bring to my people while breath

690 Still came to my lips. I sold my life
For this treasure, and I sold it well. Take
What I leave, Wiglaf, lead my people,
Help them; my time is gone. Have
The brave Geats build me a tomb,
695 When the funeral flames have burned me, and build it
Here, at the water's edge, high
On this spit of land, so sailors can see
This tower, and remember my name, and call it
Beowulf's tower, and boats in the darkness
700 And mist, crossing the sea, will know it."
    Then that brave king gave the golden
Necklace from around his throat to Wiglaf,
Gave him his gold-covered helmet, and his rings,
And his mail shirt, and ordered him to use them well:
705   "You're the last of all our far-flung family.
Fate has swept our race away,
Taken warriors in their strength and led them
To the death that was waiting. And now I follow them."
    The old man's mouth was silent, spoke
710 No more, had said as much as it could;
He would sleep in the fire, soon. His soul
Left his flesh, flew to glory.

*The men who had fled to the forest return and are reproved by
Wiglaf. Wiglaf then sends a messenger to tell of Beowulf's death.*

*The men go to the dragon's lair, where they see the bodies of the
beast and of their king. Wiglaf and seven others load a cart with the
dragon's treasure.*

Canto 43

*The people prepare a large pyre[19] and mourn Beowulf. They build a
memorial to him and remember his great deeds.*

    A huge heap of wood was ready,
Hung around with helmets, and battle
715 Shields, and shining mail shirts, all
As Beowulf had asked. The bearers brought
Their beloved lord, their glorious king,
And weeping laid him high on the wood.
Then the warriors began to kindle that greatest
720 Of funeral fires; smoke rose

---

19. **pyre.** Combustible heap for burning a dead body as a funeral rite

Above the flames, black and thick,
And while the wind blew and the fire
Roared they wept, and Beowulf's body
Crumbled and was gone. The Geats stayed,
725 Moaning their sorrow, <u>lamenting</u> their lord;
A gnarled old woman, hair wound
Tight and gray on her head, groaned
A song of misery, of infinite sadness
And days of mourning, of fear and sorrow

la • ment (lə ment´) v., express sorrow, mourning, or regret, often in a demonstrative way

730   To come, slaughter and terror and captivity.
        And Heaven swallowed the billowing smoke.
           Then the Geats built the tower, as Beowulf
        Had asked, strong and tall, so sailors
        Could find it from far and wide; working
735   For ten long days they made his monument,
        Sealed his ashes in walls as straight
        And high as wise and willing hands
        Could raise them. And the riches he and Wiglaf
        Had won from the dragon, rings, necklaces,
740   Ancient, hammered armor—all
        The treasures they'd taken were left there, too,
        Silver and jewels buried in the sandy
        Ground, back in the earth, again
        And forever hidden and useless to men.
745   And then twelve of the bravest Geats
        Rode their horses around the tower,
        Telling their sorrow, telling stories
        Of their dead king and his greatness, his glory,
        Praising him for heroic deeds, for a life
750   As noble as his name. So should all men
        Raise up words for their lords, warm
        With love, when their shield and protector leaves
        His body behind, sends his soul
        On high. And so Beowulf's followers
755   Rode, mourning their beloved leader,
        Crying that no better king had ever
        Lived, no prince so mild, no man
        So open to his people, so deserving of praise. ❖

MIRRORS & WINDOWS

In lines 125–128, Beowulf states that because he is the best warrior, it is his duty to come to the aid of Hrothgar's court. What responsibilities do leaders have to the people they represent? What roles or duties are they expected to fulfill?

Literature Connection

John Champlin Gardner (1933–1982) is perhaps best known for his novel **Grendel** (1971), a retelling of scenes from the epic poem *Beowulf* from the perspective of the monster. Gardner wrote several other novels, including *The Sunlight Dialogues* (1972), as well as poetry, literary criticism, and children's books based on medieval stories.

A teacher of creative writing and medieval studies at numerous colleges and workshops, Gardner collected his advice on writing literature in the books *On Moral Fiction*, *On Becoming a Novelist*, and *The Art of Fiction*. As you read the excerpt from *Grendel*, consider how it relates to *Beowulf*.

from

Grendel

by John Champlin Gardner

Then, with a sigh, a kind of moan, I start very carefully down the cliffs that lead to the fens and moors and Hrothgar's hall. Owls cross my path as silently as raiding ships, and at the sound of my foot, lean wolves rise, glance at me awkwardly, and, neat of step as lizards, sneak away. I used to take some pride in that—the caution of owls when my shape looms in, the alarm I stir in these giant northern wolves. I was younger then. Still playing cat and mouse with the universe.

I move down through the darkness, burning with murderous lust, my brains raging at the sickness I can observe in myself as objectively as might a mind ten centuries away. Stars, spattered out through lifeless night from end to end, like jewels scattered in a dead king's grave, tease, torment my wits toward meaningful patterns that do not exist. I can see for miles from these rock walls: thick forest suddenly still at my coming—cowering stags, wolves, hedgehogs, boars, submerged in their stifling, unmemorable fear; mute birds, pulsating,[1] thoughtless clay in hushed old trees, thick limbs interlocked to seal drab secrets in.

---

1. **pulsating.** Quickly vibrating or throbbing

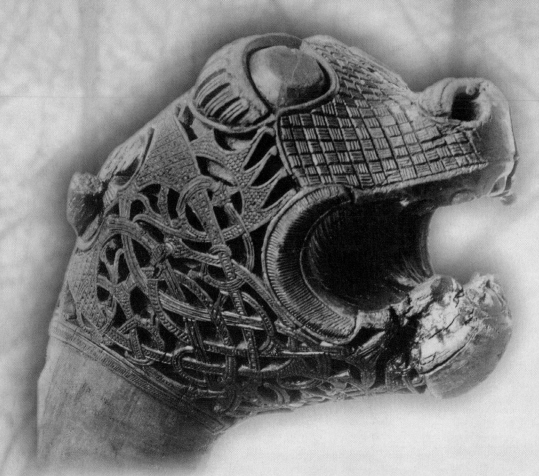

I sigh, sink into the silence, and cross it like wind. Behind my back, at the world's end, my pale slightly glowing fat mother sleeps on, old, sick at heart, in our dingy underground room. Life-bloated, baffled, long-suffering hag. Guilty, she imagines, of some unremembered, perhaps ancestral crime. (She must have some human in her.) Not that she thinks. Not that she dissects and ponders the dusty mechanical bits of her miserable life's curse. She clutches at me in her sleep as if to crush me. I break away. "Why are we here?" I used to ask her. "Why do we stand this putrid,[2] stinking hole?" She trembles at my words. Her fat lips shake. "Don't ask!" her wiggling claws implore. (She never speaks.) "Don't ask!" It must be some terrible secret, I used to think. I'd give her a crafty squint. She'll tell me, in time, I thought. But she told me nothing. I waited on. That was before the old dragon,[3] calm as winter, unveiled the truth. He was not a friend.

And so I come through trees and towns to the lights of Hrothgar's meadhall. I am no stranger here. A respected guest. Eleven years now and going on twelve I have come up this clean-mown central hill, dark shadow out of the woods below, and have knocked politely on the high oak door, bursting its hinges and sending the shock of my greeting inward like a cold blast out of a cave. "Grendel!" they squeak, and I smile like exploding spring. The old Shaper,[4] a man I cannot help but admire, goes out the back window with his harp at a single bound, though blind as a bat. The drunkest of Hrothgar's thanes come reeling and clanking down from their wall-hung beds, all shouting their meady, outrageous boasts, their

---

2. **putrid.** Rotten; foul
3. **old dragon.** Earlier in the novel, Grendel visits a dragon, who offers him advice and bits of wisdom.
4. **Shaper.** Anglo-Saxon bard, who creates and recites songs and poems

heavy swords aswirl like eagles' wings. "Woe, woe, woe!" cries Hrothgar, hoary with winters, peeking in, wide-eyed, from his bedroom in back. His wife, looking in behind him, makes a scene. The thanes in the meadhall blow out the lights and cover the wide stone fireplace with shields. I laugh, crumple over; I can't help myself. In the darkness, I alone see clear as day. While they squeal and screech and bump into each other, I silently sack up my dead and withdraw to the woods. I eat and laugh and eat until I can barely walk, my chest-hair matted with dribbled blood, and then the roosters on the hill crow, and dawn comes over the roofs of the houses, and all at once I am filled with gloom again.

"This is some punishment sent us," I hear them bawling from the hill.

My head aches. Morning nails my eyes.

"Some god is angry," I hear a woman keen. "The people of Scyld and Herogar and Hrothgar are mired[5] in sin!"

My belly rumbles, sick on their sour meat. I crawl through bloodstained leaves to the eaves of the forest, and there peek out. The dogs fall silent at the edge of my spell, and where the king's hall surmounts[6] the town, the blind old Shaper, harp clutched tight to his fragile chest, stares futilely[7] down, straight at me. Otherwise nothing. Pigs root dully at the posts of a wooden fence. A rumple-horned ox lies chewing in dew and shade. A few men, lean, wearing animal skins, look up at the gables of the king's hall, or at the vultures circling casually beyond. Hrothgar says nothing, hoarfrost-bearded, his features cracked and crazed. Inside, I hear the people praying— whimpering, whining, mumbling, pleading—to their numerous sticks and stones. He doesn't go in. The king has lofty theories of his own.

"Theories," I whisper to the bloodstained ground. So the dragon once spoke. ("They'd map out roads through Hell with their crackpot theories!" I recall his laugh.)

Then the groaning and praying stop, and on the side of the hill the dirge-slow shoveling begins. ❖

---

5. **mired.** Entangled or caught in
6. **surmounts.** Stands or lies above
7. **futilely.** Without purpose or effect

Review Questions

1. For how many years has Grendel been a visitor to Hrothgar's meadhall? How does Grendel characterize his visit? Contrast his description of the visit with the reaction of the thanes.

2. Identify the different emotions Grendel displays in this excerpt. Critique Gardner's version of the tale, which is told through Grendel's eyes. Does it seem probable? Why or why not?

3. What did the dragon once say to Grendel? Speculate what theories Hrothgar may have that differ from those of the townspeople.

TEXT ⇄ᵀᴼ TEXT CONNECTION

What scene from *Beowulf* is portrayed in this excerpt? What elements in the text reveal the scene? Do you feel differently about Grendel after reading this excerpt? Why or why not?

Refer to Text ▶ ▶ ▶ ▶ ▶	Reason with Text	
1a. Who is Beowulf? Why does he come to the land of the Danes?	**1b.** Explain what motivates Beowulf to travel across the sea to help Hrothgar.	**Understand** Find meaning
2a. List the requests that Hrothgar makes of Beowulf during the time Beowulf spends with the Danes.	**2b.** What could Hrothgar ask of Beowulf that Beowulf would refuse? Why would Beowulf refuse?	**Apply** Use information
3a. What battles are fought by Beowulf in this excerpt?	**3b.** Compare and contrast the battles, identifying similarities and differences among them.	**Analyze** Take things apart
4a. Describe Grendel's interactions with humans. Why do the Danes consider him a monster?	**4b.** Imagine that Grendel is on trial for his actions at Herot. Defend him using lines from the text as your evidence.	**Evaluate** Make judgments
5a. Identify several biblical references in the poem.	**5b.** Why were biblical events used in the retelling of this epic? Explain how the biblical elements help link parts of the story and give it greater meaning.	**Create** Bring ideas together

Analyze Literature

Alliteration and Motif

Identify five examples of alliteration in the poem. Considering that epic poems were memorized and recited for entertainment, why might alliteration have been a useful tool?

What examples of motifs did you find in *Beowulf*? In which famous literary works do they appear? Why might these motifs reappear throughout literature?

Extend the Text

Writing Options

Creative Writing Write a script for a brief scene in an adventure movie about Beowulf. Decide how to update the dialogue and action to appeal to a contemporary audience.

Expository Writing Draft an essay that analyzes how the modern *Grendel,* by John Gardner, relates to the ancient *Beowulf.* You might consider how the themes of each work relate to the Germanic society of its time; you might compare the portrayals of Grendel; or you might choose another topic to explore.

Collaborative Learning

Compare Cultures Work in small groups to analyze the boasts made by human characters in *Beowulf.* Then compare and contrast the Anglo-Saxon idea of a boast to that of modern culture. How has the concept changed?

Who in modern culture is known for boasting? Why? In a class discussion, compare your group's ideas with those of other groups.

Lifelong Learning

Conduct a Survey Working with a small group, compile a list of questions that will identify what the people around you value—for instance, What personal accomplishment are you most proud of? and What do you want to be remembered for? Then survey a random sample of people. As you listen and record their answers, seek clarification if you do not understand their responses. Separate the surveys into two groups (perhaps by gender or age) and compare the results. Discuss with the class the responses you gathered. Finally, discuss what you and your group members learned by participating in the activity.

 Go to **www.mirrorsandwindows.com** for more.

Understand the Concept

Although Anglo-Saxon literature often is considered dark in its portrayal of life's harsh realities, the poetry of the time is rich in its use of language. One commonly used literary device is the **kenning,** an imaginative combination of words coined to replace a common noun. For instance, poets created kennings such as *whale-road, swan-road,* and *seal-bath* to replace the word *ocean,* along with *battle-flame* for *sword, wave-floater* for *ship,* and *bone-house* for *body.*

Using kennings, Anglo-Saxon poets created vivid images, or word pictures, and thus portrayed common subjects in unique ways. In this sense, kennings are metaphors. The use of kennings also allowed poets to experiment with rhythm and sound. The complete *Beowulf* epic contains more than one thousand kennings. Even the word *Beowulf,* which is in Modern English *bee-wolf,* is a kenning for *bear.*

The practice of combining words has continued into modern times with the widespread use of **compound words,** in which two or more words are joined to create a single meaning. Examples of modern compounds are *newspaper, fireplace, thumbprint,* and *courthouse.* **Compound nouns** like these that are written as one word, with no space or punctuation, are called *closed compounds.* In other compound nouns, the words are joined with a hyphen, as in *runner-up* and *ten-year-old,* or left open, as in *master builder* and *high school.*

Perhaps the most commonly used compounds are **compound adjectives,** such as *part-time, two-year,* and *follow-up.* Many compound adjectives are hyphenated, but others are closed, such as *childproof* and *trustworthy.* By joining words to form compound adjectives, writers can create specific, unique descriptors, often with subtle shades of meaning. For instance, in *Beowulf,* the description of a *battle-sharp dagger* suggests the context or use of the weapon.

Compounds that are created for specific instances and used infrequently are called *temporary compounds.* Compounds that become accepted into everyday usage are called *permanent compounds* and appear in the dictionary.

Apply the Skill

Exercise A
Identify the compound adjective or adjectives in each of the following sentences. For each compound, suggest a single word that could be used in its place. For example, the single word *brave* could be substituted for *strong-hearted* in the phrase *strong-hearted king.* Explain any difference in meaning between the single adjective and the compound.

1. *Beowulf* is a symbol-laden epic poem from the Anglo-Saxon Era.
2. It was composed by an unknown poet in the northern part of present-day Great Britain.
3. Robin Lamb produced a word-for-word translation of the original epic, which was written in Old English.
4. The poem's characters are Geats and Danes from Scandinavia, which are Germanic-related peoples.
5. The character Beowulf may be based on a historical figure, but the story places him in farfetched, fantasy-filled situations.

Exercise B
Look up each of the following words in the dictionary, and find four permanent compounds that can be created using it, whether nouns or adjectives. Write down each compound in its correct form—closed (one word), open (two words), or hyphenated—and use it in a sentence.

1. first
2. new
3. bird
4. low
5. snow

SPELLING PRACTICE

Compound Words

Spelling compound words correctly means knowing which compounds are open, closed, and hyphenated. Review this list of compound words from *Beowulf,* noting which are compounds nouns versus adjectives.

battle-shield	gold-covered	ring-giver
blood-stained	high-spirited	seafarer
bloodthirsty	kinsmen	snakelike
countryside	mail shirt	steel-edged
daybreak	man-hating	strong-minded
faraway	meadhall	swampland
farewell	outcast	underground
footprint	pathway	wolf-den

The Head of Humbaba

from Gilgamesh

Verse Translation by Herbert Mason

The epic **Gilgamesh** is based on the life of an ancient Babylonian king who ruled over the city of Uruk nearly five thousand years ago. In the epic, Gilgamesh is said to be superhuman: two-thirds god and one-third human. He is a harsh ruler of his people until he befriends Enkidu, a wild boy who was born and raised among the animals of the forest. Gradually, Gilgamesh and Enkidu form a bond that transforms each into a gentler, wiser being.

After becoming bored with life in Uruk, Gilgamesh plans an adventure for Enkidu and himself. They are to travel to the famous cedar forest to collect wood for the city. In order to take the cedar, the friends will have to kill a monster named Humbaba, the keeper of the forest. Gilgamesh and Enkidu are nervous about their impending encounter with Humbaba.

The translator of this selection, **Herbert Mason,** is a professor of history and religion at Boston University. In addition to his retelling of *Gilgamesh,* Mason has written several novels; a novella; collections of essays, reflections, and poetry; a dramatic poem; and translations of various texts. *Gilgamesh: A Verse Narrative* was a nominee for the 1971 National Book Award.

Clay mask of Humbaba's head from Sippar, Southern Iraq, c. 1800 BCE. British Museum, London, Great Britain.

> At dawn Gilgamesh raised his ax
> And struck at the great cedar.
> When Humbaba heard the sound of falling trees,
> He hurried down the path that they had seen
> 5 But only he had traveled. Gilgamesh felt weak
> At the sound of Humbaba's footsteps and called
>   to Shamash[1]
> Saying, I have followed you in the way decreed;[2]
> Why am I abandoned now? Suddenly the winds
> Sprang up. They saw the great head of Humbaba
> 10 Like a water buffalo's bellowing down the path,
> His huge and clumsy legs, his flailing[3] arms
> Thrashing at phantoms in his precious trees.
> His single stroke could cut a cedar down
> And leave no mark on him. His shoulders,
> 15 Like a porter's[4] under building stones,
> Were permanently bent by what he bore;
> He was the slave who did the work for gods
> But whom the gods would never notice.
> Monstrous in his contortion,[5] he aroused
> 20 The two almost to pity.
> But pity was the thing that might have killed.
> It made them pause just long enough to show

1. **Shamash.** The sun god of Sumerian mythology. Shamash has promised Gilgamesh's mother that he will look after Gilgamesh and guide him in his conflict with Humbaba.
2. **decreed.** Ordered or commanded, as in a law
3. **flailing.** Thrashing or swinging wildly
4. **porter's.** One who transports, or carries, objects
5. **contortion.** Twisted or malformed feature; deformity

Bronze sculpture of Babylonian king (c. 2250 BCE).

How pitiless he was to them. Gilgamesh in horror saw
Him strike the back of Enkidu and beat him to the ground
25   Until he thought his friend was crushed to death.
He stood still watching as the monster leaned to make
His final strike against his friend, unable
To move to help him, and then Enkidu slid
Along the ground like a ram making its final lunge
30   On wounded knees. Humbaba fell and seemed
To crack the ground itself in two, and Gilgamesh,
As if this fall had snapped him from his daze,
Returned to life
And stood over Humbaba with his ax
35   Raised high above his head watching the monster plead
In strangled sobs and desperate appeals
The way the sea contorts under a violent squall[6]
I'll serve you as I served the gods, Humbaba said;

---

6. **squall.** Harsh storm that appears suddenly

I'll build you houses from their sacred trees.
40　Enkidu feared his friend was weakening
And called out: Gilgamesh! Don't trust him!
As if there were some hunger in himself
That Gilgamesh was feeling
That turned him momentarily to yearn
45　For someone who would serve, he paused;
And then he raised his ax up higher
And swung it in a perfect arc
Into Humbaba's neck. He reached out
To touch the wounded shoulder of his friend,
50　And late that night he reached again
To see if he was yet asleep, but there was only
Quiet breathing. The stars against the midnight sky
Were sparkling like mica[7] in a riverbed.
In the slight breeze
55　The head of Humbaba was swinging from a tree. ❖

7. **mica.** Crystal-like mineral, often characterized by a colorful luster

Based on your personal definition of *hero,* whom do you consider the hero of this passage: Gilgamesh, Enkidu, or Humbaba?

Refer and Reason

1. Analyze the individual actions of Gilgamesh, Enkidu, and Humbaba. Which character displays the most confidence? Explain your choice.

2. Evaluate Gilgamesh as a hero. What strengths and weaknesses does he have? What kind of friend is he to Enkidu? Is Gilgamesh an admirable hero? Why or why not?

3. Recall some of Beowulf's heroic traits. How might Beowulf have handled the battle with Humbaba? How might Gilgamesh have handled the situation with Grendel? Who is the greater hero: Beowulf or Gilgamesh? Explain.

Writing Options

1. The cities and communities surrounding the great cedar forest do not know that Humbaba has been slain. Write a public service announcement proclaiming his death and the facts of how he died and emphasizing that the cedar forest is now safe for humans to visit.

2. Imagine that a high school class five thousand years in the future will study an epic poem about a hero from today. Choose a person from current society, and write a brief epic poem that tells the story of a heroic episode from his or her life. Determine what qualities of modern-day society you want to represent in your epic. Include slang and sayings commonly used today, and provide a glossary with definitions and usage notes to help your readers understand the poem. Refer to a print or online dictionary of current slang, such as *The Oxford Dictionary of Slang,* for help in writing the poem and compiling the glossary.

 Go to **www.mirrorsandwindows.com** for more.

The Sumerian Civilization

The epic of Gilgamesh is an ancient Sumerian text that probably was written around 2000 BCE. The Sumerian civilization was centered in the southern part of Mesopotamia, or modern-day Iraq. It is one of the earliest examples of human civilization, existing from about 5300 BCE until 1730 BCE.

One of the greatest challenges the ancient Sumerians faced was the arid climate of Mesopotamia. This area received less than five inches of rainfall a year, making it extremely difficult to develop a sustainable agricultural system. To resolve this problem, Sumerian farmers invented the technique of irrigation. They dug ditches along the banks of the Tigris and Euphrates Rivers and funneled the water into their farmlands, providing a limitless supply of water for growing crops.

The Sumerians invented several other technologies still in use today. They were among the first people to use glue, math, wheels, boats, and beer. In addition, they divided time into the increments used in the modern world and constructed a twelve-month calendar. The Sumerians also were the first people to keep detailed statistical records of their own population, and they developed advanced legal systems to mete out justice.

The Sumerian inventive spirit was remarkable, but it ultimately led to the civilization's downfall. The dry desert soil simply could not withstand repeated harvesting, even with irrigation. Crop yields started to diminish around the end of the third millennium BCE, which devastated the Sumerian population. As Sumerian institutions began to crumble, the remaining citizens abandoned their empire and joined the Babylonians in the north.

Sumerian mosaic.

The Seafarer

An Elegy, Anonymous, Translated by Burton Raffel

The Wife's Lament

An Elegy, Anonymous, Translated by Marcelle Thiébaux

Build Background

Literary Context The poem **"The Seafarer"** probably was composed in the eighth century by a sailor. It shows extensive familiarity with the weather and wildlife experienced by a seafarer of the North Sea. It also presents the conflicting feelings of a sailor who loves the sea but hates the hardships of sea life.
   "The Wife's Lament" is unusual among Anglo-Saxon poems because it is one of the few to explore a woman's point of view. Many literary scholars have debated whether "The Wife's Lament" is secular or explores Christian themes. It is difficult to say, as the details of the plot in the poem are sketchy. Some scholars have suggested that the poem is based on a story that would have been well known to Anglo-Saxon readers and listeners.

Cultural Context Both of these poems explore the concept of *exile,* a fear that Anglo-Saxons explore repeatedly in their literature. Early Anglo-Saxons lived in small, closely knit groups, and many of the people in the groups were blood relatives. Life was harsh for those who were part of a group, but anyone who was made an outcast or otherwise cut off from the group would have had enormous difficulty surviving. Old English poems often celebrate ties to family, ruler, and community and emphasize how terrible it is not to have these connections.

Reader's Context What would it be like to live in exile, cut off from your family, friends, and community? What would you miss the most? Why?

Meet the Authors

The authors of "The Seafarer" and "The Wife's Lament" are unknown. Both literary works are contained in *The Exeter Book,* a collection of poems written in Old English and one of the few manuscripts to have survived from the Anglo-Saxon period. Two of the poems in *The Exeter Book* are attributed to a poet named Cynewulf, but no other authors are mentioned.
   Scholars have determined that one person compiled the poems in *The Exeter Book.* However this person almost certainly was not the author but rather a *scribe* (someone who copies the works of others). In the Anglo-Saxon period (449–1066), books were copied and illustrated one by one. Monks played an important role in preserving the literature of the era by laboriously copying books by hand and housing them in their monasteries.
   Despite the work of these scribes, most Anglo-Saxon literature was lost. Invasions, war, disasters, and the passing of time destroyed all but a few of the manuscripts of this period.

Compare Literature

Mood and Elegy

Mood, or atmosphere, is the emotion created in the reader by part or all of a literary work.

An **elegy** is a poem of mourning, usually about someone who has died.

Set Purpose

Life was hard during Anglo-Saxon times, and that fact is reflected in the literature of the era. As you read "The Seafarer" and "The Wife's Lament," consider each poem's mood. Jot down specific words and images that create that mood. Also consider how each poem is an elegy. Identify what each speaker mourns and how he or she expresses that loss.

Preview Vocabulary

admonish, 63
ravenous, 63
fervent, 64
chaste, 65
asunder, 67
blithe, 67
whorled, 67
hovel, 67
dreary, 68

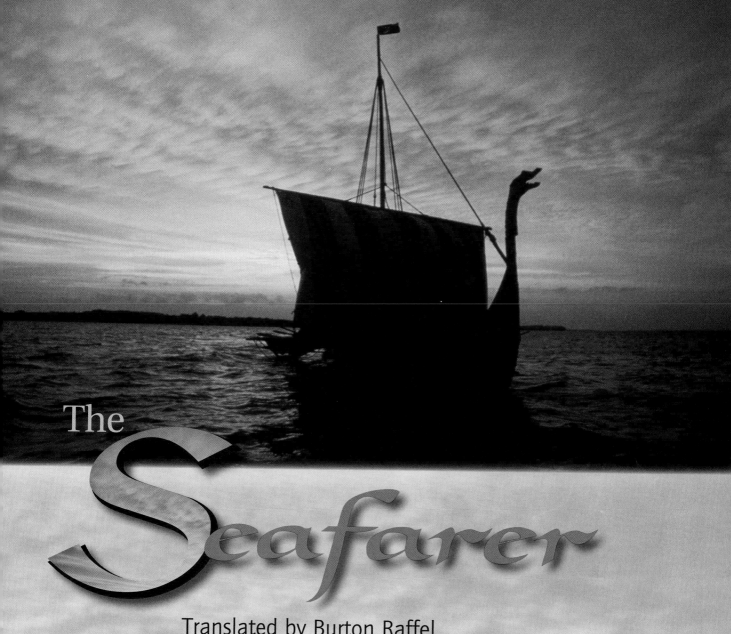

The Seafarer

Translated by Burton Raffel

This tale is true, and mine. It tells
How the sea took me, swept me back
And forth in sorrow and fear and pain,
Showed me suffering in a hundred ships,
5   In a thousand ports, and in me. It tells
Of smashing surf when I sweated in the cold
Of an anxious watch, perched in the bow
As it dashed under cliffs. My feet were cast
In icy bands, bound with frost,
10   With frozen chains, and hardship groaned

The Viking Influence

Although "The Seafarer" is an Anglo-Saxon poem, the voyage undertaken by the narrator is one only a Viking would have made. The Anglo-Saxons were not accomplished sailors and would not have had the skills to embark on a naval journey in unknown or treacherous waters. Why, then, is an Anglo-Saxon author relating a Viking experience?

From about 793 until 1066, the Vikings were the dominant civilization in Europe. They perfected warfare and seafaring technology far beyond other Europeans. The Vikings also were remarkably expansive, reaching the shores of North America in the West and the steppes of Russia in the East. Despite their abilities as explorers, the Vikings were not interested in being conquerors. Upon reaching new territory, they typically constructed a small base camp or trade settlement, raided the surrounding villages, and left before anyone could organize a counterattack. Active as traders, the Vikings often bartered with the goods they had plundered or the slaves they had captured.

Many Viking warriors had numerous wives, in part because they married women in the villages they raided. As a result of this, some Viking customs permeated other European civilizations. For example, people in foreign lands adopted aspects of the Viking religion and literary tradition in their own mythologies. Long journeys, especially across vast bodies of water, were a common element in Scandinavian stories because of their real-world connection to the Viking experience. Modern readers can identify these sorts of themes in Anglo-Saxon literature because of the Vikings' considerable cultural influence.

Around my heart. Hunger tore
At my sea-weary soul. No man sheltered
On the quiet fairness of earth can feel
How wretched I was, drifting through winter
15 On an ice-cold sea, whirled in sorrow,
Alone in a world blown clear of love,
Hung with icicles. The hailstorms flew.
The only sound was the roaring sea,
The freezing waves. The song of the swan
20 Might serve for pleasure, the cry of the sea-fowl,
The death-noise of birds instead of laughter,
The mewing[1] of gulls instead of mead.[2]
Storms beat on the rocky cliffs and were echoed
By ice-feathered terns[3] and the eagles screams;
25 No kinsman could offer comfort there,
To a soul left drowning in desolation.

---

1. **mewing.** Sounds made by gulls or other seabirds
2. **mead.** Drink similar to beer but made from honey
3. **terns.** Type of seabird similar to a gull

And who could believe, knowing but
The passion of cities, swelled proud with wine
And no taste of misfortune, how often, how wearily,
30 I put myself back on the paths of the sea.
Night would blacken; it would snow from the north;
Frost bound the earth and hail would fall,
The coldest seeds. And how my heart
Would begin to beat, knowing once more
35 The salt waves tossing and the towering sea!
The time for journeys would come and my soul
Called me eagerly out, sent me over
The horizon, seeking foreigners' homes.
        But there isn't a man on earth so proud,
40 So born in greatness, so bold with his youth,
Grown so grave, or so graced by God,
That he feels no fear as the sails unfurl,
Wondering what Fate has willed and will do.
No harps ring in his heart, no rewards,
45 No passion for women, no worldly pleasures,
Nothing, only the oceans heave;
But longing wraps itself around him.
Orchards blossom, the towns bloom,
Fields grow lovely as the world springs fresh,
50 And all these <u>admonish</u> that willing mind
Leaping to journeys, always set
In thoughts traveling on a quickening tide.
So summer's sentinel,[4] the cuckoo, sings
In his murmuring voice, and our hearts mourn
55 As he urges. Who could understand,
In ignorant ease, what we others suffer
As the paths of exile stretch endlessly on?
        And yet my heart wanders away,
My soul roams with the sea, the whales'
60 Home, wandering to the wildest corners
Of the world, returning <u>ravenous</u> with desire,
Flying solitary, screaming, exciting me

---

4. **sentinel.** Guard or sentry

> **ad • mon • ish** (ad män´ ish) *v.,* give warning or show disapproval
> **rav • e • nous** (ra´ və nəs) *adj.,* eager or greedy for satisfaction
>   or pleasure

To the open ocean, breaking oaths
On the curve of a wave.
65   Thus the joys of God
Are <u>fervent</u> with life, where life itself
Fades quickly into the earth. The wealth
Of the world neither reaches to Heaven nor remains.
No man has ever faced the dawn
70   Certain which of Fate's three threats
Would fall: illness, or age, or an enemy's
Sword, snatching the life from his soul.
The praise the living pour on the dead
Flowers from reputation: plant
75   An earthly life of profit reaped
Even from hatred and rancor,[5] of bravery
Flung in the devil's face, and death
Can only bring you earthly praise
And a song to celebrate a place
80   With the angels, life eternally blessed
In the hosts of Heaven.
                              The days are gone
When the kingdoms of earth flourished in glory;
Now there are no rulers, no emperors,
85   No givers of gold, as once there were,
When wonderful things were worked among them
And they lived in lordly magnificence.
Those powers have vanished, those pleasures are dead.
The weakest survives and the world continues,
90   Kept spinning by toil. All glory is tarnished.
The world's honor ages and shrinks.
Bent like the men who mould it. Their faces
Blanch[6] as time advances, their beards
Wither and they mourn the memory of friends.
95   The sons of princes, sown in the dust.
The soul stripped of its flesh knows nothing
Of sweetness or sour, feels no pain,
Bends neither its hand nor its brain. A brother
Opens his palms and pours down gold

---

5. **rancor.** Deep-seated ill will
6. **Blanch.** Lose color; become ashen or pale

fer • vent (fər´ vənt) *adj.*, characterized by strong feeling

100   On his kinsman's grave, strewing his coffin
    With treasures intended for Heaven, but nothing
    Golden shakes the wrath of God
    For a soul overflowing with sin, and nothing
    Hidden on earth rises to Heaven.
105   We all fear God. He turns the earth,
    He set it swinging firmly in space,
    Gave life to the world and light to the sky.
    Death leaps at the fools who forget their God.
    He who lives humbly has angels from Heaven
110   To carry him courage and strength and belief.
    A man must conquer pride, not kill it,
    Be firm with his fellows, <u>chaste</u> for himself,
    Treat all the world as the world deserves,
    With love or with hate but never with harm,
115   Though an enemy seek to scorch him in hell,
    Or set the flames of a funeral pyre[7]
    Under his lord. Fate is stronger
    And God mightier than any man's mind.
    Our thoughts should turn to where our home is,
120   Consider the ways of coming there,
    Then strive for sure permission for us
    To rise to that eternal joy,
    That life born in the love of God
    And the hope of Heaven. Praise the Holy
125   Grace of Him who honored us,
    Eternal, unchanging creator of earth. Amen. ❖

---

7. **funeral pyre.** Pile of materials on which a dead body is burned during
funeral rites

chaste (chast) *adj.,* innocent; pure in thought and action

MIRRORS & WINDOWS

The speaker describes sailors as "wondering what Fate has willed and will do."
Do you believe in fate—that people have no control over events in their lives?

The Wife's Lament

Translated by
Marcelle Thiébaux

Ingeborg's Lament. J. A. Malmström.
Scandinavian Library, University College,
London, England. (See detail on page 60.)

I tell this story about me, in my sorrow,
I sing the fate of my voyaging self. I may say that
whatever hardship I lived through since I grew up—
new griefs and old—in those days it was not worse than now.
5   Always I grieve in the pain of my torment.

First my lord went away from his people
over the tossing waves. I felt cold care in the dark before dawn,[1]
wondering where my lord of the lands might be.
Then I left on a journey to seek and serve him—
10   a friendless wanderer in my terrible need.

---

1. **cold care . . . dark before dawn.** The translator is imitating the alliteration of the original
Anglo-Saxon verse.

That man's kinsmen began to plot
with secret scheming to split us both apart,
so that we two—widely asunder in the world—
lived most wretchedly. And longing smote me.

15 My lord called to me to take up my hard dwelling here.
I had few loved ones in this country,
few devoted friends. For this my mind mourns.
Then I found myself a most husbandly man,
but a man with hard luck, brooding in his heart;
20 he hid his moods, his murderous thoughts,
yet seemed blithe in his bearing. Very often we boasted that
none but death alone would drive us apart—
not anything else! All that is whorled backward, changed;
now it's as if it never had been,
25 the loving friendship the both of us had. Far and near I must
suffer the feud[2] of my dearly loved man.
They forced me to live in a grove of wood
under an oak tree in an earth hovel.
Old is this den of earth. I am stabbed with longing.
30 The valleys are dark, the hills rise high,
bitterly sharp is my garrison[3] overgrown with brambles,
a joyless stronghold. Here very often what seizes me fiercely
is the want of my husband! There are friends on earth,
lovers living who lie clasped in their bed,
35 while I walk alone in the hours before daybreak
under the oak tree, throughout this earth cave
where I must remain the summerlong day,
where I can weep the sorrows
of my many hardships, because I never can
40 find sweet rest for that heart's grief of mine—
not for all of that longing laid on me in this life.

Always must the young be troubled in mood,
with thoughts harsh in their hearts, yet at the same time
seem blithe in bearing despite a care-burdened breast
45 and a swarm of sorrows. The young man must rely on himself

---

2. **feud.** Disdain, hatred
3. **garrison.** Military post or station; fortified place

> **asun • der** (ə sun´ dər) *adv.,* apart; separate
> **blithe** (blīth) *adj.,* cheerful; carefree
> **whorled** (wôr´ ld) *adj.,* coiled
> **hov • el** (hô´ vəl) *n.,* shed or hut

Anglo-Saxon Riddles
Anonymous

Translated by Burton Raffel

The Exeter Book, which also contains "The Seafarer" and "The Wife's Lament" (see page 60), is one of the most important surviving manuscripts of Old English verse. In addition to more traditional poems, *The Exeter Book* contains ninety-five **Anglo-Saxon riddles.** At one time, people thought that a poet named Cynewulf wrote the riddles because he is the only named poet in *The Exeter Book.* Now, it is generally believed that the riddles are the works of anonymous writers.

Anglo-Saxon riddles were written on a variety of subjects, from animals and other elements of the natural world to daily items and chores that dominated the farm-based Anglo-Saxon lifestyle. These

riddles show an interesting combination of light-hearted wordplay and a grim view of the world. As you read, keep in mind that some of these riddles provide the answer through the speaker's use of the word *I* or *me.*

RIDDLE 1

How many men are so knowing, so wise,
That their tongues can tell Who drives me into exile,
Swells me brave and strong and fierce,
Sends me roaring across the earth,
5 Wild and cruel, burning men's homes,
Wrecking their palaces? Smoke leaps up,
Gray like a wolf, and all the world
Crackles with the sounds of pain and death.
When I shake forests, uproot peaceful
10 Groves, clouds cover me; exalted
Powers hurl me far and wide.
What once protected the world, sheltered
Men, I bear on my back, bodies
And souls whirled in the mist. Where
15 Am I swallowed down, and what is my name?

Answer: An on-land storm

Riddles in Greek Mythology

Riddles have played an important role in many cultures throughout history. One of the most famous stories in Greek mythology is that of a wayward traveler named Oedipus, who encountered a Sphinx upon his return to Thebes, the city of his birth. The Sphinx had a beautiful woman's face, but her body was that of a lion, with eagle's wings protruding from her shoulders and a live serpent for a tail. She was renowned for her dazzling intellect but also her ruthless nature and insatiable thirst for blood.

Ares, the Greek god of war, ordered the Sphinx to hold the Thebans (the citizens of Thebes) captive until a hero could answer the following riddle:

What creature goes on four feet in the morning, on two at noonday, on three in the evening?

After taking some time to ponder the riddle, Oedipus decided the answer must be a *human being,* since a person crawls in childhood, walks on two feet as an adult, and uses a cane in old age. Oedipus's answer was correct, which prompted the Sphinx to immediately devour herself. Oedipus ascended to the Theban throne, marrying the widowed queen, Jocasta.

Oedipus's reign over Thebes was plagued by intense misfortune. A terrible disease befell his people, and in an effort to discover its origins, Oedipus unknowingly revealed a horrible truth about his lineage: Jocasta actually was his mother, and he had mistakenly killed his real father during his journey to Thebes. Jocasta committed suicide after hearing this news, and Oedipus blinded himself by piercing his eyes with a brooch from her dress, abdicating (resigning from) the throne in shame.

You may recognize this story as the one portrayed in the drama *Oedipus the King,* a Greek tragedy written by Sophocles and first performed in 428 BCE. The play begins with Oedipus's becoming king and ends with his blinding and exile.

The Epic of Gilgamesh

King Gilgamesh's outrages against his people are challenged by wild man Enkidu. After wrestling, the two become fast friends and go adventuring, until a jealous goddess kills Enkidu. As he mourns his friend, Gilgamesh searches for the secret of immortality. Discovered in 1839, this Sumerian epic from the third millennium BCE is one of humankind's most ancient texts.

Beowulf **translated by Seamus Heaney**

A slimy, shadow-stalking monster, his tarn-hag mother, and a sky-winging dragon are featured in this eighth-century epic recounting the heroic deeds of Geat hero Beowulf. In this new translation, Nobel Prize winner Seamus Heaney presents a quite readable version of the original poem and a compelling look into the Anglo-Saxon world, where fate and fear ruled.

Sarum: The Novel of England
by Edward Rutherfurd

Who built Stonehenge? Why was it abandoned? *Sarum* suggests answers as it follows five families, each representing a different cultural group, through ten thousand years in the history of Salisbury, England. Starting with the Stone Age, Rutherfurd chronicles major events in British history, revealing their long-term effects on these families and the land itself.

Grendel **by John Gardner**

The shadow-stalking Grendel may have been born a monster, but he possesses human emotions. As Grendel tells his story, we meet a lonely outsider who is first curious about humans and later anguished by the court bard's songs. In refashioning the Beowulf story, Gardner comments on the ideal of heroism and the human condition.

A Needle in the Right Hand of God: The Norman Conquest of 1066 and the Making and Meaning of the Bayeux Tapestry **by R. Howard Bloch**

The 230-foot-long Bayeux Tapestry, the most famous textile in the Western world, records the Battle of Hastings, in which Norman Prince William the Bastard defeated Anglo-Saxon King Harold of Britain, thus ending Scandinavian dominance of the island. Bloch presents the political history behind the tapestry, as well as its art and remarkable story of survival.

How the Irish Saved Civilization
by Thomas Cahill

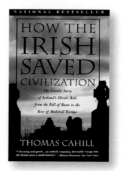

When the Roman Empire collapsed in the fifth century and the European continent fell into darkness, there was one little-known bright spot on the empire's fringes: Ireland. There, learned monks gathered and copied the treasury of Western literature, creating jewels such as the *Book of Kells,* reestablishing literacy, and helping to shape the medieval mind.

If you were *writing* about a specific place, you would describe it in detail, using sensory images and vivid language to help your readers see, hear, smell, feel, and even taste it. You should use the same strategies when describing a place in an oral presentation, or speech.

1. Choose a Place

To choose a place, start by taking a closer look at the places you go every day, such as your bedroom, your school homeroom, and the inside of your car. Think not only about the observable qualities of each place but also the mood or feeling it has.

Another possible topic is a place that has special meaning for you—perhaps a favorite park or beach or your grandparents' house. Again, think about the mood or feeling you want to convey. Think, too, about whether you can describe the place in a way that will be interesting to others.

2. Plan the Description

The most logical way to describe a place is to trace a course within it. In describing a room, for instance, you might start from the door and go around clockwise, describing the contents of the room in their order of appearance. You also might start by describing the first thing someone would see when looking into the room; then relate everything else to it.

Some places might be described using a *chronological* sequence, or according to time. In describing a place you have visited repeatedly throughout your life, you might explain how it has changed or how you have come to see it differently as you have aged.

3. Use Descriptive Language

As much as possible, provide vivid details that will appeal to listeners' senses of sight, sound, taste, smell, and touch. Use precise language to identify colors, shapes, sizes, and numbers of items. Help listeners visualize the place you are describing. In particular, focus on those sensory details that create the mood or feeling of the place, such as a certain smell or sound. Leave out details that are not important and might distract your readers from the overall sense of the place.

4. Practice Your Delivery

In preparing this assignment, be sure to allow enough time to practice your presentation. The more time you spend practicing, the more confident and relaxed you will feel when you actually deliver your speech to an audience.

As you practice, work on using your voice to help create the desired mood or feeling of the place. To create suspense, for example, lower the pitch of your voice and speak slowly. To create excitement, raise the pitch and speak more quickly. Match the qualities of your voice to the mood or feeling you want to create. Likewise, consider how to use facial expressions and gestures to enhance your description of the place.

If possible, audiotape or videotape your work and then play it back to observe your presentation. Will audience members be able to envision the place you are describing? Will they understand the sense of the place you want to convey?

5. Present the Description

Try to deliver your description using just a few notes—perhaps a brief outline of the plan you created. Focus on the place and what you want listeners to know about it. Relating the sense of the place is your primary goal.

SPEAKING & LISTENING RUBRIC

Your presentation will be evaluated on these elements:

Content

- ❏ You have identified the qualities of a place and the overall mood or feeling it has.
- ❏ You describe the place using an effective plan and a suitable amount of detail.
- ❏ You describe the place using sensory details and vivid language.

Delivery & Presentation

- ❏ You use voice, facial expressions, and gestures to enhance the description.
- ❏ You convey the mood or feeling of the place.

Many of the stories you read, the movies you watch, and even the video games you play focus on the classic struggle between good and evil. In Old English storytelling, this type of tale often was told in a narrative poem, or one that tells a story. A traditional form of narrative is the epic, a long story often told in verse that features heroes and foes and provides a portrait of a culture.

How might you apply this traditional form to a modern-day story? Contemporary heroes may not face foes such as monsters and dragons, but they encounter a variety of challenges within the culture in which they live. In this assignment, you will write a narrative poem about a contemporary hero facing a contemporary "foe."

> **Assignment** Compose a narrative poem about a modern-day hero
>
> **Purpose** To describe a contemporary hero using traditional poetic conventions
>
> **Audience** An author interested in using your narrative poem to introduce a book on your hero

❶ Prewrite

Select a Topic
Many people can be considered modern-day heroes: police and firefighters protecting lives, teachers improving minds, scientists curing diseases, and so on.

> **WRITING RUBRIC**
>
> A successful narrative poem has these qualities:
> ❑ tells the story of a hero facing a challenge
> ❑ uses poetic conventions such as stanza, meter, and rhyme
> ❑ uses imagery, sound devices, and figurative language

Make a list of three or four specific people who are possible heroes, and for each, identify a challenge he or she faces. Then choose the hero you feel you can best portray in a narrative poem.

Gather Information
Research your hero to learn more about his or her life. If the person is famous, use both library and Internet resources. If the person is not famous, talk to others about him or her or draw from your own experience with this individual. Gather information about this person's background, personal qualities, and accomplishments.

Also gather information about the foe, or challenge, your hero has faced. Is it another person or group of people? Is it a custom or law? Look into the background of the foe, and identify its qualities. Also determine how this foe has stood in opposition to your hero.

Record your research findings using a graphic organizer like the one on page 81.

Organize Ideas
Review the information you recorded on each side of the chart, "HERO" and "FOE." Which details best represent the qualities and achievements of your hero? Which details best represent those of your foe?

Put checkmarks next to five or so items on each side that you will use to tell your hero's story. Likewise, identify items from the bottom "RESULTS" section that you will use to create an overall impression of your hero and his or her challenge.

Write an Organizing Statement
Based on the items you have chosen, write one sentence that states the message you want to convey about your hero. This sentence will not appear in your narrative poem but instead will help you stay focused on your message.

Using information from the Hero Chart, one student, Sasha, wrote this organizing statement about Martin Luther King Jr.:

> *Martin Luther King Jr. was determined to bring about change using peaceful means, no matter what his opponents did to him.*

Hero Chart

HERO Martin Luther King Jr.	FOE People who oppose racial equality
Background Born in Georgia, January 15, 1929 ✓ Well educated; earned Ph.D. in Theology Became Baptist minister at age 24 ✓	**Background** Rooted in old ideas ✓ Slavery Segregation
Qualities Peaceful ✓ Inspiring Determined ✓	**Qualities** Afraid of change ✓ Prejudiced Violent ✓
Accomplishments Montgomery bus boycott (1955) March on Washington, "I Have a Dream" speech (1963) ✓ Nobel Peace Prize (1964); youngest recipient	**Opposition** Bombed King's house ✓ Imprisoned King Repressed protests Tried to frame King as communist ✓
RESULTS Growth in Civil Rights movement ✓ Civil Rights Act passed (1964) Assassinated April 4, 1968 ✓	

❷ Draft

Conventions of Poetry

Writing a poem involves using the unique conventions of poetry. For instance, whereas a work of prose, such as an essay, is written in paragraphs, a poem is written in *stanzas*. Common types of stanzas are *couplets*, comprised of two lines, and *quatrains*, comprised of four lines.

Traditional poems, like many of those in this book, also have meter and rhyme. *Meter* is a regular rhythmic pattern in poetry, as determined by the number of beats, or stresses, in each line. *Rhyme* is the repetition of sounds at the ends of words, as with *sight* and *rite*. Many poems have *end rhyme,* in which the words

rhyme at the ends of lines. A common *rhyme scheme,* or pattern of end rhymes, is to have every other line rhyme.

Other conventions of poetry relate to how words are used. Poets generally write with a limited number of words, and so they are particular to choose just the right words. By using literary devices such as imagery and figures of speech, poets can mold language in unique ways. See the Literary Terms Handbook for definitions and examples of these and other terms.

Whether you are a novice or experienced poet, focus on writing a traditional narrative poem for this assignment, one that is organized into stanzas and has both meter and rhyme. In addition, experiment with using at least two literary devices.

Structure

Unlike an essay or report, a poem does not have an introduction, body, and conclusion. However, as a story, a narrative poem should be structured to provide an opening and a closing in addition to the details of the story. Follow the three-part structure outlined below.

> **Opening stanza** Introduce your hero, and create a context for his or her story.
>
> **Middle stanza** Write one stanza for each main point you want to make about your hero.
>
> **Closing stanza** Show how the story ends, and create a final impression of your hero.

The opening stanza of your narrative poem should introduce your hero and set the stage for his or her story. The first stanza Sasha wrote during the Draft stage is shown in the left-hand column on page 83. In it, she presents Dr. King and establishes a context for his challenge, but she does not pay much attention to word choices. She will fine-tune her use of language in the Revise stage.

To write the middle stanzas, use the information you mapped out in the Prewrite stage. Look at the items you checked off in your Hero Chart. Plan to write one stanza for each main point you want to make about this person. Begin by jotting down each point in a phrase or two. Focus on the key words associated with this point, such as the person's name, and use these words in creating rhyme.

See the draft of Sasha's third stanza in the chart on page 83. It describes some of the things King's foes did to try to stop him. Note that Sasha has not followed through with the rhyme scheme of the opening stanza. Rather than struggle with the rhyme while drafting, she decided to keep writing and resolve this problem in the Revise stage.

Your final stanza should do two things: bring the story to an end and leave the reader with a final impression. Does Sasha do these two things in her final stanza? Look at her draft on page 83.

What Great Writers Do

Rita Dove, former poet laureate and Pulitzer Prize winner, notes that "poetry is language at its most distilled and most powerful." Making careful word choices is critical to poetry. Here are some of the points Sasha considered in choosing words during both the Draft and Revise stages:

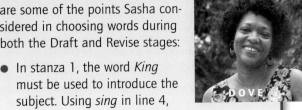

D O V E

- In stanza 1, the word *King* must be used to introduce the subject. Using *sing* in line 4, instead of *begin*, establishes rhyme and creates an image associated with civil rights. In line 2 of this stanza, replacing *Georgia* with *the South* helps restore the meter and creates alliteration (*South* and *sired*).
- In stanza 3, revising lines 1 and 4 restores the meter. Replacing the last word of line 4 with *change* creates slant rhyme, since *change* almost rhymes with *raged* (line 2) but not quite.
- In the closing stanza, making better word choices in line 1 creates alliteration (*sadly* and *some*). A metaphor is created in line 2 about people "breaking" rather than "bending." Rewording the last two lines creates consonance (*shot* and *stopped*) and also leaves the reader with a better final impression.
- Repetition of the word *dream* in the opening and closing stanzas alludes to King's famous speech and provides continuity.

❸ Revise

Evaluate Your Draft

You can evaluate your own poem or exchange poems with a classmate and evaluate each other's work. Either way, think carefully about what works well and what can be improved.

Start by looking at the content and organization. Make sure that the poem tells a story based on your organizing statement. Each stanza should present a new idea about your hero. The poem also should

DRAFT STAGE		REVISE STAGE	
Opening Stanza A dream was born one winter day. Georgia had found a King. A man set out to pave the way for civil rights to begin.	Establishes subject and context Defines challenge	A dream was born one winter day. ~~Georgia~~ the South had ~~found~~ sired ~~a~~ its King. A man set out to pave the way for civil rights to ~~begin~~ sing.	Improves meter and rhyme Creates alliteration and imagery
Third Stanza He went on and on, not one to quit while others fought and raged. They bombed his house and soiled his name but they could not make him stop.	Identifies events in hero's life Focuses on his courage	~~He went on and on,~~ On he went, not one to quit while others fought and raged. They bombed his house and soiled his name but ~~they~~ could not make him ~~stop~~ change.	Improves meter and rhyme
Final Stanza Some of the people he fought wanted him to stop. With a bullet he was killed— but his ideas, they could not end.	Brings story to end Creates final impression	Sadly, some of ~~the people~~ those he fought ~~wanted him to stop~~ would rather break than bend. With a ~~bullet~~ shot he was ~~killed~~ stopped— but his ~~ideas~~ dream, they could not end.	Creates alliteration and metaphor Improves meter and rhyme Creates better final impression

follow the poetic conventions of stanza, meter, and rhyme and use at last two literary devices, such as imagery, alliteration, and metaphor.

Evaluate your word choices. Are you using descriptive language that includes sensory details? Use a thesaurus to find more colorful synonyms to describe your experiences.

Use the Revision Checklist below to help you evaluate. Make notes directly on the poem about what changes need to be made.

REVISION CHECKLIST

Content & Organization

❏ Does the opening stanza introduce the hero and set the context for his or her story?

❏ Does each stanza relate clearly to the organizing statement?

❏ Does each stanza use stanza, rhyme, and meter?

❏ Does each stanza use literary devices, such as imagery and figures of speech?

❏ Does the closing stanza finish the story and create a final impression of the hero?

Grammar & Style

❏ Do all of your subjects and verbs agree? (page 19)

❏ Do you use pronouns correctly throughout? Do the pronouns agree with their antecedents? (page 71)

Revise for Content, Organization, and Style

Sasha evaluated her poem and found a number of things to improve. Look at the chart on page 81 (this time, the right-hand column) to see how she revised the three stanzas you looked at earlier. Also read the What Great Writers Do box on page 82 to trace the decisions she made about word choices.

Review the notes you or your partner made as you evaluated your draft. Then apply each comment in effectively revising your draft.

Proofread for Errors

The purpose of proofreading is to check for remaining errors. While you can look for errors as you evaluate your poem, you should focus on checking for errors that you might have missed or that were introduced in new material you added. Use proofreader's symbols to mark any errors you find.

To complete the assignment, print out a final draft and read it aloud before turning it in. Reading your draft aloud will not only help you catch errors you might otherwise miss, but it will also help you ensure that your meter and rhyme are correct.

Take a look at Sasha's final draft on the next page. Review how she worked through the three stages of the writing process: Prewrite, Draft, and Revise.

Writing Follow-Up

Publish and Present

● Perform your poem for the class using costumed readers, props, and musical accompaniment, or show the class a videotaped presentation of your poem.

● Enhance the storytelling aspect of your narrative poem by illustrating one stanza from it.

Reflect

● Think of several contemporary heroes from television programs, movies, and novels. How is the modern-day hero alike and different from the hero depicted in Anglo-Saxon literature? Which hero do you prefer? Why?

STUDENT MODEL

He Had a Dream
by Sasha Carlson

A dream was born one winter day,
    the South had sired its King.
A man set out to pave the way
    for civil rights to sing.

He preached the Word for all to hear,
    hoping to bring peace.
Yet in a jail was made to sit,
    waiting for release.

On he went, not one to quit,
    while others fought and raged.
They bombed his house and soiled his name
    but could not make him change.

Marching all across the land,
    he made his protests fair.
He tried his best to win it all.
    He did more than his share.

Sadly, some of those he fought
    would rather break than bend.
With a shot he was stopped—
    but his dream, they could not end.

What is the meter in stanza 1? What is the rhyme scheme in stanza 1?

What detail about King's life is presented in stanza 2?

What is the purpose of stanza 3? What words created slant rhyme?

What does stanza 4 tell about King's life?

What literary devices are used here? What final impression is created?

Reading Skills

Make Inferences

You constantly make inferences in everyday life. For example, suppose you are looking out a window and can see what is happening outside but not hear anything. You observe a dog walker stop, stomp her foot, bend over, and emphatically point her index finger at the dog, all the while quickly moving her mouth open and shut. You *infer* that the dog walker is angry at the dog and yelling at it. You cannot be sure this is the case, but the dog walker's behavior is similar to that of other angry people you have observed in the past.

Making *inferences* when reading is sometimes referred to as "reading between the lines." You use the information stated explicitly in the text along with your own knowledge as clues to meaning. You make an educated guess. The more clues, or evidence, you can find, the more likely your inference will be correct.

To make good inferences, read carefully and pay close attention to everything in the text. Be sure you understand all the words and the antecedents for pronouns, so you always know to what or whom the reference is being made. Also think about the tone of the passage, the author's perspective, and the characters' personalities and relationships. Then relate all of these clues to any prior knowledge you have that may be relevant.

As you make inferences, choose the *most likely* and *most logical* explanation from the various facts available to you. Remember that each inference should fit with all of the other clues in the text and with your prior knowledge.

TEST-TAKING TIP

In a testing situation, do your best to feel positive, confident, comfortable, relaxed, and alert. Do not be influenced by the behavior of others. Just because they are nervous does not mean you have to be.

Practice

Directions: Read the following passage from *Beowulf*, an epic poem whose author is unknown. Answer the questions after it on the basis of what is stated or implied in the passage.

> *The people prepare a large pyre and mourn Beowulf. They build a memorial to him and remember his great deeds.*

A huge heap of wood was ready,
5   Hung around with helmets, and battle
Shields, and shining mail shirts, all
As Beowulf had asked. The bearers brought
Their beloved lord, their glorious king,
And weeping laid him high on the wood.
10   Then the warriors began to kindle that greatest
Of funeral fires; smoke rose

Above the flames, black and thick,
And while the wind blew and the fire
Roared they wept, and Beowulf's body
15   Crumbled and was gone. The Geats stayed,
Moaning their sorrow, lamenting their lord;
A gnarled old woman, hair wound
Tight and gray on her head, groaned
A song of misery, of infinite sadness
20   And days of mourning, of fear and sorrow
To come, slaughter and terror and captivity.
And Heaven swallowed the billowing
     smoke.

Then the Geats built the tower, as Beowulf
Had asked, strong and tall, so sailors
25   Could find it from far and wide; working
For ten long days they made his monument,
Sealed his ashes in walls as straight
And high as wise and willing hands
Could raise them. And the riches he and
     Wiglaf

Had won from the dragon, rings, necklaces,
30 Ancient, hammered armor—all
The treasures they'd taken were left there, too,
Silver and jewels buried in the sandy
Ground, back in the earth, again
And forever hidden and useless to men.
35 And then twelve of the bravest Geats
Rode their horses around the tower,
Telling their sorrow, telling stories
Of their dead king and his greatness, his glory,

Praising him for heroic deeds, for a life
40 As noble as his name. So should all men
Raise up words for their lords, warm
With love, when their shield and protector leaves
His body behind, sends his soul
On high. And so Beowulf's followers
45 Rode, mourning their beloved leader,
Crying that no better king had ever
Lived, no prince so mild, no man
So open to his people, so deserving of praise.

Multiple Choice

1. From this excerpt, which of the following ideas can be inferred?
   A. The people are preparing a large pyre.
   B. Everyone is mourning.
   C. The warriors kindle the fire.
   D. Beowulf is dead.
   E. The people are remembering Beowulf's great deeds.

2. What is the first clue in this passage that helps you make this inference?
   A. "prepare a large pyre" (line 1)
   B. "a huge heap of wood was ready" (line 4)
   C. "As Beowulf had asked" (line 7)
   D. "Of funeral fires" (line 11)
   E. "lamenting their lord" (line 16)

3. Which of the following statements *best* summarizes the people's feelings toward Beowulf?
   A. They feared him.
   B. They respected and loved him.
   C. They coveted his treasures.
   D. They wanted to be rid of him as quickly as possible.
   E. They were sorrowful and lamenting.

4. All of the following are clues to how the people felt toward Beowulf *except*
   A. "mourn Beowulf" (lines 1–2)
   B. "remember his great deeds" (line 3)
   C. "their glorious king" (line 8)
   D. "moaning their sorrow" (line 16)
   E. "terror and captivity" (line 21)

Constructed Response

5. What inferences can you make from the repetition of the phrase "as Beowulf had asked"? (see lines 7, 23–24).

Writing Skills

Plan Your Time

For the SAT, you will have twenty-five minutes to complete the writing test. Plan your time to allow reading and considering the prompt and then outlining, writing, and revising your essay. If you know how much time to spend on each step, you will feel more in control of your writing and produce a better response.

To help manage your time, use these estimates of minutes to spend on each step:

- *Read and consider the prompt:* Spend three or four minutes evaluating the prompt. Make certain you understand what you are supposed to do.
- *Outline your response:* Take another three or four minutes to plan your response. What main points do you want to make in the essay, and in what order do you want to present them?
- *Write your response:* Start writing by the six- to eight-minute mark, and give yourself about twelve minutes overall to write your response. Spend the first three or four minutes on the introduction. This

is an important part of your essay; if it is clearly thought out and well written, the remainder of your essay will come more easily. Write the remainder of your essay in ten minutes or so.

- *Revise your response:* Allow at least five minutes to review what you have written and make changes. Cross out unnecessary words and add new ones as neatly as possible.

TEST-TAKING TIP

In outlining your response, make a rough outline, draw a web or map, or do whatever you would do to plan a piece of writing in a normal, untimed writing situation. Having a written plan of some type will help you stay focused and thus make the best use of your time.

Practice

Timed Writing: 25 minutes

Think carefully about the issue presented in the following excerpt and the assignment below.

What students are allowed to wear to school varies according to the school. At some schools, uniforms are required. At others,

certain types of clothing are banned, and at still others, almost any apparel is acceptable. What policy is best for students: uniforms, a strict dress code, or a lenient dress code?

Assignment: What type of clothing policy is best for students? Plan and write an essay in which you develop your perspective on this issue. Support your position with reasoning and examples taken from your reading, studies, experience, or observations.

Revising and Editing Skills

As part of the writing section, some standardized tests ask you to identify sentence errors involving grammar, usage, word choice, idioms, and mechanics. Being able to find mistakes in what you have written is important to being a good writer. Examples of common errors that you should watch for include the following:

- incorrect spellings and capitalization
- dangling participles

- disagreement between subject and verb
- inconsistent verb tense
- incorrect forms of irregular verbs
- incorrect use of frequently confused words such as *between* and *among*
- double negatives
- adjective/adverb confusion
- incorrect or missing punctuation

Practice

Directions: Each of the following sentences contains either a single error or no error. The error, if there is one, appears in one of the let-tered and underlined series of words. Write the letter that identifies the error in each sentence. If there is no error, write "E" for "No error." Do not write more than one letter, because no sentence contains more than one error.

Multiple Choice

1. In the middle of the (A) night when (B) she was asleep, the burglar (C) quietly broke into Mrs. Kim's (D) home and stole all her valuables. (E) No error

2. The teacher (A) said, "Work in small (B) groups, choose a leader and a recorder, and (C) come up with a consensus (D) on this issue". (E) No error

3. If you use information (A) from the Internet in your (B) paper, one needs to (C) cite it properly (D) according to the style guide. (E) No error

4. (A) People who have difficulty with (B) math, often give (C) its abstract nature as a reason for (D) their difficulty. (E) No error

The Battle of San Romano, c. 1450–1460. Paolo Uccello. National Gallery, London, England.

Medieval Period

Unit 2

1066–1485

Medieval Period 1066–1485

1066

1200

BRITISH LITERATURE BRITISH LITERATURE BRITISH LITERATURE BRITISH LI

1086
The Domesday Book, similar to a modern census, is completed

early 1100s
Benedeit writes the Anglo-Norman poem *The Voyage of St. Brendan*

1136
Geoffrey of Monmouth writes *The History of the Kings of Britain*

1155
Wace finishes the Anglo-Norman poem *Roman de Brut*

c. 1170
Thomas writes one of the first versions of *Tristan* in Anglo-Norman

c. 1200
Marie de France is writing Anglo-Norman poems, fables, and the lives of saints

c. 1265
St. Thomas Aquinas writes *Summa Theologiae*

1267
Roger Bacon sends his *Opus Majus* to Pope Clement IV

BRITISH HISTORY BRITISH HISTORY BRITISH HISTORY BRITISH HISTORY BRI

1066
At the Battle of Hastings, William the Conqueror completes the Norman Conquest of England

1096
Instruction begins at Oxford University

1135
A period of great turmoil known as the Anarchy begins

1154
Henry II becomes King of England

1170
Thomas à Becket, the Archbishop of Canterbury, is murdered

1209
Cambridge University is founded

1215
King John I signs the Magna Carta

1275
King Edward I summons the first officially sanctioned Parliament

1278
The Franciscans imprison Roger Bacon for practicing witchcraft

WORLD HISTORY WORLD HISTORY WORLD HISTORY WORLD HISTORY WORLD HISTORY WORLI

1075
The Almoravids, Muslims from North Africa, declare a jihad (holy war) against the Ghana Empire

1095
Pope Urban II launches the first Crusade

1110
The University of Paris is founded

1185
The Kamakura period begins in Japan

1206
Genghis Khan creates the Mongol Empire in central Asia

1240
Led by Sundiata Keita, the Mali Empire completes its takeover of the Ghana Empire in West Africa

1244
Jerusalem is captured by Muslims

1270
Yekuno Amlak establishes the Solomonic Dynasty in the Abyssinian highlands of eastern Africa

1271
Marco Polo arrives in Kublai Khan's court in China

1274 and 1281
The Mongolians invade Japan

1300   1400

c. 1375
Sir Gawain and the Green Knight is written

1386
Geoffrey Chaucer begins writing *The Canterbury Tales*

1390
John Gower publishes a 33,000-line poem entitled *Confessio Amantis*

c. 1400
The religious lyric "I Sing of a Maiden" is written

c. 1433
Margery Kempe dictates *The Book of Margery Kempe* to scribes

c. 1470
Sir Thomas Malory writes *Le Morte d'Arthur*

1476
William Caxton sets up the first printing press in England

1305
William Wallace, a Scottish patriot, is executed in London

1337
The Hundred Years' War begins between France and England

1348
England is ravaged by the Black Death, or bubonic plague

1381
Peasants revolt in England

1415
King Henry V fights at the Battle of Agincourt in France

1453
The Hundred Years' War ends

1455
The Wars of the Roses begin

1485
King Richard III falls in battle against Henry Tudor; Henry Tudor ascends to the British throne and becomes Henry VII

c. 1300
The Renaissance begins in Italy

1308
Dante Alighieri starts writing *The Divine Comedy*

1325
The capital of the Aztec Empire, Tenochtitlan, Mexico, is founded

1341
Petrarch becomes the poet laureate of Rome

1390s
Great Zimbabwe, a massive granite building constructed over two centuries in south-eastern Africa, is nearly completed

1424
Joan of Arc experiences a vision that orders her to drive the English from France

1431
Joan of Arc is convicted of heresy and burned at the stake

c. 1450
The Gutenberg press begins printing Bibles in Germany

1468
Sunni Ali, King of Songhai, captures Timbuktu from the Mali Empire

> *"Forbid us something,*
> *and that thing we desire."*
>
> —GEOFFREY CHAUCER

The Norman Conquest

In 1066, following the death of English King Edward the Confessor, the Anglo-Saxon council of elders chose Harold II to assume the throne. However, Duke William of Normandy (c. 1028–1087), cousin to Edward the Confessor, claimed that Edward had promised the English throne to him. With the support of the Church, Duke William left the northern region of France known as Normandy and invaded England. At the Battle of Hastings, William defeated Harold, marking the end of the Anglo-Saxon Era and ushering in the Medieval Period.

In four years of bloody fighting, the Normans killed most of the native English nobility. The rest of the populace was put under strict rule of the French-speaking barons loyal to the new ruler, who became known as William the Conqueror. To make sure the barons remained loyal, William established England's feudal system.

The Organization of Medieval Society

After declaring that all the land belonged to him, William parceled out tracts to the barons he trusted. These new landowners were obligated to be loyal to the king, to raise armies to fight in his battles, and to pay taxes to support his court. In turn, the barons granted land to lesser nobles and required service and support from them. Who owned what was recorded in the *Domesday Book* in 1086, the first doorstep taxation survey.

At the very bottom of the social order was a class of peasants called villeins or serfs, who lived and worked on the nobles' land. The serfs were considered property of feudal lords and could not leave the land or even marry without permission. The lot of the serfs generally was miserable. They lived on a meager diet, suffered from disease, and worked very hard, only to turn over much of what they produced to support the lord's household. Occasionally, a serf could earn freedom by performing some exceptional service to his or her lord. Gradually during the Medieval Period, the class of freemen grew to include many merchants, traders, laborers, and artisans.

Political Developments in the Early Medieval Period

Politically, the Medieval Period in England was one of enormous change. The feudal system introduced by William the Conqueror was solidified by his successors. Henry II, who reigned from 1154 to 1189, brought Ireland and Scotland under control of the English throne. Henry encouraged a Norman lord, "Strongbow," to invade Ireland in 1170 on behalf of a deposed local monarch, and for the next 600 years, Anglo-Normans controlled Ireland from a fortified area called the Pale. In Scotland, Henry himself defeated a revolt led by William "the Lion." In Wales, English lords held the South and West while Welsh ruled the North.

Among Henry II's civil accomplishments was the introduction of a system of traveling judges whose rulings were to make up the common law that still provides the basis for the legal systems of England

---

NOTABLE NUMBERS

- **120** Weight in pounds of a typical suit of armor
- **1 in 3** Proportion of the European population wiped out by the Black Death, or about 25 million people
- **7** Number of deadly sins identified by medieval theologians: pride, avarice, lechery, anger, gluttony, envy, and sloth
- **10,000** Number of French soldiers who died in the Battle of Crécy in 1346 due to the efficacy of the English longbow
- **20** Number of kings who ruled England during the Medieval Period

and the United States. Another innovation of the period was legislative government in the form of a Parliament, or representative ruling body.

In 1215, England's nobles forced King John, Henry II's son, to sign the Magna Carta, or "Great Charter." The document laid down sixty-three rights that a good overlord should recognize, including the right to proper justice and consent to taxation. In addition, the Magna Carta clarified relations with the Church and paved the way for constitutional rule in England.

The Black Death and Peasants' Revolt

In 1348, the Black Death, or bubonic plague, terrorized the inhabitants of England. The destructive virus [*bacterium*] spread to humans from fleas living on plague-infected rats that roamed the populated areas of England. Large crowds of people living in cities and towns and attending markets and fairs helped spread the deadly disease, which wiped out entire villages and resulted in strict quarantines. Today, the Black Death is considered the worst epidemic ever.

Those peasants who survived found their labor suddenly was much more valuable and began to negotiate higher wages. In response, Parliament enacted statutes forbidding wage hikes. Next came a poll tax, intended to fund the war with France. It imposed a flat-rate tax on everyone, no matter how poor. In 1381, the peasants revolted. Led by Jack Straw and Wat Tyler, peasants armed with stones and farming tools marched on the city of London to demand individual liberties and human rights for the common people. The revolt was brutally suppressed, and its leaders were executed. Nonetheless, this act of rebellion signaled a move toward greater independence among working-class people.

Relations with the Church

In the Medieval Period, the Catholic Church played a prominent role in the daily lives of people from all classes of English society. The king himself was considered the Pope's vassal (servant). Vast resources went into building churches, first in the squat, towered, and turreted Norman or Romanesque style and later in the grand Gothic style of Canterbury Cathedral, with its pointed arches, flying buttresses, and tall windows.

Like many political leaders of the time, Henry II frequently quarreled with the Church. When he became angry at Thomas à Becket, the Archbishop of Canterbury, for deferring to the Pope on an important issue, overzealous barons loyal to Henry II murdered

The Magna Carta.

Becket in 1170. Becket became a Christian martyr who symbolized the rift between the throne and the Church. Two centuries later, Geoffrey Chaucer documented the ritual pilgrimage to Becket's shrine at Canterbury in *The Canterbury Tales.*

"Will no one rid me of this turbulent priest?"

—KING HENRY II

From the eleventh to the thirteenth centuries, European nations embarked on a series of Crusades, or holy wars, to recapture Jerusalem from the Moslems. English King Richard I, another son of Henry II, led the Third Crusade, which ended in a truce with Moslem leader Saladin when Richard had to return to England to prevent his brother John from taking over the crown.

Europe clearly benefited from the crusaders' exposure to the Middle East's more sophisticated culture and the development of new trade relationships. However, many hundreds of thousands of Moslems, Jews, and Greek Orthodox followers were brutally killed during the Crusades, and the crusaders' ranks were decimated by disease, starvation, and warfare. The saddest episode was the Children's Crusade in 1212, in which armies of French and German children (around fifty thousand in all) fell sick, starved, or were sold into slavery on their way to the Holy Land.

The Late Medieval Period

From 1339 to 1453, England fought the Hundred Years' War over possession of French lands. In 1346, England won a decisive victory at the Battle of Crécy by using the longbow. This innovative bow and arrow had a range of up to two hundred yards and could pierce the heavy suits of armor worn by the French knights. For a time, England dominated France. In the next century, however, under the inspired leadership of Joan of Arc (1412–1431), France was able to win back its territory from England.

From 1455 to 1485, England was torn by civil war between two noble houses. The House of Lan-caster, whose crest bore a red rose, fought against the House of York, whose crest bore a white rose. The so-called Wars of the Roses started when Richard II, fearing the power of the English nobles, banished his most powerful noble, Henry Bolingbroke. When Richard was away fighting a rebellion in Ireland, Bolingbroke declared himself Henry IV. Thirty years later, the wars ended with the 1485 defeat of Yorkist Richard III by Henry Tudor, a distant relative of the Lancastrians, who became King Henry VII. The wars were brutal. One battle, at Towton in 1461, was one of the bloodiest ever fought on English soil.

The Medieval Period was not all about wars, however. Significant social and cultural changes also occurred during this time. Towns and cities grew up around mills that processed wool into cloth. The invention of the iron plowshare meant more land could be farmed and the new surplus commodities could be traded for goods. Merchants and artisans organized into guilds responsible for training apprentices and regulating business, resulting in the growth of a middle class of free merchants and tradespeople.

In the realm of education, the Universities of Oxford and Cambridge opened their doors, promoting higher learning. With the introduction of the movable-type printing press around 1450, the printed word became more widely available, particularly to common people. The spread of learning that followed contributed to the decline of the powerful aristocracy.

King Henry VII at Towton, 1860. William Dyce. City of Guildhall Art Gallery, London, England.

The Emergence of Middle English

The Norman Conquest brought about profound changes in the English language. From 1066 to the mid-1200s, the aristocratic ruling class of England spoke Norman French almost exclusively, yet few French words entered English. However, from about 1260 to the late 1300s, most English aristocrats were bilingual, speaking both Norman French and English. When speaking and writing English, these aristocrats borrowed heavily from the pronunciation, grammar, and vocabulary of their native French. As a result, the English language underwent rapid change, developing into what is now known as **Middle English.**

The vast changes that occurred in the language can be seen by comparing passages written near the beginning and near the end of the Medieval Period. The first passage below, written shortly after the Norman Conquest, is difficult for modern readers to comprehend without translation. The second passage, written in the 1300s, presents few difficulties:

English Lyric from the Early 1100s
Merie sungen ðe muneches binnin Ely
Da Cnut ching reu ðer by.
Roweð, cnites, noer the land
And here we pes muneshes sæng.

Translation
Merrily sang the monks with Ely
When Cnut the king rowed thereby.
Row, knights, nearer the land
And let us hear the monks' song.

Passage from Chaucer's Troilus and Cressida
Go, lytle [little] booke,
And for ther is so greet diversitee [great diversity]
In English and in wryting [writing] of our
    tonge [tongue],
So preye I god that noon [no one] miswryte
    [miswrite] thee.

Words Borrowed from French

As a result of the borrowing from French that began in the Medieval Period, today it is almost impossible to write an English paragraph without using words of French origin. Many of the French words added to English related to power and prestige, reflecting the Norman conquerors' ruling-class status (see the box on the next page). Fortunately, for English writers and speakers, many native English words survived alongside their French counterparts, creating a wealth of choices from among words with different levels of formality. Here are some examples of Modern English words with different origins but related meanings:

From Old English	From French
begin	commence
bloom	flower
buy	purchase
fight	battle
foe	enemy
folk	people
help	aid
house	mansion
king	emperor
wedding	marriage

Notice that the French words often carry connotations of formality or prestige not associated with the corresponding English words. This is explained by the French-speaking Normans' membership in the sophisticated ruling class. The distinction can be seen clearly in certain word pairs related to foods derived from animals. The native English people, who were forced by the Normans into a subservient lower class, had the responsibility of caring for barnyard animals. The terms that survived for describing live animals were therefore English in origin. The terms used to describe animals when killed and cooked, however, were French in origin, because it was the French-speaking Normans who were wealthy enough to eat prepared meat. Consider these examples:

English Words for Live Animals	French Terms for Prepared Meats
pig, boar, swine	pork, bacon
cow, ox	beef, veal
deer	venison
sheep	mutton

Other Changes in the Language

Changes in Pronunciation and Grammar

In addition to greatly influencing the lexicon (vocabulary) of the English language, Norman French also influenced both the pronunciation and grammar of English. In the area of pronunciation, English became much less harsh and guttural, losing some of the Germanic traits that characterized Old English. In the area of grammar, the use of English by aristocrats unfamiliar with its intricacies led to simplification of the language. For instance, the grammatical endings, or *inflections,* that were common in Old English were dropped. Syntax (sentence structure) also changed, so that the subject of a sentence generally appeared before the verb, reversing another characteristic of Old English.

Categories of Words Borrowed from French

Politics city, council, county, government, mayor, nation, parliament, tyrant

Finances account, budget, customer, estate, price, receipt, tax, value

Power relationships authority, obey, oppress, power, servant, slave

Law accuse, attorney, crime, innocent, jail, jury, justice, legal, sentence, treason, verdict

War army, attack, conquer, peace, pursue, retreat, siege, surrender, war

Manners agreeable, calm, courtesy, dangerous, gracious, honest, nice, pleasant, tender

Religion altar, angel, baptism, cathedral, faith, grace, preach, saint, sermon, vice, virtue

Architecture and furnishings aisle, balcony, castle, chair, chimney, couch, lamp, porch, table, tower

Clothing apparel, buckle, dress, fashion, garments, gown, lace, robe, satin

Arts art, color, dance, design, melody, music, ornament, painting, sculpture

Food banquet, cherries, dinner, feast, lemons, pastry, peaches, roast, salad, soup, spice, stew

---

Standardization

Throughout the Medieval Period, spoken and written English appeared in what Chaucer called a "greet diversitee" of forms, making it difficult for people of one region of England to communicate effectively with people from another region. Middle English was divided into five major dialects: Northern, East Midland, West Midland, Southeastern, and Southwestern. Within these major dialectal areas, individual communities, speakers, and writers followed their own rules for pronunciation and spelling, making communication all the more difficult.

Toward the end of the Medieval Period and during the early Renaissance, two related cultural developments brought about regularities of pronunciation and spelling in the English language. The first development was the rise in prestige of the East Midland dialect spoken in London, England's capital city. The second was the widespread availability of printed works following the introduction of printing by William Caxton in the late 1400s. Caxton printed his books in the East Midland dialect and regularized, to some extent, the spelling and vocabulary of the authors whose works he made available. The East Midland dialect of London and of Caxton developed into the Modern English spoken and written today. Refer to a history of language, such as *The Cambridge History of the English Language,* for more information on the development of the English language.

PART 1

Songs and Tales

Even when Norman French was the official language of the British court, commoners continued to produce oral poetry and songs. Many of these songs, known as *ballads,* survived for hundreds of years, long enough to be printed after the invention of the printing press or gathered by scholars from anonymous oral sources. Some ballads, such as "Lord Randall," told fantastic tales of ghosts, demons, and other strange events. Other ballads recorded important events; for instance, "Sir Patrick Spens" tells of the shipwreck of a Scottish knight and his men. Many ballads were simple tales of love or betrayal, such as "Bonny Barbara Allen." A few were humorous and even ironic, including "Get Up and Bar the Door."

The most famous work of the Medieval Period is *The Canterbury Tales,* by Geoffrey Chaucer. This lengthy narrative, begun in 1386, consists primarily of the tales told by a group of Christians during their pilgrimage (religious journey) to the cathedral at Canterbury, England. The characters are from various sectors of medieval life and are introduced roughly in order of their social rank.

The life of a medieval woman is portrayed in *The Book of Margery Kempe* (1433), the oldest surviving full-length autobiography in English. Unlike a modern autobiography, this work is not the chronological story of the writer's life but instead a spiritual history of her religious experiences. Strong spiritual themes also underlie *Everyman* (1485), a medieval morality play about the Christian struggle between good and evil.

Detail of stained glass window, Sainte-Chapelle, Paris, France.

The Ballad Defined

Dating from the twelfth century, a **ballad** is a traditional form of narrative poetry that may be recited or sung. Many of the earliest English and Scottish ballads were, in fact, songs that had been passed along orally from one generation to the next and from one region to another. *Troubadours*, entertainers who sang and recited poetry, brought the ballads with them as they traveled, strumming on mandolins and other early instruments. During this era, much of the population did not know how to read, so telling a story as a song, using rhyme and rhythm, was an effective way of ensuring people would remember it.

During the Medieval Period, ballads provided a popular form of entertainment and a way of recording events. As noted earlier, the subjects of ballads included love, betrayal, war, heroism, and tragedy. A few were meant to be humorous; many others had frightening themes. Regular in rhythm and rhyme and simple in language, the form is closely related to other works of the oral tradition.

The ballad experienced a revival with the interest in folk music that occurred during the mid-twentieth century. Folk and rock musicians adapted the form to express contemporary concerns and new musical styles. Among the best-known balladeers today is Bob Dylan, whose contemporary classic "A Hard Rain's A-Gonna Fall" appears in this unit.

Elements of the Ballad

Form and Structure

The typical ballad form is based on a simple stanza of four lines. The rhyme scheme tends to follow an *aabb* or *abab* pattern, although "Lord Randall" has an *abcd* pattern. **Slant rhyme,** in which the rhyming sounds are similar but not identical, is common to many ballads, such as "Lord Randall" and "Bonny Barbara Allan." For example, in the initial verse of "Bonny Barbara Allan," the rhymed words are *falling* and *Allan.* In "Get Up and Bar the Door," we find both slant rhyme (*then/pan*) and perfect rhyme (*see/me*).

The regular rhythm of the lines balances the variations in sound patterns, as does the frequent inclusion of a strong **refrain,** or repetition of lines, and other instances of **repetition** ("bar the door;" "For I'm sick at heart, an I fain wad lie down;" "my blue-eyed son"). The use of rhyme, refrains, and other repetition makes ballads easy to remember and recite.

Narrative Technique

A ballad conveys a dramatic story through the use of **dialogue,** often in the form of questions and answers. The question-and-answer format establishes a conversational rhythm and can build suspense, drawing in the reader or listener to speculate about answers. The effect of the dialogue can be humorous, as in the traditional "Get Up and Bar the Door," or ominous and brooding, as in the two poems about true love betrayed. For example, we learn of Lord Randall's impending death through a series of questions and answers. The young lord's mother asks him where he has been, whom he has met, on what he has dined, and where he has left his hawks and hounds. Through his terse replies, his mother recognizes that her darkest suspicions have been confirmed and that her son has been poisoned by the woman he loves.

Mood

Mood, or atmosphere, is the emotion created in the reader by part or all of a literary work. The mood of "Lord Randall" is eerie. We do not know why the lord's lover has murdered him, and this gap in understanding both moves and mystifies us. The mood of "Bonny Barbara Allan" is pitiful, caused by the lovesickness and remorse that kills first John Graeme and then his beloved Barbara Allan. Dylan's lyric, with its obvious reference to "Lord Randall," evokes an apocalyptic mood (one that brings to mind the end of the world) with its suggestions of violence and doom. A ballad need not be calamitous or melancholic, however. Consider the merry, playful mood of "Get Up and Bar the Door," in which a peasant couple banter and make an inconsequential wager about whose job it will be to close the door to holiday visitors.

See the Understanding Literary Forms in Unit 1, pages 20–21, for guidelines on how to read ballads and other forms of poetry.

Bonny Barbara Allan
Get Up and Bar the Door
Lord Randall

Anonymous Ballads

Build Background

Literary Context Like most ballads from medieval Scotland and England, the three selections that follow are of unknown origin. The verses may have been based on actual events and characters; they were passed down orally from generation to generation.

In **"Bonny Barbara Allan,"** Sir John Graeme dies because a young woman does not return his love. Note that *Bonny* is not part of her name; it is a standard title for a young woman that means "pretty." Although Sir John lies near death, Barbara Allan shows no pity. Sir John, she says, snubbed her by failing to raise a glass to her when he drank to others. Yet in the last two stanzas, Barbara cries out to her mother with a plea that is both shocking and sad.

"Get Up and Bar the Door" differs from most other medieval ballads in being amusing, even ironic, rather than serious in its subject matter. In this selection, a husband and wife, arguing about who should secure the door on a cold and windy night, decide that the first to speak must be the one to shut the door. Meanwhile, robbers enter the house and help themselves to the dinner the wife has made. Finally, the husband can bear the silence and stalemate no longer and confronts the thieves, only to hear his wife claim victory in the squabble.

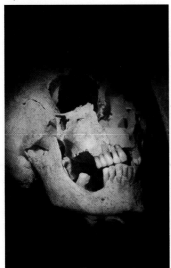

The ballad **"Lord Randall"** appears in many different versions. In this rendering, the *dialect,* or regional language variation, is Scottish. Like a number of medieval ballads, "Lord Randall" is told entirely in dialogue. The story it narrates might come from the life of Sir Thomas Randall, a Scottish war hero who, in 1332, died suddenly after supposedly being poisoned by a spy pretending to be his sweetheart. According to some historical sources, however, he suffered from a fatal disease.

Reader's Context In an age when few people could read and write, what made ballads so popular? Why are many of them still popular, even though literacy is widespread?

Analyze Literature

Rhyme Scheme and Repetition
A **rhyme scheme** is a pattern of rhymes at the ends of lines of verse. For instance, the rhyme scheme of "Bonny Barbara Allan" is *abcb;* lines 1 and 3 do not rhyme but lines 2 and 4 do.

Repetition is the intentional reuse of a sound, word, phrase, or sentence.

Set Purpose

Medieval ballads are known to readers today because they were transmitted for centuries through the oral tradition. As you read the three ballads that follow, consider how the use of rhyme and repetition helped people remember and pass on these literary works. Analyze the use of rhyme in each ballad, and determine whether it follows a pattern, or rhyme scheme. Also analyze the use of repetition, counting the instances in each selection.

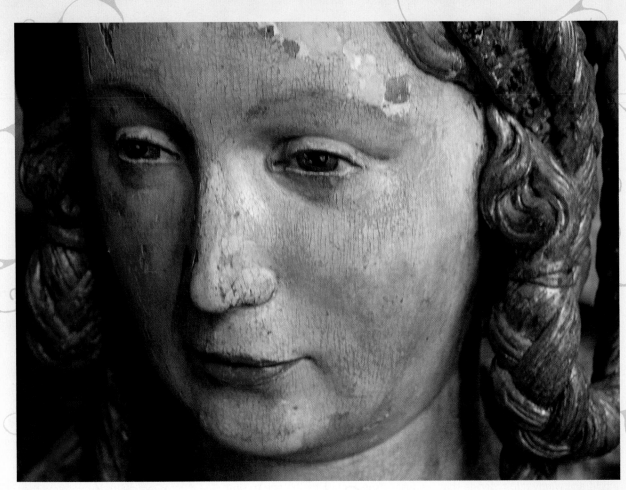

Bonny Barbara Allan

It was in and about the Martinmas[1] time,
    When the green leaves were a-fallin';
That Sir John Graeme in the West Country
    Fell in love with Barbara Allan.

5 He sent his man down through the town
    To the place where she was dwellin':
"O haste and come to my master dear,
    If you be Barbara Allan."

---

1. **Martinmas.** Feast of St. Martin, November 11

O gently, gently rose she up,
10   To the place where he was lyin',
And when she drew the curtain by:
        "Young man, I think you're dyin'."

"O it's I'm sick, and very, very sick,
        And 'tis a' for Barbara Allan."
15 "O the better for me you shall never be,
        Though your heart's blood were a-spillin'.

"O do you remember, young man," said she,
        When you the cups were fillin',
That you made the healths go round and round,
20   And slighted Barbara Allan?"

He turned his face unto the wall,
        And death with him was dealin':
"Adieu,[2] adieu, my dear friends all,
        And be kind to Barbara Allan."

25 And slowly, slowly rose she up,
        And slowly, slowly left him;
And sighing said she could not stay,
        Since death of life had reft[3] him.

She had not gone a mile but two,
30   When she heard the death-bell knellin',
And every stroke that the death-bell made,
        It cried, "Woe to Barbara Allan!"

"O mother, mother, make my bed,
        O make it soft and narrow:
35 Since my love died for me today,
        I'll die for him tomorrow." ❖

---

2. **Adieu.** [French] Good-bye
3. **reft.** Deprived; bereft

For whom do you feel more pity: Sir John or Barbara Allan? Do you usually forgive people who have wronged you, or do you tend to hold a grudge?

Get Up and Bar the Door

It fell about the Martinmas time,[1]
    And a gay time it was then,
When our goodwife got puddings to make,
    She's boild them in the pan.

5 The wind sae cauld blew south and north.
    And blew into the floor;
Quoth our goodman to our goodwife,
    "Gae out and bar the door."

"My hand is in my hussyfskap.[2]
10   Goodman, as ye may see;
An it should nae be barrd this hundred year,
    It's no be barrd for me."[3]

They made a paction[4] tween them twa.
    They made it firm and sure.
15 That the first word whaeer shoud speak,
    Shoud rise and bar the door.

Then by there came two gentlemen,
    At twelve o'clock at night,
And they could neither see house nor hall,
20   Nor coal nor candlelight.

---

1. **Martinmas.** Feast of St. Martin, November 11
2. **hussyfskap.** Housekeeping chores
3. **An it shoud nae be. . . . It's no be barrd for me.** It won't be barred for a hundred years if I'm supposed to do it.
4. **paction.** Pact or agreement

"Now whether is this a rich man's house,
 Or whether it is a poor?"
But neer a word wad ane o' them[5] speak,
 For barring of the door.

25 And first they[6] ate the white puddings,
 And then they ate the black:
Tho muckle[7] thought the goodwife to hersel,
 Yet neer a word she spake.

Then said the one unto the other,
30 "Here, man, take ye my knife;
Do ye tak aff the auld man's beard,
 And I'll kiss the goodwife."

"But there's nae water in the house,
 And what shall we do than?"
35 "What ails ye at the pudding broo,[8]
 That boils into the pan?"

O up then started our goodman,
 An angry man was he:
"Will ye kiss my wife before my een[9]
40 And scad[10] me wi pudding bree?"[11]

Then up and started our goodwife,
 Gied three skips on the floor:
"Goodman, you've spoken the foremost word;
 Get up and bar the door." ❖

---

5. **But neer a word wad ane o them speak.** But not a word
 would either of them (husband or wife) speak.
6. **they.** Refers to the two intruders
7. **muckle.** Much
8. **What ails thee at the pudding broo.** Why can't you use the
 pudding water?
9. **een.** Eyes
10. **scad.** Scald
11. **bree.** Broth

What makes people so stubborn that they do foolish things? Can stubbornness
be overcome?

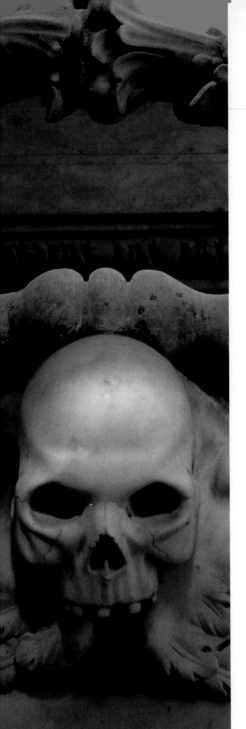

Lord Randall

"O where hae ye been, Lord Randall, my son?
O where hae ye been, my handsome young man?"
"I hae been to the wild wood; mother, make my bed soon,
For I'm weary wi' hunting, and fain[1] wald lie down."

5 "Where gat ye your dinner, Lord Randall, my son?
Where gat ye your dinner, my handsome young man?"
"I din'd wi' my true-love; mother, make my bed soon,
For I'm weary wi' hunting, and fain wald lie down."

"What gat ye to your dinner, Lord Randall, my son?
10 What gat ye to your dinner, my handsome young man?"
"I gat eels boil'd in broo;[2] mother, make my bed soon,
For I'm weary wi' hunting, and fain wald lie down."

"What became of your bloodhounds, Lord Randall, my son?
What became of your bloodhounds, my handsome young man?"
15 "O they swell'd and they died; mother, make my bed soon,
For I'm weary wi' hunting, and fain wald lie down."

"O I fear ye are poison'd, Lord Randall, my son!
O I fear ye are poison'd, my handsome young man!"
"O yes! I am poison'd; mother, make my bed soon,
20 For I'm sick at the heart, and I fain wald lie down." ❖

---

1. **fain.** Gladly
2. **broo.** Broth

MIRRORS & WINDOWS

Have you ever felt intimidated or offended by someone's questioning, such as that of a parent? Was the concern justified?

Literature Connection

Literary and musical scholars have speculated on the similarities between "Lord Randall" and the contemporary musical ballad **"A Hard Rain's A-Gonna Fall,"** composed by folk singer **Bob Dylan.** Dylan's song was first released in 1963 during a period of social and political unrest in the United States. In late 1962, tensions between the United States and the Soviet Union had led to the Cuban Missile Crisis, during which many Americans feared the outbreak of nuclear war. "A Hard Rain's A-Gonna Fall" is often considered to be a protest against nuclear war. The bleak images and worried tone convey a sense of the world coming to an end. Dylan, who was born in 1941, is perhaps best known for the protest songs he wrote in the 1960s to speak out against difficult social and political conditions, including poverty, war, and racial inequality.

A Hard Rain's A-Gonna Fall

by Bob Dylan

Oh, where have you been, my blue-eyed son?
And where have you been, my darling young one?
I've stumbled on the side of twelve misty mountains,
I've walked and I've crawled on six crooked highways,
5 I've stepped in the middle of seven sad forests,
I've been out in front of a dozen dead oceans,
I've been ten thousand miles in the mouth of a graveyard,
And it's a hard, and it's a hard, it's a hard, and it's a hard,
And it's a hard rain's a-gonna fall.

10 Oh, what did you see, my blue-eyed son?
Oh, what did you see, my darling young one?
I saw a newborn baby with wild wolves all around it
I saw a highway of diamonds with nobody on it,
I saw a black branch with blood that kept drippin',

Geoffrey Chaucer

> *"From every shire's end of England, down to Canterbury they went to seek the holy blissful martyr."*

Geoffrey Chaucer (c.1342–1400), a public servant and a poet, was one of the first authors to write in everyday English, instead of French or Latin. Today, he is probably the best-known writer of Middle English, the form of the language that emerged between the twelfth and fifteenth centuries.

The son of a London wine merchant, Chaucer was raised in a society that had a growing middle class. In 1357, the young man secured employment as a page for Elizabeth, Countess of Ulster. Two years later, he participated in an invasion of France and was captured; he was freed when a ransom was paid by a number of individuals, including English King Edward III. Throughout his life, Chaucer served as a soldier, controller of customs, justice of the peace, clerk of the king's works, member of Parliament, and diplomat to France, Italy, and Spain. In his old age, he was generously provided for by King Richard II and his successor, Henry IV. Despite Chaucer's work as a public servant, he found time to write both poetry and prose on a wide range of subjects, drawing on his varied personal experiences.

Chaucer was widely read and well educated on a variety of subjects. His first literary influences were the French allegorical poets, who were popular with the English aristocracy. One of his first works, *Book of the Duchess*, is an allegorical lament written following the death of Blanche, the wife of John of Gaunt, who helped support Chaucer financially through much of his adult life.

On a diplomatic trip to Italy in 1372, Chaucer encountered the Renaissance, the great flowering of literature, painting, music, and other humanistic efforts to revive influences from Classical Greek and Roman times. The experience provided Chaucer with ideas for subjects and forms for his own writing. Italian writers such as Dante, Boccaccio, and Petrarch made a strong impression on Chaucer, yet he developed his own unique writing style. One of his best poems, *Troilus and Criseyde*, is based on a love story by Boccaccio. In the poem, Chaucer uses seven-line stanzas, perfecting a form that is now called *rhyme royal*. The verses are composed in iambic pentameter with a rhyme scheme of *ababbcc*.

Chaucer died before he was able to finish his greatest work, *The Canterbury Tales*. As explained on the following page, his strong storytelling and character realizations in these tales have entertained readers for centuries.

Noted Works

Book of the Duchess (c. 1370)

The House of Fame (c. 1379)

Parlement of Foules (c. 1382)

Troilus and Criseyde (c. 1384)

The Canterbury Tales (c. 1386)

The Prologue
from The Canterbury Tales

A Frame Tale by Geoffrey Chaucer
Translated by Nevill Coghill

Build Background

Literary Context Geoffrey Chaucer's *The Canterbury Tales* is a **frame tale,** a narrative that provides a vehicle for telling other stories. The frame for *The Canterbury Tales* is established in **"The Prologue,"** which introduces a diverse group of characters, including the narrator. The rest of the work consists primarily of tales the characters share to pass the time during their *pilgrimage* (religious journey) to Canterbury, the site of a shrine to St. Thomas à Becket. The characters, from various sectors of medieval life, are introduced roughly in order of social rank. After being described briefly in "The Prologue," the characters are further developed throughout *The Canterbury Tales* by the discussions they conduct and the stories they tell.

In creating his characters, Chaucer drew inspiration from a number of literary forms, cultural beliefs, and everyday experiences of people during this period. The literary forms represented in *The Canterbury Tales* include medieval romances, fairy tales, folk tales, *fabliau* (comic and bawdy stories), and sermons. The topics addressed by the pilgrims' stories range from chivalry and male-female relationships to the consequences of power and greed. The interaction among the characters and the diversity of storytellers and narratives are innovations that Chaucer made to the frame tale, which was already a popular form.

Chaucer began work on *The Canterbury Tales* around 1386 but never completed the project. He had planned for each pilgrim to tell four stories, but many of those narratives likely never were written and others exist only as unfinished fragments. The order the author intended for the stories also is unclear.

Cultural Context Pilgrimages to Canterbury were common during the Medieval Period, and the shrine of St. Thomas à Becket was one of the most visited in England. For the most part, the route from London to Canterbury was well established and well traveled. The towns along the way profited from the pilgrims' journeys by providing them with meals and lodging and selling them religious items, such as relics and flasks for holy water.

Reader's Context What can you learn about individuals from their appearance, their conversation, and the stories they tell? What can you learn about someone from what others tell you?

Analyze Literature

Characterization and Irony
Characterization is the act of creating or describing a character. *Direct characterization* describes characters outright; *indirect characterization* shows what characters say, do, or think or what others say or think about them.

Irony is the difference between appearance and reality.

Set Purpose

The Canterbury Tales have entertained readers for centuries, in large part because of Chaucer's strong skills in characterization. As you read each character description, jot down details about the individual. Also look for uses of irony—for example, instances in which characters are not as respectable as their social positions would suggest.

Preview Vocabulary

solicitous, 118
prelate, 119
absolution, 120
verity, 120
accrue, 121
arbitrate, 121
sanguine, 122
superfluity, 124
scrupulosity, 126
prevarication, 129

Chaucer's Canterbury Pilgrims, Tabard Inn, 1897. Edward Henry Corbould.
Private collection. (See detail on page 113.)

The Prologue

by Geoffrey Chaucer

Translated by Nevill Coghill

Of sundry folk happening then to fall
In fellowship, and they were pilgrims all
That towards Canterbury meant to ride.

<table>
<tr><td>

1 When in April the sweet showers fall[1]
    And pierce the drought of March to
      the root, and all
  The veins are bathed in liquor of such power
  As brings about the engendering of the flower,
5 When also Zephyrus[2] with his sweet breath
  Exhales an air in every grove and heath
  Upon the tender shoots, and the young sun
  His half-course in the sign of the Ram has run,[3]
  And the small fowl are making melody
10 That sleep away the night with open eye
  (So nature pricks them and their heart engages)
  Then people long to go on pilgrimages
  And palmers long to seek the stranger strands[4]
  Of far-off saints, hallowed in sundry lands,
15 And specially, from every shire's end
  Of England, down to Canterbury they wend
  To seek the holy blissful martyr,[5] quick
  To give his help to them when they were sick.
    It happened in that season that one day
20 In Southwark,[6] at *The Tabard,* as I lay
  Ready to go on pilgrimage and start
  For Canterbury, most devout at heart,
  At night there came into that hostelry
  Some nine and twenty in a company
25 Of sundry folk happening then to fall
  In fellowship, and they were pilgrims all
  That towards Canterbury meant to ride.
  The rooms and stables of the inn were wide;
  They made us easy, all was of the best.
30 And, briefly, when the sun had gone to rest,
  I'd spoken to them all upon the trip
  And was soon one with them in fellowship,
  Pledged to rise early and to take the way
  To Canterbury, as you heard me say.
35 But none the less, while I have time and
      space,
  Before my story takes a further pace,
  It seems a reasonable thing to say
  What their condition was, the full array
  Of each of them, as it appeared to me,
40 According to profession and degree,
  And what apparel they were riding in;
  And at a Knight I therefore will begin.

</td><td>

Whan that Aprill with his shoures soote
The droghte of March hath perced to
    the roote,
And bathed every veyne in swich licour
Of which vertu engendred is the flour;
Whan Zephirus eek with his sweete breeth
Inspired hath in every holt and heeth
The tendre croppes, and the yonge sonne
Hath in the Ram his halve cours yronne,
And smale foweles maken melodye,
That slepen al the nyght with open ye
(So priketh hem nature in hir corages);
Thanne longen folk to goon on pilgrimages,
And palmeres for to seken straunge strondes,
To ferne halwes, kowthe in sondry londes;
And specially from every shires ende
Of Engelond to Caunterbury they wende,
The hooly blisful martir for to seke,
That hem hath holpen whan that they were seeke.
  Bifil that in that seson on a day,
In Southwerk at the Tabard as I lay
Redy to wenden on my pilgrymage
To Caunterbury with ful devout corage,
At nyght was come into that hostelrye
Wel nyne and twenty in a compaignye,
Of sondry folk, by aventure yfalle
In felaweshipe, and pilgrimes were they alle,

</td></tr>
</table>

Here was a *Knight,* a most distinguished man,
Who from the day on which he first began
45 To ride abroad had followed chivalry,
  Truth, honor, generousness and courtesy.

---

1. **Lines 1–26** are given here in the original Middle English (right column) and in a Modern English translation (left column). The rest of "The Prologue" appears only in the Modern English translation.
2. **Zephyrus.** West wind
3. **young . . . run.** The sun has gone halfway through its course in Aries, the Ram, the first sign of the Zodiac in the solar year.
4. **palmers . . . strands.** Pilgrims went to visit faraway shrines.
5. **holy . . . martyr.** Saint Thomas à Becket, who was murdered in Canterbury Cathedral in 1170
6. **Southwark.** Suburb of London, located south of the River Thames, and the site of the Tabard Inn

Thomas à Becket

The "hooly blisful martir" Chaucer mentions in line 17 of "The Prologue" is Thomas à Becket (c. 1118–1170), who served as chancellor of England and Archbishop of Canterbury during the reign of King Henry II. In the twelfth century, King Henry hoped to make executive decisions without interference from the pope or the Catholic Church. In his role as chancellor, Becket generally had supported the king in conflicts between church and state. Henry therefore appointed Becket Archbishop of Canterbury, assuming he would use the position to enforce the king's will. Instead, Becket became a devout follower of Church law and answered to the pope instead of King Henry.

This conflict created serious animosity between the two men. In 1170, four knights overheard Henry ranting violently about Becket. The knights interpreted this as an order to assassinate Becket (although that probably was not Henry's intention), and they murdered the archbishop in Canterbury Cathedral. In response, Henry's relatives attempted to remove him from the throne, and other Christian countries quickly became hostile to England. Henry made reparations by performing public penance at Becket's grave, which became one of the most popular pilgrimage sites in England. Pope Alexander canonized Becket three years later, establishing him as St. Thomas à Becket.

The life of Thomas à Becket has been the subject of several modern dramas. In 1938, American-British poet and playwright T. S. Eliot dramatized Becket's death in the play *Murder in the Cathedral,* which generally is considered his finest drama. In 1959, French playwright Jean Anouilh also wrote a stage version entitled *Becket.* First produced on Broadway, the play won a Tony Award for best play of the 1960–1961 season. The film version of *Becket,* starring Peter O'Toole and Richard Burton, garnered twelve Oscar nominations in 1964.

He had done nobly in his sovereign's war
And ridden into battle, no man more,
As well in Christian as in heathen places,
50 And ever honored for his noble graces.
    When we took Alexandria, he was there.
He often sat at table in the chair
Of honor, above all nations, when in Prussia.
In Lithuania he had ridden, and Russia,
55 No Christian man so often, of his rank.
When, in Granada, Algeciras sank
Under assault, he had been there, and in
North Africa, raiding Benamarin;
In Anatolia he had been as well
60 And fought when Ayas and Attalia[7] fell,
For all along the Mediterranean coast
He had embarked with many a noble host.
In fifteen mortal battles he had been
And jousted for our faith at Tramissene

---

7. **Alexandria . . . Attalia.** Sites of battles in which the Knight fought against the Muslims, Moors, and various African, Asian, and European enemies

65 Thrice in the lists,[8] and always killed his man.
This same distinguished knight had led the
    van
Once with the Bey of Balat, doing work
For him against another heathen Turk;
He was of sovereign value in all eyes.
70 And though so much distinguished,
    he was wise
And in his bearing modest as a maid.
He never yet a boorish thing had said
In all his life to any, come what might;
He was a true, a perfect gentle-knight.
75 Speaking of his equipment, he possessed
Fine horses, but he was not gaily dressed.
He wore a fustian[9] tunic stained and dark
With smudges where his armor had left mark;
Just home from service, he had joined our
    ranks
80 To do his pilgrimage and render thanks.

> *He had done nobly
> in his sovereign's war,
> And ridden into battle,
> no man more.*

He had his son with him, a fine young
    Squire,
A lover and cadet, a lad of fire
With locks as curly as if they had been pressed.
He was some twenty years of age, I guessed.
85 In stature he was of a moderate length,
With wonderful agility and strength.
He'd seen some service with the cavalry
In Flanders and Artois and Picardy
And had done valiantly in little space
90 Of time, in hope to win his lady's grace.
He was embroidered like a meadow bright
And full of freshest flowers, red and white.
Singing he was, or fluting all the day;
He was as fresh as is the month of May.
95 Short was his gown, the sleeves were long
    and wide;

He knew the way to sit a horse and ride.
He could make songs and poems and recite,
Knew how to joust and dance, to draw and
    write.
He loved so hotly that till dawn grew pale
100 He slept as little as a nightingale.
Courteous he was, lowly and serviceable,
And carved to serve his father at the table.

There was a *Yeoman* with him at his side,
No other servant; so he chose to ride.
105 This Yeoman wore a coat and hood of green,
And peacock-feathered arrows, bright and
    keen
And neatly sheathed, hung at his belt the while
—For he could dress his gear in yeoman style,
His arrows never drooped their feathers
    low—
110 And in his hand he bore a mighty bow.
His head was like a nut, his face was brown.
He knew the whole of woodcraft up and down.
A saucy brace was on his arm to ward
It from the bow-string, and a shield and sword
115 Hung at one side, and at the other slipped
A jaunty dirk,[10] spear-sharp and well-
    equipped.
A medal of St. Christopher[11] he wore
Of shining silver on his breast, and bore
A hunting-horn, well slung and burnished
    clean,
120 That dangled from a baldrick[12] of bright green.
He was a proper forester, I guess.

There also was a *Nun,* a Prioress,
Her way of smiling very simple and coy.
Her greatest oath was only "By St. Loy!"
125 And she was known as Madam Eglantyne.
And well she sang a service, with a fine
Intoning through her nose, as was most
    seemly,

---

8. **lists.** Arena for jousting tournaments
9. **fustian.** Coarse cloth
10. **dirk.** Dagger
11. **St. Christopher.** Patron saint of travelers
12. **baldrick.** Belt worn over one shoulder and across the chest

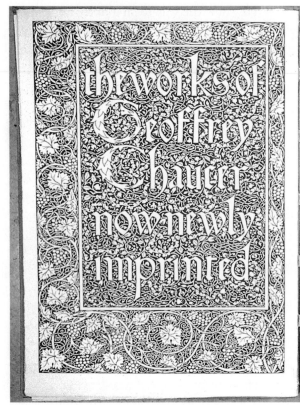

Title page of *The Works of Geoffrey Chaucer.* William Morris. Wellesley College Library, Wellesley, Massachusetts.

And she spoke daintily in French, extremely,
After the school of Stratford-atte-Bowe;[13]

130 French in the Paris style she did not know.
At meat her manners were well taught withal;
No morsel from her lips did she let fall,
Nor dipped her fingers in the sauce too deep;
But she could carry a morsel up and keep

135 The smallest drop from falling on her breast.
For courtliness she had a special zest,
And she would wipe her upper lip so clean
That not a trace of grease was to be seen
Upon the cup when she had drunk; to eat,

140 She reached a hand sedately for the meat.
She certainly was very entertaining,
Pleasant and friendly in her ways, and straining
To counterfeit a courtly kind of grace,
A stately bearing fitting to her place,

145 And to seem dignified in all her dealings.
As for her sympathies and tender feelings,

She was so charitably <u>solicitous</u>
She used to weep if she but saw a mouse
Caught in a trap, if it were dead or bleeding.

150 And she had little dogs she would be feeding
With roasted flesh, or milk, or fine white bread.
And bitterly she wept if one were dead
Or someone took a stick and made it smart;
She was all sentiment and tender heart.

155 Her veil was gathered in a seemly way,
Her nose was elegant, her eyes glass-grey;
Her mouth was very small, but soft and red,
Her forehead, certainly, was fair of spread,
Almost a span across the brows, I own;

160 She was indeed by no means undergrown.

---

13. **Stratford-atte-Bowe.** Location of a convent school where French was taught but not especially well

so • lic • i • tous (sə li´ sə təs) *adj.,* showing concern

Her cloak, I noticed, had a graceful charm.
She wore a coral trinket on her arm,
A set of beads, the gaudies[14] tricked in green,
Whence hung a golden brooch of brightest
    sheen
165 On which there first was graven a crowned A,
And lower, *Amor vincit omnia.*[15]

> ## Her way of smiling very simple and coy.

Another *Nun,* the secretary at her cell,
Was riding with her, and three *Priests*
    as well.
A *Monk* there was, one of the finest sort
170 Who rode the country; hunting was his sport.
A manly man, to be an Abbot able;
Many a dainty horse he had in stable.
His bridle, when he rode, a man might hear
Jingling in a whistling wind as clear,
175 Aye, and as loud as does the chapel bell
Where my lord Monk was Prior of the cell.
The Rule of good St. Benet or St. Maur
As old and strict he tended to ignore;
He let go by the things of yesterday
180 And took the modern world's more
    spacious way.
He did not rate that text at a plucked hen
Which says that hunters are not holy men
And that a monk uncloistered is a mere
Fish out of water, flapping on the pier,
185 That is to say a monk out of his cloister.
That was a text he held not worth an oyster;
And I agreed and said his views were sound;
Was he to study till his head went round
Poring over books in cloisters? Must he toil
190 As Austin bade and till the very soil?
Was he to leave the world upon the shelf?
Let Austin have his labor to himself.
This Monk was therefore a good man to horse;
Greyhounds he had, as swift as birds, to
    course.
195 Hunting a hare or riding at a fence

Was all his fun, he spared for no expense.
I saw his sleeves were garnished at the hand
With fine gray fur, the finest in the land,
And on his hood, to fasten it at his chin
200 He had a wrought-gold cunningly fashioned
    pin;
Into a lover's knot it seemed to pass.
His head was bald and shone like looking-
    glass;
So did his face, as if it had been greased.
He was a fat and personable[16] priest;
205 His prominent eyeballs never seemed to settle.
They glittered like the flames beneath a kettle;
Supple his boots, his horse in fine condition.
He was a prelate fit for exhibition,
He was not pale like a tormented soul.
210 He liked a fat swan best, and roasted whole.
His palfrey[17] was as brown as is a berry.

There was a *Friar,* a wanton[18] one and
    merry,
A Limiter,[19] a very festive fellow.
In all Four Orders[20] there was none so
    mellow,
215 So glib with gallant phrase and well-turned
    speech.
He'd fixed up many a marriage, giving each
Of his young women what he could afford her.
He was a noble pillar to his Order.
Highly beloved and intimate was he
220 With County folk within his boundary,
And city dames of honor and possessions;
For he was qualified to hear confessions,
Or so he said, with more than priestly scope;
He had a special license from the Pope.

---

14. **gaudies.** Every eleventh bead in a rosary marks a special prayer and is called a gaudy.
15. ***Amor vincit omnia.*** [Latin] Love conquers all
16. **personable.** Having a pleasant appearance and personality
17. **palfrey.** Horse
18. **wanton.** Unrestrained; extravagant
19. **Limiter.** Friar who could beg only in a limited, assigned area
20. **Four Orders.** There are four orders—Dominican, Franciscan, Carmelite, and Augustinian—whose friars live by begging.

> **prel • ate** (preˊlət) *n.,* high-ranking member of the clergy

Lydgate and the Canterbury Pilgrims Leaving Canterbury.
British Library, London, England.

225 Sweetly he heard his penitents at shrift[21]
  With pleasant <u>absolution</u>, for a gift.
  He was an easy man in penance-giving
  Where he could hope to make a decent living;
  It's a sure sign whenever gifts are given
230 To a poor Order that a man's well shriven,
  And should he give enough he knew in <u>verity</u>
  The penitent repented in sincerity.
  For many a fellow is so hard of heart
  He cannot weep, for all his inward smart.

235 Therefore instead of weeping and of prayer
  One should give silver for a poor Friar's care.
  He kept his tippet[22] stuffed with pins for curls,

---

21. **shrift.** Confession to a priest
22. **tippet.** Long scarf worn by a clergy

> **ab · so · lu · tion** (ab sə lü′ shən) *n.*, forgiveness, especially
> following confession
> **ver · i · ty** (ver′ ə tē) *n.*, truthfulness

And pocket-knives, to give to pretty girls.
And certainly his voice was gay and sturdy,
240 For he sang well and played the hurdy-gurdy.
At sing-songs he was champion of the hour.
His neck was whiter than a lily-flower
But strong enough to butt a bruiser down.
He knew the taverns well in every town
245 And every innkeeper and barmaid too
Better than lepers, beggars and that crew,
For in so eminent a man as he
It was not fitting with the dignity
Of his position, dealing with a scum
250 Of wretched lepers; nothing good can come
Of commerce with such slum-and-gutter
   dwellers,
But only with the rich and victual-sellers.
But anywhere a profit might <u>accrue</u>
Courteous he was and lowly of service too.
255 Natural gifts like his were hard to match.
He was the finest beggar of his batch,
And, for his begging-district, paid a rent;
His brethren did no poaching where he went.
For though a widow mightn't have a shoe,
260 So pleasant was his holy how-d'ye-do
He got his farthing from her just the same
Before he left, and so his income came
To more than he laid out. And how he
   romped,
Just like a puppy! He was ever prompt
265 To <u>arbitrate</u> disputes on settling days
(For a small fee) in many helpful ways,
Not then appearing as your cloistered scholar
With threadbare habit hardly worth a dollar,
But much more like a Doctor or a Pope.
270 Of double-worsted was the semi-cope
Upon his shoulders, and the swelling fold
About him, like a bell about its mold
When it is casting, rounded out his dress.
He lisped a little out of wantonness
275 To make his English sweet upon his tongue.
When he had played his harp, or having sung,
His eyes would twinkle in his head as bright
As any star upon a frosty night.
This worthy's name was Hubert, it appeared.

> *For many a fellow
> is so hard of heart
> He cannot weep,
> for all his inward smart.*

280 There was a *Merchant* with a forking
   beard
And motley[23] dress; high on his horse he sat,
Upon his head a Flemish beaver hat
And on his feet daintily buckled boots.
He told of his opinions and pursuits
285 In solemn tones, he harped on his increase
Of capital; there should be sea-police
(He thought) upon the Harwich-Holland
   ranges;[24]
He was expert at dabbling in exchanges.
This estimable Merchant so had set
290 His wits to work, none knew he was in debt,
He was so stately in administration,
In loans and bargains and negotiation.
He was an excellence fellow all the same;
To tell the truth I do not know his name.

295 An *Oxford Cleric,* still a student though,
   One who had taken logic long ago,
Was there; his horse was thinner than a rake,
And he was not too fat, I undertake,
But had a hollow look, a sober stare;
300 The thread upon his overcoat was bare.
He had found no preferment in the church
And he was too unworldly to make search
For secular employment. By his bed
He preferred having twenty books in red
305 And black, of Aristotle's philosophy,

---

23. **motley.** Multicolored
24. **sea-police . . . ranges.** He wanted the sea to be well monitored
   to guard his wool trade.

---

ac • crue (ə krü´) *v.,* accumulate or increase periodically
ar • bi • trate (är´ bə trāt) *v.,* settle a dispute

Than costly clothes, fiddle or psaltery.[25]
Though a philosopher, as I have told,
He had not found the stone for making gold.[26]
Whatever money from his friends he took
310 He spent on learning or another book
And prayed for them most earnestly, returning
Thanks to them thus for paying for his learning.
His only care was study, and indeed
He never spoke a word more than was need,
315 Formal at that, respectful in the extreme,
Short, to the point, and lofty in his theme.
A tone of moral virtue filled his speech
And gladly would he learn, and gladly teach.

> *Though there was nowhere
> one so busy as he,
> He was less busy
> than he seemed to be.*

A *Sergeant at the Law* who paid his calls,
320 Wary and wise, for clients at St. Paul's[27]
There also was, of noted excellence.
Discreet he was, a man to reverence,
Or so he seemed, his sayings were so wise.
He often had been Justice of Assize
325 By letters patent,[28] and in full commission.
His fame and learning and his high position
Had won him many a robe and many a fee.
There was no such conveyancer[29] as he;
All was fee-simple[30] to his strong digestion,
330 Not one conveyance could be called in
      question.
Though there was nowhere one so busy as he,
He was less busy than he seemed to be.
He knew of every judgment, case and crime
Ever recorded since King William's time.
335 He could dictate defenses or draft deeds;
No one could pinch a comma from his screeds
And he knew every statute off by rote.
He wore a homely parti-colored coat,
Girt with a silken belt of pin-stripe stuff;
340 Of his appearance I have said enough.

T here was a *Franklin*[31] with him, it
    appeared;
White as a daisy-petal was his beard.
A sanguine man, high-colored and benign,
He loved a morning sop of cake in wine.
345 He lived for pleasure and had always done,
For he was Epicurus,[32] very son,
In whose opinion sensual delight
Was the one true felicity in sight.
As noted as St. Julian was for bounty
350 He made his household free to all the County.
His bread, his ale were finest of the fine
And no one had a better stock of wine.
His house was never short of bake-meat pies,
Of fish and flesh, and these in such supplies
355 It positively snowed with meat and drink
And all the dainties that a man could think.
According to the seasons of the year
Changes of dish were ordered to appear.
He kept fat partridges in coops, beyond,
360 Many a bream and pike were in his pond.
Woe to the cook unless the sauce was hot
And sharp, or if he wasn't on the spot!
And in his hall a table stood arrayed
And ready all day long, with places laid.
365 As Justice at the Sessions none stood higher;
He often had been Member for the Shire.
A dagger and a little purse of silk
Hung at his girdle, white as morning milk.
As Sheriff he checked audit, every entry.
370 He was a model among landed gentry.

A *Haberdasher*, a *Dyer*, a *Carpenter*,
  A *Weaver* and a *Carpet-maker* were

---

25. **psaltery.** Type of harp
26. **the stone . . . gold.** Imaginary stone sought by alchemists
27. **St. Paul's.** The porch of St. Paul's Cathedral was a common meeting place for lawyers and their clients.
28. **letters patent.** Legal documents granting rights
29. **conveyancer.** Land speculator
30. **fee-simple.** Absolute and unrestricted
31. ***Franklin.*** Prosperous landowner of lower-class ancestry
32. **Epicurus.** One of the Greek philosophers who taught that pleasure should be a large part of life

san • guine (san´ gwən) *adj.,* ruddy, red; happy

Among our ranks, all in the livery[33]
Of one impressive guild-fraternity.

375 They were so trim and fresh their gear
       would pass
For new. Their knives were not tricked out[34]
       with brass
But wrought with purest silver, which
       avouches[35]
A like display on girdles and on pouches.
Each seemed a worthy burgess,[36] fit to grace
380 A guild-hall with a seat upon the dais.
Their wisdom would have justified a plan
To make each one of them an alderman;
They had the capital and revenue,
Besides their wives declared it was their due.
385 And if they did not think so, then they ought;
To be called *'Madam'* is a glorious thought,
And so is going to church and being seen
Having your mantle carried, like a queen.

Illustration of the Cook from *The Canterbury Tales*
(c. 1400s).

They had a *Cook* with them who stood
       alone
390 For boiling chicken with a marrow-bone,
Sharp flavoring-powder and a spice for savor.
He could distinguish London ale by flavor,
And he could roast and seethe and broil and
       fry,
Make good thick soup and bake a tasty pie.
395 But what a pity—so it seemed to me,
That he should have an ulcer on his knee.
As for blancmange,[37] he made it with the best.

There was a *Skipper* hailing from far west;
       He came from Dartmouth, so I
       understood.
400 He rode a farmer's horse as best he could,
In a woolen gown that reached his knee.
A dagger on a lanyard[38] falling free
Hung from his neck under his arm and down.
The summer heat had tanned his color brown,
405 And certainly he was an excellent fellow.
Many a draft of vintage, red and yellow,
He'd drawn at Bordeaux, while the trader
       snored.
The nicer rules of conscience he ignored.

If, when he fought, the enemy vessel sank,
410 He sent his prisoners home; they walked the
       plank.
As for his skill in reckoning his tides,
Currents and many another risk besides,
Moons, harbors, pilots, he had such dispatch
That none from Hull to Carthage was his
       match.
415 Hardy he was, prudent in undertaking;
His beard in many a tempest had its shaking,
And he knew all the havens as they were
From Gottland to the Cape of Finisterre,
And every creek in Brittany and Spain;
420 The barge he owned was called *The
       Maudelayne.*

A *Doctor* too emerged as we proceeded;
       No one alive could talk as well as he did
On points of medicine and of surgery,

---

33. **livery.** Uniform
34. **tricked out.** Dressed up
35. **avouches.** Gives reason to expect
36. **burgess.** Citizen of a borough or town
37. **blancmange.** Bland, custard-like dessert
38. **lanyard.** Cord worn around the neck

Page from *Canon of Medicine,* by Avicenna, a medieval Persian Islamic physician (c. 1300s).

Galen and Rhazes, Hali, Serapion,
Averroes, Avicenna, Constantine,
Scotch Bernard. John of Gaddesden,
    Gilbertine.[44]
445 In his own diet he observed some measure;
There were no <u>superfluities</u> for pleasure,
Only digestives, nutritives and such.
He did not read the Bible very much.
In blood-red garments, slashed with bluish
    gray
450 And lined with taffeta, he rode his way;
Yet he was rather close as to expenses
And kept the gold he won in pestilences.
Gold stimulates the heart, or so we're told.
He therefore had a special love of gold.

455 A worthy *woman* from beside Bath city
    Was with us, somewhat deaf, which
      was a pity.
In making cloth she showed so great a bent
She bettered those of Ypres and of Ghent.[45]
In all the parish not a dame dared stir
460 Toward the altar steps in front of her,
And if indeed they did, so wrath was she
As to be quite put out of charity.
Her kerchiefs were of finely woven ground[46]
I dared have sworn they weighed a good ten
    pound,
465 The ones she wore on Sunday, on her head.
Her hose were of the finest scarlet red

For, being grounded in astronomy,[39]
425 He watched his patient closely for the hours
When, by his horoscope, he knew the powers
Of favorable planets, then ascendant,
Worked on the images for his dependent.[40]
The cause of every malady you'd got
430 He knew, and whether dry, cold, moist or
    hot;[41]
He knew their seat, their humor and
    condition.
He was a perfect practicing physician.
These causes being known for what they were,
He gave the man his medicine then and there.
435 All his apothecaries[42] in a tribe
Were ready with the drugs he would prescribe
And each made money from the other's guile;[43]
They had been friendly for a goodish while.
He was well-versed in Aesculapius too
440 And what Hippocrates and Rufus knew
And Dioscorides, now dead and gone,

---

39. **astronomy.** Astrology
40. **He watched . . . dependent.** Effigies, or images, were made and used during the most influential hours according to the patient's horoscope.
41. **dry . . . hot.** It was believed that the human body was made up of four elements: earth, water, air, and fire. Earth was considered cold and dry; water, cold and wet; air, hot and moist; and fire, hot and dry. Disease, it was thought, was caused by an imbalance in these elements.
42. **apothecaries.** Pharmacists
43. **guile.** Slyness and cunning
44. **Aesculapius . . . Gilbertine.** Historic medical authorities
45. **Ypres and of Ghent.** Flemish cities known for cloth making
46. **ground.** Texture

su • per • flu • i • ty (sü pər´ flü ə tē) *n.,* something unnecessary or extra

And gartered tight; her shoes were soft and
    new.
Bold was her face, handsome, and red in hue.
A worthy woman all her life, what's more
470 She'd had five husbands, all at the church
    door,
Apart from other company in youth;
No need just now to speak of that, forsooth.
And she had thrice been to Jerusalem,
Seen many strange rivers and passed over
    them;
475 She'd been to Rome and also to Boulogne,
St. James of Compostella and Cologne,
And she was skilled in wandering by the way.
She had gap-teeth, set widely, truth to say.
Easily on an ambling horse she sat
480 Well wimpled up;[47] and oh her head a hat
As broad as is a buckler[48] or a shield;
She had a flowing mantle that concealed
Large hips, her heels spurred sharply under
    that.
In company she liked to laugh and chat
485 And knew the remedies for love's mischances,
An art in which she knew the oldest dances.

A holy-minded man of good renown
There was, and poor, the *Parson* to a
    town,
Yet he was rich in holy thought and work.
490 He also was a learned man, a clerk,
Who truly knew Christ's gospel and would
    preach it
Devoutly to parishioners, and teach it.
Benign and wonderfully diligent.[49]
And patient when adversity was sent
495 (For so he proved in much adversity)
He hated cursing to extort a fee,
Nay rather he preferred beyond a doubt
Giving to poor parishioners round about
Both from church offerings and his property;
500 He could in little find sufficiency.
Wide was his parish, with houses far asunder,
Yet he neglected not in rain or thunder,
In sickness or in grief, to pay a call
On the remotest, whether great or small,

Chaucer at the Court of Edward III, c. 1847–1851.
Ford Madox Brown. Art Gallery of New South Wales,
Sydney, Australia.

505 Upon his feet, and in his hand a stave.
This noble example to his sheep he gave
That first he wrought, and afterwards he
    taught;
And it was from the Gospel he had caught
Those words, and he would add this figure
    too,
510 That if gold rust, what then will iron do?
For if a priest be foul in whom we trust
No wonder that a common man should rust;
And shame it is to see—let priests take stock—
A shitten shepherd and a snowy flock.
515 The true example that a priest should give
Is one of cleanness, how the sheep should live.
He did not set his benefice[50] to hire
And leave his sheep encumbered[51] in the mire

---

47. **wimpled up.** Medieval women commonly wrapped their heads
    and necks in a cloth called a *wimple.*
48. **buckler.** Small shield
49. **diligent.** Hard-working; persevering
50. **benefice.** Endowed office
51. **encumbered.** Held back

Or run to London to earn easy bread
520　By singing masses for the wealthy dead,
Or find some Brotherhood and get enrolled.
He stayed at home and watched over his fold
So that no wolf should make the sheep
　　　miscarry.
He was a shepherd and no mercenary.
525　Holy and virtuous he was, but then
Never contemptuous of sinful men,
Never disdainful, never too proud or fine,
But was discreet in teaching and benign.
His business was to show a fair behavior
530　And draw men thus to Heaven and their
　　　Savior,
Unless indeed a man were obstinate;
And such, whether of high or low estate,
He put to sharp rebuke, to say the least.
I think there never was a better priest.
535　He sought no pomp or glory in his dealings,
No <u>scrupulosity</u> had spiced his feelings.
Christ and His Twelve Apostles and their lore
He taught, but followed it himself before.

There was a *Plowman* with him there,
　　　his brother;
540　Many a load of dung one time or other
He must have carted through the morning dew.
He was an honest worker, good and true,
Living in peace and perfect charity,
And, as the gospel bade him, so did he,
545　Loving God best with all his heart and mind
And then his neighbor as himself, repined
At no misfortune, slacked for no content,
For steadily about his work he went
To thrash his corn, to dig or to manure
550　Or make a ditch; and he would help the poor
For love of Christ and never take a penny
If he could help it, and, as prompt as any,
He paid his tithes in full when they were due
On what he owned, and on his earnings too.
555　He wore a tabard smock[52] and rode a mare.

There was a *Reeve,*[53] also a *Miller,* there
A College *Manciple*[54] from the Inns of
　　　Court,

A papal *Pardoner,*[55] and, in close consort,[56]
A Church-Court *Summoner,*[57] riding at a trot
560　And finally myself—that was the lot.

> *A wrangler and buffoon,*
> *he had a store*
> *Of tavern stories,*
> *filthy in the main.*

The *Miller* was a chap of sixteen stone,[58]
A great stout fellow big in brawn and
　　　bone.
He did well out of them, for he could go
And win the ram[59] at any wrestling show.
565　Broad, knotty and short-shouldered, he
　　　would boast
He could heave any door off hinge and post,
Or take a run and break it with his head.
His beard, like any sow or fox, was red
And broad as well, as though it were a spade;
570　And, at its very tip, his nose displayed
A wart on which there stood a tuft of hair
Red as the bristles in an old sow's ear.
His nostrils were as black as they were wide.
He had a sword and buckler at his side,
575　His mighty mouth was like a furnace door.
A wrangler[60] and buffoon, he had a store
Of tavern stories, filthy in the main.
His was a master-hand at stealing grain.

---

52. **tabard smock.** Loose jacket, sometimes bearing a lord's crest
53. ***Reeve.*** Overseer of an estate
54. ***Manciple.*** Purchasing agent
55. ***Pardoner.*** Person with authority from the pope to sell sinners pardons and indulgences
56. **consort.** Partnership
57. ***Summoner.*** Employee of the religious court who summoned those who were suspected of breaking church law
58. **stone.** Unit of weight equal to fourteen pounds
59. **win the ram.** A ram was the usual prize at the popular wrestling tournaments.
60. **wrangler.** One who provokes arguments

scru • pu • los • i • ty (skrü pyə lä´ sə tē) *n.,* moral worry or concern

He felt it with his thumb and thus he knew
580 Its quality and took three times his due—[61]
A thumb of gold, by God, to gauge an oat!
He wore a hood of blue and a white coat.
He liked to play his bagpipes up and down
And that was how he brought us out of town.

585 The *Manciple* came from the Inner Temple;
All caterers might follow his example
In buying victuals; he was never rash
Whether he bought on credit or paid cash.
He used to watch the market most precisely
590 And got in first, and so he did quite nicely.
Now isn't it a marvel of God's grace
That an illiterate fellow can outpace
The wisdom of a heap of learned men?
His masters—he had more than thirty then—
595 All versed in the abstrusest[62] legal
knowledge,
Could have produced a dozen from their
College
Fit to be stewards in land and rents and game
To any Peer in England you could name,
And show him how to live on what he had
600 Debt-free (unless of course the Peer were mad)
Or be as frugal[63] as he might desire,
And make them fit to help about the Shire
In any legal case there was to try;
And yet this Manciple could wipe their eye.

605 The *Reeve* was old and choleric and thin;
His beard was shaven closely to the skin,
His shorn hair came abruptly to a stop
Above his ears, and he was docked[64] on top
Just like a priest in front; his legs were lean,
610 Like sticks they were, no calf was to be seen.
He kept his bins and garners[65] very trim;
No auditor could gain a point on him.
And he could judge by watching drought
and rain
The yield he might expect from seed and grain.
615 His master's sheep, his animals and hens,
Pigs, horses, dairies, stores and cattle-pens
Were wholly trusted to his government,
He had been under contract to present

Illustration of the Manciple from *The Canterbury Tales.*

The accounts, right from his master's earliest
years.
620 No one had ever caught him in arrears.
No bailiff, serf or herdsman dared to kick,
He knew their dodges, knew their every trick;
Feared like the plague he was, by those
beneath.
He had a lovely dwelling on a heath,
625 Shadowed in green by trees above the sward.[66]
A better hand at bargains than his lord,
He had grown rich and had a store of treasure
Well tucked away, yet out it came to pleasure

61. **Took . . . due.** Took for himself more than the lawful
percentage
62. **abstrusest.** Most difficult to understand
63. **frugal.** Thrifty
64. **docked.** Trimmed
65. **garners.** Granaries
66. **sward.** Grassy area

Manuscript illustration of Chaucer reading his poems to the court of Richard II, c. 1400s. Corpus Christi College, Cambridge, England.

For he had carbuncles.[69] His eyes were narrow,
He was as hot and lecherous as a sparrow.
645   Black scabby brows he had, and a thin beard.
Children were afraid when he appeared.
No quicksilver, lead ointment, tartar creams,
No brimstone, no boracic, so it seems,
Could make a salve that had the power to bite,
650   Clean up or cure his whelks[70] of knobby white
Or purge the pimples sitting on his cheeks.
Garlic he loved, and onions too, and leeks,
And drinking strong red wine till all was hazy.
Then he would shout and jabber as if crazy,
655   And wouldn't speak a word except in Latin
When he was drunk, such tags as he was
        pat in;
He only had a few, say two or three,
That he had mugged up out of some decree;[71]
No wonder, for he heard them every day.
660   And, as you know, a man can teach a jay
To call out "Walter" better than the Pope.
But had you tried to test his wits and grope
For more, you'd have found nothing in the
        bag.
Then *"Questio quid juris"*[72] was his tag.
665   He was a noble varlet[73] and a kind one,
You'd meet none better if you went to find
        one.
Why, he'd allow—just for a quart of wine—
Any good lad to keep a concubine
A twelvemonth and dispense him altogether!
670   And he had finches of his own to feather:
And if he found some rascal with a maid
He would instruct him not to be afraid
In such a case of the Archdeacon's curse
(Unless the rascal's soul were in his purse)
675   For in his purse the punishment should be.
"Purse is the good Archdeacon's Hell," said he.
But well I know he lied in what he said;

His lord with subtle loans or gifts of goods,
630   To earn his thanks and even coats and hoods.
When young he'd learnt a useful trade and still
He was a carpenter of first-rate skill.
The stallion-cob he rode at a slow trot
Was dapple-grey and bore the name of Scot.
635   He wore an overcoat of bluish shade
And rather long; he had a rusty blade
Slung at his side. He came, as I heard tell,
From Norfolk, near a place called Baldeswell.
His coat was tucked under his belt and
        splayed.[67]
640   He rode the hindmost of our cavalcade.

There was a *Summoner* with us at that Inn,
His face on fire, like a cherubin,[68]

---

67. **splayed.** Spread out
68. **cherubin.** Cherubs are often depicted with red faces.
69 and 70. **carbuncles; whelks.** Pus-filled boils
71. **he had . . . decree.** He had hurriedly studied when a new law required it.
72. **Questio quid juris.** Common phrase in religious courts, Latin for "What point of law does this involve?"
73. **varlet.** Rascal

A curse should put a guilty man in dread,
For curses kill, as shriving[74] brings, salvation.
680 We should beware of excommunication.
Thus, as he pleased, the man could bring duress
On any young fellow in the diocese.
He knew their secrets, they did what he said.
He wore a garland set upon his head
685 Large as the holly-bush upon a stake
Outside an ale-house, and he had a cake,
A round one, which it was his joke to wield
As if it were intended for a shield.

> *But well I know
> he lied in what he said;
> A curse should put
> a guilty man in dread.*

He and a gentle *Pardoner* rode together,
690 A bird from Charing Cross of the same feather,
Just back from visiting the Court of Rome.
He loudly sang *"Come hither, love, come home!"*
The Summoner sang deep seconds to this song,
No trumpet ever sounded half so strong.
695 This Pardoner had hair as yellow as wax,
Hanging down smoothly like a hank of flax.
In driblets fell his locks behind his head
Down to his shoulders which they overspread;
Thinly they fell, like rat-tails, one by one.
700 He wore no hood upon his head, for fun;
The hood inside his wallet[75] had been stowed,
He aimed at riding in the latest mode;
But for a little cap his head was bare
And he had bulging eye-balls, like a hare.
705 He'd sewed a holy relic on his cap;
His wallet lay before him on his lap,
Brimful of pardons come from Rome, all hot.
He had the same small voice a goat has got.
His chin no beard had harbored, nor would harbor,

710 Smoother than ever chin was left by barber.
I judge he was a gelding, or a mare.
As to his trade, from Berwick down to Ware
There was no pardoner of equal grace,
For in his trunk he had a pillow-case
715 Which he asserted was Our Lady's veil.
He said he had a gobbet[76] of the sail
Saint Peter had the time when he made bold
To walk the waves, till Jesu Christ took hold.
He had a cross of metal set with stones
720 And, in a glass, a rubble of pigs' bones.
And with these relics, any time he found
Some poor up-country parson to astound,
In one short day, in money down, he drew
More than the parson in a month or two,
725 And by his flatteries and prevarication
Made monkeys of the priest and congregation.
But still to do him justice first and last
In church he was a noble ecclesiast.
How well he read a lesson or told a story!
730 But best of all he sang an Offertory,
For well he knew that when that song was sung
He'd have to preach and tune his honey-tongue
And (well he could) win silver from the crowd.
That's why he sang so merrily and loud.

How I have told you shortly, in a clause,
735 The rank, the array, the number and the cause
Of our assembly in this company
In Southwark, at that high-class hostelry
Known as *The Tabard,* close beside *The Bell.*
740 And now the time has come for me to tell
How we behaved that evening; I'll begin
After we had alighted at the Inn,
Then I'll report our journey, stage by stage,

---

74. **shriving**. Confessing
75. **wallet.** Knapsack
76. **gobbet.** Bit, fragment

---

pre • var • i • ca • tion (pri ver ə kā′ shən) *n.,* lie; falsehood

Howe þ[at] þ[i]s Mauuint was mayden marie
And sir his loue floure and fructifie

Al þogh his lyfe be queynt þe resemblaunce
Of him hath in me so fressh lyflynesse
Þat to putte othir men in remembraunce
Of his persone I haue heere his lyknesse
Do make to þis ende in sothfastnesse
Þat þei þat haue of him lest þought & mynde
By þis peynture may ageyn him fynde

The ymages þ[at] in þe chirche been
Maken folk þenke on god & on his seyntes
Whan þe ymages þei beholden & seen
Were oft vnsyte of hem cauffeth restreyntes
Of þoughtes gode Whan a þing depeynt is
Or entailed if men take of it heede
Thoght of þe lyknesse it wil in hym brede

Illuminated (illustrated) page from "The Prologue" of *The Canterbury Tales*.

All the remainder of our pilgrimage.
745 But first I beg of you, in courtesy,
Not to condemn me as unmannerly
If I speak plainly and with no concealings
And give account of all their words and
    dealings,
Using their very phrases as they fell.
750 For certainly, as you all know so well,
He who repeats a tale after a man
Is bound to say, as nearly as he can,
Each single word, if he remembers it,
However rudely spoken or unfit,
755 Or else the tale he tells will be untrue,

The things pretended and the phrases new.
He may not flinch although it were his brother,
He may as well say one word as another.
And Christ Himself spoke broad in Holy Writ,
760 Yet there is no scurrility[77] in it,
And Plato says, for those with power to read,
"The word should be as cousin to the deed."
Further I beg you to forgive it me
If I neglect the order and degree
765 And what is due to rank in what I've planned.
I'm short of wit as you will understand.

---

77. **scurrility.** Coarseness or indecency of language

Our *Host* gave us great welcome; everyone
Was given a place and supper was
  begun.
He served the finest victuals[78] you could think,
770 The wine was strong and we were glad to
  drink.
A very striking man our Host withal,
And fit to be a marshal in a hall.
His eyes were bright, his girth a little wide;
There is no finer burgess in Cheapside.[79]
775 Bold in his speech, yet wise and full of tact,
There was no manly attribute he lacked,
What's more he was a merry-hearted man.
After our meal he jokingly began
To talk of sport, and, among other things
780 After we'd settled up our reckonings,
He said as follows: "Truly, gentlemen,
You're very welcome and I can't think when
—Upon my word I'm telling you no lie—
I've seen a gathering here that looked so spry,
785 No, not this year, as in this tavern now.
I'd think you up some fun if I knew how.
And, as it happens, a thought has just occurred
To please you, costing nothing, on my word.
You're off to Canterbury—well, God speed!
790 Blessed St. Thomas answer to your need!
And I don't doubt, before the journey's done
You mean to while the time in tales and fun.
Indeed, there's little pleasure for your bones
Riding along and all as dumb as stones.
795 So let me then propose for your enjoyment,
Just as I said, a suitable employment.
And if my notion suits and you agree
And promise to submit yourselves to me
Playing your parts exactly as I say
800 Tomorrow as you ride along the way,
Then by my father's soul (and he is dead)
If you don't like it you can have my head!
Hold up your hands, and not another word."
  Well, our opinion was not long deferred,
805 It seemed not worth a serious debate;
We all agreed to it at any rate
And bade him issue what commands he
  would.
"My lords," he said, "now listen for your good,

And please don't treat my notion with disdain.
810 This is the point. I'll make it short and plain.
Each one of you shall help to make things slip
By telling two stories on the outward trip
To Canterbury, that's what I intend,
And, on the homeward way to journey's end
815 Another two, tales from the days of old;
And then the man whose story is best told,
That is to say who gives the fullest measure
Of good morality and general pleasure,
He shall be given a supper, paid by all,
820 Here in this tavern, in this very hall,
When we come back again from Canterbury.

> *And I don't doubt,
> before the journey's done,
> You mean to while the time
> in tales and fun.*

And in the hope to keep you bright and merry
I'll go along with you myself and ride
All at my own expense and serve as guide.
825 I'll be the judge, and those who won't obey
Shall pay for what we spend upon the way.
Now if you all agree to what you've heard
Tell me at once without another word,
And I will make arrangements early for it."
830   Of course we all agreed, in fact we swore it
Delightedly, and made entreaty too
That he should act as he proposed to do,
Become our Governor in short, and be
Judge of our tales and general referee,
835 And set the supper at a certain price.
We promised to be ruled by his advice
Come high, come low; unanimously thus
We set him up in judgment over us.
More wine was fetched, the business being
  done;

---

78. **victuals.** Prepared foods
79. **Cheapside.** Section of London; in Chaucer's day, the site of a
marketplace

Illustration of the Knight from *The Canterbury Tales* (c. 1400s).

> # Now draw for cut
> ## and then we can depart;
> ### The man who draws
> ### the shortest cut shall start.

855 Now draw for cut and then we can depart;
The man who draws the shortest cut shall
    start.
"My Lord the Knight," he said, "step up to me
And draw your cut, for that is my decree.
And come you near, my Lady Prioress,
860 And you, Sir Cleric, drop your shame-
    fastness,[81]
No studying now! A hand from every man!"
Immediately the draw for lots began
And to tell shortly how the matter went,
Whether by chance or fate or accident,
865 The truth is this, the cut fell to the Knight,[82]
Which everybody greeted with delight.
And tell his tale he must, as reason was
Because of our agreement and because
He too had sworn. What more is there to say?
870 For when this good man saw how matters lay,
Being by wisdom and obedience driven
To keep a promise he had freely given,
He said, "Since it's for me to start the game,
Why, welcome be the cut in God's good name!
875 Now let us ride, and listen to what I say."
And at the word we started on our way
And in a cheerful style he then began
At once to tell his tale, and thus it ran. ❖

840 We drank it off and up went everyone
To bed without a moment of delay.
    Early next morning at the spring of day
Up rose our Host and roused us like a cock,
Gathering us together in a flock,
845 And off we rode at slightly faster pace
Than walking to St. Thomas' watering-place;[80]
And there our Host drew up, began to ease
His horse, and said, "Now, listen if you please,
My lords! Remember what you promised me.
850 If evensong and matins will agree
Let's see who shall be first to tell a tale.
And as I hope to drink good wine and ale
I'll be your judge. The rebel who disobeys,
However much the journey costs, he pays,

---

80. **St. Thomas' watering-place.** Brook crossed by the road to
    Canterbury two miles from London
81. **shamefastness.** Shyness
82. **Whether . . . Knight.** Chance, fate, and accident play a large
    role in the Knight's tale. It is fitting that he begins the story-telling
    for the same reason he is described first: because of his social rank.

MIRRORS & **W**INDOWS

In line 766 of "The Prologue," the narrator says of himself, "I'm short of wit as you
will understand." Do you agree with his self-assessment? Based on "The Prologue,"
what kind of person does the narrator seem to be?

Refer to Text ▶ ▶ ▶ ▶ ▶ Reason with Text

1a. Name the pilgrims who are associated with the Church.

1b. Compare and contrast the Parson to the other religious figures on the trip. How are they alike and different?

Understand
Find meaning

2a. The Monk likes to hunt. What does the Church teach about hunting?

2b. *Satire* is humor intended to point out errors, falsehoods, and failings. Who does Chaucer satirize? What failings does he point out?

Apply
Use information

3a. From whose point of view is "The Prologue" told? Which pronoun in the text identifies this person?

3b. Differentiate between the character traits that are honored and those portrayed as negative qualities.

Analyze
Take things apart

4a. Recall what the narrator says will happen if he does not report every word the pilgrims speak.

4b. From what you have read in "The Prologue," is the narrator an objective reporter? Consider the motive for his comments in lines 740–766.

Evaluate
Make judgments

5a. What is the primary purpose of "The Prologue"?

5b. If you were going to create a present-day version of *The Canterbury Tales*, what people, values, and failings would you include? Why?

Create
Bring ideas together

Analyze Literature

Characterization and Irony

Review the list of details you noted for each pilgrim. What information does Chaucer provide? How much of the information comes from the characters themselves versus their fellow pilgrims? How might the source of the information affect its credibility?

Identify instances of irony in "The Prologue." What are the major targets of the irony? Use examples from the text to support your answer.

Extend the Text

Writing Options

Creative Writing Imagine that you are a pilgrim going to Canterbury. You might be the Student, the Teenager, or the Twenty-First-Century Traveler. Choose a role and then write an introduction of your character using Chaucer's style.

Expository Writing Write a one-paragraph character analysis of one of the pilgrims introduced in "The Prologue." Reread the description of this character; then imagine meeting him or her. How might he or she behave, say, at a baseball game, rock concert, or other modern-day event? Base your judgment on the details provided in "The Prologue."

Lifelong Learning

Research Social Stratification Using library and Internet sources, research social stratification (or class structure) in the Medieval Period. Identify the primary social classes and what determined membership in them. To which class does each character in "The Prologue" belong? Create a chart that identifies the primary social classes and lists the pilgrims that belong in each class.

Collaborative Learning

Illustrate the Troubadours Working with a group, briefly research medieval music. For example, what instruments commonly were played during this era? What kinds of songs did the troubadours sing? Who wrote the lyrics and the music? Create a display illustrating troubadours and medieval musical instruments.

 Go to **www.mirrorsandwindows.com** for more.

1. Which of the following lines from early in "The Pro-logue" states the basic idea underlying the frame tale?
   A. "When in April the sweet showers fall." (line 1)
   B. "As brings about the engendering of the flower." (line 4)
   C. "(So nature pricks them and their heart engages.)" (line 11)
   D. "Then people long to go on pilgrimages." (line 12)
   E. "To give his help to them when they were sick." (line 18)

2. In line 71, the Knight is described as being "modest as a maid." This is an example of what?
   A. a simile
   B. personification
   C. a metaphor
   D. irony
   E. an allusion

3. Review the descriptions of the Knight, the Squire, the Nun, and the Cleric. Chaucer uses verbal irony in describing which of these characters?
   A. Knight: "He was a true, a perfect gentle-knight." (line 74)
   B. Squire: "He was as fresh as is the month of May." (line 94)
   C. Nun: "She was all sentiment and tender heart." (line 154)
   D. Cleric: "His only care was study." (line 313)
   E. All of the above

4. From what point of view (perspective) is the story told, and what effect does this have on your reading of it?
   A. The story is told using first-person point of view, which makes it seem distant and objective.
   B. The story is told using first-person point of view, which makes it seem live and personal.
   C. The story is told using third-person point of view, which makes it seem distant and objective.
   D. The story is told using third-person point of view, which makes it seem live and personal.
   E. The story is told using both first- and third-person points of view, which provides a balanced perspective.

5. In lines 455–486, all of the following details are revealed about the Wife of Bath except what?
   A. She has had five husbands.
   B. She wears tight red hose (stockings).
   C. She is a talented weaver.
   D. She is modest and ladylike.
   E. She has traveled to Rome and Jerusalem.

6. In the contest proposed by the Host, what is the award?
   A. a supper paid for by the others
   B. being assured of going to heaven
   C. forgiveness for any wrongdoing
   D. being the judge of the pilgrims' tales
   E. the privilege of returning on horseback

7. How does the Parson compare to the other church figures: the Nun, the Monk, and the Friar?
   A. He is different from the others because he is a fraud.
   B. He is different from the others because he is caring and unselfish.
   C. He is similar to the others in terms of age.
   D. He is similar to the others in terms of being a religious and moral person.
   E. He is similar to the others in terms of being morally corrupt and un-Christian.

8. In lines 662–663, the Summoner is characterized as being what?
   A. careful with money
   B. not very smart
   C. passionately eloquent
   D. faithful and devoted
   E. coldly calculating

9. **Constructed Response:** Choose one character from "The Prologue," and summarize what the narrator reveals about him or her. Then infer what this description reveals about the character's personality, values, and beliefs. Use details from the passage to support your answer.

10. **Constructed Response:** Suppose you had the chance to spend a day with one of the individuals making the pilgrimage to Canterbury. Which pilgrim would you most like to know and why? Would your answer change if you had to spend more than a day with this individual? Explain.

Understand the Concept

Many writers sometimes make the mistake of writing sentence fragments instead of complete sentences. A **sentence fragment** is a phrase or clause that does not express a complete thought but has been capitalized and punctuated as if it were a sentence.

EXAMPLES

Phrase fragment Pilgrims on their way to Canterbury. [The verb, plus any modifiers, is missing.]

Sentence Pilgrims on their way to Canterbury told stories to each other.

Clause fragment When they reached the famous cathedral. [This is a clause, not a sentence, because it begins with a subordinating conjunction, *when*. To become a sentence, the fragment needs to be linked to a main clause.]

Sentence When they reached the famous cathedral, the pilgrims visited the tomb of Thomas à Becket.

Clause fragment Whom the plotters murdered in the cathedral in 1170. [This is a clause, not a sentence, because it begins with a relative pronoun, *whom*. The fragment needs to be linked to a main clause to become a sentence.]

Sentence It was Becket whom the plotters murdered in the cathedral in 1170.

To avoid writing fragments, make sure that every sentence has a subject and a verb. If you write a clause introduced by a subordinating conjunction or a relative pronoun, be sure to link the clause to a main clause to make a sentence. Another way to catch fragments in your writing is to proofread your work carefully.

Apply the Skill

Identify Sentence Fragments
Indicate which of the following items are *sentences* (mark *S*) and which are *fragments* (mark *F*).

1. Geoffrey Chaucer a talented, skilled writer.
2. After he produced a collection of works about life in medieval times.
3. Chaucer is best known for his collection of stories within a story, *The Canterbury Tales*.
4. The structure of a frame tale.
5. The stories for *The Canterbury Tales* are not all original creations of Chaucer.
6. Drawn from many sources, including love poems, the lives of saints, and other religious works.
7. Fables more often passed by word of mouth than written down.
8. Chosen to fit the variety of characters.
9. For example, the Pardoner gives a sample of one of the sermons.
10. Even in its unfinished state, remains a masterpiece of English literature.

Fix Sentence Fragments
The following items are all fragments. Rewrite each one to make it a sentence.

1. In the twelfth century, the first stained glass windows.
2. Stories in colorful pieces of glass.
3. Helped people learn stories from the Bible.
4. Pieces of glass with lead between them.
5. Provided brilliant images and captivated worshippers' attention.

Use Complete Sentences
Work with a partner to practice building sentences and avoiding fragments. Each of you should make a list of five phrases, including prepositional phrases (for example, *behind the building*), participial phrases (*having tried several times*), and infinitive phrases (*to complete the project on time*). Then exchange lists. From each phrase, build a sentence. (If necessary, make minor adjustments in the wording of the phrase.) Read your sentences aloud and work together to correct any fragments.

The Pardoner's Tale
The Wife of Bath's Tale
from The Canterbury Tales

A Frame Tale by Geoffrey Chaucer
Translated by Nevill Coghill

Build Background

Literary Context **"The Pardoner's Tale,"** one of the stories in Chaucer's *The Canterbury Tales,* is preceded by a brief prologue of its own, in which the Pardoner explains how he preaches against greed. In the Medieval Period, a *pardoner* was a religious authority who sold pardons and indulgences to sinners, essentially allowing people to buy forgiveness.

Like many of Chaucer's stories, "The Pardoner's Tale" has several possible origins. The most likely source is one of the many collections of **exempla,** or brief stories told to teach moral lessons, that were circulated throughout Europe during this era and often used in sermons.

Like "The Pardoner's Tale," **"The Wife of Bath's Tale"** is preceded by a prologue; in fact, the prologue is twice as long as the actual tale. In the prologue, the Wife of Bath expresses her belief that a good marriage is one in which the wife dominates the husband or, at the very least, is allowed to do what she wants.

"The Wife of Bath's Tale" has a plot device that sometimes is associated with stories of heroes: namely, the search for an answer to a question or a riddle. In Chaucer's version, a knight whom the king has sentenced to death tries to save his life by correctly answering a question posed by the queen. Given a year and a day to respond, the knight sets off on a journey to find the answer to the queen's question.

"The Wife of Bath's Tale" confronts a number of cultural assumptions made about women during this period. For instance, medieval society recognized a strict gender hierarchy, in which women were subordinate to men. Also, men typically were believed to be calm and rational, whereas women were believed to be impulsive and emotional. As you read "The Wife of Bath's Tale," consider how these assumptions regarding social status and gender differences are treated in the story.

Reader's Context Think of a story you have read or a movie you have seen that addresses an important social issue. How do such stories encourage people to discuss these issues?

Analyze Literature

Characterization and Irony
Characterization is the act of creating or describing a character.

Irony is the difference between appearance and reality.

Set Purpose

Throughout *The Canterbury Tales,* Chaucer continues to develop his characters by relying on *indirect characterization:* showing what characters say, do, or think or what others say or think about them. As you read these tales consider what beliefs and values are expressed in each story. Also look for instances of *situational irony,* in which a character does not behave according to his or her social position.

Preview Vocabulary

prudent, 140
forlorn, 144
implore, 144
reprove, 145
contemptuous, 147
abominably, 147
temporal, 148
esteem, 148
suffice, 150

Chaucer, the Knight, and the Squire, c. 1900s. Harry Mileham.
Private collection. (See detail on page 136.)

THE PARDONER'S TALE

by Geoffrey Chaucer

"What, old fool? Give place!
Why are you all wrapped up except your face?
Why live so long? Isn't it time to die?"

It's of three rioters I have to tell
Who, long before the morning service bell,
Were sitting in a tavern for a drink.
And as they sat, they heard the hand-bell clink
5 Before a coffin going to the grave;

One of them called the little tavern-knave
And said "Go and find out at once—look
      spry!—
Whose corpse is in that coffin passing by;
And see you get the name correctly too."

10 "Sir," said the boy, "no need, I promise you;
　Two hours before you came here I was told.
　He was a friend of yours in days of old,
　And suddenly, last night, the man was slain,
　Upon his bench, face up, dead drunk again.
15 There came a privy thief, they call him Death,
　Who kills us all round here, and in a breath
　He speared him through the heart, he never
　　　stirred.
　And then Death went his way without a word.
　He's killed a thousand in the present plague,
20 And, sir, it doesn't do to be too vague
　If you should meet him; you had best be
　　　wary.¹
　Be on your guard with such an adversary,
　Be primed to meet him everywhere you go,
　That's what my mother said. It's all I know."
25 The publican joined in with, "By St. Mary,
　What the child says is right; you'd best be
　　　wary,
　This very year he killed, in a large village
　A mile away, man, woman, serf at tillage,²
　Page in the household, children—all there
　　　were.
30 Yes, I imagine that he lives round there.
　It's well to be prepared in these alarms,
　He might do you dishonor." "Huh, God's
　　　arms!"
　The rioter said, "Is he so fierce to meet?
　I'll search for him, by Jesus, street by street.
35 God's blessed bones! I'll register a vow!
　Here chaps! The three of us together now,
　Hold up your hands, like me, and we'll be
　　　brothers
　In this affair, and each defend the others,
　And we will kill this traitor Death, I say!
40 Away with him as he has made away
　With all our friends. God's dignity! Tonight!"
　　They made their bargain, swore with
　　　appetite,
　These three, to live and die for one another
　As brother-born might swear to his born
　　　brother.
45 And up they started in their drunken rage
　And made towards this village which the page

And publican had spoken of before.
Many and grisly³ were the oaths they swore,
Tearing Christ's blessed body to a shred;
50 "If we can only catch him, Death is dead!"

"If we can only catch him,
Death is dead!"

　When they had gone not fully half a mile,
Just as they were about to cross a stile,⁴
They came upon a very poor old man
Who humbly greeted them and thus began,
55 "God look to you, my lords, and give you
　　　quiet!"
To which the proudest of these men of riot
Gave back the answer, "What, old fool? Give
　　　place!
Why are you all wrapped up except your face?
Why live so long? Isn't it time to die?"
60 The old, old fellow looked him in the eye
And said, "Because I never yet have found,
Though I have walked to India, searching
　　　round
Village and city on my pilgrimage,
One who would change his youth to have
　　　my age.
65 And so my age is mine and must be still
Upon me, for such time as God may will.
　"Not even Death, alas, will take my life;
So, like a wretched prisoner at strife,
Within himself, I walk alone and wait
70 About the earth, which is my mother's gate,
Knock-knocking with my staff from night to
　　　noon
And crying, 'Mother, open to me soon!
Look at me, mother, won't you let me in?
See how I wither, flesh and blood and skin!
75 Alas! When will these bones be laid to rest?

---

1. **wary.** Cautious
2. **tillage.** Land suitable for farming
3. **grisly.** Horrible; terrifying
4. **stile.** Steps used in climbing over a wall

Panel depicting a scene from "The Pardoner's Tale." Museum of London, London, England.

Mother, I would exchange—for that were
    best—
The wardrobe in my chamber, standing there
So long, for yours! Aye, for a shirt of hair
To wrap me in!' She has refused her grace,
80 Whence comes the pallor of my withered face
     "But it dishonored you when you began
To speak so roughly, sir, to an old man,
Unless he had injured you in word or deed.
It says in holy writ, as you may read,
85 'Thou shalt rise up before the hoary[5] head
And honor it.' And therefore be it said
'Do no more harm to an old man than you,
Being now young, would have another do
When you are old'—if you should live till
    then.
90 And so may God be with you, gentlemen,
For I must go whither I have to go."
    "By God," the gambler said, "you shan't
    do so,
You don't get off so easy, by St. John!
I heard you mention, just a moment gone,
95 A certain traitor Death who singles out

And kills the fine young fellows hereabout.
And you're his spy, by God! You wait a bit.
Say where he is or you shall pay for it,
By God and by the Holy Sacrament!
100 I say you've joined together by consent
To kill us younger folk, you thieving swine!"
    "Well, sirs," he said, "if it be your design
To find out Death, turn up this crooked way
Toward that grove, I left him there today
105 Under a tree, and there you'll find him waiting.
He isn't one to hide for all your prating.[6]
You see that oak? He won't be far to find.
And God protect you that redeemed mankind,
Aye, and amend you!" Thus that ancient man.
110 At once the three young rioters began
To run, and reached the tree, and there they
    found
A pile of golden florins[7] on the ground,
New-coined, eight bushels of them as they
    thought.

5. **hoary.** White or gray haired
6. **prating.** Chatter
7. **florins.** Gold coins

The Stories of *The Canterbury Tales*

In the introduction to "The Prologue," Chaucer says twenty-nine pilgrims arrive at the hostelry, but in fact, thirty-one pilgrims are mentioned. Another pilgrim, the Canon's Yeoman, joins the pilgrimage and tells a tale. These inconsistencies in *The Canterbury Tales* may be due to the fact that the stories were written over a long period of time and the collection never was finished.

The pilgrims tell their stories in the order in which they are introduced in "The Prologue." Interaction among the characters weaves a continuous thread throughout the collection. Several pilgrims tell their tales to annoy their fellow travelers or to respond in anger to others' stories. Following are some of the pilgrims and the stories they tell:

Knight: a courtly romance based on Boccaccio's *Teseida*

Miller: a humorous story of love and deception

Reeve: a *fabliau* (comic and often bawdy tale) told in response to the tale told by the Miller

Cook: a fragment of another fabliau

Sergeant at the Law: the story of the Christian Constance who is married to a sultan; a common story in medieval times

Friar: a story of a summoner and the devil who agree to split whatever they are given

Summoner: a reply to the Friar's story in which a friar is to divide a deathbed legacy

Clerk: another story based on Boccaccio, the tale of patient Griselda and her trials

Merchant: a story of a romance prone to infidelity

Squire: a story about a king's daughter who is given the gift of understanding the birds; a falcon tells her a story of desertion

Franklin: a story of lovers and magic

Doctor: a story about a daughter who is killed by her father to save her from a corrupt judge

Skipper: the tale of a woman who requests a loan from a priest who borrows the money from her merchant husband

No longer was it Death those fellows sought,
115 For they were all so thrilled to see the sight,
The florins were so beautiful and bright,
That down they sat beside the precious pile.
The wickedest spoke first after a while.
"Brothers," he said, "you listen to what I say.
120 I'm pretty sharp although I joke away.
It's clear that Fortune has bestowed this treasure
To let us live in jollity and pleasure.
Light come, light go! We'll spend it as we ought.
God's precious dignity! Who would have thought

125 This morning was to be our lucky day?
"If one could only get the gold away,
Back to my house, or else to yours, perhaps—
For as you know, the gold is ours, chaps—
We'd all be at the top of fortune, hey?
130 But certainly it can't be done by day.
People would call us robbers—a strong gang,
So our own property would make us hang.
No, we must bring this treasure back by night
Some <u>prudent</u> way, and keep it out of sight.
135 And so as a solution I propose

---

pru • dent (prü´ d'nt) *adj.,* discreet or careful

We draw for lots and see the way it goes;
The one who draws the longest, lucky man,
Shall run to town as quickly as he can
To fetch us bread and wine—but keep
      things dark—
140 While two remain in hiding here to mark
Our heap of treasure. If there's no delay,
When night comes down we'll carry it away,
All three of us, wherever we have planned."
    He gathered lots and hid them in his hand
145 Bidding them draw for where the luck
      should fall.
It fell upon the youngest of them all,
And off he ran at once towards the town.
    As soon as he had gone the first sat down
And thus began a parley with the other:
150 "You know that you can trust me as a brother;
Now let me tell you where your profit lies;
You know our friend has gone to get supplies
And here's a lot of gold that is to be
Divided equally amongst us three.
155 Nevertheless, if I could shape things thus
So that we shared it out—the two of us—
Wouldn't you take it as a friendly act?"
"But how?" the other said. "He knows the fact
That all the gold was left with me and you;
160 What can we tell him? What are we to do?"
    "Is it a bargain," said the first, "or no?
For I can tell you in a word or so
What's to be done to bring the thing about."
"Trust me," the other said, "you needn't doubt
165 My word. I won't betray you, I'll be true."
    "Well," said his friend, "you see that we
      are two,
And two are twice as powerful as one.
Now look; when he comes back, get up in fun
To have a wrestle; then, as you attack,
170 I'll up and put my dagger through his back
While you and he are struggling, as in game;
Then draw your dagger too and do the same.
Then all this money will be ours to spend,
Divided equally of course, dear friend.
175 Then we can gratify our lusts and fill
The day with dicing[8] at our own sweet will."
Thus these two miscreants[9] agreed to slay

The third and youngest, as you heard me say.
    The youngest, as he ran towards the town,
Kept turning over, rolling up and down
180 Within his heart the beauty of those bright
New florins, saying, "Lord, to think I might
Have all that treasure to myself alone!
Could there be anyone beneath the throne
Of God so happy as I then should be?"
185   And so the Fiend, our common enemy,
Was given power to put it in his thought

> "Trust me," the other said,
> "you needn't doubt
> My word. I won't betray you,
> I'll be true."

That there was always poison to be bought,
And that with poison he could kill his friends.
To men in such a state the Devil sends
190 Thoughts of this kind, and has a full
      permission
To lure them on to sorrow and perdition;[10]
For this young man was utterly content
To kill them both and never to repent.
And on he ran, he had no thought to tarry,
195 Came to the town, found an apothecary
And said, "Sell me some poison if you will,
I have a lot of rats I want to kill
And there's a polecat too about my yard
That takes my chickens and it hits me hard;
200 But I'll get even, as is only right,
With vermin that destroy a man by night."
    The chemist answered, "I've a preparation
Which you shall have, and by my soul's
      salvation
If any living creature eat or drink
205 A mouthful, ere he has the time to think,

---

8. **dicing.** Gambling
9. **miscreants.** Evildoers
10. **perdition.** Loss of soul

Though he took less than makes a grain of
    wheat,
You'll see him fall down dying at your feet;
Yes, die he must, and in so short a while
You'd hardly have the time to walk a mile,
210 The poison is so strong, you understand."
    This cursed fellow grabbed into his hand
The box of poison and away he ran
Into a neighboring street, and found a man
Who lent him three large bottles. He withdrew
215 And deftly poured poison into two.
He kept the third one clean, as well he might,
For his own drink, meaning to work all night
Stacking the gold and carrying it away.
And when this rioter, this devil's clay,
220 Had filled his bottles up with wine, all three,
Back to rejoin his comrades sauntered he.
    Why make a sermon of it? Why waste
    breath?
Exactly in the way they'd planned his death

They fell on him and slew him, two to one.
225 Then said the first of them when this was
    done,
"Now for a drink. Sit down and let's be merry,
For later on there'll be the corpse to bury."
And, as it happened, reaching for a sup,
He took a bottle full of poison up
230 And drank; and his companion, nothing loth,
Drank from it also, and they perished both.
    There is, in Avicenna's long relation[11]
Concerning poison and its operation,
Trust me, no ghastlier section to transcend
235 What these two wretches suffered at their end.
Thus these two murderers received their due,
So did the treacherous young poisoner too. ❖

---

11. **Avicenna's long relation.** Avicenna, or Ibn Sina (908–1037),
an Islamic physician and philosopher from Persia, wrote a
lengthy medical book with a detailed chapter on poisons.

MIRRORS & WINDOWS   In addition to greed, what personal qualities or emotions can lead people to act
irrationally? Do people generally get what they deserve in life?

The Infatuated Old Woman, c. 1500. Lucas Cranach, the Elder.
Musuem of Fine Arts, Budapest, Hungary.

The Wife of Bath's Tale

by Geoffrey Chaucer

*'Yet you shall live if you can answer me:
What is the thing that women most desire?'*

When good King Arthur ruled in
    ancient days
(A king that every Briton loves to praise)
This was a land brim-full of fairy folk.
The Elf-Queen and her courtiers joined and
    broke
5 Their elfin dance on many a green mead,

Or so was the opinion once, I read,
Hundreds of years ago, in days of yore.
But no one now sees fairies any more.
For now the saintly charity and prayer
10 Of holy friars seem to have purged[1] the air;

---

1. **purged.** Cleansed

They search the countryside through field
    and stream
As thick as motes that speckle a sun-beam,
Blessing the halls, the chambers, kitchens,
    bowers,
Cities and boroughs, castles, courts and
    towers,
15 Thorpes,[2] barns and stables, outhouses and
    dairies,
And that's the reason why there are no fairies.
Wherever there was wont to[3] walk an elf
To-day there walks the holy friar himself
As evening falls or when the daylight springs,
20 Saying his mattins[4] and his holy things,
Walking his limit round from town to town.
Women can now go safely up and down
By every bush or under every tree;
There is no other incubus[5] but he,
25 So there is really no one else to hurt you
And he will do no more than take your virtue.
    Now it so happened, I began to say,
Long, long ago in good King Arthur's day,
There was a knight who was a lusty liver.[6]
30 One day as he came riding from the river
He saw a maiden walking all <u>forlorn</u>
Ahead of him, alone as she was born.
And of that maiden, spite of all she said,
By very force he took her maidenhead.
35   This act of violence made such a stir,
So much petitioning to the king for her,
That he condemned the knight to lose his head
By course of law. He was as good as dead
(It seems that then the statutes took that view)
40 But that the queen, and other ladies too,
<u>Implored</u> the king to exercise his grace
So ceaselessly, he gave the queen the case
And granted her his life, and she could choose
Whether to show him mercy or refuse.
45   The queen returned him thanks with all
    her might,
And then she sent a summons to the knight
At her convenience, and expressed her will:
'You stand, for such is the position still,
In no way certain of your life,' said she,
50 'Yet you shall live if you can answer me:

What is the thing that women most desire?
Beware the axe and say as I require.
    'If you can't answer on the moment, though,
I will concede you this: you are to go
55 A twelvemonth and a day to seek and learn
Sufficient answer, then you shall return.
I shall take gages from you to extort
Surrender of your body to the court.'
    Sad was the knight and sorrowfully sighed,
60 But there! All other choices were denied,
And in the end he chose to go away
And to return after a year and day
Armed with such answer as there might be
    sent
To him by God. He took his leave and went.
65   He knocked at every house, searched
    every place,

2. **Thorpes.** Villages
3. **was wont to.** Was accustomed to
4. **mattins.** Morning prayers
5. **incubus.** Evil spirit that comes to someone who is asleep
6. **liver.** One who lives; a person

for • lorn (fər lôrn´) *adj.,* sad; lonely
im • plore (im plôr´) *v.,* beg or plead

Yes, anywhere that offered hope of grace.
What could it be that women wanted most?
But all the same he never touched a coast,
Country or town in which there seemed to be
70   Any two people willing to agree.
         Some said that women wanted wealth and
              treasure,
'Honour,' said some, some 'Jollity and
              pleasure,'
Some 'Gorgeous clothes' and others 'Fun in
              bed,'
'To be oft widowed and remarried,' said
75   Others again, and some that what most
              mattered
Was that we should be cosseted[7] and flattered.
That's very near the truth, it seems to me;
A man can win us best with flattery.
To dance attendance on us, make a fuss,
80   Ensnares us all, the best and worst of us.

> *That's very near the truth,
> it seems to me;
> A man can win us best
> with flattery.*

         Some say the things we most desire are
              these:
Freedom to do exactly as we please,
With no one to <u>reprove</u> our faults and lies,
Rather to have one call us good and wise.
85   Truly there's not a woman in ten score
Who has a fault, and someone rubs the sore,
But she will kick if what he says is true;
You try it out and you will find so too.
However vicious we may be within
90   We like to be thought wise and void of sin.
Others assert we women find it sweet
When we are thought dependable, discreet
And secret, firm of purpose and controlled,
Never betraying things that we are told.
95   But that's not worth the handle of a rake;
Women conceal a thing? For Heaven's sake!

Remember Midas?[8] Will you hear the tale?
         Among some other little things, now stale,
Ovid[9] relates that under his long hair
100   The unhappy Midas grew a splendid pair
Of ass's ears; as subtly as he might,
He kept his foul deformity from sight;
Save for his wife, there was not one that knew.
He loved her best, and trusted in her too.
105   He begged her not to tell a living creature
That he possessed so horrible a feature.
And she—she swore, were all the world to
              win,
She would not to such a villainy and sin
As saddle her husband with so foul a name;
110   Besides to speak would be to share the shame.
Nevertheless she thought she would have died
Keeping this secret bottled up inside;
It seemed to swell her heart and she, no doubt,
Thought it was on the point of bursting out.
115   Fearing to speak of it to woman or man,
Down to a reedy marsh she quickly ran
And reached the sedge. Her heart was all on
              fire
And, as a bittern[10] bumbles in the mire,
She whispered to the water, near the ground,
120   'Betray me not, O water, with thy sound!
To thee alone I tell it: it appears
My husband has a pair of ass's ears!
Ah! My heart's well, again, the secret's out!
I could no longer keep it, not a doubt.'
125   And so you see, although we may hold fast
A little while, it must come out at last,
We can't keep secrets; as for Midas, well,
Read Ovid for his story; he will tell.
         This knight that I am telling you about
130   Perceived at last he never would find out
What it could be that women loved the best.

---

7. **cosseted.** Pampered; treated as a pet
8. **Midas.** A legendary king who is granted the power to turn anything he touches to gold
9. **Ovid.** Latin poet (43 BCE–17 CE?)
10. **bittern.** Heron, a type of wading bird

---

re • prove (ri prüv´) v., correct; scold

Faint was the soul within his sorrowful breast,
As home he went, he dared no longer stay;
His year was up and now it was the day.

135   As he rode home in a dejected mood
Suddenly, at the margin of a wood,
He saw a dance upon the leafy floor
Of four and twenty ladies, nay, and more.
Eagerly he approached, in hope to learn

140 Some words of wisdom ere he should return;
But lo! Before he came to where they were,
Dancers and dance all vanished into air!
There wasn't a living creature to be seen
Save one old woman crouched upon the green.

145 A fouler-looking creature I suppose
Could scarcely be imagined. She arose
And said, 'Sir knight, there's no way on from
    here.
Tell me what you are looking for, my dear,
For peradventure[11] that were best for you;

150 We old, old women know a thing or two.'

There wasn't a living creature
to be seen,
Save one old woman
crouched upon the green.

'Dear Mother,' said the knight, 'alack
    the day!
I am as good as dead if I can't say
What thing it is that women most desire;
If you could tell me I would pay your hire.'

155 'Give me your hand,' she said, 'and swear to do
Whatever I shall next require of you
—If so to do should lie within your might—
And you shall know the answer before night.'
'Upon my honour,' he answered, 'I agree.'

160 'Then,' said the crone, 'I dare to guarantee
Your life is safe; I shall make good my claim.
Upon my life the queen will say the same.
Show me the very proudest of them all
In costly coverchief or jeweled caul[12]

165 That dare say no to what I have to teach.

Let us go forward without further speech.'
And then she crooned her gospel in his ear
And told him to be glad and not to fear.
    They came to court. This knight, in full
    array,

170 Stood forth and said, 'O Queen, I've kept my
    day
And kept my word and have my answer
    ready.'
    There sat the noble matrons and the heady
Young girls, and widows too, that have the
    grace
Of wisdom, all assembled in that place,

175 And there the queen herself was throned to
    hear
And judge his answer. Then the knight drew
    near
And silence was commanded through the hall.
    The queen gave order he should tell them
    all
What thing it was that women wanted most.

180 He stood not silent like a beast or post,
But gave his answer with ringing word
Of a man's voice and the assembly heard:
    'My liege and lady, in general,' said he,
'A woman wants the self-same sovereignty

185 Over her husband as over her lover,
And master him; he must not be above her.
That is your greatest wish, whether you kill
Or spare me; please yourself. I wait your will.'
    In all the court not one that shook her head

190 Or contradicted what the knight had said;
Maid, wife and widow cried, 'He's saved his
    life!'
    And on the word up started the old wife,
The one the knight saw sitting on the green,
And cried, 'Your mercy, sovereign lady queen!

195 Before the court disperses, do me right!
'Twas I who taught this answer to the knight,
For which he swore, and pledged his honour
    to it,
That the first thing I asked of him he'd do it,

---

11. **peradventure.** Perhaps; perchance
12. **caul.** Cowl; hood or draped neck of a garment

So far as it should lie within his might.

200 Before this court I ask you then, sir knight,
To keep your word and take me for your wife;
For well you know that I have saved your life.
If this be false, deny it on your sword!'
　　'Alas!' he said, 'Old lady, by the Lord

205 I know indeed that such was my behest,
But for God's love think of a new request,
Take all my goods, but leave my body free.'
'A curse on us,' she said, 'if I agree!
I may be foul, I may be poor and old,

210 Yet will not choose to be, for all the gold
That's bedded in the earth or lies above,
Less than your wife, nay, than your very love!'
　　'My love?' said he. 'By heaven, my
　　　　damnation!
Alas that any of my race and station

215 Should ever make so foul a misalliance!'
Yet in the end his pleading and defiance
All went for nothing, he was forced to wed.
He takes his ancient wife and goes to bed.
　　Now peradventure some may well suspect

220 A lack of care in me since I neglect
To tell of the rejoicing and display
Made at the feast upon their wedding-day.
I have but a short answer to let fall;
I say there was no joy or feast at all,

225 Nothing but heaviness of heart and sorrow.
He married her in private on the morrow
And all day long stayed hidden like an owl,
It was such torture that his wife looked foul.
　　Great was the anguish churning in his head

230 When he and she were piloted to bed;
He wallowed back and forth in desperate style.
His ancient wife lay smiling all the while;
At last she said, 'Bless us! Is this, my dear,
How knights and wives get on together here?

235 Are these the laws of good King Arthur's
　　　　house?
Are knights of his all so <u>contemptuous</u>?
I am your own beloved and your wife,
And I am she, indeed, that saved your life;
And certainly I never did you wrong.

240 Then why, this first of nights, so sad a song?
You're carrying on as if you were half-witted.

Illuminated manuscript showing a medieval marriage ceremony
(c. 1200s).

Say, for God's love, what sin have I
　　　　committed?
I'll put things right if you will tell me how.'
　　'Put right?' he cried. 'That never can be now!

245 Nothing can ever be put right again!
You're old, and so <u>abominably</u> plain,
So poor to start with, so low-bred to follow;
It's little wonder if I twist and wallow!
God, that my heart would burst within my
　　　　breast!'

250 　　'Is that,' said she, 'the cause of your unrest?'
'Yes, certainly,' he said, 'and can you
　　　　wonder?'
'I could set right what you suppose a
　　　　blunder,
That's if I cared to, in a day or two,
If I were shown more courtesy by you.

255 Just now,' she said, 'you spoke of gentle birth,

con • temp • tu • ous (kən tem[p]′ chə wəs) *adj.*, disapproving; disrespectful
abom • i • na • bly (ə bä′ mə nə blē) *adv.*, disagreeably; terribly

Illustration of the Wife of Bath from *The Ellesmere Chaucer*, 1911 facsimile edition of an early 1400s manuscript.

Such as descends from ancient wealth and
  worth.
If that's the claim you make for gentlemen
Such arrogance is hardly worth a hen.
Whoever loves to work for virtuous ends,
260 Public and private, and who most intends
To do what deeds of gentleness he can,
Take him to be the greatest gentleman.
Christ wills we take out gentleness from Him,
Not from wealth of ancestry long dim,
265 Though they bequeath their whole
  establishment
By which we claim to be of high descent.
Our fathers cannot make us bequest
Of all those virtues that became them best
And earned for them the name of gentlemen,
270 But bade us follow them as best we can.
  'Thus the wise poet of the Florentines,[13]
Dante[14] by name, has written in these lines,
For such is the opinion Dante launches:
"Seldom arises by these slender branches

275 Prowess of men, for it is God, no less,
Wills us to claim of Him our gentleness,"
For of our parents nothing can we claim
Save <u>temporal</u> things, and these may hurt
  and maim.
  'But everyone knows this as well as I;
280 For if gentility were implanted by
The natural course of lineage down the line,
Public or private, could it cease to shine
In doing the fair work of gentle deed?
No vice or villainy could then bear seed.
285 'Take fire and carry it to the darkest house
Between this kingdom and the Caucasus,[15]
And shut the doors on it and leave it there,
It will burn on, and it will burn as fair
As if ten thousand men were there to see,
290 For fire will keep its nature and degree,
I can assure you, sir, until it dies.
  'But gentleness, as you will recognize,
Is not annexed in nature to possessions.
Men fail in living up to their professions;
295 But fire never ceases to be fire.
God knows you'll often find, if you enquire,
Some lording full of villainy and shame.
If you would be <u>esteemed</u> for the mere name
Of having been by birth a gentleman
300 And stemming from some virtuous, noble
  clan,
And do not live yourself by gentle deed
Or take your father's noble code and creed,
You are no gentleman, though duke or earl.
Vice and bad manners are what make a churl.[16]
305 'Gentility[17] is only the renown
For bounty that your fathers handed down,
Quite foreign to your person, not your own;

---

13. **Florentines.** People living in Florence, Italy
14. **Dante.** Dante Alighieri (1265–1321), Italian poet, author of *Divine Comedy*
15. **Caucasus.** Region in southeastern Europe
16. **churl.** Medieval peasant
17. **gentility.** Gentry, or those of the upper or ruling class; the behavior and courtesy that guides the conduct of the gentry

tem • por • al (tem′ p[ə] rəl) *adj.*, limited to earthly life
es • teem (i stēm′) *v.*, think well of

Gentility must come from God alone.
That we are gentle come to us by grace
310 And by no means is it bequeathed with place.
    'Reflect how noble (says Valerius)
Was Tullius surnamed Hostilius,
Who rose from poverty to nobleness.
And read Boethius, Seneca[18] no less,
315 Thus they express themselves and are agreed:
"Gentle is he that does a gentle deed."
And therefore, my dear husband, I conclude
That even if my ancestors were rude,
Yet God on high—and so I hope He will—
320 Can grant me grace to live in virtue still,
A gentlewoman only when beginning
To live in virtue and to shrink from sinning.
    'As for my poverty which you reprove,
Almighty God himself in whom we move,
325 Believe and have our being, chose a life
Of poverty, and every man or wife
Nay, every child can see our Heavenly King
Would never stoop to choose a shameful
      thing.
No shame in poverty if the heart is gay,
330 As Seneca and all the learned say.
He who accepts his poverty unhurt
I'd say is rich although he lacked a shirt.
But truly poor are they who whine and fret
And covet what they cannot hope to get.
335 And he that, having nothing, covets not,
Is rich, though you may think he is a sot.

> *But truly poor are they*
> *who whine and fret*
> *And covet what they*
> *cannot hope to get.*

'True poverty can find a song to sing.
Juvenal says a pleasant little thing:
"The poor can dance and sing in the relief
340 Of having nothing that will tempt a thief."
Though it be hateful, poverty is good,
A great incentive to a livelihood,

And a great help to our capacity
For wisdom, if accepted patiently.
345 Poverty is, though wanting in estate,
A kind of wealth that none calumniate.[19]
Poverty often, when the heart is lowly,
Brings one to God and teaches what is holy,
Gives knowledge of oneself and even lends
350 A glass by which to see one's truest friends.
And since it's no offence, let me be plain;
Do not rebuke my poverty again.
    'Lastly you taxed me, sir, with being old.
Yet even if you never had been told
355 By ancient books, you gentlemen engage,
Yourselves in honour to respect old age.
To call an old man "father" shows good
      breeding,
And this could be supported from my reading.
    'You say I'm old and fouler then a fen.
360 You need not fear to be a cuckold,[20] then.
Filth and old age, I'm sure you will agree,
Are powerful wardens over chastity.
Nevertheless, well knowing your delights,
I shall fulfil your worldly appetites.
365   'You have two choices; which one will
      you try?
To have me old and ugly till I die,
But still a loyal, true, and humble wife
That never will displease you all her life,
Or would you rather I were young and pretty
370 And chance your arm what happens in a city
Where friends will visit you because of me,
Yes, and in other places too, maybe.
Which would you have? The choice is all
      your own.'
    The knight thought long, and with a
      piteous groan
375 At last he said, with all the care in life,
'My lady and my love, my dearest wife,
I leave the matter to your wise decision.

---

18. **Valerius . . . Seneca.** *Valerius Maximus* (c. 20 BCE–c. 50 CE),
    a Roman historian and moralist; *Tullius Hostilius*, a Roman king
    (c. 665 BCE); *Boethius* (c. 475–525 CE) and *Seneca* (c. 3 BCE– 65 CE),
    Roman philosophers and statesmen
19. **calumniate.** Misrepresent; falsely condemn
20. **fear . . . cuckold.** Fear that I would be an unfaithful wife

You make the choice yourself, for the
     provision
Of what may be agreeable and rich
380 In honour to us both, I don't care which;
Whatever pleases you <u>suffices</u> me.'
    'And have I won the mastery?' said she,
'Since I'm to choose and rule as I think fit?'
'Certainly, wife,' he answered her, 'that's it.'
385 'Kiss me,' she cried. 'No quarrels! On my oath
And word of honour, you shall find me both,
That is, both fair and faithful as a wife;
May I go howling mad and take my life
Unless I prove to be as good and true
390 As ever a wife was since the world was new!
And if to-morrow when the sun's above
I seem less fair than any lady-love.
Than any queen or empress east or west,
Do with my life and death as you think best.
395 Cast up the curtain, husband. Look at me!'
    And when indeed the knight had looked
        to see,

Lo, she was young and lovely, rich in charms.
In ecstasy he caught her in his arms,
400 His heart went bathing in a bath of blisses
And melted in a hundred thousand kisses,
And she responded in the fullest measure
With all that could delight or give him
     pleasure.
    So they lived ever after to the end
405 In perfect bliss; and may Christ Jesus send
Us husbands meek and young and fresh in
     bed,
And grace to overbid them when we wed.
And—Jesu hear my prayer!—cut short the
     lives
Of those who won't be governed by their
     wives;
410 And all old, angry niggards of their pence,
God send them soon a very pestilence! ❖

suf • fice (sə fīs´) v., satisfy

MIRRORS & WINDOWS

The old woman explains the benefits of having a wife who is poor, plain, and of lowly birth. Is her explanation convincing? Are the qualities that many people look for in a mate things that will make them happy?

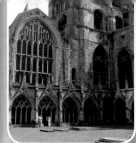

Informational Text Connection

An estimated three million people visit Canterbury Cathedral every year, hoping to glimpse some of the church's historic features. For these modern-day visitors, the greatest challenge might be to find a parking spot. One of the main challenges of medieval pilgrims, such as those in *The Canterbury Tales,* was to reach Canterbury Cathedral before the *portcullis,* or heavy gate, was lowered to protect the church from nighttime troublemakers.

As you read **"Simply Divine," Stephen Cook's** article from the newspaper *The Guardian,* consider the similarities and differences between the visits of modern-day visitors and medieval religious pilgrims.

SIMPLY DIVINE
from THE GUARDIAN

by Stephen Cook

"And specially, from every shires ende
Of Engelond, to Caunterbury they wende
The holy blisful martir for to seke
That them hath holpen, when that they were seke."

—Geoffrey Chaucer, *The Canterbury Tales*

Modern pilgrims to Canterbury, like their medieval counterparts, have to wait until the last minute to catch sight of the great cathedral where one of the most fateful murders of English history took place 831 years ago. While the spires of Salisbury or Ely are visible for miles, and Lincoln[1] sits massively on a high ridge, Canterbury is tucked away modestly in the valley of the river Stour.

And so visitors arriving from the west have already reached an unattractive roundabout in the suburb of Harbledown before the cathedral comes into view less than a mile away—the twin towers of the west front framing the taller tower of Bell Harry, with its knobbly pinnacles.

---

1. **Salisbury, Ely, Lincoln.** Three large cathedrals in England

Rising into a clear sky from the river mists of a winter's day, it is a magnificent and enticing sight.

In Chaucer's times, you'd probably be travelling at a canter—the word originates in the phrase "at Canterbury pace"—to get inside the West Gate before the portcullis came down at dusk. Nowadays your first preoccupation is likely to be the overcrowded parking facilities or the trek from either of the two railway stations to the heart of the city and the cathedral. But you keep glimpsing its creamy Caen stone, shadowed with grey patches of wear and age.

The final obstacle is the pay point at Christchurch Gate, where you'll be asked to hand over £3.50, unless you're a local person with a precinct pass or you declare that you're going in for devotional rather than rubbernecking[2] reasons. There is endless soul-searching over the imposition since 1995 of charges to enter the mother church of the Anglican Communion,[3] but the authorities seem quite content with the results.

One of the most striking things when you finally face the cathedral is that, more than most, it feels like an agglomeration of several different buildings, each with a different appearance and atmosphere. The south-east transept, for example, is an almost intact Norman edifice with multiple dog-toothed round arches and a massive, fortified feel to it, while above it soars Bell Harry tower, delicate and ornate, completed some 350 years later.

Inside, the most dramatic contrast comes between the nave, all height and light and fluted pillars from the heyday of the 14th-century perpendicular gothic, and the more sombre parts beyond. You go up the steps to the quire and presbytery and apse,[4] all built in the more florid and enclosing 12th-century French gothic style with lots of dark marble columns, or down to the huge crypt.[5] This is a shadowy and mysterious place centred on the grotto-like Chapel of Our Lady Undercroft, with its ceiling painted in stars and moons.

But what about Becket? "Everybody asks about Becket," says Barbara Toogood, one of the cathedral guides, leading you from the light and openness of the nave to a dark and hidden place near the entrance to the crypt, beside the steps leading up to the quire. It's called The Martyrdom, and marks the spot where Thomas Becket, Archbishop of Canterbury, was hacked to death by four royal knights as vespers were being sung on the stormy late afternoon of December 29, 1170.

Thomas had been Henry II's chancellor and close friend, but when he was made Archbishop he discerned a higher authority than that of the king. Their quarrels over the jurisdiction of ecclesiastical courts,[6] the appointment of bishops and the right to crown kings ended with Henry's outburst against the "drones and traitors" who allowed him to be "treated with such shameful contempt by a low-born clerk".

The knights confronted Becket in the Archbishop's Palace, and when he refused yet again to agree to the king's demands, they went off to collect their swords and axes while he went

---

2. **rubbernecking.** Sightseeing
3. **Anglican Communion.** Worldwide organization of Anglican churches (in the United States, Anglicans are called *Episcopalians*)
4. **quire, presbytery, apse.** Parts of a church. *quire* is an archaic variation of *choir*
5. **crypt.** Burial place under the main floor of a church
6. **jurisdiction . . . courts.** Power of church courts

across to the cathedral. They caught up with him on his way to the high altar, and when he turned to face them they cut him down: one blow sliced the top off his skull and spilled out his brains on the floor. The stones which were once soaked in his blood now have the word "Thomas" cut into them in red lettering, and above a simple black stone table hangs a modern sculpture of three jagged, red-tipped, downward-pointing blades. Every year it is visited after evensong on December 29 by a candle-lit procession carrying red flowers.

The simple memorial in the Martyrdom is all that is left: the gold-plated, jewel-encrusted tomb in the Trinity Chapel which housed his body for three centuries, and the casket in the Corona which contained the sliced-off part of his skull, were destroyed very deliberately by Henry VIII when he dissolved the monasteries in 1538. Twenty-six cartloads of treasure trundled off to London, and the bones were burnt.

The cathedral has many other attractions, such as the stained glass and the tomb of the Black Prince. Near the cathedral are the other two components of the Canterbury World Her-

The Canterbury Tales visitor attraction offers sounds, sights and smells from medieval pilgrimages.

itage Site—the remains of the Abbey founded in 598 by St Augustine in his Christian mission to Britain, and St Martin's Church, which dates to Roman times and is the oldest parish church still in constant use.

The Canterbury Tales visitor attraction offers sounds, sights and smells from medieval pilgrimages, and the Eastbridge Hospital, with a 12th-century wall-painting of Christ, shows you where footsore pilgrims would stay. There is a decent set of museums, pleasant punting on the river in summer, and the Marlowe[7] Theatre, named after the playwright Christopher, who was born in the town.

There is a pleasant walk with cathedral views along the city walls, past the Dane John gardens with their monument-topped mound and children's maze: the name is a corruption of the French donjon,[8] because it's near the castle. This, however, is as much a disappointment as it was in the days when it capitulated[9] to every passing attacker—the French Dauphin[10] in 1216, Wat Tyler's men in the Peasant's Revolt of 1381 and the Parliamentarians in the Civil War.[11] Any castle-seekers staying in Canterbury would do better to visit the more robust ones at nearby Dover, Bodiam and Leeds.

10 things to see in the cathedral

1. The Nave: clusters of creamy-coloured columns, thinner at the top, with rib vaults and gold ceiling bosses.
2. The ceiling of Bell Harry tower: elegant fan-vaulting and a central painted rose.
3. The Martyrdom: the spot where Archbishop Thomas Becket was murdered in 1170.
4. The Quire—especially the view from its entrance towards the Throne of St Augustine and the Apse.
5. The medieval Bible windows in the north quire aisle: three out of 14 showing Biblical stories that survived destruction by Cromwell's[12] soldiers.
6. The tomb of the Black Prince,[13] teenage warrior, complete with replicas and originals of his colourful funeral vestments.

---

7. **Marlowe.** Christopher Marlowe (1564–1593), a British dramatist
8. **donjon.** Large inner tower in a medieval castle
9. **capitulated.** Surrendered
10. **Dauphin.** Eldest son of the king and heir to the throne
11. **Parliamentarians . . . Civil War.** During the English Civil War (1642–1648), the Parliamentarians sought to limit the powers of the king
12. **Cromwell.** Oliver Cromwell (1599–1658) led the Parliamentarians in the English Civil War and assumed control of England after the king was executed in 1649
13. **Black Prince.** Edward of Woodstock, Prince of Wales (1330–1376), who died a year before the death of his father, King Edward III, thus never ascending the throne; the nickname Black Prince may refer to the armor he wore.

Portrait of a Young Woman in a Pinned Hat, c. 1435.
Rogier van der Weyden. Gelmäldegalerie, Berlin, Germany.

envious of her neighbors lest they dress as well as she did. Her whole desire was to have people admire her. She would not put up with criticism, or be content with the goods God had sent her, as her husband was, but always desired more and more.

And then out of pure greed and the wish to keep up her pride, she began to brew and was one of the greatest brewers in the town of N- for three or four years till she had lost a good deal of money, for she had never had any experience in brewing. For no matter how good her servants were and clever at brewing, yet things never went well with them. For even when the ale looked as splendid—standing under its head of froth—as anyone might see, suddenly the froth would sink down so that the ale was ruined, one brewing after another, and her servants were mortified and would not stay with her.

Then this creature thought how God had punished her already, and she refused to be warned, and now again she was punished with the loss of her goods, and then she gave up brewing and did it no more. Then she asked her husband's forgiveness for she had not followed his advice, and she said that her pride and sin had brought about her punishment and she would willingly make amends for her faults.

Yet she would not leave the world entirely, for now she thought of a new kind of house-wifely venture. She had a horse mill. She got herself two good horses and a man to grind people's corn, and in this way she felt sure she could make her living. This enterprise did not last long, for a short time after the Eve of Corpus Christi,[3] the following marvel occurred. This man was in good health of body, with two horses that were lusty and in good condition, and up till now had drawn well in the mill. Now when the man took one of these horses and put him in the mill as he had done all along, this horse would not drag a load in the mill no matter

3. **Corpus Christi.** Christian festival on the fifth Thursday or sixth Sunday after Easter

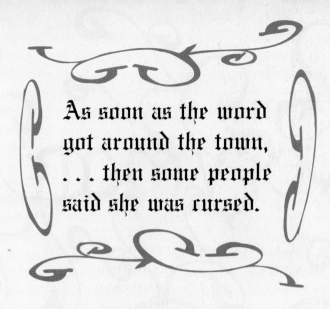

As soon as the word
got around the town,
. . . then some people
said she was cursed.

what the man did. Sometimes he led him by the head, sometimes he beat him, and sometimes he cajoled[4] him, but it was all useless because the horse would rather go backward than forward. Then this man set a pair of sharp spurs on his heels and rode on the horse's back to make him pull, but it was never any better.

When this man saw it was useless, then he put up the horse in the stable and fed him, and he ate well and freshly. Then he took the other horse and put him in the mill. And just as his fellow horse had done, so this one did, for he wouldn't pull despite anything the man did. And then this man quit his service and would no longer stay with this creature we have mentioned. As soon as the word got around the town of N- that no man or beast would work for that creature, then some people said she was cursed. Some said God took open vengeance[5] on her. Some said one thing and some said another. And some wise men whose mind was more grounded in the love of our Lord said it was the high mercy of our Lord Jesus Christ that commanded and called her from the pride and vanity of the wretched world. ❖

---

4. **cajoled.** Coaxed with flattery
5. **vengeance.** Revenge; retribution

How did the townspeople likely react to Kempe's behavior? How would people today probably react to her?

Refer and Reason

1. Why does Kempe consider herself prideful? Is her judgment of herself justified? Why or why not?

2. Identify elements of Kempe's autobiography that tell about everyday life in medieval England. What do these details reveal about women during this period?

3. Summarize Kempe's religious beliefs. How do they shape her autobiography and her opinion of herself?

Writing Options

1. A *broadside notice* is a public announcement printed on a large sheet of paper and posted on buildings, fences, and so on. Create a broadside notice from Margery Kempe that explains why she is closing the mill and will not be starting another business.

2. Write a brief article for a magazine devoted to women's interests. In your article, explain what modern-day women can learn from the example of Margery Kempe.

 Go to **www.mirrorsandwindows.com** for more.

from Everyman

CAST OF CHARACTERS

MESSENGER	KNOWLEDGE
GOD	CONFESSION
DEATH	BEAUTY
EVERYMAN	STRENGTH
FELLOWSHIP	DISCRETION
KINDRED	FIVE-WITS
COUSIN	ANGEL
GOODS	DOCTOR
GOOD DEEDS	

HERE BEGINNETH A TREATISE HOW THE HIGH FATHER OF HEAVEN SENDETH
DEATH TO SUMMON EVERY CREATURE TO COME AND GIVE ACCOUNT OF
THEIR LIVES IN THIS WORLD, AND IS IN MANNER OF A MORAL PLAY

[*Enter* MESSENGER.]

    MESSENGER.   I pray you all give your audience,
And hear this matter with reverence,
By figure[1] a moral play.
The Summoning of Everyman called it is,
5 That of our lives and ending shows
How transitory[2] we be all day.[3]
The matter is wonder precious,
But the intent of it is more gracious
And sweet to bear away.
10 The story saith: Man, in the beginning
Look well, and take good heed to the ending,
Be you never so gay.
You think sin in the beginning full sweet,
Which in the end causeth the soul to weep,
15 When the body lieth in clay.
Here shall you see how fellowship and jollity,

---

1. **figure.** Form
2. **transitory.** Temporary
3. **all day.** Always

The author of the drama
Everyman is unknown. Most
scholars believe it was written
originally in Flemish and then
translated into English sometime after 1485. Although no
manuscript of the play ever has
been found, its first printing
dates to about 1530. During
the Middle Ages, plays typically
were produced in the backs of
wagons in the
courtyards of
inns and other
public places,
with the audi-
ence standing
around the
wagon. Sets
were minimal,
but costumes
and props were
used. People would travel for
days to see a play.

    A **morality play** is a type
of medieval drama in which the
characters are *allegorical figures,* or abstract representations
of virtues, vices, and the like.
A morality play is essentially
a dramatized sermon: It delivers a clear religious message
about the Christian struggle
between good and evil. *Everyman* is considered an excellent
example of a medieval morality
play because of its lofty poetry,
its unity, the consistent and
clear message conveyed by its
characters, and its engaging
theatricality.

Le Mort et Le Boucheron, c. 1800s. Alphonse Legros.
Corcoran Gallery of Art, Washington, DC.

Both strength, pleasure, and beauty,
Will fade from thee as flower in May.
For ye shall hear how our Heaven-King
20 Calleth Everyman to a general reckoning.
Give audience and hear what he doth say.

[*Exit* MESSENGER.—*Enter* GOD.]

GOD.   I perceive, here in my majesty,
How that all creatures be to me unkind,[4]
Living without dread in worldly prosperity.
25 Of ghostly[5] sight the people be so blind,
Drowned in sin, they know me not for their God.
In worldly riches is all their mind:
They fear not of my righteousness the sharp rod;
My law that I showed when I for them died
30 They forget clean, and shedding of my blood red.

---

4. **unkind.** Thoughtless
5. **ghostly.** Spiritual

I hanged between two,[6] it cannot be denied:
To get them life I suffered to be dead.
I healed their feet, with thorns hurt was my head.
I could do no more than I did, truly—

35 And now I see the people do clean forsake me.
They use the seven deadly sins damnable,
As pride, coveitise, wrath, and lechery[7]
Now in the world be made commendable.
And thus they leave of angels the heavenly company.

40 Every man liveth so after his own pleasure,
And yet of their life they be nothing sure.
I see the more that I them forbear,
The worse they be from year to year:
All that liveth appaireth[8] fast.

45 Therefore I will, in all the haste,
Have a reckoning of every man's person.
For, and[9] I leave the people thus alone
In their life and wicked tempests,
Verily they will become much worse than beasts;

50 For now one would by envy another up eat.
Charity do they all clean forgeet.[10]
I hoped well that every man
In my glory should make his mansion,
And thereto I had them all elect.[11]

55 But now I see, like traitors deject.[12]
They thank me not for the pleasure that I to[13] them meant,
Nor yet for their being that I them have lent.
I proffered the people great multitude of mercy,
And few there be that asketh it heartily.[14]

60 They be so cumbered[15] with worldly riches
That needs on them I must do justice—
On every man living without fear.
Where art thou, Death, thou mighty messenger?

[*Enter* DEATH.]

DEATH.   Almighty God, I am here at your will,
65 Your commandment to fulfill.

---

6. **I . . . two.** Jesus was crucified between two thieves.
7. **seven . . . lechery.** The seven deadly sins are pride, avarice (greed), wrath (anger), lechery (sexual overindulgence), envy, gluttony (eating or drinking too much), and sloth (laziness).
8. **appaireth.** Degenerates
9. **and.** If
10. **forgeet.** Forgotten
11. **elect.** Chosen
12. **deject.** Abased
13. **to.** For
14. **heartily.** Sincerely
15. **cumbered.** Encumbered

GOD. Go thou to Everyman,
And show him, in my name,
A pilgrimage he must on him take,
Which he in no wise may escape;
70 And that he bring with him a sure reckoning
Without delay or any tarrying.

DEATH. Lord, I will in the world go run over all,
And cruelly out-search both great and small.

[*Exit* GOD.]

Everyman will I beset that liveth beastly
75 Out of God's laws, and dreadeth not folly.
He that loveth riches I will strike with my dart,
His sight to blind, and from heaven to depart—[16]
Except that Almsdeeds be his good friend—
In hell for to dwell, world without end.
80 Lo, yonder I see Everyman walking:
Full little he thinketh on my coming;
His mind is on fleshly lusts and his treasure,
And great pain it shall cause him to endure
Before the Lord, Heaven-King.

[*Enter* EVERYMAN.]

85 Everyman, stand still! Whither art thou going
Thus gaily? Hast thou thy Maker forgeet?

EVERYMAN. Why askest thou?
Why wouldest thou weet?[17]

DEATH. Yea, sir, I will show you:
90 In great haste I am sent to thee
From God out of his majesty.

EVERYMAN. What! sent to me?

DEATH. Yea, certainly.
Though thou have forgot him here,
95 He thinketh on thee in the heavenly sphere,
As, ere we depart, thou shalt know.

EVERYMAN. What desireth God of me?

---

16. **depart.** Separate
17. **weet.** Know

DEATH. That shall I show thee:
A reckoning he will needs have
100 Without any longer respite.[18]

EVERYMAN. To give a reckoning longer leisure I crave.
This blind[19] matter troubleth my wit.

DEATH. On thee thou must take a long journay:
Therefore thy book of count[20] with thee thou bring,
105 For turn again thou cannot by no way.
And look thou be sure of thy reckoning,
For before God thou shalt answer and shew
Thy many bad deeds and good but a few—
How thou hast spent thy life and in what wise,
110 Before the Chief Lord of Paradise.
Have ado that we were in that way,[21]
For weet thou well thou shalt make none attornay.[22]

EVERYMAN. Full unready I am such reckoning to give.
I know thee not. What messenger art thou?

115 **DEATH.** I am Death that no man dreadeth,
For every man I 'rest, and no man spareth;
For it is God's commandment
That all to me should be obedient.

EVERYMAN. O Death, thou comest when I had thee least in mind.
120 In thy power it lieth me to save:
Yet of my good[23] will I give thee, if thou will be kind,
Yea, a thousand pound shalt thou have—
And defer this matter till another day.

DEATH. Everyman, it may not be, by no way.
125 I set nought by gold, silver, nor riches,[24]
Nor by pope, emperor, king, duke, nor princes,
For, and I would receive gifts great,
All the world I might get.
But my custom is clean contrary:
130 I give thee no respite. Come hence and not tarry!

---

18. **respite.** Postponement; reprieve
19. **blind.** Unexpected
20. **count.** Accounts
21. **Have . . . way.** Let's get started right away.
22. **shalt . . . attornay.** Nobody shall go in your place.
23. **good.** Goods
24. **I . . . riches.** Riches, gold, and silver mean nothing to me.

EVERYMAN.   Alas, shall I have no longer respite?
I may say Death giveth no warning.
To think on thee it maketh my heart sick,
For all unready is my book of reckoning.
135   But twelve year and I might have a biding,[25]
My counting-book I would make so clear
That my reckoning I should not need to fear.
Wherefore, Death, I pray thee, for God's mercy,
Spare me till I be provided of remedy.

140   DEATH.   Thee availeth not to cry, weep, and pray;
But haste thee lightly[26] that thou were gone that journay
And prove[27] thy friends, if thou can.
For weet[28] thou well the tide[29] abideth no man,
And in the world each living creature
145   For Adam's sin must die of nature.[30]

EVERYMAN.   Death, if I should this pilgrimage take
And my reckoning surely make,
Show me, for saint[31] charity,
Should I not come again shortly?

150   DEATH.   No, Everyman. And thou be once there,
Thou mayst never more come here,
Trust me verily.

EVERYMAN.   O gracious God in the high seat celestial,
Have mercy on me in this most need!
155   Shall I have company from this vale terrestrial
Of mine acquaintance that way me to lead?

DEATH.   Yea, if any be so hardy
That would go with thee and bear thee company.
Hie[32] thee that thou were gone to God's magnificence,
160   Thy reckoning to give before his presence.
What, weenest[33] thou thy life is given thee,
And thy worldly goods also?

EVERYMAN.   I had weened so, verily.

---

25. **But . . . biding.** If I could put this off for just twelve years
26. **lightly.** Quickly
27. **prove.** Test
28. **weet.** Know
29. **tide.** Time
30. **of nature.** Naturally
31. **saint.** Holy
32. **Hie.** Hasten
33. **weenest.** Suppose

TWAIN

ALGER

The Everyman Archetype

In the medieval drama *Everyman,* the characters are not real people but rather representations of virtues such as beauty and strength and forces such as death. The protagonist himself is a composite of general human qualities but lacks individuality. Aptly named *Everyman,* he represents the common person in a struggle between good and evil.

Based on the character in this morality play, Everyman evolved over the centuries into an archetype that is still prevalent in modern literature. An Everyman character is an ordinary person who often is placed in extraordinary situations. In contrast to a heroic protagonist, who demonstrates remarkable skill and bravery in a difficult situation, an Everyman may respond with confusion, lack of skill, and even fear. Everyman may succeed in meeting the challenge, but he or she will do so using normal human abilities and may even get hurt in the process.

Writers often integrate an Everyman into their work because readers connect with this type of character. Readers are more likely to understand and even share the qualities of an Everyman than those of a traditional hero. When readers can make this connection, literature seems more realistic and thus appealing.

Examples of Everyman abound, especially in American literature. Many late-nineteenth-century American authors, including Horatio Alger and Mark Twain, built their careers on writing novels about ordinary people. One of the most famous Everyman characters from twentieth-century literature is Willy Loman, the protagonist of Arthur Miller's play *Death of a Salesman* (1949).

The Everyman archetype also has pervaded American politics. Thomas Jefferson, Andrew Jackson, and Abraham Lincoln all promoted themselves as common Americans. Even today, politicians look for ways to present themselves as everyday people who understand the needs, values, and lives of common folks. Like authors who create Everyman characters, these politicians hope to connect with their audiences.

DEATH.   Nay, nay, it was but lent thee.
165   For as soon as thou art go,
      Another a while shall have it and then go therefro,
      Even as thou hast done.
      Everyman, thou art mad! Thou hast thy wits[34] five,
      And here on earth will not amend thy live!
170   For suddenly I do come.

EVERYMAN.   O wretched caitiff![35] Whither shall I flee
      That I might 'scape this endless sorrow?
      Now, gentle Death, spare me till tomorrow,
      That I may amend me
175   With good advisement.[36]

---

34. **wits.** Senses
35. **caitiff.** Mean, cowardly person
36. **advisement.** Preparation

DEATH.   Nay, thereto I will not consent,
Nor no man will I respite,
But to the heart suddenly I shall smite,
Without any advisement.
180 And now out of thy sight I will me hie:
See thou make thee ready shortly,
For thou mayst say this is the day
That no man living may 'scape away.

[*Exit* DEATH.]

EVERYMAN.   Alas, I may well weep with sighs deep:
185 Now have I no manner of company
To help me in my journey and me to keep[37]
And also my writing is full unready—
How shall I do now for to excuse me?
I would to God I had never be geet![38]
190 To my soul a full great profit it had be.
For now I fear pains huge and great.

· · ·

EVERYMAN.   Alas, I am so faint I may not stand—
My limbs under me doth fold!
Friends, let us not turn again to this land,
195 Not for all the world's gold.
For into this cave must I creep
And turn to earth, and there to sleep.

BEAUTY.   What, into this grave, alas?

EVERYMAN.   Yea, there shall ye consume,[39] more and lass.[40]

200 **BEAUTY.**   And what, should I smother here?

EVERYMAN.   Yea, by my faith, and nevermore appear.
In this world live no more we shall,
But in heaven before the highest Lord of all.

BEAUTY.   I cross out all this! Adieu, by Saint John—
205 I take my tape in my lap and am gone.

EVERYMAN.   What, Beauty, whither will ye?

---

37. **keep.** Guard
38. **never be geet.** Never been begotten; never been born
39. **consume.** Decay
40. **more and lass.** More and less

BEAUTY.   Peace, I am deaf—I look not behind me,
Not and thou wouldest give me all the gold in thy chest.

[*Exit* BEAUTY.]

210   **EVERYMAN.**   Alas, whereto may I trust?
Beauty goeth fast away fro me—
She promised with me to live and die!

STRENGTH.   Everyman, I will thee also forsake and deny.
Thy game liketh[41] me not at all.

215   **EVERYMAN.**   Why then, ye will forsake me all?
Sweet Strength, tarry a little space.

STRENGTH.   Nay, sir, by the rood of grace,
I will hie me from thee fast,
Though thou weep till thy heart tobrast.[42]

---

41. **liketh.** Pleases
42. **tobrast.** Break

220   **EVERYMAN.**   Ye would ever bide by me, ye said.

    STRENGTH.   Yea, I have you far enough conveyed!
Ye be old enough, I understand,
Your pilgrimage to take on hand:
I repent me that I hither came.

225   **EVERYMAN.**   Strength, you to displease I am to blame,[43]
Yet promise is debt, this ye well wot.[44]

    STRENGTH.   In faith, I care not:
Thou art but a fool to complain;
You spend your speech and waste your brain.
230 Go, thrust thee into the ground.

    [*Exit* STRENGTH.]

    EVERYMAN.   I had weened[45] surer I should you have found.
He that trusteth in his Strength
She him deceiveth at the length.
235 Both Strength and Beauty forsaketh me—
Yet they promised me fair and lovingly.

    DISCRETION.   Everyman, I will after Strength be gone:
As for me, I will leave you alone.

    EVERYMAN.   Why Discretion, will ye forsake me?

240 **DISCRETION.**   Yea, in faith, I will go from thee.
For when Strength goeth before,
I follow after evermore.

    EVERYMAN.   Yet I pray thee, for the love of the Trinity,
Look in my grave once piteously.

245 **DISCRETION.**   Nay, so nigh will I not come
Farewell everyone!

    [*Exit* DISCRETION.]

    EVERYMAN.   O all thing faileth save God alone—
Beauty, Strength, and Discretion.
250 For when Death bloweth his blast
They all run fro me full fast.

---

43. **you . . . blame.** I'm to blame for displeasing you.
44. **wot.** Know
45. **weened.** Supposed

FIVE-WITS. Everyman, my leave now of thee I take.
I will follow the other, for here I thee forsake.

EVERYMAN. Alas, then may I wail and weep,
255 For I took you for my best friend.

FIVE-WITS. I will no longer thee keep.[46]
Now farewell, and there an end!

[*Exit* FIVE-WITS.]

EVERYMAN. O Jesu, help, all hath forsaken me!

260 **GOOD DEEDS.** Nay, Everyman, I will bide with thee:
I will not forsake thee indeed;
Thou shalt find me a good friend at need.

EVERYMAN. Gramercy, Good Deeds!
Now may I true friends see.
265 They have forsaken me every one—
I loved them better than my Good Deeds alone.
Knowledge, will ye forsake me also?

KNOWLEDGE. Yea, Everyman, when ye to Death shall go,
But not yet, for no manner of danger.

270 **EVERYMAN.** Gramercy, Knowledge, with all my heart!

KNOWLEDGE. Nay, yet will I not from hence depart
Till I see where ye shall become.[47]

EVERYMAN. Methink, alas, that I must be gone
To make my reckoning and my debts pay,
275 For I see my time is nigh spent away.
Take example, all ye that this do hear or see,
How they that I best loved do forsake me,
Except my Good Deeds that bideth truly.

GOOD DEEDS. All earthly things is but vanity.
280 Beauty, Strength, and Discretion do man forsake,
Foolish friends and kinsmen that fair spake—
All fleeth save Good Deeds, and that am I.

EVERYMAN. Have mercy on me, God most mighty,
And stand by me, thou mother and maid, holy Mary!

285 **GOOD DEEDS.** Fear not: I will speak for thee.

---

46. **keep.** Watch over
47. **Till . . . become.** Until I see what will become of you

Everyman. Here I cry God mercy!

Good Deeds. Short our end, and 'minish our pain.
Let us go, and never come again.

Everyman. Into thy hands, Lord, my soul I commend:
290 Receive it, Lord, that it be not lost.
As thou me boughtest,[48] so me defend,
And save me from the fiend's boast,
That I may appear with that blessed host
That shall be saved at the day of doom.
295 *In manus tuas,* of mights most,
Forever *commendo spiritum meum.*[49]

[Everyman *and* Good Deeds *descend into the grave.*]

Knowledge. Now hath he suffered that we all shall endure,
The Good Deeds shall make all sure.
300 Now hath he made ending,
Methinketh that I hear angels sing
And make great joy and melody
Where Everyman's soul received shall be.

Angel [*within*] Come, excellent elect[50] spouse to Jesu![51]
305 Here above thou shalt go
Because of thy singular virtue.
Now the soul is taken the body fro,
Thy reckoning is crystal clear:
Now shalt thou into the heavenly sphere—
310 Unto the which all ye shall come
That liveth well before the day of doom.

[*Enter* Doctor.]

Doctor. This memorial[52] men may have in mind:
Ye hearers, take it of worth, old and young,
315 And forsake Pride, for he deceiveth you in the end.
And remember Beauty, Five-Wits, Strength and Discretion,
They all at the last do Everyman forsake,
Save his Good Deeds there doth he take—
But beware, for and they be small,
320 Before God he hath no help at all—

---

48. **boughtest.** Redeemed
49. **In . . . meum.** [Latin] Into your hands, Almighty One, I forever commend my spirit.
50. **elect.** Chosen
51. **spouse to Jesu.** The soul is often called the "bride of Jesus."
52. **memorial.** Reminder

None excuse may be there for Everyman.
Alas, how shall he do than?[53]
For after death amends[54] may no man make,
For then mercy and pity doth him forsake.
325 If his reckoning be not clear when he doth come,
God will say, *"Ite, maledicti, in ignem eternum!"*[55]
And he that hath his account whole and sound,
High in heaven he shall be crowned,
Unto which place God bring us all thither,
330 That we may live body and soul togither.
Thereto help, the Trinity!
Amen, say ye, for saint charity. ❖

---

53. **than.** Then
54. **amends.** Acts done to make up for injury, loss, or the like
55. **Ite . . . eternum.** [Latin] Go, cursed one, into the everlasting fire.

What matters about a person's life upon his or her death? In addition to Good Deeds, what characters would you add to the play to accompany Everyman?

Refer and Reason

1. What is Everyman's state of mind as he talks with Death? Explain why Everyman feels this way.

2. Identify the primary theme in *Everyman*. Would a play like *Everyman,* even if written in Modern English, be effective in delivering this message today? Explain.

3. What request does Everyman ask of Death? What is Death's response? If you were to judge Everyman, what kind of person would you deem him to be?

Writing Options

1. Write a one-act play that has a moral (teaches a lesson) for young people. You can create the work as an *allegory,* like *Everyman,* in which the characters represent abstract qualities, such as Kindness and Equality. If you prefer, you can write a modern-style play that presents the moral lesson through action and character development.

2. You are the drama critic for the school or local newspaper and have seen a production of the classical play *Everyman.* Write a review of the play that focuses on its theme. Comment on how well the acting, set design, costumes, and other elements communicate the theme. Describe similarities and differences between the director's interpretation and the original script, and analyze how effective the director's choices were. Recommend whether people should or should not see the play. Support your opinion with details from the play.

 Go to **www.mirrorsandwindows.com** for more.

During the thirteenth and fourteenth centuries, the Christian Crusades and devotion to the Virgin Mary (the mother of Jesus) influenced the development of a unique form of literature known as a *romance*. Romance literature portrayed the standards of knightly conduct known as *chivalry*.

Although love did play a major role in early romance literature, at the root, medieval romances were stories of adventure. A typical romance presented a series of loosely connected adventures, each a trial, or test, of the knight's virtues—his loyalty, honesty, faith, skill, and courage. The most famous such trial was the quest for the Holy Grail, the cup from which Jesus offered his apostles communion at the Last Supper.

Often, a knight's trial or quest was undertaken to rescue or win the favor of a fair lady, who was represented in idealized terms as the worthy inspiration of great deeds. This idealization of women and knights' faithful service to them formed the core of *courtly love*, the code of behavior between women and their suitors. The concept of courtly love is explained in a treatise by Andreas Cappellanus.

The most well-known and enduring of the English romances are those written about the legendary King Arthur and his Knights of the Round Table, including Sir Gawain, Sir Lancelot, and Sir Galahad. One of the most famous Arthurian romances is *Sir Gawain and the Green Knight*, believed to have been written around 1370 by an unknown author called the Pearl Poet. A century later, Sir Thomas Malory compiled and retold the Arthurian legends in *Le Morte d'Arthur* (*The Death of Arthur*).

Le Livre et la vraye hystoire du bon roy Alixandre
(*The Book and the True History of the Good King Alexander*), c. 1400s. British Library, London, England.

from **Sir Gawain and the Green Knight**

A Romance by the Pearl Poet, Translated by John Gardner

from **Le Morte d'Arthur**

A Romance by Sir Thomas Malory

Build Background

Literary Context Many medieval works of literature deal with the legend of King Arthur and the Knights of the Round Table. Like most Arthurian romances, **Sir Gawain and the Green Knight** is based on **chivalry,** the code of conduct of the medieval knight. According to that code, a knight was to be a loyal servant to his lord or lady and a perfect example of virtues such as bravery, courtesy, honesty, faith, and gentleness.

When Sir Thomas Malory wrote **Le Morte d'Arthur** at the end of the Middle Ages, the popularity of romance literature was declining. Ironically, Malory's work, which is divided into twenty-one books, is the most complete retelling of the Arthurian legend. Although the title can be translated as *The Death of Arthur,* the work actually focuses on the adventures of the individual Knights of the Round Table. Most of the selection that follows is from the first book of *Le Morte d'Arthur* and chronicles the future king's birth and youth. The final section speculates that the king, who has died, will rule again. In contrast to most English authors of the Medieval Period, who wrote narratives principally in verse, Malory wrote in prose.

Reader's Context What would it have been like to have been a king, knight, or other powerful member of society during the Middle Ages? What would it have been like to have been a common person?

Meet the Authors

No one knows who the **Pearl Poet** actually was. The name given to this writer comes from the first work of a manuscript containing four narrative poems: "Pearl," "Purity," "Patience," and "Sir Gawain and the Green Knight." The poems probably were written around 1370, which would have made the poet a contemporary of Geoffrey Chaucer.

Little is known about **Sir Thomas Malory** (c. 1405–1471). By some accounts, he spent most of his later life in prison. While in his forties, he was arrested for attacking a religious house and faced further charges for escaping from prison and committing other crimes. Malory's involvement in an unsuccessful revolt against Edward IV during the Wars of the Roses (1455–1485) landed him in prison again in 1468. Scholars are certain that Malory was in prison when he completed the manuscript for *Le Morte d'Arthur* around 1469 and that he died in prison.

Compare Literature

Arthurian Romance and Alliteration

An **Arthurian romance** tells of the adventures of King Arthur and his Knights of the Round Table.

Alliteration is the repetition of initial consonant sounds, as in "And **b**oth were **b**ound up with a **b**and of **b**rilliant green."

Set Purpose

Stories of King Arthur and the Knights of the Round Table are some of the most enduring in all of literature. As you read *Sir Gawain and the Green Knight* and *Le Morte d'Arthur,* look for qualities of Arthurian romance, such as elements of fantasy and reality as well as the chivalric code. Also focus closely on the use of language, looking for examples of alliteration. Read *Sir Gawain* aloud to appreciate the effects of alliteration.

Preview Vocabulary

chagrin, 180
ingeniously, 184
reproof, 185
efficacious, 186
covetousness, 188
countenance, 193
usurp, 194
inter, 195
indignation, 197
providence, 197

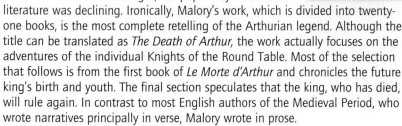

from

Sir Gawain and the Green Knight

by the Pearl Poet

Translated by John Gardner

Sir Gawain Beheads the Green Knight, c. 1300s.
British Library, London, England. (See detail on page 176.)

My head fell off at my feet, yet I never flickered;
But you! You tremble at heart before you're touched!

*King Arthur and his Knights of the Round Table are celebrating Christmas
when an enormous green man, the Green Knight, bursts through the door.*

Splendid that knight errant[1] stood in a splay of green,
And green, too, was the mane of his mighty destrier;[2]
Fair fanning tresses enveloped the fighting man's shoulders,
And over his breast hung a beard as big as a bush;
5   The beard and the huge mane burgeoning forth from his head
Were clipped off clean in a straight line over his elbows,
And the upper half of each arm was hidden underneath

---

1. **knight errant.** Knight in search of adventure
2. **destrier** [des´ trē ər]. Steed; horse

from Le Morte d'Arthur

by Sir Thomas Malory

The Death of Arthur, 1862. John Mulcaster Carrick.
Private collection.

Whoso pulleth out this sword of this stone and anvil, is rightwise King born of all England.

from Book I, Chapter 1

FIRST, HOW UTHER PENDRAGON SENT FOR
THE DUKE OF CORNWALL AND IGRAINE HIS WIFE,
AND OF THEIR DEPARTING SUDDENLY AGAIN

It befell in the days of Uther Pendragon, when he was king of all England, and so reigned, that there was a mighty duke in Cornwall that held war against him long time. And the duke was called the Duke of Tintagel. And so by means King Uther sent for this duke, charging him to bring his wife with him, for she was called a fair lady, and a passing[1] wise, and her name was called Igraine.

---

1. **passing.** Exceedingly

So when the duke and his wife were comen unto the king, by the means of great lords they were accorded both. The king liked and loved this lady well, and he made them great cheer out of measure, and desired to have lain by her. But she was a passing good woman, and would not assent unto the king. And then she told the duke her husband, and said, "I suppose that we were sent for that I should be dishonored, wherefore, husband, I counsel you that we depart from hence suddenly, that we may ride all night unto our own castle." And in like wise as she said so they departed, that neither the king nor none of his council were ware of their departing.

As soon as King Uther knew of their departing so suddenly, he was wonderly wroth.[2] Then he called to him his privy council,[3] and told them of the sudden departing of the duke and his wife. Then they advised the king to send for the duke and his wife by a great charge: "And if he will not come at your summons, then may ye do your best, then have ye cause to make mighty war upon him."

> "And if he will not come at your summons, . . . then have ye cause to make mighty war upon him."

So that was done, and the messengers had their answers, and that was this shortly, that neither he nor his wife would not come at him. Then was the king wonderly wroth. And then the king sent him plain word again, and bad him be ready and stuff him and garnish him,[4] for within forty days would fetch him out of the biggest castle that he hath.

When the duke had this warning, anon he went and furnished and garnished two strong castles of his, of the which the one hight[5] Tintagel, and the other castle hight Terrabil. So his wife Dame Igraine he put in the Castle of Tintagel, and himself he put in the Castle of Terrabil, the which had many issues and posterns[6] out. Then in all haste came Uther with a great host, and laid a siege about the Castle of Terrabil. And there he pitched many pavilions, and there was great war made on both parties, and much people slain.

Then for pure anger and for great love of fair Igraine the King Uther fell sick. So came to the King Uther Sir Ulfius, a noble knight, and asked the king why he was sick.

"I shall tell thee," said the king. "I am sick for anger and for love of fair Igraine that I may not be whole."

"Well, my lord," said Sir Ulfius, "I shall seek Merlin, and he shall do you remedy, that your heart shall be pleased."

So Ulfius departed, and by adventure he met Merlin in a beggar's array, and there Merlin asked Ulfius whom he sought. And he said he had little ado to tell him.

"Well," said Merlin, "I know whom thou seekest, for thou seekest Merlin; therefore seek no farther, for I am he, and if King Uther will well reward me, and be sworn unto me to fulfil my desire, that shall be his honor and profit more than mine, for I shall cause him to have all his desire."

"All this will I undertake," said Ulfius, "that there shall be nothing reasonable but thou shalt have thy desire."

"Well," said Merlin, "he shall have his intent and desire. And therefore," said Merlin, "ride on your way, for I will not be long behind."

---

2. **wroth.** Angry
3. **privy council.** King's group of advisors
4. **stuff . . . him.** Prepare for a siege
5. **hight.** Called; known as
6. **posterns.** Private rear entrance

Meeting of Arthur and Merlin with the Lady of the Lake,
c. 1893. Aubrey Beardsley. Private collection.

from Book I, Chapter 2

How Uther Pendragon made war on the Duke
of Cornwall, and how by the mean of Merlin
he lay by the Duchess and gat[7] Arthur

Then Ulfius was glad, and rode on more than
a pace till that he came to King Uther Pendragon, and told him he had met with Merlin.

"Where is he?" said the king.

"Sir," said Ulfius, "he will not dwell[8] long."

Therewithal Ulfius was ware where Merlin
stood at the porch of the pavilion's door. And
then Merlin was bound to come to the king.
When King Uther saw him, he said he was
welcome.

"Sir," said Merlin "I know all your heart
every deal.[9] So ye will be sworn unto me as ye

be a true king anointed, to fulfil my desire, ye
shall have your desire."

Then the king was sworn upon the four
Evangelists.

"Sir," said Merlin, "this is my desire: the
first night that ye shall lie by Igraine ye shall
get a child on her, and when that is born, that
it shall be delivered to me for to nourish there
as I will have it; for it shall be your worship,[10]
and the child's avail as mickle[11] as the child is
worth."

"I will well," said the king, "as thou wilt
have it."

"Now make you ready," said Merlin, "this
night ye shall lie with Igraine in the Castle of
Tintagel, and ye shall be like the duke her husband, Ulfius shall be like Sir Brastias, a knight
of the duke's, and I will be like a knight that
hight Sir Jordans, a knight of the duke's. But
wait[12] ye make not many questions with her
nor her men, but say ye are diseased,[13] and so
hie you to bed, and rise not on the morn till I
come to you, for the Castle of Tintagel is but
ten miles hence."

So this was done as they devised. But the
Duke of Tintagel espied how the king rode
from the siege of Terrabil, and therefore that
night he issued out of the castle at a postern
for to have distressed the king's host. And so,
through his own issue, the duke himself was
slain or-ever[14] the king came at the Castle of
Tintagel.

So after the death of the duke, King Uther
lay with Igraine more than three hours after his
death, and begat on her that night Arthur; and,
or day came, Merlin came to the king, and bad
him make him ready, and so he kissed the lady

---

7. **gat.** Begat; fathered
8. **dwell.** Delay
9. **deal.** Part
10. **worship.** Honor
11. **mickle.** Much
12. **wait.** Take care
13. **diseased.** Tired
14. **or-ever.** Before

Igraine and departed in all haste. But when the lady heard tell of the duke her husband, and by all record he was dead or-ever King Uther came to her, then she marvelled who that might be that lay with her in likeness of her lord; so she mourned privily and held her peace.

And so, through his own issue, the duke himself was slain.

Then all the barons by one assent prayed the king of accord betwixt the lady Igraine and him; the king gave them leave, for fain would he have been accorded with her. So the king put all the trust in Ulfius to entreat[15] between them, so by the entreaty at the last the king and she met together.

"Now will we do well," said Ulfius. "Our king is a lusty knight and wifeless, and my lady Igraine is a passing fair lady; it were great joy unto us all, and it might please the king to make her his queen."

Unto that they all well accorded and moved it to the king. And anon, like a lusty knight, he assented thereto with good will, and so in all haste they were married in a morning with great mirth and joy.

And King Lot of Lothian and of Orkney then wedded Margawse that was Gawain's mother, and King Nentres of the land of Garlot wedded Elaine. All this was done at the request of King Uther. And the third sister Morgan le Fay was put to school in a nunnery, and there she learned so much that she was a great clerk of necromancy,[16] and after she was wedded to King Uriens of the land of Gore, that was Sir Uwain's le Blanchemains father.

from Book I, Chapter 3

OF THE BIRTH OF KING ARTHUR AND OF HIS NURTURE

Then Queen Igraine waxed[17] daily greater and greater, so it befell after within half a year, as King Uther lay by his queen, he asked her, by the faith she ought to him, whose was the child within her body; then was she sore abashed to give answer.

"Dismay you not," said the king, "but tell me the truth, and I shall love you the better, by the faith of my body."

"Sir," said she, "I shall tell you the truth. The same night that my lord was dead, the hour of his death, as his knights record, there came into my castle of Tintagel a man like my lord in speech and in <u>countenance</u>, and two knights with him in likeness of his two knights Brastias and Jordans, and so I went unto bed with him as I ought to do with my lord, and the same night, as I shall answer unto God, this child was begotten upon me."

"That is truth," said the king, "as ye say; for it was I myself that came in the likeness, and therefore dismay you not, for I am father to the child;" and there he told her all the cause, how it was by Merlin's counsel. Then the queen made great joy when she knew who was the father of her child.

Soon came Merlin unto the king, and said, "Sir, ye must purvey you for the nourishing of your child."

"As thou wilt," said the king, "be it."

"Well," said Merlin, "I know a lord of yours in this land, that is a passing true man and a faithful, and he shall have the nourishing of your child; and his name is Sir Ector, and he is a lord

15. **entreat.** Negotiate
16. **necromancy.** Black magic; sorcery
17. **waxed.** Grew gradually larger

coun • te • nance (kaȯn´ t'n ənts) *n.*, appearance; facial features

Discovering King Arthur

Modern scholars are unsure of whether King Arthur was a real person or a figure descended from other legends. Geoffrey of Monmouth, an English clergy who lived in the twelfth century, wrote a book entitled *Historia Regum Brittaniae* that supposedly proved Arthur was a real historical figure. Monmouth claimed to have translated his history from an ancient Welsh book, but it is obvious that he drew mainly from mythological sagas. An English monk named William of Newburgh, who lived at approximately the same time as Monmouth, wrote, "It is quite clear that everything this man wrote about Arthur was made up, partly by himself and partly by others, either from an inordinate love of lying, or for the sake of pleasing the Britons."

The argument commonly offered against Arthur's existence is his remarkable similarity to Alfred the Great (849–899). Both Alfred and Arthur were strong leaders who organized a diverse population of varying ethnicities to ward off foreign invasion. Ancient Europeans used myths to explain their world, which meant historical figures sometimes were integrated into mythological narratives.

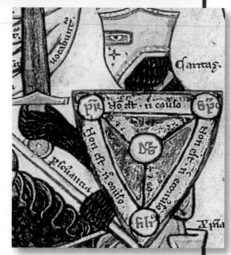

However, in 1998, archaelogists discovered a sixth-century stone among the ruins of Tintagel Castle in Cornwall (southwestern England) that may prove Arthur was a real person. The stone has the names *Artognou* and *Coll* inscribed on its surface. *Artognou* could mean "descendent of Arthur." In fact, Monmouth listed a man named Coel Hen as a descendant of Arthur. While the stone does not prove that Arthur existed or that Artognou was his descendant, it may provide a link between the Arthurian legend and the kings that ruled England before the Anglo-Saxon invasion.

---

of fair livelihood in many parts in England and Wales; and this lord, Sir Ector, let him be sent for, for to come and speak with you, and desire him yourself, as he loveth you, that he will put his own child to nourishing to another woman, and that his wife nourish yours. And when the child is born let it be delivered to me at yonder privy postern unchristened."

So like as Merlin devised it was done. And when Sir Ector was come he made fiance[18] to the king for to nourish the child like as the king desired; and there the king granted Sir Ector great rewards. Then when the lady was delivered, the king commanded two knights and two ladies to take the child, bound in a cloth of gold, "and that ye deliver him to what poor man ye meet at the postern gate of the

castle." So the child was delivered unto Merlin, and so he bare it forth unto Sir Ector, and made an holy man to christen him, and named him Arthur; and so Sir Ector's wife nourished him with her own pap.

from Book I, Chapter 4

OF THE DEATH OF KING UTHER PENDRAGON

Then within two years King Uther fell sick of a great malady. And in the meanwhile his enemies <u>usurped</u> upon him, and did a great

---

18. **fiance.** A promise

usurp (yü sərp´) *v.*, seize unlawfully, as a throne or other seat of power battle upon his men, and slew many of his people.

"Sir," said Merlin, "ye may not lie so as ye do, for ye must to the field though ye ride on an horse-litter; for ye shall never have the better of your enemies but if your person be there, and then shall ye have the victory."

So it was done as Merlin had devised, and they carried the king forth in an horse-litter with a great host toward his enemies. And at St. Albans there met with the king a great host of the north. And that day Sir Ulfius and Sir Brastias did great deeds of arms, and King Uther's men overcame the northern battle and slew many people, and put the remnant to flight. And then the king returned unto London, and made great joy of his victory.

And then he fell passing sore sick, so that three days and three nights he was speechless; wherefore all the barons made great sorrow, and asked Merlin what counsel were best.

> ## And then he fell passing sore sick, so that three days and three nights he was speechless.

"There is none other remedy," said Merlin, "but God will have his will. But look ye all, barons, be before King Uther to-morn, and God and I shall make him to speak."

So on the morn all the barons with Merlin came tofore the king; then Merlin said aloud unto King Uther, "Sir, shall I your son Arthur be king, after your days, of this realm with all the appurtenance?"[19]

Then Uther Pendragon turned him, and said in hearing of them all, "I give him God's blessing and mine, and bid him pray for my

soul, and righteously and worshipfully that he claim the crown upon forfeiture of my blessing." And therewith he yielded up the ghost, and then was he <u>interred</u> as longed to a king, wherefore the queen, fair Igraine, made great sorrow, and all the barons.

from Book I, Chapter 5

How Arthur was chosen king, and of wonders and marvels of a sword taken out of a stone by the said Arthur

Then stood the realm in great jeopardy long while, for every lord that was mighty of men made him strong, and many weened[20] to have been king. Then Merlin went to the Archbishop of Canterbury, and counselled him for to send for all the lords of the realm, and all the gentlemen of arms, that they should to London come by Christmas, upon pain of cursing; and for this cause: that Jehu, that was born on that night, that He would of his great mercy show some miracle, as He was come to be king of mankind, for to show some miracle who should be rightwise king of this realm. So the Archbishop, by the advice of Merlin, sent for all the lords and gentlemen of arms that they should come by Christmas even unto London. And many of them made them clean of their life, that their prayer might be the more acceptable unto God.

So in the greatest church of London (whether it were Paul's or not the French book maketh no mention) all the estates were long or day in the church for to pray. And when matins[21] and the first mass was done, there was seen in the churchyard, against the high altar, a great stone four square, like unto a marble stone, and in midst thereof was like an anvil

---

19. **appurtenance.** Property that belongs with, or is part of, a possession or other item
20. **weened.** Thought
21. **matins.** Morning prayers

in • ter (in tər´) v., bury

of steel a foot on high, and therein stuck a fair sword naked by the point, and letters there were written in gold about the sword that saiden thus:—WHOSO PULLETH OUT THIS SWORD OF THIS STONE AND ANVIL, IS RIGHTWISE KING BORN OF ALL ENGLAND. Then the people marvelled, and told it to the Archbishop.

"I command," said the Archbishop, "that ye keep you within your church, and pray unto God still; that no man touch the sword till the high mass be all done."

So when all masses were done all the lords went to behold the stone and the sword. And when they saw the scripture, some assayed,[22] such as would have been king. But none might stir the sword nor move it.

"He is not here," said the Archbishop, "that shall achieve the sword, but doubt not God will make him known. But this is my counsel," said the Archbishop, "that we let purvey[23] ten knights, men of good fame, and they to keep this sword."

So it was ordained, and then there was made a cry, that every man should assay that would, for to win the sword. And upon New Year's Day the barons let make a jousts and a tournament, that all knights that would joust or tourney there might play. And all this was ordained for to keep the lords together and the commons, for the Archbishop trusted that God would make him known that should win the sword.

So upon New Year's Day, when the service was done, the barons rode unto the field, some to joust and some to tourney, and so it happed that Sir Ector, that had great livelihood about London, rode unto the jousts, and with him rode Sir Kay his son, and young Arthur that was his nourished brother; and Sir Kay was made knight at All Hallowmass afore. So as they rode to the jousts-ward, Sir Kay had lost his sword, for he had left it at his father's lodging, and so he prayed young Arthur for to ride for his sword.

"I will well," said Arthur, and rode fast after the sword. And when he came home the lady and all were out to see the jousting.

Then was Arthur wroth, and said to himself, "I will ride to the churchyard, and take the sword with me that sticketh in the stone, for my brother Sir Kay shall not be without a sword this day." So when he came to the churchyard, Sir Arthur alit and tied his horse to the stile, and so he went to the tent, and found no knights there, for they were at jousting; and so he handled the sword by the handles, and lightly and fiercely pulled it out of the stone, and took his horse and rode his way until he came to his brother Sir Kay, and delivered him the sword.

And as soon as Sir Kay saw the sword, he wist[24] well it was the sword of the stone, and so he rode to his father Sir Ector, and said; "Sir, lo here is the sword of the stone, wherefore I must be king of this land."

When Sir Ector beheld the sword, he returned again and came to the church, and there they alit all three, and went into the church. And anon he made Sir Kay to swear upon a book how he came to that sword.

"Sir," said Sir Kay, "by my brother Arthur, for he brought it to me."

"How gat ye this sword?" said Sir Ector to Arthur.

"Sir, I will tell you. When I came home for my brother's sword, I found nobody at home to deliver me his sword, and so I thought my brother Sir Kay should not be swordless, and so I came hither eagerly and pulled it out of the stone without any pain."

"Found ye any knights about this sword?" said Sir Ector.

"Nay," said Arthur.

"Now," said Sir Ector to Arthur, "I understand ye must be king of this land."

"Wherefore[25] I," said Arthur, "and for what cause?"

---

22. **assayed.** Attempted
23. **let purvey.** Appoint
24. **wist.** Knew
25. **Wherefore.** Why

"Sir," said Ector, "for God will have it so, for there should never man have drawn out this sword, but he that shall be rightwise king of this land. Now let me see whether ye can put the sword there as it was, and pull it out again."

"That is no mastery," said Arthur, and so he put it in the stone; therewithal Sir Ector assayed to pull out the sword and failed.

from Book I, Chapter 6

HOW KING ARTHUR PULLED OUT
THE SWORD DIVERS TIMES

"Now assay," said Sir Ector unto Sir Kay. And anon he pulled at the sword with all his might, but it would not be.

"Now shall ye assay," said Sir Ector to Arthur.

"I will well," said Arthur, and pulled it out easily. And therewithal Sir Ector knelt down to the earth, and Sir Kay.

"Alas!" said Arthur, "my own dear father and brother, why kneel ye to me?"

"Nay, nay, my lord Arthur, it is not so, I was never your father nor of your blood, but I wot[26] well ye are of an higher blood than I weened ye were." And then Sir Ector told him all, how he was betaken[27] him for to nourish him, and by whose commandment, and by Merlin's deliverance. Then Arthur made great dole[28] when he understood that Sir Ector was not his father.

"Sir," said Ector unto Arthur, "will ye be my good and gracious lord when ye are king?"

"Else were I to blame," said Arthur, "for ye are the man in the world that I am most beholding to, and my good lady and mother your wife, that as well as her own hath fostered me and kept. And if ever it be God's will that I be king as ye say, ye shall desire of me what I may do, and I shall not fail you, God forbid I should fail you."

"Sir," said Sir Ector, "I will ask no more of you, but that ye will make my son, your foster brother, Sir Kay, seneschal[29] of all your lands."

"That shall be done," said Arthur, "and more, by the faith of my body, that never man shall have that office but he, while he and I live."

Therewithal they went unto the Archbishop, and told him how the sword was achieved, and by whom. And on Twelfthday all the barons came thither, and to assay to take the sword, who that would assay. But there afore them all, there might none take it out but Arthur; wherefore there were many lords wroth, and said it was great shame unto them all and the realm, to be over-governed with a boy of no high blood born, and so they fell out at that time, that it was put off till Candlemas,[30] and then all the barons should meet there again; but alway the ten knights were ordained to watch the sword day and night, and so they set a pavilion over the stone and the sword, and five always watched.

So at Candlemas many more great lords came thither for to have won the sword, but there might none prevail. And right as Arthur did at Christmas, he did at Candlemas, and pulled out the sword easily, whereof the barons were sore agrieved and put it off in delay till the high feast of Easter. And as Arthur sped before, so did he at Easter, yet there were some of the great lords had indignation that Arthur should be king, and put it off in a delay till the feast of Pentecost.[31] Then the Archbishop of Canterbury by Merlin's providence let purvey then of the best knights that they might get, and such knights as Uther Pendragon loved best and

---

26. **wot.** Know
27. **betaken.** Assigned to care for
28. **dole.** Lamentation; dolor
29. **seneschal.** Steward
30. **Candlemas.** A church feast on February 2
31. **Pentecost.** The seventh Sunday after Easter

---

in • dig • na • tion (in dig nā´ shən) *n.*, anger, scorn, or annoyance

prov • i • dence (prä´ və dəns) *n.*, benevolent guidance

most trusted in his days. And such knights were put about Arthur as Sir Baudwin of Britain, Sir Kay, Sir Ulfius, Sir Brastias. All these with many other, were always about Arthur, day and night, till the feast of Pentecost.

from Book I, Chapter 7

HOW KING ARTHUR WAS CROWNED,
AND HOW HE MADE OFFICERS

And at the feast of Pentecost all manner of men assayed to pull at the sword that would assay, but none might prevail but Arthur, and pulled it out afore all the lords and commons that were there, wherefore all the commons cried at once, "We will have Arthur unto our king; we will put him no more in delay, for we all see that it is God's will that he shall be our king, and who that holdeth against it, we will slay him." And therewithal they kneeled at once, both rich and poor, and cried Arthur mercy because they had delayed him so long. And Arthur forgave them, and took the sword between both his hands, and offered it upon the altar where the Archbishop was, and so was he made knight of the best man that was there.

And so anon was the coronation made. And there was he sworn unto his lords and the commons for to be a true king, to stand with true justice from thenceforth the days of this life. Also then he made all lords that held of the crown to come in, and to do service as they ought to do. And many complaints were made unto Sir Arthur of great wrongs that were done since the death of King Uther, of many lands that were bereaved lords, knights, ladies, and gentlemen.

Wherefore King Arthur made the lands to be given again unto them that ought them.[32] When this was done, that the king had stablished all the countries about London, then he let make Sir Kay Seneschal of England; and Sir Baudwin of Britain was made constable; and Sir Ulfius was made chamberlain; and Sir Brastias was made warden to wait upon the north from Trent forwards, for it was that time the most part the king's enemies. But within few years after, Arthur won all the north, Scotland, and all that were under their obeisance.[33] Also Wales, a part of it, held against Arthur, but he overcame them all, as he did the remnant, through the noble prowess of himself and his knights of the Round Table.

. . .

from Book XXI, Chapter 7

OF THE OPINION OF SOME MEN OF THE DEATH
OF KING ARTHUR; AND HOW QUEEN GUENEVER
MADE HER A NUN IN ALMESBURY

Yet some men say in many parts of England that King Arthur is not dead, but had by the will of Our Lord Jesu into another place; and men say that he shall come again, and he shall win the holy cross. I will not say that it shall be so, but rather I will say, here in this world he changed his life. But many men say that there is written upon his tomb this verse: HIC IACET ARTHURUS, REX QUONDAM REXQUE FUTURUS.[34] ❖

---

32. **ought them.** Owned them
33. **obeisance.** Authority; rule
34. **HIC . . . FUTURUS.** [Latin] Here lies Arthur, the once and future king

MIRRORS & WINDOWS

Merlin wanted the young Arthur to be raised by Sir Ector, not King Uther, his father. What might be the benefits of being raised in a humble setting? What might be the benefits of being raised in a setting of luxury and privilege?

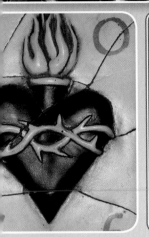

Primary Source Connection

The Art of Courtly Love, by **Andreas Cappellanus,** is a *treatise,* which is a statement defining a belief or policy about a particular topic. This excerpt from Cappellanus's treatise consists of a series of statements on the nature of love and the rules governing the pursuit of romance. Among the author's assertions are that lovers should be faithful to each other, that men should not take advantage of women, and that love is true only when the partners think constantly of each other. The author, whose name means "André the Chaplain," was recruited by a daughter of Eleanor of Aquitaine, a French ruler of the twelfth century. His assignment was to teach the young people at Eleanor's castle in Poitiers, France, how to behave.

from The Art of Courtly Love

by Andreas Cappellanus

1. Marriage is no real excuse for not loving.
2. He who is not jealous cannot love.
3. No one can be bound by a double love.
4. It is well known that love is always increasing or decreasing.
5. That which a lover takes against the will of his beloved has no relish.
6. Boys do not love until they arrive at the age of maturity.
7. When one lover dies, a widowhood of two years is required of the survivor.
8. No one should be deprived of love without the very best of reasons.
9. No one can love unless he is impelled by the persuasion of love.
10. Love is always a stranger in the home of avarice.
11. It is not proper to love any woman whom one would be ashamed to seek to marry.
12. A true lover does not desire to embrace in love anyone except his beloved.
13. When made public, love rarely endures.

14. The easy attainment of love makes it of little value; difficulty of attainment makes it prized.
15. Every lover regularly turns pale in the presence of his beloved.
16. When a lover suddenly catches sight of his beloved, his heart palpitates.
17. A new love puts to flight an old one.
18. Good character alone makes any man worthy of love.
19. If love diminishes, it quickly fails and rarely revives.
20. A man in love is always apprehensive.
21. Real jealousy always increases the feeling of love.
22. Jealousy, and therefore love, are increased when one suspects his beloved.
23. He whom the thought of love vexes, eats and sleeps very little.
24. Every act of a lover ends in the thought of his beloved.
25. A true lover considers nothing good except what he thinks will please his beloved.
26. Love can deny nothing to love.
27. A lover can never have enough of the solaces of his beloved.
28. A slight presumption causes a lover to suspect his beloved.
29. A man who is vexed by too much passion usually does not love.
30. A true lover is constantly and without intermission possessed by the thought of his beloved.
31. Nothing forbids one woman being loved by two men or one man by two women. ❖

Review Questions

1. According to Cappellanus, what does *not* constitute love? Differentiate between a "home of avarice" and one of generosity. How does this affect love?

2. What "is no real excuse" for being unloving? Interpret what Cappellanus means by this.

3. List the words and phrases that describe a lover. Summarize Cappellanus's definition of a lover.

TEXT ⇄ TEXT CONNECTION

Most educated Europeans of the era were familiar with Arthurian romances. Sir Thomas Malory, for example, based his writing on French literature and other works. Which elements of Cappellanus's treatise on love correspond to the code of chivalry suggested in Malory's *Le Morte d'Arthur* and the Pearl Poet's *Sir Gawain and the Green Knight?* Which elements seem different from the code?

Refer to Text ▶ ▶ ▶ ▶ ▶	**Reason with Text**	
1a. Identify the main elements of fantasy or magic associated with the Green Knight.	**1b.** Near the end of *Sir Gawain,* how does the Green Knight become more of a real-life character who shows human emotions?	**Understand** Find meaning
2a. In the excerpt from *Le Morte d'Arthur,* with whom does Arthur spend his childhood? How is his royal heritage discovered?	**2b.** Examine how not knowing his real identity might have affected the young Arthur.	**Apply** Use information
3a. In *Le Morte d'Arthur,* how does Arthur seek to help Sir Kay, his foster brother? In *Sir Gawain,* why does Gawain volunteer to fight with the Green Knight at the holiday banquet?	**3b.** Compare and contrast the two men who are tested, Arthur and Gawain.	**Analyze** Take things apart
4a. In the story of Gawain, how does he react when he learns that the sash belongs to the Green Knight?	**4b.** Argue whether Gawain judges himself too harshly during his final meeting with the Green Knight.	**Evaluate** Make judgments
5a. Describe Merlin's influence on young Arthur, as described in *Le Morte d'Arthur.*	**5b.** Explain why Merlin might have acted as he did.	**Create** Bring ideas together

Compare Literature

Arthurian Romance and Alliteration

Identify the features of Arthurian romance in *Sir Gawain and the Green Knight* and in *Le Morte d'Arthur.* What elements of the chivalric code are present in the behavior of Arthur and of Gawain?

Which passages in *Sir Gawain and the Green Knight* contain alliteration? How do these passages differ from those that do not use this literary device? How does the alliteration in Gawain's tale differ from that in other poetry with which you are familiar?

Extend the Text

Writing Options

Creative Writing Write a children's story for some youngsters you know that features alliteration. You may wish to illustrate the story yourself or ask for help from your intended audience.

Expository Writing The selections by Malory and the Pearl Poet are both Arthurian romances, but the two writers have distinct approaches to the Arthurian legend. Write an essay that compares and contrasts the conflicts in *Le Morte d'Arthur* and *Sir Gawain and the Green Knight.*

Critical Literacy

Create a Map of Arthur's Britain Although the location of Camelot, the site of King Arthur's court, has not been verified historically, many of the geographical locations mentioned in Arthurian legends do exist. Use a historical atlas to find landmarks mentioned in *Le Morte d'Arthur;* then create your own map of Arthurian England.

Media Literacy

Find a Modern Version Select a modern adaptation of the story of Arthur to read or watch. Possibilities include *The Once and Future King* (1958), by T. H. White; *Camelot* (film version, 1967); *The Mists of Avalon* (1983), by Marion Zimmer Bradley; and *Prince Valiant* comics, by Hal Foster. After reviewing the work, discuss in a small group how it compares to Malory's story.

 Go to **www.mirrorsandwindows.com** for more.

Robin Hood and Allen a Dale

Anonymous Ballad

Build Background

Cultural Context Like most ballads, **"Robin Hood and Allen a Dale"** has an anonymous author and was passed from generation to generation through the oral tradition. No one knows for sure when the legend of Robin Hood first developed, although the outlaw hero is mentioned in the narrative poem *Piers Plowman* as early as 1377.

Most likely, the legend of Robin Hood developed much earlier. In fact, it may have developed out of the ancient fertility rituals of the Druids (Celtic priests from Ireland and Wales) or the Teutonic (Germanic) tribes. In the Robin Hood ballads, the hero is dressed in green and lives in the greenwood, or forest. Through the centuries, Robin Hood and various figures associated with him were central characters in May festivals celebrating the coming of spring. This practice also may have survived from ancient religious rituals that have been lost.

The legend of Robin Hood has survived for centuries because it is always being retold. Each retelling may add a different perspective or twist on the tale. In the past century, Robin Hood has been featured in a number of films: the 1922 silent film *Robin Hood,* starring Douglas Fairbanks; *The Adventures of Robin Hood* (1938), starring Errol Flynn; the Disney version of *Robin Hood* (1973); *Robin Hood: Prince of Thieves* (1991), starring Kevin Costner; and Mel Brooks's film *Robin Hood: Men in Tights,* which satirizes the version in which Costner starred.

Richard Coeur de Lion (1157–1199).

Historical Context How did Robin Hood come to be the outlaw hero so familiar in English-speaking countries? In the late twelfth century, the heir apparent (next in line) to the English throne was Richard Coeur de Lion (sometimes called Richard the Lion Heart), who journeyed to the Holy Land on a Crusade. On his return home, he was held captive by the Holy Roman Emperor, ruler of parts of Europe. During Richard's absence, his brother John became the English monarch. John was a hated king who taxed his subjects severely. Many of the Robin Hood stories and ballads became popular at this time. They tell of an outlaw who is loyal to King Richard and who robs the wealthy to give to the poor.

According to historical records, many outlaws in England throughout the Middle Ages identified themselves with Robin Hood. No one knows, however, whether there was, in fact, an actual person who inspired the legend.

Reader's Context Under what circumstances can an outlaw or someone who violates society's regulations also be a protector of society?

Analyze Literature

Stanza, Quatrain, and Meter

A **stanza** is a section of lines in a poem. Ballads generally are divided into stanzas of four lines called **quatrains.** The lines of each quatrain are arranged in a specific **meter,** which is a regular rhythmic pattern determined by the number of beats, or stresses, in each line. As you read "Robin Hood and Allen a Dale," notice how the first and third lines of each quatrain have four beats, or *feet* (known as *tetrameter*), and the second and fourth lines have three feet (*trimeter*).

Set Purpose

Like the story of King Arthur, the story of Robin Hood may have been based on a real historical figure but became legendary through repeated retellings and adaptations. Analyze how the qualities of the ballad, including its form and meter, contributed to its being passed down through the oral tradition. Read aloud "Robin Hood and Allen a Dale" to listen for these qualities.

ROBIN HOOD

and

ALLEN A DALE

Sketch of Robin Hood, 1852. Richard Dadd.
Yale Center for British Art, New Haven, Connecticut.
(See detail on page 204.)

Come listen to me, you gallants so free,
    All you that love mirth for to hear,
And I will you tell of a bold outlaw,
    That lived in Nottinghamshire.

5 As Robin Hood in the forest stood,
    All under the greenwood tree,
There was he aware of a brave young man,
    As fine as fine might be.

The youngster was clothed in scarlet red,
10   In scarlet fine and gay,
And he did frisk it over the plain,
    and chanted a roundelay.[1]

---

1. **roundelay.** Joyful song

As Robin Hood next morning stood,
    Among the leaves so gay,
15 There did he spy the same young man
    Come drooping along the way.

The scarlet he wore the day before,
    It was clean cast away;
And every step he fetched a sigh,
20   "Alack and a well a day!"

Then stepped forth brave Little John,
    And Nick the miller's son,
Which made the young man bend his bow,
    When as he saw them come.

25 "Stand off, stand off," the young man said,
    "What is your will with me?"
"You must come before our master straight,
    Under yon greenwood tree."

And when he came bold Robin before,
30   Robin asked him courteously,
"O hast thou any money to spare
    For my merry men and me?"

"I have no money," the young man said,
    "But five shillings and a ring;
35 And that I have kept this seven long years,
    To have it at my wedding.

"Yesterday I should have married a maid,
    But she is now from me tane,[2]
And chosen to be an old knight's delight,
40   Whereby my poor heart is slain."

"What is thy name?" then said Robin Hood,
    "Come tell me, without any fail."
"By the faith of my body," then said the young man,
    "My name it is Allen a Dale."

45 "What wilt thou give me," said Robin Hood,
    "In ready gold or fee,
To help thee to thy true love again,
    And deliver her unto thee?"

---

2. **tane.** Taken

"I have no money," then quoth the young man,
50   "No ready gold nor fee,
But I will swear upon a book
    Thy true servant for to be."

"How many miles is it to thy true love?
    Come tell me without any guile."[3]
55 "By the faith of my body," then said the young man,
    "It is but five little mile."

Then Robin he hastened over the plain,
    He did neither stint nor lin,[4]
Until he came unto the church
60   Where Allen should keep his wedding.

"What dost thou do here?" the bishop he said,
    "I prithee now tell to me."
"I am a bold harper," quoth Robin Hood,
    "And the best in the north country."

65 "O welcome, O welcome," the bishop he said,
    "That music best pleaseth me";
"You shall have no music," quoth Robin Hood,
    "Till the bride and the bridegroom I see."

With that came in a wealthy knight,
70   Which was both grave and old,
And after him a finikin[5] lass,
    Did shine like glistering[6] gold.

"This is no fit match," quoth bold Robin Hood,
    "That you do seem to make here;
75 For since we are come unto the church,
    The bride she shall choose her own dear."

Then Robin Hood put his horn to his mouth,
    And blew blasts two or three;
When four and twenty bowmen bold
80   Come leaping over the lee.[7]

---

3. **guile.** Slyness
4. **stint nor lin.** Stop nor cease
5. **finikin.** Well dressed; fine
6. **glistering.** Shining; sparkling
7. **lee.** Sheltered, hidden place

And when they came into the churchyard,
    Marching all in a row,
The first man was Allen a Dale,
    To give bold Robin his bow.

85 "This is thy true love," Robin he said,
    "Young Allen, as I hear say;
And you shall be married at this same time,
    Before we depart away."

"That shall not be," the bishop he said,
90   "For thy word shall not stand;
They shall be three times asked in the church,[8]
    As the law is of our land."

Robin Hood pulled off the bishop's coat,
    And put it upon Little John;
95 "By the faith of my body," then Robin said,
    "This cloth doth make thee a man."

When Little John went into the choir,
    The people began for to laugh;
He asked them seven times in the church,
100   Lest three times should not be enough.

"Who gives me this maid," then said Little John;
    Quoth Robin, "That do I,
And he that doth take her from Allen a Dale
    Full dearly[9] he shall her buy."

105 And thus having ended this merry wedding,
    The bride looked as fresh as a queen,
And so they returned to the merry greenwood,
    Among the leaves so green. ❖

---

8. **three . . . church.** An intended marriage had to be announced three
   Sundays in a row.
9. **dearly.** At great cost

MIRRORS & WINDOWS

Are Robin Hood and his friends justified in interrupting the wedding ceremony and having Little John marry Allen and the bride? When is it appropriate to intervene in someone else's life?

Refer to Text ▶ ▶ ▶ ▶ ▶ ▶   Reason with Text

1a. Who is the "youngster" dressed in scarlet mentioned in stanza 3?	**1b.** Describe how the youngster's mood changes. What causes his change in mood?	**Understand** Find meaning
2a. When Robin Hood puts the bishop's coat on Little John, what *proverb*, or traditional saying, does Robin quote?	**2b.** The proverb suggests that a poor man can become a gentleman by wearing a suit. The word *cloth* often is used in referring to the clergy. Given all this, how is Robin's use of the proverb ironic?	**Apply** Use information
3a. Whom is Allen a Dale's beloved being forced to marry?	**3b.** What attitude toward the upper class is suggested by the speaker and the characters in the ballad? Infer why the common people might have had this attitude.	**Analyze** Take things apart
4a. Why is Little John able to perform the marriage rites?	**4b.** Judge whether Robin Hood is justified in stealing the bride and marrying her.	**Evaluate** Make judgments
5a. What is meant by the expression "People may sometimes take the law into their own hands"?	**5b.** Suggest under what conditions, if any, people might be justified in taking the law into their own hands. Explain your response.	**Create** Bring ideas together

Analyze Literature

Stanza, Quatrain, and Meter
How many stanzas, or quatrains, does "Robin Hood and Allen a Dale" have? Copy the first two stanzas, and mark the stressed beats in each line. What is the metric pattern?

Extend the Text

Writing Options
Creative Writing Shows like *Saturday Night Live (SNL)* have perfected the art of comic parody. With a small group, write and perform a parody of "Robin Hood and Allen a Dale," focusing on the theme of the original work and on how the characters relate to the economic ideas of their time. Keep in mind that the humor of a parody comes from closely imitating the original work while exaggerating certain elements.

Expository Writing Robin Hood seemed to have had *charisma*, the ability to attract followers. In a one-paragraph character analysis, identify the qualities that made him so appealing to so many people.

Collaborative Learning
Compare Literary Traditions How do American ballads compare with British ballads? Working in small groups, use library and Internet resources to research and compare the two literary traditions. You might examine Stith Thompson's classic work *Motifs of the Folktale*. Look for themes, characters, or stories that recur in the ballads of both countries. Share your findings.

Media Literacy
Develop a Television Pilot Over time, the legend of Robin Hood has been expressed in traditional text (prose, poetry, and drama), as well as in music, visual arts, and film (see listing on page 204). Each version of the story is unique, reflecting the social and cultural views of the period in which it was created. Suppose you and a partner were asked to develop a television pilot, or first episode, featuring Robin Hood in the twenty-first century. How would your version reflect the social and cultural views of this period? To gain a better understanding of how Robin Hood has been portrayed over the centuries, go to **http://lit.emcp.net/robinhood**. Then write a summary of your story line for the television pilot.

 Go to **www.mirrorsandwindows.com** for more.

VOCABULARY & SPELLING
WORD PARTS

Understand the Concept

When you come across an unfamiliar word, try analyzing its parts. You may be able to determine the meaning of the word if you recognize its root and affixes.

A **word root** is a central word part that cannot stand alone. In the word *mortal,* for instance, *mort* is the word root. In Latin, *mort* means "death."

An **affix** is added to a root to change its meaning. There are two kinds of affixes: **prefixes,** which are added to the beginnings of words, and **suffixes,** which are added to the ends of words. In the word *mortal,* the suffix *-al* has been added to the root *mort.* This suffix means "of" or "related to." The word *mortal,* which is an adjective, therefore means "related to death." Adding the prefix *im-,* which means "not," creates *immortal,* which means "not related to death."

Here are some commonly used prefixes and suffixes and examples of words that contain them:

Word Part	Meaning	Examples
Prefixes		
pre-	"before"	preview, precaution
post-	"after"	postgame, postmortem
non-	"not"	nonbreakable, nonsurgical
dis-	"opposite of"	disagree, discomfort
re-	"again"	revisit, remember
Suffixes		
-sion, -tion	"action" or "process"	submission, intention
-able	"capable of"	understandable, reasonable
-ance, -ence	"quality" or "state of"	performance, confidence
-ant, -ante	"one that does"	attendant, confidante
-ally, -ly	"in the manner of"	logically, quickly

The more meanings of prefixes, suffixes, and word roots you know, the more easily you will be able to determine the meanings of unfamiliar words in your reading.

Apply the Skill

Exercise A

Decode or sound out the words in each row of the preceding chart. Then write a definition for each of the words. Identify the origin of the word part listed. Use a dictionary to help you. Then use each word in a sentence in which the word's meaning is clear from the context. Work with a partner, taking turns reading your sentences aloud and listening for meaning.

Exercise B

Identify and determine the meaning of words from different subject areas using the following affixes that originated from Latin, Greek, and French. Find words beginning with these prefixes: *ab-, mal-, mis-, ante-,* and *con-, col-,* or *cor-.* Then locate words ending with these suffixes: *-et, -ia, -ious, -ment,* and *-ify.* For each word, give the meaning of the prefix or the suffix and of the word itself. Your answers can include both prefixes and suffixes.

SPELLING PRACTICE

Consonant Blends and Digraphs

Digraphs are groups of consonants that together make a new sound, such as *sh* and *th.* *Consonant blends* are groups of consonants in which each letter maintains its original sound, such as *br* and *cl.* In spelling words with consonant blends or digraphs, be sure to include all the letters in the grouping. Identify the consonant blends and digraphs in these words from "Robin Hood and Allen a Dale."

bishop	knight
bridegroom	laugh
choir	listen
churchyard	might
clothed	neither
enough	straight
glistering	wealthy
hastened	youngster

Choose another story (perhaps "The Honeysuckle: Chevrefoil," on pages 217–219) and listen while a partner reads it aloud or you play a recording of it. Write down each word that sounds like it contains a consonant blend or a digraph, keeping a separate list for each type of word. After the reading, check each word in a dictionary to see whether it was pronounced correctly and you spelled it correctly.

Federigo's Falcon
from The Decameron

by Giovanni Boccaccio

Translated by Mark Musa and Peter Bondanella

Giovanni Boccaccio (1313–1375) was an Italian poet and writer who grew up in Florence and studied in Naples. *The Decameron,* Boccaccio's masterpiece, is similar to Geoffrey Chaucer's *The Canterbury Tales* in that it is a **frame tale,** a story that provides the means for narrating other stories. In Boccaccio's collection of stories, seven ladies and three gentlemen leave Florence during the plague (a fast-spreading illness that killed many in Florence in 1348) to stay in a country villa. Over the course of ten days, the ten refugees tell each other one hundred stories. (The word part *deca-* means "ten.") **"Federigo's Falcon"** is one of the stories. A hawk-like bird, the falcon was used during the Middle Ages in *falconry,* a type of sports hunting.

The similarity in structure between Chaucer's work and Boccaccio's is no coincidence. In fact, during Chaucer's journey to Italy in 1372, he found inspiration in *The Decameron.*

F ilomena had already finished speaking, and when the Queen saw there was no one left to speak except for Dioneo, who was exempted because of his special privilege, she herself with a cheerful face said:

It is now my turn to tell a story and, dearest ladies, I shall do so most willingly with a tale similar in some respects to the preceding one, its purpose being not only to show you how much power your beauty has over the gentle heart, but also so that you yourselves may learn, whenever it is fitting, to be the donors of your favors instead of always leaving this act to the whim of Fortune,[1] who, as it happens, on most occasions bestows such favors with more abundance than discretion.[2]

You should know, then, that Coppo di Borghese Domenichi, who once lived in our city and perhaps still does, a man of great and respected authority in our times, one most illustrious and worthy of eternal fame both for his way of life and his ability much more than for the nobility of his blood, often took delight, when he was an old man, in discussing things from the past with his neighbors and with others. He knew how to do this well, for he was more logical and had a better memory and a more eloquent style of speaking than any other man. Among the many

---

1. **Fortune.** Personification of the power that supposedly distributes good and bad luck to people
2. **discretion.** Sense of carefulness and restraint in one's actions or words

Cavaliers in Court Room of Gualtiereri di Saluzzo, 1430. Francesco di Stefano Pesellino. Accademia Carrara, Bergamo, Italy.

Be the donors of your favors instead of always leaving this act to the whim of Fortune.

beautiful tales he told, there was one he would often tell about a young man who once lived in Florence named Federigo, the son of Messer Filippo Alberighi, renowned above all other men in Tuscany for his prowess in arms and for his courtliness.

As often happens to most men of gentle breeding, he fell in love, with a noble lady named Monna Giovanna, in her day considered to be one of the most beautiful and most charming ladies that ever there was in Florence; and in order to win her love, he participated in jousts and tournaments, organized and gave banquets, spending his money with-

out restraint; but she, no less virtuous than beautiful, cared little for these things he did on her behalf, nor did she care for the one who did them. Now, as Federigo was spending far beyond his means and getting nowhere, as can easily happen, he lost his wealth and was reduced to poverty, and was left with nothing to his name but his little farm (from whose revenues he lived very meagerly[3]) and one falcon, which was among the finest of its kind in the world.

More in love than ever, but knowing that he would never be able to live the way he wished to in the city, he went to live at Campi, where his farm was. There he passed his time hawking whenever he could, imposing on no one, and enduring his poverty patiently. Now one day, during the time that Federigo was

---

3. **meagerly.** Poorly; scantily

reduced to these extremes, it happened that the husband of Monna Giovanna fell ill, and realizing death was near, he made his last will: he was very rich, and he left everything to his son, who was just growing up, and since he had also loved Monna Giovanna very much, he made her his heir should his son die without any legitimate[4] children; and then he died.

Monna Giovanna was now a widow, and every summer, as our women usually do, she would go to the country with her son to one of their estates very close by to Federigo's farm. Now this young boy of hers happened to become more and more friendly with Federigo and he began to enjoy birds and dogs; and after seeing Federigo's falcon fly many times, it made him so happy that he very much wished it were his own, but he did not dare to ask for it, for he could see how precious it was to Federigo. During this time, it happened that the young boy took ill, and his mother was much grieved, for he was her only child and she loved him dearly; she would spend the entire day by his side, never ceasing to comfort him, asking him time and again if there was anything he wished, begging him to tell her what it might be, for if it was possible to obtain it, she would certainly do everything in her power to get it. After the young boy had heard her make this offer many times, he said:

"Mother, if you can arrange for me to have Federigo's falcon, I think I would get well quickly."

After seeing Federigo's falcon fly many times, it made him so happy that he very much wished it were his own.

When the lady heard this, she was taken aback for a moment, and then she began thinking what she could do about it. She knew that Federigo had been in love with her for some time now, but she had never deigned[5] to give him a second look; so, she said to herself:

"How can I go to him, or even send someone, and ask for this falcon of his, which is, as I have heard tell, the finest that ever flew, and furthermore, his only means of support? And how can I be so insensitive as to wish to take away from this nobleman the only pleasure which is left to him?"

And involved in these thoughts, knowing that she was certain to have the bird if she asked for it, but not knowing what to say to her son, she stood there without answering him. Finally the love she bore for her son persuaded her that she should make him happy, and no matter what the consequences might be, she would not send for the bird, but rather go herself to fetch it and bring it back to him; so she answered her son:

"My son, cheer up and think only of getting well, for I promise you that first thing tomorrow morning I shall go and fetch it for you."

The child was so happy that he showed some improvement that very day. The following morning, the lady, accompanied by another woman, as if they were out for a stroll, went to Federigo's modest little house and asked for him. Since the weather for the past few days had not been right for hawking, Federigo happened to be in his orchard attending to certain tasks, and when he heard that Monna Giovanna was asking for him at the door, he was so surprised and happy that he rushed there; as she saw him coming, she rose to greet him with womanly grace, and once Federigo had welcomed her most courteously, she said:

"How do you do, Federigo?" Then she continued, "I have come to make amends for the harm you have suffered on my account by loving me more than you should have, and in token of this, I intend to have a simple meal with you and this companion of mine this very day."

---

4. **legitimate.** Born of parents who are legally married to each other
5. **deigned.** Stooped or condescended

Theseus Returns in Triumph to Athens, c. 1400s. Giovanni Boccaccio.

To this Federigo humbly replied: "Madonna,[6] I have no recollection of ever suffering any harm because of you; on the contrary: so much good have I received from you that if ever I was worth anything, it was because of your worth and the love I bore for you; and your generous visit is certainly so very dear to me that I would spend all over again all that I spent in the past, but you have come to a poor host."

And having said this, he humbly led her through the house and into his garden, and because he had no one there to keep her company, he said:

"My lady, since there is no one else, this good woman, who is the wife of the farmer here, will keep you company while I see to the table."

Though he was very poor, Federigo until now had never realized to what extent he had wasted his wealth; but this morning, the fact that he had nothing in the house with which he could honor the lady for the love of whom he had in the past entertained countless people, gave him cause to reflect: in great anguish,[7] he cursed himself and his fortune, and like some-one out of his senses he started running here and there throughout the house, but unable to find either money or anything he might be able to pawn, and since it was getting late and he was still very much set on serving this noble lady some sort of meal, but unwilling to turn for help to even his own farmer (not to mention anyone else), he set his eyes upon his good falcon, which was sitting on its perch in a small room, and since he had nowhere else to turn, he took the bird, and finding it plump, he decided that it would be a worthy food for such a lady. So, without giving the matter a second thought, he wrung its neck and quickly gave it to his servant girl to pluck, prepare, and place on a spit to be roasted with care; and when he had set the table with the whitest of tablecloths (a few of which he still had left), he returned, with a cheerful face, to the lady in his garden and announced that the meal, such as he was able to prepare, was ready.

The lady and her companion rose and went to the table together with Federigo, who waited upon them with the greatest devotion, and they ate the good falcon without knowing what it was they were eating. Then, having left the table and spent some time in pleasant conversation, the lady thought it time now to say what she had come to say, and so she spoke these kind words to Federigo:

"Federigo, if you recall your former way of life and my virtue, which you perhaps mistook for harshness and cruelty, I have no doubt at all that you will be amazed by my presumption[8] when you hear what my main reason for com-

---

6. **Madonna.** Italian for "my lady," a polite form of address used in speaking to a married woman. *Monna* is a contraction of this term.
7. **anguish.** Agony
8. **presumption.** Bold or outrageous behavior

ing here is; but if you had children, through whom you might have experienced the power of parental love, I feel certain that you would, at least in part, forgive me. But, just as you have no child, I do have one, and I cannot escape the laws common to all mothers; the force of such laws compels[9] me to follow them, against my own will and against good manners and duty, and to ask of you a gift which I know is most precious to you; and it is naturally so, since your extreme condition has left you no other delight, no other pleasure, no other consolation; and this gift is your falcon, which my son is so taken by that if I do not bring it to him, I fear his sickness will grow so much worse that I may lose him. And therefore I beg you, not because of the love that you bear for me, which does not oblige[10] you in the least, but because of your own nobleness, which you have shown to be greater than that of all others in practicing courtliness, that you be pleased to give it to me, so that I may say that I have saved the life of my son by means of this gift, and because of it I have placed him in your debt forever."

When he heard what the lady requested and knew that he could not oblige her because he had given her the falcon to eat, Federigo began to weep in her presence, for he could not utter a word in reply. The lady at first thought his tears were caused more by the sorrow of having to part with the good falcon than by anything else, and she was on the verge of telling him she no longer wished it, but she held back and waited for Federigo's reply once he stopped weeping. And he said:

"My lady, ever since it pleased God for me to place my love in you, I have felt that Fortune has been hostile to me in many ways, and I have complained of her, but all this is nothing compared to what she has just done to me, and I shall never be at peace with her again, when I think how you have come here to my poor home, where, when it was rich, you never deigned to come, and how you requested but a small gift, and Fortune worked to make it

impossible for me to give it to you; and why this is so I shall tell you in a few words. When I heard that you, out of your kindness, wished to dine with me, I considered it only fitting and proper, taking into account your excellence and your worthiness, that I should honor you, according to my possibilities, with a more precious food than that which I usually serve to other people. So I thought of the falcon for which you have just asked me and of its value and I judged it a food worthy of you, and this very day I had it roasted and served to you as best I could. But seeing now that you desired it another way, my sorrow in not being able to serve you is so great that never shall I be able to console myself again."

> "My sorrow in not being able to serve you is so great that never shall I be able to console myself again."

And after he had said this, he laid the feathers, the feet, and the beak of the bird before her as proof. When the lady heard and saw this, she first reproached[11] him for having killed a falcon such as this to serve as a meal to a woman. But then to herself she commended[12] the greatness of his spirit, which no poverty was able, or would be able, to diminish; then, having lost all hope of getting the falcon and thus, perhaps, of improving the health of her son, she thanked Federigo both for the honor paid to her and for his good intentions, and then left in grief to return to her son. To his mother's extreme sorrow, whether in disappointment in not having the falcon or because his illness inevitably led to it, the boy passed from this life only a few days later.

---

9. **compels.** Urges or pressures
10. **oblige.** Make it one's duty to act
11. **reproach.** Express disapproval of or disappointment in
12. **commend.** Express approval of; praise

Writing Skills

Analyze the Prompt

Before you begin writing, analyze the prompt carefully. Determine *exactly* what it is asking. If you do not interpret the prompt correctly, you will not write on the correct topic and will not receive credit for your essay.

Evaluate the prompt for the clues it provides about what is expected of you. Some prompts contain key words that specify what is being asked. For example, the prompt may be asking you to *analyze* or *identify, describe* or *discuss, evaluate* or *argue for or against something,* or *justify* or *explain.* Underline key words like these in the prompt. You also might find it helpful to make notes in the margin as you analyze the prompt. Doing so may help you formulate a plan for writing.

Finally, be sure to read *all* of the prompt. Some prompts have more than one part and ask you to do more than one thing. After drafting your essay, go back and reread the prompt. Make sure you have addressed everything it asks.

> **TEST-TAKING TIP**
>
> In any written test response, make an obvious argument and support your claims with relevant details that are easy to understand. Consider that a judge will read your essay and assign it a score—along with thousands of other essays. He or she will not have much time to read your work, so make sure you present a clear, well-supported argument.

Practice

Timed Writing: 30 minutes

Compared to students from some other countries, U.S. students tend to score lower on achievement tests, particularly in the areas of math and science. Some people think these lower scores result from the U.S. high school curriculum being too flexible and easy. They would like to see more required courses and fewer electives. Others think students should be able to select most of their courses according to their interests, abilities, and future plans. In your opinion, should high school students' courses involve mostly required subjects or mostly elective subjects?

In your essay, take a position on this question. You may write about either one of the two perspectives given, or you may present a different perspective on this question. Use specific reasons and examples to support your position.

Revising and Editing Skills

Some standardized tests ask you to read a draft of an essay and answer questions about how to improve it. As you read the draft, watch for errors such as these:

- Incorrect spellings
- Disagreement between subject and verb; inconsistent verb tense; incorrect forms for irregular verbs; sentence fragments and run-ons; double negatives; and incorrect use of frequently confused words (such as *affect* and *effect*)

- Missing end marks, incorrect comma use, and lower-case proper nouns and proper adjectives
- Unclear purpose, unclear main ideas, and lack of supporting details
- Confusing order of ideas and missing transitions
- Language and mood that are inappropriate to the audience and purpose

After checking for errors, read each test question and decide which answer is best.

Practice

Directions: In the passage that follows, certain words and phrases are numbered and under-lined. In the questions below the passage, you will find alternatives for each underlined word or phrase. In each case, choose the alternative that best expresses the idea, that is worded most consistently with the style and tone of the rest of the passage, or that makes the text correct according to the conventions of standard written English. If you think the original version is best, choose the first alternative, MAKE NO CHANGE. To indicate your answer, circle the letter of the chosen alternative.

(1) It is human <u>nature to learn more and do better</u> with a subject that interests us. (2) As the saying <u>goes: "One shoe doesn't fit everybody."</u> (3) Therefore, it is in the <u>student's best interest to let them</u> choose some of their classes. (4) They, in turn, will perform <u>up to their potential and be better prepared for life after having graduated.</u>

Multiple Choice

1. A. MAKE NO CHANGE.
   B. nature to learn more and do best
   C. nature to learn and do better
   D. nature, learning more and doing better,

2. F. MAKE NO CHANGE.
   G. goes: "One shoe doesn't fit everybody"!
   H. goes "One shoe doesn't fit everybody."
   J. goes, "One shoe doesn't fit everybody."

3. A. MAKE NO CHANGE.
   B. students' best interest to let them
   C. student's best interest to let him or her
   D. student's best interest to let one

4. F. MAKE NO CHANGE.
   G. up to their potential and be better prepared for life after they have graduated.
   H. up to their potential and be better prepared for life after having had graduated.
   J. up to their potential and be better prepared for life after graduation.

Renaissance

Unit 3

PART 1

Courtiers

"Come live with me and be my love."

—CHRISTOPHER MARLOWE

PART 2

Mind, Body, and Spirit

"Death, be not proud,
though some have calléd thee
Mighty and dreadful,
for thou art not so."

—JOHN DONNE

1485–1625

Renaissance 1485–1625

1485   1535

BRITISH LITERATURE BRITISH LITERATURE BRITISH LITERATURE BRITISH LI

1500
Desiderius Erasmus publishes *Adages*

ERASMUS

1501
The Book of Margery Kempe is published posthumously

1513
Gavin Douglas publishes the first English translation of Virgil's *Aeneid*

1516
Thomas More publishes *Utopia*

1532
The Prince, by Niccolò Machiavelli, is published in England five years after the author's death

1539
Sir Thomas Elyot publishes *The Castel of Helth*, a popular medical book

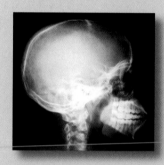

1540
Hector Boece publishes a history of Scotland entitled *Historia Scotorum*

1541
George Buchanan publishes *Baptistes and Jephtha*

1549
The Book of Common Prayer is published for the first time

BRITISH HISTORY BRITISH HISTORY BRITISH HISTORY BRITISH HISTORY BRI

1497
Michael An Gof leads Cornish rebels in a march on London

1499
Perkin Warbeck is hanged for pretending to be a successor to the English throne

1509
King Henry VII dies and is succeeded by his son, Henry VIII

1534
Henry VIII establishes the Anglican Church in order to divorce his wife, Catherine of Aragon

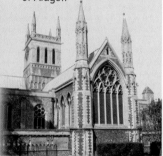

1535
Thomas More is executed for failing to approve of the king's break with the Catholic Church

MORE

1553
Edward VI dies and is succeeded by Mary Tudor

1555
Queen Mary I has some three hundred Protestants executed

1558
Mary I dies and Elizabeth I ascends to the throne

WORLD HISTORY WORLD HISTORY WORLD HISTORY WORLD HISTORY WORLD

1492
Christopher Columbus lands in the modern-day Bahamas and makes contact with the Arawaks

1517
Martin Luther initiates the Reformation in Europe, indirectly prompting a wave of emigration to North America

1521
Spanish conquistadores destroy Tenochtitlan in Mexico

1521
Ferdinand Magellan's crew completes the first successful attempt at world navigation, but their leader is killed during the voyage

c. 1529
Askia Muhammad, king of Songhai, dies; he expanded the empire to be the largest ever in West Africa and made Timbuktu a major center of Islamic learning and book trade

1539
Hernando de Soto explores North America

1543
Copernicus develops the first modern heliocentric theory of the solar system

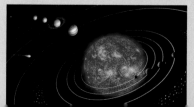

1543
Portuguese merchants make contact with the Japanese

1556
The Shaanxi earthquake, widely considered the deadliest earthquake in history, strikes China, killing approximately 830,000

BRITISH LITERATURE BRITISH LITERATURE BRITISH LITERATURE BRITISH LITERATU

1562
Gorboduc is performed for the first time before Elizabeth I

1579
Edmund Spenser publishes *The Shepheardes Calender*

1596
Sir Philip Sidney's *An Apologie for Poetrie* is published after the author's death

1597
Sir Walter Raleigh publishes *The Discoverie of the Large, Rich and Beautiful Empyre of Guiana*

RALEIGH

1600
Thomas Dekker writes *Old Fortunatus*

1607
King James I publishes his version of the Bible

1611
George Chapman translates Homer's *The Iliad* into English

1616
Ben Jonson becomes the first Poet Laureate of England

HOMER

BRITISH HISTORY BRITISH HISTORY BRITISH HISTORY BRITISH HISTORY BRITI

1562
England begins its slave trade with Africa

1567
The Northern Earls rise in England

1580
Sir Francis Drake circumnavigates the globe

1585
The Anglo-Spanish War begins

1588
English ships defeat the Spanish Armada

1601
The Treaty of London ends the Anglo-Spanish War

1603
Elizabeth I dies and is succeeded by James VI of Scotland, who becomes James I of England and merges the two kingdoms

1605
The Gunpowder Plot, a plan to assassinate James I, is thwarted

1607
English colonists found the colony of Jamestown in modern-day Virginia

JAMES I

WORLD HISTORY WORLD HISTORY WORLD HISTORY WORLD HISTORY WORLD HISTO

1571
Pope Pius V tries to dissolve Ottoman Turkish control of the Mediterranean

1572
Spanish conquistadores execute Túpac Amaru, the last Incan leader, in Peru

1580
Spain and Portugal unite kingdoms, a union that lasts until 1640

1582
Oda Nobunaga, a major *daimyo*, or feudal lord of Japan, is assassinated by a trusted vassal

1591
The Songhai Empire falls to Moroccans

1603
Tokugawa Ieyasu unifies Japan as its new shogun

1618
The Thirty Years' War begins, involving several European countries

1619
The first African slaves arrive in Jamestown, Virginia

1623
Abbas I expands Persia by capturing territory from the Ottomans and the Portuguese

"Not marble, nor the gilded monuments of princes, shall outlive this powerful rhyme."

—WILLIAM SHAKESPEARE

The Beginnings of the Tudor Dynasty

When Henry VII ascended the throne in 1485, he became the first monarch of the Tudor Dynasty, which ruled England until 1603. The new king inherited a country exhausted by the Wars of the Roses, yet he proved to be a capable leader. Henry VII rebuilt the nation's treasury, established a powerful central government, made profitable commercial treaties with other nations, and built a fleet of merchant ships that formed the basis for English power during the coming centuries. During Henry VII's reign, England began exploratory expeditions to the New World that led to the colonization of North America.

Henry VII died in 1509, leaving the throne to his son, Henry VIII, one of the most important and colorful figures in English history. Well-educated, strong-willed, self-absorbed, and charismatic, Henry VIII further increased the power of the monarchy. His desire for a male heir to carry on his successes led to the most important event of his reign: the English break with the Roman Catholic Church.

The Protestant Reformation in England

In 1517, German monk Martin Luther nailed to the door of a church in Wittenburg, Germany, his "95 Theses," a list of objections to certain beliefs and practices of the Catholic Church. Luther issued this list at a time when European monarchs were jealous of the wealth of the Church and its representatives were living very worldly lives, funded in part from collecting contributions by the sale of spiritual benefits. These factors led to a revolt against Church authority known as the Protestant Reformation.

Another central figure in the Reformation was John Calvin of Switzerland. While Luther and Calvin agreed that humans were sinful and in need of God's redemption, Calvin taught that God had preordained each individual's salvation or damnation at the beginning of time. This Calvinist doctrine, known as *predestination,* became the central belief of the Puritan movement that would strongly influence life in England and in the English colonies in North America.

In England, the Protestant Reformation resulted because of Henry VIII's inability to have his marriage to Catherine of Aragon annulled. When the pope refused his request, Henry broke with the Catholic Church and asked Parliament to declare him Supreme Head of the new Church of England, or Anglican Church. The king then dismantled the Roman Catholic

Martin Luther posts his list of objections.

Church in England and seized its land and wealth. He burned and pillaged the monasteries, thus destroying many precious manuscripts.

Some Christians did not want to leave the Catholic Church, preferring instead to correct the abuses criticized by Luther and Calvin. These followers launched the Counter-Reformation and helped restore the position of the church in many areas of Europe but not England.

The Reigns of Edward, Mary, and Elizabeth

When Henry VIII died in 1547, his sickly nine-year-old son became King Edward VI. During Edward's reign, Protestantism spread throughout England, the Anglican creed was established, and the *Book of Common Prayer* was written. In 1553, fifteen-year-old Edward died and was succeeded by his older half-sister, Mary I, child of Henry's first wife, Catherine of Aragon. Mary I was a staunch Catholic and attempted to restore the power and authority of the Roman Catholic Church in England by ordering the use of its rituals in English church services, executing many Protestants, and reestablishing the pope as head of the English church.

Perhaps the greatest monarch in all of English history was Mary's successor, Elizabeth I, daughter of Henry VIII and Anne Boleyn. Under Queen Elizabeth I,

England grew to become the most powerful nation in Europe, and English literature reached what many people consider its zenith. Elizabeth's long reign, from 1558 to 1603, is known as the Elizabethan Age.

At home, Elizabeth reestablished the monarch as head of the Church of England and ended the persecution of Protestants. She also tolerated Catholic beliefs and practices and only reluctantly agreed to the execution of Mary Stuart to prevent her cousin's Catholic supporters from overthrowing the throne. Ironically, it was Mary's heirs, the Stuart kings, who followed Elizabeth to the throne.

Abroad, English pirates such as Sir Francis Drake preyed on Spanish ships and colonies for many years with the secret blessing of Queen Elizabeth. In 1588, Spain's King Philip II, who wanted to unseat Queen Elizabeth, decided to attack England with his mighty fleet, the Spanish Armada. Having a strong navy of its own, England was able to stop the Spanish. This victory established the English Navy as a formidable force and led to the rise of the British Empire—England's commercial and territorial holdings overseas.

"Though you have had and may have many mightier and wiser princes sitting in this seat, yet you never had, nor shall have, any love you better."

—QUEEN ELIZABETH I

The First Stuart King

The death of the much-revered Queen Elizabeth I in 1603 ended the Tudor Dynasty and brought to the throne the first of the Stuart kings, James VI of Scotland, who became James I of England. While Elizabeth had been able to maintain stability amid the sweeping changes of the Reformation, James I, a Catholic, clashed frequently with the Protestant Parliament over taxes. Adding to the tension was the division of the Protestant Church of England into two factions: conservative Anglican traditionalists, who wanted to

NOTABLE NUMBERS

- **118** Length in years of the Tudor Dynasty
- **6** Number of wives King Henry VIII had over his lifetime
- **6 out of 600** Books of the Worchester Priory Library that survived Henry VIII's dissolution of the monasteries; many of the earliest Anglo-Saxon manuscripts were lost
- **45** Years of Elizabeth I's reign
- **54** Number of scholars who worked on translating the Bible into English over seven years

> *"I do not think that any language, be it whatsoever, is better able to utter all arguments, either with more pith or greater plainness, than our English tongue is."*
>
> —RICHARD MULCASTER, SIXTEENTH-CENTURY EDUCATOR

retain the rituals of Catholicism in their church services, and Puritans, who wanted to "purify" the church of everything that did not strictly adhere to the Bible. James supported the Anglicans and conflicted with the Puritans.

James believed monarchs had a right to rule without any limits on power, a philosophy known as the *divine right of kings*. This absolutist theory was rooted in the medieval concept of the king as a supreme protector of his subjects. According to the divine right of kings, rulers were chosen by God and therefore did not have to answer to anyone but God. James I believed that the best government was run by a single person— a form of government known as *autocracy*. Despite his political challenges, James is well regarded for commissioning the King James Bible, a hugely successful translation of the sacred text into English.

Renaissance Thought

Historians refer to the period between the fifteenth and early seventeenth centuries as the *Renaissance*, which means, literally, "rebirth." During this time, Europeans renewed their interest in Greek and Latin learning and began to move away from the rigid class system and deference to the Catholic Church and landholding nobles that characterized medieval society.

The writers and thinkers of ancient Greece and Rome valued individual conscience as well as the arts and works of this world. Their literature was dominated by questions related to human life: What is a good life? What is a good state? Beginning in Italy and then spreading to the rest of Europe, this focus on the arts and literature of ancient Greece and Rome sparked a renewed interest in human life on Earth, as opposed to the Christian concept of life after death. The Renaissance devotion to the Greek and Latin classics has come to be known as *Humanism*.

The Humanists were not irreligious. Humanist philosophy was based on the idea that human beings were created in the image of God. Humanists believed that human beings, sharing as they did in the divine, could perfect themselves and the institutions of this world. Out of this belief came a new emphasis on learning and a flowering of the arts, as well as religious and political debates that led to the Protestant Reformation, the decline of feudalism, and the emerging importance of vernacular languages (the normal, spoken forms of languages) and nationalism.

Amid the growing religious strife of this period, philosophers and scientists were defining new ways of looking at the world in which they lived. Previously, tradition and revelation were seen as the prime sources of knowledge. During the Renaissance, people such as Italian Galileo Galilei (1564–1642) and Englishman Francis Bacon (1561–1626) began making scientific observations and then drawing out general principles from them. In England and throughout Europe, these changes would have a profound impact on religion and on the power of monarchies—in short, on how people viewed the world.

Galileo studying the heavens.

In *The Elementarie,* a treatise on education published in 1582, Richard Mulcaster wrote, "Whatsoever shall become of the English state, the English tongue cannot prove fairer than it is at this day." Readers of Philip Sidney, Edmund Spenser, William Shakespeare, Christopher Marlowe, and the King James Bible tend to agree with Mulcaster that at no time has the English language been more beautiful or expressive than during the early Modern period.

The Emergence of Modern English

The version of English spoken today, known as *Modern English,* emerged in the two-hundred-year period from roughly 1400 to 1600. However, for the sake of convenience, the Modern English period often is dated from the publication of William Caxton's version of Malory's *Le Morte d'Arthur* in 1485. At that time, most of the changes in pronunciation, vocabulary, and grammar that transformed Middle English into Modern English were well underway.

The Great Vowel Shift

Perhaps the most important difference between Middle English and Modern English is in the sound of the language. Between 1400 and 1600, dramatic changes occurred in the pronunciations of vowels. These changes are known collectively as the *Great Vowel Shift.*

The primary effect of the Great Vowel Shift was to raise the position of articulation in the mouth of all the long vowels except *i* and *u.* Thus, the word *name,* which was pronounced in Chaucer's day as "nah-muh," was pronounced "naym" in Modern English. The word *bete,* formerly pronounced "bay-tuh," became "beet." Moreover, in both these words, the final -*e,* which was pronounced as a second syllable ("uh") in Middle English, became silent or was dropped in Modern English.

The long *i* and long *u* sounds became *diphthongs,* made of two vowels slurred together. Thus, the word *mus,* pronounced "moos" in Middle English, became *mouse,* which has a vowel that combines "ah" and "oo."

Grammatical Changes

Throughout the Medieval Period, English gradually evolved from being an *inflected language,* in which words' grammatical roles are shown by their word endings, to an *analytical language,* in which words' grammatical roles are shown by their positions in sentences. In the early Modern period, this change became fairly complete.

An important example of this kind of change was the addition of -*s* to the end of a word as the standard means of indicating plural. In Middle English, the plural form often had been shown by adding -*en.* Thus, the plural of *eye* was *eyen,* and the plural of *pea* was *pesen.* In Modern English, most plurals are formed with -*s,* but a few older forms of plurals survive in words such as *children, oxen,* and *brethren.*

Another important grammatical change that occurred during the early Modern period was the introduction of new relative pronouns, prepositions, and conjunctions. These additions increased the ability of English speakers to make precise logical distinctions and connections.

Vocabulary and the New Learning

Of great importance to the development of the language used today was the introduction by scholars during the early Modern period of thousands of new words from Latin and Greek. An estimated one-fourth of the words that appear in a standard Latin dictionary have been incorporated into English in some form. Many of these words were introduced as a result of Humanist learning during the Renaissance. New Latin words that entered the language include many terms related to literary study, such as *accent, alphabet, critic, drama, fiction, metaphor, phrase, poem, simile, sonnet,* and *stanza.* Other new Latin and Greek words that date from the Renaissance are shown in the box on the top of the next page.

Pure versus "Inkhorn" English

During the Renaissance, some writers and editors objected to the rapid influx of learned words from Latin and Greek, dubbing them "inkhorn" terms

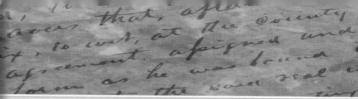

Words from Latin and Greek Introduced During the Early Modern Period

adapt	enormous	method
antipathy	enthusiasm	minor
area	erupt	numerous
benefit	exit	omen
catastrophe	external	patriot
chemist	function	precise
compatible	genius	scientific
conspicuous	habitual	skeleton
crisis	idea	system
cynic	impression	theory
dexterity	item	vacuum
disaster	machine	

Other Sources of New Words

In addition to borrowing from Latin and Greek, early Modern English borrowed heavily from other European languages, especially French, Spanish, and Italian. From French came *battery, comrade, entrance, essay, pioneer,* and *trophy.* From Spanish came *apricot, bravado, cavalier, embargo, guitar,* and *tornado.* From Italian came *balcony, bankrupt, fresco, pastel, piazza, porcelain,* and *traffic.* Some of these words, such as *pioneer, embargo,* and *traffic,* reflected the worldwide exploration and trade that began during the Renaissance. Other words added because of exploration are shown in the box below.

Printing and the Regularization of Spelling

During the early Modern period, as during the Middle Ages, spelling largely was a matter of personal preference. Most literature was written by noblemen and -women for circulation among friends, and in this literature, as in the letters, spelling varied widely. In fact, an educated person might well spell the same word several different ways in the same piece.

An example of this variety can be seen in the spelling of Shakespeare's name. Existing signatures show the great poet and dramatist signing his name variously as *Shaksp, Shakspe, Shakspeare,* and *Shakspere,* but nowhere is the spelling commonly used today. As printing became widespread and books became more common, spelling became more regularized.

because the scholars who introduced them used quill pens and ink for writing. Sir John Cheke of Cambridge University wrote, for example, "Our tongue should be written clean and pure, unmixed and unmangled with borrowing of other tongues, wherein if we take not heed by time, ever borrowing and never paying, she shall be fain to keep her house as bankrupt." A brief glance at the words from Latin and Greek (see box above) shows that English was greatly enriched by the learned additions that occurred during the Renaissance. Even so, many writers and editors to this day agree with Cheke that, in most writing, a simple word of Anglo-Saxon origin is preferable over a more elaborate one derived from a Classical language.

In English, speakers and writers often have a choice between the two. They can write *way* instead of *method, home* instead of *domicile, put out* instead of *extinguish, go* instead of *exit,* and so on. Overusing words of Latin or Greek origin can make writing or speech seem too formal, even stilted.

Fortunately for English speakers and writers, the first great translator of the Bible, William Tyndale, preferred simple words of English origin, and much of his phrasing was adopted in the King James Bible, which became the standard text in English-speaking countries for centuries. The simple Anglo-Saxon language of the King James Bible dramatically influenced the shape of spoken and written English.

New Words in Early Modern English Related to Exploration

armada	flamingo	sherry
buffalo	galleon	smuggle
cacao	harem	tattoo
canoe	hurricane	tomahawk
caravan	llama	tomato
chocolate	maize	totem
coconut	moccasin	yacht
cruise	reef	yam
dock	savannah	

Following the lead of William Caxton (c. 1422–c. 1491), who introduced printing to England, many printers during the early Tudor Period reissued works of authors from previous centuries. Few outstanding new works were produced, however.

Literary activity increased during the reign of Henry VIII, which spanned from 1509 to 1547. Notable poets included Thomas Wyatt and Henry Howard, Earl of Surrey, who generally are credited for initiating British interest in the *sonnet,* a fourteen-line form of Italian verse (see Understanding Literary Forms, pages 246–247).

The true flowering of literary creativity in the English Renaissance came during the second half of the sixteenth century with the reign of Elizabeth I, who was a great patron of the arts. The Elizabethan Age was remarkable for two kinds of literature: lyric poetry and drama. Great lyric poets of the period included *courtiers,* or attendants of the court, such as Sir Philip Sidney, Christopher Marlowe, and Ben Jonson and would-be courtiers such as Edmund Spenser. Sidney, Spenser, and Shakespeare all produced outstanding *sonnet sequences,* or collections of related sonnets. During this time, lyric poems often were written for circulation among friends and acquaintances. (See Unit 4 for a comprehensive review of Elizabethan drama.)

A defining quality of Renaissance literature was wit, which was conveyed through the use of word play and elaborate analogies and metaphors, called *conceits.* During this era, being amusing was one way to obtain favor with the queen and other powerful figures. Shakespeare actually mocked the common use of conceits in several of his sonnets.

Tapestry showing the arms of the Earl of Leicester, c. 1575–1585. Victoria and Albert Museum, London, England.

Speech to the Troops at Tilbury

A Speech by Queen Elizabeth I

Build Background

Historical Context Prince Philip of Spain, enraged by English raids on his ships and colonies and intent on unseating Queen Elizabeth, decided in 1588 to attack England with his mighty fleet, the Spanish Armada. The English Navy prepared for a battle at sea, while English lords assembled an army of 4,000 at Tilbury to fend off the possible invasion by 30,000 men of the armada and 16,000 troops from Spain's ally, Parma.

Queen Elizabeth insisted on going to Tilbury against the advice of her ministers, who feared for her safety. Her **"Speech to the Troops,"** delivered on the morning of August 9, 1588, would become one of the most famous of her reign. After hearing it, the Earl of Leiceister said her words "had so inflamed the hearts of her good subjects, as I think the weakest among them is able to match the proudest Spaniard that dares land in England." The English Navy, led by Sir Francis Drake and Lord Charles Howard, defeated the Spanish Armada, and the invasion was avoided.

Reader's Context How do you prepare yourself for a stressful or frightening situation?

Meet the Author

Queen Elizabeth I (1533–1603), daughter of Henry VIII and Anne Boleyn, was perhaps the greatest monarch in all of English history. Her long reign, from 1558 to 1603, is known as the Elizabethan Age.

Elizabeth used her navy to explore and colonize foreign lands and sent Sir Walter Raleigh to establish the colony of Virginia in North America. With Elizabeth's secret support and blessing, the pirate Sir Francis Drake preyed on Spanish ships and colonies for treasure, helping to finance the growth of England and to establish it as the greatest power in Europe.

Elizabeth's reign was unprecedented in many respects: forty-five years of stable government and internal peace, exploration of the world by her adventurous nobles, and domination of the seas by her much-feared navy. From a modern perspective, Elizabeth commanded tremendous power and respect and ruled quite capably as a single woman in an era when a woman's power normally was derived through her husband. Determined to maintain her own power, Elizabeth played off male suitors or convinced them she was on the brink of engagement, only to turn them away. She was known as the Virgin Queen. A popular ruler, she was and still is known by the people of England as Good Queen Bess.

Analyze Literature

Purpose and Parallelism
A writer's **purpose** is his or her aim, or goal. Writers usually write with one or more of the following purposes: to inform or explain, to persuade, to describe someone or something, and to express thoughts and ideas or share a story.

Parallelism is a rhetorical device in which a writer or speaker emphasizes the equal value or weight of two or more ideas by expressing them in the same grammatical form.

Set Purpose

Queen Elizabeth went to Tilbury against the advice of her ministers, apparently determined to address the troops before battle. As you read, identify the purpose or purposes of her speech. Also evaluate Elizabeth's use of parallelism in this speech. List examples of parallelism, and consider how Elizabeth uses this rhetorical device to achieve her purpose.

Preview Vocabulary

treachery, 239
concord, 240

SPEECH TO THE TROOPS AT TILBURY

by Queen Elizabeth I

The Launching of the English Ships Against the Spanish Armada [detail].
National Maritime Museum, Greenwich, England.

> I assure you I do not desire to live to distrust my faithful and loving people. Let tyrants fear.

My loving people,

We[1] have been persuaded by some that are careful of our safety, to take heed how we commit our selves to armed multitudes, for fear of <u>treachery</u>; but I assure you I do not desire to live to distrust my faithful and loving people. Let tyrants fear. I have always so behaved myself that, under God, I have placed my chiefest strength and safeguard in the loyal hearts and goodwill of my subjects; and therefore I am come amongst you, as you see, at this time, not for my recreation and disport,[2]

---

1. **We.** It is customary for a monarch to refer to himself or herself as *We* rather than *I*. This is known as the *royal We.*
2. **disport.** Fun

treach • ery (treˊ chə rē) *n.,* treason

Sir Francis Drake

During the reign of Queen Elizabeth I, England surpassed Spain as a power in both the old and new worlds. This was due, in part, to having a superior navy, which included the use of pirates to raid Spanish ports and plunder their treasures. Sir Francis Drake was the most notorious of these pirates.

Queen Elizabeth hired Drake to conduct a campaign against the Spanish in the Americas in 1577, supplying him with five ships and 150 sailors. In return, Drake agreed to share the pirated goods with the English government. Drake returned three years later after circumnavigating the globe, becoming only the second European to complete such a trip and the first to return unharmed to his homeland. (One hundred of Drake's sailors died along the way, however.) Drake's plundering produced an enormous hoard of spices, jewels, minerals, and other precious materials that originated primarily from Spanish ports. The booty Drake stole was so valuable that the English government's share was more than it had raised through taxation and other means. As a result, Queen Elizabeth knighted Drake and appointed him to a seat in Parliament.

Not surprisingly, Drake's exploits infuriated Spain's King Philip II. In 1585, Philip ordered his navy to invade England, but before they could initiate their plan, Drake sailed into the Spanish harbor of Cadiz and occupied its waters for three days, stealing even more Spanish goods. Further antagonizing the Spanish crown, Drake contributed heavily to Spain's defeat during the Spanish Armada battles in 1588.

but being resolved, in the midst and heat of the battle, to live or die amongst you all; to lay down for my God, and for my kingdom, and my people, my honor and my blood, even in the dust. I know I have the body but of a weak and feeble woman; but I have the heart and stomach of a king, and of a king of England too, and think foul scorn that Parma[3] or Spain, or any prince of Europe, should dare to invade the borders of my realm; to which rather than any dishonor shall grow by me, I myself will take up arms, I myself will be your general, judge, and rewarder of every one of your virtues in the field. I know already, for your forwardness you have deserved rewards and crowns;[4] and We do assure you in the word of a prince, they shall be duly paid you. In the mean time, my lieutenant general shall be in my stead, than whom never prince commanded a more noble or worthy subject; not doubting but by your obedience to my general, by your <u>concord</u> in the camp, and your valor in the field, we shall shortly have a famous victory over those enemies of my God, of my kingdom, and of my people. ❖

---

3. **Parma.** Parma, a city-state in Italy, had allied with Spain and was expected in the invasion.
4. **crowns.** British coins

con • cord (kän´ kôrd´) *n.,* agreement; harmony

Queen Elizabeth defied her advisers and risked her own safety by going to Tilbury to speak to the troops. What do actions like these suggest about a leader? How might people be inspired by such a leader?

Informational Text Connection

This article from the **Columbia Encyclopedia** introduces Queen Elizabeth I of England, who delivered the "Speech to the Troops" that you read in the previous selection. As the daughter of the ill-fated Anne Boleyn, one of the many wives of King Henry VIII, Elizabeth I began her life being declared illegitimate. Yet when she died in 1603 after forty-five years of reign, she was one of the most beloved and long-lasting rulers of England.

As noted earlier, Elizabeth's years as a ruler marked one of the greatest periods of England's history, a time when the country became a major European power and began establishing colonies throughout the world. As you read this selection and learn more about Elizabeth's life, think about how the time period in which she lived shaped her as a ruler.

ELIZABETH I, QUEEN OF ENGLAND
from The Columbia Encyclopedia

1533–1603, queen of England (1558–1603).

Early Life
The daughter of Henry VIII and Anne Boleyn,[1] she was declared illegitimate just before the execution of her mother in 1536, but in 1544 Parliament reestablished her in the succession after her half brother, Edward (later Edward VI), and her half sister, Mary (later Mary I). Elizabeth was well educated by a series of tutors, most notably Roger Ascham.

In 1553 she supported the claims of Mary I over Lady Jane Grey. After Mary was crowned, Elizabeth was careful to avoid implication in the plot of the younger Sir Thomas Wyatt (1554). Nevertheless, since Elizabeth's potential succession to the throne inevitably furnished a rallying point for discontented Protestants, she

was imprisoned. She later regained a measure of freedom through outward conformity to Roman Catholicism.

Reign
When Elizabeth succeeded her sister to the throne in 1558, religious strife, a huge government debt, and failures in the war with France had brought England's fortunes to a low ebb. Elizabeth came to the throne with the Tudor concept of strong rule and the realization that effective rule depended upon popular support. She was able to select and work well with the

---

1. **Anne Boleyn.** The second queen of Henry VIII, who had divorced Catherine of Aragon in order to marry her. Henry wanted a male heir to the throne, and after the birth of Elizabeth and the loss of an unborn son, Anne was charged with adultery and incest and subsequently beheaded.

most competent of counselors. Sir William Cecil (Lord Burghley) was appointed immediately, and Sir Francis Walsingham in 1573.

At her death 45 years later, England had passed through one of the greatest periods of its history—a period that produced William Shakespeare, Edmund Spenser, Francis Bacon, Walter Raleigh, Martin Frobisher, Francis Drake, and other notable figures in literature and exploration; a period that saw England, united as a nation, become a major European power with a great navy; a period in which English commerce and industry prospered and English colonization was begun.

Although Elizabeth has been accused, with some justice, of being vain, fickle, vacillating, prejudiced, and miserly, she was nonetheless exceedingly successful as a queen. Endowed with immense personal courage and a keen awareness of her responsibility as a ruler, she commanded throughout her reign the unwavering respect and allegiance of her subjects.

Domestic Developments

One of Elizabeth's first acts was to reestablish Protestantism (see England, Church of) through the acts of Supremacy and Uniformity (1559). The measures against Roman Catholics (see Penal Laws)[2] grew harsher over the course of her reign, particularly after the rebellion of the Catholic earls of Northumberland and Westmorland (1569), Elizabeth's excommunication by the pope (1570), and the coming of the Jesuit missionaries (1580). But the persecution of the Catholics was due, at least in part, to a series of plots to murder Elizabeth and seat the Catholic Mary Queen of Scots on the throne. English Puritans, like the Catholics, objected to the Established Church, and a severe law against conventicles (unauthorized religious assemblies) in 1593 kept the separatist movement underground for the time.

At the beginning of her reign, Elizabeth's government enacted needed currency reforms and took steps to mend English credit abroad. Other legislation of the reign dealt with new social and economic developments—the Statute of Apprentices (1563) to stabilize labor conditions; the poor laws (1563–1601) to attempt some remedy of widespread poverty; and various acts to encourage agriculture, commerce, and manufacturing.

Foreign Affairs and the Spanish War

Elizabeth had many suitors, including King Philip II of Spain; Francis, duke of Alençon and Anjou; and her own favorite, Robert Dudley, earl of Leicester. For a combination of personal and political reasons, she was reluctant to choose a husband and remained unmarried, although she often used the lure of marriage as a weapon of diplomacy. Elizabeth engaged in a long series of diplomatic maneuvers against England's old enemy, France, and the new enemy, Spain, but for 30 years she managed to keep the country at peace.

In 1559 she concluded a treaty ending her sister's unfortunate war with France and refused the marriage offer of Philip of Spain. The next year the Treaty of Edinburgh initiated a policy toward Scotland, successful in the long run, of supporting the Protestant lords against the Catholic party. By lending unofficial aid to French Huguenots she managed for some time to harass France and Spain without involving England in an actual war. As part of her marriage negotiations she later supported the duke of Alençon's participation in the Dutch war against Spain.

The major problem posed by Elizabeth's refusal to marry was that of the succession. The chief claimant was Mary Queen of Scots, but

---

2. **Penal Laws.** The Penal Laws in England and Ireland grew out of the English Reformation and establishment of the Church of England. The term applies to discriminatory and oppressive laws directed at Roman Catholics and Protestant nonconformists.

her Catholicism made her a threat to Elizabeth. In 1568 after Mary's forced abdication from the Scottish throne, Elizabeth gave her refuge but then kept her prisoner for nearly 19 years. Despite the numerous plots, both real and alleged, on Mary's behalf, Elizabeth resisted until 1587 her counselors' advice that Mary be executed.

By that time Spain had emerged as England's main enemy. English sailors had been unofficially encouraged to encroach on Spanish monopolies and raid Spanish shipping. In 1588, Philip launched the long-planned expedition of the Spanish Armada as a great Catholic crusade against Protestant England. The Armada was defeated by the skill of such leaders as John Hawkins and Francis Drake and by storms, rather than planning on Elizabeth's part, but the victory strengthened English national pride and lowered the prestige of Spain. An indecisive war with Spain dragged on until Elizabeth's death. From the beginning of the reign Ireland had been the scene of civil wars and severe rebellions, culminating with that of the earl of Tyrone, which was suppressed by the campaigns of Lord Mountjoy from 1600 to 1603.

Declining Years

After the Armada, Elizabeth's popularity began to wane. Parliament became less tractable and began to object to the abuse of royally granted monopolies. The rash uprising of Elizabeth's favorite, Robert Devereux, 2d earl of Essex, darkened her last years. She refused until on her deathbed to name her successor—the son of Mary Queen of Scots, James VI of Scotland, who became James I of England. ❖

Review Questions

1. What happened to Elizabeth just before her mother was executed? Why did Elizabeth's father, the king, have her mother, Anne Boleyn, killed?

2. What did Elizabeth do at the beginning of her reign that helped improve England's economy? Make a list of reforms the queen made that helped strengthen the country.

3. Infer why Elizabeth never married. What problems were associated with her refusal to marry?

TEXT $\xrightarrow{\text{TO}}$ TEXT CONNECTION

Review the details of Queen Elizabeth's life provided in this encyclopedia article and in the Build Background and Meet the Author materials that precede the speech (see page 238). What details help you understand why Elizabeth was not afraid to visit a battle site and speak to the troops? What details contributed to the British people's loving and lasting impression of Good Queen Bess?

Refer to Text ▶ ▶ ▶ ▶ ▶   **Reason with Text**

1a. Recall what Queen Elizabeth tells the crowd about her body and her heart and stomach.	**1b.** Why does she make this contrast?	**Understand** Find meaning
2a. What have some people advised the queen not to do?	**2b.** Why isn't the queen afraid to be among her subjects?	**Apply** Use information
3a. What reasons for fighting does Elizabeth give her troops? What does she say to strengthen their resolve?	**3b.** Deduce why Elizabeth's vow to join the fighting, if necessary, might have strengthened the will and passion of the troops.	**Analyze** Take things apart
4a. Make a list of adjectives that describe the queen.	**4b.** Given Elizabeth's purpose, evaluate the effectiveness of her speech.	**Evaluate** Make judgments
5a. To what values or emotions does Elizabeth appeal?	**5b.** Synthesize the ideas in this speech and compare them to other motivational speeches you have heard, for example Martin Luther King's "I Have a Dream" speech.	**Create** Bring ideas together

Analyze Literature

Purpose and Parallelism

What was Queen Elizabeth I's main purpose in this speech? Does she accomplish this purpose?

At what points in the speech does Elizabeth use parallelism? What is her goal in using this rhetorical device? How does the use of parallelism help achieve her overall purpose?

Extend the Text

Writing Options

Creative Writing Imagine that you are Queen Elizabeth, preparing to leave for Tilbury. What concerns would be foremost in your mind? Write a journal entry that Queen Elizabeth might have written on this occasion.

Persuasive Writing Think of a cause you want to promote in your school, such as academic credit for volunteer work. Write a short persuasive speech, and present your argument at a student council meeting. During your presentation, maintain good eye contact, an appropriate speaking rate and volume, and clear enunciation. Use appropriate language conventions and gestures as well.

Media Literacy

Compare Speeches Throughout history, leaders have given speeches to inspire their followers. Memorable examples are Martin Luther King Jr.'s "I've Been to the Mountaintop" speech the night before he was assassinated, and Knute Rockne's "win one for the Gipper" speech to the Notre Dame football team. An audio recording and a transcript of King's speech can be found at **http://lit.emcp.net/king**. A transcript of Rockne's speech is available at **http://lit.emcp.net/rockne**, and a dramatization is presented in the 1940 film *Knute Rockne–All American*. Choose one of these speeches, or another famous inspirational speech, and compare and contrast it with Queen Elizabeth's "Speech to the Troops at Tilbury." Consider the audience, purpose, and occasion of each speech, and evaluate how differences in formality and tone reflect variations in these factors.

Lifelong Learning

Research the Elizabethan Era As a class, conduct research about the Elizabethan Era. Have individuals or small groups research specific topics, such as clothing, food, music, literature, and drama. As a class, put on an Elizabethan fair for your school. Have authentic costumes, refreshments, and entertainment.

 Go to **www.mirrorsandwindows.com** for more.

Understand the Concept

A sentence has **parallel structure** or **parallelism** when it uses the same grammatical forms to express ideas of equal—or parallel—importance. One example of parallel structure appears in Queen Elizabeth I's "Speech to the Troops at Tilbury." Queen Elizabeth used a series of prepositional phrases—"of my God, of my kingdom, of my people"—to emphasize her strong stance against "those enemies."

Parallelism not only adds emphasis and rhythm to writing, but it also improves unity and balance. Faulty parallelism makes sentences sound awkward and can obscure their meaning.

EXAMPLES

Faulty Elizabeth used her navy for exploration and to colonize foreign lands.

Parallel Elizabeth used her navy to explore and colonize foreign lands. [*exploration* is changed to *explore* to use the same structure as *colonize*]

Faulty The English Navy prepared for sea battle while Elizabeth's lords were assembling an army of four thousand at Tilbury.

Parallel The English Navy prepared for sea battle while Elizabeth's lords assembled an army of four thousand at Tilbury. [*were assembling* is changed to *assembled* to use the same structure as *prepared*]

To correct faulty parallelism, look for series of nouns and verbs and similarly constructed clauses and phrases. Match like elements, and write them using the same grammatical structure.

Apply the Skill

Identify Parallel Structure

Find the uses of parallel structure in the following excerpt from Queen Elizabeth's speech:

> I have always so behaved myself that, under God, I have placed my chiefest strength and safeguard in the loyal hearts and goodwill of my subjects; and therefore I am come amongst you, as you see, at this time, not for my recreation and disport, but being resolved, in the midst and heat of the battle, to live or die amongst you all; to lay down for my God, and for my kingdom, and my people, my honor and my blood, even in the dust. I know I have the body but of a weak and feeble woman; but I have the heart and stomach of a king, and of a king of England too, and think foul scorn that Parma or Spain, or any prince of Europe, should dare to invade the borders of my realm; to which rather than any dishonor shall grow by me, I myself will take up arms, I myself will be your general, judge, and rewarder of every one of your virtues in the field.

Improve Parallel Structure

Rewrite each sentence using parallel structure.

1. When Elizabeth succeeded her sister to the throne in 1558, religious strife, huge government debt, and failing in the war with France had reduced England's fortunes.
2. Elizabeth came to the throne with the Tudor concept of strong rule and realizing that effective rule depended on popular support.
3. The Elizabethan Age was one of the greatest periods of its history—a period that produced William Shakespeare and other notable figures in literature; when England became a major European power; and a period in which English commerce and industry prospered.
4. Queen Elizabeth's reign also was marked by social and economic reforms, including the Statute of Apprentices to stabilize labor conditions, the Poor Laws to attempt some remedy of widespread poverty, and various acts that encouraged agriculture, commerce, and manufacturing.
5. The Spanish Armada was defeated by the skill of such leaders as John Hawkins and Francis Drake and storms.

Use Parallel Structure in Your Own Writing

Imagine you are a soldier who has heard Queen Elizabeth's "Speech to the Troops at Tilbury." Write a letter to the queen in which you thank her for offering the troops encouragement as they prepared for battle. Use five examples of parallelism in your letter. After completing your letter, read it aloud. Any errors in parallelism will sound awkward. Revise your writing to improve the use of parallelism.

The Sonnet Defined

A **sonnet** is a form of lyric poetry composed of fourteen lines in **iambic pentameter.** The two major types of sonnets are the **Petrarchan,** or Italian, **sonnet,** and the **Shakespearean,** or English, **sonnet.** A less common form is the Spenserian sonnet, originated by Sir Edmund Spenser.

The Petrarchan sonnet is named after Italian Renaissance poet Francesco Petrarch (1304–1374), who dedicated more than three hundred poems to an idealized woman named Laura. She may have been Laura de Noves, a married woman and mother who died of the plague in 1348. In any case, Laura was a rich symbol for the poet, a means through which to express the sentiments conventionally associated with courtly love. Petrarch's **sonnet sequence** influenced countless other poets and still is held in high critical esteem today.

Among poets influenced by Petrarch were Thomas Wyatt and his Elizabethan contemporary Henry Howard, the Earl of Surrey. These two men helped spark a literary movement in England that produced hundreds of sonnets, most having romantic love as a central theme. Among the most famous English sonnet sequences are the poems of Shakespeare to a fair friend and to a dark lady and Sir Philip Sidney's *Astrophil and Stella.*

> *"Loving in truth, and fain in verse my love to show, / That she (dear She) might take some pleasure of my pain."*

> —SIR PHILIP SIDNEY, FROM SONNET 1, *ASTROPHIL AND STELLA*

Elements of the Sonnet

Structure and Form

Each of the two predominant sonnet forms has a particular **rhyme scheme.** The Petrarchan sonnet consists of an **octave** (eight lines) rhyming *abbaabba* followed by a **sestet** (six lines), which may rhyme *cdecde, cdedce,* or any combination. The Shakespearean sonnet is composed of three **quatrains** (four lines) rhyming *abab cdcd efef* and a **couplet** (two lines) rhyming *gg.* The idiosyncratic Spenserian sonnet follows the rhyme scheme *abab bcbc cdcd* and is completed by a couplet rhyming *ee.*

The sonnet provides a clear example of how form creates meaning. The division of the Petrarchan sonnet follows a formula: The octave raises a question or makes an argument, which the sestet addresses, explores, or resolves. The stanza division of the Shakespearean sonnet allows for the presentation of three distinct images, united or interpreted by the couplet, or by the development of three points of an argument, resolved in the couplet.

For example, the octave of Petrarch's Sonnet 1 begs the reader to indulge his "mixed style," a combination of English vernacular and Latin, and establishes the speaker as the abject, hopeless lover of courtly tradition, penning his verses as best he can. The sestet advances the argument in new terms: Ambition, like romantic love, is nothing but a dream, and all the speaker's posturings are mere vanity.

Notice the break in thought that occurs between the octave and the sestet. This break or turn, called the *volta,* occurs at line 9, which signals in this particular poem that the speaker's mood has changed. The volta also can herald the resolution of the problem set forth in the octave.

Now consider Shakespeare's Sonnet 116. The speaker states his argument in the opening quatrain: Sincere love does not change, no matter the circumstances. The second quatrain introduces a **metaphor** to illustrate this point, characterizing love as "the star to every wandering bark." The third quatrain builds on the argument through the use of personification: Time as reaper of youth, who yet cannot conquer love. The concluding epigrammatic couplet assures the reader of the veracity of the speaker's argument. If he does not speak the truth, then he has never written a lyric poem and no man has ever experienced romantic love.

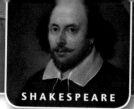

WYATT **SIDNEY** **SHAKESPEARE**

Meter

The sonnet is a precise and limited form that forces the poet to follow certain conventions. For instance, the **meter** is fixed, with ten syllables occurring in **iambic pentameter.** A line of iambic pentameter has five **iambs,** in which an unstressed syllable is followed by a stressed syllable, as in the word *insist.* The sonnet is a precise and limited form that forces the poet to follow certain conventions. When we scan the line of the sonnet, we find a rhythm that alternates between soft and loud syllables. When we read a line aloud, we hear that in every iamb, the second syllable is always pronounced more emphatically than the first. This is the case whether the iamb is one word, such as *admit,* or two, such as *O, no!*

It is easy to hear the iambic meter. In fact, it has been observed that iambic pentameter is the natural rhythm of spoken English. Try reading the final couplet of Shakespeare's Sonnet 116 aloud, according to the **scansion** (analysis of meter) shown at the top of the next column:

⌣ / ⌣ / ⌣ / ⌣ / ⌣ /
If this | be err | or and | upon | me proved,

⌣ / ⌣ / ⌣ / ⌣ / ⌣ /
I ne | ver writ, | nor no | man ev | er loved.

Of course, the object of reading a poem is to capture the natural rhythms and cadences of speech. If we read a poem in a forced manner, the result can sound awkward and artificial. As you read a sonnet, pronounce the words as you think they should be pronounced, and train your ear to identify variations in the metrical pattern and rhythm.

*"A Sonnet is a moment's monument,—
Memorial from the Soul's eternity
To one dead deathless hour."*

—DANTE GABRIEL ROSSETTI,
NINETEENTH-CENTURY BRITISH POET

HOW TO READ

A Sonnet

Read it aloud. Although formal in structure, sonnets often are written to mimic the natural sounds of speech and so are well suited for reading aloud. Reading a poem aloud also can help you recognize where the poet has used sound devices such as rhyme, assonance, consonance, and alliteration. Finally, reading a poem aloud can help you recognize the meter.

Analyze the form to discover the meaning. Determine whether a sonnet is Petrarchan or Shakespearean in form, and use that distinction to discover its meaning. In a Petrarchan sonnet, the octave asks a question or makes an argument, which the sestet addresses, explores, or resolves. In a Shakespearean sonnet, the first three stanzas present three distinct images or arguments, which are interpreted or resolved in the couplet.

Identify conceits. Sonnets, particularly those of the Renaissance, often employ *conceits,* which are elaborate and fanciful analogies or metaphors. For example, a lover might be compared to nature. Once you have identified a conceit, try to determine the vehicle and tenor of the metaphor. Doing so will help you better understand the purpose of the sonnet. If the sonnet ends in a couplet, you also may discover the message of the poem there.

See Understanding Literary Forms in Unit 1, pages 20–21, for additional guidelines on how to read poetry.

"Whoso list to hunt"

A Sonnet by Sir Thomas Wyatt

"With how sad steps" (Sonnet 31)

A Sonnet by Sir Philip Sidney

Build Background

Literary Context Sir Thomas Wyatt's **"Whoso list to hunt"** is a superb example of a Petrarchan sonnet, both technically and thematically. Wyatt may have written this sonnet about Anne Boleyn, one of the wives of Henry VIII. Wyatt had grown up in the same household with Anne and fallen deeply in love with her. He was devastated when she married Henry, and Henry quite naturally was suspicious of him. The reference in the poem to Caesar may be read as meaning "any powerful man," such as King Henry.

Sir Philip Sidney's **"With how sad steps"** (Sonnet 31) is part of the sonnet cycle *Astrophil and Stella,* which generally follows the Petrarchan rhyme scheme and subject of unrequited (unreturned) love. Sidney addresses his sonnets to the unattainable Stella, whose name means "star." The speaker, Astrophil ("star-lover"), expresses the complex emotions of someone in love. In "With how sad steps," the speaker addresses the moon, asking it if in the heavenly sphere, as on Earth, constancy (faithfulness) is considered lack of intelligence.

Reader's Context Most people have had the experience of liking or loving someone who did not return the feeling. When have you had this experience? How did you feel? What did you do?

Meet the Authors

Sir Thomas Wyatt (1502–1542) was born in Kent, England. A courtier and diplomat much of his life, Wyatt served as clerk and ambassador to King Henry VIII. Twice he was arrested and imprisoned as a result of quarrels at court. He spent most of his adult life abroad and was greatly influenced by the Italian poet Petrarch (see page 253).

Sir Philip Sidney (1554–1586) was a well-loved courtier, soldier, poet, and patron of the arts who was deeply mourned by the English after he died in battle at age thirty-two. After working for Queen Elizabeth, he retired to the estate of his sister, the Countess of Pembroke. There, at her request, he wrote the pastoral romance *Arcadia,* which is considered the greatest piece of prose fiction written in English before 1700. Also highly regarded is his "Defense of Poesy," literary criticism in which he argues that poets can improve on nature by creating worlds better than the real one.

Compare Literature

Sensory Details and Personification
Sensory details are words and phrases that describe how things look, sound, smell, taste, and feel.

Personification is a figure of speech in which an animal, thing, force of nature, or idea is described as if it were human or is given human characteristics.

Set Purpose

In writing about unrequited love, Wyatt and Sidney use many sensory details, related primarily to nature. As you read each sonnet, record the sensory words and phrases in a five-column chart, with columns labeled "Sight," "Sound," "Smell," "Taste," and "Feel." Note which sense or senses are referenced most by each poet. As you read "With how sad steps," determine what object Sidney is personifying and what human characteristics he gives it.

Preview Vocabulary

travail, 249
graven, 249
wan, 250
languished, 250
scorn, 250

WHOSO LIST TO HUNT

After the Hunt,
c. 1644. Karel Dujardin.
Michaelis Collection,
Cape Town, South Africa.
(See detail on page 248.)

by Sir Thomas Wyatt

Whoso list[1] to hunt, I know where is an hind,[2]
But as for me, alas, I may no more.
The vain <u>travail</u> hath wearied me so sore
I am of them that farthest cometh behind.
5   Yet may I, by no means, my wearied mind
Draw from the deer, but as she fleeth afore,
Fainting I follow. I leave off therefore,
Since in a net I seek to hold the wind.
Who list her hunt, I put him out of doubt,
10 As well as I, may spend his time in vain.
And <u>graven</u> with diamonds in letters plain
There is written, her fair neck round about,
"Noli me tangere, for Cæsar's I am,[3]
And wild for to hold, though I seem tame." ❖

---

1. **list.** Desires
2. **hind.** Female deer
3. **noli me tangere.** [Latin] "Do not touch me."

> **tra • vail** (trə vāl´) *n.,* very hard work
> **grav • en** (grā´ vən) *adj.,* engraved

MIRRORS & WINDOWS

The speaker in "Whoso list to hunt" laments the fact that the woman he loves belongs to someone else. Discuss what it feels like not to get what you want. How do you respond to this kind of disappointment?

A Fine Day at the Coast, 1869. Henry Moore. (See detail on page 255.)

from *Amoretti*

"One day I wrote her name upon the strand"
(Sonnet 75)

by Edmund Spenser

One day I wrote her name upon the strand,[1]
But came the waves and washèd it away:
Agayne I wrote it with a second hand,
But came the tyde, and made my paynes his pray.[2]
5 "Vayne man," sayd she, "that doest in vaine assay,[3]
A mortall thing so to <u>immortalize</u>,
For I my selve shall lyke to this decay,

Can't keep alive Forever

---

1. **strand.** Beach
2. **pray.** Prey (victim)
3. **assay.** Attempt

---

im • mor • tal • ize (i môr′ təl īz′) *v.*, make exempt from death; make lasting through fame

And eek[4] my name bee wypéd out lykewize."[5]
"Not so," quod[6] I, "let baser things devize, *She may live forever in his poetry*
10   To dy in dust, but you shall live by fame:
My verse your vertues rare shall eternize,[7]
And in the heavens wryte your glorious name.
Where whenas death shall all the world subdew,
Our love shall live, and later life renew." ❖

Poetry is eternal immortality

---

4. **eek.** Also
5. **lykewize.** Also
6. **quod.** Quoth (stated)
7. **eternize.** Make eternal

MIRRORS & WINDOWS

The speaker plans to memorialize his love's "rare vertues" in his poetry. For what personal quality or act would you like to be memorialized?

LITERARY CONNECTION

Poets' Corner

In 1400, Geoffrey Chaucer became the first poet to be buried at Westminster Abbey, the London church in which British monarchs traditionally are crowned and buried. Chaucer earned this place of honor not because he was a celebrated writer but because he had been clerk of works to the palace of Westminster. More than 150 years after his death, a more magnificent tomb was built at his gravesite, and in 1599, Edmund Spenser was buried nearby.

The burials of Chaucer and Spenser began a tradition that developed into designating the South Transept of Westminster Abbey as Poets' Corner. Some of the most famous writers buried there include poets Alfred, Lord Tennyson; John Dryden; Robert Browning; and Ben Jonson. Interestingly, Jonson is buried vertically, since his family could not afford to pay for an extended plot. Charles Dickens, Samuel Johnson, Rudyard Kipling, and Thomas Hardy are some of the most noted later English writers buried in Poets' Corner. A few nonwriters also are buried there, including composer George Frederic Handel, Shakespearean actor David Garrick, and modern-day actor Sir Laurence Olivier.

Other famous British writers are memorialized at Poets' Corner but not actually buried there. They

include poets John Milton, John Keats, William Wordsworth, Robert Burns, William Blake, and T. S. Eliot and fiction writers Jane Austen, Samuel Butler, Oliver Goldsmith, and Charlotte, Emily, and Anne Brontë. William Shakespeare is buried in the town of his birth, Stratford-on-Avon. A monument to him was built at Westminster Abbey in 1740, more than one hundred years after his death.

"Let me not to the marriage of true minds"

(Sonnet 116)

by William Shakespeare

Let me not to the marriage of true minds
Admit <u>impediments</u>. Love is not love
Which <u>alters</u> when it alteration finds,
Or bends with the remover to remove:
5 O, no! It is an ever-fixéd mark
That looks on tempests and is never shaken;
It is the star to every wandering bark,[1]
Whose worth's unknown, although his height be taken.
Love's not Time's fool, though rosy lips and cheeks
10 Within his bending sickle's compass[2] come;
Love alters not with his brief hours and weeks,
But bears it out even to the edge of doom.[3]
     If this be error and upon me proved,
     I never writ, nor no man ever loved. ❖

---

1. **star to every wandering bark.** Star that guides every wandering ship; North Star
2. **compass.** Range; scope
3. **doom.** Judgment Day

im • ped • i • ment (im peʹ də mənt) *n.*, obstacle
al • ter (ôlʹ tər) *v.*, change

MIRRORS & WINDOWS

The speaker of Sonnet 116 has a strong opinion about what constitutes true love. Based on this definition, how often do people find true love? Is it common or rare?

"My mistress' eyes are nothing like the sun"

(Sonnet 130)

by William Shakespeare

Autumn, c. 1876–1916.
Thomas Benjamin Kennington.

[handwritten annotations:]

"Uncomparing" her

Not about beauty / girlfriend

beyond possible

→ Attractive, but not the conventional type of beauty.

Not a possible model

Imagery that makes a lie of this beautiful woman

No human being can possibly be

No one has "golden" hair

– Taking to task the Petrarchan conceit

My mistress' eyes are nothing like the sun;
Coral is far more red than her lips' red;
If snow be white, why then her breasts are dun;[1]
If hairs be wires, black wires grow on her head.
5   I have seen roses damasked,[2] red and white,
But no such roses see I in her cheeks;
And in some perfumes is there more delight
Than in the breath that from my mistress reeks.[3]
I love to hear her speak, yet well I know
10 That music hath a far more pleasing sound;
I grant I never saw a goddess go;
My mistress, when she walks, treads on the ground.
    And yet, by heaven, I think my love as rare
    As any she belied with false compare. ❖

---

1. **dun.** ~~Dark~~ tan
2. **damasked.** Intermingled
3. **reeks.** Give off or exude, especially an unpleasant odor

be • lie (bē līʹ) *v.,* misrepresent

MIRRORS & WINDOWS

An old saying suggests that "Beauty is in the eye of the beholder." How important is physical appearance in meeting someone and developing a relationship?

The Sonnet, 1839. William Mulready. Victoria and Albert Museum, London, England. (See detail on page 265.)

"When, in disgrace with Fortune and men's eyes"

(Sonnet 29)

by William Shakespeare

When, in disgrace with Fortune and men's eyes,
I all alone beweep my outcast state,
And trouble deaf heaven with my bootless[1] cries,
And look upon myself and curse my fate,
5   Wishing me like to one more rich in hope,
Featured like him, like him with friends possessed,
Desiring this man's art and that man's scope,
With what I most enjoy contented least;
Yet in these thoughts myself almost despising,
10 Haply[2] I think on thee, and then my state
(Like to the lark at break of day arising
From sullen earth) sings hymns at heaven's gate;
    For thy sweet love remembered such wealth brings
    That then I scorn to change my state with kings. ❖

---

1. **bootless.** Useless
2. **Haply.** By chance or accident
luckily or fortunately

MIRRORS & WINDOWS

The speaker's discontent is resolved at the thought of a special love or friend. Who or what helps lift your spirits when you are troubled or angry?

Refer to Text ▶ ▶ ▶ ▶ ▶   Reason with Text

1a. According to the opening lines in Sonnet 29, how does the speaker sometimes feel?	**1b.** Infer what makes the speaker feel this way.	**Understand** Find meaning
2a. What does the speaker in Sonnet 116 say love is and is not?	**2b.** Based on this description of love, how old does the speaker seem to be?	**Apply** Use information
3a. In Sonnet 130, what ideal characteristics does the speaker say his love does not have?	**3b.** Suggest why the speaker points out his mistress's shortcomings.	**Analyze** Take things apart
4a. Is the speaker in each poem in love with a specific person? Explain, using details from the poem.	**4b.** Compare and contrast the three speakers' views of love.	**Evaluate** Make judgments
5a. Select the line from each poem that best states the speaker's concept of love.	**5b.** Write your own definition of *love*.	**Create** Bring ideas together

Analyze Literature

Speaker and Tone

Review the notes you made about the speaker in each sonnet. How are the speakers alike and different? Do they all have the same attitude toward love? Discuss how the speaker fits the concept of love presented in each poem.

What word or words best describe the tone of each poem? Compare and contrast the tones of the three sonnets. Explain how the tone relates to each speaker's concept of love.

Extend the Text

Writing Options

Creative Writing Your school is having a Shakespearean poetry contest. Write your own sonnet, borrowing from the themes and forms in the three Shakespearean sonnets in this grouping. Make sure your poem has fourteen lines (three quatrains and a closing couplet) and is written in iambic pentameter.

Expository Writing Write an essay in which you compare and contrast one of Shakespeare's sonnets with one of the sonnets by Wyatt, Sidney, Petrarch, or Spenser reviewed earlier in this unit. Consider the sonnet type, structure, form, and meter in addition to elements such as sensory details, speaker, tone, and theme. (Review the description of a sonnet on pages 246–247.)

Media Literacy

Illustrate a Sonnet You have been asked to create the illustrations for a collection of Shakespeare's sonnets.

Reread Sonnets 29, 116, and 130, and choose the one you feel is best suited to illustration. Consider the use of imagery, the tone, the qualities of the speaker, and so on. Then decide what media to use, such as watercolors or pen and ink. Display your finished illustration in an exhibit with the illustrations of your classmates.

Collaborative Learning

Circle Poetry Reading Have each member of the class select a favorite Shakespearean sonnet (from this text or elsewhere). Form circles of five or six, and take turns reading the poems. As you listen, try to hear and enjoy the meter and rhyme. As you read, try to recite the lines with feeling, portraying the sentiment of the speaker.

 Go to **www.mirrorsandwindows.com** for more.

No work of art is completely independent of the historical period and culture in which it is created, and every work is, in some respects, shaped by the artist's personal experience. In examining a literary text from the theory of **biographical-historical criticism,** the critic draws on the fabric of a time and place as well as details of its author's life to discover the greater context of the work. The basic premise of this theory is refreshingly clear: We examine the writer's life and influences and look for ways in which his or her experience is tied to the historical moment.

"The text is merely one of the contexts of a piece of literature, its lexical or verbal one, no more or less important than the sociological, psychological, historical, anthropological or generic."

—LESLIE FIEDLER, AMERICAN LITERARY CRITIC

Overview of Biographical-Historical Criticism

The Elizabethan Period

Shakespeare's sonnets were written during the Elizabethan Period, a fruitful time for literature. In his own time, Shakespeare was only one of a number of superior English authors. Modern audiences revere Shakespeare for his plays, but the Elizabethans valued poetry above all other forms of literature.

In composing his sonnet sequence, Shakespeare worked with a popular form adapted from the sonnets of the Italian poet Petrarch. (See Understanding Literary Forms: The Sonnet, on pages 246–247.) Shakespeare wrote the poems during an era of political instability, when advancement at court was uncertain. Because poets and artists depended on the patronage of the aristocracy, it was common practice for a work to be dedicated to a particular noble.

Perhaps that explains, in part, why Shakespeare's early sonnets were addressed to a young man of surpassing beauty and accomplishment who also was of noble birth. The identity of this nobleman is not known, but he may have been Henry Wriothesley, Earl of Southampton, a patron to whom Shakespeare dedicated his poems *Venus and Adonis* (1593) and *The Rape of Lucrece* (1594).

The Author

Certain facts about Shakespeare's life are known. In the early 1590s, he was a promising actor and playwright in London theaters. To support his young family on the money earned from his plays, he would have needed the continued patronage of the nobility. Unfortunately, an outbreak of the plague closed the London theaters in 1592. Shakespeare and his fellow actors toured playhouses outside the city but undoubtedly struggled to make a living. At this point, Shakespeare turned to writing poetry, and legend has it that the two poems he dedicated to Wriothesley earned him more money than all of his plays.

Application of Biographical-Historical Criticism

Readers might conclude that Shakespeare's sonnets, with their impassioned speaker who seems to reveal his innermost feelings, constitute a biography of their author. Readers also must consider the *persona,* the mask worn by the author. The sonnet form long has been identified with a courtly tradition, in which the beloved sometimes is merely the vehicle for the poet's verbal feats. Yet the approximate date of "When, in disgrace with Fortune" (Sonnet 29), the early 1590s, suggests a biographical link to the content.

In the same year of the plague outbreak, dramatist Robert Greene wrote an attack on Shakespeare, in which he called him "an upstart Crow" who imagines himself "in his owne conceit the only Shake-scene in a countrey." The speaker's sense of being "in disgrace with Fortune and men's eyes" may be related to the double threat to Shakespeare's livelihood and reputation.

Convention and Meaning

Because the heyday of the sonnet coincided with Shakespeare's use of the form, we cannot separate the literary convention from the content of the poem. The sonnet, a lyrical form rich in romantic associations,

tends to place the speaker in a somewhat miserable position: He pleads with the beloved, sometimes even pestering her with his declarations.

Of course, Sonnet 29 addresses a young male friend, but the role of the beloved is much the same. The speaker, lamenting his worldly status and driven nearly to self-contempt, has reached the low point of his fortunes and pours out his complaint to his esteemed friend:

> When, in disgrace with Fortune and men's eyes,
>   I all alone beweep my outcast state,
> And trouble deaf Heaven with my bootless cries,
>   And look upon myself, and curse my fate.

❏ **Analyze** Consider the literary conventions of the sonnet as well as the practical circumstances that produced this particular poem. How does Shakespeare's use of these conventions shape your expectations as a reader? How closely should the reader identify the speaker's history with that of the poet? Do you take his lament at face value, or do other factors influence your analysis? Explain.

Mood, Theme and the Historical Moment

We already have established the historical moment of Sonnet 29 as one of instability, both in Shakespeare's community of artists and in the larger society. With the author deprived of access to London audiences and attacked by a significant literary figure of the times, the initial mood of the work (and consequently of the reader) is troubled. Possibly, the poet-speaker has in mind his rivals on the literary scene as he writes:

> Wishing me like to one more rich in hope,
>   Featured like him, like him with friends possessed,
> Desiring this man's art and that man's scope,
>   With what I most enjoy contented least.

❏ **Analyze** How does information about the circumstances surrounding the writing of the poem add to your understanding of the poem's themes? How did you interpret the poem before this information was presented to you? Does it significantly change your analysis of the sonnet? Why or why not?

Conflict and Resolution

If our knowledge of Shakespeare's life and times suggests that Sonnet 29 can be read as biography, we also can see that the poet is following literary tradition in setting up his conflict in the octave and then resolving it so brilliantly in the sestet. To do so, he contrasts his mired, earthly state—the professional reversals and his relative poverty, which breed envy and discontent—with the mental state induced by thoughts of his dear friend. It is through contemplation of this influential person that the speaker rouses himself from self-pity:

> Haply I think on thee, and then my state
> (Like to the lark at break of day arising
>   From sullen earth) sings hymns at heaven's gate.

❏ **Analyze** Compare the first quatrain of the poem to the sestet. Consider the references to *fortune* (line 1) and *wealth* (line 13). How might Shakespeare's connection to a patron such as Henry Wriothesley, Earl of Southampton, have shaped the resolution of the speaker's conflict? Does the shadowy existence of such a person alter your initial reading of the poem? Why or why not?

WRITING ABOUT

Biographical-Historical Criticism

Write an essay that answers this question: To what extent is the speaker's lament motivated by biographical and historical circumstance? Use details from the sonnet to illustrate how personal and social history inform one another.

1. What is the main idea expressed in "Let me not to the marriage of true minds" (Sonnet 116)?
   A. Love is blind.
   B. Love neither changes nor ends.
   C. The love that is commonly felt is not true love.
   D. People should not get divorced but should endure through their problems.
   E. If two people really love each other, they should get married.

2. Which of the following sentences or phrases from Sonnet 116 say essentially the same thing?
   A. "Let me not to the marriage of true minds / Admit impediments" *and* "Love is not love / Which alters when it alteration finds, / Or bends with the remover to remove."
   B. "It is an ever-fixéd mark / That looks on tempests and is never shaken" *and* "It is the star to every wandering bark, / Whose worth's unknown, although his height be taken."
   C. "Love's not Time's fool, though rosy lips and cheeks / Within his bending sickle's compass come" *and* "Love alters not with his brief hours and weeks."
   D. B and C
   E. A, B, and C

3. What is the speaker saying in the last two lines of Sonnet 116?
   A. True love really does not exist.
   B. He actually did not write this poem.
   C. What he has just written is absolutely true.
   D. It is up to the reader to judge the truth of these lines.
   E. He cannot be held accountable for what he has written.

4. What is the overall tone of Sonnet 116?
   A. sincere   D. sarcastic
   B. insincere   E. familiar
   C. playful

5. In "My mistress' eyes are nothing like the sun" (Sonnet 130), Shakespeare contrasts his mistress, or parts of her, to all of the following *except*
   A. the sun.   D. a goddess.
   B. coral.   E. the ground.
   C. perfume.

6. The contrasts in Sonnet 130 are between what two things?
   A. different kinds of lies
   B. what is and what should be
   C. common like and rare love
   D. an idealistic and a realistic viewpoint
   E. the natural and the artificial worlds

7. In Sonnet 130, what is Shakespeare's attitude toward how poets in the past have described their mistresses?
   A. amusingly critical
   B. accepting as fact
   C. envious and wishful
   D. harshly disrespectful
   E. rejecting as harmful lies

8. What is most distinctive and effective in lines 3–4 of Sonnet 130?
   A. the meter
   B. the slant rhyme
   C. the parallel structure
   D. the use of descriptive words
   E. the strong criticism

9. **Constructed Response:** Based on Sonnets 116 and 130, write a description of a sonnet. What elements do these sonnets share?

10. **Constructed Response:** Which of these two sonnets do you like better? What specifically about it appeals to you? List at least three reasons for your preference.

> **TEST-TAKING TIP**
>
> Although you cannot write on the test sheet, you can make notes in the accompanying booklet. When you come across a complicated question, write out the possible responses next to the question in the booklet. Putting your thoughts on paper will help clarify your thinking. Doing so also will help you retrace your thoughts when you check your work later.

The Passionate Shepherd to His Love
A Lyric Poem by Christopher Marlowe

The Nymph's Reply to the Shepherd
A Lyric Poem by Sir Walter Raleigh

Build Background

Literary Context Best known as a Renaissance dramatist, Christopher Marlowe also was a successful poet. His **"The Passionate Shepherd to His Love"** (c. 1590) is a plea from a shepherd inviting his beloved to come live with him. Several poets wrote responses to this lyric invitation, including Sir Walter Raleigh. **"The Nymph's Reply to the Shepherd"** (1599–1600) is one of Raleigh's most popular short poems.

Marlowe wrote "The Passionate Shepherd" in **iambic tetrameter,** a straightforward, natural meter that matches the simplicity of the poem's subject. Raleigh's poem mirrors Marlowe's poem in several important ways. Both poems make many references to nature and have the same rhyme scheme, meter, and number of lines. The speakers in the two poems are quite different, however. Raleigh's speaker is thoughtful and resigned, whereas Marlowe's speaker is passionate.

Reader's Context Think about a place in which you like to spend time. If you wanted to convince someone else to go there, how would you describe it?

Meet the Authors

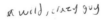
a wild, crazy guy

Christopher Marlowe (1564–1593), the son of a shoemaker, received a scholarship to attend Cambridge. In 1587, while at Cambridge, he wrote the famous play *Tamburlaine,* which dramatized the adventures of a fourteenth-century shepherd who conquered much of the known world. Marlowe went on to write five more plays. (See Unit 4, pages 336 and 442, for more on Marlowe's plays.) Marlowe's life was cut short. Only six years after his success with *Tamburlaine,* he was killed in a brawl over a tavern bill.
stabbed in head

Sir Walter Raleigh (1552–1618) led a varied life as a soldier, explorer, courtier, philosopher, colonist, poet, student of science, and historian. His accomplishments included establishing the Roanoke colony in Virginia and importing the potato to Ireland. A favorite of Queen Elizabeth, Raleigh was known for his flamboyant dress, his enthusiasm for life, and his quick temper. He did not find favor with Elizabeth's successor, King James I, who ultimately executed him for treason. In prison, Raleigh wrote his long but unfinished *History of the World.*

Compare Literature

Pastoral, Enjambment, and End-Stopped Line
A **pastoral** poem or other literary work depicts the lives of shepherds or rural life in general and often draws a comparison between the innocence and serenity of the country and the misery and corruption of the city.

Enjambment is the act of continuing a statement beyond the end of a line in a poem. This is in contrast to an **end-stopped line,** in which both the sense and grammar are complete at the end of the line.

Set Purpose

Pastorals were quite popular during the Renaissance Era, appearing in both dramatic and poetic forms. As you read these poems, note the ways in which Marlowe's poem idealizes rural life and Raleigh's takes a harsher view. Also look for examples of enjambment and end-stopped lines. Read each poem aloud to consider how enjambment affects the sound of the verse.

Preview Vocabulary

wanton, 271
gall, 271

The Passionate Shepherd to His Love

by Christopher Marlowe

The Hireling Shepherd, c. 1800s. William Holman Hunt. Manchester City Art Gallery, Manchester, England. (See detail on page 269.)

persuasive, only giving positive info

Come live with me and be my love,
And we will all the pleasures prove
That valleys, groves, hills, and fields,
Woods, or steepy mountain yields.

5   And we will sit upon the rocks,
Seeing the shepherds feed their flocks,
By shallow rivers to whose falls
Melodious birds sing madrigals.[1]

And I will make thee beds of roses
10 And a thousand fragrant posies,
A cap of flowers, and a kirtle[2]
Embroidered all with leaves of myrtle;[3]

A gown made of the finest wool
Which from our pretty lambs we pull;
15 Fair lined slippers for the cold,
With buckles of the purest gold;

A belt of straw and ivy buds,
With coral clasps and amber studs:
And if these pleasures may thee move,
20 Come live with me, and be my love.

The shepherds' swains[4] shall dance and sing
For thy delight each May morning:
If these delights thy mind may move,
Then live with me and be my love. ❖

complex songs not trendy at time

1. **madrigals.** Songs, often in several parts
2. **kirtle.** Woman's dress
3. **myrtle.** Type of plant with evergreen leaves and white or pink flowers
4. **swains.** Country youths, especially shepherds

MIRRORS & WINDOWS

The speaker describes all the "pleasures" and "delights" of life in the country. Does this life seem attractive to you? How would you respond to the invitation at the end of the poem?

The Nymph's Reply
to the Shepherd

realistic reply

by Sir Walter Raleigh

argumentative

If all the world and love were young,
And truth in every shepherd's tongue,
These pretty pleasures might me move
To live with thee and be thy love.

5 Time drives the flocks from field to fold *pen where sheep kept*
When rivers rage and rocks grow cold,
allusion and Philomel[1] becometh dumb;
The rest complains of cares to come.

The flowers do fade, and <u>wanton</u> fields *growth of fields* *changeable/ faithless*
10 To wayward winter reckoning yields;
A honey tongue, a heart of <u>gall</u>,
Is fancy's spring, but sorrow's fall.

Thy gowns, thy shoes, thy beds of roses, *listing*
Thy cap, thy kirtle, and thy posies *"chopping" argument*
15 Soon break, soon wither, soon forgotten—
In folly ripe, in reason rotten. *purposely does not flow*

Thy belt of straw and ivy buds.
Thy coral clasps and amber studs,
All these in me no means can move
20 To come to thee and be thy love.

But could youth last and love still breed,
Had joys no date nor age no need,
Then these delights my mind might move
To live with thee and be thy love. ❖

Amaryllis, or the Shepherdess, 1884.
William Holman Hunt.

1. **Philomel.** A *philomel* is a nightingale, so named for
   Philomela, a character in Greek and Roman mythology who
   was changed into a nightingale by the gods.

wan · ton (wän´ t'n) *adj.,* luxuriant
gall (gôl) *n.,* bitterness

How do you usually respond when something sounds too good to be true?
Are you eager or cautious?

Refer to Text ▶ ▶ ▶ ▶ ▶   Reason with Text

1a. To what images does Marlowe refer in the first stanza of "The Passionate Shepherd"?	**1b.** Explain how these elements of nature give pleasure to people.	**Understand** Find meaning
2a. Identify the qualities of the speaker in "The Nymph's Reply."	**2b.** Compare and contrast the attitude of Raleigh's nymph to that of Marlowe's shepherd.	**Apply** Use information
3a. In lines 13–15 of "The Nymph's Reply," what does the nymph say about beautiful clothes and flowers?	**3b.** Why might some things be "in folly ripe, in reason rotten" (line 16)? What does the nymph mean by this?	**Analyze** Take things apart
4a. In "The Passionate Shepherd," what promises does the shepherd make to his beloved?	**4b.** Argue whether the shepherd's promises are realistic.	**Evaluate** Make judgments
5a. What images does each author use to portray pastoral life?	**5b.** Write a one-sentence summary of each author's view of this life.	**Create** Bring ideas together

Compare Literature

Pastoral, Enjambment, and End-Stopped Lines

What does the shepherd in Marlowe's poem convey about pastoral life? In contrast, what does the nymph in Raleigh's poem think of pastoral life? What seems to have been Raleigh's purpose in responding to Marlowe's poem?

What examples of enjambment and end-stopped lines did you find? Refer to one example of enjambment in each poem. What idea is conveyed in these lines? Where in the poem do these lines appear? What effect does enjambment have on your reading of the poem? How does its use contribute to the overall purpose of the poem?

Extend the Text

Writing Options

Creative Writing Pastoral dramas, as well as poems, were popular during the Renaissance. Write your own short drama by creating a scene in which the shepherd and the nymph meet and exchange views on love and life. Begin by briefly describing the scenery, the characters, and the events leading up to the exchange.

Descriptive Writing Write a two-paragraph character sketch about the shepherd and the nymph (one paragraph about each). Use the images in each poem to describe who the character is, where he or she lives, what he or she likes and dislikes, and what he or she believes. Present your character description to the class.

Lifelong Learning

Interview Community Members Visit a nursing home with several classmates, and interview four or five residents about their experiences with love and romance. Prepare the interview questions in advance, and check with the nursing home staff to make sure the questions are appropriate. Also decide who from your group will conduct each interview and who will record the responses. After completing the interviews, review and summarize the residents' responses as a group and categorize individuals as representing either "nymph" attitudes or "shepherd" attitudes.

Critical Literacy

Classify Poetry Review the poetry you have read so far in this unit, and classify the poems. Create your own categories, perhaps classifying the poems by form, subject matter, or attitude of the speaker. Be sure to provide at least one example for each category you create. Some poems will fit into two or more categories.

 Go to **www.mirrorsandwindows.com** for more.

Understand the Concept

A useful technique for learning vocabulary is to classify or categorize the words. Creating associations among new words will help you understand their meanings and commit them to memory.

To use this technique, first review the list of new words and look for similarities or patterns. Perhaps some of the words pertain to the same topic or describe the same quality. Create a label for each similarity or pattern, such as *Colors* or *Words About Winter.* Write each label on a sheet of paper, and then list under it the words that fit the classification.

Examine the following classifications of words from Shakespeare's sonnets:

Words showing a negative relationship with others disgrace, outcast, despise, scorn

Words about change alter, belie

Words about movement or progress impediment, scope, reek, tread

Apply the Skill

Exercise A
Classify the following words into three categories:
(1) Musical Terms, (2) Words about Love and Courtship, and (3) Types of Trees.

1. melodious
2. madrigal
3. myrtle
4. swain
5. wanton

Exercise B
Review the following list of words from "The Passionate Shepherd to His Love" and "The Nymph's Reply to the Shepherd," looking for similarities and patterns among them. Create three classifications by which to group the words, and write the labels on a sheet of paper. Then list each word under the appropriate label.

amber	mountains
birds	myrtle
coral	rivers
fields	rocks
flowers	roses
gold	straw
groves	valleys
hills	woods
ivy buds	

Exercise C
Make a list of vocabulary words from selections in this unit you have already read. Include at least twenty words but no more than forty. Consider different ways to classify the words. For example, you could first classify them by parts of speech (Verbs, Nouns, Adjectives, Adverbs, and so on). Then you could further divide these groups based on either meaning or some other criterion. Add to this classification whenever you come across new vocabulary. Work with a partner, taking turns reading each other's words aloud and putting the words into the correct categories.

SPELLING PRACTICE

Vowel Combinations

Knowing how to spell vowel combinations correctly is challenging for many writers, because the same combination can be pronounced several different ways. Consider, for instance, the *ea* combination in *break* and *breakfast.* Working with a partner, say these two words out loud and listen for the difference in the way the letter combination *ea* is pronounced. Together, identify the vowel combinations in the following words from the lesson for "The Passionate Shepherd to His Love" and "The Nymph's Reply." Read the words aloud to each other and group them according to the sounds produced by the various vowel combinations. If you have trouble, ask your teacher to pronounce the word for you.

breed	means	shoes
complains	mountain	yields
fields	pleasures	youth
heart	reason	

Song: To Celia
On My First Son

Lyric and Elegiac Poems by Ben Jonson

Build Background

Literary Context Often sung to musical accompaniment, Ben Jonson's **"Song: To Celia"** is a lyric poem that celebrates an unattainable, goddess-like woman. Drawing from the work of Philostratus, a Greek philosopher from the third century CE, Jonson carefully reworded phrases from various passages. Each eight-line stanza has an individual rhyme scheme. Jonson uses a variety of meters in this poem, mainly *iambic,* but many lines and phrases are *dactylic,* beginning with an accented syllable. Moreover, the poem's lines are not all the same length; they vary from three to five feet, with most of the odd lines being at least one foot longer than the even lines.

Only 1st three lines *→10, tetrameter*

"On My First Son" is an **elegy,** a song or poem written to lament someone who has died. Jonson wrote this poem to mourn the loss of his eldest son, Benjamin, who died in 1603 at age seven from the plague.

Reader's Context Both of these poems are about unattainable hopes and goals. To what lengths have you gone to try to achieve a specific goal? Were you successful?

Meet the Author

Ben Jonson (1572–1637) enjoyed success in many literary roles: actor, playwright, poet, scholar, critic, and translator. Born after the death of his father, a clergyman, Jonson became the stepson of a master bricklayer. He was educated by the great classical scholar William Camden at Westminster School, worked for a short time with his stepfather, and then entered the army. He was a brave soldier in hand-to-hand combat at Flanders, where the Dutch and English fought the Spaniards. When he returned to England in 1594, he became a playwright and actor.

Jonson was a temperamental man. He nearly was hanged after killing another actor in a duel, and he was jailed for insulting the Scottish nation. As he grew older, he calmed down considerably and became a father figure to London's literary circle. Jonson's followers, known as the Sons of Ben, formed England's first literary school. A favorite of the royal court, Jonson was named England's first poet laureate by King James I in 1616.

Unlike other poets of his time, such as his friend Shakespeare, Jonson was not meek about publicizing his poems and plays, and he personally oversaw their publication in *The Works of Benjamin Jonson.* The first English author to take such a bold step, Jonson gained respect in the literary community and paved the way for future authors to make a living.

Analyze Literature

Meter and Metaphor

Meter is a regular rhythmic pattern in poetry, which is determined by the number of beats, or stresses, in each line. Stressed and unstressed syllables are divided into rhythmical units called *feet.* (See the Literary Terms Handbook for a more detailed explanation of feet.)

A **metaphor** is a figure of speech in which one thing is spoken or written about as if it were another. It invites the reader to compare the writer's actual subject, the *tenor* of the metaphor, with something else to which the subject is likened, the *vehicle* of the metaphor.

Set Purpose

Like many lyric poems, "Song: To Celia" has a highly musical quality. Read it aloud several times to feel the rhythm, or meter, that helps create this quality. Identify the stressed and unstressed syllables, noting in which lines the meter changes. In addition, identify the metaphors Jonson creates in both poems. For each metaphor, determine the tenor and the vehicle.

Preview Vocabulary

wither, 275
lament, 276

Song: To Celia

Raw Sexual Attraction

by Ben Jonson

Intoxicating power of kiss

~ to drink to someone is to pledge them

Drink to me only with thine eyes,
  And I will pledge with mine;
Or leave a kiss but in the cup,
  And I'll not look for wine.

binds a vow — Don't need the wine, promise is in the gaze

5   The thirst that from the soul doth rise *desire/love*
  Doth ask a drink divine:
But might I of Jove's nectar[1] sup,
  I would not change[2] for thine.

would rather kiss her than become immortal

hyperbole

I sent thee late[3] a rosy wreath,
10 Not so much honoring thee,
As giving it a hope that there
  It could not <u>withered</u> be.
But thou thereon didst only breathe,
  And sent'st it back to me;
15 Since when it grows and smells, I swear,
  Not of itself, but thee. ❖

roses are a gift more importantly it is to favor her, roses will not wither with her presence

Gifting them back, now they smell like her

another compliment

she is more attractive than the roses

---

1. **Jove's nectar.** Jove is a Roman god, and nectar is the drink of the gods. *Jupiter, king of the Pantheon*
2. **change.** Exchange
3. **late.** Lately; recently

with • er (with´ ər) v., wilt and shrivel

What advice would you give the speaker in this poem: to continue pursuing his beloved or to give up?

On My First Son

by Ben Jonson

Farewell, thou child of my right hand,[1] and joy;
   My sin was too much hope of thee, loved boy.
Seven years thou wert lent to me, and I thee pay,[2]
   Exacted by thy fate, on the just day.[3]
5 O, could I lose all father now![4] For why
   Will man <u>lament</u> the state he should envy?
To have so soon 'scaped world's and flesh's rage,
   And, if no other misery, yet age?
Rest in soft peace, and, asked, say here doth lie
10 Ben Jonson his[5] best piece of poetry;
For whose sake, henceforth, all his vows be such,
   As what he loves may never like too much. ❖

---

1. **child of my right hand.** The literal translation of the Hebrew name Benjamin, which implies the meaning "dexterous" or "fortunate."
2. **I thee pay.** Pay thee back
3. **on the just day.** The word *just* could mean "exact" or "complete in amount." In Jonson's time, loans were made for a period of seven years. Jonson's son died on his seventh birthday, completing exactly seven years of life.
4. **could I lose all father now.** Give up thoughts of being a father
5. **Ben Jonson his.** Possessive *Ben Jonson's*

la • ment (lə ment´) *v.*, express sorrow, mourning, or regret

The Sick Child, c. 1820. Jean Augustin Franquelin.
(See detail on page 278).

MIRRORS & **W**INDOWS

Surviving a loved one is difficult, sometimes even devastating. What would be especially difficult about surviving your own child?

Musical Elegies

The term *elegy* originally referred to a verse form: a series of couplets in which a six-beat (*hexameter*) line was followed by a five-beat (*pentameter*) line. Greek poets created the elegy in the seventh century BCE, and Latin poets continued the form during the Roman Empire. Beginning in the sixteenth century, elegies began to reflect on life and often expressed regret or lament, as when someone died. Thus, the tone of sadness and theme of remembrance became the distinctive features of the elegy.

In the nineteenth and twentieth centuries, classical composers adopted the elegiac form and wrote music that reflected the somber attitude of earlier poets. Gabriel Fauré (1845–1924), Peter Tchaikovsky (1840–1893), and Igor Stravinsky (1882–1971) all wrote musical elegies. Stravinsky, a remarkably versatile Russian composer who emigrated to the United States, put to music an elegiac poem by W. H. Auden mourning the death of President John F. Kennedy in 1963.

Igor Stravinsky.

Contemporary musicians have continued the elegiac tradition, writing works in a number of musical styles. "Goodbye Pork Pie Hat," an elegy to jazz saxophonist and clarinetist Lester Young, who died in 1959, was perhaps the most-recorded piece of jazz bassist Charles Mingus (1922–1979). More recently, Jeff Beck, Eugene Chadbourne, and Bert Jansch and John Renbourn have recorded Mingus's piece. Canadian singer/songwriter Joni Mitchell wrote lyrics for a version of the song in 1978 on an album meant as an elegy to Mingus himself.

Jazz pianist and band leader Duke Ellington (1899–1974) wrote an elegy to his mother when she passed away. When Ellington died, trumpeter Miles Davis (1926–1991) recorded a thirty-minute elegy called "He Loved Him Madly."

Duke Ellington.

Refer to Text ▷ ▷ ▷ ▶ ▶   Reason with Text

Refer to Text	Reason with Text	
1a. In "On My First Son," what sin does Jonson say he has committed?	**1b.** What does Jonson seem to suggest about having expectations?	**Understand** Find meaning
2a. In the elegy, what state does Jonson say man should "envy," rather than "lament"?	**2b.** What does Jonson describe as the advantages of dying, particularly at a young age?	**Apply** Use information
3a. In "Song: To Celia," what does the speaker ask his beloved to leave in the cup?	**3b.** What does the speaker really want? If he had this, why would he not look for wine?	**Analyze** Take things apart
4a. What does the speaker in "Song: To Celia" give his beloved? What does she do with the gift?	**4b.** Argue whether Celia's response to the gift changes the speaker's feelings about pursuing the relationship.	**Evaluate** Make judgments
5a. What loss or disappointment is described by the speaker in each poem?	**5b.** Summarize the risks associated with loving someone.	**Create** Bring ideas together

Analyze Literature

Meter and Metaphor
Review the pattern of stressed and unstressed syllables you noted in reading "Song: To Celia." What types of meter are used? How does the meter emphasize the emotions the speaker conveys in the poem?

What metaphors did you find in each poem? In each case, what is the tenor and what is the vehicle? Evaluate the effectiveness of each metaphor in creating meaning.

Extend the Text

Writing Options
Creative Writing Rejuvenation, or rebirth, is a common theme in Renaissance poetry, often symbolized by images of spring. The musical quality of the lyric enhances these images. Write a lyric poem about rejuvenation. Try mirroring the meter used in the first stanza of "Song: To Celia."

Expository Writing Write two paragraphs comparing and contrasting the speaker in "Song: To Celia" with that in "On My First Son." What loss or disappointment has each speaker experienced? What attitude does each speaker have toward this experience? How are their experiences similar and different?

Critical Literacy
Research Musical Elegies Using the Music Connection box on page 277 as a starting point, conduct library or Internet research to learn more about musical elegies and their composers. With a group of three or four classmates, locate and listen to recordings of two or three musical elegies. Critique each one, discussing about whom the elegy was written and evaluating whether the music and words (if applicable) effectively mourn him or her.

Lifelong Learning
Deliver an Oral Interpretation Choose another poem by Ben Jonson or by one of the Sons of Ben, and prepare an oral reading to convey your interpretation of it. Think about delivery issues such as tone, pace, and diction as you prepare your interpretation. Begin your presentation with a brief introduction to the poem.

 Go to **www.mirrorsandwindows.com** for more.

 JACK AND JOAN

by Thomas Campion

Thomas Campion
(1567–1620) was known primarily as a poet, but he also was a composer, theorist, physician, and law student. His first poems were published in 1591 in an edition of Sir Philip Sidney's *Astrophil and Stella.*

Eleven years later, Campion set forth a set of rules for writing poetry in a treatise entitled *Observations in the Art of English Poesie* (1602).

Interestingly, Campion broke many of the rules he proposed, including one that argued against the use of rhyme, which he described as "vulgar and unartificial." In addition to writing poetry, Campion also wrote a book on music theory and a series of *masques,* short allegorical dramas performed by masked actors, many of which were performed for King James I.

"Jack and Joan" is an *air,* or lyric poem with a musical quality. It first appeared in the second of the four books of *A Booke of Ayres to be Sung to the Lute, Orpherian and Bass Viol* (1601).

Jack and Joan they think no ill,
But loving live, and merry still;
Do their week-days' work, and pray
Devoutly on the holy day;
5   Skip and trip it on the green,
And help to choose the summer queen;
Lash out, at a country feast,
Their silver penny with the best.

Well can they judge of nappy ale,[1]
10 And tell at large a winter tale;
Climb up to the apple loft
And turn the crabs till they be soft.
Tib is all the father's joy,
And little Tom the mother's boy.
15 All their pleasure is content;
And care, to pay their yearly rent.

Joan can call by name her cows
And deck her windows with green boughs;
She can wreaths and tutties[2] make,
20 And trim with plums a bridal cake.
Jack knows what brings gain or loss,
And his long flail[3] can stoutly toss,
Makes the hedge, which others break,
And ever thinks what he doth speak.

25 Now, you courtly dames and knights,
That study only strange delights,
Though you scorn the home-spun gray
And revel in your rich array,

---

1. **nappy ale.** Strong ale drink
2. **tutties.** Small bouquets of flowers
3. **flail.** Device for thrashing grain

Though your tongues dissemble deep
30 And can your heads from danger keep,
    Yet, for all your pomp and train,
    Securer lives the silly swain. ❖

The Village Fete, c. 1870. Jean Charles Meissonier.

The characters Jack and Joan live a simple but happy life. Is simplicity the key to living a happy life? Does it take a certain type of person to appreciate the simple life?

Refer and Reason

1. Describe the title characters. What are their joys in life?

2. What is the speaker's attitude toward Jack and Joan? Given this, how would you describe the overall tone of this poem?

3. Identify whom the speaker addresses in the last stanza. How are these people described? Do you agree that "securer lives the silly swain"? Why or why not?

Writing Options

1. Taking the point of view of either Jack or Joan, write a poem in response to Campion's that states whether the speaker romanticized their lives or portrayed them accurately. Consider how Jack or Joan may feel about the "dames and knights" who are mentioned.

2. Write a paragraph that explains how "Jack and Joan" is representative of pastoral poetry, which depicts the lives of shepherds or rural life in general and often draws a comparison between the innocence and serenity of the country and the misery and corruption of the city. Present your explanation to the class.

Go to **www.mirrorsandwindows.com** for more.

PART 2

Mind, Body, and Spirit

The Renaissance sparked new interest in learning and perfecting oneself and one's world. Renaissance scholars expressed their ideas in prose, some writing in Latin and some in English.

Three prose works are particularly significant. Sir Thomas More's *Utopia* (1515–1516) suggested what society might be like if organized anew on different principles. Sir Francis Bacon's *Novum Organum* (1620) proposed the use of inductive reasoning in scientific analysis. Bacon, England's first true essayist, wrote a number of works intended to improve people's lives by sharpening their minds. By far the greatest prose work of the period, however, was the King James Bible, a translation into English of the Hebrew and Greek scriptures. Before this time, only scholars and clergy had been able to read the Bible, but now, anyone in the English-speaking world who could read could examine the work independently.

Access to the Bible awakened spiritual contemplation that found expression in both poetry and prose. The writing of John Donne epitomizes this new period of personal reflection. Donne, George Herbert, and Andrew Marvell are among a group of writers called the **Metaphysical poets.** These authors did not comprise a literary movement during their day. In fact, the label *metaphysical* was assigned to them as a criticism by Dr. Samuel Johnson in 1744, who thought their work lacked feeling. Regardless, the writing of the Metaphysical poets shares several qualities: the use of conceits, complex imagery, intellectual wit, and rational examination. The work of the Metaphysicals was rediscovered in the twentieth century and influenced poets such as T. S. Eliot. (See Unit 5 for discussions of Marvell and Johnson and Unit 8 for a discussion of Eliot.)

Sistine Madonna [detail], c. 1512–1514.
Raphael Sanzio. Gemäldegalerie Alte Meister, Dresden, Germany.

Thou preparest a table before me in the presence of mine enemies: thou <u>anointest</u> my head with oil; my cup runneth over.

Surely goodness and mercy shall follow me all the days of my life: and I will dwell in the house of the Lord for ever. ❖

anoint (ə noint´) v., apply oil as a sacred rite; choose as if by divine election

The first line of Psalm 23 is one of the most often quoted lines from the Bible. How might having religious or spiritual beliefs give people security and comfort, particularly in difficult times?

CULTURAL CONNECTION

The Story of David and Goliath

The psalms in the Old Testament of the Bible supposedly were written by King David of Israel, who ruled between 1010 and 970 BCE. Much of what is known today about King David comes from other texts in the Old Testament, including the books of Samuel I and II, Kings I, and Chronicles I. One of the most famous stories in the Bible is that of David and Goliath, which appears in Samuel I.

As the story is told, during a war between the Philistines and the Israelites, David was summoned by King Saul to the battlefield to play music. At the time, the Israelites were being taunted by an oversized Philistine named Goliath, who had gained notoriety for being a fearsome warrior. Goliath dared the Israelites to send their strongest soldier to fight him in a one-on-one battle, but no one seemed willing to volunteer. When David saw that none of the soldiers had stepped forward, he convinced Saul that he could take on Goliath. Too small to carry Saul's armor, David went into battle with only his sling, some pebbles, and his staff.

When David appeared before the monstrous man, Goliath was amused to see such a small warrior and mocked him. David responded by taking a stone out of his bag and slinging it at Goliath. The stone struck the giant's forehead, and he fell unconscious. David then took Goliath's sword and cut off his head. When the Philistines saw Goliath fall, they fled from Judah.

This same story of David and Goliath appears in the Qur'an, the central text of Islam, and this account differs only slightly from that provided in the Torah, the central text of Judaism.

The Prodigal[1] Son

from The King James Bible

Return of the Prodigal Son, c. 1668–1669.
Rembrandt Harmenszoon van Rijn.
The Hermitage Museum, St. Petersburg, Russia.

Self-Portrait as F...
Rembrandt van Rij...
Amsterdam, The Ne...

Father, I have sinned against heaven, and in thy sight and am no more worthy to be called thy son.

T hen drew near unto him all the publicans[2] and sinners for to hear him.

And the Pharisees[3] and scribes murmured, saying, This man receiveth sinners, and eateth with them.

And he spake this parable unto them, saying,

What man of you, having an hundred sheep, if he lose one of them, doth not leave the ninety and nine in the wilderness, and go after that which is lost, until he find it?

And when he hath found it, he layeth it on his shoulders, rejoicing.

And when he cometh home, he calleth together his friends and neighbors, saying unto them, Rejoice with me; for I have found my sheep which was lost.

I say unto you, that likewise joy shall be in heaven over one sinner that repenteth,[4] more than over ninety and nine just persons, which need no repentance.

Either what woman having ten pieces of silver, if she lose one piece, doth not light a candle and sweep the house, and seek <u>diligently</u> till she find it?

And when she hath found it, she calleth her friends and her neighbors together, saying, Rejoice with me for I have found the piece which I had lost.

Likewise, I say unto you, there is joy in the presence of the angels of God over one sinner that repenteth.

And he said, A certain man had two sons:

And the younger of them said to his father, Father, give me the portion of goods that falleth to me. And he divided unto them his living.

But the fat...
forth the best ...
a ring on his h...

And bring ...
and let us eat, ...

For this my...
again; he was l...
began to be me...

Now his el...
he came and dr...
music and danc...

---

1. **Prodigal.** Reckless in spending money
2. **publicans.** Tax collectors in ancient Judea
3. **Pharisees.** Members of an ancient Jewish sect known for strictly observing Old Testament law
4. **repenteth.** Repents; feels sorry for having done something wrong

dil • i • gent • ly (di´ lə jənt lē) *adv.*, carefully and steadily

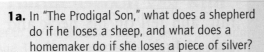

Refer to Text ▶ ▶ ▶ ▶ ▶	Reason with Text	
1a. In "The Prodigal Son," what does a shepherd do if he loses a sheep, and what does a homemaker do if she loses a piece of silver?	**1b.** How do these examples of the shepherd and homemaker introduce the story of the prodigal son?	**Understand** Find meaning
2a. List the different comforts God gives to the narrator of Psalm 23.	**2b.** Why does the narrator find comfort in these things?	**Apply** Use information
3a. In Psalm 23, God is described as a shepherd. How is God described in the parable?	**3b.** Compare and contrast the Lord in Psalm 23 and the father in "The Prodigal Son."	**Analyze** Take things apart
4a. Identify the primary qualities of each son and the nature of his relationship with the father.	**4b.** Does the father treat both sons fairly? Explain.	**Evaluate** Make judgments
5a. What lesson does "The Prodigal Son" teach?	**5b.** List situations in which a parable might be a good way to make a point.	**Create** Bring ideas together

Analyze Literature

Purpose and Imagery

For what purpose or purposes was Psalm 23 likely written? What about the parable? What purposes might religious texts typically have? Why?

Review your list of images for each selection. Which images are created using figurative language versus literal language? What function do these images serve in each selection? How do they support the purpose of the selection?

Extend the Text

Writing Options

Creative Writing Write a letter offering advice to a young child who is afraid of the dark. Suggest what he or she can do to relieve feelings of fear and find comfort.

Persuasive Writing You are running for student council president and need to state your position on whether to have an open campus, allowing students to leave school during lunch breaks and study times. Write a persuasive speech on this topic using a parable to make your point. Practice your speech in front of a group of classmates to obtain their feedback. Have them evaluate the persuasiveness of your content, evidence, rhetorical devices, and delivery (good eye contact, appropriate intonation, and purposeful gestures).

Collaborative Learning

Conduct a Survey Ask these questions of ten or so classmates: What kinds of things are they afraid of? What do they do when they are afraid? What gives them comfort and strength in times of uncertainty? Review the respondents' answers to look for similarities and differences. Write a one-page summary of your findings.

Critical Literacy

Give and Follow Oral Instructions As a group, create a reader's theater production of "The Prodigal Son." Divide the story into several scenes, and assign a scene to each person in the group. Decide how you want the actors to move during your scene. As a group, take turns acting out all the scenes. When you are directing your scene, give oral instructions about how you want the actors to move. When you are acting in someone else's scene, follow the director's instructions and monitor your understanding by asking questions if you need clarification. Then perform the complete story for the class.

 Go to **www.mirrorsandwindows.com** for more.

Of Studies
An Essay by Sir Francis Bacon

Build Background

Literary Context The root meaning of the word *essay* is "trial" or "attempt." Sir Francis Bacon was the first Englishman to use this word to describe a short piece of writing and was instrumental in popularizing the essay form. He borrowed the word from the French writer Montaigne, whose essays were mainly about himself.

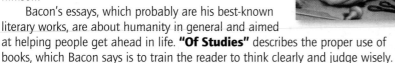

Bacon's essays, which probably are his best-known literary works, are about humanity in general and aimed at helping people get ahead in life. **"Of Studies"** describes the proper use of books, which Bacon says is to train the reader to think clearly and judge wisely.

Reader's Context How do you use books in your life? What do you read and why?

Meet the Author

Sir Francis Bacon (1561–1626) was a true Renaissance man, someone who had many interests and was an expert in several areas. He was an English philosopher, essayist, statesman, and, some say, dramatist. He was known as a great thinker whose life aim was to make the world a better place.

Born in London, Bacon was educated at Trinity College, Cambridge, and at Gray's Inn. His father was Nicholas Bacon, Lord Chancellor of England and Lord Keeper of the Great Seal, an office that Sir Francis eventually would hold. He began his adult career in law and eventually rose to the ranks of British nobility and government, serving in the House of Lords. He became quite wealthy but also was said to be in debt often because of his extravagant lifestyle.

In 1621, when Bacon was sixty years old, he was accused and found guilty of accepting bribes as lord chancellor, which ended his career as a public servant. He spent the last five years of his life thinking and writing. His work covered a broad spectrum of subjects: botany, political science, biology, physics, economics, music, architecture, constitutional law, industrial development, philosophy, mythology, religious thought, astronomy, chemistry, landscape gardening, and literature. At the end of his life, he immersed himself in the study of science. In fact, just before he died, he conducted an experiment to see if freezing a dead chicken in the snow would preserve it. In the course of the experiment, Bacon was overcome from exposure, and he died a short time later.

Analyze Literature

Thesis and Simile
A **thesis** is the main idea supported in a work of nonfiction.

A **simile** is a comparison of two dissimilar things that uses the word *like* or *as*—for example, "My heart is like a singing bird."

Set Purpose

An essay presents a main (controlling) idea, or thesis, about a particular topic and then supports, or proves, it. Identify Bacon's thesis, and write down three pieces of information he provides to support it. Then analyze the consistency and clarity of his expression of the controlling idea. Extend your analysis by writing down the similes Bacon uses. What comparisons does he make, and how do they support his thesis?

Preview Vocabulary

ornament, 290
discourse, 290
marshal, 290
sloth, 290
affectation, 290
diligence, 290
conference, 291
witty, 291
impediment, 291
wrought, 291

Could have taken blame for someone else

Of Studies

by Sir Francis Bacon

Portrait of Nicolas Kratzer [detail], 1528. Hans Holbein. The Louvre, Paris, France. (See detail on page 289.)

Reading maketh a full man.

*[handwritten margin notes: audience—young men wishing to go into politics, all advice geared to this; there are things for free time separate from work; parallelism + ellipsis; *for politicians?; like learning to drive; The use will eventually come to you. How to let it soak]*

Studies serve for delight, for <u>ornament</u>, and for ability. Their chief use for delight, is in privateness and retiring;[1] for ornament, is in <u>discourse</u>; and for ability, is in the judgment, and disposition[2] of business. For expert men can execute, and perhaps judge of particulars, one by one; but the general counsels, and the plots and <u>marshalling</u> of affairs, come best, from those that are learned. To spend too much time in studies is <u>sloth</u>; to use them too much for ornament, is <u>affectation</u>; to make judgment wholly by their rules, is the humor[3] of a scholar. They perfect nature, and are perfected by experience: for natural abilities are like natural plants, that need proyning,[4] by study; and studies themselves, do give forth directions too much at large, except they be bounded in by experience.

Crafty men contemn[5] studies, simple men admire them, and wise men use them; for they teach not their own use; but that is a wisdom without them, and above them, won by observation. Read not to contradict and confute;[6] nor to believe and take for granted; nor to find talk and discourse; but to weigh and consider.

Some books are to be tasted, others to be swallowed, and some few to be chewed and digested; that is, some books are to be read only in parts; others to be read, but not curiously;[7] and some few to be read wholly, and with <u>diligence</u> and attention. Some books also may be read by deputy, and extracts made of them by others;[8] but that would be only in the less important arguments, and the meaner[9] sort of books, else distilled books are like common distilled waters,[10] flashy[11] things.

---

1. **privateness and retiring.** Privacy and leisure
2. **disposition.** Administration; settlement
3. **humor.** Whim
4. **proyning.** Pruning; cultivating
5. **contemn.** Condemn; despise
6. **confute.** Refute; argue against
7. **curiously.** Carefully
8. **read by deputy, and extracts made of them.** Read and summarized by or reported on someone else
9. **meaner.** Average
10. **common distilled waters.** Homemade concoctions
11. **flashy.** Empty; flat

---

or • na • ment (ôr´ nə mənt) *n.*, something that lends grace or beauty
dis • course (dis´ kôrs) *n.*, conversation
mar • shal (mär´ shəl) *v.*, take form or order
sloth (slôth) *n.*, laziness
af • fec • ta • tion (a' fek tā´ shən) *n.*, artificial behavior designed to impress others
di • li • gence (di´ lə jənts) *n.*, care

The Debate Over Authorship

William Shakespeare generally is acknowledged to be the foremost dramatist in English literature. Still, literary scholars debate whether he actually wrote all the plays attributed to him. After all, he lacked education, social standing, and experience with the aristocracy and the world.

Who was the true author of Shakespeare's plays? Some scholars suggest it was Sir Francis Bacon. They point to similar phrases in both Shakespeare's plays and Bacon's essays and correspondence, to Bacon's well-rounded education, and to comments made by Renaissance poets Joseph Hall and John Marston that Bacon was the writer of Shakespeare's plays.

Scholars who dispute this theory argue that similarities in phrases suggest only that Bacon and Shakespeare were contemporaries; borrowing and refashioning material from other sources was common among Renaissance writers. And while Shakespeare had only a grammar school education, he would have been exposed to a variety of classical sources and had the skills and knowledge needed to write the plays. Finally, comments from Renaissance playwrights—including Ben Jonson, Robert Greene, and Shakespeare's editors, John Heminge and Henry Condell—suggest that it was Shakespeare who authored the plays.

SHAKESPEARE

Reading maketh a full man; <u>conference</u> a ready man; and writing an exact man. And therefore, if a man write little, he had need have a great memory; if he confer little, he had need have a present wit:[12] and if he read little, he had need have much cunning, to seem to know, that[13] he doth not. Histories make men wise; poets <u>witty</u>; the mathematics subtile; natural philosophy deep; moral grave; logic and rhetoric able to contend. *Abeunt studia in mores.*[14] Nay, there is no stond[15] or <u>impediment</u> in the wit, but may be <u>wrought</u> out by fit studies; like as diseases of the body, may have appropriate exercises. Bowling is good for the stone and reins;[16] shooting for the lungs and breast; gentle walking for the stomach; riding for the head; and the like.

So if a man's wit be wandering, let him study the mathematics; for in demonstrations, if his wit be called away never so little, he must begin again. If his wit be not apt to distinguish or find differences, let him study the Schoolmen;[17] for they are *cymini sectores.*[18] If he be not apt to beat over[19] matters, and to call up one thing to prove and illustrate another, let him study the lawyers' cases. So every defect of the mind, may have a special receipt.[20] ❖

---

12. **present wit.** Ability to think fast
13. **that.** That which
14. ***Abeunt studia in mores*** [Latin]. "Studies develop into habits"
15. **stond.** Stoppage
16. **stone and reins.** Gall bladder or testicles and kidneys
17. **Schoolmen.** Medieval philosophers
18. ***cymini sectores*** [Latin]. "Hairsplitters," or, literally, "dividers of cumin seed"
19. **beat over.** Discuss at length
20. **receipt.** Remedy

---

con • fer • ence (kän′ fər ənts) *n.,* conversation, discussion
wit • ty (wi′ tē) *adj.,* imaginative; clever
im • ped • i •ment (im pe′ də mənt) *n.,* obstruction; hindrance
wrought (rôt) *adj.,* worked

MIRRORS & WINDOWS

Bacon suggests that knowledge must be balanced with experience. What are the drawbacks of knowing about something but never having experienced it? What have you read or heard about that you would like to do?

Refer to Text ▶ ▶ ▶ ▶ ▶ **Reason with Text**

1a. To spend too much time studying is what, according to Bacon?	**1b.** What does he mean by this statement?	**Understand** Find meaning
2a. What three purposes do studies serve?	**2b.** Give examples of when you have read or studied for these purposes.	**Apply** Use information
3a. What are the different effects of studying history, poetry, and mathematics?	**3b.** Identify the analogy Bacon uses to illustrate how studying different topics affects a person differently. How does the relationship between the words in the analogy help you determine the meanings of the words?	**Analyze** Take things apart
4a. What should someone do if his or her "wit be wandering"?	**4b.** Bacon claims there is a "receipt" for "every defect of the mind." Analyze the context to determine the nuanced meaning of the word *receipt*. Do you agree? Why or why not?	**Evaluate** Make judgments
5a. What words does Bacon use to describe reading certain books?	**5b.** In what other ways can books be read? For what kind of book would each be appropriate?	**Create** Bring ideas together

Analyze Literature

Thesis and Simile

What is Bacon's thesis, and what information does he provide to support it? How does the placement of the thesis affect the development of Bacon's essay? How does it affect your ability to understand the point he is making?

What similes did you find in the essay? How appropriate are they to the subject of reading and studies? Are they effective in proving Bacon's thesis to readers? Why or why not?

Extend the Text

Writing Options

Creative Writing Toward the end of the essay, Bacon recommends doing specific exercises to cure diseases of various parts of the body. For example, he says gentle walking is good for the stomach and riding is good for the head. Make a list of axioms, or well-established principles, people follow today to remedy physical problems.

Persuasive Writing Bacon suggests that positions of leadership and authority should be filled by educated people. Does someone have to be well educated to be successful today? Develop a thesis stating your response, and support it with evidence in a persuasive essay.

Lifelong Learning

Write a How-to Guide As Bacon notes, there are different ways to approach reading and studying. Write a how-to guide on effective ways to study. Include creative ways to tackle difficult subjects and sharpen study skills in general. Test the effectiveness of the lessons by following the directions after one of your classmates reads his or her lesson. Suggest improvements as needed.

Critical Literacy

Research the Author The label *Renaissance man* still is used today to describe someone with wide-ranging skills and interests. Sir Francis Bacon may have been the original Renaissance man, given his many areas of knowledge and achievement. Conduct research to learn more about Bacon. Then write his *curriculum vitae,* or *CV,* which is similar to a résumé but longer and more detailed in terms of providing background information. European employers commonly request a CV from a job applicant, whereas American employers commonly request a résumé.

 Go to **www.mirrorsandwindows.com** for more.

Understand the Concept

A **paragraph** is a group of related sentences that develop one main idea. A paragraph can have any of several purposes: to narrate, to describe, to persuade, or to inform. In any case, an effective paragraph has two key characteristics: unity and a logical method of organization.

Most effective paragraphs have a **main idea,** a point that is developed with **supporting details,** such as examples, details, facts, and quotations. The main idea is often stated directly at the beginning of the paragraph in a **topic sentence,** which is followed by several supporting sentences.

Look at the following paragraph from Sir Francis Bacon's "Of Studies." The main idea of the paragraph is stated in the first sentence:

> Studies serve for delight, for ornament, and for ability. Their chief use for delight, is in privateness and retiring; for ornament, is in discourse; and for ability, is in the judgment, and disposition of business. For expert men can execute, and perhaps judge of particulars, one by one; but the general counsels, and the plots and marshalling of affairs, come best, from those that are learned. To spend too much time in studies is sloth; to use them too much for ornament, is affectation; to make judgment wholly by their rules, is the humor of a scholar. . . .

Note how the other sentences in the paragraph support the topic sentence, examining the various types and purposes of studies. All the sentences work together to create a unified paragraph.

The topic sentence does not always come first in a paragraph, however. Sometimes the supporting sentences come first and lead up to the topic sentence, which is stated at the end.

Apply the Skill

Identify the Main Idea and Topic Sentence

Read the last paragraph from Bacon's "Of Studies." Identify the main idea of the paragraph and where it is stated in a topic sentence.

> So if a man's wit be wandering, let him study the mathematics; for in demonstrations, if his wit be called away never so little, he must begin again. If his wit be not apt to distinguish or find differences, let him study the School-men; for they are *cymini sectores.* If he be not apt to beat over matters, and to call up one thing to prove and illustrate another, let him study the lawyers' cases. So every defect of the mind, may have a special receipt.

Revise a Paragraph to Improve Unity

Revise the following paragraph, rearranging the numbered sentences to improve organization and unity. (The first sentence is the topic sentence and should remain in that position.) After you have decided the order of the sentences, edit the paragraph to eliminate repetition, replacing *Bacon* with pronouns such as *he* and *his.*

> Sir Francis Bacon had many interests and was an expert in several areas. (1) At age sixty, Bacon's career as a public servant came to an end when he was accused and found guilty of accepting bribes. (2) As a young man, Bacon began a career in law and eventually rose to the ranks of British nobility and government. (3) Just before Bacon died, he conducted an experiment to see if freezing a dead chicken in the snow would preserve it. (4) Bacon's success brought great wealth, but he often was in debt because of his extravagant lifestyle. (5) During the experiment, Bacon was overcome from exposure, and he died a short time later. (6) Bacon spent the last five years of his life thinking and writing about a broad range of subjects, from botany to political science to music to literature.

Write a Unified Paragraph

For the following topic sentence, write four supporting sentences to create a short paragraph. Each supporting sentence should develop the main idea stated in the topic sentence, and all the sentences should be related.

> High school graduates should be required to perform one year of public service for the U.S. government, such as serving in the military or working for the Peace Corps.

John Donne

> *"No man is an island, entire of itself; every man is a piece of the continent, a part of the main."*

John Donne (1572–1631) was born into a prosperous Roman Catholic family at a time when anti-Catholic sentiment was widespread in England. His father, a well-to-do merchant, died when Donne was just four, leaving his mother, Elizabeth, to raise him and his two siblings. Donne's mother was the daughter of playwright John Heywood and a distant relative of Sir Thomas More.

Educated as a youth by Jesuits (scholarly Catholic priests), Donne went on to study at Oxford and Cambridge Universities. He never received a degree, however, because he refused to take an oath that recognized Queen Elizabeth I as supreme head of the Church of England. At the time, Catholics still held the Pope as the supreme head of the Church. Donne went on to study law and appeared destined for a career in the legal or diplomatic field.

In his twenties, Donne lived extravagantly on a generous inheritance from his father. At age twenty-six, he was appointed secretary to a high official in the court of Queen Elizabeth I. Three years later, however, Donne was fired from that position and imprisoned after secretly marrying seventeen-year-old Anne More in opposition to her powerful father. After that, Donne struggled to support his growing family.

Donne could not receive a post or preferment from the king unless he took Anglican orders.

To publicly renounce his Catholic faith, he published two anti-Catholic polemics, *Pseudo-Martyr* (in 1610) and *Ignatius His Conclave* (in 1611). In 1614, he converted to Anglicanism, and the next year, he entered the ministry and became an Anglican priest. With his deep learning, dramatic wit, and metaphorical style, Donne at once established himself as a great preacher. He was appointed dean of St. Paul's Cathedral in 1621, a position that made him one of the most influential ministers in England.

Rather than teach basic rules of morality in his sermons, Donne preferred to probe the depths of human spiritual yearnings. No one could better convey a sense of drama and direct personal experience when preaching about topics such as entering heaven. Donne's private devotions were published in 1624, but his collected poems were not published until 1633, two years after his death. Donne's poetic style influenced other Metaphysical poets, including George Herbert and Andrew Marvell, as well as twentieth-century poets such as T. S. Eliot.

Noted Works

Devotions Upon Emergent Occasions (1624)

"Love's Alchemy" (1633)

"A Valediction: Forbidding Mourning" (1633)

"Satire III, Religion" (1633)

Holy Sonnets (1633)

A Valediction: Forbidding Mourning

A Lyric Poem by John Donne

"Death, be not proud" (Holy Sonnet 10)

A Sonnet by John Donne

Build Background

Literary Context John Donne once described himself as a dual character: Jack Donne, the writer of ironic, worldly verse, and Dr. Donne, the writer of fervent religious poems. Whatever his character, Donne, in the intensely personal and immediate tone of his poetry, made a keen break from the decorative style of most Elizabethan verse. Often considered the father of the Metaphysical poets, he is noted for employing conceits that shift restlessly and dramatically between a personal and a cosmic view, probing readers to think deeply and philosophically.

Donne wrote **"A Valediction: Forbidding Mourning"** to his wife before leaving on a long trip in 1612. It addresses the subject of true love but has a subtle religious theme. The intermingled bodies and souls of the two lovers represent the religious concept of an individual's body and soul. In one of the poem's conceits, Donne likens his connection to his wife to that of the legs on a compass: As he travels, like the outer leg of a compass that draws the circle, his soul remains fixed in one place—with his wife who stays at home, like the center leg of a compass.

"Death, be not proud," or **Holy Sonnet 10** (1633), is among the most famous of Donne's later religious poems. As one of a collection of nineteen Holy Sonnets, this poem follows the conventions of the sonnet structure in terms of rhyme and meter. It breaks with tradition, however, in its bold use of paradox and unexpected use of a traditional form. Holy Sonnet 10 also reflects Donne's refusal to accept conventional ideas about death.

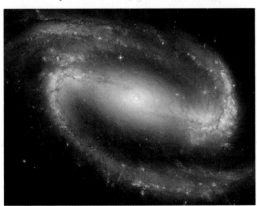

Reader's Context What are your ideas about death? Do you think of it as "mighty and dreadful," the conventional view Donne challenges in Holy Sonnet 10? Explain.

Analyze Literature

Conceit and Paradox A **conceit** is an elaborate or unusual comparison of two things. The use of conceits is characteristic of Renaissance poetry and particularly that of the Metaphysical poets.

[handwritten: does not have to be elaborate, tends to be a bit unusual, metaphysical conceits very strange]

A **paradox** is a seemingly contradictory statement, idea, or event that actually may be true.

Set Purpose

In Donne's roles as preacher and poet, he challenged others to examine old ideas in a new light, as he did. In his poems, Donne often used conceits and paradoxes to present information in unique ways. As you read "A Valediction: Forbidding Mourning," identify the conceit and determine what two things are being compared. As you read Holy Sonnet 10, look for two instances of paradox and note what seems contradictory in each one.

Preview Vocabulary

virtuous, 296
breach, 297
obliquely, 297

A Valediction:[1]
Forbidding Mourning

by John Donne

[handwritten: peacefully, quietly]

As <u>virtuous</u> men pass <u>mildly away</u>,   *[handwritten: A christian death   not]*
  And whisper to their souls to go,   *[handwritten: no commotion   troubling]*
Whilst some of their sad friends do say   *[handwritten: remeet at 2nd   at n))]*
  The breath goes now, and some say, no: *[handwritten: coming]*
[handwritten: not breaking   like ice melting]

[left margin handwritten: Simile started w/ "as"]

5 So let us melt, and make no noise,   *[handwritten: So, let's say goodbye]*
  No tear-floods, nor sigh-tempests move,   *[handwritten: w/out commotion]*
'Twere profanation[2] of our joys   *[handwritten: should not make a scene]*
  To tell the laity[3] our love.

[left margin handwritten: about movement → not terror]

Moving of th' earth[4] brings harms and fears,
  Men reckon what it did and meant,
10 But trepidation of the spheres,[5]
  Though greater far, is innocent.[6]

---

1. **Valediction.** ~~Act of farewell~~ *a farewell speech forbidding mourning*
2. **profanation.** Lack of reverence
3. **laity.** Layperson; someone unable to understand the "religion" of true love *every layperson*
4. **moving of th' earth.** Earthquake
5. **trepidation of the spheres.** Irregular movements of heavenly bodies
6. **innocent.** Unobserved and harmless compared to earthquakes

> **vir • tu • ous** (vər´ chə wəs) *adj.*, morally excellent; righteous

[left margin handwritten: A seperation that is not a breakup "Goodbye, I will be back" — Little bit of Autobiography of Donne in his poetry]

[handwritten top margin: inside heavenly sphere than contains moon, mortal]

[handwritten left margin: Some relationships (sensuality, physicality) can not last w/ separation]

[handwritten right margin: look at last p. in poetry packet]

Dull sublunary[7] lovers' love
    (Whose soul is sense[8]) cannot admit
15 Absence, because it doth remove
    Those things which elemented[9] it.

But we by a love, so much refined,
    That ourselves know not what it is,
Inter-assuréd of the mind,
20   Care less, eyes, lips, and hands to miss.

Our two souls therefore, which are one,
    Though I must go, endure not yet
A breach, but an expansion,
    Like gold to airy thinness beat.

[handwritten right margin: This relationship is not breaking, but expanding, like gold pure, valuable]

25 If they be two, they are two so
    As stiff twin compasses are two;
Thy soul, the fixed foot, makes no show
    To move, but doth, if th' other do.

[handwritten: 1 thing   perfect imagery]

And though it in the center sit,
30   Yet when the other far doth roam,
It leans and hearkens after it,
    And grows erect, as that comes home.

Such wilt thou be to me, who must
    Like th' other foot, obliquely run;
35 Thy firmness[10] makes my circle just,[11]
    And makes me end where I begun. ❖

[handwritten right margin: no cheating, will come back to her]

---

7. **sublunary.** "Sub lunar," or under the moon and thus
    subject to change
8. **soul is sense.** Essence or being is physical, not spiritual
9. **elemented.** Comprised
10. **firmness.** Fidelity
11. **just.** Complete; perfect

> **breach** (brēch) *n.,* break in an accustomed friendly
> relationship
> **oblique • ly** (ō blēk´ lē) *adv.,* moving off course

MIRRORS & WINDOWS

The word *valediction* often is associated with graduations and other occasions in which people leave one stage of life and move on to another. Do you find such occasions sad, exciting, or some mixture of the two?

The Last Look of John Donne, 1940. Marsden Hartley.
Brooklyn Museum, Brooklyn, New York.

(Holy Sonnet 10)

by John Donne

Death, be not proud, though some have callèd[1] thee
Mighty and dreadful, for thou art not so;
For those whom thou think'st thou dost[2] overthrow
Die not, poor Death, nor yet canst thou kill me.
5　From rest and sleep, which but thy pictures be,
Much pleasure; then from thee much more must flow,
And soonest our best men with thee do go,
Rest of their bones, and soul's delivery.
Thou art slave to fate, chance, kings, and desperate men,
10　And dost with poison, war, and sickness dwell,
And poppy or charms can make us sleep as well
And better than thy stroke; why swell'st thou then?[3]
One short sleep past, we wake eternally
And death shall be no more; Death, thou shalt die. ❖

---

1. **callèd.** The accent on the *e* makes the *-ed* a separate syllable: *call • ed.*
2. **dost.** Does
3. **why swell'st thou then?** Why do you puff up with pride?

MIRRORS & WINDOWS

Many religions provide for some kind of afterlife or spiritual existence after death. How might believing in an afterlife make the prospect of death more comforting?

ART CONNECTION

Marsden Hartley

Marsden Hartley (1877–1943) was born in Lewiston, Maine. He left home at age fifteen to attend the Cleveland Art Institute, and in his early twenties, he moved to New York City to attend the National Academy of Design. In New York, he associated with some of the leading writers and artists of the early twentieth century and soon established himself as one of the United States' foremost painters.

Hartley participated in two artistic movements during his life. He began as a *Regionalist* painter, portraying the common people and settings of his native Maine. Then as a young man, he embraced *Modernism,* a movement that abandoned traditional forms and explored new, often abstract modes of expression. He later returned to his Regionalist roots, painting rugged landscapes.

Hartley also created a series of abstract self-portraits in the Modernist style, along with portraits of several of his own personal heroes. One of those heroes was John Donne, whose portrait appears on page 298. Entitled *The Last Look of John Donne,* the painting is a reproduction of a portrait Donne commissioned late in his life. It depicts the poet in a burial shroud, as he envisioned he would look when meeting God upon his death.

Critical Viewing Art critics have described Hartley's portraits, including this one of Donne, as "brooding," "primitive," and "stark." How would you describe Donne's portrait? What does Hartley's portrayal of the poet suggest about him? How does the portrait relate to the theme of death often associated with Donne's poetry?

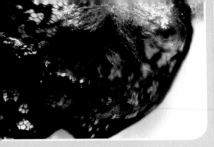

Literature Connection

An *explication* analyzes the meanings and relationships of the words, images, and literary techniques used in a literary work. The word *explicate* is derived from the Latin and means, literally, "to unfold." The further you unfold the layers of meaning in a poem, the more you will expand your ability to think analytically, intuitively, and expansively.

Anniina Jokinen's **"A Quick and Rough Explication of Donne's 'Holy Sonnet 10: Death, Be Not Proud'"** takes apart John Donne's poem, which Jokinen says "is really not such a tough nut to crack." A writer, editor, translator, actor, and poet, Jokinen is originally from Finland but now lives in Pennsylvania, where she also maintains a number of web-sites devoted to the study of Renaissance literature.

A Quick and Rough Explication of Donne's "Holy Sonnet 10: Death, Be Not Proud"

by Anniina Jokinen

"Death, be not proud, though some have
  called thee
Mighty and dreadful, for thou art not so;"

Simple. Donne is anthropomorphizing[1] Death, and addressing him as an equal, or indeed, as it becomes apparent later, as an inferior. Donne is saying that Death likes to think of himself as powerful and terrifying, and indeed some people have called him that, but he is not so in truth. In the next lines Donne explains why.

"For those, whom thou think'st thou dost
  overthrow,
Die not, poor Death, nor yet canst thou kill
  me."

Death thinks that he is "overthrowing" men when he takes them, that is, conquering, vanquishing, defeating, ruining, causing to fall. Instead, and this here is the "Holy" conceit[2] of the sonnet, a very Christian concept, he does not cause them to fall, but helps them to rise—

---

1. **anthropomorphizing.** Attributing human form or personality to something not human
2. **conceit.** Elaborate or strained metaphor

death is the means by which man finds Resurrection (literally, "rising again"), eternal life and immortality through Christ in heaven. Donne is patronizing and sarcastic with "poor Death," who is so deluded as to think himself a bane[3] on man's existence. And again, "nor yet canst thou kill me," hearkens back to the same idea that Death does not kill, but is instead the enabler of new, immortal life. Death cannot kill him, thus he holds no power over the speaker (whom we may treat as Donne).

> "From rest and sleep, which but thy
>   picture[s] be,
> Much pleasure, then from thee much more
>   must flow,
> And soonest our best men with thee do go,
> Rest of their bones, and soul's delivery."

"rest and sleep, . . . thy picture[s]" Here we have the Renaissance idea of sleep as death's image (cf. Donne, Woman's Constancy; Cowley, On the Death of Mr. William Hervey,

Wroth, "When night's black mantle . . . ," etc."), that is, death's likeness, semblance—a sleeping man looks much like a dead man, and vice versa (the parallel of sleeping/waking and dying/waking is played with later in the sonnet). Thus, if man gets much pleasure out of rest and sleep, which are but copies of death, how much more pleasure then must be gotten from death, the original? This is why, Donne posits, the best men of the era go unhesitatingly to their deaths—they have wisely realized this to be the case. They go with Death, their bones get to their rest (in the grave), and their souls get "delivered" (lit. set free), containing the meanings at the same time of 1. being freed from the human body (think: "shuffle off this mortal coil" —Hamlet), 2. freed from the fear of death, 3. delivered into heaven, and 4. delivered in the sense of being born, or reborn. Heady stuff, *n'est-ce pas*?![4]

---

3. **bane.** Source of harm or ruin
4. *n'est-ce pas.* [French] "Isn't it?"

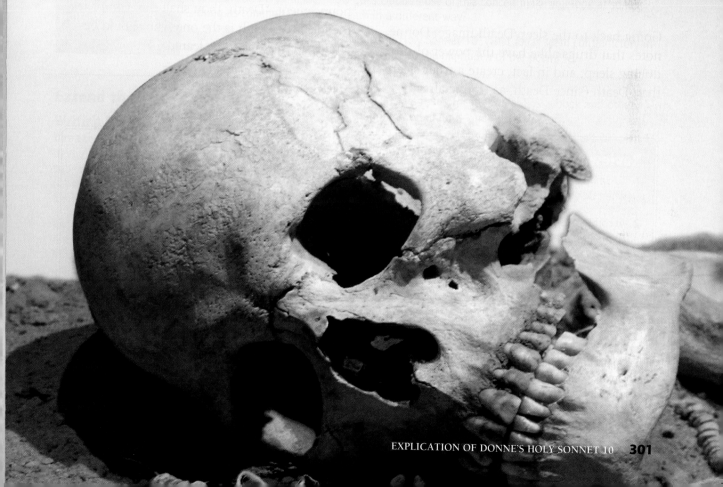

Song ("Go and catch a falling star")

by John Donne

Go and catch a falling star,
   Get with child a mandrake root,[1]
Tell me where all past years are,
   Or who cleft[2] the Devil's foot,
5 Teach me to hear mermaids singing,[3]
   Or to keep off envy's stinging,
     And find
     What wind
Serves to advance an honest mind.

10 If thou beest[4] born to strange sights,
   Things invisible to see,
Ride ten thousand days and nights,
   Till age snow white hairs on thee,
Thou, when thou return'st, wilt tell me
15 All strange wonders that befell thee,
     And swear
     No where
Lives a woman true, and fair.

If thou find'st one, let me know,
20 Such a pilgrimage were sweet;
Yet do not, I would not go,
   Though at next door we might meet;
Though she were true when you met her,
And last till you write your letter,
25   Yet she
     Will be
False, ere[5] I come, to two, or three. ❖

Woman Playing the Viola, c. 1480–1524. Andrea Solario.
Doria Pamphili, Rome, Italy. (See detail on page 305.)

1. **mandrake root.** Forked root resembling the human body
2. **cleft.** Divided; split. The devil conventionally has been
   pictured as having goatlike hooves.
3. **mermaids singing.** This reference may be to the sirens in
   Greek myth, whose song led to the destruction of all who
   heard it except Odysseus.
4. **thou beest.** You have been
5. **ere.** Before

MIRRORS & WINDOWS

Do you believe in the concept of a *soulmate*—that there is one person in the world who is a perfect match for you?

This sin of yours surmounts them all as far
80   As doth the sun another little star.

Then let us have our liberty again,
And challenge²¹ to yourselves no sovereignty.
You came not in the world without our pain,
Make that a bar against your cruelty;
85   Your fault being greater, why should you disdain
Our being your equals, free from tyranny?
     If one weak woman simply did offend,
     This sin of yours hath no excuse nor end,

To which, poor souls, we never gave consent.
90   Witness, thy wife, O Pilate, speaks for all,
Who did but dream, and yet a message sent
That thou shouldest have nothing to do at all
With that just man;²² which, if thy heart relent,
Why wilt thou be a reprobate with Saul²³
95   To seek the death of him that is so good,
     For thy soul's health to shed this dearest blood? ❖

---

21. **challenge.** Claim
22. **just man.** Jesus
23. **reprobate with Saul.** Damned like Saul, King of Israel, who wanted God's
    prophet-king, David, killed.

Lanier argues that Eve acted out of ignorance and weakness and thus cannot be blamed for what she did. Is ignorance a valid excuse for wrongdoing? Is weakness?

Refer and Reason

1. Who does Pilate represent? How does Eve represent all women in this poem? Identify the sins each of these biblical figures has committed.

2. According to the speaker, in what should women not take glory? Infer why the speaker says this.

3. What arguments does Lanier make in the second-to-last stanza about why women should be men's equals? How does the message in "Eve's Apology" support the idea that Lanier's work is protofeminist?

Writing Options

1. Write a one-paragraph apology, in which you present an argument proclaiming your innocence for something you have done. Choose something from everyday life, such as being late for an appointment. Determine to whom you should offer your explanation and how best to convince him or her of your innocence.

2. Amelia Lanier lived in a time women had few rights, yet she wrote works that championed women. After doing brief research on Lanier, write a one-paragraph biographical sketch that accurately portrays her protofeminist qualities.

Go to **www.mirrorsandwindows.com** for more.

A Man for All Seasons by Robert Bolt

Even when everyone else in court circles pledges to support King Henry VIII's 1535 Act of Succession, which declares the pope is no longer head of the Church of England, Chancellor Sir Thomas More cannot. In Bolt's play, More refuses to forsake his own private conscience for the sake of public duty, thus sealing his death warrant.

Queen of Scots: The True Life of Mary Stuart by John Guy

Crowned at age one, married at sixteen, remarried to her cousin Elizabeth's seventeen-year-old ex-lover, and later accused of his murder, Mary Stuart was at the epicenter of court drama. British historian John Guy separates truth from legend and finds a far wiser monarch than depicted at the time by the queen's enemies.

Will in the World: How Shakespeare Became Shakespeare by Stephen Greenblatt

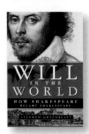

Although Stratford in the 1560s was torn by religious civil war, the medieval folk culture continued to flourish, and it was this culture that deeply influenced the childhood of William Shakespeare. Using recent scholarship and evidence from Shakespeare's poetry and plays, Greenblatt's biography helps readers imagine how a talented youth became the world's greatest dramatist.

Elizabeth I by Anne Somerset

Despite King Henry VIII's monumental attempts to sire a male heir, it was a daughter, Elizabeth I, who reigned for forty-five years, bringing political cunning and relative stability to a turbulent era. Somerset reveals the Virgin Queen as a magnetic and complex sovereign who used her gender to advantage in a man's world.

God's Secretaries: The Making of the King James Bible by Adam Nicolson

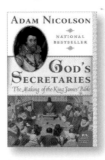

Determined to reunite his fractured realm, King James I in 1604 commissioned fifty scholars to produce a new version of the Bible. Astonishingly, the scholars, working in six committees over seven years, managed to create a rhetorical masterpiece. Nicolson sets the translation within the period's religious struggles and brings to life the diverse personalities involved.

Renaissance Women Poets edited by Danielle Clarke

Although few sixteenth-century women's voices have been preserved, three exceptions include servant Isabella Whitney, courtesan Amelia Lanier, and countess Mary Sidney. Coming from varied backgrounds, these three poets were attracted to different topics, including London life, female piety, and women's lack of social and economic power. Together, their work reveals an emergent female identity.

Reading and analyzing a speech by a prominent orator such as Winston Churchill, British prime minister during most of World War II, can give you an idea of what makes a public address memorable. (See Unit 8 for the text of one of Churchill's famous speeches.) To analyze such a speech, you might try reciting it to get a sense of what it feels like to participate in a critical moment in history. If you can, listen to an audiotape or view a videotape of the speech or speaker.

Choose a famous speech by a prominent orator, and use the following questions to analyze it.

1. How Does the Message Fit the Occasion?

Begin your analysis of the speech by establishing its *purpose,* or aim. Look for clues—some obvious, some less so—that indicate when, where, and why the address was given.

For instance, Churchill's speech was made on BBC radio in London on May 19, 1940. Why did the prime minister address the British people at that time? What was he asking his listeners to do? What information about the course of World War II did he provide as motivation? Then consider whether the address fits the historical occasion.

2. What Rhetorical Devices Does the Orator Use, and How Effective Are They?

A *rhetorical device* is a technique that a speaker or writer uses to achieve a particular effect. Frequently used devices include *repetition* (usually of words, phrases, and clauses) and *parallelism* (repetition of a grammatical form, such as sentence structure). In the Churchill speech, parallelism occurs in the opening sentence on page 1059, and repetition occurs with the phrase "side by side" on page 1062. Determine how these rhetorical devices affect the soundness of the argument and the persuasiveness of the speech.

To assess Churchill's delivery (eye contact, intonation, and gestures), go to **http://lit.emcp.net/ churchill** and listen to an audio recording of the speech. How does Churchill's delivery affect the effectiveness of the rhetorical devices and the persuasiveness of his message?

3. What Is the Tone of the Speech?

Tone is the emotional attitude toward the reader or subject implied by a literary work, such as playful or sad, serious or sarcastic. Conveying a particular tone helps an orator motivate the audience to respond to his or her call for action.

How would you characterize the tone of Churchill's speech? Does the speech use formal or informal English? How do *diction* (word choice) and the use of rhetorical devices help create the tone? What kind of response do you think the prime minister was hoping to elicit, or produce, in his audience?

4. Who Were the Other Audiences of the Speech?

Famous pictures from 1940 show ordinary citizens in homes all over Britain concentrating on the famous voice emerging from the *wireless,* a British term for *radio.* Yet clearly, Churchill also had other audiences in mind to whom he wished to send certain messages. Who were the other audiences, and what did the prime minister want them to understand?

5. How Is the Speech Similar to or Different from Other Speeches of the Era?

During World War II, many speeches were given in Parliament or from the throne; some were broadcast on the wireless. Look in published collections of famous speeches or on the Internet to find public addresses by prominent British men and women of the time. Synthesize the ideas among these speeches, noting textual evidence that supports any inferences and conclusions that you make. Examine the similarities and differences between these presentations, and consider how each one reflects its time. Which speeches might be intended to arouse a patriotic response? What other purposes might some of the orators have had when they spoke?

SPEAKING & LISTENING RUBRIC

Research

❑ You locate a well-known speech or address by a prominent orator.

Analysis

❑ You evaluate the speech as a reflection of its time, judge the effectiveness of its rhetorical devices, and consider the likely audience response.

❑ If you can view an audiotape or videotape, you evaluate the speaker's delivery.

Twentieth-century poet T. S. Eliot once said, "Genuine poetry can communicate before it is understood." After reading the Renaissance Era poetry in this unit, you probably understand what he means. Great poetry spirals and branches in many directions at once. Sometimes, however, reading a poem may give you more of a feeling than a true understanding.

Explicating a poem forces you to slow down. In an explication, you analyze the meanings and relationships of the words, images, and literary techniques used to make a poem or other work of literature. As you conduct this analysis, you will find yourself expanding and shifting your own ideas about the poem.

For this assignment, you will write an explication that explains the literary devices used in a poem in this unit and analyzes how they help create meaning.

> **Assignment** Write an explication of a poem in this unit
>
> **Purpose** To explain the meanings of and relationships among elements in the poem
>
> **Audience** Someone who has read the poem and needs help understanding it

❶ Prewrite

Select Your Topic
Review the poems in this unit, and identify the three that most intrigue you. Choose the one that you feel you can best take apart and analyze. Consider selecting a poem whose meaning is not entirely obvious to you, as slowing down to analyze the work will allow you to better comprehend it.

Gather Information
Begin by reading the poem aloud several times. Listen to the rhythms and sounds, make notes about the literary devices you identify, such as alliteration and particular meter. Next start making notes about content.

Use a graphic organizer like the one page 321 to record your notes. Include the numbers of lines from the poem you might want to use as support.

Organize Your Ideas
Review column 2, "Literary Devices," of your Poem Analysis Table to look for recurring topics. In the sample table, note that "Alliteration" and "Repetition" both appear twice, as does "Structure."

On your own table, circle the three literary devices that provide the strongest evidence of the elements and meaning of the poem. Then number them in the order you want them to appear in your explication. You can discuss the poem stanza by stanza or organize the paragraphs according to topic.

Write Your Thesis Statement
What main point do you want to make about the poem? What literary devices and themes best portray the poet's meaning? Your answer to these questions is your **thesis statement.**

One student, Jeremiah, wrote this thesis statement about Sir Walter Raleigh's "The Nymph's Reply to the Shepherd":

> *Raleigh uses imagery and repetition to illustrate his speaker's argument that life and love are not eternal and will eventually fade and die.*

WRITING RUBRIC

A successful poetry explication has these elements:

- ❑ an introduction that states the title and author of the poem and captures readers' interest
- ❑ a thesis statement that clearly expresses the main idea of the explication
- ❑ a body that analyzes the literary devices used and supports the analysis with details from the poem
- ❑ a conclusion that restates the thesis, summarizes the analysis, and provides a sense of closure

---

What Great Writers Do
You might find it helpful to read poetry explications by literary scholars. Libraries carry a number of periodicals that contain explications of literature. *PMLA,* the journal of the Modern Language Association of America, is an excellent place to start.

Poem Analysis Table: Raleigh's "The Nymph's Reply to the Shepherd"

Stanza #s	Literary Devices	Line #s	Possible Purpose/Meaning
1 and 6	Alliteration Repetition (Marlowe's phrases) Structure	1–4, 21–24 3–4, 23–24 1–4, 21–24	Musicality To connect two poems Hypothetical argument

2 and 3	Alliteration
	Metaphor
	Allusion
	
	Metaphor
		5–6, 8
		5
		7
		
		9–12
			Musicality
			Time in control; he is herding people
			Reinforces idea that all things
			    come to an end
			Season imagery reinforces tran-
			    sient nature of life/ love; all things
			    end; time destructive force

4 and 5	Alliteration
	Repetition
	Structure (list)
		13–16, 17–20 / 16
		15–16
		13–14, 17–18
			Musicality/emphasis on "rotten"
			
			Emphasize what have in common—
			    all end and rot; it will happen
			    soon
			
			Emphasizes they are insignificant
			    and fleeting

Overall	Iambic tetrameter Structure	Throughout Stanzas 1–6 Stanzas 2–5	Lyrical feel/mimic Marlowe's meter Hypothetical Main argument, make 1 and 6 look impossible

❷ Draft

Write your explication by following this three-part framework: Introduction, Body, and Conclusion.

Introduction Name the title and author of the poem, and state your thesis.

Body Elaborate on your thesis statement, supporting each point with evidence from the poem.

Conclusion Restate your thesis, summarize your analysis, and bring the explication to a close.

Draft Your Introduction

Begin the introduction to your explication by stating the poet and work to be analyzed. Also state your thesis, proposing the main idea or point of the explication.

The introduction that Jeremiah wrote during the Draft stage is shown in the first column on page 323. Jeremiah is quick to name his poet and poem in his first sentence, and in the next sentence, he states his thesis. Two sentences don't make much of an introduction, though. What else could he include?

Draft Your Body

In the body, state each point you want to make about the poem and then support or prove it using examples from the selection. Be sure to discuss poetic devices as well as content and meaning. This is information you already mapped out in the Prewrite stage.

Jeremiah decided to begin his explication by looking at imagery in the poem. Look at the draft of his first body paragraph in the left-hand column of the chart on page 323. By including examples from "A Nymph's Reply to the Shepherd" to show how the poem's imagery illustrates the effect of time on relationships, Jeremiah was able to prove his thesis.

Review the three statements you circled on your Poem Analysis Table and the order in which you planned to present them. Develop each statement into a paragraph by adding evidence gathered from your careful scrutiny of the poem. Each paragraph should clearly relate to the argument you are making, as stated in your thesis.

Draft Your Conclusion

Finally, write the conclusion for your poetry explication. A good conclusion does two things: (1) it summarizes the main point made in the body of the essay, reemphasizing the thesis without merely restating it, and (2) it brings the discussion to a close.

Does Jeremiah do both these things in his conclusion? Look at the draft of his conclusion in the chart on page 324.

❸ Revise

Evaluate Your Draft

You can evaluate your own writing or exchange essays with a classmate and evaluate each other's work. Start by looking at the content and organization. Make sure that the three parts of the essay—the introduction, body, and conclusion—work together to prove the thesis.

Use the Revision Checklist at right to help you evaluate. Make notes directly on the essay about what changes need to be made.

Next, check the language for errors. Go back through your draft to make sure you have correctly applied the guidelines in the Grammar & Style workshops in this unit. Again, use the Revision Checklist to evaluate the writing. Consider how the writing can be made more engaging.

Review the notes you made as you reviewed your draft as well as the comments you received from your partner. First, make changes to the ideas in your explication. Improve the thesis statement, if necessary, and do any reorganization needed. Add evidence where support is lacking, and improve word choices where appropriate. Make sure each sentence says exactly what you mean.

What Great Writers Do

Nineteenth-century English essayist William Hazlitt said, "Poetry is all that is worth remembering in life." Is this statement true? It could certainly be applied to the topic of Raleigh's poem, the effect of time on love. How might it apply to the poem you analyzed for your explication?

HAZLITT

REVISION CHECKLIST

Content & Organization

- ❏ Does the introduction clearly state the poet and work to be analyzed?
- ❏ Does the introduction present a clear thesis statement and generate reader interest?
- ❏ Does each paragraph in the body clearly relate back to the thesis?
- ❏ Does each body paragraph provide relevant evidence from the poem to support the thesis?
- ❏ Does the conclusion summarize the essay by restating the thesis and providing closure?

Grammar & Style

- ❏ Have you used parallelism to express similar ideas in similar grammatical forms? (page 245)
- ❏ Have you written well-unified paragraphs? (page 293)
- ❏ Are transitions used between paragraphs to help orient your reader? (page 311)

DRAFT STAGE		REVISE STAGE	
Introduction Walter Raleigh wrote "The Nymph's Reply to the Shepherd" in response to Christopher Marlowe's poem, "A Passionate Shepherd to His Mistress." In his response to Marlowe's poem, Raleigh uses imagery and repetition to illustrate his speaker's argument that life and love are not eternal and will eventually fade and die.	Establishes poet and poem States thesis	Sir Walter Raleigh wrote "The Nymph's Reply to the Shepherd" in response to Christopher Marlowe's poem~,~ "A Passionate Shepherd to His Mistress." In Marlowe's poem, a fictional shepherd woos his mistress with presents and promises to encourage her to seize the day and live with him in love's eternal bliss. In his response to Marlowe's poem, Raleigh uses imagery and repetition to illustrate his speaker's argument that life and love are not eternal and will eventually fade and die.	Eliminates unnecessary comma Adds sentence to provide context and more complete introduction
Body Paragraph In his poem, Raleigh shows the effects of time on life. To show how powerful a force time is, he describes time as a shepherd herding flocks. This comparison suggests that time is in charge and that people are merely sheep being driven through life by time. The seasonal imagery of spring and winter is reinforcing time's powerful influence over life and is suggesting that it may have a destructive influence.		~In his poem~ In the second and third stanzas of "The Nymph's Reply to the Shepherd," Raleigh shows the effects of time on life. To show how powerful a force time is, he describes time as a shepherd herding flocks and writes, "Time drives the flocks from field to fold" (5). This comparison suggests that time is in charge and that people are merely sheep being driven through life by time. In addition to the shepherd metaphor, the seasonal imagery of spring and winter in lines 9–12 ~is reinforcing~ reinforces time's powerful influence over life and ~is suggesting that~ suggests it may have a destructive influence. Beautiful flowers will fade, and spring will turn into winter. The seasonal imagery suggests this is a natural but inevitable process.	Gets more specific for first mention Provides supporting quote Adds transition Uses stronger verb Adds important detail and expands idea

DRAFT STAGE	REVISE STAGE	
Conclusion Raleigh's speaker rejects the shepherd's arguments because of the powerful influence of time. Raleigh's speaker does not believe that the shepherd can promise eternal love and asserts that all love must come to an end.	It is clear through Sir Walter Raleigh's use of imagery and repetition that the speaker rejects the shepherd's arguments because of the powerful influence of time over life and love. Raleigh's speaker does not believe that the shepherd can promise eternal love and asserts that all love must come to an end. Raleigh's poem offers the reader a pessimistic view of love and shows the reader that love is not eternal but subject to the pressures of time.	Fleshes out idea Adds first name to mirror introduction Wraps up discussion better

Revise for Content, Organization, and Style

Jeremiah read over his explication and found several things to improve. Look at the right-hand column of the chart on pages 323–324 to see how he revised the three paragraphs you looked at earlier:

- **Introduction:** Adding another sentence allowed Jeremiah to flesh out his introduction and provide more basic information about his poem.
- **Body:** Including supporting quotes and examples made this paragraph more specific and interesting.
- **Conclusion:** By adding another sentence, Jeremiah was able to bring his conclusion to a more appropriate length and more effectively close his discussion.

Review the notes you or your partner made as you evaluated your draft. Then apply each comment in effectively revising your draft.

Proofread for Errors

The purpose of proofreading is to check for remaining errors. While you can look for errors as you evaluate your essay, you should focus on checking for any you might have missed or introduced in new material you added. Use proofreader's symbols to mark any errors you find.

To complete the assignment, print out a final draft and read it aloud once before turning it in. This will enable you to catch more errors.

Take a look at Jeremiah's final draft on the next page. Note how he worked through the three stages of the writing process: Prewrite, Draft, and Revise.

Writing Follow-Up

Publish & Present

- Local coffee shops often host "poetry slams," giving local poets a chance to display their work. Hold a poetry slam of a different sort in your class, reading the poem you chose followed by your explication of it.
- Make a wall display with strings or arrows pointing from verbal images in the poems to your artistic renditions of them. This same idea could be expanded on a webpage or hypertext stack that would use links instead of strings.

Reflect

- When you study great poetry, you do much more than simply describe what happens in a work of art. You also describe how you see yourself in relationship to art and how a poem makes you think. What new perspectives did you discover as you explored this poet and poem? Try writing a poem that begins "When I read [your poet], my brain . . ."

STUDENT MODEL

The Power of Time in Raleigh's "A Nymph's Reply to the Shepherd" by Jeremiah Wagner

Sir Walter Raleigh wrote "The Nymph's Reply to the Shepherd" in response to Christopher Marlowe's poem "A Passionate Shepherd to His Mistress." In Marlowe's poem, a fictional shepherd woos his mistress with presents and promises to encourage her to seize the day and live with him in love's eternal bliss. In his response to Marlowe's poem, Raleigh uses imagery and repetition to illustrate his speaker's argument that life and love are not eternal and will eventually fade and die.

In the second and third stanzas of "The Nymph's Reply to the Shepherd," Raleigh shows the effects of time on life. To show how powerful a force time is, he describes time as a shepherd herding flocks and writes, "Time drives the flocks from field to fold" (5). This comparison suggests that time is in charge and that people are merely sheep being driven through life by time. In addition to the shepherd metaphor, the seasonal imagery of spring and winter in lines 9–12 reinforces time's powerful influence over life and suggests it may have a destructive influence. Beautiful flowers will fade, and spring will turn into winter. The seasonal imagery suggests this is a natural but inevitable process.

Lines 11 and 12 connect time's effect on life to time's effect on love. Raleigh writes, "A honey tongue, a heart of gall / Is fancy's spring, but sorrow's fall" (11–12). Here he compares fancy, or love, to spring and sorrow to the season of fall. This comparison sets up the same cyclical relationship between time's effect on the seasons—spring must inevitably turn into fall—with time's effect on relationships—fancy will inevitably turn into sorrow. This comparison to the seasons' cyclical nature reinforces the natural inevitability of progressing from being in love to falling out of love.

Stanzas four and five apply this argument of time's effect on life and relationships to the promises offered in Marlowe's poem. In lines 13–14 and 17–18, Raleigh echoes the list of presents offered by Marlowe's shepherd and states what they all have in common: Over time, they will perish and be forgotten. Raleigh repeats sounds and words to emphasize this fact. For example, the alliteration of *r* "In folly ripe, in reason rotten" (16) draws attention to the last two words, "reason" and "rotten." Both the gifts and the feeling that inspired their giving will not last and will become rotten. The repetition of "soon" in line 15, "Soon break, soon wither, soon forgotten," suggests the destruction will happen; it is just a matter of time.

It is clear through Sir Walter Raleigh's use of imagery and repetition that the speaker rejects the shepherd's arguments because of the powerful influence of time over life and love. Raleigh's speaker does not believe that the shepherd can promise eternal love and asserts that all love must come to an end. Raleigh's poem offers the reader a pessimistic view of love and shows the reader that love is not eternal but subject to the pressures of time.

How does the writer provide appropriate context?

What is the writer's thesis statement?

What is the main point of the first body paragraph? How does the writer support his claim?

What examples of imagery does the writer see? What do these examples show about the passage of time on life and love?

What types of repetition does Raleigh use? How does he use repetition to support his point?

How does the writer conclude his piece?

Reading Skills

Compare and Contrast Characters

To **compare and contrast** characters, begin by listing the features or characteristics of each. These characteristics can be located in a direct description of the character, in the character's behavior, in the character's private thoughts and emotions, or in the character's interaction with other characters—how he or she treats others or behaves with them and what others say or think about him or her. Once you have listed the traits of the characters, determine which traits they have in common.

How you format the lists of characters' traits can help you analyze the information. Try listing the features of the characters in adjacent columns. Then draw lines connecting the columns as you match the same or similar characteristics. These paired traits are the characters' similarities. All the traits left unpaired are the characters' differences.

Another way to show similarities and differences is in a Venn diagram, which uses two slightly overlapping circles. In the outer part of each circle, jot down the traits unique to each character, or their differences. In the inner, or shared, part of each circle, record the traits the two characters share.

Not all character traits are equally important. In comparing and contrasting characters, focus on a few of the most important traits. To judge whether a trait is important, think about how often it is mentioned in the selection. Also consider the result of the character being this way. Would the story change measurably if the character did not have this trait?

TEST-TAKING TIP

In responding to a multiple-choice question, remember that you are looking for the *best* answer option. It's possible that more than one option may be correct, or at least correct in some way. Be sure to look at all the options and choose the best one.

Practice

Directions: Read the following passages from *The Faerie Queen*, an epic poem by Edmund Spenser, and *The Ingenious Hidalgo Don Quixote de La Mancha*, a mock epic novel by Miguel de Cervantes. The questions that follow both passages will ask you to compare and contrast characters from these passages.

from *The Faerie Queen*

A Gentle Knight was pricking[1] on the plaine,
  Ycladd[2] in mightie armes and silver shielde,
  Wherein old dints of deepe wounds did
    remaine,
  The cruell markes of many a bloudy fielde;
5 Yet armes till that time did he never wield:
  His angry steede did chide his foming bitt,
As much disdayning to the curbe to yield:
  Full jolly[3] knight he seemd, and faire did sitt,
  As one for knightly giusts[4] and fierce
    encounters fitt.

10 But on his brest a bloudie Crosse he bore,
  The deare remembrance of his dying Lord,
  For whose sweete sake that glorious badge
    he wore,
  And dead as living ever him adored:
  Upon his shield the like was also scored,
15 For soveraine hope, which in his helpe he
    had:
  Right faithfull true he was in deede and word,
  But of his cheere did seeme too solemne sad;[5]
Yet nothing did he dread, but ever was ydrad.[6]
Upon a great adventure he was bond,
20 That greatest Gloriana to him gave,
  That greatest Glorious Queen of Faerie Lond,
  To winne him worship,[7] and her grace to
    have,
  Which of all earthly things he most did
    crave;
  And ever as he rode, his hart did earne[8]
25 To prove his puissance[9] in battell brave
  Upon his foe, and his new force to learne;
Upon his foe, a Dragon horrible and stearne.

1. **pricking.** Galloping; running
2. **Ycladd.** Dressed
3. **jolly.** Gallant
4. **giusts.** Jousts
5. **solemne sad.** Grave; serious

6. **ydrad.** Dreaded
7. **worship.** Honor
8. **earne.** Yearn
9. **puissance.** Power

from *Don Quixote*

In short, his wits being quite gone, [Don Quixote] hit upon the strangest notion that ever a madman in this world hit upon, and that was that he fancied it was right and
5 requisite, as well for the support of his own honour as for the service of his country, that he should make a knight-errant of himself, roaming the world over in full armour and on horseback in quest of adventures. . . .
10   The first thing he did was to clean up some armour that had belonged to his great-grandfather, and had been for ages lying forgotten in a corner. . . . He scoured and polished it as best he could, but he per-
15 ceived one great defect in it, that it had no closed helmet, nothing but a simple mori-on.[1] This deficiency, however, his ingenuity supplied, for he contrived a kind of half-helmet of pasteboard which, fitted on to the
20 morion, looked like a whole one. It is true that, in order to see if it was strong and fit to stand a cut, he drew his sword and gave it a couple of slashes, the first of which undid in an instant what had taken him a week to
25 do. The ease with which he had knocked it to pieces disconcerted him somewhat, and to guard against that danger he set to work again, fixing bars of iron on the inside until

he was satisfied with its strength; and then,
30 not caring to try any more experiments with it, he passed it and adopted it as a helmet of the most perfect construction.
    He next proceeded to inspect his hack,[2] which [had] more quartos[3] than a *real*.[4] . . .
35 Four days were spent in thinking what name to give him. . . .
    Having got a name for his horse so much to his taste, he was anxious to get one for himself, and he was eight days
40 more pondering over this point, till at last he made up his mind to call himself "Don Quixote." . . . Recollecting, however, that the valiant Amadis[5] was not content to call himself curtly Amadis and nothing more,
45 but added the name of his kingdom and country to make it famous, and called him-self Amadis of Gaul, he, like a good knight, resolved to add on the name of his, and to style himself Don Quixote of La Mancha,
50 whereby, he considered, he described accu-rately his origin and country, and did hon-our to it in taking his surname from it.

1. **morion.** Crested helmet without a visor
2. **hack.** Old horse
3. **quartos.** Cracks
4. *real.* Old Spanish silver coin
5. **Amadis.** Amadis of Gaul was a Renaissance knight

Multiple Choice

1. The knight in *The Faerie Queen* is character-ized as
   A. angry.
   B. happy.
   C. dying.
   D. faithful.
   E. great.

2. What do lines 10–13 reveal about the knight?
   A. He has blond hair.
   B. He is a smart dresser.
   C. He yearns for glory.
   D. He is very popular.
   E. He is religious.

3. Which of the following statements from the second passage best characterizes Don Quixote?
   A. "He next proceeded to inspect his hack." (line 33)
   B. "At last he made up his mind to call himself 'Don Quixote.'" (lines 40–42)
   C. "His wits being quite gone, . . . he fancied it was right and requisite, . . . that he should make a knight-errant of himself." (lines 1–7)
   D. "The first thing he did was to clean up some armour that had belonged to his great-grandfather." (lines 10–12)
   E. "He set to work again, fixing bars of iron on the inside until he was satisfied with its strength." (lines 27–29)

4. Which of the following best shows the contrast between the knight in *The Faerie Queen* and the character of Don Quixote?
   A. The knight is dignified, whereas Don Quixote is foolish.
   B. The knight is brave, whereas Don Quixote is cowardly.
   C. The knight is comic, whereas Don Quixote is tragic.
   D. The knight is stern, whereas Don Quixote is happy-go-lucky.
   E. The knight is honest, whereas Don Quixote sometimes hides the truth.

Constructed Response

5. Compare and contrast the knight in Spenser's poem *The Faerie Queen* with the character Don Quixote from Cervantes' novel by the same name.

Writing Skills

Plan Your Response

As soon as you have a clear understanding of the essay prompt, collect and organize your thoughts. Taking the time to plan your response before you start writing will ensure that you produce a better answer.

First, identify the main point or points you want to make. Jot them down in a list, not worrying about their order for now. For each main point, think about what you will provide for supporting details. You should be able to develop each main point into a paragraph that includes three or four supporting sentences.

Next, determine the order in which to present your main points. Number the points in your list to reflect this order. If there is a natural or logical order to these ideas, such as sequential or chronological, then follow it. When writing a persuasive essay, using a rhetorical organization, in which you lead up to your strongest point, is usually most effective. In that way, your essay builds a case, leading readers to the most important idea. Ending with that idea will help ensure readers understand and remember it.

The result of planning your response should be a rough outline of your essay. If you follow it when writing, your essay will be focused and well organized. Keep in mind that your essay response should be written in standard, formal English.

> **TEST-TAKING TIP**
>
> In planning your response, consider how much time is allotted for writing. If you cannot cover all your main ideas and supporting evidence in that time, then choose the most convincing ideas and evidence.

Practice

Timed Writing: 25 minutes

Think carefully about the issue presented in the following excerpt and assignment.

While moderation is often the best policy, it is not always possible. Some things are out of the realm of our control. Consider the weather, for example. In some places, the summers are uncomfortably hot and humid. In other places, the winters are bitterly cold. If you had to choose one of these extremes, which would you prefer: a climate that is sometimes too hot or one that is sometimes too cold?

Assignment: Which extreme is better: a too-cold climate or a too-hot one? Plan and write an essay in which you develop your perspective on this issue. Support your position with reasoning and examples taken from your reading, studies, experience, or observations.

Revising and Editing Skills

As part of the Writing section, some standardized tests ask you to improve sentences. The items in this section focus on your ability to recognize and write clear, effective, and precise sentences. These items assess correctness and effectiveness of expression—without ambiguity and awkwardness.

Practice

Directions: Each of the following items consists of a sentence, part of which is underlined. Beneath each sentence are five different ways of expressing the same idea. Choice A repeats the text of the original sentence. The other four choices provide ways to rephrase the underlined text. Select the choice that offers the best phrasing.

Multiple Choice

1. Mrs. Brown just learned to drive <u>and she was eighty years old then</u>.
   A. and she was eighty years old then.
   B. at age eighty years old.
   C. upon having had turned eighty.
   D. at the age of eighty.
   E. after she had become eighty years old.

2. T. S. Eliot, who was born in the United States but lived in England most of his <u>life, often he is studied in</u> both English and American literature courses.
   A. life, often he is studied in
   B. life, often is being studied in
   C. life, and often he is studied in
   D. life, often is studied in
   E. life, often he has been studied in

3. Their independent <u>nature and their being quiet account</u> for much of the popularity of cats.
   A. nature and their being quiet account
   B. and quiet nature account
   C. nature and the fact that they are quiet account
   D. and quiet nature accounts
   E. nature and its being quiet account

4. People say there has never been a shortage of <u>gas, this just being</u> a political maneuver.
   A. gas, this just being
   B. gas, just being
   C. gas, and this is just
   D. gas, its just being
   E. gas, it's just

Banquet Scene from Macbeth, 1840. Daniel Maclise. Guildhall Art Gallery, London, England.

Renaissance Drama

Unit 4

"Life's but a walking shadow, a poor player,
That struts and frets his hour upon the stage,
And then is heard no more. It is a tale
Told by an idiot, full of sound and fury,
Signifying nothing."

—WILLIAM SHAKESPEARE,
The Tragedy of Macbeth

1485–1642

Renaissance Drama 1485–1642

1485

1580

DRAMATIC LITERATURE

c. 1490–1501
Henry Medwall's *Fulgens and Lucrece* is performed

c. 1516
John Skelton's *Magnyfycence* is printed

1553
The first five-act plays in English are written: Nicholas Udall's *Ralph Roister Doister* and William Stevenson's *Gammer Gurton's Needle*

1562
The first English tragedy, *Tragedy of Gorboduc,* is presented before Queen Elizabeth I

1564
Christopher Marlowe is born

1564
William Shakespeare is baptized as an infant on April 26

1565
The Westminster boys' troupe presents Plautus's Latin play *Miles Gloriosus* for Queen Elizabeth I

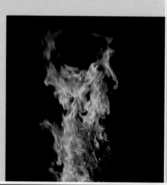

1587
Tamburlaine is the first Marlowe play known to be performed on the London stage

1588
Marlowe writes *The Tragical History of Doctor Faustus*

1592
Shakespeare's *Henry VI* is presented in perhaps the first public performance of his work

1593
Marlowe is killed in a brawl

1596
Shakespeare's *Romeo and Juliet* is first performed

1597
The first printed edition of Shakespeare's *Romeo and Juliet* appears

RENAISSANCE THEATERS

1531
James Burbage is born at Stratford-on-Avon

1576
Burbage erects the Theater in Shoreditch

1577
The Curtain Theater is built near Burbage's Theater

1594
Shakespeare becomes a shareholder in the Lord Chamberlain's Men, a theatrical company

1595
The Swan Theater is built

1597
Performance of *The Isle of Dogs* leads to the temporary closing of all London theaters

1598
The Globe Theater is built

1599
The Blackfriars Theater becomes the first theater built with a roof

1599
The Blackfriars Theater is opened

STRATFORD-ON-AVON

The Globe

c. 1601
Shakespeare's *Hamlet* is performed at both Cambridge and Oxford Universities

c. 1603
Shakespeare writes *Macbeth*

c. 1605
Shakespeare's *Macbeth* is first performed

1608
Shakespeare's *King Lear* appears in a quarto edition

1613
Shakespeare's last play, *Henry VIII*, premieres at the Globe Theater

1616
Shakespeare dies on April 23

HENRY VIII

1622
The quarto edition of Shakespeare's *Othello* is published

1623
The First Folio is published, containing thirty-six of Shakespeare's plays

1625
Shakespeare's *The Tempest* is printed for the first time

1632
A second edition of Shakespeare's First Folio is printed

1600
The Fortune Theater is built

1604
Shakespeare's company becomes the King's Men

1604
The Red Bull Theater is built

1608
Shakespeare's company purchases the Blackfriars Theater

1608
The Whitefriars Theater is built

1613
A misfired cannon burns down the Globe Theater during the premiere of *Henry VIII*

1614
The Globe Theater is rebuilt

1616
The Cockpit Theater is converted from a cockfighting arena into a playhouse

1618
The Cockpit Theater is rebuilt after being burned down and renamed the Phoenix

1621
The Fortune Theater burns down

1629
The Salisbury Court Theater is built

1642
The Puritans shut down all theaters in London

"A kingdom for a stage, princes to act, And monarchs to behold the swelling scene!"

—WILLIAM SHAKESPEARE, *HENRY V*

The Dramatic Inheritance

In the Middle Ages, plays were presented by traveling troupes of actors or by members of professional business associations called *guilds.* The guilds performed outdoors on the backs of wagons, which were used as mobile stages. Almost always, these plays dealt with religious subjects. **Miracle plays** told fantastic stories about the lives of saints, **mystery plays** told stories from the Bible, and **morality plays** dramatized the battle between good and evil for an individual's immortal soul.

In the late 1400s, at the beginning of the Renaissance, theater still was being performed in the open air by traveling troupes of actors. Performances also were held in schools and in halls in the great homes of noble men and women. As attending the theater became increasingly popular, specially designed open-air stages called *amphitheaters* were built to bring plays to eager audiences and capture larger profits for theater owners.

Renaissance plays were influenced by the Humanist philosophy popular at this time, which held that human beings were created in the image of God and could perfect themselves and their worldly institutions. Renaissance playwrights drew on a wider variety of sources than their medieval counterparts. They mined the works of classical texts and English historical chronicles for subject matter to fashion into English plays. As Renaissance plays began to incorporate more secular (nonreligious) sources, they also began to examine psychological issues more deeply and consider the inner workings of character.

The two most common types of drama during the English Renaissance were comedies and tragedies. A **comedy** progressed from initial order to a humorous misunderstanding or confusion and back to order again, and a **tragedy** told the story of the downfall of a person of high status (see also Understanding

Literary Forms, pages 337–339). Other kinds of plays produced during the Renaissance included *histories,* which addressed events from the past, and *romances,* which contained highly fantastic elements such as fairies and magical spells. Also popular were short plays called *interludes* and elaborate entertainments called *masques* that featured acting, music, and dance.

While Elizabethan theater (c. 1558–1603) provided theatergoers with a wide variety of drama, Jacobean theater (1603–1625) concentrated on comedies, tragedies, and masques. The tragedies of Jacobean playwrights such as Thomas Middleton (1580–1627)

Interior of London's Fortune Theater c. 1620.

and John Webster (c. 1580–1634) celebrated the darker side of humanity and explored issues of deception and revenge.

The Political Conditions of Theater in Renaissance London

In the late sixteenth century, London was a bustling city of about 200,000 people and the mercantile, political, and artistic center of England. City officials often frowned on theater because it brought together large crowds of people, creating the potential for lawlessness and the spread of disease as well as controversial ideas. During this period, theaters sometimes were closed due to an outbreak of plague or in response to objections about the content of a play.

Because it was illegal for women to perform on the stage, all Renaissance actors were men. Boys were hired to play the parts of female characters and would have played the roles of Lady Macduff and Lady Macbeth in Shakespeare's *Macbeth*. Women were not allowed to act on stage until the reign of King Charles II (1660–1685), almost forty-five years after Shakespeare died.

Another obstacle for players and playwrights was the presence of Puritans in Parliament. The Puritans disapproved of secular drama and made many attempts to shut down London's theaters. When actors were targeted by Puritan members of Parliament, they sought protection from members of the nobility. In effect, actors became servants of benefactors such as lords and even the queen herself and went by names such as the Lord Chamberlain's Men.

NOTABLE NUMBERS

- **1,500** Approximate audience capacity of the Globe Theater
- **37** Number of plays attributed to William Shakespeare
- **50** People in Shakespeare's lifetime who testified to his authorship
- **8** Number of sides on the Globe Theater

Despite these obstacles, theater flourished under both Queen Elizabeth I (1558–1603) and King James I (1603–1625). However, in 1642, the Puritans succeeded in closing the theaters. It was not until Charles II was restored to the throne in 1660 that drama was allowed to return to the public stage.

The Renaissance Playhouse

The first professional playhouse in England was built in 1576 by James Burbage. He located this playhouse, named the Theater, just outside the northern boundary of London, where he could avoid control by city authorities. In 1598, Burbage and other members of his theater company, the Lord Chamberlain's Men, tore down the Theater and used its materials to build a new playhouse, the Globe, south of the city on the banks of the River Thames. One of the shareholders in the Globe was William Shakespeare.

Contemporary drawings and descriptions based on evidence from Renaissance plays provide a good idea of what Shakespeare's Globe must have looked like. The building was octagonal, or eight sided. The center of this "wooden O," as Shakespeare called it, was open to the air. The stage projected into the middle of this open space. Theatergoers from the working classes, called *groundlings,* stood around three sides of the stage. More wealthy theatergoers paid an additional penny or two and sat in one of the three tiers, or stories, of seats in the walls of the theater.

The stage of the Globe was partially covered by a canopy held in place by two large pillars. Trapdoors in the stage floor allowed for mysterious events such as appearances of spirits and fairies and disappearances of bodies. Behind the stage was an inner area called the *tiring house,* which could be used for indoor scenes and costume changes. At the back of the tiring house was a door and stairway that led to a second-level playing area. Above this balcony area was a third level, which housed the musicians and sound-effects people.

Because the playhouse was open to the air, plays were presented in the daytime and had little or no artificial lighting. Scenery, in the modern sense, was nonexistent, and few properties were used beyond an

occasional table or chair. Audiences had to envision the scenes, and playwrights assisted in this by writing descriptions of scenes into characters' speeches. Audiences also interacted with the players, showing appreciation or disapproval by cheering the heroes or throwing hay at the villains.

Indoor theaters began to attract theatergoers in the 1590s. Burbage opened the Blackfriars Theater in 1596 after converting part of an old London monastery. Used initially by acting troupes and choirs during Elizabeth's reign, it eventually became the winter home for Shakespeare's company. Smaller than the Globe and with more limited seating, the Blackfriars attracted a wealthier audience who could afford the higher admission price.

Marlowe and Shakespeare

The two greatest playwrights of the Elizabethan Age were Christopher Marlowe (1564–1593) and William Shakespeare (1564–1616). Marlowe's most important innovation in English theater was his use of *blank verse,* or unrhymed iambic pentameter. Other playwrights before him had used this meter, but Marlowe used it more often and with greater skill. Marlowe also blended elements of the comic and the tragic, treated romantic themes, probed the psychology of his characters, and understood what constituted an exciting and dramatic situation.

An artist's representation of the Globe Theater.

William Shakespeare was a gifted observer of people and wrote plays that probed the range of human experience. His language tended to be dense, metaphorical, full of puns and word play, yet natural. He used a combination of prose, rhymed poetry, and blank verse, as appropriate to the character or scene at hand.

> "*Of all modern, and perhaps ancient poets, Shakespeare had the largest and most comprehensive soul. . . . He needed not the spectacles of books to read Nature; he looked inwards, and found her there.*"
>
> —JOHN DRYDEN, SEVENTEENTH-CENTURY POET AND PLAYWRIGHT

In 1623, seven years after Shakespeare's death, thirty-six of his plays were collected and printed in a folio edition. That edition, the First Folio, is a landmark publication for several reasons. Most important, it ensured the survival of many of Shakespeare's plays. Eighteen plays survive only because they were printed in the First Folio. Prior to this edition, fourteen of Shakespeare's plays had been printed in quarto editions.

The terms *folio* and *quarto* refer to book size. A folio was a larger book made by folding a sheet of paper in half, which yielded four pages. A quarto was a smaller book made by folding a sheet of paper into fourths, which yielded eight pages. Because a printer would use less paper to print a book in quarto form than in folio form, quartos were cheaper to produce and buy. Most folios were reference books or important works by famous writers such as Homer and Edmund Spenser. The 1623 First Folio was the first one to contain only plays.

Shakespeare's First Folio was assembled by actors John Heminge and Henry Condell and printed by Isaac Jaggard and Edward Blount. It must have sold reasonably well because a second edition, which included an additional play attributed to Shakespeare, was printed just nine years later in 1632.

Drama Defined

A **drama,** or play, is a story told through characters played by actors. Dramas are divided into segments called *acts* and *scenes.* The **script,** or written form, is made up of *dialogue* spoken by the characters and *stage directions* that explain the setting and tell the actors how to give expression to emotions and physical movements. Because it is meant to be performed before an audience, an important element of drama is **spectacle,** or the visual portrayal of meaning. In order to achieve spectacle, drama features unique elements such as lighting, costumes, makeup, properties (called *props*), backgrounds and sets, music, and sound effects.

Drama has always been a highly popular literary form. Grounded in religious ritual, it dates back to sixth-century BCE Greece. Centuries elapsed between the classical drama of ancient Greece and the simple plays of medieval Europe. The great drama revival occurred during the seventeenth and eighteenth centuries with Elizabethan and Restoration drama. In this period, playwrights rediscovered classical drama and restored certain dramatic conventions, such as the act and scene structure. Even so, classical drama eventually was seen as outmoded and limiting, and playwrights threw off its conventions to create more modern productions with realistic themes and characters.

"All the world's a stage,
And all the men and women merely players;
They have their exits and their entrances,
And one man in his time plays many parts."
—WILLIAM SHAKESPEARE, *AS YOU LIKE IT*

Types of Drama

The two major types of drama are comedy and tragedy. A **comedy** is a lighthearted or humorous work that typically presents characters with limitations and misunderstandings. The action in a comedy usually progresses from order, to disorder caused by a humorous misunderstanding or confusion, and back to order again. Standard elements of comedy include mistaken identities, word play, satire, and exaggerated characters and events.

A **tragedy** portrays the fall of a person of high status, such as a king or god. It celebrates the courage and dignity of a *tragic hero,* the main character, in the face of inevitable doom. Sometimes the hero's fate is determined by a *tragic flaw,* or personal weakness that brings about his or her fall. In *Macbeth,* ambition is the tragic flaw that leads to the hero's fall. Today, the term *tragedy* is used more loosely to mean any work that has a sad ending.

Many dramas are predominantly comic or tragic but contain contrary or opposite elements. Comedies, for instance, often explore serious and tragic topics and themes. Conversely, tragedies often include humorous characters and events to create *comic relief,* or a break from the serious tone of the play. In *Macbeth,* the drunken Porter who guards the gate of Macbeth's castle provides comic relief.

Elements of Drama

As you read a play, you will find many of the elements of fiction, such as character, theme, and plot, but you will also notice significant differences between the two genres. For instance, the author of a fictional novel or short story can describe a person, object, or landscape for many pages before a character utters a single word. The author of a play, or **playwright,** however, does not have this luxury. The **exposition,** or background information, and other commentary or description must be expressed by the characters through their dialogue and behavior.

Another important difference between a play and a work of fiction is that a play is meant to be performed and must create a visual picture on stage. Because of this, certain features make a play different from a novel or short story. As you read a play, examine how the playwright uses lighting and scenery to create mood, employs stage directions to direct the actors, and specifies the kinds of stage properties (props) that are to be used.

Act and Scene Division

As noted earlier, a typical play is divided into acts and scenes. An act generally comprises several scenes. Scene breaks allow the dramatist to indicate a new time or place of action.

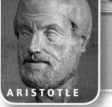

Although contemporary playwrights create their own structures, Shakespeare and his contemporaries created dramas with five acts. The structure of a typical five-act play is as follows:

- Act I, the introduction, presents the setting and main characters along with the inciting incident, or the event that sets in motion the central conflict of the play.
- Act II, the rising action, develops the central conflict.
- Act III, the crisis or climax, presents a decisive event that determines what happens in the rest of the play.
- Act IV, the falling action, presents events that happen as a result of the crisis.
- Act V, the resolution, presents the event that resolves, or ends, the central conflict.

"The Plot, then, is the first principle, and, as it were, the soul of a tragedy: Character holds the second place."

—ARISTOTLE, *POETICS*

Stage Directions

Because a play is written to be produced on stage, a reader with a playscript in hand must rely in part on his or her own imagination. The reader needs to picture the expressions on the actors' faces and imagine how they speak and move across the stage.

Stage directions are notes included in a play that describe how something should be performed on stage. Such notes help the director to guide the actors as they translate words into performance. Written notations are essential for the actors because the playwright rarely directs his or her own play. Stage directions indicate the writer's conception of setting, lighting, music, sound effects, entrances and exits, properties, and movements of characters. Stage directions usually are printed in italic type and enclosed in brackets or parentheses.

Unlike modern plays, which often have detailed stage directions, Renaissance plays had relatively few explicit directions. Much of the information now conveyed in stage directions was revealed through characters' dialogue in Renaissance plays. By convention, certain stage directions communicated specific details and actions to theatergoers. For example, the direction "Thunder and lightning" often signaled the arrival of supernatural forces and appears throughout Shakespeare's *Macbeth* and Christopher Marlowe's *The Tragical History of Doctor Faustus.*

Character

A **character** is an individual who takes part in the action of a literary work. Just as in fiction, the main character, or **protagonist,** is the most important character in a drama and is in conflict with the **antagonist.** A drama also may include a *chorus,* which may be a single character or a group of characters who comment on the action of the play. Choruses appear most frequently in Greek drama but also were used occasionally by Shakespeare and Marlowe.

Characters can be classified in other ways. *Major characters* play significant roles in a work, and *minor characters* play lesser roles. Whereas the major characters take part in the central conflict of the work, minor characters usually serve to fulfill a specific function. Such a character might play the part of a **foil,** a character whose traits contrast with and therefore highlight the traits of another character. As you read *Macbeth,* look for this type of relationship between the characters Macbeth and Banquo.

Another classification identifies static versus dynamic characters. A *static character* is one who does not change during the course of the play, and a *dynamic character* is one who does change. The scholars in Marlowe's *Doctor Faustus* are examples of static characters, while Faustus is a dynamic character.

Irony

Irony is a difference between appearance and reality. There are three types of irony: (1) *dramatic irony* is when something is known by the reader or audience but unknown to the characters; (2) *verbal irony* is when a character says one thing but means another; and (3) *irony of situation* is when an event occurs that violates the expectations of the characters, the reader, or the audience.

All three types of irony are present in *Macbeth.* The central dramatic irony, of course, is that Macbeth is someone who could have risen to prominence without committing the outrages that ultimately bloody his hands. *Macbeth* also contains many instances of verbal irony. For instance, in Act II, Scene iii, when Lennox asks Macbeth whether the king is to leave Macbeth's castle, Shakespeare phrases the question, "Goes the king hence to-day?" Macbeth replies, "He does; he did appoint so." Macbeth knows what Lennox does not: that he intends to dispatch Duncan "hence" with his own dagger. *Macbeth* also abounds with instances of situational irony. After you read the play, consider how the fulfillment of the witches' prophecy can be considered ironic.

Speech

Dialogue is a conversation between two or more characters. If you have ever watched a dramatic television program, movie, or theater play, you know that most of what you learn about characters is based on what they say and do or from what others say about them.

In addition to dialogue, the playwright can use any of several literary devices to reveal a character's thoughts and motivations. In a **monologue,** a character speaks aloud or directly addresses the audience or another character in the play. In a **soliloquy,** a character is alone on stage, speaking his or her thoughts. This device allows the author to establish the character's interior state without the use of direct commentary by a narrator. For instance, in Act IV, Scene xiii of *Dr. Faustus,* Faustus's soliloquy reveals his personal feelings about his impending doom. In an **aside,** a character literally turns to the audience and comments on the situation, a device that may have a humorous effect.

Motif

A **motif** is a recurring element or pattern, such as the notion of embarking on a quest or being transformed from one state to another. In drama, motifs can be visual, thematic, or aural. They can be used to emphasize parallels in the text and support an overarching theme of the play.

Much can be revealed by studying the motifs in a play. For example, throughout *Macbeth,* the motif of lightness and darkness is used to contrast innocence and depravity. A director who wanted to emphasize this contrast could use variations in lighting to create a visual motif to support this thematic motif. Other motifs in *Macbeth* are ambiguity, disturbances in nature, madness, and blood. While you read the play, consider what motifs draw your attention and how you could emphasize them if you were directing a performance of the play.

HOW TO READ

Drama

Read the script aloud. A play is meant to be performed. Hearing the words spoken will help you better understand dialogue that relates characters' feelings or descriptions of events and settings.

Visualize. Try to picture the elements described by stage directions, such as props, costumes, and lighting. If the stage directions contain only minimal information, imagine how you would stage the play if you were producing it.

Use the organization of the text. Plays usually are divided into acts and scenes. Each scene change indicates a change in time or place. Make note of these changes to track when and where events take place

Make inferences. It generally is not possible in a drama to provide lengthy exposition. Such explanatory information must come from the stage directions and characters' dialogue. Beyond that, you can make inferences about characters' motivations and other details. Discuss your ideas with your classmates, and read to see whether your inferences prove correct.

The Tragedy of Macbeth, Act I
A Drama by William Shakespeare

Build Background

Historical Context Shakespeare used Raphael Holinshed's 1587 edition of *Chronicles of England, Scotland, and Ireland* as the major historical source in writing *Macbeth* (see the Primary Source Connection on pages 434–437). The *Chronicles* tell of the reign of a bloodthirsty, twelfth-century Scottish king named Macbeth, as well as the murder of the Scottish King Duff by Donwald. Shakespeare combined these two tales to create the storyline of his play for a performance before King James I, who was descended from one of the characters in the play, Banquo.

Literary Context Along with *Romeo and Juliet* (1594), *Julius Caesar* (1599), *Hamlet* (1601), and *King Lear* (1603), *Macbeth* (1605–1606) is included among Shakespeare's greatest tragedies. A dark tale of a man's ambition and treachery, *Macbeth* still strikes a frighteningly familiar chord today, four centuries later. Few plays can match *Macbeth* for sheer spectacle and suspense.

Reader's Context You likely have heard the saying "The end justifies the means." What would you be willing to do to achieve a goal?

Meet the Author

William Shakespeare (1564–1616) had become a successful actor and playwright by his late twenties. His history plays *Henry VI, Parts 1, 2,* and *3,* and *Richard III* had established him as a significant presence in London theater. In 1593, when an outbreak of the plague forced the closing of the theaters, Shakespeare turned to writing narrative poetry, producing *Venus and Adonis* and *The Rape of Lucrece,* both of which were dedicated to a patron, the Earl of Southampton. When the theaters reopened, Shakespeare plunged back into his primary vocation, writing thirty-seven plays in less than twenty years.

Shakespeare's final play, *Henry VIII,* was performed in London in 1613. At that time, he probably was living again in Stratford in a large house called New Place, which he had bought in 1597. When he died in 1616, survived by his wife and two daughters, Shakespeare was a wealthy man. He was buried in the Holy Trinity Church in Stratford-on-Avon.

For a full biography of William Shakespeare, see the Author Focus in Unit 3, page 260.

Trinity Church in Stratford-on-Avon.

Analyze Literature
Conflict and Foil

The **conflict** is the struggle between two forces in a literary work. A plot introduces a conflict, develops it, and eventually resolves it. In an *external conflict,* the main character may struggle against another character, the forces of nature, society, or fate. In an *internal conflict,* the main character struggles against some element within himself or herself.

A **foil** is a character whose attributes, or qualities, contrast with and therefore highlight those of another character.

Set Purpose

Macbeth features some of Shakespeare's darkest characters. As you read Act I, identify the conflict facing Macbeth and determine whether it is internal or external. Also examine the roles of Banquo, King Duncan, and Lady Macbeth, who serve as foils for Macbeth. Record details about these characters' qualities, and think about how they are different from Macbeth.

Preview Vocabulary

flout, 344
trifle, 349
surmise, 349
recompense, 351
wanton, 352
chastise, 353
remorse, 353
pall, 354
purveyor, 355
mettle, 358

The TRAGEDY of MACBETH

by William Shakespeare

CHARACTERS IN THE PLAY

DUNCAN, *King of Scotland*

MALCOLM

DONALBAIN — *Duncan's sons*

MACBETH

BANQUO — *Generals in the king's army*

MACDUFF

LENNOX

ROSSE

MENTETH — *Scottish noblemen*

ANGUS

CATHNESS

FLEANCE, *Banquo's son*

SIWARD, *Earl of Northumberland, leader of the English troops*

YOUNG SIWARD, *Siward's son*

SEYTON, *Macbeth's servant*

BOY, *Macduff's son*

ENGLISH DOCTOR

SCOTS DOCTOR

SERGEANT

PORTER, *or* GATEKEEPER

OLD MAN

Three MURDERERS

LADY MACBETH

LADY MACDUFF

GENTLEWOMAN, *Lady Macbeth's servant*

Three WITCHES, *the Weïrd Sisters*

Three other WITCHES

HECATE, *Queen of the Witches*

APPARITIONS

LORDS, GENTLEMEN, OFFICERS, SOLDIERS, ATTENDANTS, MESSENGERS *and* BANQUO'S GHOST

SCENES: Scotland and England

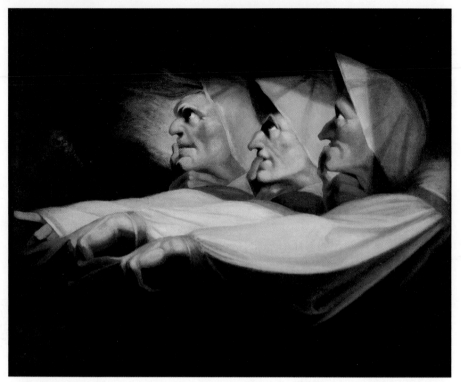

Three Witches, 1783. Johann Heinrich Füssli.
Royal Shakespeare Theater Collection, London, England.
(See detail on page 340.)

Act I

Scene i: An open place

Thunder and lightning. Enter three Witches.

1. Witch.   When shall we three meet again?
In thunder, lightning, or in rain?

2. Witch.   When the hurly-burly's[1] done,
When the battle's lost and won.

5   **3. Witch.**   That will be ere the set of sun.

1. Witch.   Where the place?

2. Witch.   Upon the heath.

3. Witch.   There to meet with Macbeth.

1. Witch.   I come, Graymalkin.[2]

2. Witch.   Paddock[3] calls.

10   **3. Witch.**   Anon.

All.   Fair is foul, and foul is fair,
Hover through the fog and filthy air.   *Exeunt.*

Act I, Scene i
1. **hurly-burly.** Commotion of the battle

2. **Graymalkin.** Gray cat; the witch's companion's name
3. **Paddock.** Toad; the second witch's companion's name

SCENE ii: A CAMP IN SCOTLAND

ACT I, SCENE ii
4. **Alarum.** Trumpet call

Alarum[4] *within. Enter* KING DUNCAN, MALCOLM, DONALBAIN, LENNOX,
with ATTENDANTS, *meeting a bleeding* SERGEANT.

DUNCAN.   What bloody man is that? He can report,
As seemeth by his plight, of the revolt
The newest state.

MALCOLM.   This is the sergeant,
Who like a good and hardy soldier fought
'Gainst my captivity. Hail, brave friend!
Say to the King the knowledge of the broil
As thou didst leave it.

SERGEANT.   Doubtful it stood,
As two spent swimmers that do cling together
And choke their art.[5] The merciless Macdonwald

5. **art.** Skill (in swimming)

(Worthy to be a rebel, for to that
The multiplying villainies of nature
Do swarm upon him) from the Western Isles
Of kerns and gallowglasses[6] is supplied,
And Fortune, on his damned quarrel[7] smiling,
Show'd like a rebel's whore. But all's too weak;
For brave Macbeth (well he deserves that name),
Disdaining Fortune, with his brandish'd steel,
Which smok'd with bloody execution,
(Like Valor's minion[8]) carv'd out his passage
Till he fac'd the slave;
Which nev'r shook hands, nor bade farewell to him,
Till he unseam'd him from the nave to th' chops,[9]
And fix'd his head upon our battlements.

6. **kerns and gallowglasses.**
Kerns—lightly armed foot
soldiers; *gallowglasses*—heavily
armed soldiers
7. **quarrel.** Cause

8. **minion.** Favorite

9. **unseam'd . . . chops.** Cut
him from navel to jaw

DUNCAN.   O valiant cousin,[10] worthy gentleman!

SERGEANT.   As whence the sun gins his reflection[11]
Shipwracking storms and direful thunders break,
So from that spring whence comfort seem'd to come
Discomfort swells. Mark, King of Scotland, mark!
No sooner justice had, with valor arm'd,
Compell'd these skipping kerns to trust their heels,
But the Norweyan lord, surveying vantage,
With furbish'd arms and new supplies of men,
Began a fresh assault.

10. **cousin.** Generic term for
a relative (Duncan and Macbeth were both grandsons of
King Malcolm)
11. **gins his reflection.**
Begins turning back (at the
vernal equinox)

DUNCAN.   Dismay'd not this
Our captains, Macbeth and Banquo?

SERGEANT.   Yes,
As sparrows eagles; or the hare the lion.
If I say sooth, I must report they were

As cannons overcharg'd with double cracks,[12] so they
Doubly redoubled strokes upon the foe.
Except they meant to bathe in reeking[13] wounds,
40 Or memorize another Golgotha,[14]
I cannot tell—
But I am faint, my gashes cry for help.

DUNCAN.   So well thy words become thee as thy wounds,
They smack of honor both. Go get him surgeons.

> *Exit* SERGEANT, *attended.*

Enter ROSSE *and* ANGUS.

Who comes here?

45 MALCOLM.   The worthy Thane[15] of Rosse.

LENNOX.   What a haste looks through his eyes! So should he look
That seems to speak things strange.

ROSSE.   God save the king!

DUNCAN.   Whence cam'st thou, worthy thane?

ROSSE.   From Fife, great King,
Where the Norweyan banners <u>flout</u> the sky
50 And fan our people cold.
Norway himself, with terrible numbers,
Assisted by that most disloyal traitor,
The Thane of Cawdor, began a dismal conflict,
Till that Bellona's bridegroom, lapp'd in proof,[16]
55 Confronted him with self-comparisons,
Point against point, rebellious arm 'gainst arm,
Curbing his lavish spirit; and to conclude,
The victory fell on us.

DUNCAN.   Great happiness!

ROSSE.   That now
Sweno, the Norways' king, craves composition;
60 Nor would we deign him burial of his men
Till he disbursed at Saint Colme's inch[17]
Ten thousand dollars to our general use.

DUNCAN.   No more that Thane of Cawdor shall deceive
Our bosom interest. Go pronounce his present[18] death,
65 And with his former title greet Macbeth.

ROSSE.   I'll see it done.

DUNCAN.   What he hath lost, noble Macbeth hath won.

> *Exeunt.*

12. cracks. Charges

13. reeking. Steaming

14. memorize . . . Golgotha. Make the place as memorable for slaughter as Golgotha, the place of skulls

15. Thane. Scottish title of nobility

flout (flout) *v.,* show scorn or contempt for

16. Bellona's . . . proof. Macbeth, who is paired with Bellona, goddess of war, is clad in tested armor.

17. Saint Colme's inch. Small island near Edinburgh, Scotland

18. present. Immediate

Jean-Philippe Lafont and Maria Guleghina perform an opera version of *Macbeth* at the Opéra National de Paris in Paris, France (1999).

SCENE iii: A HEATH

Thunder. Enter the three WITCHES.

1. WITCH.   Where hast thou been, sister?

2. WITCH.   Killing swine.[19]

3. WITCH.   Sister, where thou?

1. WITCH.   A sailor's wife had chestnuts in her lap,
5 And mounch'd, and mounch'd, and mounch'd. "Give me!" quoth I.
"Aroint[20] thee, witch!" the rump-fed ronyon[21] cries.
Her husband's to Aleppo gone, master o' th' *Tiger*;[22]
But in a sieve I'll thither sail,
And, like a rat without a tail,
10 I'll do, I'll do, and I'll do.

2. WITCH.   I'll give thee a wind.

1. WITCH.   Th' art kind.

3. WITCH.   And I another.

1. WITCH.   I myself have all the other,
15 And the very ports they blow,
All the quarters that they know
I' th' shipman's card.[23]
I'll drain him dry as hay:
Sleep shall neither night nor day

ACT I, SCENE iii
19. **killing swine.** It was commonly believed that witches killed domestic animals, especially pigs.

20. **Aroint.** Be gone
21. **rump-fed ronyon.** Fat, good-for-nothing creature
22. **Aleppo . . . Tiger.** Her husband went to Aleppo, a trading center in Syria, on a ship called the *Tiger*.

23. **shipman's card.** Compass or chart

20   Hang upon his penthouse lid;[24]
      He shall live a man forbid;[25]
      Weary sev'nnights, nine times nine,
      Shall he dwindle, peak,[26] and pine;
      Though his bark cannot be lost,
25   Yet it shall be tempest-toss'd.
      Look what I have.

      2. Witch.   Show me, show me.

      1. Witch.   Here I have a pilot's thumb,
      Wrack'd as homeward he did come.
      Drum within.

30   **3. Witch.**   A drum, a drum!
      Macbeth doth come.

      All.   The weïrd[27] sisters, hand in hand,
      Posters[28] of the sea and land,
      Thus do go, about, about,
35   Thrice to thine, and thrice to mine,
      And thrice again, to make up nine.
      Peace, the charm's wound up.

      Enter Macbeth *and* Banquo.

      Macbeth.   So foul and fair a day I have not seen.

      Banquo.   How far is't call'd to Forres? What are these
40   So wither'd and so wild in their attire,[29]
      That look not like th' inhabitants o' th' earth,
      And yet are on't? Live you? or are you aught
      That man may question? You seem to understand me,
      By each at once her choppy[30] finger laying
45   Upon her skinny lips. You should be women,
      And yet your beards forbid me to interpret
      That you are so.

      Macbeth.   Speak, if you can: what are you?

      1. Witch.   All hail, Macbeth, hail to thee, Thane of Glamis!

      2. Witch.   All hail, Macbeth, hail to thee, Thane of Cawdor!

50   **3. Witch.**   All hail, Macbeth, that shalt be King hereafter!

      Banquo.   Good sir, why do you start, and seem to fear
      Things that do sound so fair?—I' th' name of truth,
      Are ye fantastical,[31] or that indeed
      Which outwardly ye show? My noble partner
55   You greet with present grace,[32] and great prediction
      Of noble having and of royal hope,
      That he seems rapt withal; to me you speak not.
      If you can look into the seeds of time,

---

24. **penthouse lid.** Eyelid

25. **forbid.** Under a curse

26. **peak.** Become peaked, or pale and sickly

27. **weïrd.** Destiny serving; from the Old English *wyrd*, or fate

28. **Posters.** Swift travelers

29. **attire.** Dress; clothing

30. **choppy.** Chapped

31. **fantastical.** Imaginary

32. **present grace.** By his present title; that is, Thane of Glamis

Witchcraft in Early Modern Europe

Early modern Europeans believed that witches lived in their midst and feared their practices eventually would destroy Christianity. As a result, individuals accused of holding secret ceremonies and performing so-called black magic often were driven from their communities, tried in the courts, and even tortured and killed.

Although witch hunts occurred sporadically throughout the Middle Ages, they did not become prevalent until the mid-1400s. Before then, the Catholic Church had declared that even acknowledging the existence of witchcraft was a sin punishable by death. As local witch hunts became more frequent, the Church felt it had to publicly address this growing phenomenon. In 1400, the Church officially recognized the existence of witchcraft for the first time.

People in rural areas were more prone to conduct witch hunts than those in urban centers, likely because of the differences in education and experience between rural and urban dwellers. Medieval conceptions of witches and magic lingered in remote areas. Witch hunts also occurred more frequently in regions where infighting between Catholics and Protestants was prevalent. Accusing religious opponents of practicing witchcraft was an effective means of silencing them.

German woodcut depicting witches brewing up a hailstorm (1489).

Accusations of witchcraft peaked in the 1400s and early 1500s, dropped in the mid-1500s, and then increased again in the early 1600s, when Shakespeare wrote *Macbeth*. Accusations subsided in England after the Great London Fire of 1666, but they resurfaced in the American colonies with the Salem witch trials in 1692.

And say which grain will grow, and which will not,
60   Speak then to me, who neither beg nor fear
Your favors nor your hate.

    1. WITCH.   Hail!

    2. WITCH.   Hail!

    3. WITCH.   Hail!

65   **1. WITCH.**   Lesser than Macbeth, and greater.

    2. WITCH.   Not so happy, yet much happier.

    3. WITCH.   Thou shalt get kings, though thou be none.
So all hail, Macbeth and Banquo!

    1. WITCH.   Banquo and Macbeth, all hail!

70   **MACBETH.**   Stay, you imperfect[33] speakers, tell me more:
By Sinel's[34] death I know I am Thane of Glamis,
But how of Cawdor? The Thane of Cawdor lives
A prosperous gentleman; and to be king
Stands not within the prospect of belief,

33. **imperfect.** Incomplete
34. **Sinel.** Macbeth's father

75   No more than to be Cawdor. Say from whence
     You owe this strange intelligence,[35] or why
     Upon this blasted heath you stop our way
     With such prophetic greeting? Speak, I charge you.

                                        WITCHES *vanish*.

     BANQUO.   The earth hath bubbles, as the water has,
80   And these are of them. Whither are they vanish'd?

     MACBETH.   Into the air; and what seem'd corporal[36] melted,
     As breath into the wind. Would they had stay'd!

     BANQUO.   Were such things here as we do speak about?
     Or have we eaten on the insane root[37]
85   That takes the reason prisoner?

     MACBETH.   Your children shall be kings.

     BANQUO.   You shall be king.

     MACBETH.   And Thane of Cawdor too; went it not so?

     BANQUO.   To th' self-same tune and words. Who's here?

     Enter ROSSE *and* ANGUS.

     ROSSE.   The King hath happily receiv'd, Macbeth,
90   The news of thy success; and when he reads
     Thy personal venture in the rebels' fight,
     His wonders and his praises do contend
     Which should be thine or his.[38] Silenc'd with that,
     In viewing o'er the rest o' th' self-same day,
95   He finds thee in the stout Norweyan ranks,
     Nothing afeard of what thyself didst make,
     Strange images of death. As thick as tale
     Came post with post,[39] and every one did bear
     Thy praises in his kingdom's great defense,
     And pour'd them down before him.

100 ANGUS.   We are sent
     To give thee from our royal master thanks,
     Only to herald thee into his sight,
     Not pay thee.

     ROSSE.   And for an earnest[40] of a greater honor,
105 He bade me, from him, call thee Thane of Cawdor;
     In which addition, hail, most worthy thane,
     For it is thine.

     BANQUO.   What, can the devil speak true?

     MACBETH.   The Thane of Cawdor lives; why do you dress me
     In borrowed robes?

35. **owe this strange intelligence.** Possess this strange information

36. **corporal.** Of the body; bodily

37. **insane root.** Insanity-causing root, probably hemlock or henbane

38. **His wonders . . . his.** Duncan is torn between amazement and admiration

39. **post with post.** Messenger after messenger

40. **earnest.** Something given or done as an indication or assurance of what is to come

ANGUS.   Who was the thane lives yet,
110   But under heavy judgment bears that life
Which he deserves to lose. Whether he was combin'd[41]
With those of Norway, or did line[42] the rebel
With hidden help and vantage, or that with both
He labor'd in his country's wrack,[43] I know not;
115   But treasons capital, confess'd and prov'd,
Have overthrown him.

MACBETH.   [*Aside.*] Glamis, and Thane of Cawdor!
The greatest is behind.[44] [*To Rosse and Angus.*] Thanks for your
    pains.
[*Aside to Banquo.*] Do you not hope your children shall be kings,
When those that gave the Thane of Cawdor to me
Promis'd no less to them?

120   **BANQUO.**   [*Aside to Macbeth.*] That, trusted home,[45]
Might yet enkindle you unto[46] the crown,
Besides the Thane of Cawdor. But 'tis strange;
And oftentimes, to win us to our harm,
The instruments of darkness tell us truths,
125   Win us with honest <u>trifles</u>, to betray 's
In deepest consequence.—
Cousins, a word, I pray you.

MACBETH.   [*Aside.*] Two truths are told,
As happy prologues to the swelling act
Of the imperial theme.[47]—I thank you, gentlemen.
130   [*Aside.*] This supernatural soliciting
Cannot be ill; cannot be good. If ill,
Why hath it given me earnest of success,
Commencing in a truth? I am Thane of Cawdor.
If good, why do I yield to that suggestion
135   Whose horrid image doth unfix my hair
And make my seated heart knock at my ribs,
Against the use of nature? Present fears
Are less than horrible imaginings:
My thought, whose murther[48] yet is but fantastical,
140   Shakes so my single state of man that function
Is smother'd in <u>surmise</u>, and nothing is
But what is not.

BANQUO.   Look how our partner's rapt.

MACBETH.   [*Aside.*] If chance will have me king, why, chance
    may crown me
Without my stir.

---

41. **combin'd.** Allied
42. **line.** Align with, support

43. **wrack.** Ruin

44. **behind.** Right behind it; yet to come

45. **home.** Completely
46. **enkindle you unto.** Cause you to hope for

tri • fle (trī´ fəl) *n.,* something of little value or importance

47. **swelling . . . theme.** Grand idea that I will be king

48. **murther.** Murder

sur • mise (sər mīz´) *n.,* guessing; imagined action

Lawrence Olivier as Macbeth, 1955. Ruskin Spear.
Victoria and Albert Museum, London, England.

BANQUO.   New honors come upon him,
145   Like our strange garments, cleave not to their mould
But with the aid of use.[49]

MACBETH.   [*Aside.*] Come what come may,
Time and the hour runs through the roughest day.

BANQUO.   Worthy Macbeth, we stay upon your leisure.

MACBETH.   Give me your favor;[50] my dull brain was wrought
150   With things forgotten. Kind gentlemen, your pains
Are regist'red where every day I turn
The leaf to read them. Let us toward the King.
[*Aside to Banquo.*] Think upon what hath chanc'd; and at more time,
The interim having weigh'd it, let us speak
Our free hearts each to other.

155   **BANQUO.**   Very gladly.

MACBETH.   Till then, enough.—Come, friends.   *Exeunt.*

Scene iv: A room in the palace at Forres

Flourish. Enter KING DUNCAN, LENNOX, MALCOLM, DONALBAIN,
and ATTENDANTS.

DUNCAN.   Is execution done on Cawdor? Are not
Those in commission[51] yet return'd?

MALCOLM.   My liege,
They are not yet come back. But I have spoke
With one that saw him die; who did report
5   That very frankly he confess'd his treasons,
Implor'd your Highness' pardon, and set forth

49. **New honors . . . aid of use.** Banquo is saying that Macbeth needs to wear his new title a while before it will feel right, just as one needs to break in new clothes.

50. **favor.** Pardon

ACT I, SCENE iv
51. **in commission.** Delegated to oversee the execution

Tanistry

Early Gaelic clans living in Scotland, Ireland, and the Isle of Man chose their leaders using a succession system called *tanistry*. When a new king assumed power, the clan's nobles would elect a successor, whom they called the *tanist*. This individual usually was from a different branch of the clan from the king. Once a tanist became king, the nobles would fill the vacated position by electing a new tanist from another branch of the clan. This rotation of power ensured that no single branch of a clan would assume absolute control. Tanistry remained Scotland's system of succession until 1603, when James I abolished it in favor of the English hereditary system.

Based on the laws of tanistry, Macbeth had more right to the throne than Malcolm, having earned the title as a war hero. Thus, according to some interpretations, Duncan wrongs Macbeth by naming his son Malcolm as his successor. From this perspective, the play is much more sympathetic to Macbeth.

A deep repentance. Nothing in his life
Became him like the leaving it. He died
As one that had been studied in his death,
10 To throw away the dearest thing he ow'd,
As 'twere a careless trifle.

DUNCAN.   There's no art
To find the mind's construction in the face:
He was a gentleman on whom I built
An absolute trust.

Enter MACBETH, BANQUO, ROSSE, *and* ANGUS.

                    O worthiest cousin!
15 The sin of my ingratitude even now
Was heavy on me. Thou art so far before,
That swiftest wing of <u>recompense</u> is slow
To overtake thee. Would thou hadst less deserv'd,
That the proportion both of thanks and payment
20 Might have been mine![52] Only I have left to say,
More is thy due than more than all can pay.

MACBETH.   The service and the loyalty I owe,
In doing it, pays itself. Your Highness' part
Is to receive our duties; and our duties
25 Are to your throne and state children and servants;
Which do but what they should, by doing every thing
Safe toward your love and honor.

DUNCAN.   Welcome hither!
I have begun to plant thee, and will labor

> **rec • om • pense**
> (reˊ kəm pən[t]s)
> *n.,* repayment; reward

52. **Would . . . mine.** If you had been less deserving, I could have rewarded you as you deserve.

To make thee full of growing. Noble Banquo,
30   That hast no less deserv'd, nor must be known
No less to have done so, let me infold thee
And hold thee to my heart.

BANQUO.   There if I grow,
The harvest is your own.

DUNCAN.   My plenteous joys,
<u>Wanton</u> in fullness, seek to hide themselves
35   In drops of sorrow. Sons, kinsmen, thanes,
And you whose places are the nearest, know
We will establish our estate upon
Our eldest, Malcolm, whom we name hereafter
The Prince of Cumberland; which honor must
40   Not unaccompanied invest him only,
But signs of nobleness, like stars, shall shine
On all deservers. From hence to Enverness,[53]
And bind us further to you.

MACBETH.   The rest is labor, which is not us'd for you.
45   I'll be myself the harbinger,[54] and make joyful
The hearing of my wife with your approach;
So humbly take my leave.

DUNCAN.   My worthy Cawdor!

MACBETH.   [*Aside.*] The Prince of Cumberland! that is a step
On which I must fall down, or else o'erleap,
50   For in my way it lies. Stars, hide your fires,
Let not light see my black and deep desires;
The eye wink at the hand;[55] yet let that be
Which the eye fears, when it is done, to see.

Exit.

DUNCAN.   True, worthy Banquo! he is full so valiant,
55   And in his commendations I am fed;
It is a banquet to me. Let's after him,
Whose care is gone before to bid us welcome:
It is a peerless kinsman.

Flourish. Exeunt.

SCENE V: A ROOM IN MACBETH'S CASTLE AT INVERNESS

Enter MACBETH'S WIFE *alone with a letter.*

LADY MACBETH. [*Reads.*] "They met me in the day of success; and
I have learn'd by the perfect'st report, they have more in them
than mortal knowledge. When I burnt in desire to question them
further, they made themselves air, into which they vanish'd.

wan • ton (wän´ t'n)
adj., undisciplined;
unmanageable

53. **Enverness.** Inverness,
Macbeth's castle

54. **harbinger.** Something or
someone that arrives before

55. **The eye . . . hand.** Be
blind to what the hand does

5 Whiles I stood rapt in the wonder of it, came missives[56] from the
 King, who all-hail'd me 'Thane of Cawdor,' by which title, before,
 these weïrd sisters saluted me, and referr'd me to the coming on
 of time with 'Hail, King that shalt be!' This have I thought good
10 to deliver thee, my dearest partner of greatness, that thou mightst
 not lose the dues of rejoicing by being ignorant of what greatness
 is promis'd thee. Lay it to thy heart, and farewell."
 Glamis thou art, and Cawdor, and shalt be
 What thou art promis'd. Yet do I fear thy nature,
15 It is too full o' th' milk of human kindness
 To catch the nearest way. Thou wouldst be great,
 Art not without ambition, but without
 The illness[57] should attend it. What thou wouldst highly,
 That wouldst thou holily; wouldst not play false,
20 And yet wouldst wrongly win. Thou'ldst have, great Glamis
 That which cries, "Thus thou must do," if thou have it;
 And that which rather thou dost fear to do
 Than wishest should be undone. Hie thee hither,
 That I may pour my spirits in thine ear,
25 And chastise with the valor of my tongue
 All that impedes[58] thee from the golden round,
 Which fate and metaphysical[59] aid doth seem
 To have thee crown'd withal.

 Enter MESSENGER.

        What is your tidings?

MESSENGER. The King comes here tonight.

LADY MACBETH.   Thou'rt mad to say it!
 Is not thy master with him? who, were't so,
30 Would have inform'd for preparation.

MESSENGER. So please you, it is true; our thane is coming.
 One of my fellows had the speed of him,
 Who, almost dead for breath, had scarcely more
 Than would make up his message.

LADY MACBETH.   Give him tending,
 He brings great news.   *Exit* MESSENGER.
35   The raven himself is hoarse
 That croaks the fatal entrance of Duncan
 Under my battlements. Come, you spirits
 That tend on mortal[60] thoughts, unsex me here,
 And fill me from the crown to the toe topful
40 Of direst cruelty! Make thick my blood,
 Stop up th' access and passage to remorse,

56. **missives.** Messengers

57. **illness.** Wickedness

chas • tise (chas['] tīz´)
v., scold or condemn sharply

58. **impedes.** Obstructs or delays
59. **metaphysical.** Supernatural

60. **mortal.** Deadly

re • morse (ri môrs´)
n., pity; compassion

That no compunctious visitings of nature[61]
Shake my fell[62] purpose, nor keep peace between
Th' effect and it! Come to my woman's breasts,
45 And take my milk for gall,[63] you murth'ring ministers,
Wherever in your sightless substances
You wait on nature's mischief! Come, thick night,
And <u>pall</u> thee in the dunnest smoke of hell,
That my keen knife see not the wound it makes,
50 Nor heaven peep through the blanket of the dark
To cry, "Hold, hold!"

Enter MACBETH.

                       Great Glamis! worthy Cawdor!
Greater than both, by the all-hail hereafter!
Thy letters have transported me beyond
This ignorant present, and I feel now
The future in the instant.

55 MACBETH.   My dearest love,
Duncan comes here tonight.

LADY MACBETH.   And when goes hence?

57 MACBETH.   Tomorrow, as he purposes.

LADY MACBETH.   O, never
Shall sun that morrow see!
Your face, my thane, is as a book, where men
60 May read strange matters. To beguile the time,[64]
Look like the time; bear welcome in your eye,
Your hand, your tongue; look like th' innocent flower,
But be the serpent under't. He that's coming
Must be provided for; and you shall put
65 This night's great business into my dispatch,[65]
Which shall to all our nights and days to come
Give solely sovereign sway and masterdom.

MACBETH.   We will speak further.

LADY MACBETH.   Only look up clear:[66]
To alter favor ever is to fear.
70 Leave all the rest to me.   *Exeunt.*

SCENE vi: IN FRONT OF MACBETH'S CASTLE

Hoboys and torches. Enter KING DUNCAN, MALCOLM, DONALBAIN,
BANQUO, LENNOX, MACDUFF, ROSSE, ANGUS, *and* ATTENDANTS.

DUNCAN.   This castle hath a pleasant seat,[67] the air
Nimbly and sweetly recommends itself
Unto our gentle senses.

---

61. **compunctious . . .
nature.** Natural feelings
of pity
62. **fell.** Cruel
63. **gall.** Bile

pall (pôl) *v.*, cloak in
darkness

64. **beguile the time.** Deceive
everybody

65. **dispatch.** Management

66. **look up clear.** Seem
innocent

ACT I, SCENE vi
67. **seat.** Location

BANQUO.   This guest of summer,
The temple-haunting marlet,[68] does approve,
5   By his lov'd mansionry,[69] that the heaven's breath
Smells wooingly here; no jutty, frieze,
Buttress, nor coign of vantage,[70] but this bird
Hath made his pendant bed and procreant cradle.
Where they most breed and haunt, I have observ'd
The air is delicate.

Enter LADY MACBETH.

10   **DUNCAN.**   See, see, our honor'd hostess!
The love that follows us sometime is our trouble,
Which still we thank as love. Herein I teach you
How you shall bid God 'ield us for your pains,
And thank us for your trouble.[71]

LADY MACBETH.   All our service
15   In every point twice done, and then done double,
Were poor and single[72] business to contend
Against those honors deep and broad wherewith
Your Majesty loads our house. For those of old,
And the late dignities heap'd up to them,
We rest your ermites.[73]

20   **DUNCAN.**   Where's the Thane of Cawdor?
We cours'd him at the heels, and had a purpose
To be his <u>purveyor</u>; but he rides well,
And his great love, sharp as his spur, hath holp[74] him
To his home before us. Fair and noble hostess,
We are your guest tonight.

25   **LADY MACBETH.**   Your servants ever
Have theirs, themselves, and what is theirs, in compt,[75]
To make their audit at your Highness' pleasure,
Still[76] to return your own.

DUNCAN.   Give me your hand.
Conduct me to mine host, we love him highly,
30   And shall continue our graces towards him.
By your leave, hostess.   *Exeunt.*

SCENE vii: A ROOM IN MACBETH'S CASTLE

Hoboys, torches. Enter a SEWER[77] *and divers* SERVANTS *with dishes and service over the stage. Then enter* MACBETH.

MACBETH.   If it were done, when 'tis done, then 'twere well
It were done quickly. If th' assassination
Could trammel up the consequence, and catch
With his surcease, success;[78] that but this blow

---

68. temple-haunting marlet. Bird that nests around churches
69. mansionry. Nest
70. no jutty . . . vantage. No projecting structure or convenient corner

71. The love . . . trouble. Although my visit is an inconvenience to you, you should ask God to reward me for your pains because I came out of love for you.
72. single. Feeble

73. We . . . ermites. We shall be your hermits (that is, we shall always pray for you).

pur • vey • or
(pur' vā´ ər) *n.,* one who supplies or provides

74. holp. Helped

75. compt. Trust

76. Still. Always

ACT I, SCENE vii
77. Sewer. Butler

78. If . . . success. If the assassination could be successful and without consequence

5 Might be the be-all and the end-all—here,
  But here, upon this bank and shoal of time,
  We'd jump the life to come. But in these cases
  We still have judgment here, that we but teach
  Bloody instructions, which, being taught, return
10 To plague th' inventor. This even-handed justice
  Commends[79] th' ingredience of our poison'd chalice
  To our own lips. He's here in double trust:
  First, as I am his kinsman and his subject,
  Strong both against the deed; then, as his host,
15 Who should against his murtherer shut the door,
  Not bear the knife myself. Besides, this Duncan
  Hath borne his faculties[80] so meek, hath been
  So clear[81] in his great office, that his virtues
  Will plead like angels, trumpet-tongu'd, against
20 The deep damnation of his taking-off;
  And pity, like a naked new-born babe,
  Striding the blast, or heaven's cherubin, hors'd
  Upon the sightless couriers[82] of the air,
  Shall blow the horrid deed in every eye,
25 That tears shall drown the wind. I have no spur
  To prick the sides of my intent, but only
  Vaulting ambition, which o'erleaps itself,
  And falls on th' other—

  Enter LADY MACBETH.

     How now? what news?

79. **Commends.** Offers

80. **faculties.** Royal powers
81. **clear.** Blameless

82. **sightless couriers.**
Invisible messengers; the wind

LADY MACBETH.   He has almost supp'd. Why have you left the
chamber?

MACBETH.   Hath he ask'd for me?

30 **LADY MACBETH.**   Know you not he has?

MACBETH.   We will proceed no further in this business:
He hath honor'd me of late, and I have bought[83]
Golden opinions from all sorts of people,
Which would be worn now in their newest gloss,
Not cast aside so soon.

35 **LADY MACBETH.**   Was the hope drunk
Wherein you dress'd yourself? Hath it slept since?
And wakes it now to look so green and pale
At what it did so freely? From this time
Such I account thy love. Art thou afeard
40 To be the same in thine own act and valor
As thou art in desire? Wouldst thou have that
Which thou esteem'st the ornament of life,[84]
And live a coward in thine own esteem,
Letting "I dare not" wait upon, "I would,"
Like the poor cat i' th' adage?[85]

45 **MACBETH.**   Prithee peace!
I dare do all that may become a man;
Who dares do more is none.

LADY MACBETH.   What beast was't then
That made you break[86] this enterprise to me?
When you durst do it, then you were a man;
50 And to be more than what you were, you would
Be so much more the man. Nor time, nor place,
Did then adhere,[87] and yet you would make both:
They have made themselves, and that their fitness now
Does unmake you. I have given suck, and know
55 How tender 'tis to love the babe that milks me;
I would, while it was smiling in my face,
Have pluck'd my nipple from his boneless gums,
And dash'd the brains out, had I so sworn as you
Have done to this.

MACBETH.   If we should fail?

LADY MACBETH.   We fail?
60 But[88] screw your courage to the sticking place,[89]
And we'll not fail. When Duncan is asleep
(Whereto the rather shall his day's hard journey
Soundly invite him), his two chamberlains
Will I with wine and wassail[90] so convince,

83. **bought.** Earned

84. **ornament of life.** Crown

85. **cat . . . adage.** Refers to
an old saying about a cat who
wants to eat fish without getting its paws wet

86. **break.** Broach

87. **Did then adhere.** Were
then suitable

88. **But.** Only
89. **the sticking place.**
Notch that holds the string
of a crossbow

90. **wassail.** Carousing

65 That memory, the warder of the brain,
  Shall be a fume, and the receipt of reason
  A limbeck[91] only. When in swinish sleep
  Their drenched natures lies as in a death,
  What cannot you and I perform upon
70 Th' unguarded Duncan? what not put upon
  His spungy[92] officers, who shall bear the guilt
  Of our great quell?[93]

  MACBETH.   Bring forth men-children only!
  For thy undaunted <u>mettle</u> should compose
  Nothing but males. Will it not be receiv'd,
75 When we have mark'd with blood those sleepy two
  Of his own chamber, and us'd their very daggers,
  That they have done't?

  LADY MACBETH. Who dares receive it other,
  As we shall make our griefs and clamor roar
  Upon his death?

  MACBETH. I am settled, and bend up
80 Each corporal agent to this terrible feat.
  Away, and mock the time[94] with fairest show:
  False face must hide what the false heart doth know.

            Exeunt. ❖

91. **That . . . limbeck.**
Fumes of wine would rise
from the stomach and confuse
the brain.

92. **spungy.** Spongy with
drink; drunk
93. **quell.** Murder

met • tle (me´ t'l) *n.*,
spirit; courage

94. **mock the time.** Deceive
the world

MIRRORS & WINDOWS Do you believe in supernatural predictions and prophecies? Do you read your horoscope? What appeal do these things have to some people?

Refer to Text ▶ ▶ ▶ ▶ ▶ **Reason with Text**

1a. In Macbeth's first statement in the play (Scene iii, line 38), how does he describe the day of the battle?

1b. Why is line 38 ominous? Explain what it foreshadows, or hints, about Macbeth's future associations.

Understand
Find meaning

2a. List the predictions the witches make when talking to Macbeth and Banquo in Scene iii. Which of these predictions comes true almost immediately?

2b. How do Macbeth and Banquo differ in their reactions to the witches' prophecies? Suggest what these differences reveal about the two characters.

Apply
Use information

3a. What reasons does Macbeth have for killing Duncan? What reasons does he have for not killing him?

3b. Point out the character traits that could lead Macbeth to kill Duncan anyway.

Analyze
Take things apart

4a. How does Lady Macbeth react to her husband's letter? What does she make up her mind to do?

4b. Why do Macbeth and Lady Macbeth argue in Scene vii? Compare and contrast their feelings about the planned assassination of Duncan.

Evaluate
Make judgments

5a. How does Lady Macbeth get her husband to change his mind about killing Duncan? Evaluate the notion of manliness she presents.

5b. Explain how the concept of manliness is different or the same in modern society.

Create
Bring ideas together

Analyze Literature

Conflict and Foil
What is the primary struggle, or conflict, facing Macbeth? Is it an internal or external conflict? Explain using details from the text.

Review the details you recorded about Banquo, King Duncan, and Lady Macbeth. What quality or qualities make each of these characters a foil for Macbeth? How are they different from Macbeth?

Extend the Text

Writing Options
Creative Writing Imagine you are Banquo and write a letter to your wife detailing the events of the day from your point of view.

Descriptive Writing Write a character sketch of Macbeth and Lady Macbeth. Cite specific line numbers in the text that support your description of each character.

Collaborative Learning
Understand Dramatic Conventions An aside is a statement made by a character in a play, intended to be heard by the audience but not by other characters in the play. With a partner, locate the parts of Scene iii that

are spoken as asides, and list the information revealed in each aside. What do Macbeth's and Banquo's asides reveal about their characters? Share your responses with the class.

Critical Literacy
Analyze Speeches Review Macbeth's soliloquy in Act I, Scene vii, lines 1–28. Outline Macbeth's speech and list the pros and cons he considers for acting immediately to kill King Duncan. What does he decide? How does this decision influence his course of action, in Scene vii? Discuss your findings with a partner.

 Go to **www.mirrorsandwindows.com** for more.

Understand the Concept

A **contraction** is formed by combining a pronoun and a verb or the words in a verb phrase. One or more letters are omitted and replaced with an apostrophe. For instance, combining the pronoun *I* with the verb *am* creates the contraction *I'm,* and combining the words *is* and *not* creates *isn't.*

Shakespeare used contractions frequently but often in ways now considered archaic or obsolete. For the sake of pronunciation (remember that dramas are meant to be performed), he created many past-tense verbs by adding *-d* instead of *-ed,* such as *murther'd* (*murdered*) in the following example. Words such as *it, us, his,* and *the* also were frequently contracted.

> **EXAMPLE**
>
> If't be so, For Banquo's issue have I fil'd my mind, For them the gracious Duncan have I murther'd. (Act III, Scene i, lines 64–65)

In a less archaic and contracted form, this sentence would read, "If it be so, for Banquo's issue I have defiled my mind, for them the gracious Duncan have I murdered."

In modern usage, the use of contractions generally is considered informal and thus acceptable in everyday conversation and personal writing. Commonly used contractions formed from the pronouns *I, you, we,* and *they* include the following:

I'm (I am)	we're (we are)
I've (I have)	we've (we have)
I'll (I will)	we'll (we will)
you're (you are)	they're (they are)
you've (you have)	they've (they have)
you'll (you will)	they'll (they will)

Commonly used contractions formed from verb phrases with *not* include these:

isn't (is not)	don't (do not)
wasn't (was not)	didn't (did not)
won't (will not)	doesn't (does not)
wouldn't (would not)	couldn't (could not)

Several other commonly used contractions are sometimes mistakenly used as possessives to show ownership. The word *it's* is a contraction that means "it is"; the possessive *its* is written without an apostrophe. Similarly, the word *who's* is a contraction meaning "who is"; the possessive of *who* is *whose.*

EXAMPLES
Contraction *It's* time to leave for the play.
Possessive The car was due for *its* tune-up.
Contraction You decide *who's* coming.
Possessive *Whose* turn is next?

Apply the Skill

Exercise A
Write these sentences on a sheet of paper. Then underline the contractions and circle the possessives.

1. Theater wasn't performed indoors until almost 1600, well into the Renaissance.
2. Early outdoor dramas used few props and didn't include much scenery or artificial lighting.
3. Women weren't allowed on stage during the Renaissance, so women's roles typically were performed by boys.
4. Acting troupes often were named for their noble benefactors, such as the Lord Chamberlain's Men and the Lord Admiral's Men.
5. Shakespeare's acting troupe used the Blackfriars Theater as a winter home.

Exercise B
Revise the sentences in Exercise A, writing out each contraction above the line. Note the difference in formality between the original and revised sentences.

SPELLING PRACTICE

Vowel Combinations *ei* or *ie*
To decide whether to use *ei* or *ie,* many people repeat the saying "*I* before *e,* except after *c,* or when sounded long *a* as in *neighbor* or *weigh.*" Another rule states that if the combination is pronounced with a long *e,* it should be spelled *ie,* as in *thief.* But if the syllable starts with the sound "see," it should be spelled *ei,* as in *receipt.* If the syllable contains the "shuh" sound, the correct spelling is *ie,* as in *ancient.* Which rule fits each of these words from *Macbeth,* Act I? Working with a partner, say each word aloud, listen for the correct sound, and agree on the rule that applies. Ask your teacher to pronounce the word correctly if you are not able to reach consensus.

belief	grief	neither	sovereign
deceive	leisure	receive	weird
friends	mischief	sieve	yield

The Tragedy of Macbeth, Act II

A Drama by William Shakespeare

Build Background

Literary Context Playwrights and directors often use repetition to reinforce messages and themes in the play. When an audience sees a series of similar images, hears a similar line spoken by different characters, or witnesses a repeated action performed by one or several characters, it is likely the playwright or director is trying to draw your attention to this detail.

Two questions are introduced in Act I: Is Macbeth's decision to kill King Duncan a natural or an unnatural act? Is Macbeth acting in accordance with his own free will, or is he simply a pawn of fate? In Act II, Shakespeare continues to focus on these questions, repeating specific words and images that foreshadow and react to Macbeth's dark deed.

For instance, throughout Act II, the characters make numerous references to different kinds of animals. Some animals, such as crows and owls, would have been associated superstitiously with death by the Jacobean audience. More alarming are the omens and strange signs reported by the lords and servants at Macbeth's castle. The animals' strange behavior and the fears their behavior provokes in their human keepers are reported by many characters.

Accounts of strange weather are given by Macduff, Macbeth, and Rosse, and prophetic dreams or prophecies are alluded to by Macbeth, Macduff, and Banquo. Even individual words are repeated by different characters and in different contexts. For instance, the words *sleep, daggers, murther,* and *bloody* are uttered multiple times through Act II. Shakespeare's deliberate repetition of words, omens, and strange occurrences runs throughout the act.

Reader's Context When have you found it difficult to act on a decision you had made? Why did you have second thoughts?

Analyze Literature

Comic Relief and Hyperbole

Comic relief is a technique used to relieve the seriousness or emotional intensity of a literary work by introducing a humorous character or situation.

A **hyperbole** (hī pʉr´ bō lē) is a deliberate exaggeration made for effect.

Set Purpose

Even though *Macbeth* is one of Shakespeare's grimmest plays, it contains a famous example of comic relief. As you read Act II, look for the scene containing a humorous situation and consider Shakespeare's purpose for including it. In Scene ii, identify lines containing hyperbole. Consider what is being exaggerated and why.

Preview Vocabulary

augment, 363
palpable, 363
stealthy, 364
multitudinous, 367
equivocator, 367
scruples, 371

Macbeth Instructing the Murderers Employed to Kill Banquo, c. 1850.
George Cattermole. Victoria and Albert Museum, London, England.
(See detail on page 361.)

ACT II

SCENE i: OPEN COURT WITHIN MACBETH'S CASTLE

Enter BANQUO, *and* FLEANCE *with a torch before him.*

BANQUO.   How goes the night, boy?

FLEANCE.   The moon is down; I have not heard the clock.

BANQUO.   And she goes down at twelve.

FLEANCE.   I take't, 'tis later, sir.

BANQUO.   Hold, take my sword. There's husbandry[1] in heaven,
5   Their candles are all out. Take thee that too.
                    Gives him his belt and dagger.
A heavy summons[2] lies like lead upon me,
And yet I would not sleep. Merciful powers,
Restrain in me the cursed thoughts that nature
Gives way to in repose!

Enter MACBETH, *and a* SERVANT *with a torch.*

                    Give me my sword.
10   Who's there?

MACBETH.   A friend.

BANQUO.   What, sir, not yet at rest? the King's a-bed.
He hath been in unusual pleasure, and

ACT II, SCENE i
1. **husbandry.** Thrift

2. **heavy summons.**
Sleepiness

Sent forth great largess to your offices.[3]

15 This diamond he greets your wife withal,
By the name of most kind hostess, and shut up[4]
In measureless content.

MACBETH.   Being unprepar'd,
Our will became the servant to defect,
Which else should free have wrought.[5]

BANQUO.   All's well.
20 I dreamt last night of the three weïrd sisters:
To you they have show'd some truth.

MACBETH.   I think not of them.
Yet when we can entreat an hour to serve,
We would spend it in some words upon that business,
If you would grant the time.

BANQUO.   At your kind'st leisure.

25 MACBETH.   If you shall cleave to my consent, when 'tis,[6]
It shall make honor for you.

BANQUO.   So I lose none
In seeking to <u>augment</u> it, but still keep
My bosom franchis'd[7] and allegiance clear,
I shall be counsell'd.

MACBETH.   Good repose the while!

30 BANQUO.   Thanks, sir; the like to you!

Exit BANQUO *with* FLEANCE.

MACBETH.   Go bid thy mistress, when my drink is ready,
She strike upon the bell. Get thee to bed.

Exit SERVANT.

Is this a dagger which I see before me,
The handle toward my hand? Come, let me clutch thee:
35 I have thee not, and yet I see thee still.
Art thou not, fatal vision, sensible[8]
To feeling as to sight? or art thou but
A dagger of the mind, a false creation,
Proceeding from the heat-oppressed brain?
40 I see thee yet, in form as <u>palpable</u>
As this which now I draw.
Thou marshal'st[9] me the way that I was going,
And such an instrument I was to use.
Mine eyes are made the fools o' th' other senses,
45 Or else worth all the rest. I see thee still;
And on thy blade and dudgeon[10] gouts of blood,

---

3. **largess . . . offices.** Gifts to your servants' quarters

4. **shut up.** Concluded

5. **Being . . . wrought.** Because we were not prepared, we were not able to entertain as fully as we would have liked.

6. **cleave . . . 'tis.** Support my cause when the time comes

aug • ment (ôg´ ment')
v., add to; supplement

7. **franchis'd.** Free from guilt

8. **sensible.** Perceptible by the senses

pal • pa • ble
(pal´ pə bəl) *adj.,* tangible

9. **Thou marshal'st.** You lead

10. **dudgeon.** Handle of a dagger

Which was not so before. There's no such thing:
It is the bloody business which informs[11]
Thus to mine eyes. Now o'er the one half world
50 Nature seems dead, and wicked dreams abuse[12]
The curtain'd sleep; witchcraft celebrates
Pale Hecate's off'rings;[13] and wither'd Murther,
Alarum'd by his sentinel, the wolf,
Whose howl's his watch, thus with his <u>stealthy</u> pace,
55 With Tarquin's[14] ravishing strides, towards his design
Moves like a ghost. Thou sure and firm-set earth,
Hear not my steps, which way they walk, for fear
The very stones prate of my whereabout,
And take the present horror from the time,
60 Which now suits with it. Whiles I threat, he lives:
Words to the heat of deeds too cold breath gives.

A bell rings.

I go, and it is done; the bell invites me.
Hear it not, Duncan, for it is a knell,
That summons thee to heaven or to hell.

Exit.

Scene ii: Open court within Macbeth's castle

Enter Lady Macbeth.

Lady Macbeth.   That which hath made them drunk hath made
   me bold;
What hath quench'd them hath given me fire. Hark! Peace!
It was the owl that shriek'd, the fatal bellman,
Which gives the stern'st good-night.[15] He is about it:
5   The doors are open; and the surfeited grooms[16]
Do mock their charge with snores. I have drugg'd their possets,[17]
That death and nature do contend about them,
Whether they live or die.

Macbeth.   [*Within.*]   Who's there? What ho?

Lady Macbeth.   Alack, I am afraid they have awak'd,
10 And 'tis not done; th' attempt, and not the deed,
Confounds[18] us. Hark! I laid their daggers ready,
He could not miss 'em. Had he not resembled
My father as he slept, I had done't.

Enter Macbeth.

My husband!

Macbeth.   I have done the deed. Didst thou not hear a noise?

11. **informs.** Takes shape

12. **abuse.** Deceive
13. **Hecate's off'rings.** Offerings to Hecate, goddess of witchcraft

stealthy (stel´ thē)
adj., slow, deliberate, and secretive

14. **Tarquin.** Roman tyrant

Act II, Scene ii
15. **owl . . . good-night.** The owl's cry was a sign of death, as was the midnight ringing of the bell outside of a prisoner's cell.
16. **surfeited grooms.** Overfed servants
17. **possets.** Bedtime drinks of wine and hot milk

18. **attempt . . . Confounds.** A failed attempt ruins us

Costumes for the Renaissance Stage

A modern-day theatergoer attending a performance of *Macbeth* likely would see actors dressed in kilts and traditional Scottish dress, reflecting the historical setting of the play. This would not have been the case for an audience seeing the play four hundred years earlier on an Elizabethan or Jacobean stage. The actors would not have worn kilts but rather English dress.

Actors' costumes had to comply with English *sumptuary laws,* which established strict rules for what was and was not appropriate for certain people to wear. The intent of these laws was to allow identifying people by their clothes. Certain colors, such as purple, were reserved for royalty, while certain styles and fabrics were allowed for nobility, artisans, and peasants. Interestingly, actors were exempt from sumptuary laws because they were servants of the queen. Because of the strict enforcement of these rules (violators could be fined and jailed), clothing became symbolic in English society.

During the Renaissance, the characters in a play wore the clothing appropriate to their stations in English society, allowing audience members to instantly identify the characters' backgrounds. Each character's status, wealth, and place in the world of the drama would have been understood instantly when he or she walked onto the stage.

Costumes were quite costly and thus represented a significant investment for a theatrical company. Due to the high turnover of plays performed in the theaters, costumes had to be reused, regardless of the setting of the play. Unlike Victorian theatergoers, who expected to see realistic visual re-creations of time and place, Renaissance audiences relied on the description of the setting in the dialogue to distinguish, for instance, between Verona, Italy, and Inverness, Scotland.

---

15   **LADY MACBETH.**   I heard the owl scream and the crickets cry.
Did not you speak?

      MACBETH.   When?

      LADY MACBETH.   Now.

      MACBETH.   As I descended?

      LADY MACBETH.   Aye.

      MACBETH.   Hark! Who lies i' th' second chamber?

      LADY MACBETH.   Donalbain.

      MACBETH.   This is a sorry sight.

                          Looking on his hands.

      LADY MACBETH.   A foolish thought, to say a sorry sight.

20   **MACBETH.**   There's one did laugh in 's sleep, and one cried,
   "Murther!"
That they did wake each other. I stood and heard them;
But they did say their prayers, and address'd them
Again to sleep.

LADY MACBETH.   There are two[19] lodg'd together.

MACBETH.   One cried, "God bless us!" and "Amen!" the other,
25   As they had seen me with these hangman's hands.
List'ning their fear, I could not say "Amen,"
When they did say "God bless us!"

LADY MACBETH.   Consider it not so deeply.

MACBETH.   But wherefore could not I pronounce "Amen"?
I had most need of blessing, and "Amen"
Stuck in my throat.

30   **LADY MACBETH.**   These deeds must not be thought
After these ways; so, it will make us mad.

MACBETH.   Methought I heard a voice cry, "Sleep no more!
Macbeth does murther sleep"—the innocent sleep,
Sleep that knits up the ravell'd sleave[20] of care,
35   The death of each day's life, sore labor's bath,
Balm of hurt minds, great nature's second course,[21]
Chief nourisher in life's feast.

LADY MACBETH.   What do you mean?

MACBETH.   Still it cried, "Sleep no more!" to all the house;
"Glamis hath murther'd sleep, and therefore Cawdor
40   Shall sleep no more—Macbeth shall sleep no more."

LADY MACBETH.   Who was it that thus cried? Why, worthy thane,
You do unbend[22] your noble strength, to think
So brain-sickly of things. Go get some water,
And wash this filthy witness[23] from your hand.
45   Why did you bring these daggers from the place?
They must lie there. Go carry them, and smear
The sleepy grooms with blood.

MACBETH.   I'll go no more.
I am afraid to think what I have done;
Look on't again I dare not.

LADY MACBETH.   Infirm of purpose!
50   Give me the daggers. The sleeping and the dead
Are but as pictures; 'tis the eye of childhood
That fears a painted devil. If he do bleed,
I'll gild[24] the faces of the grooms withal,
For it must seem their guilt.   *Exit. Knock within.*

MACBETH.   Whence is that knocking?
55   How is't with me, when every noise appalls me?
What hands are here? Hah! they pluck out mine eyes.
Will all great Neptune's ocean wash this blood

---

19. **two.** The two are the grooms described in Act I, Scene vii, line 75.

20. **knits . . . sleave.** Straightens the tangled threads
21. **nature's second course.** Nature has two courses: food and sleep.

22. **unbend.** Relax

23. **witness.** Evidence

24. **gild.** Blood was often referred to as golden.

Clean from my hand? No; this my hand will rather
The <u>multitudinous</u> seas incarnadine,[25]

60   Making the green one red.

mul • ti • tu • di • nous
(mul′ tə tüd′ nəs) *adj.*,
numerous; infinite

Enter LADY MACBETH.

LADY MACBETH.   My hands are of your color; but I shame
To wear a heart so white. (*Knock.*) I hear a knocking
At the south entry. Retire we to our chamber.
A little water clears us of this deed;

65   How easy is it then! Your constancy
Hath left you unattended.[26] (*Knock.*) Hark, more knocking.
Get on your night-gown, lest occasion call us
And show us to be watchers.[27] Be not lost
So poorly in your thoughts.

70   MACBETH.   To know my deed, 'twere best not know myself. *Knock.*
Wake Duncan with thy knocking! I would thou couldst! *Exeunt.*

25. **incarnadine.** To turn red

26. **constancy . . .
unattended.** Firmness of purpose has abandoned you.
27. **watchers.** People who
stay up late

SCENE iii: OPEN COURT WITHIN MACBETH'S CASTLE

Enter a PORTER. *Knocking within.*

PORTER.   Here's a knocking indeed! If a man were porter of Hell
Gate, he should have old[28] turning the key. (*Knock.*) Knock, knock,
knock! Who's there, i' th' name of Belzebub?[29] Here's a farmer,
that hang'd himself on th' expectation of plenty. Come in time!

5   Have napkins enow about you, here you'll sweat for't. (*Knock.*)
Knock, knock! Who's there, in th' other devil's name? Faith, here's
an <u>equivocator</u>, that could swear in both the scales against either
scale, who committed treason enough for God's sake, yet could not
equivocate to heaven. O, come in, equivocator. (*Knock.*) Knock,

10   knock, knock! Who's there? Faith, here's an English tailor come
hither for stealing out of a French hose.[30] Come in, tailor, here you
may roast your goose.[31] (*Knock.*) Knock, knock! Never at quiet!
What are you? But this place is too cold for hell. I'll devil-porter
it no further. I had thought to have let in some of all professions

15   that go the primrose way to th' everlasting bonfire. (*Knock.*) Anon,
anon! [*Opens the gate.*] I pray you remember the porter.

ACT II, SCENE iii
28. **he should have old.** He
would get tired of
29. **Belzebub.** Chief devil

equiv • o • ca • tor
(i kwi′ və kā′ tər) *n.*, one
who speaks ambiguously

30. **tailor . . . hose.** The tailor stole cloth while making
French hose.
31. **roast your goose.** Heat
your iron

Enter MACDUFF *and* LENNOX.

MACDUFF.   Was it so late, friend, ere you went to bed, That you
do lie so late?

PORTER.   Faith, sir, we were carousing till the second cock;[32] and

20   drink, sir, is a great provoker of three things.

32. **second cock.** 3:00 AM

MACDUFF.   What three things does drink especially provoke?

PORTER.   Marry, sir, nose-painting, sleep, and urine. Lechery, sir,
it provokes, and unprovokes: it provokes the desire, but it takes

Portrait of Beerbohm Tree as Macbeth, 1911–1914. Charles Buchel.
Victoria and Albert Museum, London, England.

away the performance. Therefore much drink may be said to be
25 an equivocator with lechery: it makes him, and it mars him; it sets
him on, and it takes him off; it persuades him, and disheartens
him; makes him stand to, and not stand to; in conclusion, equivo-
cates him in a sleep, and giving him the lie, leaves him.

MACDUFF. I believe drink gave thee the lie[33] last night.

33. **gave thee the lie.**
Knocked you out

30 PORTER. That it did, sir, i' the very throat on me; but I requited
him for his lie, and (I think) being too strong for him, though he
took up my legs sometime, yet I made a shift to cast him.[34]

34. **cast him.** Pun meaning
both "throw him off," as in
wrestling, and "throw him
up," as in vomit him (the
drink) up

MACDUFF. Is thy master stirring?

Enter MACBETH.

Our knocking has awak'd him; here he comes.

LENNOX. Good morrow, noble sir.

35 MACBETH. Good morrow, both.

MACDUFF. Is the King stirring, worthy thane?

MACBETH.   Not yet.

MACDUFF. He did command me to call timely on him, I have almost slipp'd the hour.

MACBETH.   I'll bring you to him.

40 **MACDUFF.** I know this is a joyful trouble to you; But yet 'tis one.

MACBETH. The labor we delight in physics pain.[35] This is the door.

MACDUFF.   I'll make so bold to call, For 'tis my limited service.

>   *Exit* MACDUFF.

LENNOX. Goes the King hence to-day?

MACBETH.   He does; he did appoint so.

45 **LENNOX.** The night has been unruly. Where we lay, Our chimneys were blown down, and (as they say) Lamentings heard i' th' air; strange screams of death, And prophesying, with accents terrible, Of dire combustion[36] and confus'd events
50 New hatch'd to th' woeful time. The obscure bird Clamor'd the livelong night. Some say, the earth Was feverous, and did shake.

MACBETH.   'Twas a rough night.

LENNOX. My young remembrance cannot parallel A fellow to it.

> *Enter* MACDUFF.

55 **MACDUFF.** O horror, horror, horror! Tongue nor heart Cannot conceive nor name thee!

MACBETH AND LENNOX.   What's the matter?

MACDUFF. Confusion now hath made his masterpiece! Most sacrilegious murther hath broke ope The Lord's anointed temple,[37] and stole thence The life o' th' building!

60 **MACBETH.**   What is't you say—the life?

LENNOX. Mean you his Majesty?

MACDUFF. Approach the chamber, and destroy your sight With a new Gorgon.[38] Do not bid me speak; See, and then speak yourselves.

>   *Exeunt* MACBETH *and* LENNOX.

35. **The labor . . . pain.** The work we enjoy cures the pain of labor.

36. **combustion.** Confusion

37. **Lord's anointed temple.** Body of the king

38. **Gorgon.** Mythological monster who turned to stone everyone who looked at it

Awake, awake!

65　Ring the alarum-bell! Murther and treason!
　　Banquo and Donalbain! Malcolm, awake!
　　Shake off this downy sleep, death's counterfeit,
　　And look on death itself! Up, up, and see
　　The great doom's image![39] Malcolm! Banquo!
70　As from your graves rise up, and walk like sprites,
　　To countenance this horror! Ring the bell.

Bell rings.

Enter LADY MACBETH.

LADY MACBETH.　　What's the business,
　　That such a hideous trumpet calls to parley
　　The sleepers of the house? Speak, speak!

MACDUFF.　　　　　　　　　　O gentle lady,
75　'Tis not for you to hear what I can speak:
　　The repetition in a woman's ear
　　Would murther as it fell.

Enter BANQUO.

　　　　　　　　　　O Banquo, Banquo,
　　Our royal master's murther'd!

LADY MACBETH.　　　　　　Woe, alas!
　　What, in our house?

BANQUO.　　　　Too cruel any where.
80　Dear Duff, I prithee contradict thyself,
　　And say, it is not so.

Enter MACBETH, LENNOX, ROSSE.

MACBETH.　　Had I but died an hour before this chance,
　　I had liv'd a blessed time; for from this instant
　　There's nothing serious in mortality:[40]
85　All is but toys:[41] renown and grace is dead,
　　The wine of life is drawn, and the mere lees[42]
　　Is left this vault to brag of.

Enter MALCOLM *and* DONALBAIN.

DONALBAIN.　　What is amiss?

MACBETH.　　　　　　　You are, and do not know't.
　　The spring, the head, the fountain of your blood
90　Is stopp'd, the very source of it is stopp'd.

MACDUFF.　　Your royal father's murther'd.

MALCOLM.　　　　　　　　O, by whom?

39. **great doom's image.**
Likeness of Doomsday

40. **serious in mortality.**
Worthwhile in human life
41. **toys.** Trifles
42. **lees.** Dregs

LENNOX.   Those of his chamber, as it seem'd, had done't.
Their hands and faces were all badg'd[43] with blood;
So were their daggers, which unwip'd we found
95   Upon their pillows. They star'd and were distracted;
No man's life was to be trusted with them.

MACBETH.   O, yet I do repent me of my fury,
That I did kill them.

MACDUFF.   Wherefore did you so?

MACBETH.   Who can be wise, amaz'd, temp'rate, and furious,
100   Loyal, and neutral, in a moment? No man.
Th' expedition[44] of my violent love
Outrun the pauser, reason. Here lay Duncan,
His silver skin lac'd with his golden blood,
And his gash'd stabs look'd like a breach in nature
105   For ruin's wasteful entrance; there, the murtherers,
Steep'd in the colors of their trade, their daggers
Unmannerly breech'd with gore.[45] Who could refrain,
That had a heart to love, and in that heart
Courage to make 's love known?

LADY MACBETH.   Help me hence, ho!

MACDUFF.   Look to the lady.

110   **MALCOLM.**   [*Aside to* DONALBAIN.] Why do we hold our
      tongues,
That most may claim this argument for ours?

DONALBAIN.   [*Aside to* MALCOLM.] What should be spoken here,
      where our fate,
Hid in an auger-hole,[46] may rush and seize us?
Let's away,
Our tears are not yet brew'd.

115   **MALCOLM.**   [*Aside to* DONALBAIN.] Nor our strong sorrow
Upon the foot of motion.

BANQUO.   Look to the lady.

               LADY MACBETH *is carried out.*

And when we have our naked frailties hid,[47]
That suffer in exposure, let us meet
And question this most bloody piece of work,
120   To know it further. Fears and <u>scruples</u> shake us.
In the great hand of God I stand, and thence
Against the undivulg'd pretense[48] I fight
Of treasonous malice.

MACDUFF.   And so do I.

43. **badg'd.** Marked

44. **expedition.** Haste

45. **breech'd with gore.** Covered with blood

46. **auger-hole.** Small hole, an unlikely hiding place

47. **naked frailties hid.** Gotten dressed

scru • ples (skrü´ pəlz) *n.*, doubts; qualms

48. **undivulg'd pretense.** Secret purpose

ALL. So all.

MACBETH. Let's briefly put on manly readiness,
And meet i' th' hall together.

125 **ALL.** Well contented.

Exeunt all but MALCOLM *and* DONALBAIN.

MALCOLM. What will you do? Let's not consort with them;
To show an unfelt sorrow is an office
Which the false man does easy. I'll to England.

DONALBAIN. To Ireland, I; our separated fortune
130 Shall keep us both the safer. Where we are,
There's daggers in men's smiles; the near in blood,
The nearer bloody.[49]

MALCOLM. This murtherous shaft that's shot
Hath not yet lighted,[50] and our safest way
Is to avoid the aim. Therefore to horse,
135 And let us not be dainty of leave-taking,
But shift away. There's warrant in that theft
Which steals itself,[51] when there's no mercy left.

Exeunt.

SCENE iv: OUTSIDE MACBETH'S CASTLE

Enter ROSSE *with an* OLD MAN.

OLD MAN. Threescore and ten I can remember well,
Within the volume of which time I have seen
Hours dreadful and things strange; but this sore[52] night
Hath trifled former knowings.

ROSSE. Ha, good father,
5 Thou seest the heavens, as troubled with man's act,
Threatens his bloody stage. By th' clock 'tis day,
And yet dark night strangles the travelling lamp.[53]
Is't night's predominance, or the day's shame,
That darkness does the face of earth entomb,
When living light should kiss it?

OLD MAN. 'Tis unnatural,
10 Even like the deed that's done. On Tuesday last,
A falcon, tow'ring in her pride of place,
Was by a mousing owl hawk'd at, and kill'd.

ROSSE. And Duncan's horses (a thing most strange and certain),
15 Beauteous and swift, the minions of their race,
Turn'd wild in nature, broke their stalls, flung out,
Contending 'gainst obedience, as they would make
War with mankind.

49. **the near . . . bloody.**
The closer we are related to Duncan, the greater the danger of being murdered ourselves.
50. **lighted.** Hit its mark

51. **steals itself.** Sneaks away

ACT II, SCENE iv
52. **sore.** Dreadful

53. **travelling lamp.** Sun

OLD MAN.   'Tis said, they eat[54] each other.

ROSSE.   They did so—to th' amazement of mine eyes
That look'd upon't.

Enter MACDUFF.

20   Here comes the good Macduff.
How goes the world, sir, now?

MACDUFF.   Why, see you not?

ROSSE.   Is't known who did this more than bloody deed?

MACDUFF.   Those that Macbeth hath slain.

ROSSE.   Alas the day,
What good could they pretend?

MACDUFF.   They were suborned.[55]
25 Malcolm and Donalbain, the King's two sons,
Are stol'n away and fled, which puts upon them
Suspicion of the deed.

ROSSE.   'Gainst nature still!
Thriftless ambition, that will ravin up[56]
Thine own live's means! Then 'tis most like
30 The sovereignty will fall upon Macbeth.

MACDUFF.   He is already nam'd, and gone to Scone[57]
To be invested.

ROSSE.   Where is Duncan's body?

MACDUFF.   Carried to Colmekill,[58]
The sacred store-house of his predecessors
And guardian of their bones.

35 **ROSSE.**   Will you to Scone?

MACDUFF.   No, cousin, I'll to Fife.[59]

ROSSE.   Well, I will thither.

MACDUFF.   Well, may you see things well done there: adieu,
Lest our old robes sit easier than our new!

ROSSE.   Farewell, father.

40 **OLD MAN.**   God's benison[60] go with you, and with those
That would make good of bad, and friends of foes!

                        Exeunt omnes. ❖

---

54. **eat.** Ate (pronounced "et")

55. **suborned.** Bribed

56. **ravin up.** Eat ravenously

57. **Scone.** Where Scottish kings were crowned

58. **Colmekill.** Where Scottish kings were buried

59. **Fife.** Macduff's castle

60. **benison.** Blessing

MIRRORS & WINDOWS

Think about how you handle feelings of guilt. Do you get angry or depressed? Do you dwell on these feelings or try to overcome them? Do you try to make up for whatever is causing your guilt?

Refer to Text ▶ ▶ ▶ ▶ ▶   **Reason with Text**

Refer to Text	Reason with Text	
1a. What does Macbeth imagine he sees in Scene i? To what does he attribute this illusion?	**1b.** Describe Macbeth's state of mind immediately before the murder.	**Understand** Find meaning
2a. At the end of Scene ii, what does Macbeth imagine a voice crying out?	**2b.** State the consequences Macbeth might face for having murdered Duncan.	**Apply** Use information
3a. In Scenes iii and iv, what strange disturbances in nature do Lennox, Rosse, and the old man note on the night of the murder?	**3b.** In what sense is Macbeth's deed unnatural? How does the murder affect the natural order?	**Analyze** Take things apart
4a. At the end of the act, what does Rosse say about Malcolm and Donalbain?	**4b.** Evaluate the truth of these lines when applied to Macbeth.	**Evaluate** Make judgments
5a. Describe Macbeth's state of mind after murdering Duncan, using examples from the text to support your answer.	**5b.** Propose what the future holds as Macbeth takes the throne and attempts to rule Scotland.	**Create** Bring ideas together

Analyze Literature

Comic Relief and Hyperbole

Scene iii, involving the Porter, is a famous example of comic relief. Why might Shakespeare have added this scene at this point in the play?

Reread lines 57–60 in Scene ii, in which Macbeth laments having killed Duncan. What is being exaggerated? What effect does this use of hyperbole have on readers?

Extend the Text

Creative Writing In the role of Macbeth, newly named king, write a funeral elegy for Duncan. In it, honor the king by summarizing his finest qualities. What can you say to your subjects to reassure them about the future?

Persuasive Writing Write a persuasive essay arguing whether the Porter's scene (Act II, Scene iii) adds to or detracts from the play's serious mood. Present your argument using elements of a classical persuasive speech: an introduction that states your opinion, a body that outlines your arguments and evidence, and a conclusion that summarizes your points. Use logical transitions to help listeners follow your arguments, and include rhetorical devices, such as parallelism and repetition, to emphasize your points and sway listeners.

Media Literacy

Record a Television Show Write the script for a television program about unsolved crimes or mysteries that focuses on the murder of Duncan. Provide a brief account of the murder along with interviews of witnesses close to the action and theories of who committed the crime. Videotape your television show and show it to the class.

Lifelong Learning

Research the Effects of an Assassination Choose an assassination that took place in American or world history. Research the events that took place immediately after the leader's death, and discuss the emotional, political, and social impact the assassination had on the community. Based on this information, predict what might happen to Scotland after the murder of King Duncan.

 Go to **www.mirrorsandwindows.com** for more.

1. Near the beginning of the play, Macbeth is characterized as
   A. brave and noble.
   B. upset and envious.
   C. fearful and scheming.
   D. greedy and revengeful.
   E. confused and vulnerable.

2. Which of the following is *not* an example of one of the many *paradoxes,* or contradictions, in *Macbeth?*
   A. "So foul and fair a day" (Act I, Scene iii, line 38)
   B. "Lesser than Macbeth, and greater." (I.iii.65)
   C. "Thou shalt get kings, though thou be none" (I.iii.67)
   D. "th' milk of human kindness" (I.v.14)
   E. "this is a joyful trouble" (II.iii.39)

3. Line 49 in Act I, Scene ii—"Where the Norweyan banners flout the sky"—is an example of
   A. irony.
   B. a simile.
   C. personification.
   D. alliteration.
   E. an oxymoron.

4. What or whom is Banquo describing in Act I, Scene iii, lines 40–47?
   A. the witches
   B. Duncan's guards
   C. Macbeth's visions
   D. the men coming from the battlefield
   E. Macbeth, when acting unmanly, and Lady Macbeth

5. What is the third prediction the witches make?
   A. that Macbeth will live forever
   B. that Macbeth will win the battle
   C. that Macbeth will become king
   D. that Macbeth will commit murder
   E. that Macbeth will be unable to sleep

6. Review Act I, Scene iii, lines 130–139. What does Macbeth mean when he states in lines 134–136, "If good, why do I yield to that suggestion / Whose horrid image doth unfix my hair / And make my seated heart knock at my ribs"?
   A. Terror has caused his hair to fall out and his heart to stop.
   B. The idea makes his hair stand on end and his heart pound.
   C. He is losing heart at the thought, and his hair is losing its curl.
   D. He must stop and reconsider what he has done.
   E. He cannot overcome his fear.

7. In Act I, Scene iii, lines 130–139, what does Macbeth reveal about himself?
   A. He fears he is going mad.
   B. He has not been entirely truthful.
   C. He has been experiencing visions.
   D. He wants to be the Thane of Cawdor.
   E. He is contemplating committing murder.

8. In Act II, Scene ii, lines 43–44, what is "this filthy witness" to which Lady Macbeth refers?
   A. dirt
   B. blood
   C. his visions
   D. the stained dagger
   E. whoever saw Duncan killed

9. **Constructed Response:** In Act II, Scene i, line 16, Banquo refers to Lady Macbeth as the "most kind hostess." Given what you know about Lady Macbeth, what is your reaction to having her described this way? Is she truly a "most kind hostess"? Support your analysis with details from the play.

10. **Constructed Response:** Explain to what extent the witches' predictions near the beginning of the play are self-fulfilling prophecies. Is what happens fate or something else? Again, support your explanation with details from the text.

Understand the Concept

To bring descriptions to life and help readers experience what they are describing, writers use **sensory details:** words and phrases that describe how things look, sound, smell, taste, and feel. Good descriptive writing relies on sensory details to make it vivid and real.

In a drama, the playwright incorporates sensory details into the characters' dialogue in order to help the audience better visualize what is happening. For example, in *Macbeth,* Shakespeare uses details of sight and sound to describe the sleeping grooms who guard King Duncan. Lady Macbeth's description in Act II, Scene ii, lines 5–6 allows the audience to know that the king sleeps unprotected:

EXAMPLE

"The doors are open; and the surfeited grooms
Do mock their charge with snores."

In Act II, Shakespeare uses details of sound to create a tense and foreboding atmosphere. Owls screech, crickets chirp, and the bell tolls as Macbeth goes to murder the king:

EXAMPLES

"I go, and it is done; the bell invites me." (II.i.62)

"I heard the owl scream and the crickets cry."
(II.ii.15)

Try to incorporate sensory details in your own writing to make it more clear, interesting, and believable. Choose details that are appropriate to your subject, purpose, and audience. For example, in Act II, Scene iii, lines 102–107, Duncan is murdered off stage and the audience must rely on Macbeth's description to visualize the crime scene:

Here lay Duncan,
His silver skin lac'd with his golden blood,
And his gash'd stabs look'd like a breach in
    nature
For ruin's wasteful entrance; there, the mur-
    therers,
Steep'd in the colors of their trade, their daggers
Unmannerly breech'd with gore.

From this description, we learn that Duncan is covered in his own blood. His grooms and their daggers also are drenched in the king's blood.

Apply the Skill

Identify Sensory Details

On a sheet of paper, create a simple chart in which you can record the sensory details you identify in Lennox's speech from Act II, Scene iii, lines 45–52:

The night has been unruly. Where we lay,
Our chimneys were blown down, and (as
    they say)
Lamentings heard i' th' air; strange screams
    of death,
And prophesying, with accents terrible,
Of dire combustion and confus'd events
New hatch'd to th' woeful time. The obscure
    bird
Clamor'd the livelong night. Some say, the
    earth
Was feverous, and did shake.

Improve Use of Sensory Details

For each of the following scenarios, write a short paragraph that incorporates at least four sensory details. Appeal to at least three different senses with the details you choose.

1. Jake took a walk in the cemetery on a September night.
2. Marianna cried at her grandmother's funeral.
3. The farmer arrived home in the evening and had dinner.
4. The student walked in the door of his or her brand-new school.

The Tragedy of Macbeth, Act III

A Drama by William Shakespeare

Build Background

Literary Context Shakespeare often uses the structure of language to highlight aspects of characters' personalities. For most of *Macbeth,* the characters speak in **iambic pentameter,** a type of meter in which a line of poetry has five iambic feet, each comprising one unstressed syllable followed by one stressed syllable, as in the word *insist.* However, at times, the characters do not speak in this meter. These deviations from iambic pentameter in *Macbeth* are interesting because they often reveal something about a character.

One of the most noticeable changes is when a character speaks in prose, not verse. For example, in Act II, Scene iii, the Porter speaks in prose while the other characters address him in iambic pentameter. Some literary scholars have suggested that the Porter's use of prose reflects his drunken state. His speech stands in contrast to the formal, ordered iambic pentameter of the sober Scottish lords. Other instances of prose in *Macbeth* occur in informal situations, such as Lady Macbeth's reading of the letter in Act I, Scene v. Shakespeare's use of prose often indicates a shift in formality or a character that is different from those around him or her.

The three witches speak in **trochaic tetrameter,** a meter in which a line of poetry has four trochaic feet, each comprising one stressed syllable followed by one unstressed syllable, as in the word *freedom.* With this distinctive meter, the witches' speech essentially is opposite that of the other characters in the play. This different speech pattern effectively sets them apart from the rest of the characters and reinforces their supernatural nature.

Woodcut depicting Macbeth's first meeting with the three witches (c. 1600s).

Reader's Context

What can you tell about someone by the way he or she speaks? What does your use of language reveal about you?

Analyze Literature

Climax and Motif

The **climax** is the high point of interest or suspense in a work of drama or fiction. Sometimes called the *crisis,* it is the point in the plot at which a decisive event causes the main character's situation to become better or worse.

A **motif** is any element that recurs in one or more works of literature or art. Motifs in *Macbeth* include ambition, deception, disturbances in nature, blood, madness, and sleep.

Set Purpose

In a traditional five-act tragedy, the climax occurs in the third act. In the first two acts, the fortunes of the protagonist steadily improve, and in the last two acts, they decline. As you read Act III, identify the climax. Determine how this event will affect Macbeth, both immediately and in the long run. Also note the use of motifs in this act. Write down examples of *deception* motifs.

Preview Vocabulary

verity, 378
dauntless, 379
jocund, 383
nonpareil, 385
malevolence, 392

Lady Macbeth Approaching the Murdered Duncan, c. 1800s.
William Blake. Agnew and Sons, London, England. (See detail on page 377.)

ACT III

SCENE i: A ROOM IN THE PALACE AT FORRES

Enter BANQUO.

BANQUO.   Thou hast it now: King, Cawdor, Glamis, all,
As the weïrd women promis'd, and I fear
Thou play'dst most foully for't; yet it was said
It should not stand in thy posterity,[1]

5   But that myself should be the root and father
Of many kings. If there come truth from them—
As upon thee, Macbeth, their speeches shine[2]—
Why, by the <u>verities</u> on thee made good,
May they not be my oracles as well,

10   And set me up in hope? But hush, no more.

Sennet[3] *sounded. Enter* MACBETH *as King,* LADY MACBETH *as Queen,*
LENNOX, ROSSE, LORDS, *and* ATTENDANTS.

MACBETH.   Here's our chief guest.

LADY MACBETH.   If he had been forgotten,
It had been as a gap in our great feast,
And all-thing unbecoming.

MACBETH.   To-night we hold a solemn supper, sir,
And I'll request your presence.

15   BANQUO.   Let your Highness
Command upon me, to the which my duties
Are with a most indissoluble tie
For ever knit.

ACT III, SCENE i
1. **posterity.** Succeeding
generations

2. **shine.** Are fulfilled

ver • i • ty (ver´ ə tē)
n., truth

3. **Sennet.** Trumpet call

MACBETH.   Ride you this afternoon?

BANQUO.   Aye, my good lord.

20 MACBETH.   We should have else desir'd your good advice
(Which still hath been both grave and prosperous)[4]
In this day's council; but we'll take tomorrow.
Is't far you ride?

BANQUO.   As far, my lord, as will fill up the time
25 'Twixt this and supper. Go not my horse the better,
I must become a borrower of the night[5]
For a dark hour or twain.

MACBETH.   Fail not our feast.

BANQUO.   My lord, I will not.

MACBETH.   We hear our bloody cousins are bestow'd[6]
30 In England and in Ireland, not confessing
Their cruel parricide,[7] filling their hearers
With strange invention. But of that tomorrow,
When therewithal we shall have cause of state
Craving us jointly.[8] Hie you to horse; adieu,
35 Till you return at night. Goes Fleance with you?

BANQUO.   Aye, my good lord. Our time does call upon 's.[9]

MACBETH.   I wish your horses swift and sure of foot;
And so I do commend you to their backs.
Farewell.
                                        Exit BANQUO.
40 Let every man be master of his time
Till seven at night. To make society
The sweeter welcome, we will keep ourself
Till supper-time alone; while[10] then, God be with you!

                    Exeunt LORDS *with* LADY MACBETH *and others.*

                Manent MACBETH *and a* SERVANT.

Sirrah, a word with you. Attend those men
45 Our pleasure?

SERVANT.   They are, my lord, without the palace gate.

MACBETH.   Bring them before us.   *Exit* SERVANT.
                              To be thus[11] is nothing,
But to be safely thus. Our fears in Banquo
Stick deep, and in his royalty of nature[12]
50 Reigns that which would be fear'd. 'Tis much he dares,
And to that <u>dauntless</u> temper of his mind,
He hath a wisdom that doth guide his valor
To act in safety. There is none but he
Whose being I do fear; and under him

4. grave and prosperous.
Serious and profitable

5. Go . . . night. If my horse
doesn't go faster, I will have to
ride on at night.

6. are bestow'd. Living

7. parricide. Murder of a
parent or other close relative

8. Craving us jointly.
Requiring attention from
both of us

9. Our . . . upon 's. Our
business is urgent.

10. while. Until

11. thus. *i.e.,* King

12. royalty of nature.
Natural kingliness

daunt • less (dônt´ ləs)
adj., fearless

55 My Genius is rebuk'd, as it is said
Mark Antony's was by Caesar. He chid the sisters
When first they put the name of king upon me,
And bade them speak to him; then prophet-like
They hail'd him father to a line of kings.

60 Upon my head they plac'd a fruitless crown,
And put a barren sceptre in my gripe,[13]
Thence to be wrench'd with an unlineal hand,
No son of mine succeeding. If't be so,
For Banquo's issue have I fil'd[14] my mind,

65 For them the gracious Duncan have I murther'd,
Put rancors in the vessel of my peace
Only for them, and mine eternal jewel[15]
Given to the common enemy of man,
To make them kings—the seeds of Banquo kings!

70 Rather than so, come fate into the list,[16]
And champion me to th' utterance![17] Who's there?

Enter SERVANT *and two* MURDERERS.

Now go to the door, and stay there till we call.

Exit SERVANT.

Was it not yesterday we spoke together?

MURDERERS.   It was, so please your Highness.

MACBETH.   Well then, now
75 Have you consider'd of my speeches?—know
That it was he in the times past which held you
So under fortune, which you thought had been
Our innocent self? This I made good[18] to you
In our last conference, pass'd in probation[19] with you:

80 How you were borne in hand, how cross'd, the instruments,
Who wrought with them, and all things else that might
To half a soul and to a notion craz'd[20]
Say, "Thus did Banquo."

1. MURDERER.   You made it known to us.

MACBETH.   I did so; and went further, which is now
85 Our point of second meeting. Do you find
Your patience so predominant in your nature
That you can let this go? Are you so gospell'd,[21]
To pray for this good man, and for his issue,
Whose heavy hand hath bow'd you to the grave,
And beggar'd yours for ever?

90 **1. MURDERER.**   We are men, my liege.

13. **gripe.** Grip

14. **fil'd.** Defiled

15. **eternal jewel.** Immortal soul

16. **list.** Arena for combat
17. **champion . . . utterance.** Fight me to the death

18. **made good.** Demonstrated
19. **pass'd in probation.** Reviewed and proved

20. **half . . . craz'd.** A half wit and crazed mind

21. **so gospell'd.** Such good followers of the Gospel

MACBETH.   Aye, in the catalogue ye go for men,
As hounds and greyhounds, mungrels, spaniels, curs,
Shoughs, water-rugs, and demi-wolves[22] are clipt[23]
All by the name of dogs; the valued file[24]
95 Distinguishes the swift, the slow, the subtle,
The house-keeper, the hunter, every one,
According to the gift which bounteous nature
Hath in him clos'd; whereby he does receive
Particular addition, from the bill
100 That writes them all alike: and so of men.
Now, if you have a station in the file,
Not i' th' worst rank of manhood, say't,
And I will put that business in your bosoms,
Whose execution takes your enemy off,
105 Grapples you to the heart and love of us,
Who wear our health but sickly in his life,
Which in his death were perfect.

2. MURDERER.   I am one, my liege,
Whom the vile blows and buffets of the world
Hath so incens'd that I am reckless what
I do to spite the world.

110 1. MURDERER.   And I another,
So weary with disasters, tugg'd with fortune,
That I would set my life on any chance,
To mend it, or be rid on't.

MACBETH.   Both of you
Know Banquo was your enemy.

MURDERERS.   True, my lord.

115 MACBETH.   So is he mine; and in such bloody distance,[25]
That every minute of his being thrusts
Against my near'st of life;[26] and though I could
With barefac'd power sweep him from my sight,
And bid my will avouch[27] it, yet I must not,
120 For certain friends that are both his and mine,
Whose loves I may not drop, but wail his fall[28]
Who I myself struck down. And thence it is
That I to your assistance do make love,
Masking the business from the common eye
For sundry weighty reasons.

125 2. MURDERER.   We shall, my lord,
Perform what you command us.

1. MURDERER.   Though our lives—

---

22. **Shoughs . . . demi-wolves.**
Types of dogs
23. **clipt.** Called
24. **valued file.** List of the
values of each

25. **distance.** Hostilities

26. **near'st of life.** Life itself

27. **avouch.** Justify

28. **wail his fall.** Must seem
to be lamenting his death

MACBETH.   Your spirits shine through you. Within this hour, at
    most,
I will advise you where to plant yourselves,
Acquaint you with the perfect spy o' th' time,[29]
130 The moment on't, for't must be done tonight,
And something[30] from the palace; always thought
That I require a clearness: and with him—
To leave no rubs[31] nor botches in the work—
Fleance his son, that keeps him company,
135 Whose absence is no less material to me
Than is his father's, must embrace the fate
Of that dark hour. Resolve yourselves apart,[32]
I'll come to you anon.

MURDERERS.   We are resolv'd, my lord.

MACBETH.   I'll call upon you straight; abide within.

                                        Exeunt MURDERERS.

140 It is concluded: Banquo, thy soul's flight,
If it find heaven, must find it out tonight.

                                                    Exit.

SCENE ii: ANOTHER ROOM IN THE PALACE

Enter MACBETH'S LADY *and a* SERVANT.

LADY MACBETH.   Is Banquo gone from court?

SERVANT.   Aye, madam, but returns again tonight.

LADY MACBETH.   Say to the King, I would attend his leisure
For a few words.

SERVANT.   Madam, I will.   *Exit.*

LADY MACBETH.   Nought's had, all's spent,
5 Where our desire is got without content;
'Tis safer to be that which we destroy
Than by destruction dwell in doubtful joy.

Enter MACBETH.

How now, my lord, why do you keep alone,
Of sorriest fancies your companions making,
10 Using those thoughts which should indeed have died
With them they think on? Things without all remedy
Should be without regard: what's done, is done.

MACBETH.   We have scorch'd[33] the snake, not kill'd it;
She'll close[34] and be herself, whilest our poor malice
15 Remains in danger of her former tooth.[35]
But let the frame of things disjoint, both the worlds suffer,[36]

29. **perfect . . . time.** Precise
moment

30. **something.** Some
distance

31. **rubs.** Imperfections

32. **Resolve yourselves apart.**
Go and make up your minds.

ACT III, SCENE ii
33. **scorch'd.** Lightly
wounded
34. **close.** Heal
35. **our . . . tooth.** Despite
our hatred our danger is the
same as before.
36. **both . . . suffer.** Heaven
and earth fall apart

Ere we will eat our meal in fear, and sleep
In the affliction of these terrible dreams
That shake us nightly. Better be with the dead,
20 Whom we, to gain our peace, have sent to peace,
Than on the torture of the mind to lie
In restless ecstasy.[37] Duncan is in his grave;
After life's fitful fever he sleeps well.
Treason has done his worst; nor steel, nor poison,
25 Malice domestic, foreign levy, nothing,
Can touch him further.

LADY MACBETH.   Come on;
Gentle my lord, sleek o'er your rugged looks,
Be bright and jovial among your guests tonight.

MACBETH.   So shall I, love, and so, I pray, be you.
30 Let your remembrance apply to Banquo,
Present him eminence both with eye and tongue:
Unsafe the while, that we
Must lave our honors in these flattering streams,[38]
And make our faces vizards[39] to our hearts,
Disguising what they are.

35 **LADY MACBETH.**   You must leave this.

MACBETH.   O, full of scorpions is my mind, dear wife!
Thou know'st that Banquo and his Fleance lives.

LADY MACBETH.   But in them nature's copy's not eterne.[40]

MACBETH.   There's comfort yet, they are assailable.
40 Then be thou <u>jocund</u>; ere the bat hath flown
His cloister'd flight, ere to black Hecate's summons
The shard-borne[41] beetle with his drowsy hums
Hath rung night's yawning peal, there shall be done
A deed of dreadful note.

LADY MACBETH.   What's to be done?

45 **MACBETH.**   Be innocent of the knowledge, dearest chuck,[42]
Till thou applaud the deed. Come, seeling[43] night,
Scarf up the tender eye of pitiful day,
And with thy bloody and invisible hand
Cancel and tear to pieces that great bond[44]
50 Which keeps me pale! Light thickens, and the crow
Makes wing to th' rooky[45] wood;
Good things of day begin to droop and drowse,
Whiles night's black agents to their preys do rouse.
Thou marvel'st at my words, but hold thee still:
55 Things bad begun make strong themselves by ill.
So prithee go with me.   *Exeunt.*

37. **restless ecstasy.** Agitated frenzy

38. **Unsafe . . . streams.** We are unsafe, so we must wash our honors in streams of flattery.
39. **vizards.** Masks

40. **in . . . eterne.** They are not eternal.

joc • und (jä´ kənd) *adj.,* cheerful; merry

41. **shard-borne.** Carried on scaly wings

42. **chuck.** A term of endearment
43. **seeling.** Blinding

44. **great bond.** Promise made to Banquo by the witches
45. **rooky.** Gloomy

SCENE iii: A ROAD LEADING TO THE PALACE

Enter three MURDERERS.

1. MURDERER.   But who did bid thee join with us?

3. MURDERER.   Macbeth.

2. MURDERER.   He needs not our mistrust, since he delivers
Our offices,[46] and what we have to do,
To the direction just.[47]

1. MURDERER.   Then stand with us.
5   The west yet glimmers with some streaks of day;
Now spurs the lated[48] traveller apace
To gain the timely inn, and near approaches
The subject of our watch.

3. MURDERER.   Hark, I hear horses.

BANQUO.   (*Within.*) Give us a light there, ho!

2. MURDERER.   Then 'tis he; the rest
10   That are within the note of expectation
Already are i' th' court.

1. MURDERER.   His horses go about.

3. MURDERER.   Almost a mile; but he does usually,
So all men do, from hence to th' palace gate
Make it their walk.

Enter BANQUO, *and* FLEANCE *with a torch.*

2. MURDERER.   A light, a light!

3. MURDERER.   'Tis he.

15   **1. MURDERER.**   Stand to't.

BANQUO.   It will be rain tonight.

1. MURDERER.   Let it come down.

They attack BANQUO.

BANQUO.   O, treachery! Fly, good Fleance, fly, fly, fly!
Thou mayst revenge. O slave!

BANQUO *dies.* FLEANCE *escapes.*

3. MURDERER.   Who did strike out the light?

1. MURDERER.   Was't not the way?[49]

3. MURDERER.   There's but one down; the son is fled.

20   **2. MURDERER.**   We have lost
Best half of our affair.

1. MURDERER.   Well, let's away, and say how much is done.

Exeunt.

ACT III, SCENE iii
46. **offices.** Duties

47. **To . . . just.** Exactly as
Macbeth ordered

48. **lated.** Belated

49. **Was't not the way?**
Wasn't that the right thing
to do?

SCENE iv: A BANQUET ROOM IN THE PALACE

Banquet prepar'd. Enter MACBETH, LADY MACBETH, ROSSE, LENNOX, LORDS, *and* ATTENDANTS.

MACBETH.   You know your own degrees,[50] sit down. At first
And last, the hearty welcome.

LORDS.   Thanks to your Majesty.

MACBETH.   Ourself will mingle with society,
And play the humble host.

5   Our hostess keeps her state,[51] but in best time
We will require her welcome.

LADY MACBETH.   Pronounce it for me, sir, to all our friends,
For my heart speaks they are welcome.

Enter FIRST MURDERER *to the door.*

MACBETH.   See, they encounter thee with their hearts' thanks.

10   Both sides are even; here I'll sit i' th' midst.
Be large in mirth;[52] anon we'll drink a measure[53]
The table round.—   *Goes to the door.*
There's blood upon thy face.

MURDERER.   'Tis Banquo's then.

MACBETH.   'Tis better thee without than he within.[54]
Is he dispatch'd?

15   MURDERER.   My lord, his throat is cut;
That I did for him.

MACBETH.   Thou art the best o' th' cut-throats,
Yet he's good that did the like for Fleance.
If thou didst it, thou art the <u>nonpareil</u>.

MURDERER.   Most royal sir, Fleance is scap'd.

20   MACBETH.   Then comes my fit again. I had else been perfect,
Whole as the marble, founded as the rock,
As broad and general[55] as the casing[56] air;
But now I am cabin'd, cribb'd, confin'd, bound in
To saucy doubts and fears. But Banquo's safe?[57]

25   MURDERER.   Aye, my good lord; safe in a ditch he bides,
With twenty trenched gashes on his head,
The least a death to nature.

MACBETH.   Thanks for that:
There the grown serpent lies; the worm[58] that's fled
Hath nature that in time will venom breed,
30   No teeth for th' present. Get thee gone; tomorrow
We'll hear ourselves[59] again.

Exit MURDERER.

ACT III, SCENE iv
50. **degrees.** Order of seating based on rank

51. **state.** Seat

52. **large in mirth.** Very merry
53. **measure.** Large glass

54. **better . . . within.** Better on your face than in his body

non • pa • reil
(nän' pə rel´) *n.,* someone unequaled

55. **broad and general.** Free and unrestrained
56. **casing.** Surrounding
57. **safe.** No longer a threat

58. **worm.** The little serpent, Fleance

59. **hear ourselves.** Talk to each other

The Third Murderer

The appearance of the third murderer in Scene iii has led to much speculation among literary scholars. Some believe the murderer must have been introduced in a short scene that was later cut when Shakespeare edited the script before the play was performed for James I. No version of the script exists to verify this theory, however. Other scholars suggest the third murderer is Macbeth, since the character possesses keen hearing and utters the word *Macbeth* upon introduction. Still others identify Lady Macbeth as the third murderer, because the mysterious assassin is overtly secretive and has intimate knowledge of Banquo and the castle.

A remaining possibility is that Shakespeare intended the identity of the third murderer to be ambiguous. He may have used the unnamed killer to further the plot or encourage multiple interpretations of the scene. Accordingly, directors sometimes identify an existing character as the third murderer to add complexity and intrigue to the play. Director Roman Polanski made such a decision in his 1971 film adaptation of *Macbeth*. His interpretations of Act II, Scene iii, and Act IV, Scene ii, add an entirely different twist to the plot and darken the mood of the play.

LADY MACBETH.   My royal lord,
You do not give the cheer. The feast is sold
That is not often vouch'd, while 'tis a-making,
'Tis given with welcome.[60] To feed were best at home;
35   From thence, the sauce to meat is ceremony,
Meeting were bare without it.

Enter the GHOST OF BANQUO *and sits in* MACBETH'S *place.*

MACBETH.   Sweet remembrancer!
Now good digestion wait on appetite,
And health on both!

LENNOX.   May't please your Highness sit.

MACBETH.   Here had we now our country's honor roof'd,[61]
40   Were the grac'd person of our Banquo present,
Who may I rather challenge for unkindness
Than pity for mischance.[62]

ROSSE.   His absence, sir,
Lays blame upon his promise. Please't your Highness
To grace us with your royal company?

MACBETH.   The table's full.

45   **LENNOX.**   Here is a place reserv'd, sir.

MACBETH.   Where?

LENNOX.   Here, my good lord. What is't that moves your Highness?

60. The feast . . . welcome. Unless the guests feel welcome, a feast is no better than a dinner one buys.

61. roof'd. Under one roof

62. Who . . . mischance. Who I hope is absent due to discourtesy and not due to an accident

MACBETH.   Which of you have done this?

LORDS.   What, my good lord?

MACBETH.   Thou canst not say I did it, never shake
50 Thy gory locks at me.

ROSSE.   Gentlemen, rise, his Highness is not well.

LADY MACBETH.   Sit, worthy friends; my lord is often thus,
And hath been from his youth. Pray you keep seat.
The fit is momentary, upon a thought[63]

55 He will again be well. If much you note him,
You shall offend him and extend his passion.
Feed, and regard him not.—Are you a man?

MACBETH.   Aye, and a bold one, that dare look on that
Which might appall the devil.

LADY MACBETH.   O proper stuff!
60 This is the very painting of your fear;
This is the air-drawn dagger which you said
Led you to Duncan. O, these flaws[64] and starts
(Impostors to true fear) would well become
A woman's story at a winter's fire,
65 Authoriz'd by her grandam. Shame itself,
Why do you make such faces? When all's done,
You look but on a stool.

MACBETH.   Prithee see there!
Behold! look! lo! how say you?
Why, what care I? if thou canst nod, speak too.
70 If charnel-houses[65] and our graves must send
Those that we bury back, our monuments
Shall be the maws of kites.[66]   *Exit* GHOST.

LADY MACBETH.   What? quite unmann'd in folly?

MACBETH.   If I stand here, I saw him.

LADY MACBETH.   Fie, for shame!

MACBETH.   Blood hath been shed ere now, i' th' olden time,
75 Ere humane statute purg'd the gentle weal;[67]
Aye, and since too, murthers have been perform'd
Too terrible for the ear. The time has been,
That when the brains were out, the man would die,
And there an end; but now they rise again
80 With twenty mortal murthers on their crowns,[68]
And push us from our stools. This is more strange
Than such a murther is.

LADY MACBETH.   My worthy lord,
Your noble friends do lack you.

63. **upon a thought.** Momentarily

64. **flaws.** Emotional outbursts

65. **charnel-houses.** Storage spaces for human bones

66. **maws of kites.** Stomachs of birds of prey

67. **Ere . . . weal.** Before human laws cleansed and civilized the state

68. **mortal . . . crowns.** Deadly wounds to the head

Ellen Terry as Lady Macbeth, 1885–1886.
John Singer Sargent. Tate Gallery, London, England.

MACBETH. I do forget.
Do not muse at me, my most worthy friends,
85 I have a strange infirmity, which is nothing
To those that know me. Come, love and health to all,
Then I'll sit down. Give me some wine, fill full.

Enter GHOST.

I drink to th' general joy o' th' whole table,
And to our dear friend Banquo, whom we miss;
90 Would he were here! to all, and him, we thirst,
And all to all.

LORDS. Our duties, and the pledge.

MACBETH. Avaunt, and quit my sight! let the earth hide thee!

Thy bones are marrowless, thy blood is cold;
Thou hast no speculation in those eyes
Which thou dost glare with!

95 **LADY MACBETH.**   Think of this, good peers,
But as a thing of custom. 'Tis no other;
Only it spoils the pleasure of the time.

MACBETH.   What man dare, I dare.
Approach thou like the rugged Russian bear,
100 The arm'd rhinoceros, or th' Hyrcan[69] tiger,
Take any shape but that,[70] and my firm nerves
Shall never tremble. Or be alive again,
And dare me to the desert[71] with thy sword;
If trembling I inhabit then,[72] protest me
105 The baby of a girl. Hence, horrible shadow!
Unreal mock'ry, hence!   *Exit* GHOST.
                    Why, so; being gone,
I am a man again. Pray you sit still.

LADY MACBETH.   You have displac'd the mirth, broke the good
   meeting,
With most admir'd[73] disorder.

MACBETH.   Can such things be,
110 And overcome us like a summer's cloud,
Without our special wonder? You make me strange
Even to the disposition that I owe,[74]
When now I think you can behold such sights,
And keep the natural ruby of your cheeks,
When mine is blanch'd with fear.

115 **ROSSE.**   What sights, my lord?

LADY MACBETH.   I pray you speak not. He grows worse and worse,
Question enrages him. At once, good night.
Stand not upon the order of your going,[75]
But go at once.

LENNOX.   Good night, and better health
Attend his Majesty!

120 **LADY MACBETH.**   A kind good night to all!

                    Exeunt LORDS *and* ATTENDANTS.

MACBETH.   It will have blood, they say; blood will have blood.
Stones have been known to move and trees to speak;
Augures and understood relations[76] have
By maggot-pies and choughs[77] and rooks brought forth
125 The secret'st man of blood. What is the night?

69. **Hyrcan.** From Hyrcania, a
desert near the Caspian Sea
70. **that.** The shape of Banquo

71. **Desert.** Deserted area
where nobody would
intervene
72. **If . . . then.** If I feel fear
then

73. **admir'd.** Attention-
getting

74. **You . . . owe.** You make
me feel like a stranger to the
courageous person I thought
I was.

75. **Stand . . . going.**
Dispense with formality as
you leave.

76. **Augures . . . relations.**
Omens and the meanings
associated with them
77. **maggot-pies and
choughs.** Magpies and crows

LADY MACBETH.   Almost at odds with morning, which is which.

MACBETH.   How say'st thou, that Macduff denies his person
At our great bidding?

LADY MACBETH.   Did you send to him, sir?

MACBETH.   I hear it by the way; but I will send.
130 There's not a one of them but in his house
I keep a servant fee'd.[78] I will tomorrow
(And betimes I will) to the weïrd sisters.
More shall they speak; for now I am bent to know,
By the worst means, the worst. For mine own good
135 All causes shall give way. I am in blood
Stepp'd in so far that, should I wade no more,
Returning were as tedious as go o'er.
Strange things I have in head, that will to hand,
Which must be acted ere they may be scann'd.[79]

140 **LADY MACBETH.**   You lack the season[80] of all natures, sleep.

MACBETH.   Come, we'll to sleep. My strange and self-abuse[81]
Is the initiate fear that wants hard use:
We are yet but young in deed.[82]   *Exeunt.*

SCENE V: THE HEATH

Thunder. Enter the three WITCHES, *meeting* HECATE.

1. WITCH.   Why, how now, Hecate? you look angerly.

HECATE.   Have I not reason, beldams[83] as you are?
Saucy and overbold, how did you dare
To trade and traffic with Macbeth
5 In riddles and affairs of death;
And I, the mistress of your charms,
The close contriver[84] of all harms,
Was never call'd to bear my part,
Or show the glory of our art?
10 And which is worse, all you have done
Hath been but for a wayward son,
Spiteful and wrathful, who (as others do)
Loves for his own ends, not for you.
But make amends now. Get you gone,
15 And at the pit of Acheron[85]
Meet me i' th' morning; thither he
Will come to know his destiny.
Your vessels and your spells provide,
Your charms and every thing beside.
20 I am for th' air; this night I'll spend

78. **fee'd.** Paid as a spy

79. **ere . . . scann'd.** Before
they can be properly
examined
80. **season.** Preservative
81. **strange and self-abuse.**
Strange self-delusion

82. **young in deed.**
Inexperienced in crime

ACT III, SCENE v
83. **beldams.** Hags

84. **close contriver.** Secret
inventor

85. **pit of Acheron.** Place of
a passage through the earth
to Hell

Unto a dismal and a fatal end.
Great business must be wrought ere noon:
Upon the corner of the moon
There hangs a vap'rous drop profound,
25　I'll catch it ere it come to ground;
And that, distill'd by magic sleights,
Shall raise such artificial sprites
As by the strength of their illusion
Shall draw him on to his confusion.[86]

30　He shall spurn fate, scorn death, and bear
His hopes 'bove wisdom, grace, and fear;
And you all know, security[87]
Is mortals' chiefest enemy.

　　　　Music, and a song. Sing within: "Come away, come away, etc."

Hark, I am call'd; my little spirit, see,
35　Sits in a foggy cloud, and stays for me.　　　　　　*Exit.*

1. WITCH.　Come, let's make haste, she'll soon be back again.
　　　　　　　　　　　　　　　　　　　Exeunt.

SCENE vi: A PLACE IN SCOTLAND

Enter LENNOX *and another* LORD.

LENNOX.　My former speeches have but hit your thoughts,
Which can interpret farther;[88] only I say
Things have been strangely borne.[89] The gracious Duncan
Was pitied of Macbeth; marry, he was dead.
5　And the right valiant Banquo walk'd too late,
Whom you may say (if't please you) Fleance kill'd,
For Fleance fled. Men must not walk too late.
Who cannot want the thought,[90] how monstrous
It was for Malcolm and for Donalbain
10　To kill their gracious father? Damned fact!
How it did grieve Macbeth! Did he not straight
In pious rage the two delinquents tear,
That were the slaves of drink and thralls[91] of sleep?
Was not that nobly done? Aye, and wisely too;
15　For 'twould have anger'd any heart alive
To hear the men deny't. So that, I say,
He has borne all things well, and I do think
That had he Duncan's sons under his key
(As, and't please heaven, he shall not), they should find
20　What 'twere to kill a father; so should Fleance.
But peace! for from broad words,[92] and 'cause he fail'd
His presence at the tyrant's feast, I hear

86. **confusion.** Ruin

87. **security.** False sense of security; overconfidence

ACT III, SCENE vi
88. **interpret farther.** Draw more conclusions
89. **borne.** Handled

90. **Who . . . thought.** Who can help thinking

91. **thralls.** Slaves

92. **Broad words.** Out-spokenness

Macduff lives in disgrace. Sir, can you tell
Where he bestows himself?

LORD.   The son of Duncan
25 (From whom this tyrant holds the due of birth[93])
Lives in the English court, and is receiv'd
Of the most pious Edward[94] with such grace
That the <u>malevolence</u> of fortune nothing
Takes from his high respect. Thither Macduff
30 Is gone to pray the holy king, upon his aid[95]
To wake Northumberland and warlike Siward,
That by the help of these (with Him above
To ratify the work) we may again
Give to our tables meat, sleep to our nights;
35 Free from our feasts and banquets bloody knives;[96]
Do faithful homage and receive free honors;
All which we pine for now. And this report
Hath so exasperate the King[97] that he
Prepares for some attempt of war.

LENNOX.   Sent he to Macduff?

40 LORD.   He did; and with an absolute "Sir, not I,"
The cloudy[98] messenger turns me his back,
And hums, as who should say, "You'll rue the time
That clogs me with this answer."[99]

LENNOX.   And that well might
Advise him to a caution, t' hold what distance
45 His wisdom can provide.[100] Some holy angel
Fly to the court of England, and unfold
His message ere he come, that a swift blessing
May soon return to this our suffering country
Under a hand accurs'd!

LORD.   I'll send my prayers with him.

Exeunt. ❖

93. **Holds . . . birth.** With-
holds the birthright; i.e., the
crown
94. **Edward.** King Edward
the Confessor (1003?–1066),
considered to be a saintly
person

ma • lev • o • lence
(mə le´ və len[t]s) *n.*,
malice; spitefulness

95. **upon his aid.** On Malcolm's behalf
96. **Free . . . knives.** Restore
order so that violence is not
a common occurrence at
banquets
97. **the King.** Macbeth

98. **cloudy.** Surly, scowling

99. **hums . . . answer.** Har-
rumphs, as if to say, "You'll
regret making me waste my
time trying to get an answer."
(The messenger probably
realizes that Macduff will not
answer.)
100. **Advise him . . . provide.** Warn him to keep as
far out of Macbeth's way as
he can

MIRRORS & WINDOWS

Macbeth tells Lady Macbeth that "For mine own good / All causes shall give way."
What is the difference between *ambition* and *greed*?

Literature Connection

William Hazlitt (1778–1830), born in Kent, England, was well known for his works of literary criticism. This essay on *Macbeth* was published in 1817 in his book **Characters of Shakespeare's Plays.** In addition to being a well-respected essayist, Hazlitt worked as a painter, journalist, and theater critic. He especially loved the theater. "Wherever there is a play house," he wrote in 1817, "the world will go on not amiss. The stage not only refines the manners, but it is the best teacher of morals, for it is the truest and most intelligible picture of life." From 1818 to 1820, Hazlitt presented a series of lectures on English writers, many of whom were Elizabethan dramatists.

HAZLITT

Macbeth, from Characters of Shakespeare's Plays

by William Hazlitt

"The poet's eye in a fine
  frenzy rolling
Doth glance from heaven to
  earth, from earth to heaven;
And as imagination bodies forth
The forms of things
  unknown, the poet's pen
Turns them to shape, and
  gives to airy nothing
A local habitation and a name."[1]

Macbeth and *Lear, Othello* and *Hamlet,* are usually reckoned Shakespeare's four principal tragedies. *Lear* stands first for the profound intensity of the passion; *Macbeth* for the wildness of the imagination and the rapidity of the action; *Othello* for the progressive interest and powerful alternations of feeling; *Hamlet* for the refined development of thought and sentiment. If the force of genius shown in each of these works is astonishing, their variety is not less so. They are like different creations of the same mind, not one of which has the slightest reference to the rest. This distinctness and originality is indeed the necessary consequence of truth and nature. Shakespeare's genius alone appeared to possess the resources of nature. He is "your only *tragedy maker.*" His plays have the force of things upon the mind. What he represents is brought home to the bosom as a part of our experience, implanted in the memory as if

---

1. **"The poet's . . . name."** From Shakespeare's *A Midsummer Night's Dream,* Act V, Scene i

we had known the places, persons, and things of which he treats. *Macbeth* is like a record of a preternatural and tragical event. It has the rugged severity of an old chronicle with all that the imagination of the poet can engraft upon traditional belief. The castle of Macbeth, round which "the air smells wooingly," and where "the temple-haunting martlet builds," has a real subsistence in the mind; the Weird Sisters meet us in person on "the blasted heath"; the "air-drawn dagger" moves slowly before our eyes; the "gracious Duncan," the "blood-boltered Banquo" stand before us; all that passed through the mind of Macbeth passes, without the loss of a tittle, through ours. All that could actually take place, and all that is only possible to be conceived, what was said and what was done, the workings of passion, the spells of magic, are brought before us with the same absolute truth and vividness.

Shakespeare excelled in the openings of his plays: that of *Macbeth* is the most striking of any. The wildness of the scenery, the sudden shifting of the situations and characters, the bustle, the expectations excited, are equally extraordinary. From the first entrance of the Witches and the description of them when they meet Macbeth:

> *What are these*
> *So wither'd and so wild*
> *   in their attire,*
> *That look not like the*
> *   inhabitants of th' earth*
> *And yet are on't?*

the mind is prepared for all that follows.

This tragedy is alike distinguished for the lofty imagination it displays, and for the tumultuous vehemence of the action; and the one is made the moving principle of the other. The overwhelming pressure of preternatural agency urges on the tide of human passion with redoubled force. Macbeth himself appears driven along by the violence of his fate like a vessel drifting before a storm: he reels to and fro like a drunken man; he staggers under the weight of his own purposes and the suggestions of others; he stands at bay with his situation; and from the superstitious awe and breathless suspense into which the communications of the Weird Sisters throw him is hurried on with daring impatience to verify their predictions, and with impious and bloody hand to tear aside the veil which hides the uncertainty of the future. He is not equal to the struggle with fate and conscience. He now "bends up each corporal instrument to the terrible feat"; at other times his heart misgives him, and he is cowed and abashed by his success. "The deed, no less than the attempt, confounds him." His mind is assailed by the stings of remorse, and full of "preternatural solicit-

ings." His speeches and soliloquies are dark riddles on human life, baffling solution, and entangling him in their labyrinths. In thought he is absent and perplexed, sudden and desperate in act, from a distrust of his own resolution. His energy springs from the anxiety and agitation of his mind. His blindly rushing forward on the objects of his ambition and revenge, or his recoiling from them, equally betrays the harassed state of his feelings. This part of his character is admirably set off by being brought in connection with that of Lady Macbeth, whose obdurate strength of will and masculine firmness give her the ascendancy over her husband's faltering virtue. She at once seizes on the opportunity that offers for the accomplishment of all their wished-for greatness, and never flinches from her object till all is over. The magnitude of her resolution almost covers the magnitude of her guilt. She is a great bad woman, whom we hate, but whom we fear more than we hate. She does not excite our loathing and abhorrence like Regan and Goneril.[2] She is only wicked to gain a great end and is perhaps more distinguished by her commanding presence of mind and inexorable self-will, which do not suffer her to be diverted from a bad purpose, when once formed, by weak and womanly regrets, than by the hardness of her heart or want of natural affections. The impression which her lofty determination of character makes on the mind of Macbeth is well described where he exclaims:

> Bring forth men children only;
> For thy undaunted mettle should compose
> Nothing but males!

Nor do the pains she is at to "screw his courage to the sticking-place," the reproach to him, not to be "lost so poorly in himself," the assurance that "a little water clears them of this deed," show anything but her greater consistency in depravity. Her strong-nerved ambition furnishes ribs of steel to "the sides of his intent"; and she is herself wound up to the execution of her baneful project with the same unshrinking fortitude in crime, that in other circumstances she would probably have shown patience in suffering. The deliberate sacrifice of all other considerations to the gaining "for their future days and nights sole sovereign sway and masterdom," by the murder of Duncan, is gorgeously expressed in her invocation on hearing of "his fatal entrance under her battlements":

> Come all you spirits
> That tend on mortal thoughts, unsex me here:
> And fill me, from the crown to th' toe, top-full
> Of direst cruelty; make thick my blood,
> Stop up the access and passage to remorse,
> That no compunctious visitings of nature
> Shake my fell purpose, nor keep peace between
> The effect and it. Come to my woman's breasts,
> And take my milk for gall, you murthering
>   ministers,
> Wherever in your sightless substances
> You wait on nature's mischief. Come, thick night!
> And pall thee in the dunnest smoke of hell,
> That my keen knife see not the wound it makes,
> Nor heav'n peep through the blanket of the dark,
> To cry, hold, hold!

When she first hears that "Duncan comes there to sleep" she is so overcome by the news, which is beyond her utmost expectations, that she answers the messenger, "Thou 'rt mad to say it"; and on receiving her husband's account of the predictions of the Witches, conscious of his instability of purpose, and that her presence is necessary to goad him on to the consummation of his promised greatness, she exclaims:

> Hie thee hither,
> That I may pour my spirits in thine ear,
> And chastise with the valor of my tongue
> All that impedes thee from the golden round,
> Which fate and metaphysical aid doth seem
> To have thee crowned withal.

---

2. **Regan and Goneril.** Two evil daughters in Shakespeare's *King Lear*

This swelling exultation and keen spirit of triumph, this uncontrollable eagerness of anticipation, which seems to dilate her form and take possession of all her faculties, this solid, substantial flesh and blood display of passion, exhibit a striking contrast to the cold, abstracted, gratuitous, servile malignity of the Witches, who are equally instrumental in urging Macbeth to his fate for the mere love of mischief, and from a disinterested delight in deformity and cruelty. They are hags of mischief, obscene panders to iniquity, malicious from their impotence of enjoyment, enamored of destruction, because they are themselves unreal, abortive, half-existences, who become sublime from their exemption from all human sympathies and contempt for all human affairs, as Lady Macbeth does by the force of passion! Her fault seems to have been an excess of that strong principle of self-interest and family aggrandizement,[3] not amenable to the common feelings of compassion and justice, which is so marked a feature in barbarous nations and times. A passing reflection of this kind, on the resemblance of the sleeping king to her father, alone prevents her from slaying Duncan with her own hand. . . .

Macbeth (generally speaking) is done upon a stronger and more systematic principle of contrast than any other of Shakespeare's plays. It moves upon the verge of an abyss and is a constant struggle between life and death. The action is desperate and the reaction is dreadful. It is a huddling together of fierce extremes, a war of opposite natures, which of them shall destroy the other. There is nothing but what has a violent end or violent beginnings. The lights and shades are laid on with a determined hand; the transitions from triumph to despair, from the height of terror to the repose of death, are sudden and startling; every passion brings in its fellow-contrary, and the thoughts pitch and jostle against each other as in the dark. The whole play is an unruly chaos of strange and forbidden things, where the ground rocks under our feet. Shakespeare's genius here took its full swing, and trod upon the farthest bounds of nature and passion. ❖

---

3. **family aggrandizement.** Enhancement of the power, wealth, or reputation of her family

Review Questions

1. According to Hazlitt, which plays usually are considered the four principal Shakespearean tragedies? Why is *Macbeth* counted among them? Name three things that distinguish *Macbeth* from Shakespeare's other plays.

2. Identify what motivates Lady Macbeth to drive Macbeth to his fate, according to Hazlitt. Also identify what motivates the witches. How are Macbeth and Lady Macbeth different, in Hazlitt's view? How are Lady Macbeth and the three witches different?

3. Select three quotes from Hazlitt that support his argument that *Macbeth* is a play of passion. What main point is Hazlitt making about *Macbeth*?

TEXT ^{TO} TEXT CONNECTION

Suppose you are writing a review of *Macbeth*. What will you say you like about the play? What will you say you do not like? What lines from the play will you quote to support each of these points? Overall, will your review be favorable or unfavorable? Why?

Refer to Text ▶ ▶ ▶ ▶ ▶   Reason with Text

Refer to Text	Reason with Text	
1a. What is the result of the murder plot against Banquo and his son?	**1b.** Describe how Macbeth reacts to the news of the outcome of the murder plot.	**Understand** Find meaning
2a. At the end of Scene iv, how does Macbeth indicate that he will kill anyone who stands in his way?	**2b.** What does Macbeth seem to have planned for Macduff? Predict what will happen to Macduff in the next act.	**Apply** Use information
3a. How does Lady Macbeth explain her husband's behavior at the banquet to the guests and to Macbeth himself?	**3b.** Infer why Macbeth cannot sleep and how his sleeplessness affects him.	**Analyze** Take things apart
4a. According to Hecate in Scene v, who or what is Macbeth's worst enemy?	**4b.** Argue whether Macbeth is on a course from which he cannot turn back.	**Evaluate** Make judgments
5a. State the reason Macbeth offers for killing Duncan.	**5b.** What characteristics can lead to a character's downfall? Describe the downfall of a character from a television show or movie.	**Create** Bring ideas together

Analyze Literature

Climax and Motif

What is the climax? How does this event affect Macbeth? How might it bring about his downfall? Support your answers with details from the play. (Keep in mind that readers and critics disagree about the answers to these questions.)

What examples of the *deception* motif did you find? How are they used to reinforce the theme of deception in Act III? What other motifs did you observe? Discuss how the various motifs are interrelated.

Extend the Text

Creative Writing Imagine that you are one of the Scottish lords present at the banquet when Macbeth sees the ghost of Banquo. Write a letter to your wife discussing the king's strange behavior.

Persuasive Writing In the role of a prosecuting attorney, write a position statement or argument that will convince a jury to convict Macbeth for murdering Banquo. Build a logical case by providing examples of Macbeth's behavior. State your case in an oral presentation that includes elements of classical speeches: a clear introduction that states your position, a body that presents valid evidence and addresses any counterarguments; and a conclusion that summarizes your argument. Use logical transitions to help listeners follow your arguments, and include rhetorical devices, such as parallelism and repetition, to help emphasize your points and to sway listeners.

Collaborative Learning

Reveal Hypocrisy The word *hypocrisy* means pretending to be what one is not. With a partner, list examples of hypocrisy in Act III. What do these examples reveal about the true nature of Macbeth and Lady Macbeth? Imagine that you and your partner can ask Macbeth one question that will expose his hypocrisy. What would that question be? Share your question with your classmates.

Lifelong Learning

Study Transitions to Power In medieval Europe, the death of a monarch frequently set off civil war between factions vying for the throne. Sometimes this occurred even when there was a clear, legitimate successor. Research a European king or queen's transition to power. Give an oral report on your findings.

 Go to **www.mirrorsandwindows.com** for more.

Understand the Concept

An **allusion** is a reference to a well-known person, place, event, or work of art, music, or literature. The reference may be obvious or obscure, but in either case, it is not explained. Rather, the readers or listeners are left to identify the reference and infer its meaning, based on their own background knowledge. An allusion may present a situation that is parallel to the one being described, or it may serve to emphasize the universal nature of a specific situation.

Writers use allusions to forge connections that enrich and illuminate the contexts in which they occur. For example, if you refer to the house you lived in as a child as a "Camelot," you are making an allusion to the stories of King Arthur and the Knights of the Round Table, who held court at Camelot. In doing so, you are suggesting that your childhood home or the time you lived there had an atmosphere of idyllic happiness.

Allusions are common in literature. Look at the following passage from *Macbeth,* Act III, Scene i, lines 53–56, in which Macbeth contemplates murdering Banquo:

> There is none but he
> Whose being I do fear; and under him
> My Genius is rebuk'd, as it is said
> Mark Antony's was by Caesar.

This passage alludes to ancient Roman leaders Mark Antony and Octavius (Augustus) Caesar, whose story is told in Shakespeare's play *Antony and Cleopatra.* The two men were friends and corulers of Rome but then went to war with one another. Caesar was the victor and became the first emperor of the Roman Empire. Macbeth fears Banquo will defeat him as Caesar did Antony.

Apply the Skill

Explain the Allusions

For each of the following sentences from *Macbeth,* identify who or what is referenced by the underlined allusion. Then explain what the allusion means in this context. You might want to work with a partner to pool your knowledge.

1. Except they meant to bathe in reeking wounds, / Or memorize another <u>Golgotha</u>. (Act I, Scene ii, lines 39–40)
2. . . . and wither'd Murther, / Alarum'd by his sentinel, the wolf, / Whose howl's his watch, thus with his stealthy pace, / With <u>Tarquin's</u> ravishing strides, towards his design / Moves like a ghost. (II.i.52–56)
3. Will all great <u>Neptune's</u> ocean wash this blood / Clean from my hand? (II.ii.57–58)
4. Approach the chamber, and destroy your sight / With a new <u>Gorgon</u>. (II.iii.62–63)
5. Get you gone, / And at the pit of <u>Acheron</u> / Meet me i' th' morning. (III.v.14–16)

Use Allusions in Your Writing

Write a diary entry about a typical day at school, and in it, include at least four allusions. Draw the allusions from people, places, or events in history, music, art, or literature. Also include an allusion to *Macbeth*—for instance, the cunning cruelty of Lady Macbeth, the rhyming incantations of the Weird Sisters, or the "vaulting ambition" of Macbeth. Your allusion also could refer to one of the play's famous lines, such as "Screw your courage to the sticking place."

The Tragedy of Macbeth, Act IV

A Drama by William Shakespeare

Build Background

Historical Context Shakespeare was one of a number of playwrights who made their living by their pens during the English Renaissance. The plays of Thomas Kyd (1558–1594), Christopher Marlowe (1564–1593), and Robert Greene (1558–1592) delighted Elizabethan audiences with tragic tales of thwarted kings and fallen friars. Satirical comedies by Thomas Dekker (c. 1570–1632) and Thomas Middleton (1580–1627) and the grim revenge tragedies of John Webster (c. 1580–1634) entertained later Jacobean theatergoers.

Copyright laws did not exist in Renaissance England, and the playwriting culture of that period was very different from that of today. During the Renaissance, it was quite common for playwrights to share the same sources; revise, adapt, and incorporate material from earlier plays; make additions to existing plays; and collaborate with other playwrights on a single work. This culture of collaboration helps to explain why similar material sometimes appears in plays by different playwrights.

The content of plays also was affected by competition among theaters for audience members. If a play was successful at one theater, other theaters would likely produce a play with a similar theme or setting to attract theatergoers.

Nineteenth-century engraving of William Shakespeare.

Given these conditions of collaboration and competition, modern-day scholars sometimes find it difficult to agree on who wrote specific Renaissance plays. Records regarding performance dates and spectator accounts are incomplete, and many plays never were printed. Although many scholars agree that Shakespeare collaborated with John Fletcher (1579–1629) on his last two plays, *Henry VIII* and *The Two Noble Kinsman,* the issue of collaboration on the Bard's other plays is hotly debated.

Reader's Context When have you interpreted a situation to fit what you wanted to believe? What happened when you found out your interpretation was incorrect?

Analyze Literature

Characterization and Paradox
Characterization is the act of creating or describing a character. Using *direct characterization,* the writer tells what the character is like by describing him or her directly. Using *indirect characterization,* the writer shows what a character is like through portraying his or her own thoughts and actions or those of other characters.

A **paradox** is a seemingly contradictory statement, idea, or event that actually may be true.

Set Purpose

Shakespeare's extraordinary ability to create characters is evident in Act IV, in which he introduces Lady Macduff (Scene ii) and further develops the characters Macduff and Malcolm (Scene iii). Record examples from the text that demonstrate the different characterization techniques Shakespeare uses. Also look for examples of paradox in the statements by the apparitions in Scene i.

Preview Vocabulary

pernicious, 404
homely, 407
impediment, 410
stanchless, 411
abjure, 412
teem, 413
doff, 414

The Witches in Macbeth, c. 1841–1842. Alexandre-Gabriel Decamps.
Wallace Collection, London, England. (See detail on page 399.)

ACT IV

SCENE i: A CAVE

Thunder. Enter the three WITCHES.

1. WITCH.   Thrice the brinded[1] cat hath mew'd.

2. WITCH.   Thrice, and once the hedge-pig whin'd.

3. WITCH.   Harpier[2] cries, "'Tis time, 'tis time."

1. WITCH.   Round about the cauldron go;
5   In the poison'd entrails throw;
Toad, that under cold stone
Days and nights has thirty-one
Swelt'red venom sleeping got,
Boil thou first i' th' charmed pot.

10   **ALL.**   Double, double, toil and trouble;
Fire burn, and cauldron bubble.

2. WITCH.   Fillet of a fenny snake,[3]
In the cauldron boil and bake;
Eye of newt and toe of frog,

ACT IV, SCENE i
1. **brinded.** Brindled; striped

2. **Harpier.** Third witch's
spirit

3. **fenny snake.** Swamp
snake

Thomas Middleton

Because of the Renaissance culture of collaboration and the difficulty of accurately dating when plays were written and performed in Renaissance England, scholars dispute the authorship of sections of Shakespeare's *Macbeth*. Some scholars argue that Thomas Middleton (1580–1627), a contemporary of Shakespeare, adapted portions of Shakespeare's *Macbeth*.

Macbeth is thought to have been written and performed around 1606, although this date is debated. The first printed copy of the play appeared seventeen years later in 1623 with publication of the First Folio. Around 1616, Middleton is thought to have written a play titled *The Witch*. Some scholars argue that certain characters, songs, and lines from Middleton's *The Witch* were incorporated into

Shakespeare's *Macbeth*, suggesting that Middleton adapted the version of *Macbeth* that appears in the First Folio.

For instance, the witch scenes appearing within the First Folio *Macbeth* include references to two songs and a number of lines that also appear in Middleton's *The Witch*. One of these songs appears in Act III, Scene v, line 33, after the witch Hecate makes her first appearance in the play. The second song appears in Act IV, Scene i, line 43, just before Macbeth arrives to consult the witches.

It seems likely these additions were made to make the play more popular, for they increase the level of spectacle and length of the drama. If these excerpts were indeed written by Middleton, it remains unclear whether Shakespeare asked Middleton to collaborate on *Macbeth* or the Middleton excerpts were added after Shakespeare's death.

15 Wool of bat and tongue of dog,
    Adder's fork and blind-worm's[4] sting,
    Lizard's leg and howlet's[5] wing,
    For a charm of pow'rful trouble,
    Like a hell-broth boil and bubble.

20 **ALL.** Double, double, toil and trouble;
    Fire burn, and cauldron bubble.

    3. WITCH. Scale of dragon, tooth of wolf,
    Witch's mummy,[6] maw and gulf
    Of the ravin'd salt-sea shark,[7]
25 Root of hemlock digg'd i' th' dark,
    Liver of blaspheming Jew,[8]
    Gall of goat, and slips of yew
    Sliver'd in the moon's eclipse,
    Nose of Turk and Tartar's lips,[9]
30 Finger of birth-strangled babe
    Ditch-deliver'd by a drab,
    Make the gruel thick and slab.
    Add thereto a tiger's chawdron,[10]
    For th' ingredience of our cau'dron.

4. **blind-worm.** Small legless lizard
5. **howlet.** Small owl

6. **Witch's mummy.** Medicinal substance made from parts of a mummy
7. **maw . . . shark.** Stomach and gullet of the voracious shark
8. **Liver . . . Jew.** This line reflects anti-Semitic attitudes that existed in Shakespeare's England.
9. **Nose . . . lips.** This line reflects a similar prejudice against Turkish people and natives of Eastern Europe and Asia.
10. **chawdron.** Entrails

35   **ALL.**   Double, double, toil and trouble;
      Fire burn, and cauldron bubble.

      2. WITCH.   Cool it with a baboon's blood,
      Then the charm is firm and good.

      Enter HECATE *and the other three* WITCHES.

      HECATE.   O, well done! I commend your pains,
40   And every one shall share i' th' gains.
      And now about the cauldron sing,
      Like elves and fairies in a ring,
      Enchanting all that you put in.

      Music and a song: "Black spirits, etc." *Exeunt* HECATE *and singers.*

      2. WITCH.   By the pricking of my thumbs,
45   Something wicked this way comes.   (*Knocking.*)
                     Open, locks,
                     Whoever knocks!

      Enter MACBETH.

      MACBETH.   How now, you secret, black, and midnight hags?
      What is't you do?

      ALL.   A deed without a name.

50   **MACBETH.**   I conjure you, by that which you profess[11]
      (How e'er you come to know it), answer me:
      Though you untie the winds, and let them fight
      Against the churches; though the yesty[12] waves
      Confound[13] and swallow navigation up;
55   Though bladed corn be lodg'd,[14] and trees blown down;
      Though castles topple on their warders' heads;
      Though palaces and pyramids do slope
      Their heads to their foundations; though the treasure
      Of nature's germains[15] tumble all together,
60   Even till destruction sicken; answer me
      To what I ask you.

      1. WITCH.   Speak.

      2. WITCH.   Demand.

      3. WITCH.   We'll answer.

      1. WITCH.   Say, if th' hadst rather hear it from our mouths,
      Or from our masters'?

      MACBETH.   Call 'em; let me see 'em.

      1. WITCH.   Pour in sow's blood, that hath eaten
65   Her nine farrow;[16] grease that's sweaten
      From the murderer's gibbet[17] throw
      Into the flame.

11. **that . . . profess.** Your witchcraft

12. **yesty.** Foamy
13. **Confound.** Destroy
14. **bladed . . . lodg'd.** Ripe wheat is beaten down

15. **germains.** Seeds

16. **nine farrow.** Nine offspring in a litter of pigs
17. **gibbet.** Gallows where executed criminals were left hanging as a warning

ALL. Come high or low;
Thyself and office deftly show!

Thunder. FIRST APPARITION, *an* ARMED HEAD.[18]

MACBETH. Tell me, thou unknown power—

1. WITCH. He knows thy thought:
70 Hear his speech, but say thou nought.

1. APPARITION. Macbeth! Macbeth! Macbeth! beware Macduff,
Beware the Thane of Fife. Dismiss me. Enough. *He descends.*

MACBETH. What e'er thou art, for thy good caution, thanks;
Thou hast harp'd[19] my fear aright. But one word more—

75 **1. WITCH.** He will not be commanded. Here's another,
More potent than the first.

Thunder. SECOND APPARITION, *a* BLOODY CHILD.[20]

2. APPARITION. Macbeth! Macbeth! Macbeth!

MACBETH. Had I three ears, I'ld hear thee.

2. APPARITION. Be bloody, bold, and resolute: laugh to scorn
80 The pow'r of man; for none of woman born
Shall harm Macbeth. *Descends.*

MACBETH. Then live, Macduff; what need I fear of thee?
But yet I'll make assurance double sure,
And take a bond of fate:[21] thou shalt not live,
85 That I may tell pale-hearted fear it lies,
And sleep in spite of thunder.

Thunder. THIRD APPARITION, *a* CHILD CROWNED, *with a tree in his hand.*[22]

What is this
That rises like the issue of a king,
And wears upon his baby-brow the round
And top of sovereignty?[23]

ALL. Listen, but speak not to't.

90 **3. APPARITION.** Be lion-mettled, proud, and take no care
Who chafes, who frets, or where conspirers are:
Macbeth shall never vanquish'd be until
Great Birnan wood to high Dunsinane hill
Shall come against him. *Descends.*

MACBETH. That will never be.
95 Who can impress[24] the forest, bid the tree
Unfix his earth-bound root? Sweet bodements![25] good!
Rebellious dead, rise never till the wood
Of Birnan rise, and our high-plac'd Macbeth
Shall live the lease of nature,[26] pay his breath

18. **armed Head.** Signifies Macduff

19. **harp'd.** Hit upon

20. **bloody Child.** Signifies Macduff at birth

21. **bond of fate.** Force fate to keep the agreement to kill Macduff

22. **Child . . . hand.** Signifies Malcolm and foreshadows Malcolm's soldiers carrying boughs to Dunsinane

23. **round . . . sovereignty.** The crown

24. **impress.** Force into service
25. **bodements.** Prophecies

26. **lease of nature.** Natural life span

100	To time and mortal custom.[27] Yet my heart
	Throbs to know one thing: tell me, if your art
	Can tell so much, shall Banquo's issue ever
	Reign in this kingdom?

ALL. Seek to know no more.

MACBETH. I will be satisfied. Deny me this,

105 And an eternal curse fall on you! Let me know.
Why sinks that cauldron? and what noise[28] is this? *(Hoboys.)*[29]

1. WITCH. Show!

2. WITCH. Show!

3. WITCH. Show!

110 **ALL.** Show his eyes, and grieve his heart;
Come like shadows, so depart.

A show of eight KINGS, *the eighth with a glass*[30] *in his hand, and*
BANQUO *last.*

MACBETH. Thou art too like the spirit of Banquo; down!
Thy crown does sear mine eyeballs. And thy hair,
Thou other gold-bound brow, is like the first.

115 A third is like the former. Filthy hags,
Why do you show me this?—A fourth? Start, eyes!
What, will the line stretch out to th' crack of doom?
Another yet? A seventh? I'll see no more.
And yet the eighth appears, who bears a glass

120 Which shows me many more; and some I see
That twofold balls and treble sceptres[31] carry.
Horrible sight! Now I see 'tis true,
For the blood-bolter'd[32] Banquo smiles upon me,
And points at them for his. APPARITIONS *vanish.*
What? is this so?

125 **1. WITCH.** Aye, sir, all this is so. But why
Stands Macbeth thus amazedly?
Come, sisters, cheer we up his sprites,[33]
And show the best of our delights.
I'll charm the air to give a sound,

130 While you perform your antic round;[34]
That this great king may kindly say
Our duties did his welcome pay.

Music. The WITCHES *dance and vanish.*

MACBETH. Where are they? Gone? Let this <u>pernicious</u> hour
Stand aye accursed in the calendar!

135 Come in, without there!

---

27. **mortal custom.** Natural death

28. **noise.** Music
29. **Hoboys.** Oboes

30. **show . . . glass.** Silent procession of eight kings, the last holding a mirror

31. **twofold . . . sceptres.** English coronation regalia. The treble sceptres also symbolize Ireland, Scotland, and England, united when James VI of Scotland became James I of England.
32. **blood-bolter'd.** Hair matted with blood

33. **sprites.** Spirits

34. **antic round.** Fantastic circular dance

per • ni • cious
(pər ni´ shəs) *adj.,*
causing ruin and death

Enter LENNOX.

LENNOX.   What's your Grace's will?

MACBETH.   Saw you the weïrd sisters?

LENNOX.   No, my lord.

MACBETH.   Came they not by you?

LENNOX.   No indeed, my lord.

MACBETH.   Infected be the air whereon they ride,
And damn'd all those that trust them! I did hear
140   The galloping of horse. Who was't came by?

LENNOX.   'Tis two or three, my lord, that bring you word
Macduff is fled to England.

MACBETH.   Fled to England!

LENNOX.   Aye, my good lord.

MACBETH.   [*Aside.*] Time, thou anticipat'st my dread exploits:
145   The flighty purpose never is o'ertook
Unless the deed go with it.[35] From this moment
The very firstlings[36] of my heart shall be
The firstlings of my hand. And even now,
To crown my thoughts with acts, be it thought and done:
150   The castle of Macduff I will surprise,
Seize upon Fife, give to th' edge o' th' sword
His wife, his babes, and all unfortunate souls
That trace[37] him in his line. No boasting like a fool;
This deed I'll do before this purpose cool.
155   But no more sights!—Where are these gentlemen?
Come bring me where they are.   *Exeunt.*

SCENE ii: MACDUFF'S CASTLE IN FIFE

Enter MACDUFF'S WIFE, *her* SON, *and* ROSSE.

LADY MACDUFF.   What had he done, to make him fly the land?

ROSSE.   You must have patience, madam.

LADY MACDUFF.   He had none;
His flight was madness. When our actions do not,
Our fears do make us traitors.

ROSSE.   You know not
5   Whether it was his wisdom or his fear.

LADY MACDUFF.   Wisdom? to leave his wife, to leave his babes,
His mansion and his titles,[38] in a place
From whence himself does fly? He loves us not,
He wants the natural touch;[39] for the poor wren,

35. **flighty . . . it.** Purpose is
always fleeing unless it is done
immediately.
36. **firstlings.** First-born (first
thoughts; impulses)

37. **trace.** Follow

ACT IV, SCENE ii
38. **titles.** Properties
39. **wants . . . touch.** Lacks
natural feelings toward his
family

10   The most diminutive of birds, will fight,
      Her young ones in her nest, against the owl.
      All is the fear, and nothing is the love;
      As little is the wisdom, where the flight
      So runs against all reason.

      ROSSE.   My dearest coz,[40]   40. **coz.** Cousin, kin
15   I pray you school[41] yourself. But for your husband,   41. **school.** Control
      He is noble, wise, judicious, and best knows
      The fits o' th' season.[42] I dare not speak much further,   42. **fits . . . season.** Distur-
      But cruel are the times when we are traitors,   bances of the time
      And do not know ourselves;[43] when we hold rumor   43. **know ourselves.** Recog-
20   From what we fear, yet know not what we fear,   nize ourselves as traitors
      But float upon a wild and violent sea
      Each way, and move. I take my leave of you;
      'Shall not be long but I'll be here again.
      Things at the worst will cease, or else climb upward
25   To what they were before. My pretty cousin,
      Blessing upon you!

      LADY MACDUFF.   Father'd he is, and yet he's fatherless.

      ROSSE.   I am so much a fool, should I stay longer,
      It would be my disgrace and your discomfort.
      I take my leave at once.   *Exit* ROSSE.

30   LADY MACDUFF.   Sirrah, your father's dead,
      And what will you do now? How will you live?

      SON.   As birds do, mother.

      LADY MACDUFF.   What, with worms and flies?

      SON.   With what I get, I mean, and so do they.

      LADY MACDUFF.   Poor bird, thou'dst never fear the net nor lime,[44]   44. **lime.** Birdlime, used to
35   The pitfall nor the gin.[45]   catch birds
                                                                            45. **gin.** Snare
      SON.   Why should I, mother? Poor birds they are not set for.
      My father is not dead, for all your saying.

      LADY MACDUFF.   Yes, he is dead. How wilt thou do for a father?

      SON.   Nay, how will you do for a husband?

40   LADY MACDUFF.   Why, I can buy me twenty at any market.

      SON.   Then you'll buy 'em to sell[46] again.   46. **sell.** Betray

      LADY MACDUFF.   Thou speak'st with all thy wit, and yet, i' faith,
      With wit enough for thee.[47]   47. **With . . . thee.** You are
                                                                            clever for a child.
      SON.   Was my father a traitor, mother?

45   LADY MACDUFF.   Aye, that he was.

      SON.   What is a traitor?

LADY MACDUFF. Why, one that swears and lies.

SON. And be all traitors that do so?

LADY MACDUFF. Every one that does so is a traitor, and must be
50 hang'd.

SON. And must they all be hang'd that swear and lie?

LADY MACDUFF. Every one.

SON. Who must hang them?

LADY MACDUFF. Why, the honest men.

55 **SON.** Then the liars and swearers are fools; for there are liars and
swearers enow[48] to beat the honest men and hang up them.

LADY MACDUFF. Now God help thee, poor monkey! But how wilt
thou do for a father?

SON. If he were dead, you'd weep for him; if you would not, it
60 were a good sign that I should quickly have a new father.

LADY MACDUFF. Poor prattler, how thou talk'st!

Enter a MESSENGER.

MESSENGER. Bless you, fair dame! I am not to you known
Though in your state of honor I am perfect.[49]
I doubt[50] some danger does approach you nearly.
65 If you will take a <u>homely</u> man's advice,
Be not found here; hence with your little ones.
To fright you thus, methinks I am too savage;
To do worse to you were fell[51] cruelty,
Which is too nigh your person. Heaven preserve you!
I dare abide no longer.   *Exit* MESSENGER.

70 **LADY MACDUFF.**   Whither should I fly?
I have done no harm. But I remember now
I am in this earthly world—where to do harm
Is often laudable, to do good sometime
Accounted dangerous folly. Why then, alas,
75 Do I put up that womanly defense,
To say I have done no harm?

Enter MURDERERS.

                 What are these faces?

1. MURDERER. Where is your husband?

LADY MACDUFF. I hope, in no place so unsanctified
Where such as thou mayst find him.

1. MURDERER.   He's a traitor.

SON. Thou li'st, thou shag-ear'd villain!

48. **enow.** Enough

49. **in . . . perfect.** I know
you are an honored person.
50. **doubt.** Fear

home • ly (hōmʹ lē) *adj.*,
simple; unpretentious

51. **fell.** Savage

Poster for 1884 theater production of *Macbeth*.

80   **1. MURDERER.**   What, you egg!⁵² [*Stabbing him.*]
Young fry of treachery!

SON.   He has kill'd me, mother:
Run away, I pray you!   [*Dies.*]

> *Exit* LADY MACDUFF *crying* "Murther!"
> *and pursued by the* MURDERERS.

52. **egg.** Traitor to be

SCENE iii: ENGLAND, THE KING'S PALACE

Enter MALCOLM *and* MACDUFF.

MALCOLM.   Let us seek out some desolate shade, and there
Weep our sad bosoms empty.

MACDUFF.   Let us rather
Hold fast the mortal sword, and like good men
Bestride our downfall birthdom.[53] Each new morn
5 New widows howl, new orphans cry, new sorrows
Strike heaven on the face, that it resounds
As if it felt with Scotland, and yell'd out
Like syllable of dolor.[54]

MALCOLM.   What I believe, I'll wail,
What know, believe; and what I can redress,
10 As I shall find the time to friend,[55] I will
What you have spoke, it may be so perchance.
This tyrant, whose sole name blisters our tongues,
Was once thought honest;[56] you have lov'd him well;
He hath not touch'd you yet. I am young, but something
15 You may discern of him through me, and wisdom[57]
To offer up a weak, poor, innocent lamb
T' appease an angry god.

MACDUFF.   I am not treacherous.

MALCOLM.   But Macbeth is.
A good and virtuous nature may recoil
20 In an imperial charge.[58] But I shall crave your pardon;
That which you are, my thoughts cannot transpose:
Angels are bright still, though the brightest[59] fell.
Though all things foul would wear the brows of grace,
Yet grace must still look so.[60]

MACDUFF.   I have lost my hopes.

25 MALCOLM.   Perchance even there where I did find my doubts.
Why in that rawness[61] left you wife and child,
Those precious motives,[62] those strong knots of love,
Without leave-taking? I pray you,
Let not my jealousies be your dishonors,
30 But mine own safeties.[63] You may be rightly just,
What ever I shall think.

MACDUFF.   Bleed, bleed, poor country!
Great tyranny, lay thou thy basis sure,
For goodness dare not check thee; wear thou thy wrongs,
The title is affeer'd![64] Fare thee well, lord,
35 I would not be the villain that thou think'st
For the whole space that's in the tyrant's grasp,
And the rich East to boot.

MALCOLM.   Be not offended;
I speak not as in absolute fear of you.
I think our country sinks beneath the yoke:

ACT IV, SCENE iii

53. **Bestride . . . birthdom.** Fight to protect our down-fallen country

54. **Like . . . dolor.** Similar shout of pain

55. **to friend.** Favorable

56. **honest.** Honorable

57. **You . . . wisdom.** You may see a way to help yourself by betraying me; it is the worldly way.

58. **imperial charge.** Order from the king

59. **the brightest.** Lucifer

60. **Though . . . so.** Even if wickedness takes on the appearance of virtue, virtue must keep its appearance.

61. **rawness.** Unprotected state
62. **motives.** People who inspire your love and protection

63. **Let . . . safeties.** My suspicions are not meant to dishonor you, but rather to protect me.

64. **affeer'd.** Confirmed

40	It weeps, it bleeds, and each new day a gash
	Is added to her wounds. I think withal
	There would be hands uplifted in my right;
	And here from gracious England[65] have I offer
	Of goodly thousands. But, for all this,
45	When I shall tread upon the tyrant's head,
	Or wear it on my sword, yet my poor country
	Shall have more vices than it had before,
	More suffer, and more sundry ways than ever,
	By him that shall succeed.

MACDUFF.   What should he be?

50	**MALCOLM.** It is myself I mean; in whom I know
	All the particulars of vice so grafted
	That, when they shall be open'd, black Macbeth
	Will seem as pure as snow, and the poor state
	Esteem him as a lamb, being compar'd
	With my confineless[66] harms.

55	**MACDUFF.** Not in the legions
	Of horrid hell can come a devil more damn'd
	In evils to top Macbeth.

MALCOLM.   I grant him bloody,
Luxurious,[67] avaricious, false, deceitful,
Sudden, malicious, smacking of every sin

60	That has a name; but there's no bottom, none,
	In my voluptuousness. Your wives, your daughters,
	Your matrons, and your maids could not fill up
	The cestern of my lust, and my desire
	All continent <u>impediments</u> would o'erbear
65	That did oppose my will. Better Macbeth
	Than such an one to reign.

MACDUFF.   Boundless intemperance
In nature is a tyranny; it hath been
Th' untimely emptying of the happy throne,
And fall of many kings. But fear not yet

70	To take upon you what is yours. You may
	Convey your pleasures in a spacious plenty,[68]
	And yet seem cold,[69] the time you may so hoodwink.
	We have willing dames enough; there cannot be
	That vulture in you to devour so many
75	As will to greatness dedicate themselves,
	Finding it so inclin'd.

MALCOLM.   With this, there grows
In my most ill-compos'd affection[70] such

---

65. **England.** King of England, Edward the Confessor

66. **confineless.** Limitless

67. **Luxurious.** Lustful

im • ped • i • ment
(im pe′ də mənt) *n.*,
obstacle

68. **Convey . . . plenty.** Find plenty of space to indulge secretly in your pleasures

69. **cold.** Chaste

70. **ill-composed affection.** Immoral character

A <u>stanchless</u> avarice that, were I king,
I should cut off the nobles for their lands,
80 Desire his jewels, and this other's house,
And my more-having would be as a sauce
To make me hunger more, that I should forge
Quarrels unjust against the good and loyal,
Destroying them for wealth.

MACDUFF.   This avarice
85 Sticks deeper, grows with more pernicious root
Than summer-seeming[71] lust; and it hath been
The sword of our slain kings. Yet do not fear,
Scotland hath foisons[72] to fill up your will
Of your mere own.[73] All these are portable,[74]
90 With other graces weigh'd.

MALCOLM.   But I have none. The king-becoming graces,
As justice, verity, temp'rance, stableness,
Bounty, perseverance, mercy, lowliness,
Devotion, patience, courage, fortitude,
95 I have no relish of them, but abound
In the division of each several crime,
Acting it many ways. Nay, had I pow'r, I should
Pour the sweet milk of concord into hell,
Uproar the universal peace, confound
All unity on earth.

100 **MACDUFF.**   O Scotland, Scotland!

MALCOLM.   If such a one be fit to govern, speak.
I am as I have spoken.

MACDUFF.   Fit to govern?
No, not to live. O nation miserable!
With an untitled tyrant bloody-sceptred,
105 When shalt thou see thy wholesome days again,
Since that the truest issue of thy throne
By his own interdiction[75] stands accus'd,
And does blaspheme his breed?[76] Thy royal father
Was a most sainted king; the queen that bore thee,
110 Oft'ner upon her knees than on her feet,
Died every day she liv'd.[77] Fare thee well,
These evils thou repeat'st upon thyself
Hath banish'd me from Scotland. O my breast,
Thy hope ends here!

MALCOLM.   Macduff, this noble passion,
115 Child of integrity, hath from my soul
Wip'd the black scruples,[78] reconcil'd my thoughts

stanch · less (stänch′ ləs) *adj.,* unstoppable (modern form: *staunchless*)

71. **summer-seeming.** Lasting only for the summer or prime of life
72. **foisons.** Plenty
73. **mere own.** Royal property
74. **portable.** Bearable

75. **interdiction.** Legal restriction
76. **blaspheme his breed.** Slander his ancestors

77. **Died . . . liv'd.** Died to the world (prepared for heaven) every day, and so lived in a state of grace

78. **scruples.** Doubts

To thy good truth and honor. Devilish Macbeth
By many of these trains[79] hath sought to win me
Into his power, and modest wisdom plucks me
120 From over-credulous haste. But God above
Deal between thee and me! for even now
I put myself to thy direction, and
Unspeak mine own detraction; here abjure
The taints and blames I laid upon myself,
125 For strangers to my nature. I am yet
Unknown to woman, never was forsworn,
Scarcely have coveted what was mine own,
At no time broke my faith, would not betray
The devil to his fellow, and delight
130 No less in truth than life. My first false speaking
Was this upon myself. What I am truly
Is thine and my poor country's to command:
Whither indeed, before thy here-approach,
Old Siward, with ten thousand warlike men
135 Already at a point, was setting forth.
Now we'll together, and the chance of goodness
Be like our warranted quarrel![80] Why are you silent?

MACDUFF.   Such welcome and unwelcome things at once
'Tis hard to reconcile.

Enter a DOCTOR.

140 MALCOLM.   Well, more anon.—Comes the King forth, I pray you?

DOCTOR.   Aye, sir; there are a crew of wretched souls
That stay his cure.[81] Their malady convinces
The great assay of art;[82] but at his touch,
Such sanctity hath heaven given his hand,
They presently amend.

145 MALCOLM.   I thank you, doctor.   *Exit* DOCTOR.

MACDUFF.   What's the disease he means?

MALCOLM.   'Tis call'd the evil:[83]
A most miraculous work in this good king,
Which often, since my here-remain in England,
I have seen him do. How he solicits heaven,
150 Himself best knows; but strangely-visited people,
All swoll'n and ulcerous, pitiful to the eye,
The mere despair of surgery, he cures,
Hanging a golden stamp[84] about their necks,
Put on with holy prayers, and 'tis spoken,
155 To the succeeding royalty he leaves
The healing benediction. With this strange virtue,

79. **trains.** Devices

ab • jure (ab jūr´)
v., renounce

80. **chance . . . quarrel.** May
our luck be as good as our
cause is just.

81. **stay his cure.** Wait for
him to cure them
82. **convinces . . . art.**
Defeats even the highest
medical skill

83. **the evil.** Scrofula, tuberculosis of the lymph nodes,
was thought to be cured by
the touch of royalty.

84. **stamp.** Coin

He hath a heavenly gift of prophecy,
And sundry blessings hang about his throne
That speak him full of grace.

Enter Rosse.

Macduff.   See who comes here.

160 **Malcolm.**   My countryman; but yet I know him not.

Macduff.   My ever gentle[85] cousin, welcome hither.

Malcolm.   I know him now. Good God betimes remove
The means that makes us strangers![86]

Rosse.   Sir, amen.

Macduff.   Stands Scotland where it did?

Rosse.   Alas, poor country,
165 Almost afraid to know itself! It cannot
Be call'd our mother, but our grave; where nothing,
But who knows nothing, is once seen to smile;
Where sighs, and groans, and shrieks that rent the air
Are made, not mark'd;[87] where violent sorrow seems
170 A modern ecstasy.[88] The dead man's knell
Is there scarce ask'd for who, and good men's lives
Expire before the flowers in their caps,
Dying or ere[89] they sicken.

Macduff.   O relation!
Too nice,[90] and yet too true.

Malcolm.   What's the newest grief?

175 **Rosse.**   That of an hour's age doth hiss the speaker;[91]
Each minute <u>teems</u> a new one.

Macduff.   How does my wife?

Rosse.   Why, well.

Macduff.   And all my children?

Rosse.   Well too.

Macduff.   The tyrant has not batter'd at their peace?

Rosse.   No, they were well at peace when I did leave 'em.

180 **Macduff.**   Be not a niggard[92] of your speech; how goes't?

Rosse.   When I came hither to transport the tidings,
Which I have heavily[93] borne, there ran a rumor
Of many worthy fellows that were out,[94]
Which was to my belief witness'd the rather,[95]
185 For that I saw the tyrant's power[96] afoot.
Now is the time of help; your eye in Scotland

---

85. **gentle.** Noble

86. **betimes . . . strangers.** Soon remove Macbeth who has caused our separation

87. **mark'd.** Noticed
88. **modern ecstasy.** Common emotion

89. **or ere.** Before

90. **relation! / Too nice.** Tale all too accurate

91. **hiss the speaker.** Cause the speaker to be hissed for telling old news

teem (tēm) *v.*, bring forth

92. **niggard.** Stingy

93. **heavily.** Very sadly
94. **out.** Out in arms
95. **witness'd the rather.** Made more believable
96. **tyrant's power.** Armed forces

Would create soldiers, make our women fight,
To <u>doff</u> their dire distresses.

MALCOLM.　　　　　　　Be't their comfort
We are coming thither. Gracious England hath
190　Lent us good Siward, and ten thousand men;
An older and a better soldier none
That Christendom gives out.

ROSSE.　　　　　　　　Would I could answer
This comfort with the like! But I have words
That would be howl'd out in the desert air,
Where hearing should not latch[97] them.

97. **latch.** Catch

195　**MACDUFF.**　　　　　　　What concern they?
The general cause? or is it a fee-grief
Due to some single breast?[98]

98. **fee-grief . . . breast.** Private sorrow to be held by just one person

ROSSE.　　　　　　　No mind that's honest
But in it shares some woe, though the main part
Pertains to you alone.

MACDUFF.　　　　If it be mine,
200　Keep it not from me, quickly let me have it.

ROSSE.　　Let not your ears despise my tongue for ever,
Which shall possess them with the heaviest sound
That ever yet they heard.

MACDUFF.　　　　　Humh! I guess at it.

ROSSE.　　Your castle is surpris'd; your wife, and babes,
205　Savagely slaughter'd. To relate the manner,
Were on the quarry[99] of these murther'd deer
To add the death of you.

99. **quarry.** Heap of slaughtered bodies, like game from a hunting expedition

MALCOLM.　　　　　Merciful heaven!
What, man, ne'er pull your hat upon your brows;
Give sorrow words. The grief that does not speak
210　Whispers the o'er-fraught heart,[100] and bids it break.

100. **Whispers the o'er-fraught heart.** Whispers to the overburdened heart

MACDUFF.　My children too?

ROSSE.　　　　　　Wife, children, servants, all
That could be found.

MACDUFF.　　　　And I must be from thence![101]
My wife kill'd too?

101. **from thence.** Away from there

ROSSE.　　　　I have said.

MALCOLM.　　　　　Be comforted.
Let's make us med'cines of our great revenge
215　To cure this deadly grief.

MACDUFF.   He has no children. All my pretty ones?
Did you say all? O hell-kite! All?
What, all my pretty chickens, and their dam,[102]
At one fell swoop?

MALCOLM.   Dispute[103] it like a man.

220 **MACDUFF.**   I shall do so;
But I must also feel it as a man:
I cannot but remember such things were,
That were most precious to me. Did heaven look on,
And would not take their part? Sinful Macduff,
225 They were all strook for thee! naught[104] that I am,
Not for their own demerits, but for mine,
Fell slaughter on their souls. Heaven rest them now!

MALCOLM.   Be this the whetstone of your sword, let grief
Convert to anger; blunt not the heart, enrage it.

230 **MACDUFF.**   O, I could play the woman with mine eyes,
And braggart with my tongue! But, gentle heavens,
Cut short all intermission. Front to front[105]
Bring thou this fiend of Scotland and myself;
Within my sword's length set him; if he scape,
Heaven forgive him too!

235 **MALCOLM.**   This tune goes manly.
Come go we to the King, our power is ready,
Our lack is nothing but our leave. Macbeth
Is ripe for shaking, and the pow'rs above
Put on their instruments.[106] Receive what cheer you may,
240 The night is long that never finds the day.   *Exeunt.* ❖

102. **dam.** Mother

103. **Dispute.** Revenge

104. **naught.** Wicked

105. **Front to front.** Face to face

106. **Put . . . instruments.** Prepare for action by arming themselves

MIRRORS & WINDOWS

What qualities of a leader inspire loyalty? What qualities of a leader can turn others against him or her?

Refer to Text ▶ ▶ ▶ ▶ ▶ Reason with Text

1a. In Scene ii, what does Lady Macduff say to her son about her husband?

1b. Explain why Shakespeare might have included this exchange between Lady Macduff and her son. How does it affect the audience's feelings about the outcome of Scene ii?

Understand
Find meaning

2a. List the lies Malcolm tells Macduff in Scene iii.

2b. Suggest why Malcolm misleads Macduff. What does he accomplish by doing so?

Apply
Use information

3a. What apparitions do the witches show Macbeth, and what do they tell him?

3b. How does Macbeth interpret the statements of the apparitions? What other interpretations are possible?

Analyze
Take things apart

4a. In Scene iii, how do Malcolm and Macduff describe the condition of Scotland under Macbeth's rule?

4b. Compare and contrast the condition of England under Edward, as described in this act, to that of Scotland under Macbeth.

Evaluate
Make judgments

5a. What does Macbeth plan to do to Macduff?

5b. Explain why Macbeth chooses this course of action. Has he become more accustomed to doing evil than good? Support your opinion with details from the play.

Create
Bring ideas together

Analyze Literature

Characterization and Paradox

Review the examples of characterization techniques you recorded. Which techniques does Shakespeare use in creating Lady Macduff in Scene ii? Which techniques does he use to develop the characters Macduff and Malcolm in Scene iii? Create a simple chart or web-type diagram to compare the character traits of these two men. What traits do they have in common?

In Scene i, which statements made by the apparitions are examples of paradox? For each statement, explain what seems to be contradictory but actually may be true.

Extend the Text

Creative Writing As Macduff, write a journal entry about your reaction to the massacre of your family and your reasons for supporting Malcolm over Macbeth.

Expository Writing The word *weird* is derived from the Old English *wyrd,* meaning "fate." Some literary scholars say that the predictions of the "weïrd sisters" represent Macbeth's fate, which arises out of his character. Others note that Shakespeare's audience would have believed in witches, so they represent the evil that causes Macbeth's downfall. Write an essay evaluating these two positions, using details from the play to support your analysis.

Collaborative Learning

Design a Scene Working with a small group, choose one scene from Act IV to adapt to film. Create a plan for the scenery, lighting, props, music, and costumes. Present your scene design and explain your decisions to the class.

Lifelong Learning

Research Superstitions Shakespeare's audience would have found the witches to be believable and frightening. Research a popular superstition in Elizabethan or Jacobean England, and locate one example in *Macbeth* that alludes to that superstition. Present your information in an oral report to the class.

 Go to **www.mirrorsandwindows.com** for more.

1. In Act III, Scene i, lines 1–3, what does Banquo think about the current situation?
   A. The witches' predictions have not come true.
   B. The witches were just kidding but in an unkind way.
   C. There is something suspicious about how all the witches' predictions came true.
   D. Macbeth now has everything he ever wanted and can relax.
   E. The witches have killed Duncan and will now have to pay the consequences.

2. Macbeth's feelings of guilt explain all of the following *except* his
   A. sleeplessness.
   B. tortured mind.
   C. obsession with blood.
   D. seeing the ghost of Banquo.
   E. being shown three apparitions by the witches.

3. Which of the following reveals the most about Lady Macbeth's character?
   A. what she says
   B. what she looks like
   C. how she acts when she is alone
   D. how she interacts with others
   E. what others say about her

4. In Act IV, Lady Macduff states, "I am in this earthly world—where to do harm / Is often laudable, to do good sometime / Accounted dangerous folly" (IV.ii.72–74). These lines are an example of what literary element?
   A. a foil
   B. an aside
   C. a simile
   D. a paradox
   E. a hyperbole

5. What is meaning of the following lines? "Good men's lives / Expire before the flowers in their caps, / Dying or ere they sicken." (IV.iii.171–173)
   A. Good people die young.
   B. There is beauty in death.
   C. Goodness lives on after death.
   D. Being sick is better than dying.
   E. Dying is better than being sick.

6. Which literary device does Shakespeare use in the line "To doff their dire distresses" (IV.iii.188)?
   A. irony
   B. metaphor
   C. assonance
   D. consonance
   E. alliteration

7. Upon hearing of the deaths of his wife and children, Macduff states, "My children too? / . . . / My wife kill'd too? / . . . / All my pretty ones? / Did you say all? O hell-kite! All? / What, all my pretty chickens, and their dam, / At one fell swoop?" (IV.iii.211, 213, 216–219) What is the most likely reason for Macduff's repetitious questioning?
   A. He is hard of hearing.
   B. He is in a state of shock and disbelief.
   C. He is trying to divert his anger and be calm.
   D. He is emphasizing what happened so nobody will forget it.
   E. He is trying to get Rosse or Malcolm to reveal their guilt in their responses.

8. At the end of Act IV, what does Malcolm mean when he says, "Macbeth / Is ripe for shaking" (IV.iii.37–38)?
   A. Macbeth is getting old.
   B. Macbeth is vulnerable.
   C. Macbeth is traitorous.
   D. Macbeth is afraid.
   E. Macbeth is overconfident.

9. Constructed Response: In Act III, Scene iv, lines 111–115, Macbeth says to his wife, "You make me strange / Even to the disposition that I owe, / When now I think you can behold such sights, / And keep the natural ruby of your cheeks, / When mine is blanch'd with fear." What is different about the appearances of Macbeth and Lady Macbeth? What do these lines reveal about Macbeth's feelings about the murders and his character in general?

10. Constructed Response: Discuss why Macbeth avoids using the word *murder* (or *murther*) and instead usually refers to the act of killing as "it" or "the deed."

Understand the Concept

Synonyms are words that have the same or similar meanings. **Antonyms** are words that have opposite meanings. Knowing both the synonyms and antonyms of a word can help you expand your vocabulary and thus add variety, accuracy, and interest to your writing.

Consider *wisdom,* as used by Rosse to explain Macduff's flight in Act IV, Scene ii, lines 4–5: "You know not / Whether it was his wisdom or his fear." Synonyms and antonyms for the noun *wisdom* are as follows:

Synonyms intelligence, knowledge, understanding
Antonyms foolishness, stupidity, ignorance

Note that the words in each group have slightly different meanings. For instance, the synonym *intelligence* seems more clinical or objective than *knowledge,* and *understanding* implies a broader sense of perception or intuition. Among the antonyms, *foolishness* suggests a lack of experience or judgment and is less critical or negative than *ignorance. Stupidity* seems the harshest.

To choose the appropriate synonym or antonym, you need to know the exact meaning or context of the original word. For instance, the word *light,* used as an adjective, has different meanings. It can refer to either the level of brightness or the weight of something. The antonym for *light,* therefore, could be *dark* or *heavy,* depending on the context. Likewise, you would need to know in what context *light* is used to choose from among the synonyms *pale, bright,* and *insubstantial.*

A useful source of information about synonyms and antonyms is a *thesaurus,* a reference book organized much like a dictionary that lists words with alternative and opposite meanings by part of speech. Keep a thesaurus nearby as you write, and use it to find more specific and interesting words. Dictionaries also list synonyms and antonyms with the definitions.

Apply the Skill

Exercise A

Read the following lines from Act IV of *Macbeth.* Analyze the textual context of the scene to draw conclusions about nuances in the meanings of the words. Then write two synonyms and two antonyms for each word, referring to a thesaurus as needed. Finally, write a different sentence for each underlined word, synonym, and antonym. As you write, keep in mind the subtle differences in meaning between the related words.

1. "You must have <u>patience</u>, madam." (Scene ii, line 2)
2. "But cruel are the times when we are <u>traitors</u>, / And do not know ourselves." (ii.18–19)
3. "Let us seek out some <u>desolate</u> shade, and there / Weep our sad bosoms empty." (iii.1–2)
4. "Such welcome and unwelcome things at once / 'Tis hard to <u>reconcile</u>." (iii.138–139)
5. "I cannot but remember such things were, / That were most <u>precious</u> to me." (iii.222–223)

Exercise B

Knowing synonyms and antonyms can help you *paraphrase* a piece of writing, or rewrite it in your own words. This is a useful skill when doing research. Practice paraphrasing a passage of about ten lines from *Macbeth.* Compare your work with that of a classmate.

Keep in mind that paraphrasing is different from *summarizing,* in which you condense information to identify the main ideas in a few sentences. When you paraphrase, you essentially translate the original language line by line or sentence by sentence, maintaining the level of detail. (See the Grammar & Style workshop on paraphrasing and summarizing in Unit 9.)

SPELLING PRACTICE

Words Ending in *-ous/-ious* and *-tion/-sion*
Many new words can be made by adding the suffix *-ous/-ious* or *-tion/-sion* to an existing word. Adding *-ous* or *-ious* to a noun creates an adjective meaning "full of" or "having the qualities of," such as *poisonous.* Adding *-tion* or *-sion* to a verb creates a noun meaning "the process or result of," such as *emission.* For each word below from *Macbeth,* Act IV, identify the original and new forms and determine the new meaning. Look for patterns in how each suffix is added. For instance, when the suffix *-tion* is added to a word ending with *t,* the final *t* is dropped, as in *prediction.*

apparition	caution	pernicious
avaricious	foundation	judicious
benediction	intermission	malicious

The Tragedy of Macbeth, Act V

A Drama by William Shakespeare

Build Background

Cultural Context Examining how theater and film productions have approached Shakespeare's *Macbeth* often highlights some of the central questions raised by the play. For instance, decisions about the relationship between Macbeth and Lady Macbeth, two central characters, often shape the presentation of the play.

The 1955 Glen Byam Shaw production at Stratford, England, chose to highlight the change in the couple's behavior over the course of the drama. At the beginning of the play, Lady Macbeth is strong and ruthless, whereas her husband is indecisive and wracked by his conscience. By the end of the play, the dynamic has shifted. It is Macbeth who is bold and resolute and Lady Macbeth who is consumed by guilt. This crossover interpretation commonly underlies presentations of the play that focus on the dynamics in the relationship between Macbeth and Lady Macbeth.

In his nineteenth-century operatic adaptation of *Macbeth,* Giuseppe Verdi presented a different portrait of Lady Macbeth. He closely linked Lady Macbeth to the witches by making her the head of a coven (assembly of thirteen witches) that manipulates Macbeth into seizing the throne. This presentation emphasizes that Lady Macbeth is a significant evil factor in driving her husband to act.

The 1971 Roman Polanski film version of *Macbeth* focused the attention not on Macbeth and Lady Macbeth but on the corrupt society in which they lived. Polanski chose to address the responsibility society has in the murders and portrays Macbeth and Lady Macbeth simply as products of society. In Polanski's medieval Scotland, it does not matter if Macbeth is defeated, because another man just like him will rise to take his place.

These different interpretations of the same play encourage readers and viewers to reexamine their own interpretations.

Reader's Context How can looking at a situation or event from several perspectives increase your understanding of it?

Kathleen Broderick in the role of Lady Macbeth in the Verdi Opera presentation of *Macbeth* (2000).

Analyze Literature

Tragedy and Theme
A **tragedy** is a work of literature that tells the story of the fall of a person of high status. It celebrates the courage and dignity of a *tragic hero* in the face of inevitable doom. Sometimes, that doom is made inevitable by a *tragic flaw,* a personal weakness that leads to the hero's downfall.

A **theme** is a central message or perception about life revealed in a literary work. A *stated theme* is presented directly, whereas an *implied theme* must be inferred.

Set Purpose

As noted elsewhere, Shakespeare's *Macbeth* is one of the most famous tragedies in all of literature. Before you read this final act, reflect on the character Macbeth and what has been revealed about him thus far in the play. What qualities of a tragic hero does he possess? As you read Act V, identify Macbeth's tragic flaw. Also think about how Shakespeare uses Macbeth to reveal the central theme of the drama.

Preview Vocabulary

taint, 424
ague, 428
harbinger, 429
usurper, 432

The Death of Lady Macbeth, 1875. Dante Gabriel Rossetti.
Ashmolean Museum, University of Oxford, England.
(See detail on page 419.)

Act V

Scene i: A castle at Dunsinane

Enter a Doctor of Physic *and a* Waiting-Gentlewoman.

Doctor.   I have two nights watch'd with you, but can perceive no truth in your report. When was it she last walk'd?

Gentlewoman.   Since his Majesty went into the field,[1] I have seen her rise from her bed, throw her nightgown upon her, unlock her
5   closet, take forth paper, fold it, write upon't, read it, afterwards seal it, and again return to bed; yet all this while in a most fast sleep.

Doctor.   A great perturbation in nature, to receive at once the benefit of sleep and do the effects of watching![2] In this slumb'ry agitation, besides her walking and other actual performances, what,
10   at any time, have you heard her say?

Gentlewoman.   That, sir, which I will not report after her.

Doctor.   You may to me, and 'tis most meet you should.

Act V, Scene i
1. **went . . . field.** Went to battle

2. **do . . . watching.** Do activities one normally does while awake

Dante Gabriel Rossetti

Dante Gabriel Rossetti (1828–1882) was born in London to a family of Italian academics. He had graduated from King's College by age fourteen, and by the time he was twenty, he had translated a number of Italian poems into English.

Although Rossetti initially planned to pursue a literary career, his love for painting took hold in 1845 when he became a full-time student at the Royal Academy. At the academy, Rossetti and fellow students William Holman Hunt and John Everett Millais developed a great admiration for Medieval Italian art. Together, the three formed the Pre-Raphaelite Brotherhood in 1848.

Rossetti and his companions felt British painters had established a boring and uninspired artistic climate. They formed the Pre-Raphaelite Brotherhood with the intention of returning passion to the art community, using early Renaissance models as their guides. The Pre-Raphaelites heralded the Medieval Period as a time of greater beauty and simplicity. This artistic vision was somewhat influenced by the Romantic poets, including William Blake and William Wordsworth (see Unit 6). Like the Romantics, the Pre-Raphaelites saw a transcendent beauty in the natural world that they often framed in religious terms. The two groups also shared the belief that art should act as a moral compass for its audience.

The Industrial Revolution also had a strong influence on Rossetti's nostalgia for the past. Poor living conditions and frequent social unrest made life unpleasant for most Londoners during this time, and many yearned for a life without industrialization. In fact, Rossetti suffered from chronic health problems, probably due to London's high level of industrial pollutants. He died in 1882 at the relatively young age of fifty-three.

Critical Viewing As you look at Rossetti's *The Death of Lady Macbeth* on page 420, identify some of its passionate, religious, and moral characteristics. How are some of Rossetti's principles reflected in this drawing?

GENTLEWOMAN. Neither to you nor any one, having no witness to confirm my speech.

Enter LADY MACBETH *with a taper.*

15 Lo you, here she comes! This is her very guise,[3] and upon my life, fast asleep. Observe her, stand close.[4]

DOCTOR. How came she by that light?

GENTLEWOMAN. Why, it stood by her. She has light by her continually, 'tis her command.

20 DOCTOR. You see her eyes are open.

GENTLEWOMAN. Aye, but their sense are shut.

DOCTOR. What is it she does now? Look how she rubs her hands.

GENTLEWOMAN. It is an accustom'd action with her, to seem thus washing her hands. I have known her continue in this a quarter of
25 an hour.

3. **her very guise.** Precisely what she has been doing
4. **close.** Hidden

LADY MACBETH. Yet here's a spot.

DOCTOR. Hark, she speaks. I will set down what comes from her, to satisfy my remembrance the more strongly.

LADY MACBETH. Out, damn'd spot! out, I say! One—two—why
30 then 'tis time to do't. Hell is murky. Fie, my lord, fie, a soldier, and afeard? What need we fear who knows it, when none can call our pow'r to accompt?[5] Yet who would have thought the old man to have had so much blood in him?

DOCTOR. Do you mark that?

35 **LADY MACBETH.** The Thane of Fife had a wife; where is she now? What, will these hands ne'er be clean? No more o' that, my lord, no more o' that; you mar all with this starting.[6]

DOCTOR. Go to, go to; you have known what you should not.

GENTLEWOMAN. She has spoke what she should not, I am sure of
40 that; heaven knows what she has known.

LADY MACBETH. Here's the smell of the blood still. All the perfumes of Arabia will not sweeten this little hand. O, O, O!

DOCTOR. What a sigh is there! The heart is sorely charg'd.[7]

GENTLEWOMAN. I would not have such a heart in my bosom for
45 the dignity of the whole body.

DOCTOR. Well, well, well.

GENTLEWOMAN. Pray God it be, sir.

DOCTOR. This disease is beyond my practice; yet I have known those which have walk'd in their sleep who have died holily in
50 their beds.

LADY MACBETH. Wash your hands, put on your nightgown, look not so pale. I tell you yet again, Banquo's buried; he cannot come out on 's grave.

DOCTOR. Even so?

55 **LADY MACBETH.** To bed, to bed; there's knocking at the gate. Come, come, come, come, give me your hand. What's done cannot be undone. To bed, to bed, to bed.

Exit LADY.

DOCTOR. Will she go now to bed?

GENTLEWOMAN. Directly.

60 **DOCTOR.** Foul whisp'rings are abroad. Unnatural deeds
Do breed unnatural troubles; infected minds
To their deaf pillows will discharge their secrets.
More needs she the divine than the physician.

5. **call our pow'r to accompt.** Call to account anyone so powerful as we

6. **starting.** Sudden, startled movements

7. **charg'd.** Burdened

God, God, forgive us all! Look after her,
65 Remove from her the means of all annoyance,
And still keep eyes upon her. So good night.
My mind she has mated, and amaz'd my sight.[8]
I think, but dare not speak.

GENTLEWOMAN.   Good night, good doctor.   *Exeunt.*

8. **My . . . sight.** She has confused my mind and bewildered my sight.

SCENE ii: COUNTRYSIDE NEAR DUNSINANE

Drum and Colors. Enter MENTETH, CATHNESS, ANGUS, LENNOX, SOLDIERS.

MENTETH.   The English pow'r is near, led on by Malcolm,
His uncle Siward, and the good Macduff.
Revenges burn in them; for their dear causes
Would to the bleeding and the grim alarm[9]
Excite the mortified[10] man.

ACT V, SCENE ii
9. **bleeding . . . alarm.** Bloody and horrible battle
10. **mortified.** Almost dead

5 **ANGUS.**   Near Birnan wood
Shall we well meet them; that way are they coming.

CATHNESS.   Who knows if Donalbain be with his brother?

LENNOX.   For certain, sir, he is not; I have a file[11]
Of all the gentry. There is Siward's son,
10 And many unrough[12] youths that even now
Protest their first of manhood.[13]

11. **file.** List

12. **unrough.** Unbearded

13. **Protest . . . manhood.** Show their manhood for the first time

MENTETH.   What does the tyrant?

CATHNESS.   Great Dunsinane he strongly fortifies.
Some say he's mad; others that lesser hate him
Do call it valiant fury; but for certain
15 He cannot buckle his distemper'd cause
Within the belt of rule.[14]

14. **He . . . rule.** He cannot confine his corrupt cause within self-control.

ANGUS.   Now does he feel
His secret murthers sticking on his hands;
Now minutely revolts[15] upbraid his faith-breach;
Those he commands move only in command,
20 Nothing in love. Now does he feel his title
Hang loose about him, like a giant's robe
Upon a dwarfish thief.

15. **minutely revolts.** New revolts every minute

MENTETH.   Who then shall blame
His pester'd senses to recoil and start,
When all that is within him does condemn
Itself for being there?

25 **CATHNESS.**   Well, march we on
To give obedience where 'tis truly ow'd.

Lady Macbeth Sleepwalking, 1781. Henry Fuseli.
The Louvre, Paris, France.

Meet we the med'cine of the sickly weal,[16]
And with him pour we, in our country's purge,
Each drop of us.

LENNOX.   Or so much as it needs
30   To dew the sovereign flower[17] and drown the weeds.
Make we our march towards Birnan.

Exeunt marching.

SCENE iii: THE CASTLE AT DUNSINANE

Enter MACBETH, DOCTOR, *and* ATTENDANTS.

MACBETH.   Bring me no more reports, let them fly all.
Till Birnan wood remove to Dunsinane
I cannot <u>taint</u> with fear. What's the boy Malcolm?
Was he not born of woman? The spirits that know
5   All mortal consequences[18] have pronounc'd me thus:
"Fear not, Macbeth, no man that's born of woman
Shall e'er have power upon thee." Then fly, false thanes,
And mingle with the English epicures![19]

16. **med'cine . . . weal.**
Malcolm is the medicine that
can cure the state.

17. **sovereign flower.**
Malcolm

taint (tānt) *v.,* infect

ACT V, SCENE iii
18. **mortal consequences.**
Human destinies

19. **epicures.** Those who like
easy living, not soldiers

The mind I sway[20] by, and the heart I bear,
10   Shall never sag with doubt, nor shake with fear.

Enter SERVANT.

The devil damn thee black,[21] thou cream-fac'd loon!
Where got'st thou that goose-look?

SERVANT.   There is ten thousand—

MACBETH.   Geese, villain?

SERVANT.   Soldiers, sir.

MACBETH.   Go prick thy face, and over-red thy fear,
15   Thou lily-liver'd boy. What soldiers, patch?[22]
Death of thy soul! those linen cheeks of thine
Are counsellors to fear. What soldiers, whey-face?

SERVANT.   The English force, so please you.

MACBETH.   Take thy face hence.   [*Exit* SERVANT.]
                                Seyton!—I am sick at heart
20   When I behold—Seyton, I say!—This push[23]
Will cheer me ever, or disseat[24] me now.
I have liv'd long enough: my way of life
Is fall'n into the sear,[25] the yellow leaf,
And that which should accompany old age,
25   As honor, love, obedience, troops of friends,
I must not look to have; but in their stead,
Curses, not loud but deep, mouth-honor,[26] breath,
Which the poor heart would fain[27] deny, and dare not.
Seyton!

Enter SEYTON.

SEYTON.   What's your gracious pleasure?

30   MACBETH.   What news more?

SEYTON.   All is confirm'd, my lord, which was reported.

MACBETH.   I'll fight, till from my bones my flesh be hack'd.
Give me my armor.

SEYTON.   'Tis not needed yet.

MACBETH.   I'll put it on.
35   Send out moe[28] horses, skirr[29] the country round,
Hang those that talk of fear. Give me mine armor.
How does your patient, doctor?

DOCTOR.   Not so sick, my lord,
As she is troubled with thick-coming fancies,
That keep her from her rest.

20. **sway.** Control myself

21. **devil . . . black.** Damned souls were said to turn black

22. **patch.** Fool

23. **push.** Surge of effort
24. **disseat.** Dethrone (with wordplay on *cheer*, pronounced *chair*)
25. **sear.** Dried and withered

26. **mouth-honor.** Honored in words but not in actions
27. **fain.** Gladly, eagerly

28. **moe.** More
29. **skirr.** Scour

Sleepwalking

In Scene i of Act V, Lady Macbeth's sleepwalking functions effectively as a literary device, exposing her subconscious feelings of guilt and suggesting she may have gone insane. In real life, however, it is unlikely that someone would speak and act in this manner while sleepwalking.

Sleepwalking, the common name for a medical condition called *somnambulism,* is a sleep disorder that causes people to perform everyday functions while sleeping. Behaviors can range from simply sitting up in bed and looking around to getting up, walking around, and performing simple tasks. In rare instances, sleepwalkers have been reported to drive cars and perform hostile, violent actions.

Contrary to popular belief, most somnambulists sleepwalk with their eyes open, but they appear confused or dazed. They also tend to mumble and rarely say anything coherent during an episode of sleepwalking. In most cases, sleepwalkers cannot respond or converse during an episode and do not remember the episode upon awakening.

Sleepwalking typically occurs during the first one-third of the sleep cycle, the stages of deep sleep. Children are especially likely to display signs of sleepwalking early in their sleep, and the condition is more common in males than females. Sleepwalking and other sleep disturbances can be prompted by stress and anxiety. Scientists estimate that nearly one in five people is prone to some form of this sleep disorder.

  MACBETH.   Cure her of that.
40 Canst thou not minister to a mind diseas'd,
  Pluck from the memory a rooted sorrow,
  Raze out[30] the written troubles of the brain,
  And with some sweet oblivious antidote[31]
  Cleanse the stuff'd bosom of that perilous stuff
  Which weighs upon the heart?

45 DOCTOR.   Therein the patient
  Must minister to himself.

  MACBETH. Throw physic[32] to the dogs, I'll none of it.
  Come, put mine armor on; give me my staff.
  Seyton, send out. Doctor, the thanes fly from me.—
50 Come, sir, dispatch.—If thou couldst, doctor, cast
  The water of my land, find her disease,[33]
  And purge it to a sound and pristine health,
  I would applaud thee to the very echo,
  That should applaud again.—Pull't off, I say.—
55 What rhubarb, cyme, or what purgative drug,
  Would scour these English hence? Hear'st thou of them?

  DOCTOR. Aye, my good lord; your royal preparation
  Makes us hear something.

30. **Raze out.** Erase

31. **oblivious antidote.** Medicine that causes forgetfulness

32. **physic.** Medical science

33. **cast . . . disease.** Diagnose the disease

MACBETH.   Bring it after me.—

I will not be afraid of death and bane,[34]

60   Till Birnan forest come to Dunsinane.

34. **bane.** Destruction

Exeunt all but the DOCTOR.

DOCTOR.   Were I from Dunsinane away and clear,

Profit again should hardly draw me here.

Exit.

SCENE iv: COUNTRYSIDE NEAR DUNSINANE

Drum and Colors. Enter MALCOLM, SIWARD, MACDUFF, SIWARD'S SON,
MENTETH, CATHNESS, ANGUS, LENNOX, ROSSE, *and* SOLDIERS, *marching.*

MALCOLM.   Cousins, I hope the days are near at hand

That chambers will be safe.

MENTETH.   We doubt it nothing.

SIWARD.   What wood is this before us?

MENTETH.   The wood of Birnan.

MALCOLM.   Let every soldier hew him down a bough,

5   And bear't before him, thereby shall we shadow

The numbers of our host,[35] and make discovery[36]

Err in report of us.

ACT V, SCENE iv

35. **shadow . . . host.**
Camouflage our numbers

36. **discovery.** Reports of
scouts

SOLDIERS.   It shall be done.

SIWARD.   We learn no other but the confident tyrant

Keeps still in Dunsinane, and will endure

Our setting down before't.[37]

MALCOLM.   'Tis his main hope;

10   For where there is advantage[38] to be given,

Both more and less[39] have given him the revolt,

And none serve with him but constrained things,

Whose hearts are absent too.

37. **setting down before't.**
Laying siege to

38. **advantage.** Opportunity

39. **more and less.** Nobles
and common people

MACDUFF.   Let our just censures

15   Attend the true event,[40] and put we on

Industrious soldiership.

40. **Let . . . event.** Let our
judgments wait for the actual
event.

SIWARD.   The time approaches

That will with due decision make us know

What we shall say we have, and what we owe.

Thoughts speculative their unsure hopes relate,

20   But certain issue strokes must arbitrate,[41]

Towards which advance the war.

41. **Thoughts . . . arbitrate.**
Talking about an event is just
dealing with hopes; issues are
only solved through action.

Exeunt marching.

SCENE V: THE CASTLE AT DUNSINANE

Enter MACBETH, SEYTON, *and* SOLDIERS, *with Drum and Colors.*

MACBETH.   Hang out our banners on the outward walls,
The cry is still, "They come!" Our castle's strength
Will laugh a siege to scorn; here let them lie
Till famine and the <u>ague</u> eat them up.
5   Were they not forc'd with those that should be ours,[42]
We might have met them dareful, beard to beard,
And beat them backward home.

(A cry within of women.)

What is that noise?

SEYTON.   It is the cry of women, my good lord.   *Exit.*

MACBETH.   I have almost forgot the taste of fears.
10   The time has been, my senses would have cool'd
To hear a night-shriek, and my fell of hair[43]
Would at a dismal treatise[44] rouse and stir
As life were in't. I have supp'd full with horrors;
Direness, familiar to my slaughterous thoughts,
Cannot once start me.[45]

Enter SEYTON.

15   Wherefore was that cry?

SEYTON.   The Queen, my lord, is dead.

MACBETH.   She should have died hereafter;[46]
There would have been a time for such a word.
Tomorrow, and tomorrow, and tomorrow,
20   Creeps in this petty pace from day to day,
To the last syllable of recorded time;
And all our yesterdays have lighted fools
The way to dusty death. Out, out, brief candle!
Life's but a walking shadow, a poor player,
25   That struts and frets his hour upon the stage,
And then is heard no more. It is a tale
Told by an idiot, full of sound and fury,
Signifying nothing.

Enter a MESSENGER.

                    Thou com'st to use thy tongue;
Thy story quickly.

MESSENGER.   Gracious my lord,
30   I should report that which I say I saw,
But know not how to do't.

MACBETH.   Well, say, sir.

ACT V, SCENE V

> **ague** (ā′ gyü[']) *n.,* fever and chills

42. **forc'd . . . ours.** Reinforced with traitors from our side

43. **my . . . hair.** Hair on my skin
44. **treatise.** Story

45. **once start me.** Ever startle me

46. **should . . . hereafter.** Was bound to die eventually

[Handwritten marginal notes:]
Or – well she picked a hell of a time to die! Not the right time
Or – I can't face this now
wants to mourn her but he is in overload, can not handle it

Most depressed speech he gives throughout the play

–Life is a bitch, and then you die

–nothing has meaning

He has hit rockbottom

MESSENGER.   As I did stand my watch upon the hill,
I look'd toward Birnan, and anon methought
The wood began to move.

MACBETH.   Liar and slave!   *—Freaks out*   *Prophecy is fulfilling itself*

35   **MESSENGER.**   Let me endure your wrath, if't be not so.
Within this three mile may you see it coming;
I say, a moving grove.

MACBETH.   If thou speak'st false,
Upon the next tree shall thou hang alive,
Till famine cling[47] thee; if thy speech be sooth,[48]
40   I care not if thou dost for me as much.
I pull in[49] resolution, and begin
To doubt th' equivocation of the fiend
That lies like truth. "Fear not, till Birnan wood
Do come to Dunsinane," and now a wood
45   Comes toward Dunsinane. Arm, arm, and out!
If this which he avouches[50] does appear,
There is nor flying hence, nor tarrying here.
I gin to be a-weary of the sun,
And wish th' estate o' th' world were now undone.
50   Ring the alarum-bell! Blow wind, come wrack,[51]   *—Bravery still in Macbeth—*
At least we'll die with harness[52] on our back.

                                        Exeunt.

SCENE vi: FIELD AT DUNSINANE

Drum and Colors. Enter MALCOLM, SIWARD, MACDUFF, *and their army,
with boughs.*   *Status order*

MALCOLM.   Now near enough; your leavy[53] screens throw down,
And show like those you are.[54] You, worthy uncle,
Shall with my cousin, your right noble son,
Lead our first battle.[55] Worthy Macduff and we
5   Shall take upon 's what else remains to do,
According to our order.

SIWARD.   Fare you well.
Do we but find the tyrant's power tonight,
Let us be beaten, if we cannot fight.

MACDUFF.   Make all our trumpets speak, give them all breath,
10   Those clamorous <u>harbingers</u> of blood and death.

launches the battle
but he is not enthusiastic
                        Exeunt. Alarums continued.

47. **cling.** Wither
48. **sooth.** Truth

49. **pull in.** Rein in

50. **avouches.** Affirms

51. **wrack.** Ruin
52. **harness.** Armor

ACT V, SCENE vi
53. **leavy.** Leafy

54. **show . . . are.** Show
yourselves as you are

55. **battle.** Battalion

har • bin • ger
(här´ bən jər) *n.,* person
or thing that comes before
and ~~hints at~~ what is to
follow *announces*

SCENE vii: FIELD AT DUNSINANE

Enter MACBETH.

MACBETH.   They have tied me to a stake; I cannot fly,
But bear-like I must fight the course.[56] What's he
That was not born of woman? Such a one
Am I to fear, or none.

Enter YOUNG SIWARD.

YOUNG SIWARD.   What is thy name?

5   MACBETH.   Thou'lt be afraid to hear it.

YOUNG SIWARD.   No; though thou call'st thyself a hotter name
Than any is in hell.

MACBETH.   My name's Macbeth.

YOUNG SIWARD.   The devil himself could not pronounce a title
More hateful to mine ear.

MACBETH.   No; nor more fearful.

10   YOUNG SIWARD.   Thou liest, abhorred tyrant, with my sword
I'll prove the lie thou speak'st.

[*Fight, and* YOUNG SIWARD *slain.*]

MACBETH.   Thou wast born of woman.
But swords I smile at, weapons laugh to scorn,
Brandish'd by man that's of a woman born.

Exit.

Alarums. Enter MACDUFF.

MACDUFF.   That way the noise is. Tyrant, show thy face!
15   If thou beest slain and with no stroke of mine,
My wife and children's ghosts will haunt me still.
I cannot strike at wretched kerns,[57] whose arms
Are hir'd to bear their staves;[58] either thou, Macbeth,
Or else my sword with an unbattered edge
20   I sheathe again undeeded.[59] There thou shouldst be;
By this great clatter, one of greatest note
Seems bruited.[60] Let me find him, Fortune!
And more I beg not.   *Exit. Alarums.*

Enter MALCOLM *and* SIWARD.

SIWARD.   This way, my lord, the castle's gently rend'red:[61]
25   The tyrant's people on both sides do fight,
The noble thanes do bravely in the war,
The day almost itself professes yours,
And little is to do.

ACT V, SCENE vii
56. **bear-like . . . course.** It was a common sport to tie a bear to a stake and make it fight with dogs.

57. **kerns.** Foot soldiers
58. **staves.** Spears

59. **undeeded.** Unused

60. **bruited.** Announced

61. **castle's gently rend'red.** Surrendered easily

(handwritten note:) very chivalrous only get Macbeth

MALCOLM.   We have met with foes
That strike beside us.[62]

SIWARD.   Enter, sir, the castle.   *Exeunt. Alarum.*

SCENE viii: FIELD AT DUNSINANE

Enter MACBETH.

MACBETH.   Why should I play the Roman fool, and die
On mine own sword?[63] Whiles I see lives,[64] the gashes
Do better upon them.

Enter MACDUFF.

MACDUFF.   Turn, hell-hound, turn! *not honorable to stab a man in the back*

MACBETH.   Of all men else I have avoided thee.
5   But get thee back, my soul is too much charg'd
With blood of thine already.

MACDUFF.   I have no words,
My voice is in my sword, thou bloodier villain
Than terms can give thee out!

                              Fight. Alarum.

MACBETH.   Thou losest labor.
As easy mayst thou the intrenchant[65] air
10 With thy keen sword impress as make me bleed.
Let fall thy blade on vulnerable crests,
I bear a charmed life, which must not yield
To one of woman born.

MACDUFF.   Despair thy charm,
And let the angel whom thou still hast serv'd
15 Tell thee, Macduff was from his mother's womb
Untimely ripp'd.[66]

MACBETH.   Accursed be that tongue that tells me so,
For it hath cow'd my better part of man!
And be these juggling fiends no more believ'd,
20 That palter[67] with us in a double sense,
That keep the word of promise to our ear,
And break it to our hope. I'll not fight with thee.

MACDUFF.   Then yield thee, coward,
And live to be the show and gaze o' th' time!
25 We'll have thee, as our rarer monsters are,
Painted upon a pole,[68] and underwrit,
"Here may you see the tyrant."

MACBETH.   I will not yield,
To kiss the ground before young Malcolm's feet,
And to be baited with the rabble's curse. *Common people*

62. **strike beside us.** Fight on our side

ACT V, SCENE viii
63. **Roman fool . . . sword.** Commit suicide like a Roman soldier faced with defeat
64. **Whiles . . . lives.** As long as I see others alive

65. **intrenchant.** Incapable of being cut

66. **Untimely ripp'd.** Delivered prematurely and by Caesarean section—not "of woman born" in the natural way

67. **palter.** Equivocate, speak deceitfully

68. **Painted . . . pole.** Portrait carried on a pole

30 Though Birnan wood be come to Dunsinane,
And thou oppos'd, being of no woman born,
Yet I will try the last. Before my body
I throw my warlike shield. Lay on, Macduff,
And damn'd be him that first cries, "Hold, enough!"

ignore stage directions   *Exeunt fighting. Alarums.*

Enter fighting, and MACBETH *slain.* MACDUFF *carries off* MACBETH'S *body.*

SCENE ix: CASTLE AT DUNSINANE

Retreat and flourish. Enter, with Drum and Colors, MALCOLM, SIWARD, ROSSE, THANES, *and* SOLDIERS.

MALCOLM. I would the friends we miss were safe arriv'd.

SIWARD. Some must go off;[69] and yet, by these I see,
So great a day as this is cheaply bought.[70]

MALCOLM. Macduff is missing, and your noble son.

5 ROSSE. Your son my lord, has paid a soldier's debt.
He only liv'd but till he was a man,
The which no sooner had his prowess confirm'd
In the unshrinking station where he fought,[71]
But like a man he died.

SIWARD.   Then he is dead?

10 ROSSE. Aye, and brought off the field. Your cause of sorrow
Must not be measur'd by his worth, for then
It hath no end.

SIWARD.   Had he his hurts before? *Brave warriors have wounds on front faced enemies*

ROSSE. Aye, on the front.

SIWARD.   Why then, God's soldier be he!
Had I as many sons as I have hairs,

15 I would not wish them to a fairer death.
And so his knell is knoll'd.

MALCOLM.   He's worth more sorrow,
And that I'll spend for him.

SIWARD. *spoke man of manhood code* He's worth no more;
They say he parted well, and paid his score,
And so God be with him! Here comes newer comfort.

Enter MACDUFF *with* MACBETH'S *head.* *happened frequently*

20 MACDUFF. Hail, King! for so thou art. Behold where stands
Th' usurper's cursed head: the time is free.[72]
I see thee compass'd with thy kingdom's pearl,[73]

ACT V, SCENE ix
69. **go off.** Die
70. **cheaply bought.** Marked with few casualties

71. **unshrinking . . . fought.** Spot from which he did not retreat

usurp • er (yü sʉr´ pər) *n.*, one who assumes power without right

72. **time is free.** Freedom reigns now
73. **compass'd . . . pearl.** Surrounded by the most noble in your realm

That speak my salutation in their minds;
Whose voices I desire aloud with mine:
Hail, King of Scotland!

acclamation
—he is king officially

25   **ALL.**   Hail, King of Scotland!   *Flourish.*

MALCOLM.   We shall not spend a large expense of time
Before we reckon with your several loves,
And make us even with you.[74] My thanes and kinsmen,
Henceforth be earls, the first that ever Scotland

30   In such an honor nam'd. What's more to do,
Which would be planted newly with the time,
As calling home our exil'd friends abroad
That fled the snares of watchful tyranny,
Producing forth[75] the cruel ministers

35   Of this dead butcher and his fiend-like queen,
Who (as 'tis thought) by self and violent hands[76]
Took off her life; this, and what needful else
That calls upon us, by the grace of Grace,
We will perform in measure, time, and place.

40   So thanks to all at once and to each one,
Whom we invite to see us crown'd at Scone.

74. **make . . . you.** Reward as
you deserve

75. **Producing forth.** Bringing forward to trial

76. **self . . . hands.** The
violence of her own hands

Flourish. Exeunt omnes. ❖

All is well
in Scotland

Rennaisance attitude

MIRRORS & WINDOWS

Macbeth proclaims his invincibility by saying "The mind I sway by, and the heart
I bear, / Shall never sag with doubt, nor shake with fear." When have you felt
invincible? What made you feel this way? How did it affect the way you interacted with others?

In writing historical plays about the kings of England and particularly in writing *Macbeth*, Shakespeare drew extensively from the 1587 edition of Raphael Holinshed's **Chronicles of England, Scotland, and Ireland.** Because of the unique features of drama, it was necessary for Shakespeare to adapt the information in *Chronicles* for the stage. Even so, he did not merely dramatize the events that *Chronicles* recorded but rather refashioned them to achieve his own purpose for the play. As you read the following discussion of Holinshed's *Chronicles,* consider the dramatic choices Shakespeare made and what effect they had on *Macbeth.* Note that the spellings of words have been modernized in the excerpts from the Holinshed text, with the exception of the names of characters and locations.

Comparing Shakespeare's *Macbeth* to Holinshed's *Chronicles of England, Scotland, and Ireland*

The following excerpt is Holinshed's account of Macbeth's meeting with the three witches. Shakespeare represents this passage in the play in Act I, Scene iii, lines 38–155. Note that, aside from the small differences in setting, Shakespeare decided to present the incident largely as Holinshed recorded it. In *Macbeth*, Shakespeare chose to keep the supernatural and unearthly quality of the witches and the presentation of their prophecy to Macbeth and Banquo. Because Shakespeare was adapting this passage for the stage, he incorporated Holinshed's descriptive information in the dialogue of his characters. For instance, in the following excerpt, note that Banquo describes the witches' appearance to the audience (I.iii.39–47), and

Macbeth states that he is Sinel's heir and thus the Thane of Glamis (I.iii.71):

Shortly after happened a strange and un-couth[1] wonder, which afterward was the cause of much trouble in the realm of Scotland, as ye shall after hear. It fortuned[2] as Makbeth and Banquho journeyed towards Fores, where the king then lay, they went sporting by the way together[3] without other company, save only themselves, passing thorough the woods and fields, when suddenly in the midst of a laund,[4]

---

1. **uncouth.** Mysterious and uncanny
2. **fortuned.** Happened; occurred
3. **sporting by . . . together.** Traveling together
4. **laund.** Open space in the woods, clearing

*there met them three women in strange and
wild apparel, resembling creatures of elder
world, whom when they attentively beheld,
wondering much at the sight, the first of them
spake and said: "All hail, "Makbeth, thane of
Glammis!" (for he had lately entered into that
dignity and office by the death of his father
Sinell). The second of them said: "Hail, Makbeth, thane of Cawder!" But the third said: "All
hail, Makbeth, that hereafter shalt be king of
Scotland!"*

*Then Banquho: "What manner of women"
(saith he) "are you, that seem so little favorable unto me, whereas to my fellow here,
besides high offices, ye assign also the kingdom,
appointing forth nothing for me at all?" "Yes"
(saith the first of them) "we promise greater
benefits unto thee, than unto him, for he shall
reign in deed, but with an unlucky end: neither
shall he leave any issue behind him to succeed
in his place, where contrarily thou in deed
shalt not reign at all, but of thee those shall be
borne which shall govern the Scottish kingdom
by long order of continual descent." Herewith
the foresaid women vanished immediately out
of their sight. This was reputed at the first but
some vain fantastical illusion by Makbeth and
Banquho, insomuch that Banquho would call
Makbeth in jest, king of Scotland; and Makbeth again would call him in sport[5] likewise,
the father of many kings. But afterwards the
common opinion was, that these women were
either the weird sisters, that is (as ye would
say) the goddesses of destiny, or else some
nymphs or fairies, indued[6] with knowledge
of prophecy by their necromantical[7] science,
because every thing came to pass as they had
spoken.*

Shakespeare took more liberty in presenting the information in the following passage:

*A certain witch, whom he had in great trust,
had told that he should never be slain with
man borne of any woman, nor vanquished[8] till*

*the wood of Bernane came to the castle of Dun-
sinane. By this prophecy Makbeth put all fear
out of his heart, supposing he might do what
he would, without any fear to be punished for
the same, for by the one prophecy he believed
it was impossible for any man to vanquish him,
and by the other impossible to slay him. This
vain hope caused him to do many outrageous
things, to the grievous oppression of his subjects. At length Makduffe, to avoid peril of life,
purposed with himself[9] to pass into England,
to procure[10] Malcolme Cammore to claim the
crown of Scotland.*

Throughout Act IV, Scene i, Shakespeare
chose to include the following information
from this short passage: (1) the witches' prophecy that Macbeth cannot be killed by any man
born of woman and (2) their prophecy that
Macbeth cannot be defeated until Birnan Wood
marches on Dunsinane Castle, along with the
fact that (3) this information causes Macbeth
to become more fearless and ruthless and
(4) Macbeth's increased cruelty causes Macduff
to flee for his life. To dramatize the presentation of this information, Shakespeare created
the three witches and three apparitions. The
character Lennox delivered the news that
Macduff has fled, and Macbeth's fearlessness
was presented in his dialogue with the witches.
Further proof of his ruthless nature was shown
in the next scene, when he ordered the slaughter of everyone remaining at Macduff's castle.
What was not included in Holinshed but was
emphasized by Shakespeare (IV.i.110–124) was
the reminder that Banquo's descendants will
be kings.

---

5. **in sport.** In jest; jokingly
6. **indued.** Endowed or possessed
7. **necromantical.** Use of sorcery to conjure spirits to predict the future
8. **vanquished.** Defeated
9. **purposed with himself.** Caused himself
10. **procure.** Get

One of the most striking differences between Holinshed's text and Shakespeare's play is the representation of the characters Macbeth, Lady Macbeth, and Banquo. The following excerpts show Holinshed's presentation of Macbeth before he became king, after he became king, and after he was killed:

One Makbeth a valiant gentlemen, and one that if he had not been somewhat cruel of nature, might have been thought most worthy the government of a realm. On the other part, Duncane was so soft and gentle of nature, that the people wished the inclinations and manners of these two cousins to have been so tempered[11] and interchangably bestowed betwixt them,[12] that where the one had too much of clemency,[13] and the other of cruelty, the mean virtue betwixt these two extremities might have reigned by indifferent partition in them both, so should Duncane have proved a worthy king, and Makbeth an excellent captain.

. . .

To be brief, such were the worthy doings and princely acts of this Makbeth in the administration of the realm, that if he had attained there unto by rightful means, and continued in uprightness of justice as he began, till the end of his reign, he might well have been numbered amongst the most noble princes that anywhere had reigned. He made many wholesome laws and statutes for the public weal[14] of his subjects. . . . These and the like commendable laws Makbeth caused to be put as then in use, governing the realm for the space of ten years in equal justice. . . . But this was but a counterfeit zeal of equity showed by him, partly against his natural inclination, to purchase thereby the favor of the people. Shortly after, he began to show what he was, instead of equity practicing cruelty. For the prick of conscience (as it chance to occur in tyrants, and such as attain to any estate by unrighteous means) caused him ever to fear, least he should be served

of the same cup, as he had ministered to his predecessor. The words also of the three weird sisters would not out of his mind, which as they promised him the kingdom, so likewise did they promise it at the same time unto the posterity[15] of Banquho. He willed therefore the same Banquho, with his son named Fleance, to come to a supper that he had prepared for them: which was in deed as he had devised, present death at the hands of certain murderers, whom he hired to execute that deed; appointing them to meet with the same Banquho and his son without the palace, as they returned to their lodgings, and there to slew them.

. . .

This was the end of Makbeth, after he had reigned 17 years over the Scotsmen. In the beginning of his reign he accomplished many worthy acts, very profitable to the commonwealth (as ye have heard) but afterward, by illusion of the devil, he defamed the same with most terrible cruelty.

Although Shakespeare initially presented a Macbeth who is respected by others for his prowess in battle and struggles with his decision to murder the king, he omitted Macbeth's ten years of peaceful and ordered rule and instead immediately set his protagonist down the dark path of ambition, cruelty, and tyranny. Shakespeare did not directly address Duncan's weak rule, so readers cannot rationalize that Macbeth actually could be a stronger leader than Duncan and perhaps have sympathy for him. Holinshed, like Shakespeare, suggests that the witches' prophecy continues to haunt the new king and is, in part, the cause of his increased ruthlessness.

---

11. **tempered.** Make more moderate
12. **interchangeably . . . them.** Exchanged between them
13. **clemency.** Full of mercy
14. **public weal.** Welfare, or common good
15. **posterity.** Future generations

In addition to adapting the character of Macbeth, Shakespeare also adapted the characters of Lady Macbeth and Banquo. The following passage from Holinshed explains the roles of Lady Macbeth and Banquo in the murder of King Duncan:

The words of the three weird sisters also (of whom before ye have heard) greatly encouraged him here unto, but especially his wife lay sore upon him to attempt the thing, as she that was very ambitious, burning in unquenchable desire to bear the name of a queen. At length therefore, communicating his purposed intent with his trusty friends, amongst whom Banquho was the chiefest, upon confidence of their promised aid, he slew the king at Inverness . . . in the sixth year of his reign. Then having a company about him of such as he had made privy to his enterprise,[16] he caused himself to be proclaimed king, and forthwith went unto Scone,[17] where (by common consent) he received the investiture[18] of the kingdom according to the accustomed manner.

This passage contains Holinshed's only mention of Macbeth's wife and suggests that Banquo participated in the murder of Duncan. From this meager information, Shakespeare created one of his most merciless female characters and gave her a far greater role than did Holinshed. Shakespeare also omitted any suggestion that Banquo had knowledge of Macbeth's plot to seize the throne. Instead, Shakespeare painted Banquo as an unceasingly loyal thane to Duncan, who was shocked by the extent of Macbeth's ambition. ❖

---

16. **privy to his enterprise.** Aware of his secret plan
17. **Scone.** Scottish city where coronations occurred
18. **investiture.** Ceremonial and official investing of a person with an office

Review Questions

1. What details does Holinshed provide about Macbeth? What details in Shakespeare's play support or contradict Holinshed's description? Compare and contrast the two descriptions.

2. In Holinshed's text, what roles are played by Lady Macbeth and Banquo? In the play, what roles do these characters play in the downfall of Macbeth?

3. Review the excerpts from Holinshed and identify examples of bias, editorializing, and foreshadowing. Synthesize the ideas in the two pieces to determine how the accuracy or objectivity of modern historical accounts might also be affected by these issues. Argue whether it is possible to write an entirely unbiased historical account.

TEXT ⇄ TO ⇄ TEXT CONNECTION

Evaluate the ways in which Shakespeare adapted Holinshed's text. What might have been his purpose in making these changes? Was he trying to rewrite history by altering the facts, or was he simply trying to create an interesting play? Support your explanation with details from both texts.

from

The Analects

by Confucius
Translated by Arthur Waley

Confucius (551–479 BCE) is the Anglicized (English) name of K'ung Ch'iu, the most famous teacher and philosopher in Chinese history. Orphaned at an early age, he devoted himself to education in the six practical arts (ritual, music, archery, charioteering, calligraphy, and arithmetic) as well as in classical history and poetry. He became the most learned man of his era and believed that learning should serve the practical ends of public service.

The teachings of Confucius were collected by his disciples in the **Lun-yü,** or **Analects,** meaning "miscellaneous excerpts." His teachings stress the moral order of the universe, as reflected in the proper behavior and interaction of people from various parts of society. Important themes in Confucian teaching include duty, loyalty, obligation, ritual, social norms, and action befitting one's place in society. Today, more than two thousand years after the life of Confucius, his teachings still permeate thought and codes of behavior throughout the Asian world.

BOOK I, SECTION 5
The Master said, A country of a thousand war-chariots cannot be administered unless the ruler attends strictly to business, punctually observes his promises, is economical in expenditure,[1] shows affection toward his subjects in general, and uses the labor of the peasantry only at the proper times of year.

BOOK I, SECTION 6
The Master said, A young man's duty is to behave well to his parents at home and to his elders abroad, to be cautious in giving promises and punctual in keeping them, to have kindly feelings toward everyone, but seek the intimacy of the Good. If, when all that is done, he has any energy to spare, then let him study the polite arts.

BOOK I, SECTION 8
The Master said, If a gentleman is frivolous, he will lose the respect of his inferiors and lack firm ground on which to build his education. First and foremost, he must learn to be faithful to his superiors, to keep promises, to refuse the friendship of all who are not like him. And if he finds he has made a mistake, then he must not be afraid of admitting the fact and amending his ways.

BOOK II, SECTIONS 1–3
1. The Master said, He who rules by moral force is like the pole star, which remains in its place while all the lesser stars do homage[2] to it.

---

1. **expenditure.** Disbursement of money
2. **homage.** Expression of high regard or tribute

2. The Master said, If out of the three hundred Songs I had to take one phrase to cover all my teaching, I would say, "Let there be no evil in your thoughts."

3. The Master said, Govern the people by regulations, keep order among them by chastisements,[3] and they will flee from you, and lose all self-respect. Govern them by moral force, keep order among them by ritual, and they will keep their self-respect and come to you of their own accord. ❖

---

3. **chastisement.** Punishment or censure

 Which precept, or saying, in this excerpt from *The Analects* do you choose to live by?

Refer and Reason

1. Which precept best sums up Confucius's teaching? Explain why this is the most important precept.

2. How should a ruler act, according to Confucius? Describe the relationship that should exist between a ruler and his or her subjects.

3. What methods of government do not work? On what principles should a government be based? Explain the kind of government Confucius seems to promote.

Writing Options

1. Write a code of conduct for high school teachers and students based on precepts from *The Analects.*

2. Confucius lived more than two thousand years ago and in a time of great social and political unrest. How are his teachings still relevant today? Write an essay that responds to this question. Support your response using examples from *The Analects.*

 Go to **www.mirrorsandwindows.com** for more.

from The Tragical History of Doctor Faustus

A Drama by Christopher Marlowe

Build Background

Literary Context Christopher Marlowe's *The Tragical History of Doctor Faustus* is based on a medieval legend that, in the sixteenth century, became associated with a German *necromancer* (someone who called on the spirits of the dead to predict the future). This German version first appeared in the *Faustbuch,* published in Germany in 1587, and soon was translated into English.

Marlowe set his play in the German university town of Wittenberg at the end of the sixteenth century. Dr. Faustus, a brilliant scholar, makes a deal with the devil: Faustus will receive the powers of black magic and the services of the devil's servant, Mephastophilis, in exchange for his soul. Throughout the remainder of the play, Faustus agonizes over his decision, yearning for forgiveness but believing that ultimately he cannot be saved. This selection, which is the final scene of the play, begins as Faustus confesses his bargain to fellow scholars.

Reader's Context When have you regretted a decision you made? Why did you regret it? What were the consequences?

Meet the Author

Christopher Marlowe (1564–1593) was the son of a Canterbury shoemaker. He attended Cambridge University, where he studied a wide range of subjects and earned bachelor's and master's degrees. He may have begun his studies with the intention of becoming an Anglican priest, but the actual course of his life was quite different. Evidence suggests that, while still in school, Marlowe may have been a spy for the British government. After graduating, he immediately began a career in the theater. He wrote his first great play, *Tamburlaine,* in 1587 and continued producing plays over the next six years.

In 1593, Marlowe's friend and fellow dramatist Thomas Kyd, author of *The Spanish Tragedy,* was arrested. Under torture, he confessed that some radical papers found in his quarters had been written by Marlowe. Conservatives accused Marlowe of atheism (not believing in God), but the government interceded to protect him from prosecution, perhaps because he was still serving as a spy.

Later that year, Marlowe was killed in a tavern brawl. The Puritans slandered the dead playwright, calling him impious and immoral and pointing to the manner of his death as proof. Literary scholars have been more accepting of Marlowe, celebrating the tender sincerity of his lyric poetry and the moral fervor of such works as *The Tragical History of Doctor Faustus.*

Analyze Literature

Chorus and Soliloquy

A **chorus** is a group of actors who speak directly to the audience between scenes, commenting on the action of the play.

A **soliloquy** is a speech delivered by a lone character that reveals the speaker's thoughts and feelings.

Set Purpose

In classical Greek drama, a chorus often was used to comment on moral and social issues or advise the characters in the play. Identify Marlowe's purpose in using a chorus at the end of this play. Determine what comment the chorus makes on Faustus's soliloquy. Make a web-type chart that identifies the alternatives Faustus imagines to get out of his pact with the devil.

Preview Vocabulary

surfeit, 444
abjure, 444
blaspheme, 444
felicity, 444
firmament, 446
rend, 446
ireful, 446
incessant, 446
exhort, 447
entice, 447

from
The Tragical History of Doctor Faustus

by Christopher Marlowe

Scene xiii

[*Enter* Faustus *with the* Scholars.]

Faustus. Ah, gentlemen!

1 Scholar. What ails Faustus?

Faustus. Ah, my sweet chamber-fellow, had I lived with thee, then had I lived still; but now I die eternally. Look, comes he not, comes he not?

2 Scholar. What means Faustus?

3 Scholar. Belike he is grown into some sickness, by being oversolitary.

1 Scholar.   If it be so, we'll have physicians to cure him; 'tis but
a surfeit: never fear, man.

Faustus.   A surfeit of deadly sin, that hath damned both body
and soul.

2 Scholar.   Yet Faustus, look up to heaven; remember God's
mercies are infinite.

Faustus.   But Faustus' offense can ne'er be pardoned! The serpent that tempted Eve[1] may be saved, but not Faustus. Ah gentlemen, hear me with patience, and tremble not at my speeches,
though my heart pants and quivers to remember that I have been
a student here these thirty years—O would I had never seen Wittenberg,[2] never read book—and what wonders I have done, all
Wittenberg can witness—yea, all the world; for which Faustus
hath lost both Germany and the world—yea, heaven itself—
heaven, the seat of God, the throne of the blessed, the kingdom of joy; and must remain in hell for ever—hell, ah, hell for
ever! Sweet friends, what shall become of Faustus, being in hell
for ever?

3 Scholar.   Yet Faustus, call on God.

Faustus.   On God, whom Faustus hath abjured? On God,
whom Faustus hath blasphemed? Ah my God—I would weep,
but the devil draws in my tears! gush forth blood, instead of
tears—yea, life and soul! O, he stays my tongue! I would lift up
my hands, but see, they hold them, they hold them!

All.   Who, Faustus?

Faustus.   Lucifer and Mephastophilis![3] Ah gentlemen, I gave
them my soul for my cunning.

All.   God forbid!

Faustus.   God forbade it indeed, but Faustus hath done it: for
the vain pleasure of four-and-twenty years hath Faustus lost eternal joy and felicity. I writ them a bill with mine own blood, the
date is expired, the time will come, and he will fetch me.

1 Scholar.   Why did not Faustus tell us of this before, that
divines might have prayed for thee?

Faustus.   Oft have I thought to have done so, but the devil
threatened to tear me in pieces if I named God, to fetch both
body and soul, if I once gave ear to divinity; and now 'tis too late.
Gentlemen away, lest you perish with me!

2 Scholar.   O what shall we do to save Faustus?

3 Scholar.   God will strengthen me. I will stay with Faustus.

---

sur • feit (sur′ fət)
n., overabundance

1. **The serpent . . . Eve.** In
the Bible's book of Genesis,
the serpent tempted Eve to eat
from the tree of knowledge,
bringing the first sin into the
world.
2. **Wittenberg.** Famous
university in Germany

ab • jure (ab jür′)
v., renounce; give up

blas • pheme (blas′ fēm′
or blas fēm′) *v.,* show
contempt or irreverence for
something sacred

3. **Lucifer and Mepha-
stophilis.** Devils

fe • li • ci • ty
(fi li′ sə tē) *n.,* happiness

The Faustian Bargain

In writing *The Tragical History of Dr. Faustus*, Christopher Marlowe drew on a German folk story. He followed the plot of the story closely, but his interpretation of the main character was quite different. Translations of the German Faust story were well known in London at the time Marlowe wrote his play, and he is said to have used a translation called *The History of the Damnable Life and Deserved Death of Doctor John Faustus*. The text of Marlowe's play often is very close to the text of this source. In fact, Marlowe even preserves some of the factual errors made by the translator.

Marlowe is not the only writer to have drawn on the German Faust story. Its influence on literature has been enormous, giving rise to many similar stories about people who make bargains with the devil in a quest for knowledge, power, beauty, fame, or fortune. Literary scholars consider Johann Wolfgang von Goethe's drama *Faust,* written and revised between 1806 and 1832, one of the greatest achievements in Western literature. Perhaps the most famous retelling in American literature is Washington Irving's "The Devil and Tom Walker," published in 1824.

Musical composers have been inspired by the Faust story and Goethe's drama, as well. In the mid-1800s, Richard Wagner, Hector Berlioz, and Franz Liszt all wrote orchestral works after being inspired by Goethe's drama. A more recent Faust story can be found in the musical *Damn Yankees!* by Richard Adler and Jerry Ross, which premiered on Broadway in 1955 and was made into a movie three years later.

---

50 **1 Scholar.** Tempt not God, sweet friend, but let us into the next room, and there pray for him.

Faustus. Aye, pray for me, pray for me; and what noise soever ye hear, come not unto me, for nothing can rescue me.

2 Scholar. Pray thou, and we will pray, that God may have mercy upon thee.

55 **Faustus.** Gentlemen, farewell. If I live till morning, I'll visit you; if not, Faustus is gone to hell.

All. Faustus, farewell.

[*Exeunt* Scholars.]

[*The clock strikes eleven.*]

Faustus. Ah Faustus,
Now hast thou but one bare hour to live,
60 And then thou must be damned perpetually.
Stand still, you ever-moving spheres of heaven,
That time may cease, and midnight never come.
Fair Nature's eye, rise, rise again, and make
Perpetual day, or let this hour be but
65 A year, a month, a week, a natural day,

That Faustus may repent and save his soul.
O lente, lente currite noctis equi![4]
The stars move still, time runs, the clock will strike,
The devil will come, and Faustus must be damned.

70   O, I'll leap up to my God! Who pulls me down?
See, see where Christ's blood streams in the <u>firmament</u>!
One drop would save my soul, half a drop: ah my Christ—
Ah, <u>rend</u> not my heart for naming of my Christ;
Yet will I call on him—O spare me, Lucifer!

75   Where is it now? 'Tis gone: and see where God
Stretcheth out his arm, and bends his <u>ireful</u> brows!
Mountains and hills, come, come and fall on me,
And hide me from the heavy wrath of God.
No, no?

80   Then will I headlong run into the earth:
Earth, gape![5] O no, it will not harbor[6] me.
You stars that reigned at my nativity,[7]
Whose influence hath allotted death and hell,
Now draw up Faustus like a foggy mist

85   Into the entrails of yon laboring cloud,
That when you vomit forth into the air,
My limbs may issue from your smoky mouths,
So that my soul may but ascend to heaven.

[*The watch strikes.*]

Ah, half the hour is past: 'twill all be past anon.

90   O God, if thou wilt not have mercy on my soul,
Yet for Christ's sake, whose blood hath ransomed me,
Impose some end to my <u>incessant</u> pain:
Let Faustus live in hell a thousand years,
A hundred thousand, and at last be saved.

95   O, no end is limited to damned souls!
Why wert thou not a creature wanting soul?
Or why is this immortal that thou hast?
Ah, Pythagoras' *metempsychosis*[8]—were that true,
This soul should fly from me, and I be changed

100   Unto some brutish beast:
All beasts are happy, for when they die,
Their souls are soon dissolved in elements;
But mine must live still[9] to be plagued in hell.
Cursed be the parents that engendered me:

105   No, Faustus, curse thy self, curse Lucifer,
That hath deprived thee of the joys of heaven.

[*The clock strikes twelve.*]

---

4. *O lente . . . equi.* [Latin] Slowly, slowly run, O horses of the night.

fir • ma • ment (fŭr′ mə mənt) *n.*, sky

rend (rend) *v.*, rip apart

ire • ful (īr′ fəl) *adj.*, angry

5. **gape.** Open wide
6. **harbor.** Provide protection to
7. **nativity.** Birth

in • cess • ant (in[′] se′ s'nt) *adj.*, continuous; never ending

8. *metempsychosis.* Pythagoras's theory that souls pass from one body to another at death

9. **still.** Always

O it strikes, it strikes! Now body, turn to air,
Or Lucifer will bear thee quick[10] to hell.

10. **quick.** Alive

[*Thunder and lightning.*]

110 O soul, be changed into little water drops,
And fall into the ocean, ne'er be found.
My God, my God, look not so fierce on me!

[*Enter* DEVILS.]

Adders and serpents, let me breathe awhile!
Ugly hell gape not! Come not, Lucifer!
I'll burn my books—ah, Mephastophilis!

[*Exeunt with him.*]

EPILOGUE

[*Enter* CHORUS.]

Cut is the branch that might have grown full straight,
And burnéd is Apollo's laurel bough,[11]
That sometime grew within this learned man.
Faustus is gone! Regard his hellish fall,
5 Whose fiendful fortune[12] may <u>exhort</u> the wise
Only to wonder at unlawful things:
Whose deepness doth <u>entice</u> such forward wits,
To practice more than heavenly power permits.

[*Exit.*]

Terminat hora diem, terminat author opus.[13] ❖

11. **laurel bough.** The laurel bough is a conventional symbol of achievement; in this case, it symbolizes the attainment of wisdom or learning.
12. **fiendful fortune.** Devilish fate

ex • hort (ig zôrt´)
v., warn; plead with

en • tice (en tīs´)
v., tempt

13. *Terminat . . . opus.* [Latin] The hour ends the day; the author ends his work.

MIRRORS & WINDOWS

What would you be willing to sacrifice to receive a gift of, say, a million dollars? For instance, would you betray someone? Would you lie? Would you give up a personal goal or dream?

Refer to Text ▶ ▶ ▶ ▶ ▶ **Reason with Text**

1a. What does Faustus tell the scholars he has done to himself? What do the scholars urge Faustus to do?	**1b.** Describe the scholars' attitudes toward Faustus and the sin he confesses.	**Understand** Find meaning
2a. Why does Faustus beg for the mountains and hills to fall on him? What does he want to become?	**2b.** Examine how Faustus feels about the decision he made. Why does he want to be turned into something else?	**Apply** Use information
3a. Identify what will happen to Faustus now that "the date is expired" on his contract with the devil.	**3b.** Who is to blame for Faustus's situation?	**Analyze** Take things apart
4a. What aspects of Faustus's personality make him a sympathetic character?	**4b.** Interpret what Faustus's thoughts and feelings reveal about his character.	**Evaluate** Make judgments
5a. How does Faustus imagine God will judge him?	**5b.** Assume the role of Marlowe, and argue how modern technological and scientific advances overstep the limits God has set on humans. What is your position?	**Create** Bring ideas together

Analyze Literature

Chorus and Soliloquy

What likely was Marlowe's purpose for using the chorus at the end of the play? Is it necessary or helpful? Do you agree or disagree with the viewpoint the chorus expresses? Explain.

Review the chart you created. What alternatives does Faustus imagine? What does this information reveal about him? When he recites his soliloquy, what is his state of mind? Explain your answer using details from the play.

Extend the Text

Writing Options

Creative Writing Imagine that you are Faustus and are writing to your colleagues from hell. Write a memo explaining what happened to you and giving advice that will help your fellow scholars avoid the mistakes you made.

Narrative Writing Write a one-page narrative that develops the storyline for a science fiction film based on *The Tragical History of Doctor Faustus*. For example, change the devils in Marlowe's play to aliens that give some of their power or knowledge to an earthling in exchange for giving up life on Earth after a certain period of time. Practice and present your narration to the class.

Critical Literacy

Compare Soul-Selling Themes The theme of selling one's soul to the devil is common in Western art and literature. Pick another version of the Faust story to research, such as Washington Irving's short story "The Devil and Tom Walker" (1824); Stephen Vincent Benét's "The Devil and Daniel Webster" (1937); the film *Damn Yankees!* (1958); or the song "The Devil Went Down to Georgia" (1979), by the Charlie Daniels Band. As a class, discuss how each is similar and different from what you read of Marlowe's play.

Collaborative Learning

Hold a Mock Trial Determine whether the punishment Faustus receives is fair. With a group of four to eight classmates, assign people to play the roles of Faustus, the defense attorney, the prosecuting attorney, and the judge. You also may want to present several witnesses. Then conduct a mock trial and evaluate its outcome.

 Go to **www.mirrorsandwindows.com** for more.

Monologues and Soliloquies from Shakespeare's Plays

from The Tragedy of Hamlet

In this tragedy, Hamlet's father, the king of Denmark, has recently died, and Hamlet's uncle, Claudius, has taken the throne. The ghost of Hamlet's father appears to Hamlet, accuses Claudius of murdering him, and asks Hamlet to seek revenge.

In the first selection, Polonius, an elderly government minister, is saying goodbye to his son, Laertes, who is leaving for college.

In the second selection, Hamlet is alone and thinking aloud about what makes people willing to face the many difficulties of life. The speech follows a conversation in which the king and queen discuss their fears that Hamlet is deranged.

Hamlet persuades a group of actors to perform for King Claudius a play about *regicide* (the killing of a king) to see if the king's reaction confirms his suspicion. In the third selection, Hamlet is giving the actors directions prior to the performance. His speech to the actors provides superb advice about the craft of acting—advice that has stood the test of time.

FROM ACT I, SCENE iii

POLONIUS.   And these few precepts in thy memory
Look thou character.[1] Give thy thoughts no tongue,
Nor any unproportion'd thought his act.
Be thou familiar, but by no means vulgar:
5   Those friends thou hast, and their adoption tried,
Grapple them unto thy soul with hoops of steel,
But do not dull thy palm with entertainment
Of each new-hatch'd, unfledg'd courage. Beware
Of entrance to a quarrel, but being in,
10   Bear't that th' opposed may beware of thee.
Give every man thy ear, but few thy voice,
Take each man's censure, but reserve thy judgment.
Costly thy habit as thy purse can buy,
But not express'd in fancy, rich, not gaudy,
15   For the apparel oft proclaims the man,
And they in France of the best rank and station
[Are] of a most select and generous chief in that.
Neither a borrower nor a lender [be],
For [loan] oft loses both itself and friend,
20   And borrowing dulleth [th'] edge of husbandry.[2]
This above all: to thine own self be true,

ACT 1, SCENE iii
1. **character.** Inscribe

2. **husbandry.** Thrifty management; frugality

And it must follow, as the night the day,
Thou canst not then be false to any man.
Farewell, my blessing season this in thee!

FROM ACT III, SCENE i

HAMLET.   To be, or not to be, that is the question:
Whether 'tis nobler in the mind to suffer
The slings and arrows of outrageous fortune,
Or to take arms against a sea of troubles,
5   And by opposing, end them. To die, to sleep—
No more, and by a sleep to say we end
The heart-ache and the thousand natural shocks
That flesh is heir to; 'tis a consummation
Devoutly to be wish'd. To die, to sleep—
10   To sleep, perchance to dream—ay, there's the rub,
For in that sleep of death what dreams may come,
When we have shuffled off this mortal coil,
Must give us pause; there's the respect
That makes calamity of so long life:
15   For who would bear the whips and scorns of time,
Th' oppressor's wrong, the proud man's contumely,
The pangs of despis'd love, the law's delay,
The insolence of office, and the spurns
That patient merit of th' unworthy takes,
20   When he himself might his quietus³ make
With a bare bodkin;⁴ who would fardels⁵ bear,
To grunt and sweat under a weary life,
But that the dread of something after death,
The undiscover'd country, from whose bourn⁶
25   No traveller returns, puzzles the will,
And makes us rather bear those ills we have,
Than fly to others that we know not of?
Thus conscience does make cowards [of us all],
And thus the native hue of resolution
30   Is sicklied o'er with the pale cast of thought,
And enterprises of great pitch and moment
With this regard their currents turn awry,
And lose the name of action.

FROM ACT III, SCENE ii

HAMLET.   Speak the speech, I pray you, as I pronounc'd it to
you, trippingly on the tongue, but if you mouth it, as many of
our players do, I had as live⁷ the town-crier spoke my lines. Nor
do not saw the air too much with your hand, thus, but use all
5   gently, for in the very torrent, tempest, and, as I may say, whirl-

ACT III, SCENE i
3. **quietus.** Release from an obligation
4. **bodkin.** Dagger
5. **fardels.** Burdens

6. **bourn.** Domain

ACT III, SCENE ii
7. **had as live.** Would prefer

Hamlet, c. 1970. Juan Carlos Liberti.
Galería Zuburbán, Buenos Aires, Argentina.

wind of your passion, you must acquire and beget a temperance
that may give it smoothness. O, it offends me to the soul to hear
a robustious periwig-pated fellow tear a passion to totters, to very
rags, to spleet[8] the ears of the groundlings,[9] who for the most
10 part are capable of nothing but inexplicable dumb shows and
noise. I would have such a fellow whipt for o'erdoing Termagant,
it out-Herods Herod,[10] pray you avoid it.

[1] PLAYER.   I warrant your honor.

HAMLET.   Be not too tame neither, but let your own discretion
15 be your tutor. Suit the action to the word, the word to the action,
with this special observance, that you o'erstep not the modesty[11]
of nature: for any thing so o'erdone is from the purpose of playing, whose end, both at the first and now, was and is, to hold as
'twere the mirror up to nature: to show virtue her feature, scorn
20 her own image, and the very age and body of the time his form
and pressure.[12] Now this overdone, or come tardy[13] off, though it
makes the unskillful laugh, cannot but make the judicious grieve;
the censure of which one must in your allowance o'erweigh a
whole theatre of others. O, there be players that I have seen
25 play—and heard others [praise], and that highly—not to speak
it profanely,[14] that, neither having th' accent of Christians or the
gait of Christian, pagan, nor man, have so strutted and bellow'd

8. **spleet.** Split
9. **groundlings.** Spectators
who stood on the ground in
the pit of the theater
10. **Termagant . . . Herod.**
Both Termagant and Herod
were noisy, violent characters
in medieval drama.

11. **modesty.** Moderation

12. **pressure.** Exact image
13. **tardy.** Inadequately

14. **profanely.** Irreverently

that I have thought some of Nature's journeymen had made men, and not made them well, they imitated humanity so abominably.

30 [1] PLAYER.   I hope we have reform'd that indifferently with us, [sir].

HAMLET.   O, reform it altogether. And let those that play your clowns speak no more than is set down for them, for there be of them that will themselves laugh to set on some quantity of barren
35 spectators to laugh too, though in the mean time some necessary question of the play be then to be considered. That's villainous, and shows a most pitiful ambition in the fool that uses it. Go make you ready. ❖

Polonius advises, "This above all: To thine own self be true." How easy is it to think and act for yourself? What can make it difficult?

from **The Tragedy of King Richard the Second**

Shakespeare's *Richard the Second* tells of the fall of a king who rules arbitrarily, willfully, and selfishly yet is someone with whom many readers can sympathize. When Richard's uncle, John of Gaunt, dies, Richard unjustly confiscates Gaunt's estates to finance a campaign to put down a rebellion. Eventually, Richard is deposed by Gaunt's son, the fiercely ambitious Bullingbrook (Bolingbroke), who would later become King Henry IV.

In the first selection, John of Gaunt, near death from illness, has stated a desire to advise his nephew Richard, whom he views as a reckless youth.

In the second selection, Richard, facing defeat by Bolingbroke, ponders how even the greatest individual must meet his or her end. Richard's claim that some kings are "haunted by the ghosts they have deposed" often reminds readers of *Macbeth*.

FROM ACT II, SCENE i

GAUNT.   Methinks I am a prophet new inspir'd,
And thus expiring do foretell of him:[1]
His rash fierce blaze of riot cannot last,
For violent fires soon burn out themselves;
5   Small show'rs last long, but sudden storms are short;
He tires betimes that spurs too fast betimes;
With eager feeding food doth choke the feeder;
Light vanity, insatiate cormorant,[2]
Consuming means, soon preys upon itself.
10   This royal throne of kings, this sceptred isle,

ACT II, SCENE i
1. **him.** Gaunt is referring to King Richard.

2. **cormorant.** In this context, a glutton

Richard II at Stratford, Ontario, c. 1970.
Franklin McMahon.

This earth of majesty, this seat of Mars,[3]
This other Eden, demi-paradise,
This fortress built by Nature for herself
Against infection and the hand of war,
15   This happy breed of men, this little world,
This precious stone set in the silver sea,
Which serves it in the office of a wall,
Or as [a] moat defensive to a house,
Against the envy of less happier lands;
20   This blessed plot, this earth, this realm, this England,
This nurse, this teeming womb of royal kings,
Fear'd by their breed, and famous by their birth,
Renowned for their deeds as far from home,
For Christian service and true chivalry,
25   As is the sepulchre in stubborn Jewry
Of the world's ransom, blessed Mary's Son;
This land of such dear souls, this dear dear land,
Dear for her reputation through the world,
Is now leas'd out—I die pronouncing it—
30   Like to a tenement or pelting farm.
England, bound in with the triumphant sea,
Whose rocky shore beats back the envious siege

3. **Mars.** Roman god of war and protector of the nation

Of wat'ry Neptune,[4] is now bound in with shame,
With inky blots and rotten parchment bonds;
35 That England, that was wont to conquer others,
Hath made a shameful conquest of itself.
Ah, would the scandal vanish with my life,
How happy then were my ensuing death!

4. **Neptune.** Roman god of the sea

FROM ACT III, SCENE ii

RICHARD.   Let's talk of graves, of worms, and epitaphs,
Make dust our paper, and with rainy eyes
Write sorrow on the bosom of the earth.
Let's choose executors and talk of wills;
5 And yet not so, for what can we bequeath
Save our deposed bodies to the ground?
Our lands, our lives, and all are Bullingbrook's,[5]
And nothing can we call our own but death,
And that small model of the barren earth
10 Which serves as paste and cover to our bones.
For God's sake let us sit upon the ground
And tell sad stories of the death of kings:
How some have been depos'd, some slain in war,
Some haunted by the ghosts they have deposed,
15 Some poisoned by their wives, some sleeping kill'd,
All murthered—for within the hollow crown
That rounds the mortal temples of a king
Keeps Death his court, and there the antic sits,
Scoffing his state and grinning at his pomp,[6]
20 Allowing him a breath, a little scene,
To monarchize, be fear'd, and kill with looks,
Infusing him with self and vain conceit,
As if this flesh which walls about our life
Were brass impregnable; and humor'd thus,
25 Comes at the last and with a little pin
Bores thorough his castle wall, and farewell king!
Cover your heads, and mock not flesh and blood
With solemn reverence, throw away respect,
Tradition, form, and ceremonious duty,
30 For you have but mistook me all this while.
I live with bread like you, feel want,
Taste grief, need friends: subjected thus,
How can you say to me I am a king? ❖

ACT III, SCENE ii
5. **Bullingbrook.** Bullingbrook (or Bolingbroke) is the surname of Henry, Duke of Herford, who later became King Henry IV.

6. **antic . . . pomp.** The antic is a jester who makes fun of the ceremonious regality of the king.

MIRRORS & WINDOWS Gaunt laments the harm a bad king can inflict on his country, and Richard speaks of the burdens a king must carry. What obligations do leaders have to the people they serve? Do people tend to expect too much from their leaders?

The Three Caskets: The Merchant of Venice, Act III, Scene ii, c. 1860–1880.
Robert Alexander Hillingford.

from **The Merchant of Venice**

In *The Merchant of Venice,* Antonio has borrowed money from a prosperous Venetian merchant named Shylock for the purpose of helping a friend. Shylock agrees to lend the money without interest but holds as part of the bargain that if the loan cannot be repaid, he can collect on it by cutting a pound of flesh from Antonio's body. When the ships carrying Antonio's merchandise are lost at sea, Antonio is left bankrupt, and Shylock comes to close his part of the bargain.

In the selection, Antonio's friend Portia tries to appeal to Shylock's sense of mercy to save Antonio.

FROM ACT IV, SCENE i

PORTIA.   The quality of mercy is not strain'd,[1]
It droppeth as the gentle rain from heaven
Upon the place beneath. It is twice blest:
It blesseth him that gives and him that takes.
5   'Tis mightiest in the mightiest, it becomes
The throned monarch better than his crown.
His sceptre shows the force of temporal power,
The attribute to awe and majesty,
Wherein doth sit the dread and fear of kings;
10   But mercy is above this sceptred sway,
It is enthroned in the hearts of kings,
It is an attribute to God himself;
And earthly power doth then show likest God's
When mercy seasons justice. ❖

ACT IV, SCENE i

1. **strain'd.** Constrained, forced

MIRRORS & WINDOWS

Portia speaks eloquently about reasons to be merciful. When might showing mercy be difficult or even inappropriate?

THE MERCHANT OF VENICE   **455**

A Scene from Shakespeare's **The Tempest** [detail of Caliban],
c. 1730–1735. William Hogarth. Nostell Priory, Wakefield, England.

from **The Tempest**

The Tempest, a highly poetic work of fantasy, is thought to be the last play Shakespeare wrote before retiring to Stratford. In this play, the magician Prospero has been exiled to an enchanted island, home to many spirits as well as the savage Caliban. Prospero is the rightful Duke of Milan, but his brother, Antonio, has usurped his rule. When a ship carrying Antonio passes the island, Prospero stirs up a storm that capsizes the vessel and washes Antonio and his party ashore. Eventually, Caliban and Antonio plot to kill Prospero, who becomes aware of their scheme.

In the selection, Prospero's speech closes an episode in which the spirits have been performing. Prospero, remembering the schemes against him, has called an end to the festivities.

FROM ACT IV, SCENE i

PROSPERO.   Our revels now are ended. These our actors
(As I foretold you) were all spirits, and
Are melted into air, into thin air,
And like the baseless fabric of this vision,
5   The cloud-capp'd tow'rs, the gorgeous palaces,

The solemn temples, the great globe itself,
Yea, all which it inherit, shall dissolve,
And like this insubstantial pageant faded
Leave not a rack[1] behind. We are such stuff
10 As dreams are made on; and our little life
Is rounded with a sleep. Sir, I am vex'd;
Bear with my weakness, my old brain is troubled.
Be not disturb'd with my infirmity.
If you be pleas'd, retire into my cell,
15 And there repose. A turn or two I'll walk
To still my beating mind. ❖

ACT IV, SCENE i
1. **rack.** Wisp of cloud

 **MIRRORS & WINDOWS** What are the benefits of having a vivid imagination? What might be the drawbacks?

Refer and Reason

1. Refer to the speech from *Hamlet,* Act III, Scene i. Identify the words Hamlet uses to describe the misfortunes of life. What is Hamlet contemplating? What points does he weigh on each side?

2. In the passage from *The Merchant of Venice,* what is Portia advocating? Analyze how her manner of appealing to Shylock reveals her character.

3. Identify one or two lines in each speech that demonstrate the character of the speaker. What sort of person do you envision playing the character? What direction would you give an actor delivering this character's lines?

Writing Options

1. Plan a series of greeting cards using lines from the speeches. Choose several lines from a speech from each play (four speeches in all) to place on the front of a card. Then draw or write suggestions for an artist who will illustrate each card. Finally, write the sentiment that will appear inside each card.

2. Find and view a modern film version of one of the Shakespeare plays you just sampled. Compare and contrast the movie's presentation of each monologue or soliloquy with the lines from original play. Consider how well the acting, set design, costumes, and other elements communicate the central message of the passage. Describe similarities and differences between the actor's interpretations and the original script, and analyze the effectiveness of the actor's delivery.

 Go to **www.mirrorsandwindows.com** for more.

A Midsummer Night's Dream
by William Shakespeare

A royal wedding, love triangles, a feud between the fairy king and queen, and a clutch of bumbling, would-be thespians are the stuff of dreams and comedic chaos in this popular Shakespearean drama. When trickster Puck produces a magical juice to induce love at first sight, there's no telling who will fall for whom or what. (EMC Access Edition)

Volpone, or The Fox by Ben Jonson

Feigning illness, con artist Volpone plans to get even with his supposed friends by pretending to name each as heir to his fortune. All goes well until his crafty servant Mosca turns the tables on Volpone and everyone lands in court. Jonson's satire is peopled with comic characters whose perversity have made it a perennial favorite.

Shakespeare and Co.: Christopher Marlowe, Thomas Dekker, Ben Jonson, Thomas Middleton, John Fletcher and the Other Players in His Story
by Stanley Wells

Shakespeare was embedded in a lively circle of theater people, including Kit Marlow (the theater's biggest name), lead actor Richard Burbage, and rivals Ben Jonson and Thomas Kyd. Wells reveals the economic and social milieu within which they worked and describes Shakespeare's luck in entering his maturity as a playwright at just the right moment.

Doctor Faustus by Christopher Marlowe

The brilliant scholar Doctor Faustus has mastered traditional forms of knowledge, but he thirsts for even more and the power it will bring. After learning the black arts, he summons up the devil Mephastophilis and agrees to exchange his soul for twenty-four years of service. But when it is time to pay up, will Faustus repent?

Playing Shakespeare: An Actor's Guide by John Barton

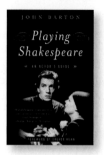

Thespians intent on playing Shakespeare will be interested in this thoughtful guide. Barton, who was associate director of London's Royal Shakespeare Company for thirty-five years, offers performers advice on understanding and handling the Bard's work, including his soliloquies, irony, sometimes tongue-twisting prose, and nuanced characters (especially the challenging Shylock). Barton's advice comes from television workshops with some of Britain's foremost actors.

Hamlet, Prince of Denmark by William Shakespeare

One bitterly cold night, at a lonely guard station, the ghost of the dead king of Denmark appears. He is there to tell his son, Prince Hamlet, of "a foul and most unnatural murder"—and to plead for revenge. Thus begins a tale of ghosts, swordplay, love, treachery, and madness.

Whether you write a critique of a movie or theatrical production or give your review as an oral presentation, you should provide facts and evaluations that accomplish two goals. First, the critique should help readers or listeners decide whether to see the film or play, and second, it should help those who do see the work better comprehend and appreciate it.

1. Select a Film or Play to Review

Commercial video and CD outlets offer a wide selection of movies, and some libraries have videos and CDs in circulation. If you prefer to critique a play, you might watch the tape or CD of a drama on television (for example, on public television). Some theatrical productions originally presented on Broadway or elsewhere in the United States also may be available on tape or CD. If you are not sure how to locate theatrical tapes or CDs, check with your teacher or a librarian or look on the Internet.

You might critique a movie you have not seen yet—perhaps one based on a novel you have enjoyed. You might choose a play by a writer whose comedies or dramas you are familiar with or a musical based on a novel you have read.

2. View the Work from a Critical Perspective

As you watch the movie or theatrical production you have selected, keep in mind that you will be presenting a review of it. By all means, enjoy the work, but think of your experience as more than entertainment. As you watch, ask yourself critical questions such as the following; the answers should help you evaluate what you are seeing (explain each yes/no answer):

- If the work is fantasy, such as science fiction, does it hold your interest? If the work is a comedy, is it amusing? If the film is animated, are the design and production appealing?
- Do the characters change or develop—for example, gain self-knowledge?
- Are the actors well suited to the roles they play?
- Does the set, or location, of the play contribute to the story? Does the *cinematography* (filming technique) enhance the work?
- If you have read the novel (or other written work) on which the movie or play is based, does the adapted version do justice to the original form?

These are just some of the critical questions you can explore. If possible, watch the work twice: the first time, to gain an overall impression and to consider preliminary questions and answers, and the second time, to focus on details you may have missed and to understand how elements of the work relate to each other.

3. Develop Your Critique and Prepare Notes

Develop a main idea and supporting evidence that express, in brief form, your evaluation of the film or play. Make sure your critique is unified. Concentrate on one or two important points, such as character development or actors' performances, and provide convincing supporting details. Make sure to include an attention-getting introduction, key transitions, and a strong conclusion. Prepare notes containing your key ideas. (Avoid writing out your presentation in full.) Use persuasive rhetorical devices and delivery techniques to communicate your ideas to your audience.

4. Practice Your Oral Presentation Using Notes

As you rehearse your presentation, time yourself. If your delivery is longer than the assigned limit, delete the less important material. Practice with your notes. For feedback, practice in front of a mirror or ask a friend or family member to be your practice audience.

5. Listen Actively to Presentations

As you listen to your classmates' presentations, identify the positions taken and supporting evidence. Ask questions to clarify your understanding of the content. Assess the persuasiveness of the presentation based on content, diction, rhetorical strategies, and delivery.

SPEAKING & LISTENING RUBRIC

Your movie or play critique will be evaluated on these elements:

Content

- ❏ You have selected an appropriate film or production of a play to critique.
- ❏ Your review presents a critical examination of one or two important features of the work.

Delivery & Presentation

- ❏ Your enunciation (clarity of speaking), voice level, and hand gestures contribute to your presentation.
- ❏ You maintain eye contact with your audience, especially as a way to gauge their response.

A well-written character captures your attention. You may come to empathize with him or her, as you would a friend, or you may come to despise this individual, as you may Lady Macbeth.

Writing a character description can help you understand a character. Whether your reaction is based on like or dislike, your aim in writing the description is to understand the character intimately.

For this assignment, you will write a character description to try to understand a character.

Assignment Write a description of one character in this unit

Purpose To come to understand him or her

Audience Yourself

① Prewrite

Select Your Topic
Review the characters from the selections you have read in this unit. List three to five that you have reacted to, either positively or negatively. Choose the one that most intrigues you.

Gather Information
Jot down details from the selection that led to your understanding of the character. Consider the character's appearance, actions, motives, words, and thoughts. With a complex character, some details may conflict, so that he or she is likable in some ways and detestable in others.

WRITING RUBRIC

A successful character description has these qualities:

❏ an introduction that contains a thesis statement about the character

❏ body paragraphs that provide details to support the thesis and explain the character

❏ a conclusion that restates the thesis and synthesizes understanding of the character

Organize Your Ideas
Review your notes. Group in clusters those details that relate to one another or convey a certain character trait. Identify the trait. Number the clusters in the order in which you will present them, such as order of importance or order of events in the selections.

Write Your Thesis Statement
Based on the details, form an impression of the character's dominant quality or behavior. Put that impression into a one-sentence statement. This is your *thesis statement*—for example, *Lady Macbeth is a conniving individual who influences her husband to perform evil acts.*

② Draft

Write your character description by following this three-part framework: Introduction, Body, and Conclusion.

Introduction Name your character, along with the selection and author, and state what trait or traits you will address.

Body Give details from the selection to support your impression of your character.

Conclusion Restate your thesis and summarize your understanding of the character.

Draft Your Introduction
Write your introduction as if you were introducing your character to someone. Identify the character, along with the selection and its author, early in the introduction. Also state your thesis.

Draft Your Body
In the body, support your thesis by providing the details from the selection that led to the impression you formed. This is the information you mapped out in the Prewrite stage. Follow the order you decided on earlier. Make sure each body paragraph connects to your thesis.

Draft Your Conclusion
Use the conclusion to close your case. Restate your thesis and summarize how the details you have presented show the nature of the character.

❸ Revise

Evaluate Your Draft

Evaluate your own draft or exchange papers with a classmate and evaluate each other's work. Determine if the description shows a clear understanding of the character. What works well and what can be improved?

Look at the content and organization. Make sure the introduction, body, and conclusion support the characterization set down in the thesis statement. Verify that enough relevant details are provided to support the thesis. Every paragraph should relate directly to the thesis statement, and the paragraphs should flow one from the next.

Pay attention to your word choices. Are you using descriptive language that includes sensory details? Use a thesaurus to find more colorful synonyms to describe your character.

Use the Revision Checklist below to help you evaluate the character description. Make notes about changes directly on the draft.

Next check each sentence for mistakes. Make sure you have correctly used the concepts outlined in the Grammar & Style workshops in this unit. If you are unsure if you have used a word or phrase correctly, consult a specialized language usage dictionary such as Fowler's *Modern English Usage*. Again, use the Revision Checklist to assess the writing.

What Great Writers Do

When writing your character description, choose vivid words. Make sure your choices are meeting a purpose, not a length requirement. Twentieth-century American writer Ernest Hemingway, who is known for his minimalist style, once noted, "Prose is architecture, not interior decoration."

HEMINGWAY

Revise for Content, Organization, and Style

Read the comments you or your partner made on your draft, and make changes as you revise your character description.

Proofread for Errors

Now look for remaining mistakes, using proofreader's symbols to mark any you find. Print out a final draft and read it aloud. This will allow you to slow down to catch errors you normally might miss.

Writing Follow-Up

Publish and Present

● Create a collage, or a visual depiction of your character. Look for images that represent the character's traits, not necessarily his or her physical appearance, such as marionettes to show how controlling Lady Macbeth is.

Reflect

● If you were to write a character description about yourself, what trait or traits would you feature? How might this description change if it were written by a friend? A sibling? Your parents?

REVISION CHECKLIST

Content & Organization

❏ Does the introduction identify the character, the work, and the author and state a thesis about the character's dominant traits?

❏ Does the body give sufficient details to illustrate the character's traits?

❏ Does the conclusion restate and thesis show an understanding of the character?

Grammar & Style

❏ Have you included sensory details to make your descriptions vivid and real? (page 376)

❏ Have you used allusions to literature, the arts, and history? (page 398)

Reading Skills

Analyze Elements of Plot

The **plot** is a series of events related to a central **conflict,** or struggle. The cause of this conflict is the *inciting force,* which can be an event or a character. Hints about what will happen later in the plot are called **foreshadowing.**

Usually, a plot follows a structured format that consists of an exposition, an inciting incident, rising action, a climax, falling action, and a resolution. The **exposition** introduces the main characters and setting, provides background information, and sets the tone, or mood. On a line graph, the exposition is a flat line.

The *inciting incident* introduces a central conflict, such as one character versus another, a character versus himself or herself, or a character versus nature or society. During the **rising action,** the conflict develops and intensifies, with one or more characters being faced with a crisis, or turning point. On a graph, the line now slopes upward.

The action keeps rising to the **climax,** where the conflict is most intense and something decisive happens. At this point, readers feel the highest interest, emotion, or suspense and usually can predict the outcome of the conflict or how the story will end. Graphically, this is the peak of the mountain; everything after it slopes downhill.

The **falling action** details the events that follow the climax. The **resolution,** or *dénouement,* marks the point at which the central conflict is ended or resolved. This final section ties up any loose ends and provides a sense of closure.

TEST-TAKING TIP

In responding to a multiple-choice question, don't go back and change your answer unless you are sure you have misread or misinterpreted the item. Usually, your first choice is best. Second-guessing often is caused by nervousness and lack of confidence.

Practice

Directions: Read the following passage. The questions that come after it will ask you to analyze elements of the plot.

DRAMA: These excerpts are from Act I of Shakespeare's play *The Tragedy of Macbeth.*

> MACBETH. Speak, if you can: what are you?
>
> 1. WITCH. All hail, Macbeth, hail to thee, Thane of Glamis!
>
> 2. WITCH. All hail, Macbeth, hail to thee, Thane of Cawdor!
>
> 3. WITCH. All hail, Macbeth, that shalt be King hereafter!
>
> 5 BANQUO. Good sir, why do you start, and seem to fear
> Things that do sound so fair?—I' th' name of truth,
>
> Are ye fantastical, or that indeed
> Which outwardly ye show? My noble partner
> You greet with present grace, and great
> 10   prediction
> Of noble having and of royal hope,
> That he seems rapt withal; to me you speak
>   not.
> If you can look into the seeds of time,
> And say which grain will grow, and which
>   will not,
> 15 Speak then to me, who neither beg nor fear
> Your favors nor your hate.
>
> 1. WITCH. Hail! . . . Lesser than Macbeth, and greater.
>
> 2. WITCH. Not so happy, yet much happier.
>
> 3. WITCH. Thou shalt get kings, though thou be none.
> 20 So all hail, Macbeth and Banquo! . . .
>
> MACBETH. Stay, you imperfect speakers, tell me more:

By Sinel's death I know I am Thane of Glamis,
But how of Cawdor? The Thane of Cawdor
    lives
A prosperous gentleman; and to be king
25 Stands not within the prospect of belief,
No more than to be Cawdor.

      . . .

Enter MACBETH'S WIFE *alone with a letter.*

LADY MACBETH.   [*Reads.*] . . . Glamis thou
    art, and Cawdor, and shalt be
What thou art promis'd. Yet do I fear thy
    nature,
It is too full o' th' milk of human kindness
30 To catch the nearest way. Thou wouldst be great,
Art not without ambition, but without
The illness should attend it. What thou
    wouldst highly,
That wouldst thou holily; wouldst not play
    false,
And yet wouldst wrongly win. Thou'ldst have,
    great Glamis
35 That which cries, "Thus thou must do," if
    thou have it;

And that which rather thou dost fear to do
Than wishest should be undone. Hie thee
    hither,
That I may pour my spirits in thine ear,
And chastise with the valor of my tongue
40 All that impedes thee from the golden round,
Which fate and metaphysical aid doth seem
To have thee crown'd withal. . . .
               The raven himself is hoarse
That croaks the fatal entrance of Duncan
Under my battlements. Come, you spirits
45 That tend on mortal thoughts, unsex me here,
And fill me from the crown to the toe topful
Of direst cruelty! Make thick my blood,
Stop up th' access and passage to remorse,
That no compunctious visitings of nature
50 Shake my fell purpose, nor keep peace between
Th' effect and it! . . . Come, thick night,
And pall thee in the dunnest smoke of hell,
That my keen knife see not the wound it
    makes,
Nor heaven peep through the blanket of the
    dark
55 To cry, "Hold, hold!"

Multiple Choice

1. What is the inciting incident of the play, as revealed in this excerpt?
   A. Macbeth kills Duncan.
   B. The witches make a prophecy.
   C. The witches disappear.
   D. Lady Macbeth tells what she is going to do.

2. Lady Macbeth's thoughts, which she reveals starting in line 27, are an example of
   F. a climax.   H. a dénouement.
   G. falling action.   J. foreshadowing.

3. What central conflict does Macbeth face?
   A. a fear of the witches and the future
   B. the desire to be a good person and the ambition to be king

   C. a struggle against the witches and forces of nature
   D. a fight with his wife and Banquo

4. Based on this excerpt, who do you think will commit murder?
   F. Macbeth   H. Lady Macbeth
   G. the witches   J. the Thane of Cawdor

Constructed Response

5. Create a simple diagram of the plot of *Macbeth*, as revealed or foreshadowed in these excerpts. Draw and label the various plot elements and describe what occurs at each point, if possible. (Note that you will not be able to describe all the main events in the plot from the limited material provided in the excerpts, but include all you can.)

Writing Skills

Write a Good Introduction

Once you have outlined your essay, you will be ready to start writing. In your first paragraph, the **introduction,** your goals are to capture your reader's attention and establish your subject and position.

An effective introduction hooks the reader and makes him or her want to keep reading. When you are writing an essay for a standardized test, you will not have the opportunity to look for a quotation or any interesting facts—both common types of introductory "hooks." Nonetheless, try to introduce the subject in an engaging way that takes the intended audience into consideration. You might ask a question or relate the subject to the reader in some way.

Even more important than getting your reader's attention in a persuasive essay is providing a clear thesis statement. When planning your response, you should have identified the main point or points you want to make. This will become your thesis. Your **thesis statement** is a single sentence that sums up your answer to the essay prompt. It should be specific, clear, matter of fact, yet strong. Your thesis should include your assertion or argument about the topic and a brief indication of the kind of evidence that will support your claim.

In most cases, the introductory paragraph also should indicate the order in which you will present the evidence. In a short essay that makes good use of transitions, this explanation sometimes can be eliminated.

TEST-TAKING TIP

If you find yourself stuck when trying to write an introduction, proceed with the rest of the essay and add the introduction later. Writing the rest of the essay should help clarify your approach to the topic, making it easier to write the introduction.

Practice

Timed Writing: 30 minutes

Obesity is an increasingly serious problem among children in the United States. Some people favor serving only healthful, fairly low-calorie food in school cafeterias. Others contend that a choice of food items should be offered so students can select according to their preference, whether it be a salad or a hamburger and fries. In your opinion, should school cafeteria food be limited to foods that will not contribute to the obesity of today's youth?

In your essay, take a position on this question. You may write about either one of the two perspectives given, or you may present a different perspective on this question. Use specific reasons and examples to support your position.

Revising and Editing Skills

Some standardized tests ask you to read a draft of an essay and answer questions about how to improve it. As you read the draft, watch for errors like these:

- incorrect spellings
- disagreement between subject and verb; inconsistent verb tense; incorrect forms for irregular verbs; sentence fragments and run-ons; double negatives; and incorrect use of frequently confused words, such as *affect* and *effect*

- missing end marks, incorrect comma use, and lowercased proper nouns and proper adjectives
- unclear purpose, unclear main ideas, and lack of supporting details
- confusing order of ideas and missing transitions
- language that is inappropriate to the audience and purpose, and mood that is inappropriate for the purpose

Practice

Directions: In the passage that follows, certain words and phrases are numbered and underlined. In the questions below the passage, you will find alternatives for each underlined word or phrase. In each case, choose the alternative that best expresses the idea, that is worded most consistently with the style and tone of the rest of the passage, or that makes the text correct according to the conventions of standard written English. If you think the original version is best, choose the first alternative, Make no change. To indicate your answer, circle the letter of the chosen alternative.

(1) Although many American kids <u>maybe fat, meals in the school lunch program play</u> only a small role in contributing to this fact. (2) Restricting the foods served in the cafeteria to <u>healthful, low-calorie ones aren't</u> the answer. (3) <u>Besides, it undoubtly would have</u> negative results. (4) Kids <u>won't learn how to make wise decisions, compromise, nor</u> consider the future.

Multiple Choice

1. A. Make no change.
   B. maybe fat, meals in the school lunch program plays
   C. maybe fat meals in the school lunch program play
   D. may be fat, meals in the school lunch program play

2. F. Make no change.
   G. healthfull, low-calorie ones aren't
   H. healthful, low-calorie ones isn't
   J. healthful low-calorie ones aren't

3. A. Make no change.
   B. Besides, it undoubtedly would have
   C. Beside it undoubtly would have
   D. Besides, it undoubtly would be having

4. F. Make no change.
   G. won't learn how to make wise decisions, compromize, nor
   H. would not learn how to make wise decisions, compromise, nor
   J. won't learn how to make wise decisions, compromise, or

A View of the Thames with the York Buildings Water Tower, c. 1760. Samuel Scott. Tate Gallery, London, England.

Seventeenth and Eighteenth

Unit 5

Centuries 1625–1798

Seventeenth and Eighteenth Centuries 1625–1798

1625

1660

BRITISH LITERATURE BRITISH LITERATURE BRITISH LITERATURE BRITISH L

1639
William Davenant publishes
The Spanish Lovers

1651
Thomas Hobbes publishes
Leviathan

1654
John Milton attempts to read
everything in the English
language and goes blind in
the process

1659
Robert Boyle publishes
Seraphic Love

1667
John Milton publishes
Paradise Lost

1678
John Bunyan publishes
The Pilgrim's Progress

1687
Isaac Newton publishes
Principia, redefining the
scientific world

1688
Aphra Behn publishes
Oroonoko

1690
John Locke publishes *Two
Treatises of Government*

1694
Jonathan Swift is ordained
a clergyman

BRITISH HISTORY BRITISH HISTORY BRITISH HISTORY BRITISH HISTORY BR

1630
Approximately seventy
thousand Puritans emigrate
from England to North
America during the Great
Migration

1642
Civil war breaks out in
England

1649
Charles I is beheaded at
Whitehall Gate

1653
Oliver Cromwell declares
himself Lord Protector over
Great Britain

1658
Cromwell dies of malaria

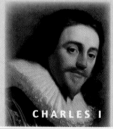

CHARLES I

1660
Charles II assumes the
throne, beginning the
Restoration period

1665
The Great Plague of London
kills one-fifth of the city's
population

1666
The London Fire burns over
80 percent of the city

1675
English settlers harass the
Wampanoag population in
New England, prompting
King Philip's War

1689
The Dutch Protestant William
of Orange becomes King of
England, deposing Catholic
King James II during the
Glorious Revolution

WORLD HISTORY WORLD HISTORY WORLD HISTORY WORLD HISTORY WORI

1626
Construction is completed
on St. Peter's Basilica in the
Vatican in Rome

1644
China's last
imperial
dynasty, the
Qing Dynasty,
begins with
the capture
of Beijing by
an invading
Manchu army

1648
The Peace of Westphalia
ends several religious wars
in Europe

1648
The Taj Mahal is
completed in India

1656
The Quaker religious
movement begins in
England

1674
Shivaji founds the Maratha
Empire in India

1685
The Edict of Fontainebleau
outlaws Protestantism in
France

1688
The Nine Years' War, also
known as the War of the
Great Alliance, begins in
continental Europe

1692
The Salem witch trials begin
in Salem, Massachusetts

1695
Osei Tutu founds the Asanti
Empire in West Africa

BRITISH LITERATURE BRITISH LITERATURE BRITISH LITERATURE BRITISH LITERA

1702
The Daily Courant becomes the first daily newspaper printed in English

1711
Alexander Pope publishes "An Essay on Criticism"

1719
Daniel Defoe publishes *Robinson Crusoe*

1726
Jonathan Swift publishes *Gulliver's Travels*

1728
John Gay writes *The Beggar's Opera*

1749
Henry Fielding publishes *Tom Jones*

1755
Dr. Samuel Johnson completes his *Dictionary*

1764
Horace Walpole publishes *The Castle of Otranto*

1776
Adam Smith publishes *The Wealth of Nations*

1784
Charlotte Smith publishes the first of eleven editions of *Elegiac Sonnets and Other Essays*

ORY BRITISH HISTORY BRITISH HISTORY BRITISH HISTORY BRITISH HISTORY BRIT

1707
The Act of Union unites Scotland and England, creating the Kingdom of Great Britain

1715
Catholics sympathetic to James II incite the First Jacobite Rebellion

1746
Jacobite leader Charles Edward Stuart is defeated at the Battle of Culloden, ending hope of a Stuart restoration

1754
The French and Indian War erupts between English and French colonists over territory disputes in North America

1769
James Watt patents the steam engine

1770
British explorer James Bruce finds the source of the Blue Nile River in Africa

1775
The Revolutionary War begins between Great Britain and the North American colonies

1783
The Treaty of Paris is signed, ending the Revolutionary War and granting independence to the North American colonies

WORLD HISTORY WORLD HISTORY WORLD HISTORY WORLD HISTORY WORLD HISTO

c. 1700
The last Dodo bird perishes on Mauritius Island

1702
Forty-seven Samurai avenge their master's death in Japan, an event that becomes popularized through *kabuki* theater

1703
Peter the Great founds St. Petersburg in Russia

1715
Louis XIV, known as the "Sun King," dies in France after a seventy-two-year reign

1741
Danish sailor Vitus Bering discovers Alaska

1762
Catherine the Great becomes Empress of Russia

1767
The Burmese conquer Ayutthaya in Thailand

1768
The Gurkhas conquer Nepal and establish Hinduism as the state religion

1770
The Bengal famine kills one-third of India's population

1788
The city of Sydney becomes the first permanent European settlement in Australia

1789
The French Revolution begins

> ## "Curiosity is one of the permanent and certain characteristics of a vigorous mind."
>
> —SAMUEL JOHNSON

The House of Stuart and Oliver Cromwell

The House of Stuart was marked by one of the most turbulent periods in the history of England. The monarchy swung from nearly absolute power in the first part of the seventeenth century, to complete dissolution at midcentury, to vastly reduced power later in the century. Much of this turbulence was sparked by conflicts over religion, as various Protestant sects split off from the Anglican Church of England.

Charles I ascended the throne in 1625. Like his father, James I, he continued to clash with Parliament over taxes and religion. He also was an advocate of the divine right of kings, going so far as to dismiss Parliament in 1629 to secure his absolute power. In 1640, Charles had to reconvene Parliament to fund a war against religious freedom in Scotland. By this time, an angry Parliament had a long list of complaints against Charles. Parliament demanded more power, including control of the army.

In response, Charles invaded the Parliamentary House of Commons with three hundred soldiers. Civil war broke out between his supporters, the Cavaliers, and those who sided with Parliament, the Roundheads. Led by Puritan Oliver Cromwell, the Roundheads triumphed, and Charles surrendered in 1646. Parliament dissolved the monarchy and beheaded Charles in 1649.

Cromwell, too, soon conflicted with Parliament. He wanted to impose Puritan ideas of morality on England. Cromwell and his Puritan supporters took over Parliament; then Cromwell disbanded Parliament and ruled as a dictator. This period is referred to as the Commonwealth, or the *Interregnum* (Latin for "between reigns").

Cromwell transformed England into a Puritan state, and he succeeded in conquering Ireland and Scotland. When he died in 1658, power passed to his son, who proved to be a weak leader. By 1660, Parliament had reconvened and asked Charles II, son of Charles I, to reclaim the throne. This event is called the Restoration.

> ## "Keep your faith in God, but keep your powder dry."
>
> —OLIVER CROMWELL

The Restoration and the Glorious Revolution

With the monarchy restored and Parliament meeting again, Charles II attempted to establish toleration of Catholics; however, Parliament did not approve of these measures. James II succeeded his older brother Charles in 1685. A staunch Catholic, James made a series of moves to promote Catholicism.

When James's second wife gave birth to a boy in 1688, Parliament wanted to prevent this Catholic son from becoming the next ruler. Toward this goal, Parliament invited James's Protestant daughter, Mary, and her Dutch husband, William of Orange, to England, setting off a series of events known as the Glorious Revolution.

With few political supporters, the unpopular James was forced to flee to France. Parliament decided that, in fleeing, James had abdicated, or given up the throne. In 1689, Parliament offered the throne to William and Mary, along with several conditions laid out in the Bill of Rights. This document officially shifted power from the monarchy to Parliament, moving England toward a democratic form of government known as a constitutional monarchy, which remains in place to this day.

Despite James's efforts to reestablish himself and his male heirs to the monarchy, he was unable

to regain the throne. Following the deaths of Mary in 1694 and William in 1702, Anne, Mary's sister, became queen. Under Anne's reign, the nation of Great Britain was formed in 1707 by the Act of Union between England and Scotland. Anne died without leaving an heir, marking the end of the House of Stuart. Since the Bill of Rights barred Catholics from ever ascending the throne, Anne was succeeded in 1714 by George I, a distant relative by marriage, from Hanover, Germany.

The House of Hanover

During the reign of George I (1714–1727), the governmental ministries and political parties, Whigs and Tories, grew more powerful. Under George II (1727–1760), the position and power of prime minister was formalized.

George II appointed statesman William Pitt the Elder as secretary of state during the Seven Years' War (1756–1760), a worldwide conflict in which Britain battled France for colonial supremacy. Under Pitt's leadership, Britain asserted imperial dominance in East India and North America, gaining land from France and creating a British trading empire. An important part of this empire was the slave trade, which involved shipping cheap manufactured goods from Britain to Africa, trading them for slaves, carrying the slaves to the West Indies, and selling the slaves for sugar and molasses.

With its expanded empire, Britain found it had increased the financial burden of defending its territories. To help cover the cost, George III, who had inherited the throne in 1760, required the North American colonists to pay a series of taxes. The colonists felt the taxes were unfair and grew increasingly dissatisfied with British rule. The American Revolution erupted with the battles at Lexington and Concord in 1775 and ended with the British surrender in 1781.

In 1789, the success of the American Revolution helped spark the French Revolution, which attempted to replace the monarchy with a representative form of government. While the French rebels did not immediately achieve all of their goals, they set off a shockwave that reverberated throughout Europe and that began the long process of establishing democracy in France.

The Industrial Revolution

Even before the American and French Revolutions, a revolution of a different sort had begun in Britain: the Industrial Revolution. The Industrial Revolution comprised the period of economic development that

NOTABLE NUMBERS

- **2 of 3** Workers in water-powered Scottish textile factories who were children in 1788

- **13,000** Homes burned in the Great Fire of London in 1666

- **609** Number of slaves carried on the *Brookes,* a British ship built to carry a maximum of 451 people

- **12,000** Estimate of people beheaded by guillotine during the Reign of Terror (1793–1794) after the French Revolution

Nat-Y-Glo Ironworks, Wales, c. 1788. George Robertson. Private collection.

began in the mid-1700s. A number of innovations in farming and industry occurred during this period, including crop rotation, improved methods of transportation, and the enclosure of several small plots of land to produce large farms. The cloth trade also was revolutionized with inventions that sped up the spinning of wool and weaving of cloth. Steam- and coal-powered factories were built in and around London, drawing people from outlying communities who wanted jobs and money. New towns sprang up near factories in northern England, attracting people from the countryside in search of work.

While these innovations made entrepreneurs wealthy, they caused great hardships for people who were displaced. Families lost the common rights land they had farmed for generations when new laws allowed landlords to enclose fields and operate them as private, for-profit farms that employed a much smaller labor force. People who had spun wool and woven cloth in their homes for extra income were put out of work. Moreover, life in factory towns was grim. Because of children's small size, they were made to crawl beneath large pieces of machinery and perform other dangerous works. Families across Great Britain earned barely enough to survive. The nation would

continue to struggle with the effects of industrialization over the next century.

The Age of Reason and Empiricism

The ideals that set off the revolutionary movements in France and North America had been evolving throughout the seventeenth and eighteenth centuries, a period sometimes referred to as the Enlightenment, or Age of Reason. During this period, philosophers, writers, and scientists across Europe were applying the findings of scientific discoveries made during the Renaissance and forming new theories and ideas about humans, the world, and the universe. A new philosophy, *Empiricism,* suggested that by repeatedly observing phenomena, people could reasonably predict natural events.

Soon Empiricist principles were applied to communal life, where many social problems, it was assumed, could be solved with the application of reason. In England, economist Adam Smith proposed that economics is governed by *laissez faire* ("let it be"), a system of natural laws that work in an ordered and rational way, if not interfered with by governments or monopolies. However, philosopher Thomas Hobbes observed the unrest of the times and concluded that humans were naturally brutish and needed a strong government to keep them in line. John Locke, a fellow philosopher, disagreed and saw all humans as equal, entering life as *tabula rasa,* or "blank sheets," that learned by observation. Locke also disputed the divine right of kings and popularized the idea of natural rights.

"No one ought to harm another in his life, health, liberty or possessions."

—JOHN LOCKE

Locke's thinking, as well as that of Frenchmen Voltaire and Jean-Jacques Rousseau, inspired ideas of tolerance, democracy, and equality. These ideas, in turn, fed the revolutions in France and North America and helped shape the language in Thomas Jefferson's Declaration of Independence.

John Freeth and His Circle, 1792. John Eckstein. Birmingham Museum, Birmingham, England.

Ideas Old and New

During the first half of the seventeenth century, a group of poets known as the Cavaliers reflected old ideals mixed with a new secular lifestyle. As courtiers who supported Charles I during the English Civil War, the **Cavalier poets** wrote about love, honor, and loyalty to their king, and they lived a cavalier, or sumptuous and courtly, lifestyle. The Cavalier poets include John Suckling, Richard Lovelace, and Robert Herrick.

In contrast to the lighthearted Cavaliers, two Puritan writers, John Milton and John Bunyan, wrote about spiritual themes, creating some of the greatest literature in the English language. Milton is best remembered for the Christian epic poem *Paradise Lost.* Bunyan's masterpiece of Christian allegory, *The Pilgrim's Progress,* was, until the nineteenth century, the most widely read book in English after the Bible.

By the eighteenth century, religious thought was giving way to a more rational and reasoned view of the world. The Age of Pope (1700–1750) represented the peak of **Neoclassical** literature, which adapted Classical forms and allusions used during the early Roman Empire to promote ideals of harmony, tradition, and reason. Alexander Pope, after whom the period is named, employed wit, reason, and balance in his poetry. His mock epic *The Rape of the Lock* satirizes the historical conflict between men and women. In contrast to Pope's work, Jonathan Swift's *Gulliver's Travels* and "A Modest Proposal" are famous for their pointed, sharp satire of the European political and intellectual landscape.

The seventeenth and eighteenth centuries also saw an increase in the number of women writers, such as Margaret Cavendish and Aphra Behn. Behn's *Oroonoko* (1688), a prose work about slavery in the West Indies, was one of the first English novels.

John Middleton with his family in his drawing room (1796). Museum of London, London, England.

473

Song ("Why so pale and wan")

A Lyric Poem by Sir John Suckling

Build Background

Literary Context Sir John Suckling was one of the Cavalier poets, loyalists to King Charles I who wrote about love, honor, and loyalty to their king. Suckling was known for his wit and extravagance. One of Suckling's best-known poems is "Ballade Upon a Wedding."

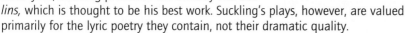

The poem **"Song"** ("Why so pale and wan") comes from the play *Aglaura,* for which Suckling paid for an extravagant production in 1638. That same year, Suckling produced the comedy *The Goblins,* which is thought to be his best work. Suckling's plays, however, are valued primarily for the lyric poetry they contain, not their dramatic quality.

Most of Suckling's work appeared after he died. Some literary scholars believe he never committed himself to the serious study of literature and, as a result, produced an irregular body of work.

Reader's Context How well do you receive criticism? How would you respond if someone told you that what you are doing is not going to work?

Meet the Author

Sir John Suckling (1609–1642) was born to a wealthy family at Whitton, England, on February 10, 1609. His mother died when he was four years old. Suckling enrolled at Trinity College, Cambridge, at age fourteen, but he left in 1626 before completing a degree.

Suckling's father died that year, leaving him to inherit vast estates. He was admitted to Gray's Inn, part of the English justice system, in 1627. He pursued a military and ambassadorial career and, while in Germany, joined the army of Sweden's king Gustavus Adolphus during the Thirty Years' War. He was knighted in 1630.

Suckling was quite popular in the English court because of his wealth and charm. He was considered a gamester and is said to have invented the game of cribbage. In 1639, Suckling helped recruit and equip the cavalry to help King Charles I in his war against religious freedom in Scotland. According to some accounts, the poet was ridiculed for outfitting his troops in scarlet uniforms and plumed hats.

In 1641, Suckling was implicated in a plot against Parliamentary forces. England was headed toward civil war, and Suckling was pressed by Parliament to account for his actions. Shortly thereafter he fled to Paris and, fearing poverty, died there a few months later.

Analyze Literature

Repetition and Speaker Repetition is a writer's intentional reuse of a sound, word, phrase, or sentence. Writers often use repetition to emphasize ideas or, especially in poetry, to create a musical effect.

The **speaker** is the character who speaks in, or narrates, a poem—the voice assumed by the writer. The speaker and the writer of a poem are not necessarily the same person.

Set Purpose

In the English court, Suckling was well known for his lyric poems: musical types of poems that express the emotions of a speaker. Poets often create musical effects through the use of repetition. As you read Suckling's lyric poem, list the instances of repetition and identify what kind of repetition each involves (sound, word, phrase, or sentence). Consider for what purpose or purposes Suckling uses repetition in "Song." Also identify the speaker of the poem. Determine what details help you identify the poem's speaker and his attitude toward love.

Preview Vocabulary

wan, 475
prevail, 475
mute, 475

Concert à Huit Personnages, c. 1600s. Valentin de Boulogne. The Louvre, Paris, France. (See detail on page 474.)

Song ("Why so pale and wan")

by Sir John Suckling

Why so pale and <u>wan</u>, fond lover?
    Prithee,[1] why so pale?
Will, when looking well can't move her,
    Looking ill <u>prevail</u>?
5   Prithee, why so pale?

Why so dull and <u>mute</u>, young sinner?
    Prithee, why so mute?
Will, when speaking well can't win her,
    Saying nothing do 't?
10   Prithee, why so mute?

Quit, quit, for shame; this will not move,
    This cannot take her.
If of herself she will not love,
    Nothing can make her:
15   The devil take her! ❖

---

1. **prithee.** Please

> **wan** (wän) *adj.,* sickly; pallid
> **pre · vail** (pri vāl´) *v.,* be greater in influence or strength
> **mute** (myüt) *adj.,* refraining from producing speech or a vocal sound

MIRRORS & WINDOWS

Assume the role of the speaker of the poem. What advice would you give the subject?

seasons, and for days, and years: And let them be for lights in the firmament of the heaven to give light upon the earth": And it was so. And God made two great lights; the greater light to rule the day, and the lesser light to rule the night: He made the stars also. And God set them in the firmament of the heaven to give light upon the earth, and to rule over the day and over the night, and to divide the light from the darkness: And God saw that it was good. And the evening and the morning were the fourth day.

And God said, "Let the waters bring forth abundantly[4] the moving creature[5] that hath life, and fowl that may fly above the earth in the open firmament of heaven." And God created great whales, and every living creature that moveth, which the waters brought forth abundantly, after their kind, and every winged fowl after his kind: And God saw that it was good. And God blessed them, saying, "Be fruitful, and multiply, and fill the waters in the seas, and let fowl multiply in the earth." And the evening and the morning were the fifth day.

And God said, "Let the earth bring forth the living creature after his kind, cattle, and creeping thing, and beast of the earth after his kind": And it was so. And God made the beast of the earth after his kind, and cattle after their kind, and every thing that creepeth upon the earth after his kind: And God saw that it was good. And God said, "Let us make man in our image,[6] after our likeness: And let them have dominion over the fish of the sea, and over the fowl of the air, and over the cattle, and over all the earth, and over every creeping thing that creepeth upon the earth." So God created man in his own image, in the image of God created he him; male and female created he them. And God blessed them, and God said unto them, "Be fruitful, and multiply, and replenish the earth, and subdue it: And have dominion over the fish of the sea, and over the fowl of the air, and over every living thing that moveth upon the earth." And God said, "Behold, I have given

you every herb bearing seed, which is upon the face of all the earth, and every tree, in which is the fruit of a tree yielding seed; to you it shall be for meat.[7] And to every beast of the earth, and to every fowl of the air, and to every thing that creepeth upon the earth, wherein there is life, I have given every green herb for meat": And it was so. And God saw every thing that he had made, and, behold, it was very good. And the evening and the morning were the sixth day.

Thus the heavens and the earth were finished, and all the host of them. And on the seventh day God ended his work which he had made; and he rested on the seventh day from all his work which he had made. And God blessed the seventh day, and sanctified it: because in it he had rested from all his work which God created and made.

These are the generations of the heavens and of the earth when they were created, in the day that the LORD God made the earth and the heavens, and every plant of the field before it was in the earth, and every herb of the field before it grew: for the LORD God had not caused it to rain upon the earth, and there was not a man to till the ground. But there went up a mist from the earth, and watered the whole face of the ground. And the LORD God formed man of the dust of the ground, and breathed into his nostrils the breath of life; and man became a living soul. And the LORD God planted a garden eastward in Eden; and there he put the man whom he had formed. And out of the ground made the LORD God to grow every tree that is pleasant to the sight, and good for food; the tree of life also in the midst of the garden, and the tree of knowledge of good and

---

4. **abundantly.** Plentifully; amply
5. **creature.** Created being; animal, plant, or environment
6. **our image.** God refers to himself using *we* and *our* as a sign of power.
7. **meat.** Food

Creation of the Animals, c. 1550. Jacopo Tintoretto.

caused a deep sleep to fall upon Adam, and he slept: And he took one of his ribs, and closed up the flesh instead thereof; and the rib, which the LORD God had taken from man, made he a woman, and brought her unto the man. And Adam said, "This is now bone of my bones, and flesh of my flesh: She shall be called Woman, because she was taken out of Man." Therefore shall a man leave his father and his mother, and shall cleave[11] unto his wife: And they shall be one flesh. And they were both naked, the man and his wife, and were not ashamed.

evil. And a river went out of Eden to water the garden; and from thence it was parted, and became into four heads. The name of the first is Pison:[8] That is it which compasseth the whole land of Havilah, where there is gold; and the gold of that land is good: There is bdellium and the onyx[9] stone. And the name of the second river is Gihon: The same is it that compasseth the whole land of Ethiopia. And the name of the third river is Hiddekel: That is it which goeth toward the east of Assyria. And the fourth river is Euphrates. And the LORD God took the man, and put him into the garden of Eden to dress it and to keep it. And the LORD God commanded the man, saying, "Of every tree of the garden thou mayest freely eat: But of the tree of the knowledge of good and evil, thou shalt not eat of it: For in the day that thou eatest thereof thou shalt surely die"

And the LORD God said, "It is not good that the man should be alone; I will make him an help meet[10] for him." And out of the ground the LORD God formed every beast of the field, and every fowl of the air; and brought them unto Adam to see what he would call them: And whatsoever Adam called every living creature, that was the name thereof. And Adam gave names to all cattle, and to the fowl of the air, and to every beast of the field; but for Adam there was not found an help meet for him. And the LORD God

Now the serpent[12] was more subtil than any beast of the field which the LORD God had made. And he said unto the woman, "Yea, hath God said, 'Ye shall not eat of every tree of the garden'?" And the woman said unto the serpent, "We may eat of the fruit of the trees of the garden: But of the fruit of the tree which is in the midst of the garden, God hath said, 'Ye shall not eat of it, neither shall ye touch it, lest ye die.'" And the serpent said unto the woman, "Ye shall not surely die: For God doth know that in the day ye eat thereof, then your eyes shall be opened, and ye shall be as gods, knowing good and evil." And when the woman saw that the tree was good for food, and that it was pleasant to the eyes, and a tree to be desired to make one wise, she took of the fruit thereof, and did eat, and gave also unto her husband with her; and he did eat. And the eyes of them both were opened, and they knew that they were naked; and they sewed fig leaves together, and made themselves aprons. And they heard the voice of the LORD God walking in the garden in the cool of the day: And Adam and his wife hid themselves from the presence of the LORD God amongst the trees of the garden. And the

---

8. **Pison.** One of many place names that have led biblical scholars to place Eden in Mesopotamia, or what is now Iraq.
9. **bdellium and the onyx.** Two precious substances
10. **help meet.** Helpmate, or companion and helper
11. **cleave.** Join and stay with loyally
12. **serpent.** Satan in another form

LORD God called unto Adam, and said unto him, "Where art thou?" And he said, "I heard thy voice in the garden, and I was afraid, because I was naked; and I hid myself." And he said, "Who told thee that thou wast naked? Hast thou eaten of the tree, whereof I commanded thee that thou shouldest not eat?" And the man said, "The woman whom thou gavest to be with me, she gave me of the tree, and I did eat." And the LORD God said unto the woman, "What is this that thou hast done?" And the woman said, "The serpent beguiled[13] me, and I did eat." And the LORD God said unto the serpent, "Because thou hast done this, thou art cursed above all cattle,[14] and above every beast of the field; upon thy belly shalt thou go, and dust shalt thou eat all the days of thy life: And I will put enmity[15] between thee and the woman, and between thy seed and her seed; it shall bruise thy head, and thou shalt bruise his heel." Unto the woman he said, "I will greatly multiply thy sorrow and thy conception;[16] in sorrow thou shalt bring forth children; and thy desire shall be to thy husband, and he shall rule over thee." And unto Adam he said, "Because thou hast hearkened unto[17] the voice of thy wife, and hast eaten of the tree, of which I commanded thee, saying, 'Thou shalt not eat of it': Cursed is the ground

for thy sake; in sorrow shalt thou eat of it all the days of thy life; thorns also and thistles shall it bring forth to thee; and thou shalt eat the herb of the field; in the sweat of thy face shalt thou eat bread, till thou return unto the ground; for out of it wast thou taken: For dust thou art, and unto dust shalt thou return." And Adam called his wife's name Eve; because she was the mother of all living. Unto Adam also and to his wife did the LORD God make coats of skins, and clothed them.

And the LORD God said, "Behold, the man is become as one of us, to know good and evil: and now, lest he put forth his hand, and take also of the tree of life, and eat, and live for ever": Therefore the LORD God sent him forth from the garden of Eden, to till the ground from whence he was taken. So he drove out the man; and he placed at the east of the garden of Eden cherubims,[18] and a flaming sword which turned every way, to keep the way of[19] the tree of life. ❖

---

13. **beguiled.** Deceived; used wiles to trick
14. **cattle.** Animals
15. **enmity.** Active hatred or ill will; hostility
16. **conception.** Childbirth pains
17. **hearkened unto.** Listened to and did as told
18. **cherubims.** Fierce angels
19. **keep the way of.** Block the path to

Review Questions

1. On the sixth day, what did God decree man should have? Explain how an interpretation of this decree may have led to environmental abuse over the centuries.

2. What did the serpent say would happen if Adam and Eve ate the fruit of the tree of knowledge? Why might the knowledge of good and evil be considered evil or dangerous and thus require removal from paradise?

3. How were Adam and Eve punished? Suggest how their punishments have been reflected in human society throughout the centuries.

TEXT $\xleftrightarrow{\text{TO}}$ TEXT CONNECTION

Compare the biblical story of Adam and Eve's fall from grace to Milton's version in *Paradise Lost*. What aspects of the story did Milton clearly create or embellish? Do your feelings toward the characters differ from one version to the other? Does one version have a stronger moral than the other? Explain.

Refer to Text ▷ ▶ ▶ ▶ ▶	Reason with Text	
1a. In lines 1–5, what does the speaker say the subject of the epic will be?	**1b.** What theme does this suggest for the epic?	**Understand** Find meaning
2a. In lines 173–216, whose point of view is presented? What attitude does he express toward the people he views?	**2b.** What is surprising about this view? Describe what it suggests about the nature of evil.	**Apply** Use information
3a. What happens to Satan in Book 1?	**3b.** Describe the parallel experience between Satan and Adam and Eve.	**Analyze** Take things apart
4a. List the traits Satan displays.	**4b.** How effectively does Milton portray Satan? Use details from the epic to support your opinion.	**Evaluate** Make judgments
5a. In lines 25–26, what purpose does Milton set for his epic?	**5b.** Relate this purpose to the concerns that Milton expresses in Sonnets VII and XIX.	**Create** Bring ideas together

Analyze Literature

Motivation and Apostrophe

What motivates Satan to tempt Adam and Eve? What motivation does he reveal in the last section of the selection? How does this motivation compare to what motivated him to the actions that got him expelled from heaven?

Whom does Milton address in an apostrophe in line 17? What does Milton ask? How does this apostrophe relate to Milton's purpose in *Paradise Lost*?

Extend the Text

Writing Options

Creative Writing Suppose you have been asked "to justify the ways of God to men" to a modern audience. Choose one or more of the excerpts from *Paradise Lost,* and retell it in a form that will appeal to modern readers, such as a situation/comedy (sitcom) television show or action movie. Write a brief scene in the form you choose.

Expository Writing Choose another poem with a religious theme, such as George Herbert's "Easter Wings," Amelia Lanier's "Eve's Apology in Defense of Women," or a psalm from the Bible (see Unit 3). Read the poem carefully. Then write a paragraph comparing the theme and tone of the poem to that of the excerpts you have read from *Paradise Lost.*

Collaborative Learning

Discuss Gender Roles Review Milton's descriptions of Adam and Eve in lines 107–128. Then discuss these questions with a small group: How are Adam and Eve portrayed? How do they represent men and women? What similarities and differences do you find between the characterizations of men and women? Do you agree with these characterizations? Are these characterizations still relevant today? Use details from the text to support your response.

Media Literacy

Prepare a Talk Show Interview With two or three other students, prepare a talk show interview with Satan or with Adam and Eve, portraying the character or characters as they are represented in *Paradise Lost.* Begin by writing out the questions the interviewer will ask and the answers the interviewee or interviewees will provide. Include details from the epic to lend realism to the interview. Then role-play the interview for the class.

 Go to **www.mirrorsandwindows.com** for more.

1. What is the "forbidden tree" referred to in the first three lines from *Paradise Lost?*
  A. a poisonous apple tree in Paradise
  B. a weed that has sprung up in the garden
  C. any tree growing in the Garden of Eden
  D. the tree of the knowledge of good and evil
  E. a metaphor for anything people cannot have

2. In line 6 of the excerpt from *Paradise Lost,* the speaker addresses "Heavenly Muse." What other term from this epic poem is synonymous with "Heavenly Muse"?
  A. greater Man
  B. Oreb
  C. O Spirit
  D. Eternal Providence
  E. Almighty Power

3. Review lines 12 and 13 from *Paradise Lost.* What is a simpler way of saying "I thence / Invoke thy aid to my adventurous song"?
  A. Now sing along with me.
  B. Please help me write this poem.
  C. I beseech you to keep me safe during my adventures.
  D. I call upon divine intervention to make me a better singer.
  E. Thus, I request your powers to make my trip more exciting.

4. What is the answer to the questions asked in lines 28–33 of *Paradise Lost?*
  A. Eve
  B. Satan
  C. the Most High
  D. Adam
  E. Nature

5. What two things are being contrasted in the following lines (lines 81–83) from *Paradise Lost?* "Farewell, happy fields, / Where joy forever dwells! Hail, horrors! hail, / Infernal world!"
  A. good and evil
  B. heaven and hell
  C. coming and going
  D. the sky and the earth
  E. the external world (nature) and internal world (emotions)

6. Review lines 186–192 from *Paradise Lost.* Which adjectives best describe how Satan feels watching the newly created Adam and Eve?
  A. hateful but happy
  B. fierce but fulfilled
  C. scheming and evil
  D. blissful and desirous
  E. envious and resentful

7. According to the excerpt from Genesis, what did God create on the fourth day?
  A. heaven
  B. the earth
  C. two lamps
  D. day and night
  E. the sun and the moon

8. According to the last paragraph of the excerpt from Genesis, what does God think might happen if Adam and Eve remain in the Garden of Eden?
  A. They might acquire eternal life.
  B. They might be tempted by the servant.
  C. They might recognize good and evil.
  D. They might be killed by the flaming sword.
  E. They might become ashamed.

9. Constructed Response: Discuss Milton's use of slant rhyme in *Paradise Lost,* in which rhyming sounds are similar but not identical (as in *rave* and *rove*). Identify examples of slant rhyme and discuss how using this type of rhyme affects the sound and rhythm of the poem. Infer Milton's purpose for using slant rhyme in this epic work.

10. Constructed Response: Compare and contrast Milton's *Paradise Lost* and the book of Genesis from the Bible in terms of written style. Consider such elements of style as word choice (or *diction*), sentence structure and length, and other recurring features. Which selection did you find more difficult to read and understand? Explain why, using details from the selection.

from The Pilgrim's Progress

An Allegory by John Bunyan

Build Background

Literary Context John Bunyan's ***The Pilgrim's Progress, from This World to That Which Is to Come,*** is one of the most popular allegories in English literature and has been translated into more than one hundred languages. It tells the story of the life journey of a pilgrim named Christian. In this passage from the beginning of the work, the narrator has a dream in which he sees Christian, who is weeping and wondering what to do.

Bunyan modeled his writing style in *The Pilgrim's Progress* on the prose of the English Bible, intending to allow even the most humble reader to share the experiences of Christian and the travelers he meets. Published in 1678, *The Pilgrim's Progress* became a household book and thus contributed many colloquial phrases to the English language, including "the house beautiful," "Mr. Worldly-Wiseman," and "Vanity Fair."

Reader's Context How can taking a trip, whether to a new or familiar place, help you see life in a different way?

Meet the Author

John Bunyan (1628–1688), the son of a Bedfordshire tinker (someone who makes and mends metal pots), received only a meager education before adopting his father's trade. From 1644 to 1646, Bunyan served in the Parliamentary army.

After his marriage in 1648, Bunyan turned his thoughts to religion and experienced a period of spiritual struggle. In 1653, he converted faiths and joined the Baptist church at Bedford. Like many other men and women in his day, Bunyan answered the call to preach. However, England's Anglican Church viewed these lay preachers as dissenters and worked to persecute and silence them.

Bunyan was imprisoned from 1660 to 1672 for refusing to obey a royal ban on nonconformist preaching. While in prison, he wrote his spiritual auto-biography, *Grace Abounding the Chief of the Sinners,* which uses details of his early life to reveal the purposes of divine Providence. After being released from prison, Bunyan became minister of the Bedford nonconformist church. Imprisoned again in 1675, he wrote *The Pilgrim's Progress,* his most celebrated work; it was published three years later. Prompted by the success of his allegory, Bunyan published Part II of *The Pilgrim's Progress* in 1684, but it never captured the popularity of his original work.

Analyze Literature

Allegory and Point of View
An **allegory** is a work in which characters, events, or settings symbolize, or represent, something else. A *naive allegory* is one in which these elements are personifications of abstractions such as good deeds or beauty.

Point of view is the vantage point, or perspective, from which the story is told. In *first-person point of view,* the narrator participates in or witnesses the action. In *third-person point of view,* the narrator usually stands outside the action and observes.

Set Purpose

As a naive allegory, Bunyan's *The Pilgrim's Progress* contains many symbolic elements. List the elements you find in the work, including personifications of abstractions. Identify what each allegorical element represents. Also consider Bunyan's decision to tell the story in third-person point of view. How might the meaning of the story be different if Bunyan had written it from, say, first-person point of view?

Preview Vocabulary

plight, 512
obstinate, 514
pliable, 514
incorruptible, 514
undefiled, 514
revile, 514
contrive, 515
raiment, 517

from

The Pilgrim's Progress

by John Bunyan

"What shall I do to be saved?"

Engraving from *The Pilgrim's Progress* showing Pilgrim entering the wicket gate, opened by Good-Will (1778). (See detail on page 511.)

From this World to That Which Is to Come: Delivered Under the Similitude[1] of a Dream

[Christian Sets out for the Celestial City]

As I walked through the wilderness of this world, I lighted on a certain place where was a Den, and I laid me down in that place to sleep; and, as I slept, I dreamed a dream. I dreamed, and behold I saw a man clothed with rags, standing in a certain place, with his face from his own house, a book in his hand, and a great burden upon his back (Isaiah lxiv.6; Luke xiv.33; Psalms xxxviii.4; Habakkuk ii.2; Acts xvi.31). I looked and saw him open the book and read therein; and, as he read, he wept, and trembled; and not being able longer to contain, he brake out with a lamentable cry, saying, "What shall I do?" (Acts ii.37).

In this <u>plight</u>, therefore, he went home and refrained himself as long as he could, that his wife and children should not perceive his distress; but he could not be silent long, because that his trouble increased. Wherefore at length he brake his mind to his wife and children; and thus he began to talk to them. O my dear wife, said he, and you the children of my bowels, I your dear friend am in myself

---

1. **Similitude.** Allegory

plight (plīt) *n.*, unfortunate situation

undone by reason of a burden that lieth hard upon me; moreover, I am for certain informed that this our city will be burned with fire from heaven, in which fearful overthrow both myself, with thee, my wife, and you, my sweet babes, shall miserably come to ruin, except (the which yet I see not) some way of escape can be found, whereby we may be delivered. At this his relations were sore amazed; not for that they believed that what he had said to them was true, but because they thought that some frenzy distemper[2] had got into his head; therefore, it drawing towards night, and they hoping that sleep might settle his brains, with all haste they got him to bed; but the night was as troublesome to him as the day; wherefore, instead of sleeping, he spent it in sighs and tears. So when the morning was come, they would know how he did. He told them, Worse and worse; he also set to talking to them again, but they began to be hardened. They also thought to drive away his distemper by harsh and surly carriages[3] to him: sometimes they would deride, sometimes they would chide, and sometimes they would quite neglect him. Wherefore he began to retire himself to his chamber, to pray for and pity them, and also to condole his own misery; he would also walk solitarily in the fields, sometimes reading, and sometimes praying; and thus for some days he spent his time.

Now I saw, upon a time, when he was walking in the fields, that he was (as he was wont[4]) reading in this book, and greatly distressed in his mind; and as he read, he burst out, as he had done before, crying, "What shall I do to be saved?"

I saw also that he looked this way and that way, as if he would run; yet he stood still, because (as I perceived) he could not tell which way to go. I looked then, and saw a man named Evangelist[5] coming to him, who asked, Wherefore dost thou cry? (Job xxxiii.23). He answered, Sir, I perceive by the book in my hand that I am condemned to die, and after that to come to judgment (Hebrews ix.27), and I find that I am not willing to do the first (Job xvi.21), nor able to do the second (Ezekiel xxii.14). . . .

Then said Evangelist, Why not willing to die, since this life is attended with so many evils? The man answered, Because I fear that this burden that is upon my back will sink me lower than the grave, and I shall fall into Tophet[6] (Isaiah xxx.33). And, sir, if I be not fit to go to prison, I am not fit to go to judgment, and from thence to execution; and the thoughts of these things make me cry.

Then said Evangelist, If this be thy condition, why standest thou still? He answered, Because I know not whither to go. Then he gave him a parchment roll, and there was written within, "Fly from the wrath to come" (Matthew iii.7).

The man therefore read it, and looking upon Evangelist very carefully,[7] said, Whither must I fly? Then said Evangelist, pointing with his finger over a very wide field, Do you see yonder wicketgate? (Matthew vii.13, 14.) The man said, No. Then said the other, Do you see yonder shining light? (Psalms cxix.105; II Peter i.19.) He said, I think I do. Then said Evangelist, Keep that light in your eye, and go up directly thereto; so shalt thou see the gate; at which when thou knockest it shall be told thee what thou shalt do.

So I saw in my dream that the man began to run. Now, he had not run far from his own door, but his wife and children perceiving it, began to cry after him to return; but the man put his fingers in his ears, and ran on, crying, Life! life! eternal life! (Luke xiv.26.) So he

---

2. **frenzy distemper.** Illness causing madness
3. **carriages.** Behavior
4. **wont.** Accustomed
5. **Evangelist.** One who preaches the Christian Gospel
6. **Tophet.** Name for hell
7. **carefully.** In this context, sorrowfully

looked not behind him, but fled towards the middle of the plain (Genesis xix.17).

The neighbors also came out to see him run (Jeremiah xx.10); and as he ran some mocked, others threatened, and some cried after him to return; and, among those that did so, there were two that resolved to fetch him back by force. The name of the one was Obstinate, and the name of the other Pliable. Now by this time the man was got a good distance from them; but, however, they were resolved to pursue him, which they did, and in a little time they overtook him. Then said the man, Neighbors, wherefore are ye come? They said, To persuade you to go back with us. But he said, That can by no means be; you dwell, said he, in the City of Destruction (the place also where I was born) I see it to be so; and, dying there, sooner or later, you will sink lower than the grave, into a place that burns with fire and brimstone;[8] be content, good neighbors, and go along with me.

OBSTINATE.　What! said Obstinate, and leave our friends and our comforts behind us?

CHRISTIAN.　Yes, said Christian (for that was his name), because that ALL which you shall forsake is not worthy to be compared with a little of that which I am seeking to enjoy (II Corinthians v.17); and, if you will go along with me, and hold it, you shall fare as I myself; for there, where I go, is enough and to spare (Luke xv.17). Come away, and prove my words.

"All which you shall forsake is not worthy to be compared with a little of that which I am seeking to enjoy."

OBSTINATE.　What are the things you seek, since you leave all the world to find them?

CHRISTIAN.　I seek an inheritance incorruptible, undefiled, and that fadeth not away (I Peter i.4), and it is laid up in heaven, and safe there (Hebrews xi.16), to be bestowed, at the time appointed, on them that diligently seek it. Read it so, if you will, in my book.

OBSTINATE.　Tush! said Obstinate, away with your book; will you go back with us or no?

CHRISTIAN.　No, not I, said the other, because I have laid my hand to the plow (Luke ix.62).

OBSTINATE.　Come, then, neighbor Pliable, let us turn again, and go home without him; there is a company of these crazed-headed coxcombs, that, when they take a fancy[9] by the end, are wiser in their own eyes than seven men that can render a reason (Proverbs xxvi.16).

PLIABLE.　Then said Pliable, Don't revile; if what the good Christian says is true, the things he looks after are better than ours; my heart inclines to go with my neighbor.

OBSTINATE.　What! more fools still? Be ruled by me, go back; who knows whither such a brain-sick fellow will lead you? Go back, go back, and be wise.

CHRISTIAN.　Nay, but do thou come with thy neighbor, Pliable; there are such things to be had which I spoke of, and many more glories besides. If you believe not me, read here in this book; and for the truth of what is expressed therein, behold, all is confirmed by the blood of Him that made it (Hebrews ix.17–22; xiii.20).

PLIABLE.　Well, neighbor Obstinate, said Pliable, I begin to come to a point, I intend to go along with this good man, and to cast in my

---

8. **brimstone.** Sulfur; fire and brimstone are associated with hell.
9. **coxcombs . . . fancy.** Fools that become deluded

> **ob • sti • nate** (äb´ stə nət) *adj.,* stubborn; not easily persuaded
> **pli• able** (plī´ ə bəl) *adj.,* yields easily to others
> **in • cor • rupt • i • ble** (in´ kə rup´ tə bəl) *adj.,* incapable of being contaminated or debased
> **un • de • filed** (un də fīld´) *adj.,* unspoiled; honorable
> **re • vile** (ri vīl´) *v.,* subject to verbal abuse

The Tower of Babel

In *The Pilgrim's Progress,* Bunyan alludes to the biblical story of the Tower of Babel (Genesis 11:1–9) when he says the merchants "from one end of the fair to the other . . . seemed barbarians [foreigners speaking different languages] each to the other." This biblical parable attempts to explain why the people of the world speak so many different languages.

In the beginning of the story, all of humanity speaks one language and uses its unified communication to build an enormous tower in the kingdom of Babylon. As this tower looms closer and closer to the kingdom of Heaven, God becomes increasingly enraged, believing people will attempt to challenge his power. In response, God destroys the towering structure and divides people's common language into hundreds of different languages. Doing so effectively ends people's potential challenge to God's

authority. Interestingly, variations of this tale, as well as other well-known biblical tales, also can be found in the Islamic, Aztec, and O'odham literary traditions.

---

lot with him: but, my good companion, do you know the way to this desired place?

CHRISTIAN.   I am directed by a man, whose name is Evangelist, to speed me to a little gate that is before us, where we shall receive instructions about the way.

PLIABLE.   Come, then, good neighbor, let us be going. Then they went both together.

[VANITY FAIR]¹⁰

Then I saw in my dream, that when they were got out of the wilderness, they presently saw a town before them, and the name of that town is Vanity; and at the town there is a fair kept, called Vanity Fair; it is kept all the year long; it beareth the name of Vanity Fair because the town where it is kept is lighter than vanity; and also because all that is there sold, or that cometh thither, is vanity. As is the saying of the wise, "All that cometh is vanity" (Ecclesiastes i.2, 14; ii.11, 17; xi.8; Isaiah xl.17).

This fair is no new-erected business, but a thing of ancient standing; I will show you the original of it.

Almost five thousand years agone, there were pilgrims walking to the Celestial City, as these two honest persons are; and Beelzebub, Apollyon, and Legion,¹¹ with their companions, perceiving by the path that the pilgrims made, that their way to the city lay through this town of Vanity, they <u>contrived</u> here to set up a fair; a fair wherein should be sold all sorts of vanity, and that it should last all the year long. Therefore at this fair are all such merchandise sold, as houses, lands, trades, places, honors, preferments,¹² titles, countries, kingdoms, lusts, pleasures, and delights of all sorts, as whores, bawds, wives, husbands, children, masters,

---

10. **Vanity Fair.** *Vanity* means "excessive pride" or "arrogance." Local fairs were annual events in England. Vanity Fair is an allegory of the corruption of religious life through worldly attractions.

11. **Beelzebub . . . Legion.** Prince of Devils, the Destroyer, and the Unclean Spirit

12. **preferments.** Appointments to political or ecclesiastical positions

---

con • trive (kən trīv´) *v.,* scheme

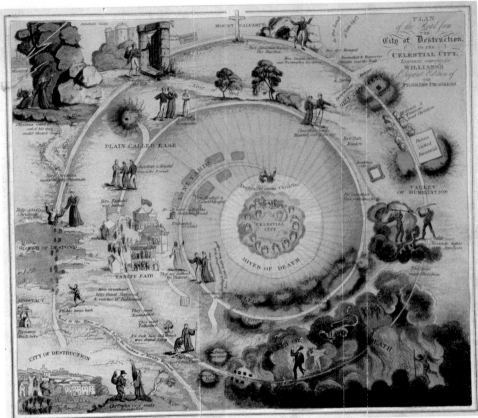

This nineteenth-century engraving shows the spiral road leading from the City of Destruction (bottom left) to the Celestial City (middle). Notice how the road travels through Vanity Fair (middle left).

the ware of Rome and her merchandise[13] is greatly promoted in this fair; only our English nation, with some others, have taken a dislike threat.

Now, as I said, the way to the Celestial City lies just through this town where this lusty fair is kept; and he that will go to the City, and yet not go through this town, must needs "go out of the world" (I Corinthians v.10). The Prince of princes himself, when here, went through this town to his own country, and that upon a fair-day too,[14] yea, and as I think, it was Beelzebub, the chief lord of this fair, that invited him to buy of his vanities; yea, would have made him lord of the fair, would he but have done him reverence as he went through the town. (Matthew iv.8; Luke iv.5–7.) Yea, because he was such a person of honor, Beelzebub had him from street to street, and showed him all the kingdoms of the world in a little time, that he might, if possible, allure the Blessed One to cheapen[15] and buy some of his vanities; but he had no mind to the merchandise, and therefore left the town, without laying out so much as one farthing upon these vani-

servants, lives, blood, bodies, souls, silver, gold, pearls, precious stones, and what not.

And, moreover, at this fair there is at all times to be seen jugglings, cheats, games, plays, fools, apes, knaves, and rogues, and that of every kind.

Here are to be seen, too, and that for nothing, thefts, murders, adulteries, false swearers, and that of a blood-red color.

And as in other fairs of less moment, there are the several rows and streets, under their proper names, where such and such wares are vended; so here likewise you have the proper places, rows, streets (viz., countries and kingdoms), where the wares of this fair are soonest to be found. Here is the Britain Row, the French Row, the Italian Row, the Spanish Row, the German Row, where several sorts of vanities are to be sold. But, as in other fairs, some one commodity is as the chief of all the fair, so

---

13. **Rome . . . merchandise.** Refers to the temporal power of the Roman Catholic Church
14. **Prince . . . too.** Refers to the temptation of Jesus in the wilderness
15. **cheapen.** Ask the price

ties. This fair, therefore, is an ancient thing, of long standing, and a very great fair.

Now these pilgrims, as I said, must needs go through this fair. Well, so they did; but, behold, even as they entered into the fair, all the people in the fair were moved, and the town itself as it were in a hubbub about them; and that for several reasons: for

First, The pilgrims were clothed with such kind of <u>raiment</u> as was diverse from the raiment of any that traded in that fair. The people, therefore, of the fair, made a great gazing upon them: some said they were fools, some they were bedlams, and some they are outlandish men.[16] (I Corinthians ii.7, 8.)

Secondly, And as they wondered at their apparel, so they did likewise at their speech; for few could understand what they said, they naturally spoke the language of Canaan,[17] but they that kept the fair were the men of this world; so that, from one end of the fair to the other, they seemed barbarians each to the other.

Thirdly, But that which did not a little amuse the merchandisers was that these pilgrims set very light by all their wares; they cared not so much as to look upon them; and if they called upon them to buy, they would put their fingers in their ears, and cry, "Turn away mine eyes from beholding vanity," and look upwards, signifying that their trade and traffic was in heaven.(Psalms cxix.37; Philippians iii.19, 20.)

One chanced mockingly, beholding the carriages of the men, to say unto them, What will ye buy? But they, looking gravely upon him, said, "We buy the truth" (Proverbs xxiii.23). At that there was an occasion taken to despise the men the more; some mocking, some taunting, some speaking reproachfully, and some calling upon others to smite[18] them. At last things came to an hubbub and great stir in the fair, insomuch that all order was confounded. Now was word presently brought to the great one of the fair, who quickly came down, and deputed some of his most trusty friends to take these men into examination, about whom the fair was almost overturned. So the men were brought to examination; and they that sat upon them[19] asked them whence they came, whither they went, and what they did there, in such an unusual garb? The men told them that they were pilgrims and strangers in the world, and that they were going to their own country, which was the Heavenly Jerusalem (Hebrews xi.13–16); and that they had given no occasion to the men of the town, nor yet to the merchandisers, thus to abuse them, and to let[20] them in their journey, except it was for that, when one asked them what they would buy, they said they would buy the truth. But they that were appointed to examine them did not believe them to be any other than bedlams and mad, or else such as came to put all things into a confusion in the fair. Therefore they took them and beat them, and besmeared them with dirt, and then put them into the cage, that they might be made a spectacle to all the men of the fair. ❖

---

16. **bedlams . . . outlandish men.** *Bedlams* were lunatics from an insane asylum in London; *outlandish men* were foreigners.
17. **Canaan.** Promised Land
18. **smite.** Strike sharply or heavily
19. **sat upon them.** Questioned and tried them
20. **let.** Hinder

rai • ment (rā´ mənt) *n.,* clothing; garments

When asked to accompany Christian, Obstinate replies, "What! . . . and leave our friends and comforts behind us?" What would you be willing to give up for a cause you strongly believed in?

Refer to Text ▶ ▶ ▶ ▶ ▶ **Reason with Text**

1a. What is the only way to the Celestial City, besides passing through the fair? *die*

1b. What is symbolized by the pilgrims' passage through the ancient fair? *tempation*

Understand
Find meaning

2a. What does Christian tell Obstinate he seeks? *incoruptable inheritance*

2b. Would people today likely set off on a similar journey? Suggest what kind of journey people today might seek.

Apply
Use information

3a. What does Christian do when his family and neighbors beg him to return? How do the pilgrims react to the merchants in Vanity Fair? *puts fingers in ear, ignores them*

3b. Determine what personal characteristics will help Christian and the other pilgrims reach their goal. *steadfast*

Analyze
Take things apart

4a. Who decides to make the pilgrimage with Christian? Who refuses to go? *Pliable; obstinate*

4b. Explain why this person likely decided to go with Christian. *easily swayed*

Evaluate
Make judgments

5a. List the kinds of temptations the fair holds for the pilgrims.

5b. Describe the temptations or trials the pilgrims may have faced in the wilderness before entering the fair.

Create
Bring ideas together

Analyze Literature

Allegory and Point of View

Review the list of allegorical elements you made. Explain what each of these elements represents: Christian, the burden he carries on his back, Evangelist, the wicket gate, the journey to the Celestial City, and Vanity Fair.

Why might Bunyan have decided to use a narrator from outside the story? What does this third-person perspective lend to the story? How might the allegory have been different if Christian had narrated the events?

Extend the Text

Writing Options

Creative Writing Write a short newspaper story describing the pilgrims' experience in Vanity Fair from the point of view of a townsperson. Consider what the pilgrims looked like, how they acted, how they were treated, and so on. Include a quote from a fictional townsperson.

Expository Writing Use a Bible to look up three of the many biblical allusions Bunyan makes in *The Pilgrim's Progress*. Then write a footnote to explain each reference to a modern reader who is not well versed in Christian writings. Provide enough information to help the reader understand the allusion in the context of the selection.

Collaborative Learning

Create a Board Game With a small group, plan a board game that involves taking a journey like that in *The Pilgrim's Progress*. Design a game board that includes places such as Vanity Fair and the Celestial City and characters such as Obstinate and Pliable. Write a set of rules for the game and create any other pieces necessary to play. Then the groups will trade games and play one of the games created by another group. Assign one person from your group to verbally explain the directions to the new players.

Lifelong Learning

Research the Puritan Interregnum The English Puritans overthrew the monarchy and, under Oliver Cromwell, governed the country from 1649 to 1660 during a period known as the *Interregnum*. Work with other students to research the changes to British society during the Interregnum. Produce a skit or video to share your findings with the class.

 Go to **www.mirrorsandwindows.com** for more.

Matsuo Bashō (1644–1694) was the pen name of Matsuo Munefusa, considered by many the greatest Japanese haiku poet. A **haiku** is a traditional Japanese three-line poem containing five syllables in the first line, seven in the second, and five again in the third. A haiku presents a single vivid image, often of nature or the seasons, intended to evoke in the reader a specific emotional or spiritual response.

Influenced by his study of Zen philosophy, Bashō led a simple, reclusive life. He adopted the name *Bashō* from *Bashō-an,* the word for the simple hut in which he lived. *The Narrow Road to the Deep North and Other Travel Sketches,* written in 1694, describes one of the many journeys Bashō took. It has become one of the classics of world literature not only for the beauty of its prose descriptions but also for the lovely verse it contains. Bashō's poetry finds beauty and meaning in the simplest of natural phenomena.

from
— The Narrow Road — to the Deep North
and Other Travel Sketches

by Matsuo Bashō
Translated by Nobuyuki Yuasa

1

God of this mountain,
May you be kind enough
To show me your face
Among the dawning blossoms?

2

Together let us eat
Ears of wheat,
Sharing at night
A grass pillow.

3

Just as a stag's antlers
Are split into tines,
So I must go willy-nilly[1]
Separated from my friend.

4

In the days
Of the ancient gods,
A mere seedling
This pine must have been. ❖

---

1. **willy-nilly.** No matter what; regardless

MIRRORS & WINDOWS

Think of a place that has special meaning for you, whether indoors or outdoors. What three words or phrases would you use to describe the place to someone who has never been there?

Statue of Matsuo Bashō at the Kehi Jingu Shrine in Tsuruga, Japan.

Refer and Reason

1. Identify the main image in each haiku. Which image do you find most vivid or meaningful? Why?

2. In the first haiku, what does the speaker ask of the "God of this mountain"? Infer what this haiku suggests about the relationship between nature and spirituality.

3. In the fourth haiku, what thought does the speaker have upon viewing a pine tree? What kind of person do you envision the speaker to be? Briefly describe him or her.

Writing Options

1. Write a haiku about humans' relationship with nature. Choose a natural object, place, or phenomenon that has meaning for you and to which others likely can relate. Choose words carefully to create a vivid image and convey your theme about the relationship between humans and nature.

2. Write a one-page travelogue chronicling a trip you have taken or would like to take to a natural area, such as a national park or wilderness area. Include vivid images and other sensory details that will help readers share your experience.

Go to **www.mirrorsandwindows.com** for more.

from Gulliver's Travels

A Novel by Jonathan Swift

A Modest Proposal

An Essay by Jonathan Swift

Build Background

Literary Context Jonathan Swift's novel ***Gulliver's Travels*** (1726) is a wicked satire of eighteenth-century British politics. Originally titled *Travels into Several Remote Nations of the World, by Lemuel Gulliver,* the book tells of Gulliver's experiences in four lands. The selection that follows includes excerpts from Part I, "A Voyage to Lilliput," where the people are one-twelfth Gulliver's size and proportionally small minded and petty, and from Part II, "A Voyage to Brobdingnag," where the people are twelve times Gulliver's size and view Europeans as "a pernicious race of little odious vermin."

Swift wrote the satirical essay **"A Modest Proposal"** in 1729 to express his sympathy for the plight of the oppressed Irish peasants and his anger at the English ruling class, whom he faulted for creating that plight. "A Modest Proposal" is the longest-sustained piece of irony in the English language. Many critics have attacked the essay because they have missed Swift's ironic tone.

Reader's Context What are the best and worst qualities of the society in which you live?

Meet the Author

Jonathan Swift (1667–1745), an Englishman, grew up in Dublin, Ireland. His father died before he was born, but a generous uncle funded his education. He earned bachelor's and master's degrees from Trinity College, despite being a marginal and headstrong student.

In 1688, Swift went to England to serve as secretary for Sir William Temple, a position he disliked but nonetheless held for eleven years. Upon returning to Ireland in 1699, Swift rededicated himself to writing—this time writing prose. He produced biting commentaries and satires, reflecting the sentiment that he "liked individuals but hated humanity."

Swift's essays soon became popular in England, and from 1702 to 1714, during the reign of Queen Anne, he was a key figure in London's literary and political worlds. He also served as an official writer for the government, but when the Tories fell out of power with the accession of King George I in 1714, Swift's political writing career in England ended and he returned to Ireland.

Swift suffered a stroke in 1742, after which he was no longer able to care for himself. He died three years later. His self-written epitaph reads "Where fierce indignation no longer tears the heart."

Analyze Literature

Satire and Irony

Satire is humorous writing or speech intended to point out errors, falsehoods, foibles, or failings. It is written for the purpose of reforming human behavior or institutions.

Irony is a difference between appearance and reality.

Set Purpose

Swift once defined *satire* as "a sort of [looking] glass, wherein beholders do generally discover everybody's face but their own." Keep this definition in mind as you read the excerpts from *Gulliver's Travels* and the essay "A Modest Proposal." In reading each selection, determine what elements in society Swift is satirizing and what changes he seems to be recommending. Also consider how Swift's use of irony contributes to the satire. Write down examples of irony from each selection. What is the effect of the use of irony?

Preview Vocabulary

infallibly, 523
confounded, 523
pernicious, 525
impotent, 527
melancholy, 528
prodigious, 529
rudiment, 529
deference, 531
scrupulous, 531
emulation, 533

Gulliver's Travels diorama. St. Patrick's Trian, Armagh, Northern Ireland. (See detail on page 521.)

from Gulliver's Travels

by Jonathan Swift

> "You have clearly proved that ignorance, idleness, and vice are the proper ingredients for qualifying a legislator."

from A Voyage to Lilliput

CHAPTER 5. THE AUTHOR BY AN EXTRAORDINARY STRATAGEM PREVENTS AN INVASION. A HIGH TITLE OF HONOR IS CONFERRED UPON HIM. . . .

The empire of Blefuscu is an island situated to the north north-east side of Lilliput, from whence it is parted only by a channel of eight hundred yards wide. I had not yet seen it, and upon this notice of an intended inva-sion, I avoided appearing on that side of the coast, for fear of being discovered by some of the enemy's ships, who had received no intel-ligence of me; all intercourse between the two empires having been strictly forbidden during the war, upon pain of death; and an embargo[1] laid by our Emperor upon all vessels whatso-ever. I communicated to his Majesty a project I had formed of seizing the enemy's whole fleet;

---

1. **embargo.** Government order prohibiting the entry or departure of ships

which, as our scouts assured us, lay at anchor in the harbor ready to sail with the first fair wind. I consulted the most experienced seamen upon the depth of the channel, which they had often plumbed; who told me, that in the middle at high water it was seventy *glumgluffs* deep, which is about six foot of European measure; and the rest of it fifty *glumgluffs* at most. I walked to the northeast coast over against Blefuscu; where, lying down behind a hillock, I took out my small pocket perspective glass,[2] and viewed the enemy's fleet at anchor, consisting of about fifty men of war, and a great number of transports: I then came back to my house, and gave order (for which I had a warrant) for a great quantity of the strongest cable and bars of iron. The cable was about as thick as packthread, and the bars of the length and size of a knitting-needle. I trebled the cable to make it stronger, and for the same reason I twisted three of the iron bars together, bending the extremities into a hook. Having thus fixed fifty hooks to as many cables, I went back to the northeast coast, and putting off my coat, shoes, and stockings, walked into the sea in my leathern jerkin,[3] about half an hour before high water. I waded with what haste I could, and swam in the middle about thirty yards until I felt the ground; I arrived at the fleet in less than half an hour. The enemy was so frighted when they saw me, that they leaped out of their ships, and swam to shore, where there could not be fewer than thirty thousand souls. I then took my tackling, and fastening a hook to the hole at the prow of each, I tied all the cords together at the end. While I was thus employed, the enemy discharged several thousand arrows, many of which stuck in my hands and face; and besides the excessive smart, gave me much disturbance in my work. My greatest apprehension was for my eyes, which I should have <u>infallibly</u> lost, if I had not suddenly thought of an expedient. I kept, among other little necessaries, a pair of spectacles in a private pocket, which, as I observed before, had escaped the Emperor's searchers. These I

took out, and fastened as strongly as I could upon my nose; and thus armed went on boldly with my work in spite of the enemy's arrows; many of which struck against the glasses of my spectacles, but without any other effect, further than a little to discompose them. I had now fastened all the hooks, and taking the knot in my hand, began to pull; but not a ship would stir, for they were all too fast by their anchors, so that the boldest part of my enterprise remained. I therefore let go the cord, and leaving the hooks fixed to the ships, I resolutely cut with my knife the cables that fastened the anchors, receiving about two hundred shots in my face and hands; then I took up the knotted end of the cables to which my hooks were tied; and with great ease drew fifty of the enemy's largest men-of-war after me.

> The enemy was so frighted when they saw me, that they leaped out of their ships, and swam to shore.

The Blefuscudians, who had not the least imagination of what I intended, were at first <u>confounded</u> with astonishment. They had seen me cut the cables, and thought my design was only to let the ships run adrift, or fall foul on each other: but when they perceived the whole fleet moving in order, and saw me pulling at the end, they set up such a scream of grief and despair, that it is almost impossible to describe or conceive. When I had got out of danger, I stopped a while to pick out the arrows that stuck in my hands and face, and rubbed on some of the same ointment that was given me

---

2. **perspective glass.** Telescope
3. **jerkin.** Vest or sleeveless jacket

---

in • fal • li • bly (in faˊ lə blē) *adv.,* certainly
con • found • ed (kən founˊ dəd) *adj.,* confused

Gulliver in Lilliput captures the invading fleet. Illustration from *Gulliver's Travels* (c. 1800s).

shallower every step I made, I came in a short time within hearing; and holding up the end of the cable by which the fleet was fastened, I cried in a loud voice, Long live the most puissant[4] Emperor of Lilliput! This great prince received me at my landing with all possible encomiums,[5] and created me a *Nardac* upon the spot, which is the highest title of honor among them.

His Majesty desired I would take some other opportunity of bringing all the rest of his enemy's ships into his ports. And so unmeasurable is the ambition of princes, that he seemed to think of nothing less than reducing the whole empire of Blefuscu into a province, and governing it by a viceroy; of destroying the Big-Endian exiles, and compelling that people to break the smaller end of their eggs,[6] by which he would remain sole monarch of the whole world. But I endeavored to divert him from this design, by many arguments drawn from the topics of policy as well as justice: and I plainly protested, that I would never be an instrument of bringing a free and brave people into slavery. And when the matter was debated in council, the wisest part of the ministry were of my opinion.

at my first arrival, as I have formerly mentioned. I then took off my spectacles, and waiting about an hour until the tide was a little fallen, I waded through the middle with my cargo, and arrived safe at the royal port of Lilliput.

The Emperor and his whole court stood on the shore, expecting the issue of this great adventure. They saw the ships move forward in a large half-moon, but could not discern me, who was up to my breast in water. When I advanced to the middle of the channel, they were yet more in pain, because I was under water to my neck. The Emperor concluded me to be drowned, and that the enemy's fleet was approaching in a hostile manner: but he was soon eased of his fears, for the channel growing

> I plainly protested, that I would never be an instrument of bringing a free and brave people into slavery.

This open bold declaration of mine was so opposite to the schemes and politics of his

---

4. **puissant.** Powerful
5. **encomiums.** Expressions of high praise
6. **Big-Endian . . . eggs.** In Chapter 4, Gulliver explains that this dispute started with the emperor's decree that all his subjects must break their eggs at the small end. This dispute is Swift's satiric allegory of the schism between Catholics and Protestants during his time.

Imperial Majesty, that he could never forgive me; he mentioned it in a very artful manner at council, where I was told that some of the wisest appeared, at least by their silence, to be of my opinion; but others, who were my secret enemies, could not forbear some expressions, which by a side-wind[7] reflected on me. And from this time began an intrigue between his Majesty and a junta[8] of ministers maliciously bent against me, which broke out in less than two months, and had like to have ended in my utter destruction. Of so little weight are the greatest services to princes, when put into the balance with a refusal to gratify their passions.

. . .

from A Voyage to Brobdingnag

FROM CHAPTER 6

His Majesty in another audience was at the pains to recapitulate[9] the sum of all I had spoken; compared the questions he made with the answers I had given; then taking me into his hands, and stroking me gently, delivered himself in these words, which I shall never forget, nor the manner he spoke them in. "My little friend Grildrig, you have made a most admirable panegyric[10] upon your country. You have clearly proved that ignorance, idleness, and vice are the proper ingredients for qualifying a legislator. That laws are best explained, interpreted, and applied by those whose interests and abilities lie in perverting,[11] confounding, and eluding them. I observe among you some lines of an institution which in its original might have been tolerable; but these half erased, and the rest wholly blurred and blotted by corruptions. It doth not appear from all you have said how any one virtue is required towards the procurement of any one station among you; much less that men are ennobled on account of their virtue, that priests are advanced for their piety or learning, soldiers for their conduct or valor, judges for their integrity, senators for the love of their country, or

"Laws are best explained, interpreted, and applied by those whose interests and abilities lie in perverting, confounding, and eluding them."

counselors for their wisdom. As for yourself," continued the King, "who have spent the greatest part of your life in traveling, I am well disposed to hope you may hitherto have escaped many vices of your country. But by what I have gathered from your own relation, and the answers I have with much pains wringed and extorted from you, I cannot but conclude the bulk of your natives to be the most <u>pernicious</u> race of little odious vermin that nature ever suffered to crawl upon the surface of the earth."

. . .

FROM CHAPTER 7

In hopes to ingratiate myself farther into his Majesty's favor, I told him of an invention discovered between three and four hundred years ago, to make a certain powder, into an heap of which the smallest spark of fire falling would kindle the whole in a moment, although it were as big as a mountain, and make it all fly up in the air together, with a noise and agitation greater than thunder. That a proper quantity of this powder rammed into an hollow tube of brass or iron, according to its bigness, would drive a ball of iron or lead with such violence and speed as nothing was able to sustain its

---

7. **side-wind.** Indirect means, method, or manner
8. **junta.** Council
9. **recapitulate.** Summarize
10. **panegyric.** High praise
11. **perverting.** Distorting; misinterpreting

per • ni • cious (pər niˊ shəs) *adj.,* wicked

Interior of a School for Orphan Girls, 1850. François Bonvin.
Musée St. Didier, Langres, France.

age they will not yield above three pounds, or three pounds and half a crown at most on the Exchange; which cannot turn to account either to the parents or the kingdom, the charge of nutriment and rags having been at least four times that value.

I shall now therefore humbly propose my own thoughts, which I hope will not be liable to the least objection.

I have been assured by a very knowing American of my acquaintance in London, that a young healthy child well nursed is at a year old a most delicious, nourishing, and whole-some food, whether stewed, roasted, baked, or boiled; and I make no doubt that it will equally serve in a fricassee or a ragout.

I do therefore humbly offer it to public consideration that of the hundred and twenty thousand children, already computed, twenty thousand may be reserved for breed, whereof only one fourth part to be males, which is more than we allow to sheep, black cattle, or swine; and my reason is that these children are seldom the fruits of marriage, a circumstance not much regarded by our savages, there-fore one male will be sufficient to serve four females. That the remaining hundred thousand may at a year old be offered in sale to the per-sons of quality and fortune through the king-dom, always advising the mother to let them suck plentifully in the last month, so as to render them plump and fat for a good table. A child will make two dishes at an entertainment for friends; and when the family dines alone, the fore or hind quarter will make a reason-able dish, and seasoned with a little pepper or salt will be very good boiled on the fourth day, especially in winter.

[handwritten annotations: "stock breeding", "meant to be offensive and dehumanizing", "Ironic"]

A child will make two dishes at an entertainment for friends.

I have reckoned upon a medium that a child just born will weigh twelve pounds, and in a solar year if tolerably nursed increaseth to twenty-eight pounds.

[handwritten: not average tells us this is Fishy and Fantasy]

I grant this food will be somewhat dear, and therefore very proper for landlords, who, as they have already devoured most of the parents, seem to have the best title to the children.

[handwritten: irony overcomes the person]

[handwritten: hunt the teenagers]

Infant's flesh will be in season throughout the year, but more plentiful in March, and a little before and after. For we are told by a grave author, an eminent French physician,[6] that fish being a prolific diet, there are more children born in Roman Catholic countries about nine months after Lent than at any other season; therefore, reckoning a year after Lent, the markets will be more glutted than usual, because the number of popish infants is at least three to one in this kingdom; and therefore it will have one other collateral advantage, by lessening the number of Papists among us.

I have already computed the charge of nursing a beggar's child (in which list I reckon all cottagers, laborers, and four fifths of the farmers) to be about two shillings per annum, rags included; and I believe no gentleman would repine to give ten shillings for the carcass of a good fat child, which, as I have said, will make four dishes of excellent nutritive meat, when he hath only some particular friend or his own family to dine with him. Thus the squire will learn to be a good landlord, and grow popular among the tenants; the mother will have eight shillings net profit, and be fit for the work till she produces another child.

Those who are more thrifty (as I must confess the times require) may flay the carcass; the skin of which artificially dressed will make admirable gloves for ladies, and summer boots for fine gentlemen.

As to our city of Dublin, shambles[7] may be appointed for this purpose in the most convenient parts of it, and butchers we may be assured will not be wanting; although I rather recommend buying the children alive, and dressing them hot from the knife as we do roasting pigs.

A very worthy person, a true lover of his country, and whose virtues I highly esteem, was lately pleased in discoursing on this matter to offer a refinement upon my scheme. He said that many gentlemen of this kingdom, having of late destroyed their deer, he conceived that the want of venison might be well supplied by the bodies of young lads and maidens, not exceeding fourteen years of age nor under twelve, so great a number of both sexes in every county being now ready to starve for want of work and service; and these to be disposed of by their parents, if alive, or otherwise by their nearest relations. But with due deference to so excellent a friend and so deserving a patriot, I cannot be altogether in his sentiments; for as to the males, my American acquaintance assured me from frequent experience that their flesh was generally tough and lean, like that of our schoolboys, by continual exercise, and their taste disagreeable; and to fatten them would not answer the charge. Then as to the females, it would, I think with humble submission, be a loss to the public, because they soon would become breeders themselves; and besides, it is not improbable that some scrupulous people might be apt to censure such a practice (although indeed very unjustly) as a little bordering upon cruelty; which I confess, hath always been with me the strongest objection against any project, how well soever intended.

---

6. **grave . . . physician.** Refers to François Rabelais, a French satirist
7. **shambles.** Slaughterhouses

---

def • er • ence (de´ fə rən[t]s) *n.*, respect for an elder or superior
scru • pu • lous (skrü´ pyə ləs) *adj.*, possessing moral integrity, upright

But in order to justify my friend, he confessed that this expedient was put into his head by the famous Psalmanazar,[8] a native of the island Formosa, who came from thence to London above twenty years ago, and in conversation told my friend that in his country when any young person happened to be put to death, the executioner sold the carcass to persons of quality as a prime dainty; and that in his time the body of a plump girl of fifteen, who was crucified for an attempt to poison the emperor, was sold to his Imperial Majesty's prime minister of state, and other great mandarins of the court,[9] in joints from the gibbet,[10] at four hundred crowns. Neither indeed can I deny that if the same use were made of several plump young girls in this town, who without one single groat to their fortunes cannot stir abroad without a chair, and appear at the playhouse and assemblies in foreign fineries which they never will pay for, the kingdom would not be the worse.

Irony
Don't worry about the cripples, they are dying fast enough

Some persons of a desponding[11] spirit are in great concern about that vast number of poor people who are aged, diseased, or maimed, and I have been desired to employ my thoughts what course may be taken to ease the nation of so grievous an encumbrance. But I am not in the least pain upon that matter, because it is very well known that they are every day dying and rotting by cold and famine, and filth and vermin, as fast as can be reasonably expected. And as to the younger laborers, they are now in almost as hopeful a condition. They cannot get work, and consequently pine away for want of nourishment to a degree that if at any time they are accidentally hired to common labor, they have not strength to perform it; and thus the country and themselves are happily delivered from the evils to come.

I have too long digressed, and therefore shall return to my subject. I think the advantages by the proposal which I have made are obvious and many, as well as of the highest importance.

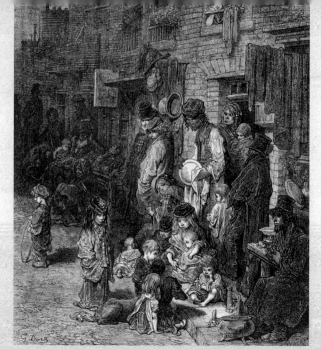

Wentworth Street, Whitechapel, 1872. Gustave Doré.

Cut down on Catholic population

For first, as I have already observed, it would greatly lessen the number of Papists, with whom we are yearly overrun, being the principal breeders of the nation as well as our most dangerous enemies; and who stay at home on purpose to deliver the kingdom to the Pretender, hoping to take their advantage by the absence of so many good Protestants, who have chosen rather to leave their country than stay at home and pay tithes against their conscience to an Episcopal curate.

Secondly, the poorer tenants will have something valuable of their own, which by law may be made liable to distress, and help to pay their landlord's rent, their corn and cattle being already seized and money a thing unknown.

can sell the baby

Thirdly, whereas the maintenance of an hundred thousand children, from two years old and upwards, cannot be computed at less than

help the economy

---

8. **Psalmanazar.** George Psalmanazar was a famous imposter; he was a Frenchman who pretended to be a Formosan and wrote fictitious accounts of Formosa (now Taiwan) in which he describes human sacrifices and cannibalism.
9. **great . . . court.** Powerful officials
10. **gibbet.** Gallows
11. **desponding.** Despairing

ten shillings a piece per annum, the nation's stock will be thereby increased fifty thousand pounds per annum, besides the profit of a new dish introduced to the tables of all gentlemen of fortune in the kingdom who have any refinement in taste. And the money will circulate among ourselves, the goods being entirely of our own growth and manufacture.

Fourthly, the constant breeders, besides the gain of eight shillings sterling per annum by the sale of their children, will be rid of the charge of maintaining them after the first year.

Fifthly, this food would likewise bring great custom to taverns, where the vintners will certainly be so prudent as to procure the best receipts for dressing it to perfection, and consequently have their houses frequented by all the fine gentlemen, who justly value themselves upon their knowledge in good eating; and a skillful cook, who understands how to oblige his guests, will contrive to make it as expensive as they please.

Sixthly, this would be a great inducement to marriage, which all wise nations have either encouraged by rewards or enforced by laws and penalties. It would increase the care and tenderness of mothers toward their children, when they were sure of a settlement for life to the poor babes, provided in some sort by the public, to their annual profit instead of expense. We should see an honest <u>emulation</u> among the married women, which of them could bring the fattest child to the market. Men would become as fond of their wives during the time of their pregnancy as they are now of their mares in foal, their cows in calf, or sows when they are ready to farrow; nor offer to beat or kick them (as is too frequent a practice) for fear of a miscarriage.

Many other advantages might be enumerated. For instance, the addition of some thousand carcasses in our exportation of barreled beef, the propagation of swine's flesh, and improvement in the art of making good bacon, so much wanted among us by the great destruction of pigs, too frequent at our tables, which are no way comparable in taste or magnificence to a well-grown, fat, yearling child, which roasted whole will make a considerable figure at a lord mayor's feast or any other public entertainment. But this and many others I omit, being studious of brevity.

Supposing that one thousand families in this city would be constant customers for infants' flesh, besides others who might have it at merry meetings, particularly weddings and christenings, I compute that Dublin would take off annually about twenty thousand carcasses, and the rest of the kingdom (where probably they will be sold somewhat cheaper) the remaining eighty thousand.

I can think of no one objection that will probably be raised against this proposal, unless it should be urged that the number of people will be thereby much lessened in the kingdom. This I freely own, and it was indeed one principal design in offering it to the world. I desire the reader will observe, that I calculate my remedy for this one individual kingdom of Ireland and for no other that ever was, is, or I think ever can be upon earth. Therefore let no man talk to me of other expedients: of taxing our absentees at five shillings a pound: of using neither clothes nor household furniture except what is of our own growth and manufacture: of utterly rejecting the materials and instruments that promote foreign luxury: of curing the expensiveness of pride, vanity, idleness, and gaming in our women: of introducing a vein of parsimony,[12] prudence, and temperance: of learning to love our country, in the want of which we differ even from Laplanders and the inhabitants of Topinamboo:[13] of quitting our animosities

---

12. **parsimony.** Thriftiness; stinginess
13. **in learning to love our country . . . Topinamboo.** The Anglo-Irish do not love Ireland the way the Laplanders love their frozen land or the Topinamboo love the wild jungles of Brazil.

em • u • la • tion (em′ yə lā′ shən) *n.,* imitation

and factions, nor acting any longer like the Jews, who were murdering one another at the very moment their city was taken:[14] of being a little cautious not to sell our country and conscience for nothing: of teaching landlords to have at least one degree of mercy toward their tenants: lastly, of putting a spirit of honesty, industry, and skill into our shopkeepers; who, if a resolution could now be taken to buy only our native goods, would immediately unite to cheat and exact upon us in the price, the measure, and the goodness, nor could ever yet be brought to make one fair proposal of just dealing, though often and earnestly invited to it.[15]

Swift's own opinion

Therefore I repeat, let no man talk to me of these and the like expedients, till he hath at least some glimpse of hope that there will ever be some hearty and sincere attempt to put them in practice.

But as to myself, having been wearied out for many years with offering vain, idle, visionary thoughts, and at length utterly despairing of success, I fortunately fell upon this proposal, which, as it is wholly new, so it hath something solid and real, of no expense and little trouble, full in our own power, and whereby we can incur no danger in disobliging England. For this kind of commodity will not bear exportation, the flesh being of too tender a consistence to admit a long continuance in salt, although perhaps I could name a country which would be glad to eat up our whole nation without it.

After all, I am not so violently bent upon my own opinion as to reject any offer proposed by wise men, which shall be found equally innocent, cheap, easy, and effectual. But before something of that kind shall be advanced in contradiction to my scheme, and offering a better, I desire the author or authors will be pleased maturely to consider two points. First,

as things now stand, how they will be able to find food and raiment for an hundred thousand useless mouths and backs. And secondly, there being a round million of creatures in human figure throughout this kingdom, whose sole subsistence put into a common stock would leave them in debt two millions of pounds sterling, adding those who are beggars by profession to the bulk of farmers, cottagers, and laborers, with their wives and children who are beggars in effect; I desire those politicians who dislike my overture, and may perhaps be so bold to attempt an answer, that they will first ask the parents of these mortals whether they would not at this day think it a great happiness to have been sold for food at a year old in the manner I prescribe, and thereby have avoided such a perpetual sense of misfortunes as they have since gone through by the oppression of landlords, the impossibility of paying rent without money or trade, the want of common sustenance, with neither house nor clothes to cover them from the inclemencies of the weather, and the most inevitable prospect of entailing the like or greater miseries upon their breed forever.

I profess, in the sincerity of my heart, that I have not the least personal interest in endeavoring to promote this necessary work, having no other motive than the public good of my country, by advancing our trade, providing for infants, relieving the poor, and giving some pleasure to the rich. I have no children by which I can propose to get a single penny; the youngest being nine years old, and my wife past childbearing. ❖

---

14. **Jews . . . taken.** Fighting factions of Jews destroyed Jerusalem during the siege by the Roman emperor Titus in 70 CE.
15. **being . . . to it.** These are all proposals Swift had made in pamphlets.

MIRRORS & WINDOWS

Is satire an appropriate means of dealing with a serious issue? Can it be effective in promoting social change?

Refer to Text ▶ ▶ ▶ ▶ ▶   Reason with Text

1a. Define the problem Swift is trying to solve in "A Modest Proposal." What does he propose?	**1b.** Discuss what the proposal suggests about the attitudes of the English to the plight of the Irish.	**Understand** Find meaning
2a. According to the Brobdingnagian King in *Gulliver's Travels,* what are the qualifications of a legislator? What is the proper purpose of government?	**2b.** Does Gulliver feel more at home politically in Lilliput or Brobdingnag? What would he likely think of modern American politics?	**Apply** Use information
3a. Give examples to show how the Lilliputians are small and the Brobdingnagians are large.	**3b.** Infer why Swift plays with size in this way.	**Analyze** Take things apart
4a. In "A Modest Proposal," what are the six arguments Swift makes to support his view?	**4b.** Evaluate Swift's proposal in terms of both its logical and emotional appeals.	**Evaluate** Make judgments
5a. What one objection does Swift say can be made about his proposal?	**5b.** What other objections might people raise? How might the Lilliputian Emperor and Brobdingnagian King react to Swift's proposal?	**Create** Bring ideas together

Analyze Literature

Satire and Irony
What aspects of society does Swift satirize in the excerpts from *Gulliver's Travels?* Whom does he satirize in "A Modest Proposal"? What changes does he want to bring about in British society?

How is the Brobdingnagian King being ironic when he says to Gulliver, "You have made a most admirable panegyric upon your country"? Explain two other examples of irony from each selection. Discuss how the use of irony contributes to Swift's satiric purpose.

Extend the Text

Writing Options
Creative Writing Imagine that you are writing a continuation of *Gulliver's Travels* for a modern audience. Choose some fault of modern society, and satirize it using a fictitious land and people. Write a scene describing this land and its people and how Gulliver interacts with them.

Expository Writing Write an essay analyzing Swift's use of satire and irony in *Gulliver's Travels* and "A Modest Proposal." Using examples from both selections, explain how Swift uses irony to create satire. Also evaluate the effectiveness of each satire in bringing attention to a social problem.

Lifelong Learning
Write a Problem/Solution Essay Although well known as a satire, "A Modest Proposal" is actually a problem/solution essay, because it identifies a problem and

presents a possible solution. Identify a problem in your school and write a short problem/solution essay for the school or local newspaper. Consider your audience and purpose when deciding the tone and details. Also address questions or issues your audience may have.

Media Literacy
Explore Contemporary Satire You will find satirical commentaries on social and political issues in a variety of media today. View episodes of satirical shows, such as *The Simpsons* or *The Daily Show*, or read several modern satirical articles, perhaps from *The Onion*. Then, with several classmates, connect these works to "A Modest Proposal." Analyze elements such as theme, tone, and purpose, and support your response with textual evidence (see "Draft Your Body," page 1269, for information).

 Go to **www.mirrorsandwindows.com** for more.

1. In which of the following quotations from *Gulliver's Travels* does Gulliver seem to be speaking on behalf of Swift?
   A. "I communicated to his Majesty a project I had formed of seizing the enemy's whole fleet, which, as our scouts assured us, lay at anchor in the harbor ready to sail with the first fair wind."
   B. "While I was thus employed, the enemy discharged several thousand arrows, many of which stuck in my hands and face; and besides the excessive smart, gave me much disturbance in my work."
   C. "This great prince received me at my landing with all possible encomiums, and created me a *Nardac* upon the spot, which is the highest title of honor among them."
   D. "Of so little weight are the greatest services to princes, when put into the balance with a refusal to gratify their passions."
   E. "Thus I humbly offered to his Majesty as a small tribute of acknowledgement in return of so many marks that I had received of his royal favor and protection."

2. What is significant about the physical size of the King of the Brobdingnag?
   A. He is small, which suggests he is secretive and selfish.
   B. He is large, which suggests he is slow and clumsy.
   C. He is small, which suggests he is agile and fast.
   D. He is large, which suggests he is compassionate and generous.
   E. He is large, which suggests he is ruthless and ambitious.

3. In "A Modest Proposal," what social problem is Swift trying to solve?
   A. people refusing to pay taxes
   B. corruption of Irish politicians
   C. people's lack of charity
   D. political instability in Ireland
   E. the existence of too many poor children

4. What does Swift propose to solve this problem?
   A. selling babies as meat
   B. making young children work
   C. expelling English landlords from Ireland
   D. giving food to the poor
   E. distributing the wealth more evenly

5. What is the first hint in "A Modest Proposal" that Swift is not being serious?
   A. use of the word *Modest* in the title
   B. the section in all capital letters at the beginning
   C. the words *great* and *dear* in the first paragraph
   D. the description in paragraph 9 that "a young healthy child is . . . a most delicious, nourishing and wholesome food"
   E. the details in paragraph 9 about cooking children: "whether stewed, roasted, baked, or boiled; and I make no doubt that it will equally serve in a fricassee or a ragout"

6. In "A Modest Proposal," toward whom in particular does Swift seem bitter?
   A. women
   B. children
   C. the poor
   D. the nobility
   E. landlords

7. In "A Modest Proposal" what does Swift mean by the phrase "a child just dropped by its dam"?
   A. a newborn child
   B. a baby animal
   C. an abused child
   D. a child who has fallen
   E. a nearly drowned child

8. The vocabulary words *pernicious* and *prodigious* both contain the adjective suffix *-ious*, originating from Old French. Adjective suffixes are added to nouns to form descriptive adjectives. Choose the best set of definitions for these words as they are used in the selections.
   A. *pernicious*—anxious; *prodigious*—probing
   B. *pernicious*—lighthearted; *prodigious*—stable
   C. *pernicious*—harmful; *prodigious*—sizeable
   D. *pernicious*—beneficial; *prodigious*—insignificant
   E. *pernicious*—generous; *prodigious*—foreboding

9. **Constructed Response:** Compare and contrast the Emperor of Lilliput with the King of Brobdingnag in *Gulliver's Travels*. Address the physical qualities of these rulers as well as their social and political beliefs. What does Swift find to satirize about each one?

10. **Constructed Response:** In "A Modest Proposal," Swift never quite directly states his whole proposal but rather reveals bits of it here and there. Analyze his purpose in doing so. How does this technique affect your understanding of and reaction to the proposal he makes?

Understand the Concept

Most fields of study and lines of work have terms specific to their topics and practices. For example, in studying political science or history, you will encounter many terms related to government. You also may see or hear some of these terms in the news, in historical fiction, or in documentaries related to these fields. Because Swift's *Gulliver's Travels* is a political satire, you encountered several terms from politics and history in your reading.

Words enter English through many channels. They may be adopted from other languages, made by combining common words or word parts, or shortened from other words. Most dictionaries provide information about how a word entered English, which is called the **etymology.** Consider these examples:

Word	How It Entered the Language
czar	From another language: Russian for *tsar*
bicameral	Combines prefix *bi-*, meaning "two," and Latin word for *room*
pol	Shortened from word *politician*

A dictionary also can help you understand the meaning of a new word, but often, you can get the meaning without looking up the definition. When you encounter a new word, you can use context clues and word parts to help you understand its meaning. Knowing these word parts may help you understand political terms:

Word Part	Meaning	Example
capit	head	capital
crac, crat	power	democratic
mand, mend	entrust or order	mandate
polis, polit	city	policy, politicize

Apply the Skill

Exercise A

Determine the meaning of each of the following underlined words based on context clues and the word's affixes. Then use a dictionary to clarify the meaning and identify the etymology (origin) of each word and affix.

1. According to recent news reports, the ruler has rejected the advice of his junta.

2. An oligarchy of nobles took over the country to preserve their land rights and other powers.
3. Because of the grain embargo, many farmers could not sell their crops abroad.
4. The people revolted to depose the despot, but the next leader also was a tyrant.
5. The gubernatorial debates gave the candidates who hoped to lead the state a chance to share their positions.

Exercise B

Use context clues, word parts, and prior knowledge to find the meanings of these underlined terms from *Gulliver's Travels.* Write a definition for each word that could be used in the glossary of a book about history or politics.

1. The empire of Blefuscu is an island situated to the north north-east side of Lilliput.
2. He seemed to think nothing less than reducing the whole empire of Blefuscu into a province.
3. Twenty or thirty of which tubes, charted with the proper quantity of powder and balls, would batter down the walls of the strongest town in his dominion.

SPELLING PRACTICE

Words Ending in -able/-ible

Adding suffixes to words sometimes complicates their spelling, as is the case with -able and -ible, both of which mean "capable or worthy of." The general rule is to use -able with whole words and -ible with word parts—for instance, *prefer* + -able = *preferable* and *vis* + -ible = *visible*. However, there are many exceptions to this rule, such as *capable*. Familiarize yourself with the spellings and meanings of these words from *Gulliver's Travels* and "A Modest Proposal."

admirable	infallible
comparable	inevitable
deplorable	reasonable
disagreeable	sensible
impossible	tolerable
improbable	valuable

The Age of Absolutism

Philosophers during the Enlightenment Period thought about issues such as the rights of individuals and social contracts between people and rulers to maintain order in society. These ideas influenced European monarchs and emperors. While England decreased the power of monarchs after the execution of Charles I in the mid-seventeenth century, other places in Europe saw an increase in the power of monarchs. These rulers, sometimes referred to as *Enlightened Absolutists,* became concerned with making their countries better places to live.

Leaders such as Frederick II of Prussia and Charles III of Spain chose to modernize their countries' infrastructures (roadways, utilities, and so on). Doing so bolstered the nation's economy and increased the citizens' quality of life. Tired of constant religious feuding, some leaders initiated reforms to prevent hysteria. For example, Maria Theresa of Austria outlawed witch burning and torture. Some rulers invested more heavily in the arts than their predecessors had. Catherine the Great of Russia became famous for her generous donations to museums and artistic circles.

Virtually every Absolutist, however, remained uninterested in political reform. Most believed that their subjects were incapable of making political decisions and that instituting any form of representative government ultimately would condemn the state. Moreover, these rulers believed in the divine right of kings and did not want their subjects to interfere with their power. When Russian intellectuals proposed governing by an elected assembly, Catherine the Great famously told them they were dreaming of "castles in the air." In sum, while the Enlightened Absolutists encouraged reforms that propelled their countries forward, many of their ideas about power and government remained entrenched in traditional beliefs and policies.

Catherine the Great.

CHAPTER II

WHAT HAPPENED TO CANDIDE
AMONG THE BULGARIANS

Candide, expelled from the earthly paradise, wandered for a long time without knowing where he was going, turning up his eyes to Heaven, gazing back frequently at the noblest of castles which held the most beautiful of young Baronesses; he lay down to sleep supperless between two furrows[9] in the open fields; it snowed heavily in large flakes. The next morning the shivering Candide, penniless, dying of cold and exhaustion, dragged himself towards the neighboring town, which was called Waldberghoff-trarbk-dikdorff. He halted sadly at the door of an inn. Two men dressed in blue noticed him. "Comrade," said one, "there's a well-built young man of the right height." They went up to Candide and very civilly invited him to dinner. "Gentlemen," said Candide with charming modesty, "you do me a great honor, but I have no money to pay my share." "Ah, sir," said one of the men in blue, "persons of your figure and merit never pay anything; are you not five feet five tall?" "Yes, gentlemen," said he, bowing, "that is my height." "Ah, sir, come to table; we will not only pay your expenses, we will never allow a man like you to be short of money; men were only made to help each other." "You are in

---

9. **furrow.** Groove in the earth made by a plow

the right," said Candide, "that is what Doctor Pangloss was always telling me, and I see that everything is for the best." They begged him to accept a few crowns, he took them and wished to give them an IOU; they refused to take it and all sat down to table. "Do you not love tenderly . . ." "Oh, yes," said he. "I love Mademoiselle Cunegonde tenderly." "No," said one of the gentlemen. "We were asking if you do not tenderly love the King of the Bulgarians." "Not a bit," said he, "for I have never seen him." "What! He is the most charming of Kings, and you must drink his health." "Oh, gladly, gentlemen." And he drank. "That is sufficient," he was told. "You are now the support, the aid, the defender, the hero of the Bulgarians; your fortune is made and your glory assured." They immediately put irons on his legs and took him to a regiment.[10] He was made to turn to the right and left, to raise the ramrod[11] and return the ramrod, to take aim, to fire, to double up, and he was given thirty strokes with a stick; the next day he drilled not quite so badly, and received only twenty strokes; the day after, he only had ten and was looked on as a prodigy[12] by his comrades. Candide was completely mystified and could not make out how he was a hero. One fine spring day he thought he would take a walk, going straight ahead, in the belief that to use his legs as he pleased was a privilege of the human species as well as of animals. He had not gone two leagues when four other heroes, each six feet tall, fell upon him, bound him and dragged him back to a cell. He was asked by his judges whether he would rather be thrashed thirty-six times by the whole regiment or receive a dozen lead bullets at once in his brain. Although he protested that men's wills are free and that he wanted neither one nor the other, he had to make a choice; by virtue of that gift of God which is called *liberty,* he determined to run the gauntlet[13] thirty-six times and actually did so twice. There were two thousand men in the regiment. That made four thousand strokes which laid

Candide was completely mystified and could not make out how he was a hero.

bare the muscles and nerves from his neck to his backside. As they were about to proceed to a third turn, Candide, utterly exhausted, begged as a favor that they would be so kind as to smash his head; he obtained this favor; they bound his eyes and he was made to kneel down. At that moment the King of the Bulgarians came by and inquired the victim's crime; and as this King was possessed of a vast genius, he perceived from what he learned about Candide that he was a young metaphysician[14] very ignorant in worldly matters, and therefore pardoned him with a clemency[15] which will be praised in all newspapers and all ages. An honest surgeon healed Candide in three weeks with the ointments recommended by Dioscorides. He had already regained a little skin and could walk when the King of the Bulgarians went to war with the King of the Abares.[16]

CHAPTER III

HOW CANDIDE ESCAPED FROM THE BULGARIANS
AND WHAT BECAME OF HIM

Nothing could be smarter, more splendid, more brilliant, better drawn up than the two armies. Trumpets, fifes, hautboys, drums, cannons, formed a harmony such as has never

---

10. **regiment.** Unit of soldiers
11. **ramrod.** Poker used for loading a muzzle-loaded rifle
12. **prodigy.** Person with talent or genius
13. **run the gauntlet.** Face an ordeal, in this case passing by soldiers, each of whom will strike him
14. **metaphysician.** One who studies the branch of philosophy that deals with ultimate realities and the nature of being
15. **clemency.** Leniency, mercy
16. **Bulgarians . . . Abares.** Voltaire's Bulgarians and Abarians represent, respectively, the Prussians under Frederick the Great and the French.

been heard even in hell. The cannons first of all laid flat about six thousand men on each side; then the musketry removed from the best of worlds some nine or ten thousand blackguards[17] who infested its surface. The bayonet also was the sufficient reason for the death of some thousands of men. The whole might amount to thirty thousand souls. Candide, who trembled like a philosopher, hid himself as well as he could during this heroic butchery. At last, while the two Kings each commanded a Te Deum[18] in his camp, Candide decided to go elsewhere to reason about effects and causes. He clambered over heaps of dead and dying men and reached a neighboring village, which was in ashes; it was an Abare village which the Bulgarians had burned in accordance with international law.

. . .

Candide fled to another village as fast as he could; it belonged to the Bulgarians, and Abarian heroes had treated it in the same way. Candide, stumbling over quivering limbs or across ruins, at last escaped from the theatre of war,

carrying a little food in his knapsack, and never forgetting Mademoiselle Cunegonde. His provisions were all gone when he reached Holland; but, having heard that everyone in that country was rich and a Christian, he had no doubt at all but that he would be as well treated as he had been in the Baron's castle before he had been expelled on account of Mademoiselle Cunegonde's pretty eyes. He asked an alms of several grave persons, who all replied that if he continued in that way he would be shut up in a house of correction to teach him how to live. He then addressed himself to a man who had been discoursing on charity in a large assembly for an hour on end. This orator, glancing at him askance, said: "What are you doing here? Are you for the good cause?" "There is no effect without a cause," said Candide modestly. "Everything is necessarily linked up and arranged for the best. It was necessary that I should be expelled from the company of Mademoiselle Cunegonde, that I ran the gauntlet, and that I beg my bread until I can earn it; all this could not have happened differently." "My friend," said the orator, "do you believe that the Pope is Anti-Christ?" "I had never heard so before," said Candide, "but whether he is or isn't, I am starving." "You don't deserve to eat," said the other. "Hence, rascal; hence, you wretch; and never come near me again." The orator's wife thrust her head out of the window and seeing a man who did not believe that the Pope was Anti-Christ, she poured on his head

"Everything is necessarily linked up and arranged for the best."

17. **blackguards.** Scoundrels or villains
18. **Te Deum.** Hymn of thanksgiving

a full . . . O Heavens! To what excess religious zeal is carried by ladies! A man who had not been baptized, an honest Anabaptist[19] named Jacques, saw the cruel and ignominious treatment of one of his brothers, a featherless two-legged creature with a soul; he took him home, cleaned him up, gave him bread and beer, presented him with two florins,[20] and even offered to teach him to work at the manufacture of Persian stuffs which are made in Holland. Candide threw himself at the man's feet, exclaiming: "Doctor Pangloss was right in telling me that all is for the best in this world, for I am vastly more touched by your extreme generosity than by the harshness of the gentleman in the black cloak and his good lady." The next day when he walked out he met a beggar covered with sores, dull-eyed, with the end of his nose fallen away, his mouth awry, his teeth black, who talked huskily, was tormented with a violent cough and spat out a tooth at every cough.

CHAPTER IV

HOW CANDIDE MET HIS OLD MASTER IN PHILOSOPHY, DOCTOR PANGLOSS, AND WHAT HAPPENED

Candide, moved even more by compassion than by horror, gave this horrible beggar the two florins he had received from the honest Anabaptist, Jacques. The phantom gazed fixedly at him, shed tears and threw its arms round his neck. Candide recoiled in terror. "Alas!" said the wretch to the other wretch, "don't you recognize your dear Pangloss?" ❖

---

19. **Anabaptist.** Member of a radical Protestant sect that opposed infant baptism
20. **florins.** Coins

 Candide is taught that "everything is necessarily for the best end." What are the advantages of having such an accepting, optimistic outlook? What might be the disadvantages?

Refer and Reason

1. List three unfortunate events that befall Candide. How does this evidence contradict the idea that all things are connected in a series of causes and effects to create "the best of all possible worlds"?

2. In Chapter II, how does Candide explain his actions to the Bulgarians? What is the result? What does this suggest about Candide's life philosophy?

3. Summarize Pangloss's philosophy about the nature of things. In which ways are his ideas positive? In which ways are they dangerous?

Writing Options

1. Make a comic strip of Candide's adventures. You may focus on one event, such as his conscription into the army or his interchange with the orator, or you may create a longer strip that shows his story from expulsion to meeting Pangloss again. Use captions and speech bubbles to convey what happens to him.

2. Finish the dialogue you imagine would take place between Candide and Pangloss. Imagine that your dialogue would be read by readers of *Candide*. What would Candide have to say to his old teacher? What would he tell Pangloss about his experiences since they last saw one another? What would Pangloss have to say about Candide's current state?

 Go to **www.mirrorsandwindows.com** for more.

from **The Rape of the Lock**
from **An Essay on Man**
Poems by Alexander Pope

Build Background

Literary Context *The Rape of the Lock: An Heroi-Comical Poem* is based on a quarrel between two families that erupted when a lord cut off a lock of hair from a young woman. Pope wrote the poem at the suggestion of his friend John Caryll, who hoped that the humor Pope would bring to the incident would help heal bad feelings between the two families. Written as a mock epic, *The Rape of the Lock* is

a parody of such epics as *The Aeneid, The Iliad,* and *Paradise Lost.* The "war" in this case is the battle between the sexes.

   An Essay on Man is an unfinished philosophical poem that is written in heroic couplets. Divided into four epistles, or letters, the poem is an examination of human nature, society, and morals. It features the optimism of Pope's age regarding the nature of the universe and humans' place in it. The poem attempts to warn people that, despite what they think, they are not the center of the universe and must seek salvation through God. In this selection from Epistle 2, Pope cautions against intellectual pride by vividly describing the uncertain "middle state" in which humans have been placed.

Reader's Context Make some generalizations about human nature. What qualities do most poeple share?

Meet the Author

The insight and wisdom **Alexander Pope** (1688–1744) was able to capture in epigrams from his verses makes him one of the most frequently quoted authors in the English language. Pope was educated primarily at home by Catholic priests. He learned Greek, Latin, French, and Italian, and at the age of twelve, he produced some of his first poetry, imitating the styles of the poets he was reading.

   By young adulthood, Pope had begun his extensive output of literary work, which included numerous volumes of verse and ambitious projects—complete translations of Homer's *The Iliad* and *The Odyssey.* In his mature years, Pope lived and wrote on his country estate on the River Thames outside London and befriended many noteworthy writers, including Jonathan Swift. By the end of his life, Pope was immersed in a multitude of literary endeavors, although his death left some work, such as *An Essay on Man,* unfinished.

   Pope frequently wrote in **iambic pentameter.** An *iamb* is a poetic foot with one weakly stressed syllable and one strongly stressed syllable, as in the word *alone.* A *pentameter* line has five feet.

Analyze Literature

Mock Epic and Couplet
A **mock epic** is a form of satire in which the writer uses the structure, style, and classical elements of an epic poem but chooses a trivial social issue to be the poem's subject.

A **couplet** is two lines of verse that rhyme. A pair of rhyming iambic pentameter lines is also known as a *heroic couplet.*

Set Purpose

Pope is noted for the range of styles in which he wrote and for his mastery in writing poetry, particularly couplets. Think about the epics you have read, such as *Beowulf* and *Paradise Lost,* and brainstorm a list of elements that appear in an epic. While you read *The Rape of the Lock,* look for these elements and note where they appear in Pope's poem. Also determine whether either selection uses heroic couplets.

Preview Vocabulary

ogle, 548
oblique, 548
verdant, 549
destitute, 550
promiscuous, 550
prostrate, 551
exulting, 551
radiant, 551
pungent, 554

from *The Rape of the Lock*

An Heroi-Comical Poem

by Alexander Pope

Hearts and Trumps, c. 1800s. George G. Kilburne.
Private collection. (See detail on page 546.)

Canto III

> Close by those Meads for ever crown'd with Flow'rs,
> Where *Thames*[1] with Pride surveys his rising Tow'rs,
> There stands a Structure of Majestick Frame,
> Which from the neighb'ring *Hampton*[2] takes its Name.
> 5 Here *Britain*'s Statesmen oft the Fall foredoom
> Of Foreign Tyrants, and of Nymphs at home;
> Here Thou, great *Anna*! whom three Realms obey,[3]
> Dost sometimes Counsel take—and sometimes *Tea*.
>
> Hither the Heroes and the Nymphs resort,
> 10 To taste awhile the Pleasures of a Court;
> In various Talk th' instructive hours they past,
> Who gave the *Ball*, or paid the *Visit* last:

---

1. *Thames.* River that runs through London
2. *Hampton.* Location of the royal palace
3. **great *Anna*! whom three Realms obey.** Refers to Queen Anne who
   ruled England, Ireland, and Scotland from 1702 to 1714

tedious voyage, and at last arrived at the mouth of the river of Surinam, a colony belonging to the King of England, and where they were to deliver some part of their slaves. There the merchants and gentlemen of the country going on board to demand those lots of slaves they had already agreed on, and, amongst those, the overseers of those plantations where I then chanced to be, the captain, who had given the word, ordered his men to bring up those noble slaves in fetters whom I have spoken of; and having put 'em some in one and some in other lots, with women and children . . . they sold 'em off as slaves to several merchants and gentlemen; not putting any two in one lot, because they would separate 'em far from each other, not daring to trust 'em together, lest rage and courage should put 'em upon contriving some great action, to the ruin of the colony.

Oroonoko was first seized on, and sold to our overseer, who had the first lot, with seventeen more of all sorts and sizes, but not one of quality with him. When he saw this, he found what they meant, for, as I said, he understood English pretty well; and being wholly unarmed and defenseless, so as it was in vain to make any resistance, he only beheld the captain with a look all fierce and disdainful, upbraiding him with eyes that forced blushes on his guilty cheeks; he only cried, in passing over the side of the ship, "Farewell, sir. 'Tis worth my suffering, to gain so true a knowledge both of you and of your gods by whom you swear." And desiring those that held him to forbear their pains, and telling 'em he would make no resistance, he cried, "Come, my fellow slaves; let us descend, and see if we can meet with more honor and honesty in the next world we shall touch upon." So he nimbly leaped into the boat, and showing no more concern, suffered himself to be rowed up the river with his seventeen companions. ❖

 **MIRRORS & WINDOWS**

When has someone deceived you? How did it affect you in the short term and in the long term?

Refer and Reason

1. Identify the main characteristics Behn presents of the Africans and the slave traders. Explain the role these differences had in Oroonoko's capture.

2. Which characteristics of a novel are present in this excerpt? How can *Oroonoko* be considered an antislavery piece? Evaluate how well the excerpt holds up in both regards.

3. List the main events that occur in the excerpt. In the eighteenth century, James Thomson wrote these lyrics for a popular song: "Rule, Britannia, rule the waves; Britons never will be slaves." To what extent can *Oroonoko* be seen as a repudiation of such imperialist attitudes?

Writing Options

1. Write a dramatic adaptation of part of this selection from *Oroonoko*. Remember that the characters will have to convey meaning by words and actions with little help from a narrator. You can use the words of *Oroonoko* or adapt them, as needed, to make the dialogue flow.

2. Earlier in the novel, Behn writes, "And these People represented to me an absolute *Idea* of the first state of Innocence, before *Man* knew how to sin." How does Behn view the African people? What can you infer about her view based on her portrayal of Oroonoko and the captain? Write a paragraph explaining how objective Behn is in her portrayal of people and events.

 Go to **www.mirrorsandwindows.com** for more.

The literature of the Enlightenment is well known for its wit and emphasis on social interaction. It flourished in many different forms, such as the essay, satire, parody, novel, diary, journal, and formal letter, or *epistle.* Joseph Addison collaborated with other writers on *The Tatler* and *The Spectator,* both groundbreaking examples of a new literary medium: the periodical. Other notable prose works of the time include Samuel Pepys's *Diary,* a journal of daily events in Pepys's life from 1660 to 1669, and Daniel Defoe's *A Journal of the Plague Year.* Both these works illustrate life during the plague outbreak of 1665, which killed approximately 20 percent of London's population.

The final period in Enlightenment literature was the Age of Johnson (1750–1798). Named after Samuel Johnson, the most famous writer of his generation, this period bridges the Enlightenment and the Romantic Era. During this time, some writers began to move away from the ideals of Neoclassicism toward the more free, emotional, and natural style of the Romantics.

Johnson, a master of many forms of poetry, literary criticism, and prose fiction, is best known for his *A Dictionary of the English Language.* This was the first definitive dictionary of English, containing more than 40,000 words and 114,000 quotations. Johnson also started his own periodical, *The Rambler,* which contained essays, allegories, and literary criticism written primarily by him. In 1763, he met James Boswell, whose *The Life of Samuel Johnson, LL.D.,* presents the actions and opinions of the great man. Boswell's book is considered the first great modern English biography.

Saints Anthony Abbot and Francis of Assisi, c. 1627. Andrea Sacchi. National Gallery, London, England.

The Diary and Journal Defined

Diaries and journals are personal forms of expression and reflection. A **diary** is a day-to-day record of a person's activities, experiences, thoughts, and feelings. A **journal,** like a diary, is a similar day-to-day record. In contrast to the word *diary*, the word *journal* connotes an outward, rather than an inward, focus.

Diaries and journals often are considered one genre, since both are first-person narratives written without the clear intent of publication. Even so, journals may be more likely than diaries to reference newsworthy topics, such as wars, changes in government, and important discoveries. While history has preserved the works of notable record keepers such as Samuel Pepys, Samuel Johnson, and Fanny Burney, giving them an enduring audience, the authors could not assume that publication would follow. In fact, some of the diary and journal selections you will encounter were not published until long after they were written.

This does not mean, however, that published diaries and journals differ in literary merit from novels and essays. The literary diarist or journalist brings the same keen powers of observation and construction to the writing process. One finds in a well-written diary or journal accurate description, profound analysis, and often specific historical facts about the period in which the writer lived. This is history written in the first-person singular. The intimacy of the writer's tone speaks to us, conjuring up images and scenes from earlier times and sparking our interest in the author who lived through them.

Elements of Diaries and Journals

Voice and Tone

Voice is the way a writer uses language to reflect his or her unique personality and attitude toward topic, form, and audience. A writer expresses voice through tone, word choice, and sentence structure. **Tone** is the emotional attitude implied by a literary work toward the reader or the subject. Examples of the different tones that a work may have include *familiar, ironic, playful, sarcastic, serious*, and *sincere*. Voice and tone guide our experience of reading a work and shape our responses to it.

The narrative voice we encounter in this genre naturally varies a great deal, depending on the character and aims of the writer. For example, in reading Fanny Burney's diary, we hear the voice of an eighteenth-century society lady, as interested as any Jane Austen heroine in matters of courtship and manners.

> *"Knowledge is of two kinds. We know a subject ourselves, or we know where we can find information on it."*
>
> —SAMUEL JOHNSON

Audience

In a diary or journal, the writer and audience are supposedly one and the same, so the writer is not obligated to provide background information. In many respects, the diary or journal entry is a **monologue,** a long speech made by one person. Even when the entry is written partly as **dialogue,** as in the Burney passage, the diarist uses the blank page as a captive audience.

However, the act of writing usually assumes there is an external audience of some kind. Who is this audience? That depends on the author. The diarist might imagine an ideal reader of his or her own time or attempt to speak to future generations. The journalist might imagine a reader eager to know the circumstances of a king's coronation or the worth of a new production of a Shakespeare play.

Sincerity and Authenticity

How sincere and reliable is the diarist or journalist? Should we take this writer at face value, assuming there is no deception or pretense in the literary work? This certainly seems to be true of Pepys's diaries. Along with the awe-inspiring details of the plague and the devastating London fire, Pepys writes candidly

PEPYS   BURNEY   DEFOE

of his petty concerns about sums of money and the contents of his wardrobe. On the other hand, in Daniel Defoe's *A Journal of the Plague Year,* a fictional narrator describes real events in 1665, when Defoe was a five-year-old child.

Consider, too, the diary excerpts allegedly penned by a young lady of fashion and reprinted by editor Joseph Addison in *The Spectator.* These excerpts are meant to reveal the triviality of the society woman. "Clarinda" allows herself to be wooed by the inconsequential Mr. Froth, while passing the rest of the day in the company of people such as Lady Blithe. Of course, Addison was parodying the uselessness of the diary when it serves only as a vehicle for trivialities, but his gentle satire points to a problem raised by the genre: Once we perceive the journal or diary entry as containing at least some elements of fiction, we can no longer experience it as a natural and spontaneous expression. Or perhaps the literary merit of some journals stems from that very manipulation of the facts.

The Eyewitness Account

We read a diary from an earlier century for what it tells us about a distant past and for its ability to draw us into the moment. Samuel Pepys kept a continuous diary from 1660 to 1669 that is a rich source of historical and cultural material. His detailed descriptions of the Great Fire of London, for example, have an immediacy and personal interest for us. We experience something of the writer's shock and horror at the destruction of his city, which moves us in a way that a factual historical account may fail to do. The substance of the narrative, with its mixture of homely detail and grand spectacle, is a balancing of the personal and the historical.

"True happiness arises, in the first place, from the enjoyment of one's self, and in the next, from the friendship and conversation of a few select companions."

—JOSEPH ADDISON

from The Diary of Samuel Pepys

A Diary by Samuel Pepys

from A Journal of the Plague Year

A Fictional Journal by Daniel Defoe

Build Background

Historical Context Samuel Pepys and Daniel Defoe both wrote accounts the Great Plague, which spread through London in 1665. (See the History Connection box on page 573.)

    The Diary of Samuel Pepys, published for the first time in 1825, is an interesting account of the daily life of a successful, middle-class Englishman. Pepys writes about important events such as the plague and the Great London Fire of 1666 and mundane issues such as fashion and entertainment.

    Although fictional, Defoe's ***A Journal of the Plague Year*** often is believed to be an actual journal because of its realism. Events are told from the point of view of an individual who does not, like many Londoners, flee the infected city. Defoe was only five during the epidemic, so many of the details he provides come from research rather than experience.

Reader's Context What important social and historical events have you experienced? Why might a journal recording the events of these times be interesting in the future?

Meet the Authors

Samuel Pepys (1633–1703) was the son of a tailor. Pepys (pronounced "Peeps") earned two degrees from Cambridge University. He had a successful naval career and eventually won a seat in Parliament by promoting sea power. Pepys also was interested in theater, art, and literature. He counted among his friends such luminaries as scientist Sir Isaac Newton and writer John Dryden. Today, Pepys's diary makes him a literary luminary and gives readers a vivid view of life in England during the seventeenth century.

Daniel Defoe (1660–1731) faced financial, political, and religious woes over the course of his life. He participated in a rebellion against King James II and was forced to live in hiding for two years to avoid prosecution. Arrested because his satiric works were read literally, Defoe became a spy and wrote propaganda for the government after a politician helped him get out of prison. His best-known work is the novel *Robinson Crusoe,* which tells the story of a man stranded on a desert island. Defoe was also a journalist and pamphlet writer.

Compare Literature

Diction and Narrator
Diction refers to the author's choice of words.

A **narrator** is a character or speaker who tells a story. The writer's choice of narrator determines how much and what kind of information readers will be given about events and other characters.

Set Purpose

Consider the kind of diction you would expect to find in a diary or journal, particularly from this time period. Examine Pepys's and Defoe's diction as you read. What inferences about the author's attitude and personality can you make based on the diction used in the diary or journal? Also think about what limitations you would expect of the narrator of a diary or journal.

Preview Vocabulary

ague, 574
endeavor, 575
mortal, 580
inimitable, 580
discourse, 583
importune, 584
prodigious, 584
divert, 585
abate, 586
calamitous, 586

Great Fire of London, 1666. (See detail on page 570.)

from
The Diary of Samuel Pepys
by Samuel Pepys

first person narratives
was written for himself
was translated centuries later
probably wished for someone to figure it out, but not right away

> *The people die so, that now it seems they are fain to carry the dead to be buried by daylight, the nights not sufficing to do it.*

Have to pull the emotion out of this

— he is feeling the emotions as he is writing it —

— have to dramatize it in your mind) —

On Seeing a Play by Shakespeare
MARCH 1, 1662

This morning I paid Sir Wm. Batten 40*l*, which I have owed him this half year, having borrowed it of him.

Then to the office all the morning. So dined at home. And after dinner comes my uncle Thomas, with whom I have some high words of difference; but ended quietly, though I fear I shall do no good by fair means upon him.

Then my wife and I by coach, first to see my little picture that is a-drawing, and thence to the Opera and there saw *Romeo and Julett*, the first time it was ever acted.[1] But it is the play of itself the worst that ever I heard in my life, and the worst acted that ever I saw these people do; and I am resolved to go no more to see the first time of acting, for they were all of them out more or less. Thence home, and after supper and wrote by the post—I settled to what I have long entended, to cast up my accounts with myself; and after much pains to do it and great fear, I do find that I am 500*l* in money beforehand in the world, which I was afeared I was not. But I find that I have spent above 250*l* this last half year, which troubles me much. But by God's blessing, I am now resolved to take up, having furnished myself

---

1. ***Romeo and Julett . . . acted.*** Pepys saw *Romeo and Juliet* acted for the first time since the Restoration.

with all things for a great while, and tomorrow to think upon some rules and obligations upon myself to walk by.

So with my mind eased of a great deal of trouble, though with no great content to find myself above 100*l* worse now then I was half a year ago, I went to bed.

The Plague of 1665
JUNE 7, 1665

[handwritten: trying to block the smell incase that is how it spreads]

This day, much against my Will, I did in Drury-lane see two or three houses marked with a red cross[2] upon the doors, and "Lord have mercy upon us" writ there—which was a sad sight to me, being the first of that kind that to my remembrance I ever saw. It put me into an ill conception of myself and my smell, so that I was forced to buy some roll-tobacco to smell to and chaw—which took away the apprehension.[3]

AUGUST 3, 1665

Up, and betimes to Deptford to Sir G. Carteret's; where not liking the horse which had been hired by Mr. Uthwayt for me, I did desire Sir G. Carteret to let me ride his new 40*l* horse; which he did and so I left my hacquenee[4] behind. And so after staying a good while in their bedchamber while they were dressing themselfs, discoursing merrily, I parted and to the Ferry, where I was forced to stay a great while before I could get my horse brought over. And then mounted and rode very finely to Dagenham's—all the way, people, Citizens, walking to and again to enquire how the plague is in the City this week by the Bill—which by chance at Greenwich I had heard was 2010 of the plague, and 3000 and odd of all diseases; but methought it was a sad question to be so often asked me. Coming to Dagenham's, I there met our company coming out of the house, having stayed as long as they could for me. So I let them go a little before, and went and took leave of my Lady Sandwich—good woman, who seems very sensible of my service and this late business—and having her direc-tions in some things; among others, to get Sir G. Carteret and my Lord to settle the portion and what Sir G. Carteret is to settle into land as soon as may be; she not liking that it should lie long undone, for fear of death on either side. So took leave of her, and then down to the buttery and eat a piece of cold venison-pie and drank and took some bread and cheese in my hand; and so mounted after them, Mr. Marr very kindly staying to lead me the way. By and by met my Lord Crew returning, after having accompanied them a little way. And so after them, Mr. Marr telling me by the way how a maid-servant of Mr. John Wrights (who lives thereabouts), falling sick of the plague, she was removed to an out-house, and a nurse appointed to look to her—who being once absent, the maid got out of the house at the window and run away. The nurse coming and knocking, and having no answer, believed she was dead, and went and told Mr. Wright so; who, and his lady, were in great strait what to do to get her buried. At last resolved to go to Burntwood hard by, being in that parish, and there get people to do it—but they would not; so he went home full of trouble, and in the way met the wench walking over the Common, which frighted him worse then before. And was forced to send people to take her; which he did, and they got one of the pest Coaches and put her into it to carry her to a pest-house. And passing in a narrow lane, Sir Anthony Browne, with his brother and some friends in the coach, met this coach with the Curtains drawn close. The brother being a young man, and believing

> *Falling sick of the plague, she was removed to an out-house, and a nurse appointed to look to her.*

---

2. **red cross.** Quarantine mark used during the plague
3. **roll-tobacco . . . apprehension.** In Pepys's time, tobacco was believed to have medicinal value.
4. **hacquenee.** Horse for riding

The Great Plague

London's Great Plague of 1665–1666 actually was much less destructive than earlier outbreaks of the bubonic plague during the Middle Ages. Even so, the pandemic terrorized London, killing nearly one hundred thousand people in just over a year. Dutch trading ships probably were responsible for reintroducing the plague to England during the winter of 1664, given that the Netherlands had experienced outbreaks earlier that year.

A bacterium called *Yersinia pestis* transmitted the bubonic plague through infected fleas. These fleas lodged on rats, which inhabited ships in great numbers during the seventeenth century. When a ship would land in port, the rats and fleas would move on land and spread throughout the immediate area. The thatched roofs typical of many houses provided ideal living conditions for the rodents, and the excessive amounts of garbage in urban neighborhoods gave them plenty to eat. In London, another contributing factor was that most of the city's population lived in cramped living conditions. This allowed the fleas to move easily among hosts, families, and communities.

All of these factors contributed to the rapid dissemination of the plague in London. When it reached its zenith in September 1665, it killed seven thousand people a week.

Although cold weather caused the outbreak to subside, the plague was ultimately quashed by the Great Fire of London, which burned seven-eighths of London's residential districts in September 1666. Most of the rats that carried the plague lived within these districts, so they, too, perished in the fire. After the fire, the city was rebuilt with more open spaces and with better sanitation systems. Thatched roofs, a fire hazard as well as a nesting site for vermin, were outlawed.

Engraving of a physician wearing clothing to protect against the plague (1656).

---

there might be some lady in it that would not be seen, and the way being narrow, he thrust his head out of his own into her coach to look, and there saw somebody look very ill, and in a sick dress and stunk mightily; which the coachman also cried out upon. And presently they came up to some people that stood looking after it; and told our gallants that it was a maid of Mr. Wrights carried away sick of the plague—which put the young gentleman into a fright had almost cost him his life, but is now well again.

August 12, 1665

The people die so, that now it seems they are fain to carry the dead to be buried by daylight, the nights not sufficing to do it in. And my

Lord Mayor commands people to be within at 9 at night, all (as they say) that the sick may have liberty to go abroad for ayre. There is one also dead out of one of our ships at Deptford, which troubles us mightily—the *Providence* fire-ship, which was just fitted to go to sea. But they tell me today, no more sick on board. And this day W Bodham tells me that one is dead at Woolwich, not far from the Ropeyard. I am told too, that a wife of one of the groomes at Court is dead at Salsbury, so that the King and Queene are speedily to be all gone to Milton. God preserve us.

September 3, 1665

Lords day. Up, and put on my coulour silk suit, very fine, and my new periwigg, bought a good while since, but darst not wear it because the plague was in Westminster when I bought it. And it is a wonder what will be the fashion after the plague is done as to periwigs, for nobody will dare to buy any haire for fear of the infection—that it had been cut off of the heads of people dead of the plague. . . .

Church being done, my Lord Brouncker, Sir J. Mennes, and I up to the Vestry at the desire of the Justices of the Peace, Sir Th Bidolph and Sir W Boreman and Alderman Hooker—in order to the doing something for the keeping of the plague from growing; but Lord, to consider the madness of people of the town, who will (because they are forbid) come in Crowds along with the dead Corps to see them buried. But we agreed on some orders for the prevention thereof.[5] Among other stories, one was very passionate methought—of a complaint brought against a man in the town for taking a child from London from an infected house. Alderman Hooker told us it was the child of a very able citizen in Gracious-street, a saddler, who had buried all the rest of his children of the plague; and himself and wife now being shut up, and in despair of escaping, did desire only to save the life of this little child; and so prevailed to have it received stark-naked into the arms of a friend, who brought it (having put it into new fresh clothes) to Grenwich; where, upon hearing the story, we did agree it should be [permitted to be] received and kept in the town. Thence with my Lord Brouncker to Captain Cockes, where we mighty merry, and supped; and very late, I by water to Woolwich, in great apprehensions of an Ague. Here was my Lord Brouncker's lady of pleasure, who I perceive goes everywhere with him, and he I find is obliged to carry her and make all the Courtship to her that can be.

The Great Fire of London
SEPTEMBER 2, 1666

Lords day. Some of our maids sitting up late last night to get things ready against our feast today, Jane called us up, about 3 in the morning, to tell us of a great fire they saw in the City.[6] So I rose, and slipped on my nightgown and went to her window, and thought it to be on the back side of Markelane at the furthest; but being unused to such fires as fallowed, I thought it far enough off, and so went to bed again and to sleep. About 7 rose again to dress myself, and there looked out at the window and saw the fire not so much as it was, and further off. So to my closet to set things to rights after yesterday's cleaning. By and by Jane comes and tells me that she hears that above 300 houses have been burned down tonight by the fire we saw, and that it was now burning down all Fishstreet by London Bridge. So I made myself ready presently, and walked to the Tower and there got up upon one of the high places, Sir J Robinsons little son going up with me; and there I did see the houses at that end of the bridge all on fire, and an infinite great fire on this and the other side the end of the bridge—which, among other people, did trouble me for poor little Michell and our Sarah on the Bridge. So down, with my heart full of trouble, to the Lieutenant of the Tower, who tells me that it begun this morning in the King's bakers house in Pudding-lane, and that it hath burned down St. Magnes Church and most part of Fishstreete already. So I down to the water-side and there got a boat and through bridge, and there saw a lamentable fire. Poor Michells house, as far as the Old Swan, already

> **Above 300 houses have been burned down tonight by the fire we saw.**

5. **orders . . . thereof.** Laws were made forbidding funeral processions during the Plague.
6. **fire . . . City.** Great Fire of London, which burned for four days and nights

ague (ā´ gyü) *n.,* fever and chills

Eighteenth-century woodcut depicting the disposal of bodies during the Great Plague.

burned that way and the fire running further, that in a very little time it got as far as the Still-yard while I was there. Everybody endeavouring to remove their goods, and flinging into the River or bringing them into lighters that lay off. Poor people staying in their houses as long as till the very fire touched them, and then running into boats or clambering from one pair of stair by the water-side to another. And among other things, the poor pigeons I perceive were loath to leave their houses, but hovered about the windows and balconies till they were some of them burned, their wings, and fell down.

Having stayed, and in an hour's time seen the fire rage every way, and nobody to my sight endeavouring to quench it, but to remove their goods and leave all to the fire; and having seen it get as far as the Steeleyard, and the wind mighty high and driving it into the city, and everything, after so long a drough, proving combustible, even the very stones of churches, and among other things, the poor steeple by which pretty Mrs. _____ lives, and whereof my old school-fellow Elborough is parson, taken fire in the very top and there burned till it fall down—I to Whitehall with a gentleman with me who desired to go off from the Tower to see the fire in my boat—to White-hall, and there up to the King's closet in the chapel, where people came about me and I did give them an account dismayed them all; and word was carried in to the King, so I was called for and did tell the King and Duke of York what I saw, and that unless his Majesty did command houses to be pulled down, nothing could stop the fire. They seemed much troubled, and the King commanded me to go to my Lord Mayor from him and command him to spare no houses but to pull down before the fire every way. The Duke of York bid me tell him that if he would have any more soldiers, he shall; and so did my Lord Arlington afterward, as a great secret. Here meeting with Captain Cocke, I in his coach, which he lent me, and Creed with me, to Pauls; and there walked along Watling-street as well as I could, every creature coming away loaden with goods to save—and here and there sick people carried away in beds. Extraordinary good goods carried in carts and on backs. At last met my Lord Mayor in Canning Streete, like a man spent, with a hankercher about his neck. To the King's message, he cried like a fainting woman, "Lord, what can I do? I am

en · deav · or (in de´ vər) v., try; attempt

Detail from the Great Fire of London Mural in London, England. This scene depicts King Charles II's reaction to the news that the fire was destroying the city.

By this time it was about 12 a-clock, and so home and there find my guests, which was Mr. Wood and his wife, Barbary Shelden, and also Mr. Moone—she mighty fine, and her husband, for aught I see, a likely man. But Mr. Moones design and mine, which was to look over my closet and please him with the sight thereof, which he hath long desired, was wholly disappointed, for we were in great trouble and disturbance at this fire, not knowing what to think of it. However, we had an extraordinary good dinner, and as merry as at this time we could be.

While at dinner, Mrs. Batelier came to enquire after Mr. Woolfe and Stanes (who it seems are related to them), whose houses in Fishstreet are all burned, and they in a sad condition. She would not stay in the fright.

As soon as dined, I and Moone away and walked through the City, the streets full of nothing but people and horses and carts loaden with goods, ready to run over one another, and removing goods from one burned house to another—they now removing out of Canning-street (which received goods in the morning) into Lumbard Streete and further; and among others, I now saw my little goldsmith Stokes receiving some friend's goods, whose house itself was burned the day after. We parted at Pauls, he home and I to Pauls-Wharf, where I had appointed a boat to attend me; and took in Mr. Carcasse and his brother, whom I met in the street, and carried them below and above bridge, to and again, to see the fire, which was now got further, both below and above, and no likelihood of stopping it. Met with the King and Duke of York in their Barge, and with

spent. People will not obey me. I have been pull[ing] down houses. But the fire overtakes us faster then we can do it." That he needed no more soldiers; and that for himself, he must go and refresh himself, having been up all night. So he left me, and I him, and walked home—seeing people all almost distracted and no manner of means used to quench the fire. The houses too, so very thick thereabouts, and full of matter for burning, as pitch and tar, in Thames-street—and warehouses of oyle and wines and Brandy and other things. Here I saw Mr. Isaccke Houblon, that handsome man—prettily dressed and dirty at his door at Dowgate, receiving some of his brothers things whose houses were on fire; and as he says, have been removed twice already, and he doubts (as it soon proved) that they must be in a little time removed from his house also—which was a sad consideration. And to see the churches all filling with goods, by people who themselfs should have been quietly there at this time.

them to Queen-Hith and there called Sir Rd. Browne to them. Their order was only to pull down houses apace, and so below bridge at the water-side; but little was or could be done, the fire coming upon them so fast. Good hopes there was of stopping it at the Three Cranes above, and at Buttolphs-Wharf below bridge, if care be used; but the wind carries it into the City, so as we know not by the water-side what it doth there. River full of lighter[s] and boats taking in goods, and good goods swimming in the water; and only, I observed that hardly one lighter or boat in three that had the goods of a house in, but there was a pair of virginalls[7] in it. Having seen as much as I could now, I away to White-hall by appointment, and there walked to St. James's Park, and there met my wife and Creed and Wood and his wife and walked to my boat, and there upon the water again, and to the fire up and down, it still increasing and the wind great. So near the fire as we could for smoke; and all over the Thames, with one's face in the wind you were almost burned with a shower of Firedrops—this is very true—so as houses were burned by these drops and flakes of fire, three or four, nay five or six houses, one from another. When we could endure no more upon the water, we to a little alehouse on the Bankside over against the Three Cranes, and there stayed till it was dark almost and saw the fire grow; and as it grow darker, appeared more and more, and in Corners and upon steeples and between churches and houses, as far as we could see up the hill of the City, in a most horrid malicious bloody flame, not like the fine flame of an ordinary fire. Barbary and her husband away before us. We stayed till, it being darkish, we saw the fire as only one entire arch of fire from this to the

All over the Thames, with one's face in the wind you were almost burned with a shower of Firedrops.

other side the bridge, and in a bow up the hill, for an arch of above a mile long. It made me weep to see it. The churches, houses, and all on fire and flaming at once, and a horrid noise the flames made, and the cracking of houses at their ruine. So home with a sad heart, and there find everybody discoursing and lamenting the fire; and poor Tom Hater came with some few of his goods saved out of his house, which is burned upon Fish-street hill. I invited him to lie at my house, and did receive his goods: but was deceived in his lying there, the noise coming every moment of the growth of the Fire, so as we were forced to begin to pack up our own goods and prepare for their removal. And did by Moone-shine (it being brave, dry, and moon-shine and warm weather) carry much of my goods into the garden, and Mr. Hater and I did remove my money and Iron-chests into my cellar—as thinking that the safest place. And got my bags of gold into my office ready to carry away, and my chief papers of accounts also there, and my tallies into a box by themselfs. So great was our fear, as Sir W. Batten had carts come out of the country to fetch away his goods this night. We did put Mr. Hater, poor man, to bed a little; but he got but very little rest, so much noise being in my house, taking down of goods.

SEPTEMBER 5, 1666

I lay down in the office again upon W. Hewer's quilt, being mighty weary and sore in my feet with going till I was hardly able to stand. About 2 in the morning my wife calls me up and tells of new Cryes of "Fyre!"—it being come to Barkeing Church, which is the bottom of our lane. I up; and finding it so, resolved presently to take her away; and did, and took my gold (which was about 2350*l*), W. Hewer, and Jane down by Poundy's boat to Woolwich. But Lord, what a sad sight it was by moonlight to see the whole City almost on fire—that you

---

7. **pair of virginalls.** Rectangular keyboard instruments

might see it plain at Woolwich, as if you were by it. There when I came, I find the gates[8] shut, but no guard kept at all; which troubled me, because of discourses now begun that there is plot in it and that the French had done it.[9] I got the gates open, and to Mr. Shelden's, where I locked up my gold and charged my wife and W. Hewer never to leave the room without one of them in it night nor day. So back again, by the way seeing my goods well in the lighters at Deptford and watched well by people. Home, and whereas I expected to have seen our house on fire, it being now about 7 a-clock, it was not. But to the Fyre, and there find greater hopes then I expected; for my confidence of finding our office on fire was such, that I durst not ask anybody how it was with us, till I came and saw it not burned. But going to the fire, I find, by the blowing up of houses and the great help given by the workmen out of the King's yards, sent up by Sir W. Penn, there is a good stop given to it, as well at Marke-lane end as ours—it having only burned the Dyall of Barkeing Church, and part of the porch, and was there quenched. I up to the top of Barkeing steeple, and there saw the saddest sight of desolation that I ever saw. Everywhere great fires. Oyle-cellars and brimstone and other things burning. I became afeared to stay there long; and therefore down again as fast as I could, the fire being spread as far as I could see it, and to Sir W. Penn's and there eat a piece of cold meat, having eaten nothing since Sunday but the remains of Sunday's dinner.

Here I met with Mr. Young and Whistler; and having removed all my things, and received good hopes that the fire at our end is stopped, they and I walked into the town and find Fanchurch street, Gracious-street, and Lumbard-street all in dust. The Exchange a sad sight, nothing standing there of all the statues or pillars but Sir Tho. Gresham's picture in the corner.[10] Walked into Moore-fields (our feet ready to burn, walking through the town among the hot coles) and find that full of people, and poor wretches carrying their goods there, and everybody keeping his goods together by themselfs (and a great blessing it is to them that it is fair weather for them to keep abroad night and day); drank there, and paid twopence for a plain penny loaf.

Thence homeward, having passed through Cheapside and Newgate-market, all burned—and seen Anthony Joyces house in fire. And took up (which I keep by me) a piece of glass of Mercer's chapel in the street, where much more was, so melted and buckled with the heat of the fire, like parchment. I also did see a poor Catt taken out of a hole in the chimney joyning to the wall of the Exchange, with the hair all burned off the body and yet alive. So home at night, and find there good hopes of saving our office—but great endeavours of watching all night and having men ready; and so we lodged them in the office, and had drink and bread and cheese for them. And I lay down and slept a good night about midnight—though when I rose, I hear that there had been a great alarme of French and Duch being risen—which proved nothing. But it is a strange thing to see how long this time did look since Sunday, having been alway full of variety of actions, and little sleep, that it looked like a week or more. And I had forgot almost the day of the week. ❖

---

8. **gates.** Dockyard gates
9. **discourses . . . it.** Rumors that the French had started the fire and were now entering the city
10. **Exchange . . . corner.** The stock exchange was destroyed except for the statue of Gresham, the founder.

MIRRORS & WINDOWS In his diary, Pepys records a mixture of trivial and catastrophic events. What does this suggest about how people tend to deal with tragedies and disasters?

Saint Jerome [detail], c. 1605. Michelangelo Merisi da Caravaggio. Galleria Borghese, Rome, Italy.

from

A Journal of the Plague Year

by Daniel Defoe — *a dissenter (protestants without vestments)*

traitor, writer, spy

dramatization

> I had many dismal scenes before my eyes, as particularly od persons falling dead in the streets.

— making the plague come alive for the next generation —

— he was 5 during the plague — critical (developmental) period

1. The Infection Spreads

Here the opinion of the physicians agreed with my observation afterward, namely, that the danger was spreading insensibly, for the sick could infect none but those that came within reach of the sick person; but that one man who may have really received the infection and knows it not, but goes abroad and about

Very medical and scientific

COMPARING LITERATURE COMPARING LITERATURE COMPARING LITERATURE COMPARING as a sound person, may give the plague to a thousand people, and they to greater numbers in proportion, and neither the person giving the infection or the persons receiving it know anything of it, and perhaps not feel the effects of it for several days after.

For example, many persons in the time of this visitation never perceived that they were infected till they found to their unspeakable surprise, the tokens come out upon them; after which they seldom lived six hours; for those spots they called the tokens were really gangrene spots, or mortified flesh[1] in small knobs as broad as a little silver penny, and hard as a piece of callus or horn; so that, when the disease was coming up to that length, there was nothing could follow but certain death; and yet, as I said, they knew nothing of their being infected, nor found themselves so much as out of order, till those <u>mortal</u> marks were upon them. But everybody must allow that they were infected in a high degree before, and must have been so some time, and consequently their breath, their sweat, their very clothes, were contagious for many days before. . . .

2. Dismal Scenes   *maybe dramatizing generic happenings of the time*

I had some little obligations, indeed, upon me to go to my brother's house, which was in Coleman Street[2] parish and which he had left to my care, and I went at first every day, but afterward only once or twice a week.

In these walks I had many dismal scenes before my eyes, as particularly of persons falling dead in the streets, terrible shrieks and screechings of women, who, in their agonies, would throw open their chamber windows and cry out in a dismal, surprising manner. It is impossible to describe the variety of postures in which the passions of the poor people would express themselves.

Passing through Tokenhouse Yard, in Lothbury, of a sudden a casement[3] violently opened just over my head, and a women gave three frightful screeches, and then cried, "Oh! death, death, death!" in a most <u>inimitable</u> tone, and which struck me with horror and a chillness in my very blood. There was nobody to be seen in the whole street, neither did any other window open, for people had no curiosity now in any case, nor could anybody help one another, so I went on to pass into Bell Alley.

Just in Bell Alley, on the right hand of the passage, there was a more terrible cry than that, though it was not so directed out at the window; but the whole family was in a terrible fright, and I could hear women and children run screaming about the rooms like distracted, when a garret window opened and somebody from a window on the other side of the alley called and asked, "What is the matter?" upon which, from the first window, it was answered, "Oh Lord, my old master has hanged himself!" The other asked again, "Is he quite dead?" and the first answered, "Ay, ay, quite dead; quite dead and cold!" This person was a merchant and a deputy alderman,[4] and very rich. I care not to mention the name, though I knew his name too, but that would be an hardship to the family, which is now flourishing again.

But this is but one; it is scarce credible what dreadful cases happened in particular families every day. People in the rage of the distemper, or in the torment of their swellings, which was indeed intolerable, running out of their own government,[5] raving and distracted, and oftentimes laying violent hands upon themselves, throwing themselves out at their windows, shooting themselves, etc.; mothers

---

1. **tokens . . . flesh.** Symptoms of the plague included decaying flesh, often called *tokens*.
2. **Coleman Street.** This street, like most of the places to which Defoe refers, are in London.
3. **casement.** Window with hinges
4. **deputy alderman.** City official
5. **out of their own government.** Out of control

---

mor • tal (môr´ t'l) *adj.*, deadly
in • im • it • able (i' ni´ mə tə bəl) *adj.*, difficult to imitate

murdering their own children in their lunacy, some dying of mere grief as a passion, some of mere fright and surprise without any infection at all, others frighted into idiotism and foolish distractions, some into despair and lunacy, others into melancholy madness.

The pain of the swelling was in particular very violent, and to some intolerable; the physicians and surgeons may be said to have tortured many poor creatures even to death. The swellings in some grew hard, and they applied violent drawing plasters or poultices to break them, and if these did not do they cut and scarified[6] them in a terrible manner. In some those swellings were made hard partly by the force of the distemper and partly by their being too violently drawn, and were so hard that no instrument could cut them, and then they burnt them with caustics, so that many died raving mad with the torment, and some in the very operation. In these distresses, some, for want of help to hold them down in their beds, or to look to them, laid hands upon themselves as above. Some broke out into the streets, perhaps naked, and would run directly down to the river if they were not stopped by the watchman or other officers, and plunge themselves into the water wherever they found it.

It often pierced my very soul to hear the groans and cries of those who were thus tormented, but of the two this was counted the most promising particular in the whole infection, for if these swellings could be brought to a head, and to break and run, or, as the surgeons call it, to digest, the patient generally recovered; whereas those who, like the gentlewoman's daughter, were struck with death at the beginning, and had the tokens come out upon them, often went about indifferent easy till a little before they died, and some till the moment they dropped down, as in apoplexies[7] and epilepsies is often the case. Such would be taken suddenly very sick, and would run to a bench or bulk, or any convenient place

that offered itself, or to their own houses if possible, as I mentioned before, and there sit down, grow faint, and die. This kind of dying was much the same as it was with those who die of common mortifications,[8] who die swooning, and, as it were, go away in a dream. Such as died thus had very little notice of their being infected at all till the gangrene was spread through their whole body; nor could physicians themselves know certainly how it was with them till they opened their breasts or other parts of their body and saw the tokens.

> *If these swellings could be brought to head, and to break and run, . . . the patient generally recovered.*

3. Escape from Quarantine

I remember one citizen who, having thus broken out of his house in Aldersgate Street or thereabout, went along the road to Islington;[9] he attempted to have gone in at the Angel Inn, and after that the White Horse, two inns known still by the same signs, but was refused; after which he came to the Pied Bull, an inn also still continuing the same sign. He asked them for lodging for one night only, pretending to be going into Lincolnshire,[10] and assuring them of his being very sound and free from the infection, which also at that time had not reached much that way.

They told him they had no lodging that they could spare but one bed up in the garret, and that they could spare that bed for one

---

6. **drawing plasters . . . scarified.** Treatments for plague swellings included hot packs to soften sores and draw out infections and cutting or puncturing the sores.
7. **apoplexies.** Strokes
8. **common mortifications.** Gangrene
9. **Islington.** Northern suburb of London
10. **Lincolnshire.** County on England's eastern coast

The Diseases and Casualties this Week.

Disease	Count		Disease	Count
Abortive	4		Imposthume	8
Aged	45		Infants	22
Breeding	1		Kingsevil	4
Broken legge	1		Lethargy	1
Broke her skull by a fall in the street at St. Mary Woolchurch	1		Livergrown	1
			Meagrome	1
Childbed	28		Palsie	1
Chrisomes	9		Plague	4237
Consumption	126		Purples	2
Convulsion	89		Quinsie	5
Cough	1		Rickets	23
Dropsie	53		Rising of the Lights	18
Feaver	348		Rupture	1
Flox and Small-pox	11		Scurvy	3
Flux	1		Shingles	1
Frighted	2		Spotted Feaver	166
Gowt	1		Stilborn	4
Grief	3		Stone	2
Griping in the Guts	79		Stopping of the stomach	17
Head-mould-shot	1		Strangury	3
Jaundies	7		Suddenly	2
			Surfeit	74
			Teeth	111
			Thrush	6
			Tissick	9
			Ulcer	1
			Vomiting	10
			Winde	4
			Wormes	20

Christned { Males — 90, Females — 81, In all — 171 } Buried { Males — 2777, Females — 2791, In all — 5568 } Plague — 4237

Increased in the Burials this Week ——— 249

Parishes clear of the Plague ——— 27   Parishes Infected ——— 103

The Assize of Bread set forth by Order of the Lord Major and Court of Aldermen, A penny Wheaten Loaf to contain Nine Ounces and a half, and three half-penny White Loaves the like weight.

Death bill for London's dead during one week in August 1665. The total number of deaths recorded this week was 5,568. Deaths caused by the plague are noted separately in the bottom-right corner.

night, some drovers being expected the next day with cattle; so, if he would accept of that lodging, he might have it, which he did. So a servant was sent up with a candle with him to show him the room. He was very well dressed, and looked like a person not used to lie in a garret; and when he came to the room he fetched a deep sigh, and said to the servant, "I have seldom lain in such a lodging as this." However, the servant assuring him again that they had no better, "Well," says he, "I must make shift; this is a dreadful time; but it is but for one night."

So he sat down upon the bedside, and bade the maid, I think it was, fetch him up a pint of warm ale. Accordingly the servant went for the ale, but some hurry in the house, which perhaps employed her other ways, put it out of her head, and she went up no more to him.

The next morning, seeing no appearance of the gentleman, somebody in the house asked the servant that had showed him upstairs what was become of him. She started. "Alas!" says she, "I never thought more of him. He bade me carry him some warm ale, but I forgot." Upon which, not the maid, but some other person was sent up to see after him, who, coming into the room, found him stark dead and almost cold, stretched out across the bed. His clothes were pulled off, his jaw fallen, his eyes open in a most frightful posture, the rug of the bed being grasped hard in one of his hands, so that it was plain he died soon after the maid left him; and 'tis probable, had she gone up with the ale, she had found him dead in a few minutes after he sat down upon the bed. The alarm was great in the house, as anyone may suppose, they having been free from the distemper till that disaster, which, bringing the infection to the house, spread it immediately to other houses round about it. . . .

4. Burial Pits and Dead-Carts

he is obsessed with the burial pits

There was a strict order to prevent people coming to those pits, and that was only to prevent infection. But after some time that order was more necessary, for people that were infected and near their end, and delirious also, would run to those pits, wrapped in blankets or rugs, and throw themselves in, and, as they said, bury themselves. . . .

This may serve a little to describe the dreadful condition of that day, though it is impossible to say anything that is able to give a true idea of it to those who did not see it, other than this, that it was indeed very, very, very dreadful, and such as no tongue can express.

I got admittance into the churchyard by being acquainted with the sexton who attended; who, though he did not refuse me at all, yet earnestly persuaded me not to go, telling me very seriously (for he was a good, religious, and sensible man) that it was indeed their business and duty to venture, and to run all hazards, and that in it[11] they might hope to be preserved; but that I had no apparent call to it but my own curiosity, which, he said, he believed I would not pretend was sufficient to justify my running that hazard. I told him I had been pressed in my mind to go, and that per-

Protestants – being led by Holy Spirit

haps it might be an instructing sight, that might not be without its uses. "Nay," says the good man, "if you will venture upon that score, name of God go in; for, depend upon it, 'twill be a sermon to you, it may be, the best that ever you heard in your life. 'Tis a speaking sight," says he, "and has a voice with it, and a loud one, to call us all to repentance," and with that he opened the door and said, "Go, if you will."

> **People that were infected and near their end, and delirious also, would run to these pits . . . and bury themselves.**

His discourse had shocked my resolution a little, and I stood wavering for a good while, but just at that interval I saw two links[12] come over from the end of the Minories, and heard the bell-man,[13] and then appeared a dead-cart, as they called it, coming over the streets; so I could no longer resist my desire of seeing it, and went in. There was nobody, as I could perceive at first, in the churchyard, or going into it, but the buriers and the fellow that drove the cart, or rather led the horse and cart; but when they came up to the pit they saw a man go to and again, muffled up in a brown cloak, and making motions with his hands under his cloak, as if he was in great agony, and the buriers immediately gathered about him, supposing he was one of those poor delirious or desperate creatures that used to pretend, as I have said, to bury themselves. He said nothing as he walked about, but two or three times groaned very deeply and loud, and sighed as he would break his heart.

---

11. **in it.** Going up to the edge of the pits
12. **links.** Torches
13. **bell-man.** Man who rang a bell by the dead cart

---

dis • course (dis′ kôrs′) *n.,* formal expression of thought

When the buriers came up to him they soon found he was neither a person infected and desperate, as I have observed above, or a person distempered in mind, but one oppressed with a dreadful weight of grief indeed, having his wife and several of his children all in the cart that was just come in with him, and he followed in an agony and excess of sorrow. He mourned heartily, as it was easy to see, but with a kind of masculine grief that could not give itself vent by tears; and calmly defying the buriers to let him alone, said he would only see the bodies thrown in and go away, so they left <u>importuning</u> him. But no sooner was the cart turned round and the bodies shot into the pit promiscuously, which was a surprise to him, for he at least expected they would have been decently laid in, though indeed he was afterward convinced that was impracticable; I say, no sooner did he see the sight but he cried out aloud, unable to contain himself. I could not hear what he said, but he went backward two or three steps and fell down in a swoon. The buriers ran to him and took him up, and in a little while he came to himself, and they led him away to the Pie Tavern over against the end of Houndsditch, where, it seems the man was known, and where they took care of him. He looked into the pit again as he went away, but the buriers had covered the bodies so immediately with throwing in earth, that though there was light enough, for there were lanterns, and candles in them, placed all night round the sides of the pit, upon heaps of earth, seven or eight, or perhaps more, yet nothing could be seen.

This was a mournful scene indeed, and affected me almost as much as the rest; but the other was awful and full of terror. The cart had in it sixteen or seventeen bodies; some were wrapped up in linen sheets, some in rags, some little other than naked, or so loose that what covering they had fell from them in the shooting out of the cart, and they fell quite naked among the rest; but the matter was not much to them, or the indecency much to anyone else, seeing they were all dead, and were to be huddled together into the common grave of mankind, as we may call it, for here was no difference made, but poor and rich went together; there was no other way of burials, neither was it possible there should, for coffins were not to be had for the <u>prodigious</u> numbers that fell in such a calamity as this.

> *They were all dead, and were to be huddled together into the common grave of mankind.*

5. A Poor Piper

. . . John Hayward . . . was at that time undersexton of the parish of St. Stephen, Coleman Street. By undersexton was understood at that time gravedigger and bearer of the dead. This man carried, or assisted to carry, all the dead to their graves which were buried in that large parish, and who were carried in form;[14] and after that form of burying was stopped, went with the dead-cart and the bell to fetch the dead bodies from the houses where they lay. . . .

It was under this John Hayward's care, and within his bounds, that the story of the piper, with which people have made themselves so merry, happened, and he assured me that it was true. It is said that it was a blind piper; but, as John told me, the fellow was not blind, but an ignorant, weak, poor man, and usually walked his rounds about ten o'clock at night and went piping along from door to door, and the people usually took him in at public

---

14. **in form.** Following the usual burial customs

im • por • tune (im′ pər tün′) *v.*, demand
pro • di • gious (prə di′ jəs) *adj.*, extremely large

houses[15] where they knew him, and would give him drink and victuals, and sometimes farthings;[16] and he in return would pipe and sing and talk simply, which <u>diverted</u> the people; and thus he lived. It was but a very bad time for this diversion while things were as I have told, yet the poor fellow went about as usual, but was almost starved; and when anybody asked how he did he would answer, the dead-cart had not taken him yet, but that they had promised to call for him next week.

It happened one night that this poor fellow, whether somebody had given him too much to drink or no—John Hayward said he had not drink in his house, but that they had given him a little more victuals than ordinary at the public house in Coleman Street—and the poor fellow, having not usually had a bellyful for perhaps not a good while, was laid all along upon the top of a bulk or stall, and fast asleep, at a door in the street near London Wall, towards Cripplegate; and that upon the same bulk or stall the people of some house, in the alley of which the house was a corner, hearing a bell which they always rang before the cart came, had laid a body really dead of the plague just by him, thinking, too, that this poor fellow had been a dead body, as the other was, and laid there by some of the neighbors.

Accordingly, when John Hayward with his bell and the cart came along, finding two dead bodies lie upon the stall, they took them up with the instrument they used and threw them into the cart, and all this while the piper slept soundly.

From hence they passed along and took in other dead bodies, till, as honest John Hayward told me, they almost buried him alive in the cart; yet all this while he slept soundly. At length the cart came to the place where the bodies were to be thrown into the ground, which, as I do remember, was at Mount Mill; and as the cart usually stopped some time before they were ready to shoot out the melancholy load they had in it, as soon as the cart stopped the

fellow awaked and struggled a little to get his head out from among the dead bodies, when, raising himself up in the cart, he called out, "Hey! where am I?" This frighted the fellow that attended about the work; but after some pause John Hayward, recovering himself, said, "Lord, bless us! There's somebody in the cart not quite dead!" So another called to him and said, "Who are you?" The fellow answered, "I am the poor piper. Where am I?" "Where are you?" says Hayward. "Why, you are in the dead-cart, and we are going to bury you." "But I an't dead though, am I?" says the piper, which made them laugh a little—though, as John said, they were heartily frighted at first; so they helped the poor fellow down, and he went about his business.

I know the story goes he set up his pipes in the cart and frighted the bearers and others so that they ran away; but John Hayward did not tell the story so, nor say anything of his piping at all; but that he was a poor piper, and that he was carried away as above I am fully satisfied of the truth of. . . .

6. A Violent Cure

I heard of one infected creature who, running out of his bed in his shirt in the anguish and agony of his swellings, of which he had three upon him, got his shoes on and went to put on his coat; but the nurse resisting, and snatching the coat from him, he threw her down, ran over her, ran downstairs and into the street, directly to the Thames in his shirt, the nurse running after him, and calling to the watch to stop him; but the watchman, frighted at the man, and afraid to touch him, let him go on; upon which he ran down to the Stillyard stairs, threw away his shirt, and plunged into the Thames, and, being a good swimmer, swam

---

15. **public houses.** Taverns
16. **farthing.** Former British coin worth less than a cent

di • vert (də vʉrt´) v., entertain; amuse

quite over the river; and the tide being coming in, as they call it (that is, running westward) he reached the land not till he came about the Falcon stairs, where landing, and finding no people there, it being in the night, he ran about the streets there, naked as he was, for a good while, when, it being by that time high water,[17] he takes the river again, and swam back to the Stillyard, landed, ran up the streets again to his own house, knocking at the door, went up the stairs and into his bed again; and that this terrible experiment cured him of the plague, that is to say, that the violent motion of his arms and legs stretched the parts where the swellings he had upon him were, that is to say, under his arms and his groin, and caused them to ripen and break; and that the cold of the water abated the fever in his blood. . . .

7. The Plague Diminishes

. . . The contagion despised all medicine; death raged in every corner; and had it gone on as it did then, a few weeks more would have cleared the town of all, and everything that had a soul. Men everywhere began to despair; every heart failed them for fear; people were made desperate through the anguish of their souls, and the terrors of death sat in the very faces and countenances of the people.

In that very moment when we might very well say, "Vain was the help of man,"—I say, in that very moment it pleased God, with a most agreeable surprise, to cause the fury of it to abate, even of itself; and the malignity declining, as I have said, though infinite numbers were sick, yet fewer died, and the very first weeks' bill[18] decreased 1,843; a vast number indeed!

It is impossible to express the change that appeared in the very countenances of the people that Thursday morning when the weekly bill came out. It might have been perceived in their countenances that a secret surprise and smile of joy sat on everybody's face. They shook one another by the hands in the streets, who would hardly go on the same side of the way with one another before. Where the streets were not too broad they would open their windows and call from one house to another, and ask how they did, and if they had heard the good news that the plague was <u>abated</u>. Some would return, when they said good news, and ask, "What good news?" and when they answered that the plague was abated and the bills decreased almost two thousand, they would cry out, "God be praised!" and would weep aloud for joy, telling them they had heard nothing of it; and such was the joy of the people that it was, as it were, life to them from the grave. I could almost set down as many extravagant things done in the excess of their joy as of their grief; but that would be to lessen the value of it. . . .

8. I'm Alive!

. . . I shall conclude the account of this <u>calamitous</u> year . . . with a coarse but sincere stanza of my own, which I placed at the end of my ordinary memorandums the same year they were written:

> A dreadful plague in London was
> In the year sixty-five,
> Which swept an hundred thousand souls
> Away; yet I alive! ❖

---

17. **high water.** High tide
18. **weeks' bill.** Every week during the plague, a count of the dead was published.

abate (ə bāt´) *v.,* lessen
ca • lam • i • tous (kə la´ mə təs) *adj.,* accompanied by misery and loss

---

MIRRORS & **W**INDOWS

Defoe describes people's tremendous joy and relief when the plague diminished. How else might they have felt about surviving a disaster that killed so many people? Why might the survivors of a disaster or accident feel guilty?

Refer to Text ▶ ▶ ▶ ▶ ▶   Reason with Text

Refer to Text	Reason with Text	
1a. How did Pepys describe the fire seen from the alehouse? What did he describe next?	**1b.** Explain how describing a specific event increases the horror of the whole event.	**Understand** Find meaning
2a. According to Defoe, how did people react as the plague dragged on?	**2b.** Examine what this reaction suggests about human nature in the face of adversity.	**Apply** Use information
3a. What anecdotes and specific details does Pepys record about the plague?	**3b.** What mood does Pepys's description of the plague create? Compare the mood to that in *A Journal of the Plague Year*.	**Analyze** Take things apart
4a. According to Defoe, how were the dead buried?	**4b.** Evaluate the authenticity of Defoe's journal based on your knowledge of the plague.	**Evaluate** Make judgments
5a. What does Pepys say people will be afraid to do after the plague? What does Defoe's narrator say about the end of the plague?	**5b.** Specify the usefulness and the limitations of diaries, journals, and historical fiction for learning about a certain time period.	**Create** Bring ideas together

Compare Literature

Diction and Narrator

Does the diction of Pepys and Defoe reflect the informal language of a typical diary or journal entry? Explain your answer. How would you compare Defoe's diction to Pepys's use of language?

Who is the narrator in each excerpt? How is each narrator's knowledge limited? How does the choice of narrator affect the content of each selection?

Extend the Text

Writing Options

Creative Writing Write a fictionalized journal for teens about a major historical event that happened during your lifetime. Choose a narrator other than yourself and adopt the voice and diction of this narrator. Then freewrite about your memories related to your chosen event.

Persuasive Writing Write a one-paragraph analysis of *The Diary of Samuel Pepys* and *A Journal of the Plague Year* to be used by social studies teachers to determine if these works would be good for their class on seventeenth-century England.

Lifelong Learning

Analyze Documents About Diseases The Centers for Disease Control (CDC), World Health Organization (WHO), and others provide information about infectious diseases. Gather information about a specific disease using the Internet, the public health department, or newspapers. What is the purpose of each piece of information? How is that reflected in the piece's diction and tone?

Media Literacy

Analyze Health Documents The Centers for Disease Control and the World Health Organization provide infor-mation about infectious diseases. Gather information about a specific disease from their websites: **http://lit.emcp.net/cdc** and **http://lit.emcp.net/who**. Also research other sources on the Internet, the public health department, and newspapers. Determine the purpose, diction, and tone of each piece of information. Then write a report in which you synthesize the ideas from all your sources, citing textual evidence to support your inferences and conclusions.

Research Blogs Online blogs are modern versions of diaries and journals, sharing views about public and private events. Search online for blogs about a recent pandemic (widespread outbreak of disease), such as the H1N1 flu outbreak in 2009. One good source of such information is *The New York Times* news blog The Lede, at **http://lit.emcp.net/blog**. What parallels can you draw between Defoe's account of misinformation about the plague—for example, when he refers to the "terrible experiment" of a victim running and swimming to "ripen and break" the swellings—and bloggers' comments on misinformation they are getting? Discuss with your class-mates other similarities and differences among blogs, dia-ries, and journals in terms of content and layout. Address how the blog techniques of using images and sounds affect the meaning of the text.

A Young Lady's Diary

by Joseph Addison

Lady Chambers, 1756. Sir Joshua Reynolds. Iveagh Bequest, Kenwood, England. (See detail on page 589.)

I find that I am at a loss to know whether I pass my time well or ill.

The Spectator, No. 323: Tuesday, March 11, 1712.

Modo vir, modo femina.[1]—OVID

The Journal with which I presented my readers on Tuesday last has brought me in several letters with accounts of many private lives cast into that form. I have the Rake's Journal, the Sot's Journal, the Whore-master's Journal, and among several others a very curious piece, entitled, The Journal of a Mohock.[2] By these instances I find that the intention of my last Tuesday's paper has been mistaken by many of my readers. I did not design so much to expose vice as idleness, and aimed at those persons who pass away their time rather in

---

1. *Modo vir, modo femina.* Quote from Ovid's *Metamorphoses,* meaning "sometimes a man, sometimes a woman"
2. **Mohock.** Term Mohock or Mohawk referred to London street thugs.

trifles and impertinence, than in crimes and immoralities. Offenses of this later kind are not to be dallied with, or treated in so ludicrous a manner. In short, my journal only holds up folly to the light, and shows the disagreeableness of such actions as are indifferent in themselves, and blamable only as they proceed from creatures endowed with reason.

> *In short, my journal only holds up folly to the light.*

My following correspondent, who calls herself Clarinda, is such a journalist as I require: she seems by her letter to be placed in a modish state of indifference between vice and virtue, and to be susceptible of either, were there proper pains taken with her. Had her journal been filled with gallantries, or such occurrences as had shown her wholly divested of her natural innocence, notwithstanding it might have been more pleasing to the generality of readers, I should not have published it; but as it is only the picture of a life filled with a fashionable kind of gayety and laziness, I shall set down five days of it, as I have received it from the hand of my correspondent.

Dear Mr. Spectator,

You having set your readers an exercise in one of your last week's papers, I have performed mine according to your orders and herewith send it you enclosed. You must know, Mr. Spectator, that I am a maiden lady of a good fortune, who have had several matches offered me for these ten years last past, and have at present warm applications made to me by a very pretty fellow. As I am at my own disposal, I come up to town every winter and pass my time after the manner you will find in the following journal, which I began to write upon the very day after your *Spectator* upon that subject.

TUESDAY *night.* Could not go to sleep till one in the morning for thinking of my journal.

WEDNESDAY. *From eight till ten.* Drank two dishes of chocolate in bed, and fell asleep after them.

From ten to eleven. Eat a slice of bread and butter, drank a dish of bohea,[3] read *The Spectator.*

From eleven to one. At my toilette, tried a new head. Gave orders for Veny[4] to be combed and washed. Mem.[5] I look best in blue.

From one till half an hour after two. Drove to the Change. Cheapened[6] a couple of fans.

Till four. At dinner. Mem. Mr. Froth passed by in his new liveries.

From four to six. Dressed, paid a visit to old Lady Blithe and her sister, having before heard they were gone out of town that day.

From six to eleven. At basset.[7] Mem. Never set again upon the ace of diamonds.

THURSDAY. *From eleven at night to eight in the morning.* Dreamed that I punted to[8] Mr. Froth.

From eight to ten. Chocolate. Read two acts in *Aurenzebe* a-bed.

From ten to eleven. Tea-table. Sent to borrow Lady Faddle's Cupid for Veny. Read the play-bills. Received a letter from Mr. Froth. Mem. Locked it up in my strong box.

Rest of the morning. Fontange,[9] the tire-woman, her account of my Lady Blithe's wash. Broke a tooth in my little tortoise-shell comb.

---

3. **bohea.** Type of tea
4. **Veny.** Nickname for Clarinda's dog, Venice
5. **Mem.** Abbreviation used throughout to mean "I must remember"
6. **Cheapened.** Priced
7. **basset.** Card game
8. **punted to.** Gambled with
9. **Fontange.** Fashionable hairdresser in London

---

tri • fle (trī′ fəl) *n.,* something of little value or importance
lu • di • crous (lü′ də krəs) *adj.,* foolish and worthy of scorn

from
A Dictionary of the English Language

by Samuel Johnson

A

DICTIONARY

OF THE

ENGLISH LANGUAGE:

IN WHICH

The WORDS are deduced from their ORIGINALS,

AND

ILLUSTRATED in their DIFFERENT SIGNIFICATIONS

BY

EXAMPLES from the best WRITERS.

TO WHICH ARE PREFIXED,

A HISTORY of the LANGUAGE,

AND

AN ENGLISH GRAMMAR.

BY SAMUEL JOHNSON, A.M.

IN TWO VOLUMES.

VOL. I.

Cum tabulis animum cenforis fumet honefti :
Audebit quæcunque parum fplendoris habebunt,
Et fine pondere erunt, et honore indigna ferentur.
Verba movere loco; quamvis invita recedant,
Et verfentur adhuc intra penetralia Veftæ;
Obfcurata diu populo bonus eruet, atque
Proferet in lucem fpeciofa vocabula rerum,
Quæ prifca memorata Catonibus atque Cethegis,
Nunc fitus informis premit et deferta vetuftas.   HOR.

LONDON,
Printed by W. STRAHAN,
For J. and P. KNAPTON; T. and T. LONGMAN; C. HITCH and L. HAWES;
A. MILLAR; and R. and J. DODSLEY.
MDCCLV.

ANTHO´LOGY. *n.*

 1. A collection of flowers.

GANG. *n.*

 A number herding together; a troop; a company; a tribe; a herd. It is seldom used but in contempt or <u>abhorrence</u>.

---

ab · hor · rence (əb hôr´ ən[t]s) *n.,* loathing

LEXICO´GRAPHER. *n.*

A writer of dictionaries; a harmless <u>drudge</u>, that busies himself in tracing the original, and detailing the signification of words.

NA´TURE. *n.*

1. An imaginary being supposed to preside over the material and animal world.

> Though, *nature,* art my goddess; to thy law
> My services are bound.—*Shakespeare*

2. The native state or properties of anything, by which it is discriminated from others.

3. The constitution of an animated body.

4. <u>Disposition</u> of mind; temper.

5. The regular course of things.

6. The compass of natural existence.

7. Natural affection, or reverence; native sensations.

8. The state or operation of the material world.

9. Sort; species.

10. Sentiments or images adapted to nature, or comfortable to truth and reality.

11. Physics; the science which teaches the qualities of things.

> *Nature* and *nature's* laws lay hid in night,
> God said, Let Newton be, and all was light.—*Pope.*

OATS. *n.*

A grain, which in England is generally given to horses, but in Scotland supports the people.

PA´TRON. *n.*

1. One who countenances, supports, or protects. Commonly a wretch who supports with <u>insolence</u>, and is paid with flattery. ❖

---

drudge (drŭj) *n.,* person who does tedious work
dis • po • si • tion (dis pə zi´ shən) *n.,* tendency; habit
in • so • lence (in´ sōl ənts) *n.,* disrespect; contempt

MIRRORS & WINDOWS

How and when should new words be added to the dictionary? What guidelines would you propose for deciding whether to add a word to a modern dictionary?

A BRIEF TO FREE A SLAVE

by Samuel Johnson

NO MAN IS BY NATURE THE PROPERTY OF ANOTHER.

I t must be agreed that in most ages many countries have had part of their inhabitants in a state of slavery; yet it may be doubted whether slavery can ever be supposed the natural condition of man. It is impossible not to conceive that men in their original state were equal; and very difficult to imagine how one would be subjected to another but by violent <u>compulsion</u>. An individual may, indeed, forfeit his liberty by a crime; but he cannot by that crime forfeit the liberty of his children. What is

true of a criminal seems true likewise of a captive. A man may accept life from a conquering enemy on condition of perpetual servitude; but it is very doubtful whether he can <u>entail</u> that servitude on his descendants; for no man can <u>stipulate</u> without commission for another. The

---

com • pul • sion (kəm pul´ shən) *n.,* coercion; driving force
en • tail (in tāl´) *v.,* pass on
stip • u • late (sti´ pyə lāt´) *v.,* specify conditions of an
    agreement

The British Slave Trade

The European slave trade started at the beginning of the sixteenth century, when European colonies needed manual labor to excavate and till America's newly discovered resources. The slave trade soon became an integral part of the British economy, and the wealth it generated helped build the British colonial empire.

Between 1500 and 1850, European countries enslaved approximately twelve million Africans. During this same time, 250 documented uprisings occurred on slave ships as they journeyed across the Atlantic Ocean. European slave trafficking reached its peak in the eighteenth century, when six million Africans were shipped across the Atlantic.

The British imported some Africans to Britain to personally serve the wealthy elite. However, the British did not barter slaves, and the law did not explicitly outline their legal status. This ambiguity led to placing limits on slavery in 1772. A runaway slave named James Somerset escaped from Jamaica that year and landed in England.

His owner attempted to recapture him, but abolitionists intervened and demanded a trial. The presiding judge decided that since British law did not consider Somerset property, his owner had no right to detain him. This landmark decision immediately freed the fourteen thousand slaves living in Britain.

Nonetheless, slavery persisted in Britain's colonies overseas. British abolitionists, led by the Quakers and a freed slave named Olaudah Equiano, continued lobbying for the British government to ban the institution entirely. In 1833, Parliament passed the Slavery Abolition Act, which effectively put an end to slavery throughout the British Empire.

---

condition which he himself accepts, his son or grandson perhaps would have rejected. If we should admit, what perhaps may with more reason be denied, that there are certain relations between man and man which may make slavery necessary and just, yet it can never be proved that he who is now suing for his freedom ever stood in any of those relations. He is certainly subject by no law, but that of violence, to his present master, who pretends no claim to his obedience, but that he bought him from a merchant of slaves, whose right to sell him never was examined. It is said that, according to the constitutions of Jamaica, he was legally enslaved; these constitutions are merely positive; and apparently injurious to the rights of mankind, because whoever is exposed to sale is condemned to slavery without appeal; by whatever fraud or violence he might have been originally brought into the merchant's power. In our own time princes have been sold, by wretches to whose care they were entrusted, that they might have an European education; but when once they were brought to a market in the plantations, little would <u>avail</u> either their dignity or their wrongs. The laws of Jamaica afford a Negro no <u>redress</u>. His color is considered as a sufficient testimony against him. It is to be lamented that moral right should ever give way to political convenience. But if temptations of interest are

IT MAY BE DOUBTED WHETHER SLAVERY CAN EVER BE SUPPOSED THE NATURAL CONDITION OF MAN.

avail (ə vāl´) v., be of use; help
re · dress (ri dres´) n., compensation for wrongdoing

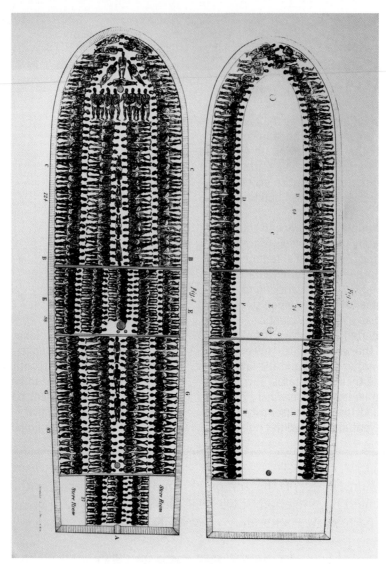

Lithograph of the hold of a slave ship (c. 1790).

sometimes too strong for human virtue, let us at least retain a virtue where there is no temptation to quit it. In the present case there is apparent right on one side, and no convenience on the other. Inhabitants of this island can neither gain riches nor power by taking away the liberty of any part of the human species. The sum of the argument is this:—No man is by nature the property of another: The defendant is, therefore, by nature free: The rights of nature must be some way forfeited before they can be justly taken away: That the defendant has by any act forfeited the rights of nature we require to be proved; and if no proof of such forfeiture can be given, we doubt not but the justice of the court will declare him free. ❖

Johnson presents a rational argument for freeing a slave. Would his argument be stronger if it were more emotional—for instance, describing the horrors of slavery? Which type of argument do you generally find more convincing: one based on reason or emotion?

Refer to Text ▶ ▶ ▶ ▶ ▶   Reason with Text

1a. According to Johnson's "A Brief to Free a Slave," why might slavery seem attractive to some people?	**1b.** Why does Johnson believe that any reasons that make slavery attractive cannot apply to Joseph Knight's case?	**Understand** Find meaning
2a. In his dictionary, how does Johnson define *gang?*	**2b.** How would you define the word? What might explain differences in definitions?	**Apply** Use information
3a. Identify the arguments in favor of slavery that Johnson includes in his brief.	**3b.** Analyze how Johnson uses these arguments in making his own case against slavery.	**Analyze** Take things apart
4a. How does Johnson define *lexicographer* in his dictionary?	**4b.** Judge whether Johnson fits this definition. What does this definition tell you about him?	**Evaluate** Make judgments
5a. What does Johnson say about slavery in the opening sentence of "A Brief to Free a Slave"?	**5b.** How might Johnson define *slavery* in his *Dictionary of the English Language?*	**Create** Bring ideas together

Analyze Literature

Denotation, Connotation, and Argument

What are the denotation and connotations of *gang* in Johnson's dictionary? Does this word have the same connotations for you? What connotations does Johnson include in his definition of *oats?*

What is Johnson's thesis, or the main or controlling idea he supports, in "A Brief to Free a Slave"? Review your list of arguments that Johnson uses to support his thesis. Analyze the consistency and clarity of Johnson's expression of that idea. How effective is his argument? Why?

Extend the Text

Writing Options

Creative Writing Imagine you are creating your own dictionary. Choose three words that have specific connotations for you. Write definitions for the words in which you include a serious denotation and your own connotations. Use quotations from literature or songs to illustrate the meaning of at least one word.

Expository Writing Write an editorial about Johnson's brief that might have been published in an eighteenth-century newspaper. Write from the point of view of a slave owner or an abolitionist. Address the specific points Johnson makes, critiquing his brief and its chances of succeeding.

Media Literacy

Analyze Reports on Human Rights With a small group, find two editorials or other opinion pieces about a human rights issue. Analyze the arguments made by the writers of these pieces, and identify the arguments and counterarguments in each piece. Then discuss these questions: What is the thesis of each piece? What arguments does each writer use? Do the writers use facts to support their ideas? Do they try to manipulate emotions? Does either writer use features such as ambiguity or contradictory messages? How do these devices contribute to the effectiveness of the essays?

Lifelong Learning

Conduct Interviews Choose five words that likely have different meanings to different people. Write your own definition and contextual sentence for each word. Interview several people and ask each to define the word and use it in a sentence. Encourage people to give multiple meanings. Compile the responses in a chart. Discuss your findings with the class.

 Go to **www.mirrorsandwindows.com** for more.

Understand the Concept

When we think about the meanings of words, we typically think of dictionary definitions. But words also have more subjective, subtle meanings that can cause confusion or even insult. Consider, for instance, the difference between the words *cheap* and *inexpensive.* Both mean essentially the same thing: "of low cost." However, which word would you likely use to describe a gift you have purchased for someone important to you?

The two types of word meanings are denotation and connotation. The **denotation** of a word is its dictionary definition; this meaning is objective and generally agreed on. The **connotation** of a word is the emotional association or implication it makes; this meaning is subjective and often personal.

Connotations often are positive (favorable) or negative (unfavorable). For example, the adjectives *unique* and *freakish* both mean "different from what is typical." But *unique* suggests that something is original and distinctive, having a positive connotation. In contrast, *freakish* suggests that something is strange or abnormal and has a negative connotation. *Different* is neutral, having neither a positive nor a negative connotation.

Connotations also sometimes express degrees of intensity, or depth of feeling. Notice the increase in intensity among these words: *startled, surprised, shocked, outraged.* Where would you insert *stunned*?

When you are reading, try to determine the connotations of unfamiliar words from the context. Use clues from the surrounding text to help identify the emotional associations that words have. Consider, too, the overall tone of a passage to determine connotative word meanings. Look at the following sentences:

EXAMPLES

I hadn't realized how illness had ravaged Jorge's body until I saw his *emaciated,* skeletal figure.

Vince was a *scrawny* kid who was always getting picked on.

You can tell from these sentences that the words *emaciated* and *scrawny* both mean "thin." However, in the first sentence, you can infer that the thinness is the result of illness, and in the second sentence, that being thin is associated with being small and weak.

When you are writing and speaking, be aware of connotations. Choose words that have the specific meanings you intend. Although a dictionary won't include the connotative meanings, you can use the denotative definitions and examples of usage provided to distinguish between words. A thesaurus, which lists synonyms, near synonyms, and antonyms, also can be helpful in understanding the connotations of words.

Apply the Skill

Exercise A

On your own paper, identify the denotation of each pair of words. Then explain the differences between the connotations of the two words.

1. tenacious, stubborn
2. economical, cheap
3. inquisitive, prying
4. childlike, immature
5. showy, ostentatious

Write two sentences for each word pair above (one sentence using each word). Then discuss with a partner how the meaning of the sentence changes depending on which word is used. For each pair of words, write a word analogy to help explain the differences in connotation. For example: "Cute is to lovely as daisy is to rose."

Exercise B

In the last paragraph of "A Brief to Free a Slave," Johnson states, "No man is by nature the property of another." Analyze the textual context of *nature* to draw conclusions about nuances in the word's meaning. Write the definition that you think Johnson had in mind.

SPELLING PRACTICE

Commonly Misspelled Words

Many of the following words from Samuel Johnson's dictionary and "A Brief to Free a Slave" present challenges to spellers. Study the list and see if you can determine a spelling rule to help you remember how to spell each word. Write the words and rules on a separate sheet of paper.

abhorrence	countenance	necessary
accept	descendants	obedience
apparently	existence	reverence
condemned	injurious	servitude
convenience	insolence	sufficient

from The Life of Samuel Johnson, LL.D.

A Biography by James Boswell

Build Background

Literary Context Soon after befriending Samuel Johnson in 1763, James Boswell conceived a plan to write a new type of biography: one that told less about dates and observable events and more about the subject's thoughts and personality. **The Life of Samuel Johnson, LL.D.** (1791) shows Boswell's genius for drawing out Johnson and for recognizing and selecting quotations and anecdotes that depict his subject intimately. In fact, many of Johnson's famous quotations are recorded in Boswell's biography of him.

Boswell's biography draws on research, interviews, and his own conversations with Johnson. Boswell says of his writing style, "I draw him in the style of a Flemish painter. I am not satisfied with hitting the large features. I must be exact as to every hair, or even every spot on his countenance." Boswell's willingness to reveal his own foibles made the work a surpassing novelty when it appeared.

Reader's Context If you were writing a biography about your best friend, what would you want people to know about him or her?

Meet the Author

James Boswell (1740–1795) was the son of a judge. His father's title allowed Boswell to enter high society in London and Edinburgh. Although Boswell studied law and even opened a successful practice, he had literary and political ambitions.

One of Boswell's major goals was to befriend noted writers. On a tour of Europe as a young man, he met with the French Enlightenment philosophers Jean-Jacques Rousseau and Voltaire. His meeting with Samuel Johnson in 1763 proved to be the most influential, however. Knowing that Johnson did not like the Scots, Boswell implored the person who introduced them not to say where he was from. When it was announced he was from Scotland, he apologized to Johnson, saying he could not help it. Johnson quipped, "Sir, that, I find, is what a great many of your countrymen cannot help." Thirty years separated the two men in age, but after a shaky beginning, they became lifelong friends.

After Johnson's death, Boswell completed *The Life of Samuel Johnson, LL.D.*, which stands today as his greatest literary accomplishment. Boswell was working on another volume of the biography when he died in 1795. Long after his death, his diaries were published. With these, Boswell's reputation grew from one of the premier biographers in English to one of the great diarists in English, as well.

Analyze Literature

Characterization and Anecdote

Characterization is the act of creating or describing a character. *Indirect characterization* shows what characters say, do, or think and what other characters say or think about them. *Direct characterization* shows what physical features, dress, and personality the characters display.

An **anecdote** is a short narrative of an interesting, amusing, or biographical incident.

Set Purpose

Boswell uses characterization techniques to create a vivid account of Samuel Johnson's life and personality. While you read this excerpt, list specific examples of the techniques Boswell uses and label them accordingly. How do these examples contribute to your understanding of Johnson's character? Also consider Boswell's use of anecdotes in the selection. How do they help readers better understand Johnson's character?

Preview Vocabulary

arduous, 614
eminent, 615
prodigious, 615
implicitly, 615
insinuate, 616
conciliate, 616
solicit, 616
posterity, 616
cynical, 617
asperity, 617

Dr. Johnson in the Ante-Room of the Lord Chesterfield Waiting for an Audience, 1748, 1845.
Edward Matthew Ward. (See detail on page 613.)

from
The Life of
Samuel Johnson, LL. D.

by James Boswell

Praise, in general, was pleasing to him; but by praise from a man of rank and elegant accomplishments, he was peculiarly gratified.

But the year 1747 is distinguished as the epoch,[1] when Johnson's <u>arduous</u> and important work, his *Dictionary of the English Language,* was announced to the world, by the publication of its *Plan* or *Prospectus.*

How long this immense undertaking had been the object of his contemplation, I do not know. I once asked him by what means he had attained to that astonishing knowledge of our language, by which he was enabled to realize a design of such extent, and accumulated difficulty. He told me, that "it was not the effect of particular study; but that it had grown up in his mind insensibly." I have been informed

---

1. **epoch.** Period of time

ar • du • ous (är´ jə wəs) *adj.,* extremely difficult

by Mr. James Dodsley, that several years before this period, when Johnson was one day sitting in his brother Robert's shop, he heard his brother suggest to him, that a Dictionary of the English Language would be a work that would be well received by the publick; that Johnson seemed at first to catch at the proposition, but, after a pause, said, in his abrupt decisive manner, "I believe I shall not undertake it." That he, however, had bestowed much thought upon the subject, before he published his *Plan,* is evident from the enlarged, clear, and accurate views which it exhibits and we find him mentioning in that tract, that many of the writers whose testimonies were to be produced as authorities, were selected by Pope; which proves that he had been furnished, probably by Mr. Robert Dodsley, with whatever hints that <u>eminent</u> poet had contributed towards a great literary project, that had been the subject of important consideration in a former reign.

. . .

Dr. Adams found him one day busy at his *Dictionary,* when the following dialogue ensued. "ADAMS. This is a great work, Sir. How are you to get all the etymologies?[2] JOHNSON. Why, Sir, here is a shelf with Junius, and Skinner, and others; and there is a Welch gentleman who has published a collection of Welch proverbs, who will help me with the Welch. ADAMS. But, Sir, how can you do this in three years? JOHNSON. Sir, I have no doubt that I can do it in three years. ADAMS. But the French Academy, which consists of forty members, took forty years to compile their Dictionary. JOHNSON. Sir, thus it is. This is the proportion. Let me see; forty times forty is sixteen hundred. As three to sixteen hundred, so is the proportion of an Englishman to a Frenchman." With so much ease and pleasantry could he talk of that <u>prodigious</u> labor which he had undertaken to execute.

. . .

Lord Chesterfield, to whom Johnson had paid the high compliment of addressing

With so much ease and pleasantry could he talk of the prodigious labor which he had undertaken to execute.

to his Lordship the *Plan* of his *Dictionary,* had behaved to him in such a manner as to excite his contempt and indignation. The world has been for many years amused with a story confidently told, and as confidently repeated with additional circumstances, that a sudden disgust was taken by Johnson upon occasion of his having been one day kept long in waiting in his Lordship's antechamber, for which the reason assigned was, that he had company with him; and that at last, when the door opened, out walked Colley Cibber;[3] and that Johnson was so violently provoked when he found for whom he had been so long excluded, that he went away in a passion, and never would return. I remember having mentioned this story to George Lord Lyttelton, who told me, he was very intimate with Lord Chesterfield; and holding it as a well-known truth, defended Lord Chesterfield, by saying, that "Cibber, who had been introduced familiarly by the backstairs, had probably not been there above ten minutes." It may seem strange even to entertain a doubt concerning a story so long and so widely current, and thus <u>implicitly</u> adopted, if not sanctioned, by the authority which I have mentioned; but Johnson himself assured me, that there was not the least foundation for it. He told me, that there never was any particular incident which produced a quarrel between Lord Chesterfield and him; but that his Lordship's continued neglect was the

---

2. **etymologies.** Origins of words
3. **Colley Cibber.** Minor English poet ridiculed by Pope

em • i • nent (e´ mə nənt) *adj.,* noteworthy
pro • di • gious (prə di´ jəs) *adj.,* amazing; huge
im • plic • it • ly (im pli´ sət lē) *adv.,* doubtlessly

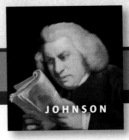

JOHNSON

Development of the Biography

The literary genre of the *biography* first emerged in ancient Greece, when a historian named Herodotus detailed the lives of ancient Persian kings during the fifth century BCE. The Classic Mediterranean literary world featured many notable biographers, whom historians still reference when studying ancient civilizations and cultures.

English biographies first became popular during the reign of King Henry VIII, but they gained particular prominence during the time of James Boswell. At age twenty-three, Boswell attached himself to Samuel Johnson. A skilled observer with a highly precise memory, Boswell rarely took notes during his meetings with Johnson. Only later would Boswell write down what he had seen and heard.

Johnson also wrote two biographies. Before these works, most English biographies either praised or scandalized their subjects. In contrast, Johnson included the defects as well as the strengths of his subjects, believing that a biography should get as close to the truth of the living person as possible.

---

reason why he resolved to have no connection with him. When the *Dictionary* was upon the eve of publication, Lord Chesterfield, who, it is said, had flattered himself with expectations that Johnson would dedicate the work to him, attempted, in a courtly manner, to sooth, and <u>insinuate</u> himself with the Sage, conscious, as it should seem, of the cold indifference with which he had treated its learned author; and further attempted to <u>conciliate</u> him, by writing two papers in *The World,* in recommendation of the work; and it must be confessed, that they contain some studied compliments, so finely turned, that if there had been no previous offense, it is probable that Johnson would have been highly delighted. Praise, in general, was pleasing to him; but by praise from a man of rank and elegant accomplishments, he was peculiarly gratified.

. . .

This courtly device failed of its effect. Johnson, who thought that "all was false and hollow," despised the honeyed words, and was even indignant that Lord Chesterfield should, for a moment, imagine that he could be the dupe of such an artifice. His expression to me concerning Lord Chesterfield, upon this occasion, was, "Sir, after making great professions, he had, for many years, taken no notice of me; but when my *Dictionary* was coming out, he fell a scribbling in *The World* about it. Upon which, I wrote him a letter expressed in civil terms, but such as might shew him that I did not mind what he said or wrote, and that I had done with him."

This is that celebrated letter of which so much has been said, and about which curiosity has been so long excited, without being gratified. I for many years <u>solicited</u> Johnson to favor me with a copy of it, that so excellent a composition might not be lost to <u>posterity</u>. He delayed from time to time to give it me; till at last in 1781, when we were on a visit at Mr. Dilly's, at Southill in Bedfordshire, he was pleased to dictate it to me from memory. He afterwards

in • sin • u • ate (in sin´ yū āt) *v.,* work into gradually
con • cil • i • ate (kən si´ lē āt') *v.,* win over
so • lic • it (sə li´ sət) *v.,* ask or seek pleadingly
pos • ter • i • ty (pä ster´ ə tē) *n.,* succeeding generations

found among his papers a copy of it, which he had dictated to Mr. Baretti, with its title and corrections, in his own handwriting. This he gave to Mr. Langton; adding that if it were to come into print, he wished it to be from that copy. By Mr. Langton's kindness, I am enabled to enrich my work with a perfect transcript of what the world has so eagerly desired to see.

To The Right Honorable
the Earl of Chesterfield

'My Lord,   February 1755

"I have been lately informed, by the proprietor of *The World*, that two papers, in which my Dictionary is recommended to the publick, were written by your Lordship. To be so distinguished, is an honor, which, being very little accustomed to favors from the great, I know not well how to receive, or in what terms to acknowledge.

"When, upon some slight encouragement, I first visited your Lordship, I was overpowered, like the rest of mankind, by the enchantment of your address; and could not forbear to wish that I might boast myself *Le vainqueur du vainqueur de la terre;*[4]—that I might obtain that regard for which I saw the world contending; but I found my attendance so little encouraged, that neither pride nor modesty would suffer me to continue it. When I had once addressed your Lordship in publick, I had exhausted all the art of pleasing which a retired and uncourtly scholar can possess. I had done all that I could; and no man is well pleased to have his all neglected, be it ever so little.

"Seven years, my Lord, have now passed, since I waited in your outward rooms, or was repulsed from your door; during which time I have been pushing on my work through difficulties, of which it is useless to complain, and have brought it, at last, to the verge of publication, without one act of assistance, one word of encouragement, or one smile of favor. Such treatment I did not expect, for I never had a Patron before.

"The shepherd in Virgil grew at last acquainted with Love, and found him a native of the rocks.

"Is not a Patron, my Lord, one who looks with unconcern on a man struggling for life in the water, and, when he has reached ground, encumbers him with help? The notice which you have been pleased to take of my labors, had it been early, had been kind; but it has been delayed till I am indifferent, and cannot enjoy it; till I am solitary, and cannot impart it; till I am known, and do not want it. I hope it is no very cynical asperity not to confess obligations where no benefit has been received, or to be unwilling that the Publick should consider me as owing that to a Patron, which Providence has enabled me to do for myself.

"Having carried on my work thus far with so little obligation to any favorer of learning, I shall not be disappointed though I should conclude it, if less be possible, with less; for I have been long wakened from that dream of hope, in which I once boasted myself with so much exultation, my Lord, your Lordship's most humble, most obedient servant,

'Sam. Johnson.' ❖

---

4. *Le vainqueur . . . terre.* [French] "The conqueror of the conqueror of the world."

cyn • i • cal (sĭ´ ni kəl) *adj.*, believing that people are insincere or selfish; sarcastic
as • per • i • ty (ă sper´ ə tē) *n.*, harshness

Mirrors & Windows

Johnson's letter to Lord Chesterfield makes it clear that he produced his dictionary without the help of a patron. When can it be helpful to have other people contribute to a large project? When can it be a hindrance?

Refer to Text ▶ ▶ ▶ ▶ ▶ Reason with Text

1a. How long did Johnson expect he would need to complete his dictionary? How long did the French Academy take?

1b. What did Johnson think of the French?

Understand
Find meaning

2a. Name the obstacles Dr. Adams saw in Johnson's dictionary plan. What did Johnson's response show?

2b. How would you react if somebody pointed out potential obstacles in your path?

Apply
Use information

3a. Outline why people thought there was a rift between Johnson and Lord Chesterfield. How did Johnson describe the situation?

3b. Compare the two versions. Why was the original story Boswell conveyed likely so popular?

Analyze
Take things apart

4a. Identify three details Boswell includes about Johnson.

4b. Evaluate Boswell's treatment of Johnson. Does it seem evenhanded? Why?

Evaluate
Make judgments

5a. What does Johnson say about patrons in his letter to Lord Chesterfield?

5b. Compare what Johnson says about patrons in his letter to Lord Chesterfield with the definition he includes in his dictionary.

Create
Bring ideas together

Analyze Literature

Characterization and Anecdote

Which characterization techniques does Boswell use to bring Johnson to life for the reader? Refer to your list, and identify examples of direct and indirect characterization. Explain what you learn about Johnson from it.

Why does Boswell include anecdotes? How does each anecdote support his characterization of Johnson? Examine the Lord Chesterfield anecdote. Discuss what details are and are not included. How does this anecdote contribute to your understanding of Johnson's character?

Extend the Text

Writing Options

Creative Writing Write a biographical essay about somebody you know well that will be read or distributed at a celebratory event, such as a milestone birthday. Also write a second essay that you would like to give to the person you have chosen; focus less on events and dates and more on the personality of the individual.

Persuasive Writing Boswell's biography is considered one of the greatest in English literature. Write a review of the biography explaining why it does or does not deserve this description. You may wish to read more of Boswell's biography or compare it to other biographies.

Media Literacy

Deliver a Narrative Presentation Prepare a narrative presentation about someone you know to be given at a roast or award ceremony honoring the person. Include a few anecdotes and choose a tone, such as humorous or reverent. Practice using varied volume, pacing, gestures, and facial expressions. Then deliver the presentation to your class or in a setting where your subject is present.

Collaborative Learning

Report on Noteworthy Citizens Work in groups to prepare reports on noteworthy figures in your community. If the person is living, try to conduct an interview. Identify a place to display your finished project, such as a library, bank, or other business, and write a letter requesting permission to do so. Ask if there are any guidelines for such a display. Check facts and make necessary corrections before installing your project.

 Go to **www.mirrorsandwindows.com** for more.

READING ASSESSMENT
for A Dictionary of the English Language;
A Brief to Free a Slave; *and* The Life of Samuel Johnson, LL.D.

1. Which general statement best describes Johnson's *A Dictionary of the English Language,* based on the two excerpts you read?
   A. It is a regular dictionary.
   B. It contains only humorous definitions, no real ones.
   C. It is a combination of real definitions and humorous ones.
   D. It defines all the words in Johnson's writings in the ways they are used there.
   E. It is a historic dictionary that contains the definitions of words as they were used in the past.

2. Which of Johnson's definitions of *nature* comes closest to how the word is used in the following sentence: She is by nature even tempered?
   A. "2. The native state or properties of anything, by which it is discriminated from others."
   B. "6. The compass of natural existence."
   C. "7. Natural affection, or reverence, native sensations."
   D. "8. The state or operation of the material world."
   E. "10. Sentiments or images adapted to nature, or comfortable to truth and reality."

3. In the title "A Brief to Free a Slave," what does the word *brief* mean?
   A. short
   B. abrupt
   C. a legal outline
   D. an official letter
   E. precise instructions

4. In "A Brief to Free a Slave," which of the following states the main point?
   A. "It must be agreed that in most ages many countries have had part of their inhabitants in a state of slavery."
   B. "A man may accept life from a conquering enemy on condition of perpetual servitude."
   C. "No man can stipulate without commission for another."
   D. "There are certain relations between man and man which may make slavery necessary and just."
   E. "No man is by nature the property of another."

5. In "A Brief to Free a Slave," why does Johnson always use masculine words in referring to people—for example, *man* and *he?*
   A. Only males could be slaves.
   B. Johnson was not concerned with female slaves.
   C. That was the language convention of the time.
   D. Johnson is addressing a group of men.
   E. What Johnson writes does not apply to females.

6. In his biography of Johnson, Boswell writes, "Johnson was so violently provoked when he found for whom he had been so long excluded, that he went away in a passion, and never would return." What do *excluded* and *in a passion* mean?
   A. excited; offended
   B. kept waiting; very upset
   C. denied admittance; depressed
   D. expelled; emotional
   E. prevented from participating; in love

7. Based on these three selections, why were Johnson and Boswell likely considered friends?
   A. They were both biographers.
   B. They were complete opposites.
   C. They had similar attitudes and interests.
   D. They were just being polite to each other.
   E. They were isolated from society and just had each other.

8. **Constructed Response:** Discuss what is interesting or ironic about Johnson's definition of *lexicographer.*

9. **Constructed Response:** Compare Johnson's definition of *patron* in his dictionary to the question about patrons in his letter to the Earl of Chesterfield: "Is not a Patron, my Lord, one who looks with unconcern on a man struggling for life in the water, and, when he has reached ground, encumbers him with help?"

Elegy Written in a Country Churchyard

An Elegy by Thomas Gray

Build Background

Literary Context A long, formal poem about death and loss, Thomas Gray's **"Elegy Written in a Country Churchyard"** is perhaps the most well-known and beloved tribute to common people in English poetry. Even Gray's harshest critics have acknowledged the importance of this poem. The universality of this work—its applicability to all time and places—makes it one of the masterpieces of world literature.

"Elegy Written in a Country Churchyard" took Gray many years to write, and he revised and edited it extensively, honing the language, imagery, rhythm, style, and tone. In 1751, the poem was published (although it is unclear if Gray was satisfied with it) to avoid pirated versions from being distributed.

The poem is likely set in the churchyard at Stoke Poges, where Gray's ancestors are buried and thus he often visited. The poem combines Neoclassical elements, such as the elegy form and references to the Muse, with Romantic elements, including the celebration of the common person. Gray is considered a forerunner of the Romantic movement.

Reader's Context For what would you like to be remembered?

Meet the Author

Thomas Gray (1716–1771) was born in London to middle-class parents. His father was a scrivener (public secretary), and his mother and aunt ran a milliner's (hat) shop. Educated at Eton and later at Cambridge, Gray left the university without a degree to travel in Europe. He returned to Cambridge in 1742, where he began to write poetry. His first odes were published in 1747.

Gray did not produce a great volume of verse, but he wrote carefully, bringing each poem to a level of perfection rarely achieved before or since. Characteristics that distinguish Gray's verse include a unique sensitivity to landscape and a strain of melancholy that shows him to have had a dignified, tragic view of life.

Continuing to write poetry through 1769, Gray lived the life of a Cambridge scholar, traveling and devoting himself to the study of pre-Elizabethan poetry and Old Norse and Welsh literature. He enjoyed art and music. A careful observer of nature, he sought refuge each summer in the wild and beautiful landscapes of Scotland and England's Lake District.

After his death in 1771, Gray was buried in the country churchyard that inspired his elegy. He is honored by monuments there, at Cambridge and Eton, and in Poets' Corner in Westminster Abbey.

Analyze Literature

Elegy and Speaker

An **elegy** is a poem of mourning, usually about someone who has died. *an elegy can be about anything that has died*

A **speaker** is the character who speaks in a poem—the voice assumed by the writer. You can learn about the speaker based on his or her diction, actions, and interests.

Set Purpose

Gray probably wrote the poem after the death of a friend and a favorite aunt, but the poem is not about either of them. While you read "An Elegy Written in a Country Churchyard," determine for whom or what the speaker grieves. Make a list of the images about death and loss that appear in the poem. How do these images help you understand for whom or what the speaker grieves? Also consider the speaker in the poem. What can you infer about the speaker's values and attitude toward life based on the ideas presented in the poem?

Preview Vocabulary

jocund, 622
obscure, 622
impute, 623
provoke, 623
ingenuous, 624
ignoble, 624
dirge, 626

[handwritten: A transitional piece]

[handwritten: - leaning towards the Romantic attitude]

Elegy Written in a Country Churchyard

[handwritten: ~ from Graveyard class of poetry]

by Thomas Gray

[handwritten: metaphor The death bell of the dying day is the curfew "the day is dying"]

The curfew tolls the knell of parting day, *[handwritten: cattle]*
   The lowing herd wind slowly o'er the lea,[1]
The plowman homeward plods his weary way,
   And leaves the world to darkness and to me.

5 Now fades the glimmering landscape on the sight, *[handwritten: the soft sounds are]*
   And all the air a solemn stillness holds, *[handwritten: all that can be heard]*
Save where the beetle wheels his droning flight, *[handwritten: showing it is very quiet]*
   And drowsy tinklings lull the distant folds; *[handwritten: sound of bell of lead cow / sheep]*

---

1. **lea.** Meadow

Romantic obsession with ruins

Save that from yonder ivy-mantled tower
10   The moping owl does to the moon complain
Of such, as wandering near her secret bower,
        Molest her ancient solitary reign.

Beneath those rugged elms, that yew tree's shade,
        Where heaves the turf in many a moldering heap,
15   Each in his narrow cell forever laid,
        The rude[2] forefathers of the hamlet[3] sleep.

The breezy call of incense-breathing Morn,
        The swallow twittering from the straw-built shed,
The cock's shrill clarion, or the echoing horn,
20   No more shall rouse them from their lowly bed.

For them no more the blazing hearth shall burn,   *they are dead*
        Or busy housewife ply her evening care;   *all the common nice*
No children run to lisp their sire's return,   *things they will not*
        Or climb his knees the envied kiss to share.   *enjoy anymore*

25   Oft did the harvest to their sickle yield,   *a valarizing of*
        Their furrow oft the stubborn glebe[4] has broke;   *peasant farmers*
How <u>jocund</u> did they drive their team afield!
        How bowed the woods beneath their sturdy stroke!

Let not Ambition mock their useful toil,   *don't make fun*
30   Their homely joys, and destiny <u>obscure</u>;   *of these ordinary*
Nor Grandeur hear with a disdainful smile   *people*
        The short and simple annals of the poor.   *interrogating the way*
                                                              of life

The boast of heraldry, the pomp of power,
        And all that beauty, all that wealth e'er gave,
35   Awaits alike the inevitable hour.
        The paths of glory lead but to the grave.   *all gonna die*
                                                              equalizer

2. **rude.** Ignorant – *uneducated, un sophisticated*
3. **hamlet.** Small village
4. **glebe.** Soil

> **jo • cund** (jä´ kənd) *adv.,* cheerfully (the correct form of this word is *jocundly*)
> **ob • scure** (äb skyŭr´) *adj.,* faint; undefined

Indian Summer, 1891. George Inness Jr. Private collection.

Nor you, ye proud, <u>impute</u> to these the fault,
    If Memory o'er their tomb no trophies raise,
Where through the long-drawn aisle and fretted[5] vault
40   The pealing anthem swells the note of praise.

[handwritten: Can't blame the poor if they do not have the fancy tombs]

Can storied urn or animated bust
    Back to its mansion call the fleeting breath?
Can Honor's voice <u>provoke</u> the silent dust,
    Or Flattery soothe the dull cold ear of Death?

[handwritten: the fancy tomb will not bring the dead back]

45 Perhaps in this neglected spot is laid *[handwritten: Holy spirit]*
    Some heart once pregnant with celestial fire;
Hands that the rod of empire might have swayed,
    Or waked to ecstasy the living lyre. *[handwritten: bard/poetry comes to mind]*

[handwritten: a person full of inspiration could be buried here]

But Knowledge to their eyes her ample page
50   Rich with the spoils of time did ne'er unroll;
Chill Penury[6] repressed their noble rage,
    And froze the genial current of the soul.

[handwritten: poor because of lack of knowledge and poverty]

---

5. **fretted.** Decorated with a raised design of intersecting lines
6. **Penury.** Poverty

im • pute (im pyüt´) *v.,* attribute
pro • voke (prə vōk´) *v.,* stir up action or feeling

Full many a gem of purest ray serene,
The dark unfathomed caves of ocean bear:
55 Full many a flower is born to blush unseen,
And waste its sweetness on the desert air.

[handwritten: just because you do not see the power does not mean it doesn't exist]

Some village Hampden,[7] that with dauntless breast
The little tyrant of his fields withstood;
Some mute inglorious Milton[8] here may rest,
60 Some Cromwell[9] guiltless of his country's blood.

[handwritten left: held back from commiting crimes]

[handwritten right: —Hampden— stood up for common rights]

[handwritten right: magnificent poetry]

The applause of listening senates to command,
The threats of pain and ruin to despise,
To scatter plenty o'er a smiling land,
And read their history in a nation's eyes,

65 Their lot forbade: nor circumscribed alone
Their growing virtues, but their crimes confined;
Forbade to wade through slaughter to a throne,
And shut the gates of mercy on mankind,

The struggling pangs of conscious truth to hide,
70 To quench the blushes of ingenuous shame,
Or heap the shrine of Luxury and Pride
With incense kindled at the Muse's flame.[10]

Far from the madding crowd's ignoble strife,
Their sober wishes never learned to stray;
75 Along the cool sequestered vale of life
They kept the noiseless tenor of their way.

[handwritten: protection]

Yet even these bones from insult to protect
Some frail memorial still erected nigh,
With uncouth rhymes and shapeless sculpture decked,
80 Implores the passing tribute of a sigh.

[handwritten right: even these people have their gravestones]

[handwritten right: everyone wants to be remembered]

---

7. **Hampden.** John Hampden (1594–1643) was a member of Parliament who defended the rights of the people.
8. **Milton.** English poet; author of *Paradise Lost*
9. **Cromwell.** Oliver Cromwell, ruler of England during the Commonwealth Period, or Puritan Interregnum, 1653–1658
10. **incense . . . flame.** Poems written to praise them

---

in • gen • u • ous (in jen´ yü əs) *adj.,* artless; naive
ig • no • ble (ig nō´ bəl) *adj.,* dishonorable; mean

June, 1882. George Inness Sr. Brooklyn Museum of Art, Brooklyn, New York.

Their name, their years, spelt by the unlettered Muse,
    The place of fame and elegy supply:
And many a holy text around she strews,
    That teach the rustic moralist to die.

85 For who to dumb Forgetfulness a prey,
    This pleasing anxious being e'er resigned,
Left the warm precincts of the cheerful day,
    Nor cast one longing lingering look behind?

On some fond breast the parting soul relies,
90   Some pious drops the closing eye requires;
Even from the tomb the voice of Nature cries,
    Even in our ashes live their wonted fires.

For thee,[11] who mindful of the unhonored dead
    Dost in these lines their artless tale relate;
95 If chance, by lonely contemplation led,
    Some kindred spirit shall inquire thy fate,

Haply[12] some hoary-headed swain[13] may say,
    "Oft have we seen him at the peep of dawn
Brushing with hasty steps the dews away
100   To meet the sun upon the upland lawn.

we leave this life reluctantly
Everybody wants to be
*   remembered*

---

11. **thee.** Gray himself
12. **Haply.** Perhaps
13. **hoary-headed swain.** White-haired peasant

Pressed by the Moon, Mute Arbitress of Tides

by Charlotte Smith

Charlotte (Turner) Smith (1749–1806) began her literary career relatively late in life. Married at age sixteen, she raised ten children. She began writing novels and poetry to earn money when her husband was sent to debtor's prison. Influenced by Jean-Jacques Rousseau and the ideals of the French Revolution, Smith was criticized for writing novels that were too egalitarian and too political for a woman. Her book of poems *Elegiac Sonnets* (1784) was so popular that it eventually went through eleven editions. It also influenced later Romantic poets, such as Samuel Taylor Coleridge, William Wordsworth, and Elizabeth Barrett Browning.

"Pressed by the Moon, Mute Arbitress of Tides" is a *sonnet,* a fourteen-line poem that follows one of several rhyme schemes. On the surface, the poem is about a natural event, but a close reading shows that it also contains elements of inward reflection.

Written in the churchyard at Middleton in Sussex

Pressed by the moon, mute arbitress[1] of tides,
    While the loud equinox[2] its power combines,
    The sea no more its swelling surge confines,
But o'er the shrinking land sublimely rides.
5 The wild blast, rising from the western cave,
    Drives the huge billows from their heaving bed,
    Tears from their grassy tombs the village dead,
And breaks the silent sabbath[3] of the grave!
With shells and seaweed mingled, on the shore
10   Lo! their bones whiten in the frequent wave;
    But vain to them the winds and waters rave;
They hear the warring elements no more:
While I am doomed—by life's long storm oppressed,
To gaze with envy on their gloomy rest. ❖

---

1. **arbitress.** Archaic feminine form of *arbiter,* a person selected to judge a dispute; the moon affects the changing tides of the ocean.
2. **equinox.** Occurs when the sun crosses the equator, making night and day of equal length
3. **sabbath.** Rest

MIRRORS & WINDOWS

In her poem, Smith uses the image of a stormy sea as a metaphor for life. What natural image would you choose to describe an aspect of your life?

Northern Sea by Moonlight, c. 1800s. Caspar David Friedrich.
National Gallery, Prague, Czech Republic.

Refer and Reason

1. Identify the natural elements Smith refers to in the sonnet. What do these elements suggest about the speaker's attitude toward nature?

2. Evaluate Smith's descriptions of nature. How does she relate those descriptions to the human experience?

3. Review the last six lines of the sonnet. Why might Charlotte Smith feel that life is a "long storm" that oppresses her? In your answer, consider the biographical and historical information you know about Smith.

Writing Options

1. Write a newspaper article about the events described by the speaker of this poem. In your article, answer the questions *who, what, when, why,* and *how.* Use an objective tone. You may want to include a quote from the speaker. How might she answer your questions?

2. Both this poem and Thomas Gray's "Elegy Written in a Country Churchyard" were composed in church-yards. Write a brief comparison-and-contrast essay about the two poems. For each poem, consider the tone, the speaker, and the attitudes toward life and death it expresses.

 Go to **www.mirrorsandwindows.com** for more.

Waverly, or 'Tis Sixty Years Since
by Sir Walter Scott

Bookish Edward Waverly is sent to Scotland after joining the army in 1745. There, he encounters the wild Highland chieftain Fergus and his passionate daughter Flora, who pull him into a plot to place Bonny Prince Charlie Stuart on the English throne. With *Waverly,* Sir Walter Scott established the historical novel form as it critiqued forms of Romanticism.

Oroonoko: or, the Royal Slave
by Aphra Behn

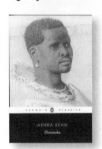

African prince Oroonoko loves Imoinda, a general's daughter, and together, they plot her escape from his grandfather's harem. When caught, they are put on a slave trader's ship headed for the New World, where Oroonoko leads a slave revolt. Behn's novel, one of the first in the English language, provides a sixteenth-century perspective on colonialism and kingship.

The History of Tom Jones, a Foundling by Henry Fielding

Taken in and raised by Squire Allworthy, Tom Jones grows into a mischievous, lusty young man; however, he cannot escape the ill will of the squire's nephew. When Tom is disinherited by the squire and refused the neighbor's daughter in marriage, he goes off on a series of adventures that have made this comic novel a favorite among generations of readers.

The Way of the World
by William Congreve

The rogue Mirabell plots to win the lovely and wealthy but forbidden Millamant—a plot that becomes entangled in his jealous opponents' strategies. Peopled with rakes, fops, aristocrats, and servants who mimic their masters, this Restoration comedy holds a mirror to common human foibles, then and now.

Journals and Letters by Fanny Burney

Fanny Burney was a member of Queen Charlotte's staff, witness to the Napoleonic Wars, and successful novelist and playwright in an age when women were not accepted as writers. Her journals and letters, written over seventy-two years, contain witty observations of London and Parisian life, as well as portraits of Mad King George III, the charismatic Napoleon, and admirer Dr. Samuel Johnson.

The Life of Samuel Johnson, LL.D.
by James Boswell

For over twenty years, Boswell, a Scottish lawyer, struggled over his biographical *Life,* often rushing home after an evening with Dr. Johnson to transcribe the best bits of conversation. Boswell's magnificent portrait of the essayist and author of the eighteen-inch-thick, 42,773-entry *Dictionary of the English Language* depicts the genuine Johnson in speech and action, demonstrating both his wit and common sense.

A small-group discussion or meeting might contain between three and fifteen people, interacting in a face-to-face situation, who have a sense of group identity. At some small-group sessions, participants meet one or more times to discuss a particular project, issue, or event—for example, to plan a volunteer effort sponsored by the class. Meetings of this type are sometimes called *ad hoc* sessions. At other small-group sessions, members of a club or similar organization meet, usually on a regular schedule, to conduct club business, such as holding elections.

Group leaders, sometimes called *facilitators,* have the task of keeping the discussion flowing smoothly. Professional facilitators, such as social workers, may have special training in conducting discussion groups. For instance, a facilitator would reduce tensions among group members in ways that can help members learn to handle interpersonal conflict. As a student leader or facilitator, you might sometimes find yourself encouraging shy participants to join the discussion or tactfully discouraging other group members from taking over the meeting.

1. Understand the Tasks of Group Leader/Facilitator

As a group leader/facilitator, you probably will play several roles. Understanding each function, and feeling at ease performing it, will benefit you and the other group members:

- The primary role of the leader/facilitator is to direct the work of the group or the ad hoc session. If you are the leader/facilitator of a club meeting, your tasks might include introducing topics for discussion; calling on members to speak; ensuring that members with certain responsibilities do their jobs (for example, that the secretary keeps minutes of the meeting or that the treasurer gives a financial report); making sure that the procedures for voting on motions or electing club officers are conducted fairly; following the *agenda,* or list of tasks to be done or topics to be covered at the meeting; and *adjourning,* or closing, the meeting.
- If you are leading or facilitating an ad hoc session, your chief task is likely to be keeping the discussion on track so that the group can achieve its goal.

- Regardless of the type of meeting group you are leading or facilitating, try to maintain a sense of order and purpose. As *gatekeeper,* you keep communication open and moving ahead, by reminding participants of the focus of the session. As *harmonizer,* you help resolve conflicts or reduce tension between group members.

2. Learn How to Work with Less Cooperative Group Members

In general, participants will cooperate to make the discussion productive. Some participants, however, may choose to play destructive roles. As a leader/facilitator, you might encourage these participants to turn their negative contributions into constructive ones.

Disruptive types include the *joker,* who distracts the group by engaging in horseplay; the *dominator,* who tries to control the group for his or her own advantage; the *blocker,* who belittles the ideas of others; and the *deserter,* who withdraws from the group and refuses to participate.

3. Serve as a Role Model for Group Members

Most groups have *norms* (unwritten rules) or written rules governing appropriate behavior for their members. For example, participants are expected to arrive promptly, be courteous to each other, and follow through on tasks they have offered to do. As leader/facilitator, you may function as a role model for other members, so be sure you are familiar with and respectful of the group's written and unwritten rules.

SPEAKING & LISTENING RUBRIC

Your role as group leader/facilitator will be evaluated on these elements:

Performance as Conductor of Meetings

- ❏ You conduct the group's work by making sure the group stays focused on the topic or agenda and by ensuring that everyone has a chance to speak and that no one monopolizes the discussion.

Behavior as Role Model for Other Members

- ❏ You function as a role model for other members by being familiar with and respectful of the group's written and unwritten rules.

Wit and sarcasm can be effective tools for offering criticism in a nonthreatening manner. Taking a light-hearted or flippant approach to a problem allows delivering the intended message but without the tension or conflict.

Satire is a form of writing or speech that uses wit and sarcasm to point out errors, falsehoods, shortcomings, or failings. Often, the target of satire is a social behavior or institution and the intent is to bring about change. Some satires are clever and funny, whereas others are cutting and sarcastic.

Perhaps the best-known example of satire in British literature is Jonathan Swift's "A Modest Proposal." In it, Swift attacks insensitive politicians and greedy landlords for their treatment of the poor. He offers an outlandish solution to the problem of poverty, drawing attention to the issue and the need for reform.

For this assignment, you will write a satire on a current social behavior or institution you feel needs to be changed.

Assignment Write a satire about a contemporary social issue or institution

Purpose To challenge the ideas of your audience

Audience Someone who is unaware of your topic as a problem, disagrees with your point of view, or is undecided about your topic

WRITING RUBRIC

A successful satire has these elements:

- ❏ an introduction that poses a problem and offers a solution in the form of a thesis statement
- ❏ a body that supports the writer's thesis with appropriate details and examples
- ❏ a tone that enables the reader to recognize the writer's satirical intent
- ❏ a conclusion that restates the thesis and offers a tongue-in-cheek moral, call to action, or logical close

① Prewrite

Select Your Topic

Much in modern society deserves to be satirized, from the celebrity-obsessed tabloid culture to fanatical diet and exercise fads. List topics from several different areas of modern life, such as politics, education, advertising, and health. Think about specific issues or problems within each area that stir controversy or criticism. Also think about likely solutions to these problems. What must happen to bring about change? Choose an issue or problem that you feel strongly about and can recommend how to solve.

One student, Adam, focused on the problem of *senioritis:* the impatient, sometimes bored attitude of high school seniors who are ready to move beyond high school. Adam wanted to defend the importance of the senior year and recommend that students continue to work hard during that final year.

> ### What Great Writers Do
>
> Avoid choosing a topic that either has been sensationalized or is disparaging to a certain viewpoint, person, or culture. As contemporary American journalist Molly Ivins has noted, "Satire is traditionally the weapon of the powerless against the powerful. I only aim at the powerful. When satire is aimed at the powerless, it is not only cruel—it's vulgar."

IVINS

Gather Information

Once you have identified a problem and formulated a solution, think about how to satirize it. State your solution in as original and absurd a way as possible—for instance, in terms that are opposite your actual opinion. Part of what makes satire successful is its ability to examine even an old topic from a new perspective. In addition, pointing out what is ridiculous or absurd in a situation can be an effective way of persuading others to your point of view.

For example, Adam's intent was to motivate high school seniors to work hard in school, so he decided to propose just the opposite: that seniors skip their final year. With this idea in mind, he brainstormed a list of reasons in support of skipping the senior year. Some of the reasons seemed ridiculous, such as suggesting that students could develop higher-level thinking skills from watching daytime TV. Other reasons seemed to have some practical merit, such as considering the resources schools could save by eliminating the twelfth-grade year.

Brainstorm your own list of reasons in support of your solution. Consider both serious and outlandish ideas. Remember that your goal is to motivate readers to consider your topic in a new way.

Organize Your Ideas

Review your list of reasons and look for some pattern among them. For instance, Adam recognized that some of his reasons were things that would benefit the students and others were things that would benefit the school. He created the chart below to sort the reasons into these two categories. Then he numbered the reasons in the order in which he decided to present them in his satire.

There are several other options for organizing your reasons. If there is a time sequence or cause/effect relationship among the ideas, arrange them in that order. If one of your reasons is particularly important or thought provoking, present it first or last. Consider in what position it will have the most impact on your readers: at the start or the finish of your piece. Number your reasons in the order that will be most effective in persuading readers of your point of view.

Write Your Thesis Statement

The solution you have proposed to an issue or problem is your **thesis statement.** As noted earlier, in a satire, the solution offered to a problem or issue is often outlandish or even opposite the point the writer wants to make. By proposing an outrageous solution, the writer draws attention to the issue and gets readers to consider it from a unique perspective.

After thinking about his purpose for writing and reviewing his chart of reasons, Adam wrote this thesis statement:

> *Skipping the senior year would benefit both the seniors and the school.*

❷ Draft

Write your essay by following this three-part framework: Introduction, Body, and Conclusion.

Introduction Introduce the topic of your satire, creating a context, piquing interest, and stating your thesis.

Body Elaborate on your topic, giving reasons that will support your thesis.

Conclusion Bring your satire to a logical close, perhaps with a lesson or moral that emphasizes your thesis.

Satire Planning Chart

Student Benefits	School Benefits
② College plans already made	④ Save resources: eliminate teachers, classes
③ Transition to college easier	⑤ Underclassmen: smaller classes, no bad example
① Develop skills at home via TV, computer games, movies	

Draft Your Introduction

To orient readers to your topic and convince them of the problem it poses, provide some context. To establish common ground, consider sharing a personal anecdote or describing a situation to which readers can relate.

Next, establish the basis for your satire. Offer an absurd observation or tongue-in-check comment to get readers to see your topic in a new light. Then state your thesis, in which you offer an outlandish solution to the problem you have posed.

Also use your introduction to establish the appropriate tone. In an effective satire, the writer's tone fits his or her approach to the topic, be it ridiculously funny, bitingly sarcastic, or somewhere in between.

The introduction Adam wrote during the Draft stage is shown in the left-hand column on page 635. Note that he establishes context in the first two sentences by describing a common experience: senioritis. He uses the third sentence to recommend students' need for rest, and he states his thesis in the fourth sentence. How well does Adam establish a satiric tone?

Draft Your Body

In the body, your goal is to prove your thesis. Present the reasons you listed in your planning chart in the order in which you determined would be most effective. Develop each reason into a paragraph by adding details, examples, and other types of support. Again, focus on the tone you want to create.

Look at the draft of one of Adam's body paragraphs in the the chart on page 635 (left-hand column). In it, he addresses how schools would benefit from seniors skipping their final year of school. Using the information from his planning chart, he discusses saving resources and having smaller classes. His sarcasm comes through in the comments about letting go of teachers, eliminating supposedly unnecessary classes, and allowing better-educated students in other countries to take available jobs.

Draft Your Conclusion

A good conclusion does two things: (1) it reemphasizes the solution or thesis without merely restating it, and (2) it brings discussion to a logical close. In this case, the close might offer a tongue-in-cheek moral, a call to action, or a purposely misinterpreted quote.

Does Adam do both these things in his conclusion? Look his draft in the chart on page 636.

❸ Revise

Evaluate Your Draft

You can evaluate your own writing or exchange essays with a classmate and evaluate each other's work. Either way, think carefully about what works well and what needs to be improved.

Begin with content and organization. Make sure that the three parts of the essay—the introduction, body, and conclusion—work together to support your thesis. Every paragraph should clearly relate to the thesis. Use the Revision Checklist on page 636 to help you evaluate. Make notes directly on the essay about changes to be made.

Next, focus on the tone of the essay. Is your goal to be funny, sarcastic, or some combination of the two? Again, your tone should fit the approach to your topic. Consider where you can revise the language to make it more effective.

Read the notes you made as you reviewed your draft as well as the comments you got from your partner. First, address any problems in content or structure. Add evidence where support is lacking. Then look at each sentence to ensure that it conveys the proper tone. Make adjustments or change wording where necessary.

Revise for Content, Organization, and Style

Adam reviewed his satire and noted many areas that could use improvement. Look at the right-hand column of the chart on pages 635–636 to see how he revised the three paragraphs presented earlier:

- **Introduction:** Adam added several sentences to introduce the idea of students needing change and to lead to his thesis statement about skipping the final year. He also fine-tuned the language to make the tone more light and humorous.
- **Body:** To clarify the shift from discussing benefits to students to discussing benefits to the school, Adam added a topic sentence to the beginning of the paragraph. He also added several sarcastic rhetorical questions to enhance the satiric tone and get readers thinking.
- **Conclusion:** Adam added descriptive details to further develop the idealized graduation ceremony and to ensure readers would understand his sarcastic intent. He also added a final rhetorical question to lead readers to the final lesson or point: that the senior year is important.

DRAFT STAGE		REVISE STAGE	
Introduction Completing eleven years of school is a long, hard road. By the time most students reach their final year of high school, they are more than ready to be done. To prepare them for what lies ahead, the senior year of high school should be devoted to rest and relaxation. Skipping the senior year would benefit both the seniors and the school.	Establishes context States thesis	Completing eleven years of school is a long, hard road. By the time most students reach their final year of high school, they are more than ready to be done. Whether they have plans to go to college or to begin a career, they are ready for change. To prepare them for ~~what lies ahead~~ that change, the senior year of high school should ~~be devoted to rest and relaxation~~ —a sort of extended Senior Skip Day. Seniors deserve some beach time, some sleep-in time, and some late-night movie time. Skipping the senior year would benefit both the seniors and the school.	Adds sentence to introduce idea of change Adds humorous detail to help create tone Adds sentence to create drama and lead into thesis
Body Paragraph Think of the resources schools would save if seniors were allowed to check in by phone every few days. Teachers who have been around too long could be let go. And with computers and today's global marketplace, students don't need all of those reading and math classes. Students from other countries can fill the jobs that require a solid education. Without those sleepy seniors around, underclassmen would enjoy smaller classes.	Addresses benefits to schools; ties directly to thesis	Additional benefits would accrue directly to the high school. Think of the resources schools would save if seniors were allowed to check in by phone every few days to rattle off the list of thoughts they have had. Teachers who have been around too long could be let go. Who needs Brit Lit? And with computers and today's global marketplace, who needs ~~students don't need~~ all of those reading and math classes?~~.~~ Students from other countries can fill the jobs that require a solid education. Without those sleepy seniors around, underclassmen would enjoy smaller classes and avoid the bad example of poor attendance during ski or beach season.	Adds topic sentence about benefits to school Adds detail to maintain tone Asks rhetorical questions to pique readers' interest Continues to develop satiric tone

DRAFT STAGE		REVISE STAGE	
Conclusion I can see it now: rows of graduates at commencement on a perfect evening in June. Confident they had learned it all during their eleven years of schooling, they would be ready to take on the world.	Creates hypothetical scene Returns to idea from introduction	I can see it now: rows of eager graduates at commencement on a perfect evening in June, refreshed and smiling, arms around one another, with perfect handshakes and a joke for every occasion. Confident they had learned it all during their eleven years of schooling, they would be ready to take on the world. What difference could one more year have made?	Adds adjectives and details to enhance description of scene Adds rhetorical question to lead readers to final point

Also review the tone of your satire. Achieving the appropriate tone is critical to its effectiveness. Keep in mind that your purpose in writing is to persuade others to some point of view or course of action. Although you may achieve that by shocking readers, you may also offend them and risk your credibility. The response to Jonathan Swift's "A Modest Proposal" has historically been mixed; many readers have found the work in poor taste and missed the point of the satire.

Review the notes you or your partner made as you evaluated your draft. Then apply each comment as you revise your draft.

Proofread for Errors

Proofreading your work before handing it in is essential. Use proofreader's symbols to mark any errors you find. Print out a final draft and read it aloud before turning it in. This will help you catch mistakes.

Take a look at Adam's final draft on page 637. Note how he worked through the three stages of the writing process: Prewrite, Draft, and Revise.

Writing Follow-Up

Publish & Present

- Approach debaters in your school to discuss the issue that your satire addresses.
- See if your school newspaper is interested in a series of editorial satires.

Reflect

- Read a satire produced in your class. Did it make you change your mind? Why or why not?
- Is satire an appropriate tool for bringing about social change? Why or why not?

REVISION CHECKLIST

Content & Organization

- ❏ Does the introduction pose a problem and offer a solution in the form of a thesis statement?
- ❏ Does the body support the thesis with appropriate details and examples?
- ❏ Does the conclusion restate the thesis and offer a final lesson or moral?
- ❏ Is the tone of the satire appropriate for the approach to the subject, be it humorous, sarcastic, or some of both?

Grammar & Style

- ❏ Are verb tenses used correctly? (page 483)
- ❏ Are proper nouns and adjectives properly capitalized? (page 489)
- ❏ Have modifiers been chosen carefully and placed appropriately? (page 558)
- ❏ Do word choices reflect precise and lively use of language? (page 604)

STUDENT MODEL

Skipping Ahead
by Adam Costello

Completing eleven years of school is a long, hard road. By the time most students reach their final year of high school, they are more than ready to be done. Whether they have plans to go to college or to begin a career, they are ready for change. To prepare them for that change, the senior year of high school should be devoted to rest and relaxation—a sort of extended Senior Skip Day. Seniors deserve some beach time, some sleep-in time, and some late-night movie time. Skipping the senior year would benefit both the seniors and the school.

Seniors would benefit in several ways. A daily diet of television, video-tapes, movies, and computer games would keep their critical-thinking skills sharp. Daytime soaps and talk shows would keep them grounded in reality and teach valuable lessons about problem solving in everyday life. In addition, strategizing skills would be sharpened through playing computer games and watching reality programs.

Also, it's a known fact that, at the start of the senior year, most students already know what they're going to do after that golden Graduation Day. True, some persnickety colleges hold applicants in limbo, waiting for senior-year transcripts, but they aren't the colleges most seniors end up going to anyway. Statistics have proven this: Very few high school graduates go to these picky colleges.

Regardless of where graduates want to go, the transition to college would be smoother if the senior year was devoted to rest. As college freshmen, these students would be better able to cope with the targeted socializing required during their first year. Contacts. It's all about contacts. These well-rested students would be ready to succeed!

Additional benefits would accrue directly to the high school. Think of the resources schools would save if seniors were allowed to check in by phone every few days to rattle off the list of thoughts they have had. Teachers who have been around too long could be let go. Who needs Brit Lit? And with computers and today's global marketplace, who needs all of those reading and math classes? Students from other countries can fill the jobs that require a solid education. Without those sleepy seniors around, underclassmen would enjoy smaller classes and avoid the bad example of poor attendance during ski or beach season.

I can see it now: rows of eager graduates at commencement on a perfect evening in June, refreshed and smiling, arms around one another, with perfect handshakes and a joke for every occasion. Confident they had learned it all during their eleven years of schooling, they would be ready to take on the world. What difference could one more year have made?

How does the writer provide a context for the topic of his satire?

How does the writer lead up to his thesis statement?

What is the purpose of this first body paragraph?

How does the writer use "facts" to support his argument?

What is the tone of this satire? How does the writer create the tone?

What is the purpose of this paragraph?

How does the writer bring his satire to a close? What tongue-in-cheek comment are readers left with?

Reading Skills

Identify the Author's Purpose

Being able to determine an author's **purpose** is an important reading skill. To determine the writer's goal, ask yourself these questions: Why did the author write this piece? What is he or she trying to do? What is the intended response from the reader?

An author may write with one or more of the following purposes:

- to inform or explain (*expository writing*)
- to portray a person, place, object, or event *(descriptive writing)*
- to convince people to accept a position and respond in some way *(persuasive writing)*
- to tell a story (*narrative writing*)

A writer's purpose corresponds to a specific mode, or type, of writing. The purpose of descriptive writing, such as that found in a character sketch or lyric poem, tends to be to reflect on an experience or event. Short stories, biographies, myths, and historical accounts

tell a story, or narrate. The writers of news articles, research reports, expository essays, and book reviews want to inform the reader about a certain subject. Editorials, petitions, political speeches, persuasive essays, and other forms of argumentative writing are intended to persuade.

Once you identify what the author is trying to do, you can evaluate how well the author achieved that purpose. For example, if a convincing argument is made in a persuasive essay, then the writer was effective. A news article that is written in a confusing manner so that you cannot understand it is not an effective informative piece.

TEST-TAKING TIP

With a multiple-choice question, if you have no idea of the correct answer, look to see whether two of the choices are similar or directly opposite. Chances are that one of these is the correct answer.

Practice

Directions: Read the following passage. The questions that come after it will ask you to identify the author's purpose.

POETRY: This poem is "The Introduction," by Anne Finch (1661–1720).

Did I my lines intend for public view,
How many censures would their faults pursue,
Some would, because such words they do affect,
Cry they're insipid, empty, uncorrect.
5   And many have attained, dull and untaught,
The name of wit only by finding fault.
True judges might condemn their want of wit,
And all might say they're by a woman writ.
Alas! a woman that attempts the pen
10 Such an intruder on the rights of men,

Such a presumptuous creature is esteemed,
The fault can by no virtue be redeemed.
They tell us we mistake our sex and way;
Good breeding, fashion, dancing, dressing, play
15 Are the accomplishments we should desire;
To write, or read, or think, or to enquire
Would cloud our beauty, and exhaust our time,
And interrupt the conquests of our prime;
Whilst the dull manage of a servile house
20 Is held by some our utmost art, and use.
   Sure 'twas not ever thus, nor are we told
Fables, of women that excelled of old;
To whom, by the diffusive hand of Heaven
Some share of wit and poetry was given.
25 On that glad day on which the Ark returned, . . .
Here holy virgins in the concert join,
The louder notes to soften and refine,
And with alternate verse complete the hymn divine.

Lo! the young poet, after God's own heart,
30 By Him inspired, and taught the Muses' art,
Returned from conquest, a bright chorus
       meets,
That sing his slain ten thousand in the streets.
In such loud numbers they his acts declare,
Proclaim the wonders of his early war,
35 That Saul upon the vast applause does frown,
And feels its mighty thunder shake the crown.
What, can the threatened judgment now
       prolong?
Half of the kingdom is already gone;
The fairest half, whose influence guides the
       rest,
40 Have David's empire o'er their hearts
       confessed.
    A woman here leads fainting Israel on,
She fights, she wins, she triumphs with a
       song,
Devout, majestic, for the subject fit,

And far above her arms exalts her wit,
45 Then to the peaceful, shady palm withdraws,
And rules the rescued nation with her laws.
How are we fallen, fallen by mistaken rules?
And education's, more than nature's fools,
Debarred from all improvements of the mind,
50 And to be dull, expected and designed;
And if some one would soar above the rest,
With warmer fancy and ambition pressed,
So strong th' opposing faction still appears.
The hopes to thrive can ne'er outweigh the
       fears.
55 Be cautioned then my Muse, and still retired;
Nor be despised, aiming to be admired;
Conscious of wants, still with contracted wing,
To some few friends and to thy sorrows sing;
For groves of laurel thou wert never meant;
60 Be dark enough thy shades, and be thou there
       content.

Multiple Choice

1. What is the purpose of the first few lines in
   this poem?
   A. to involve the reader
   B. to offer a criticism
   C. to persuade the reader to take her side
   D. to reveal her reluctance to publish
   E. to plea innocent of the charges against her

2. In line 30, the poet refers to the Muses because
   A. women inspire poets.
   B. women love poetry and the arts.
   C. historically women have been involved in
      the arts.
   D. she is better educated than many women
      of her time.
   E. her education included the study of
      mythology.

3. Finch's purpose for writing this poem is to
   A. express her theories about poetry.
   B. persuade readers that women have the
      ability and right to be poets.

   C. become famous for her great talents, as
      evidenced in this poem.
   D. entertain and enrich the reader's life by
      providing a sweet-sounding poem.
   E. inform people of the rich tradition of
      women writers and leaders in history.

4. How is this poem different from much
   poetry of this time in its purpose?
   A. It rhymes, but some of the rhymes are
      imperfect.
   B. It uses words unfamiliar to us today.
   C. It takes a strong, controversial stand on
      an issue.
   D. It contains examples of alliteration.
   E. It makes references to mythology and
      Christianity.

Constructed Response

5. Discuss how the poet's choice of words in
   "The Introduction" furthers her purpose.

Writing Skills

Provide Support for Your Opinion

Once you have a thesis statement, the next step is to provide several main ideas to support your thesis statement. For each main idea, list several supporting details—statements, facts, examples, quotes, and illustrations that explain or demonstrate your idea.

Devote one paragraph to each major point of support for your thesis statement. Continue to write quickly, and do not spend too much time on any one paragraph. At the same time, however, provide adequate coverage of each point.

When writing the body of an essay, refer to your outline. Each heading in your outline will become the main idea of one of your paragraphs.

To move smoothly from one idea to another, use transitional words and phrases. They will help the reader see how one point relates to another and alert him or her to the organization of the essay. Transitions in a persuasive essay may be as simple as *first, next, another reason,* and *in contrast.*

Present ideas logically and precisely. Be knowledgeable and fair in your presentation of evidence. Aim to be convincing but not conniving. You want the reader to believe you and be on your side. Use a balance of reason and emotion. It is all right to use personal experience as support, but if possible, also include some objective evidence. Keep in mind that your essay response should be written in standard, formal English.

TEST-TAKING TIP

Use transitions to connect your points. Otherwise, your essay will seem disjointed, and the reader will have difficulty following your points to the conclusion you reach.

Practice

Timed Writing: 25 minutes

Think carefully about the issue presented in the following excerpt and assignment.

The speed limits on major highways in different places differ. In some areas, there are no restrictions at all on how fast you can drive. In the United States, highway speed limits fluctu-ate according to the dominant consideration of the time, be it the number of highway fatalities or gas availability. Is the current speed limit on highways best, or should it be changed?

Assignment: Should the present speed limits be increased, decreased, or maintained? Plan and write an essay in which you develop your perspective on this issue. Support your position with reasoning and examples taken from your reading, studies, experience, or observations.

Revising and Editing Skills

As part of the Writing section, some standardized tests ask you to improve paragraphs. You will be presented with a draft of a short essay. Then you will be asked questions regarding how the sentences and paragraphs fit together. To answer, you will make revisions by combining sentences and changing structures within sentences.

Practice

Directions: The following passage is an early draft of an introductory paragraph of an essay. Some parts of the passage need to be rewritten. Read the passage and select the best answers for the questions that follow. Some questions deal with particular sentences or parts of sentences, asking you to consider the sentence structure or word choice. Other questions address the structure of the paragraph.

(1) High speed limits suit people's tendency to be in a hurry. (2) We're always in such a rush to get wherever we're headed. (3) Speed gets us somewhere more quickly, which is what's most important. (4) Isn't it? (5) I think the most important issue is getting there safely. (6) Driving really fast is dangerous and may increase the risk of being in a car accident. (7) Then there is also the issue of how much more gas it takes to operate a motor vehicle at high speeds.

Multiple Choice

1. Which sentence would it be best to add to the end of this paragraph?
   A. We're not just talking saving money but also conserving energy here.
   B. Although 40 mph, the speed at which a vehicle consumes the least amount of gas, is too slow, our current speed limits are too high.
   C. The current highway speed limits are optimal: They are a compromise between the desire for safety and energy conservation and the need for speed.
   D. In my opinion, the posted speed limits now in effect should remain unchanged.
   E. I think the current highway speed limits need to be reexamined.

2. In context, what is the best version of the underlined portions of sentences 3 and 4?
   A. (As it is now)
   B. quickly. Which is what's most important. Isn't it?
   C. quickly, which is what's most important, isn't it?
   D. quickly, the most important thing—not!
   E. quickly; which is what's most important. Isn't it?

3. What sentence should be deleted?
   A. 1
   B. 2
   C. 4
   D. 5
   E. 6

4. In context, what is the best way to rewrite sentence 7?
   A. (As it is now)
   B. Another issue being the amount of gas it takes to operate vehicles at high speeds.
   C. It also takes more gas to travel at high speeds.
   D. Finally, we should consider the issue of how much more gas it takes to drive fast.
   E. Let's not forget energy conservation.

Study of Boatsmen on River, c. 1800s. John Constable.
Private collection.

Romantic Period

Unit 6

1798–1832

Romantic Period 1798–1832

1798   1805

BRITISH LITERATURE BRITISH LITERATURE BRITISH LITERATURE BRITISH LI

1798
William Wordsworth and Samuel Taylor Coleridge jointly publish *The Lyrical Ballads*

1800
Sir Walter Scott publishes *Ballads*

1802
William Wordsworth writes "Preface to The Lyrical Ballads" in a second edition of the original work

1804
William Blake publishes *Jerusalem*

1811
Percy Bysshe Shelley publishes *The Necessity of Atheism*

1812
Lord Byron publishes *Childe Harold's Pilgrimage*

1813
Jane Austen publishes *Pride and Prejudice*

1813
Poet Robert Southey publishes Lord Nelson's autobiography

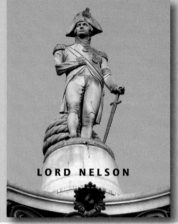

LORD NELSON

BRITISH HISTORY BRITISH HISTORY BRITISH HISTORY BRITISH HISTORY BRI

1799
The Napoleonic Wars begin between France and Britain

1801
The Act of Union merges the Kingdom of Ireland with Great Britain, creating the United Kingdom

1802
The Treaty of Amiens results in a brief peace between Britain and France

1802
Marie Tussaud opens her world-famous wax museum in London

1805
Lord Nelson dies at the Battle of Trafalgar

1807
The British end the slave trade

1811
King George III goes insane and is removed from the throne

1812
The War of 1812 begins between the United States and the United Kingdom

1813
The United Kingdom and Russia engage in a conflict over central Asia generally referred to as the "Great Game"

WORLD HISTORY WORLD HISTORY WORLD HISTORY WORLD HISTORY WORL

1799
Napoleon stages a coup d'etat and becomes dictator of France

1801
The United States engages in the Barbary Wars with the piratical city-states of northern Africa

1803
The United States purchases the Louisiana Territory from France

1804
The Republic of Haiti is founded

1806
The Holy Roman Empire is dissolved

1810
The first Oktoberfest takes place in Munich, Germany

1805
Colombia declares independence from Spain

1811
The Battle of Tippecanoe takes place between the United States and the American Indian Confederation

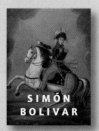

SIMÓN BOLIVAR

1815   1820

1817
John Keats publishes his epic poem "Endymion"

1818
Mary Shelley publishes *Frankenstein*

1819
Percy Bysshe Shelley publishes "Ode to the West Wind"

1819
Lord Byron publishes the first two cantos of "Don Juan" anonymously

1820
John Keats publishes "Ode on a Grecian Urn"

1821
John Keats dies of tuberculosis at age twenty-five

1822
Percy Bysshe Shelley drowns one month before his thirtieth birthday

1824
Lord Byron dies before completing "Don Juan"

1826
Mary Shelley publishes *The Last Man*

1827
William Blake dies

1815
British troops are repelled by General Andrew Jackson during the Battle of New Orleans

DUKE OF WELLINGTON

1815
The Duke of Wellington defeats Napoleon at the Battle of Waterloo

1817
During the Pentrich Rising, working class British march to Nottingham with revolutionary intentions

1819
The British East India Company establishes the city of Singapore

1823
The first Anglo-Burmese War begins

1826
The British Empire wins the first Anglo-Burmese War, which results in the erosion of Burmese sovereignty

1829
The Catholic Emancipation Act passes, removing all legal restrictions for Roman Catholics

1832
The Reform Act of 1832 extends voting and representation rights for male British subjects

1816
Argentina gains its independence from Spain

SHAKA ZULU

1816
Shaka Zulu's kingdom becomes the largest in southern Africa

1817
Andrew Jackson leads a campaign against Seminole and Creek Native North Americans in the First Seminole War

1817
In Brazil, rebels fight against the Portuguese imperial forces during the Pernambucan Revolt

1820
Liberia is founded by freed American slaves

1827
Greece wins independence from the Ottoman Empire

1828
The Persian Empire wins the Russo-Persian War

1830
France invades Algeria

1830
The Belgian Revolution results in the formation of Belgium

> ## "Death is nothing; but to live defeated and inglorious is to die daily."
>
> —NAPOLEON BONAPARTE

The Aftermath of the French Revolution

The violent overthrow of the French monarchy in 1789 sent shockwaves throughout Europe. During the 1790s, Britain joined forces with several other European countries whose absolutist monarchs opposed the French Revolution and republican ideals.

In France, amid the tumult of internal rebellions and foreign invasions, a brilliant military dictator named Napoleon Bonaparte seized power in 1799. Napoleon restored order and began invading surrounding countries, with the ultimate goal of creating a French Empire across the European continent. The British Navy blocked the flow of trade goods to and from French ports. In 1805, at the Battle of Trafalgar on the coast of Spain, the British Navy gained a major victory against Napoleon that ended his power on the seas and his hope of invading Britain.

The Napoleonic Wars dragged on until 1815, when the British Duke of Wellington finally defeated Napoleon and the French Army at the Battle of Waterloo in Belgium. Napoleon surrendered to the British and was exiled to the remote island of St. Helena, where he spent the last six years of his life.

In 1799 and 1800, Parliament responded to the fear that British workers would follow the example set by French revolutionaries by enacting a series of laws known as the Combination Acts, which limited free speech and outlawed the gathering of workers in groups. Anyone calling for change in the political system could be charged with treason, as was Thomas Paine, author of *The Rights of Man*.

In 1801, the second Act of Union formally united Britain and Ireland as the United Kingdom of Great Britain and Ireland. British Prime Minister William Pitt achieved the union by recognizing the need to support civil rights for Irish Catholics. King George III, however, vetoed the Catholic Emancipation Act. It would not be passed until 1829, after a massive but nonviolent popular campaign led by Irishman Daniel O'Connell.

In 1811, George III was declared insane and his brother George IV took over as regent and then king until his death in 1830. His brother, William IV, succeeded him and ruled until 1837.

The end of the Napoleonic Wars in 1815 brought economic depression to Britain because it no longer had to supply troops with food and other provisions. With an oversupply of goods, farms and manufacturers needed fewer workers. Furthermore, for the last half-century, the Industrial Revolution had already been

Napoleon at St. Bernard, 1800. Jacques-Louis David. The Louvre, Paris, France.

disrupting age-old ways of life. The British troops who had fought at Waterloo came home hoping to find work but instead found domestic turmoil. Craftsmen thrown out of work by the new industrial advances attacked factories and smashed machinery. Those who took factory jobs worked long hours for low wages and

"Men of England, wherefore plough
For the lords who lay ye low?
Wherefore weave with toil and care
The rich robes which your tyrants wear?"

—PERCY BYSSHE SHELLEY

had little to show for their lifetime of labor.

In 1804 and 1815, Parliament passed the so-called Corn Laws, which set the price of all grains, making food much more expensive for people who were poor and greatly benefiting those in the landed class. A series of protests against these conditions were put down with armed force. In an 1819 demonstration, workers gathered at St. Peter's Fields in Manchester, England, to protest the Corn Laws and lobby

NOTABLE NUMBERS

73 Age at which King George III was declared insane

71,947 French soldiers who faced an Allied army of 67,661 at the Battle of Waterloo

9 Minimum age of child laborers in cotton mills set by the Factory Act of 1819; the act also established twelve hours as the maximum workday for those under age sixteen

30,000 to 150,000 Number of people who participated in the reform meeting in Manchester that ended with the Peterloo Massacre; eleven were killed

72% Members of Parliament (MPs) selected by just 180 powerful landlords before the passage of the Reform Act of 1832

for representation in Parliament. They were met by the British cavalry, resulting in injuries and death in the Peterloo Massacre. Soon, Parliament enacted a series of even more stringent restrictions on the freedoms of speech and assembly.

Reform Comes to Britain

Representation in Parliament had long been skewed toward the landholding aristocrats, with large industrial cities often having no representation. Landlords owned one or more "pocket boroughs," for which they handpicked two people to represent the borough in Parliament. The populations of some boroughs had shrunk so much since the start of the Industrial Revolution that they were known as "rotten boroughs," yet the landlords of these boroughs still nominated two people to serve in Parliament. This unbalanced representation had been the subject of bitter debate for decades. In general, members of the Tory political party opposed reform, while the Whigs supported it.

When Lord Earl Grey, a Whig, became prime minister in 1830, he pressed for change. After Parliament defeated his Reform Act in 1831, riots broke out in several British towns. Fears of a civil war convinced enough Members of Parliament to vote for and pass the Reform Act in 1832. The act redistributed parliamentary seats more equitably and gave the right to vote to men of the middle class, which increased the number of voters by 50 percent. Rural landlords still held control of Parliament, but the passage of the Reform Act signaled that change would come to Britain not through violent revolution but through legislation.

Some other reforms of the period concerned child labor and the slave trade. The first of the factory laws, passed in 1802, restricted children to no more than twelve hours a day of labor, although there was no enforcement mechanism. By 1833, the number was reduced to nine hours and by 1844, to six and a half hours. Although the slave trade was outlawed in 1807, owning slaves was not abolished throughout the British Empire until 1833.

The Rise of Romanticism

The early phases of Romanticism began in eighteenth-century Germany and quickly spread throughout Europe, affecting the literature, music, art, and philosophy of the age. The term *Romantic* comes from the word *romance,* which refers to a medieval heroic narrative. This type of narrative centered on a heroic individual and incorporated elements of the exotic and mysterious. German writer Friedrich Schlegel (1772–1829) was the first to adopt the term *Romantic* to describe literature that broke away from the classical traditions of the eighteenth century.

Throughout the late-eighteenth and early nineteenth centuries, artists, philosophers, and writers rebelled against the rational, orderly forms that had been popular during the previous era. They created instead works that celebrated emotion over reason, nature over human artifice, ordinary people over aristocrats, and spontaneity and freedom over decorum and control. At the heart of these changes was an emphasis on the individual and a growing reverence for the power of the creative imagination. In British poetry, the writer's ability to feel and experience life intensely was valued, and many poems and novels explored the passionate struggles and internal turmoil of the individual.

"The poet thinks and feels in the spirit of the passions of men."

—WILLIAM WORDSWORTH

This emphasis on the unique experiences of the individual also led to an interest in the historical and cultural heritage of various nations. Composers linked music to folktales and legends or attempted to capture the unique spirit of their countries through music.

English painters John Constable and J. M. W. Turner turned to the English landscape for inspiration and created scenes that inspired awe and celebrated the beauty of nature. Poets and writers such as William Wordsworth also found inspiration in the English countryside and bustling cities.

The shift toward these new sentiments led to political uprisings throughout Europe and the Mediterranean. Few historical eras have seen such political and social tumult as the shift from monarchy to republic—government free from hereditary rule, with popular control of the state. As British novelist Charles Dickens characterized the times half a century later, they were "the best of times and the worst of times"—the best because they saw the birth of freedom and equality, the worst because the cost of freedom and equality was terrible bloodshed.

Weymouth Bay, c. 1816. John Constable.

Toward the end of the late eighteenth century, poets showed tendencies toward **Romanticism** in their emotional explorations and perceptions of nature as wild and untamed. However, they followed the **Neoclassical** model of imitating traditional literary forms. Among the most noted of these transitional poets were Robert Burns and William Blake. Burns, who won acclaim as the national poet of Scotland, avoided the formal language of Neoclassical writers, favoring instead his native Scots dialect. Blake

was a poet, painter, mystic, and visionary. Much of his writing attacks the complacent rationality and orderliness of the eighteenth century.

The shift from Neoclassicism to Romanticism also reflected a newfound respect for ordinary people as opposed to the nobility. This thinking owed much to the American and French Revolutions and to the writings of French philosopher Jean-Jacques Rousseau. A few writers even believed that the rights of the common man should be extended to women. In the landmark essay *A Vindication of the Rights of Woman,* Mary Wollstonecraft argued for the education and equality of women.

The true beginning of the Romantic Era came in 1798 with publication of *The Lyrical Ballads,* by William Wordsworth and Samuel Taylor Coleridge. Worried about how critics would respond to their experimental verse, the authors left their names off the title page in the first edition. In a second edition published in 1801, the authors added their names, and Wordsworth provided a preface explaining that poetry should be about common people and events that are expressed in ordinary language.

Water Meadows Near Salisbury, 1829. John Constable.
Victoria and Albert Museum, London, England.

The Lyric Poem Defined

A **lyric poem** is a highly musical type of poetry that expresses the emotions of a speaker. The modern lyric evolved from an ancient Greek form of poetry that was recited or sung to the accompaniment of a stringed instrument called a *lyre.* Types of lyric poetry include the sonnet, ode, ballad, elegy, and dramatic monologue.

The lyric mode exemplifies William Wordsworth's belief that "poetry is the spontaneous overflow of powerful feelings." The tone of the lyric poem tends to be personal and meditative. The form was perfectly suited to the Romantic Era, in which writers turned away from industrialization and depersonalization to find beauty and solace in the idealization of nature and personal relationships.

Forms of the Lyric Poem

A **ballad** is a poem that tells a story and typically is written in four-line stanzas. Most ballads have a regular rhythm and rhyme scheme and feature a *refrain,* or repetition of lines. Samuel Coleridge's "Rime of the Ancient Mariner" is an example of a ballad. (See the discussion of the ballad in Unit 2, page 100.)

> *"Poetry lifts the veil from the hidden beauty of the world, and makes familiar objects be as if they were not familiar."*
>
> —PERCY BYSSHE SHELLEY

An **ode** is a lyric poem on a serious theme, usually with varying line lengths and complex stanzas. The classical Greek ode was a tight form with a strict meter. In the looser Romantic ode, nature is a vehicle for meditation on a serious subject, which culminates in a flash of insight or resolution. Some examples are Percy Bysshe Shelley's "Ode to the West Wind" and John Keats's "Ode to a Nightingale."

A **sonnet** is a fourteen-line poem, usually in *iambic pentameter,* that follows one of several different rhyme schemes. The *English, Elizabethan,* or *Shakespearean* sonnet is divided into four parts: three

quatrains and a final couplet. The *Italian* or *Petrarchan* sonnet is divided into two parts: an octave and a sestet. John Keats's "When I Have Fears" is written in the sonnet form. (See the discussion of the sonnet in Unit 3, pages 246–247.)

Elements of the Lyric Poem

Allegory and Symbolism

An **allegory** is a work in which characters, events, or settings **symbolize,** or represent, something else. The work of William Blake is highly allegorical. For instance, in "The Lamb," the animal typifies Jesus and the pure innocence of childhood. In the paired poem "The Tyger," the tiger symbolizes the darker forces of life, or what Blake conceived of as experience. Read together, the two poems form an allegory of human consciousness in its progress from naivete to an awareness of the world's complexity.

Narrative Voice

As noted earlier, the Romantic lyric poets had broken away from the restraints of Neoclassicism. The narrative **voice** had become self-consciously liberated and self-aware, the speaker seeking emotional intimacy with the reader. Keats's lyric opens with the line "When I have fears that I may cease to be." Then, within the formal structure of the traditional sonnet, the poet explores his own emotional depths instead of appealing to his beloved. The repeated use of first-person pronouns underscores the heightened subjectivity of the narrative voice.

Dialect and Diction

The Romantic poets rejected the artificial language of eighteenth-century literature, preferring syntax that sounded more like natural speech. In the poems of Robert Burns, the traditional Scots **dialect** replaces the King's English. In Wordsworth's "Tintern Abbey," the tone is colloquial (everyday), primarily because the **diction,** or word choice, is much less formal than that of much pre-Romantic verse.

See the Understanding Literary Forms in Unit 1, pages 20–21, for guidelines on how to read poetry.

To a Mouse

A Lyric Poem by Robert Burns

Build Background

Literary Context The poem **"To a Mouse, on Turning Her Up in Her Nest with the Plough"** was collected in Robert Burns's first poetry book, *Poems, Chiefly in the Scottish Dialect* (1786). With publication of this book, Burns found almost instant success in Scotland's literary and aristocratic circles.

Written as a speaker directly addressing a mouse, "To a Mouse" is steeped in Burns's background as a *cotter,* or Scottish farmer, and reveals his gentle attitude toward animals, a trait exhibited in several of his other works. Written in the Scots dialect, the language of the working class, the poem celebrates those who are of humble origins. Both the subject matter and style of "To a Mouse" show a break from Neoclassicism. Burns drew inspiration from the oral tradition of Scottish songs and folklore.

Reader's Context Think about a time when your presence scared a wild animal, such as a bird, a squirrel, or a deer. How did you feel about the incident? How did the animal react?

Meet the Author

Robert Burns (1759–1796), the national poet of Scotland, was the son of an unsuccessful farmer who valued education and was partly responsible for the education of his children. At fifteen, Burns fell in love for the first time and soon afterward began to write poetry. By age twenty-seven, he had written the renowned "Kilmarnock edition" of his verse (so called because it was published in the town of Kilmarnock) and had become famous among intellectuals.

Burns's best poetry is written in Scots, his native dialect. He chose his style deliberately from the Scottish folkloric and literary traditions. During his lifetime, he wrote hundreds of songs about love, work, friendship, patriotism, and the nobility of common men and women. A supporter of the revolutions in America and France, Burns sympathized with democratic causes.

In his late twenties, Burns settled down, got married, and began working as a tax inspector in Dumfries. Extremely patriotic and passionate about Scotland, he worked feverishly during his last years to preserve his country's music in published form. Although often in need of money, Burns would take no financial compensation for his work on these volumes of Scottish lyrics. He continued to work on the Scottish anthologies until he died of heart disease at age thirty-seven.

Analyze Literature

Dialect and Meter

Dialect is a version of a language spoken by the people of a particular place, time, or social group.

Meter is a regular rhythmic pattern in poetry. The pattern is determined by the number of beats, or stresses, in each line. Stressed and unstressed syllables are divided into rhythmical units called *feet*.

Set Purpose

The Romantic period saw a growing interest in national traditions and culture, and much of Burns's poetry was influenced by traditional Scottish folklore and literary tradition. "To a Mouse" is written in Scots, a northern dialect of English spoken by Scottish peasants. You may find it helpful to read the poem through once, using the footnotes, and then again for fluidity. If you have difficulty understanding the dialect, read each line aloud to hear what the words sound like when spoken. While you read, consider the effect the dialect has on your understanding and appreciation of the poem. Also notice the meter Burns uses throughout the poem.

Preview Vocabulary

dominion, 653
ensue, 653

The Trespassers Surprised, 1829. E. Morley.
Private collection. (See detail on page 651.)

To a Mouse

by Robert Burns

*On Turning Her Up in Her Nest
with the Plow, November, 1785*

Wee, sleekit,[1] cow'rin',[2] tim'rous[3] beastie,
O, what panic's in thy breastie!
Thou need na[4] start awa[5] sae[6] hasty,
    Wi' bickering brattle!
5 I wad[7] be laith[8] to rin[9] an' chase thee
    Wi' murd'ring pattle![10]

---

1. **sleekit.** Sleek
2. **cow'rin.** Cowering
3. **tim'rous.** Timorous, which means nervous or fearful
4. **na.** Not
5. **awa.** Away
6. **sae.** So
7. **wad.** Would
8. **laith.** Loath
9. **rin.** Run
10. **pattle.** Paddle; farm tool for plow

I'm truly sorry man's <u>dominion</u>
Has broken Nature's social union,
An' justifies that ill opinion,
10   Which makes thee startle,
At me, thy poor, earth-born companion,
     An' fellow-mortal!

I doubt na, whyles,[11] but thou may thieve;
What then? poor beastie, thou maun[12] live!
15 A daimen icker in a thrave[13]
     'S a sma'[14] request:
I'll get a blessin' wi' the lave,[15]
     And never miss't!

Thy wee bit housie, too, in ruin!
20 Its silly wa's[16] the win's[17] are strewin'!
An' naething, now, to big[18] a new ane,[19]
     O' foggage[20] green!
An' bleak December's winds <u>ensuin'</u>,
     Baith[21] snell[22] an' keen!

25 Thou saw the fields laid bare and waste,
An' weary winter comin' fast,
An' cozie here, beneath the blast,
     Thou thought to dwell,
Till crash! the cruel coulter[23] past
30   Out through thy cell.

---

11. **whyles.** Sometimes
12. **maun.** Must
13. **A daimen . . . thrave.** Only one ear of corn from a bundle
14. **sma'.** Small
15. **lave.** Rest
16. **wa's.** Walls
17. **win's.** Winds
18. **big.** Build
19. **ane.** One
20. **foggage.** Autumn grass
21. **Baith.** Both
22. **snell.** Bitter
23. **coulter.** Sharp blade on a plow

do • min • ion (də miʹ nyən) *n.,* authority or control over
en • sue (in süʹ) *v.,* come after

The Burns Supper

The Scots celebrate their most famous native poet through a ritual called the *Burns Supper*. It typically is held on Burns's birthday, January 25, which Scotland observes as a national holiday.

The supper begins with bagpipe music and the guests' recitation of Burns's "Selkirk Grace," a Scottish prayer. The host then serves a Scottish soup as an appetizer. Once the guests have finished the soup, they rise to welcome the *haggis,* a traditional Scottish dish that consists of sheep organs, oatmeal, spices, and vegetables stuffed in a sheep stomach. The host delivers the Burns poem "Address to a Haggis" in a comical tone while brandishing a dinner knife. After the host finishes, the diners toast to the haggis and devour it.

After they have eaten, the guests are expected to "do a turn" and provide some entertainment. Some will offer a short speech, make a joke, or read a Burns poem. The evening ends with everyone clasping hands and singing "Auld Lang Syne."

That wee bit heap o' leaves an' stibble,
Has cost thee mony[24] a weary nibble!
Now thou's turned out, for a' thy trouble,
   But[25] house or hald,[26]
35 To thole[27] the winter's sleety dribble,
   An' cranreuch[28] cauld![29]

But Mousie, thou art no thy lane,[30]
In proving foresight may be vain:
The best laid schemes o' mice an' men
40   Gang aft a-gley,[31]
An' lea'e us nought but grief an' pain,
   For promised joy.

Still, thou art blest, compared wi' me!
The present only toucheth thee:
45 But, och! I backward cast my e'e
   On prospects drear!
An' forward, though I canna[32] see,
   I guess an' fear! ❖

---

24. **mony.** Many
25. **But.** Without
26. **hald.** Hold, landholding
27. **thole.** Endure
28. **cranreuch.** Frost
29. **cauld.** Cold
30. **no thy lane.** Not alone
31. **Gang aft a-gley.** Go often awry
32. **canna.** Cannot

MIRRORS & WINDOWS

Mice do not have to recall the past or worry about the future. How might this be an advantage? What other advantages are there to living in the present?

Refer to Text ▶ ▶ ▶ ▶ ▶   **Reason with Text**

1a. In the first stanza, whom does the speaker address with the words *thou* and *thee?*	**1b.** Determine the speaker's purpose in addressing this subject.	**Understand** Find meaning
2a. In lines 37–42, what famous statement does Burns make about foresight?	**2b.** Relate this statement to a situation or experience in your own life.	**Apply** Use information
3a. According to the speaker, what problems does the mouse face?	**3b.** How are the speaker's problems similar to and different from the mouse's problems?	**Analyze** Take things apart
4a. State the specific apology the speaker makes to the mouse in stanza 2.	**4b.** Is Burns's apology to the mouse made in earnest or to be humorous? Explain.	**Evaluate** Make judgments
5a. List five examples of Burns's Scots dialect.	**5b.** Find a song that uses regional dialect or slang. Compare this modern use of dialect and slang to Burns's use of dialect?	**Create** Bring ideas together

Analyze Literature

Dialect and Meter

In "To a Mouse," Burns uses the Scots dialect, or the language of the working class in Scotland. Refer to the footnotes on pages 652–654 for examples of this dialect. How does the use of the Scots dialect affect the poem? How would a change in the formality of the language affect the purpose and audience of the poem? In what ways does the use of dialect add to or detract from your enjoyment and understanding of the poem?

Describe the patterns of stressed and unstressed syllables in "To a Mouse." What term would you use to identify the meter of "To a Mouse"?

Extend the Text

Writing Options

Creative Writing In "To a Mouse," Robert Burns apologizes to a mouse for destroying its home right before winter. Write a letter in response to the poet explaining how you, as the mouse, feel about the poet's actions and apology.

Expository Writing Write a paragraph explaining how the poem "To a Mouse" reflects the ideals and principles emphasized during the Romantic Era. Share your paragraph with several classmates in a small group, and compare interpretations of the poem and of Romanticism.

Collaborative Learning

Update Burns's Style Robert Burns abandoned the classical style of writing poetry in favor of a more informal, contemporary style. In a small group, determine what Burns's style would be like if he were a student in your school today. Identify the dialect (including slang and sayings) of your peers, and together write a brief poem about a current subject using this language. Share your poem with the class, and compare each group's interpretation of the popular language in your area. If you prefer, write your poem in a dialect from another part of the United States or another English-speaking country or time period. Use an electronic or print dialect dictionary, such as the *Dictionary of American Regional English*, to find accurate, powerful words and phrases.

Media Literacy

Illustrate the Poem Imagine that you have been hired as an illustrator of a children's book that includes "To a Mouse." Create a design for a spread in a book (two pages that face one another) that includes the poem and graphic illustrations. As you design your layout, keep in mind that your audience will be elementary schoolchildren.

 Go to **www.mirrorsandwindows.com** for more.

The Lamb
The Tyger
London

Lyric Poems by William Blake

Build Background

Literary Context Both **"The Lamb"** and **"The Tyger"** are included in William Blake's *Songs of Innocence* and *Songs of Experience.* The two poems are almost mirror images of one another in structure. One uses a symbol for innocence; the other uses a symbol for experience. Blake considered these poems representative of "two contrary states of the human soul."

The poem **"London,"** like "The Tyger," also is a song of experience. In this poem, Blake writes poignantly about some of the evils of urban life. In *Songs of Innocence,* he presents a vision of the world through the naïve eyes of innocence. In *Songs of Experience,* he presents this same world in all the truth of its ugliness and fearsomeness. After viewing life through both lenses, one might then reach a mature vision of the world and of life that incorporates both, a state he called "organized innocence."

Reader's Context Throughout history, certain animals have been associated with certain traits. What animals have symbolic meanings for you?

Meet the Author

Born to a middle-class family in London, **William Blake** (1757–1827) received his formal education in art, studying at the Royal Academy of Arts. When he was fourteen, he was apprenticed to James Basire, a well-known engraver. During his free time, Blake wrote poetry and read.

As a child, Blake had a number of visions. The earliest one was of God looking through his bedroom window—a vision that left Blake screaming in fear. Other visions followed, and Blake later explained that his poetry and drawings were "copied" from the visions he saw. Thus, Blake's experience of the world was intensely visual and reflected in the imagery of his poetry and in his paintings and drawings.

One wealthy patron of the arts who once supported Blake and his wife tried to convince the artist to work with a more conventional style. Blake refused, insisting that his poems reflected a passionate, spiritual world that must be kept separate from the corporeal (physical) world. Consequently, he lived for a time in poverty and isolation because his work was so contrary to the tastes and conventions of his day.

In his sixties, Blake left his poetry behind to concentrate on his visual art. He died at the age of seventy.

Analyze Literature

Synesthesia and Parallelism
Synesthesia is a figure of speech that combines in a single expression images related to two or more senses.

Parallelism is a rhetorical device in which a writer emphasizes the equal value or weight of two or more ideas by expressing them in the same grammatical form.

Set Purpose

According to recent studies, creative people often have a medical condition called *synesthesia,* in which they experience a sensation other than the sense being stimulated. This blending of senses influences their work. As you read, note figures of speech that are connected to more than one sense. In addition, look for lines that share grammatical structure, both within each poem and between the poems. What effect does this structure have on your understanding of each poem?

Preview Vocabulary

aspire, 658
sinew, 658
manacle, 659
hapless, 659
blight, 659

The Lamb

by William Blake

The Infant Saint John with the Lamb, c. 1660.
Bartolomé Esteban Murillo. National Gallery, London, England.

Little Lamb, who made thee?
Dost thou know who made thee?
Gave thee life & bid thee feed,
By the stream & o'er the mead;[1]
5 Gave thee clothing of delight,
Softest clothing wooly bright;
Gave thee such a tender voice,
Making all the vales[2] rejoice!
Little Lamb who made thee?
10 Dost thou know who made thee?

Little Lamb I'll tell thee,
Little Lamb I'll tell thee!
He is calléd[3] by thy name,
For he calls himself a Lamb;[4]
15 He is meek & he is mild,
He became a little child;
I a child & thou a lamb,
We are calléd by his name.
Little Lamb God bless thee.
20 Little Lamb God bless thee. ❖

1. **mead.** Meadow
2. **vales.** Valleys
3. **calléd.** The accent over the *e* indicates that the /ed/ is
   a stressed syllable, making this a two-syllable word, in
   order to fit the meter of the poem.
4. **Lamb.** Jesus is often referred to as the "Lamb of God."

MIRRORS & WINDOWS

Blake uses a young child and lamb as symbols of innocence. What animal would
be an appropriate symbol for the teenage years?

The Tyger

by William Blake

Tyger! Tyger! burning bright
In the forests of the night,
What immortal hand or eye
Could frame thy fearful symmetry?

5 In what distant deeps or skies
Burnt the fire of thine eyes?
On what wings dare he <u>aspire</u>?
What the hand dare seize the fire?

And what shoulder, & what art,
10 Could twist the <u>sinews</u> of thy heart?
And when thy heart began to beat,
What dread hand? & what dread feet?

What the hammer? what the chain?
In what furnace was thy brain?
15 What the anvil? what dread grasp
Dare its deadly terrors clasp?
When the stars threw down their spears[1]
And water'd heaven with their tears,
Did he smile his work to see?
20 Did he who made the Lamb make thee?

Tyger! Tyger! burning bright
In the forests of the night,
What immortal hand or eye
Dare frame thy fearful symmetry? ❖

---

1. **stars . . . spears.** Reference to the angels who fell with
Satan and threw down their spears after losing the war in
heaven (Revelation 12:7–9)

as • pire (ə spīr´) *v.*, seek to achieve lofty goals
si • new (sin´ yü[']) *n.*, tendon or nerve

MIRRORS & WINDOWS

How is childhood a time of innocence? Are children in modern times more grown up or worldly than children from times past?

Applicants for Admission to a Casual Ward, 1874. Sir Samuel Luke Fildes.
Royal Holloway Collection, University of London, London, England.

by William Blake

I wander thro' each charter'd[1] street,
Near where the charter'd Thames does flow,
And mark in every face I meet
Marks of weakness, marks of woe.

5 In every cry of every Man,
In every Infant's cry of fear,
In every voice, in every ban,[2]
The mind-forg'd <u>manacles</u> I hear:

How the Chimney-sweeper's cry
10 Every blackning Church appalls,
And the <u>hapless</u> Soldier's sigh
Runs in blood down Palace walls.

But most thro' midnight streets I hear
How the youthful Harlot's curse
15 Blasts the new-born Infant's tear,
And <u>blights</u> with plagues the Marriage hearse. ❖

---

1. **charter'd.** Established or created as a free entity, as in "given a charter," but also bound, or rented out to someone by its owner, as in "to charter a hall or carriage"
2. **ban.** Proclamation, prohibition, or announcement of marriage

man • a • cle (maˊ ni kəl) *n.,* handcuff; shackle
hap • less (haˊ pləs) *adj.,* having no luck
blight (blīt) *v.,* destroy; prevent growth

MIRRORS & WINDOWS

Think about the city or town in which you live. What about it do you like and dislike? What about it would you change if you could?

Title page created
by William Blake for
Songs of Innocence
(1789).

William Blake's Engravings

William Blake not only was an immensely talented poet but also an accomplished visual artist. While writing *Songs of Innocence* and *Songs of Experience,* he integrated illustrations of his poems within the lines of the selections, so that the images and words became inseparable.

To achieve this, Blake invented a method of relief etching called *illuminated printing,* in which he engraved a set of images and text onto a copper plate covered with wax. After applying acid to bring the design into relief, he printed the page. He later hand-colored each page with watercolors and stitched together the pages to create an *illuminated book.* This method limited Blake's production, but each book was a work of art.

Blake also illustrated the works of other authors, including Mary Wollstonecraft (1759–1797), a leading female writer of the era, and Dante Alighieri (1265–1321), an early Italian Renaissance poet. British abolitionist J. G. Stedman asked Blake to illustrate his book on the slave trade in the West Indies. Blake, an ardent abolitionist, readily agreed. The grisly images he produced helped propel the British abolitionist movement and contributed to the eventual ban of slavery in 1833.

Critical Viewing The poems in Songs of Innocence were written for children and examine the world from an innocent, uncorrupted perspective. Examine the title page from Songs of Innocence (above). How does Blake use light, color, and imagery to capture and reinforce the theme of innocence? Extend your analysis of Blake's work by finding a contemporary poem that integrates illustrations with the text, and compare and contrast the graphics in the two poems. Evaluate similarities and differences in the graphics themselves as well as in the ways they are used.

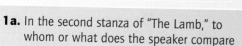

Refer to Text ▶ ▶ ▶ ▶ ▶	Reason with Text	
1a. In the second stanza of "The Lamb," to whom or what does the speaker compare the lamb?	**1b.** Identify the similarities that form the basis of this comparison. In other words, how are the two things alike?	**Understand** Find meaning
2a. In "The Tyger," what characteristics of the tiger are described in stanzas 2 and 3?	**2b.** What impression do you have of the tiger? How does this description make you feel about experience?	**Apply** Use information
3a. In stanza 3 of "London," what two people are mentioned? What two social institutions are juxtaposed with these people?	**3b.** Analyze the people who are wronged in this poem. What sort of people are they? Who or what is accused of the wrongdoing?	**Analyze** Take things apart
4a. Identify the three main life events discussed in the last stanza of "London."	**4b.** What judgment is Blake making about urban life during the Romantic period? Is this view consistent with Romantic ideals? Explain.	**Evaluate** Make judgments
5a. List the words used to describe the lamb and those used to describe the tiger.	**5b.** Explain how innocence differs from experience.	**Create** Bring ideas together

Analyze Literature

Synesthesia and Parallelism

What examples of synesthesia did you find in "London"? How do these multisensual images affect your experience of the poem?

In which of these poems does Blake use parallelism to present ideas? Which lines illustrate the technique?

Extend the Text

Writing Options

Creative Writing Write an allegorical poem about an animal. Consider what that animal might symbolize for you. Then use details that will appeal to your reader's senses of touch, taste, sight, smell, and hearing to describe the animal and develop the symbolic association.

Expository Writing Imagine you are a nineteenth-century social reformer who has observed the conditions portrayed by Blake in "London." Write an *exposé* (a formal statement of facts) for a newspaper, pointing out these conditions and offering a proposal for correcting them.

Media Literacy

Compile an Anthology Research other Romantic poets who wrote poems about London, as well as Romantic authors who wrote fiction set in the city. (For example, see Wordsworth's poem "Composed Upon Westminster Bridge," on page 673.) Choose several pieces of literature to include in an anthology about the Romantics' view of London. Then create a book of poems, using unique fonts and graphics for each selection.

Collaborative Learning

Research Graphic Elements in Poetry In a small group, research changes in graphic elements used in British poetry across time periods. Graphic elements in poetry include unconventional capitalization or type styles, varying line lengths, unusual word placement, and integrated illustrations (like William Blake's engravings). Choose three poems from different time periods, and compare and contrast how the graphic elements work together with the text to express the theme of each poem. Cite examples from the poems to support your inferences and conclusions.

 Go to **www.mirrorsandwindows.com** for more.

1. Which of the following statements does *not* correctly describe the two stanzas in the poem "The Lamb"?
   A. Both stanzas directly address the lamb.
   B. The two stanzas are parallel in structure.
   C. The first stanza asks a question, and the second stanza provides the answer.
   D. The mood of the first stanza is peaceful, and the mood of the second is turbulent.
   E. The first stanza describes a lamb, and the second stanza describes the Lamb of God.

2. Review lines 3–8 in "The Lamb." The details that Blake includes in these lines treat the lamb and its life in what way?
   A. idealized, better than it truly is
   B. realistic, just as it actually is
   C. indifferent or unemotional
   D. villainized, worse than it really is
   E. inconsistent, sometimes one way and sometimes another

3. Which of the following lines from "The Tyger" has *slant rhyme,* in which the rhyming sounds are similar but not identical?
   A. "Tyger! Tyger! burning bright / In the forests of the night,"
   B. "What immortal hand or eye / Could frame thy fearful symmetry?"
   C. "In what distant deeps or skies / Burnt the fire of thine eyes?"
   D. "On what wings dare he aspire? / What the hand dare seize the fire?"
   E. "And when thy heart began to beat, / What dread hand? & what dread feet?"

4. Which of the following statements correctly describes the dominant sounds in "The Lamb" and "The Tyger"?
   A. Smooth, peaceful sounds dominate in both poems.
   B. Hard, almost violent sounds dominate in both poems.
   C. The dominant sounds in "The Lamb" come from the rhyming words; this is not the case in "The Tyger."
   D. The questioning inflection, with the voice going up at the end of the sentences, dominates in "The Lamb"; the beginning sounds in sentences dominate in "The Tyger."
   E. Many of the initial consonants, especially *l* in "The Lamb," sound soft and melodic; many of the initial consonants in "The Tyger," such as *t* and *b,* have harsh sounds.

5. Which of the following details from "London" does *not* contribute to creating the same mood as all the others?
   A. "each charter'd street"
   B. "marks of woe"
   C. "cry of fear"
   D. "mind-forg'd manacles"
   E. "blackning Church"

6. Which of the following nouns that are capitalized in "London" belongs with *Church* as something being criticized in the poem?
   A. Man
   B. Infant
   C. Chimney-sweeper
   D. Soldier
   E. Palace

7. How do the last two stanzas of "London" differ from the first two?
   A. mood and tone
   B. rhyme scheme and meter
   C. subject matter and mood
   D. meter and absence of repetition
   E. number and kind of poetic devices used

8. What is the poet's attitude toward most of what he describes in "London"?
   A. calm
   B. violent
   C. critical
   D. sarcastic
   E. indifferent

9. **Constructed Response:** Compare and contrast "The Lamb" and "The Tyger." Identify at least three ways in which the two poems are similar and different.

10. **Constructed Response:** Discuss Blake's choices of verbs in the last two stanzas of "London." What verbs might you expect to be used in the sentences, and what is the effect of the verbs that are used?

Understand the Concept

Parallelism, or **parallel structure,** is achieved by repeating grammatical forms to express ideas of equal, or *parallel,* importance. Poets often use parallelism to give equal weight to ideas expressed in lines of verse. Consider, for instance, lines 5–8 from William Blake's "London":

> In every cry of every Man,
> In every Infant's cry of fear,
> In every voice, in every ban,
> The mind-forg'd manacles I hear:

Notice how Blake repeats the construction of a prepositional phrase that begins with the words "In every." By using parallelism in these lines, the poet gives equal importance to the ideas that follow these two words.

Likewise, in everyday writing, a sentence has parallelism when it uses the same grammatical structure to express ideas of equal, or parallel, importance.

EXAMPLES

Not parallel The puppy likes *to chew on socks* and *jumping.*

Parallel The puppy likes *to chew on socks* and *to jump.*

Parallel The puppy likes *chewing on socks* and *jumping.*

The first of these examples presents an infinitive and a gerund to express two equal ideas. To achieve parallelism, two infinitives should be used, as in the second example, or two gerunds, as in the final example.

Using parallel structure will help you better express your ideas and make your writing more organized and clear. When you edit sentences during revision, verify that you have used parallelism effectively.

Apply the Skill

Identify Parallelism

Write the following lines of poetry on a separate piece of paper, and underline the parallel language in each one. If the lines do not contain parallelism, write *No.*

1. And the coming wind did roar more loud,
   And the sails did sigh like sedge;
   And the rain poured down from one black cloud;
   The Moon was at its edge.
   —Samuel Taylor Coleridge, "The Rime of the Ancient Mariner"

2. One shade the more, one ray the less,
   Had half impair'd the nameless grace
   —Lord Byron, "She Walks in Beauty"

3. Or at the casement seen her stand?
   Or is she known in all the land,
   The Lady of Shalott?
   —Alfred, Lord Tennyson, "The Lady of Shalott"

4. I love thee freely, as men strive for Right;
   I love thee purely, as they turn from Praise.
   —Elizabeth Barrett Browning, "Sonnet 43"

5. Was it cowardice, that I dared not kill him?
   Was it perversity, that I longed to talk to him?
   Was it humility, to feel so honored?
   I felt so honored.
   —D. H. Lawrence, "Snake"

Fix Errors in Parallelism

Rewrite each of the following sentences to use parallel structure.

1. The wind was howling past the windows and knocked on the door.
2. We plan on driving to the beach, walking on the sand, and swim in the ocean.
3. In the house, I washed the clothes, and I hung them in the yard.
4. To prepare for the party, I baked a cake and am wrapping presents.
5. I agree with the speaker's opinions, and with her concerns I empathize.

Use Parallelism in Your Writing

Write a paragraph about the town or city in which you live. Try to capture the city's character or your attitude toward it, instead of just giving facts and other objective information. Make sure you use parallelism in your sentences.

from A Vindication of the Rights of Woman

An Essay by Mary Wollstonecraft

Build Background

Cultural Context Mary Wollstonecraft lived in a time when women had few rights under the law. They could neither vote nor sue in court. They had limited educational opportunities and were not allowed to attend universities. When they married, their husbands inherited all of their property. They had few opportunities for work except as servants, nurses, seamstresses, or governesses (who performed tutoring and child care duties).

In *A Vindication of the Rights of Woman,* Wollstonecraft argues that such inequities reduce women to the dependent state of children; rob them of self-sufficiency; make them weak, docile, and overly emotional; and keep them from becoming fully human. In contemporary terms, one might state Wollstonecraft's argument as follows: Lack of opportunity and education make it impossible for women to achieve their full potential.

Reader's Context What happens to people when they are denied the right to education, ownership of property, or participation in the government or workforce?

Meet the Author

Mary Wollstonecraft (1759–1797) is widely recognized as one of the first great feminist writers and thinkers. At age nineteen, she took a position as a companion to an older woman but had to give it up to care for her mother during a protracted terminal illness. In 1784, Wollstonecraft helped her sister escape from a cruel husband. The two sisters, along with a friend, then started a school at Newington Green. Although the school initially was a success, financial difficulties resulted in its closing.

Wollstonecraft wrote her first book, *Thoughts on the Education of Daughters,* in 1786. This work was followed in 1788 by a novel, *Mary, a Fiction;* in 1790 by a book on the French Revolution, *A Vindication of the Rights of Men;* and in 1792 by Wollstonecraft's masterpiece, *A Vindication of the Rights of Woman.* During the years 1793–1794, Wollstonecraft went to France to observe the French Revolution firsthand. After adventures and misadventures, she returned to London and married radical social philosopher William Godwin. The couple's child, Mary Wollstonecraft Godwin, grew up to write an astonishing Romantic novel, *Frankenstein.*

Unfortunately, Wollstonecraft never knew her daughter, for she died as a result of childbirth. Her work was suppressed after her death. However, twentieth-century women's rights advocates have come to view *A Vindication of the Rights of Woman* as a pioneering work on the necessity of equal education and opportunity for women.

Analyze Literature

Argument and Epithet
An **argument** is a form of persuasion that makes a case to the audience for accepting or rejecting a proposition or a course of action.

An **epithet** is a characteristic word or phrase used alongside the name of a person, place, or thing.

Set Purpose

Wollstonecraft's persuasive essay is a landmark in the struggle for women's rights and points out how both sexes benefit when women are encouraged to achieve their full potential. As you read, list Wollstonecraft's beliefs and note how she turns them into an argument. What techniques does she use to persuade readers to change their perspective? Look closely at the language she uses to emphasize her argument. Write down those words and phrases you find particularly compelling. Also consider how Wollstonecraft uses epithets to support her argument.

Preview Vocabulary

specious, 666
caprice, 666
satirize, 666
scrupulous, 666
puerile, 666
propriety, 666
insinuate, 666
ignoble, 667
indefeasible, 667
expostulate, 667

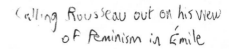
Calling Rousseau out on his view of Feminism in Émile

from

A Vindication of the

Rights of Woman

by Mary Wollstonecraft

persuasive essay

How grossly do they insult us who thus advise us only to render ourselves gentle, domestic brutes!

answering Rousseau's

Day Dream, 1880. Dante Gabriel Rossetti. Victoria and Albert Museum, London, England. (See detail on page 664.)

All humanity should attain the same kind of virtue

To account for, and excuse the tyranny of man, many ingenious arguments have been brought forward to prove, that the two sexes, in the acquirement of virtue, ought to aim at attaining a very different character: or, to speak explicitly, women are not allowed to have sufficient strength of mind to acquire what really deserves the name of virtue. Yet it *> ironic* should seem, allowing them to have souls, that there is but one way appointed by Providence to lead *mankind* to either virtue or happiness.

Three Children, c. 1806–1809. Rembrandt Peale.

If then women are not a swarm of ephemeron[1] triflers, why should they be kept in ignorance under the <u>specious</u> name of innocence? Men complain, and with reason, of the follies and <u>caprices</u> of our sex, when they do not keenly <u>satirize</u> our headstrong passions and groveling vices.—Behold, I should answer, the natural effect of ignorance! The mind will ever be unstable that has only prejudices to rest on, and the current will run with destructive fury when there are no barriers to break its force. Women are told from their infancy, and taught by the example of their mothers, that a little knowledge of human weakness, justly termed cunning, softness of temper, *outward* obedience, and a <u>scrupulous</u> attention to a <u>puerile</u> kind of <u>propriety</u>, will obtain for them the pro-

tection of man; and should they be beautiful, every thing else is needless, for, at least, twenty years of their lives.

Thus Milton describes our first frail mother; though when he tells us that women are formed for softness and sweet attractive grace,[2] I cannot comprehend his meaning, unless, in the true Mahometan strain,[3] he meant to deprive us of souls, and <u>insinuate</u> that we were beings only designed by sweet attractive grace, and docile blind obedience, to gratify the senses of man when he can no longer soar on the wing of contemplation.

How grossly do they insult us who thus advise us only to render ourselves gentle, domestic brutes! For instance, the winning softness so warmly, and frequently, recommended, that governs by obeying. What childish expressions, and how insignificant is the being—can it be an immortal one? who will condescend to govern by such sinister methods! "Certainly," says

---

1. **ephemeron.** Insect that only lives one day
2. **Milton . . . grace.** In *Paradise Lost* (IV. 297–299), Milton wrote that men were formed for "contemplation" and "valor," while women were made for "softness" and "sweet attractive grace."
3. **Mahometan strain.** Wollstonecraft is referring to an eighteenth-century understanding of an Islamic law (where Mahomet is another name for Mohammed, the Islamic prophet) that suggests women are soulless.

spe • cious (spē´ shəs) *adj.*, seeming sound or logical while not really being so
ca • price (kə prēs´) *n.*, whim
sat • i • rize (sa´ tə rīz´) *v.*, attack or ridicule with satire
scru • pu • lous (skrü´ pyə ləs) *adj.*, extremely careful
pue • rile (pyür´ əl) *adj.*, childish; immature
pro • pri • e • ty (prə prī´ ə tē) *n.*, quality of acting in a proper or socially correct manner
in • sin • u • ate (in sin´ yə wāt´) *v.*, suggest; imply

beauty has a shelf life
traded in for a newer model when old

these girls are at their husband's mercy

Lord Bacon,[4] "man is of kin to the beasts by his body; and if he be not of kin to God by his spirit, he is a base and <u>ignoble</u> creature!" Men, indeed, appear to me to act in a very unphilosophical manner when they try to secure the good conduct of women by attempting to keep them always in a state of childhood. Rousseau was more consistent when he wished to stop the progress of reason in both sexes, for if men eat of the tree of knowledge, women will come in for a taste; but, from the imperfect cultivation which their understandings now receive, they only attain a knowledge of evil.

Children, I grant, should be innocent; but when the epithet is applied to men, or women, it is but a civil term for weakness. For if it be allowed that women were destined by Providence to acquire human virtues, and by the exercise of their understandings, that stability of character which is the firmest ground to rest our future hopes upon, they must be permitted to turn to the fountain of light, and not forced to shape their course by the twinkling of a mere satellite. Milton, I grant, was of a very different opinion; for he only bends to the <u>indefeasible</u> right of beauty, though it would be difficult to render two passages which I now mean to contrast, consistent. But into similar inconsistencies are great men often led by their senses.

> To whom thus Eve with *perfect beauty*
>   adorned.
> My Author and Disposer, what thou bidst
> *Unargued* I obey; So God ordains;
> God is thy *law, thou mine:*—to know no
>   more
> Is Woman's *happiest* knowledge and her
>   praise.[5]

[handwritten] God → Adam's law →
Eve to Adam's law

These are exactly the arguments that I have used to children; but I have added, your reason is now gaining strength, and, till it arrives at some degree of maturity, you must look up to me for advice—then you ought to *think*, and only rely on God.

Yet in the following lines Milton seems to coincide with me; when he makes Adam thus <u>expostulate</u> with his Maker.

> Hast thou not made me here thy substitute,
> And these inferior far beneath me set?
> Among *unequals* what society
> Can sort, what harmony or true delight?
> Which must be mutual, in proportion due
> Giv'n and *received;* but in *disparity*
> The one intense, the other still remiss
> Cannot well suit with either, but soon
>   prove
> Tedious alike: of *fellowship* I speak
> Such as I seek, fit to participate
> All rational delight—[6]

In treating, therefore, of the manners of women, let us, disregarding sensual arguments, trace what we should endeavor to make them in order to cooperate, if the expression be not too bold, with the supreme Being. ❖

---

4. **Lord Bacon.** The following quote is from English thinker Francis Bacon's (1561–1626) essay "Of Atheism."
5. **To whom . . . praise.** *Paradise Lost* IV. 634–638; Wollstonecraft has added italics to emphasize her point
6. **Hast . . . delight.** *Paradise Lost* VII. 381–392; Wollstonecraft has added italics to show the inconsistency between this and the previous passage

ig • no • ble (ig nō´ bəl) *adj.,* not noble; common; low class
in • de • fea • si • ble (in di fē´ zə bəl) *adj.,* impossible to undo or void
ex • pos • tu • late (ik späs´ chə lāt´) *v.,* discuss

MIRRORS & WINDOWS

Why might women want to be known for more than beauty and gentleness? Why might innocence and docility be considered negative attributes?

Refer to Text ▶ ▶ ▶ ▶ ▶ Reason with Text

1a. What reason did Wollstonecraft's contemporaries give to support the belief that women cannot acquire virtue?	**1b.** Summarize Wollstonecraft's feelings about the contention that women are incapable of attaining virtue.	**Understand** Find meaning
2a. To what two British writers does Wollstonecraft allude to make her point?	**2b.** With which argument from the two separated passages does Wollstonecraft agree? Why would some agree with the other argument?	**Apply** Use information
3a. Paraphrase the two passages from Milton to which Wollstonecraft refers.	**3b.** Identify the contradictions between the two passages.	**Analyze** Take things apart
4a. In what state were women kept? In Wollstonecraft's opinion, what must women be allowed if they are to be virtuous?	**4b.** Evaluate Wollstonecraft's argument. What does she want for women? What reasons does she give? How effective is her argument?	**Evaluate** Make judgments
5a. According to Wollstonecraft, what is assumed about women's intellectual ability?	**5b.** Compare the similarities in the arguments against educating women with those against educating African slaves, Native Americans, and others. Why were these arguments used?	**Create** Bring ideas together

Analyze Literature

Argument and Epithet

What are the main points of Wollstonecraft's argument? How do her language and tone support her argument? Describe how she makes her argument effective.

To whom is the epithet of innocence connected in this excerpt? Describe the effect of these word associations on Wollstonecraft's argument.

Extend the Text

Writing Options

Creative Writing In this excerpt, Wollstonecraft singles out the writings of John Milton to explain her point. Write a letter from John Milton to Wollstonecraft responding to her use of his words in her essay. If necessary, research Milton to better understand his belief system.

Expository Writing Suppose that you were a critic at a literary magazine during the time that *A Vindication of the Rights of Woman* was published. Write a one-page analysis of Wollstonecraft's argument for this magazine. Identify and evaluate her main points and the details that support them.

Collaborative Learning

Debate Gender Equality Do social norms, including attitudes and behaviors, still favor the development of men's abilities over those of women? Do men still have more opportunities than women? Hold a class debate on these issues. Choose an equal number of men and women from among your classmates to represent each debate team. Your teacher can act as moderator.

Lifelong Learning

Research Writing About Women's Rights Divide into small groups and choose one of these major works on women's rights: Mary Wollstonecraft, *A Vindication of the Rights of Woman;* John Stuart Mill, *On the Subjugation of Women;* Simone de Beauvoir, *The Second Sex;* Betty Friedan, *The Feminine Mystique;* or Susan Faludi, *Backlash.* Study and discuss the major ideas of the work with your group. Then report to the class about the social conditions of the time in which the work was produced.

 Go to **www.mirrorsandwindows.com** for more.

Understand the Concept

A **phrase** is a group of words that does not contain a subject and a verb but functions as one part of speech. The most common type of phrase in the English language is the **prepositional phrase.** A **preposition** is a word that gives meaning to a noun by linking it with other words in the sentence. Some common prepositions are *to, from, after, about,* and *for.* A prepositional phrase begins with a preposition and includes the preposition's object and any modifiers. A prepositional phrase can function either as an adverb or an adjective.

> EXAMPLES
>
> Mary Wollstonecraft died *after childbirth.* [Functions as an adverb]
>
> She wrote a famous essay *about women's rights.* [Functions as an adjective]

Another type of phrase in the English language is the **gerund phrase,** a verbal phrase that functions as a noun. A gerund phrase begins with a **gerund,** or a word that ends in *-ing* and acts as a noun.

> EXAMPLE
>
> *Raising awareness* was important to Wollstonecraft.

A second type of verbal phrase, the **infinitive phrase,** can function as a noun, adjective, or adverb. It includes an **infinitive,** or the word *to* plus a verb.

> EXAMPLES
>
> *To express her beliefs* was one of Wollstonecraft's goals. [Noun]
>
> The work *to begin with* is her *A Vindication of the Rights of Woman.* [Adjective]
>
> I have tried *to tell others about her writing.* [Adverb]

A participial phrase is a verbal phrase that functions as an adjective. It includes a **participle,** which is described as an "action adjective."

> EXAMPLE
>
> *Wollstonecraft's eloquently worded* essay has impressed scholars throughout the ages.

Do not confuse a phrase with a **clause,** which is a group of words that contains a subject and a verb.

Apply the Skill

Identify Types of Phrases

Copy the following sentences on a separate sheet of paper. Then underline the phrase or phrases in each sentence. Also identify the type of phrase by labeling each *AJ* (adjectival prepositional phrase), *AV* (adverbial prepositional phrase), *G* (gerund phrase), *I* (infinitive phrase), or *P* (participial phrase).

1. Mary Wollstonecraft envisioned a future with more equality.
2. Her thought-provoking essay gained widespread recognition.
3. Writing intelligent essays helped her express her opinions.
4. She believed strongly in women's learning abilities.
5. Some scholars believe she used a rich vocabulary to support her argument.
6. Reduced to a dependent state, many women of her time lacked self-sufficiency.
7. Lacking opportunity and education, women were not considered fully human.
8. Mary Wollstonecraft gave up her position as governess to care for her mother.
9. In 1784, she helped her sister escape from a cruel husband.
10. A memoir written by Godwin after Wollstonecraft's death scandalized the public.

Improve the Use of Phrases

Write a sentence using each of the following phrases.

1. made by a professional
2. smiling to himself
3. to sail around the world
4. influenced by flattery
5. like a hungry beast
6. from the pocket of her coat
7. chosen at random
8. yawning surreptitiously
9. to conceal his dark secret
10. creeping through the hedges

Use a Variety of Phrases in Your Writing

Write a paragraph about a social issue you would like to see remedied. In your paragraph, try to write a sentence using each type of phrase: prepositional phrase (adverb), gerund phrase, participial phrase, prepositional phrase (adjective), and infinitive phrase.

William Wordsworth

> *"Come forth into the light of things,*
> *Let Nature be your teacher."*

William Wordsworth (1770–1850), the father of the Romantic Movement in England, had more influence on English poetry than any other writer since Shakespeare. Before Wordsworth, people generally viewed nature as something to be controlled and tamed for human uses. A tree was to be chopped down and turned into a house or a bridge. Wordsworth taught people to see the tree as a thing of beauty that could inspire elevated emotions.

Wordsworth was born in the English Lake District to parents who both died before he was thirteen years old. In his early childhood, he developed a deep love for the Lake District countryside. He attended Cambridge but did not take to academic life. After leaving school in 1791, he lived for a year in France, where he became a strong supporter of the democratic ideals of the French Revolution.

Wordsworth met fellow poet Samuel Taylor Coleridge in 1795. Together, they walked through the Dorsetshire countryside, spoke of poetry and philosophy, and conceived radical new ideas about verse. These ideas would find fruit in *Lyrical Ballads* (1798), the collection of poems they coauthored. Wordsworth's controversial Preface to *Lyrical Ballads* argues that poetry should be written not in flowery, formal language but in the voice of the common person. The verse in *Lyrical Ballads* contains portraits of nature and of ordinary but noble people. In addition, it avoids the use of artificial, mechanical devices of style in favor of "a selection of the language actually used by men." Finally, it records moments of spontaneous emotions enhanced by "a certain coloring of the imagination."

The period from 1797 to 1807 saw the creation of Wordsworth's finest poems, most of which dealt with the elevation of the soul through communion with nature. During this period, he also married Mary Hutchinson, with whom he had five children. Thereafter, Wordsworth's poetic powers declined as his conservatism, derived from bitterness over the failures of the French Revolution, increased. This conservatism earned him the scorn of younger, more radical poets, including Shelley, Byron, Keats, and Robert Browning, a scorn most famously expressed in Browning's poem "The Lost Leader."

In 1843, Wordsworth accepted the position of Poet Laureate of England under the condition that he not be required to write occasional or official verse. In his later years, he cared patiently and devotedly for his beloved sister, Dorothy, who suffered from dementia. When Wordsworth himself died, he was buried in Grasmere Churchyard in the Lake District that he had immortalized in his work.

Noted Works

Lyrical Ballads (1798)

"Tintern Abbey" (1798)

The Prelude (1799)

"Ode: Intimations of Immortality" (1807)

"I Wandered Lonely as a Cloud"
   (revised version, 1815)

The World Is Too Much with Us
Composed Upon Westminster Bridge
Sonnets by William Wordsworth

Build Background

Literary Context **"The World Is Too Much with Us"** and **"Composed Upon Westminster Bridge"** are both **sonnets,** a poetic form that had fallen out of favor during the Neoclassical Period but saw a revival in the Romantic Era. Wordsworth uses the Petrarchan, or Italian, sonnet form. It contains an **octave** (group of eight lines)

with the rhyme scheme *abbaabba* followed by a **sestet** (group of six lines) with the rhyme scheme *cdcdcd*. Also characteristic of the Petrarchan form, each sonnet presents a problem in the octave and then gives a response to it in the sestet.

"The World Is Too Much with Us," which is reminiscent of Blake's poem "London," was written in 1807, during an inspired and productive period in Wordsworth's poetic career. The poem bemoans humanity's separation from nature, suggesting that people who have become inspired by material things might be happier if they were still in touch with the values of pagan times—namely, the exultation of the natural world. In many of his poems, Wordsworth chooses to explore the relationship between nature and humanity and the impact this relationship has on the human condition. His reverence for the natural world helped spark the Romantic Movement in literature.

According to the journals of his sister, Dorothy, Wordsworth wrote the sonnet "Composed Upon Westminster Bridge" in the summer of 1802 while passing through London upon returning from France. In the poem "Composed

Another impressive London landmark is the Tower of London, constructed in 1078 by William the Conqueror. Over the centuries, the tower has served many purposes, including as a fortress, a royal residence, and a prison.

Upon Westminster Bridge," the speaker acknowledges the beauty found in an early morning view of London from West-minster Bridge. This beauty is a surprise to the speaker, who seems to have asso-ciated city life with noise, clutter, and pollution. The revelation is in line with the Romantic idea that a divine endow-ment of beauty is not only present in the natural world but also in the parts of the world modified by humans.

Reader's Context Do you enjoy spending time in nature, or do you prefer being in a city setting? Explain your feel-ings about each.

Analyze Literature
Theme and Allusion

A **theme** is a central message or perception about life that is revealed through a literary work. A *stated theme* is presented directly; whereas an *implied theme* must be inferred. A *uni-versal theme* can be understood by people of most cultures.

An **allusion** is a reference to a well-known person, event, object, or work from history or literature.

Set Purpose

Poets from the Romantic Era often examine the relationship between humanity and nature, but they do not always regard this relationship in the same way. Think about the message, or theme, revealed in each of these Wordsworth poems. For each poem, consider whether the theme is stated or implied and whether it could be clas-sified as universal. In addi-tion, look for instances where Wordsworth uses allusions to emphasize an idea he is present-ing. Consider how the use of allusions supports Wordsworth's theme.

Preview Vocabulary

sordid, 672

The Heart of the Empire, c. 1800s. Niels Moiler Lund. Guildhall Art Gallery, London, England.

The World Is Too Much with Us

by William Wordsworth

The world is too much with us; late and soon,
Getting and spending, we lay waste our powers:
Little we see in Nature that is ours;
We have given our hearts away, a <u>sordid</u> boon![1]
5   This Sea that bares her bosom to the moon;
The winds that will be howling at all hours,
And are up-gathered now like sleeping flowers;
For this, for every thing, we are out of tune;
It moves us not.—Great God! I'd rather be
10 A Pagan suckled in a creed outworn;
So might I, standing on this pleasant lea,[2]
Have glimpses that would make me less forlorn;
Have sight of Proteus[3] rising from the sea;
Or hear old Triton[4] blow his wreathéd horn. ❖

---

1. **boon.** Gift
2. **lea.** Meadow
3. **Proteus.** In *The Odyssey,* Proteus was an old man of the sea who could change his shape at will.
4. **Triton.** Sea god, often shown blowing on a shell

sor • did (sôr´ dəd) *adj.,* ignoble; wretched

MIRRORS & WINDOWS

What aspects of modern life distance you from nature? How could you get more in touch with nature without altering your lifestyle too much?

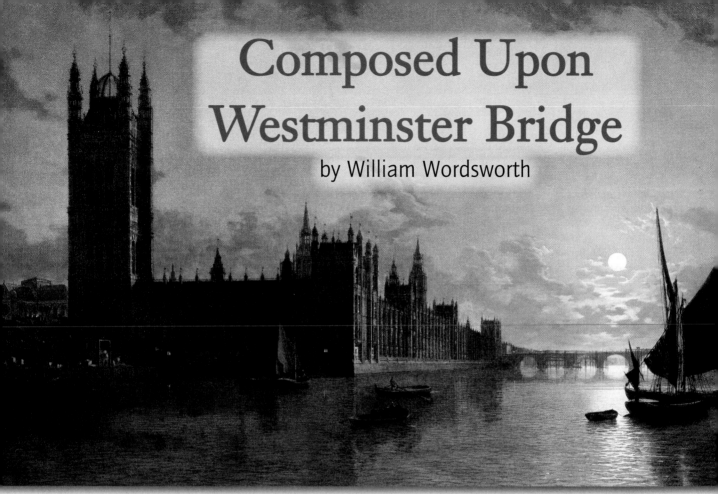

Composed Upon Westminster Bridge

by William Wordsworth

Westminster Abbey and the Houses of Parliament, 1859. Henry Pether. Private collection. (See detail on page 671.)

Nature

How he feels about the city

loving its beauty

September 3, 1802

Earth has not anything to show more fair:
Dull would he be of soul who could pass by
A sight so touching in its majesty:
This City now doth, like a garment, wear
5 The beauty of the morning; silent, bare,
Ships, towers, domes, theaters, and temples lie
Open unto the fields, and to the sky;
All bright and glittering in the smokeless air.
Never did sun more beautifully steep
10 In his first splendor, valley, rock, or hill;
Ne'er saw I, never felt, a calm so deep!
The river glideth at his own sweet will:
Dear God! the very houses seem asleep;
And all that mighty heart is lying still! ❖

MIRRORS & WINDOWS

In describing Westminster Bridge, Wordsworth writes, "Earth has not anything to show more fair." Do you tend to be more impressed with works of nature or humans? What human creation has impressed you?

Westminster Bridge

The Westminster Bridge that inspired William Wordsworth to write his heartfelt poem is not the same structure that today runs across the River Thames in London. Wordsworth's bridge, built in 1750, was a simple stone structure. By the mid-1800s, the bases of this bridge were crumbling more quickly than masons could repair them. In 1862, Britain commissioned Sir Charles Barry to design a new bridge made of wrought iron. Barry also had been commissioned in 1834 to rebuild Westminster Palace, home of the British Parliament, after much of it was destroyed by fire; that project spanned some thirty years.

Westminster Bridge has seven arches and runs in an east/west direction, linking the London burrows of Westminster and Lambeth. It provides avenues for both pedestrians and motor traffic. The bridge's wrought iron is the same green as the seats in Parliament's House of Commons, the branch of government that meets within the northern part of Westminster Palace, closest to the bridge. The Lambeth Bridge, which crosses the Thames slightly south of the Westminster, is red iron, corresponding to the red seats in the House of Lords, which meets at the southern end of the palace.

Westminster Bridge has been the subject of many famous paintings, most notably, works by John Sutton and Daniel Turner. The bridge also has appeared prominently in many movies, including the James Bond film *Die Another Day* (2002).

Westminster Bridge and the Houses of Parliament in London, England.

Primary Source Connection

This selection is an excerpt from the **Preface** to Wordsworth and Coleridge's **Lyrical Ballads, with a Few Other Poems.** For the book's first publication in 1798, neither author included his name on the title page for fear the public would scorn the work. A few years later, Wordsworth wrote this Preface to explain the authors' intentions in writing *Lyrical Ballads.* In the Preface, Wordsworth proposes that poetry should be written in the voice of the ordinary person. In other words, poetry should be natural, not artificial. Wordsworth's championing of the common person and nature reflects his belief in natural rights, as embodied in the rhetoric of the French Revolution. The ideas contained in Wordsworth's Preface helped shaped the way poetry was analyzed and discussed throughout the eighteenth and nineteenth centuries.

from

Preface to Lyrical Ballads

by William Wordsworth

The principal object, then, which I myself proposed in these poems was to choose incidents and situations from common life, and to relate or describe them, throughout, as far as was possible in a selection of language really used by men; and, at the same time to throw over them a certain coloring of imagination, whereby ordinary things should be presented to the mind in an unusual way; and, further, and above all, to make these incidents and situations interesting by tracing in them, truly though not ostentatiously, the primary laws of our nature: chiefly, as far as regards the manner in which we associate ideas in a state of excitement. Humble and rustic life was generally chosen, because in that condition, the essential passions of the heart find a better soil in which they can attain their maturity, are less under restraint, and speak a plainer and more emphatic language; because in that condition of life our elementary feelings coexist in a state of greater simplicity, and, consequently, may be more accurately contemplated, and more forcibly communicated.

. . .

Not that I . . . always began to write with a distinct purpose formally conceived; but I believe that habits of meditation have so formed my feelings that my descriptions of such objects as strongly excite those feelings will be found to carry along with them a *purpose*. If this opinion be erroneous,[1] I can have little right to the name of a poet. For all good poetry is the spontaneous overflow of powerful feelings: but though this be true, poems to which any value can be attached were never produced on any variety of subjects but by a man who, being possessed of more than usual organic[2] sensibility had also thought long and deeply.

. . .

The reader will find that personifications of abstract ideas rarely occur in these volumes; and are utterly rejected, as an ordinary device, to elevate the style and raise it above prose. My purpose was to imitate, and, as far as possible, to adopt the very language of men; and assuredly such personifications do not make any natural or regular part of that language.

They are, indeed, a figure of speech occasionally prompted by passion, and I have made use of them as such; but have endeavored utterly to reject them as a mechanical device of style, or as a family language which writers in meter seem to lay claim to by prescription. I have wished to keep the reader in the company of flesh and blood, persuaded that by so doing I shall interest him.

I have said that poetry is the spontaneous overflow of powerful feelings: it takes its origin from emotion recollected in tranquillity; the emotion is contemplated till, by a species of reaction, the tranquillity gradually disappears, and an emotion, kindred to that which was before the subject of contemplation, is gradually produced, and does itself actually exist in the mind. ❖

---

1. **erroneous.** Based on error; wrong
2. **organic.** Inherent; inborn

Review Questions

1. What kinds of situations and language does Wordsworth propose to use in the poems in *Lyrical Ballads?* How does he feel about other kinds of topics and language used in poetry? Explain why Wordsworth feels strongly about the type of situation and language used in poetry.

2. What does Wordsworth try to imitate in his poetry? What device does he reject? Outline the process Wordsworth describes for writing of good poetry, and describe the qualities of a good poem.

3. According to Wordsworth, what is poetry? How might the philosophies of the French Revolution have influenced Wordsworth's ideals and conception of poetry? Consider that the revolution began in 1789, when common folk stormed the Bastille Prison to protest their treatment by the monarchy and to demand equality.

TEXT ⇄ᵀᴼ TEXT CONNECTION

William Wordsworth wrote "The World Is Too Much with Us" in 1806 and "Composed Upon Westminster Bridge" in 1802—both after he wrote this Preface. Did Wordsworth continue writing poetry according to the principles he set forth in the Preface? How do these two poems reflect or contradict the ideas expressed in the Preface?

Refer to Text ▶ ▶ ▶ ▶ ▶	Reason with Text	
1a. Determine the "sight" line 3 of "Composed Upon Westminster Bridge."	**1b.** How is line 1 of the poem shocking given Wordsworth's status as a Romantic poet?	**Understand** Find meaning
2a. According to "The World Is Too Much with Us," how do we "lay waste our powers"?	**2b.** What might be wrong with focusing too much on "getting and spending"?	**Apply** Use information
3a. List the specific elements of the "sight" in "Composed Upon Westminster Bridge."	**3b.** Classify these elements into two categories: *Natural World* and *Humanmade World*.	**Analyze** Take things apart
4a. In "The World Is Too Much with Us," what have we "given . . . away"?	**4b.** How does the poet feel about humans' relationship to nature?	**Evaluate** Make judgments
5a. What does and does not move the speakers of the two poems?	**5b.** Are the messages of the poems contradictory? Why or why not?	**Create** Bring ideas together

Analyze Literature

Theme and Allusion

How would you describe the themes of "The World Is Too Much with Us" and "Composed Upon Westminster Bridge"? Are the themes stated or implied? Are they universal themes? Explain.

Identify two allusions in "The World Is Too Much with Us." Why might Wordsworth have wanted to call to readers' minds these figures from the past? What is the effect of this technique?

Extend the Text

Writing Options

Creative Writing Your firm has been hired to create an advertising campaign promoting nature conservation. Write a slogan that raises awareness and persuades people to take better care of the natural world. Your target audience for this ad campaign is your peers.

Expository Writing Write a brief essay that compares Wordsworth's "Composed Upon Westminster Bridge" to Blake's "London" (page 659). What is the central message of each poem? What is each speaker's attitude toward the city? Share your essay with your classmates.

Lifelong Learning

Research Romanticism Research how the ideals of Romanticism revealed themselves in the music and visual art of the period. Then pair one song or one piece of visual art with one of Wordsworth's poems. If you choose a song, draw parallels between the music's melody, lyrics, and instrumental choices and the Romantic ideals of the poetry. If you choose a piece of visual art, such as a painting or sculpture, make connections between the imagery, subjects, emotions, materials, and techniques of the artwork and the Romantic ideals of the poetry. Present your ideas to your classmates.

Media Literacy

Participate in a Panel Discussion Many people agree with Wordsworth that industrialization is still wrong for humankind. Others argue that technology only enhances the human experience. Form teams to discuss the issue. As a group, prepare and give a presentation using elements of a classical persuasive speech: an introduction that states your team's opinion; a body that addresses your arguments, evidence, and any counterarguments; and a conclusion that summarizes your points. Use logical transitions to help listeners follow your arguments. Include rhetorical devices, such as parallelism and repetition, to help emphasize your points and to sway listeners. Allow time for questions.

Go to **www.mirrorsandwindows.com** for more.

1. What does Wordsworth mean in line 2 of "The World Is Too Much with Us"?
   A. A penny saved is a penny earned.
   B. The more money we make, the more power we have.
   C. You first have to earn money before you can spend it.
   D. Our concern for material things makes us lesser human beings.
   E. We have to work so hard for a living that there is little time to sleep.

2. In the "The World Is Too Much with Us," what would be another term for what Wordsworth calls "the world"?
   A. nature
   B. people
   C. modern-day life
   D. financial affairs
   E. intellectual concerns

3. In lines 6–7 from "The World Is Too Much with Us," to what are the winds compared?
   A. a dog or wolf
   B. an unspecified howler
   C. someone who is sleeping
   D. a person who cannot sleep
   E. a flower

4. In "The World Is Too Much with Us," the speaker says he would rather be "a Pagan suckled in a creed outworn" than what?
   A. "Great God"
   B. a victim of unrequited love
   C. "Proteus rising from the sea"
   D. a person out of touch with nature
   E. someone "standing on this pleasant lea"

5. In line 2 of "Composed Upon Westminster Bridge," to whom does *he* refer?
   A. Earth
   B. any person
   C. Westminster Bridge
   D. the narrator of the poem
   E. a man the poet sees on the bridge

6. What is Wordsworth describing in the poem "Composed Upon Westminster Bridge"?
   A. Earth
   B. the city (London)
   C. Westminster Bridge
   D. life in general
   E. a person's heart

7. Review lines 9–10 in "Composed Upon Westminster Bridge." In these lines, how does Wordsworth personify the sun?
   A. by using the word his instead of its
   B. by using the word I instead of it
   C. by using metaphors
   D. by using onomatopoeia
   E. by using the words *beautifully* and *sweet*

8. **Constructed Response:** Identify the line from "Composed Upon Westminster Bridge" that you find most powerful or moving. Explain what about the line makes it so compelling.

9. **Constructed Response:** Read the following passage from Wordsworth's Preface to *Lyrical Ballads*. Discuss how this aim applies either to "The World Is Too Much with Us" or "Composed Upon Westminster Bridge."

The principal object, then, which I myself proposed in these poems was to choose incidents and situations from common life, and to relate or describe them, throughout, as far as was possible in a selection of language really used by men; and, at the same time to throw over them a certain coloring of imagination, whereby ordinary things should be presented to the mind in an unusual way; and, further, and above all, to make these incidents and situations interesting by tracing in them, truly though not ostentatiously, the primary laws of our nature: chiefly, as far as regards the manner in which we associate ideas in a state of excitement.

Lines Composed a Few Miles Above Tintern Abbey

A Lyric Poem by William Wordsworth

Build Background

memory of a young man, not childhood memory

Literary Context **"Lines Composed a Few Miles Above Tintern Abbey"** was published in 1798 as one of the "other poems" in the first edition of *Lyrical Ballads, with a Few Other Poems.* Composed in blank verse, "Tintern Abbey" is very different in style from the ballads, which are written in the voice of an ordinary person. Wordsworth himself noted "the impassioned music of the versification" in "Tintern Abbey," which is more like an ode than a ballad. Whereas a ballad is typically short and tells a story, an ode is elaborate and stately.

"Tintern Abbey" was inspired by a four- or five-day walk that Wordsworth took from Tintern to Bristol with his sister, Dorothy. This area, known as the Wye River Valley, informally separates Wales from England. At that time, as it is now, Tintern Abbey was merely a ruin of a once-functioning abbey. Built in 1131, the abbey held a community of nearly four hundred monks at the height of its functioning. The abbey was abandoned in the mid-1500s, after which the roof fell and other parts of the building crumbled. This nearly nine-hundred-year-old ruin still inspires awe in those who visit it—not only for its idyllic placement among hills, woods, and the River Wye but also for the history held within its open walls.

In the 1790s, the picturesque ruin was the highlight of a popular walking tour through the Wye Valley. On reading "Tintern Abbey," Wordsworth's contemporaries would have recognized it as a travel poem. Tourism and an appreciation for the beauty of the natural world were relatively new at this time.

The poem's speaker reflects on a memory of an earlier visit to Tintern Abbey, acknowledging that childhood memories of nature are at once both permanent and fleeting. In other words, childhood experiences of nature cannot be replaced by recreating the experience in adulthood—an adult experiences life differently than a child does. However, new memories can exist among the old ones and work together to bring peace and happiness when recalled.

The Wye River runs along the border of England and Wales.

Reader's Context Recall a place in nature you visited as a young child. Describe how this place looked and how it made you feel then, and imagine how you might react to it now.

See the Author Focus on page 670 for biographical information about William Wordsworth.

Analyze Literature

Voice and Blank Verse
Voice is the way a writer uses language to reflect his or her unique personality and attitude toward a topic, form, and audience. A writer expresses voice through tone, word choice, and sentence structure.

Blank verse is unrhymed poetry written in iambic pentameter.

Set Purpose

Wordsworth's poetry often is described as meditative or introspective—a trait found in much of the *Lyrical Ballads,* which helped establish a new era of more personal and reflective poetry. As you read "Tintern Abbey," notice how this tone influences the speaker's voice. Make a list of distinctive words, phrases, and lines that help create the speaker's voice. Also determine how the use of blank verse affects your reading and understanding of this poem. Consider how Wordsworth's use of blank verse further contributes to the development of the speaker's voice.

Preview Vocabulary

secluded, 680
repose, 680
copse, 681
vagrant, 681
beauteous, 681
tranquil, 681
sublime, 681
corporeal, 681
recompense, 683
exhortation, 685

Lines Composed a Few Miles
Above Tintern Abbey

Tintern Abbey, c. 1800. Frederick Waters Watts.
Private collection.

[handwritten annotations:]
How beautiful the country is
contrast to Epistle to Miss Blount

Blank verse
Iambic pentameter no rhyme

Brother bringing his little sister

by William Wordsworth — went 1793
and Dorothy at Tintern Abbey Coming back 1798

[handwritten: Setting the scene / enjambment / hardly end stop line]

Five years have past; five summers, with the length
Of five long winters! and again I hear
These waters, rolling from their mountain-springs
With a soft inland murmur. Once again
5   Do I behold these steep and lofty cliffs,
That on a wild <u>secluded</u> scene impress
Thoughts of more deep seclusion; and connect
The landscape with the quiet of the sky.
The day is come when I again <u>repose</u>
10   Here, under this dark sycamore, and view
These plots of cottage ground, these orchard tufts,
Which at this season, with their unripe fruits,

---

se • clud • ed (si klüd´ əd) *adj.,* hidden from public view
re • pose (ri pōz´) *v.,* lie quietly; rest

Are clad in one green hue, and lose themselves
'Mid groves and copses. Once again I see
15 These hedgerows, hardly hedgerows, little lines
Of sportive wood run wild; these pastoral farms,
Green to the very door; and wreaths of smoke
Sent up, in silence, from among the trees!
With some uncertain notice, as might seem
20 Of vagrant dwellers in the houseless woods,
Or of some Hermit's cave, where by his fire
The Hermit sits alone.

These beauteous forms,
Through a long absence, have not been to me
As is a landscape to a blind man's eye;
25 But oft, in lonely rooms, and 'mid the din
Of towns and cities, I have owed to them
In hours of weariness, sensations sweet,
Felt in the blood, and felt along the heart;
And passing even into my purer mind,
30 With tranquil restoration—feelings too
Of unremembered pleasure; such, perhaps,
As have no slight or trivial influence
On that best portion of a good man's life,
His little, nameless, unremembered, acts
35 Of kindness and of love. Nor less, I trust,
To them I may have owed another gift,
Of aspect more sublime; that blessed mood,
In which the burthen of the mystery,
In which the heavy and the weary weight
40 Of all this unintelligible world,
Is lightened—that serene and blessed mood,
In which the affections gently lead us on—
Until, the breath of this corporeal frame
And even the motion of our human blood
45 Almost suspended, we are laid asleep
In body, and become a living soul;
While with an eye made quiet by the power
Of harmony, and the deep power of joy,
We see into the life of things.

he meditates upon this landscape
brings him tranquility

talking about the physical
response to the calming from
the thought of the sitting landscape
Imagining it brings him new pleasure
it restores him
feeds him spiritually

talking about prayer or meditation
prayer brings a different
state of mind

Sounds like enlightenment

has a noticeable effect

---

copse (käps) *n.,* thicket of small trees or bushes
va • grant (vā´ grənt) *adj.,* nomadic; wandering
beau • te • ous (byü´ tē əs) *adj.,* beautiful
tran • quil (traŋ´ kwəl) *adj.,* peaceful; calm
sub • lime (sə blīm´) *adj.,* majestic
cor • po • re • al (kôr pôr´ ē əl) *adj.,* of a bodily or physical nature

Dorothy Wordsworth

In William Wordsworth's "Lines Composed a Few Miles Above Tintern Abbey," the "Dear, dear sister" mentioned in line 121 is Dorothy Wordsworth (1771–1855). Almost two years apart in age, Dorothy and William did not share a typical sibling relationship. They lived together for most of their adult lives and rarely traveled without one another. Their close connection as adults may have resulted from being separated for much of their childhood, due first to the death of their mother in 1778 and then that of their father in 1783. After being shuttled among relatives for many years, William and Dorothy finally were reunited in 1795, when William came into some money and Dorothy moved into his home to care for him.

Dorothy spent much of her time writing poetry and composing entries in her diary, but she did not aspire to publish her work. For nearly eighty years after her death, she was known only for her role in William's life. Then in 1931, children's author Beatrix Potter purchased Dove Cottage, where Dorothy and William had lived, and discovered Dorothy's journals among some papers in the barn. She published the work two years later as *The Grasmere Journal.*

The writing in Dorothy's journal included accounts of daily life as well as encounters with literary figures of the day, such as Samuel Taylor Coleridge. Not only was Dorothy's writing impressive on its own, but it also revealed the powerful influence she had on her brother's poetry. The vivid descriptions Dorothy provides of nature hikes with her brother contain many reflections and images used by William in his work. For instance, William's poems "Daffodils" and "Beggars" contain exact phrases used by Dorothy in her journals. Discovering the journals of Dorothy Wordsworth helped redefine women's contribution to Romantic literature. Several other collections of her poems, journals, and letters also were published well after her death.

[handwritten: he expects criticism this paragraph is saying "so what", it works]

                                        If this
50 Be but a vain[1] belief, yet, oh! how oft—
    In darkness and amid the many shapes
    Of joyless daylight; when the fretful stir
    Unprofitable, and the fever of the world
    Have hung upon the beatings of my heart—
55 How oft, in spirit, have I turned to thee,
    O sylvan Wye![2] thou wanderer thro' the woods,
    How often has my spirit turned to thee!

[handwritten: Brings us back to Tintern abbey]

    And now, with gleams of half-extinguished thought,
    With many recognitions dim and faint,
60 And somewhat of a sad perplexity,
    The picture of the mind revives again:

---

1. **vain.** Empty, worthless
2. **Wye.** River in England

While here I stand, not only with the sense
Of present pleasure, but with pleasing thoughts
That in this moment there is life and food
65 For future years. And so I dare to hope,
Though changed, no doubt, from what I was when first
I came among these hills; when like a roe[3]
I bounded o'er the mountains, by the sides
Of the deep rivers, and the lonely streams,
70 Wherever nature led—more like a man
Flying from something that he dreads, than one
Who sought the thing he loved. For nature then
(The coarser pleasures of my boyish days,
And their glad animal movements all gone by)
75 To me was all in all.—I cannot paint
What then I was. The sounding cataract
Haunted me like a passion; the tall rock,
The mountain, and the deep and gloomy wood,
Their colors and their forms, were then to me
80 An appetite; a feeling and a love,
That had no need of a remoter charm,
By thought supplied, nor any interest
Unborrowed from the eye.—That time is past,
And all its aching joys are now no more,
85 And all its dizzy raptures. Not for this
Faint[4] I, nor mourn nor murmur; other gifts
Have followed; for such loss, I would believe,
Abundant <u>recompense</u>. For I have learned
To look on nature, not as in the hour
90 Of thoughtless youth; but hearing oftentimes
The still, sad music of humanity,
Nor harsh nor grating, though of ample power
To chasten and subdue. And I have felt
A presence that disturbs me with the joy
95 Of elevated thoughts; a sense sublime
Of something far more deeply interfused,
Whose dwelling is the light of setting suns,
And the round ocean and the living air,
And the blue sky, and in the mind of man:
100 A motion and a spirit, that impels

Handwritten annotations:
- It was asthetic appreciation when he went the 1st time
- Just experiencing (sensory) no thinking
- Can't go back into adolescent stage
- Now he is philosophizing as an adult
- emotions are raw as adolescent
- he isn't sad about it because now he sees the big picture
- the reward of growing up

---

3. **roe.** Type of deer
4. **Faint.** Lose heart

rec • om • pense (re´ kəm pen[t]s') *n.,* repayment; reward

Llanberis Lake in Wales.

[handwritten: talking about God sees the holy Spiritualness]

All thinking things, all objects of all thought,
And rolls through all things. Therefore am I still
A lover of the meadows and the woods,
And mountains; and of all that we behold
105 From this green earth; of all the mighty world

[handwritten: a relationship where spiritual understanding comes from aesthetic beginning]

Of eye, and ear—both what they half create,
And what perceive; well pleased to recognize
In nature and the language of the sense,
The anchor of my purest thoughts, the nurse,
110 The guide, the guardian of my heart, and soul
Of all my moral being.

                Nor perchance,
If I were not thus taught, should I the more
Suffer my genial spirits[5] to decay:
For thou art with me here upon the banks
115 Of this fair river; thou my dearest Friend,[6]
My dear, dear Friend; and in thy voice I catch
The language of my former heart, and read
My former pleasures in the shooting lights
Of thy wild eyes. Oh! yet a little while
120 May I behold in thee what I was once,
My dear, dear Sister! and this prayer I make,
Knowing that Nature never did betray
The heart that loved her; 'tis her privilege,

[handwritten: sees his sister as he was and hopes the view will help her in time]

[handwritten: hopes it develops in the way like he has]

---

5. **genial spirits.** Creative spirit; from the noun *genius*
6. **dearest Friend.** Dorothy, his sister

Through all the years of this our life, to lead
125 From joy to joy: for she can so inform
The mind that is within us, so impress
With quietness and beauty, and so feed
With lofty thoughts, that neither evil tongues,
Rash judgments, nor the sneers of selfish men,
130 Nor greetings where no kindness is, nor all
The dreary intercourse of daily life,
Shall e'er prevail against us, or disturb
Our cheerful faith, that all which we behold
Is full of blessings. Therefore let the moon
135 Shine on thee in thy solitary walk;
And let the misty mountain winds be free
To blow against thee: and, in after years,
When these wild ecstasies shall be matured
Into a sober pleasure; when thy mind
140 Shall be a mansion for all lovely forms,
Thy memory be as a dwelling place
For all sweet sounds and harmonies; oh! then,
If solitude, or fear, or pain, or grief
Should be thy portion, with what healing thoughts
145 Of tender joy wilt thou remember me,
And these my exhortations! Nor, perchance—
If I should be where I no more can hear
Thy voice, nor catch from thy wild eyes these gleams
Of past existence—wilt thou then forget
150 That on the banks of this delightful stream
We stood together; and that I, so long
A worshiper of Nature, hither came
Unwearied in that service; rather say
With warmer love—oh! with far deeper zeal[7]
155 Of holier love. Nor wilt thou then forget,
That after many wanderings, many years
Of absence, these steep woods and lofty cliffs,
And this green pastoral landscape, were to me
More dear, both for themselves and for thy sake! ❖

---

7. **zeal.** Passion; fervor

ex • hor • ta • tion (ek' sôr' tā´ shən) n., strong urging

IRRORS & WINDOWS

Where do you go when you are upset or worried? Why does that place make you feel safe and calm? How would you describe it to a friend?

Refer to Text 	**Reason with Text**	
1a. How does the speaker describe his attitude toward nature when he was a child? As an adult?	**1b.** Describe how the speaker feels about the change in his relationship with nature. What has grown to be important to him as an adult?	**Understand** Find meaning
2a. Paraphrase lines 62–65, restating them in your own words.	**2b.** Do these lines discuss the past, the present, or the future? Find another example in the poem where the speaker focuses on these time states.	**Apply** Use information
3a. Recall the period of the speaker's life described in lines 66–83 and lines 88–111.	**3b.** Compare the two different descriptions, and analyze the change in his relationship to nature.	**Analyze** Take things apart
4a. Whom does the speaker address in line 115? How do you know?	**4b.** Assess the importance of the presence of this "friend" to the message of the poem. What role does this direct address play?	**Evaluate** Make judgments
5a. Identify two lines of the poem that express great emotion.	**5b.** Find other evidence of "the spontaneous overflow of powerful feelings" in "Tintern Abbey." What evidence contradicts this idea?	**Create** Bring ideas together

Analyze Literature

Voice and Blank Verse

Describe the speaker's voice in "Tintern Abbey." Refer to your list of distinctive words, phrases, and lines. How do these words and phrases contribute to the creation of the speaker's voice?

What specific aspects of the poem make it blank verse? How does Wordsworth's use of blank verse contribute to the speaker's voice?

Extend the Text

Writing Options

Creative Writing Write a free verse poem of at least two stanzas about a childhood memory, such as a place, a family event, a person, or a special possession. What did it mean to you at the time? What is its significance to you now? Has its significance changed?

Descriptive Writing Write a paragraph describing your favorite place to relax. As you write, imagine yourself in that place, and try to identify how each of your senses experiences it. Include in your description as many of the five senses as possible.

Collaborative Learning

Compare Poets' Attitudes In small groups, discuss how William Blake's views of youth and adulthood relate to Wordsworth's views as presented in "Tintern Abbey." Does Wordsworth draw a line between innocence and experience? What might Blake say about Wordsworth's comparison of his youthful experience at Tintern Abbey and his adult experience?

Media Literacy

Analyze Media and Society Wordsworth believed that mass culture has the effect of spreading mental dullness by overwhelming people with trivial details and sensationalism. Think about Wordsworth's opinion in relation to your own life and today's media culture. What are the effects of the avalanche of trivia to which we are exposed daily in the mass media? Write notes outlining your thoughts on these questions, and share them with the class.

 Go to **www.mirrorsandwindows.com** for more.

Kubla Khan
The Rime of the Ancient Mariner

Narrative Poems by Samuel Taylor Coleridge

Build Background

Literary Context Both "Kubla Khan" and "The Rime of the Ancient Mariner" are **narrative poems,** which tell stories. In the preface to **"Kubla Khan,"** Coleridge wrote that he awoke from a dream with the poem fully formed in his mind. In ill health and taking medication, he had fallen asleep while reading *Purchas His Pilgrimage,* by Samuel Purchas, which contains the line "In Xanadu did Cublai Can build a stately Palace." Kubla Khan founded the Mongol Dynasty in China in the thirteenth century.

The supernatural ballad **"The Rime of the Ancient Mariner"** first appeared in 1798 in *Lyrical Ballads,* the collection Coleridge coauthored with his friend William Wordsworth (see page 670). With its chilling narrative, consistent rhyme scheme, and regular rhythm, this poem is an excellent example of the ballad form. The formal, classical aspects of the poem's language do not reflect Wordsworth's belief that poetry should be in the language of the common person. In later versions of the poem, however, Coleridge edited some of the archaic language, making the poem more accessible to less scholarly readers.

Reader's Context If you could imagine a paradise for yourself and include any real or imaginary mystical elements, how would you describe such a place?

Meet the Author

Samuel Taylor Coleridge (1772–1834) was born in rural Devonshire. He attended school in London and later in Cambridge, but he never completed his degree.

In 1795, Coleridge met William Wordsworth, the friend and fellow poet with whom he would collaborate on the influential *Lyrical Ballads.* Coleridge suffered from rheumatism and took laudanum (an opium derivative), following the standard medical procedures of the day. He became addicted to the drug around 1800, soon after becoming estranged (separated) from his wife. In 1810, at his lowest point, he had a terrible argument with Wordsworth. Despite his agonies, Coleridge continued to write, lecture, and publish. After finding a caring physician who reduced the strength of his addiction, Coleridge regained his tranquility, reconciled with Wordsworth, and made peace with his former wife.

Perhaps because of his tragic addiction, many of Coleridge's most intense work efforts, including "Kubla Khan," were never finished and exist today only in the form of scrawled notes. Nonetheless, Coleridge is considered one of the great poets of the Romantic Era and an influential literary theorist.

Analyze Literature

Imagery and Personification
Imagery is the figurative or descriptive language used to create an image, or word picture—a word or phrase that names something that can be seen, heard, touched, tasted, or smelled.

Personification is a figure of speech in which an animal, a thing, a force of nature, or an idea is described as if it were human or is given human characteristics.

Set Purpose

As you read each poem, list the images you find most striking. How does each image help you visualize what the speaker is describing? Also look for examples of personification in "The Rime of the Ancient Mariner." Consider what impact Coleridge's use of personification has on your understanding of the events in the poem.

Preview Vocabulary

cavern, 688
chasm, 689
meander, 689
tumult, 689
sprite, 696
agape, 697
flecked, 697
wan, 702
discern, 704
abate, 706

Kubla Khan

by Samuel Taylor Coleridge

[handwritten: - Romantic poetry]

[handwritten: - Conquerers of Asia]

[handwritten: - taken on a journey not instructional]

[handwritten: - Kubla khan - powerful and wealthy leader]

[handwritten: gives an esthetic experience not a story]

In Xanadu did Kubla Khan *[handwritten: exotic]*
A stately pleasure dome decree:
Where Alph,[1] the sacred river, ran
Through <u>caverns</u> measureless to man *[handwritten: a mysterious ending]*
5   Down to a sunless sea.
So twice five miles of fertile ground *[handwritten: varied vegetation]*
With walls and towers were girdled round:
And there were gardens bright with sinuous rills,[2]
Where blossomed many an incense-bearing tree;
10 And here were forests ancient as the hills,
Enfolding sunny spots of greenery.

[handwritten: vivid imagery]

1. **Alph.** Probably the Alpheus River in Greece
2. **sinuous rills.** Winding streams

cav • ern (kaˊ vərn *or* kaˊ vrən) *n.*, cave

But oh! that deep romantic <u>chasm</u> which slanted
Down the green hill athwart a cedarn cover![3]
A savage place! as holy and enchanted
15 As e'er beneath a waning moon was haunted
By woman wailing for her demon lover!
And from this chasm, with ceaseless turmoil seething,
As if this earth in fast thick pants were breathing,
A mighty fountain momently was forced:[4]
20 Amid whose swift half-intermitted burst
Huge fragments vaulted like rebounding hail,
Or chaffy grain beneath the thresher's flail:
And 'mid these dancing rocks at once and ever
It flung up momently the sacred river.
25 Five miles <u>meandering</u> with a mazy motion
Through wood and dale the sacred river ran,
Then reached the caverns measureless to man,
And sank in <u>tumult</u> to a lifeless ocean:
And 'mid this tumult Kubla heard from far
30 Ancestral voices prophesying war!
    The shadow of the dome of pleasure
    Floated midway on the waves;
    Where was heard the mingled measure
    From the fountain and the caves.
35 It was a miracle of rare device,
A sunny pleasure dome with caves of ice!

    A damsel with a dulcimer
    In a vision once I saw:
    It was an Abyssinian maid,
40   And on her dulcimer she played
    Singing of Mount Abora.[5]

---

3. **athwart a cedarn cover.** Chasm cut across the cedar-covered hill on a
downward slant
4. **A . . . forced.** Waters springing from underground have long been a
symbol for poetic inspiration.
5. **Mount Abora.** Apparently, a reference to Milton's *Paradise Lost*, Book IV,
Lines 280–282, in which he refers to "Mount Amara," where Abyssinian
kings were believed to have built a palatial paradise

chasm (ka´ z'm) *n.,* deep cleft in the earth
me • an • der (mē an´ dər) *v.,* follow a winding course
tu • mult (tü´ mult') *n.,* loud commotion

Could I revive within me
Her symphony and song,
To such a deep delight 'twould win me,
45 That with music loud and long,
I would build that dome in air,
That sunny dome! those caves of ice!
And all who heard should see them there, *imagery of the Bard as he is composing*
And all should cry, Beware! Beware!
50 His flashing eyes, his floating hair!
Weave a circle round him thrice,[6] *beware, he has been somewhere we can not go*
And close your eyes with holy dread,
For he on honeydew hath fed,
And drunk the milk of Paradise. ❖

Yep, I'm a poet   *makes audience have*

6. **Weave . . . thrice.** Magical ritual   *the experience*

shows power of the poet

MIRRORS & WINDOWS

The story Coleridge tells in "Kubla Khan" reportedly came from a highly detailed dream. What do you dream about? What story could you tell based on one of your dreams?

HISTORY CONNECTION

The Travels of Marco Polo

The subject of Samuel Taylor Coleridge's poem "Kubla Khan" was Kublai Khan (1214–1294), the fifth ruler of the Mongol Empire and grandson of Genghis Khan, the empire's founder. Under Kublai Khan, sometimes called the Great Khan, Chinese civilization flourished.

Italian explorer Marco Polo (c. 1254–c. 1324) traveled to Cathay (China) in 1271, then capital of the empire, and spent seventeen years as a friend and adviser to Kublai Khan. Polo later recorded his experiences in a travel narrative called *Il Milione;* it was the first written account of the Mongol Empire by a European. The title of Polo's work, which means "the million" in Italian, fits the lavish language he used in the narrative to describe the empire's vast army, wealth, and resources.

Although *Il Milione* is considered one of the most important travel narratives ever written, historians do not consider it reliable. Polo had a reputation for exaggerating, which made some Europeans skeptical of his account. In fact, critics called *Il Milione* "the Million Lies." The manner in which the book was written also raised questions of credibility. Polo had dictated his travel stories to a fellow inmate while in prison some twenty years after returning from China. The book first was written in Old French and then translated into many different languages. However, the original manuscript was lost, and the translations that have survived contradict one another on many important points.

Even so, *Il Milione* was widely popular. Marco Polo's words inspired fellow Italian explorer Christopher Columbus (1451–1506) to traverse the Atlantic. Columbus reportedly brought a copy of Polo's book with him on his journey.

The Rime of the Ancient Mariner

Head of an Old Man, c. 1500s. Hans Baldung-Grien.
Galleria e Museo Estense, Modena, Italy.

by Samuel Taylor Coleridge

Part I

It is an ancient Mariner
And he stoppeth one of three.
"By thy long gray beard and glittering eye,
Now wherefore stopp'st thou me?

5 The Bridegroom's doors are opened wide,
And I am next of kin;
The guests are met, the feast is set:
May'st hear the merry din."

*An ancient Mariner
meeteth three Gallants
bidden to a wedding feast,
and detaineth one.*

Refer to Text ▶ ▶ ▶ ▶ ▶	**Reason with Text**	
1a. In the second stanza of "Kubla Khan," how is the "chasm" described? What issues out of the chasm?	**1b.** Describe what is happening in the second stanza. How does that scene compare to the scene of the first stanza?	**Understand** Find meaning
2a. Who tells the story in "The Rime of the Ancient Mariner"? To whom is the story being told?	**2b.** Why might Coleridge have chosen to create this framework around the poem, instead of having the mariner be the only speaker?	**Apply** Use information
3a. What sounds are repeated in lines 59–62 of "The Rime of the Ancient Mariner"?	**3b.** Analyze Coleridge's use of rhyme, rhythm, and repetition to complement the images he is presenting. Give one example of each use.	**Analyze** Take things apart
4a. List the elements of "The Rime of the Ancient Mariner" that seem supernatural or characteristic of science fiction.	**4b.** Would the mariner's story have the same effect if these elements were not present? Explain your answer.	**Evaluate** Make judgments
5a. Identify parts of "Kubla Khan" that seem dreamlike or supernatural.	**5b.** How does the progression of the poem compare to that of a dream?	**Create** Bring ideas together

Analyze Literature

Imagery and Personification

Choose three images from your list for each poem. What does Coleridge's use of these images indicate about the theme in each poem?

What examples of personification are in "The Rime of the Ancient Mariner"? How does the use of personification bring to life the eerie aspects of the story?

Extend the Text

Writing Options

Creative Writing If the pleasure dome were a real place, it would be a wonder to see. Write a travel brochure designed to entice tourists of all ages to visit Kubla Kahn's paradise.

Applied Writing Summarize the main plot of "The Rime of the Ancient Mariner" in writing. Then retell the story in graphic novel format, with the goal of visually capturing the poem's more chilling moments. Where possible, include the poem's original dialogue in the drawings. Share the poem with friends who have not read it.

Lifelong Learning

Research the Rime Some scholars believe that Coleridge was inspired to write "The Rime of the Ancient Mariner" after learning about one of the voyages of British seaman Captain James Cook. Using a variety of sources, find out more about this and other possible origins for the story of "The Rime of the Ancient Mariner." Then write a brief introduction to the poem based on your research.

Collaborative Learning

Create a Dictionary Working in a small group, choose ten words from the footnotes for "The Rime of the Ancient Mariner" and create a dictionary of archaic language to help students who will study the poem next year. For each entry, include the word or phrase, its definition, and an original example of the word or phrase used in context.

 Go to **www.mirrorsandwindows.com** for more.

Understand the Concept

Scholars who study language have classified European languages into two major categories: inflected languages and syntactic languages. The words of **inflected languages** change form to tell speakers how a word is used, and word order is not particularly important to meaning. Latin and German are examples of inflected languages. English, however, is a **syntactic language,** in which word order is very important. In English, the word order, or **syntax,** determines meaning.

In English, words are arranged in specific patterns to create a sentence. The most common sentence pattern first tells *who* and then tells *what:*

EXAMPLE
The teacher writes the assignment on the board.

In this example, *The teacher* is the who and *writes the assignment on the board* is the what.

When the word order changes, the meaning of the sentence changes, as well. If the accepted patterns or rules are ignored, then the sentence may become awkward or even meaningless.

EXAMPLE
The assignment board on the writes teacher.

Positioning the same word in different places in a sentence also results in different meanings.

EXAMPLES
The flag *flies* triumphantly in the breeze.

Flies were swarming the screen.

In the first sentence, the word *flies* is a verb that describes an action. In the second sentence, *flies* is a noun that names something—a type of bug. In both sentences, the word form of *flies* is the same, but the different positions signal different meanings.

Occasionally, writers alter the syntax to achieve a certain effect. This technique often is used in poetry, allowing the poet to maintain rhythm or create rhyme.

> The souls did from their bodies fly,—
> They fled to bliss or woe!
> And every soul, it passed me by,
> Like the whizz of my crossbow!

In this example from lines 220–223 of "The Rime of the Ancient Mariner," Coleridge rearranges the syntax of the first line to preserve the rhythm of the poem and to create a rhyme with the word *by* in the third line.

Apply the Skill

Exercise A

Rewrite each of the following lines from "The Rime of the Ancient Mariner" using conventional syntax.

1. At length did cross an Albatross / Through the fog it came. (lines 63–64)
2. Ah wretch! said they, the bird to slay, / That made the breeze to blow! (lines 95–96)
3. The many men, so beautiful! / And they all dead did lie. (lines 236–237)
4. But swift as dreams, myself I found / Within the Pilot's boat. (lines 554-555)
5. How long in that same fit I lay, / I have not to declare. (lines 393–394)

Exercise B

Each of the following words can have two meanings. To illustrate those different meanings, write two sentences for each word using different syntax.

1. close
2. bow
3. lead
4. lie
5. wound

SPELLING PRACTICE

Doubling the Final Consonant

When you add a suffix such as *-ed, -est,* or *-ing* to a word that ends with the pattern consonant/vowel/consonant (CVC), you need to double the last consonant. For example, the word *sad* has the CVC pattern, so when you add *-er* or *-est,* you need to double the last letter to make *sadder* or *saddest.* These words from "Kubla Khan" and "The Rime of the Ancient Mariner" are examples of words that have doubled the final consonant.

averred	ribbed	stirred
dipping	rotting	stunned
dogged	sadder	sunny
fanned	setting	upper
intermitted	stepped	winning

CASABIANCA[1]

by Felicia Dorothea Hemans

Felicia Dorothea Hemans
(1793–1835), who is best
known for her Romantic lyric
poetry, was much admired as
a poet by William Wordsworth
and Sir Walter Scott. Her first
collection of
poetry, titled
Poems, was
first published
in 1808 and is
believed to have
been written
when she was
between eight
and thirteen
years old. Over the next twenty
years, she produced twenty-
three more volumes of poetry.
After separating from her husband in 1819, she helped support her five children by selling
her poems.
    "Casabianca" is set
during the Napoleonic Wars
between France and England
during the Battle of the Nile
on August 1, 1798. The battle
was a significant victory for
the British, but both sides suffered heavy casualties. "Casabianca" tells the story of a
young doomed soldier and also
contains many elements of a
ballad.

The boy stood on the burning deck
    Whence all but he had fled;
The flame that lit the battle's wreck
    Shone round him o'er the dead.

5 Yet beautiful and bright he stood,
    As born to rule the storm;
A creature of heroic blood,
    A proud, though childlike form.

The flames roll'd on—he would not go
10   Without his father's word;
That father, faint in death below,
    His voice no longer heard.

He call'd aloud:—"Say, Father, say
    If yet my task is done?"
15 He knew not that the chieftain lay
    Unconscious of his son.

"Speak, Father!" once again he cried,
    "If I may yet be gone!"
And but the booming shots replied,
20   And fast the flames roll'd on.

---

1. **Casabianca.** Thirteen-year-old boy who remained at his post
on the *Orient* after it had been abandoned during the Battle of
the Nile, August 1, 1798

Painting of the Battle of the Nile, by Arnald George (1763–1841), showing the explosion of the French flagship *L'Orient*.

Upon his brow he felt their breath,
  And in his waving hair,
And look'd from that lone post of death
  In still, yet brave despair.

25 And shouted but once more aloud,
  "My Father! must I stay?"
While o'er him fast, through sail and shroud,
  The wreathing fires made way.

The Rising of the Skylark, c. 1839. Samuel Palmer.
National Museum and Gallery of Wales, Cardiff, Wales.
(See detail on page 731).

To a Skylark

by Percy Bysshe Shelley

Hail to thee, <u>blithe</u> spirit!
 Bird thou never wert,[1]
That from heaven, or near it,
 Pourest thy full heart
5 In <u>profuse</u> strains of <u>unpremeditated</u> art.

---

1. **wert.** Were *(archaic)*

> **blithe** (blīth) *adj.,* carefree and happy
> **pro • fuse** (prō fyüs´) *adj.,* plentiful; freely flowing
> **un • pre • med • i • ta • ted** (un prē med´ ə tā' təd) *adj.,* unplanned;
>   spontaneous

Hallstatter-See, c. 1800s. Ferdinand Georg Waldmüller.
Museum Karlsplatz, Vienna, Austria.

What objects are the fountains
   Of thy happy strain?
What fields, or waves, or mountains?
   What shapes of sky or plain?
75 What love of thine own kind? what ignorance of pain?

With thy clear keen joyance
   <u>Languor</u> cannot be—
Shadow of annoyance
   Never came near thee;
80 Thou lovest—but ne'er knew love's sad <u>satiety</u>.

lan • guor (laŋ´ gər) *n.,* weakness or listlessness
sa • ti • e • ty (sə tī´ ə tē) *n.,* state of being full or satisfied

Waking or asleep,
   Thou of death must deem[7]
Things more true and deep
   Than we mortals dream,
85 Or how could thy notes flow in such a crystal stream?

We look before and after,
   And pine for what is not;
Our sincerest laughter
   With some pain is <u>fraught</u>;
90 Our sweetest songs are those that tell of saddest thought.

Yet if we could scorn
   Hate, and pride, and fear;
If we were things born
   Not to shed a tear,
95 I know not how thy joy we ever should come near.

Better than all measures
   Of delightful sound,
Better than all treasures
   That in books are found,
100 Thy skill to poet were,[8] thou Scorner of the ground!

Teach me half the gladness
   That thy brain must know,
Such harmonious madness
   From my lips would flow,
105 The world should listen then, as I am listening now. ❖

---

7. **deem.** Think about or consider
8. **were.** Would be

---

fraught (frôt) *adj.,* accompanied by (used with the word *with*)

What lessons can the natural world teach us? How might life be different for humans if we learned these lessons? What troubles may arise from ignoring the lessons of nature?

Refer to Text ▶ ▶ ▶ ▶ ▶ **Reason with Text**

1a. When the speaker introduces the skylark in the first stanza, what is the bird doing?

1b. Interpret the meaning of "unpremeditated art" in line 5. How does this description differentiate the skylark from a poet?

Understand
Find meaning

2a. According to the speaker in lines 76–80, from what is the skylark's experience free?

2b. Explain the contradiction between this assertion and the idea the speaker expresses in lines 88–90.

Apply
Use information

3a. Recall what the speaker says in line 31 about the definition of the skylark.

3b. To what does the speaker compare the skylark? Identify the literary technique Shelley uses to create the comparisons.

Analyze
Take things apart

4a. Restate what the speaker says of the greatest human songs in comparison to the skylark's song in lines 61–70.

4b. Do you agree with the speaker's opinion about human songs versus the skylark's song? Why or why not? How effectively does he clarify his opinion?

Evaluate
Make judgments

5a. Paraphrase the final two stanzas of the poem.

5b. Does the speaker seem to believe that his song can have the same effect as the skylark's? Was his prophecy correct? Explain.

Create
Bring ideas together

Analyze Literature

Sensory Details and Hyperbole

Find examples of sensory details in lines 15–30. To what senses does the poet appeal? How do the sensory details enhance his description of the experience?

What examples of hyperbole can you find in "To a Skylark"? What was Shelley's goal in using such exaggeration? What effect does the use of hyperbole have on your experience of the poem?

Extend the Text

Writing Options

Creative Writing If the skylark could speak English, what might it have to say in its song? Write the lyrics to the skylark's song, using details from the poem to place the bird in a setting and to understand its actions. Share your lyrics with a partner, and discuss your different interpretations.

Persuasive Writing Is it important to know about a writer's life experiences to understand his or her writing? Write a brief persuasive essay either for or against the necessity of biographical knowledge in understanding an author's work. Share your essay with classmates.

Collaborative Learning

Compile an Anthology With a small group, collect at least ten poems that provide lessons in what humankind can learn from nature. A library or Internet search for nature poems may yield results. For each selection, write a paragraph that states the title, author, and publication date, along with a brief analysis of what the lesson is. Gather the selections together in an anthology.

Critical Literacy

Analyze Themes In small groups, discuss the themes that run through each of Shelley's poems included in this unit. Identify shared themes as well as those that are unique to each poem. Then, discuss how these themes reflect the major ideas of the Romantic Movement. In what ways do the poems explore themes outside of this realm?

 Go to **www.mirrorsandwindows.com** for more.

1. Review lines 10–14 in "Ozymandias." What is *most* ironic or contradictory about these lines?
   A. Ozymandias feels the need to explain who he is.
   B. The "King of Kings" uses the word *Mighty*.
   C. The word *Wreck* is capitalized.
   D. Ozymandias's works no longer exist; only nature remains.
   E. The desert sands are described as boundless and level.

2. Based on the details provided about the king in "Ozymandias," which of the following pairs of adjectives best describes him?
   A. cruel, deceitful
   B. friendly, old
   C. powerful, vain
   D. fair, kindhearted
   E. mocking, unhappy

3. Why does Ozymandias think that someone who looks at his works should despair?
   A. They are not well preserved and therefore are decaying.
   B. Ozymandias wants everyone else to be miserable.
   C. The viewer would like more time to look at them.
   D. They are so great and so numerous as to be intimidating.
   E. Ozymandias thinks they are beautiful enough to make viewers cry.

4. What is the rhyme scheme of "Ode to the West Wind"?
   A. *aba cdc efe ghg ii*
   B. *aba bcb cdc ded ee*
   C. *aba aba aba aba aa*
   D. *ababcdcdefefgg*
   E. *aaa bbb ccc ddd*

5. What is the main effect of the rhyme scheme of "Ode to the West Wind"?
   A. It unites the stanzas.
   B. It creates many slant rhymes.
   C. It sounds choppy when read aloud.
   D. It means that many lines do not rhyme.
   E. It makes the poem harder to understand.

6. In "Ode to the West Wind," what or who is the *thou* the poet is addressing?
   A. the reader
   B. the west wind
   C. a divine being
   D. the poet's beloved
   E. everything in nature

7. What is the mood of "To a Skylark"?
   A. joyful
   B. anticipatory
   C. mysterious
   D. melancholic
   E. sometimes joyful, sometimes a bit sad

8. Which line in "To a Skylark" seems to be a paradox, or contradiction?
   A. "With music sweet as love, which overflows her bower." (line 45)
   B. "That panted forth a flood of rapture so divine." (line 65)
   C. "Our sweetest songs are those that tell of saddest thought." (line 90)
   D. "I know not how thy joy we ever should come near." (line 95)
   E. "The world should listen then, as I am listening now." (line 105)

9. **Constructed Response:** Compare and contrast the subject matter and main ideas in "Ode to the West Wind" and "To a Skylark." Argue whether the two poems have more similarities or differences, using details from the works to support your point.

10. **Constructed Response:** Which of the three poems by Shelley do you like best? Why? Support your response with details from the poem.

Understand the Concept

Literal language presents the actual meanings of words—the meanings found in a dictionary. **Figurative language,** however, is meant to be understood imaginatively.

Consider the statement *That load is too heavy to carry.* In the literal sense, this statement means that the physical weight of something makes it impossible to pick up or move. In the figurative sense, however, the statement might refer to an overwhelming sense of sorrow or guilt.

One of the most common types of figurative language (sometimes called *figures of speech*) is the **metaphor,** in which one thing is spoken or written about as if it were another. This figure of speech invites the reader to make a comparison between the two things: the writer's actual subject, or the *tenor* of the metaphor, and another thing to which the subject is likened, the *vehicle* of the metaphor. In Shelley's "To a Skylark," the line "Or how could thy notes flow in such a crystal stream?" (line 85) contains a metaphor in which the skylark's song is compared to a stream. In this instance, the tenor is "thy notes," referring to the bird's song, and the vehicle is a "crystal stream."

A **simile** is a comparison using *like* or *as.* "From the earth thou springest / Like a cloud of fire" (lines 7–8) is an example of a simile describing how the skylark takes flight.

Personification is a figure of speech in which an idea, animal, or object is described as if it were a person. "The *moon* rains out *her* beams" (line 30) is an example of personification.

A **hyperbole** is an exaggeration made for rhetorical effect. In Shelley's poem, an example of hyperbole is "All the earth and air / With thy voice is loud" (lines 26–27). It is unrealistic to believe that the entire sky could be filled with the sound of one bird's song.

In contrast, an **understatement** is an ironic expression in which something of importance is spoken of as though it were not important. An example of understatement would be if after writing his poem "To a Skylark," Shelley described to a friend that he thought the skylark's song was a "nice melody."

Synesthesia is a figure of speech that combines in a single expression images related to two or more different senses, as in Shelley's line "As from thy presence showers a rain of melody" (line 35). Here, the senses of sound and sight are used to describe the bird's song.

Apply the Skill

Exercise A

Write a possible literal explanation and a figurative interpretation of each of the following items.

1. Suddenly, the sunlight shone through the clouds.
2. I tiptoed on the edge.
3. He was lost and he did not think anyone would try to find him.
4. He paced quietly in his cage.
5. It stretched for miles in front of me.

Exercise B

Try your hand at creating figurative language. Using each of the following suggested topics, create a figure of speech of the type noted in parentheses.

1. laughter (metaphor)
2. strength (hyperbole)
3. tree (personification)
4. smoke (simile)
5. hurricane (synesthesia)

SPELLING PRACTICE

Digraphs

A *digraph* is two or three consonants that together make a new sound, such as *sh* or *th*. A digraph differs from a *consonant blend*, which is a cluster of consonants in which each letter in the blend maintains its original sound, such *br* or *cl*. When spelling words with digraphs, be sure to remember each letter in the grouping. Identify the digraphs in these words from "Ozymandias," "Ode to the West Wind," and "To the Skylark."

antique	pestilence
approaching	prophecy
atmosphere	sepulcher
blithe	strength
chasms	thieves
crystalline	triumphal
languor	unextinguished
laughter	

John Keats

"A thing of beauty is a joy for ever"

John Keats (1795–1821), the son of a livery stableman, came from the least privileged background of all the major British poets. The eldest of five children, he was an energetic, boisterous child. One of his teachers encouraged him to write and read poetry, including the work of Edmund Spenser.

By the time Keats was fifteen, both of his parents had died. He was taken out of school and apprenticed to a surgeon and apothecary. He later qualified to study medicine but decided to pursue poetry instead. He worked with great urgency, in part because he always believed he would die young. At twenty-one, he published "On First Looking Into Chapman's Homer." Soon after, he began work on the epic poem *Hyperion*, modeled on John Milton's *Paradise Lost*.

Keats was concerned not to imitate other poets and steered away from friendship with Percy Shelley to avoid the latter's powerful poetic influence. Another Romantic poet, Lord Byron, had a strained relationship with Keats, as Byron did not value Keats's poetic style and took offense at Keats's disregard of Alexander Pope, one of Byron's literary idols.

In 1818, Keats became mortally ill with tuberculosis. Despite his illness, he was extremely creative and prolific during the year that followed. He published a series of masterpieces, including his great odes and sonnets. Critics have compared Keats's language to that of William Shakespeare because of its richness of detail and its celebration of existence.

Keats's respiratory illness intensified in 1820. A year later, he died in Rome at age twenty-five. Some people, including Shelley, attributed his sickness and death to the criticism he received in the literary press after publishing *Hyperion*. Upon Keats's death, Lord Byron renounced his own criticism of the young poet's work and suggested that Keats may have honed his craft and realized his genius if only he had lived longer.

After Keats's death, several of his contemporaries honored him in their writing. In the summer of 1821, Shelley published the poem "Adonais: An Elegy on the Death of John Keats." Lord Byron, in his masterpiece *Don Juan*, wrote, "John Keats, who was kill'd off by one critique, / Just as he really promised something great" (stanza 60 of Canto XI).

Noted Works

"On First Looking Into Chapman's Homer" (1816)

Endymion (1817)

The Fall of Hyperion (1819)

Odes (1819–1820)

The Eve of St. Agnes (1820)

Ode to a Nightingale
Ode on a Grecian Urn

Lyric Poems by John Keats

Build Background

Literary Context John Keats's odes are deemed by many literary scholars to be among the most beautiful short poems ever written. **"Ode to a Nightingale"** was reportedly written over the course of two or three hours while the poet sat under a plum tree in a friend's yard and observed a nightingale that had nested in the yard. Keats wrote this poem during a time of much upheaval in his life. His beloved brother had just died, and his relationship with his fiancée was troubled. Perhaps because of these circumstances, "Ode to a Nightingale" carefully explores the borders between life and death, consciousness and unconsciousness, and peace and anxiety. Each of the poem's eight stanzas is composed of a quatrain that rhymes *abab* and a sestet that rhymes *cdecde*.

Keats used this same verse structure, with some irregularities, in **"Ode on a Grecian Urn."** Upon first reading, "Ode on a Grecian Urn" is an exploration of the value and purpose of art. The skilled potters of ancient Greece made urns for various purposes, including storage of wine and a variety of foods. These urns often were decorated with figures. In Keats's poem, the speaker addresses a Grecian urn and the various figures that appear on it: a bride, men or gods, maidens, a pipe-playing youth, a lover, and a priest leading a cow to sacrifice. When read more closely, however, the poem reveals its desperate contemplation of life and death and the passage of time—themes that are central to many of Keats's finest works.

Mosaic of a Greek poet.

Reader's Context

What do you daydream about? Do you find that your daydreams take you to the past, the present, the future, or some other moment in time?

Analyze Literature

Apostrophe and Paradox
An **apostrophe** is a method by which a speaker turns from the audience as a whole to address a single person or thing.

A **paradox** is a seemingly contradictory statement, idea, or event that actually may be true. Some paradoxes, however, present irresolvable contradictory ideas.

Set Purpose

Keats strove to create an original poetic style and to avoid the stylistic influence of other poets, such as Shelley and Byron. In "Ode on a Grecian Urn" and "Ode to a Nightingale," Keats addressed two unusual subjects to explore themes of death and beauty. As you read each poem, note who or what Keats addresses directly. Consider why the speaker might be drawn to these subjects and what meaning they have for him. Also list the paradoxes you find in "Ode on a Grecian Urn." What effect do they have on your understanding of the poem?

Preview Vocabulary

verdurous, 743
requiem, 744
plaintive, 745
deity, 746
adieu, 747
citadel, 747

The Avenue of Chestnut Trees at La Celle-Saint-Cloud, 1867. Alfred Sisley. Southampton City Art Gallery, Hampshire, England. (See detail on page 741.)

Ode to a Nightingale

wrote this after death of his brother, knows he is next

by John Keats

died of tuberculosis tragically young, 26

wants to drink and fade into nature

He can't court his girlfriend since he knows he will die, has to give her up

— psychological journey

feeling near forgetfulness

the song is too happy for situation

yearns for forgetfulness

My heart aches, and a drowsy numbness pains
   My sense, as though of hemlock[1] I had drunk,
Or emptied some dull opiate[2] to the drains
   One minute past, and Lethe-wards[3] had sunk:
5 'Tis not through envy of thy happy lot,
   But being too happy in thine happiness—
     That thou, light-wingéd Dryad[4] of the trees,
      In some melodious plot
   Of beechen green, and shadows numberless,
10   Singest of summer in full-throated ease.

1. **hemlock.** Poisonous herb used to create a toxic drink
2. **opiate.** Drug made from the opium poppy
3. **Lethe-wards.** The River Lethe flows through Hades in Greek mythology. It is associated with forgetfulness because, as part of their journey through the after-life, people drank from the river Lethe to forget their lives on Earth.
4. **Dryad.** Tree spirits in Greek mythology

2

O, for a draught of vintage![5] that hath been
    Cool'd a long age in the deep-delvéd earth,
Tasting of Flora[6] and the country green,
    Dance, and Provençal song,[7] and sunburnt mirth!
15 O for a beaker full of the warm South,
    Full of the true, the blushful Hippocrene,[8]
      With beaded bubbles winking at the brim,
        And purple-stainéd mouth;
That I might drink, and leave the world unseen,
20   And with thee fade away into the forest dim:

3

Fade far away, dissolve, and quite forget
    What thou among the leaves hast never known,
The weariness, the fever, and the fret
    Here, where men sit and hear each other groan;
25 Where palsy[9] shakes a few, sad, last gray hairs,
    Where youth grows pale, and spectre-thin,[10] and dies;
      Where but to think is to be full of sorrow
        And leaden-eyed despairs,
Where Beauty cannot keep her lustrous eyes,
30   Or new Love pine at them beyond to-morrow.

4

Away! away! for I will fly to thee,
    Not charioted by Bacchus and his pards,[11]
But on the viewless wings of Poesy,[12]
    Though the dull brain perplexes and retards:
35 Already with thee! tender is the night,
    And haply the Queen-Moon is on her throne,
      Cluster'd around by all her starry Fays;[13]
        But here there is no light,
Save what from heaven is with the breezes blown
40   Through <u>verdurous</u> glooms and winding mossy ways.

[handwritten annotation:] rejecting alcohol and will forget through poetry

[handwritten annotation:] Conjuring the nighttime feeling

---

5. **draught of vintage.** Drink of wine
6. **Flora.** Goddess of flowers in Roman mythology
7. **Provençal song.** Refers to the French troubadours of medieval times
8. **Hippocrene.** Fountain revered by the Muses for its powers of creative inspiration in Greek mythology
9. **palsy.** Condition characterized by muscle weakness and shaking
10. **spectre-thin.** *Spectre* is another word for *ghost*
11. **Bacchus and his pards.** God of wine and celebration in Roman mythology. Bacchus was often depicted in a chariot driven by leopards, or "pards."
12. **Poesy.** Poetry
13. **Fays.** Fairies

> **ver • dur • ous** (ver´ jə rəs) *adj.,* green with thick plant growth

5

> I cannot see what flowers are at my feet,
>> Nor what soft incense hangs upon the boughs,
> But, in embalméd darkness, guess each sweet
>> Wherewith the seasonable month endows

45 The grass, the thicket, and the fruit-tree wild;
>> White hawthorn, and the pastoral eglantine;[14]
>>> Fast fading violets cover'd up in leaves;
>>> And mid-May's eldest child,
> The coming musk-rose, full of dewy wine,
>>> The murmurous haunt of flies on summer eves.

brings to total darkness

6

> Darkling[15] I listen; and, for many a time
>> I have been half in love with easeful Death,
> Call'd him soft names in many a muséd rhyme,
>> To take into the air my quiet breath;

55 Now more than ever seems it rich to die,
>> To cease upon the midnight with no pain,
>>> While thou art pouring forth thy soul abroad
>>> In such an ecstasy!
> Still wouldst thou sing, and I have ears in vain—
>>> To thy high <u>requiem</u> become a sod.[16]

wishes he could die this way, not in pain

→ painless, peaceful death

---

14. **White hawthorn . . . eglantine.** Keats is referring to types of bushes and their flowers.
15. **Darkling.** In the dark
16. **sod.** Section of turf. Keats is suggesting that he would become a part of the earth once he died and could no longer enjoy the nightingale's song.

> **re • qui • em** (reʹ kwē əm) *n.,* song for the dead

7

Thou wast not born for death, immortal Bird!
　No hungry generations tread thee down;
The voice I hear this passing night was heard
　In ancient days by emperor and clown. *← country person/peasant*

65 Perhaps the self-same song that found a path
　Through the sad heart of Ruth,[17] when, sick for home,
　　She stood in tears amid the alien corn;
　　The same that oft-times hath
　Charm'd magic casements,[18] opening on the foam
70 　Of perilous seas, in faery lands forlorn.

imaginative/magic from the song of nightingale

Symbolism of nightingale

8

Forlorn! the very word is like a bell
　To toil me back from thee to my sole self!
Adieu! the fancy cannot cheat so well
　As she is fam'd to do, deceiving elf.
75 Adieu! adieu! thy <u>plaintive</u> anthem fades
　Past the near meadows, over the still stream,
　　Up the hill-side; and now 'tis buried deep
　　In the next valley-glades:
　Was it a vision, or a waking dream?
80 　Fled is that music:—Do I wake or sleep? ❖

---

17. **Ruth.** Biblical figure known for her loyalty in the midst of hardship
18. **casements.** Window sashes

plain • tive (plān´ tiv) *adj.,* sorrowful; grieving

Keats's speaker asks, "Was it a vision, or a waking dream? . . . Do I wake or sleep?" Does it matter whether the nightingale's song was real or imagined?

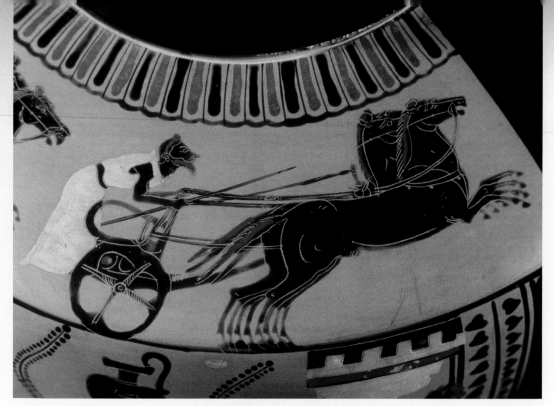

Ode on a
GRECIAN URN

by John Keats

1

Thou still unravish'd bride of quietness,
    Thou foster-child of silence and slow time,
Sylvan[1] historian, who canst thus express
    A flowery tale more sweetly than our rhyme:
5 What leaf-fring'd legend haunts about thy shape
    Of <u>deities</u> or mortals, or of both,
      In Tempe or the dales of Arcady?[2]
    What men or gods are these? What maidens loth?
What mad pursuit? What struggle to escape?
10   What pipes and timbrels?[3] What wild ecstasy?

---

1. **Sylvan.** Rustic
2. **Tempe . . . Arcady.** Tempe and Arcadia are both places in Greece that have become symbols for ideal rural beauty.
3. **timbrels.** Ancient tambourines

de • i • ty (dē´ ə tē) *n.*, god

2

Heard melodies are sweet, but those unheard
    Are sweeter; therefore, ye soft pipes, play on;
Not to the sensual ear,[4] but, more endear'd,
    Pipe to the spirit ditties of no tone:
15 Fair youth, beneath the trees, thou canst not leave
    Thy song, nor ever can those trees be bare;
      Bold lover, never, never canst thou kiss,
Though winning near the goal—yet, do not grieve;
      She cannot fade, though thou hast not thy bliss,
20   For ever wilt thou love, and she be fair!

3

Ah, happy, happy boughs! that cannot shed
    Your leaves, nor ever bid the Spring adieu;
And, happy melodist, unwearied,
    For ever piping songs for ever new;
25 More happy love! more happy, happy love!
    For ever warm and still to be enjoy'd,
      For ever panting, and for ever young;
All breathing human passion far above,
    That leaves a heart high-sorrowful and cloy'd,[5]
30   A burning forehead, and a parching tongue.

4

Who are these coming to the sacrifice?
    To what green altar, O mysterious priest,
Lead'st thou that heifer lowing at the skies,
    And all her silken flanks with garlands drest?
35 What little town by river or sea shore,
    Or mountain-built with peaceful citadel,
      Is emptied of this folk, this pious morn?
And, little town, thy streets for evermore
    Will silent be; and not a soul to tell
40   Why thou art desolate, can e'er return.

---

4. **sensual ear.** Ear that actually hears, not that of imagination
5. **cloy'd.** Have had too much; surfeited

> **adieu** (ə dyü´) *adj.*, goodbye in French
> **cit • a • del** (si´ tə del') *n.*, fortress; safe place

Mount Olympus, the highest mountain in Greece, is the home of the mythological Greek gods and goddesses.

5

O Attic[6] shape! Fair attitude! with brede[7]
　Of marble men and maidens overwrought,
With forest branches and the trodden weed;
　Thou, silent form, dost tease us out of thought
45 As doth eternity: Cold Pastoral!
　　When old age shall this generation waste,
　　　Thou shalt remain, in midst of other woe
　　Than ours, a friend to man, to whom thou say'st,
"Beauty is truth, truth beauty,"—that is all
50 　　Ye know on earth, and all ye need to know. ❖

---

6. **Attic.** Characteristic of Attica, the region of Greece where Athens is located
7. **brede.** Archaic word meaning an embroidered or braided edge

Keats writes, "Beauty is truth, truth beauty." When might beauty not be truth? How do you define *beauty*?

Draft Your Introduction

The introduction of a personal essay hooks readers. Consider beginning with a scene. For example, if you are writing about an interest in sports, you might start with a tense scene that shows your fanaticism. Make clear the trait this scene reveals and indicate that the whole essay will address that trait.

Draft Your Body

In the body, clarify how this trait is an important part of who you are. Use information that you already mapped out in the prewrite stage: events, encounters, conversations, details, and feelings. Develop each paragraph by writing a topic sentence and supporting it with details that reveal who you are. Each paragraph should relate clearly to your organizing statement.

Draft Your Conclusion

Finally, write the conclusion for your personal essay. Leave readers with a clear picture of who you are, ending perhaps with a comment about yourself.

❸ Revise

Evaluate Your Draft

Evaluate your draft or exchange drafts with a classmate and evaluate each other's work. See if the piece uses supporting details to present one personal aspect or trait. Determine what works well and what needs improvement.

Start by looking at the content and organization. Make sure the introduction, body, and conclusion function together to support the organizing statement. Every paragraph should relate clearly to it. Use the Revision Checklist to help you evaluate the essay. Make notes directly on the essay about what changes need to be made.

Now look at the language. Go back through the draft to make sure the guidelines in the Grammar & Style workshops in this unit have been correctly applied. Again, use the Revision Checklist to assess the writing. Consider how you can make the writing more engaging by using exact, fresh details.

Revise for Content, Organization, and Style

Review the notes you or your partner made in evaluating your draft. Then apply each comment in effectively revising your draft.

REVISION CHECKLIST

Content & Organization

❑ Does the introduction start with a scene, comment, or other detail that focuses on a primary personality trait?

❑ Does the body create a snapshot of you and your reflections, providing details to engage the reader?

❑ Does the conclusion leave your reader with a fuller sense of who you are?

Grammar & Style

❑ Have you employed parallel structure to give your sentences an even, balanced feel? (page 663)

❑ Have you used gerund, infinitive, participial, and prepositional phrases correctly, checking their placement and agreement? (page 669)

Proofread for Errors

In this stage, check for remaining errors. Use proofreader's symbols to mark any you find.

To complete the assignment, print out a final draft and read it aloud. Reading aloud will help you slow down and catch mistakes.

Writing Follow-Up

Publish and Present

● Although personal essays are just that—personal— they are meant to be shared. Give your essay to a relative or friend, perhaps someone for whom it will also have personal significance. Or give your essay to a new friend as a way to introduce yourself.

Reflect

● Compare your personal essay with one or more of the literature selections from this unit. Point out similarities among the themes, thoughts, or feelings.

Reading Skills

Evaluate an Argument

To evaluate the author's argument, ask yourself the following questions:

- Is the argument logically valid? If not, where is the problem? Compare the argument with what you know.
- Are all the premises on which the argument is based true? Are they commonly accepted generalizations? Are they actually true in all cases, or can you think of exceptions?
- Is the author credible? Does he or she seem knowledgeable about the subject and ethical or fair? Does the author make a connection to the audience? Does this connection seem good, or do you feel manipulated?
- How much evidence does the author provide to support his or her position?
- What type of evidence is provided: mostly facts or mostly opinions? Does the author rely heavily on personal experience?
- Are the argument and support details presented in a convincing way? What strategies does the author use? How effective are they? Is the order in which the writer presents the evidence coherent?
- Is there a balance between reason and emotion? Does the author appeal to your sense of right and wrong, common feelings of nostalgia or pity, or the desire to be popular?
- Does the argument stay focused and on track, or are you being presented with irrelevant or vague issues in an attempt by the author to cover up some weakness in the argument and support offered?

TEST-TAKING TIP

Learn to think like a test developer. Spend time practicing with sample items to familiarize yourself with types of questions and responses. Also determine which types of questions and responses seem most difficult for you, and focus on improving your ability to answer them.

Practice

Directions: Read the following passage. The questions that come after it will ask you to evaluate an argument.

NONFICTION: This excerpt is from the Preface to *Lyrical Ballads*, by William Wordsworth.

Having thus explained a few of my reasons for writing in verse, and why I have chosen subjects from common life, and endeavored to bring my language near to the real lan-
5   guage of men, if I have been too minute in pleading my own cause, I have at the same time been treating a subject of general interest; and for this reason a few words shall be added with reference solely to these particu-
10 lar poems and to some defects which will probably be found in them.

I am sensible that my associations must have sometimes been particular instead of general, and that, consequently, giving to
15 things a false importance, I may have sometimes written upon unworthy subjects; but I am less apprehensive on this account than that my language may frequently have suffered from those arbitrary connections of
20 feelings and ideas with particular words and phrases from which no man can altogether protect himself. Hence, I have no doubt, that in some instances, feelings, even of the ludicrous, may be given to my readers by
25 expressions which appeared to me tender and pathetic. Such faulty expressions, were

I convinced they were faulty at present and that they must necessarily continue to be so, I would willingly take all reasonable
30 pains to correct. But it is dangerous to make these alterations on the simple authority of a few individuals, or even of certain classes of men; for where the understanding of an author is not convinced, or his feelings
35 altered, this cannot be done without great

injury to himself; for his own feelings are his stay and support; and if he set them aside in one instance, he may be induced to repeat this act till his mind shall lose all confidence
40 in itself, and become utterly debilitated. To this it may be added that the critic ought never to forget that he is himself exposed to the same errors as the poet, and perhaps, in a much greater degree.

Multiple Choice

1. What is *not* an example of the writer acknowledging a criticism of his argument?
   A. "endeavored to bring my language" (lines 3–4)
   B. "if I have been too minute in pleading my own cause" (lines 5–6)
   C. "I am sensible that my associations" (line 12)
   D. "I may have sometimes written" (lines 15–16)

2. Based on the excerpt, what is the writer's thesis, or argument?
   A. Critics are subject to the same errors as poets.
   B. My poems admittedly have many faults in them.
   C. I have good reasons for writing the poems that I do.
   D. It is dangerous to make changes based on the opinions of only a few people.

3. Most of this excerpt is concerned with
   A. addressing other viewpoints.
   B. using subjects from everyday life.
   C. evoking emotion in the reader.

   D. issuing a warning to critics.

4. What technique for writing a conclusion does the writer use at the end of this excerpt?
   A. restating the thesis statement
   B. summarizing the main points in the essay
   C. providing specific details as evidence
   D. broadening the subject to refer to the reader

Constructed Response

5. Evaluate how effectively Wordsworth makes his argument in this excerpt. Support your evaluation with details from the text.

Writing Skills

Address Alternative Viewpoints

In the body of your essay, you often will want to acknowledge different viewpoints. Doing so demonstrates that you have thought about the subject and that your response is not uninformed or strictly emotional. The opening sentence or sentences of your introduction can briefly mention one or more alternative viewpoints. Then your thesis statement will dismiss them and state what you believe.

Another way to address other viewpoints is within each paragraph of the body of the essay. When giving each reason for holding a certain opinion, you can compare and contrast the supporting evidence for your opinion with other viewpoints. What do various viewpoints have in common? What fallacies (faulty arguments) have you seen in other points of view?

Try to think of what viewpoints the reader might have and what evidence he or she would offer as sup-

port. Then address each of these points. Otherwise, the reader will be thinking "But what about . . . ?"

Be careful not to spend all your time criticizing other viewpoints. Although you want to provide reasons you dismissed other perspectives and opinions, your focus should be on presenting and supporting your point of view. You may easily lose the reader's sympathy and support if you are too negative in your discussion of other alternative viewpoints.

TEST-TAKING TIP

Think of your reader. Anticipate questions and objections he or she may have. Don't talk down to the reader, but don't assume he or she knows everything you do.

Practice

Timed Writing: 30 minutes

Being a good student council president requires certain qualifications and personality traits. Imagine that someone you know has suggested you run for student council president. When you mention the idea to someone else, he or she says that you do not seem like a good candidate.

With which of these two positions do you agree: Would or would you not make a good student council president?

In your essay, take a position on this question. You may write about either one of the perspectives given, or you may present a different perspective on this question. Use specific reasons and examples to support your position.

Revising and Editing Skills

Some standardized tests ask you to read a draft of an essay and answer questions about how to improve it. As you read the draft, watch for errors such as these:

- incorrect spellings
- disagreement between subject and verb; inconsistent verb tense; incorrect forms for irregular verbs; sentence fragments and run-ons; double negatives; and incorrect use of frequently confused words, such as *affect* and *effect*
- missing end marks, incorrect comma use, and lowercased proper nouns and proper adjectives

- unclear purpose, unclear main ideas, and lack of supporting details
- confusing order of ideas and missing transitions
- language that is inappropriate to the audience and purpose, and mood that is inappropriate for the purpose

After checking for errors, read each test question and decide which answer is best.

Practice

Directions: In the passage that follows, certain words and phrases are numbered and underlined. In the questions below the passage, you will find alternatives for each underlined word or phrase. In each case, choose the alternative that best expresses the idea, that is worded most consistently with the style and tone of the rest of the passage, or that makes the text correct according to the conventions of standard written English. If you think the original version is best, choose the first alternative, MAKE NO CHANGE. To indicate your answer, choose the letter of the best alternative.

(1) The members of the <u>student council, but especially the president, has</u> an important role in a high school. (2) <u>He needs to be respected, outgoing, and an assertive person.</u> (3) <u>None of these characteristics are an accurate description of me.</u> (4) Many people have noted that I have very good <u>ideas, and am responsible but that</u> only goes so far.

Multiple Choice

1. A. MAKE NO CHANGE.
   B. student council, but especially the President, has
   C. student council, but especially the president, have
   D. student council, but especially the President, have

2. A. MAKE NO CHANGE.
   B. He needs to be respected, outgoing, and a assertive person.
   C. He needs to be respectable, outgoing, and assertive.
   D. The president needs to be respected, outgoing, and assertive.

3. A. MAKE NO CHANGE.
   B. None of these characteristics are an acurate description of me.
   C. None of these characteristics are an accurate description of myself.
   D. None of these characteristics is an acurate description of me.

4. A. MAKE NO CHANGE.
   B. ideas and am responsible, but that
   C. ideas, and that I am responsible but that
   D. ideas, and am responsible; but that

Country Party, 1885. Anselmo Guinea y Ugalde.
Private collection.

Victorian Era

Unit 7

1832–1901

Victorian Era 1832–1901

1832

1850

BRITISH LITERATURE

1835
Mary Shelley publishes *Lodore*

1837
Charles Dickens begins the serialization of *Oliver Twist*

1843
Charles Dickens publishes *A Christmas Carol*

1847
Charlotte Brontë publishes *Jane Eyre*

1847
Emily Brontë publishes *Wuthering Heights*

1848
Elizabeth Gaskell publishes *Mary Barton* anonymously

1850
Alfred Lord Tennyson publishes *In Memoriam*

1855
Anthony Trollope publishes *The Warden*

1857
Joseph Conrad is born

1859
Charles Dickens begins the serialization of *A Tale of Two Cities*

1859
Mary Anne Evans publishes her first novel, *Adam Bede*, under the pseudonym George Eliot

ELIOT

BRITISH HISTORY

1833
The Slavery Abolition Act bans slavery in the British Empire

1837
Victoria becomes Queen of the United Kingdom

QUEEN VICTORIA

1839
The first Opium War begins between the United Kingdom and China

1845
The Irish potato famine kills one million people over a span of three years

1849
A cholera epidemic breaks out across England, killing more than fourteen thousand people in London

1851
The first world's fair, called the Great Exhibition, is held in London's Hyde Park

1853
Scottish missionary David Livingstone begins a trek across Africa

1854
The Crimean War begins between the United Kingdom and Russia

1856
The United Kingdom enters into the second Opium War

1857
Indian troops revolt against the British East India Company in the Indian Mutiny

1859
Charles Darwin introduces his theory of natural selection

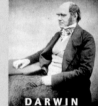

DARWIN

WORLD HISTORY

1846
The Mexican-American War begins over border disputes between Texas and Mexico

1846
Belgian musician Adolph Sax invents the saxophone

1847
Liberia declares independence from the American Colonization Society

1848
Karl Marx and Frederick Engels publish *The Communist Manifesto*

MARX

1851
The Taiping Rebellion begins in China and becomes one of the bloodiest conflicts of the century

1852
Napoleon III becomes the third emperor of France

NAPOLEON III

1859
The country of Romania is formed in eastern Europe

1859
The second Italian war for independence begins between the Italian kingdom of Sardinia and the Austrian Empire

BRITISH LITERATURE BRITISH LITERATURE BRITISH LITERATURE BRITISH LITERATU

1862
Christina Rossetti publishes *Goblin Market and Other Poems*

1864
Robert Browning publishes *The Ring and the Book*

1865
Lewis Carroll publishes *Alice in Wonderland*

1869
John Stuart Mill publishes *On the Subjection of Women*

1874
Thomas Hardy publishes *Far from the Madding Crowd*

1883
Robert Louis Stevenson publishes *Treasure Island*

1890
Oscar Wilde publishes *The Picture of Dorian Gray*

1894
Rudyard Kipling publishes *The Jungle Book*

1895
H. G. Wells publishes *The Time Machine*

1897
Bram Stoker publishes *Dracula*

BRITISH HISTORY BRITISH HISTORY BRITISH HISTORY BRITISH HISTORY BRITIS

1861
Queen Victoria's husband, Prince Albert, dies of typhoid fever

1864
Scottish physicist James Clerk Maxwell presents his equations proving the connection between electricity and magnetism

1865
The London Fire Department is established

1867
The British North America Act establishes Canada as a self-governing dominion

1875
The United Kingdom purchases Egypt's shares in the Suez Canal

1882
Egypt becomes a protectorate of the United Kingdom

1887
A massive riot, later dubbed "Bloody Sunday," breaks out in London's Trafalgar Square between police and socialist demonstrators

1888
A serial killer nicknamed "Jack the Ripper" begins to murder women in the streets of London

1891
Amendments to the Elementary Education Act, initially passed in 1870, provide free education for British children

WORLD HISTORY WORLD HISTORY WORLD HISTORY WORLD HISTORY WORLD HISTO

1861
The American Civil War begins

1863
The French begin their occupation of Mexico

1867
Diamonds are discovered in South Africa

1867
Swedish chemist Alfred Nobel invents dynamite

1868
Emperor Meiji of Japan restores himself to full power, ushering in a dramatic wave of Westernization

1877
The last of the Samurai class rebel against Westernization in Japan during the Satsuma Rebellion

1880
The First Boer War begins between Britain and the Dutch inhabitants (Boers) of South Africa

1883
The volcanic island Krakatoa erupts, killing thirty-six thousand people

1893
New Zealand becomes the first country to grant women the right to vote

1899
Chinese peasants attempt to drive out all foreigners in the Boxer Rebellion

"We are not interested in the possibilities of defeat. They do not exist."

—QUEEN VICTORIA

Impacts of Industrialization

The Industrial Revolution that had begun in the mid-eighteenth century continued through the nineteenth century. During this time, the population of Great Britain increased rapidly. This population increase helped supply labor for the nation's growing industries, while innovations in farm machinery increased the production of food, helping feed the growing population. Although the shift to industrialization forced difficult changes on people, it also allowed many to rise to the middle class.

As the middle class grew, it gained a greater voice to demand political, social, and economic rights. Under the Whig, or Liberal, leadership of Prime Minister Earl Grey, Parliament made some significant strides during the reign of William IV (1830–1837). The greatest change was the Reform Act of 1832, which allowed more men to vote and distributed seats in Parliament more evenly among the population. By this time, Britain's political leadership lay not with the monarchy but with the prime minister and the elected members of the two bodies of Parliament.

Reform continued under Lord Melbourne, another Liberal prime minister who mentored Queen Victoria when she ascended the throne in 1837 at age eighteen. In 1840, Victoria married a German prince, Albert. Queen Victoria would reign for sixty-four years, longer than any monarch in British history, in a period now referred to as the Victorian Era.

The early years of Victoria's reign were turbulent, with fears that riots might erupt in the poorest, most crowded industrial cities of the North. When economic depression, high unemployment, and crop failures occurred in the 1840s, the working class was especially hard hit. During this time, the Anti-Corn Law League worked to repeal the Corn Laws, legislation that restricted imports and exports of grain and kept the price of wheat so high that poor people could not afford bread. The poor learned to survive on potatoes instead. When a potato blight swept across Ireland from 1845 to 1849, an estimated one million Irish people died and two million more emigrated to the United States.

The Irish famine helped convince Prime Minister Robert Peel, leader of the Conservative (Tory) party, that the only way to divert disaster when crops failed was to import cheap grain. Parliament repealed the Corn Laws in 1846, which helped pacify the working class. The end of the Corn Laws also resulted in opening up trade, thus ushering in a period of prosperity. Landowners found that with free trade, agriculture thrived along with trade and industry.

"No minister ever stood, or could stand, against public opinion."

—ROBERT PEEL

Victims of Ireland's potato famine beg for work (c. 1846–1847).

The Late Nineteenth Century

Two statesmen dominated British politics in the late nineteenth century: Benjamin Disraeli, an author and progressive leader of the Conservative party, and William Gladstone, a gifted orator and leader of the Liberal party. When Disraeli became prime minister briefly in 1868, he secured enough support to pass the second Reform Act. This major step toward democracy extended the vote to working-class men who lived in towns and cities, giving them a majority in many areas. During a later second ministry (1874–1880), Disraeli passed reforms in housing, public health, and factories. In foreign policy, he supported traditional Conservative goals, extending imperialism and expanding the British Empire.

Disraeli's rival, Gladstone, served as prime minister four times between 1868 and 1894. He expanded elementary education, legalized trade unions, and required civil service workers to be hired based on ability rather than patronage. In addition, Gladstone instituted the secret ballot to prevent employers and landlords from pressuring working-class men to vote for certain measures, and he limited the amount of money candidates could spend on campaigns.

Gladstone also supported Irish Catholics, bringing them some economic gains, but he was unsuccessful in achieving Irish home rule, a movement led by

Charles Stewart Parnell to give the Irish greater control of their local government. With the Reform Act of 1884, Gladstone extended the vote to men who worked on farms. As the working class gained more political power, members argued that they needed their own political party. In 1893, they formed the Independent Labour party.

Growth of the British Empire

As the first country to experience the Industrial Revolution, Great Britain was in a superior position to increase trade as it increased the production of manufactured goods. For centuries, Britain had been building a large navy and merchant fleet for the purposes of trade and colonization. From overseas, it imported raw materials, such as cotton from the Americas and silk from China, and it exported finished goods made at home. Britain's merchant fleet—the largest in the world—traveled the globe. When other countries threatened to encroach on land or trade routes that served imperialist British interests, the navy exerted its military power.

By the end of the 1800s, the British Empire held territories on every continent. Great Britain was the world's wealthiest nation, and London served as the world's banker. The empire invested its profits in development projects in far-flung places. In 1875, Britain became the largest shareholder in one of these projects, the Suez Canal in Egypt, which had opened in 1869. Connecting the Mediterranean Sea and the Red Sea, the Suez Canal allowed two-way water transportation between Europe and Asia without circumnavigating Africa, shortening the trip from Great Britain to India by four thousand miles.

Yet while prosperous Victorians basked in the wealth of the British Empire, threats to Britain's status arose in the final decades of the Victorian Era. Germany asserted itself as a military and imperial power in 1871 by defeating France in the Franco-Prussian War. By the end of the 1800s, both Germany and the United States had surpassed Britain's level of industrial production.

NOTABLE NUMBERS

- **1 million** Irish people who starved to death during the potato famine of 1845–1849
- **42,000** Prisoners who died in British concentration camps following the Anglo-Boer War in South Africa
- **1,400** Tons of opium sold by the British to China in 1839
- **11** Minimum age at which a child could work, as decreed by the Factory Act of 1891
- **10** Hours an employee could work each day, as decreed by the Factory Act of 1844

Victorian Thought

Significant scientific discoveries during the Victorian Era added to the social upheaval of the Industrial Revolution. Astronomers already had proven that space extended much farther than anyone had fathomed. Charles Lyell showed that geological features on Earth had developed continuously and slowly over long periods of time. This influenced Charles Darwin's theory of evolution, which held that Earth's many species of animals and plants had evolved from common ancestors; through the process of natural selection, the most fit species had survived. These findings threatened Europeans' understanding of the order of the universe, and they struggled to reconcile the tension between science and religion.

Despite the questioning spurred by discovery and change, the Victorian Era often is portrayed as stuffy and moralistic. Much of this character can be attrib-

Charles Darwin.

uted to the evangelical movement, which emphasized a Protestant faith in personal salvation through God and living according to a strict moral code. The movement led to an enormous outpouring of philanthropic and charitable work and the foundation of both the Salvation Army and the Young Men's Christian Association (YMCA). In addition, the Oxford movement, or Tractarians, led by John Henry Newman, attempted to revive the earlier traditions and power of the Anglican Church of England.

For many Victorians, so-called separate spheres dictated the events of daily life: the private sphere of the home and family and the public sphere of business and politics. Women were to make the home a peaceful and moral refuge, whereas men wrestled with the competitive, amoral public sphere and protected women from it. This notion was, in fact, unattainable for many working-class individuals, who struggled in both spheres to make ends meet, but the concept had a profound impact on social relations in the Victorian Era.

Biologist and philosopher Herbert Spencer also influenced social relations. He applied Darwin's theory of natural selection to social ethics, arguing that the strongest and fittest people should survive and thrive in society, while the weak and unfit should be left to die. Many Victorians used Spencer's social Darwinism to justify inequalities based on race or ethnicity, social or economic class, and gender. Social Darwinists also favored a laissez-faire policy of little or no government intervention.

In contrast, philosopher and economist John Stuart Mill popularized the Utilitarianism of Jeremy Bentham, who argued that the object of moral action was to bring about the greatest good for the greatest number of people. Mill also championed Liberalism, a political and social philosophy that limits the power of government and upholds individual rights. More radical thinkers, the Socialists, believed in far-reaching government control and in replacing private property with publicly or communally owned lands and businesses. These debates about the proper role of government in public affairs continue into our own time.

Literary expression during the Victorian Era reflected, in large part, the difficult conditions in many British cities during this time. Victorian writers such as poets Robert Browning and Elizabeth Barrett Browning and novelist Charles Dickens embraced **Realism,** portraying authentic, detailed descriptions of everyday life, especially its darker aspects. This approach appealed to many readers who were disillusioned by the social, cultural, and political developments of the time. In *Great Expectations* and other novels, Dickens used Realism to satirize social issues.

A similar literary movement that developed during the Victorian Era was **Naturalism,** which is based on the theory that actions and events result inevitably from biological and natural forces, many of which are beyond human comprehension and control. Like the Realists, the Naturalists wrote about subjects and themes common to the lower and middle classes and strived for accuracy and authenticity. Although Naturalism was more popular in the United States and France than in Great Britain, elements of it appear in British literature. Characters who are hapless victims of fate appear in *The Mayor of Casterbridge* and other novels by Thomas Hardy and in Rudyard Kipling's short story "The Mark of the Beast."

Elements of **Romanticism** also continued to appear in Victorian literature. For example, the dark, foreboding, and mysterious influence of Gothic novels such as Mary Shelley's *Frankenstein* (Unit 6) is present in Charlotte Brontë's *Jane Eyre*, Dickens's *Great Expectations*, Kipling's "The Mark of the Beast," and other works of the Victorian Era.

Windsor—The Parade, c. 1880. Louise Rayner.
Private collection.

My Last Duchess
Porphyria's Lover

Dramatic Poems by Robert Browning

Build Background

Literary Context Originally titled "I. Italy," **"My Last Duchess"** first appeared as one of sixteen poems in *Dramatic Lyrics*, one of Robert Browning's *Bells and Pomegranates* pamphlets, published between 1841 and 1846. The speaker of the poem is Alfonso II, Duke of Ferrara, Italy. His wife, Lucrezia, has died. In the poem, he is addressing an agent who is negotiating his next marriage. The characters in the poem were real people from the late 1500s. In this sense, the poem is based on historical fact; however, what takes place in the poem is Browning's interpretation of events. "My Last Duchess" shows Browning's gift for allowing characters to speak in their own voices, inadvertently exposing their innermost conflicts and desires.

"Porphyria's Lover," published in 1836, taps into the popularity of stories about illicit relationships, violence, and insanity that fascinated Victorian readers, in part because their culture condemned what was presumed immoral behavior. Browning explored evil in many of his works and thus became known as a psychological poet, distinguishing him from other nineteenth-century writers.

Reader's Context What would you do if you suspected someone of having committed a horrible crime? Why?

Meet the Author

Robert Browning (1812–1889) was tutored at home and became one of the most learned men in Europe. While still quite young, he published two volumes of poetry, but neither met with success. He also failed in his first attempt at writing for the stage. His play *Strafford,* produced in 1837, closed after running only five nights. In subsequent years, Browning gained some reputation as a writer of verse in which characters speak in their own voices, without narrative commentary.

In 1846, Robert married Elizabeth Barrett, a poet six years older than he who had a far greater literary reputation. Elizabeth and Robert moved to Italy, in part because of Elizabeth's poor health but also to escape her domineering father. The Brownings had an exceedingly happy marriage and lived in Italy for thirteen years until Elizabeth's death in 1861. Robert then returned to England to teach and write.

In his own day, many people considered Browning's verse unpoetic and obscure. In the twentieth century, however, Browning's reputation grew enormously. His poetry is modern in its use of realistic speech and portrayal of the psychological states of characters.

Analyze Literature

Dramatic Monologue and Mood
A **dramatic monologue** is a dramatic poem written in the form of a speech of a single character to an imaginary audience.

Mood, or atmosphere, is the emotion created in the reader by part or all of a literary work.

Set Purpose

Robert Browning's dramatic monologues offer readers subtle insights into the psychological states of their speakers. To be effective, a dramatic monologue, like a play, requires both a speaker and an audience. In reading both "My Last Duchess" and "Porphyria's Lover," determine who is the speaker and who is the audience. What information is revealed over the course of the monologue? Pay attention, as well, to the emotions you feel as you read. Consider how Browning creates these moods.

Preview Vocabulary

countenance, 782
earnest, 782
officious, 782
munificence, 783
sullen, 784
vex, 784
wary, 785

Indecision, c. 1884. Charles Sillem Lidderdale.
Private collection. (See detail on page 780.)

My Last Duchess

by Robert Browning

That's my last Duchess painted on the wall,
Looking as if she were alive. I call
That piece a wonder, now: Frà Pandolf's[1] hands
Worked busily a day, and there she stands.
5 Will 't please you sit and look at her? I said
"Frà Pandolf" by design, for never read

---

1. **Frà Pandolf.** Imaginary painter. *Frà* is short for *Fratello,* Italian for *brother.*
   The painter was a monk.

Strangers like you that pictured <u>countenance</u>,
The depth and passion of its <u>earnest</u> glance,
But to myself they turned (since none puts by
10 The curtain I have drawn for you, but I)
And seemed as they would ask me, if they durst,
How such a glance came there; so, not the first
Are you to turn and ask thus. Sir, 'twas not
Her husband's presence only, called that spot
15 Of joy into the Duchess' cheek: perhaps
Frà Pandolf chanced to say "Her mantle laps
Over my lady's wrist too much," or "Paint
Must never hope to reproduce the faint
Half-flush that dies along her throat": such stuff
20 Was courtesy, she thought, and cause enough
For calling up that spot of joy. She had
A heart—how shall I say?—too soon made glad,
Too easily impressed; she liked whate'er
She looked on, and her looks went everywhere.
25 Sir, 'twas all one! My favor at her breast,
The dropping of the daylight in the West,
The bough of cherries some <u>officious</u> fool
Broke in the orchard for her, the white mule
She rode with round the terrace—all and each
30 Would draw from her alike the approving speech,
Or blush, at least. She thanked men—good! but thanked
Somehow—I know not how—as if she ranked
My gift of a nine-hundred-years-old name
With anybody's gift. Who'd stoop to blame
35 This sort of trifling? Even had you skill
In speech—(which I have not)—to make your will
Quite clear to such an one, and say, "Just this
Or that in you disgusts me; here you miss,
Or there exceed the mark"—and if she let
40 Herself be lessoned so, nor plainly set
Her wits to yours, forsooth, and made excuse
—E'en then would be some stooping; and I choose
Never to stoop. Oh sir, she smiled, no doubt,
Whene'er I passed her; but who passed without
45 Much the same smile? This grew; I gave commands;
Then all smiles stopped together. There she stands
As if alive. Will 't please you rise? We'll meet

coun • te • nance (kaun´ t'n ən[t]s) *n.,* look on a person's face
ear • nest (ər´ nəst) *adj.,* full of intense, serious feeling
of • fi • cious (ə fi´ shəs) *adj.,* meddlesome

The company below, then. I repeat,
The Count your master's known <u>munificence</u>
50 Is ample warrant that no just pretense
Of mine for dowry will be disallowed;
Though his fair daughter's self, as I avowed
At starting, is my object. Nay, we'll go
Together down, sir. Notice Neptune, though,
55 Taming a sea horse, thought a rarity,
Which Claus of Innsbruck[2] cast in bronze for me! ❖

---

2. **Claus of Innsbruck.** Imaginary sculptor

mu • nif • i • cence (myŭ niˊ fə sən[t]s) *n.*, generosity

MIRRORS & WINDOWS

Think of a time you revealed to someone more about yourself than you had intended, perhaps in a moment of joy or anger. How did you feel? What were the consequences, if any?

Porphyria's Lover

by Robert Browning

Young Woman Asleep in a Chair, c. 1880.
Marie Louise Catherine Breslau. Private collection.

The rain set early in tonight,
    The <u>sullen</u> wind was soon awake,
It tore the elm tops down for spite,
    And did its worst to <u>vex</u> the lake:
5   I listened with heart fit to break.
When glided in Porphyria; straight
    She shut the cold out and the storm,
And kneeled and made the cheerless grate
    Blaze up, and all the cottage warm;
10   Which done, she rose, and from her form
Withdrew the dripping cloak and shawl,
    And laid her soiled gloves by, untied
Her hat and let the damp hair fall,
    And, last, she sat down by my side
15   And called me. When no voice replied,
She put my arm about her waist,
    And made her smooth white shoulder bare,
And all her yellow hair displaced,
    And, stooping, made my cheek lie there,
20   And spread, o'er all, her yellow hair,
Murmuring how she loved me—she
    Too weak, for all her heart's endeavor,
To set its struggling passion free
    From pride, and vainer ties dissever,[1]
25   And give herself to me forever.

---

1. **dissever.** Separate

sul • len (suʹ lən) *adj.*, gloomily or resentfully silent or repressed
vex (veks) *v.*, agitate; bring trouble or distress

But passion sometimes would prevail,
    Nor could tonight's gay feast restrain
A sudden thought of one so pale
    For love of her, and all in vain:
30   So, she was come through wind and rain.
Be sure I looked up at her eyes
    Happy and proud; at last I knew
Porphyria worshipped me: Surprise
    Made my heart swell, and still it grew
35   While I debated what to do.
That moment she was mine, mine, fair,
    Perfectly pure and good: I found
A thing to do, and all her hair
    In one long yellow string I wound
40   Three times her little throat around,
And strangled her. No pain felt she;
    I am quite sure she felt no pain.
As a shut bud that holds a bee,
    I <u>warily</u> oped[2] her lids: again
45   Laughed the blue eyes without a stain.
And I untightened next the tress
    About her neck; her cheek once more
Blushed bright beneath my burning kiss:
    I propped her head up as before,
50   Only, this time my shoulder bore
Her head, which droops upon it still:
    The smiling rosy little head,
So glad it has its utmost will,
    That all it scorned at once is fled,
55   And I, its love, am gained instead!
Porphyria's love: She guessed not how
    Her darling one wish would be heard.
And thus we sit together now,
    And all night long we have not stirred,
60   And yet God has not said a word! ❖

---

2. **oped.** Archaic form of *opened*

wary (wer´ ē) *adj.,* cautious; careful

MIRRORS & WINDOWS

The speaker's desire to possess his love leads him to a drastic decision. When have you felt jealous about someone or something? How did your feelings influence your actions?

Refer to Text ▶ ▶ ▶ ▶ ▶   Reason with Text

1a. In "My Last Duchess," identify the causes the Duke attributes to the Duchess's smile in the painting.	**1b.** Why does the Duke dislike the Duchess's smile? What does this suggest about the Duke's personality?	**Understand** Find meaning
2a. In "Porphyria's Lover," what does Porphyria do when she first arrives at the cottage?	**2b.** How do her actions inside the cottage contrast with the weather outside? How is the speaker's psychological state similar to the weather?	**Apply** Use information
3a. In lines 22–30 of "My Last Duchess," what about the Duchess bothers the Duke? In lines 30–35 of "Porphyria's Lover," what does the speaker discover? What does this lead him to do?	**3b.** Compare the speakers of the poems. What similarities do they share?	**Analyze** Take things apart
4a. Describe what happens at the end of "Porphyria's Lover."	**4b.** Evaluate the explanation the speaker gives for his actions. According to the speaker, why are his actions logical?	**Evaluate** Make judgments
5a. What about the Duchess's portrait makes people ask questions about it?	**5b.** If the portrait could talk, what would the Duchess say about the Duke?	**Create** Bring ideas together

Analyze Literature

Dramatic Monologue and Mood

Identify the speaker and audience in each poem. Choose either "My Last Duchess" or "Porphyria's Lover," and explain the situation that prompts the dramatic monologue. What information does the speaker reveal about himself?

How does Browning's use of dramatic monologue establish the mood you experience as a reader? Use details from each poem to support your explanation.

Extend the Text

Writing Options

Creative Writing Imagine that you are either the Duke's visitor or Porphyria. Write a dramatic monologue in response to the speaker of the poem. Evaluate the dramatic structure used in Browning's nineteenth-century monologue, and either match it or adopt the structure of a monologue from an earlier or a later period.

Expository Writing Write a one-paragraph character analysis of either the Duke or Porphyria's lover. Include examples from the monologue that illustrate the personality of the speaker about whom you are writing.

Critical Literacy

Write a Public Service Announcement Write a public service announcement (PSA) about domestic abuse or dating violence. Research the subject to get statistics and other facts. Narrow the topic to a specific message you wish to convey. After crafting your message, record your PSA for a radio spot or videotape it for television.

Collaborative Learning

Perform a Dramatic Skit Collaborate with one or two other students to write a five-minute dramatic skit presenting a confrontation between the Duke in "My Last Duchess" and his former wife or the speaker in "Porphyria's Lover" and Porphyria. In your skit, portray the characters (all still alive) as they are portrayed in the poem. Write parts for each student in your group. Rehearse your skit and present it to the rest of the class.

 Go to **www.mirrorsandwindows.com** for more.

1. In "My Last Duchess," who is the duchess to whom the speaker refers?
   A. his late wife
   B. his stepmother
   C. a former girlfriend
   D. the last royal person he knew
   E. the subject in one of his paintings

2. In lines 17–19 of "My Last Duchess," which two words are used in the most unusual way?
   A. *paint* and *hope*
   B. *must* and *half-flush*
   C. *reproduce* and *faint*
   D. *hope* and *dies*
   E. *reproduce* and *along*

3. In "My Last Duchess," which of the following, if any, does the speaker feel the duchess should have liked the most?
   A. "The dropping of the daylight in the West"
   B. "The bough of cherries some officious fool / Broke in the orchard for her"
   C. "The white mule / She rode with round the terrace"
   D. "My gift of a nine-hundred-years-old name"
   E. None of these; he likes that the duchess is impartial, regarding everything the same.

4. What is the narrator's tone during most of "My Last Duchess"?
   A. familiar
   B. critical
   C. indifferent
   D. approving
   E. lighthearted

5. In "My Last Duchess," what is the order of the nature of the speaker's subject matter?
   A. personal, impersonal
   B. fairly impersonal, somewhat personal
   C. very impersonal, extremely personal
   D. fairly personal, personal, extremely personal
   E. fairly impersonal, increasingly personal, impersonal

6. Which of the following is an example of the use of personification in "Porphyria's Lover"?
   A. "The sullen wind was soon awake"
   B. "I listened with heart fit to break"
   C. "She shut the cold out and the storm"
   D. "That moment she was mine, mine, fair"
   E. "Three times her little throat around"

7. Review lines 36–42 of "Porphyria's Lover." What is most distinctive about line 41, which can be considered the climax of the poem?
   A. It is the only line that does not rhyme.
   B. It is short, containing fewer total syllables than the other lines.
   C. It is the only line with a sentence break in the middle.
   D. Its words are all single syllables, with one exception.
   E. It is the only line in which words are reversed from their usual order.

8. Based on the earlier mention of eyes and other details in "Porphyria's Lover," what likely is meant by the word *stain* in line 45?
   A. pain
   B. pride
   C. happiness
   D. any emotion
   E. unrequited love

9. **Constructed Response:** Describe the narrator in "My Last Duchess," identifying at least three qualities or traits. Does your impression of the narrator change throughout the poem? If so, how does it change and why? Support your description and analysis using details from the poem.

10. **Constructed Response:** Discuss whether the climax of "Porphyria's Lover" (see question 7) comes as a total surprise or whether there are hints that something like that is going to happen. In responding, discuss such elements as word choice, mood, and tone in addition to what is said directly.

"How do I love thee?" (Sonnet 43)

A Sonnet by Elizabeth Barrett Browning

Build Background

Literary Context **"How do I love thee?" (Sonnet 43)** comes from Elizabeth Barrett Browning's book *Sonnets from the Portuguese* (1850), which is a sequence of forty-five sonnets she wrote to chronicle the stages of her love for her husband, Robert. "The Portuguese" was one of Robert's pet names for Elizabeth.

Because of the deeply personal nature of the poems, Browning initially did not intend for them to be published and read by the general public. She later decided to publish the collection as *Sonnets from the Portuguese*, believing this title would imply the poems were translations of Portuguese poems, not her original work.

Until Browning's time, the best-known sonnet sequences all had been written by men, and it was unusual to use the sonnet form to tell a love story from the point of view of a woman. Sonnet 43 is by far the most famous of any of the poems in Browning's sequence.

Reader's Context What are some of the different types of love? Whom do you love in different ways?

Meet the Author

In her own era, **Elizabeth Barrett Browning** (1806–1861) was one of Britain's best-known female poets. She is most often associated with the love poetry she wrote for her husband, Robert Browning. However, at the time she wrote it, she already was respected as a scholarly poet, and her large body of work raised many moral and political issues.

During her early years, Browning received a thorough education in Latin and Greek, philosophy, and literature. As a child, she began to write poetry, and at age fourteen, she composed an epic poem that her father had printed privately. Elizabeth's father, although supportive of his daughter's obvious talent, was overprotective and kept careful watch over her. This was especially true when Elizabeth's health began to fail, and she later was confined to her home.

Browning was an invalid, living in the family home in London, when her literary career began to thrive. In 1844, at age thirty-nine, she received her first letter from Robert Browning, an unknown poet who admired her work. She wrote back, and the two began one of the most famous romances in literary history, marrying in 1846. Although Elizabeth and Robert were supportive of one another in their individual literary careers, at the time of Elizabeth's death in 1861, her work was much more popular than his.

Analyze Literature

Catalog and Repetition
A **catalog** is a list of people or things.

Repetition is the writer's intentional reuse of a sound, word, phrase, or sentence. Writers often use repetition to emphasize ideas or, especially in poetry, to create a musical effect.

Set Purpose

Although published fairly late in Browning's literary career, the poems in *Sonnets from the Portuguese* are among some of her best-known works. The line "How do I love thee? Let me count the ways" is one of the most recognized lines of love poetry, but most people do not remember what those ways are. As you read, list the reasons offered by the speaker. Determine the cumulative effect of the catalog that identifies the ways the loved one is loved. In addition, notice how the repeated phrase in Sonnet 43 emphasizes the main idea and creates a musical effect. What other examples of repetition can you find in the poem?

"How do I love thee?"
(SONNET 43)

The Market Stall, 1870. Petrus van Schendel.
Private collection. (See detail on page 788.)

by Elizabeth Barrett Browning

How do I love thee? Let me count the ways.
I love thee to the depth and breadth and height
My soul can reach, when feeling out of sight
For the ends of Being and ideal Grace.
5 I love thee to the level of everyday's

Most quiet need, by sun and candle-light.
I love thee freely, as men strive for Right;
I love thee purely, as they turn from Praise.
I love thee with the passion put to use
10   In my old griefs,[1] and with my childhood's faith.
I love thee with a love I seemed to lose
With my lost saints,—I love thee with the breath,
Smiles, tears, of all my life!—and, if God choose,
I shall but love thee better after death. ❖

---

1. **passion . . . old griefs.** Natural reserve of passion that had been directed to grief but that now is directed to love

How are the feelings Browning describes about love similar to or different from your own feelings?

LITERARY CONNECTION

Writing About Social Injustice

BROWNING

Although Elizabeth Barrett Browning is most famous for her Sonnet 43, a love poem, most of her poetry was intended as a vehicle for social activism. For instance, Browning harshly rebuked British mining and milling companies for their child labor practices with her poem "The Cry of the Children" (1841). Similarly, she argued for the abolition of slavery in "The Runaway Slave at Pilgrim's Point" (1847), despite her father's involvement with sugar plantations and the Atlantic slave trade. Browning also took a keen interest in women's rights, publishing an epic poem entitled *Aurora Leigh* (1857) that challenged traditional assumptions about the female character.

After settling in Florence, Italy, in 1846, Browning wrote extensively about the Italian struggle for independence from Austria. "Casa Guidi Windows" (1851), often considered her most significant work, poeticized this fight for liberty. In "Poems Before Congress" (1860), written just a year before her death, Browning criticized the British government's lack of involvement in Italy's struggle for independence.

Refer to Text ▶ ▶ ▶ ▶ ▶ Reason with Text

1a. In line 6, how does the speaker refer to night and day?	**1b.** Explain what the speaker means by saying that she loves "to the level of everyday's / Most quiet need."	**Understand** Find meaning
2a. Identify the answers the speaker gives to her initial question "How do I love thee?"	**2b.** What do these things have in common?	**Apply** Use information
3a. Cite what the speaker says about death in the last line of the poem.	**3b.** What can you infer about the speaker's love from the last three lines of the poem?	**Analyze** Take things apart
4a. Locate two specific lines that are effective in conveying the depth of the speaker's love.	**4b.** How does the poet's use of language or imagery support her statements?	**Evaluate** Make judgments
5a. List the references the speaker makes to religion.	**5b.** Explain why the speaker makes these references. What is the speaker's attitude toward religion? What is her attitude toward love?	**Create** Bring ideas together

Analyze Literature

Catalog and Repetition
Refer to your list of reasons given by the speaker. How does Browning use the catalog technique in her poem? How does her use of this technique affect your reading and understanding of the poem?

Identify examples of repetition. How does the use of repetition emphasize the poem's theme?

Extend the Text

Writing Options
Creative Writing Imagine someone has just written a poem for you. Write a journal entry describing what the poem says and how you react to it.

Expository Writing Write an essay in which you compare and contrast Elizabeth Barrett Browning's Sonnet 43 with one of the sonnets in Unit 3; those sonnets were published about 250 years earlier. Discuss how the language and tone of the poems differ.

Collaborative Learning
Create a Media Collage How have expressions of love changed since Browning professed her love for her husband? With a partner, look for words and pictures that relay images of love to use in a media collage addressing that question. To understand how society viewed love in Browning's time, refer to "How Do I Love Thee?" as well as these nineteenth-century texts: Lord Byron's "She Walks in Beauty" (page 719) and John Keats's "Ode to a Gre-

cian Urn" (page 746). As you plan your collage, respond to these questions: How have the expressions of love in song lyrics and in television and movie scripts changed from those in the traditional texts of the nineteenth century? How do the images of love in these media reflect the social and cultural views of their time? What general observations can you make about the portrayals of love now and in Browning's time?

Critical Literacy
Conduct an Interview Imagine you are asked to interview Robert Browning about his relationship with his wife for a celebrity talk show. How does he feel about the poem his wife wrote about her love for him? Can he list ways in which he loves her? Write a list of five additional questions about Robert Browning's relationship with his wife that would interest your audience, and then write Browning's possible response to each question.

 Go to **www.mirrorsandwindows.com** for more.

The Novel Defined

A **novel** may be defined most simply as a long work of fiction that often has an involved plot, many characters, and numerous settings. Although the novel shares many features with the short story (see Unit 9, Understanding Literary Forms, pages 1182–1183), it is a much more extended form of narrative.

The novel developed gradually from the prose writings of the sixteenth and seventeenth centuries. Some literary historians suggest that *Don Quixote de la Mancha,* published by Miguel de Cervantes between 1605 and 1615, is the first real novel because Cervantes presented his characters' adventures as a continuous tale, rather than as the series of disjointed episodes common in prose fiction of the time. The novel as an acknowledged genre did not really flourish until the late eighteenth century, however, when works of various kinds began to appear. Some were intended to teach a moral, and others, to shock and scandalize. By the nineteenth century, the genre was well established.

In this unit, you will read excerpts from the novels of Charles Dickens, Emily Brontë, Gustave Flaubert, and Thomas Hardy. All these novels reflect the social and economic concerns of the Victorian Era. Dickens frequently wrote about people living in slums, suffering hunger and disease, and dying anonymously in London. Thomas Hardy depicted the plight of farming families and itinerant workers and the alienation of those who did not seem to fit the existing social structure.

In many respects, Dickens's works represent early-nineteenth-century fiction, which was still greatly influenced by the characteristics of the eighteenth-century novel: comical, often satirical, rambling, and full of physical details. Hardy, a late Victorian novelist, offers a more somber style and reveals the late Victorian anxiety over change. For instance, in his *The Mayor of Casterbridge,* Michael Henchard's rise in the social hierarchy from agricultural worker to mayor is both a sign and a result of the social and cultural upheaval of the late nineteenth century.

Elements of the Novel

As you read a novel, notice how it is structured. A long prose work usually is divided into chapters and some-times into parts. The Victorian novel typically was published in parts or installments called *serials.* Because readers would have to wait quite awhile between installments, authors tended to construct elaborate plots, with each installment ending in the suspense of a cliffhanger. Notice how the complex structure of the novel supports the development of the plot and characters. Many Victorian novelists created multiple subplots, or secondary conflicts, that, when skillfully handled, contributed to the interest and drama of the main plot's development and resolution.

Plot

The **plot** is the series of events related to a central conflict, or struggle. The plot typically introduces a conflict, develops it, and eventually resolves it. The plot often contains the following elements (see diagram below), although it may not include all of them and they may not appear in precisely this order:

- The **exposition,** or introduction, sets the tone or mood, introduces the characters and setting, and provides necessary background information.
- In the **rising action,** the conflict is developed and intensified.
- The **climax** is the high point of interest or suspense.
- The **falling action** consists of all the events that follow the climax.
- The **resolution,** or denouement (dā' nü män´), is the point at which the central conflict is ended, or resolved.

Elements of Plot

Setting and Mood

The **setting** is the time and place of the unfolding action together with all the details used to create a sense of a particular time and place. The details that create the setting also create a **mood,** or atmosphere, the emotion created in the reader by part or all of a

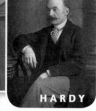

DICKENS   BRONTË   HARDY

"A boy's story is the best that is ever told."
— CHARLES DICKENS

literary work. For instance, in Dickens's *Great Expectations,* the details of Miss Havisham's musty room, where the clock had stopped at twenty minutes to nine, suggest a mood of stasis and death.

Character and Conflict

A **character** is an individual that takes part in the action of a literary work. The main character, or **protagonist,** is the most important character in the work and is in conflict with the **antagonist.** A character also may struggle against nature, society, or self. In Flaubert's *Madame Bovary,* consider the forces with which Emma Bovary is in conflict: her unassuming husband, who represents a social embarrassment; a highly stratified society; and her own ambition, which threatens to disrupt her respectable life as the wife of a village doctor.

Narrative Voice and Point of View

A **narrator** is a character or speaker who tells a story. He or she may be a major or minor character or simply someone who witnessed or heard about the events being related.

Point of view is the vantage point, or perspective, from which the story is told. *First-person narrators* are story characters; their point of view is limited to what they can directly observe about other characters and situations. For example, Jane, who tells the story in *Jane Eyre,* does not know what her charge, Adèle, or her employer, Mr. Rochester, are thinking. *Third-person narrators* may have a limited point of view or they may be omniscient, revealing the thoughts of all the characters, as in *Madame Bovary.*

Tone

Tone is the emotional attitude toward the reader or toward the subject implied by a literary work. In *The Mayor of Casterbridge,* consider how Hardy's compassionate description of the weary Susan Henchard allows readers to identify with an empathetic tone, drawing them into the emotional lives of characters.

Theme

A **theme** is a central message or perception about life that is revealed through a literary work. Themes may be stated or implied. A *stated theme* is presented directly, whereas an *implied theme* must be inferred. Often, several major themes recur in a work of literature.

HOW TO READ

The Novel

Identify the point of view. Knowing who is telling the story is a key to understanding it. The author's choice of narrator determines how much and what kind of information readers will be given. Identify who is telling the story, and determine how this person's perspective may be limited or biased.

Trace the sequence of events. As you read, trace the sequence of events, including the main plot of the story and any subplots that may be unfolding. In particular, identify the central conflict and trace its development to the climax. Predict how the conflict might be resolved to bring the story to a satisfying end.

Identify themes. Without reducing the novel to a single moral or lesson, look for its central message. Think about what is suggested by the resolution of the story's main conflict. Also consider the outcome for the various characters, especially the protagonist. Has he or she changed in some way? Several themes may be central in a novel.

from **Great Expectations**

A Novel by Charles Dickens

Build Background

Literary Context The novel *Great Expectations* first appeared as a serial in the magazine *Year Round* between 1860 and 1861. Publishing in this format, Charles Dickens reached a wide audience and thus became wildly popular in his day.

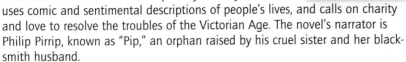

Great Expectations is considered one of Dickens's most influential novels. It is typical of his fiction in that it attacks social indifference to poverty and injustice, uses comic and sentimental descriptions of people's lives, and calls on charity and love to resolve the troubles of the Victorian Age. The novel's narrator is Philip Pirrip, known as "Pip," an orphan raised by his cruel sister and her blacksmith husband.

In this excerpt, Pip is invited to the home of the well-to-do Miss Havisham, a bitter old woman who has given up on life after being abandoned on her wedding day many years before, and her adopted daughter, Estella. Through these visits, Pip develops the taste for a better life.

Reader's Context How would your life be different if you were suddenly wealthy or poor? How would it be better or worse?

Meet the Author

Much of the life of **Charles Dickens** (1812–1870) appeared in fictional form in his literary work. His childhood began happily but changed dramatically in his eleventh year, when the family moved from Chatham, a port town, to the city of London. Soon after the move, Dickens's father was sent to prison for unpaid debts. Young Charles was taken out of school and eventually put to work in a warehouse. The mark these two experiences left on Dickens was profound. Later in life, he became an ardent social critic on behalf of the poor and downtrodden people who filled London's streets in the mid-nineteenth century.

Eventually, Dickens returned to school. When he was twenty-one, he began contributing stories, many of them humorous, to newspapers and magazines. His unique writing style and themes of social awareness won him wide popularity, both in England and the United States. Many of his novels sympathetically described the poverty and insecurity of children, clerks, and small merchants struggling on their own in the city.

A Christmas Carol (1843), featuring the character Ebenezer Scrooge, is perhaps Dickens's best-known work. Other major works include *A Tale of Two Cities* (1859), *Oliver Twist* (1838), *Nicholas Nickleby* (1839), *Bleak House* (1853), and *Hard Times* (1854).

Analyze Literature

Setting and Characterization

The **setting** of a literary work is the time and place in which it occurs, together with all the details used to create a sense of a particular time and place.

Characterization is the act of creating a character. *Direct characterization* describes characters' physical features, dress, and personality. *Indirect characterization* shows what characters say, do, or think or what others say or think about them.

Set Purpose

Among the talents for which Dickens is known today is his ability to capture the feel of nineteenth-century England. Look for clues to the specific setting as you read this selection. List the details Dickens provides that help you visualize the scene. Accompanying Dickens's evocative settings are his memorable characters. As you read this excerpt, make note of examples of direct and indirect characterization.

Preview Vocabulary

mortifying, 795
penitential, 795
propound, 796
self-possessed, 797
ghastly, 799
diversion, 799
concede, 799
disdain, 800
transfixed, 801
spurn, 802

from Great Expectations

by Charles Dickens

The Madwoman, c. 1819. Theodore Gericault. Musée des Beaux-Arts de Lyon, Lyon, France. (See detail on page 794.)

"I was so humiliated, hurt, spurned, offended, angry, sorry . . . that tears started to my eyes."

Chapter 8

Mr. Pumblechook and I breakfasted at eight o'clock in the parlor behind the shop, while the shopman took his mug of tea and hunch[1] of bread-and-butter on a sack of peas in the front premises. I considered Mr. Pumblechook wretched company. Besides being possessed by my sister's idea that a <u>mortifying</u> and <u>penitential</u> character ought to be imparted to my diet—besides giving me as much crumb as possible in combination with as little butter, and putting such a quantity of warm water into my milk that it would have been more candid to have left the milk out altogether—his conversation consisted of noth-

---

1. **hunch.** Chunk

> **mor • ti • fy • ing** (môr´ tə fī´ iŋ) *adj.,* humbling; embarrassing
> **pen • i • ten • tial** (pe´ nə ten[t]´ shəl) *adj.,* expressing sorrow or shame for wrongdoing

ing but arithmetic. On my politely bidding him good morning, he said pompously, "Seven times nine, boy?" And how should *I* be able to answer, dodged in that way, in a strange place, on an empty stomach! I was hungry but before I had swallowed a morsel, he began a running sum that lasted all through the breakfast. "Seven?" "And four?" "And eight?" "And six?" "And two?" "And ten?" And so on. And after each figure was disposed of, it was as much as I could do to get a bite or a sup before the next came; while he sat at his ease guessing nothing, and eating bacon and hot roll in (if I may be allowed the expression) a gorging and gormandizing[2] manner.

———— ❖ ————

Within a quarter of an hour we came to Miss Havisham's house, which was of old brick, and dismal, and had a great many iron bars to it.

———— ❖ ————

For such reasons I was very glad when ten o'clock came and we started for Miss Havisham's; though I was not at all at my ease regarding the manner in which I should acquit[3] myself under that lady's roof. Within a quarter of an hour we came to Miss Havisham's house, which was of old brick, and dismal, and had a great many iron bars to it. Some of the windows had been walled up; of those that remained, all the lower were rustily barred. There was a courtyard in front, and that was barred; so, we had to wait, after ringing the bell, until someone should come to open it. While we waited at the gate, I peeped in (even then Mr. Pumblechook said, "And fourteen?" but I pretended not to hear him), and saw that at the side of the house there was a large brewery. No brewing was going on in it, and none seemed to have gone on for a long long time.

A window was raised, and a clear voice demanded "What name?" To which my conductor replied, "Pumblechook." The voice returned, "Quite right," and the window was shut again, and a young lady came across the courtyard, with keys in her hand.

"This," said Mr. Pumblechook, "is Pip."

"This is Pip, is it?" returned the young lady, who was very pretty and seemed very proud; "come in, Pip."

Mr. Pumblechook was coming in also, when she stopped him with the gate.

"Oh!" she said. "Did you wish to see Miss Havisham?"

"If Miss Havisham wished to see me," returned Mr. Pumblechook, discomfited.[4]

"Ah!" said the girl; "but you see, she don't."

She said it so finally, and in such an undiscussible way, that Mr. Pumblechook, though in a condition of ruffled dignity, could not protest. But he eyed me severely—as if *I* had done anything to him!—and departed with the words reproachfully delivered: "Boy! Let your behavior here be a credit unto them which brought you up by hand!" I was not free from apprehension that he would come back to propound through the gate, "And sixteen?" But he didn't.

My young conductress locked the gate, and we went across the courtyard. It was paved and clean, but grass was growing in every crevice. The brewery buildings had a little lane of communication with it; and the wooden gates of that lane stood open, and all the brewery beyond stood open, away to the high enclosing wall; and all was empty and disused. The cold wind seemed to blow colder there than outside the gate; and it made a shrill noise in howling

---

2. **gormandizing.** Eating like a glutton
3. **acquit.** Conduct
4. **discomfited.** Made uneasy

pro • pound (prə paúnd´) *v.,* put forth for consideration

in and out at the open sides of the brewery, like the noise of wind in the rigging of a ship at sea.

She saw me looking at it, and she said, "You could drink without hurt all the strong beer that's brewed there now, boy."

"I should think I could, miss," said I, in a shy way.

"Better not try to brew beer there now, or it would turn out sour, boy; don't you think so?"

"It looks like it, miss."

"Not that anybody means to try," she added, "for that's all done with, and the place will stand as idle as it is, till it falls. As to strong beer, there's enough of it in the cellars already to drown the Manor House."

"Is that the name of this house, miss?"

"One of its names, boy."

"It has more than one, then, miss?"

"One more. Its other name was Satis; which is Greek, or Latin, or Hebrew, or all three—or all one to me—for enough."

"Enough House!" said I; "that's a curious name, miss."

"Yes," she replied; "but it meant more than it said. It meant, when it was given, that whoever had this house could want nothing else. They must have been easily satisfied in those days, I should think. But don't loiter, boy."

Though she called me "boy" so often, and with a carelessness that was far from complimentary, she was of about my own age. She seemed much older than I, of course, being a girl, and beautiful and <u>self-possessed</u>; and she

> **self • pos • sessed** (self pə zesd′) *adj.,* in full control of one's feelings and actions

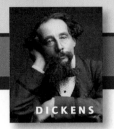

DICKENS

Dickens and Copyright Law

The concept of intellectual property was just beginning to emerge when Charles Dickens's work became popular. While British publishers compensated the famous author for his book sales, U.S. publishers printed copies of his books without paying him anything. Dickens discovered this during a journey to the United States in 1842 and denounced the practice in his travelogue *American Notes for General Circulation*. Moreover, he actively began demanding that the U.S. government put an end to literary bootlegging.

Many American authors, including Henry Wadsworth Longfellow and Washington Irving, sympathized with Dickens, since they had experienced similar issues with the sales of their work in England. The U.S. Congress, however, criticized Dickens for challenging the integrity of U.S. publishers and did nothing to prevent the illegal publication of his work. It was not until 1891 that Congress entered into an international copyright agreement with other countries.

> **She seemed much older than I, of course, being a girl, and beautiful and self-possessed; and she was as scornful of me as if she had been one-and-twenty, and a queen.**

---

was as scornful of me as if she had been one-and-twenty, and a queen.

We went into the house by a side door—the great front entrance had two chains across it outside—and the first thing I noticed was that the passages were all dark, and that she had left a candle burning there. She took it up, and we went through more passages and up a staircase, and still it was all dark, and only the candle lighted us.

At last we came to the door of a room, and she said, "Go in."

I answered, more in shyness than politeness, "After you, miss."

To this, she returned: "Don't be ridiculous, boy; I am not going in." And scornfully walked away, and—what was worse—took the candle with her.

This was very uncomfortable, and I was half-afraid. However, the only thing to be done being to knock at the door, I knocked, and was told from within to enter. I entered, therefore, and found myself in a pretty large room, well lighted with wax candles. No glimpse of daylight was to be seen in it. It was a dressing room, as I supposed from the furniture, though much of it was of forms and uses then quite unknown to me. But prominent in it was a draped table with a gilded looking glass,[5] and that I made out at first sight to be a fine lady's dressing table.[6]

Whether I should have made out this object so soon if there had been no fine lady sitting at it, I cannot say. In an armchair, with an elbow resting on the table and her head leaning on that hand, sat the strangest lady I have ever seen, or shall ever see.

She was dressed in rich materials—satins, and lace, and silks—all of white. Her shoes were white. And she had a long white veil

---

5. **looking glass.** Mirror
6. **dressing table.** Low table with a mirror for use while grooming

dependent from her hair, and she had bridal flowers in her hair, but her hair was white. Some bright jewels sparkled on her neck and on her hands, and some other jewels lay sparkling on the table. Dresses less splendid than the dress she wore, and half-packed trunks, were scattered about. She had not quite finished dressing, for she had but one shoe on—the other was on the table near her hand—her veil was but half arranged, her watch and chain were not put on, and some lace for her bosom lay with those trinkets, and with her handkerchief, and gloves, and some flowers, and a prayer book, all confusedly heaped about the looking glass.

It was not in the first few moments that I saw all these things, though I saw more of them in the first moments than might be supposed. But I saw that everything within my view which ought to be white had been white long ago, and had lost its luster, and was faded and yellow. I saw that the bride within the bridal dress had withered like the dress, and like the flowers, and had no brightness left but the brightness of her sunken eyes. I saw that the dress had been put upon the rounded figure of a young woman, and that the figure upon which it now hung loose had shrunk to skin and bone. Once I had been taken to see some <u>ghastly</u> waxwork at the fair, representing I know not what impossible personage lying in state.[7] Once I had been taken to one of our old marsh churches to see a skeleton in the ashes of a rich dress that had been dug out of a vault under the church pavement. Now, waxwork and skeleton seemed to have dark eyes that moved and looked at me. I should have cried out, if I could.

"Who is it?" said the lady at the table.

"Pip, ma'am."

"Pip?"

"Mr. Pumblechook's boy, ma'am. Come—to play."

"Come nearer; let me look at you. Come close."

It was when I stood before her, avoiding her eyes, that I took note of the surrounding objects in detail, and saw that her watch had stopped at twenty minutes to nine, and that a clock in the room had stopped at twenty minutes to nine.

"Look at me," said Miss Havisham. "You are not afraid of a woman who has never seen the sun since you were born?"

I regret to state that I was not afraid of telling the enormous lie comprehended in the answer "No."

"Do you know what I touch here?" she said, laying her hands, one upon the other, on her left side.

"Yes, ma'am." (It made me think of the young man.)

"What do I touch?"

"Your heart."

"Broken!"

She uttered the word with an eager look, and with strong emphasis, and with a weird smile that had a kind of boast in it. Afterwards, she kept her hands there for a little while, and slowly took them away as if they were heavy.

"I am tired," said Miss Havisham. "I want <u>diversion</u>, and I have done with men and women. Play."

I think it will be <u>conceded</u> by my most disputatious[8] reader that she could hardly have directed an unfortunate boy to do anything in the wide world more difficult to be done under the circumstances.

"I sometimes have sick fancies," she went on, "and I have a sick fancy that I want to see some play. There there!" with an impatient

---

7. **lying in state.** Placed in public view for honors prior to burial
8. **disputatious.** Fond of arguing

---

ghast • ly (gast´ lē) *adj.*, horrible; ghostlike
di • ver • sion (dī vʉr´ zhən) *n.*, entertaining type of distraction
con • cede (kən sēd´) *v.*, acknowledge

movement of the fingers of her right hand; "play, play, play!"

For a moment, with the fear of my sister's working[9] me before my eyes, I had a desperate idea of starting round the room in the assumed character of Mr. Pumblechook's chaise-cart. But I felt myself so unequal to the performance that I gave it up, and stood looking at Miss Havisham in what I suppose she took for a dogged manner, inasmuch as she said, when we had taken a good look at each other:

"Are you sullen and obstinate?"

"No, ma'am, I am very sorry for you, and very sorry I can't play just now. If you complain of me I shall get into trouble with my sister, so I would do it if I could; but it's so new here, and so strange, and so fine—and melancholy—" I stopped, fearing I might say too much, or had already said it, and we took another look at each other.

Before she spoke again, she turned her eyes from me, and looked at the dress she wore, and at the dressing table, and finally at herself in the looking glass.

"So new to him," she muttered, "so old to me; so strange to him, so familiar to me; so melancholy to both of us! Call Estella."

As she was still looking at the reflection of herself, I thought she was still talking to herself, and kept quiet.

"Call Estella," she repeated, flashing a look at me. "You can do that. Call Estella. At the door."

To stand in the dark in a mysterious passage of an unknown house, bawling Estella to a scornful young lady neither visible nor responsive, and feeling it a dreadful liberty so to roar out her name, was almost as bad as playing to order. But she answered at last, and her light came along the dark passage like a star.

Miss Havisham beckoned her to come close, and took up a jewel from the table, and tried its effect upon her fair young bosom and against her pretty brown hair. "Your own, one day, my dear, and you will use it well. Let me see you play cards with this boy."

"With this boy? Why, he is a common laboring-boy!"

I thought I overheard Miss Havisham answer—only it seemed so unlikely, "Well? You can break his heart."

"What do you play, boy?" asked Estella of myself, with the greatest disdain.

"Nothing but Beggar my Neighbor, miss."

"Beggar him," said Miss Havisham to Estella. So we sat down to cards.

"She sat, corpse-like, as we played at cards; the frillings and trimmings on her bridal dress looking like earthy paper."

It was then I began to understand that everything in the room had stopped, like the watch and the clock, a long time ago. I noticed that Miss Havisham put down the jewel exactly on the spot from which she had taken it up. As Estella dealt the cards, I glanced at the dressing table again, and saw that the shoe upon it, once white, now yellow, had never been worn. I glanced down at the foot from which the shoe was absent, and saw that the silk stocking on it, once white, now yellow, had been trodden[10] ragged. Without this arrest of everything, this standing still of all the pale decayed objects, not even the withered bridal dress on the collapsed form could have looked so like graveclothes, or the long veil so like a shroud.

So she sat, corpse-like, as we played at cards; the frillings and trimmings on her bridal

---

9. **working.** Beating
10. **trodden.** Worn from walking

dis • dain (dis dān´) *n.,* scorn

She won the game, and I dealt. I misdealt, as was only natural, when I knew she was lying in wait for me to do wrong; and she denounced me for a stupid, clumsy laboring-boy.

"You say nothing of her," remarked Miss Havisham to me, as she looked on. "She says many hard things of you, yet you say nothing of her. What do you think of her?"

"I don't like to say," I stammered.

"Tell me in my ear," said Miss Havisham, bending down.

"I think she is very proud," I replied, in a whisper.

"Anything else?"

"I think she is very pretty."

"Anything else?"

"I think she is very insulting." (She was looking at me then with a look of supreme aversion.)

"Anything else?"

"I think I should like to go home."

"And never see her again, though she is so pretty?"

"I am not sure that I shouldn't like to see her again, but I should like to go home now."

"You shall go soon," said Miss Havisham aloud. "Play the game out."

Saving for the one weird smile at first, I should have felt almost sure that Miss Havisham's face could not smile. It had dropped into a watchful and brooding expression—most likely when all the things about her had become <u>transfixed</u>—and it looked as if nothing could ever lift it up again. Her chest had dropped, so that she stooped; and her voice

dress looking like earthy paper. I knew nothing then of the discoveries that are occasionally made of bodies buried in ancient times, which fall to powder in the moment of being distinctly seen; but I have often thought since that she must have looked as if the admission of the natural light of day would have struck her to dust.

"He calls the knaves jacks, this boy!" said Estella with disdain, before our first game was out. "And what coarse hands he has! And what thick boots!"

I had never thought of being ashamed of my hands before; but I began to consider them a very indifferent pair. Her contempt for me was so strong that it became infectious, and I caught it.

---

trans · fixed (tran[t]s fikst´) *adj.,* motionless; fixed in one position

---

had dropped, so that she spoke low, and with a dead lull upon her; altogether, she had the appearance of having dropped, body and soul, within and without, under the weight of a crushing blow.

I played the game to an end with Estella, and she beggared[11] me. She threw the cards down on the table when she had won them all, as if she despised them for having been won of me.

"When shall I have you here again?" said Miss Havisham. "Let me think."

I was beginning to remind her that today was Wednesday when she checked me with her former impatient movement of the fingers of her right hand.

"There, there! I know nothing of days of the week; I know nothing of weeks of the year. Come again after six days. You hear?"

"Yes, ma'am."

"Estella, take him down. Let him have something to eat, and let him roam and look about him while he eats. Go, Pip."

I followed the candle down, as I had followed the candle up, and she stood it in the place where we had found it. Until she opened the side entrance, I had fancied, without thinking about it, that it must necessarily be nighttime. The rush of the daylight quite confounded me, and made me feel as if I had been in the candlelight of the strange room many hours.

"You are to wait here, you boy," said Estella, and disappeared and closed the door.

I took the opportunity of being alone in the courtyard to look at my coarse hands and my common boots. My opinion of those accessories was not favorable. They had never troubled me before, but they troubled me now, as vulgar appendages. I determined to ask Joe why he had ever taught me to call those picture-cards jacks which ought to be called knaves. I wished Joe had been rather more genteelly[12] brought up, and then I should have been so, too.

She came back, with some bread and meat and a little mug of beer. She put the mug down on the stones of the yard, and gave me the bread and meat without looking at me, as insolently as if I were a dog in disgrace. I was so humiliated, hurt, spurned, offended, angry, sorry—I cannot hit upon the right name for the smart—God knows what its name was—that tears started to my eyes. The moment they sprang there, the girl looked at me with a quick delight in having been the cause of them. This gave me power to keep them back and to look at her: so, she gave a contemptuous toss—but with a sense, I thought, of having made too sure that I was so wounded—and left me.

But, when she was gone, I looked about me for a place to hide my face in, and got behind one of the gates in the brewery-lane, and leaned my sleeve against the wall there, and leaned my forehead on it and cried. As I cried, I kicked the wall, and took a hard twist at my hair; so bitter were my feelings, and so sharp was the smart without a name, that it needed counteraction. ❖

---

11. **beggared.** Beat at "Beggar My Neighbor"
12. **genteelly.** Politely; elegantly

spurn (spʉrn) v., reject

MIRRORS & WINDOWS

Pip describes Miss Havisham's dressing room by saying "everything in the room had stopped, like the watch and the clock, a long time ago." What are the disadvantages of clinging to things from the past? What from your past have you found difficult to give up?

Refer to Text ▶ ▶ ▶ ▶ ▶   Reason with Text

1a. How does Pip describe the company of Mr. Pumblechook?

1b. Explain why he might feel that way, and cite specific details to support your answer.

Understand
Find meaning

2a. How does Pip describe Miss Havisham?

2b. What does this description suggest about Miss Havisham's personality?

Apply
Use information

3a. Quote Estella's comments about the brewery. What is significant about the brewery? How does Pip describe the building and the surrounding courtyard?

3b. How do Estella's comments and Pip's description set the tone for Pip's encounter with Miss Havisham?

Analyze
Take things apart

4a. Recall the name of the manor house. According to Estella, what does the name mean?

4b. What does Estella think about the name? From reading this excerpt from *Great Expectations*, are Estella and Miss Havisham satisfied with what they have? Why or why not?

Evaluate
Make judgments

5a. What does Pip notice about Miss Havisham's watch and clock?

5b. Describe all the things Pip compares to the watch and the clock as he surveys the room. To what does he compare Miss Havisham's things? How does this comparison relate to the overall mood of the excerpt?

Create
Bring ideas together

Analyze Literature

Setting and Characterization
Briefly describe the setting of the excerpt from *Great Expectations*. What details does Dickens use to make the setting reflect the personality of Miss Havisham?

Give specific examples of how Dickens uses both direct and indirect characterization techniques to create Miss Havisham and Estella. How effective is Dickens in creating these characters?

Extend the Text

Writing Options
Creative Writing In the role of Miss Havisham, write one page of a memoir. Describe what has made her so bitter and sad. What does she think about her life right now? What does she think about the people around her?

Expository Writing Write an essay analyzing the character of Pip. Explain why he is so bothered by the way Estella treats him. Support your analysis using details from the novel.

Media Literacy
Create a Comic Strip Dickens often portrayed tragic characters and situations in a humorous light. With this in mind, create a comic strip that portrays Pip's initial visit to Miss Havisham's home. Think about the tone you want to express and how you want to reflect or comment on the tone in Dickens's excerpt.

Lifelong Learning
Write a Journal Article Research how Dickens influenced the development of the British novel, and report your findings in the form of an article for a literary journal. Begin your article with a one-paragraph *abstract*, or summary of the main points, and include a Works Cited page, listing the sources you used in writing the article.

 Go to **www.mirrorsandwindows.com** for more.

Understand the Concept

To *coordinate* things means to join them in an equal or a balanced way. In writing, **coordination** is a strategy for combining related ideas of the same importance.

Ideas are combined using **coordinating conjunctions.** The most common coordinating conjunctions are *and, or, nor, for, but, yet,* and *so.* Each conjunction indicates a different relationship between the words or groups of words that it connects. For instance, the conjunction *or* indicates a choice. The conjunctions *but* and *yet* indicate a contrast or variation.

Coordinating conjunctions can be used to connect several words, such as nouns, verbs, adjectives, and adverbs. They also can be used to connect groups of words, such as phrases, clauses, and sentences. When a coordinating conjunction joins two or more independent clauses (or sentences), a **compound sentence** is formed. A comma is placed before the coordinating conjunction joining the two clauses.

In the following examples from *Great Expectations,* Dickens uses several coordinating conjunctions to describe Miss Havisham at her dressing table. Notice how Dickens's frequent use of *and* reflects the character's eccentric nature.

> Some bright jewels sparkled on her neck *and* on her hands, *and* some other jewels lay sparkling on the table.

In this example, the first coordinating conjunction, *and,* connects two prepositional phrases; the second conjunction, *and,* joins the two independent clauses to form a compound sentence.

> She had not quite finished dressing, *for* she had but one shoe on. . . . Her watch *and* chain were not put on, *and* some lace for her bosom lay with those trinkets, *and* with her handkerchief, *and* gloves, *and* some flowers, *and* a prayer book, all confusedly heaped about the looking glass.

In this example, the coordinating conjunction *for* connects two independent clauses; the second conjunction, *and,* joins two nouns to form a compound subject; the third conjunction, *and,* connects two independent clauses; and the rest of the coordinating conjunctions join objects of the preposition *with.*

Apply the Skill

Identify Coordinating Conjunctions

Identify the coordinating conjunctions in the following sentences.

1. Dickens's father could not pay his family's debts, so he was sent to prison.
2. As a boy, Dickens was taken out of school and put to work in a warehouse.
3. During England's Victorian Age, widespread poverty forced many children to work in factories and shops.
4. Dickens's childhood struggles left their mark on his consciousness, for he became a social critic on behalf of the poor.
5. His novels include *A Tale of Two Cities* and *Oliver Twist,* but *A Christmas Carol* is probably his best-known work.

Correct Coordinating Conjunctions

Write the following sentences on a piece of paper. In each sentence, underline the coordinating conjunctions. Some sentences may have more than one. If the coordinating conjunction links two independent clauses, insert a comma before it.

1. *Great Expectations* attacks social indifference to poverty and injustice.
2. Pip helps an escaped convict yet he treats him with kindness and understanding.
3. Neither Miss Havisham's waxen complexion nor her skeletal figure could evoke a scream from the stunned Pip.
4. Pip's visits to Miss Havisham made him ashamed of his appearance but his social status would soon change.
5. Estella's uncharitable treatment of Pip made him tearful for he felt humiliated and angry at her obvious pleasure in his reaction.

Use Coordination in Your Writing

As readers, we make judgments about Miss Havisham based on her appearance and surroundings. If an unexpected visitor saw you in the familiar surroundings of your room, what would the objects reveal about you? Write a descriptive paragraph and then review your writing to identify the coordinating conjunctions used.

from Jane Eyre

A Novel by Charlotte Brontë

Build Background

Literary Context Charlotte Brontë's novel *Jane Eyre* is a coming-of-age tale set in nineteenth-century England. The book was first published in 1847 in London under the title *Jane Eyre: An Autobiography* and the pseudonym Currer Bell. After the book's almost instant success, Brontë revealed herself as the author.

Jane Eyre, the narrator and main character of the novel, is a poor orphan who leads an unhappy life. Her wealthy aunt raises her out of duty, not compassion. She is unkind to Jane and eventually sends her to Lowood, a boarding school run by another cruel character, Mr. Brocklehurst. Eventually, Jane is employed as a governess for the daughter of a wealthy businessman, Edward Rochester. A Byronic figure, Rochester is a brooding and scornful man who is nonetheless capable of deep affection. Jane's life changes dramatically after she falls in love with her employer and discovers he has a secret that jeopardizes their relationship.

The following excerpt contains Jane's initial meeting with Mr. Rochester.

Reader's Context What stories do you remember from your childhood? Why do you think you remember them?

Meet the Author

Charlotte Brontë (1816–1854) was born and raised in the Yorkshire district of northern England. Her father, a rector (clergyman) from Ireland, moved the family to Haworth, Yorkshire, in 1820. After the death of her mother in 1821, Brontë and her siblings were left almost entirely on their own in the moorland rectory. The children were educated at home and spent a great deal of time reading and writing.

In 1841, Brontë and her sister Emily traveled to Brussels, Belgium, to study languages and school management. They were hoping to establish a school for girls in England. After the death of one of their aunts, however, the sisters returned home.

In 1845, Brontë, Emily, and another sister, Anne, published a collection of their poetry under the pseudonyms Currer Bell, Ellis Bell, and Acton Bell. The book was unsuccessful at the time; however, it now is being looked at with new respect, mainly because of contemporary scholars' appreciation of Emily's poetry. Emily's only novel and greatest artistic achievement, *Wuthering Heights*, appeared two years later, along with Charlotte's classic work *Jane Eyre.*

After the success of *Jane Eyre*, Charlotte Brontë published two more novels in her lifetime: *Shirley* (1849) and *Vilette* (1853). Her novel *The Professor* was published posthumously in 1857.

Analyze Literature

Narrator and Tone
A **narrator** is a character or speaker who tells a story. The writer's choice of narrator determines how much and what kind of information readers will be given about events and other characters.

Tone is the emotional attitude toward the reader or the subject implied by a literary work—for instance, familiar, ironic, playful, sarcastic, serious, or sincere.

Set Purpose

Jane Eyre is one of the most famous female characters in British literature. She narrates her tale, thus giving readers a "Jane's-eye" view of events and characters and insights into her mind. Determine whether the narration is *omniscient,* in which the thoughts of all the characters are revealed, or *limited,* in which the thoughts of the speaker or a single character are revealed. As you read, note Jane's tone. Think about the effect it has on you and what it indicates about Jane.

Preview Vocabulary

indulge, 806
vivacious, 807
vapid, 807
pliable, 807
covet, 808
prostrate, 809
officious, 809
endeavour, 811
monotonous, 811
stagnation, 812

Rochester and Jane Eyre, c. 1840–1875. Frederick Walter.
(See detail on page 805.)

from *Jane Eyre*

by Charlotte Brontë

*The incident had occurred and was gone for me, . . . yet it marked
with change one single hour of a monotonous life.*

Chapter 12

The promise of a smooth career, which my first calm introduction to Thornfield Hall seemed to pledge, was not belied on a longer acquaintance with the place and its inmates. Mrs. Fairfax turned out to be what she appeared, a placid-tempered, kind-natured woman, of competent education and average intelligence. My pupil was a lively child, who had been spoilt and <u>indulged</u>, and therefore was sometimes wayward; but as she was committed entirely to my care, and no injudicious interference from any quarter ever thwarted my plans for her improvement, she soon forgot her

> **in · dulge** (in dulj´) *v.,* yield to; give in to the desires and whims to an excessive degree

little freaks,[1] and became obedient and teachable. She had no great talents, no marked traits of character, no peculiar development of feeling or taste which raised her one inch above the ordinary level of childhood; but neither had she any deficiency or vice which sunk her below it. She made reasonable progress, entertained for me a <u>vivacious</u>, though perhaps not very profound, affection; and by her simplicity, gay prattle, and efforts to please, inspired me, in return, with a degree of attachment sufficient to make us both content in each other's society.

This, *par parenthèse*,[2] will be thought cool language by persons who entertain solemn doctrines about the angelic nature of children, and the duty of those charged with their education to conceive for them an idolatrous[3] devotion: but I am not writing to flatter paternal egotism, to echo cant,[4] or prop up humbug; I am merely telling the truth. I felt a conscientious solicitude[5] for Adèle's welfare and progress, and a quiet liking to her little self; just as I cherished towards Mrs. Fairfax a thankfulness for her kindness, and a pleasure in her society proportionate to the tranquil regard she had for me, and the moderation of her mind and character.

. . .

The other members of the household, viz., John and his wife, Leah the housemaid, and Sophie the French nurse, were decent people; but in no respect remarkable: with Sophie I used to talk French, and sometimes I asked her questions about her native country; but she was not of a descriptive or narrative turn, and generally gave such <u>vapid</u> and confused answers as were calculated rather to check than encourage inquiry.

October, November, December passed away. One afternoon in January, Mrs. Fairfax had begged a holiday for Adèle, because she had a cold; and, as Adèle seconded the request with an ardour that reminded me how precious occasional holidays had been to me in my own childhood, I accorded it, deeming that I did well in showing <u>pliability</u> on the point. It was a fine, calm day, though very cold; I was tired of sitting still in the library through a whole long morning: Mrs. Fairfax had just written a letter which was waiting to be posted, so I put on my bonnet and cloak and volunteered to carry it to Hay; the distance, two miles, would be a pleasant winter afternoon walk. Having seen Adèle comfortably seated in her little chair by Mrs. Fairfax's parlour fireside, and given her best wax doll (which I usually kept enveloped in silver paper in a drawer) to play with, and a story-book for change of amusement; and having replied to her "Revenez bientôt, ma bonne amie, ma chère Mdlle. Jeannette,"[6] with a kiss, I set out.

. . .

On the hill-top above me sat the rising moon; pale yet as a cloud, but brightening momently: she looked over Hay, which, half lost in trees, sent up a blue smoke from its few chimneys; it was yet a mile distant, but in the absolute hush I could hear plainly its thin murmurs of life. My ear too felt the flow of currents; in what dales and depths I could not tell: but there were many hills beyond Hay, and doubtless many becks threading their passes. That evening calm betrayed alike the tinkle of the nearest streams, the sough[7] of the most remote.

A rude noise broke on these fine ripplings and whisperings, at once so far away and so clear: a positive tramp, tramp; a metallic clatter, which effaced the soft wave-wanderings; as, in a picture, the solid mass of a crag, or the rough boles of a great oak, drawn in dark and strong

---

1. **freaks.** Sudden or capricious turns of mind; whims
2. **par parenthèse.** [French] Parenthetically
3. **idolatrous.** Excessive, almost worshipful, admiration
4. **cant.** Slang
5. **solicitude.** Concern
6. **Revenez bientôt . . . Jeannette.** [French] I'll come back soon, my little friend, my dear Miss Jeannette.
7. **sough.** Soft murmuring or rustling sound

---

vi • va • cious (vī vā′ shəs) *adj.*, filled with animation and spirit
vap • id (va′ pəd) *adj.*, lacking liveliness, zest, or interest
pli • a • bility (plī′ ə bil′ ə tē) *n.*, flexibility; state of being easily influenced

on the foreground, efface the aërial distance of azure hill, sunny horizon, and blended clouds, where tint melts into tint.

The din was on the causeway: a horse was coming; the windings of the lane yet hid it, but it approached. I was just leaving the stile; yet, as the path was narrow, I sat still to let it go by. In those days I was young, and all sorts of fancies bright and dark tenanted my mind: the memories of nursery stories were there amongst other rubbish; and when they recurred, maturing youth added to them a vigour and vividness beyond what childhood could give. As this horse approached, and as I watched for it to appear through the dusk, I remembered certain of Bessie's tales, wherein figured a North-of-England spirit, called a "Gytrash"; which, in the form of horse, mule, or large dog, haunted solitary ways, and sometimes came upon belated travellers, as this horse was now coming upon me.

It was very near, but not yet in sight; when, in addition to the tramp, tramp, I heard a rush under the hedge, and close down by the hazel stems glided a great dog, whose black and white colour made him a distinct object against the trees. It was exactly one mask of Bessie's Gytrash,—a lion-like creature with long hair and a huge head: it passed me, however, quietly enough; not staying to look up, with strange pretercanine eyes, in my face, as I half expected

Joan Fontaine as Jane and Margaret O'Brien as Adèle in the 1944 film adaptation of *Jane Eyre*.

> *In those days I was young, and all sorts of fancies bright and dark tenanted my mind.*

it would. The horse followed,—a tall steed, and on its back a rider. The man, the human being, broke the spell at once. Nothing ever rode the Gytrash: it was always alone; and goblins, to my notions, though they might tenant the dumb carcasses of beasts, could scarce <u>covet</u> shelter in the common-place human form. No Gytrash

cov • et (kuʹ vet) *v.*, feel envious of or desire for something that belongs to someone else was this,—only a traveler taking the short cut to Millcote. He passed, and I went on; a few steps, and I turned: a sliding sound and an exclamation of "What the deuce is to do now?" and a clattering tumble, arrested my attention. Man and horse were down; they had slipped on the sheet of ice which glazed the causeway. The dog came bounding back, and seeing his master in a predicament, and hearing the horse groan, barked till the evening hills echoed the sound, which was deep in proportion to his magnitude. He snuffed round the <u>prostrate</u> group, and then he ran up to me; it was all he could do,—there was no other help at hand to summon. I obeyed him, and walked down to the traveller, by this time struggling himself free of his steed. His efforts were so vigorous, I thought he could not be much hurt; but I asked him the question:—

"Are you injured, sir?"

I think he was swearing, but am not certain; however, he was pronouncing some formula which prevented him from replying to me directly.

"Can I do anything?" I asked again.

"You must just stand on one side," he answered as he rose, first to his knees, and then to his feet. I did; whereupon began a heaving, stamping, clattering process, accompanied by a barking and baying which removed me effectually some yards distance; but I would not be driven quite away till I saw the event. This was finally fortunate; the horse was re-established, and the dog was silenced with a "Down, Pilot!" The traveller, now stooping, felt his foot and leg, as if trying whether they were sound; apparently something ailed them, for he halted to the stile whence I had just risen, and sat down.

I was in the mood for being useful, or at least <u>officious</u>, I think, for I now drew near him again.

"If you are hurt, and want help, sir, I can fetch some one either from Thornfield Hall or from Hay."

"Thank you; I shall do: I have no broken bones,—only a sprain;" and again he stood up and tried his foot, but the result extorted an involuntary "Ugh!"

> Had he been a handsome, heroic-looking young gentleman, I should not have dared to stand thus questioning him against his will, and offering my services unasked.

Something of daylight still lingered, and the moon was waxing bright: I could see him plainly. His figure was enveloped in a riding cloak, fur collared, and steel clasped; its details were not apparent, but I traced the general points of middle height, and considerable breadth of chest. He had a dark face, with stern features and a heavy brow; his eyes and gathered eyebrows looked ireful and thwarted just now; he was past youth, but had not reached middle age; perhaps he might be thirty-five. I felt no fear of him, and but little shyness. Had he been a handsome, heroic-looking young gentleman, I should not have dared to stand thus questioning him against his will, and offering my services unasked. I had hardly ever seen a handsome youth; never in my life spoken to one. I had a theoretical reverence and homage for beauty, elegance, gallantry, fascination; but had I met those qualities incarnate in masculine shape, I should have known instinctively that they neither had nor could have sympathy with anything in me, and should have shunned them as one would fire, lightning, or anything else that is bright but antipathetic.[8]

If even this stranger had smiled and been good-humoured to me when I addressed him; if he had put off my offer of assistance gaily and with thanks, I should have gone on my

---

8. **antipathetic.** Hostile

---

pros • trate (prä′ strāt′) adj., lying face down
of • fi • cious (ə fi′ shəs) adj., dutiful or obliging

The Emergence of Feminism

Some modern-day literary scholars have argued that *Jane Eyre* represents one of the earliest examples of feminist ideology in literature. *Feminism* is a social and political theory that emerged in the mid-1800s as part of the women's suffrage movement. The theory states that gender does not determine a person's worth in society and that women are equally capable of handling tasks traditionally performed by men.

While this idea may seem obvious to modern readers, traditional Victorians did not believe in gender equality. In fact, many Victorians of both genders felt women were best suited for passive and domestic responsibilities, such as cooking and child rearing. Many Victorians believed that more intellectual and vigorous tasks, such as jobs in economics, politics, and the military, required a level of energy only men possessed. A minority Christian sect called the Society of Friends, or Quakers, challenged these assumptions, but most Victorians did not take the Quakers seriously.

Brontë's famous novel brought gender issues to a wider audience and, in doing so, generated a substantial amount of controversy. The outspoken behavior of the character Jane Eyre went far

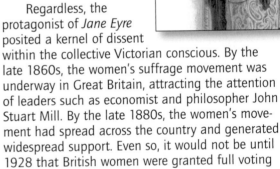

beyond that of any literary figure who had preceded her. Eyre's assertion that she was unhappy with her limited position as a woman in Victorian England horrified many Victorian readers. They found it unfathomable that a woman could be dissatisfied with a role considered so basic to femininity. Most literary critics reacted similarly, publishing negative reviews of the novel.

Regardless, the protagonist of *Jane Eyre* posited a kernel of dissent within the collective Victorian conscious. By the late 1860s, the women's suffrage movement was underway in Great Britain, attracting the attention of leaders such as economist and philosopher John Stuart Mill. By the late 1880s, the women's movement had spread across the country and generated widespread support. Even so, it would not be until 1928 that British women were granted full voting rights.

way and not felt any vocation[9] to renew inquiries: but the frown, the roughness of the traveller set me at my ease: I retained my station when he waved to me to go, and announced:—

"I cannot think of leaving you, sir, at so late an hour, in this solitary lane, till I see you are fit to mount your horse."

He looked at me when I said this: he had hardly turned his eyes in my direction before.

"I should think you ought to be at home yourself," said he, "if you have a home in this neighbourhood; where do you come from?"

"From just below; and I am not at all afraid of being out late when it is moonlight: I will run over to Hay for you with pleasure, if you wish it; indeed, I am going there to post a letter."

"You live just below—do you mean at that house with the battlements?"—pointing

to Thornfield Hall, on which the moon cast a hoary[10] gleam, bringing it out distinct and pale from the woods, that, by contrast with the western sky, now seemed one mass of shadow.

"Yes, sir."

"Whose house is it?"

"Mr. Rochester's."

"Do you know Mr. Rochester?"

"No, I have never seen him."

"He is not resident, then?"

"No."

"Can you tell me where he is?"

"I cannot."

"You are not a servant at the hall, of course. You are—" He stopped, ran his eye over my

---

9. **felt any vocation.** Felt compelled to act out of a sense of duty
10. **hoary.** Silvery

dress, which, as usual, was quite simple: a black merino cloak, a black beaver bonnet; neither of them half fine enough for a lady's maid. He seemed puzzled to decide what I was: I helped him.

"I am the governess."

> He seemed puzzled to decide what I was: I helped him.

"Ah, the governess!" he repeated; "deuce take me, if I had not forgotten! The governess!" and again my raiment[11] underwent scrutiny. In two minutes he rose from the stile: his face expressed pain when he tried to move.

"I cannot commission you to fetch help," he said; "but you may help me a little yourself, if you will be so kind."

"Yes, sir."

"You have not an umbrella that I can use as a stick?"

"No."

"Try to get hold of my horse's bridle and lead him to me: you are not afraid?"

I should have been afraid to touch a horse when alone, but when told to do it, I was disposed to obey. I put down my muff on the stile, and went up to the tall steed; I endeavoured to catch the bridle, but it was a spirited thing, and would not let me come near its head; I made effort on effort, though in vain: meantime, I was mortally afraid of its trampling forefeet. The traveller waited and watched for some time, and at last he laughed.

"I see," he said, "the mountain will never be brought to Mahomet, so all you can do is to aid Mahomet to go to the mountain; I must beg of you to come here."

I came. "Excuse me," he continued, "necessity compels me to make you useful." He laid a heavy hand on my shoulder, and leaning on me with some stress, limped to his horse. Having once caught the bridle, he mastered it directly, and sprang to his saddle; grimacing

grimly as he made the effort, for it wrenched his sprain.

"Now," said he, releasing his under lip from a hard bite, "just hand me my whip; it lies there under the hedge."

I sought it and found it.

"Thank you; now make haste with the letter to Hay, and return as fast as you can."

A touch of a spurred heel made his horse first start and rear, and then bound away; the dog rushed in his traces: all three vanished,

> "Like heath that, in the wilderness,
> The wild wind whirls away."

I took up my muff and walked on. The incident had occurred and was gone for me: it *was* an incident of no moment, no romance, no interest, in a sense; yet it marked with change one single hour of a <u>monotonous</u> life. My help had been needed and claimed; I had given it: I was pleased to have done something; trivial, transitory though the deed was, it was yet an active thing, and I was weary of an existence all passive. The new face, too, was like a new picture introduced to the gallery of memory; and it was dissimilar to all the others hanging there: firstly, because it was masculine; and, secondly, because it was dark, strong, and stern. I had it still before me when I entered Hay, and slipped the letter into the post-office; I saw it as I walked fast down hill all the way home. When I came to the stile, I stopped a minute, looked round and listened, with an idea that a horse's hoofs might ring on the causeway again, and that a rider in a cloak, and a Gytrash-like Newfoundland dog, might be again apparent: I saw only the hedge and a pollard willow before me, rising up still and straight to meet the moonbeams; I heard only the faintest waft of wind roaming fitful among the trees round Thornfield, a mile dis-

---

11. **raiment.** Garments

en • deav • our (in dēˊ vər) v., attempt to achieve through strong effort
mo • not • o • nous (mə näˊ tə nəs) adj., repetitiously dull

tant; and when I glanced down in the direction of the murmur, my eye, traversing the hallfront, caught a light kindling in a window: it reminded me that I was late, and I hurried on.

I did not like re-entering Thornfield. To pass its threshold was to return to <u>stagnation</u>; to cross the silent hall, to ascend the darksome staircase, to seek my own lonely little room, and then to meet tranquil Mrs. Fairfax, and spend the long winter evening with her, and her only, was to quell wholly the faint excitement wakened by my walk,—to slip again over my faculties the viewless fetters of an uniform and too still existence; of an existence whose very privileges of security and ease I was becoming incapable of appreciating. What good it would have done me at that time to have been tossed in the storms of an uncertain struggling life, and to have been taught by rough and bitter experience to long for the calm amidst which I now repined! Yes, just as much good as it would do a man tired of sitting still in a "too easy chair" to take a long walk: and

just as natural was the wish to stir, under my circumstances, as it would be under his.

. . .

I hastened to Mrs. Fairfax's room: there was a fire there too, but no candle, and no Mrs. Fairfax. Instead, all alone, sitting upright on the rug, and gazing with gravity at the blaze, I beheld a great black and white long-haired dog, just like the Gytrash of the lane. It was so like it that I went forward and said,—

"Pilot," and the thing got up and came to me and snuffed me. I caressed him, and he wagged his great tail: but he looked an eerie creature to be alone with, and I could not tell whence he had come. I rang the bell, for I wanted a candle; and I wanted, too, to get an account of this visitant. Leah entered.

"What dog is this?"

"He came with master."

"With whom?"

"With master—Mr. Rochester—he is just arrived."

"Indeed! and is Mrs. Fairfax with him?"

"Yes, and Miss Adela; they are in the dining-room, and John is gone for a surgeon: for master has had an accident; his horse fell and his ankle is sprained."

"Did the horse fall in Hay Lane?"

"Yes, coming down the hill; it slipped on some ice."

"Ah! Bring me a candle, will you, Leah?"

Leah brought it; she entered, followed by Mrs. Fairfax, who repeated the news; adding that Mr. Carter the surgeon was come, and was now with Mr. Rochester: then she hurried out to give orders about tea, and I went upstairs to take off my things. ❖

> **stag • na • tion** (stag nā´ shən) *n.*, state of no progress or development

---

MIRRORS & WINDOWS

After helping Rochester, Jane says she feels good because she has been useful. Why is it important for people to feel productive? Why does it make them feel good?

Refer to Text ▶ ▶ ▶ ▶ ▶   **Reason with Text**

1a. What is Jane Eyre's career?

1b. How does Jane Eyre describe Adèle? What can you infer about Jane Eyre's attitude toward her charge based on her description?

Understand
Find meaning

2a. List the beliefs of the type of reader Jane says will find her language "cool."

2b. Explain how Jane's beliefs differ from those listed. Is she proud of this difference? What does this suggest about her character?

Apply
Use information

3a. Identify the story that Jane remembers when she hears the clatter of an approaching horse on her way to the village.

3b. Analyze the effect this memory has on the mood of the story. How does it create tension and suspense?

Analyze
Take things apart

4a. What reasons does Jane give for being reluctant to return to Thornfield?

4b. Compare and contrast her reactions to the encounter with Mr. Rochester and her experience at Thornfield. What do these reactions reveal about Jane?

Evaluate
Make judgments

5a. Describe Jane's initial meeting with Mr. Rochester.

5b. Suggest how meeting under different circumstances would have changed each character's perception of the other.

Create
Bring ideas together

Analyze Literature

Narrator and Tone

Identify the narrator, and determine whether he or she is omniscient or limited in knowledge. How does this affect your reading of the excerpt and your understanding of the events?

Describe the narrator's tone. How does it affect your reading of the novel? Provide specific examples from the text to support your answer.

Extend the Text

Writing Options

Creative Writing Imagine that you are Mr. Rochester and you have just had an accident with your horse. Write a one-paragraph description of the incident on top of the hill from Mr. Rochester's point of view. Recall what you know about his personality from Jane's account, and incorporate his voice into your description.

Expository Writing This excerpt reveals that Jane is a governess for a wealthy businessman she meets unknowingly one day. Write an essay analyzing the character of Jane. Cite evidence of her character from the excerpt.

Critical Literacy

Analyze Film Adaptations You have been asked to help create an exhibit called "*Jane Eyre* in Modern Society" for a local museum. Research film adaptations of *Jane Eyre* (such as the 2006 television miniseries directed

by Susanna White and produced by the British Broadcasting Company). Write a paragraph analyzing each adaptation. Evaluate how the dialogue, set design, costumes, sound effects, and other dramatic elements reflect the purpose of the adaptation and affect the intended audience, as well as how closely the director followed the original text. Discuss any biases you discover in the director's interpretation. Compile your work in a scrapbook, including photos and other visual elements.

Collaborative Learning

Perform a Scene Jane says that if Mr. Rochester had been handsome and heroic, she probably would not have had the courage to help him. With several classmates, role-play a scene in which Mr. Rochester is a young and dashing man. How does Jane react to the situation? What evidence from the text supports your group's interpretation?

 Go to **www.mirrorsandwindows.com** for more.

Understand the Concept

An **appositive** is a noun or noun phrase that is placed next to or near another noun to identify it or add information about it. If the information in an appositive specifically identifies the noun that precedes it, then the appositive is **essential** (or *restrictive*) and is not set off with commas. In the following example, the proper noun *Charlotte Brontë* specifically identifies the noun phrase *British writer:*

> **EXAMPLE**
>
> This selection was written by British writer *Charlotte Brontë*.

If the information in the appositive does not specifically identify the noun that precedes it, then the appositive is **nonessential** (or *nonrestrictive*) and is set off with commas. In the following example, *a British writer* could describe any number of writers, not just Charlotte Brontë:

> **EXAMPLE**
>
> This selection was written by Charlotte Brontë, *a British writer.*

An **appositive phrase** is a group of words that includes an appositive and the words that modify it, such as adjectives and prepositional phrases. The group of words adds information about the noun it modifies. In the next example, the appositive phrase *who was born in the Yorkshire district of northern England* gives further information about the proper noun *Brontë:*

> **EXAMPLE**
>
> Brontë, *who was born in the Yorkshire district of northern England,* was educated at home.

Apply the Skill

Identify Appositives

For each of the following sentences from *Jane Eyre,* identify the appositive or appositive phrases. Then identify the noun the appositive identifies or renames.

1. The other members of the household, viz., John and his wife, Leah the housemaid, and Sophie the French nurse, were decent people; but in no respect remarkable.
2. The man, the human being, broke the spell at once.
3. With master—Mr. Rochester—he is just arrived.
4. Leah brought it [the candle]; she entered, followed by Mrs. Fairfax, who repeated the news; adding that Mr. Carter the surgeon was come.

Correct the Punctuation with Appositives

Copy the following paragraph onto a separate sheet of paper. Underline all the appositive and appositive phrases. Then insert commas where they are needed to set off nonessential information.

> Jane Eyre a poor orphan is the main character of Charlotte Brontë's novel by the same name. Jane's wealthy aunt a despicable woman attempts to raise Jane but shuttles her off to Lowood a boarding school when she tires of the responsibility. Jane finds employment as a governess for a wealthy businessman Edward Rochester. Soon after, she falls in love with Rochester her employer and discovers a startling secret that jeopardizes their relationship.

Use Appositives in Your Writing

Jane's serendipitous encounter with Mr. Rochester after his riding accident changes her life. Write a story in which a chance meeting with someone leads to new discoveries or adventures. After drafting your story, look for appositives in your writing. Which type of appositive did you use more often: essential (restrictive) or nonessential (nonrestrictive)? Check to make sure you used commas to set off nonrestrictive appositives but not restrictive appositives.

from Madame Bovary

by Gustave Flaubert

Chapter 8

Gustave Flaubert (1821–1880), who was born in Rouen, France, showed an interest in literature at an early age, particularly the work of Romantic novelists. He was a meticulous writer who sometimes spent days trying to find the precise word or formulate a flawless sentence. He spent five years writing his best-known work, *Madame Bovary,* a novel about a young married woman, who, stirred by romantic ideals and dissatisfaction with marriage, rebels against her middle-class lifestyle by having love affairs and trying to live extravagantly.

When *Madame Bovary* was first published as a magazine serial in 1856, the public was shocked by its subject matter. Flaubert was brought to trial for publishing a work deemed morally offensive. He defended himself by arguing that the tragic results of Emma Bovary's extravagance would serve as a lesson in using good moral judgment. Flaubert was acquitted in 1857, and the story was released in book form that same year.

The château, a modern building in Italian style, with two projecting wings and three flights of steps, lay at the foot of an immense greensward, on which some cows were grazing among groups of large trees set out at regular intervals, while large beds of arbutus, rhododendron, syringas, and guelder roses bulged out their irregular clusters of green along the curve of the gravel path. A river flowed under a bridge; through the mist one could distinguish buildings with thatched roofs scattered over the field bordered by two gently sloping well-timbered hillocks, and in the background amid the trees rose in two parallel lines the coach houses and stables, all that was left of the ruined old château.

Charles's dogcart pulled up before the middle flight of steps; servants appeared; the Marquis came forward, and offering his arm to the doctor's wife, conducted her to the vestibule.

It was paved with marble slabs, was very lofty, and the sound of footsteps and that of voices reechoed through it as in a church. Opposite rose a straight staircase, and on the left a gallery overlooking the garden led to the billiard room, through whose door one could hear the click of the ivory balls. As she crossed it to go to the drawing room, Emma saw standing around the table men with grave faces, their chins resting on high cravats.[1] They all wore orders, and smiled silently as they made their strokes. On the dark wainscoting of the walls large gold frames bore at the bottom names written in black letters. She read: "Jean-Antoine

---

1. **cravats.** Neckerchiefs or scarves; neckties

The Marquis opened the drawing-room door; one of the ladies, the Marchioness herself, came to meet Emma. She made her sit down by her on an ottoman, and began talking to her as amicably[3] as if she had known her a long time. She was a woman of about forty, with fine shoulders, a hook nose, a drawling voice, and on this evening she wore over her brown hair a simple guipure fichu[4] that fell in a point at the back. A fair young woman was by her side in a high-backed chair, and gentlemen with flowers in their buttonholes were talking to ladies around the fire.

At seven dinner was served. The men, who were in the majority, sat down at the first table in the vestibule; the ladies at the second in the dining room with the Marquis and Marchioness.

Emma, on entering, felt herself wrapped around by the warm air, a blending of the perfume of flowers and of the fine linen, of the fumes of the viands, and the odor of the truffles. The silver dish covers reflected the lighted wax candles in the candelabra, the cut crystal covered with light steam reflected from one to the other pale rays; bouquets were placed in a row the whole length of the table; and in the large bordered plates each napkin, arranged after the fashion of a bishop's miter,[5] held between its two gaping folds a small oval-shaped roll. The red claws of lobsters hung over the dishes; rich fruit in open baskets was piled up on moss; there were quails in their plumage; smoke was rising; and in silk stockings, knee breeches, white cravat, and frilled shirt, the steward, grave as a judge, offering ready carved dishes between the shoulders of the guests, with a touch of the spoon gave you the piece chosen. On the large stove of porcelain inlaid with copper baguettes the statue of a woman, draped to the chin, gazed motionless on the room full of life.

d'Andervilliers d'Yverbonville, Count de la Vaubyessard and Baron de la Fresnaye, killed at the battle of Coutras on the 20th of October 1587." And on another: "Jean-Antoine-Henri-Guy d'Andervilliers de la Vaubyessard, Admiral of France and Chevalier of the Order of St. Michael, wounded at the battle of the Hougue-Saint-Vaast on the 29th of May 1692; died at Vaubyessard on the 23rd of January 1693." One could hardly make out those that followed, for the light of the lamps lowered over the green cloth threw a dim shadow around the room. Burnishing the horizontal pictures, it broke up against these in delicate lines where there were cracks in the varnish and from all these great black squares framed in with gold stood out here and there some lighter portion of the painting—a pale brow, two eyes that looked at you, perukes[2] flowing over and powdering red-coated shoulders, or the buckle of a garter above a well-rounded calf.

2. **perukes.** Powdered wigs worn by men in the 1600s and 1700s
3. **amicably.** In a friendly manner
4. **guipure fichu.** Lace cape worn with the ends crossed or fastened in front
5. **miter.** Headdress; tall ornamental cap with peaks in front and back

Madame Bovary noticed that many ladies had not put their gloves in their glasses.

But at the upper end of the table, alone among all these women, bent over his full plate, and his napkin tied around his neck like a child, an old man sat eating, letting drops of gravy drip from his mouth. His eyes were bloodshot, and he wore a little queue[6] tied with a black ribbon. He was the Marquis' father-in-law, the old Duke de Laverdière, once on a time favorite of the Count d'Artois, in the days of the Vaudreuil hunting parties at the Marquis de Conflans', and had been, it was said, the lover of Queen Marie Antoinette, between Monsieur de Coigny and Monsieur de Lauzun. He had lived a life of noisy debauch, full of duels, bets, elopements; he had squandered his fortune and frightened all his family. A servant behind his chair named aloud to him in his ear the dishes that he pointed to stammering, and constantly Emma's eyes turned involuntarily to this old man with hanging lips, as to something extraordinary. He had lived at court and slept in the bed of queens!

Bent over his full plate, and his napkin tied around his neck like a child, an old man sat eating, letting drops of gravy drip from his mouth.

Iced champagne was poured out. Emma shivered all over as she felt it cold in her mouth. She had never seen pomegranates nor tasted pineapples. The powdered sugar even seemed to her whiter and finer than elsewhere.

The ladies afterwards went to their rooms to prepare for the ball.

Emma made her toilet with the fastidious care of an actress on her début. She did her hair according to the directions of the hairdresser, and put on the barège dress spread out upon the bed. Charles's trousers were tight across the belly.

"My trouser-straps will be rather awkward for dancing," he said.

"Dancing?" repeated Emma.

"Yes!"

"Why, you must be mad! They would make fun of you; keep your place. Besides, it is more becoming for a doctor," she added.

Charles was silent. He walked up and down waiting for Emma to finish dressing.

He saw her from behind in the glass between two lights. Her black eyes seemed blacker than ever. Her hair, undulating[7] towards the ears, shone with a blue luster; a rose in her chignon[8] trembled on its mobile stalk, with artificial dewdrops on the tip of the leaves. She wore a gown of pale saffron trimmed with three bouquets of pompon roses mixed with green.

Charles came and kissed her on her shoulder.

"Let me alone!" she said; "you are tumbling me."

One could hear the flourish of the violin and the notes of a horn. She went downstairs restraining herself from running.

Dancing had begun. Guests were arriving. There was some crushing. She sat down on a form near the door.

The quadrille[9] over, the floor was occupied by groups of men standing up and talking and servants in livery bearing large trays. Along the line of seated women painted fans were fluttering, bouquets half hid smiling faces, and gold stoppered scent bottles were turned in partly closed hands, whose white gloves outlined the nails and tightened on the flesh at the wrists. Lace trimmings, diamond brooches, medallion bracelets trembled on bodices, gleamed on breasts, clinked on bare arms. The hair, well smoothed over the temples and knotted at the nape, bore crowns, or bunches, or sprays of myosotis, jasmine, pomegranate blossoms, ears of corn, and cornflowers. Calmly seated in their

---

6. **queue.** Braid of hair at the back of the head
7. **undulating.** Moving in a wavy or flowing manner
8. **chignon.** Knot or coil of hair worn at the back of the neck
9. **quadrille.** Dance performed by four couples

places, mothers with forbidding countenances were wearing red turbans.

Emma's heart beat rather faster when, her partner holding her by the tips of the fingers, she took her place in a line with the dancers, and waited for the first note to start. But her emotion soon vanished, and, swaying to the rhythm of the orchestra, she glided forward with slight movements of the neck. A smile rose to her lips at certain delicate phrases of the violin, that sometimes played alone while the other instruments were silent; one could hear the clear clink of the louis d'or that were being thrown down upon the card tables in the next room; then all struck in again, the cornet-a-piston uttered its sonorous note, feet marked time, skirts swelled and rustled, hands touched and parted; the same eyes falling before you met yours again.

A few men (some fifteen or so) of twenty-five to forty, scattered here and there among the dancers or talking at the doorways, distinguished themselves from the crowd by a certain air of breeding, whatever their differences in age, dress or face.

Their clothes, better made, seemed of finer cloth, and their hair, brought forward in curls towards the temples, glossy with more delicate pomades.[10] They had the complexion of wealth—that clear complexion that is heightened by the pallor of porcelain, the shimmer of satin, the veneer of old furniture, and that an ordered regimen of exquisite nurture main-

tains at its best. Their necks moved easily in their low cravats, their long whiskers fell over their turned-down collars, they wiped their lips upon handkerchiefs with embroidered initials that gave forth a subtle perfume. Those who were beginning to grow old had an air of youth, while there was something mature in the faces of the young. In their unconcerned looks was the calm of passions daily satiated,[11] and through all their gentleness of manner pierced that peculiar brutality, the result of a command of half easy things, in which force is exercised and vanity amused—the management of thoroughbred horses and the society of loose women.

A few steps from Emma a gentleman in a blue coat was talking of Italy with a pale young woman wearing a parure of pearls.

They were praising the breadth of the columns of St. Peter's, Tivoli, Vesuvius, Castellamare, and Cassines, the roses of Genoa, the Coliseum by moonlight. With her other ear Emma was listening to a conversation full of words she did not understand. A circle gathered round a very young man who the week before had beaten "Miss Arabella" and "Romolus," and won two thousand louis jumping a ditch in England. One complained that his race horses were growing fat; another of the printers' errors that had disfigured the name of his horse.

The atmosphere of the ball was heavy; the lamps were growing dim. Guests were flocking to the billiard room. A servant got upon a chair and broke the window panes. At the crash of the glass Madame Bovary turned her head and saw in the garden the faces of peasants pressed against the window looking in at them. Then the memory of the Bertaux came back to her. She saw the farm again, the muddy pond, her father in a blouse under the apple trees, and she saw herself again as formerly, skimming with her finger the cream off the milk pans in the dairy. But in the refulgence[12] of the present hour her past life, so distinct until then, faded

---

10. **pomades.** Perfumed ointments for the hair
11. **satiated.** Satisfied fully or to excess
12. **refulgence.** Brilliance

away completely, and she almost doubted having lived it. She was there; beyond the ball was only shadow overspreading all the rest. . . .

After supper, where were plenty of Spanish and Rhine wines, soups *à la bisque* and *au lait d'amandes,* puddings *à la Trafalgar,* and all sorts of cold meats with jellies that trembled in the dishes, the carriages one after the other began to drive off. Raising the corners of the muslin[13] curtain, one could see the light of their lanterns glimmering through the darkness. The seats began to empty, some card players were still left; the musicians were cooling the tips of their fingers on their tongues. Charles was half asleep, his back propped against a door.

At three o'clock the cotillion[14] began. Emma did not know how to waltz. Everyone was waltzing, Mademoiselle d'Andervilliers herself and the Marquis; only the guests staying at the castle were still there, about a dozen persons.

One of the waltzers, however, who was familiarly called Viscount, and whose low cut waist-coat seemed molded to his chest, came a second time to ask Madame Bovary to dance, assuring her that he would guide her, and that she would get through it very well.

They began slowly, then went more rapidly. They turned; all around them was turning—the lamps, the furniture, the wainscoting, the floor, like a disc on a pivot. On passing near the doors the bottom of Emma's dress caught against his trousers. Their legs commingled; he looked down at her; she raised her eyes to his. A torpor[15] seized her; she stopped. They started again, and with a more rapid movement; the Viscount, dragging her along, disappeared with her to the end of the gallery, where, panting, she almost fell, and for a moment rested her head upon his breast. And then, still turning, but more slowly, he guided her back to her seat. She leaned back against the wall and covered her eyes with her hands.

When she opened them again, in the middle of the drawing-room three waltzers were kneeling before a lady sitting on a stool. She chose the Viscount, and the violin struck up once more.

Everyone looked at them. They passed and repassed, she with rigid body, her chin bent downward, and he always in the same pose, his figure curved, his elbow rounded, his chin thrown forward. That woman knew how to waltz! They kept up a long time, and tired out all the others.

Then they talked a few moments longer, and after the good nights, or rather good mornings, the guests of the château retired to bed.

Charles dragged himself up by the balusters. His "knees were going up into his body." He had spent five consecutive hours standing bolt upright at the card tables, watching them play whist, without understanding anything about it, and it was with a deep sigh of relief that he pulled off his boots.

Emma threw a shawl over her shoulders, opened the window, and leaned out.

The night was dark; some drops of rain were falling. She breathed in the damp wind that refreshed her eyelids. The music of the ball was still murmuring in her ears, and she tried to keep herself awake in order to prolong the illusion of this luxurious life that she would soon have to give up.

Day began to break. She looked long at the windows of the château, trying to guess which were the rooms of all those she had noticed the evening before. She would fain[16] have known their lives, have penetrated, blended with them. But she was shivering with cold. She undressed, and cowered down between the sheets against Charles, who was asleep.

There were a great many people to luncheon. The repast lasted ten minutes; no liquors were served, which astonished the doctor. Next, Mademoiselle d'Andervilliers collected some pieces of roll in a small basket to take them to the swans on the ornamental waters, and they went to walk in the hot houses, where strange plants, bristling with

---

13. **muslin.** Strong and sheer cotton cloth of plain weave
14. **cotillion.** Formal ball
15. **torpor.** Extreme sluggishness; lethargy
16. **fain.** With pleasure; gladly

Young Woman in Evening Dress, 1879. Berthe Morisot.
Musée d'Orsay, Paris, France.

hairs, rose in pyramids under hanging vases, where, as from overfilled nests of serpents, fell long green cords interlacing. The orangery, which was at the other end, led by a covered way to the outhouses of the château. The Marquis, to amuse the young woman, took her to see the stables. Above the basketshaped racks porcelain slabs bore the names of the horses in black letters. Each animal in its stall whisked its tail when anyone went near and said "Tchk! tchk!" The boards of the harness room shone like the flooring of a drawing-room. . . .

Charles, meanwhile, went to ask a groom to put his horse to. The dogcart was brought to the foot of the steps, and all the parcels being crammed in, the Bovarys paid their respects to the Marquis and Marchioness and set out again for Tostes.

Emma watched the turning wheels in silence. Charles, on the extreme edge of the seat, held the reins with his two arms wide apart, and the little horse ambled along in the shafts that were too big for him. The loose reins hanging over his crupper[17] were wet with foam, and the box fastened on behind the chaise gave great regular bumps against it.

They were on the heights of Thibourville when suddenly some horsemen with cigars between their lips passed laughing. Emma thought she recognized the Viscount, turned back, and caught on the horizon only the movement of the heads rising or falling with the unequal cadence of the trot or gallop.

A mile farther on they had to stop to mend with some string the traces that had broken.

But Charles, giving a last look to the harness, saw something on the ground between his horse's legs, and he picked up a cigar case with a green silk border and emblazoned in the center like the door of a carriage.

"There are even two cigars in it," said he; "they'll do for this evening after dinner."

"Why, do you smoke?" she asked.

"Sometimes, when I get a chance."

He put his find in his pocket and whipped up the nag.

When they reached home the dinner was not ready. Madame lost her temper. Natasie answered rudely.

"Leave the room!" said Emma. "You are forgetting yourself. I give you warning."

For dinner there was onion soup and a piece of veal with sorrel. Charles, seated opposite Emma, rubbed his hands gleefully.

"How good it is to be at home again!"

Natasie could be heard crying. He was rather fond of the poor girl. She had formerly, during the wearisome time of his widowhood, kept him company many an evening. She had been his first patient, his oldest acquaintance in the place.

---

17. **crupper.** Part of a padded leather saddle-strap passed around the base of a horse's tail to keep the saddle from moving forward

"Have you given her warning for good?" he asked at last.

"Yes. Who is to prevent me?" she replied.

Then they warmed themselves in the kitchen while their room was being made ready. Charles began to smoke. He smoked with lips protruding, spitting every moment, recoiling at every puff.

"You'll make yourself ill," she said scornfully.

He put down his cigar and ran to swallow a glass of cold water at the pump. Emma seizing hold of the cigar case threw it quickly to the back of the cupboard.

The next day was a long one. She walked about her little garden, up and down the same walks, stopping before the beds, before the espalier,[18] before the plaster curate, looking with amazement at all these things of once-on-a-time that she knew so well. How far off the ball seemed already! What was it that thus set so far asunder the morning of the day before yesterday and the evening of today? Her jour-ney to Vaubyessard had made a hole in her life, like one of those great crevasses that a storm will sometimes make in one night in mountains. Still she was resigned. She devoutly put away in her drawers her beautiful dress, down to the satin shoes whose soles were yellowed with the slippery wax of the dancing floor. Her heart was like these. In its friction against wealth something had come over it that could not be effaced.[19]

The memory of this ball, then, became an occupation for Emma. Whenever the Wednesday came round she said to herself as she awoke, "Ah! I was there a week—a fortnight—three weeks ago." And little by little the faces grew confused in her remembrance. She forgot the tune of the quadrilles; she no longer saw the liveries and appointments so distinctly; some details escaped her, but the regret remained with her. ❖

18. **espalier.** Lattice or trellis on which shrubs are trained to grow flat
19. **effaced.** Eliminated; vanished

MIRRORS & WINDOWS

A common saying tells us that "Money can't buy happiness." Do you agree or disagree?

Refer and Reason

1. Describe Emma's reaction upon seeing the Marquis' father-in-law, the Duke de Laverdière, at the ball. What does her reaction suggest about her attitude toward prominent people in society? What does this suggest about her character?

2. Describe Emma's treatment of Charles at the ball and at home. What can you infer about Emma's feelings for her husband, based on her actions?

3. What is Charles doing just before the ball ends? What is the first thing Charles and Emma do when they return to the room? Critique the reactions of Charles and Emma at the end of the dance and at home. What do these reactions reveal about their individual perspectives on their lives and their relationship?

Writing Options

1. Choose a character, other than Emma, from the selection. Write a diary entry from that character's point of view, describing his or her experience at the ball or his or her interactions with Emma after the ball.

2. Write a character sketch of Emma Bovary. Pay particular attention to what her interactions with the other characters reveal about her personality. Be sure to include specific examples and other evidence from the text to support your description.

 Go to **www.mirrorsandwindows.com** for more.

from
The Mayor of Casterbridge

by Thomas Hardy

"I don't think I can ever meet Mr Henchard.
He is not how I thought he would be—he overpowers me!"

Mother Anthony's Tavern, 1866. Pierre Auguste Renoir.
Nationalmuseum, Stockholm, Sweden.

Chapter 3

The highroad into the village of Weydon-Priors was again carpeted with dust. The trees had put on as of yore their aspect of dingy green, and where the Henchard family of three had once walked along, two persons not unconnected with the family walked now.

The scene in its broad aspect had so much of its previous character, even to the voices and rattle from the neighbouring village down, that it might for that matter have been the afternoon following the previously recorded episode. Change was only to be observed in details; but here it was obvious that a long procession of years had passed by. One of the two who walked the road was she who had figured as the young wife of Henchard on the previous occasion; now her face had lost much of its rotundity; her skin had undergone a textural change; and though her hair had not lost colour it was considerably thinner than heretofore. She was dressed in the mourning clothes of a widow. Her companion, also in black, appeared as a well-formed young woman about eighteen, completely possessed of that ephemeral[1] precious essence youth, which is itself beauty, irrespective of complexion or contour.

A glance was sufficient to inform the eye that this was Susan Henchard's grown-up daughter. While life's middle summer had set its hardening mark on the mother's face, her

---

1. **ephemeral.** Short lived; transitory

former spring-like specialities were transferred so dexterously by Time to the second figure, her child, that the absence of certain facts within her mother's knowledge from the girl's mind would have seemed for the moment, to one reflecting on those facts, to be a curious imperfection in Nature's powers of continuity.

> While life's middle summer had set its hardening mark on the mother's face, her former spring-like specialities were transferred so dexterously by Time to the second figure, her child.

They walked with joined hands, and it could be perceived that this was the act of simple affection. The daughter carried in her outer hand a withy[2] basket of old-fashioned make; the mother a blue bundle, which contrasted oddly with her black stuff gown.

Reaching the outskirts of the village they pursued the same track as formerly, and ascended to the fair. Here, too it was evident that the years had told. Certain mechanical improvements might have been noticed in the round-abouts and high-fliers, machines for testing rustic strength and weight, and in the erections devoted to shooting for nuts. But the real business of the fair had considerably dwindled. The new periodical great markets of neighbouring towns were beginning to interfere seriously with the trade carried on here for centuries. The pens for sheep, the tie-ropes for horses, were about half as long as they had been. The stalls of tailors, hosiers, coopers, linen-drapers, and other such trades had almost disappeared, and the vehicles were far less numerous. The mother and daughter threaded the crowd for some little distance, and then stood still.

"Why did we hinder our time by coming in here? I thought you wished to get onward?" said the maiden.

"Yes, my dear Elizabeth-Jane," explained the other. "But I had a fancy for looking up here."

"Why?"

"It was here I first met with Newson—on such a day as this."

"First met with father here? Yes, you have told me so before. And now he's drowned and gone from us!" As she spoke the girl drew a card from her pocket and looked at it with a sigh. It was edged with black, and inscribed within a design resembling a mural tablet were the words, "In affectionate memory of Richard Newson, mariner, who was unfortunately lost at sea, in the month of November 184–, aged forty-one years."

"And it was here," continued her mother, with more hesitation, "that I last saw the relation we are going to look for—Mr Michael Henchard."

"What is his exact kin to us, mother? I have never clearly had it told me."

"He is, or was—for he may be dead—a connection by marriage," said her mother deliberately.

"That's exactly what you have said a score[3] of times before!" replied the young woman, looking about her inattentively. "He's not a near relation, I suppose?"

"Not by any means."

"He was a hay-trusser, wasn't he, when you last heard of him?"

"He was."

"I suppose he never knew me?" the girl innocently continued.

Mrs Henchard paused for a moment, and answered uneasily, "Of course not, Elizabeth-Jane. But come this way." She moved on to another part of the field.

"It is not much use inquiring here for anybody, I should think," the daughter observed, as she gazed round about. "People at fairs change like the leaves of trees; and I daresay

---

2. **withy.** Long, flexible twigs
3. **score.** Large number

dex • ter • ous (dek′ st[ə] rəs) *adj.,* skillful
as • cend (ə send′) *v.,* go or move upward

you are the only one here to-day who was here all those years ago."

"I am not so sure of that," said Mrs Newson, as she now called herself, keenly eyeing something under a green bank a little way off. "See there."

The daughter looked in the direction signified. The object pointed out was a tripod of sticks stuck into the earth; from which hung a three-legged crock, kept hot by a smouldering wood fire beneath. Over the pot stooped an old woman <u>haggard</u>, wrinkled, and almost in rags. She stirred the contents of the pot with a large spoon, and occasionally croaked in a broken voice, "Good furmity[4] sold here!"

It was indeed the former mistress of the furmity tent—once thriving, cleanly, white-aproned, and chinking with money—now tentless, dirty, owning no tables or benches, and having scarce any customers except two small whity-brown boys, who came up and asked for "A ha'p'orth, please—good measure," which she served in a couple of chipped yellow basins of commonest clay.

"She was here at that time," resumed Mrs Newson, making a step as if to draw nearer.

"Don't speak to her—it isn't respectable!" urged the other.

> "Don't speak to her—it isn't respectable!" urged the other.

"I will just say a word—you, Elizabeth-Jane, can stay here."

The girl was not loth,[5] and turned to some stalls of coloured prints while her mother went forward. The old woman begged for the latter's custom as soon as she saw her, and responded to Mrs Henchard-Newson's request for a penny-worth with more <u>alacrity</u> than she had shown in selling six-pennyworths in her younger days. . . .

Her customer . . . pretended to eat a little of the furmity with the leaden spoon offered, and as she did so said blandly to the hag, "You've seen better days?"

"Ah, ma'am—well ye may say it!" responded the old woman, opening the sluices[6] of her heart forthwith. "I've stood in this fairground, maid, wife, and widow, these nine-and-thirty years, and in that time have known what it was to do business with the richest stomachs in the land! Ma'am you'd hardly believe that I was once the owner of a great pavilion-tent that was the attraction of the fair. Nobody could come, nobody could go, without having a dish of Mrs Goodenough's furmity. I knew the clergy's taste, the dandy gent's taste; I knew the town's taste, the country's taste. I even knowed the taste of the coarse shameless females. But Lord's my life—the world's no memory; straightforward dealings don't bring profit—'tis the sly and the underhand that get on in these times!"

Mrs Newson glanced round—her daughter was still bending over the distant stalls. "Can you call to mind," she said cautiously to the old woman, "the sale of a wife by her husband in your tent eighteen years ago to-day?"

The hag reflected, and half shook her head. "If it had been a big thing I should have minded it in a moment," she said. "I can mind every serious fight o' married parties, every murder, every manslaughter, even every pocket-picking—leastwise large ones—that 't has been my lot to witness. But a selling? Was it done quiet-like?"

"Well, yes. I think so."

The furmity woman half shook her head again. "And yet," she said, "I do. At any rate, I can mind a man doing something o' the sort—a man in a cord jacket, with a basket of tools; but, Lord bless ye, we don't gi'e it headroom, we don't, such as that. The only reason why I can mind the man is that he came back here to the

---

4. **furmity.** Type of porridge made from wheat
5. **loth.** Reluctant or unwilling
6. **sluices.** Valves

hag • gard (ha´ gərd) *adj.*, worn, pale, and exhausted
alac • ri • ty (ə la´ krə tē) *n.*, eagerness

Chapter 4

Henchard's wife acted for the best, but she had involved herself in difficulties. A hundred times she had been upon the point of telling her daughter Elizabeth-Jane the true story of her life, the tragical crisis of which had been the transaction at Weydon Fair, when she was not much older than the girl now beside her. But she had refrained. An innocent maiden had thus grown up in the belief that the relations between the <u>genial</u> sailor and her mother were the ordinary ones that they had always appeared to be. The risk of endangering a child's strong affection by disturbing ideas which had grown with her growth was to Mrs Henchard too fearful a thing to contemplate. It had seemed, indeed folly to think of making Elizabeth-Jane wise. . . .

The history of Susan Henchard's adventures in the interim can be told in two or three sentences. Absolutely helpless she had been taken off to Canada where they had lived several years without any great worldly success, though she worked as hard as any woman could to keep their cottage cheerful and well-provided. When Elizabeth-Jane was about twelve years old the three returned to England, and settled at Falmouth, where Newson made a living for a few years as boatman and general handy shoreman.

He then engaged in the Newfoundland trade, and it was during this period that Susan had an

next year's fair, and told me quite private-like that if a woman ever asked for him I was to say he had gone to—where?—Casterbridge—yes—to Casterbridge, said he. But, Lord's my life, I shouldn't ha' thought of it again!"

Mrs Newson would have rewarded the old woman as far as her small means afforded had she not discreetly borne in mind that it was by that <u>unscrupulous</u> person's liquor her husband had been degraded. She briefly thanked her informant, and rejoined Elizabeth, who greeted her with, "Mother, do let's get on—it was hardly respectable for you to buy refreshments there. I see none but the lowest do."

"I have learned what I wanted, however," said her mother quietly. "The last time our relative visited this fair he said he was living at Casterbridge. It is a long, long way from here, and it was many years ago that he said it, but there I think we'll go."

With this they descended out of the fair, and went onward to the village, where they obtained a night's lodging.

---

un • scru • pu • lous (ən' skrü´ pyə ləs) *adj.*, unprincipled
ge • nial (jēn´ nē əl) *adj.*, friendly and pleasant

awakening. A friend to whom she confided her history ridiculed her grave acceptance of her position; and all was over with her peace of mind. When Newson came home at the end of one winter he saw that the <u>delusion</u> he had so carefully sustained had vanished for ever.

When Newson came home at the end of one winter he saw that the delusion he had so carefully sustained had vanished for ever.

There was then a time of sadness, in which she told him her doubts if she could live with him longer. Newson left home again on the New-foundland trade when the season came round. The vague news of his loss at sea a little later on solved a problem which had become torture to her meek conscience. She saw him no more.

Of Henchard they heard nothing. To the liege[7] subjects of Labour, the England of those days was a continent, and a mile a geographical degree. . . .

It was on a Friday evening, near the middle of September and just before dusk, that they reached the summit of a hill within a mile of the place they sought. There were high banked hedges to the coach-road here, and they mounted upon the green turf within, and sat down. The spot commanded a full view of the town and its environs.

"What an old-fashioned place it seems to be!" said Elizabeth-Jane, while her silent mother mused on other things than topography. "It is huddled all together; and it is shut in by a square wall of trees, like a plot of garden ground by a box-edging."

Its squareness was, indeed, the characteristic which most struck the eye in this antiquated borough, the borough of Casterbridge—at that time, recent as it was, untouched by the faint-est sprinkle of modernism. It was compact as a box of dominoes. It had no suburbs—in the ordinary sense. Country and town met at a mathematical line. . . .

Chapter 5

A few score yards brought them to the spot where the town band was now shaking the window-panes with the strains of "The Roast Beef of Old England."

The building before whose doors they had pitched their music-stands was the chief hotel in Casterbridge—namely, the King's Arms. A spacious bow-window projected into the street over the main portico, and from the open sashes came the babble of voices, the jingle of glasses, and the drawing of corks. The blinds, more-over, being left unclosed, the whole interior of this room could be surveyed from the top of a flight of stone steps to the road-waggon office opposite, for which reason a knot of idlers had gathered there.

"We might, perhaps, after all, make a few inquiries about—our relation Mr Henchard," whispered Mrs Newson who, since her entry into Casterbridge, had seemed strangely weak and agitated, "And this, I think, would be a good place for trying it—just to ask, you know, how he stands in the town—if he is here, as I think he must be. You, Elizabeth-Jane, had bet-ter be the one to do it. I'm too worn out to do anything—pull down your fall first."

She sat down upon the lowest step, and Elizabeth-Jane obeyed her directions and stood among the idlers.

"What's going on to-night?" asked the girl, after singling out an old man and standing by him long enough to acquire a neighbourly right of converse.

"Well, ye must be a stranger sure," said the old man, without taking his eyes from the window. "Why, 'tis a great public dinner of the gentle-people and such like leading volk—wi' the Mayor in the chair. As we plainer fellows bain't invited, they leave the winder-shutters

---

7. **liege.** Owing allegiance and services to a sovereign or lord

de • lu • sion (dē lü′ zhən) *n.*, false belief held in spite of invalidating evidence

open that we may get jist a sense o't out here. If you mount the steps you can see em. That's Mr Henchard, the Mayor, at the end of the table, a facing ye; and that's the Council men right and left. . . . Ah, lots of them when they begun life were no more than I be now!"

"Henchard!" said Elizabeth-Jane, surprised, but by no means suspecting the whole force of the revelation. She ascended to the top of the steps.

Her mother, though her head was bowed, had already caught from the inn-window tones that strangely riveted her attention, before the old man's words, "Mr Henchard, the Mayor," reached her ears. She arose, and stepped up to her daughter's side as soon as she could do so without showing exceptional eagerness.

The interior of the hotel dining-room was spread out before her, with its tables, and glass, and plate, and inmates. Facing the window, in the chair of dignity, sat a man about forty years of age; of heavy frame, large features, and commanding voice; his general build being rather coarse than compact. He had a rich complexion, which verged on <u>swarthiness</u>, a flashing black eye, and dark, bushy brows and hair. When he indulged in an occasional loud laugh at some remark among the guests, his large mouth parted so far back as to show to the rays of the chandelier a full score or more of the two-and-thirty sound white teeth that he obviously still could boast of.

That laugh was not encouraging to strangers, and hence it may have been well that it was rarely heard. Many theories might have been built upon it. It fell in well with conjectures of a temperament which would have no pity for weakness, but would be ready to yield ungrudging admiration to greatness and strength. Its producer's personal goodness, if he had any, would be of a very fitful cast—an occasional almost oppressive generosity rather than a mild and constant kindness.

Susan Henchard's husband—in law, at least—sat before them, matured in shape, stiffened in line, exaggerated in traits; disciplined, thought-marked—in a word, older. Elizabeth, <u>encumbered</u> with no recollections as her mother was, regarded him with nothing more than the keen curiosity and interest which the discovery of such unexpected social standing in the long-sought relative naturally begot. He was dressed in an old-fashioned evening suit, an expanse of frilled shirt showing on his broad breast; jewelled studs, and a heavy gold chain. Three glasses stood at his right hand; but, to his wife's surprise, the two for wine were empty, while the third, a tumbler, was half full of water.

Susan Henchard's husband—in law, at least—sat before them, matured in shape, stiffened in line, exaggerated in traits; disciplined, thought-marked—in a word, older.

When last she had seen him he was sitting in a corduroy jacket, fustian[8] waistcoat and breeches, and tanned leather leggings, with a basin of hot furmity before him. Time, the magician, had wrought much here. Watching him, and thus thinking of past days, she became so moved that she shrank back against the jamb of the waggon-office doorway to which the steps gave access, the shadow from it conveniently hiding her features. She forgot her daughter till a touch from Elizabeth-Jane aroused her. "Have you seen him, mother?" whispered the girl.

"Yes, yes," answered her companion hastily. "I have seen him, and it is enough for me! Now I only want to go—pass away—die."

"Why—O what?" She drew closer, and whispered in her mother's ear, "Does he seem to you not likely to befriend us? I thought he looked a generous man. What a gentleman he is, isn't he? and how his diamond studs shine!

---

8. **fustian.** Coarse, sturdy cloth of cotton and flax

swar • thy (swôr´ thē) *adj.,* having a dark color or complexion
en • cum • ber (in kum´ bər) *v.,* burden or weigh down

How strange that you should have said he might be in the stocks, or in the workhouse, or dead! Did ever anything go more by contraries! Why do you feel so afraid of him? I am not at all; I'll call upon him—he can but say he don't own such remote kin."

"I don't know at all—I can't tell what to set about. I feel so down."

"Don't be that, mother, now we have got here and all! Rest there where you be a little while—I will look on and find out more about him."

"I don't think I can ever meet Mr Henchard. He is not how I thought he would be—he overpowers me! I don't wish to see him any more."

"But wait a little time and consider."

Elizabeth-Jane had never been so much interested in anything in her life as in their present position, partly from the natural <u>elation</u> she felt at discovering herself akin to a coach; and she gazed again at the scene. The younger guests were talking and eating with animation; their elders were searching for titbits, and sniffing and grunting over their plates like sows nuzzling for acorns. Three drinks seemed to be sacred to the company—port, sherry, and rum; outside which old-established trinity few or no palates ranged.

A row of ancient rummers with ground figures on their sides, and each primed with a spoon, was now placed down the table, and these were promptly filled with grog at such high temperatures as to raise serious considerations for the articles exposed to its vapours. But Elizabeth-Jane noticed that, though this filling went on with great promptness up and down the table, nobody filled the Mayor's glass, who still drank large quantities of water from the tumbler behind the clump of crystal vessels intended for wine and spirits.

"They don't fill Mr Henchard's wineglasses," she ventured to say to her elbow acquaintance, the old man.

"Ah, no; don't ye know him to be the celebrated abstaining worthy of that name? He scorns all tempting liquors; never touches nothing. O yes, he've strong qualities that way. I have heard tell that he sware a gospel oath in bygone times, and has bode by it ever since. So they don't press him, knowing it would be unbecoming in the face of that: for yer gospel oath is a serious thing."

Another elderly man, hearing this discourse, now joined in by inquiring, "How much longer have he got to suffer from it, Solomon Longways?"

"Another two year, they say. I don't know the why and the wherefore of his fixing such a time, for 'a never has told anybody. But 'tis exactly two calendar years longer, they say. A powerful mind to hold out so long!"

"True. . . . But there's great strength in hope. Knowing that in four-and-twenty months' time ye'll be out of your bondage, and able to make up for all you've suffered, by partaking without stint—why, it keeps a man up, no doubt."

"No doubt, Christopher Coney, no doubt. And 'a must need such reflections—a lonely widow man," said Longways.

"When did he lose his wife?" asked Elizabeth.

"I never knowed her. 'Twas afore he came to Casterbridge," Solomon Longways replied with terminative emphasis, as if the fact of his ignorance of Mrs Henchard were sufficient to deprive her history of all interest. ❖

---

ela • tion (i lā´ shən) *n.,* joy; excitement

People sometimes withhold information from others with the goal of protecting them. Is this a fair or kind thing to do?

Refer to Text ▶ ▶ ▶ ▶ ▶ Reason with Text

1a. How does the author describe the road to Weydon-Prior? Why does the author describe the scene's "previous character"?

1b. Discuss other ways the author signals the passage of time in this excerpt. What effect does this have on the narrative?

Understand
Find meaning

2a. Whom does Susan Henchard-Newson talk with at the fair? What does she learn?

2b. Describe the effect this information has on the development of the narrative in this excerpt.

Apply
Use information

3a. Summarize the description of the mayor of Casterbridge.

3b. What characteristics of the mayor can you infer from this description? What kind of man is Michael Henchard?

Analyze
Take things apart

4a. Identify the reason Susan gives for not telling her daughter the truth about her tragic past.

4b. Evaluate Susan's reason. Would it have been better for Elizabeth-Jane to know the truth? Explain.

Evaluate
Make judgments

5a. Why is Susan unwilling to reward the old woman at the fair for her information? Why do the waiters not refill the mayor's wineglass?

5b. Based on these observations, construct a possible reason the mayor refuses to drink alcohol.

Create
Bring ideas together

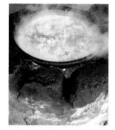

Analyze Literature

Description and Exposition
What specific sensory details does Hardy include in his description of the woman who sold furmity? What does the description tell you about this woman's life?

What does the exposition reveal about Mrs. Newson's past? How does knowing this further your understanding of the different emotions Mrs. Newson and Elizabeth-Jane feel as they watch the mayor's public dinner from the street?

Extend the Text

Writing Options

Creative Writing Imagine that you are Susan Henchard, and you have just been sold at the country fair by your drunken husband. Write a diary entry that details your thoughts and feelings upon being sold.

Expository Writing Dickens and Hardy approached storytelling in different ways. Compare their different forms of narration in *Great Expectations* and *The Mayor of Casterbridge*. Read or reread just the first few pages of the excerpts in your text, then write a brief essay explaining the authors' different approaches. You may want to focus on differences in one literary element, such as point of view or tone. Include examples from the stories to support your position.

Collaborative Learning

Plan a Website Design a website for teenagers about Thomas Hardy's life and works, which will be hosted by a local library. Break into small groups, and brainstorm a list of categories of important information about Hardy's life and his works that teenage readers should know. Under each item, briefly describe what information the category will contain. Then brainstorm ideas for visual images your group can incorporate with the information to make the website more interesting.

Media Literacy

Create an Advertisement Write an advertisement for the local Weydon-Priors paper that Michael Henchard might place to find his wife and daughter. To whom might he address the advertisement? How would he explain the circumstances in which he lost his wife and daughter?

 Go to **www.mirrorsandwindows.com** for more.

The Darkling Thrush
Ah, Are You Digging on My Grave?

Poems by Thomas Hardy

Build Background

Literary Context Written on December 31, 1899, the last day of the nineteenth century, **"The Darkling Thrush"** originally was published with the subtitle "By the Century's Deathbed." The poem reflects Hardy's disillusionment with the age in which he lived and contrasts it with a message of hope from a source in nature. The verse is composed of four *octets* (or *octaves*), which are eight-line stanzas, each rhyming *ababcdcd*. It demonstrates Thomas Hardy's ability to create a somber mood through a few deft strokes of his poetic brush.

"Ah, Are You Digging on My Grave?" is a good example of a writer's use of irony. The work is a humorous poem in which a dead woman asks who is digging on her grave. A voice answers her questions, and she finally finds that the voice belongs to her dog. Each of the poem's six *sestets*, or six-line stanzas, follows the rhyme scheme *abcccb*. The first two lines of each sestet pose a question to identify the digger, to which a humorous denial is offered; finally, in stanza 4, the dog admits the deed. After the dead woman praises the dog's loyalty in stanza 5, the dog sets her straight in stanza 6: He is just burying a bone and has forgotten that she is buried there.

Both of these poems recall Romantic lyrics on similar subjects written by John Keats: "Ode to a Nightingale" and "When I Have Fears" (see Unit 6, pages 742–745 and 753).

Reader's Context Are you a temperamental person—someone who has wide and sudden mood swings? Do you know someone who is? How do moody people affect those around them?

See the Author Focus on page 822 for biographical information about Thomas Hardy.

Analyze Literature

Slant Rhyme and Irony
A **slant rhyme** is one in which the rhyming sounds are similar but not identical, as in *rave* and *rove*.

Irony is the difference between appearance and reality. Types of irony include *dramatic irony*, in which something is known by the reader or audience but not the characters; *verbal irony*, in which a character says one thing but means another; and *irony of situation*, in which an event violates the expectations of the characters, the reader, or the audience.

Set Purpose

The two poems that follow—one somber and the other humorous—demonstrate Hardy's versatility as a writer. As you read "The Darkling Thrush," identify its *rhyme scheme*, or pattern of end rhymes, and list the examples of slant rhyme you find. Determine which stanza has the most uses of slant rhyme. In reading "Ah, Are You Digging on My Grave?" look for words and phrases that are ironic. Determine which of the three types of irony this poem most clearly demonstrates.

Preview Vocabulary

desolate, 833
gaunt, 834
ecstatic, 834

Thrushes, c. 1900s. Frederick Cuming.
Private collection.

The Darkling[1] Thrush

by Thomas Hardy

I leant upon a coppice gate[2]
   When Frost was spectre-gray,
And Winter's dregs made <u>desolate</u>
   The weakening eye of day.
5 The tangled bine-stems[3] scored the sky
   Like strings of broken lyres,[4]
And all mankind that haunted nigh
   Had sought their household fires.

---

1. **Darkling.** In the dark
2. **coppice gate.** Gate leading into a wooded area
3. **tangled bine-stems.** Intertwined stems of shrubs
4. **lyres.** Small stringed instruments like harps

> **des • o • late** (deˊ sə lət) *adj.,* barren, lifeless, or deserted

The land's sharp features seemed to be
10   The Century's corpse outleant,[5]
His crypt the cloudy canopy,
    The wind his death-lament.
The ancient pulse of germ and birth
    Was shrunken hard and dry,
15 And every spirit upon earth
    Seemed fervourless[6] as I.

At once a voice arose among
    The bleak twigs overhead
In a full-hearted evensong
20   Of joy illimited;
An aged thrush, frail, <u>gaunt</u>, and small,
    In blast-beruffled plume,
Had chosen thus to fling his soul
    Upon the growing gloom.

25 So little cause for carolings
    Of such <u>ecstatic</u> sound
Was written on terrestrial things
    Afar or nigh around,
That I could think there trembled through
30   His happy good-night air
Some blessed Hope, whereof he knew
    And I was unaware. ❖

---

5. **Century's corpse outleant.** The poem was written on
December 31, 1899, the final day of the nineteenth century; figuratively, the century was dead.
6. **fervourless.** Without passion

> **gaunt** (gônt) *adj.,* haggard; emaciated
> **ec • stat • ic** (ek staˊtik) *adj.,* thrilled; overjoyed

MIRRORS & WINDOWS

Hardy wrote this somber poem on the last day of the nineteenth century. How do
you feel at the end of the year? Do you make plans for the year to come, or do
you tend to dwell on what happened during the previous year?

AH, ARE YOU DIGGING ON MY GRAVE?

by Thomas Hardy

"Ah, are you digging on my grave
   My loved one?—planting rue?"[1]
—"No: yesterday he went to wed
One of the brightest wealth has bred.
5 'It cannot hurt her now,' he said,
   'That I should not be true.'"

"Then who is digging on my grave?
   My nearest dearest kin?"
—"Ah, no: they sit and think, 'What use!
10 What good will planting flowers produce?
No tendance of her mound can loose
   Her spirit from Death's gin.'"[2]

"But some one digs upon my grave?
   My enemy?—prodding sly?"
15 —"Nay: when she heard you had passed the Gate
That shuts on all flesh soon or late,
She thought you no more worth her hate,
   And cares not where you lie."

"Then, who is digging on my grave?
20   Say—since I have not guessed!"
—"O it is I, my mistress dear,
Your little dog, who still lives near,
And much I hope my movements here
   Have not disturbed your rest?"

25 "Ah yes! *You* dig upon my grave . . .
   Why flashed it not to me
That one true heart was left behind!
What feeling do we ever find
To equal among human kind
30   A dog's fidelity!"[3]

"Mistress, I dug upon your grave
   To bury a bone, in case
I should be hungry near this spot
When passing on my daily trot.
35 I am sorry, but I quite forgot
   It was your resting-place."

---

1. **rue.** Herb with yellow flowers used as an emblem of sorrow; also, an
  archaic word for *sorrow*
2. **gin.** Trap
3. **fidelity.** Faithfulness

MIRRORS & WINDOWS

This poem touches on a fear shared by many people: that they will be forgotten after they die. Are you afraid of being forgotten? For what would you like to be remembered?

Refer to Text ▶ ▶ ▶ ▶ ▶ Reason with Text

1a. List the details of the environment the speaker describes in stanza 1 of "The Darkling Thrush."

1b. Infer what time of day and in what season of the year this poem is set.

Understand
Find meaning

2a. In the first three stanzas of "Ah, Are You Digging on My Grave?" who does the speaker think is digging?

2b. Show how those responses indicate the people's feelings about the dead woman.

Apply
Use information

3a. State who is digging on the grave, and explain why the digger is digging.

3b. How does the dead woman react at first to finding out the identity of the digger? How does the digger's response reflect the meaning of the poem?

Analyze
Take things apart

4a. What elements create a gloomy or grim mood throughout most of these two poems?

4b. Argue whether these two poems are optimistic or pessimistic.

Evaluate
Make judgments

5a. Identify what surprises the speaker in "The Darkling Thrush."

5b. What if the speaker had heard the thrush on a sunny day? Would it have had the same effect? Why or why not?

Create
Bring ideas together

Analyze Literature

Slant Rhyme and Irony

What is the rhyme scheme of "The Darkling Thrush"? Which stanza contains the most occurrences of slant rhyme? Why might Hardy want to emphasize these words in this stanza?

Which of the three types of irony is most clearly demonstrated by "Ah, Are You Digging on My Grave"? What is the appearance and what is the reality that makes this situation ironic?

Extend the Text

Writing Options

Creative Writing How would the dead woman have responded to the dog in a seventh stanza, after the dog told her he had forgotten about her? Write a new final verse for "Ah, Are You Digging on My Grave?" in which the dead woman responds to her dog. Try to re-create Hardy's rhyme scheme and rhythm as much as possible.

Expository Writing The speaker in "The Darkling Thrush" comes across the bird on a gray, desolate day. What if the day had been sunny and warm? Write a one-paragraph analysis about how the poem would change if the setting were different.

Critical Literacy

Conduct Literary Criticism Literary critics using the theory of biographical-historical criticism analyze a text within the context of the author's life and histori-

cal period (see Understanding Literary Criticism, Unit 3, pages 266–267). Using the Author Focus on page 822 and other sources, apply biographical-historical literary theory to Hardy's "The Darkling Thrush" and write a short analysis of the poem. Identify events in the author's life and time period that likely influenced his work.

Collaborative Learning

Form a Poetry Discussion Group In small groups, discuss the following questions about the theme of "The Darkling Thrush": (1) What does the speaker of this poem make of "terrestrial things" both "Afar" and "nigh around"? (2) What two possible references might the word *His* in line 30 have? (3) Whose air might this be? (4) What words in the last stanza have connotations of spirituality or religion? (5) What hope might the speaker be intimating by these references?

 Go to **www.mirrorsandwindows.com** for more.

1. Which of the following is *not* a clue that the mother in *The Mayor of Casterbridge* is being deliberately vague to her daughter about the identity of Mr. Michael Henchard?
   A. [The daughter asked,] "'What is his exact kin to us, mother? I have never clearly had it told me.'"
   B. "'[A] connection by marriage,' said the mother deliberately."
   C. "'That's exactly what you have said a score of times before!' replied the young woman."
   D. "'I suppose he never knew me?' the girl innocently continued."
   E. "Mrs. Henchard paused for a moment, and answered uneasily, 'Of course not, Elizabeth-Jane.'"

2. Which of the following phrases from *The Mayor of Casterbridge* means "to confide"?
   A. "was sufficient to inform the eye"
   B. "it was evident that the years had told"
   C. "opening the sluices of her heart forthwith"
   D. "have known what it was to do business"
   E. "I should have minded it in a moment"

3. In *The Mayor of Casterbridge,* the mayor character is all of the following *except*
   A. a former mariner.
   B. Mr. Michael Henchard.
   C. Mrs. Newson's husband.
   D. the man who sold his wife at the fair.
   E. someone connected by marriage with Mrs. Henchard.

4. What is the subject of the poem "The Darkling Thrush"?
   A. birds
   B. a darkling thrush
   C. being all alone outdoors
   D. the loneliness and ignorance of the poem's narrator
   E. hope and despair

5. In "The Darkling Thrush," which of the following words or phrases does *not* help establish the dominant mood?
   A. "spectre-gray"
   B. "dregs made desolate"
   C. "death-lament"
   D. "full-hearted"
   E. "growing doom"

6. Which of the following statements is true of the poem "The Darkling Thrush"?
   A. It sharply contrasts two attitudes.
   B. It is written in the third-person point of view.
   C. Its main purpose is to persuade.
   D. It describes nothing but bleakness.
   E. Its tone is informal and lighthearted.

7. In "Ah, Are You Digging on My Grave?" who are the two speakers?
   A. a dead man and God
   B. a dying person and the poet
   C. a dead woman and her dog
   D. a corpse and a never-revealed person
   E. a grave-digger and a never-revealed person

8. What is most ironic about "Ah, Are You Digging on My Grave?"
   A. the identity of the first speaker
   B. the digger and reason for the digging
   C. the rhyme scheme and the poetic techniques used
   D. the repetition of the question in the title, with changes
   E. the fact that digging other than for burial is taking place in a graveyard

9. **Constructed Response:** Given the details that Hardy provides in *The Mayor of Casterbridge*, discuss how the mayor is a suitable representative of the town of Casterbridge. What does this tell the reader about the mayor's character?

10. **Constructed Response:** Describe your reaction to the revelation at the end of "Ah, Are You Digging on My Grave?" and explain why you responded this way. What about the poem contributed to your reaction? Was your reaction immediate, or did you have to reflect on the poem?

The Mark of the Beast

A Short Story by Rudyard Kipling

Build Background

Historical Context Set in colonial India in the late-nineteenth century, Rudyard Kipling's **"The Mark of the Beast"** describes the relationship between the colonizers and the colonized. Kipling, who spent much of his early life in India, was part of the British ruling class there and witnessed the conflicts that occur when two cultures are brought together through force. This affiliation lost him some respect as a writer toward the end of his life. Even today, he is considered by some as a supporter of British colonialism.

"The Mark of the Beast" was published in July 1890 in three different periodicals. The story is about a British civil service officer in India who desecrates the statue of a Hindu god. Consequently, a leper grabs him and touches his head to the officer's chest. The attack leaves a mark on the officer's chest that curses him.

Reader's Context When has someone treated you as if you were inferior? How did it make you feel, and how did it affect your opinion of this person?

Meet the Author

Rudyard Kipling (1865–1936) was born in Bombay (now called Mumbai), India, the son of John Lockwood Kipling and Alice Macdonald Kipling. Kipling's father was an artist and taught architectural sculpture at the University of Bombay. The first years of Kipling's life were spent in India, but as was the custom of British families living abroad, he was sent at age five to Southsea, England, to stay with a foster family while being educated. This was an unhappy time for him, and it colored some of his later writing.

In 1882, Kipling returned to Lahore, India, where his parents were living. There, he worked on the newspaper *Civil and Military Gazette* and later on its sister paper, the *Pioneer,* in Allahabad. He became popular for his stories, as well as for his sketches and poems, which were published in newspapers and in cheap books sold at Indian railroad stations.

When Kipling returned to England in 1889, he published *Barrack-Room Ballads,* a collection of poems. The book was so popular it went into three printings in its first year. In 1892, he married Carrie Balestier, and they moved to her family home in Brattleboro, Vermont. That is where he wrote *The Jungle Books*. Today, Kipling is known mostly for his children's books, but while alive, he was revered as a poet.

Analyze Literature

Plot and Style

A **plot** is the series of events related to a central conflict, or struggle. The plot typically introduces the conflict, develops it, and eventually resolves it.

Style is the manner in which something is written. Word choice (or *diction*), sentence structure and length, and other recurring features help distinguish one author's work from that of another.

Set Purpose

Kipling's stories set in India are quite well known and often examine issues relating to colonialism. In "Mark of the Beast," Kipling uses the plot to explore the tension between the British colonizers and the Indians. As you read this selection, identify the conflict, the climax (the highest point of interest or suspense), and the resolution of the conflict. Also note elements that seem unique to Kipling's style, paying special attention to his diction.

Preview Vocabulary

genial, 839
riotous, 840
divinity, 841
baffle, 841
distraught, 842
degradation, 847
delusion, 848
dispassionate, 848

The Mark of the Beast

by Rudyard Kipling

"When men foregather from the uttermost ends of the Empire they have a right to be riotous."

Your Gods and my Gods—do you or I know which are the stronger?
—Indian Proverb

East of Suez, some hold, the direct control of Providence[1] ceases; Man being there handed over to the power of the Gods and Devils of Asia, and the Church of England Providence only exercising an occasional and modified supervision in the case of Englishmen.

This theory accounts for some of the more unnecessary horrors of life in India; it may be stretched to explain my story.

My friend Strickland of the Police, who knows as much of natives of India as is good for any man, can bear witness to the facts of the case. Dumoise, our doctor, also saw what Strickland and I saw. The inference which he drew from the evidence was entirely incorrect. He is dead now; he died in a rather curious manner, which has been elsewhere described.

When Fleete came to India he owned a little money and some land in the Himalayas, near a place called Dharmsala. Both properties had been left him by an uncle, and he came out to finance them. He was a big, heavy, <u>genial</u>, and inoffensive man. His knowledge of natives was, of course, limited, and he complained of the difficulties of the language.

He rode in from his place in the hills to spend New Year in the station, and he stayed with Strickland. On New Year's Eve there was a big dinner at the club, and the night was excusably wet. When men foregather from the utter-

---

1. **Providence.** God

ge • ni • al (jē´ nē əl) *adj.,* pleasant or friendly

most ends of the Empire they have a right to be <u>riotous</u>. The Frontier had sent down a contingent o' Catch-'em-Alive-O's[2] who had not seen twenty white faces for a year, and were used to ride fifteen miles to dinner at the next Fort at the risk of a Khyberee[3] bullet where their drinks should lie. They profited by their new security, for they tried to play pool with a curled-up hedgehog found in the garden, and one of them carried the marker round the room in his teeth. Half a dozen planters had come in from the south and were talking "horse" to the Biggest Liar in Asia, who was trying to cap all their stories at once. Everybody was there, and there was a general closing up of ranks and taking stock of our losses in dead or disabled that had fallen during the past year. It was a very wet night, and I remember that we sang "Auld Lang Syne" with our feet in the Polo Championship Cup, and our heads among the stars, and swore that we were all dear friends. Then some of us went away and annexed[4] Burma, and some tried to open up the Sudan and were opened up by Fuzzies[5] in that cruel scrub outside Suakim, and some found stars and medals, and some were married, which was bad, and some did other things which were worse, and the others of us stayed in our chains and strove to make money on insufficient experiences.

Fleete began the night with sherry and bitters, drank champagne steadily up to dessert, then raw, rasping Capri with all the strength of whiskey, took benedictine with his coffee, four or five whiskeys and sodas to improve his pool strokes, beer and bones[6] at half-past two, winding up with old brandy. Consequently, when he came out, at half-past three in the morning,

Promenade on an Indian Street, c. 1890. Edwin Lord Weeks.

into fourteen degrees of frost, he was very angry with his horse for coughing, and tried to leapfrog into the saddle. The horse broke away and went to his stables; so Strickland and I formed a Guard of Dishonor to take Fleete home.

2. **Catch-'em-Alive-O's.** Soldiers who were forced into service
3. **Khyberee.** People who lived in the Khyber region of what is now Pakistan and Afghanistan
4. **annexed.** Incorporated into Britain's territory
5. **Fuzzies.** Natives of Sudan; they were given this name because of their frizzy hair.
6. **bones.** Dice

ri • o • tous (rī′ ə təs) *adj.,* unrestrained; disorderly

Our road lay through the bazaar, close to a little temple of Hanuman, the Monkey-god, who is a leading divinity worthy of respect. All gods have good points, just as have all priests. Personally, I attach much importance to Hanuman, and am kind to his people—the great gray apes of the hills. One never knows when one may want a friend.

There was a light in the temple, and as we passed we could hear voices of men chanting hymns. In a native temple the priests rise at all hours of the night to do honor to their god. Before we would stop him, Fleete dashed up the steps, patted two priests on the back, and was gravely grinding the ashes of his cigar butt in to the forehead of the red stone image of Hanuman. Strickland tried to drag him out, but he sat down and said solemnly:

"Shee that? Mark of the B—beasht! *I* made it. Ishn't it fine?"

In half a minute the temple was alive and noisy, and Strickland, who knew what came of polluting gods, said that things might occur. He, by virtue of his official position, long residence in the country, and weakness for going among the natives, was known to the priests and he felt unhappy. Fleete sat on the ground and refused to move. He said that "good old Hanuman" made a very soft pillow.

Then, without any warning, a Silver Man came out of a recess behind the image of the god. He was perfectly naked in that bitter, bitter cold, and his body shone like frosted silver, for he was what the Bible calls "a leper[7] as white as snow." Also he had no face, because he was a leper of some years' standing, and his disease was heavy upon him. We two stooped to haul Fleete up, and the temple was filling and filling with folk who seemed to spring from the earth, when the Silver Man ran in under our arms, making a noise exactly like the mewing of an otter, caught Fleete round the body and dropped his head on Fleete's breast before we could wrench him away. Then he retired to a corner and sat mewing while the crowd blocked all the doors.

The priests were very angry until the Silver Man touched Fleete. That nuzzling seemed to sober them.

At the end of a few minutes' silence one of the priests came to Strickland and said, in perfect English, "Take your friend away. He has done with Hanuman but Hanuman has not done with him." The crowd gave room and we carried Fleete into the road.

Strickland was very angry. He said that we might all three have been knifed, and that Fleete should thank his stars that he had escaped without injury.

Fleete thanked no one. He said that he wanted to go to bed. He was gorgeously[8] drunk.

We moved on, Strickland silent and wrathful, until Fleete was taken with violent shivering fits and sweating. He said that the smells of the bazaar were overpowering, and he wondered why slaughterhouses were permitted so near English residences. "Can't you smell the blood?" said Fleete.

Strickland hates being mystified by natives, because his business in life is to overmatch them with their own weapons.

We put him to bed at last, just as the dawn was breaking, and Strickland invited me to have another whiskey and soda. While we were drinking he talked of the trouble in the temple, and admitted that it baffled him completely. Strickland hates being mystified by natives, because his business in life is to overmatch them with their own weapons. He has not yet succeeded in doing this, but in fifteen or twenty years he will have made some small progress.

---

7. **leper.** Person with leprosy, a bacterial disease that affects the skin, nerves, and mucous membranes and may lead to severe disfigurement

8. **gorgeously.** Magnificently; incredibly

di • **vin** • i • **ty** (də vi´ nə tē) *n.*, god or deity
baf • **fle** (ba´ fəl) *v.*, puzzle or confuse

"They should have mauled us," he said, "instead of mewing at us. I wonder what they meant. I don't like it one little bit."

I said that the Managing Committee of the temple would in all probability bring a criminal action against us for insulting their religion. There was a section of the Indian Penal Code which exactly met Fleete's offense. Strickland said he only hoped and prayed that they would do this. Before I left I looked into Fleete's room, and saw him lying on his right side, scratching his left breast. Then I went to bed cold, depressed, and unhappy, at seven o'clock in the morning.

At one o'clock I rode over to Strickland's house to inquire after Fleete's head. I imagined that it would be a sore one. Fleete was break-fasting and seemed unwell. His temper was gone, for he was abusing the cook for not sup-plying him with an underdone chop. A man who can eat raw meat after a wet night is a curiosity. I told Fleete this and he laughed.

"You breed queer mosquitoes in these parts," he said. "I've been bitten to pieces, but only in one place."

"Let's have a look at the bite," said Strickland. "It may have gone down since this morning."

While the chops were being cooked, Fleete opened his shirt and showed us, just over his left breast, a mark, the perfect double of the black rosettes—the five or six irregular blotches arranged in a circle—on a leopard's hide. Strickland looked and said, "It was only pink this morning. It's grown black now."

Fleete ran to a glass.

"By Jove!" he said, "this is nasty. What is it?"

We could not answer. Here the chops came in, all red and juicy, and Fleete bolted three in a most offensive manner. He ate on his right grinders only, and threw his head over his right shoulder as he snapped the meat. When he had finished, it struck him that he had been behav-ing strangely, for he said apologetically, "I don't think I ever felt so hungry in my life. I've bolted like an ostrich."

After breakfast Strickland said to me, "Don't go. Stay here, and stay for the night."

Seeing that my house was not three miles from Strickland's, this request was absurd. But Strickland insisted, and was going to say something, when Fleete interrupted him by declaring in a shamefaced way that he felt hun-gry again. Strickland sent a man to my house to fetch over my bedding and a horse, and we three went down to Strickland's stables to pass the hours until it was time to go out for a ride. The man who has a weakness for horses never wearies of inspecting them; and when two men are killing time in this way they gather knowl-edge and lies the one from the other.

There were five horses in the stables, and I shall never forget the scene as we tried to look them over. They seemed to have gone mad. They reared and screamed and nearly tore up their pickets; they sweated and shivered and lathered and were <u>distraught</u> with fear. Strick-land's horses used to know him as well as his dogs; which made the matter more curious.

dis • traught (di strôt´) *adj.,* anxious; worried

We left the stable for fear of the brutes throwing themselves in their panic. Then Strickland turned back and called me. The horses were still frightened, but they let us "gentle" and make much of them, and put their heads in our bosoms.

"They aren't afraid of *us*," said Strickland. "D'you know, I'd give three months' pay if *Outrage* here could talk."

But *Outrage* was dumb, and could only cuddle up to his master and blow out his nostrils, as is the custom of horses when they wish to explain things but can't. Fleete came up when we were in the stalls, and as soon as the horses saw him, their fright broke out afresh. It was all that we could do to escape from the place unkicked. Strickland said, "They don't seem to love you, Fleete."

"Nonsense," said Fleete; "my mare will follow me like a dog." He went to her; she was in a loose box; but as he slipped the bars she plunged, knocking him down, and broke away into the garden. I laughed, but Strickland was not amused. He took his moustache in both fists and pulled at it till it nearly came out. Fleete, instead of going off to chase his property, yawned, saying that he felt sleepy. He went to the house to lie down, which was a foolish way of spending New Year's Day.

Strickland sat with me in the stables and asked if I had noticed anything peculiar in Fleete's manner. I said that he ate his food like a beast; but that this might have been the result of living alone in the hills out of reach of society as refined and elevating as ours for instance. Strickland was not amused. I do not think that he listened to me, for his next sentence referred to the mark on Fleete's breast, and I said that it might have been caused by blister flies, or that it was possibly a birthmark newly born and now visible for the first time. We both agreed that it was unpleasant to look at, and Strickland found occasion to say that I was a fool.

"I can't tell you what I think now," said he, "because you would call me a madman; but you must stay with me for the next few days, if you can. I want you to watch Fleete, but don't tell me what you think till I have made up my mind."

"But I am dining out tonight," I said.

"So am I," said Strickland, "and so is Fleete. At least that is if he doesn't change his mind."

We walked about the garden smoking, but saying nothing—because we were friends, and talking spoils good tobacco—till our pipes were out. Then we went to wake up Fleete. He was wide awake and fidgeting about his room.

"I say, I want some more chops," he said. "Can I get them?"

We laughed and said, "Go and change. The ponies will be round in a minute."

"All right," said Fleete. "I'll go when I get the chops—underdone ones, mind."

All three horses were unmanageable—mad with fear.

He seemed to be quite in earnest. It was four o'clock, and we had had breakfast at one; still, for a long time, he demanded those underdone chops. Then he changed into riding clothes and went out into the veranda.[9] His pony—the mare had not been caught—would not let him come near. All three horses were unmanageable—mad with fear—and finally Fleete said that he would stay at home and get something to eat. Strickland and I rode out wondering. As we passed the Temple of Hanuman the Silver Man came out and mewed at us.

"He is not one of the regular priests of the temple," said Strickland. "I think I should peculiarly like to lay my hands on him."

There was no spring in our gallop on the racecourse that evening. The horses were stale, and moved as though they had been ridden out.

"The fright after breakfast has been too much for them," said Strickland.

That was the only remark he made through the remainder of the ride. Once or twice, I think, he swore to himself; but that did not count.

---

9. **veranda.** Open-air patio

esting phenomena; invented for the occasion, I must confess; but what of that? His wife always knew when to expect a little specimen of her husband's literary talent by a peculiar cough, which served as prelude; and, judging from this encouraging sign, and the high-pitched and emphatic voice in which he read them, she was inclined to think, that an "Ode to an Early Rosebud," in the corner devoted to original poetry, and a letter in the correspondence department, signed "Pro Bono Publico,"[3] were her husband's writing, and to hold up her head accordingly.

I never could find out what it was that occasioned the Hodgsons to lodge in the same house as the Jenkinses. Jenkins held the same office in the Tory Paper as Hodgson did in the *Examiner,* and, as I said before, I leave you to give it a name. But Jenkins had a proper sense of his position, and a proper reverence for all in authority, from the king down to the editor and sub-editor. He would as soon have thought of borrowing the king's crown for a nightcap, or the king's scepter[4] for a walking-stick as he would have thought of filling up any spare corner with any production of his own; and I think it would have even added to his contempt of Hodgson (if that were possible), had he known of the "productions of his brain," as the latter fondly alluded to the paragraphs he inserted, when speaking to his wife.

Jenkins had his wife too. Wives were wanting to finish the completeness of the quarrel which existed one memorable Christmas week, some dozen years ago, between the two neigh-

John and Dot Peerybingle, 1924. Harold Copping. Private collection.

bors, the two compositors. And with wives, it was a very pretty, a very complete quarrel. To make the opposing parties still more equal, still more well-matched, if the Hodgsons had a baby ("such a baby!—a poor, puny little thing"), Mrs. Jenkins had a cat ("such a cat! a great, nasty, miowling tom-cat, that was always stealing the milk put by for little Angel's sup-

---

3. **Pro Bono Publico.** [Latin] For the public good
4. **scepter.** Royal staff or rod

per"). And now, having matched Greek with Greek, I must proceed to the tug of war.[5] It was the day before Christmas; such a cold east wind! such an inky sky! such a blue-black look in people's faces, as they were driven out more than usual, to complete their purchases for the next day's festival.

Before leaving home that morning, Jenkins had given some money to his wife to buy the next day's dinner.

"My dear, I wish for turkey and sausages. It may be a weakness, but I own I am partial to sausages. My deceased mother was. Such tastes are hereditary. As to the sweets—whether plum-pudding or mince-pies—I leave such considerations to you; I only beg you not to mind expense. Christmas comes but once a year."

> *"I only beg you not to mind expense. Christmas comes but once a year."*

And again he called out from the bottom of the first flight of stairs, just close to the Hodgsons' door ("such ostentatiousness,"[6] as Mrs. Hodgson observed), "You will not forget the sausages, my dear!"

"I should have liked to have had something above common, Mary," said Hodgson, as they too made their plans for the next day; "but I think roast beef must do for us. You see, love, we've a family."

"Only one, Jem! I don't want more than roast beef, though, I'm sure. Before I went to service, mother and me would have thought roast beef a very fine dinner."

"Well, let's settle it, then, roast beef and a plum-pudding; and now, good-bye. Mind and take care of little Tom. I thought he was a bit hoarse this morning."

And off he went to his work.

Now, it was a good while since Mrs. Jenkins and Mrs. Hodgson had spoken to each other, although they were quite as much in possession of the knowledge of events and opinions as though they did. Mary knew that Mrs. Jenkins despised her for not having a real lace cap, which Mrs. Jenkins had; and for having been a servant, which Mrs. Jenkins had not; and the little occasional pinchings which the Hodgsons were obliged to resort to, to make both ends meet, would have been very patiently endured by Mary, if she had not winced under Mrs. Jenkins's knowledge of such economy. But she had her revenge. She had a child, and Mrs. Jenkins had none. To have had a child, even such a puny baby as little Tom, Mrs. Jenkins would have worn commonest caps, and cleaned grates, and drudged her fingers to the bone. The great unspoken disappointment of her life soured her temper, and turned her thoughts inward, and made her morbid and selfish.

"Hang that cat! he's been stealing again! he's gnawed the cold mutton in his nasty mouth till it's not fit to set before a Christian; and I've nothing else for Jem's dinner. But I'll give it him now I've caught him, that I will!"

So saying, Mary Hodgson caught up her husband's Sunday cane, and despite pussy's cries and scratches, she gave him such a beating as she hoped might cure him of his thievish propensities; when, lo! and behold, Mrs. Jenkins stood at the door with a face of bitter wrath.

"Aren't you ashamed of yourself, ma'am, to abuse a poor dumb animal, ma'am, as knows no better than to take food when he sees it, ma'am? He only follows the nature which God has given, ma'am; and it's a pity your nature, ma'am, which I've heard is of the stingy saving species, does not make you shut your cupboard door a little closer. There is such a thing as law

5. **Greek with . . . war.** Reference to the saying "When Greek joins Greek, then is the tug of war," meaning that when two strong opponents face each other, a difficult battle will result
6. **ostentatiousness.** State of being flashy or showy

Everything was to go wrong with Mary today. Now baby was awake, who was to take her husband's dinner to the office? She took the child in her arms and tried to hush him off to sleep again, and as she sung she cried, she could hardly tell why,—a sort of reaction from her violent angry feelings. She wished she had never beaten the poor cat; she wondered if his leg was really broken. What would her mother say if she knew how cross and cruel her little Mary was getting? If she should live to beat her child in one of her angry fits?

It was of no use lullabying while she sobbed so; it must be given up, and she must just carry her baby in her arms, and take him with her to the office, for it was long past dinner-time. So she pared the mutton carefully, although by so doing she reduced the meat to an infinitesimal quantity, and taking the baked potatoes out of the oven, she popped them piping hot into her basket, with the etceteras of plate, butter, salt, and knife and fork.

It was, indeed, a bitter wind. She bent against it as she ran, and the flakes of snow were sharp and cutting as ice. Baby cried all the way, though she cuddled him up in her shawl. Then her husband had made his appetite up for a potato pie, and (literary man as he was) his body got so much the better of his mind, that he looked rather black at the cold mutton. Mary had no appetite for her own dinner when she arrived at home again. So, after she had tried to feed baby, and he had fretfully refused to take his bread and milk, she laid him down as usual on his quilt, surrounded by playthings, while she sided away, and chopped suet[8] for the next day's pudding. Early in the afternoon a parcel came, done up first in brown paper, then in such a white, grass-bleached, sweet-smelling towel, and a note from her dear, dear mother; in which quaint writing she endeavored to tell her daughter that she was not for-

for brute animals. I'll ask Mr. Jenkins, but I don't think them Radicals has done away with that law yet, for all their Reform Bill, ma'am. My poor precious love of a Tommy, is he hurt? and is his leg broke for taking a mouthful of scraps, as most people would give away to a beggar—if he'd take 'em!" wound up Mrs. Jenkins, casting a contemptuous look on the remnant of a scrag end of mutton.

Mary felt very angry and very guilty. For she really pitied the poor limping animal as he crept up to his mistress, and there lay down to bemoan himself; she wished she had not beaten him so hard, for it certainly was her own careless way of never shutting the cupboard-door that had tempted him to his fault. But the sneer at her little bit of mutton turned her penitence[7] to fresh wrath, and she shut the door in Mrs. Jenkins's face, as she stood caressing her cat in the lobby, with such a bang, that it wakened little Tom, and he began to cry.

---

7. **penitence.** State of feeling sorry or regretful
8. **suet.** Animal fat

gotten at Christmas time; but that, learning that Farmer Burton was killing his pig, she had made interest for some of his famous pork, out of which she had manufactured some sausages, and flavored them just as Mary used to like when she lived at home.

"Dear, dear mother!" said Mary to herself. "There never was any one like her for remembering other folk. What rare sausages she used to make! Home things have a smack with 'em no bought things can ever have. Set them up with their sausages! I've a notion if Mrs. Jenkins had ever tasted mother's she'd have no fancy for them townmade things Fanny took in just now."

And so she went on thinking about home, till the smiles and the dimples came out again at the remembrance of that pretty cottage, which would look green even now in the depth of winter, with its pyracanthus,[9] and its holly-bushes, and the great Portugal laurel that was her mother's pride. And the back path through the orchard to Farmer Burton's, how well she remembered it! The bushels of unripe apples she had picked up there and distributed among his pigs, till he had scolded her for giving them so much green trash!

She was interrupted—her baby (I call him a baby, because his father and mother did, and because he was so little of his age, but I rather think he was eighteen months old,) had fallen asleep some time before among his playthings; an uneasy, restless sleep; but of which Mary had been thankful, as his morning's nap had been too short, and as she was so busy. But now he began to make such a strange crowing noise, just like a chair drawn heavily and gratingly along a kitchen floor! His eyes were open, but expressive of nothing but pain.

"Mother's darling!" said Mary, in terror, lifting him up. "Baby, try not to make that noise. Hush, hush, darling; what hurts him?" But the noise came worse and worse.

"Fanny! Fanny!" Mary called in mortal fright, for her baby was almost black with his gasping breath, and she had no one to ask for

> "Dear, dear mother!" said Mary to herself. "There never was any one like her for remembering other folk."

aid or sympathy but her landlady's daughter, a little girl of twelve or thirteen, who attended to the house in her mother's absence, as daily cook in gentlemen's families. Fanny was more especially considered the attendant of the upstairs lodgers (who paid for the use of the kitchen, "for Jenkins could not abide the smell of meat cooking"), but just now she was fortunately sitting at her afternoon's work of darning stockings, and hearing Mrs. Hodgson's cry of terror, she ran to her sitting-room, and understood the case at a glance.

"He's got the croup![10] O Mrs. Hodgson, he'll die as sure as fate. Little brother had it, and he died in no time. The doctor said he could do nothing for him—it had gone too far. He said if we'd put him in a warm bath at first, it might have saved him; but, bless you! he was never half so bad as your baby." Unconsciously there mingled in her statement some of a child's love of producing an effect; but the increasing danger was clear enough.

"Oh, my baby! my baby! Oh, love, love! don't look so ill! I cannot bear it. And my fire so low! There, I was thinking of home, and picking currants, and never minding the fire. O Fanny! what is the fire like in the kitchen? Speak."

"Mother told me to screw it up, and throw some slack[11] on as soon as Mrs. Jenkins had done with it, and so I did. It's very low and

---

9. **pyracanthus.** Evergreen shrub related to the rose
10. **croup.** Condition, especially affecting infants, marked by coughing fits and trouble breathing
11. **slack.** Small pieces of coal

black. But, oh, Mrs. Hodgson! let me run for the doctor—I cannot abear to hear him, it's so like little brother."

Through her streaming tears Mary motioned her to go; and trembling, sinking, sick at heart, she laid her boy in his cradle, and ran to fill her kettle.

Mrs. Jenkins, having cooked her husband's snug little dinner, to which he came home; having told him her story of pussy's beating, at which he was justly and dignifiedly (?) indignant, saying it was all of a piece with that abusive *Examiner;* having received the sausages, and turkey, and mince pies, which her husband had ordered; and cleaned up the room, and prepared everything for tea, and coaxed and duly bemoaned her cat (who had pretty nearly forgotten his beating, but very much enjoyed the petting); having done all these and many other things, Mrs. Jenkins sat down to get up the real lace cap. Every thread was pulled out separately, and carefully stretched: when—what was that? Outside, in the street, a chorus of piping children's voices sang the old carol she had heard a hundred times in the days of her youth—

> "As Joseph was a walking he heard an angel
> sing,
> 'This night shall be born our heavenly King.
> He neither shall be born in housen nor in hall,
> Nor in the place of Paradise, but in an ox's
> stall.
> He neither shall be clothed in purple nor in
> pall,[12]
> But all in fair linen, as were babies all:
> He neither shall be rocked in silver nor in gold,
> But in a wooden cradle that rocks on the
> mould,'"&c.

She got up and went to the window. There, below, stood the group of black little figures, relieved[13] against the snow, which now enveloped everything. "For old sake's sake," as she phrased it, she counted out a halfpenny apiece for the singers, out of the copper bag, and threw them down below.

The room had become chilly while she had been counting out and throwing down her money, so she stirred her already glowing fire, and sat down right before it—but not to stretch her lace; like Mary Hodgson, she began to think over long past days, on softening remembrances of the dead and gone, on words long forgotten, on holy stories heard at her mother's knee.

She began to think over long past days, on softening remembrances of the dead and gone, on words long forgotten, on holy stories heard at her mother's knee.

"I cannot think what's come over me tonight," said she, half aloud, recovering herself by the sound of her own voice from her train of thought—"My head goes wandering on them old times. I'm sure more texts have come into my head with thinking on my mother within this last half-hour, than I've thought on for years and years. I hope I'm not going to die. Folks says, thinking too much on the dead betokens[14] we're going to join 'em; I should be loth[15] to go just yet—such a fine turkey as we've got for dinner tomorrow too!"

Knock, knock, knock, at the door, as fast as knuckles could go. And then, as if the comer could not wait, the door was opened, and Mary Hodgson stood there as white as death.

---

12. **pall.** Type of cloth; often refers to cloth draped over a coffin
13. **relieved.** Silhouetted; set off by contrast
14. **betokens.** Suggests or predicts
15. **loth.** Loath; unwilling

"Mrs. Jenkins!—oh, your kettle is boiling, thank God! Let me have the water for my baby, for the love of God! He's got croup, and is dying!"

Mrs. Jenkins turned on her chair with a wooden, inflexible look on her face, that (between ourselves) her husband knew and dreaded for all his pompous dignity.

"I'm sorry I can't oblige you, ma'am; my kettle is wanted for my husband's tea. Don't be afeared, Tommy, Mrs. Hodgson won't venture to intrude herself where she's not desired. You'd better send for the doctor, ma'am, instead of wasting your time in wringing your hands, ma'am—my kettle is engaged."

CHRISTMAS STORMS AND SUNSHINE **867**

Mary clasped her hands together with passionate force, but spoke no word of entreaty to that wooden face—that sharp, determined voice; but, as she turned away, she prayed for strength to bear the coming trial, and strength to forgive Mrs. Jenkins.

Mrs. Jenkins watched her go away meekly, as one who has no hope, and then she turned upon herself as sharply as she ever did on any one else. "What a brute I am, Lord forgive me! What's my husband's tea to a baby's life? In croup, too, where times is everything. You crabbed old vixen, you!—any one may know you never had a child!"

She was downstairs (kettle in hand) before she had finished her self-upbraiding;[16] and when in Mrs. Hodgson's room, she rejected all thanks (Mary had not the voice for many words), saying, stiffly, "I do it for the poor baby's sake, ma'am, hoping he may live to have mercy to poor dumb beasts, if he does forget to lock his cupboards."

But she did everything, and more than Mary, with her young inexperience, could have thought of. She prepared the warm bath, and tried it with her husband's own thermometer (Mr. Jenkins was as punctual as clockwork in noting down the temperature of every day). She let his mother place her baby in the tub, still preserving the same rigid, affronted[17] aspect, and then she went upstairs without a word. Mary longed to ask her to stay, but dared not; though, when she left the room, the tears chased each other down her cheeks faster than ever. Poor young mother! how she counted the minutes till the doctor should come. But, before he came, down again stalked Mrs. Jenkins, with something in her hand.

"I've seen many of these croup-fits, which, I take it, you've not, ma'am. Mustard plasters[18] is very sovereign,[19] put on the throat; I've been up and made one, ma'am, and, by your leave, I'll put it on the poor little fellow."

Mary could not speak, but she signed her grateful assent.

It began to smart while they still kept silence; and he looked up to his mother as if seeking courage from her looks to bear the stinging pain; but she was softly crying to see him suffer, and her want of courage reacted upon him, and he began to sob aloud. Instantly Mrs. Jenkins's apron was up, hiding her face: "Peep-bo, baby," said she, as merrily as she could. His little face brightened, and his mother having once got the cue, the two women kept the little fellow amused, until his plaster had taken effect.

He looked up to his mother as if seeking courage from her looks to bear the stinging pain.

"He's better—oh, Mrs. Jenkins, look at his eyes! how different! And he breathes quite softly"—

As Mary spoke thus, the doctor entered. He examined his patient. Baby was really better.

"It has been a sharp attack, but the remedies you have applied have been worth all the Pharmacopoeia[20] an hour later.—I shall send a powder," &c. &c.

Mrs. Jenkins stayed to hear this opinion; and (her heart wonderfully more easy) was going to leave the room, when Mary seized her hand and kissed it; she could not speak her gratitude.

Mrs. Jenkins looked affronted and awkward, and as if she must go upstairs and wash her hand directly.

---

16. **self-upbraiding.** Criticizing oneself
17. **affronted.** Insulted
18. **mustard plasters.** Paste made from ground mustard seed used as a folk remedy to ease respiratory conditions
19. **sovereign.** In this sense, having the ability to cure
20. **Pharmacopoeia.** Group of drugs suggested as treatment for a specific condition

But, in spite of these sour looks, she came softly down an hour or so afterwards to see how baby was.

The little gentleman slept well after the fright he had given his friends; and on Christmas morning, when Mary awoke and looked at the sweet little pale face lying on her arm, she could hardly realize the danger he had been in.

When she came down (later than usual), she found the household in a commotion. What do you think had happened? Why, pussy had been traitor to his best friend, and eaten up some of Mr. Jenkin's own especial sausages; and gnawed and tumbled the rest so, that they were not fit to be eaten! There were no bounds to that cat's appetite! he would have eaten his own father if he had been tender enough. And now Mrs. Jenkins stormed and cried—"Hang the cat!"

Christmas Day, too! and all the shops shut! "What was turkey without sausages?" gruffly asked Mr. Jenkins.

"O Jem!" whispered Mary, "hearken what a piece of work he's making about sausages— I should like to take Mrs. Jenkins up some of mother's; they're twice as good as bought sausages."

"I see no objection, my dear. Sausages do not involve intimacies, else his politics are what I can no ways respect."

"But, oh, Jem, if you had seen her last night about baby! I'm sure she may scold me forever, and I'll not answer. I'd even make her cat welcome to the sausages." The tears gathered to Mary's eyes as she kissed her boy.

"Better take 'em upstairs, my dear, and give them to the cat's mistress." And Jem chuckled at his saying.

Mary put them on a plate, but still she loitered.

"What must I say Jem? I never know."

"Say—I hope you'll accept of these sausages, as my mother—no, that's not grammar;— say what comes uppermost, Mary, it will be sure to be right."

So Mary carried them upstairs and knocked at the door; and when told to "come in," she looked very red, but went up to Mrs. Jenkins, saying, "Please take these. Mother made them." And was away before an answer could be given.

Just as Hodgson was ready to go to church, Mrs. Jenkins came downstairs, and called Fanny. In a minute, the latter entered the Hodgsons' room, and delivered Mr. and Mrs. Jenkin's compliments, and they would be particular glad if Mr. and Mrs. Hodgson would eat their dinner with them.

"And carry baby upstairs in a shawl, be sure," added Mrs. Jenkins's voice in the passage, close to the door, whither she had followed her messenger. There was no discussing the matter, with the certainty of every word being overheard.

Mary looked anxiously at her husband. She remembered his saying he did not approve of Mr. Jenkins's politics.

"Do you think it would do for baby?" asked he.

"Oh, yes," answered she eagerly; "I would wrap him up so warm."

"And I've got our room up to sixty-five already, for all it's so frosty," added the voice outside.

Now, how do you think they settled the matter? The very best way in the world. Mr. and Mrs. Jenkins came down into the Hodgsons' room and dined there. Turkey at the top, roast beef at the bottom, sausages at one side, potatoes at the other. Second course, plum pudding at the top, and mince pies at the bottom.

And after dinner, Mrs. Jenkins would have baby on her knee, and he seemed quite to take to her; she declared he was admiring the real lace on her cap, but Mary thought (though she did not say so) that he was pleased by her kind looks and coaxing words. Then he was wrapped up and carried carefully upstairs to tea, in Mrs. Jenkins's room. And after tea, Mrs. Jenkins, and Mary, and her husband, found out each other's mutual liking for music, and sat singing old glees and catches,[21] till I don't

---

21. **glees and catches.** Types of songs written for several voices to join in harmony, such as songs sung in rounds

know what o'clock, without one word of politics or newspapers.

Before they parted, Mary had coaxed pussy on to her knee; for Mrs. Jenkins would not part with baby, who was sleeping on her lap.

"When you're busy bring him to me. Do, now, it will be a real favor. I know you must have a deal to do, with another coming; let him come up to me. I'll take the greatest of cares of him; pretty darling, how sweet he looks when he's asleep!"

When the couples were once more alone, the husbands unburdened their minds to their wives.

Mr. Jenkins said to his—"Do you know, Burgess tried to make me believe Hodgson was such a fool as to put paragraphs into the *Examiner* now and then; but I see he knows his place, and has got too much sense to do any such thing."

Hodgson said—"Mary, love, I almost fancy from Jenkins's way of speaking (so much civiler than I expected), he guesses I wrote that 'Pro Bono' and the 'Rosebud,'—at any rate, I've no objection to your naming it, if the subject should come uppermost; I should like him to know I'm a literary man."

Well! I've ended my tale; I hope you don't think it too long; but, before I go, just let me say one thing.

If any of you have any quarrels, or misunderstandings, or coolnesses, or cold shoulders, or shynesses, or tiffs, or miffs, or huffs, with anyone else, just make friends before Christmas,—you will be so much merrier if you do.

I ask it of you for the sake of that old angelic song, heard so many years ago by the shepherds, keeping watch by night, on Bethlehem Heights. ❖

How do you usually treat someone whose beliefs or values are different from your own? Do you treat him or her differently from someone who shares your values?

Refer and Reason

1. Identify how Mrs. Jenkins and Mrs. Hodgson feel about each other at the beginning of the story and at the end. What was the turning point in their relationship?

2. Describe the event that brought together the Jenkins and Hodgson families. Given the history between the Jenkins and the Hodgsons, determine if this event serves as a realistic plot device.

3. What two political parties are represented by the Jenkins and Hodgson families? If this story were set in the modern-day United States, how would it be different or similar?

Writing Options

1. Write a short story that celebrates how a certain holiday affects people, good or bad. Try to capture the spirit of the holiday, either by drawing on realistic experiences or by creating fictitious ones.

2. Imagine that you are a teacher and want to assess your students' understanding of "Christmas Storms and Sunshine." Write five questions that ask students to identify the main ideas of the story and think about what they mean.

 Go to **www.mirrorsandwindows.com** for more.

Elements of Romanticism, Naturalism, and Realism continued to appear throughout the novels and poetry of the late nineteenth century. For instance, Alfred, Lord Tennyson's early works reflect a more Romantic and stylized use of language than the simpler language and Realism of Matthew Arnold's poems.

The enormous changes to social, political, and religious institutions in Victorian society brought with them a crisis of faith and feelings of anxiety and disillusionment. Arnold, Thomas Hardy, Christina Rossetti, and A. E. Housman addressed these feelings in their poetry as they struggled to reconcile the ideals of the era with the realities of everyday life.

Publication in 1859 of Charles Darwin's *On the Origin of Species,* which stated the theory of evolution, was perceived as a challenge to traditional religion, and individuals responded to it in different ways. As described by Arnold, some people turned against traditional religion and looked to scientific principles for guidance, while others, such as Gerard Manley Hopkins, believed God was responsible for creation on some level. Still others followed the approach taken by Tennyson, who struggled to find some middle ground, reconciling his faith with the scientific discoveries of the age.

In sum, the writing of the Victorians is pervaded by questions about faith, individual roles and responsibilities, social and political reform, and the purpose of science. In some cases, the mood is one of disillusionment, and in others, there is a careful balance of optimism and pessimism.

Gathering Wild Flowers, 1896. Alfred Augustus Glendening. Private collection.

Alfred, Lord Tennyson

"Dreams are true while they last, and do we not live in dreams?"

Alfred, Lord Tennyson (1809–1892), was born at Somersby, Lincolnshire, to George and Elizabeth Tennyson, the fourth of twelve children. He grew up in a troubled home, as poverty and mental illness haunted the family.

While attending Trinity College in Cambridge, Tennyson collaborated with his brother Charles on a book of verse, *Poems by Two Brothers*, published in 1827. At Cambridge, Tennyson won a Chancellor's medal for poetry and joined a group of talented undergraduates who called themselves the Apostles.

During his Cambridge years, Tennyson often did not write down his work. He had terrible eyesight, which made reading and writing difficult, so he created his poetry by composing it in his head, sometimes working on a poem for years. Arthur Hallam, a close friend of Tennyson, transcribed the piece "The Lotos-Eaters" while Tennyson recited it at one of the Apostles meetings. In 1833, Hallam died suddenly, sending Tennyson into a deep depression. Over the next decade, Tennyson wrote most of his best poetry, including *In Memoriam*, "The Passing of Arthur," "Ulysses," and "Tithonus." Tennyson's depression eventually resulted in his being hospitalized for a few weeks.

In 1836, Tennyson fell in love with Emily Sellwood but was unable to marry her because he was poor. The success of the volume *Poems*, published in 1842, gained Tennyson popularity, and in 1845, he began receiving a small payment from the government. His fortune improved greatly in 1850, when William Wordsworth, England's poet laureate, died and Tennyson was named to replace him. Tennyson married Emily, and his fame as a poet continued to grow steadily.

In 1884, Queen Victoria made Tennyson a peer, bestowing on him the aristocratic title Lord. When the well-loved poet died in 1892 at age eighty-three, he was buried in Westminster Abbey in the section known as Poets' Corner.

Tennyson is considered by many to be the greatest poet of the Victorian Era. Patriotic themes and subjects from medieval romance are common in his work. Using language that appeals strongly to all the senses, he articulated the ideas and values of his era, including a concern about the effects of materialism and scientific knowledge in an industrial age and a longing for spiritual faith.

Noted Works

"The Lady of Shalott" (1830)

"Ulysses" (1842)

In Memoriam (1850)

Maud (1855)

Idylls of the King (1859)

"Tithonus" (1860)

The Lady of Shalott

A Narrative Poem by Alfred, Lord Tennyson

Ulysses

A Dramatic Poem by Alfred, Lord Tennyson

Build Background

Literary Context **"The Lady of Shalott"** tells a story set in the legendary days of King Arthur and his knights of the Round Table. The city of Camelot, mentioned repeatedly in the poem, was the capital of Arthur's kingdom. Sir Lancelot, also mentioned, was one of Arthur's most capable knights. Lancelot is the hero of many medieval romances and is portrayed as a nearly perfect knight: handsome, brave, strong, courteous, persevering, and devout. However, he has some failings that keep him from being pure enough to acquire the Holy Grail, a holy Christian relic for which many knights searched in several medieval legends.

The Lady in "The Lady of Shalott" is based on Elaine of Astolat. According to Arthurian legend, Elaine of Astolat fell in love with Sir Lancelot, but he did not return her love. When she died of unrequited love, she was, as requested, placed in a boat in the Thames River and steered to Camelot.

Ulysses was the Roman name for Odysseus, a hero from the ancient Greek epic poems attributed to Homer, *The Iliad* and *The Odyssey*. Ulysses fought in the Trojan War and returned to his kingdom, Ithaca. On the decade-long return journey, he saw many strange lands and had many marvelous, heroic adventures. In Tennyson's poem **"Ulysses,"** the aged king longs for one last adventure to culminate his career.

"The Lady of Shalott" is quite musical and has end rhymes and refrains. "Ulysses," in contrast, reads more like a dramatic speech and uses blank verse and elevated language. **Blank verse,** which is unrhymed poetry written in **iambic pentameter,** characterizes many of the great tragic and heroic works in the English language, including much of Shakespeare's *Macbeth* and all of Milton's *Paradise Lost*. Because blank verse is unrhymed, it sounds more like ordinary speech than poetry often does. Because of its regular metrical pattern, however, blank verse sounds more formal or lofty than ordinary speech. By writing in blank verse, a poet can elevate realistic characters to a lofty plane.

Reader's Context Isolation can be physical or psychological. When have you felt isolated? What caused the feelings, and how did you deal with them?

Ulysses.

Analyze Literature

Foil and Archetype

A **foil** is a character whose traits contrast with and therefore highlight the traits of another character.

An **archetype** is a type of character, image, theme, symbol, plot, or other element that appears in literature throughout the world. One example is the story of a quest or journey in which someone experiences adventure and danger and becomes wiser.

Set Purpose

As you read "The Lady of Shalott," chart the differences between the portrayals of the Lady of Shalott and Sir Lancelot. Consider how these differences highlight different aspects of their personalities. In reading "Ulysses," consider which character acts as a foil to Ulysses. After reading both poems, think about what archetypes the Lady of Shalott and Ulysses may represent.

Preview Vocabulary

surly, 876
amble, 876
wane, 878
countenance, 878
yearn, 881
discern, 881

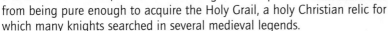

The Lady of Shalott

The Lady of Shalott, 1888. John William Waterhouse.
Tate Gallery, London, England. (See detail on page 873.)
Romantic painting

by Alfred, Lord Tennyson

(modified) tail-rhyme stanza

sounds medieval

tetrameter line is bouncy/
(lighthearted)

☆ chain is not symbolic
at all
– literal chain

candles are symbolic though
–symbolize her
life

Part 1

On either side the river lie
Long fields of barley and of rye,
That clothe the wold¹ and meet the sky;
And through the field the road runs by
     To many-towered Camelot;

5

---

1. **wold.** Plains

And up and down the people go,
Gazing where the lilies blow
Round an island there below,
    The island of Shalott.

10 Willows whiten, aspens quiver,
Little breezes dusk and shiver
Through the wave that runs forever
By the island in the river
    Flowing down to Camelot:
15 Four gray walls, and four gray towers,
Overlook a space of flowers,
And the silent isle imbowers[2]
    The Lady of Shalott.

By the margin, willow-veiled,
20 Slide the heavy barges trailed
By slow horses; and unhailed
The shallop[3] flitteth silken-sailed
    Skimming down to Camelot:
But who hath seen her wave her hand?
25 Or at the casement seen her stand?
Or is she known in all the land,
    The Lady of Shalott?

Only reapers, reaping early
In among the bearded barley,
30 Hear a song that echoes cheerly
From the river winding clearly,
    Down to towered Camelot;
And by the moon the reaper weary,
Piling sheaves in uplands airy,
35 Listening, whispers "'Tis the fairy
    Lady of Shalott."

Part 2

There she weaves by night and day
A magic web with colors gay.
She has heard a whisper say,
40 A curse is on her if she stay
    To look down to Camelot.
She knows not what the curse may be,
And so she weaveth steadily,
And little other care hath she,
45   The Lady of Shalott.

---

2. **imbowers.** Encloses or shelters
3. **shallop.** Open boat

[Handwritten margin notes:]

medieval

She is a maker of art
— weaves
works from the reflections of the outside world
When she looks out window, curse comes upon her
mirror cracks
weave comes apart

Sir Lancelot is so beautiful, she has to look outside

Knows she is doomed, but sings til her last breath
— power to the lady — Anglo-saxon

John William Waterhouse

John William Waterhouse (1849–1917) was an eclectic painter who was inspired by other Victorian artists and incorporated both Classical and Romantic qualities in his work. One of the strongest influences on his painting was an artistic movement of the mid-1800s called the Pre-Raphaelite Brotherhood (see Art Connection, Unit 4, page 421). Although the first wave of this movement had ended before Waterhouse began his career, he and several other British artists resumed the tradition and carried it into the twentieth century.

One of the most famous paintings of this second Pre-Raphaelite wave was Waterhouse's *The Lady of Shalott* (see page 874), based on Tennyson's poem. In his painting, Waterhouse re-creates the scene in Part 4 of the poem, in which the Lady of Shalott leaves the island in a boat and floats toward Camelot. Waterhouse places her in a setting surrounded by nature, which reflects the Pre-Raphaelites' emphasis on nature's beauty and power. The Lady is captivated by the crucifix mounted on the bow of the boat, indicating the Pre-Raphaelites' intense spirituality and the connection they saw between religion and nature. The flickering candles and the woman's weak hold on the chain symbolize her waning life force.

Waterhouse was one of many Victorian artists to be inspired by Tennyson's poem. Although they focused on different scenes in the narrative, these artists shared the purpose of portraying the ideal Victorian woman. Like Tennyson's Lady of Shalott, that woman was perceived as beautiful, pure, spiritual, and nurturing—a view consistent with traditional female roles, such as wife and mother. However, Victorian women were becoming aware of the world beyond the home, and their desire to experience life directly conflicted with these traditional roles. Some of the artists who depicted the Lady of Shalott indicated this conflict in scenes of imprisonment and escape.

Critical Viewing Evaluate Waterhouse's portrayal of Victorian women, based on *The Lady of Shalott*. What physical, spiritual, and emotional characteristics can you infer from the painting? Compare and contrast Waterhouse's portrayal of women with that provided in Tennyson's poem.

And moving through a mirror clear[4]
That hangs before her all the year,
Shadows of the world appear.
There she sees the highway near
50   Winding down to Camelot;
There the river eddy whirls,
And there the <u>surly</u> village churls,[5]
And the red cloaks of market girls,
        Pass onward from Shalott.

55 Sometimes a troop of damsels glad,
An abbot on an <u>ambling</u> pad,[6]

---

4. **mirror clear.** Weavers often use mirrors to see the progress of their work.
5. **churls.** Peasants
6. **pad.** Horse with an easy pace

> **sur • ly** (sʉr´ lē) *adj.,* rude; irritable
> **am • ble** (am´ bəl) *v.,* move with a smooth, easy gait

Sometimes a curly shepherd lad,
Or long-haired page in crimson clad,
    Goes by to towered Camelot;
60 And sometimes through the mirror blue
The knights come riding two and two:
She hath no loyal knight and true,
    The Lady of Shalott.

But in her web she still delights
65 To weave the mirror's magic sights,
For often through the silent nights
A funeral, with plumes and lights
    And music, went to Camelot;
Or when the moon was overhead,
70 Came two young lovers lately wed:
"I am half sick of shadows," said
    The Lady of Shalott.

Part 3

A bowshot from her bower eaves,
He rode between the barley sheaves,
75 The sun came dazzling through the leaves,
And flamed upon the brazen greaves[7]
    Of bold Sir Lancelot.
A red-cross knight forever kneeled
To a lady in his shield,
80 That sparkled on the yellow field,
    Beside remote Shalott.

The gemmy bridle glittered free,
Like to some branch of stars we see
Hung in the golden Galaxy.
85 The bridle bells rang merrily
    As he rode down to Camelot;
And from his blazoned baldric[8] slung
A mighty silver bugle hung,
And as he rode his armor rung,
90   Beside remote Shalott.

All in the blue unclouded weather
Thick-jeweled shone the saddle leather,
The helmet and the helmet-feather
Burned like one burning flame together,
95   As he rode down to Camelot;
As often through the purple night,

---

7. **greaves.** Pieces of armor that protect the lower leg
8. **baldric.** Ornamented belt used to support a sword or bugle

Ulysses Deriding Polyphemus, 1829. Joseph Mallord William Turner. National Gallery, London, England.

Ulysses

by Alfred, Lord Tennyson

[handwritten: dramatic monologue]

[handwritten: – blank verse unrhymed iambic pentameter]

[handwritten: – exciting Victorian spirit mainstream feeling on progress at the time]

[handwritten: – The Victorian poet – well known for mythological poetry]

It little profits that an idle king,
By this still hearth, among these barren crags, *[handwritten: not very positive]*
Matched with an aged wife, I mete and dole *[handwritten: he has been so transformed, his love for family + country is now gone]*
Unequal laws[1] unto a savage race,
5   That hoard, and sleep, and feed, and know not me.
> I cannot rest from travel; I will drink
Life to the lees.[2] All times I have enjoyed *[handwritten: emphasizing to take good and bad tog thro drink it all]*
Greatly, have suffered greatly, both with those
That loved me, and alone; on shore, and when *[handwritten: recklessness]*
10   Through scudding drifts the rainy Hyades[3]
Vexed the dim sea. I am become a name;
For always roaming with a hungry heart *[handwritten: everything he has been doing]*
Much have I seen and known—cities of men
And manners, climates, councils, governments,

[handwritten left margin: Describing himself / nonaction / moment of decision / he is not content]

---

1. **mete . . . laws.** Give out rewards and punishments
2. **lees.** ~~Dregs~~ *[handwritten: sludge at bottom of wine > not desirable]*
3. **Through . . . Hyades.** Through driving rain showers which were said to follow the rising of the group of stars known as the Hyades

15 Myself not least, but honored of them all—
And drunk delight of battle with my peers,
Far on the ringing plains of windy Troy, *quoted*
I am a part of all that I have met;
Yet all experience is an arch wherethrough

> *what he is going through*
> *to experience more*

20 Gleams that untraveled world whose margin fades
Forever and forever when I move.
How dull it is to pause, to make an end,
To rust unburnished, not to shine in use! *sword needs to be polished   talking of his transformation*
As though to breathe were life! Life piled on life *Just breathing is not living*
25 Were all too little, and of one to me
Little remains; but every hour is saved
From that eternal silence, something more,
A bringer of new things; and vile it were
For some three suns to store and hoard myself,
30 And this gray spirit <u>yearning</u> in desire
To follow knowledge like a sinking star,
Beyond the utmost bound of human thought.

This is my son, mine own Telemachus,
To whom I leave the scepter and the isle—

- About his son —he loves him, but they have nothing in common
says he is a good leader   kind of sad
totally focused, does nothing wrong

35 <u>Well-loved of me</u>, <u>discerning</u> to fulfill
This labor, by slow prudence to make mild
A rugged people, and through soft degrees
Subdue them to the useful and the good.

> *what a good king does*

Most blameless is he, centered in the sphere
40 Of common duties, decent not to fail
In offices of tenderness, and pay
Meet adoration to my household gods,
When I am gone. He works his work, I mine.

he can leave because he has such a great son to leave everything to

There lies the port, the vessel puffs her sail;
45 There gloom the dark, broad seas. My mariners,
Souls that have toiled, and wrought, and thought with me—
That ever with a frolic welcome took
The thunder and the sunshine, and opposed
Free hearts, free foreheads—you and I are old;
50 Old age hath yet his honor and his toil.
Death closes all; but something ere the end,
Some work of noble note, may yet be done,
Not unbecoming men that strove with Gods.

> *they are old now, but they still have something more to do*

The lights begin to twinkle from the rocks;
55 The long day wanes; the slow moon climbs; the deep

yearn (yɐrn) *v.*, filled with longing
dis • cern (di sɐrn´) *v.*, show good judgment

Ulysses embracing his son, Telemachus, as the goddess Athena looks on. Nineteenth-century wood engraving by Charles Baude.

Moans round with many voices. Come, my friends,
'Tis not too late to seek a newer world.
Push off, and sitting well in order smite
The sounding furrows; for my purpose holds

60 To sail beyond the sunset, and the baths
Of all the western stars, until I die.
It may be that the gulfs will wash us down;
It may be we shall touch the Happy Isles,[4]
And see the great Achilles,[5] whom we knew.

65 Though much is taken, much abides; and though
We are not now that strength which in old days
Moved earth and heaven, that which we are, we are—
One equal temper of heroic hearts,
Made weak by time and fate, but strong in will

70 To strive, to seek, to find, and not to yield. ❖

[handwritten: the day is coming to a close]

[handwritten: life is at twilight for them]

[handwritten: symbolic, west is where dead go, they are going beyond]

[handwritten: a ringing heroic ending]

---

4. **Happy Isles.** Paradise islands of perpetual summer located in the western ocean according to Greek myth

5. **Achilles.** Greek warrior in the Trojan War whose only vulnerable spot was his heel

MIRRORS & WINDOWS

Define the word *hero.* How does your modern-day concept of a hero compare to that in "Ulysses"?

Refer to Text ▶ ▶ ▶ ▶ ▶   Reason with Text

Refer to Text	Reason with Text	
1a. How does the Lady of Shalott see what is going on in the outside world? What art does she practice? What does she portray in her art?	**1b.** Explain how the Lady of Shalott's practice of art demonstrates her distance from the world.	**Understand** Find meaning
2a. Name the knight that the Lady of Shalott sees before going to the window and "looking down to Camelot."	**2b.** What motivates the Lady of Shalott to look toward Camelot despite the curse placed on her?	**Apply** Use information
3a. Make two lists: one of Telemachus's qualities and one of Ulysses' qualities.	**3b.** Compare and contrast Telemachus and Ulysses. Who would make the best king? Cite evidence to support your answer.	**Analyze** Take things apart
4a. In lines 1–5, about what specific aspect of his life is Ulysses unhappy?	**4b.** Judge whether Ulysses is still a hero or just an old man reluctant to give up the pleasures of his youth.	**Evaluate** Make judgments
5a. Describe the Lady of Shalott's and Ulysses' relationship with the outside world.	**5b.** How does the contrast between the Lady of Shalott's and Ulysses' relationship with the outside world illustrate different attitudes toward the theme of isolation?	**Create** Bring ideas together

Analyze Literature

Foil and Archetype

What differences did you observe in the portrayals of the Lady of Shalott and Sir Lancelot? How does Sir Lancelot serve as a foil for the Lady of Shalott? In the poem "Ulysses," how does Ulysses' son Telemachus serve as a foil for Ulysses?

What archetype does the Lady of Shalott embody? What archetype does Ulysses embody? Name other works of literature incorporating these same archetypes.

Extend the Text

Writing Options

Creative Writing In Tennyson's poem, Ulysses sails off into the sunset on his last voyage. Write an adventure story about the events that occur on Ulysses' last journey.

Expository Writing Write one paragraph that explains why the Lady of Shalott gave up her life in the tower. Support your explanation with details from the poem.

Collaborative Learning

Compare Dramatic Monologues "Ulysses" is a poem that consists of a dramatic monologue, which is a speech by one character. Ulysses was the Roman name for Odysseus, a hero from two ancient Greek epic poems attributed to Homer. Working with a partner, compare and contrast the dramatic elements of Tennyson's

"Ulysses" (published in 1842 CE) with those of a monologue or speech made by Odysseus in Homer's *The Odyssey* (written around 800 BCE). What differences do you notice in language and form? Evaluate these changes in dramatic structure, citing examples from both texts to support your inferences and conclusions.

Lifelong Learning

Prepare an Oral History Older people have acquired a lifetime of knowledge and experience, and one can learn much from them. Ask an older person to tell you one or two stories about a specific period in his or her past. If possible, record the stories and then transcribe them. If you cannot record the stories, take detailed notes and retell them or write a report on them.

 Go to **www.mirrorsandwindows.com** for more.

from
IN MEMORIAM

by Alfred, Lord Tennyson

Canto 5

I sometimes hold it half a sin
   To put in words the grief I feel;
   For words, like Nature, half reveal
And half conceal the Soul within.

5   But, for the unquiet heart and brain,
   A use in measured language lies;
   The sad mechanic exercise,
Like dull narcotics, numbing pain.

In words, like weeds,[1] I'll wrap me o'er,
10   Like coarsest clothes against the cold;
   But that large grief which these enfold
Is given in outline and no more.

. . .

Canto 54

O, yet we trust that somehow good
   Will be the final goal of ill,
15   To pangs of nature, sins of will,
Defects of doubt, and taints of blood;

That nothing walks with <u>aimless</u> feet;
   That not one life shall be destroyed,
   Or cast as rubbish to the void,
20   When God hath made the pile complete;

That not a worm is cloven in vain;
   That not a moth with vain desire
   Is shriveled in a fruitless fire,
Or but subserves another's gain.

Portrait of a Man Writing, c. 1880. F. Fry.
Private collection. (See detail on page 885.)

---

1. **weeds.** Clothes appropriate for mourning

aim • less (ām´ ləs) *adj.,* without purpose or intention

> 25   Behold, we know not anything;
>   I can but trust that good shall fall
>   At last—far off—at last, to all,
>   And every winter change to spring.
>
>   So runs my dream; but what am I?
> 30   An infant crying in the night;
>   An infant crying for the light,
>   And with no language but a cry.

     . . .

Canto 59

>   O Sorrow, wilt thou live with me
>   No casual mistress, but a wife,
> 35   My bosom friend and half of life;
>   As I confess it needs must be?
>
>   O Sorrow, wilt thou rule my blood,
>   Be sometimes lovely like a bride,
>   And put thy harsher moods aside,
> 40 If thou wilt have me wise and good?
>
>   My centered passion cannot move,
>   Nor will it lessen from today;
>   But I'll have leave at times to play
>   As with the creature of my love;
>
> 45 And set thee forth, for thou art mine,
>   With so much hope for years to come,
>   That, howsoe'er I know thee, some
>   Could hardly tell what name were thine.

     . . .

Canto 75

> 50 I leave thy praises unexpressed
>   In verse that brings myself relief,
>   And by the measure of my grief
>   I leave thy greatness to be guessed.
>
>   What practice howsoe'er expert
> 55   In fitting aptest words to things,
>   Or voice the richest-toned that sings,
>   Hath power to give thee as thou wert?
>
>   I care not in these fading days
>   To raise a cry that lasts not long,
> 60   And round thee with the breeze of song
>   To stir a little dust of praise.

Thy leaf has perished in the green,
    And, while we breathe beneath the sun,
    The world which credits what is done
Is cold to all that might have been.

65 So here shall silence guard thy fame;
    But somewhere, out of human view,
    Whate'er thy hands are set to do
Is wrought with <u>tumult</u> of acclaim.

. . .

Canto 130

Thy voice is on the rolling air
70   I hear thee where the waters run;
    Thou standest in the rising sun,
And in the setting thou art fair.

What art thou then? I cannot guess;
    But though I seem in star and flower
75   To feel thee some <u>diffusive</u> power,
I do not therefore love thee less.

My love involves the love before;
    My love is <u>vaster</u> passion now;
    Tho' mix'd with God and Nature thou,
80 I seem to love thee more and more.

Far off thou art, but ever nigh;
    I have thee still, and I rejoice;
    I prosper, circled with thy voice;
I shall not lose thee tho' I die. ❖

---

tu • mult (tu´ mult') *n.*, commotion; agitation
dif • fu • sive (di fyü´ siv) *adj.*, tending to disperse
vast (vast) *adj.*, enormous; huge

MIRRORS & WINDOWS

In canto 5, the speaker states, "I sometimes hold it half a sin / To put in words the grief I feel." How might it be helpful for someone to write or talk about his or her grief? How might it help someone come to terms with his or her sorrow?

Refer to Text ▶ ▶ ▶ ▶ ▶ Reason with Text

1a. In canto 5, what purpose does the speaker give for writing these poems?	**1b.** Explain how effective the speaker feels the words will be in conveying his feelings.	**Understand** Find meaning
2a. In canto 75, what does the speaker say the world praises? To what is the world cold?	**2b.** How do these lines explain the speaker's choice to not praise his friend in verse?	**Apply** Use information
3a. List the ways the speaker describes and personifies sorrow in canto 59.	**3b.** Choose one description from your list. How does the description show the depth of the speaker's sorrow?	**Analyze** Take things apart
4a. In canto 54, identify the event in nature that symbolizes, for the speaker, the idea that good can come of ill.	**4b.** Has the speaker accepted the idea that everything happens for a reason and that good will come of ill? Explain your answer.	**Evaluate** Make judgments
5a. Define the main ideas in cantos 5, 54, 59, 75, and 130.	**5b.** Summarize the development you see through the cantos. What conclusions does the speaker come to in them?	**Create** Bring ideas together

Analyze Literature

Elegy and Imagery

Cite passages that reflect the three stages of grief that are characteristic of an elegy. How has Tennyson's grief been transformed from the beginning to the end of the poem?

What imagery appears in stanza 3 of canto 75 (lines 57–60)? How has the poet's imagery been affected by death?

Extend the Text

Writing Options

Creative Writing Write a descriptive paragraph about a friend. Use sensory details and allusions to songs, stories, or experiences that remind you of that friend.

Applied Writing Choose someone you admire who died within the last twenty years. It may be someone you knew personally or someone you never met whose life you admire. Gather some information about the person and write an obituary for him or her.

Collaborative Learning

Write a Research Report With two or three other classmates, prepare a research report on ways in which people around the world memorialize others who have died. You may wish to focus on two cultures, such as yours and one other country, and compare and contrast memorial rituals in those countries. For example, you might compare and contrast what people do after someone dies in Japan and in the United States.

Media Literacy

Undertake a Media Death Watch Some people think death is so commonplace on television, in movies, and in the news that people have become desensitized to it. For one week, monitor what you see in the media. Determine the intended audience and purpose for each type of media piece, and evaluate any differences in formality and tone related to these factors. Then take notes on how often death is shown, whether it is shown realistically, and what you see after the death has taken place. Finally, determine how the words, images, graphics, and sounds of each piece impact meaning. Use your findings to write an essay evaluating the role that the media play in the public's response to death. Cite evidence from your research to support your conclusions.

 Go to **www.mirrorsandwindows.com** for more.

1. In "The Lady of Shalott," which set of rhymes below emphasizes an important connection in the poem?
   A. *lie, rye, sky,* and *by*
   B. *go, blow,* and *below*
   C. *quiver, shiver, forever,* and *river*
   D. *space, face,* and *grace*
   E. *Camelot, Shalott,* and *Lancelot*

2. In "The Lady of Shalott," the disconnectedness of the Lady of Shalott from the outside world is emphasized by all of the following *except*
   A. she lives on an island.
   B. she weaves elegant tapestries.
   C. she lives alone.
   D. she is called the "the fairy Lady of Shalott."
   E. she views the outside world through a mirror.

3. In "The Lady of Shalott," what distinguishes Lancelot from the other people who have been reflected in the mirror?
   A. His horse and armor are covered in jewels and he seems to radiate light.
   B. He is a knight riding toward Camelot.
   C. He is singing as he rides.
   D. He rides slowly and looks exhausted from doing great deeds.
   E. He is young, strong, and handsome.

4. In "Ulysses," which of the following lines contain an example of *internal rhyme,* or the use of rhyming words within lines?
   A. "That hoard, and sleep, and feed, and know not me."
   B. "Vexed the dim sea. I am become a name;"
   C. "And drunk delights of battle with my peers,"
   D. "Souls that have toiled, and wrought, and thought with me—"
   E. "Moved earth and heaven, that which we are, we are— / One equal temper of heroic hearts."

5. In "Ulysses," which of the following quotations from the poem best summarizes Ulysses' main goal in life?
   A. "I cannot rest from travel."
   B. "I am a part of all that I have met;"
   C. "This is my son, mine own Telemachus;"
   D. "It may be we shall touch the Happy Isles,"
   E. "To strive, to seek, to find, and not to yield."

6. Ulysses' "hungry heart" is the cause of all the following actions and behaviors *except*
   A. "I cannot rest from travel."
   B. "always roaming."
   C. "Much have I seen and known."
   D. "Made weak by time and fate."
   E. "To follow knowledge like a sinking star."

7. In which of the following lines from "Ulysses" does Tennyson employ the most *assonance,* or repetition of vowel sounds?
   A. "Matched with an aged wife, I mete and dole"
   B. "That hoard, and sleep, and feed, and know not me,"
   C. "Vexed the dim sea. I am become a name;"
   D. "And drunk delight of battle with my peers,"
   E. "As though to breathe were life! Life piled on life"

8. In lines 21–24 of canto 54 of *In Memoriam,* to what purpose are the examples of the worm and moth used?
   A. to show the senseless cruelty of human nature
   B. to emphasize that good comes out of every act
   C. to show that Tennyson will eventually overcome his grief
   D. to show Nature's indifference toward human pain
   E. to illustrate the belief that every act has a purpose in the grand scheme of things

9. **Constructed Response:** Identify the rhyme scheme of "The Lady of Shalott." How does Tennyson's use of this rhyme scheme affect your reading and understanding of the poem?

10. **Constructed Response:** Discuss the common threads running through the excerpts from *In Memoriam.*

Dover Beach

A Lyric Poem by Matthew Arnold

Build Background

Literary Context No work more typifies the struggle between faith and doubt faced by men and women of the Victorian Era than Matthew Arnold's **"Dover Beach."** Arnold lived in a time when religion was per-  ceived as coming under attack from science and many people were questioning their faith. He felt the loss of his own faith keenly and wrote about it in this famous poem. The poem fully meets Arnold's own criteria for poetry: that it have a "high seriousness" and provide a "criticism of life."

Many literary critics have called Arnold's poetry severe and melancholic, and indeed, "Dover Beach" is one of the most melancholic poems ever written. However, a close reading of the selection reveals that Arnold did have some optimism, for the poem offers as a stay against the anarchy and confusion of life the possibility that people can be "true / To one another."

Reader's Context What sights or sounds make you feel melancholy, or blue?

Meet the Author

Matthew Arnold (1822–1888) was a multitalented man: a great scholar of the Classics, a distinguished poet and lit- erary critic, and a commentator on education, religion, and culture. He attended Oxford University and received the Newdigate Prize for a poem about Oliver Cromwell, leader of England during the Puritan Interregnum (1649–1660). After graduating, Arnold took a government post as inspector of schools, a position he held for the rest of his working life. In 1851, he married Fanny Lucy Wightman, with whom he would have six children. Two years later, he published a book entitled *Poems*, which established his reputation as a writer of verse. In 1857, Arnold was appointed to the poetry chair at Oxford, a position he held for ten years. In 1859, he became foreign assistant commissioner on education, traveling to Europe to observe school systems there, which he held up as a model to improve educa- tion in England.

Arnold's collection *New Poems*, which contained "Dover Beach," appeared in 1867, but by that time, he was devoting his writing primarily to critical essays on literary, educational, and social topics. He admired the calmness, clarity, and restraint of the great writers of Classical Greece and Rome and believed that culture was the proper antidote for the worries, materialism, and decay of his times.

Analyze Literature

Allusion and Symbol An **allusion** is a reference to a well-known person, event, object, or work from history or literature.

A **symbol** is anything that stands for or represents both itself and something else. *Conventional symbols* are tradi- tional, well-known associations, such as a dove for peace. A *personal* or *idiosyncratic symbol* is one that assumes its second- ary meaning because of the special use to which it is put by a writer.

Set Purpose

Poets and writers often use allusions to connect their ideas to others that may be more familiar to their audiences. While you read "Dover Beach," note the allusion Arnold makes in the second stanza. Consider for what purpose Arnold includes this allusion. In "Dover Beach," Arnold begins his poem with a detailed description of the ocean. As you read, consider what the sea symbolizes in the poem. Does Arnold use it to rep- resent more than one thing?

Preview Vocabulary

tranquil, 892
tremulous, 893
turbid, 893
certitude, 893

The Undercliff, 1828. Richard Parkes Bonington.
Nottingham City Museums and Galleries, Nottingham, England.
(See detail on page 891.)

Dover Beach

the poetic persona

by Matthew Arnold

Free verse

— Cliffs are chalk
— no sand on beach,
* pebbles*

The sea is calm tonight.
The tide is full, the moon lies fair
Upon the straits—on the French coast the light
Gleams and is gone; the cliffs of England stand,
5 Glimmering and vast, out in the <u>tranquil</u> bay.
Come to the window, sweet is the night air!
Only, from the long line of spray
Where the sea meets the moon-blanched land,
Listen! you hear the grating roar
10 Of pebbles which the waves draw back, and fling,
At their return, up the high strand,[1]

scene

melancholy
tranquil
calm

---

1. **strand.** Shore

tran • quil (traŋ´ kwəl) *adj.,* calm and peaceful

Begin, and cease, and then again begin,
With <u>tremulous</u> cadence slow, and bring
The eternal note of sadness in.

15 Sophocles[2] long ago
Heard it on the Aegean, and it brought
Into his mind the <u>turbid ebb and flow</u>
Of human misery; we
Find also in the sound a thought,
20 Hearing it by this distant northern sea.

The Sea of Faith
Was once, too, at the full, and round earth's shore
Lay like the folds of a bright girdle furled.[3]
But now I only hear
25 Its melancholy, long, withdrawing roar,
Retreating, to the breath
Of the night wind, down the vast edges drear
And naked shingles[4] of the world.

Ah, love, let us be true
30 To one another! for the world, which seems
To lie before us like a land of dreams,
So various, so beautiful, so new,
Hath really neither joy, nor love, nor light,
Nor <u>certitude</u>, nor peace, nor help for pain;
35 And we are here as on a darkling plain
Swept with confused alarms of struggle and flight,
Where ignorant armies clash by night. ❖

Annotations (handwritten):
- Sea metaphor
- Speaker and his beloved addressing her — she is the audience
- +se
- the tide is out, when is it coming back?
- Turned from sea metaphor to clinginess — only have eachother
- Senses the loss of human faith
- clinging to beloved like a liferaft

---

2. **Sophocles** (496–406 BCE). Greek playwright
3. **Lay . . . furled.** At high tide, the sea tightly envelopes the land like
a girdle.
4. **shingles.** Rocky beaches

---

trem • u • lous (trem´ yə ləs) *adj.,* trembling
tur • bid (tur´ bəd) *adj.,* muddled
cer • ti • tude (sur´ tə tüd´) *n.,* absolute sureness

MIRRORS & WINDOWS How is modern-day society still struggling with similar issues of faith and doubt that the Victorians faced? How has modern-day society addressed these issues?

The White Cliffs of Dover

The "glimmering and vast" cliffs to which Arnold refers in "Dover Beach" are the white cliffs of Dover, one of England's most famous natural landmarks. This expanse of chalky white limestone rises up 350 feet from the Strait of Dover, the narrow sea passage at the eastern end of the English Channel, the waterway separating England and France. At this narrowest stretch of the channel, England is just twenty-one miles from the European mainland. On a clear day, observers standing on the Dover cliffs can see the beaches of France across the strait.

Given England's vulnerability to invasion at the English Channel, the Dover cliffs have played an integral role in the nation's military defense. During the Roman invasion in 55 BCE, Julius Caesar noted the difficulty of landing at Dover and elected to come ashore farther up the channel at Deal. The Romans later built two lighthouses near Dover to guide ships carrying additional legions of forces. During the Middle Ages, the English dug an extensive network of tunnels beneath the cliffs to help thwart advancements from hostile invaders. The military reused these tunnels during the Napoleonic wars and World War II.

In addition to Arnold's poem, many other works of literature have referenced the Dover cliffs. The most famous is Shakespeare's *King Lear*, in which one of the characters asks to be taken to "a cliff whose high and bending head looks fearfully in the confined deep." That cliff, which is west of Dover, later was named Shakespeare Cliff in honor of the bard. Rudyard Kipling also wrote of the Dover cliffs in his 1902 poem "The Broken Men," reflecting on the melancholy feelings of British exiles.

In one of the best-loved songs of World War II, "The White Cliffs of Dover," Vera Lynn brought hope to war-weary Brits by singing of a peaceful future. In years since, the Dover cliffs have been mentioned in songs by a diverse group of artists, including Indie rockers the Decembrists, electronic musician Fatboy Slim, jazz trumpeter Louis Prima, and Reggae singer Jimmy Cliff.

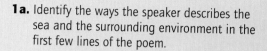

Refer to Text ▶ ▶ ▶ ▶ ▶ **Reason with Text**

1a. Identify the ways the speaker describes the sea and the surrounding environment in the first few lines of the poem.	**1b.** Explain what mood is created by this description of the environment. How does this mood change?	**Understand** Find meaning
2a. Quote the thought Sophocles has while listening to the sea.	**2b.** What connection does the speaker make to Sophocles' thought?	**Apply** Use information
3a. State what the speaker asks of his love in the last stanza. Why does he ask this?	**3b.** Compare and contrast the world as it seems to be and the way it really is according to the speaker.	**Analyze** Take things apart
4a. List the ways the speaker describes the world throughout the poem.	**4b.** Critique the speaker's attitude toward the world. Do you agree or disagree with the speaker's assessment of the world? Why or why not?	**Evaluate** Make judgments
5a. Name what the speaker says has swept the world in the last stanza.	**5b.** Explain how the speaker's description of the world reflects his personal struggle between doubt and faith. In what has the speaker lost faith? Why?	**Create** Bring ideas together

Analyze Literature

Allusion and Symbol

Identify the allusion the speaker makes in the second stanza of this poem. What is the purpose of this allusion? What idea does the allusion introduce?

How does Arnold use the sea as a symbol in the poem? What does the ebb and flow of the sea represent? What other symbolic significance does the sea have for the speaker? Explain how these representations are related.

Extend the Text

Writing Options

Creative Writing Choose a sound that you hear often. Make a connection between this sound and a feeling or idea. For example, a dripping faucet might keep you up at night like a nagging worry. Write a personal essay in which you explore the connection.

Persuasive Writing Write an editorial expressing your opinion about the state of the world. Whether you choose a positive or negative outlook, support your response with examples and offer reasons for your perception of the state of the world.

Lifelong Learning

Research Dover Dover, England, is known for its white cliffs. Using guidebooks, travel magazines, and the Internet, research Dover. Then, write a brief description of the city and create an itinerary of what you would do if you visited Dover.

Media Literacy

Evaluate the Media For several days in a row, watch the news on television, or read the news sections of the paper. How many stories are about negative events? positive events? How many "negative" stories have positive elements or slants, such as people reaching out to help flood victims? Do these news stories create an accurate portrait of what the world is like today? Present your findings to your class in a five-minute oral presentation.

 Go to **www.mirrorsandwindows.com** for more.

Pied Beauty
Spring and Fall: To a Young Child

Lyric Poems by Gerard Manley Hopkins

Build Background

Literary Context Gerard Manley Hopkins brought many changes to poetry. He created a rhythmic structure he called **sprung rhythm,** which appears in both **"Pied Beauty"** and **"Spring and Fall: To a Young Child."** Hopkins recognized this rhythm in Greek, Latin, Old English, and Welsh verse. In particular, Welsh language and literature had a very strong influence on him.

Hopkins wrote "Pied Beauty" while he was studying to become a Catholic priest. It is a curtal (shortened) sonnet, a form Hopkins created, with eleven lines rhyming *abcabc dbcdc*. The poem celebrates Hopkins's ecstasy in the beauty of nature as a symbol of the spiritual beauty of God.

"Spring and Fall" was written a few years later, while Hopkins worked in parishes in the slums of industrial cities. The speaker of the poem sympathizes with a young child's sorrow, telling her that we all must decline and die. This poem has several examples of Hopkins's practice of creating new words and compound adjectives to build concentrated images.

Reader's Context What examples from nature could be used to symbolize aspects of the human condition, such as growing up or dying?

Meet the Author

Gerard Manley Hopkins (1844–1889) grew up in a political, literary, and artistic family. He attended Oxford University and was attracted to the Oxford Movement, which, in response to the increased skepticism of the age, attempted to connect the Anglican Church to the tenets and rituals of the early Christian church. Like John Henry Newman, one of the founders of the Oxford Movement, Hopkins found himself concluding that the Roman Catholic Church was the true heir of early Christianity, and he converted to Catholicism.

In 1868 he joined the Society of Jesus, or Jesuits, and in 1877 he was ordained a priest, after which he burned the poetry he had written as a youth, considering it unworthy of his high vocation. Although some of his superiors encouraged him to resume writing poetry, only a few of Hopkins's poems were published during his lifetime because most readers could not understand his unusual words, highly compressed images, and odd rhythms. His poetry is among the most beautiful but also the oddest in the English language. It has strongly influenced a number of twentieth-century poets.

Analyze Literature

Sprung Rhythm and Alliteration

Sprung rhythm is a system in which metrical feet vary in length from one to four syllables, with just one of the syllables being stressed. The lines of a poem, therefore, can be of unequal lengths and several strong stresses can occur in a row.

Alliteration is the repetition of consonant sounds. Although alliteration usually refers to sounds at the beginning of words, it can also be used to refer to repetition of sounds on stressed syllables.

Set Purpose

Poetry, like music, has its own rhythms. Hopkins drew from Welsh techniques, especially *cynghanedd*, which is the arrangement of sounds within a line of poetry, using stress, alliteration, and rhyme, so that sound and sense are in perfect harmony. As you read Hopkins's poems, notice the irregular rhythms. Also, look for examples of alliteration in his poems. You may find it helpful to read the poems aloud to identify the placement of the stresses and instances of alliteration.

Preview Vocabulary

dappled, 897
stipple, 897

Pied Beauty[1]

by Gerard Manley Hopkins

Glory be to God for <u>dappled</u> things—
    For skies of couple-colour as a brinded[2] cow;
        For rose-moles all in <u>stipple</u> upon trout that swim;
Fresh-firecoal chestnut-falls,[3] finches' wings;
5   Landscape plotted and pieced—fold, fallow, and plough;[4]
    And áll trádes, their gear and tackle and trim.

All things counter, original, spare,[5] strange;
    Whatever is fickle, freckled (who knows how?)
      With swift, slow; sweet, sour; adazzle, dim;
10 He fathers-forth whose beauty is past change:
                Praise him. ❖

---

1. **Pied.** Marked with blotches of color
2. **brinded.** Brownish orange streaked with gray
3. **Fresh-firecoal chestnut-falls.** Freshly fallen chestnuts, red as coals
4. **fold . . . plough.** The land is colored in patches from the pastures or folds, fallow, unplowed fields, and plowed land.
5. **spare.** Rare

> **dap • pled** (da´ pəld) *adj.,* marked with spots
> **stip • ple** (sti´ pəl) *adj.,* fleck; speckle

MIRRORS & WINDOWS What unusual things do you find beautiful? What about these things makes them beautiful?

Spring and Fall
To a Young Child

by Gerard Manley Hopkins

Márgarét, áre you gríeving
Over Goldengrove unleaving?
Leáves, líke the things of man, you
With your fresh thoughts care for, can you?
5 Áh! ás the heart grows older
It will come to such sights colder
By and by, nor spare a sigh
Though worlds of wanwood leafmeal[1] lie;
And yet you *will* weep and know why.
10 Now no matter, child, the name:
Sórrow's spríngs áre the same.
Nor mouth had, no nor mind, expressed
What heart heard of, ghost guessed:
It ís the blight man was born for,
15 It is Márgarét you mourn for. ❖

---

1. **wanwood leafmeal.** Leaves that have fallen and begun to decay

Lilies, 1885. Frederick Morgan.
Private collection.

Mirrors & Windows

How differently might a child and an older person view the changing of the seasons and the passage of time? What is meant by the expression "Perspective comes with age"?

The University of Oxford

Gerard Manley Hopkins received his education from Balliol College, one of the many constituent colleges of the University of Oxford, the oldest university in England and the oldest English-speaking university in the world. Although an exact date of origin is unknown, evidence suggests that instruction began at Oxford around 1100. In the early 1200s, a master scholar, or chancellor, was appointed and the school was formally organized as a university. The first of the constituent colleges—University, Balliol, and Merton—were established between 1249 and 1264. By 1300, Oxford was recognized by academic, political, and religious leaders worldwide as a leading educational center.

Oxford has retained that reputation and today is considered among the top five academic institutions in the world. Among the approximately 7,000 professors who teach at Oxford's thirty-nine constituent colleges are some of the world's leading scientists, including biologist Richard Dawkins and physicist Stephen Hawking. Oxford's research facilities regularly produce cutting-edge technology, particularly in the field of medicine.

Competition is fierce for admission to Oxford. Of the approximately 12,000 students who apply each year, only about 3,000 (1 in 4) are admitted. Despite pressure to admit more British residents, Oxford makes a concerted effort to draw international scholars, and one-quarter of its 18,000 students are from overseas. Under the Rhodes Scholarship program, ninety highly qualified foreign students are invited to attend Oxford each year. Famous past recipients of this honor have included former president Bill Clinton and country musician Kris Kristofferson.

In addition to these famous alumni, Oxford has graduated forty-seven Nobel Prize winners, twenty-eight foreign presidents, and twenty-five British prime ministers. In addition to Hopkins, many British authors attended Oxford, including Philip Sydney, John Donne, Richard Lovelace, Jonathan Swift, Percy Shelley, Samuel Johnson, T. S. Eliot, A. E. Housman, J. R. R. Tolkien, and Graham Greene.

Refer to Text ▶ ▶ ▶ ▶ ▶ **Reason with Text**

1a. In "Pied Beauty" list the things from nature that are mentioned in the first stanza.	**1b.** Explain what these things have in common and why the speaker finds them so impressive.	**Understand** Find meaning
2a. How do the fields mentioned in line 5 of "Pied Beauty" differ from the things mentioned in lines 1–4?	**2b.** Explain how these things show the aspect of God that the speaker wants the reader to see as worthy of praise.	**Apply** Use information
3a. Identify the question the speaker asks in lines 1–2 of "Spring and Fall."	**3b.** Outline the speaker's argument.	**Analyze** Take things apart
4a. Find a quote that supports a main theme of "Spring and Fall."	**4b.** Critique the speaker's argument. Do you agree with his or her position?	**Evaluate** Make judgments
5a. List examples of nature imagery that Hopkins uses in "Pied Beauty" and "Spring and Fall."	**5b.** How does Hopkins's use of nature imagery support each poem's message or theme?	**Create** Bring ideas together

Analyze Literature

Sprung Rhythm and Alliteration

Review the definition of sprung rhythm. Choose one of the poems to scan. Write each line and mark the stressed syllables. At what point do several strongly stressed syllables appear in a row? What effect does this have?

Circle instances of alliteration in the poem you chose to scan. What effect does the alliteration have? Look at line 9 of "Pied Beauty" or line 9 of "Spring and Fall." How do stressed syllables and alliteration converge in this line? What effect does that convergence have?

Extend the Text

Writing Options

Creative Writing Review the definition of sprung rhythm on page 896. Then write your own poem about nature using Hopkins's sprung rhythm.

Expository Writing Does life get harder as we age? Or is life harder when you are young? Write a one-paragraph analysis of the argument in "Spring and Fall."

Media Literacy

Create a Nature Guide Make a nature guide celebrating pied beauty. Choose animals that show distinctive coloring or markings. Use encyclopedias, field guides, and other resources to learn more about the animals you choose. Write a brief description of the animal, its habitat, habits, and other key points. Include an illustration to show the pied beauty of each beast in your guide.

Collaborative Learning

Hold a Debate In "Spring and Fall," Hopkins argues, "It is the blight man was born for, / It is Márgarét you mourn for." As a class, identify what the "blight" is and what Hopkins is saying in these lines. Once you have come to an agreement, break into two groups to debate whether Hopkins's statement is true or false. Present your team's side of the argument by using elements of a classical persuasive speech: an introduction that states your team's position, a body that outlines the arguments and evidence from the poem as well as any counterarguments, and a conclusion that summarizes your team's points. Use logical transitions to help listeners follow your arguments, and include rhetorical devices, such as parallelism and repetition, to emphasize your points and sway listeners.

 Go to **www.mirrorsandwindows.com** for more.

When I Was One-and-Twenty
To an Athlete Dying Young

Lyric Poems by A. E. Housman

Build Background

Literary Context Both **"When I Was One-and-Twenty"** and **"To an Athlete Dying Young"** appear in Housman's first book, *A Shropshire Lad* (1896). Although initially not very successful, the volume gained popularity for its patriotic and military verse after the outbreak of the Boer War (1899–1902), and Housman became a famous poet.

The poems in this unit, like his others, are written in a simple style, one which expresses Housman's common theme of the transience of youth, beauty, and friendship. "When I Was One-and-Twenty" is bittersweet. A twenty-two-year-old man looks back to when he was a youthful twenty-one and foolish enough not to heed the advice of a wise man: Don't give yourself over to love. "To an Athlete Dying Young" harkens back to classical elegies of Greece and Rome, which often dealt with the death of a young athlete or hero.

Reader's Context What attitudes do you and your peers have toward love and fame?

Meet the Author

Alfred Edward Housman (1859–1936) was a classical scholar and distinguished poet. Although Housman did not produce a large body of work, his polished, simple style has influenced a great many other poets. Housman was born in Worcestershire, near the Shropshire countryside that often appears in his poetry. His mother died when he was twelve, and he began to question his religious faith, eventually becoming an atheist. He attended Oxford University. Although he was a brilliant student, Housman failed his final examination and went to work as a clerk in the Patent Office, where he spent ten years.

During this time, he spent evenings at the British Museum reading room studying Latin texts. He wrote articles about his studies and sent them to scholarly journals. Fellow scholars eventually took notice of his work, and in 1892 he was appointed professor of Latin at University College, London. Housman's major scholarly work was an annotated edition of the writings of Manilius, a Roman poet from the first century CE. Housman's volumes of poetry are *A Shropshire Lad*, which appeared in 1896, and *Last Poems*, which appeared nearly twenty-five years later. After Housman's death, his brother published another volume called *More Poems*.

Analyze Literature

Tone and Speaker
Tone is the emotional attitude toward the reader or toward the subject implied by a literary work. Examples of different types of tones that a work may have include familiar, ironic, playful, sarcastic, serious, and sincere.

The **speaker** is the character who speaks in, or narrates, a poem—the voice assumed by the writer. The speaker and the writer of a poem are not necessarily the same person.

Set Purpose

Housman was noted for his simple style in writing poetry, and he crafted his poems to convey a specific tone to emphasize the poem's theme. As you read each poem, pay attention to the tone Housman uses. For each poem, make a cluster chart listing words and phrases that illustrate the tone of the poem. In addition, determine who is speaking in each of the poems. How does the choice of speaker affect your understanding of the poem?

Preview Vocabulary

rue, 902
renown, 904

When I Was One-and-Twenty

by A. E. Housman

Portrait of Dr. Gachet, 1890. Vincent van Gogh.
Musée d'Orsay, Paris, France. (See detail on page 901.)

When I was one-and-twenty
 I heard a wise man say,
"Give crowns and pounds and guineas[1]
 But not your heart away;
5 Give pearls away and rubies
 But keep your fancy free."
But I was one-and-twenty,
 No use to talk to me.

When I was one-and-twenty
10 I heard him say again,
"The heart out of the bosom
 Was never given in vain;
'Tis paid with sighs a plenty
 And sold for endless <u>rue</u>."
15 And I am two-and-twenty,
 And oh, 'tis true, 'tis true. ❖

---

1. **crowns and pounds and guineas.** British monetary
 units

rue (rü) *n.*, sorrow; regret

MIRRORS & WINDOWS   The speaker admits that it was "no use" to give him advice when he was twenty-one. What things must a young person experience, rather than be told about? When does it make sense to take advice?

The Rising of the Moon

by Lady Augusta Gregory

PERSONS

SERGEANT.
POLICEMAN X.
POLICEMAN B.
A RAGGED MAN.

SCENE

Side of a quay[1] in a seaport town. Some posts and chains. A large barrel. Enter three policemen. Moonlight.

(SERGEANT, who is older than the others, crosses the stage to right and looks down steps. The others put down a pastepot and unroll a bundle of placards.)

POLICEMAN B.   I think this would be a good place to put up a notice. (*He points to barrel.*)

POLICEMAN X.   Better ask him. (*calls to SERGEANT*) Will this be a good place for a placard?

(*no answer*)

POLICEMAN B.   Will we put up a notice here on the barrel?

(*no answer*)

SERGEANT.   There's a flight of steps here that leads to the water. This is a place that should be minded well. If he got down here, his friends might have a boat to meet him; they might send it in here from outside.

POLICEMAN B.   Would the barrel be a good place to put a notice up?

SERGEANT.   It might; you can put it there.

(*They paste the notice up.*)

SERGEANT. (*reading it*)   Dark hair—dark eyes, smooth face, height five feet five—there's not much to take hold of in that—It's a pity I had no chance of seeing him before he broke out of

---

1. **quay.** Wharf.

gaol.[2] They say he's a wonder, that it's he makes all the plans for the whole organization. There isn't another man in Ireland would have broken gaol the way he did. He must have some friends among the gaolers.

POLICEMAN B. A hundred pounds is little enough for the Government to offer for him. You may be sure any man in the force that takes him will get promotion.

SERGEANT. I'll mind this place myself. I wouldn't wonder at all if he came this way. He might come slipping along there (*points to side of quay*), and his friends might be waiting for him there (*points down steps*), and once he got away it's little chance we'd have of finding him; it's maybe under a load of kelp he'd be in a fishing boat, and not one to help a married man that wants it to the reward.

POLICEMAN X. And if we get him itself, nothing but abuse on our heads for it from the people, and maybe from our own relations.

SERGEANT. Well, we have to do our duty in the force. Haven't we the whole country depending on us to keep law and order? It's those that are down would be up and those that are up would be down, if it wasn't for us. Well, hurry on, you have plenty of other places to placard yet, and come back here then to me. You can take the lantern. Don't be too long now. It's very lonesome here with nothing but the moon.

The Bulls-Eye, 1872. Gustave Doré.

POLICEMAN B. It's a pity we can't stop with you. The Government should have brought more police into the town, with *him* in gaol, and at assize[3] time too. Well, good luck to your watch.

(*They go out.*)

SERGEANT. (*walks up and down once or twice and looks at placard*) A hundred pounds and

---

2. **gaol.** British spelling of *jail*

3. **assize.** Periodic court session held in each county

promotion sure. There must be a great deal of spending in a hundred pounds. It's a pity some honest man not to be better of that.[4]

(A **Ragged Man** *appears at left and tries to slip past.* **Sergeant** *suddenly turns.*)

Sergeant. Where are you going?

Man. I'm a poor ballad-singer, your honor. I thought to sell some of these (*holds out bundle of ballads*) to the sailors.

(*He goes on.*)

Sergeant. Stop! Didn't I tell you to stop? You can't go on there.

Man. Oh, very well. It's a hard thing to be poor. All the world's against the poor!

Sergeant. Who are you?

Man. You'd be as wise as myself if I told you, but I don't mind. I'm one Jimmy Walsh, a ballad-singer.

Sergeant. Jimmy Walsh? I don't know that name.

Man. Ah, sure, they know it well enough in Ennis.[5] Were you ever in Ennis, sergeant?

Sergeant. What brought you here?

Man. Sure, it's to the assizes I came, thinking I might make a few shillings here or there. It's in the one train with the judges I came.

Sergeant. Well, if you came so far, you may as well go farther, for you'll walk out of this.

Man. I will, I will; I'll just go on where I was going.

(*goes towards steps*)

Sergeant. Come back from those steps; no one has leave to pass down them tonight.

Man. I'll just sit on the top of the steps till I see will some sailor buy a ballad off me that would give me my supper. They do be late going back to the ship. It's often I saw them in Cork[6] carried down the quay in a hand-cart.

Sergeant. Move on, I tell you. I won't have any one lingering about the quay tonight.

Man. Well, I'll go. It's the poor have the hard life! Maybe yourself might like one, sergeant. Here's a good sheet now. (*turns one over*) "Content and a pipe"—that's not much. "The Peeler and the goat"—you wouldn't like that. "Johnny Hart"—that's a lovely song.

Sergeant. Move on.

Man. Ah, wait till you hear it. (*sings*)
> There was a rich farmer's daughter lived
>   near the town of Ross;
> She courted a Highland soldier, his name
>   was Johnny Hart;
> Says the mother to her daughter, "I'll go
>   distracted mad
> If you marry that Highland soldier dressed
>   up in Highland plaid."

Sergeant. Stop that noise.

(**Man** *wraps up his ballads and shuffles towards the steps.*)

Sergeant. Where are you going?

Man. Sure you told me to be going, and I am going.

Sergeant. Don't be a fool. I didn't tell you to go that way; I told you to go back to the town.

Man. Back to the town, is it?

Sergeant. (*taking him by the shoulder and shoving him before him*) Here, I'll show you the way. Be off with you. What are you stopping for?

Man. (*who has been keeping his eye on the notice, points to it*) I think I know what you're waiting for, Sergeant.

Sergeant. What's that to you?

Man. And I know well the man you're waiting for—I know him well—I'll be going.

(*He shuffles on.*)

Sergeant. You know him? Come back here. What sort is he?

---

4. **It's a pity . . . that.** It's a pity some honest man doesn't benefit from the money.
5. **Ennis.** Town in County Clare
6. **Cork.** County in southern Ireland

The Irish Language

Although most modern Irish people use English as their primary language, some of them also speak the native Irish language, or Gaelic. Like the development of the English language, the development of the Irish language can be divided into three periods: Old Irish, from the seventh to the ninth centuries CE; Middle Irish, from the tenth to the sixteenth centuries; and Modern Irish, from the sixteenth century to the present.

The earliest surviving inscriptions of Old Irish date from sometime between the fifth and sixth centuries CE. They are written in an ancient Runic alphabet that was used by druids, or Celtic priests. Literature in the Irish language reached its peak during the Middle Ages, when Christian monks living in Ireland recorded the island's indigenous mythology.

After the English conquest of Ireland, the use of Irish declined steadily. It experienced a revival in the late nineteenth century, however, during the movement for home rule, or Irish self-government.

The leaders of this movement were ardent nationalists and encouraged the Irish to learn their native language as a way of creating an identity separate from England. The efforts of William Butler Yeats, Lady Augusta Gregory, and Edward Martyn to establish the Irish Literary Theater (later the Abbey Theater) contributed to the revival of Irish language and culture.

Today, only about 3 percent of Irish people, mostly along the western coast, use their native tongue in everyday conversation, but the nation's government is trying to revive Gaelic as a primary language. Irish public schools are required to teach the language to their students, and the European Union recognizes Irish as one of its official languages.

MAN. Come back is it, Sergeant? Do you want to have me killed?

SERGEANT. Why do you say that?

MAN. Never mind. I'm going. I wouldn't be in your shoes if the reward was ten times as much. (*goes on off stage to left*) Not if it was ten times as much.

SERGEANT. (*rushing after him*) Come back here, come back. (*drags him back*) What sort is he? Where did you see him?

MAN. I saw him in my own place, in the County Clare. I tell you you wouldn't like to be looking at him. You'd be afraid to be in the one place with him. There isn't a weapon he doesn't know the use of, and as to strength, his muscles are as hard as that board (*slaps barrel*).

SERGEANT. Is he as bad as that?

MAN. He is then.

SERGEANT. Do you tell me so?

MAN. There was a poor man in our place, a sergeant from Ballyvaughan.[7]—It was with a lump of stone he did it.

SERGEANT. I never heard of that.

MAN. And you wouldn't, sergeant. It's not everything that happens gets into the papers. And there was a policeman in plain clothes, too. . . . It is in Limerick he was. . . . It was after the time of the attack on the police barrack at Kilmallock[8]. . . Moonlight . . . just like

---

7. **Ballyvaughan.** Another town in County Clare
8. **Limerick . . . Kilmallock.** Kilmallock is a town in County Limerick.

this . . . waterside. . . . Nothing was known for certain.

SERGEANT.   Do you say so? It's a terrible county to belong to.

MAN.   That's so, indeed! You might be standing there, looking out that way, thinking you saw him coming up this side of the quay (*points*), and he might be coming up this other side (*points*), and he'd be on you before you knew where you were.

SERGEANT.   It's a whole troop of police they ought to put here to stop a man like that.

MAN.   But if you'd like me to stop with you, I could be looking down this side. I could be sitting up here on this barrel.

SERGEANT.   And you know him well, too?

MAN.   I'd know him a mile off, sergeant.

SERGEANT.   But you wouldn't want to share the reward?

MAN.   Is it a poor man like me, that has to be going the roads and singing in fairs, to have the name on him that he took a reward? But you don't want me. I'll be safer in the town.

SERGEANT.   Well, you can stop.

MAN. (*getting up on barrel*)   All right, sergeant. I wonder, now, you're not tired out, sergeant, walking up and down the way you are.

SERGEANT.   If I'm tired I'm used to it.

MAN.   You might have hard work before you tonight yet. Take it easy while you can. There's plenty of room up here on the barrel, and you see farther when you're higher up.

SERGEANT.   Maybe so. (*Gets up beside him on barrel, facing right. They sit back to back, looking different ways.*) You made me feel a bit queer with the way you talked.

MAN.   Give me a match, sergeant. (*He gives it, and Man lights pipe.*) Take a draw yourself? It'll quiet you. Wait now till I give you a light, but you needn't turn round. Don't take your eye off the quay for the life of you.

SERGEANT.   Never fear, I won't. (*Lights pipe. They both smoke.*) Indeed it's a hard thing to be in the force, out at night and no thanks for it, for all the danger we're in. And it's little we get but abuse from the people, and no choice but to obey our orders, and never asked when a man is sent into danger, if you are a married man with a family.

MAN. (*sings*)—

As through the hills I walked to view the
  hills and shamrock plain,
I stood awhile where nature smiles to view
  the rocks and streams,
On a matron fair I fixed my eyes beneath a
  fertile vale,
And she sang her song: it was on the wrong
  of poor old Granuaile.[9]

SERGEANT.   Stop that; that's no song to be singing in these times.

MAN.   Ah, sergeant, I was only singing to keep my heart up. It sinks when I think of him. To think of us two sitting here, and he creeping up the quay, maybe, to get to us.

SERGEANT.   Are you keeping a good lookout?

MAN.   I am; and for no reward too. Amn't I the foolish man? But when I saw a man in trouble, I never could help trying to get him out of it. What's that? Did something hit me? (*rubs his heart*)

SERGEANT. (*patting him on the shoulder*)   You will get your reward in heaven.

MAN.   I know that, I know that, sergeant, but life is precious.

SERGEANT.   Well, you can sing if it gives you more courage.

MAN. (*sings*)—

Her head was bare, her hands and feet with
  iron bands were bound,

---

9. **Granuaile** (gran ü´ āl). Grace O'Malley (1530–1603), an Irish woman who fought against the English in the sixteenth century; and whose deeds became legendary.

City Docks by Moonlight, c. 1850. John Atkinson Grimshaw.
Christie's, London, England.

Her pensive strain and plaintive wail min-
    gled with the evening gale,
And the song she sang with mournful air, I
    am old Granuaile.
Her lips so sweet that monarchs kissed . . .

SERGEANT.   That's not it . . . "Her gown she
wore was stained with gore. . . ." That's it—you
missed that.

MAN.   You're right, sergeant, so it is; I missed
it. (*repeats line*) But to think of a man like you
knowing a song like that.

SERGEANT.   There's many a thing a man might
know and might not have any wish for.

MAN.   Now, I daresay, sergeant, in your
youth, you used to be sitting up on a wall,
the way you are sitting up on this barrel now,
and the other lads beside you, and you singing
"Granuaile"? . . .

SERGEANT.   I did then.

MAN.   And the "Shan Van Vocht"? . . .

SERGEANT.   I did then.

MAN.   And the "Green on the Cape"?

SERGEANT.   That was one of them.

MAN.   And maybe man you are watching for
tonight used to be sitting on the wall, when he
was young, and singing those same songs . . .
It's a queer world . . .

SERGEANT.   Whisht! . . . I think I see something coming. . . . It's only a dog.

MAN.   And isn't it a queer world? . . .Maybe
it's one of the boys you used to be singing with
that time you will be arresting today or tomorrow, and sending into the dock. . . .

SERGEANT.   That's true indeed.

MAN.   And maybe one night, after you had
been singing, if the other boys had told you
some plan they had, some plan to free the
country, you might have joined with them . . .
and maybe it is you might be in trouble now.

SERGEANT.   Well, who knows but I might? I
had a great spirit in those days.

MAN. It's a queer world, sergeant, and it's little any mother knows when she sees her child creeping on the floor what might happen to it before it has gone through its life, or who will be who in the end.

SERGEANT. That's a queer thought now, and a true thought. Wait now till I think it out. . . . If it wasn't for the sense I have, and for my wife and family, and for me joining the force the time I did, it might be myself now would be after breaking gaol and hiding in the dark, and it might be him that's hiding in the dark and that got out of gaol would be sitting up here where I am on this barrel. . . . And it might be myself would be creeping up trying to make my escape from himself, and it might be himself would be keeping the law, and myself would be breaking it, and myself would be trying to put a bullet in his head, or to take up a lump of stone the way you said he did . . . no, that myself did. . . . Oh! (*gasps . . . after a pause*) What's that? (*grasps man's arm*)

MAN. (*jumps off barrel and listens, looking out over water*) It's nothing, sergeant.

SERGEANT. I thought it might be a boat. I had a notion there might be friends of his coming about the quays with a boat.

MAN. Sergeant, I am thinking it was with the people you were, and not with the law you were, when you were a young man.

SERGEANT. Well, if I was foolish then; that time's gone.

MAN. Maybe, sergeant, it comes into your head sometimes, in spite of your belt and your tunic, that it might have been as well for you to have followed Granuaile.

SERGEANT. It's no business of yours what I think.

MAN. Maybe, sergeant, you'll be on the side of the country yet.

SERGEANT. (*gets off barrel*) Don't talk to me like that. I have my duties and I know them.

(*looks round*) That was a boat; I hear the oars. (*Goes to the steps and looks down.*)

MAN. (*sings*)—
O, then, tell me, Shawn O'Farrell,
    Where the gathering is to be.
In the old spot by the river
    Right well known to you and me!

SERGEANT. Stop that! Stop that, I tell you!

MAN. (*sings louder*)—
One word more, for signal token,
    Whistle up the marching tune,
With your pike upon your shoulder,
    At the Rising of the Moon.

SERGEANT. If you don't stop that, I'll arrest you.

(*A whistle from below answers, repeating the air.*)

SERGEANT. That's a signal. (*stands between him and steps*) You must not pass this way. . . . Step farther back. . . . Who are you? You are no ballad-singer.

MAN. You needn't ask who I am; that placard will tell you. (*points to placard*)

SERGEANT. You are the man I am looking for.

MAN. (*Takes off hat and wig.* SERGEANT *seizes them.*) I am. There's a hundred pounds on my head. There is a friend of mine below in a boat. He knows a safe place to bring me to.

SERGEANT. (*looking still at hat and wig*) It's a pity! It's a pity. You deceived me. You deceived me well.

MAN. I am a friend of Granuaile. There is a hundred pounds on my head.

SERGEANT. It's a pity, it's a pity!

MAN. Will you let me pass, or must I make you let me?

SERGEANT. I am in the force. I will not let you pass.

MAN. I thought to do it with my tongue. (*puts hand in breast*) What is that?

(*voice of* POLICEMAN X *outside*). Here, this is where we left him.

SERGEANT. It's my comrades coming.

MAN. You won't betray me . . . the friend of Granuaile. (*slips behind barrel*)

(*voice of* **POLICEMAN B**). That was the last of the placards.

POLICEMAN X. (*as they come in*) If he makes his escape it won't be unknown he'll make it.

(**SERGEANT** *puts hat and wig behind his back.*)

POLICEMAN B. Did any one come this way?

SERGEANT. (*after a pause*) No one.

POLICEMAN B. No one at all?

SERGEANT. No one at all.

POLICEMAN B. We had no orders to go back to the station; we can stop along with you.

SERGEANT. I don't want you. There is nothing for you to do here.

POLICEMAN B. You bade us to come back here and keep watch with you.

SERGEANT. I'd sooner be alone. Would any man come this way and you making all that talk? It is better the place to be quiet.

POLICEMAN B. Well, we'll leave you the lantern anyhow.

(*hands it to him*)

SERGEANT. I don't want it. Bring it with you.

POLICEMAN B. You might want it. There are clouds coming up and you have the darkness of the night before you yet. I'll leave it over here on the barrel. (*goes to barrel*)

SERGEANT. Bring it with you I tell you. No more talk.

POLICEMAN B. Well, I thought it might be a comfort to you. I often think when I have it in my hand and can be flashing it about into every dark corner (*doing so*) that it's the same as being beside the fire at home, and the bits of bogwood blazing up now and again.

(*flashes it about, now on the barrel, now on* **SERGEANT**)

SERGEANT. (*furious*) Be off the two of you, yourselves and your lantern!

(*They go out.* **MAN** *comes from behind barrel. He and* **SERGEANT** *stand looking at one another.*)

SERGEANT. What are you waiting for?

MAN. For my hat, of course, and my wig. You wouldn't wish me to get my death of cold? (**SERGEANT** *gives them.*)

MAN. (*going towards steps*) Well, good-night, comrade, and thank you. You did me a good turn tonight, and I'm obliged to you. Maybe I'll be able to do as much for you when the small rise up and the big fall down . . . when we all change places at the Rising (*waves his hand and disappears*) of the Moon.

SERGEANT. (*turning his back to audience and reading placard*) A hundred pounds reward! A hundred pounds! (*turns towards audience*) I wonder, now, am I as great a fool as I think I am?

Curtain. ❖

Many works of literature deal sympathetically with outlaws who struggle against a government they see as unjust. Why are stories of outlaws who win their struggle or are let free to continue their battle popular?

YEATS

Primary Source Connection

While vacationing near Galway on the Irish coast, **Lady Augusta Gregory** met **William Butler Yeats** on a rainy afternoon in 1898, and the two developed a plan to found an Irish national theater that would feature works by Irish playwrights. Together, Gregory and Yeats wrote the following solicitation letter, **"Needed: An Irish National Theater,"** to ask for funds to start such a theater. Over the next year, Gregory and Yeats were able to raise the necessary funds.

On May 8, 1899, the first productions of the Irish Literary Theater, Yeats's *Countess Cathleen* and Edward Martyn's *Heather Field,* were held in Dublin. In 1903, this theater group became the Irish National Theater Society, and in 1904, it acquired its own theater, the Abbey. To this day, the Abbey Theater continues to feature plays by Irish playwrights.

Needed: An *Irish* National Theater

by Lady Augusta Gregory and William Butler Yeats

We propose to have performed in Dublin, in the spring of every year certain Celtic and Irish plays, which whatever be their degree of excellence will be written with a high ambition, and so to build up a Celtic and Irish school of dramatic literature. We hope to find in Ireland an uncorrupted and imaginative audience trained to listen by its passion for oratory, and believe that our desire to bring upon the stage the deeper thoughts and emotions of Ireland will ensure for us a tolerant welcome, and that freedom to experiment which is not found in theatres of England, and without which no new movement in art or literature can succeed. We will show that Ireland is not the home of buffoonery and of easy sentiment, as it has been represented, but the home of an ancient idealism. We are confident of the support of all Irish people, who are weary of misrepresentation, in carrying out a work that is outside all the political questions that divide us. ❖

The Abbey Theater in Dublin, Ireland.

Review Questions

1. State the reasons the writers give for establishing a national theater. How will Ireland benefit from such a theater? According to the writers, why is it important that the plays performed at this theater be written by Irish playwrights?

2. Locate a quotation that shows how Gregory and Yeats believe the English view Irish culture. Based on this quotation, infer what attitudes toward Irish culture the writers believe the English have. Do the writers agree with this attitude? How do they hope establishing an Irish theater will affect English attitudes toward Irish culture?

3. What purpose do Gregory and Yeats have in writing the letter? What strategies do they use to accomplish this purpose? How persuasive is the letter? Does the organization of the letter help or hinder their purpose and ability to persuade? How? Support your response with details from the letter.

TEXT ^{TO} TEXT CONNECTION

Why did Gregory and Yeats seek to establish an Irish national theater? Which of these aims are reflected in *The Rising of the Moon?*

Refer to Text ▶ ▶ ▶ ▶ ▶ Reason with Text

1a. At the beginning of *The Rising of the Moon*, for whom are the police looking? What do the officers discuss as they work?	**1b.** Do the police want to catch the man? Explain.	**Understand** Find meaning
2a. How does the ragged man identify himself to the police? Recall the important information the man says he knows.	**2b.** Show what is ironic about the information the man provides.	**Apply** Use information
3a. What is the source of the play's title? List other references to the moon that appear in the play.	**3b.** Infer what the moon symbolizes in the play. How is the title appropriate for the play?	**Analyze** Take things apart
4a. Why does the man sing the ballads? What do the songs suggest? What is learned about the officer while he talks to the man?	**4b.** Is the Sergeant's reasoning in deciding to let the man go convincing? Why or why not?	**Evaluate** Make judgments
5a. Why does the Sergeant refuse the lantern?	**5b.** Explain the symbolism in the Sergeant's act of refusing the lantern. How is this action related to the title of the play?	**Create** Bring ideas together

Analyze Literature

Stage Directions, Dialogue, and Monologue

Identify the various stage directions in the script. What kinds of information do they provide? How do they help you visualize the characters and their actions?

What is the purpose of dialogue in a play? How does dialogue in a play differ from dialogue in a short story or novel?

What does the monologue by the Sergeant illuminate about his feelings?

Extend the Text

Writing Options

Creative Writing Imagine you are the police officer responsible for tracking down fugitives. Write a wanted poster for the fugitive in the play. Use your imagination to expand what you know from the play to provide a legal charge and a description of the escapee.

Expository Writing Lady Gregory stated that this play, though Irish-based, has meaning for people "in Oxford or London or Chicago," or in many other places. Write an analysis of the play, explaining its relevance to a particular community today. The community could be the people of Ireland, another country, or someplace closer to home, such as your school.

Collaborative Learning

Write an Editorial With a group, look on the Internet or in the library for information on the status of Northern Ireland today. Then write an editorial for a local or school newspaper to appear on St. Patrick's Day. Take a stand on whether you think Northern Ireland should remain under British rule or should be united with the Republic of Ireland.

Lifelong Learning

Present the Play as Reader's Theater Work with a group to present a reader's theater performance of *The Rising of the Moon*. Since the play has few characters, group members can take turns playing these roles. You may also add characters to the play, along with suitable dialogue.

 Go to **www.mirrorsandwindows.com** for more.

1. At the beginning of the play on page 936, the Sergeant says to the other officers, "It's those that are down would be up and those that are up would be down." Which of the following statements expresses the same idea?
   A. Sergeant: "There isn't another man in Ireland would have broken gaol the way he did. He must have some friends among the gaolers."
   B. Man: "They [the sailors] do be late going back to the ship. It's often I saw them in Cork carried down the quay in a hand-cart."
   C. Man: "I'm going. I wouldn't be in your shoes if the reward was ten times as much."
   D. Sergeant: "There's many a thing a man might know and might not have any wish for."
   E. Man: "Maybe I'll be able to do as much for you when the small rise up and the big fall down . . . when we all change places at the Rising of the Moon."

2. Review the Sergeant's lines on page 937. What is another way to say "There must be a great deal of spending in a hundred pounds"?
   A. A hundred pounds will buy a lot.
   B. Many people have a hundred pounds to spend.
   C. It takes much longer to earn a hundred pounds than to spend it.
   D. Many people would like the chance to spend a hundred pounds.
   E. A reward of a hundred pounds could be divided up among many people.

3. What weapon does the fugitive use on the Sergeant?
   A. a gun
   B. his fists
   C. a knife
   D. his tongue
   E. a lump of stone

4. Which of the following lines offers the strongest foreshadowing of the revelation near the end of this play?
   A. Man: "I'm a poor ballad-singer, your honor." (page 937)
   B. Man: "And I know well the man you're waiting for—I know him well—I'll be going." (page 937)
   C. Sergeant: "Whisht! . . . I think I see something coming." (page 940)
   D. Sergeant: "Well, if I was foolish then, that time's gone." (page 940)
   E. Man: "You won't betray me . . . the friend of Granuaile." (page 941)

5. Why doesn't the Sergeant turn in the fugitive and collect the reward?
   A. He cannot catch him.
   B. He is afraid that the fugitives' friends will kill him.
   C. He comes to identify with the fugitive and his cause.
   D. He wants to hear more ballads while waiting in the moonlight.
   E. He is interrupted by the other police officers and does not want to share the reward.

6. Which of the following words is most significant to the meaning of the play?
   A. moon
   B. rising
   C. trickery
   D. fugitive
   E. placard

7. In the letter by Gregory and Yeats, they write, "We hope to find in Ireland an *uncorrupted* and imaginative audience trained to listen by its passion for oratory." What does the word *uncorrupted* mean as used here?
   A. moral
   B. honest
   C. innocent
   D. scrupulous
   E. open-minded

8. **Constructed Response:** Analyze the Man's choices of songs. Do the songs have something in common? Is there a reason he sings them in a particular order?

9. **Constructed Response:** Discuss at least three characteristics of *The Rising of the Moon* that make it a distinctly Irish play. Use details from the selection to support your explanation.

The Soldier

A Sonnet by Rupert Brooke

Build Background

Literary Context **"The Soldier,"** the final poem in a sonnet sequence by Rupert Brooke entitled *1914*, was written early in World War I. Like much of Brooke's poetry, "The Soldier" presents an idealized view of the war and a stirring heroism. Drawing on themes that appear in the other five sonnets in the sequence, "The Soldier" touches on spiritual cleansing, memories of the dead, and immortal legacies. In addition, this poem paints these themes in the context of English nationalism.

Speaking after Brooke's death, Winston Churchill, who would serve as prime minister during World War II, said that the thoughts in the writer's sonnets "will be shared by many thousands of young men moving resolutely and blithely forward into this, the hardest, the cruelest, and the least rewarded of all the wars that men have fought." The poet's early death made him a tragic symbol for the British people, even though much of his poetry is joyful. In the decade after Brooke's death, two volumes of his works—*1914 and Other Poems* and *Collected Poems*—were highly popular among the reading public.

Reader's Context How is patriotism an admirable feeling? How can such emotion be destructive?

Meet the Author

Of all the young Englishmen who died in World War I, perhaps the most romanticized as a hero was **Rupert Brooke** (1887–1915). He seemed, in many respects, an ideal young man. Intelligent and athletic, he performed well in his classes and on the cricket and football (soccer) fields at Rugby School, a boarding school where his father was housemaster.

In 1906, Brooke entered King's College, a part of Cambridge University, where he made many friends and became active in campus life, including a socialist organization called the Fabian Society. Later, he studied in Europe and sailed to Canada and the South Seas, writing travel articles and publishing a book, *Poems,* in 1911. When World War I started, Brooke joined the Royal Navy. The sequence of patriotic, idealistic sonnets called *1914* (the year the conflict began) made him famous.

After participating in a disastrous battle in the North Sea, Brooke was on his way to fight in the Gallipoli campaign, the invasion of Turkey planned by Winston Churchill, then a high naval officer. The young writer contracted fatal blood poisoning and was buried on the Greek island of Skyros. Churchill wrote an obituary describing Brooke as "all that one would wish England's noblest sons to be."

Analyze Literature

Mood and Sonnet

The **mood,** or atmosphere, is the emotion brought out in the reader by a literary work.

A **sonnet** is a fourteen-line poem, usually in iambic pentameter, that follows a specific rhyme scheme, or pattern. *English*, or *Shakespearean*, sonnets are divided into three quatrains and a final couplet with a rhyme scheme of *abab cdcd efef gg*. *Italian*, or *Petrarchan*, sonnets are divided into an octave that rhymes *abbaabba* and a sestet that may have a rhyme scheme of *cdecde, cdcdcd,* or *cdedce*.

Set Purpose

Brooke's poem, written in the early years of World War I, was intended to be stirring. Evaluate what kind of mood the poem evokes and how Brooke creates this mood. List the specific words, phrases, details, and images Brooke uses. Also consider the effect of the structure of the poem. What information is conveyed in each of the sonnet's parts? How does this structure contribute to the mood and purpose of the poem?

THE SOLDIER

by Rupert Brooke

If I should die, think only this of me:
    That there's some corner of a foreign field
That is forever England. There shall be
    In that rich earth a richer dust concealed;
5 A dust whom England bore, shaped, made aware,
    Gave, once, her flowers to love, her ways to roam,
A body of England's, breathing English air,
    Washed by the rivers, blest by suns of home.

And think, this heart, all evil shed away,
10   A pulse in the Eternal mind, no less
      Gives somewhere back the thoughts by England given,
Her sights and sounds; dreams happy as her day;
    And laughter, learnt of friends; and gentleness,
      In hearts at peace, under an English heaven. ❖

In this poem, the speaker shows his love for his country. How would you describe your feelings for your country? What are you proud of about your country? What are you not proud of about your country?

McCRAE

Literature Connection

In May 1915, **Dr. John McCrae** (1872–1918), a lieutenant colonel in the Canadian Army, was caring for the injured at a medical station in the Flanders region of western Belgium, where several battles took place in World War I. That spring, the Germans tried unsuccessfully to penetrate the British *salient,* or exposed line of defense at the town of Ypres. Overwhelmed by the suffering of the soldiers he treated—many of whom he buried in the cemetery nearby—McCrae wrote **"In Flanders Fields."**

McCrae's poem was published in *Punch* in December 1915 and became one of the most popular poems about World War I. It was translated into many languages and even used in advertising and recruitment posters for the war. Three years after publication of his famous poem, McCrae died of pneumonia and meningitis.

IN FLANDERS FIELDS
by John McCrae

In Flanders fields the poppies blow
Between the crosses, row on row,
That mark our place; and in the sky
The larks, still bravely singing, fly
5   Scarce heard amid the guns below.

We are the Dead. Short days ago
We lived, felt dawn, saw sunset glow,
Loved and were loved, and now we lie
In Flanders fields.

10   Take up our quarrel with the foe:
To you from failing hands we throw
The torch; be yours to hold it high.
If ye break faith with us who die
We shall not sleep, though poppies grow
15   In Flanders fields. ❖

Review Questions

1. Describe the setting of the poem. What images does McCrae present in the first stanza? In what ways do these images contrast with the setting of the poem? What mood does this contrast help create?

2. Identify the speaker's tone in the poem. Show what details the poet uses to create this tone. Evaluate how these details contribute to the overall tone of the poem.

3. What does the poet urge his audience to do? What does he say will happen if his audience does not do this? This poem became wildly popular after its publication in 1915. To which emotions does the poem appeal? How does the poem appeal to these emotions? Why was the poem so effective in rallying people to support the Canadian soldiers in World War I?

TEXT ^{TO} TEXT CONNECTION

Compare and contrast the mood, tone, attitude toward war, and perspective on the dead troops presented in McCrae's "In Flanders Fields" and Brooke's "The Soldier." Which poem do you find more compelling? Explain.

Posters such as these were issued by the British government during World War I to recruit volunteers into the military and create support for the war among citizens.

Refer to Text ▷ ▷ ▷ ▶ ▶ **Reason with Text**

1a. What would the speaker in "The Soldier" like the reader to think of if he dies? What is the "richer dust" buried in the foreign earth?	**1b.** Explain why the speaker believes that the dust is "richer."	**Understand** Find meaning
2a. Outline what England has done for the speaker.	**2b.** Show how the first eight lines before the stanza break differ from the six lines following the break.	**Apply** Use information
3a. In line 9, to what does "this heart" refer?	**3b.** Why does the speaker believe that "this heart" will become a "pulse in the Eternal mind"? Does the poet necessarily believe there is an "English heaven"? Explain.	**Analyze** Take things apart
4a. Identify the speaker's attitude toward his situation.	**4b.** Do you agree with the speaker's attitude? Why would he and other young Englishmen in World War I feel this way?	**Evaluate** Make judgments
5a. Describe the speaker's feelings for England.	**5b.** Does Brooke share the attitude in Shakespeare's *Richard II*: "This happy breed of men, this little world, . . . / This blessed plot, this earth, this realm, this England"? Explain.	**Create** Bring ideas together

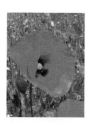

Analyze Literature

Mood and Sonnet

How would you describe the mood of "The Soldier"? Refer to your list and choose three words, phrases, and ideas. Explain how these contribute to the mood of the poem.

Why might Brooke have chosen the sonnet form for this poem? What is the rhyme scheme and what effect does this structure create?

Extend the Text

Writing Options

Creative Writing Imagine that to boost public support, the Ministry of Defense has decided to distribute copies of "The Soldier" throughout England. Write a series of slogans capturing the same spirit as "The Soldier" that the ministry can distribute with the poem.

Persuasive Writing You have been invited by a group of young veterans to discuss Brooke's attitude toward World War I, as revealed in "The Soldier." In an analytical essay, discuss the views expressed in this poem and explain why you agree or disagree with these feelings.

Collaborative Learning

Compile a Poetry Booklet With a partner, select poems for a booklet of verse about World War I. You can organize the collection chronologically or thematically. Before each poem, write a short biography of the poet and an introduction to the work itself. Share the collection by reading some of the poems to the rest of the class.

Critical Literacy

Explicate the Poem An *explication* is a detailed study of a work of literature. Reread Brooke's poem, "The Soldier," and write an explication of the poem focusing on Brooke's use of imagery and word choice. When you are done, exchange essays with a partner and compare and contrast the two explications.

 Go to **www.mirrorsandwindows.com** for more.

The Rear-Guard

A Lyric Poem by Siegfried Sassoon

Dulce et Decorum Est

A Lyric Poem by Wilfred Owen

Build Background

Literary and Historical Context The formal structure of Siegfried Sassoon's **"The Rear-Guard"** and Wilfred Owen's **"Dulce et Decorum Est"** follow complicated rhyme schemes, revealing the technical skill of these two poets. Although the poems follow traditional forms, they also represent a new style in war poetry: realism. Gruesome images of the dehumanization wrought by World War I reveal the brutality of newly invented weapons, including poison gas and tanks. Civilians at home were not told of these horrors, and patriotic sentiments of the glories of war remained strong. Meanwhile, poets on the warfront became increasingly disillusioned.

The antiwar message of "The Rear-Guard" and "Dulce et Decorum Est" stand in stark contrast to the war-as-heroism theme of Rupert Brooke's "The Soldier." Both Sassoon and Owen used irony to shock readers with the reality of war. The ironic title of Owen's poem comes from an ode by the Roman poet Horace, written in Latin: *Dulce et decorum est pro patria mori,* or "It is sweet and proper to die for your country."

Reader's Context Are poems, whether antiwar or prowar, likely to have an effect on political leaders? Explain your response.

Meet the Authors

Siegfried Sassoon (1886–1967) was born in Kent, England. He began his literary career during World War I, writing antiwar poems, but later became known for his prose works. During his tour of military duty, he was awarded the Military Cross for bravery. Later, while on leave recovering from a wound, Sassoon threw his Military Cross into the River Mersey. When he refused to return to duty, he was sent to the Craiglockhart War Hospital, where he was treated for what was then called *shell shock,* now known as posttraumatic stress disorder (PTSD).

Wilfred Owen (1893–1918), born in Shropshire, England, wrote lyric poetry influenced by Keats and Shelley (see Unit 6). In 1915, Owen enlisted in the army and began writing angrily about the horrors of war. In 1917, suffering from shell shock, he was sent to Craiglockhart, where he met Sassoon, who encouraged his writing. Owen returned to the front in August 1918 and won the Military Cross. Soon thereafter he was killed in action, just a week before the war's end. After his death, Sassoon arranged to have Owen's poems published.

Compare Literature

Irony and Description
Irony is the difference between appearance and reality. *Verbal irony* occurs when a writer or speaker says one thing but means another.

A **description** is a picture in words that portrays a character, object, or scene. Descriptions include *sensory details*—words and phrases that appeal to one or more of the five senses.

Set Purpose

Sassoon and Owen use irony in their war poems. As you read the two selections, note words and phrases that convey irony. Look for irony in the title of Owen's poem. Sassoon and Owen also present very striking images. Make a list of sensory details, noting to which sense each appeals. What effect do the descriptions have on your understanding of the poems? Consider whether the images Owen presents support the title of his poem.

Preview Vocabulary

pry, 953
unwholesome, 953
livid, 954
muffle, 954
ecstasy, 955
gutter, 956
obscene, 956
ardent, 956

THE REAR-GUARD

by Siegfried Sassoon

(Hindenburg Line,[1] April 1917)

Groping along the tunnel, step by step,
He winked his <u>prying</u> torch[2] with patching glare
From side to side, and sniffed the <u>unwholesome</u> air.
Tins, boxes, bottles, shapes too vague to know;
5 A mirror smashed, the mattress from a bed;
And he, exploring fifty feet below
The rosy gloom of battle overhead.

---

1. **Hindenburg Line.** Defensive barricade, erected across northern France
   by the Germans and constructed of massive barbed-wire entanglements
   and deep trenches
2. **torch.** British English for "flashlight"

> **pry** (prī) *v.*, look at closely or curiously
> **un • whole • some** (un′ hōl′səm) *adj.*, harmful to the physical or
> mental well-being

British tanks advance toward the front lines (c. 1914–1918).

Tripping, he grabbed the wall; saw someone lie
Humped at his feet, half-hidden by a rug,
10 And stooped to give the sleeper's arm a tug.
"I'm looking for headquarters." No reply.
"God blast your neck!" (For days he'd had no sleep)
"Get up and guide me through this stinking place."
Savage, he kicked a soft, unanswering heap,
15 And flashed his beam across the <u>livid</u> face
Terribly glaring up, whose eyes yet wore
Agony dying hard ten days before;
And fists of fingers clutched a blackening wound.

Alone he staggered on until he found
20 Dawn's ghost that filtered down a shafted stair
To the dazed, muttering creatures underground
Who hear the boom of shells in <u>muffled</u> sound.
At last, with sweat of horror in his hair,
He climbed through darkness to the twilight air,
25 Unloading hell behind him step by step. ❖

> **liv • id** (li´ vəd) *adj.*, pale and colorless, or ashen; also, very angry
> **muf • fle** (mu´ fəl) *v.*, suppress or make quieter

MIRRORS & WINDOWS

Sassoon writes that the soldier leaves the trenches with the "sweat of horror in his hair." When have you been in a situation that you found horrifying? How did you respond?

British troops march to the trenches (c. 1914–1918).

Dulce et Decorum Est

by Wilfred Owen

Bent double, like old beggars under sacks,
Knock-kneed, coughing like hags, we cursed through sludge,
Till on the haunting flares we turned our backs
And towards our distant rest began to trudge.
5 Men marched asleep. Many had lost their boots
But limped on, blood-shod. All went lame; all blind;
Drunk with fatigue; deaf even to the hoots
Of tired, outstripped Five-Nines[1] that dropped behind.

Gas! GAS! Quick, boys!—An <u>ecstasy</u> of fumbling,
10 Fitting the clumsy helmets just in time;
But someone still was yelling out and stumbling,
And floundr'ing like a man in fire or lime . . .
Dim, through the misty panes and thick green light,
As under a green sea, I saw him drowning.

---

1. **Five-Nines.** Common artillery shells

> **ec • sta • sy** (ek´ stə sē) *n.,* medical state in which the mind can focus only on one idea; also, a state of intense emotion

handwritten margin notes:
- when glory has drained out of war
- Gas warfare – horrific death not glorified
- Meant to be graphic and horrifying
- speech of the soldiers
- Personal commentary of speaker

15 In all my dreams, before my helpless sight,
     He plunges at me, <u>guttering</u>, choking, drowning.

     If in some smothering dreams you too could pace
     Behind the wagon that we flung him in,
     And watch the white eyes writhing in his face,
20 His hanging face, like a devil's sick of sin;
     If you could hear, at every jolt, the blood
     Come gargling from the froth-corrupted lungs,
     <u>Obscene</u> as cancer, bitter as the cud
     Of vile, incurable sores on innocent tongues,—
25 My friend, you would not tell with such high zest
     To children <u>ardent</u> for some desperate glory,
     The old Lie: Dulce et decorum est
     Pro patria mori.[2] ❖

(handwritten margin note, left): capitalized →

(handwritten margin note, right): A bent sonnet form / 2 sonnet rhyme scemes

---

2. **Dulce . . . mori.** Latin sentence from an ode by Horace: "It is sweet and proper to die for your country."

> **gut • ter** (guˊ tər) v., gurgle and sputter
> **ob • scene** (äb sēnˊ) adj., repulsive or disgusting
> **ar • dent** (ärˊ d'nt) adj., intensely enthusiastic or devoted; zealous

MIRRORS & WINDOWS

Owen calls the saying "It is sweet and proper to die for your county" the "old Lie." Why might some people want to believe this statement? Do you believe it?

MUSIC CONNECTION

Benjamin Britten

When Wilfred Owen died in World War I, he was largely unknown as a poet. In later years, however, his work became essential reading throughout most of Western Europe, and his legacy influenced the musical aspirations of a British composer named Benjamin Britten.

Britten was born in Suffolk County in 1913, shortly before the war began. His most famous piece is *War Requiem,* which he wrote in 1962. It combines orchestral music with choral arrangements for nine of Owen's poems and a Latin mass for the dead. Somber in mood and mournful in its melodies, *War Requiem* harshly condemns war as an impossible obstacle to peace.

To perform the piece, Britten hired singers from Russia, Germany, and England as a symbolic gesture of solidarity among countries that were growing increasingly apart due to Cold War tensions. He hoped his music could help the West and the East solve their problems without resorting to armed conflict.

Primary Source Connection

During his three years of service in the British Army, Wilfred Owen frequently wrote letters to his family back home in England. Most of these letters were addressed to his mother, Susan. Owen's last letter to his mother was written October 31, 1918, four days before he was killed in action. News of his death reached his family on November 11, 1918, the same day the armistice was signed and World War I officially ended. As you read the following **essay about the letters of Wilfred Owen,** consider how the information provided in the letters affects your understanding of Owen's war poetry.

The War Letters of Wilfred Owen

Some of the most revealing and moving examples of wartime literature are found in the collections of letters written by soldiers to family and friends at home. Among several published collections of war letters from World War I is *Wilfred Owen: Selected Letters,* edited by John Bell (1985). In reviewing these letters, readers can trace a change in Owen's attitude toward the war. The initial excitement he feels at the start of the war quickly gives way to shock and horror and eventually to an appreciation of life and the living.

In September 1915, Owen left a teaching position in France to return to England and enlist in the army. He had become increasingly concerned about the magnitude of the war, and his early letters reveal a sense of idealism and excitement about enlisting. During the first several months of officer training, he is impressed by the precision of the formation training and inspired by the music of the marching bands.

A letter of April 2, 1916, recounts Owen's first brush with the enemy, which occurred, ironically, while he was still training in England. A German zeppelin, or armed air blimp, was sighted approaching the training camp. Owen describes how he and the rest of the guard watched as the zeppelin crept closer, only to turn away and disappear. Owen characterizes his first contact with the enemy as "altogether a highly entertaining 15 minutes."

After being stationed in France in January 1917, Owen finds little exciting or impressive about the war. The cheerful tone of the early letters to his mother shifts to reveal the shock at what he encounters. On January 17, after returning from the front lines for the first time, he writes, "I can see no excuse for deceiving you about these last 4 days. I have suffered seventh hell." In this description, Owen alludes to Dante's *Inferno,* in which the seventh circle of hell is where the violent are punished. Owen tells his mother, "I have not been at the front. I have been in front of it."

In the same letter, Owen describes how his company trudged through fields in mud several feet deep. Water more than two feet deep flooded the trench where the troops were positioned, and they

British soldiers share stories by lamplight (c. 1915).

were under constant fire. A company fighting near Owen was almost completely wiped out, whereas his own company suffered only one casualty. Owen tells his mother, "We are wretched beyond my previous imagination."

Owen also describes in vivid detail the environment in which he fights. Although poetic, his descriptions present a grim, ugly landscape. In a letter dated January 19, 1917, he writes that the land "is pock-marked like a body of foulest disease and its odour the breath of cancer. . . . [It] is like the face of the moon chaotic, crater-ridden, uninhabitable, awful, the abode of madness."

Owen's experiences over the coming months continue to shock him. On February 4, 1917, he writes, "Since my last letter I have had another strong dose of the advanced Front line. . . . I have no mind to describe all the horrors of this last Tour." Although he tries to reassure his mother that he is safe and no longer in danger, Owen does not shy away from telling her about his horrifying experiences. He says he is particularly demoralized by the presence of unburied bodies on the battlefield.

He writes, "In poetry we call them the most glorious. But to sit with them all day, all night . . . and a week later come back and find them still sitting there, in motionless groups, THAT is what saps the 'soldierly spirit.'" Here, Owen alludes to the ideal of the glorious dead and suggests that these silent companions do not represent glory and honor but are instead grim reminders of danger and death.

Owen lost men in his company to both the bitter cold and the constant artillery fire and shelling. On February 4, 1917, he wrote, "I supposed I can endure cold, and fatigue, and the face-to-face death, as well as another; but extra for me there is the pervasion of Ugliness. Hideous landscapes, vile noises, foul language . . . everything unnatural, broken, blasted."

In May 1917, Owen's unit was caught in the explosion of a shell. When the men finally were relieved, Owen was diagnosed as having shell shock (now known as posttraumatic stress disorder [PTSD]). He was evacuated to England in June and then transferred to Craiglockhart Hospital in Scotland, where he was treated for this condition.

Surprisingly, the letters Owen writes during his hospitalization do not reflect any anger or bitterness about his experiences at the front. Those feelings were reflected in his poetry, however. Owen wrote many of his most famous poems during this period of hospitalization. He was encouraged to write by poet Siegfried Sassoon, who also was a patient at Craiglockhart Hospital. The two poets became friends, and Sassoon served as a mentor to the novice writer.

After a year of hospitalization, Owen rejoined his unit in England, and in August 1918, the men returned to the front lines in France. The letters from this period reflect a different perspective about the war. In contrast to his earlier letters from the front lines, which told of harsh conditions, barren landscapes, and ever-present reminders of death, Owen now expresses his admiration for the living. He writes to his mother affectionate descriptions of the men with whom he serves. This is most apparent in the last letter he sends her, dated October 31, 1918, just four days before he was killed in action. Owen writes:

So thick is the smoke in cellar that I can hardly see by candle 12 ins. away, and so thick are the inmates that I can hardly write for pokes, nudges & jolts. . . . Splashing my hand, an old soldier with a walrus moustache peels & drops potatoes into the pot. By him, Keyes, my cook, chops wood; another feeds the smoke with damp wood. It is a great life. I am more oblivious than alas! yourself, dear mother, of the ghastly glimmering of the guns outside, and the hollow crashing of the shells. There is no danger here, or, if any, it will be well over before you read these lines. I hope you are as warm as I am; as serene in your room as I am here. . . . Of this I am certain you could not be visited by a band of friends half so fine as surround me here.

Owen's shift in the focus from the dead to the living suggests that he had come to accept the conditions of the war. As he told his mother in his last letter, he had become "oblivious" to the danger and death of the battlefield, finding serenity in the people around him. ❖

Review Questions

1. What is the intended audience of Owen's letter? Evaluate how his choice of audience might affect the information he chose to present in his letters. Imagine Owen had kept a journal and recorded the same experiences he describes in his letters. What information might have been presented in the same fashion? What information might have been different? What accounts for this possible difference?

2. Review the excerpts from Owen's letters cited in the essay. How would you describe the tone of these excerpts?

3. Identify the information you learn about Owen's war letters in this essay. How does the essay affect your understanding of Owen's poem? What further questions do you have about Owen, his life, his letters, and his poetry after reading this essay? What sources could you use to find the answers to these questions?

TEXT ^{TO} TEXT CONNECTION

Compare and contrast the letter excerpts and Owen's "Dulce et Decorum Est." Make a list of the similar images and attitudes you find in both selections. What is different between the two selections? What might be the reason for this difference?

Refer to Text ▶ ▶ ▶ ▶ ▶	**Reason with Text**	
1a. In "Dulce et Decorum Est," where are the troops headed? Why do they have difficulty walking?	**1b.** What does this description suggest about the soldiers in the army? What effect does this image have on the reader?	**Understand** Find meaning
2a. Count the number of lines in each stanza of "The Rear-Guard."	**2b.** Discuss how this unusual stanza organization intensifies the impact of the poem.	**Apply** Use information
3a. In "Dulce et Decorum Est," list the words Owen chooses to describe the death of the soldier who is unable to get his mask on.	**3b.** Analyze the poet's word choice in this account. How effective are these words in relaying his experience? Why?	**Analyze** Take things apart
4a. The speakers in both poems have similar, although not identical, experiences. Describe what happens to each of them.	**4b.** Compare and contrast the endings of both poems. Which ending do you find more effective? Why?	**Evaluate** Make judgments
5a. In "The Rear-Guard," identify the effect the setting and location has on your understanding of the poem.	**5b.** Explain in what ways the survivors of the war and the families of the dead are similar to members of the rear guard.	**Create** Bring ideas together

Compare Literature

Irony and Description

Explain how the title of Owen's poem is an example of irony. How do the images in the rest of the poem make a mockery of the title?

Refer to your list of sensory details and identify the sense to which Sassoon and Owen most often appeal. How are the descriptions appropriate to the subject of war? How do they affect your understanding of the purpose of each poem?

Extend the Text

Writing Options

Creative Writing Poems can express bitterness, fear, and other unpleasant emotions. Try writing a poem about a difficult experience—one you have had, heard about, or imagined. Be sure to use concrete images and sensory details, so your readers can share the experience.

Expository Writing Imagine you were with Sassoon and Owen when they met at the war hospital in Scotland. If you had asked them what their purpose was in writing their poems, how might they have replied? Reread the selections; then prepare a one-paragraph analysis explaining why you think the poets created these works.

Collaborative Learning

Hold a Panel Discussion With a group, hold a panel discussion on the subject of wartime propaganda, not limited to World War I. To prepare, research the topic in the library or on the Internet. Members of the panel can explore the reasons for and against, and the effects of, government control of the media during wartime.

Media Literacy

Review a Film About World War I Watch a film about World War I, such as *All Quiet on the Western Front* (1932), *A Farewell to Arms* (1932 or 1957), or *The Guns of August* (1964). Then write a review in which you discuss how the film compares with the selections by Rupert Brooke, Siegfried Sassoon, and Wilfred Owen. Analyze the perspectives of the film and poems, and note any biases in the depiction of war. Determine any common underlying themes.

 Go to **www.mirrorsandwindows.com** for more.

1. In "The Rear-Guard," what is most unusual and note-worthy about the stanzas?
   A. They all have the same rhyme scheme.
   B. Each has one more line than the previous stanza.
   C. They are not in the expected chronological order.
   D. None of them uses traditional poetic techniques.
   E. They all are in the third-person point of view.

2. Which of the following words or phrases does *not* describe the prevailing mood of "The Rear-Guard"?
   A. prying
   B. unwholesome
   C. rosy gloom of battle
   D. stinking
   E. agony dying hard

3. In "The Rear-Guard," which of the following would be the least likely reason that the soldier is staggering?
   A. "his prying torch with patching glare" (line 2)
   B. "he exploring fifty feet below" (line 6)
   C. "For days he'd had no sleep" (line 12)
   D. "dawn's ghost that filtered down" (line 20)
   E. "with sweat of horror in his hair" (line 23)

4. In lines 19–22 of "The Rear-Guard," what is likely the main reason that the poet uses the word *creatures?*
   A. The word provides an example of assonance.
   B. The use of *creatures* creates emphasis on that line.
   C. The word fits best with the meter of the poem.
   D. The word is more poetic sounding than *soldiers* or *men.*
   E. The conditions make the soldiers seem like animals.

5. In "Dulce et Decorum Est," the use of first-person point of view makes the poem seem
   A. more real and personal.
   B. more distant and less real.
   C. more imaginary and untruthful.
   D. less strong and memorable.
   E. less poetic and more violent.

6. In "Dulce et Decorum Est," what message does Owen's overall word choice help to convey?
   A. War brings glory to soldiers.
   B. War is ugly and totally awful.
   C. There is a certain ecstasy in war.
   D. War is natural and unavoidable.
   E. It is sweet and proper to die for your country.

7. In line 9 of "Dulce et Decorum Est," the words *Gas! Gas! Quick, boys!* stand out for all of the following reasons *except*
   A. the exclamation marks.
   B. the repetition.
   C. the internal rhyme.
   D. the words all being one syllable.
   E. the simple, straightforward language.

8. Review lines 21–28 of "Dulce et Decorum Est." Which of the following words from this passage seems the most unusual and possibly ironic?
   A. gargling
   B. obscene
   C. innocent
   D. friend
   E. Lie

9. Constructed Response: Discuss the significance of the title "Dulce et Decorum Est," which means "It is sweet and proper." Why is it in Latin? Why does the title include only part of the longer quotation at the end of the poem, which translates as "It is sweet and proper to die for your country"?

10. Constructed Response: Compare and contrast "The Rear-Guard" and "Dulce et Decorum Est." Include at least two main similarities and two main differences in your analysis.

Pablo Neruda (1904–1973), born in Chile, was both a Nobel Prize–winning poet and a diplomat. While still in his late teens, he published his first book of poems, and with the release of his second book, he became famous as a writer. In 1933, Neruda became the Chilean consul to Buenos Aires, Argentina, and soon after, he took an assignment in Madrid, Spain.

By 1936, Spain was engulfed in civil war between the left-wing Loyalists, many of them working class, and the right-wing Nationalists, led by General Francisco Franco. Because Neruda supported the Loyalists, the Chilean government asked him to leave Madrid. After World War II, Neruda was elected to the Chilean Senate as a communist, but following a crackdown against leftists, he left his native land. In 1952, he returned and, for the next two decades, continued to write poetry and serve on diplomatic missions. Two years before his death, in 1971, he received the Nobel Prize for literature.

"I Explain a Few Things" reflects the poet's observations in Madrid during the Spanish Civil War. Writing in a conversational style, as if addressing friends, the first-person speaker asserts that, in time of war, readers cannot expect poetry to be about the beauty of nature and similar hopeful ideas. Rather, readers must expect poetry to depict the brutality of human nature.

I Explain a Few Things

by Pablo Neruda
Translated by John Felstiner

You'll ask: And where are the lilacs?
The metaphysics matted with poppies?
The rain that kept drumming
his words full of
5 pinholes and birds?
I'll tell you how it is with me.

I was living on the outskirts
of Madrid, with bells
with clocks with trees.

10 From there we looked out
on Castile's[1] dry face
like an ocean of leather.
My house was called
House of the Flowers because everywhere
15 geraniums were bursting: it was
a fine house
with dogs and children.
Raúl, remember?
You remember, Rafael?[2]

---

1. **Castile.** A region of Spain
2. **Rafael.** Rafael Alberti (1902–1999), Spanish poet

20 Federico,[3] do you remember
   from under the ground,
   remember my house and its balconies
   where June light drowned flowers in your mouth?
   Brother, my brother!

25 Everything
   was loud voices, coarse-cut salt,
   piles of palpitating bread,
   market stalls of my Argüelles quarter[4] with its statue
   a pale inkstand amidst the cod:
30 oil rose up in the spoons,
   a deep pulsing
   of feet and hands filled the streets,
   meters, liters, keen
   essence of life,
35 fish all stacked up,

---

3. **Federico.** Federico García Lorca (1898–1936), Spanish poet and dramatist,
   assassinated in the Spanish Civil War
4. **Argüelles quarter.** Located in the northwest district of Madrid

Pablo Picasso

Pablo Picasso (1881–1973), one of the most celebrated and influential artists of the twentieth century, was born in Málaga, Spain. As a child, he was recognized as an artistic prodigy and received formal instruction from his father, himself a painter and art instructor. The young Picasso also attended several distinguished art academies, including those in Barcelona and Madrid.

Like many artists and writers of the Modern Era, Picasso went to Paris to develop his talent. He lived off and on in the French capital beginning in 1900. As a struggling artist in his twenties, Picasso lived in extreme poverty. He burned many of his early paintings to keep warm in the winter.

Picasso was remarkably versatile and prolific. He created an estimated 22,000 artworks in his lifetime, ranging from drawings and paintings to prints, ceramics, and sculptures. He is best known, however, for developing a new artistic style called *Cubism.* Cubism was rooted in the idea of taking objects apart, reducing them to geometric shapes, and presenting the shapes in reorganized fashion. Many Cubist works of art also have qualities of *Surrealism,* depicting fantastic, dreamlike images and employing extensive symbolism.

Guernica, which appears on page 965, displays both Cubist and Surrealist elements and is perhaps Picasso's most famous artwork. It depicts the horrific bombing of Guernica, an unprotected village in northeastern Spain, during the Spanish Civil War in 1937. An outspoken pacifist, Picasso dedicated the work, which is a large mural, to the bombing's estimated 1,600 victims.

Critical Viewing When asked to explain the symbolism in his paintings, Picasso remarked, "It isn't up to the painter to define the symbols. . . . The public who look at the picture must interpret the symbols as they understand them." What images in this painting seem symbolic? What might they suggest about the horrors of war? Compare and contrast Picasso's depiction of war with Neruda's in "I Explain a Few Things."

rooftops woven under cold sun
that wears down the weathervane,
fine ivory delirium of potatoes,
tomatoes in waves out to the sea.

40 And one morning all this was blazing
and one morning bonfires
shot from the earth
burning up life,
and since then fire,
45 gunpowder since then,
and since then blood.
Bandits with planes and Moors,[5]
bandits with gold rings and duchesses,

---

5. **Moors.** Arabs and Berbers (North Africans) who conquered and
occupied Spain during the Middle Ages

Guernica, 1937. Pablo Picasso.
Museo Nacional Centro de Arte Reina Sofía, Madrid, Spain.

bandits with black friars blessing
50 came out of the sky to kill children,
and in the streets the blood of the children
flowed easily, like children's blood.

Jackals the jackal would reject,
stones the thistle would spit out,
55 vipers vipers would despise.

Against you I've seen the blood
of Spain rise up
to flood you in a single wave
of pride and knives!

60 Traitor
generals:
look at my dead house,
look at broken Spain:
yet from every dead house burning metal flows
65 instead of flowers,

from every crater in Spain
emerges Spain,
from every dead child a gun with eyes,
from every crime bullets
70 that one day will track down
your heart.

So you ask why his poems
don't tell us of dreams, and leaves,
and great volcanoes in his native land?

75 Come see the blood in the streets,
come see
the blood in the streets,
come see the blood
in the streets! ❖

 How would you describe the purpose of poetry? Should poetry celebrate the positive and beautiful things in the world, or should it also look at the ugly and horrible aspects of life?

Refer and Reason

1. In lines 10–24, what is the speaker describing? What is he describing in lines 25–39? Describe the tone, or emotional attitude, of these descriptions.

2. Beginning in line 40, what historical event is described? What is the effect of the last eight lines?

3. List the main points Neruda makes in the poem. How might Neruda have responded to the poems by Brooke, McCrae, Sassoon, and Owen? How might these men have responded to Neruda's poem? What similarities and differences do you see between these poems?

Writing Options

1. One of the most famous paintings of the twentieth century is *Guernica,* by the Spanish artist Pablo Picasso (1881–1973). The work was inspired by the destruction of the Spanish city Guernica in April 1937. Refer to the reproduction of this painting and describe your responses to it. How does its visual message about war compare with Neruda's thoughts in "I Explain a Few Things"?

2. If you have lived in a war-torn locality, write a descriptive essay about your experiences. If you have not witnessed war, interview a relative, friend, or other person who has fought in or lived through a bloody conflict. Record their experience in a descriptive essay.

 Go to **www.mirrorsandwindows.com** for more.

Birds on the Western Front

by Saki

Hector Hugh Munro (1870–1916), who wrote under the pen name **Saki,** was well known for his witty and biting satire. Born in Burma (now called Myanmar) to British parents, Munro and his two siblings were raised, after the death of their mother in 1872, by several aunts in England.

As a young man, Munro followed in his father's footsteps and joined the Burma police, but after a few years, he took up a writing career. As a political journalist, historian, and travel writer, he worked in several European cities, including London, Paris, and Warsaw. After enlisting in World War I, he served in France, where he was killed.

Like many of Saki's stories, **"Birds on the Western Front"** has an ironic tone. Among the frequent targets of his satire are the manners and morals of upper-class Edwardian society. In this selection, however, Saki takes a serious topic, World War I, and portrays it, quite literally, from a bird's-eye view, turning readers' expectation of a war story upside down.

Considering the enormous economic dislocation which the war operations have caused in the regions where the campaign[1] is raging, there seems to be very little corresponding disturbance in the bird life of the same districts. Rats and mice have mobilized and swarmed into the fighting line, and there has been a partial mobilization of owls, particularly barn owls, following in the wake of the mice, and making laudable[2] efforts to thin out their numbers. What success attends their hunting one cannot estimate; there are always sufficient mice left over to populate one's dug-out and make a parade-ground and race-course of one's face at night. In the matter of nesting accommodation the barn owls are well provided for; most of the still intact barns in the war zone are requisitioned[3] for billeting[4] purposes, but there is a wealth of ruined houses, whole streets and clusters of them, such as can hardly have been available at any previous moment of the world's history since Nineveh and Babylon[5] became humanly desolate. Without human occupation and cultivation there can have been no corn, no refuse, and consequently very few mice, and the owls of Nineveh cannot have enjoyed very

---

1. **campaign.** Battles being fought against the Germans during World War I
2. **laudable.** Worthy of praise
3. **requisitioned.** Asked for or requested
4. **billeting.** Made into sleeping quarters, by order of the military
5. **Nineveh and Babylon.** Two ancient cultures that were destroyed

good hunting; here in Northern France the owls have desolation and mice at their disposal in unlimited quantities, and as these birds breed in winter as well as in summer, there should be a goodly output of war owlets to cope with the swarming generations of war mice.

Apart from the owls one cannot notice that the campaign is making any marked difference in the bird life of the country-side. The vast flocks of crows and ravens that one expected to find in the neighborhood of the fighting line are nonexistent, which is perhaps rather a pity. The obvious explanation is that the roar and crash and fumes of high explosives have driven the crow tribe in panic from the fighting area; like many obvious explanations, it is not a correct one. The crows of the locality are not attracted to the battlefield, but they certainly are not scared away from

it. The rook[6] is normally so gun-shy and nervous where noise is concerned that the sharp banging of a barn door or the report of a toy pistol will sometimes set an entire rookery in commotion; out here I have seen him sedately busy among the refuse heaps of a battered village, with shells bursting at no great distance, and the impatient-sounding, snapping rattle of machine-guns going on all round him; for all the notice that he took he might have been in some peaceful English meadow on a sleepy Sunday afternoon. Whatever else German frightfulness may have done it has not frightened the rook of North-Eastern France; it has made his nerves steadier than they have ever been before, and future generations of small boys, employed in scaring rooks away from the

---

6. **rook.** Type of crow

The buzzard, that earnest seeker after mice, does not seem to be taking any war risks, at least I have never seen one out here.

sown crops in this region, will have to invent something in the way of super-frightfulness to achieve their purpose. Crows and magpies are nesting well within the shell-swept area, and over a small beech-copse I once saw a pair of crows engaged in hot combat with a pair of sparrow-hawks, while considerably higher in the sky, but almost directly above them, two Allied battle-planes were engaging an equal number of enemy aircraft.

Unlike the barn owls, the magpies have had their choice of building sites considerably restricted by the ravages of war; the whole avenues of poplars, where they were accustomed to construct their nests, have been blown to bits, leaving nothing but dreary-looking rows of shattered and splintered trunks to show where once they stood. Affection for a particular tree has in one case induced a pair of magpies to build their bulky, domed nest in the battered remnants[7] of a poplar of which so little remained standing that the nest looked almost bigger than the tree; the effect rather suggested an archiepiscopal enthronement[8] taking place in the ruined remains of Melrose Abbey. The magpie, wary and suspicious in his wild state, must be rather intrigued at the change that has come over the erst-while[9] fearsome not-to-be-avoided human, stalking everywhere over the earth as its possessor, who now creeps about in screened and sheltered ways, as chary of showing himself in the open as the shyest of wild creatures.

The buzzard, that earnest seeker after mice, does not seem to be taking any war risks, at

least I have never seen one out here, but kestrels[10] hover about all day in the hottest parts of the line, not in the least disconcerted,[11] apparently, when a promising mouse-area suddenly rises in the air in a cascade of black or yellow earth. Sparrow-hawks are fairly numerous, and a mile or two back from the firing line I saw a pair of hawks that I took to be red-legged falcons, circling over the top of an oak-copse. According to investigations made by Russian naturalists, the effect of the war on bird life on the Eastern front has been more marked than it has been over here. "During the first year of the war rooks disappeared, larks no longer sang in the fields, the wild pigeon disappeared also." The skylark in this region has stuck tenaciously to the meadows and croplands that have been seamed and bisected with trenches and honeycombed with shell-holes. In the chill, misty hour of gloom that precedes a rainy dawn, when nothing seemed alive except a few wary waterlogged sentries and many scuttling rats, the lark would suddenly dash skyward and pour forth a song of ecstatic jubilation that sounded horribly forced and insincere. It seemed scarcely possible that the bird could carry its insouciance[12] to the length of attempting to rear a brood in that desolate wreckage of shattered clods and gaping shell-

---

7. **remnants.** Remainder; what is left over
8. **archiepiscopal enthronement.** Inauguration of an archbishop
9. **erst-while** (usually *erstwhile*). Formerly
10. **kestrels.** Small falcons
11. **disconcerted.** Embarrassed or confused
12. **insouciance.** Calm, untroubled attitude

Soldiers walk through the destruction in Ypres, Belgium (c. 1914–1918).

holes, but once, having occasion to throw myself down with some abruptness on my face, I found myself nearly on the top of a brood of young larks. Two of them had already been hit by something, and were in rather a battered condition, but the survivors seemed as tranquil and comfortable as the average nestling.

At the corner of a stricken wood (which has had a name made for it in history, but shall be nameless here), at a moment when lyddite and shrapnel[13] and machine-gun fire swept and raked and bespattered that devoted spot as though the artillery of an entire Division had suddenly concentrated on it, a wee hen-chaffinch[14] flitted wistfully to and fro, amid splintered and falling branches that had never a green bough left on them. The wounded lying there, if any of them noticed the small bird, may well have wondered why anything having wings and no pressing reason for remaining should have chosen to stay in such a place. There was a battered orchard alongside the stricken wood, and the probable explanation of the bird's presence was that it had a nest of

---

13. **lyddite and shrapnel.** Explosive and the sharp bits of materials it shoots out
14. **hen-chaffinch.** Female finch, a type of songbird

young ones whom it was too scared to feed, too loyal to desert. Later on, a small flock of chaffinches blundered into the wood, which they were doubtless in the habit of using as a highway to their feeding-grounds; unlike the solitary hen-bird, they made no secret of their desire to get away as fast as their dazed wits would let them. The only other bird I ever saw there was a magpie, flying low over the wreckage of fallen tree-limbs; "one for sorrow," says the old superstition. There was sorrow enough in that wood.

The English gamekeeper, whose knowledge of wild life usually runs on limited and perverted lines, has evolved a sort of religion as to the nervous debility of even the hardiest game birds; according to his beliefs a terrier trotting across a field in which a partridge is nesting, or a mouse-hawking kestrel hovering over the hedge, is sufficient cause to drive the distracted bird off its eggs and send it whirring into the next county.

The partridge of the war zone shows no signs of such sensitive nerves. The rattle and rumble of transport, the constant coming and going of bodies of troops, the incessant rattle of musketry and deafening explosions of artillery, the night-long flare and flicker of star-shells, have not sufficed to scare the local birds away from their chosen feeding grounds, and to all appearances they have not been deterred from raising their broods. Gamekeepers who are serving with the colors might seize the opportunity to indulge in a little useful nature study. ❖

When have you witnessed an event in the natural world that mirrored an event in human society? When have you seen an event that provided a stark contrast to that of human society? What were your reactions to these events?

Review Questions

1. Summarize what Saki discusses in "Birds on the Western Front." What is the effect of Saki's unusual, unexpected narrative of World War I? Is he mocking human behavior by focusing on winged creatures? Explain.

2. In paragraph 2, what does the narrator say is not the reason for the absence of crows and ravens in the battle zone? What is ironic about this explanation? What other image in the paragraph is ironic?

3. Choose three birds that Saki discusses. For each bird, briefly describe what impact the war has on it. Some narratives, including stories, animated cartoons, and songs, feature animals instead of humans as the main characters. Why might writers and other artists use nonhuman creatures to tell a story? What might be the difference in the impact on the reader?

Writing Options

1. How is nature affected during war or other catastrophe, such as an epidemic? Write a brief narrative—from your own point of view or that of an animal—describing the impact of the disaster on the natural world.

2. How does Saki's story differ, in tone, mood, and style, from the poems by Sassoon and Owen? In your opinion, which genre—prose or poetry—is more effective for expressing an antiwar message? Explain your answer in a one-paragraph response.

 Go to **www.mirrorsandwindows.com** for more.

Understand the Concept

A **comma** is a punctuation mark used to separate words and groups of words. Commas clarify meaning by showing the relationships among parts of a sentence.

For instance, one of the most common uses of commas is to separate items in a series. A *series* may comprise words, phrases, or clauses, as shown by the following examples from Saki's short story "Birds on the Western Front."

EXAMPLES

Words in a series "In the chill, misty hour of gloom that precedes a rainy dawn . . ."

Phrases in a series "Without human occupation and cultivation there can have been no corn, no refuse, and consequently very few mice . . ."

Clauses in a series "The rattle and rumble of transport, the constant coming and going of bodies of troops, the incessant rattle of musketry and deafening explosions of artillery . . ."

A comma also is used to combine independent clauses (that is, complete sentences) to form a compound sentence. The comma is added before the coordinating conjunction (*and, but, or, nor, yet, so,* or *for*) that joins the clauses.

EXAMPLE

"Rats and mice have mobilized and swarmed into the fighting line, and there has been a partial mobilization of owls."

Finally, commas generally are used to set off introductory words, phrases, and clauses at the beginnings of sentences and subordinate words and phrases within sentences.

EXAMPLES

Introductory clause set off "According to investigations made by Russian naturalists, the effect of the war on bird life on the Eastern front has been more marked than it has been over here."

Subordinate phrase set off "The vast flocks of crows and ravens that one expected to find in the neighborhood of the fighting line are nonexistent, which is perhaps rather a pity."

Apply the Skill

Identify Uses of Commas

In the following sentence from "Birds on the Western Front," identify how each comma is used: (a) to separate items in a series, (b) to combine sentences, or (c) to set off elements.

> Crows and magpies are nesting well within the shell-swept area, and over a small beech-copse I once saw a pair of crows engaged in hot combat with a pair of sparrow-hawks, while considerably higher in the sky, but almost directly above them, two Allied battle-planes were engaging an equal number of enemy aircraft.

Fix Errors in Comma Use

Copy the following sentences on a sheet of paper, inserting commas in the correct places. Then identify how each comma is used: (a) to separate items in a series, (b) to combine sentences, or (c) to set off elements.

1. In "Birds on the Western Front" Saki writes about the war's effect on magpies larks barn owls buzzards and other birds.
2. According to Saki the rodent population has adapted well to the battlefield and has increased its numbers.
3. The birds must deal with incessant machine-gun fire exploding shells and the complete destruction of their breeding grounds.
4. Despite these horrifying conditions Saki finds a lark's nest which appears to be relatively unscathed.
5. Not all birds are as battle-hardy as these brave larks and Saki writes that he is surprised not to see any buzzards or crows on the battlefield.

Use Commas in Your Writing

Choose a conflict in your life, and write a humorous paragraph describing it. Try to include one example of each use of commas: to separate items in a series, to combine two independent clauses, and to set off elements. When you are finished, exchange paragraphs with a classmate and check each other's use of commas.

Modernism

As writers began to abandon the conventions of an older age, they embraced a new style of expression that captured the fractured, alienated, cynical reality of the modern world. Their work reflected the loss of confidence in modern society that permeated the early twentieth century and explored how to cope with this loss. **Modernism** refers to a number of trends during this period, including extensive experimentation with form, language, and purpose.

One trend focused on creating specific images to evoke a particular mood, a technique used extensively by poets T. S. Eliot and William Butler Yeats. Eliot exhibited other Modernist trends, as well, such as bleak settings, sudden shifts in context and language, and intellectual allusions to other literature and historical events. In meter, too, the Modernists were innovators. They rejected conventions of rhythm, rhyme, and stanza form in favor of *vers libre*, or free verse, which conformed more readily to the speaker's thoughts.

Innovations in fiction also emerged during this era. Novelists played with abrupt jumps in time. Authors such as James Joyce, Virginia Woolf, and D. H. Lawrence turned the focus of their novels inward. Joyce and Woolf experimented with a new literary technique called *stream of consciousness*, revealing through jumbled thoughts the inner workings of a character's mind. Lawrence's fiction explored the influence of society on basic human impulses and reflected the interest in psychology and psychoanalysis popular during this time.

The Unfortunate Land of Tyrol, 1913. Franz Marc. Solomon R. Guggenheim Museum, New York, New York.

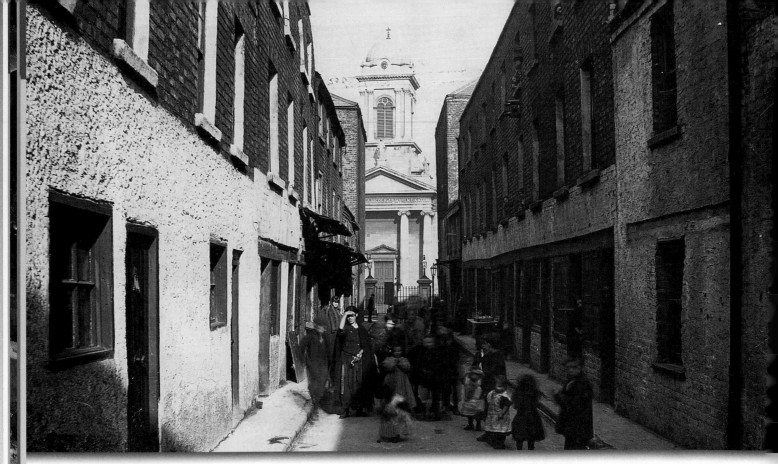

Among these I found a few paper-covered books, the pages of which were curled and damp: *The Abbot,* by Walter Scott, *The Devout Communicant,* and *The Memoirs of Vidocq.*[1] I liked the last best because its leaves were yellow. The wild garden behind the house contained a central apple-tree and a few straggling bushes under one of which I found the late tenant's rusty bicycle-pump. He had been a very charitable priest; in his will he had left all his money to institutions and the furniture of his house to his sister.

When the short days of winter came dusk fell before we had well eaten our dinners. When we met in the street the houses had grown somber. The space of sky above us was the color of ever-changing violet and towards it the lamps of the street lifted their feeble lanterns. The cold air stung us and we played till our bodies glowed. Our shouts echoed in the silent street. The career of our play brought us through the dark muddy lanes behind the houses where we ran the gauntlet of the rough tribes from the cottages, to the back doors of the dark dripping gardens where odors arose from the ashpits, to the dark <u>odorous</u> stables where a coachman smoothed and combed the horse or shook music from the buckled harness. When we returned to the street light from the kitchen windows had filled the areas. If my uncle was seen turning the corner we hid in the shadow until we had seen him safely housed. Or if Mangan's sister came out on the doorstep to call her brother in to his tea we watched her from our shadow peer up and down the street. We waited to see whether she would remain or go in and, if she remained, we left our shadow and walked up to Mangan's steps resignedly. She was waiting for us, her figure defined by the light from the half-opened door. Her brother

---

1. *The Devout Communicant . . . Vidocq.* The first work is a religious manual from 1813; the second work, the story of a French criminal.

odor • ous (ō´ də rəs) *adj.,* having a strong smell; fragrant

always teased her before he obeyed and I stood by the railings looking at her. Her dress swung as she moved her body and the soft rope of her hair tossed from side to side.

Every morning I lay on the floor in the front parlor watching her door. The blind was pulled down to within an inch of the sash so that I could not be seen. When she came out on the doorstep my heart leaped. I ran to the hall, seized my books, and followed her. I kept her brown figure always in my eye and, when we came near the point at which our ways <u>diverged</u>, I quickened my pace and passed her. This happened morning after morning. I had never spoken to her, except for a few casual words, and yet her name was like a summons to all my foolish blood.

Her image accompanied me even in places the most hostile to romance. On Saturday evenings when my aunt went marketing I had to go to carry some of the parcels. We walked through the flaring streets, jostled by drunken men and bargaining women, amid the curses of laborers, the shrill litanies of shop-boys who stood on guard by the barrels of pigs' cheeks, the nasal chanting of street-singers, who sang a *come-all-you* about O'Donovan Rossa,[2] or a ballad about the troubles in our native land. These noises converged in a single sensation of life for me: I imagined that I bore my chalice safely through a throng of foes. Her name sprang to my lips at moments in strange prayers and praises which I myself did not understand. My eyes were often full of tears (I could not tell why) and at times a flood from my heart seemed to pour itself out into my bosom. I thought little of the future. I did not know whether I would ever speak to her or not or, if I spoke to her, how I could tell her of my confused adoration. But my body was like a harp and her words and gestures were like fingers running upon the wires.

One evening I went into the back drawing-room in which the priest had died. It was a dark rainy evening and there was no sound in the house. Through one of the broken panes I heard the rain <u>impinge</u> upon the earth, the fine incessant needles of water playing in the sodden beds. Some distant lamp or lighted window gleamed below me. I was thankful that I could see so little. All my senses seemed to desire to veil themselves and, feeling that I was about to slip from them, I pressed the palms of my hands together until they trembled, murmuring: *O love! O love!* many times.

> My body was like a harp and her words and gestures were like fingers running upon the wires.

At last she spoke to me. When she addressed the first words to me I was so confused that I did not know what to answer. She asked me was I going to *Araby*. I forget whether I answered yes or no. It would be a splendid bazaar, she said; she would love to go.

—And why can't you? I asked.

While she spoke she turned a silver bracelet round and round her wrist. She could not go, she said, because there would be a retreat that week in her convent. Her brother and two other boys were fighting for their caps and I was alone at the railings. She held one of the spikes, bowing her head towards me. The light from the lamp opposite our door caught the white curve of her neck, lit up her hair that rested there and, falling, lit up the hand upon the railing. It fell over one side of her dress and caught the white border of a petticoat, just visible as she stood at ease.

—It's well for you,[3] she said.

—If I go, I said, I will bring you something.

What <u>innumerable</u> follies laid waste my waking and sleeping thoughts after that evening! I

---

2. **come-you-all . . . Rossa.** Type of Irish ballad. O'Donovan Rossa refers to Jeremiah O'Donovan, a nineteenth-century rebel against British rule.

3. **It's well for you.** "You're lucky."

di • verge (dī vʉrj′) v., go in different ways; separate
im • pinge (im pinj′) v., strike, as if with a sharp impact
in • nu • mer • a • ble (i nüm′ rə bəl) adj., countless

wished to <u>annihilate</u> the <u>tedious</u> intervening days. I chafed against the work of school. At night in my bedroom and by day in the classroom her image came between me and the page I strove to read. The syllables of the word *Araby* were called to me through the silence in which my soul luxuriated and cast an Eastern enchantment over me. I asked for leave to go to the bazaar on Saturday night. My aunt was surprised and hoped it was not some Freemason[4] affair. I answered few questions in class. I watched my master's face pass from <u>amiability</u> to sternness; he hoped I was not beginning to idle. I could not call my wandering thoughts together. I had hardly any patience with the serious work of life which, now that it stood between me and my desire, seemed to me child's play, ugly monotonous child's play.

On Saturday morning I reminded my uncle that I wished to go to the bazaar in the evening. He was fussing at the hallstand, looking for the hat-brush, and answered me curtly:

—Yes, boy, I know.

As he was in the hall I could not go into the front parlor and lie at the window. I left the house in bad humor and walked slowly towards the school. The air was pitilessly raw and already my heart misgave me.

When I came home to dinner my uncle had not yet been home. Still it was early. I sat staring at the clock for some time and, when its ticking began to irritate me, I left the room. I mounted the staircase and gained the upper part of the house. The high cold empty gloomy rooms liberated me and I went from room to room singing. From the front window I saw my companions playing below in the street. Their cries reached me weakened and indistinct and, leaning my forehead against the cool glass, I looked over at the dark house where she lived. I may have stood there for an hour, seeing nothing but the brown-clad figure cast by my imagination, touched discreetly by the lamplight at the curved neck, at the hand upon the railings and at the border below the dress.

When I came downstairs again I found Mrs. Mercer sitting at the fire. She was an old <u>garrulous</u> woman, a pawnbroker's widow, who collected used stamps for some pious purpose. I had to endure the gossip of the tea-table. The meal was prolonged beyond an hour and still my uncle did not come. Mrs. Mercer stood up to go: she was sorry she couldn't wait any longer, but it was after eight o'clock and she did not like to be out late, as the night air was bad for her. When she had gone I began to walk up and down the room, clenching my fists. My aunt said:

—I'm afraid you may put off your bazaar for this night of Our Lord.

At nine o'clock I heard my uncle's latchkey in the halldoor. I heard him talking to himself and heard the hallstand rocking when it had received the weight of his overcoat. I could interpret these signs. When he was midway through his dinner I asked him to give me the money to go to the bazaar. He had forgotten.

—The people are in bed and after their first sleep now, he said.

I did not smile. My aunt said to him energetically:

—Can't you give him the money and let him go? You've kept him late enough as it is.

My uncle said he was very sorry he had forgotten. He said he believed in the old saying: *All work and no play makes Jack a dull boy*. He asked me where I was going and, when I had told him a second time he asked me did I know *The Arab's Farewell to his Steed*.[5] When I left the kitchen he was about to recite the opening lines of the piece to my aunt.

---

4. **Freemason.** Reference to a social organization, whose members were mostly Protestant men, that conducts certain secret rituals
5. ***The Arab's Farewell to his Steed.*** The uncle's referring to and then reciting a shallow poem whose title is similar to the word *Araby* suggests that he is confused or perhaps intoxicated.

---

an · ni · hi · late (ə nī′ ə lāt′) *v.,* destroy; eliminate
te · dious (tē′ dē əs) *adj.,* boring; tiresome
ami · a · bil · i · ty (ā′ mē ə bi′ lə tē) *n.,* friendliness; pleasantness
gar · ru · lous (ger′ ə ləs) *adj.,* talkative

I held a florin[6] tightly in my hand as I strode down Buckingham Street towards the station. The sight of the streets thronged with buyers and glaring with gas recalled to me the purpose of my journey. I took my seat in a third-class carriage of a deserted train. After an <u>intolerable</u> delay the train moved out of the station slowly. It crept onward among ruinous houses and over the twinkling river. At Westland Row Station a crowd of people pressed to the carriage doors; but the porters moved them back, saying that it was a special train for the bazaar. I remained alone in the bare carriage. In a few minutes the train drew up beside an improvised wooden platform. I passed out on to the road and saw by the lighted dial of a clock that it was ten minutes to ten. In front of me was a large building which displayed the magical name.

I could not find any sixpenny entrance and, fearing that the bazaar would be closed, I passed in quickly through a turnstile, handing a shilling to a weary-looking man. I found myself in a big hall girdled at half its height by a gallery. Nearly all the stalls were closed and the greater part of the hall was in darkness. I recognized a silence like that which pervades a church after a service. I walked into the center of the bazaar timidly. A few people were gathered about the stalls which were still open. Before a curtain, over which the words *Café Chantant*[7] were written in colored lamps, two men were counting money on a salver.[8] I listened to the fall of the coins.

Remembering with difficulty why I had come I went over to one of the stalls and examined porcelain vases and flowered tea-sets. At the door of the stall a young lady was talking and laughing with two young gentlemen. I remarked[9] their English accents and listened vaguely to their conversation.

—O, I never said such a thing!

—O, but you did!

—O, but I didn't!

—Didn't she say that?

—Yes. I heard her.

—O, there's a . . . fib!

Observing me the young lady came over and asked me did I wish to buy anything. The tone of her voice was not encouraging; she seemed to have spoken to me out of a sense of duty. I looked humbly at the great jars that stood like eastern guards at either side of the dark entrance to the stall and murmured:

—No, thank you.

The young lady changed the position of one of the vases and went back to the two young men. They began to talk of the same subject. Once or twice the young lady glanced at me over her shoulder.

I lingered before her stall, though I knew my stay was useless, to make my interest in her wares seem the more real. Then I turned away slowly and walked down the middle of the bazaar. I allowed the two pennies to fall against the sixpence in my pocket. I heard a voice call from one end of the gallery that the light was out. The upper part of the hall was now completely dark.

Gazing up into the darkness I saw myself as a creature driven and derided by vanity; and my eyes burned with anguish and anger. ❖

---

6. **florin.** Coin worth about half a dollar at the time
7. *Café Chantant.* Restaurant in which entertainers sing; the words on the curtain were probably intended to suggest a romantic atmosphere.
8. **salver.** Plate for serving
9. **remarked.** Noticed

in • tol • er • a • ble (in [ʹ] täl´ rə bəl) *adj.*, unbearable

MIRRORS & WINDOWS

The boy's experience at the bazaar was not as he had hoped. When have you looked forward to an event with great anticipation, only to be disappointed by it at the end? Why were your expectations so high?

Refer to Text ▶ ▶ ▶ ▶ ▶   Reason with Text

1a. Recall how the narrator describes the house at the blind end of the street. How do the other houses gaze at each other?

1b. Explain how the house at the blind end symbolizes the narrator. What might the other houses suggest about him?

Understand
Find meaning

2a. Locate a quotation that shows how the narrator characterizes the streets through which he and his aunt walk after shopping.

2b. Why might this atmosphere motivate the boy to focus on his love for a girl he hardly knows?

Apply
Use information

3a. Define what the name of the bazaar, *Araby*, suggests to the narrator. What effect does his anticipation of the bazaar have on him?

3b. What motivates the girl to tell the narrator about the bazaar, even though the two have rarely spoken to each other?

Analyze
Take things apart

4a. Who rides on the third-class carriage of the train with the narrator?

4b. Describe how the boy's journey to Araby could be likened to a dream.

Evaluate
Make judgments

5a. With whom does the boy apparently live?

5b. The boy never mentions his parents. What might that fact suggest about the British–Irish conflict at the time?

Create
Bring ideas together

Analyze Literature

Epiphany and Point of View
Identify the epiphany the narrator has about his much-longed-for visit to the bazaar. What does he suddenly understand about the reality of human relations?

From what point of view is the story told? How does the point of view make the story suspenseful and intense? What details does the narrator provide and not provide? How would the use of a third-person point of view change the telling of the story?

Extend the Text

Writing Options
Creative Writing In cartoons, a light bulb can be a symbol for an epiphany, or sudden understanding about life. Create a comic strip narrating an epiphany that you have had or that you imagine. Your audience will be a young person who has asked for a story.

Expository Writing You would like to know more about the narrator of "Araby," who does not reveal much about himself. Why did Joyce provide so little information about the boy? Discuss the question in a one-paragraph analysis that helps you understand the author's literary technique.

Collaborative Learning
Prepare Flyers Advertising Araby Before the bazaar arrives in town, flyers must be handed out to residents to publicize the exciting event. Working with a group, prepare the advertising copy, or text, for the leaflet. Use your imagination to furnish the details. Include a suitable illustration if you wish.

Lifelong Learning
Host an Irish Cultural Festival As a class, hold a scaled-down, cultural version of the bazaar. In preparation, briefly research the artistic heritage of Ireland, such as the Celtic religion, folktales, ballads and music, visual arts, and traditional customs. Students can share their findings on posters, as illustrations, or as oral presentations.

 Go to **www.mirrorsandwindows.com** for more.

Understand the Concept

A **colon** is a punctuation mark used to mean "note what follows." It can be used to introduce a series of items or a quotation or show a close connection between clauses within a sentence. Observe how colons are used in these examples from James Joyce's short story "Araby":

EXAMPLES

To introduce a list Among these I found a few paper-covered books, the pages of which were curled and damp: *The Abbot,* by Walter Scott, *The Devout Communicant,* and *The Memoirs of Vidocq.*

To introduce a quotation My aunt said: —I'm afraid you may put off your bazaar for the night of Our Lord.

A colon also can be used between two independent clauses when the second clause explains or summarizes the first clause.

EXAMPLE

These noises converged in a single sensation of life for me: I imagined that I bore my Chalice safely through a throng of foes.

A **semicolon** is used to join the independent clauses of a compound sentence if no coordinating conjunction is used (*and, but, so, or, nor, for,* and *yet*). In addition to joining together closely related clauses, doing so adds emphasis to the second clause.

EXAMPLE

I watched my master's face pass from amiability to sternness; he hoped I was not beginning to idle.

A second use of semicolons is to separate the items in a series when the items themselves contain commas.

EXAMPLE

In addition to living in Dublin, Ireland, Joyce also lived in Paris, France; Zürich, Switzerland; and Trieste, Italy.

Apply the Skill

Identify Uses of Colons and Semicolons

For each of these sentences from "Araby," determine whether Joyce uses a colon to (a) introduce a list, (b) introduce a quotation, or (c) offer an explanation or summary or if he uses a semicolon to (d) join two independent clauses or (e) separate items in a series.

1. The tone of her voice was not encouraging; she seemed to have spoken to me out of a sense of duty.
2. I pressed the palms of my hands together until they trembled, murmuring: *O love! O love!* many times.
3. He had been a very charitable priest; in his will he had left all his money to institutions and the furniture of his house to his sister.
4. It would be a splendid bazaar, she said; she would love to go.
5. He said he believed in the old saying: *All work and no play makes Jack a dull boy.*

Use Colons and Semicolons Correctly

For each of the following sentences, insert the proper punctuation, whether a colon or semicolon. Then explain how the colon or semicolon is being used in the sentence.

1. Joyce wrote the following books *The Dubliners, Ulysses,* and *Finnegan's Wake.*
2. Joyce is known for an experimental style of writing that became popular in the earlier twentieth century stream-of-consciousness writing.
3. Reading Joyce's short stories is like falling into the mind of the narrator the narrator's thoughts and feelings are laid bare for all to see.
4. I confessed to my brother how much I liked James Joyce's writing and all he said was "Well, that's nice."
5. Schools in Salem, Massachusetts Northfield, Minnesota San Rafael, California and Charlottesville, Virginia, have read excerpts from James Joyce's stories.

Use Colons and Semicolons in Your Writing

Write a paragraph about a time in your childhood when you took a risk or got hurt. Describe the scene using sensory details, and explain the relationships between the people involved. Use colons and semicolons to connect closely related ideas, to set off items in lists, and to emphasize important ideas and quotations.

The Essay Defined

An **essay** is a short nonfiction work that presents a single main idea, or **thesis,** about a particular topic. Free of the limitations that shape other literary forms, the essay is uniquely designed for reflection. An essayist does not have to describe characters, as a novelist does, or convey information only through dialogue, as the dramatist does.

Although the essay form dates back to ancient Roman times, the first self-acknowledged essayist was Michel de Montaigne, an important figure in the French Renaissance. His complete *Essais,* published in 1588, explore a wide range of topics, including friendship, faith, knowledge, and mortality. The author described these brief works as attempts, or "trials," of his own judgment, and it still seems appropriate to describe the essay as a mode of working out one's thoughts and beliefs on a specific issue.

"If you do not tell the truth about yourself you cannot tell it about other people."

—VIRGINIA WOOLF, TWENTIETH-CENTURY
ESSAYIST AND NOVELIST

Types of Essays

If you have ever read the editorial section of a newspaper or a magazine article with a clearly personal tone, you already have encountered the essay form. Its author confidently attacks a controversial topic or explores a matter of absorbing personal interest. The writer asks What do I think about this matter? and Why? The audience is encouraged to follow the argument or perhaps simply enjoy the narrative.

There are three broad categories of essays, which may overlap in some instances. The type of essay is determined by the writer's **purpose,** or what he or she hopes to accomplish through the work.

An **expository,** or informative, essay explores a topic with the goal of informing or enlightening the reader. T. S. Eliot's "The Music of Poetry" is an example of this type of essay. Consider such statements as "the music of poetry is not something which exists apart from the meaning" and "Dissonance, even cacophony, has its place." The narrative voice is authoritative, and the writer's aim is to teach the reader how to perceive an important element of poetry.

A **persuasive** essay aims to convince the reader to accept a certain point of view. The writer often reveals his or her perspective through bold declarations. For example, in "A Room of One's Own," an essay on Shakespeare's sister, Virginia Woolf writes, "For it needs little skill in psychology to be sure that a highly gifted girl who had tried to use her gift for poetry would have been so thwarted and hindered by other people . . . that she must have lost her health and sanity to a certainty." To support her viewpoint and persuade the reader to accept her logic, Woolf provides a narrative of what would have happened had Shakespeare had a talented sister.

A *personal essay* explores a topic related to the life or interests of the writer. This type of essay is characterized by an intimate and informal style or tone. The writer makes no pretense that his or her experience or viewpoint is universal. D. H. Lawrence's essay "Reflections on the Death of a Porcupine" is highly personal and subjective in tone and content. Throughout the essay, Lawrence expresses his experiences with and reactions to nature, such that the work becomes less about the porcupine's death than about the author's psyche.

Elements of the Essay

Introduction

Whether an essay is formal or informal, it includes an *introduction*. The introductory paragraph or paragraphs engage the reader's attention, state the topic, and establish the background for the discussion. It is here that the author usually states the thesis of the essay.

WOOLF   ELIOT   LAWRENCE

Thesis Statement

The **thesis** is the main idea supported in a work of nonfiction. It identifies the topic of the essay and states the argument that will be made about it. The writer typically plants this central statement within the first paragraph or two of the essay, but in some instances, readers must look elsewhere for the sentence that best states the main idea. The thesis of the literary work may be stated directly or implied.

> *"The man who writes about himself and his own time is the only man who writes about all people and all time."*
>
> —GEORGE BERNARD SHAW, TWENTIETH-CENTURY CRITIC, ESSAYIST, AND PLAYWRIGHT

Argument

An **argument** is a form of persuasion that makes a case to readers for accepting or rejecting a proposition or course of action. The writer appeals to readers by citing authorities and statistics, using logic, and referring to personal experience. In analyzing the author's viewpoint, readers look at the language and the content of the essay. They identify opinions, facts, and possible bias in the argument. Then readers can formulate a response.

Rhetoric

The essayist may employ **rhetorical devices**, techniques used to achieve particular effects, especially to persuade or influence. Common rhetorical devices include parallelism, repetition, and rhetorical questions.

Parallelism emphasizes the equal value of two or more ideas by expressing them in the same grammatical format. **Repetition** is the intentional reuse of a sound, word, phrase, or sentence; writers often use repetition to emphasize words and ideas. A **rhetorical question** is one asked for effect but not meant to be answered because the answer is clear from context. For example, when Woolf asks "How could she disobey him? How could she break his heart?" she phrases the questions to strike a sympathetic chord in readers.

Conclusion

The *conclusion* of the essay returns to the thesis. In this final section of the essay, the writer underscores the significance of the argument. It is an opportunity to summarize the main points and deliver some powerful remarks on which readers can reflect. The conclusion even may be designed to startle readers, forcing them to reconsider the topic from a new vantage point.

HOW TO READ

An Essay

Find the main idea. Ask yourself what the writer wants you to know, think, or feel after reading the essay. Then look for details to support what he or she says. Evaluate the details to see if they make sense.

Distinguish fact from opinion. The details that support a writer's main idea are facts and opinions. A *fact* is a statement that can be proven either true or false, whereas an *opinion* expresses an attitude or desire. You can agree or disagree with an opinion but not prove it true or false.

Recognize bias. *Bias* is a personal judgment about something, a mental leaning in one direction or the other. Bias can be evident in what the writer says directly or in the details he or she leaves out.

Question the author. If you do not understand something the writer is telling you, ask questions: What does the writer mean here? Why does the writer say this? What support does the writer give for this statement? Keep track of your questions in a notebook or question log.

Virginia Woolf

"You cannot find peace by avoiding life."

Virginia Woolf (1882–1941) was born in London and educated at home by her father, Sir Leslie Stephen. There, young Virginia made good use of her father's extensive library and met many of the outstanding literary and intellectual figures of the time. After Sir Leslie's death, Virginia and her sister, Vanessa, continued to live in Gordon Square, in the Bloomsbury section of London. They hosted gatherings of writers and artists, a circle of Cambridge-educated friends that came to be known as the Bloomsbury Group.

In 1912, Virginia married one of these friends, Leonard Woolf, a writer on politics and economics. Five years later, Virginia and Leonard Woolf founded the Hogarth Press, which became a successful publishing house. The press published works by English authors Katherine Mansfield, E. M. Forster, T. S. Eliot, and Virginia Woolf and also introduced English translations of Sigmund Freud's works to the British public.

After publication of Woolf's first two novels, *The Voyage Out* (1915) and *Night and Day* (1919), she began to experiment with various elements of fiction, particularly interior monologue and stream-of-consciousness writing. Like James Joyce and French writer Marcel Proust (1871–1922), Woolf also challenged the notion of storytelling as the creation of a chronological narrative. In *Mrs. Dalloway* (1925), for instance, she explores Clarissa Dalloway's emotional ups and downs as she goes about her errands in response to a world that may not be as ordered as it appears.

The troubling memories that haunt Clarissa may reflect Woolf's own reactions to the stresses of life. The death of her mother when Virginia was just thirteen traumatized her and resulted in severe depression. Over the next few years, the deaths of her older half-sister and brother caused her to relapse into depression, and the death of her father in 1904 caused Woolf to experience an emotional breakdown. Throughout the remainder of her life, Woolf would continue to struggle with severe depression.

In addition to being a successful novelist, Woolf was one of the most distinguished literary critics of her time. She published numerous essays and works of literary analysis, including *The Common Reader* and *A Room of One's Own*. In 1953, twelve years after his wife's death, Leonard Woolf edited and published *A Writer's Diary*, which contained extracts from Virginia's journal.

Noted Works

Mrs. Dalloway (1925)

To the Lighthouse (1927)

The Common Reader (1925)

A Room of One's Own (1929)

The Waves (1931)

The Death of the Moth and Other Essays (1942)

from A Room of One's Own
Mr Sassoon's Poems

Essays by Virginia Woolf

Build Background

Literary Context Although Virginia Woolf may be best known as a novelist, she also was a perceptive critic. These two selections indicate the depth and breadth of Woolf's literary interests.

In a series of lectures presented in 1928 at Newnham College for women at Cambridge University, Woolf examined "the question of women and fiction." Her belief that the role of women as novelists remained in question suggests her feminist concerns. What social and economic factors prevented women from having the same freedom as men to create an imaginative world for readers? Ironically, one answer was to be found on the Cambridge campus: At that time, women were not allowed to use the university library. Woolf's lectures were published in 1929 as *A Room of One's Own,* one of the writer's most famous works of nonfiction.

According to Woolf, the title of the volume refers not simply to privacy and space but also to *independence*—women's right to pursue intellectual and artistic endeavors beyond the boundaries established by men. *A Room of One's Own* discusses the Elizabethan Age, the period of extraordinary creativity during the reign of Queen Elizabeth I (1558–1603). In the excerpt that follows, Woolf explores this question: If Shakespeare had had a wonderfully gifted sister (Woolf has imagined her as Judith), how would she have fared as a dramatist?

The second essay by Woolf, **"Mr Sassoon's Poems,"** originally appeared in the *Times Literary Supplement* on May 31, 1917, as a review of Siegfried Sassoon's volume *The Old Huntsman and Other Poems,* published around the same time. In the view of some critics, Sassoon wrote most of the poems in the collection before he served in combat. These works differ markedly from those written after Sassoon encountered the enemy face to face. Although Woolf speaks favorably of Sassoon's poetry in this review, she also observes that he "deserted art in a compulsion to express the intolerable." While evaluating Sassoon's strengths as a poet, Woolf also considers what it means to be a poet.

Courtyard in Newnham College at Cambridge University.

Reader's Context How can the historical period in which someone lives help determine what that person does with his or her talents?

Analyze Literature

Argument and Rhetorical Question

An **argument** is a form of persuasion that makes a case to the audience for accepting or rejecting a proposition or course of action.

A **rhetorical question** is one asked for effect but not meant to be answered because the answer is clear from context. It is a device used to persuade or influence the reader.

Set Purpose

A well-written essay not only presents a clear argument but also supports it with appropriate details and evidence. As you read the essays that follow, consider how Woolf develops her argument in each one. Identify what she is proposing, and then list the evidence she provides to support that perspective. Also look for examples of rhetorical questions in *A Room of One's Own*. Write them down and consider how Woolf uses them to develop or support her argument.

Preview Vocabulary

escapade, 1001
guffaw, 1001
beguile, 1003
pinnacle, 1006
incongruous, 1007
insinuation, 1007
sordid, 1007
loathing, 1007

Mein Wohnzimmer (My Living Room), 1903. Carl Moll.
Wien Museum Karlsplatz, Vienna, Austria.
(See detail on page 999.)

FROM A ROOM OF ONE'S OWN

by Virginia Woolf

Who shall measure the heat and violence of the poet's heart when caught and tangled in a woman's body?

Let me imagine, since facts are so hard to come by, what would have happened had Shakespeare had a wonderfully gifted sister, called Judith, let us say. Shakespeare himself went, very probably—his mother was an heiress—to the grammar school, where he may have learnt Latin—Ovid, Virgil and Horace—and the elements of grammar and logic. He was, it is well known, a wild boy who poached[1] rabbits, perhaps shot a deer, and had, rather sooner than he should have done, to marry a woman in the neighborhood, who bore him a child rather quicker than was right. That escapade sent him to seek his fortune in London. He had, it seemed, a taste for the theatre; he began by holding horses at the stage door. Very soon he got work in the theatre, became a successful actor, and lived at the hub of the universe, meeting everybody, knowing everybody, practicing his art on the boards, exercising his wits in the streets, and even getting access to the palace of the queen. Meanwhile his extraordinarily gifted sister, let us suppose, remained at home. She was as adventurous, as imaginative, as agog[2] to see the world as he was. But she was not sent to school. She had no chance of learning grammar and logic, let alone of reading Horace and Virgil. She picked up a book now and then, one of her brother's perhaps, and read a few pages. But then her parents came in and told her to mend the stockings or mind the stew and not moon about with books and papers. They would have spoken sharply but kindly, for they were substantial people who knew the conditions of life for a woman and loved their daughter—indeed, more likely than not she was the apple of her father's eye. Perhaps she scribbled some pages up in an apple loft on the sly, but was careful to hide them or set fire to them. Soon, however, before she was out of her teens, she was to be betrothed to the son of a neighboring wool-stapler. She cried out that marriage was hateful to her, and for that she was severely beaten by her father. Then he ceased to scold her. He begged her instead not to hurt him, not to shame him in this matter of her marriage. He would give her a chain of beads or a fine petticoat, he said; and there were tears in his eyes. How could she disobey him? How could she break his heart? The force of her own gift alone drove her to it. She made up a small parcel of her belongings, let herself down by a rope one summer's night and took the road to London. She was not seventeen. The birds that sang in the hedge were not more musical than she was. She had the quickest fancy, a gift like her

Perhaps she scribbled some pages up in an apple loft on the sly, but was careful to hide them or set fire to them.

brother's, for the tune of words. Like him, she had a taste for the theatre. She stood at the stage door; she wanted to act, she said. Men laughed in her face. The manager—a fat, loose-lipped man—guffawed. He bellowed something about poodles dancing and women acting—no

---

1. **poached.** Hunted illegally
2. **agog.** Eager and excited

> es • ca • pade (es´ kə pād') *n.,* reckless adventure
> guf • faw (gu´ fô') *v.,* let out a short burst of laughter

Preludes

by T. S. Eliot

T. S. Eliot, 1949. Patrick Heron.
Private collection. (See detail on page 1019.)

I

The winter evening settles down
With smell of steaks in passageways.
Six o'clock.
The burnt-out ends of smoky days.
5　And now a gusty shower wraps
The grimy scraps
Of withered leaves about your feet
And newspapers from vacant lots;
The showers beat
10　On broken blinds and chimney-pots,
And at the corner of the street
A lonely cab-horse steams and stamps.

And then the lighting of the lamps.

II

The morning comes to consciousness
15　Of faint stale smells of beer
From the sawdust-trampled street
With all its muddy feet that press
To early coffee-stands.

With the other masquerades[1]
20　That time resumes,
One thinks of all the hands
That are raising <u>dingy</u> shades
In a thousand furnished rooms.

---

1. **masquerades.** Parties or dances at which masks and fancy
costumes or disguises are worn

din • gy (din´ jē) *adj.*, dirty and shabby

III

You tossed a blanket from the bed,
25 You lay upon your back, and waited;
You dozed, and watched the night revealing
The thousand <u>sordid</u> images
Of which your soul was <u>constituted</u>;
They flickered against the ceiling.
30 And when all the world came back
And the light crept up between the shutters
And you heard the sparrows in the gutters,
You had such a vision of the street
As the street hardly understands;
35 Sitting along the bed's edge, where
You curled the papers from your hair,
Or clasped the yellow soles of feet
In the palms of both soiled hands.

IV

His soul stretched tight across the skies
40 That fade behind a city block,
Or trampled by insistent feet
At four and five and six o'clock;
And short square fingers stuffing pipes,
And evening newspapers, and eyes
45 Assured of certain certainties,
The conscience of a blackened street
Impatient to assume the world.

I am moved by fancies that are curled
Around these images, and cling:
50 The notion of some infinitely gentle
Infinitely suffering thing.

Wipe your hand across your mouth, and laugh;
The worlds revolve like ancient women
Gathering fuel in vacant lots. ❖

---

sor • did (sôr´ dəd) *adj.,* dirty; filthy
con • sti • tute (kän[t]´ stə tüt') *v.,* form or compose

MIRRORS & WINDOWS

When have you experienced a moment of compassion? How did this experience affect your view of society and the world at large?

Mistah Kurtz[1]—he dead.
A penny for the Old Guy[2]

I

We are the hollow men
We are the stuffed men
Leaning together
Headpiece filled with straw. Alas!
5 Our dried voices, when
We whisper together
Are quiet and meaningless
As wind in dry grass
Or rats' feet over broken glass
10 In our dry cellar

Shape without form, shade without color,
Paralyzed force, gesture without motion;

Those who have crossed
With direct eyes, to death's other Kingdom[3]
15 Remember us—if at all—not as lost
Violent souls, but only
As the hollow men
The stuffed men.

II

Eyes I dare not meet in dreams
20 In death's dream kingdom
These do not appear:
There, the eyes are
Sunlight on a broken column
There, is a tree swinging
25 And voices are
In the wind's singing
More distant and more solemn
Than a fading star.

Let me be no nearer
30 In death's dream kingdom
Let me also wear

Handwritten annotations:
Collection of imagery
— lack of worth
— no substance

Modernism

by T. S. Eliot
— moving to become member of church of England

Depressing

— Feeling that Faith isn't there to grasp
Focus on end of world
everything is frustrated

fragmentation, no train of thought

there is no eye contact for them

no desire for contact

False, did not intend to → help Africans

---

1. **Mistah Kurtz.** Character in Joseph Conrad's novel *Heart of Darkness,* a European who ends up dominating rather than helping the Africans he had intended to help

2. **A . . . Guy.** "Old Guy" refers to Guy Fawkes, who tried to blow up the British Parliament buildings in 1605. Each year on November 5, the British celebrate Guy Fawkes Day by burning straw dummies of Fawkes.

3. **Those . . . Kingdom.** In *Paradiso,* by the Italian author Dante Alighieri (1265–1321), God blesses individuals with "direct eyes."

Such deliberate disguises
Rat's coat, crowskin, crossed staves
In a field[4]
35 Behaving as the wind behaves
No nearer—

pushing aside connection

Not that final meeting
In the twilight kingdom

III

This is the dead land
40 This is cactus land
Here the stone images
Are raised, here they receive
The supplication[5] of a dead man's hand
Under the twinkle of a fading star.

45 Is it like this
In death's other kingdom
Waking alone

showing lack of connection again

At the hour when we are
Trembling with tenderness
50 Lips that would kiss
Form prayers to broken stone.

IV

The eyes are not here
There are no eyes here
In this valley of dying stars
55 In this hollow valley
This broken jaw of our lost kingdoms

In this last of meeting places
We grope together
And avoid speech
60 Gathered on this beach of the tumid river[6]

Sightless, unless
The eyes reappear
As the perpetual star
Multifoliate rose[7]

empty hope
no comfort

65 Of death's twilight kingdom
The hope only
Of empty men.

---

4. **Rat's . . . field.** Scarecrows
5. **supplication.** Act of praying or pleading
6. **tumid river.** Swollen river; a reference to Dante's *Inferno* in which the dead must cross a river on their way to Hell
7. **Multifoliate rose.** Rose with many leaves, perhaps a symbol of the Virgin Mary

V

Here we go round the prickly pear[8]
Prickly pear prickly pear
70 Here we go round the prickly pear
At five o'clock in the morning.[9]

Between the idea
And the reality
Between the motion
75 And the act[10]
Falls the Shadow

For Thine is the Kingdom[11]

Between the conception
And the creation
80 Between the emotion
And the response
Falls the Shadow

Life is very long[12]

Between the desire
85 And the spasm
Between the potency
And the existence
Between the essence
And the descent
90 Falls the Shadow

For Thine is the Kingdom

For Thine is
Life is
For Thine is the

95 *This is the way the world ends*
This is the way the world ends
This is the way the world ends
Not with a bang but a whimper. ❖

*Shadow cutting
of any
accomplishments*

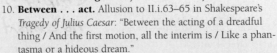

---

8. **prickly pear.** Type of cactus
9. **Here . . . morning.** Parody of children's rhyme
10. **Between . . . act.** Allusion to II.i.63–65 in Shakespeare's
   Tragedy of Julius Caesar: "Between the acting of a dreadful
   thing / And the first motion, all the interim is / Like a phan-
   tasma or a hideous dream."
11. **For . . . Kingdom.** Phrase from the Lord's Prayer
12. **Life . . . long.** From Joseph Conrad's *An Outcast of the Islands*

MIRRORS & WINDOWS

Eliot writes, "This is a dead land / This is a cactus land." How is today's society a "dead land"? How is this description overly critical of today's society?

Refer to Text ▶ ▶ ▶ ▶ ▶ Reason with Text

1a. What setting does the speaker describe in stanza 1 of "Preludes"?	**1b.** Describe the mood of this poem. What images help create this mood?	**Understand** Find meaning
2a. Identify two similes used to describe the hollow men in the first stanza of "The Hollow Men."	**2b.** Show what these images suggest about the hollow men.	**Apply** Use information
3a. Describe the different descriptions of people presented in "Preludes."	**3b.** How is the speaker moved by the people and the settings? What emotion do they evoke in him?	**Analyze** Take things apart
4a. State the attitudes toward humanity Eliot presents in "Preludes" and "The Hollow Men."	**4b.** Critique Eliot's views of humanity. Do you agree with his views? Why or why not?	**Evaluate** Make judgments
5a. Make a list of the allusions you find in the "The Hollow Men."	**5b.** Is one allusion more compelling than others? If so, how does it help further your understanding? If not, what purpose do you think Eliot hopes to achieve with his use of allusions?	**Create** Bring ideas together

Analyze Literature

Free Verse and Objective Correlative

What elements of free verse did you find in "Preludes" and "The Hollow Men"? How does the use of free verse affect your reading and understanding of each poem? Explain.

What instances of objective correlatives did you find in "Preludes" and "The Hollow Men"? How do these images enhance your response to the poems? What emotion does each objective correlative evoke? How do these emotions support the overall meaning of the poem?

Extend the Text

Writing Options

Creative Writing Recall a nursery rhyme or locate one in the library or on the Internet. Then create a parody of the rhyme. Exchange parodies with a partner and discuss each other's work. What ideas or themes can you identify in the parodied nursery rhymes?

Expository Writing You have been invited to a panel discussion of Modernist poems. First, write a definition of the term *Modernist*. Then prepare a one-paragraph explanation of why "Preludes" and "The Hollow Men" can be considered Modernist works.

Collaborative Learning

Give an Oral Interpretation of a Poem With a partner or small group, practice an oral interpretation of one of the two poems by Eliot. Take turns reciting lines from the poem or recite the lines together. In your interpretation, try to bring the poem to life.

Lifelong Learning

Illustrate the Poems Call on your organizational and artistic skills by illustrating the two selections. First, decide what the illustrations will be: (1) photographs or works of fine art (legally downloadable from the Internet) or (2) drawings, paintings, photographs, or any other appropriate artwork created by you or your classmates. Decide whether to illustrate literal images from the poem or simply suggest the mood and general setting. Then assemble your artwork together with the poems and present it to the class.

 Go to **www.mirrorsandwindows.com** for more.

from **Reflections on the Death of a Porcupine**

An Essay by D. H. Lawrence

Build Background

Literary Context The essay **"Reflections on the Death of a Porcupine"** is one of the works based on D. H. Lawrence's stay at his ranch in Taos, New Mexico, where he lived for two years. Originally published in *Reflections on the Death of a Porcupine and Other Essays* (1925), the selection focuses on the place of humans in the natural world.

Although Lawrence had always opposed the killing of any living creature, he experiences a *volte-face,* or about face, after struggling with the presence of the quilled beast making its awkward way around the ranch. As you read the essay, be alert to the vivid, sometimes wry portrayals of the animals and humans as they engage in a small-scale battle of the species.

Reader's Context In what circumstances, if any, is it acceptable to kill an animal? Why do you feel this way?

Meet the Author

David Herbert (D. H.) Lawrence (1885–1930) led a restless, colorful, and controversial life. Born in Nottinghamshire, England, he was the son of a rough coal miner and a genteel mother. Mrs. Lawrence, in fact, longed to have her children rise above their working-class origins, and the young Lawrence identified strongly with her. As an adult, however, Lawrence came to appreciate the primitive, natural integrity of his father and others of his class, as opposed to the smothering, conventional aspirations of his mother and other members of the upper class.

In 1909, Lawrence published his first poems, and in the following year, he published a novel. He taught school for a while but quit this work after meeting Frieda von Richthofen, a German woman; the two were married in 1914. Lawrence had completed the autobiographical novel *Sons and Lovers* the previous year. The work deals with a boy's attempt to break away from a domineering mother and establish his own identity.

Lawrence contracted tuberculosis, always fatal in those days, shortly after his mother's death from cancer in 1910, and he was acutely aware that his life would be short. Evidently, he spent his life resisting the bounds of conventional society's expectations in order to live fully. His literary output often explores the struggle of a character to escape the spiritual death of the modern world. Despite his early death, Lawrence produced numerous works of fiction, poetry, drama, and nonfiction, including literary criticism and travel books.

Analyze Literature

Style and Tone

Style is the manner in which something is said or written. A writer's style is characterized by elements such as word choice, sentence structure and length, and other recurring features that distinguish his or her work.

Tone is the emotional attitude toward the reader or subject implied by a literary work.

Set Purpose

Lawrence's essay "Reflections on the Death of a Porcupine" is an example of a personal narrative essay. Unlike the previous essays by Woolf and Eliot, Lawrence's primary goal is not to advocate a position or explain a theory, but to reflect on a significant incident in his life. While you read this essay, consider how Lawrence's purpose for writing influences his style and the tone of the essay. Look for a sentence or passage that best exemplifies Lawrence's writing style. Also identify the tone of this essay. Consider the relationship between Lawrence's style and the tone of the essay.

Preview Vocabulary

emit, 1028
lumbering, 1028
squalid, 1028
repugnant, 1028
protrude, 1030
pallid, 1031
sinister, 1031

from *Reflections on the Death of a Porcupine*

by D. H. Lawrence

*Wherever man establishes himself, upon the earth,
he has to fight for his place, against the lower orders of life.*

There are many bare places on the little pine trees, towards the top, where the porcupines have gnawed the bark away and left the white flesh showing. And some trees are dying from the top.

Everyone says, porcupines should be killed; the Indians, Mexicans, Americans all say the same.

At full moon a month ago, when I went down the long clearing in the brilliant moonlight, through the poor dry herbage a big porcupine began to waddle away from me, towards the trees and the darkness. The animal had raised all its hairs and bristles, so that by the light of the moon it seemed to have a tall, swaying, moonlit aureole[1] arching its back as it went. That seemed curiously fearsome, as if the animal were <u>emitting</u> itself demon-like on the air.

It waddled very slowly, with its white spiky spoon-tail steering flat, behind the round bear-like mound of its back. It had a <u>lumbering</u>, beetle's, <u>squalid</u> motion, unpleasant. I followed it into the darkness of the timber, and there, squat like a great

tick, it began scrapily to creep up a pine-trunk. It was very like a great aureoled tick, a bug, struggling up.

I stood near and watched, disliking the presence of the creature. It is a duty to kill the things. But the dislike of killing him was greater than the dislike of him. So I watched him climb.

And he watched me. When he had got nearly the height of a man, all his long hairs swaying with a bristling gleam like an aureole, he hesitated, and slithered down. Evidently he had decided, either that I was harmless, or else that it was risky to go up any further, when I could knock him off so easily with a pole. So he slithered podgily down again, and waddled away with the same bestial, stupid motion of that white-spiky repulsive spoon-tail. He was as big as a middle-sized pig: or more like a bear.

I let him go. He was <u>repugnant</u>. He made a certain squalor[2] in the moonlight of the Rocky Mountains. As all savagery has a touch of squa-

lor, that makes one a little sick at the stomach. And anyhow, it seemed almost more squalid to pick up a pine bough and push him over, hit him and kill him.

A few days later, on a hot, motionless morning when the pine trees put out their bristles in stealthy, hard assertion; and I was not in a good temper, because Black-eyed Susan, the cow, had disappeared into the timber, and I had had to ride hunting her, so it was nearly nine o'clock before she was milked: Madame[3] came in suddenly out of the sunlight, saying: "I

---

1. **aureole.** Radiant light. Originally the term referred to light cast on a religious object, but the term came to apply, as well, to ordinary objects.
2. **squalor.** Filth, often from neglect and suggesting immorality
3. **Madame.** Apparent reference to Lawrence's wife

---

emit (ē mit´) *v.*, send out or voice
lum • ber • ing (lum´ bər iŋ) *adj.*, walking slowly and heavily
squal • id (skwä´ ləd) *adj.*, dirty; filthy
re • pug • nant (ri pug´ nənt) *adj.*, repulsive; disgusting

got such a shock! There are two strange dogs, and one of them has got the most awful beard, all round his nose."

She was frightened, like a child, at something unnatural.

"Beard! Porcupine quills, probably! He's been after a porcupine."

"Ah!" she cried in relief. "Very likely! Very likely!"—then with a change of tone: "Poor thing, will they hurt him?"

"They will. I wonder when he came."

"I heard dogs bark in the night."

"Did you? Why didn't you say so? I should have known Susan was hiding—"

The ranch is lonely, there is no sound in the night, save the innumerable noises of the night, that you can't put your finger on; cosmic noises in the far deeps of the sky, and of the earth.

I went out. And in the full blaze of sunlight in the field, stood two dogs, a black-and-white, and a big, bushy, rather handsome sandy-red dog, of the collie type. And sure enough, this latter did look queer and a bit horrifying, his whole muzzle set round with white spines, like some ghastly growth; like an unnatural beard.

The black-and-white dog made off as I went through the fence. But the red dog whimpered and hesitated, and moved on hot bricks. He was fat and in good condition. I thought he might belong to some shepherds herding sheep in the forest ranges, among the mountains.

He waited while I went up to him, wagging his tail and whimpering, and ducking his head, and dancing. He daren't rub his nose with his paws any more: it hurt too much. I patted his head and looked at his nose, and he whimpered loudly.

He must have had thirty quills, or more, sticking out of his nose, all the way round; the white, ugly ends of the quills protruding an inch, sometimes more, sometimes less, from his already swollen, blood-puffed muzzle.

The porcupines here have quills only two or three inches long. But they are devilish; and a dog will die if he does not get them pulled out. Because they work further and further in, and will sometimes emerge through the skin away in some unexpected place.

Then the fun began. I got him in the yard: and he drank up the whole half-gallon of the chickens' sour milk. Then I started pulling out the quills. He was a big, bushy, handsome dog, but his nerve was gone, and every time I got a quill out, he gave a yelp. Some long quills were fairly easy. But the shorter ones, near his lips, were deep in, and hard to get hold of, and hard to pull out when you did get hold of them. And with every one that came out, came a little spurt of blood and another yelp and writhe.

The dog wanted the quills out: but his nerve was gone. Every time he saw my hand coming to his nose, he jerked his head away. I quieted him, and stealthily managed to jerk out another quill, with the blood all over my fingers. But with every one that came out, he grew more tiresome. I tried and tried and tried to get hold of another quill, and he jerked and jerked, and writhed and whimpered, and ran under the porch floor.

It was a curiously unpleasant, nerve-trying job. The day was blazing hot. The dog came out and I struggled with him again for an hour or more. Then we blindfolded him. But either he smelled my hand approaching his nose, or some weird instinct told him. He jerked his head, this way, that way, up, down, sideways, round-wise, as one's fingers came slowly, slowly, to seize a quill.

The quills on his lips and chin were deep in, only about a quarter of an inch of white

end of his bushy, foxy tail, which moved when we came near. Towards noon he emerged, ate up the chicken-food, and stood with that dog-gish look of dejection, and fear, and friendli-ness, and greediness, wagging his tail.

But I had had enough.

"Go home!" I said. "Go home! Go home to your master, and let him finish for you."

He would not go. So I led him across the blazing hot clearing, in the way I thought he should go. He followed a hundred yards, then stood motionless in the blazing sun. He was not going to leave the place.

And I! I simply did not want him.

So I picked up a stone. He dropped his tail, and swerved towards the house. I knew what he was going to do. He was going to dive under the porch, and there stick, haunting the place.

I dropped my stone, and found a good stick under the cedar tree. Already in the heat was that sting-like biting of electricity, the thunder gathering in the sheer sunshine, with-out a cloud, and making one's whole body feel dislocated.

I could not bear to have that dog around any more. Going quietly to him, I suddenly gave him one hard hit with the stick, crying: "Go home!" He turned quickly, and the end of the stick caught him on his sore nose. With a fierce yelp, he went off like a wolf, downhill,

stub <u>protruding</u> from the swollen, blood-oozed, festering black skin. It was very difficult to jerk them out.

We let him lie for an interval, hidden in the quiet cool place under the porch floor. After half an hour, he crept out again. We got a rope round his nose, behind the bristles, and one held while the other got the stubs with the pli-ers. But it was too trying. If a quill came out, the dog's yelp startled every nerve. And he was frightened of the pain, it was impossible to hold his head still any longer.

After struggling for two hours, and extract-ing some twenty quills, I gave up. It was im-possible to quiet the creature, and I had had enough. His nose on the top was clear: a punc-tured, puffy, blood-darkened mess; and his lips were clear. But just on his round little chin, where the few white hairs are, was still a bunch of white quills, eight or nine, deep in.

We let him go, and he dived under the porch, and there he lay invisible: save for the

> **pro • trude** (prō trüd´) v., project; stick out from

The Legacy of D. H. Lawrence

Most modern literary critics consider D. H. Lawrence an important contributor to the Modernist movement. However, Lawrence had a very limited readership during his own lifetime, and a number of countries banned his work from publication.

This resulted, in part, because Lawrence frequently criticized the British government's involvement in World War I. When Britain passed the Defense of the Realm Act (DORA) in 1914, the government gained the power to censor any material and deport any individual it believed was inhibiting the war effort. Given this power, British officials banned Lawrence's manuscripts and forced the author to leave his native country in 1919.

Soon after Lawrence's death in 1930, writers E. M. Forster and Aldous Huxley defended Lawrence's literary contributions, arguing that his work deserved praise regardless of his feelings about the war. Their advocacy eventually convinced the British government to relent and allow publication of Lawrence's work.

---

like a flash, gone. And I stood in the field full of pangs of regret, at having hit him, unintentionally, on his sore nose.

But he was gone.

And then the present moon came, and again the night was clear. But in the interval there had been heavy thunder-rains, the ditch was running with bright water across the field, and the night, so fair, had not the terrific, mirror-like brilliancy, touched with terror, so startling bright, of the moon in the last days of June.

We were alone on the ranch. Madame went out into the clear night, just before retiring. The stream ran in a cord of silver across the field, in the straight line where I had taken the irrigation ditch. The pine tree in front of the house threw a black shadow. The mountain slope came down to the fence, wild and alert.

"Come!" said she excitedly. "There is a big porcupine drinking at the ditch. I thought at first it was a bear."

When I got out he had gone. But among the grasses and the coming wild sunflowers, under the moon, I saw his greyish halo, like a <u>pallid</u> living bush, moving over the field, in the distance, in the moonlit *clair-obscur*.[4]

We got through the fence, and following, soon caught him up. There he lumbered, with his white spoon-tail spiked with bristles, steering behind almost as if he were moving backwards, and this was his head. His long, long hairs above the quills quivering with a dim grey gleam, like a bush.

And again I disliked him.

"Should one kill him?"

She hesitated. Then with a sort of disgust: "Yes!"

I went back to the house, and got the little twenty-two rifle. Now never in my life had I shot at any live thing: I never wanted to. I always felt guns very repugnant: <u>sinister</u>, mean. With difficulty I had fired once or twice at a target: but resented doing even so much. Other people could shoot if they wanted to. Myself, individually, it was repugnant to me even to try.

But something slowly hardens in a man's soul. And I knew now, it had hardened in mine.

---

4. ***clair-obscur.*** [French] Clear-obscure or bright-dark

pal • lid (pa´ ləd) *adj.,* dull
sin • is • ter (si´ nəs tər) *adj.,* evil or ominous

> *But something slowly hardens in a man's soul.*
> *And I knew now, it had hardened in mine.*

I found the gun, and with rather trembling hands, got it loaded. Then I pulled back the trigger and followed the porcupine. It was still lumbering through the grass. Coming near, I aimed.

The trigger stuck. I pressed the little catch with a safety-pin I found in my pocket, and released the trigger. Then we followed the porcupine. He was still lumbering towards the trees. I went sideways on, stood quite near to him, and fired, in the clear-dark of the moonlight.

And as usual I aimed too high. He turned, went scuttling back whence he had come.

I got another shell in place, and followed. This time I fired full into the mound of his round back, below the glistening grey halo. He seemed to stumble on to his hidden nose, and struggled a few strides, ducking his head under like a hedgehog.

"He's not dead yet! Oh, fire again!" cried Madame.

I fired, but the gun was empty.

So I ran quickly, for a cedar pole. The porcupine was lying still, with subsiding halo. He stirred faintly. So I turned him and hit him hard over the nose; or where, in the dark, his nose should have been. And it was done. He was dead.

And in the moonlight, I looked down on the first creature I had ever shot.

"Does it seem mean?" I asked aloud, doubtful.

Again Madame hesitated. Then: "No!" she said resentfully.

And I felt she was right. Things like the porcupine, one must be able to shoot them, if they get in one's way.

One must be able to shoot. I, myself, must be able to shoot, and to kill.

For me, this is a *volte-face*.[5] I have always preferred to walk round my porcupine, rather than kill it.

Now, I know it's no good walking round. One must kill.

I buried him in the adobe hole. But some animal dug down and ate him; for two days later there lay the spines and bones spread out, with the long skeletons of the porcupine-hands.

The only nice thing about him—or her, for I believe it was a female, by the dugs on her belly—were the feet. They were like longish, alert black hands, paw-hands. That is why a porcupine's tracks in the snow look almost as if a child had gone by, leaving naked little human foot-prints, like a little boy.

So, he is gone: or she is gone. But there is another one, bigger and blacker-looking, among the west timber. That too is to be shot. It is part of the business of ranching: even when it's only a little half-abandoned ranch like this one.

Wherever man establishes himself, upon the earth, he has to fight for his place, against the lower orders of life. Food, the basis of existence, has to be fought for even by the most idyllic of farmers. You plant, and you protect your growing crop with a gun. Food, food, how strangely it relates man with the animal and vegetable world! How important it is! And how fierce is the fight that goes on around it. ❖

---

5. ***volte-face.*** [French] About face

At the end of the essay, Lawrence says, "I have always preferred to walk round my porcupine, rather than kill it." When does it make sense to avoid difficult decisions or situations? When is it best to face them?

Refer to Text ▶ ▶ ▶ ▶ ▶   **Reason with Text**

1a. What is Lawrence's complaint about porcupines at the beginning of the essay? Who does the author say supports the killing of these animals?

1b. Discuss why Lawrence begins the essay with this information.

Understand
Find meaning

2a. Why does Lawrence attempt to pull the quills from the dog's nose? How does the dog react?

2b. What effect does the dog's reaction have on the author's later actions?

Apply
Use information

3a. Quote what Lawrence says to Madame when they see the porcupine that night. What is her response?

3b. How does Lawrence's early ambiguity about the killing of porcupines impact the central message of his essay?

Analyze
Take things apart

4a. Summarize the justification Lawrence gives for killing the porcupine.

4b. Evaluate Lawrence's reasoning. Do you find it a compelling argument? Why or why not?

Evaluate
Make judgments

5a. Which signs tell Lawrence that another animal has dug up the buried porcupine and eaten it? What else does he observe on the property?

5b. How do these discoveries affect Lawrence's attitude toward the role of humans in the natural world? Do you agree with his attitude? Explain.

Create
Bring ideas together

Analyze Literature

Style and Tone
Locate a passage or a sentence that is a strong example of Lawrence's writing style. What specific elements in this passage help create Lawrence's writing style?

Describe the tone of the essay. What specific words and phrases contribute to tone? How does Lawrence's writing style affect the tone of the essay?

Extend the Text

Writing Options
Creative Writing If you were the porcupine, how would you feel about the way Lawrence was treating you? Write a brief account of the experience from the porcupine's point of view.

Persuasive Writing Your community has a controversy: Should troublesome animals be killed? Decide which side you are on and write a letter to the editor of a newspaper outlining your views. Include convincing details to support your view and make suggestions about how the community can deal with the problem creatures other than killing them.

Collaborative Learning
Analyze Human Impact on the Environment As cities and towns continue to expand, wildlife is often pushed out of its natural habitat. In small groups, choose an animal that is affected by human population growth, such as deer, mountain lions, rabbits, pheasants, or bears. Prepare an oral report that describes how the animal is affected by human population growth and evaluates any laws that regulate how the animal may be treated.

Media Literacy
Create a Website No matter where you live, agriculture is probably an important issue for your community. For instance, where can city dwellers buy fruits and vegetables from nearby farmers? What information do city and suburban dwellers need to plant a garden? Create a website on agriculture, providing information most useful for residents in your community.

 Go to **www.mirrorsandwindows.com** for more.

The Rocking-Horse Winner

A Short Story by D. H. Lawrence

Build Background

Literary Context Throughout his career as a novelist, poet, and essayist, **D. H. Lawrence** also wrote short stories. In one of these, **"The Rocking-Horse Winner,"** a small boy finds a way to ease his family's money problems by predicting horse-race winners, hoping that he will please his cold, unfriendly mother. Although the story seems realistic in some ways, it contains elements of the supernatural, as well.

Fiction that combines the realistic and the fantastic sometimes is referred to as **Magical Realism.** This term was coined in 1925 by German art critic Franz Roh, who used it to describe a new objectivity that he found in certain German paintings of the time. In these artworks, imaginary, unbelievable, or fantastic images were portrayed in a realistic, natural way. The term came to be associated with literature, as well as art, especially with works by some Latin American authors of the twentieth century.

The term Magical Realism can be applied to Lawrence's story, in which unexplainable events, such as Paul's inspiration when he rides his toy pony, are treated as if they were ordinary. In distinguishing between the realistic and the fantastic, readers may wonder whether, in everyday life, there is a neat line between these two elements or whether imagination and emotion sometimes play a role in the outcome of events.

Reader's Context If you could be lucky in only one aspect of your life, which would it be? Why?

See the Meet the Author on page 1026 for biographical information about D. H. Lawrence.

Analyze Literature

Character and Climax

A **character** is an individual who takes part in the action of a literary work. The main character, or *protagonist*, is the most important character and is in conflict with the *antagonist*.

The **climax** is the high point of interest and suspense in a literary work. The term sometimes refers to the turning point, or point at which the rising action ends and the falling action begins.

Set Purpose

Fiction writers use a variety of techniques to engage readers in a story, including strong characterization and a solid plot structure. While you read "The Rocking-Horse Winner," consider how Lawrence creates the main character, Paul, using description, dialogue, and action. Look closely at Paul's interaction with the other characters, and consider what these interactions reveal about him. Also look for the climax of "The Rocking-Horse Winner." Consider the events in the plot that precede and follow the climax.

Preview Vocabulary

career, 1037
parry, 1038
obscure, 1038
uncanny, 1041
remonstrate, 1043

The Rocking-Horse Winner

by D. H. Lawrence

He knew the horse could take him to where there was luck, if only he forced it.

There was a woman who was beautiful, who started with all the advantages, yet she had no luck. She married for love, and the love turned to dust. She had bonny[1] children, yet she felt—they had been thrust upon her, and she could not love them. They looked at her coldly, as if they were finding fault with her. And hurriedly she felt she must cover up some fault in herself. Yet what it was that she must cover up she never knew. Nevertheless, when her children were present she always felt the center of her heart go hard. This troubled her, and in her manner she was all the more gentle and anxious for her children, as if she loved them very much. Only she herself knew that at the center of her heart was a hard little place that could not feel love, no, not for anybody. Everybody else said of her: "She is such

a good mother. She adores her children." Only she herself, and her children themselves, knew it was not so. They read it in each other's eyes.

There were a boy and two little girls. They lived in a pleasant house, with a garden, and they had discreet servants, and felt themselves superior to anyone in the neighborhood.

Although they lived in style, they felt always an anxiety in the house. There was never enough money. The mother had a small income, and the father had a small income, but not nearly enough for the social position which they had to keep up. The father went into town to some office. But though he had good prospects, these prospects never materialized. There was always the grinding sense of the short-

---

1. **bonny.** [Scottish] Attractive; healthy or robust

age of money, though the style was always kept up.

At last the mother said: "I will see if *I* can't make something." But she did not know where to begin. She racked her brains, and tried this thing and the other, but could not find anything successful. The failure made deep lines come into her face. Her children were growing up; they would have to go to school. There must be more money; there must be more money. The father, who was always very handsome and expensive in his tastes, seemed as if he never *would* be able to do anything worth doing. And the mother, who had a great belief in herself, did not succeed any better, and her tastes were just as expensive.

And so the house came to be haunted by the unspoken phrase: There must be more money! There must be more money! The children could hear it all the time, though nobody said it aloud. They heard it at Christmas, when the expensive and splendid toys filled the nursery. Behind the shining modern rocking-horse, behind the smart doll's house, a voice would start whispering: *"There must be more money! There must be more money!"* And the children would stop playing, to listen for a moment. They would look into each other's eyes, to see if they had all heard. And each one saw in the eyes of the other two that they too had heard. "There *must* be more money! There *must* be more money!"

It came whispering from the springs of the still-swaying rocking-horse, and even the horse, bending his wooden, champing head, heard it. The big doll, sitting so pink and smirking in her new pram,[2] could hear it quite plainly, and seemed to be smirking all the more self-consciously because of it. The foolish puppy, too, that took the place of the teddybear, he was looking so extraordinarily foolish for no other reason but that he heard the secret whisper all over the house: "There *must* be more money!"

Yet nobody ever said it aloud. The whisper was everywhere, and therefore no one spoke it. Just as no one ever says: "We are breathing!" in spite of the fact that breath is coming and going all the time.

"Mother," said the boy Paul one day, "why don't we keep a car of our own? Why do we always use uncle's, or else a taxi?"

"Because we're the poor members of the family," said the mother.

"But why *are* we, mother?"

"Well—I suppose," she said slowly and bitterly, "it's because your father has no luck."

The boy was silent for some time.

"Is luck money, mother?" he asked, rather timidly.

"No, Paul. Not quite. It's what causes you to have money."

"Oh!" said Paul vaguely. "I thought when Uncle Oscar said *filthy lucker,* it meant money."

"*Filthy lucre* does mean money," said the mother. "But it's lucre, not luck."

"Oh!" said the boy. "Then what *is* luck, mother?"

"It's what causes you to have money. If you're lucky you have money. That's why it's better to be born lucky than rich. If you're rich,

---

2. **pram.** Short for *perambulator,* a British word for baby carriage

If you're lucky you have money. That's why it's better to be born lucky than rich.

you may lose your money. But if you're lucky, you will always get more money."

"Oh! Will you? And is father not lucky?"

"Very unlucky, I should say," she said bitterly.

The boy watched her with unsure eyes.

"Why?" he asked.

"I don't know. Nobody ever knows why one person is lucky and another unlucky."

"Don't they? Nobody at all? Does *nobody* know?"

"Perhaps God. But He never tells."

"He ought to, then. And aren't you lucky either, mother?"

"I can't be, if I married an unlucky husband."

"But by yourself, aren't you?"

"I used to think I was, before I married. Now I think I am very unlucky indeed."

"Why?"

"Well—never mind! Perhaps I'm not really," she said.

The child looked at her to see if she meant it. But he saw, by the lines of her mouth, that she was only trying to hide something from him.

"Well, anyhow," he said stoutly, "I'm a lucky person."

"Why?" said his mother, with a sudden laugh.

He stared at her. He didn't even know why he had said it.

"God told me," he asserted, brazening it out.[3]

"I hope He did, dear!" she said, again with a laugh, but rather bitter.

"He did, mother!"

"Excellent!" said the mother, using one of her husband's exclamations.

The boy saw she did not believe him; or rather, that she paid no attention to his asser-tion. This angered him somewhere, and made him want to compel her attention.

He went off by himself, vaguely, in a childish way, seeking for the clue to "luck." Absorbed, taking no heed of other people, he went about with a sort of stealth, seeking inwardly for luck. He wanted luck, he wanted it, he wanted it. When the two girls were play-ing dolls in the nursery, he would sit on his big rocking-horse, charging madly into space, with a frenzy that made the little girls peer at him uneasily. Wildly the horse <u>careered</u>, the wav-ing dark hair of the boy tossed, his eyes had a strange glare in them. The little girls dared not speak to him.

When he had ridden to the end of his mad little journey, he climbed down and stood in front of his rocking-horse, staring fixedly into its lowered face. Its red mouth was slightly open, its big eye was wide and glassy-bright.

"Now!" he would silently command the snorting steed. "Now, take me to where there is luck! Now take me!"

And he would slash the horse on the neck with the little whip he had asked Uncle Oscar for. He *knew* the horse could take him to where there was luck, if only he forced it. So he would mount again and start on his furious ride, hoping at last to get there. He knew he could get there.

"You'll break your horse, Paul!" said the nurse.

"He's always riding like that! I wish he'd leave off!" said his elder sister Joan.

But he only glared down on them in silence. Nurse gave him up. She could make nothing of him. Anyhow, he was growing beyond her.

One day his mother and his Uncle Oscar came in when he was on one of his furious rides. He did not speak to them.

---

3. **brazening it out.** Acting boldly, without shame

ca • reer (kə rir´) *v.,* move at full speed

"Hallo, you young jockey! Riding a winner?" said his uncle.

"Aren't you growing too big for a rocking-horse? You're not a very little boy any longer, you know," said his mother.

But Paul only gave a blue glare from his big, rather close set eyes. He would speak to nobody when he was in full tilt. His mother watched him with an anxious expression on her face.

At last he suddenly stopped forcing his horse into the mechanical gallop and slid down.

"Well, I got there!" he announced fiercely, his blue eyes still flaring, and his sturdy long legs straddling apart.

"Where did you get to?" asked his mother.

"Where I wanted to go," he flared back at her.

"That's right, son!" said Uncle Oscar. "Don't you stop till you get there. What's the horse's name?"

"He doesn't have a name," said the boy.

"Gets on without, all right?" asked the uncle.

"Well, he has different names. He was called Sansovino last week."

"Sansovino, eh? Won the Ascot.[4] How did you know this name?"

"He always talks about horse-races with Bassett," said Joan.

The uncle was delighted to find that his small nephew was posted with all the racing news. Bassett, the young gardener who had been wounded in the left foot in the war and had got his present job through Oscar Cresswell, whose batman[5] he had been, was a perfect blade of the "turf."[6] He lived in the racing events, and the small boy lived with him.

Oscar Cresswell got it all from Bassett.

"Master Paul comes and asks me, so I can't do more than tell him, sir," said Bassett, his face terribly serious, as if he were speaking of religious matters.

"And does he ever put anything on a horse he fancies?"

"Well—I don't want to give him away—he's a young sport, a fine sport, sir. Would you mind asking him himself? He sort of takes a pleasure in it, and perhaps he'd feel I was giving him away, sir, if you don't mind."

Bassett was serious as a church.

The uncle went back to his nephew and took him off for a ride in the car.

"Say, Paul, old man, do you ever put anything on a horse?" the uncle asked.

The boy watched the handsome man closely.

"Why, do you think I oughtn't to?" he parried.

"Not a bit of it! I thought perhaps you might give me a tip for the Lincoln."

The car sped on into the country, going down to Uncle Oscar's place in Hampshire.

"Honor bright?"[7] said the nephew.

"Honor bright, son!" said the uncle.

"Well, then, Daffodil."

"Daffodil! I doubt it, sonny. What about Mirza?"

"I only know the winner," said the boy. "That's Daffodil."

"Daffodil, eh?"

There was a pause. Daffodil was an obscure horse comparatively.

"Uncle!"

"Yes, son?"

"You won't let it go any further, will you? I promised Bassett."

"Bassett be damned, old man! What's he got to do with it?"

"We're partners. We've been partners from the first. Uncle, he lent me my first five shil-

---

4. **Ascot.** Prestigious horse race
5. **batman.** Orderly for a military officer
6. **turf.** Sport of horse racing
7. **honor bright.** Saying meaning, "on my honor" or "on your honor"

par • ry (per´ ē) *v.*, reply in a clever or evasive way, as if warding off a verbal attack

ob • scure (äb skyür´) *adj.*, relatively unknown; not prominent or famous

lings, which I lost. I promised him, honor bright, it was only between me and him; only you gave me that ten-shilling note I started winning with, so I thought you were lucky. You won't let it go any further, will you?"

The boy gazed at his uncle from those big, hot, blue eyes, set rather close together. The uncle stirred and laughed uneasily.

"Right you are, son! I'll keep your tip private. Daffodil, eh? How much are you putting on him?"

"All except twenty pounds," said the boy. "I keep that in reserve." The uncle thought it a good joke.

"You keep twenty pounds in reserve, do you, you young romancer? What are you betting, then?"

"I'm betting three hundred," said the boy gravely. "But it's between you and me, Uncle Oscar! Honor bright?"

The uncle burst into a roar of laughter. "It's between you and me all right, you young Nat Gould,"[8] he said, laughing. "But where's your three hundred?"

"Bassett keeps it for me. We're partners."

"You are, are you! And what is Bassett putting on Daffodil?"

"He won't go quite as high as I do, I expect. Perhaps he'll go a hundred and fifty."

"What, pennies?" laughed the uncle.

"Pounds," said the child, with a surprised look at his uncle. "Bassett keeps a bigger reserve than I do."

Between wonder and amusement Uncle Oscar was silent. He pursued the matter no further, but he determined to take his nephew with him to the Lincoln races.

"Now, son," he said, "I'm putting twenty on Mirza, and I'll put five on for you on any horse you fancy. What's your pick?"

"Daffodil, uncle."

"No, not the fiver on Daffodil!"

"I should if it was my own fiver," said the child.

"Good! Good! Right you are! A fiver for me and a fiver for you on Daffodil." The child had

never been to a race-meeting before, and his eyes were blue fire. He pursed his mouth tight and watched. A Frenchman just in front had put his money on Lancelot. Wild with excitement, he flayed his arms up and down, yelling *"Lancelot! Lancelot!"* in his French accent.

The child had never been to a race—meeting before, and his eyes were blue fire.

Daffodil came in first, Lancelot second, Mirza third. The child, flushed and with eyes blazing, was curiously serene. His uncle brought him four five-pound notes, four to one.

"What am I to do with these?" he cried, waving them before the boy's eyes.

"I suppose we'll talk to Bassett," said the boy. "I expect I have fifteen hundred now; and twenty in reserve; and this twenty."

His uncle studied him for some moments.

"Look here, son!" he said. "You're not serious about Bassett and that fifteen hundred, are you?"

"Yes, I am. But it's between you and me, uncle. Honor bright?"

"Honor bright all right, son! But I must talk to Bassett."

"If you'd like to be a partner, uncle, with Bassett and me, we could all be partners. Only, you'd have to promise, honor bright, uncle, not to let it go beyond us three. Bassett and I are lucky, and you must be lucky, because it was your ten shillings I started winning with. . . ."

Uncle Oscar took both Bassett and Paul into Richmond Park for an afternoon, and there they talked.

"It's like this, you see, sir," Bassett said. "Master Paul would get me talking about racing events, spinning yarns, you know, sir. And he was always keen on knowing if I'd made or if I'd lost. It's about a year since, now, that

---

8. **Nat Gould.** Authority on horse racing

I put five shillings on Blush of Dawn for him: and we lost. Then the luck turned, with that ten shillings he had from you: that we put on Singhalese. And since that time, it's been pretty steady all things considering. What do you say, Master Paul?"

"We're all right when we're sure," said Paul. "It's when we're not quite sure that we go down."

"Oh, but we're careful then," said Bassett.

"But when are you *sure?*" smiled Uncle Oscar.

"It's Master Paul, sir," said Bassett in a secret, religious voice. "It's as if he had it from heaven. Like Daffodil, now, for the Lincoln. That was as sure as eggs."

"Did you put anything on Daffodil?" asked Oscar Cresswell.

"Yes, sir. I made my bit."

"And my nephew?"

Bassett was obstinately silent, looking at Paul.

"I made twelve hundred, didn't I, Bassett? I told uncle I was putting three hundred on Daffodil."

"That's right," said Bassett, nodding.

"But where's the money?" asked the uncle.

"I keep it safe locked up, sir. Master Paul he can have it any minute he likes to ask for it."

"What, fifteen hundred pounds?"

"And twenty! And *forty,* that is, with the twenty he made on the course."

"It's amazing!" said the uncle.

"If Master Paul offers you to be partners, sir, I would, if I were you: if you'll excuse me," said Bassett.

Oscar Cresswell thought about it.

"I'll see the money," he said.

They drove home again, and, sure enough, Bassett came round to the garden-house with fifteen hundred pounds in notes. The twenty pounds reserve was left with Joe Glee, in the Turf Commission deposit.

"You see, it's all right, uncle, when I'm *sure!* Then we go strong, for all we're worth. Don't we, Bassett?"

"We do that, Master Paul."

"And when are you sure?" said the uncle, laughing.

"Oh, well, sometimes I'm *absolutely* sure, like about Daffodil," said the boy; "and sometimes I have an idea; and sometimes I haven't even an idea, have I, Bassett? Then we're careful, because we mostly go down."

"You do, do you! And when you're sure, like about Daffodil, what makes you sure, sonny?"

"Oh, well, I don't know," said the boy uneasily. "I'm sure, you know, uncle; that's all."

"It's as if he had it from heaven, sir," Bassett reiterated.

"I should say so!" said the uncle.

But he became a partner. And when the Leger was coming on Paul was "sure" about Lively Spark, which was a quite inconsiderable horse. The boy insisted on putting a thousand on the horse, Bassett went for five hundred, and Oscar Cresswell two hundred. Lively Spark came in first, and the betting had been ten to one against him. Paul had made ten thousand.

"You see," he said, "I was absolutely sure of him."

"You see," he said, "I was absolutely sure of him."

Even Oscar Cresswell had cleared two thousand.

"Look here, son," he said, "this sort of thing makes me nervous."

"It needn't, uncle! Perhaps I shan't be sure again for a long time."

"But what are you going to do with your money?" asked the uncle.

"Of course," said the boy, "I started it for mother. She said she had no luck, because father is unlucky, so I thought if *I* was lucky, it might stop whispering."

"What might stop whispering?"

"Our house. I *hate* our house for whispering."

"What does it whisper?"

---

9. **writs.** Legal notices

"Why—why"—the boy fidgeted—"why, I don't know. But it's always short of money, you know, uncle."

"I know it, son, I know it."

"You know people send mother writs,[9] don't you, uncle?"

"I'm afraid I do," said the uncle.

"And then the house whispers, like people laughing at you behind your back. It's awful, that is! I thought if I was lucky—"

"You might stop it," added the uncle.

The boy watched him with big blue eyes, that had an <u>uncanny</u> cold fire in them, and he said never a word.

"Well, then!" said the uncle. "What are we doing?"

"I shouldn't like mother to know I was lucky," said the boy.

"Why not, son?"

"She'd stop me."

"I don't think she would."

"Oh!"—and the boy writhed in an odd way—"I *don't* want her to know, uncle."

"All right, son! We'll manage it without her knowing."

They managed it very easily. Paul, at the other's suggestion, handed over five thousand pounds to his uncle, who deposited it with the family lawyer, who was then to inform Paul's mother that a relative had put five thousand pounds into his hands, which sum was to be paid out a thousand pounds at a time, on the mother's birthday, for the next five years.

"So she'll have a birthday present of a thousand pounds for five successive years," said Uncle Oscar. "I hope it won't make it all the harder for her later."

Paul's mother had her birthday in November. The house had been "whispering" worse than ever lately, and, even in spite of his luck, Paul could not bear up against it. He was very anxious to see the effect of the birthday letter, telling his mother about the thousand pounds.

When there were no visitors, Paul now took his meals with his parents, as he was beyond the nursery control. His mother went into town nearly every day. She had discovered that she had an odd knack of sketching furs and dress materials, so she worked secretly in the studio of a friend who was the chief "artist" for the leading drapers. She drew the figures of ladies in furs and ladies in silk and sequins for the newspaper advertisements. This young woman artist earned several thousand pounds a year, but Paul's mother only made several hundreds, and she was again dissatisfied. She so wanted to be first in something, and she did not succeed, even in making sketches for drapery advertisements.

She was down to breakfast on the morning of her birthday. Paul watched her face as she read her letters. He knew the lawyer's letter. As his mother read it, her face hardened and became more expressionless. Then a cold, determined look came on her mouth. She hid the letter under the pile of others, and said not a word about it.

"Didn't you have anything nice in the post for your birthday, mother?" said Paul.

"Quite moderately nice," she said, her voice cold and absent.

She went away to town without saying more.

But in the afternoon Uncle Oscar appeared. He said Paul's mother had had a long interview with the lawyer, asking if the whole five thousand could not be advanced at once, as she was in debt.

"What do you think, uncle?" said the boy.

"I leave it to you, son."

"Oh, let her have it, then! We can get some more with the other," said the boy.

"A bird in the hand is worth two in the bush, laddie!" said Uncle Oscar.

"But I'm sure to *know* for the Grand National; or the Lincolnshire; or else the Derby. I'm sure to know for *one* of them," said Paul.

So Uncle Oscar signed the agreement, and Paul's mother touched the whole five thousand.

un • can • ny (un' ka´ nē) *adj.,* seeming to have a supernatural or mysterious quality

Then something very curious happened. The voices in the house suddenly went mad, like a chorus of frogs on a spring evening. There were certain new furnishings, and Paul had a tutor. He was *really* going to Eton, his father's school, in the following autumn. There were flowers in the winter, and a blossoming of the luxury Paul's mother had been used to. And yet the voices in the house, behind the sprays of mimosa and almond blossom, and from under the piles of iridescent cushions, simply trilled and screamed in a sort of ecstasy: "There *must* be more money! Oh-h-h; there *must* be more money. Oh, now, now-w! Now-w-w—there *must* be more money!—more than ever! More than ever!"

It frightened Paul terribly. He studied away at his Latin and Greek with his tutor. But his intense hours were spent with Bassett. The Grand National had gone by: he had not "known," and had lost a hundred pounds. Summer was at hand. He was in agony for the Lincoln. But even for the Lincoln he didn't "know," and he lost fifty pounds. He became wild-eyed and strange, as if something were going to explode in him.

"Let it alone, son! Don't you bother about it!" urged Uncle Oscar. But it was as if the boy couldn't really hear what his uncle was saying.

"I've got to know for the Derby! I've got to know for the Derby!" the child reiterated, his big blue eyes blazing with a sort of madness.

His mother noticed how overwrought he was.

"You'd better go to the seaside. Wouldn't you like to go now to the seaside, instead of waiting? I think you'd better," she said, looking down at him anxiously, her heart curiously heavy because of him.

But the child lifted his uncanny blue eyes.

"I couldn't possibly go before the Derby, mother!" he said. "I couldn't possibly!"

"Why not?" she said, her voice becoming heavy when she was opposed. "Why not? You can still go from the seaside to see the Derby with your Uncle Oscar, if that's what you wish. No need for you to wait here. Besides, I think you care too much about these races. It's a bad sign. My family has been a gambling family, and you won't know till you grow up how much damage it has done. But it has done damage. I shall have to send Bassett away, and ask Uncle Oscar not to talk racing to you, unless you promise to be reasonable about it: go away to the seaside and forget it. You're all nerves!"

"I'll do what you like, mother, so long as you don't send me away till after the Derby," the boy said.

"Send you away from where? Just from this house?"

"Yes," he said, gazing at her.

"Why, you curious child, what makes you care about this house so much, suddenly? I never knew you loved it."

He gazed at her without speaking. He had a secret within a secret, something he had not divulged, even to Bassett or to his Uncle Oscar.

But his mother, after standing undecided and a little bit sullen for some moments, said:

"Very well, then! Don't go to the seaside till after the Derby, if you don't wish it. But promise me you won't let your nerves go to pieces. Promise you won't think so much about horse-racing and *events*, as you call them!"

"Oh no," said the boy casually. "I won't think much about them, mother. You needn't worry. I wouldn't worry, mother, if I were you."

"If you were me and I were you," said his mother, "I wonder what we *should* do!"

"But you know you needn't worry, mother, don't you?" the boy repeated.

"I should be awfully glad to know it," she said wearily.

"Oh, well, you *can,* you know. I mean, you *ought* to know you needn't worry," he insisted.

"Ought I? Then I'll see about it," she said. Paul's secret of secrets was his wooden horse, that which had no name. Since he was emancipated from a nurse and a nursery-governess, he had had his rocking-horse removed to his own bedroom at the top of the house.

"Surely you're too big for a rocking-horse!" his mother had <u>remonstrated</u>.

"Well, you see, mother, till I can have a *real* horse, I like to have *some* sort of animal about," had been his quaint answer.

"Do you feel he keeps you company?" she laughed.

"Oh yes! He's very good, he always keeps me company, when I'm there," said Paul.

So the horse, rather shabby, stood in an arrested prance in the boy's bedroom.

The Derby was drawing near, and the boy grew more and more tense. He hardly heard what was spoken to him, he was very frail, and his eyes were really uncanny. His mother had sudden strange seizures of uneasiness about him. Sometimes, for half an hour, she would feel a sudden anxiety about him that was almost anguish. She wanted to rush to him at once, and know he was safe.

The Derby was drawing near, and the boy grew more and more tense.

Two nights before the Derby, she was at a big party in town, when one of her rushes of anxiety about her boy, her first-born, gripped her heart till she could hardly speak. She fought with the feeling, might and main, for she believed in common sense. But it was too strong. She had to leave the dance and go downstairs to telephone to the country. The children's nursery-governess was terribly sur-

prised and startled at being rung up in the night.

"Are the children all right, Miss Wilmot?"

"Oh yes, they are quite all right."

"Master Paul? Is he all right?"

"He went to bed as right as a trivet.[10] Shall I run up and look at him?"

"No," said Paul's mother reluctantly. "No! Don't trouble. It's all right. Don't sit up. We shall be home fairly soon." She did not want her son's privacy intruded upon.

"Very good," said the governess.

It was about one o'clock when Paul's mother and father drove up to their house. All was still. Paul's mother went to her room and slipped off her white fur cloak. She had told her maid not to wait up for her. She heard her husband downstairs, mixing a whisky and soda.

And then, because of the strange anxiety at her heart, she stole upstairs to her son's room. Noiselessly she went along the upper corridor. Was there a faint noise?

What was it?

She stood, with arrested muscles, outside his door, listening. There was a strange, heavy, and yet not loud noise. Her heart stood still. It was a soundless noise, yet rushing and powerful. Something huge, in violent, hushed motion. What was it? What in God's name was it? She ought to know. She felt that she knew the noise. She knew what it was.

Yet she could not place it. She couldn't say what it was. And on and on it went, like a madness.

Softly, frozen with anxiety and fear, she turned the door handle.

The room was dark. Yet in the space near the window, she heard and saw something plunging to and fro. She gazed in fear and amazement.

---

10. **right . . . trivet.** Idiomatic expression that means something is secure and comfortable; a *trivet* is a metal stand with short feet for use under a hot dish on a table.

re • mon • strate (re´ mən strāt´) *v.,* say in protest; object to

Then suddenly she switched on the light, and saw her son, in his green pajamas, madly surging on the rocking-horse. The blaze of light suddenly lit him up, as he urged the wooden horse, and lit her up, as she stood, blonde, in her dress of pale green and crystal, in the doorway.

"Paul!" she cried. "Whatever are you doing?"

"It's Malabar!" he screamed in a powerful, strange voice. "It's Malabar!"

His eyes blazed at her for one strange and senseless second, as he ceased urging his wooden horse. Then he fell with a crash to the ground, and she, all her tormented motherhood flooding upon her, rushed to gather him up.

But he was unconscious, and unconscious he remained, with some brain fever. He talked and tossed, and his mother sat stonily by his side.

"Malabar! It's Malabar! Bassett, Bassett, I *know*! It's Malabar!"

So the child cried, trying to get up and urge the rocking-horse that gave him his inspiration.

"What does he mean by Malabar?" asked the heart-frozen mother.

"I don't know," said the father stonily.

"What does he mean by Malabar?" she asked her brother Oscar.

"It's one of the horses running for the Derby," was the answer.

And, in spite of himself, Oscar Cresswell spoke to Bassett, and himself put a thousand on Malabar: at fourteen to one.

The third day of the illness was critical: they were waiting for a change. The boy, with his rather long, curly hair, was tossing ceaselessly on the pillow. He neither slept nor regained consciousness, and his eyes were like blue stones. His mother sat, feeling her heart had gone, turned actually into a stone.

In the evening, Oscar Cresswell did not come, but Bassett sent a message, saying could he come up for one moment, just one moment? Paul's mother was very angry at the intrusion, but on second thoughts she agreed. The boy was the same. Perhaps Bassett might bring him to consciousness.

The gardener, a shortish fellow with a little brown moustache and sharp little brown eyes, tiptoed into the room, touched his imaginary cap to Paul's mother, and stole to the bedside, staring with glittering, smallish eyes at the tossing, dying child.

"Master Paul!" he whispered. "Master Paul! Malabar came in first all right, a clean win. I did as you told me. You've made over seventy thousand pounds, you have; you've got over eighty thousand. Malabar came in all right, Master Paul."

"Malabar! Malabar! Did I say Malabar, mother? Did I say Malabar? Do you think I'm lucky, mother? I knew Malabar, didn't I? Over eighty thousand pounds! I call that lucky, don't you, mother? Over eighty thousand pounds! I knew, didn't I know I knew? Malabar came in all right. If I ride my horse till I'm sure, then I tell you, Bassett, you can go as high as you like. Did you go for all you were worth, Bassett?"

"I went a thousand on it, Master Paul."

"I never told you, mother, that if I can ride my horse, and *get there,* then I'm absolutely sure—oh, absolutely! Mother, did I ever tell you? I *am* lucky!"

"No, you never did," said his mother.

But the boy died in the night.

And even as he lay dead, his mother heard her brother's voice saying to her: "My God, Hester, you're eighty-odd thousand to the good, and a poor devil of a son to the bad. But, poor devil, he's best gone out of a life where he rides his rocking-horse to find a winner." ❖

Refer to Text ▶ ▶ ▶ ▶ ▶ **Reason with Text**

1a. Quote the phrase that haunts the house. What does the boy's mother say causes people to have money?

1b. Describe the effect this has on the boy's actions.

Understand
Find meaning

2a. Recall what happens as a result of Paul's arranging to have half of his winnings sent to his mother.

2b. Despite Paul's efforts, why does the house continue to be haunted with the phrase?

Apply
Use information

3a. In Magical Realism, elements of fantasy are treated as though they are realistic. Identify an example of Magical Realism in the story.

3b. Analyze the significance of this example and what it symbolizes. What does the symbolism suggest about the boy and the family?

Analyze
Take things apart

4a. List the secrets kept by Paul and his mother.

4b. How do these secrets increase the household's problems? Judge whether Paul and his mother were right to keep these secrets.

Evaluate
Make judgments

5a. Why does Paul's mother need the full five thousand pounds instead of just one thousand?

5b. What motivates Paul's mother to continue to spend money? How can this attitude cause social and financial harm?

Create
Bring ideas together

Analyze Literature

Character and Climax

How does Lawrence use description, dialogue, and action to create the main character? What does Paul's interaction with other characters tell us about him?

What is the climax of the story? How did secondary conflicts, such as Paul's relationship with his mother and his mother's dealings with money, impact the climax of the story?

Extend the Text

Writing Options

Creative Writing Imagine you are a newspaper reporter assigned to cover the recent death of Paul. As the reporter, interview Bassett, Uncle Oliver, and the boy's mother. From your reading of the story, infer what they might have been willing to tell you. Include these details in your newspaper article.

Expository Writing Read a short story by the Colombian writer Gabriel García Márquez. Pay special attention to the elements of Magical Realism; then write an essay in which you compare and contrast Magical Realism in the stories by García Márquez and Lawrence.

Collaborative Learning

Hold a Debate Many states have set up lotteries instead of raising taxes. Some people oppose these lotteries.

Working in two teams of three students each, debate the proposition *States should end their lotteries.* One team can take the *pro* side (agreeing with the proposition) and the other team, the *con* side (against the proposition). In preparation, teams should briefly research the topic and create a chart of the pros and cons.

Media Literacy

Analyze Nonprint Media If Paul were alive today, in the electronic age, where could he find material on support groups specializing in compulsive (addicted) gambling? Working with a partner or small group, make a list of available websites, television programs, and other electronic resources. Evaluate which media you found to be the most helpful.

 Go to **www.mirrorsandwindows.com** for more.

The Garden-Party

by Katherine Mansfield

"The Garden-Party" is considered to be one of the finest stories by New Zealand–born author **Katherine Mansfield** (1888–1923). Mansfield wrote the story at a time when she was looking back at her childhood experiences. One of the events on which she focused was a garden party her mother gave in the spring of 1907. The core of her story was a fatal street accident involving a neighbor that occurred in the midst of festivities at the Mansfield home. The selection shows the writer's ability to combine incident, image, symbol, and structure to clarify her protagonist, Laura, and to capture the essential poignancy, or affecting quality, of the situation. This technique is a hallmark of Mansfield's work.

Although Mansfield spent her adult life in England and mainland Europe, she drew from her childhood in New Zealand for many of her stories. She was the first writer in English to be influenced by Anton Chekhov (1860–1904), a Russian writer whom she greatly admired.

And after all the weather was ideal. They could not have had a more perfect day for a garden-party if they had ordered it. Windless, warm, the sky without a cloud. Only the blue was veiled with a haze of light gold, as it is sometimes in early summer. The gardener had been up since dawn, mowing the lawns and sweeping them, until the grass and the dark flat rosettes where the daisy plants had been seemed to shine. As for the roses, you could not help feeling they understood that roses are the only flowers that impress people at garden-parties; the only flowers that everybody is certain of knowing. Hundreds, yes, literally hundreds, had come out in a single night; the green bushes bowed down as though they had been visited by archangels.

Breakfast was not yet over before the men came to put up the marquee.[1]

"Where do you want the marquee put, mother?"

"My dear child, it's no use asking me. I'm determined to leave everything to you children this year. Forget I am your mother. Treat me as an honored guest."

But Meg could not possibly go and supervise the men. She had washed her hair before breakfast, and she sat drinking her coffee in a green turban, with a dark wet curl stamped on each cheek. Jose, the butterfly, always came down in a silk petticoat and a kimono jacket.

"You'll have to go, Laura; you're the artistic one."

Away Laura flew, still holding her piece of bread-and-butter. It's so delicious to have an excuse for eating out of doors, and besides, she loved having to arrange things; she always felt she could do it so much better than anybody else.

---

1. **marquee** (mär kē´). Large tent with open sides, for hosting a party

Grez-Sur-Loing, c. 1880. Robert William Vonnoh.
Private collection.

Four men in their shirt-sleeves stood grouped together on the garden path. They carried staves[2] covered with rolls of canvas, and they had big tool-bags slung on their backs. They looked impressive. Laura wished now that she had not got the bread-and-butter, but there was nowhere to put it, and she couldn't possibly throw it away. She blushed and tried to look severe and even a little bit short-sighted as she came up to them.

"Good morning," she said, copying her mother's voice. But that sounded so fearfully affected that she was ashamed, and stammered like a little girl, "O—er—have you come—is it about the marquee?"

"That's right, miss," said the tallest of the men, a lanky, freckled fellow, and he shifted his tool-bag, knocked back his straw hat and smiled down at her. "That's about it."

His smile was so easy, so friendly that Laura recovered. What nice eyes he had, small, but such a dark blue! And now she looked at the others, they were smiling too. "Cheer up, we won't bite," their smile seemed to say. How very nice workmen were! And what a beautiful morning! she mustn't mention the morning; she must be businesslike. The marquee.

"Well, what about the lily-lawn? Would that do?"

And she pointed to the lily-lawn with the hand that didn't hold the bread-and-butter. They turned, they stared in the direction. A little fat chap thrust out his under-lip, and the tall fellow frowned.

"I don't fancy it," said he. "Not conspicuous enough. You see, with a thing like a marquee," and he turned to Laura in his easy way, "you

2. **staves.** Poles

want to put it somewhere where it'll give you a bang slap in the eye, if you follow me."

Laura's upbringing made her wonder for a moment whether it was quite respectful of a workman to talk to her of bangs slap in the eye. But she did quite follow him.

"A corner of the tennis-court," she suggested. "But the band's going to be in one corner."

"H'm, going to have a band, are you?" said another of the workmen. He was pale. He had a haggard[3] look as his dark eyes scanned the tennis-court. What was he thinking?

"Only a very small band," said Laura gently. Perhaps he wouldn't mind so much if the band was quite small. But the tall fellow interrupted.

"Look here, miss, that's the place. Against those trees. Over there. That'll do fine."

Against the karakas. Then the karaka-trees would be hidden. And they were so lovely, with their broad, gleaming leaves, and their clusters of yellow fruit. They were like trees you imagined growing on a desert island, proud, solitary, lifting their leaves and fruits to the sun in a kind of silent splendor. Must they be hidden by a marquee?

They must. Already the men had shouldered their staves and were making for the place. Only the tall fellow was left. He bent down, pinched a sprig of lavender, put his thumb and forefinger to his nose and snuffed up the smell. When Laura saw that gesture she forgot all about the karakas in her wonder at him caring for things like that— caring for the smell of lavender. How many men that she knew would have done such a thing? Oh, how extraordinarily nice workmen were, she thought. Why couldn't she have workmen for friends rather than the silly boys she danced with and who came to Sunday night supper? She would get on much better with men like these.

It's all the fault, she decided, as the tall fellow drew something on the back of an envelope, something that was to be looped up or left to hang, of these absurd class distinctions. Well, for her part, she didn't feel them. Not a bit, not an atom. . . . And now there came the chock-chock of wooden hammers. Some one whistled,

some one sang out, "Are you right there, matey?" "Matey!" The friendliness of it, the—the—Just to prove how happy she was, just to show the tall fellow how at home she felt, and how she despised stupid conventions, Laura took a big bite of her bread-and-butter as she stared at the little drawing. She felt just like a work-girl.

"Laura, Laura, where are you? Telephone, Laura!" a voice cried from the house.

"Coming!" Away she skimmed, over the lawn, up the path, up the steps, across the veranda,[4] and into the porch. In the hall her father and Laurie were brushing their hats ready to go to the office.

"I say, Laura," said Laurie very fast, "you might just give a squiz at my coat before this afternoon. See if it wants pressing."

"I will," said she. Suddenly she couldn't stop herself. She ran at Laurie and gave him a small, quick squeeze. "Oh, I do love parties, don't you?" gasped Laura.

"Ra-ther," said Laurie's warm, boyish voice, and he squeezed his sister too, and gave her a gentle push. "Dash off to the telephone, old girl."

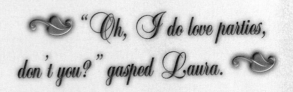

"Oh, I do love parties, don't you?" gasped Laura.

The telephone. "Yes, yes; oh yes. Kitty? Good morning, dear. Come to lunch? Do, dear. Delighted of course. It will only be a very scratch meal—just the sandwich crusts and broken meringue-shells and what's left over. Yes, isn't it a perfect morning? Your white? Oh, I certainly should. One moment—hold the line. Mother's calling." And Laura sat back. "What, mother? Can't hear."

Mrs. Sheridan's voice floated down the stairs. "Tell her to wear that sweet hat she had on last Sunday."

---

3. **haggard.** Worn, weary, gaunt
4. **veranda.** Open porch

"Mother says you're to wear that *sweet* hat you had on last Sunday. Good. One o'clock. Bye-bye."

Laura put back the receiver, flung her arms over her head, took a deep breath, stretched and let them fall. "Huh," she sighed, and the moment after the sigh she sat up quickly. She was still, listening. All the doors in the house seemed to be open. The house was alive with soft, quick steps and running voices. The green baize[5] door that led to the kitchen regions swung open and shut with a muffled thud. And now there came a long, chuckling absurd sound. It was the heavy piano being moved on its stiff castors. But the air! If you stopped to notice, was the air always like this? Little faint winds were playing chase, in at the tops of the windows, out at the doors. And there were two tiny spots of sun, one on the inkpot, one on a silver photograph frame, playing too. Darling little spots. Especially the one on the inkpot lid. It was quite warm. A warm little silver star. She could have kissed it.

The front door bell pealed, and there sounded the rustle of Sadie's print skirt on the stairs. A man's voice murmured; Sadie answered, careless, "I'm sure I don't know. Wait. I'll ask Mrs. Sheridan."

"What is it, Sadie?" Laura came into the hall.

"It's the florist, Miss Laura."

It was, indeed. There, just inside the door, stood a wide, shallow tray full of pots of pink lilies. No other kind. Nothing but lilies—canna lilies, big pink flowers, wide open, radiant, almost frighteningly alive on bright crimson stems.

"O-oh, Sadie!" said Laura, and the sound was like a little moan. She crouched down as if to warm herself at that blaze of lilies; she felt they were in her fingers, on her lips, growing in her breast.

"It's some mistake," she said faintly. "Nobody ever ordered so many. Sadie, go and find mother."

But at that moment Mrs. Sheridan joined them.

"It's quite right," she said calmly. "Yes, I ordered them. Aren't they lovely?" She pressed Laura's arm. "I was passing the shop yesterday, and I saw them in the window. And I suddenly thought for once in my life I shall have enough canna lilies. The garden-party will be a good excuse."

"But I thought you said you didn't mean to interfere," said Laura. Sadie had gone. The florist's man was still outside at his van. She put her arm round her mother's neck and gently, very gently, she bit her mother's ear.

"My darling child, you wouldn't like a logical mother, would you? Don't do that. Here's the man."

He carried more lilies still, another whole tray.

"Bank them up, just inside the door, on both sides of the porch, please," said Mrs. Sheridan. "Don't you agree, Laura?"

"Oh, I *do* mother."

In the drawing-room Meg, Jose and good little Hans had at last succeeded in moving the piano.

"Now, if we put this chesterfield against the wall and move everything out of the room except the chairs, don't you think?"

"Quite."

"Hans, move these tables into the smoking-room, and bring a sweeper to take these marks off the carpet and—one moment, Hans—" Jose loved giving orders to the servants, and they loved obeying her. She always made them feel they were taking part in some drama. "Tell mother and Miss Laura to come here at once."

"Very good, Miss Jose."

She turned to Meg. "I want to hear what the piano sounds like, just in case I'm asked to sing this afternoon. Let's try over 'This life is Weary.'"

Pom! Ta-ta-ta *Tee*-ta! The piano burst out so passionately that Jose's face changed. She clasped her hands. She looked mournfully and enigmatically[6] at her mother and Laura as they came in.

---

5. **baize.** Woolen or cotton fabric that resembles felt
6. **enigmatically.** In a manner that is perplexing or difficult to interpret

poverty-stricken. Little rags and shreds of smoke, so unlike the great silvery plumes that uncurled from the Sheridans' chimneys. Washerwomen lived in the lane and sweeps and a cobbler, and a man whose house-front was studded all over with minute bird-cages. Children swarmed. When the Sheridans were little they were forbidden to set foot there because of the revolting language and of what they might catch. But since they were grown up, Laura and Laurie on their prowls sometimes walked through. It was disgusting and sordid. They came out with a shudder. But still one must go everywhere; one must see everything. So through they went.

"And just think of what the band would sound like to that poor woman," said Laura.

"Oh, Laura!" Jose began to be seriously annoyed. "If you're going to stop a band playing every time some one has an accident, you'll lead a very strenuous life. I'm every bit as sorry about it as you. I feel just as sympathetic." Her eyes hardened. She looked at her sister just as she used to when they were little and fighting together. "You won't bring a drunken work-

man back to life by being sentimental," she said softly.

"Drunk! Who said he was drunk?" Laura turned furiously on Jose. She said, just as they had used to say on those occasions, "I'm going straight up to tell mother."

"Do, dear," cooed Jose.

"Mother, can I come into your room?" Laura turned the big glass doorknob.

"Of course, child. Why, what's the matter? What's given you such a color?" And Mrs. Sheridan turned round from her dressing-table. She was trying on a new hat.

"Mother, a man's been killed," began Laura.

"*Not* in the garden?" interrupted her mother.

"No, no!"

"Oh, what a fright you gave me!" Mrs. Sheridan sighed with relief, and took off the big hat and held it on her knees.

"But listen, mother," said Laura. Breathless, half-choking, she told the dreadful story. "Of course, we can't have our party, can we?" she pleaded. "The band and everybody arriving. They'd hear us, mother; they're nearly neighbors!"

To Laura's astonishment her mother behaved just like Jose; it was harder to bear because she seemed amused. She refused to take Laura seriously.

"But, my dear child, use your common sense. It's only by accident we've heard of it. If some one had died there normally—and I can't understand how they keep alive in those poky little holes—we should still be having our party, shouldn't we?"

Laura had to say "yes" to that, but she felt it was all wrong. She sat down on her mother's sofa and pinched the cushion frill.

"Mother, isn't it really terribly heartless of us?" she asked.

"Darling!" Mrs. Sheridan got up and came over to her, carrying the hat. Before Laura could stop her she had popped it on. "My child!" said her mother, "the hat is yours. It's made for you. It's much too young for me. I have never seen you look such a picture. Look at yourself!" And she held up her hand-mirror.

"But, mother," Laura began again. She couldn't look at herself; she turned aside.

This time Mrs. Sheridan lost patience just as Jose had done.

"People like that don't expect sacrifices from us."

"You are being very absurd, Laura," she said coldly. "People like that don't expect sacrifices from us. And it's not very sympathetic to spoil everybody's enjoyment as you're doing now."

"I don't understand," said Laura, and she walked quickly out of the room into her own bedroom. There, quite by chance, the first thing she saw was this charming girl in the mirror, in her black hat trimmed with gold daisies, and a long black velvet ribbon. Never had she imagined she could look like that. Is mother right? she thought. And now she hoped her mother was right. Am I being extrava-

gant? Perhaps it was extravagant. Just for a moment she had another glimpse of that poor woman and those little children, and the body being carried into the house. But it all seemed blurred, unreal, like a picture in the newspaper. I'll remember it again after the party's over, she decided. And somehow that seemed quite the best plan. . . .

Lunch was over by half-past one. By half-past two they were all ready for the fray. The green-coated band had arrived and was established in a corner of the tennis-court.

"My dear!" trilled Kitty Maitland, "aren't they too like frogs for words? You ought to have arranged them round the pond with the conductor in the middle on a leaf."

Laurie arrived and hailed them on his way to dress. At the sight of him Laura remembered the accident again. She wanted to tell him. If Laurie agreed with the others, then it was bound to be all right. And she followed him into the hall.

"Laurie!"

"Hallo!" He was half-way upstairs, but when he turned round and saw Laura he suddenly puffed out his cheeks and goggled his eyes at her. "My word, Laura; you do look stunning," said Laurie. "What an absolutely topping hat!"

Laura said faintly "Is it?" and smiled up at Laurie, and didn't tell him after all.

Soon after that people began coming in streams. The band struck up; the hired waiters ran from the house to the marquee. Wherever you looked there were couples strolling, bending to the flowers, greeting, moving on over the lawn. They were like bright birds that had alighted in the Sheridans' garden for this one afternoon, on their way to—where? Ah, what happiness it is to be with people who all are happy, to press hands, press cheeks, smile into eyes.

"Darling Laura, how well you look!"

"What a becoming hat, child!"

"Laura, you look quite Spanish. I've never seen you look so striking."

And Laura, glowing, answered softly, "Have you had tea? Won't you have an ice? The passion-fruit ices really are rather special." She ran to her father and begged him. "Daddy darling, can't the band have something to drink?"

And the perfect afternoon slowly ripened, slowly faded, slowly its petals closed.

"Never a more delightful garden party . . ." "The greatest success . . ." "Quite the most . . ."

Laura helped her mother with the good-byes. They stood side by side in the porch till it was all over.

"All over, all over, thank heaven," said Mrs. Sheridan. "Round up the others, Laura. Let's go and have some fresh coffee. I'm exhausted. Yes, it's been very successful. But oh, these parties, these parties! Why will you children insist on giving parties!" And they all of them sat down in the deserted marquee.

"Have a sandwich, daddy dear. I wrote the flag."

"Thanks." Mr. Sheridan took a bite and the sandwich was gone. He took another. "I suppose you didn't hear of a beastly accident that happened today?" he said.

"My dear," said Mrs. Sheridan, holding up her hand, "we did. It nearly ruined the party. Laura insisted we should put it off."

"Oh, mother!" Laura didn't want to be teased about it.

"It was a horrible affair all the same," said Mr. Sheridan. "The chap was married too. Lived just below in the lane, and leaves a wife and half a dozen kiddies, so they say."

An awkward little silence fell. Mrs. Sheridan fidgeted with her cup. Really, it was very tactless of father . . .

Suddenly she looked up. There on the table were all those sandwiches, cakes, puffs, all uneaten, all going to be wasted. She had one of her brilliant ideas.

"I know," she said. "Let's make up a basket. Let's send that poor creature some of this perfectly good food. At any rate, it will be the greatest treat for the children. Don't you agree? And she's sure to have neighbors calling in and so on. What a point to have it all ready

prepared Laura!" She jumped up. "Get me the big basket out of the stairs cupboard."

"But, mother, do you really think it's a good idea?" said Laura.

Again, how curious, she seemed to be different from them all. To take scraps from their party. Would the poor woman really like that?

"Of course! What's the matter with you today? An hour or two ago you were insisting on us being sympathetic, and now—"

Oh, well! Laura ran for the basket. It was filled, it was heaped by her mother.

"Take it yourself, darling," said she. "Run down just as you are. No, wait, take the arum lilies too. People of that class are so impressed by arum lilies."

"The stems will ruin her lace frock," said practical Jose.

So they would. Just in time. "Only the basket, then. And, Laura!"—her mother followed her out of the marquee—"don't on any account—"

"What, mother?"

No, better not put such ideas into the child's head! "Nothing! Run along."

It was just growing dusky as Laura shut their garden gates. A big dog ran by like a shadow. The road gleamed white, and down below in the hollow the little cottages were in deep shade. How quiet it seemed after the afternoon. Here she was going down the hill to somewhere where a man lay dead, and she couldn't realize it. Why couldn't she? She stopped a minute. And it seemed to her that kisses, voices, tinkling spoons, laughter, the smell of crushed grass were somehow inside her. She had no room for anything else. How strange! She looked up at the pale sky, and all she thought was, "Yes, it was the most successful party."

Now the broad road was crossed. The lane began, smoky and dark. Women in shawls and men's tweed caps hurried by. Men hung over the palings; the children played in the doorways. A low hum came from the mean little cottages. In some of them there was a flicker of light, and a shadow, crab-like, moved across the window. Laura bent her head and hurried on. She wished now she had put on a coat. How her frock shone! And the big hat with the velvet streamer—if only it was another hat! Were the people looking at her? They must be. It was a mistake to have come; she knew all along it was a mistake. Should she go back even now?

No, too late. This was the house. It must be. A dark knot of people stood outside. Beside the gate an old, old woman with a crutch sat in a chair, watching. She had her feet on a news-paper. The voices stopped as Laura drew near. The group parted. It was as though she was expected, as though they had known she was coming here.

Laura was terribly nervous. Tossing the velvet ribbon over her shoulder, she said to a woman standing by, "Is this Mrs. Scott's house?" and the woman, smiling queerly, said, "It is, my lass."

Oh, to be away from this! She actually said, "Help me, God," as she walked up the tiny path and knocked. To be away from those star-ing eyes, or to be covered up in anything, one of those women's shawls even. I'll just leave the basket and go, she decided. I shan't even wait for it to be emptied.

Then the door opened. A little woman in black showed in the gloom.

Laura said, "Are you Mrs. Scott?" But to her horror the woman answered, "Walk in please, miss," and she was shut in the passage.

"No," said Laura, "I don't want to come in. I only want to leave this basket. Mother sent—"

The little woman in the gloomy passage seemed not to have heard her. "Step this way, please, miss," she said in an oily voice, and Laura followed her.

She found herself in a wretched little low kitchen, lighted by a smoky lamp. There was a woman sitting before the fire.

"Em," said the little creature who had let her in. "Em! It's a young lady." She turned to Laura. She said meaningly, "I'm 'er sister, Miss. You'll excuse 'er, won't you?"

"Oh, but of course!" said Laura. "Please, please don't disturb her. I—I only want to leave—"

But at that moment the woman at the fire turned round. Her face, puffed up, red, with swollen eyes and swollen lips, looked terrible. She seemed as though she couldn't understand why Laura was there. What did it mean? Why was this stranger standing in the kitchen with a basket? What was it all about? And the poor face puckered up again.

Why was this stranger standing in the kitchen with a basket?

"All right, my dear," said the other. "I'll thank the young lady."

And again she began, "You'll excuse her, miss, I'm sure," and her face, swollen too, tried an oily smile.

Laura only wanted to get out, to get away. She was back in the passage. The door opened. She walked straight through into the bedroom, where the dead man was lying.

"You'd like a look at 'im, wouldn't you?" said Em's sister, and she brushed past Laura over to the bed. "Don't be afraid, my lass—" and now her voice sounded fond and sly, and fondly she drew down the sheet—" 'e looks a picture. There's nothing to show. Come along, my dear."

Laura came.

There lay a young man, fast asleep—sleeping so soundly, so deeply, that he was far, far away from them both. Oh, so remote, so peaceful. He was dreaming. Never wake him up again. His head was sunk in the pillow, his eyes were closed; they were blind under the closed eye-lids. He was given up to his dream. What did garden-parties and baskets and lace frocks matter to him? He was far from all those things. He was wonderful, beautiful. While they were laughing and while the band was playing, this marvel had come to the lane. Happy . . . happy.

. . . All is well, said that sleeping face. This is just as it should be. I am content.

But all the same you had to cry, and she couldn't go out of the room without saying something to him. Laura gave a loud childish sob.

"Forgive my hat," she said.

And this time she didn't wait for Em's sister. She found her way out of the door, down the path, past all those dark people. At the corner of the lane she met Laurie.

He stepped out of the shadow. "Is that you, Laura?"

"Yes."

"Mother was getting anxious. Was it all right?"

"Yes, quite. Oh, Laurie!" She took his arm, she pressed up against him.

"I say, you're not crying, are you?" asked her brother.

Laura shook her head. She was.

Laurie put his arm round her shoulder. "Don't cry," he said in his warm, loving voice. "Was it awful?"

"No," sobbed Laura. "It was simply marvelous. But, Laurie—" She stopped, she looked at her brother. "Isn't life," she stammered, "isn't life—" But what life was she couldn't explain. No matter. He quite understood.

"*Isn't* it, darling?" said Laurie. ❖

 Although Laura is initially uncomfortable visiting the Scott family, she later describes the experience as "marvelous." How can learning about other people's lives give you insight into your own?

Refer and Reason

1. What is Mrs. Sheridan's brilliant idea about the leftover food from the party? What does her decision reveal about her character?

2. Compare and contrast the attitudes of Laura, Jose, and Mrs. Sheridan toward the workers and the servants. How does Mansfield reveal these attitudes for the reader?

3. Describe how Laura feels about bringing the leftovers to Mrs. Scott, the widow of the dead worker. If you were Mrs. Scott, how might you feel toward Laura as she enters the cottage bearing a basket of leftover party food? Why?

Writing Options

1. The Sheridans have asked you to create an invitation to the garden party. (Keep in mind that the event takes place in New Zealand in 1907.) Create a suitable invitation; you can use your imagination to provide any needed information.

2. As the society reporter for a local newspaper, you have been assigned to cover two events: the Sheridans' garden party and a modern-day outdoor party, such as a barbeque, picnic, or block party. After time-traveling from one festive event to the other, write a newspaper article in which you describe similarities and differences between the two parties.

 Go to **www.mirrorsandwindows.com** for more.

As World War II wore on and London rumbled under German air raids, it appeared that William Butler Yeats's grim prediction of the world falling apart had come true. Once again, Great Britain found itself embroiled in another bloody conflict, and once again, Britons were called on to sacrifice for their country. Paper was rationed and the artistic and literary experimentation of the interwar years was temporarily put on hold. Several emerging new poets, such as Sidney Keyes and Keith Douglas, wrote about their experiences on the battlefield and explored the role of the war poet. Sadly, most of their works were published posthumously, as both poets were killed in the war.

The feelings of cynicism and pessimism that preceded the outbreak of World War II continued throughout the war, as Britons struggled to make sense of the chaotic world around them. Prime Minister Winston Churchill's war speeches urged Britons to fight and defend their nation against the attacking Germans. Mohandas Gandhi, spiritual leader of India while it was still under British colonial rule, presented a different view of how to resist an enemy through nonviolence.

Writers such as Vera Brittain and Elizabeth Bowen revealed how daily life changed for British citizens at home. W. H. Auden explored society's perceived indifference to human suffering in many of his poems, and Stephen Spender tapped into the feelings of disillusionment and disappointment experienced by Britons during this turbulent era.

In the Outskirts of Moscow in 1941, 1941. Aleksandr Dejneka. Tretyakov Gallery, Moscow, Russia. Art © Estate of Aleksandr Dejneka / RAO, Moscow / VAGA, New York.

Wartime Speech, May 19, 1940

A Speech by Winston Churchill

Build Background

Historical Context In May 1940, the Germans had overrun most of western Europe. Great Britain and France continued to hold off the Nazis, but France soon would fall.

In addressing the nation on May 19, 1940, Prime Minister Winston Churchill wanted to give the British people the
latest news of the war. In addition, he wanted to reassure
listeners that Britain and France, fighting a common enemy,
could meet any challenge and to ask the British to support
the men and women in battle. In his **Wartime Speech,** which was broadcast
by BBC Radio in London, Churchill seemed to be speaking directly to every
Briton.

Reader's Context In what situations would you like to hear an encouraging
speech from your leader? What would you like to hear?

Meet the Author

Winston Churchill (1874–1965) was one of the greatest figures of the twentieth century. In his early public life,
he was elected to Parliament, served as first lord of the
admiralty in the British Navy, and held other cabinet posts.
After returning to private life in the 1930s, Churchill issued
warnings against the impending Nazi threat, but they were
ignored.

In 1938, Prime Minister Neville Chamberlain drew
severe criticism for trying to appease Adolf Hitler by agreeing to German
demands for additional territory (most notably, Czechoslovakia). Early in 1940,
not long after the start of World War II (September 1939), Churchill became
prime minister. When the United States entered the war after the bombing of
Pearl Harbor in 1941, Churchill worked closely with U.S. President Franklin D.
Roosevelt.

Despite Churchill's tireless commitment to and achievement of the Allied
victory over the Axis powers, he was defeated for reelection by the Labour Party
candidate in 1945. He viewed his rejection at the ballot box as a stinging
rebuke of his leadership. Within six years, however, voters returned Churchill to
power. In 1953, he became Sir Winston when the nation conferred on him its
most prestigious honor: knighthood.

That same year, Churchill received the Nobel Prize for literature for his
writings and speeches. Among his most notable published works were two mul-
tivolume histories: one of World War II and the other of the English-speaking
people. He retired from public life in 1955, devoting his time to writing and, as
a hobby, to painting.

Analyze Literature

Speech and Rhetorical Device

A **speech** is a formal address
given on a particular occasion,
often for the purpose of persuading listeners to accept a
proposition or to take a certain
action.

A **rhetorical device** is a
technique used by a speaker or
writer to achieve a particular
effect, especially to persuade or
influence.

Set Purpose

Winston Churchill gave a number of broadcast radio speeches
throughout World War II. As
you read the following speech,
determine the prime minister's
purpose and how the audience
may have reacted to his address.
Write down specific phrases and
statements from the speech that
may have helped persuade listeners or appealed to their emotions. Also write down examples
of rhetorical devices, such as
parallelism, repetition, and rhetorical questions. Consider how
Churchill used these devices
to accomplish his purpose in
speaking.

Preview Vocabulary

formidable, 1060
adversary, 1060
invincible, 1060
unrelenting, 1060
retaliate, 1060
imperious, 1061
indomitable, 1061

Wartime Speech, May 19, 1940

by Winston Churchill

Now one bond unites us all—to wage war until victory is won.

[handwritten: German's have broken the Maginot line — terrible moment — Maginot Line was supposed to be last defense — this is a setback]

[handwritten: He must let the people know it is not time to despair]

Winston Churchill delivers a recruiting speech at the Mansion House, May 8, 1939.

I speak to you for the first time as Prime Minister in a solemn hour for the life of our country, of our Empire, of our Allies, and, above all, of the cause of Freedom. A tremendous battle is raging in France and Flanders.[1] The Germans, by a remarkable combination of air bombing and heavily armored tanks, have broken through the French defenses north of the Maginot Line,[2] and strong columns of their armored vehicles are ravaging the open country, which for the first day or two was without defenders. They have penetrated deeply and spread alarm and confusion in their track. Behind them there are now appearing infantry in lorries,[3] and behind them, again, the large masses are moving forward. The regroupment of the French armies to make head against, and also to strike at, this intruding wedge has been proceeding for several days, largely assisted by the magnificent efforts of the Royal Air Force.

[handwritten: parallelism / ellipsis]

[handwritten: builds up the sense of the extreme seriousness]

---

1. **Flanders.** Area located primarily in parts of Belgium
2. **Maginot** (ma´ zhə nō′) **Line.** Extended line of fortifications set up to protect France from invasion from the east
3. **lorries.** British English for "trucks"

more rhetorical mastery shown here

hope

possibilities to hope for

We must not allow ourselves to be intimidated by the presence of these armored vehicles in unexpected places behind our lines. If they are behind our Front, the French are also at many points fighting actively behind theirs. Both sides are therefore in an extremely dangerous position. And if the French Army, and our own Army, are well handled, as I believe they will be; if the French retain that genius for recovery and counter-attack for which they have so long been famous; and if the British Army shows the dogged endurance and solid fighting power of which there have been so many examples in the past—then a sudden transformation of the scene might spring into being.

It would be foolish, however, to disguise the gravity of the hour.

emotional rollercoaster

Speaking of the danger again

It would be foolish, however, to disguise the gravity of the hour. It would be still more foolish to lose heart and courage or to suppose that well-trained, well-equipped armies numbering three or four millions of man can be overcome in the space of a few weeks, or even months, by a scoop, or raid of mechanized vehicles, however formidable. We may look with confidence to the stabilization of the Front in France, and to the general engagement of the masses, which will enable the qualities of the French and British soldiers to be matched squarely against those of their adversaries. For myself, I have invincible confidence in the French Army and its leaders. Only a very small part of that splendid army has yet been heavily engaged; and only a very small part of France has yet been invaded. There is good evidence to show that practically the whole of the specialized and mechanized forces of the enemy have been already thrown into the battle; and we know that very heavy losses have been inflicted upon them. No officer or man, no brigade or division, which grapples at close quar-

saying its small

putting heart into it

being positive

(using) very precise diction

using intense words

ters with the enemy, wherever encountered, can fail to make a worthy contribution to the general result. The Armies must cast away the idea of resisting behind concrete lines or natural obstacles, and must realize that mastery can only be regained by furious and unrelenting assault. And this spirit must not only animate the High Command, but must inspire every fighting man.

In the air—often at serious odds—often at odds hitherto thought overwhelming—we have been clawing down three or four to one of our enemies; and the relative balance of the British and German Air Forces is now considerably more favorable to us than at the beginning of the battle. In cutting down the German bombers, we are fighting our own battle as well as that of France. My confidence in our ability to fight it out to the finish with the German Air Force has been strengthened by the fierce encounters which have taken place and are taking place. At the same time, our heavy bombers are striking nightly at the taproot of German mechanized power, and have already inflicted serious damage upon the oil refineries on which the Nazi effort to dominate the world directly depends.

We must expect that as soon as stability is reached on the Western Front, the bulk of that hideous apparatus of aggression which gashed Holland into ruin and slavery in a few days, will be turned upon us. I am sure I speak for all when I say we are ready to face it; to endure it; and to retaliate against it—to any extent that the unwritten laws of war permit. There will be many men, and many women, in this island who when the ordeal comes upon them, as come it will, will feel comfort, and even a pride—that they are sharing the perils of our

german army

---

for · mi · da · ble (fôr′ mə də bəl) *adj.,* hard to overcome
ad · ver · sary (ad′ və[r] ser′ ē) *n.,* enemy
in · vin · ci · ble (in[′] vin[t]′ sə bəl) *adj.,* unconquerable
un · re · lent · ing (un′ ri len′ tiŋ) *adj.,* not weakening in determination; firm
re · tal · i · ate (ri ta′ lē āt′) *v.,* respond, especially with stronger force

---

infuses energy into the listeners → to prepare for whats coming

The Enigma Machine

During World War II, British intelligence officers developed a code-breaking apparatus called the enigma machine, which helped them decipher secret Nazi transmissions. British Prime Minister Winston Churchill credited the enigma with winning the war, although the British government did not disclose its existence until after the Axis powers had surrendered.

The enigma machine used a complicated mathematical formula to break down the numerical codes the Nazis used to relay military commands, intelligence, and other highly secretive information. The Nazis broadcast these codes using radio signals, so even though anyone could hear them, only people with the proper knowledge could determine what they meant.

Using the enigma machine, the British Navy discovered the German Navy's intentions, which allowed Britain to claim victory in the Battle of the Atlantic. Doing so cleared the way for the Normandy invasion in 1944, which signaled the end of Germany's control over western Europe.

[handwritten note: positive spin on England being invaded]

lads at the Front—soldiers, sailors and airmen, God bless them—and are drawing away from them a part at least of the onslaught they have to bear. Is not this the appointed time for all to make the utmost exertions in their power? If the battle is to be won, we must provide our men with ever-increasing quantities of the weapons and ammunition they need. We must have, and have quickly, more airplanes, more tanks, more shells, more guns. There is <u>imperious</u> need for these vital munitions. They increase our strength against the powerfully armed enemy. They replace the wastage of the obstinate struggle; and the knowledge that wastage will speedily be replaced enables us to draw more readily upon our reserves and throw them in now that everything counts so much.

Our task is not only to win the battle— but to win the War. After this battle in France abates[4] its force, there will come the battle for our island—for all that Britain is, and all that Britain means. That will be the struggle. In that supreme emergency we shall not hesitate to take every step, even the most drastic, to call forth from our people the last ounce and the last inch of effort of which they are capable. The interests of property, the hours of labor, are nothing compared with the struggle for life and honor, for right and freedom, to which we have vowed ourselves.

I have received from the Chiefs of the French Republic, and in particular from its <u>indomitable</u> Prime Minister, M. Reynaud, the most sacred pledges that whatever happens they will fight to the end, be it bitter or be it glorious. Nay, if we fight to the end, it can only be glorious.

Having received His Majesty's commission, I have found an administration of men and women of every party and of almost every point of view. We have differed and quarreled in the past; but now one bond unites

[handwritten note centered: Sharing danger, helping out the Front]

> ### Our task is not only to win the battle—but to win the War.

[handwritten note: Struggle for life + honor edging into sacredness]

[handwritten note: Moral responsibility]

[handwritten margin notes: Shows he is a quality leader – Able to rally his people]

[handwritten margin note: His government is unified]

---

4. **abates.** Reduces

im • pe • ri • ous (im pir´ ē əs) *adj.,* urgent; vital
in • dom • i • ta • ble (in dä´ mə tə bəl) *adj.,* incapable of being defeated

In his speech, Churchill praises the efforts of Britain's Royal Air Force (RAF) (c. March 1940).

us all—to wage war until victory is won, and never to surrender ourselves to servitude and shame, whatever the cost and the agony may be. This is one of the most awe-striking periods in the long history of France and Britain. It is also beyond doubt the most sublime. Side by side, unaided except by their kith and kin in the great Dominions and by the wide Empires which rest beneath their shield—side by side, the British and French peoples have advanced to rescue not only Europe but mankind from the foulest and most soul-destroying tyranny which has ever darkened and stained the pages of history. Behind them—behind us—behind the armies and fleets of Britain and France—gather a group of shattered States and bludgeoned races: the Czechs, the Poles, the Norwegians, the Danes, the Dutch, the Belgians—upon all of whom the long night of barbarism will descend, unbroken even by a star of hope, unless we conquer, as conquer we must; as conquer we shall.

Today is Trinity Sunday. Centuries ago words were written to be a call and a spur to the faithful servants of Truth and Justice; "Arm yourselves, and be ye men of valor, and be in readiness for the conflict; for it is better for us to perish in battle than to look upon the outrage of our nation and our altar. As the Will of God is in Heaven, even so let it be." ❖

MIRRORS & WINDOWS

For what purposes does a leader need to communicate with the people he or she represents? Why is this communication especially important in a time of war or other crisis?

N D H I

Literature Connection

Mohandas K. Gandhi (1869–1948) delivered the speech **"Defending Nonviolent Resistance"** in court in 1922 after being convicted of inciting hatred or contempt against the British government, an action that violated section 124-A of the Indian Penal Code. He was sentenced to six years in prison for this offense. As a young lawyer, Gandhi became active in the resistance movement against British rule of India, which had begun in the 1850s. He earned tremendous respect for his commitment to nonviolence and so-called passive resistance, in which he and his followers refused to use any violent means to further their cause.

India was granted independence from Great Britain in 1947. However, the nation was divided into two parts: the primarily Hindu India and the primarily Muslim Pakistan. Gandhi was assassinated just one year later.

Defending Nonviolent Resistance

by Mohandas K. Gandhi

Before I read this statement, I would like to state that I entirely endorse the learned advocate general's remarks in connection with my humble self. I think that he was entirely fair to me in all the statements that he has made, because it is very true, and I have no desire whatsoever to conceal from this court the fact that to preach disaffection[1] toward the existing system of government has become almost a passion with me; and the learned advocate general is also entirely in the right when he says that my preaching of disaffection did not commence with my connection with *Young India,* but that it commenced much earlier; and in the statement that I am about to read, it will be my painful duty to admit before this court that it commenced much earlier than the period stated by the advocate general. It is the most painful duty with me, but I have to discharge

---

1. **disaffection.** Discontent

that duty knowing the responsibility that rests upon my shoulders, and I wish to endorse all the blame that the learned advocate general has thrown on my shoulders, in connection with the Bombay occurrences, Madras occurrences, and the Chauri Chaura occurrences.[2] Thinking over these deeply and sleeping over them night after night, it is impossible for me to dissociate myself from the diabolical crimes of Chauri Chaura or the mad outrages of Bombay. He is quite right when he says that as a man of responsibility, a man having received a fair share of education, having had a fair share of experience of this world, I should have known the consequences of every one of my acts. I know that I was playing with fire. I ran the risk, and if I was set free, I would still do the same. I have felt it this morning that I would have failed in my duty, if I did not say what I said here just now.

Nonviolence is the first article of my faith. It is also the last article of my creed.

I wanted to avoid violence, I want to avoid violence. Nonviolence is the first article of my faith. It is also the last article of my creed. But I had to make my choice. I had either to submit to a system which I considered had done an irreparable harm to my country, or incur the risk of the mad fury of my people bursting forth, when they understood the truth from my lips. I know that my people have sometimes gone mad. I am deeply sorry for it, and I am therefore here to submit not to a light penalty but to the highest penalty. I do not ask for mercy. I do not plead any extenuating[3] act. I am here, therefore, to invite and cheerfully submit to the highest penalty that can be inflicted upon me for what in law is a deliberate crime and what appears to me to be the highest duty of a citizen. The only course open to you, the judge, is, as I am just going to say in my state-ment, either to resign your post or inflict on me the severest penalty, if you believe that the system and law you are assisting to administer are good for the people. I do not expect that kind of conversation, but by the time I have finished with my statement, you will perhaps have a glimpse of what is raging within my breast to run this maddest risk which a sane man can run.

I owe it perhaps to the Indian public and to the public in England to placate which this prosecution is mainly taken up[4] that I should explain why from a staunch loyalist and cooperator I have become an uncompromising disaffectionist and non-cooperator. To the court too I should say why I plead guilty to the charge of promoting disaffection toward the government established by law in India.

My public life began in 1893 in South Africa in troubled weather. My first contact with British authority in that country was not of a happy character. I discovered that as a man and as an Indian I had no rights. More correctly, I discovered that I had no rights as a man because I was an Indian.

But I was not baffled. I thought that this treatment of Indians was an excrescence[5] upon a system that was intrinsically and mainly good. I gave the government my voluntary and hearty cooperation, criticizing it freely where I felt it was faulty but never wishing its destruction.

Consequently, when the existence of the empire was threatened in 1899 by the Boer challenge,[6] I offered my services to it, raised a volunteer ambulance corps, and served at

---

2. **Chauri Chaura occurrences.** Reference to violence taking place in an Indian village
3. **extenuating.** Providing justification for
4. **the public in England . . . taken up.** The public in England, whose anger at my behavior this prosecution has mainly been set up to soothe
5. **excrescence.** Unpleasant mark or outgrowth
6. **Boer challenge.** During the Boer War (1899–1902), parts of South Africa rebelled against British rule. Although the British responded with harsh tactics, the protesters agreed to remain loyal to the monarchy, as long as London treated South Africa fairly.

As part of Gandhi's passive resistance campaign, Indians boycotted British goods in 1931.

The first shock came in the shape of the Rowlatt Act, a law designed to rob the people of all the real freedom. I felt called upon to lead an intensive agitation against it. Then followed the Punjab horrors beginning with the massacre at Jallianwala Bagh and culminating in crawling orders, public floggings, and other indescribable humiliations. I discovered too that the plighted word of the prime minister to the Mussulmans of India regarding the integrity of Turkey and the holy places of Islam was not likely to be fulfilled. But in spite of the forebodings and the grave warnings of friends, at the Amritsar Congress in 1919, I fought for cooperation and working with the Montagu-Chelmsford reforms,[7] hoping that the prime minister would redeem his promise to the Indian Mussulmans, that the Punjab wound would be healed, and that the reforms, inadequate and unsatisfactory though they were, marked a new era of hope in the life of India.

But all that hope was shattered. The Khilafat promise was not to be redeemed. The Punjab crime was whitewashed, and most culprits went not only unpunished but remained in service and in some cases continued to draw pensions from the Indian revenue, and in some cases were even rewarded. I saw too that not only did the reforms not mark a change of heart, but they were only a method of further draining India of her wealth and of prolonging her servitude.

I came reluctantly to the conclusion that the Brittish connection had made India more helpless than she ever was before, politically and economically. A disarmed India has no

several actions that took place for the relief of Ladysmith. Similarly in 1906, at the time of the Zulu revolt, I raised a stretcher-bearer party and served till the end of the "rebellion." On both these occasions I received medals and was even mentioned in dispatches. For my work in South Africa I was given by Lord Hardinge a Kaiser-i-Hind Gold Medal. When the war broke out in 1914 between England and Germany, I raised a volunteer ambulance corps in London consisting of the then resident Indians in London, chiefly students. Its work was acknowledged by the authorities to be valuable. Lastly, in India, when a special appeal was made at the War Conference in Delhi in 1918 by Lord Chelmsford for recruits, I struggled at the cost of my health to raise a corps in Kheda, and the response was being made when the hostilities ceased and orders were received that no more recruits were wanted. In all these efforts at service I was actuated by the belief that it was possible by such services to gain a status of full equality in the empire for my countrymen.

---

7. **Montagu-Chelmsford reforms.** Measures enacted in 1919 that were intended to transfer some power from Britain to India

power of resistance against any aggressor if she wanted to engage in armed conflict with him. So much is this the case that some of our best men consider that India must take generations before she can achieve the dominion status. She has become so poor that she has little power of resisting famines. Before the British advent, India spun and wove in her millions of cottages just the supplement she needed for adding to her meager agricultural resources. This cottage industry, so vital for India's existence, has been ruined by incredibly heartless and inhuman processes as described by English witnesses. Little do town dwellers know how the semistarved masses of India are slowly sinking to lifelessness. Little do they know that their miserable comfort represents the brokerage they get for the work they do for the foreign exploiter, that the profits and the brokerage are sucked from the masses. Little do they realize that the government established by law in British India is carried on for this exploitation of the masses. No sophistry,[8] no jugglery in figures can explain away the evidence that the skeletons in many villages present to the naked eye. I have no doubt whatsoever that both England and the town dwellers of India will have to answer, if there is a God above, for this crime against humanity which is perhaps unequaled in history. The law itself in this country has been used to serve the foreign exploiter. My unbiased examination of the Punjab Martial Law cases has led me to believe that at least 95 percent of convictions were wholly bad. My experience of political cases in India leads me to the conclusion that in nine out of every ten the condemned men were totally innocent. Their crime consisted in the love of their country. In ninety-nine cases out of a hundred justice has been denied to Indians as against Europeans in the courts of India. This is not an exaggerated picture. It is the experience of almost every Indian who has had anything to do with such cases. In my opinion, the administration of the law is thus prostituted consciously or unconsciously for the benefit of the exploiter.

> My experience of political cases in India leads me to the conclusion that in nine out of every ten the condemned men were totally innocent.

The greatest misfortune is that Englishmen and their Indian associates in the administration of the country do not know that they are engaged in the crime I have attempted to describe. I am satisfied that many Englishmen and Indian officials honestly believe that they are administering one of the best systems devised in the world and that India is making steady though slow progress. They do not know that a subtle but effective system of terrorism and an organized display of force, on the one hand, and the deprivation of all powers of retaliation or self-defense, on the other, have emasculated the people and induced in them the habit of simulation. This awful habit has added to the ignorance and the self-deception of the administrators. Section 124-A, under which I am happily charged, is perhaps the prince among the political sections of the Indian Penal Code designed to suppress the liberty of the citizen. Affection cannot be manufactured or regulated by law. If one has an affection for a person or system, one should be free to give the fullest expression to his disaffection, so long as he does not contemplate, promote, or incite to violence. But the section under which Mr. Banker [a colleague in non-violence] and I are charged is one under which mere promotion of disaffection is a crime. I have studied some of the cases tried under it, and I know that some of the most loved of India's patriots have been convicted under it. I consider it a privilege, therefore, to be charged

---

8. **sophistry.** Slyly misleading argument

under that section. I have endeavored to give in their briefest outline the reasons for the disaffection. I have no personal ill will against any single administrator, much less can I have any disaffection toward the king's person. But I hold it to be a virtue to be disaffected toward a government which in its totality has done more harm to India than any previous system. India is less manly under the British rule than she ever was before. Holding such a belief, I consider it to be a sin to have affection for the system. And it has been a precious privilege for me to be able to write what I have in the various articles, tendered in evidence against me.

In fact, I believe that I have rendered a service to India and England by showing in non-cooperation the way out of the unnatural state in which both are living. In my humble opinion, non-cooperation with evil is as much a duty as is cooperation with good. But in the past, non-cooperation has been deliberately expressed in violence to the evildoer. I am endeavoring to show to my countrymen that violent non-cooperation only multiplies evil and that as evil can only be sustained by violence, withdrawal of support of evil requires complete abstention from violence. Nonviolence implies voluntary submission to the penalty for non-cooperation with evil. I am here, therefore, to invite and submit cheerfully to the highest penalty that can be inflicted upon me for what in law is a deliberate crime and what appears to me to be the highest duty of a citizen. The only course open to you, the judge, is either to resign your post, and thus dissociate yourself from evil if you feel that the law you are called upon to administer is an evil and that in reality I am innocent, or to inflict on me the severest penalty if you believe that the system and the law you are assisting to administer are good for the people of this country and that my activity is therefore injurious to the public weal.[9] ❖

9. **weal.** Well-being

Review Questions

1. Identify the examples of injustice against the Indian people that Gandhi cites in his speech. How does he describe the relationship between Britain and India? What support does he give for this description? What did Gandhi believe about the British system prior to these events? How did these events change his attitude toward that system?

2. Gandhi made several seemingly paradoxical or sarcastic statements, such as "I am happily charged"; "I consider it a privilege, therefore, to be charged"; and "I...submit cheerfully to the highest penalty." Analyze the effect of his use of these types of statements on his audience. Would his argument have been stronger or weaker without these statements? Give reasons and textual evidence to support your position.

3. Make an outline of Gandhi's argument. Briefly summarize the information he presents in the opening two paragraphs and the closing two paragraphs. What is his main purpose, and why might he have chosen to organize his argument in this way? How effective is this organizational pattern? Support your response.

TEXT ⇄ TEXT CONNECTION

Identify similarities and differences between Churchill's 1940 speech to the British people and Gandhi's 1922 address to the Indian court. Consider the reasoning behind each work, as well as the content; tone; use of rhetorical devices, ambiguity, contradiction, and paradox; and appropriateness of appeals to the audience. Which speech do you find most compelling? Why?

Destroyed buildings in Hamburg, Germany (1945).

WAR POET

by Sidney Keyes

I am the man who looked for peace and found
My own eyes barbed.
I am the man who groped for words and found
An arrow in my hand.
5 I am the builder whose firm walls surround
A slipping land.
When I grow sick or mad
Mock me not nor chain me:
When I reach for the wind
10 Cast me not down:
Though my face is a burnt book
And a wasted town. ❖

March 1942

The speaker describes himself as a man who "looked for peace" and "groped for words." What did he find instead? What is ironic about the title "War Poet"?

WORDS

by Keith Douglas

Words are my instruments but not my servants;
by the white pillar of a prince I lie in wait
for them. In what the hour or the minute invents,
in a web formally meshed or inchoate,[1]
5   these fritillaries[2] are come upon, trapped:
hot-coloured, or the cold scarabs[3] a thousand years
old, found in cerements[4] and unwrapped.
The catch and the ways of catching are diverse.
For instance this stooping man, the bones of whose face are
10 like the hollow birds' bones, is a trap for words.
And the pockmarked house bleached by the glare
whose insides war has dried out like gourds[5]
attracts words. There are those who capture them
in hundreds, keep them prisoners in back.
15 But I keep words only a breath of time
turning in the lightest of cages—uncover
and let them go: sometimes they escape for ever. ❖

El Ballah, 1943

---

1. **inchoate** (in kō´ət). Existing only in part; imperfectly formed
2. **fritillaries** (fri´ tə ler' ēs). Types of butterflies
3. **scarabs** (ska´ rəbs). Beetles, types of insects; also, in ancient Egypt, beetles made of stone or pottery, which are considered good luck charms
4. **cerements.** Shrouds, or cloths to cover the dead
5. **gourds.** Inedible members of the pumpkin and squash family; often dried and used as containers

MIRRORS & WINDOWS

The speaker says that if words are uncovered and released, "sometimes they escape for ever." How does this idea relate to the fact that this poem has long survived the man who wrote it?

Refer to Text ▶ ▶ ▶ ▶ ▶   **Reason with Text**

1a. In lines 1–2 of "War Poet," how does the speaker describe himself?

1b. Explain the contrast the speaker is making in this description.

Understand
Find meaning

2a. What metaphors are used in lines 1 and 9–10 of "Words"?

2b. Show how these metaphors indicate the speaker's feelings toward *words*. What might words represent to the speaker?

Apply
Use information

3a. In lines 7–10 of "War Poet," what does the speaker indicate will happen to him? In the last two lines, what will his face become?

3b. Infer why these things will happen to him. What do they suggest about a war poet?

Analyze
Take things apart

4a. From which point of view are both poems narrated: first person or third person?

4b. Compare and contrast the two speakers' attitudes toward writing poetry in wartime.

Evaluate
Make judgments

5a. In Douglas's poem, how do some soldiers handle words? How long does the speaker keep the words? What happens to some of the words?

5b. Why do some soldiers bring out words only at certain times? Why does the speaker handle words the way he does?

Create
Bring ideas together

Compare Literature

Metaphor and Simile
Review your list of metaphors and similes from the two poems. Select two metaphors and two similes, and identify for each what things are being compared. Evaluate how effectively each author uses these figures of speech. How does the use of figurative language enhance your understanding of the poem?

Extend the Text

Writing Options
Creative Writing Imagine yourself in a violent, grim situation, such as a war zone or a category 5 hurricane. Write a poem about your response to the event.

Expository Writing Write a comparison and contrast essay that examines the use of imagery in Douglas's and Keyes's poems. You can organize your essay by discussing one poem at a time, or you can follow a point-by-point organization, comparing specific images in the poems.

Collaborative Learning
Research Songs from World War II World War II produced a number of popular songs, such as "The White Cliffs of Dover." Famous entertainers sang some of the lyrics as they toured military bases to cheer up the soldiers and sailors. Research the music that helped win the war. Present your findings to the class in an oral report.

Media Literacy
Compare Coverage of World War II A vast archive of newspaper and magazine articles, documents, films, speeches, and radio transcripts from World War II is available in libraries and on the Internet. For access to some of these types of media, go to **http://lit.emcp.net/ ww2**. Then select one aspect of the conflict—for example, British and American perspectives on staying the course to achieve victory—and examine the media coverage in terms of its intended effect on audience and purpose. Evaluate how differences in formality and tone reflect these factors. In addition, analyze how the words, images, graphics, and perspective affect meaning. For example, compare and contrast your understanding of "War Poet" and "Words" with the messages in other media pieces that use the eyewitness perspective. Report your findings in an analytical essay.

 Go to **www.mirrorsandwindows.com** for more.

COMPARING LITERATURE COMPARING LITERATURE COMPARING LITERATURE COMPARIN

1. In lines 1–2 of "War Poet," what does the word *barbed* mean?
   A. lost
   B. fierce or barbaric
   C. equipped with a sharp point
   D. drugged so as to become sleepy
   E. blindfolded or somehow unable to see

2. Which of the following is *not* a contrasted pair in "War Poet"?
   A. peace and a barb
   B. groped for words and found an arrow in my hand
   C. firm walls and slipping land
   D. sick and mad
   E. reach and cast down

3. In lines 1 and 3 of "War Poet," Keyes repeats the phrase "I am the man who." In lines 1, 3, and 5, he repeats the phrase "I am." What seems to be the main purpose of this repetition?
   A. to tell the reader about the narrator
   B. to make the poem sound more poetic
   C. to serve as the subject of the sentences
   D. to add one-syllable words so the meter of the poem is regular
   E. to provide emphasis and a strong sound that goes along with the idea of war

4. Review lines 4, 5, 6, and 9 of "War Poet." In these lines, the words *hand, surround, land,* and *wind* are examples of
   A. assonance.
   B. consonance.
   C. alliteration.
   D. sight rhyme.
   E. poetic rhythm.

5. Lines 11–12 of "War Poet" contain which two poetic devices?
   A. alliteration and metaphor
   B. personification and simile
   C. assonance and onomatopoeia
   D. internal rhyme and consonance
   E. figure of speech and slant rhyme

6. Which word or words from Keith Douglas's poem "Words" mean the opposite of *inchoate?*
   A. not my servants
   B. formally meshed
   C. fritillaries
   D. trapped
   E. hot-colored

7. Who or what is *El Ballah,* which appears at the end of the poem "Words"?
   A. the pen name of the poet
   B. the person for whom the poem was written
   C. the place where the poem was written
   D. the subtitle or alternative title for the poem
   E. the person who translated the poem into English

8. Which three poetic devices are used in lines 9–10 of "Words"?
   A. simile, alliteration, and metaphor
   B. consonance, assonance, and onomatopoeia
   C. metaphor, personification, and internal rhyme
   D. sight rhyme, alliteration, and assonance
   E. onomatopoeia, simile, and personification

9. **Constructed Response:** The word *war* appears only in the title of "War Poet" and only once in "Words." Explain what the poems "War Poet" and "Words" have to do with the subject of war. Is it significant to the poem "Words" that *war* and *word* are similar-sounding words? Explain.

10. **Constructed Response:** Compare and contrast the use of rhyme in these two poems. Identify at least three points of comparison, and provide examples from the poems for support.

Musée des Beaux Arts
The Unknown Citizen

Lyric Poems by W. H. Auden

Build Background

Literary Context The two selections that follow were collected in *Another Time,* a volume of W. H. Auden's poetry published in 1940. It includes shorter poems written during the later 1930s, many of which are among his best known.

"Musée des Beaux Arts" reflects on the sixteenth-century Flemish painting *Landscape with the Fall of Icarus,* by Pieter Brueghel (c. 1525–1569), which is in the collection of the Royal Museum of Fine Arts (Musée Royaux des Beaux-Arts) in Brussels, Belgium. In Greek mythology, Icarus and his father, the architect Daedalus, try to escape from prison by flying with wings made of wax and feathers. Ignoring his father's warnings, Icarus flies too near the sun, which melts his wings and sends him plunging into the sea. Auden uses the poem to comment on the place of suffering in human life.

"The Unknown Citizen" is an ironic listing of the achievements of an ordinary person in the mid-twentieth century. The voice of the bureaucratic speaker intones the characteristics of this modern-day Everyman, whose primary identity is marked by his conformity to society's expectations. In both diction and rhythm, the work is more prosaic than poetic.

Reader's Context How should society treat its members when they are in trouble?

Meet the Author

Wystan Hugh (W. H.) Auden (1907–1973) was born in York, England, and moved to Birmingham as a child. While a student at Oxford University, he became lifelong friends with novelist and playwright Christopher Isherwood and poet Stephen Spender (see page 1081). Witty, intellectual, and widely read, Auden was influenced by the writing of Robert Frost, Thomas Hardy, William Blake, and Emily Dickinson.

Publication of his second collection of poems in 1930 made Auden famous. During the next ten years, he also wrote drama, light verse, and political observations, sometimes working with other writers. A prolific writer, Auden was noted for his technical versatility and ability to work in nearly every form of verse.

In 1939, Auden moved to the United States, where he spent more than thirty years and eventually became a citizen. His poetry collection *The Age of Anxiety* won the Pulitzer Prize in 1948, and from 1954 to 1973, he was the Chancellor of the American Academy of Poets.

Analyze Literature

Diction and Rhyme
Diction, when applied to writing, refers to the author's choice of words.

Rhyme is the repetition of sounds at the ends of words. Types of rhyme include *end rhyme,* or the use of rhyming words at the end of lines; *internal rhyme,* or the use of rhyming words within lines; and *slant rhyme,* or the use of rhyming sounds that are similar but not identical.

Set Purpose

W. H. Auden wrote about many topics and themes from popular culture and everyday life. As you read, consider how his diction fits those topics and themes. Jot down words from the poems that you feel are typical of the diction he uses. Also note Auden's use of rhyme. Specifically, identify the different types of rhyme he uses and for what effect.

Landscape with the Fall of Icarus, c. 1555. Pieter Brueghel the Elder. Musée Royaux des Beaux-Arts, Brussels, Belgium. (See detail on page 1074.)

Musée des Beaux Arts

by W. H. Auden

About suffering they were never wrong,
The Old Masters:[1] how well they understood
Its human position; how it takes place
While someone else is eating or opening a window or just walking dully along;

---

1. **Old Masters.** Collective name for great European artists before the eighteenth century

5   How, when the aged are reverently,[2] passionately waiting
    For the miraculous birth, there always must be
    Children who did not specially want it to happen, skating
    On a pond at the edge of the wood:
    They never forgot
10 That even the dreadful martyrdom[3] must run its course
    Anyhow in a corner, some untidy spot
    Where the dogs go on with their doggy life and the torturer's horse
    Scratches its innocent behind on a tree.
    In Brueghel's *Icarus*,[4] for instance: how everything turns away
15 Quite leisurely from the disaster; the ploughman may
    Have heard the splash, the forsaken cry,
    But for him it was not an important failure; the sun shone
    As it had to on the white legs disappearing into the green
    Water; and the expensive delicate ship that must have seen
20 Something amazing, a boy falling out of the sky,
    Had somewhere to get to and sailed calmly on. ❖

---

2. **reverently.** With respect and awe
3. **martyrdom.** Death or suffering for a religious, political, or other cause
4. **Brueghel's *Icarus*.** Reference to a painting by the Flemish artist Pieter Brueghel; it depicts the legend of Icarus, who flew too close to the sun with wings made of wax and as a result fell into the sea.

MIRRORS & WINDOWS

Do people tend to turn "quite leisurely from the disaster"? How concerned are most people with what happens in others' lives?

THE UNKNOWN CITIZEN

by W. H. Auden

(To JS/07/M/378

This Marble Monument Is Erected by the State)

He was found by the Bureau of Statistics to be
One against whom there was no official complaint,
And all the reports on his conduct agree
That, in the modern sense of an old-fashioned word, he was a saint,

5 For in everything he did he served the Greater Community.
Except for the War till the day he retired
He worked in a factory and never got fired,
But satisfied his employers, Fudge Motors Inc.
Yet he wasn't a scab[1] or odd in his views,
10 For his Union reports that he paid his dues,
(Our report on his Union shows it was sound)
And our Social Psychology workers found
That he was popular with his mates and liked a drink.
The Press are convinced that he bought a paper every day
15 And that his reactions to advertisements were normal in every way.
Policies taken out in his name prove that he was fully insured,
And his Health-card shows he was once in a hospital but left it cured.
Both Producers Research and High-Grade Living declare
He was fully sensible to the advantages of the Installment Plan
20 And had everything necessary to the Modern Man,
A phonograph, a radio, a car, and a frigidaire.
Our researchers into Public Opinion are content
That he held the proper opinions for the time of year;
When there was peace, he was for peace; when there was war, he went.
25 He was married and added five children to the population,
Which our Eugenist[2] says was the right number for a parent of his generation,
And our teachers report that he never interfered with their education.
Was he free? Was he happy? The question is absurd:
Had anything been wrong, we should certainly have heard. ❖

---

1. **scab.** Person who refuses to join a union or who replaces a union worker during a strike
2. **Eugenist.** Scientist who conducts experiments in human reproduction, in an effort to improve hereditary (genetic) factors

MIRRORS & WINDOWS

The speaker of this poem suggests that a "good citizen" is one who complies with the expectations and conventions of society. Do you agree with this definition?

Refer to Text ▶ ▶ ▶ ▶ ▶ **Reason with Text**

1a. To whom is "The Unknown Citizen" dedicated? Who erected the marble monument?

1b. To what does the dedication refer? Explain why the title of the poem is ironic.

Understand
Find meaning

2a. According to the speaker in "Musée des Beaux Arts," how does Brueghel's painting portray people's reactions to the fall of Icarus?

2b. What do the people's reactions indicate about human compassion?

Apply
Use information

3a. List the details of modern life mentioned in lines 14–21 of "The Unknown Citizen."

3b. What do these details suggest about the speaker's view of modern life? What is missing from the speaker's view?

Analyze
Take things apart

4a. How does the ploughman respond to the disaster in "Musée des Beaux Arts"?

4b. Do you agree with Auden that suffering often goes unnoticed because other things are happening? Why or why not?

Evaluate
Make judgments

5a. Summarize the speakers' views of modern society presented in these poems.

5b. How are these views similar to other views presented in Modern poetry? What can we learn from these poems that can help us improve the conditions of modern life?

Create
Bring ideas together

Analyze Literature

Diction and Rhyme
Describe the diction Auden uses in each poem. How do his word choices reinforce the meaning of the poem?

How does Auden use rhyme in each poem? What types of rhyme does he use? Which type of rhyme does he use most often? Suggest how Auden's use of rhyme reinforces the purpose of each poem.

Extend the Text

Writing Options
Creative Writing In "Musée des Beaux Arts," Auden uses his response to a painting to express his feelings about human suffering. Choose a photograph or a painting to which you respond. Write a poem or short essay in which you use the image as a springboard for conveying your thoughts or ideas.

Expository Writing What poetic devices, such as rhyme, appear in "The Unknown Citizen"? Which devices, such as regular rhythm, are not present? In a one-page literary analysis, explain Auden's use of poetic techniques.

Collaborative Learning
Examine the Works of Brueghel In the library or on the Internet, locate other paintings by the Flemish master

Brueghel. Working with a partner, examine the works and discuss what life was like for ordinary people in sixteenth-century northern Europe. For a modern-day literary look at another Old Master, Jan Vermeer (1632–1675), you might read the novel *Girl with a Pearl Earring,* by Tracy Chevalier, or watch a video of the film (2003).

Media Literacy
Create a Poster About Computer Privacy Today, individuals using computers should be aware of the possibility of electronic invasion of their privacy. Briefly research this topic, in the library or on the Internet, and create a poster that warns computer users to take precautions against the threat of electronic invasion of privacy.

 Go to **www.mirrorsandwindows.com** for more.

1. In lines 1 and 9 of "Musée des Beaux Arts," to whom or what does *they* refer?
   A. positions
   B. sufferings
   C. elderly people
   D. humans in general
   E. great European artists

2. Which of the following best states the primary theme of "Musée des Beaux Arts"?
   A. Art is important in everyday life.
   B. With age comes wisdom, and with wisdom comes beauty.
   C. The young and the old are very different, but they each have their strengths.
   D. People are involved in their own lives and pay little attention to what happens around them.
   E. People should enjoy life's small moments instead of always being in a hurry.

3. What activity would *not* fit with those mentioned in line 4 of "Musée des Beaux Arts"?
   A. sleeping
   B. watching TV
   C. witnessing a miracle
   D. reading the newspaper
   E. working at a routine job

4. In lines 12–13 of "Musée des Beaux Arts," what two things are contrasted?
   A. the dogs and the horse
   B. the torturer and the horse
   C. where the dogs go and on a tree
   D. the doggy life and a behind
   E. life and a tree

5. Which of the following quotations from "The Unknown Citizen" best describes the *he* referred to throughout the poem?
   A. "The Unknown Citizen" (title)
   B. "One against whom there was no official complaint" (line 2)
   C. "he was a saint" (in line 4)
   D. "he served the Greater Community" (in line 5)
   E. "He worked in a factory" (in line 7)

6. In plain language, how could the *he* in "The Unknown Citizen" best be described?
   A. as a hero
   B. as an ordinary person
   C. as a perfect individual
   D. as a friend of the poet's
   E. as a poetic figure

7. What is the tone of "The Unknown Citizen," especially as revealed in lines 28–29?
   A. critical and ironic
   B. sincere and serious
   C. proud and patriotic
   D. respectful and reverent
   E. anxious and questioning

8. Which of the following describes the rhyme scheme in "The Unknown Citizen"?
   A. *abab*
   B. *aabb*
   C. a mixture of *abab*, couplets, and one triplet
   D. a mixture of *abab*, *aabb*, *abcabc*, and *abcdabcd*
   E. There is no rhyme scheme.

9. **Constructed Response:** Evaluate Auden's choice of title for the poem "Musée des Beaux Arts." What does the title mean? To what does it refer? What does the title add to your understanding of the poem? Use details from the poem to support your answer.

10. **Constructed Response:** Discuss the significance of Auden's never identifying the *he* in "The Unknown Citizen." What do you know about *him* from the poem? What generalizations can you make about this individual? Suggest why *he* remains nameless.

What I Expected

A Lyric Poem by Stephen Spender

Build Background

Cultural Context Stephen Spender was part of the generation of British writers who grew up between the two world wars, a period of political upheaval in Europe. His poetry represents a bridge between the work of early Modernist poets such as T. S. Eliot and that of poets who began writing after World War II. Rapid changes in technology and politics, along with a worldwide economic depression, made the interwar years an edgy, uneasy period. As a result, many writers of this period turned to private, personal subjects.

Literary Context In **"What I Expected,"** the speaker presents a stark contrast between anticipation and reality—his visions of his future as a poet, unrealized because of human physical and emotional frailty in the face of time. As you read the selection, consider the impact, in particular, of the poem's short lines. (Reading the poem aloud may make the effect clearer.)

Reader's Context In which ways can the passage of time erode our expectations?

Meet the Author

Stephen Spender (1909–1995) was born in London to a liberal journalist father and a mother of German Jewish heritage. He attended University College, Oxford, where he became friends with other authors, including W. H. Auden (see page 1074).

During the 1930s, Spender was a leading member of a group of socially conscious British writers who supported communist policies and worked for social reform. His autobiography, *World Within World,* published in 1951, recounts the political and social atmosphere of the 1930s. Spender's political loyalties shifted away from leftist causes when he reportedly served as a firefighter in London during the Blitz, the relentless German bombing of the city during World War II. That shift was chronicled in *The God That Failed: Six Studies in Communism* (1950), for which Spender contributed one of the six essays.

By the 1950s, Spender turned his attention from poetry to literary criticism and lecturing in Britain and the United States. From 1953 to 1967, he edited the literary review *Encounter.* In 1972, he helped found the *Index on Censorship,* a journal dedicated to monitoring free expression throughout the world and publishing works by suppressed authors.

Spender's poems were published in several volumes during his life. His *Collected Poems* first came out in 1955, and an updated version appeared in 1986.

Analyze Literature

Speaker and Paradox

The **speaker** is the character who speaks in, or narrates, a poem—the voice assumed by the writer. The speaker and the author are not necessarily the same person.

A **paradox** is a seemingly contradictory statement, idea, or event that may actually be true. Some paradoxes can be resolved into coherent and noncontradictory ideas, while others present irresolvable contradictory ideas.

Set Purpose

Some of Spender's poetry reflects sentiments similar to those of writers who fought on the battlefields of World War II. As you read "What I Expected," consider how you would characterize the speaker. Identify specific lines, words, and phrases that help create the speaker's voice and convey his attitude. Also look for examples of paradox. Write down the line numbers in which Spender presents paradoxes. Consider what effect each paradox has on your understanding of the poem.

What I Expected

by Stephen Spender

What I expected, was
Thunder, fighting,
Long struggles with men
And climbing.
5 After continual straining
I should grow strong;
Then the rocks would shake,
And I rest long.

What I had not foreseen
10 Was the gradual day
Weakening the will
Leaking the brightness away,
The lack of good to touch,
The fading of body and soul
15 —Smoke before wind,
Corrupt, unsubstantial.

The wearing of Time,
And watching of cripples pass
With limbs shaped like questions
20 In their odd twist,
The pulverous[1] grief
Melting the bones with pity,
The sick falling from earth—
These, I could not foresee.

25 Expecting always
Some brightness to hold in trust,
Some final innocence
Exempt from dust,
That, hanging solid,
30 Would dangle through all,
Like the created poem,
Or faceted crystal.[2] ❖

1. **pulverous.** Reduced to dust
2. **faceted crystal.** Crystal cut with many flat planes

MIRRORS & WINDOWS Does the speaker of the poem seem disappointed or disillusioned? What is the difference between the two?

Refer to Text ▶ ▶ ▶ ▶ ▶ **Reason with Text**

1a. In lines 1–4, what does the speaker say he expected to happen? In lines 5–8, what condition did he expect to be in at the end of the events?

1b. Explain how the rest of the poem shows that these expectations were not fulfilled.

Understand
Find meaning

2a. In stanzas 1 and 2, which lines include the partial use of repetition?

2b. What does this use of repetition emphasize? How does it affect your understanding of the poem?

Apply
Use information

3a. In stanza 2, locate examples of alliteration, or the repetition of initial sounds.

3b. Analyze how this use of repeated sounds emphasizes the meaning of the poem.

Analyze
Take things apart

4a. In lines 25–28, what does the speaker say he always expected? In lines 31–32, which two examples does he provide?

4b. Compare and contrast these images. How effective are these images in supporting the main purpose of the poem? Why?

Evaluate
Make judgments

5a. List the events the speaker did not anticipate.

5b. Which events are specific to the time and place in which the speaker lived? Which of these events can be considered universal? Why?

Create
Bring ideas together

Analyze Literature

Speaker and Paradox

Describe the speaker of the poem. What attitude does the speaker present? Cite specific lines, words, and phrases that help support your answer.

In what lines did you find examples of paradox? Copy each paradox on a sheet of paper and restate it in your own words. Explain how the paradox is seemingly contradictory. For what purpose does Spender seem to use paradoxes?

Extend the Text

Writing Options

Creative Writing Write a personal letter to someone you care about that describes a time when your expectations clashed with the reality. Divide your letter into four sections, and begin each section with one of the following lines from Spender's poem: "What I expected, was . . ."; "What I had not foreseen . . ."; "The wearing of Time . . ."; and "Expecting always . . .".

Expository Writing "What I Expected" contains some striking uses of imagery, such as "smoke before wind." What do the images suggest? How do they increase the emotional impact of the poem? Write an essay that examines the meaning and effect of Spender's use of imagery.

Collaborative Learning

Interview a Firefighter During the Blitz Imagine that it is 1940, and conduct an interview with the local London firefighters. One or two group members of a small group can act as interviewers; others can role-play off-duty firefighters, taking a break after struggling all night to keep up with the flames. If time allows, present your interview to the class.

Lifelong Learning

Prepare a Brochure on Crystal Making How are "faceted crystals" made, and how are they used? Do simple research on the crystal-glass making, and present your findings in a brochure.

 Go to **www.mirrorsandwindows.com** for more.

The Demon Lover

A Short Story by Elizabeth Bowen

Build Background

Literary Context **"The Demon Lover"** can be read and appreciated on several levels. On one level, it is a ghost story, in which a number of apparently unexplainable events frighten the main character, Kathleen Drover. Yet the mystery that seems to haunt Mrs. Drover's visit to her London house during the Blitz may originate in her memory and her imagination. Interpreted at this level, the story is a psychological study of a woman who has retained the emotional scars suffered in the earlier war. On yet another level, Mrs. Drover may symbolize the lasting suffering inflicted on the generation that experienced two world wars.

Reader's Context What do you find more frightening: real or imaginary events?

Meet the Author

Elizabeth Bowen (1899–1973) was born in Dublin, Ireland, of Welsh heritage. Following her father's illness and her mother's death, the teenage Elizabeth was moved from relative to relative and sent to school in England. The insecurity she felt during these early years left her feeling like an outsider in both England and Ireland—a theme that runs throughout her writing.

During World War I, Bowen returned to Ireland to work in a hospital. After that, she moved to London, where she met and married her husband, Alan Cameron, in 1923. As an employee at the Ministry of Information during World War II, Bowen lived in London and endured the Blitz, which inspired many of her best short stories.

After the death of her husband in 1952, the writer moved to Bowen's Court, the family's ancestral home in Ireland, which she inherited after her father's death in 1927. Even though lecturing and other projects helped her earn money, Bowen eventually had to sell the house, which was then torn down.

As a member of the Bloomsbury Group—the circle of writers, artists, and intellectuals active in London in the early twentieth century—Bowen met Virginia Woolf. Like the older author, Bowen wrote about how women were affected by their surroundings. Bowen published a number of novels, including *The Death of the Heart* (1938), and several short story collections, among them *The Demon Lover* (1945).

Analyze Literature

Flashback and Foreshadowing
A **flashback** interrupts the chronological sequence of a literary work to present an event that occurred earlier. Writers often use flashbacks to provide background information about characters or situations.

Foreshadowing is the presentation of hints to events that will occur later in a story.

Set Purpose

As noted in Build Background, "The Demon Lover" has multiple levels of meaning. As you read this story, consider what information or insight the flashback provides to help you better understand the character of Mrs. Drover. Consider, as well, how and why Bowen uses foreshadowing in the story. Take note where in the story examples of foreshadowing appear. In particular, consider how Bowen's portrayal of the ghostly atmosphere in the house foreshadows what will happen during Mrs. Drover's brief stay there.

Preview Vocabulary

prosaic, 1085
contemptuous, 1086
stealthily, 1086
plight, 1087
fumble, 1088
acuteness, 1089
impassive, 1089

THE DEMON LOVER

by Elizabeth Bowen

SHE COULD NOT HAVE PLIGHTED A MORE SINISTER TROTH.

Toward the end of her day in London Mrs. Drover went round to her shut-up house to look for several things she wanted to take away. Some belonged to herself, some to her family, who were by now used to their country life. It was late August; it had been a steamy, showery day: at the moment the trees down the pavement glittered in an escape of humid yellow afternoon sun. Against the next batch of clouds, already piling up ink-dark, broken chimneys and parapets stood out. In her once familiar street, as in any unused channel, an unfamiliar queerness has silted up; a cat wove itself in and out of railings, but no human eye watched Mrs. Drover's return. Shifting some parcels under her arm, she slowly forced round her latchkey in an unwilling lock, then gave the door, which had warped, a push with her knee. Dead air came out to meet her as she went in.

The staircase window having been boarded up, no light came down into the hall. But one door, she could just see, stood ajar, so she went quickly through into the room and unshuttered the big window in there. Now the <u>prosaic</u> woman, looking about her, was more perplexed than she knew by everything that she saw, by traces of her long former habit of life— the yellow smoke stain up the white marble mantle-piece, the ring left by a vase on the top of the escritoire,[1] the bruise in the wallpaper where, on the door being thrown open widely, the china handle had always hit the wall. The piano, having gone away to be stored, had left what looked like claw marks on its part of the parquet.[2] Though not much dust had seeped in, each object wore a film of another kind; and, the only ventilation being the chimney, the whole drawing room smelled of the cold hearth. Mrs. Drover put down her parcels on the escri-

---

1. **escritoire** (es´ krə twär'). Desk
2. **parquet** (pär kā´). Patterned wood surface, often flooring

pro • sa • ic (prō zā´ ik) *adj.,* ordinary

toire and left the room to proceed upstairs; the things she wanted were in a bedroom chest.

She had been anxious to see how the house was—the part-time caretaker she shared with some neighbors was away this week on his holiday, known to be not yet back. At the best of times he did not look in often, and she was never sure that she trusted him. There were some cracks in the structure, left by the last bombing, on which she was anxious to keep an eye. Not that one could do anything—

A shaft of refracted daylight now lay across the hall. She stopped dead and stared at the hall table—on this lay a letter addressed to her.

She thought first—then the caretaker *must* be back. All the same, who, seeing the house shuttered, would have dropped a letter in at the box? It was not a circular, it was not a bill. And the post office redirected, to the address in the country, everything for her that came through the post. The caretaker (even if he *were* back) did not know she was due in London today—her call here had been planned to be a surprise—so his negligence in the manner of this letter, leaving it to wait in the dusk and the dust, annoyed her. Annoyed, she picked up the letter, which bore no stamp. But it cannot be important, or they would know. . . . She took the letter rapidly upstairs with her, without a stop to look at the writing till she reached what had been her bedroom, where she let in light. The room looked over the garden and other gardens: the sun had gone in; as the clouds sharpened and lowered, the trees and rank lawns seemed already to smoke with dark. Her reluctance to look again at the letter came from the fact that she felt intruded upon—and by someone <u>contemptuous</u> of her ways. However, in the tenseness preceding the fall of rain she read it: it was a few lines.

DEAR KATHLEEN,
You will not have forgotten that today is our anniversary, and the day we said. The years have gone by at once slowly and fast. In view of the fact that nothing has changed, I shall rely upon you to keep your promise. I was sorry to see you leave London, but was satisfied that you would be back in time. You may expect me, therefore, at the hour arranged.
Until then . . . K.

Mrs. Drover looked for the date: it was today's. She dropped the letter onto the bedsprings, then picked it up to see the writing again—her lips, beneath the remains of lipstick, beginning to go white. She felt so much the change in her own face that she went to the mirror, polished a clear patch in it and looked at once urgently and <u>stealthily</u> in. She was confronted by a woman of forty-four, with eyes starting out under a hatbrim that had been rather carelessly pulled down. She had not put on any more powder since she left the shop where she ate her solitary tea. The pearls her husband had given her on their marriage hung loose round her now rather thinner throat, slipping into the V of the pink wool jumper her sister knitted last autumn as they sat round the fire. Mrs. Drover's most normal expression was one of controlled worry, but of assent. Since the birth of the third of her little boys, attended by a quite serious illness, she had had an intermittent muscular flicker to the left of her mouth, but in spite of this she could always sustain a manner that was at once energetic and calm.

---

con • temp • tu • ous (kən tem[p]´ chə wəs) *adj.,* expressing disgust
stealth • i • ly (stel´ thə lē) *adv.,* slowly and secretly

Turning from her own face as precipitately[3] as she had gone to meet it, she went to the chest where the things were, unlocked it, threw up the lid and knelt to search. But as rain began to come crashing down she could not keep from looking over her shoulder at the stripped bed on which the letter lay. Behind the blanket of rain the clock of the church that still stood struck six—with rapidly heightening apprehension she counted each of the slow strokes. "The hour arranged . . . My God," she said, "*What hour?* How should I . . . ? After twenty-five years. . . ."

MRS. DROVER'S MOST NORMAL EXPRESSION WAS ONE OF CONTROLLED WORRY.

The young girl talking to the soldier in the garden had not ever completely seen his face. It was dark; they were saying good-bye under a tree. Now and then—for it felt, from not seeing him at this intense moment, as though she had never seen him at all—she verified his presence for these few moments longer by putting out a hand, which he each time pressed, without very much kindness, and painfully, on to one of the breast buttons of his uniform. That cut of the button on the palm of her hand was, principally, what she was to carry away. This was so near the end of a leave from France that she could only wish him already gone. It was August 1916. Being not kissed, being drawn away from and looked at intimidated Kathleen till she imagined spectral glitters in the place of his eyes. Turning away and looking back up the lawn she saw, through the branches of trees, the drawing-room window alight; she caught a breath for the moment when she could go running back there into the safe arms of her mother and sister, and cry: "What shall I do, what shall I do? He has gone."

Hearing her catch her breath, her fiancé said, without feeling: "Cold?"

"You're going away such a long way."

"Not so far as you think."

"I don't understand?"

"You don't have to," he said. "You will. You know what we said."

"But that was—suppose you—I mean, suppose."

"I shall be with you," he said, "sooner or later. You won't forget that. You need do nothing but wait."

Only a little more than a minute later she was free to run up the silent lawn. Looking in through the window at her mother and sister, who did not for the moment perceive her, she already felt that unnatural promise drive down between her and the rest of all humankind. No other way of having given herself could have made her feel so apart, lost and foresworn. She could not have <u>plighted</u> a more sinister troth.

Kathleen behaved well when, some months later, her fiancé was reported missing, presumed killed. Her family not only supported her but were able to praise her courage without stint because they could not regret, as a husband for her, the man they knew almost nothing about. They hoped she would, in a year or two, console herself—and had it been only a question of consolation things might have gone much straighter ahead. But her trouble, behind just a little grief, was a complete dislocation from everything. She did not reject other lovers, for these failed to appear: for years she failed to attract men—and with the approach of her thirties she became natural enough to share her family's anxiousness on this score. She began to put herself out, to wonder; and at thirty-two she was very greatly relieved to find herself being courted by William Drover. She married him, and the two of them settled down in this quiet, arboreal[4] part of Kensington; in this house the years piled up, her children were

---

3. **precipitately.** Suddenly
4. **arboreal.** Filled with trees

plight (plīt) *v.*, engage in

born and they all lived till they were driven out by the bombs of the next war. Her movements as Mrs. Drover were circumscribed,[5] and she dismissed any idea that they were still watched.

As things were—dead or living the letter writer sent her only a threat. Unable, for some minutes, to go on kneeling with her back exposed to the empty room, Mrs. Dover rose from the chest to sit on an upright chair whose back was firmly against the wall. The desuetude[6] of her former bedroom, her married London home's whole air of being a cracked cup from which memory, with its reassuring power, had either evaporated or leaked away, made a crisis—and at just this crisis the letter writer had, knowledgeably, struck. The hollowness of the house this evening canceled years on years of voices, habits and steps. Through the shut windows she only heard rain fall on the roofs around. To rally herself, she said she was in a mood—and, for two or three seconds shutting her eyes, told herself that she imagined the letter. But she opened them—there it lay on the bed.

On the supernatural side of the letter's entrance she was not permitting her mind to dwell. Who, in London, knew she meant to call at the house today? Evidently, however, this had been known. The caretaker, *had* he come back, had had no cause to expect her: he would have taken the letter in his pocket, to forward it, at his own time, through the post. There was no other sign that the caretaker had been in—but, if not? Letters dropped in at doors of deserted houses do not fly or walk to tables in halls. They do not sit on the dust of empty tables with the air of certainty that they will be found. There is needed some human hand—but nobody but the caretaker had a key. Under circumstances she did not care to consider, a house can be entered without a key. It was possible that she was not alone now. She might be being waited for, downstairs. Waited for—until when? Until "the hour arranged." At least that was not six o'clock; six had struck.

She rose from the chair and went over and locked the door.

The thing was, to get out. To fly? No, not that: she had to catch her train. As a woman whose utter dependability was the keystone of her family life she was not willing to return to the country, to her husband, her little boys and her sister, without the objects she had come up to fetch. Resuming work at the chest she set about making up a number of parcels in a rapid, <u>fumbling</u>-decisive way. These, with her shopping parcels, would be too much to carry; these meant a taxi—at the thought of the taxi her heart went up and her normal breathing resumed. I will ring up the taxi now; the taxi cannot come too soon; I shall hear the taxi out there running its engine, till I walk calmly down to it through the hall. I'll ring up—But no: the telephone is cut off. . . She tugged at a knot she had tied wrong.

The idea of flight. . . He was never kind to me, not really. I don't remember him kind at all. Mother said he never considered me. He was set on me, that was what it was—not love. Not love, not meaning a person well. What did he do, to make me promise like that? I can't remember—But she found that she could.

---

5. **circumscribed.** Carefully defined or limited; showing little variation
6. **desuetude** (de´ swi tüd´). Disuse

fum • ble (fəm´ bəl) *v.,* handle clumsily

She remembered with such dreadful <u>acuteness</u> that the twenty-five years since then dissolved like smoke and she instinctively looked for the weal left by the button on the palm of her hand. She remembered not only all that he said and did but the complete suspension of *her* existence during that August week. I was not myself—they all told me so at the time. She remembered—but with one white burning blank as where acid has dropped on a photograph: *under no conditions* could she remember his face.

So wherever he may be waiting, I shall not know him. You have no time to run from a face you do not expect.

The thing was to get to the taxi before any clock struck what could be the hour. She would slip down the street and round the side of the square to where the square gave on the main road. She would return in the taxi, safe, to her own door, and bring the driver into the house with her to pick up the parcels from room to room. The idea of the taxi driver made her decisive, bold; she unlocked her door, went to the top of the staircase and listened down.

She heard nothing—but while she was hearing nothing the passé[7] air of the staircase was disturbed by a draft that traveled up to her face. It emanated from the basement: down there a door or window was being opened by someone who chose this moment to leave the house.

The rain had stopped; the pavements steamily shone as Mrs. Drover let herself out by inches from her own front door into the empty street. The unoccupied houses opposite continued to meet her looks with their damaged stare. Making toward the thoroughfare and the taxi, she tried not to keep looking behind. Indeed, the silence was so intense—one of those creeks of London silence exaggerated this summer by the damage of war—that no tread could have gained on hers unheard. Where her

street debouched[8] on the square where people went on living, she grew conscious of, and checked, her unnatural pace. Across the open end of the square two buses <u>impassively</u> passed each other; women, a perambulator, cyclists, a man wheeling a barrow signalized, once again, the ordinary flow of life. At the square's most populous corner should be—and was—the short taxi rank. This evening, only one taxi—but this, although it presented its blank rump, appeared already to be alertly waiting for her. Indeed, without looking round the driver started his engine as she panted up from behind and put her hand on the door. As she did so, the clock struck seven. The taxi faced the main road. To make the trip back to her house it would have to turn—she had settled back on the seat and the taxi *had* turned before she, surprised by its knowing movement, recollected that she had not "said where." She leaned forward to scratch at the glass panel that divided the driver's head from her own.

The driver braked to what was almost a stop, turned round and slid the glass panel back. The jolt of this flung Mrs. Drover forward till her face was almost into the glass. Through the aperture[9] driver and passenger, not six inches between them, remained for an eternity eye to eye. Mrs. Dover's mouth hung open for some seconds before she could issue her first scream. After that she continued to scream freely and to beat with her gloved hands on the glass all round as the taxi, accelerating without mercy, made off with her into the hinterland of deserted streets. ❖

---

7. **passé** (pa sā´). [French] Outdated; past its prime
8. **debouched.** Emerged
9. **aperture.** Opening

> **acute • ness** (ə kyüt´ nəs) *n.,* state of high awareness
> **im • pas • sive** (im[´] pa´ siv) *adj.,* without emotion; expressionless

Mirrors & Windows

Filmmaker Alfred Hitchcock, known for his thrillers, once said, "There is no terror in the bang, only in the anticipation of it." What is frightening about the unknown?

from Testament of Experience

by Vera Brittain

For **Vera Brittain** (1893–1970), as for so many people in the United Kingdom, World War I brought a lifetime of loss—of her brother, her fiancé, and many friends. In 1925, Brittain married George Catlin, the "G" she refers to in the selection; they had two children, Shirley and John. Not long before World War II, the author joined the Anglican Pacifist Fellowship.

Among Brittain's best-known works are the memoirs *Testament of Youth* (1933) and *Testament of Friendship* (1940). The selection is from ***Testament of Experience: An Autobiographical Story of the Years 1925–1950*** (1957). In this excerpt, Brittain remembers how she (and probably much of Europe) felt on hearing that yet another world war had begun. She is aware not only of a sense of disbelief but also of the feeling that, at least in the early days of the war, "the first quality to move into the shadows was truth."

CHAPTER SIX
THE CLOUDS DESCEND

The purple asters lift their heads
Beneath the azure autumn skies;
Above the sunflowers golden cup
Hover the scarlet butterflies.

Not in the sandbagged city street
Where London's silver guardians soar,
But through the cottage garden throbs
The aching grief of England's war.

V.B., September, 1939.

1

When the echo of Neville Chamberlain's trembling voice[1] had died away, the paralysis which held us motionless in the study suddenly broke. John and Shirley—bored as children always are by the anxieties of their elders—vanished into the Forest and the rest of us dispersed.

Escaping from the crowded cottage, which now held eight people, I too set out on a Forest trail. Everything had changed, yet nothing was different. No counterpart of the first siren—a false alarm which startled London within twenty minutes of war's declaration—disturbed the quiet glades round Southampton. When at last I sat down to write an article—"Lift up your Hearts and keep your Heads!"—which had been asked of me in the event of war, its urgency seemed as unreal as the news.

Only when the radio next morning announced the sinking of the liner *Athenia* did we realise that war had indeed begun.

---

1. **Neville Chamberlain's trembling voice.** Chamberlain, the prime minister at the start of World War II, resigned in spring 1940 and was succeeded by Winston Churchill.

St. Paul's Cathedral stands among the burning rubble of London buildings after an air raid on December 29, 1940.

My diary for September 4 gives the news as originally reported: "She remained afloat for some hours and everyone was saved except those killed by the explosion." Actually 112 passengers were lost, including twenty-eight Americans. In the Twilight War, as Churchill afterwards called it, the first quality to move into the shadows was truth.

On Sunday night I had sent a letter to catch G. in London.

"As I write this date, I think to myself incredulously that before long it will be as familiar as August 4th, 1914,[2] and stand for as great significance—but what significance? More misery? A longer or shorter period of terror? Victory or defeat or revolution?"

We were to wait six years for the answers to those questions. Meanwhile we could only live for the moment and its emotions, which permeated the first broadcast speeches.

"Chamberlain's actually making the declaration of war I found moving because he was obviously so greatly upset," I wrote. "But everyone else might have been back in 1914. The same 'devil' who is to blame for everything; the same invocation of 'God and the right'—as though either had anything whatever to do with this business. I had the impression that nobody really meant quite what they were saying and were repeating parts like parrots for the benefit of history. It is so quiet here tonight—unbelievable that we are on the edge of chaos."

In the persistent sunshine of the next few days the wireless announcements seemed grotesque, but they made a bitter mockery of the belated summer. To G. I commented sadly on "the utter failure of all the sincere efforts made for peace through twenty years," and could not yet imagine how time would reveal that this ostensible failure had not been "utter."

Failure is only complete if the hearts and minds of men remain totally untouched. But in September 1939 the Nazis racing towards Warsaw in perfect campaigning weather appeared to have defeated much more than Poland.[3]

2

Submerged in the sunny quiet of gorse and heather, I tried vainly to take in the size of the catastrophe. War came closer when searchlights from the coast flashed meteor-wise across the midnight sky, brilliant streamers which briefly outlined the black beeches outside my bedroom window. Along the pitch-dark country roads, newly-painted white lines sprang suddenly to life as bemused drivers ran into the open beneath the stars, but became part of

---

2. **August 4th, 1914.** Beginning of World War I
3. **September 1939 . . . Poland.** World War II officially started on September 1, when the German army invaded Poland, whose capital is Warsaw.

The Somme **by Lyn MacDonald**

Presented to soldiers as "the Big Push" that would end World War I, the first day of the Battle of the Somme resulted in carnage. MacDonald allows the Tommies (British soldiers) who "went over the top" on that day to tell their stories of initial patriotism—and then the unrelenting horror of the campaign's 142 days.

Cathleen Ni Houlihan **by William Butler Yeats and Lady Augusta Gregory**

It is 1798, the year of a failed Irish rebellion. A mysterious old woman visits the peasant cottage of Michael Gillane, who is about to be married, and invites him to follow her. Early twentieth-century Irish audiences knew the phrase *Cathleen ni Houlihan* as code for "Mother Ireland" and immediately understood the play as a call to the Nationalist cause.

A Portrait of the Artist as a Young Man **by James Joyce**

Joyce's young artist is Stephen Daedelus, so named to evoke the magical craftsman of myth. Stephen's trials at boarding school, his family's political debates, and his growing isolation reveal his intellectual awakening and eventual rebellion against his upbringing. Semiautobiographical, this novel pioneers the Modernist techniques Joyce developed in his later works.

James Joyce **by Edna O'Brien**

Irish novelist O'Brien's spirited biography introduces readers to the child caught in the Joyce family's downward spiral into poverty, as well as the rebellious student, the passionate lover, the embittered émigré from Dublin to the continent, and finally, the semiblind artist lucky enough to discover a wealthy patron to support his Modernist work *Ulysses.*

Troublesome Young Men: The Rebels Who Brought Churchill to Power and Helped Save England **by Lynne Olson**

Not all British politicians supported Prime Minister Neville Chamberlain's policy of appeasing Adolf Hitler in the late 1930s. A number of young Tory politicians clearly understood the menace facing England as Austria, Czechoslovakia, and Poland fell to the Nazis. Rebelling against party leaders, these young men risked their own political futures to bring Churchill to power.

Mrs. Dalloway **by Virginia Woolf**

As Clarissa Dalloway prepares for her party, we observe her through the eyes of acquaintances, a former suitor, and her own musings. Meanwhile, Lucrezia Smith is about to send her husband, a shell-shocked war veteran, to an asylum. By focusing on the seemingly trivial details of her characters' lives, Woolf reveals the soul behind each person's facade.

Conducting an informational interview with a professional about his or her job is a good way to learn about the day-to-day realities of a particular occupation. When planning this type of informational interview, first do some background research on the occupation and then make a list of the questions you would like to ask. You may think of additional questions during the interview, but use your draft to start and structure the session.

1. Use Role-Playing to Prepare for the Interview

To practice interviewing skills, role-play an interview on a topic that does not require much specific knowledge, such as what to do on a Friday night. With a partner, alternate being the *interviewer*, the person who asks the questions, and the *interviewee*, the person who answers the questions. Practice the strategies listed in the following steps.

2. Set Up an Appointment for the Interview

Call or write the person you will interview, and make arrangements to meet in a quiet place. Explain to the interviewee the purpose of your interview and how long you expect the meeting to last. Doing so will help the individual be prepared to answer your questions.

3. Ask Mostly Open-Ended Questions

Avoid asking *closed questions,* which can be answered with a yes or no. Instead, ask *open-ended questions,* which call for an explanation and allow the interviewee to express his or her point of view. Examples of open-ended questions include "What do you find most challenging about being an architect?" and "What advice would you give to a beginning architect?"

At the end of the interview, ask "What would you like to add that I haven't asked about?" This question not only allows the interviewee to provide information you may not have thought of but also gives him or her the chance to share professional insights or experiences.

4. If Possible, Record the Interview

Recording the interview will enable you to replay it later. Be sure to ask the interviewee whether you may record the session before you actually do so. If the answer is no, accept the response graciously.

5. Take Notes During the Interview

Regardless of whether you record the interview, you should take notes. Write down main points and key words from the interviewee's responses to help you remember details. Also write down the interviewee's most important statements word for word. Ask permission to quote his or her statements in any report or oral presentation you will prepare based on the interview.

6. End the Interview on Time

Do not extend the interview beyond the time limits of your appointment. The interviewee has been courteous enough to give you his or her time, so be respectful of the schedule.

7. Write Up the Results of the Interview Promptly

Organize your notes as soon as you can after the interview, and write a brief summary of the information you learned. It is important to do this while your memory of the interview is fresh and you can make sense of all your notes.

If you do not understand an important note or think of another question to ask, contact the interviewee and politely ask for clarification. Make your request as brief as possible to avoid taking too much of the interviewee's time.

SPEAKING & LISTENING RUBRIC

Your interview will be evaluated on these elements:

Preparation

❑ You choose a profession you are interested in and do background research about it.

❑ You make an appointment with someone in that profession, and prepare a list of questions to ask him or her.

❑ You practice interviewing skills by role-playing with a partner.

Content

❑ You ask mostly open-ended questions and take detailed and accurate notes during the interview.

❑ You organize your notes and write a summary of the information you obtained in the interview.

In this unit, you have examined speeches, poems, and posters that the British government used to encourage citizens to support the war effort. These materials were crafted to appeal to the emotions. This purpose also underlies contemporary advertisements, which attempt to persuade people to buy a product or join a cause. With only seconds to gain a consumer's interest, advertisers often rely on emotion to grab attention, appealing to people's need to feel attractive, loved, successful, and respected.

For this assignment, you will analyze an advertisement and write a brief analysis of the techniques used to achieve the intended objective.

> **Assignment** Write an analysis of an advertisement.
>
> **Purpose** To highlight the advertising techniques used to achieve a certain objective
>
> **Audience** Consumers interested in the advertisement's product, service, or cause

❶ Prewrite

Select Your Topic
Flip through magazines, newspapers, or catalogs to find advertisements that are rich in image and message. Choose one that appeals most to you.

Gather Information
Once you have chosen an ad, jot down details to describe what it looks like, including people, figures, and background. Examine how the ad uses wording,

> ### WRITING RUBRIC
>
> A successful media analysis has these qualities:
>
> - ❏ an introduction that paints a vivid picture of the advertisement and states a thesis about its primary theme or objective
> - ❏ a body that identifies and explains the ad's use of advertising techniques and emotional appeals
> - ❏ a conclusion that restates the thesis and offers a final comment about the ad's effectiveness

imagery, composition, type, and colors to elicit a specific reaction or create a particular emotion.

Also consider: What is the advertisement's intended objective? Who might the advertisement be targeting? What should viewers be aware of as they consider their purchase or support? What can you see as a media analyzer that they may not see as a consumer?

Organize Your Ideas
Review your notes and group the related information together. For example, you could cluster all the details that give an overall picture of what is in the advertisement. Then cluster more in-depth information and observations about the model(s) or figures in the advertisement.

Next, prioritize your information and decide which sets of details provide the most insight into the ad. Number the sets of information accordingly. You probably should plan to describe the ad first and then follow with your comments on each advertising technique.

Write Your Thesis Statement
Review your organized information to determine what point you would like to make about the ad and the techniques it employs. Write this point in a single sentence. This will be your **thesis statement.** For example, "The strong visual images of the toys in the advertisement will appeal to impressionable children."

❷ Draft

Write your analysis by following this three-part framework: Introduction, Body, and Conclusion.

> **Introduction** Describe the advertisement and present your thesis statement.
>
> **Body** Outline the advertising techniques used and how they affect the consumer.
>
> **Conclusion** Restate the thesis and summarize how the advertisement achieves its purpose.

Introduction
Describe the visual and sensory details present in the advertisement so your reader will know what it looks like. Weave your thesis statement into the introduction, showing the dominant impact of this image.

Body

Present in detail the various advertising techniques you noted in the Prewrite stage. Follow the order you have already decided. Refer to your thesis statement as you present details.

Conclusion

Tie all the information together, stating clearly how the advertising techniques achieve the intended objective. For example, "The advertisement's use of bold color, shocking imagery, and provocative wording should reach out and grab teens by the neck and cause them to think twice about drinking and driving."

What Great Writers Do

It can seem overwhelming to take on a writing project with as many components as your advertisement analysis. John Gardner, a twentieth-century American novelist, offered this advice: "Writing . . . is like heading out over the open sea in a small boat. It helps if you have a plan and a course laid out."

GARDNER

---

❸ Revise

Evaluate Your Draft

Evaluate your advertisement analysis or exchange it with a classmate's to evaluate each other's work.

Start by looking at the content and organization. Can readers visualize the ad from the description given? Will they understand the thesis statement and know how it fits with the description? Does the body give specific examples of advertising techniques to clarify the thesis statement? Are details presented in an order that readers can easily follow? Are clusters of related details set in separate paragraphs, each introduced by a clear transition and topic sentence? Does the conclusion tie all of the information together to reinforce the thesis statement?

Use the Revision Checklist on this page to help you evaluate the analysis. Make notes directly on the draft about changes to be made. Check each sentence for grammar, spelling, and wording mistakes. Make sure you have correctly used the concepts outlined in the Grammar & Style workshops in this unit.

Revise for Content, Organization, and Style

Read the comments made on your draft; implement applicable comments as you revise your draft.

Proofread for Errors

Now look for remaining mistakes, using proofreader's symbols to mark any you find. Then print out a final draft and read it aloud before turning it in; this will help you catch remaining errors.

Writing Follow-Up

Publish and Present

- Create your own ad. Use some of the techniques you detailed in your analysis. When you are finished, bind the class's ads together. Do you notice any common subjects and techniques?

Reflect

- What have you learned about advertising? How might you use this information to help you make better purchasing decisions in the future?
- What do you think about the larger effects of advertising? Do ads plant unhealthy desires? Or do they motivate people to improve their lives?

REVISION CHECKLIST

Content & Organization

- ❏ Does the description of the ad create a clear picture for someone unfamiliar with it?
- ❏ Is the thesis statement regarding the advertisement and its impact clear?
- ❏ Is the ad's objective identified? Does the writer use sufficient details to reveal the techniques used to achieve this objective?
- ❏ Is the analysis thorough? Does it include an introduction with a thesis, a body that scrutinizes the advertising techniques, and a conclusion that ties the argument together?

Grammar & Style

- ❏ Have you correctly placed commas, using them only where necessary? (page 972)
- ❏ Are other forms of punctuation—colons, semicolons, hyphens, ellipses, and dashes—applied appropriately? (pages 995 and 1091)

Reading Skills

Analyze Point of View

Point of view is the perspective from which a story is told. There are three main points of view. In **first-person** point of view, the narrator uses words such as *I* and *we*. In **second-person** point of view, the narrator uses *you*. In **third-person** point of view, the narrator uses words such as *he, she, it,* and *they*.

Most literature is written from either the first-person point of view or the third-person point of view. In stories written from first-person point of view, the narrator may be a participant or a witness of the action. In stories told from a third-person point of view, the narrator generally stands outside the action. In some stories the narrator's point of view is **limited,** meaning that the narrator can reveal only his or her private, internal thoughts or the thoughts of a single character. In other stories, the narrator's point of view is **omniscient.** In such stories, the narrator can reveal the private thoughts of any character.

Stream of consciousness is a literary technique that describes a character's point of view by revealing his or her's thought processes. With this style of writing, readers need to synthesize fragmentary feelings and thoughts. One of its advantages is that it is more true to life because people's own thoughts do not tend to occur in an orderly, logical fashion. It also provides a feeling of intimacy so readers can get closer to a character.

Once you have identified which point of view the author is using, then you can analyze how effective it is. Consider what the author was able to relate by using this point of view and how the work would be different if another point of view had been used.

> **TEST-TAKING TIP**
>
> Do what you can to reduce test anxiety, but don't despair if you still find yourself somewhat anxious when starting the test. A little nervousness can work in your favor by making you more alert and careful.

Practice

Directions: Read the following passage from *A Portrait of the Artist as a Young Man*, a novel by James Joyce. The questions that come after it will ask you to analyze the point of view.

Once upon a time and a very good time it was there was a moocow coming down along the road and this moocow that was coming down along the road met a nicens
5 little boy named baby tuckoo. . . .

His father told him that story: his father looked at him through a glass: he had a hairy face.

He was baby tuckoo. The moocow came
10 down the road where Betty Byrne lived: she sold lemon platt.

O, the wild rose blossoms
On the little green place.

15 He sang that song. That was his song.

O, the green wothe botheth.

When you wet the bed first it is warm then it gets cold. His mother put on the oilsheet. That had the queer smell.

His mother had a nicer smell than his
20 father. She played on the piano the sailor's hornpipe for him to dance. He danced:

Tralala lala
Tralala tralaladdy
Tralala lala
25 *Tralala lala.*

Uncle Charles and Dante clapped. They were older than his father and mother but uncle Charles was older than Dante.

Dante had two brushes in her press. The
30 brush with the maroon velvet back was for Michael Davitt and the brush with the green velvet back was for Parnell. Dante gave him a cachou every time he brought her a piece of tissue paper.
35 The Vances lived in number seven. They had a different father and mother. They were Eileen's father and mother. When they were grown up he was going to marry Eileen. He hid under the table. His mother said:

40 —O, Stephen will apologise.

Dante said:

—O, if not, the eagles will come and pull out his eyes.

Pull out his eyes,
45 *Apologise,*
Apologise,
Pull out his eyes.

Apologise,
Pull out his eyes,
50 *Pull out his eyes,*
Apologise.

Multiple Choice

1. In lines 1–15, who is the observer?
   A. a young child
   B. a moocow
   C. a father
   D. Dante

2. The main reason song lines are included in this piece is because they
   F. provide a historical perspective.
   G. are what pops into the mind of the observer.
   H. offer relief from the other text.
   J. reveal all that is happening in the scene.

3. In lines 1–15, what is the point of view?
   A. first person
   B. second person
   C. third person
   D. stream of consciousness

4. What purpose does stream-of-consciousness writing serve here?
   F. It keeps the action moving.
   G. It helps the reader understand the plot.
   H. It reveals Stephen's abstract thoughts.
   J. It keeps the audience distanced from the subject.

Constructed Response

5. In this selection, Joyce does not use the usual format for dialogue—that is, with tag lines that identify the speaker and with quotation marks. Using evidence from the excerpt, discuss why he might have made this decision.

Writing Skills

Write a Good Conclusion

Because the conclusion is the last thing the reader will encounter, it is crucial to the essay. In the conclusion, you should bring together the main ideas and create a sense of closure to the issue you raised in your thesis statement.

There are many possible ways to do this. Depending on your essay, some techniques might work better than others, but there is no one correct way of writing a good conclusion. Think about what would be effective for your essay when considering the following options:

- *Summarizing or restating your main points* is probably the easiest technique. Its strength is that the reader is left with a clear understanding of your main points. Try to use different, interesting, and strong words.
- *Generalizing or linking your main idea to a broader issue* has the advantage of increasing the relevance of your subject. If using this technique, be sure that you do not make too big a leap.
- *Expanding on your main idea by connecting it to the reader's own interests* is similar to the previous technique but makes the subject of your essay seem even more relevant. You need to have a thorough understanding of your reader to make this technique work well, however.
- *Calling on the reader to adopt a view or take an action* is a forceful way to end an essay. It is a plea or an order, addressed directly to the reader.

> **TEST-TAKING TIP**
>
> Do not write an overly long conclusion that states the same ideas in several ways.

Practice

Timed Writing: 30 minutes

For various reasons, including the cost of building and maintaining schools, there is increasingly more talk about schools having classes year round rather than closing during the summer. Some people think a twelve-month school year is a good idea. Others are opposed to lengthening the school year. In your opinion, should the school year be extended?

In your essay, take a position on this question. You may write about either one of the two perspectives given, or you may present a different perspective on this question. Use specific reasons and examples to support your position.

Revising and Editing Skills

Some standardized tests ask you to read a draft of an essay and answer questions about how to improve it. As you read the draft, watch for errors such as these:

- incorrect spellings
- disagreement between subject and verb; inconsistent verb tense; incorrect forms for irregular verbs; sentence fragments and run-ons; double negatives; and incorrect use of frequently confused words, such as *affect* and *effect*
- missing end marks, incorrect comma use, and lowercased proper nouns and proper adjectives

- unclear purpose, unclear main ideas, and lack of supporting details
- confusing order of ideas and missing transitions
- language that is inappropriate to the audience and purpose, and mood that is inappropriate for the purpose

After checking for errors, read each test question and decide which answer is best.

Practice

Directions: In the passage that follows, certain words and phrases are numbered and underlined. In the questions below the passage, you will find alternatives for each underlined word or phrase. In each case, choose the alternative that best expresses the idea that is worded most consistently with the style and tone of the rest of the passage, or that makes the text correct according to the conventions of standard written English. If you think the original version is best, choose the first alternative, MAKE NO CHANGE. To indicate your answer, circle the letter of the chosen alternative.

(1) Another point is that time-off is important in the <u>lives of my fellow students and I</u>. (2) Vacation is necessary <u>for it's relaxing and rejuvenating effects</u>. (3) Just a week <u>or two don't provide enough time off for</u> this purpose. (4) All education does not take place at <u>school; much is learned elsewhere</u>.

Multiple Choice

1. A. MAKE NO CHANGE.
   B. life of my fellow students and I
   C. lifes of my fellow students and I
   D. lives of my fellow students and me

2. F. MAKE NO CHANGE.
   G. for its relaxing and rejuvenating effects
   H. for it's relaxing and rejuvenating affects
   J. since it's relaxing and rejuvenating effects

3. A. MAKE NO CHANGE.
   B. or two will not provide enough time off for
   C. or two doesn't provide enough time off for
   D. or two don't provide enough time off for

4. F. MAKE NO CHANGE.
   G. school, much is learned elsewhere
   H. school; much is learned else where
   J. school; much are learned elsewhere

Drosie in Malindi, 1992. Richard Onyango

Postmodern Era

Unit 9

PART 1

Realizations

*"Do not go gentle into that good night.
Rage, rage against the dying of the light."*

—DYLAN THOMAS

PART 2

Colonial Voices

*"He had many wonderful ideas and this was
an opportunity to put them into practice."*

—CHINUA ACHEBE

1945–Present

Postmodern Era 1945–Present

1945   1960

BRITISH LITERATURE BRITISH LITERATURE BRITISH LITERATURE BRITISH LIT

1948
T. S. Eliot is awarded the Nobel Prize for literature

1949
George Orwell publishes *1984*

1950
C. S. Lewis publishes *The Lion, the Witch and the Wardrobe*

1951
Graham Greene publishes *The End of the Affair*

1952
Samuel Beckett publishes *Waiting for Godot*

1954
William Golding publishes *Lord of the Flies*

1954
Iris Murdoch publishes *Under the Net*

1959
Chinua Achebe publishes *Things Fall Apart*

1962
Anthony Burgess publishes *A Clockwork Orange*

1966
Tom Stoppard's *Rosencrantz & Guildenstern Are Dead* is performed for the first time at the Edinburgh Fringe Festival

1969
John Fowles publishes *The French Lieutenant's Woman*

1971
V. S. Naipaul publishes *In a Free State*

1972
John Berger publishes *G*

STOPPARD

BRITISH HISTORY BRITISH HISTORY BRITISH HISTORY BRITISH HISTORY BRIT

1947
India gains independence from the United Kingdom

1948
Parliament founds the National Health Service, providing free health care to all British citizens

1948
Malaysians rebel against British rule

1951
The Mau-Mau rebellion erupts between Kenyans and British soldiers in Kenya

1952
Elizabeth II becomes Queen of Britain

1956
The Suez Crisis occurs as Britain, Israel, and France fight against Egypt

1960
The United Kingdom joins the European Free Trade Association

1969
The Irish Republican Army (IRA) splits into the Official IRA and the Provisional IRA

1973
The United Kingdom joins the European Community (now the European Union)

1974
The British government legalizes Sinn Féin, a nationalist party in Northern Ireland

Northern Ireland (UK)

Republic of Ireland

WORLD HISTORY WORLD HISTORY WORLD HISTORY WORLD HISTORY WORLD

1948
Mohandas Gandhi is assassinated in India

1948
The state of Israel is founded

1949
The Communist People's Republic of China, led by Mao Zedong, assumes control of China

1957
The USSR launches *Sputnik I*, the first artificial satellite

1959
The Vietnam War begins

1959
Fidel Castro leads the Cuban revolution and assumes leadership of the nation

MAO

1960
Seventeen African states gain independence from European colonial rule

1961
The Berlin Wall is built between East and West Germany

1963
Martin Luther King Jr. delivers his "I Have a Dream" speech in a Civil Rights march on Washington, DC

1969
U.S. astronauts are the first humans to land on the moon

1971
Idi Amin seizes power in Uganda, resulting in years of internal bloodshed and turmoil

1975
The Vietnam War ends

BRITISH LITERATURE BRITISH LITERATURE BRITISH LITERATURE BRITISH LITERATU

1980
Salman Rushdie publishes *Midnight's Children*

1983
William Golding is awarded the Nobel Prize for literature

1984
Anita Desai publishes *In Custody*

1985
Margaret Atwood publishes *The Handmaid's Tale*

1986
Wole Soyinka is awarded the Nobel Prize for literature

1989
Kazuo Ishiguro publishes *The Remains of the Day*

DESAI

1991
Nadine Gordimer is awarded the Nobel Prize for literature

1995
Seamus Heaney is awarded the Nobel Prize for literature

1997
J. K. Rowling publishes *Harry Potter and the Sorcerer's Stone*

2000
Matthew Kneale publishes *English Passengers*

2001
V. S. Naipaul is awarded the Nobel Prize for literature

2005
Harold Pinter is awarded the Nobel Prize for literature

2007
Doris Lessing is awarded the Nobel Prize for literature

ORY BRITISH HISTORY BRITISH HISTORY BRITISH HISTORY BRITISH HISTORY BRITIS

1979
Margaret Thatcher becomes prime minister; she holds the position until 1990

1981
The British Social Democratic party is founded

1981
The Brixton Riot breaks out under severe racial and economic tensions in south London

1982
The United Kingdom fights Argentina for control of the Falkland Islands

1984
A year-long miners' strike begins in the United Kingdom

1992
Devaluation of the British pound on September 16, Black Wednesday, puts the economy into the worst financial condition since the 1930s

1994
The "Chunnel," an underwater rail link between Britain and the European mainland, is completed

1997
Great Britain returns Hong Kong to China

1998
The Good Friday Agreement provides a major step toward peace in Northern Ireland

1999
The House of Lords Act is passed, mostly removing its members' right of inheritance

2007
Gordon Brown succeeds Tony Blair as prime minister

ORLD HISTORY WORLD HISTORY WORLD HISTORY WORLD HISTORY WORLD HISTOR

1980
Mount St. Helens erupts in the United States

1985
The Nevado del Ruiz volcano erupts in Colombia, killing 23,000 people

1986
Swedish Prime Minister Olof Palme is assassinated

1989
The Tiananmen Square protests result in violence between the Chinese government and political activists

1989
The Berlin Wall comes down, reuniting East and West Germany

1991
The Soviet Union collapses, ending the Cold War

1993
The World Wide Web opens for public use

1994
The apartheid government ends in South Africa

2001
Al-Qaeda attacks the United States on September 11

2004
Countries bordering the Indian Ocean are devastated by a major earthquake and resulting tsunamis

"This last year has reminded us that this world is not always an easy or safe place to live in."

—QUEEN ELIZABETH II (2005)

The Cold War

As World War II was ending in 1945, Great Britain, the Soviet Union, and the United States—represented by Winston Churchill, Joseph Stalin, and Franklin Roosevelt and Harry Truman, respectively—divided Germany into spheres of influence. Eastern Germany came under Soviet control, which solidified the Soviet Union's position in Eastern Europe.

Subsequently, the Soviets were able to install communist dictatorships over much of Eastern Europe and the Balkan states. Speaking in the United States in 1946, Prime Minister Winston Churchill declared that an "iron curtain" had fallen across the continent, dividing East and West. Symbolic of the division of Europe was the Berlin Wall in Germany, which the communists erected in 1961 to divide Soviet-controlled East Berlin from West Berlin.

For the next several decades, world politics was dominated by struggles between communist states, especially the Soviet Union, and democratic countries in Western Europe and North America. By the late

1980s, however, the Soviet Union had begun to disintegrate. In December 1991, the Soviet Union officially was dissolved and replaced by the far smaller Commonwealth of Independent States, consisting of Russia and most of the former republics. To many people's amazement, the Cold War had ended.

Postwar Britain

Following World War II, British voters rejected the Conservative Party of Prime Minister Winston Churchill. Believing that private companies had failed abysmally during the 1930s, the new Labour government took over basic industries, including coal, steel, electricity, and the railroads, and instituted free health care and education. Economic recovery was slow, however, and wartime rationing of meat, sugar, butter, eggs, and clothing continued.

In 1951, the Festival of Britain celebrated the centenary of the Great Exhibition, the first world's fair, which had been held in London's Hyde Park in 1851. The festival focused on promoting good design in rebuilding war-ravaged cities and presenting an optimistic outlook for the future. A year later, Queen Elizabeth II was crowned after the death of her father, King George VI. While the monarchy was viewed primarily as a ceremonial institution, most Britons continued to support it for the sake of tradition.

Britain's diminishing international power was revealed by the Suez Crisis in 1956. Intent on collecting the tariffs charged for passage through the Suez Canal, Egypt nationalized the waterway, converting it from private to state ownership. This action drew concern worldwide, as two-thirds of Europe's oil supply was being moved through the Suez Canal. In addition, British banks had a substantial investment in the waterway. To regain control, Great Britain, France, and Israel sent troops into the area.

NOTABLE NUMBERS

40 Years the Indian National Congress struggled for independence from Great Britain

500,000 People killed in antipartition riots in India before 1947

28 Years the Berlin Wall divided West and East Germany

15,000 Workers who produced the thirty-one-mile Channel Tunnel, or "Chunnel," connecting England and France in 1994

500 Deaths from violence in Northern Ireland in 1972, the peak year of unrest

Although the invasion was a military success, it was a political disaster. Large numbers of British citizens protested, the Soviet Union threatened to bomb London, and the United States demanded withdrawal while withholding a much needed billion-dollar loan. Humiliated, Britain withdrew from Egypt.

Independence for Britain's Colonies

Under pressure from nationalist movements within its colonies, Great Britain began dismantling its empire over the postwar decades. India gained independence in 1947, following successful nonviolent protests led by Mohandas Gandhi. Although Gandhi advocated for a single independent state, the British partitioned the territory into a Hindu state, India, and a Muslim state, Pakistan. The partition left millions on the wrong side of a border and resulted in deadly riots and a massive transfer of population. Transition also led to conflict in Malaya (now Malaysia), where Britain found itself fighting communist guerrillas, and in Palestine, which Britain ultimately handed over to the United Nations.

In Africa, the British spent six years putting down the Mau-Mau rebellion in Kenya before granting the colony independence in 1963. In southern Africa, white settlers resisted British efforts to enact universal suffrage (voting rights) and majority rule. Both southern Rhodesia (now Zimbabwe) and South Africa severed ties with Great Britain and established apartheid

Nigerians celebrate their independence on December 16, 1959, a few months before the official declaration.

(segregation) policies. Other colonies in Africa and Asia also became independent, including Burma (now Myanmar), Ceylon (now Sri Lanka), Ghana, Nigeria, Sudan, northern Rhodesia (now Zambia), Trinidad and Tobago, and Uganda. The last colonial war occurred in 1982, when Great Britain sent troops to retake the tiny Falkland Islands from Argentina. Finally, in 1997, Britain handed over Hong Kong to China.

The Commonwealth became the successor to the British Empire. Headed by the British monarch, the Commonwealth is a loose affiliation of nations formerly ruled by Great Britain. It was created to foster peace, democracy, and equal rights and to eliminate poverty, ignorance, and disease.

"The wind of change is blowing through [Africa]. Whether we like it or not, this growth of national consciousness is a political fact."

— PRIME MINISTER HAROLD MACMILLAN

Domestic Issues

The 1960s and 1970s saw a radical revolt among British youth, who challenged the values and traditions of their elders. In the early sixties, British rock 'n' roll groups such as the Beatles and the Rolling Stones became extremely popular, and teenagers around the globe imitated the hairstyles and dress of these groups in what became known as the "British invasion."

Throughout this period, neither Labour nor Conservative party policies were able to produce consistent economic recovery in Great Britain. In 1973, Britain joined the European Community (EC), an organization of western European states formed to oversee trade between member countries.

In 1979, when a public service workers' strike shut down much of Great Britain, voters turned to the Conservatives, led by Margaret Thatcher. As prime minister, she returned to private ownership industries that had been taken over by the government after World War II. During her term, Parliament passed legislation that made it more difficult for workers to strike, broke the miners' union, and cut back social programs.

Massive protests erupted in response to Thatcher's 1990 poll tax to fund local services, under which rich and poor paid the same rate. This move, coupled with a significant economic downturn, led to her resignation in 1992. Her successor, Conservative Prime Minister John Major, repealed the poll tax but faced conflict over Britain's participation in the European Union (EU, formerly the EC).

Beginning in 1997, the Labour party, led by Prime Minister Tony Blair, enacted minimum-wage legislation, increased spending on health and education, and allowed citizens in Scotland and Wales to vote on increased self-governance. Scotland established its own parliament, and Wales set up an assembly.

The Blair government strongly supported the United States in its declared War on Terror, participating in the invasions of Afghanistan in 2001 and Iraq in 2003. Blair lost favor, however, for his continued support of the U.S. mission in Iraq and in 2007 was succeeded by the new Labour party leader, Gordon Brown.

Northern Ireland

In 1968, violence erupted during a march for Catholic civil rights in Northern Ireland, where manipulation of voting districts had kept Protestants in power. When

British auto workers strike in Birmingham (1979).

rioting became widespread, the Northern Ireland government called in British troops, which were unable to restore peace. The Irish Republican Army (IRA), which wanted to reunite Northern Ireland with the Republic of Ireland in a single independent state, had waged periodic attacks on both sides of the border in the years since the 1922 partition. Outlawed by both Irish governments, the IRA had gone underground.

After the outbreak of violence in 1968, the IRA split into a nonterrorist wing and a terrorist organization known as the Provisionals. Violence spiraled as the Provisional IRA began a bombing campaign and Protestant paramilitary groups retaliated.

In 1972, Britain dissolved the Northern Ireland Parliament. A year later, the British prime minister, the Irish Republic's prime minister, and Northern Ireland's executive started power-sharing talks between Catholics and Protestants. Negotiations spanned decades, while the violence continued. Finally, in 1998, the Good Friday Agreement established a timetable to achieve power sharing and to disarm paramilitary groups. Since then, militant groups have vacillated between violating and following the accord.

Advances in Science and Technology

Amazing developments in medicine and technology were made during the 1990s. One of the most significant was the availability of a vast amount of information and entertainment on the Internet. The World Wide Web opened for public use in 1993, and soon users were zooming across cyberspace.

With funding from the international Human Genome Project, scientists began mapping all of the genes on human DNA, discovering new genes and the roles they play in disease. In 1997, British researchers announced they had successfully cloned a lamb named Dolly from the single cell of an adult sheep.

The 1990s also brought increased awareness of environmental hazards, such as global warming and acid rain, and recognition that the world's most difficult problems are tied to the world population explosion. As people work to address these issues, twenty-first century society reflects an increasingly global community.

As a result of war, economic depression, a pervasive sense that technology is out of control, and a cynicism about culture itself, much of the literature in the latter part of the twentieth century is marked by themes of alienation, negation, and emptiness. A notable exception, however, is the work of Dylan Thomas, which focuses on timeless themes of youth, aging, and death.

Isolation is seen in the poetry of Stevie Smith and Philip Larkin, in the plays of Harold Pinter, and in the stories of Graham Greene. In "Not Waving but Drowning," Smith portrays the drowning man's ill-fated attempts to connect with people onshore; Larkin examines human alienation in "Home Is So Sad." Pinter's plays reflect the inability of people to communicate effectively with each other, with characters often becoming more isolated through their speech and actions. Greene addresses the isolation that results from emotional pain.

A sense of alienation also caused some writers to reexamine the roles people had created for themselves. Margaret Atwood questions the traditional ideas of ownership and explores the relationship between humanity and the natural world in "The Moment." In the essay "Shooting an Elephant," George Orwell focuses on how British imperialism affected the relationships between people. Poet Seamus Heaney explores the effect of the past on the lives of the people living in the present. As British society in the twentieth century continued to change, these realizations helped people understand their role in a changing world.

Untitled, 1987. Susan Rowland.
Chisholm Gallery, West Palm Beach, Florida.

Shooting an Elephant
An Essay by George Orwell

Build Background

Literary Context **"Shooting an Elephant"** is an essay in which the author recalls an incident that took place in Burma during his years as a police officer of the Imperial British government. An elephant has run mad and trampled a man to death. The author is called on to respond and finds he must choose between doing what he feels is right and doing what he believes the natives expect of him as a representative of the power of the British crown.

Reader's Context Recall a time when you felt peer pressure. How did you respond to the pressure? Did your choice lead to feelings of regret or satisfaction? Why?

Meet the Author

George Orwell (1903–1950), the pseudonym of Eric Arthur Blair, is well known for his satirical and political writings. He was born in India, where his father was a British official in the Indian civil service. The young Orwell won a scholarship to Eton, one of England's leading secondary schools, but was financially unable to continue his university education at Oxford or Cambridge.

From 1922 to 1927, Orwell worked for the imperial police in Burma (now known as Myanmar); the experience provided much of the material for his early work, including the novel *Burmese Days* (1934). It also led to his dislike of imperialism, a feeling he reiterates throughout "Shooting an Elephant" (1936).

After resigning from the imperial police, Orwell worked for several years at menial, low-paying jobs. He described his experiences with poverty in *Down and Out in Paris and London* (1933). His experiences in the Spanish Civil War, in which he fought on the Republican side against General Francisco Franco, are recounted in *Homage to Catalonia* (1939).

An early convert to socialism, Orwell was angered not only by imperialism but also by sociopolitical systems that undermine human freedom, which also included fascism, capitalism, and Stalinism (the ruthless authoritarian policies of the Soviet Union under Vladimir Lenin and Joseph Stalin). Orwell's two best-known novels, *Animal Farm* (1945) and *Nineteen Eighty-Four* (1949), are attacks on Soviet-style totalitarianism. Orwell's other works include *Keep the Aspidistra Flying* (1936), *Coming Up for Air* (1939), and the posthumously published *Collected Essays, Journalism and Letters* (1968). Orwell died of tuberculosis in London at the age of forty-six.

Analyze Literature

Thesis and Irony
A **thesis** is a main idea that is supported in a work of nonfiction. It may be directly stated or inferred.

Irony is a difference between appearance and reality. Types of irony include *dramatic irony*, in which something is known by the reader but unknown to the characters; *verbal irony*, in which a character says one thing but means another; and *situational irony*, in which an event occurs that violates the expectations of the characters or reader.

Set Purpose

Orwell's experiences working for the imperial police in Burma influenced his attitude toward imperialism, which he explores in the essay "Shooting an Elephant." While you read, identify Orwell's thesis and look for the evidence he presents to support it. Also list the examples of irony in the selection. Consider what types of irony Orwell uses and how the use of irony supports his thesis.

Preview Vocabulary

supplant, 1114
prostrate, 1114
despotic, 1115
labyrinth, 1115
squalid, 1115
garish, 1117
futility, 1117
resolute, 1117
senility, 1119
pretext, 1119

African Elephants, c. 1800s. Charles Emile de Tournemine. Musée d'Orsay, Paris, France. (See detail on page 1112.)

Shooting an Elephant

by George Orwell

*When the white man turns tyrant
it is his own freedom that he destroys.*

In Moulmein, in Lower Burma, I was hated by large numbers of people—the only time in my life that I have been important enough for this to happen to me. I was subdivisional police officer of the town, and in an aimless, petty kind of way anti-European feeling was very bitter. No one had the guts to raise a riot, but if a European woman went through the bazaars alone somebody would probably spit betel juice[1] over her dress. As a police officer I was an obvious target and was baited whenever it seemed safe to do so. When a nimble Burman tripped me up on the football field and the referee (another Burman) looked the other way, the crowd yelled with hideous laughter. This happened more than once. In the end the sneering yellow faces of young men that met me everywhere, the insults hooted after me when I was at a safe distance, got badly on my

---

1. **betel juice.** Juice of the nuts and leaves of the betel palm, a tree in Asia

Shwe-zee-gon Pagoda in Myanmar (formerly Burma).

nerves. The young Buddhist priests were the worst of all. There were several thousands of them in the town and none of them seemed to have anything to do except stand on street corners and jeer at Europeans.

All this was perplexing and upsetting. For at that time I had already made up my mind that imperialism was an evil thing and the sooner I chucked up my job and got out of it the better. Theoretically—and secretly, of course—I was all for the Burmese and all against their oppressors, the British. As for the job I was doing, I hated it more bitterly than I can perhaps make clear. In a job like that you see the dirty work of Empire at close quarters. The wretched prisoners huddling in the stinking cages of the lock-ups, the grey, cowed faces of the long-term convicts, the scarred buttocks of the men who had been flogged with bamboos—all these oppressed me with an intolerable sense of guilt. But I could get nothing into perspective. I was young and ill-educated and I had had to think out my problems in the utter silence that is imposed on every Englishman in the East. I did not even know that the British Empire is dying, still less did I know that it is a great deal better than the younger empires that are going to <u>supplant</u> it. All I knew was that I was stuck between my hatred of the empire I served and my rage against the evil-spirited little beasts who tried to make my job impossible. With one part of my mind I thought of the British Raj[2] as an unbreakable tyranny, as something clamped down, *in saecula saeculorum*,[3] upon the will of <u>prostrate</u> peoples; with another part I thought that the greatest joy in the world would be to

---

2. **Raj.** Rule
3. ***in saecula saeculorum.*** [Latin] Forever and ever

---

sup • plant (sə plant´) *v.*, take the place of and serve as a substitute for
pros • trate (prä´ strāt') *adj.*, completely overcome and lacking the will or power to rise

drive a bayonet into a Buddhist priest's guts. Feelings like these are the normal by-products of imperialism; ask any Anglo-Indian official, if you can catch him off duty.

I did not know what I could do, but I wanted to see what was happening.

One day something happened which in a roundabout way was enlightening. It was a tiny incident in itself, but it gave me a better glimpse than I had had before of the real nature of imperialism—the real motives for which despotic governments act. Early one morning the sub-inspector at a police station at the other end of the town rang me up on the 'phone and said that an elephant was ravaging the bazaar. Would I please come and do something about it? I did not know what I could do, but I wanted to see what was happening and I got on to a pony and started out. I took my rifle, an old .44 Winchester and much too small to kill an elephant, but I thought the noise might be useful *in terrorem.*[4] Various Burmans stopped me on the way and told me about the elephant's doings. It was not, of course, a wild elephant, but a tame one which had gone "must."[5] It had been chained up, as tame elephants always are when their attack of "must" is due, but on the previous night it had broken its chain and escaped. Its mahout,[6] the only person who could manage it when it was in that state, had set out in pursuit, but had taken the wrong direction and was now twelve hours' journey away, and in the morning the elephant had suddenly reappeared in the town. The Burmese population had no weapons and were quite helpless against it. It had already destroyed somebody's bamboo hut, killed a cow and raided some fruit-stalls and devoured the stock; also it had met the municipal rubbish van and, when the driver jumped out and took to his heels, had turned the van over and inflicted violences upon it.

The Burmese sub-inspector and some Indian constables were waiting for me in the quarter where the elephant had been seen. It was a very poor quarter, a labyrinth of squalid bamboo huts, thatched with palm-leaf, winding all over a steep hillside. I remember that it was a cloudy, stuffy morning at the beginning of the rains. We began questioning the people as to where the elephant had gone and, as usual, failed to get any definite information. That is invariably the case in the East; a story always sounds clear enough at a distance, but the nearer you get to the scene of the events the vaguer it becomes. Some of the people said that the elephant had gone in one direction, some said that he had gone in another, some professed not even to have heard of any elephant. I had almost made up my mind that the whole story was a pack of lies, when we heard yells a little distance away. There was a loud, scandalized cry of "Go away, child! Go away this instant!" and an old woman with a switch in her hand come round the corner of a hut, violently shooing away a crowd of naked children. Some more women followed, clicking their tongues and exclaiming; evidently there was something that the children ought not to have seen. I rounded the hut and saw a man's dead body sprawling in the mud. He was an Indian, a black Dravidian[7] coolie,[8] almost naked, and he could not have been dead many minutes. The people said that the elephant had come suddenly upon him round the corner of the hut, caught him with its trunk, put its foot on his

---

4. *in terrorem.* [Latin] In order to frighten
5. **must.** Mating period for male elephants, characterized by dangerous frenzies
6. **mahout.** Elephant trainer or keeper
7. **Dravidian.** One of a race of people living in southern India
8. **coolie.** Worker or laborer

---

des • pot • ic (des pä′ tik) *adj.,* of, relating to, or characteristic of a tyrant
lab • y • rinth (la′ bə rin[t]th′) *n.,* place full of intricate pathways and blind alleys
squal • id (skwä′ ləd) *adj.,* marked by filthiness from neglect or poverty

1984 and Stalin

George Orwell's most famous work is his final novel, *1984*, which explores a disheartingly bleak future society. In the novel's fictional universe, a totalitarian government controls every aspect of its citizens' lives. The government is personified through a single figure, called simply "Big Brother," and uses its advanced technology to enslave its citizens, thereby perpetuating its own ruling power.

Orwell's inspiration for writing *1984* came in part from his observations of Stalinist Russia in the 1930s and 1940s. This dark era of history began after the death of Soviet leader Vladimir Lenin in 1924, when Josef Stalin, a high-ranking government official, began consolidating all of the state's power. He denounced and deposed all opposition as traitors to the Soviet cause.

Once Stalin had ascended to the top of the Soviet government, he created a secret police force that tortured and killed dissenters. He also took over all forms of media and censored any printed material he deemed contrary to the party agenda. Perhaps most sadistically, Stalin initiated a famine in 1933 that killed more than six million peasants because he suspected they were planning to revolt. During his rule, Stalin was responsible for approximately twenty million deaths, according to historians.

Orwell grew concerned about the increasing expansion of the Soviet Empire after the end of World War II, and he wanted to expose some of the atrocious human rights violations taking place within it. He believed that the United Kingdom, with its increasingly stratified classes and growing centralized power, was becoming more like the despotic government that had been terrorizing Russians for decades. Although the Stalinist regime has long since vanished, many people still regard *1984* as an extremely relevant warning about the consequences of unchecked power.

---

back and ground him into the earth. This was the rainy season and the ground was soft, and his face had scored[9] a trench a foot deep and a couple of yards long. He was lying on his belly with arms crucified and head sharply twisted to one side. His face was coated with mud, the eyes wide open, the teeth bared and grinning with an expression of unendurable agony. (Never tell me, by the way, that the dead look peaceful. Most of the corpses I have seen looked devilish.) The friction of the great beast's foot had stripped the skin from his back as neatly as one skins a rabbit. As soon as I saw the dead man I sent an orderly to a friend's house nearby to borrow an elephant rifle. I had already sent back the pony, not wanting it to go mad with fright and throw me if it smelt the elephant.

The orderly came back in a few minutes with a rifle and five cartridges, and meanwhile some Burmans had arrived and told us that the elephant was in the paddy fields[10] below, only a few hundred yards away. As I started forward practically the whole population of the quarter flocked out of the houses and followed me. They had seen the rifle and were all shouting excitedly that I was going to shoot the elephant. They had not shown much interest in the elephant when he was merely ravaging their homes, but it was different now that he was going to be shot. It was a bit of fun to them, as it would be to an English crowd; besides they wanted the meat. It made me vaguely uneasy. I had no intention of shooting the elephant—I merely sent for the rifle to defend myself if necessary—and it is always unnerving to have a crowd following you. I marched down the hill, looking and feeling a fool, with the rifle over my shoulder and an ever-growing army of people jostling at my heels. At the bottom, when you got away from the huts, there was a metalled road[11]

---

9. **scored.** Marked
10. **paddy fields.** Rice fields
11. **metalled road.** Road reinforced with metal strips

and beyond that a miry waste of paddy fields a thousand yards across, not yet ploughed but soggy from the first rains and dotted with coarse grass. The elephant was standing eight yards from the road, his left side towards us. He took not the slightest notice of the crowd's approach. He was tearing up bunches of grass, beating them against his knees to clean them and stuffing them into his mouth.

I had halted on the road. As soon as I saw the elephant I knew with perfect certainty that I ought not to shoot him. It is a serious matter to shoot a working elephant—it is comparable to destroying a huge and costly piece of machinery—and obviously one ought not to do it if it can possibly be avoided. And at that distance, peacefully eating, the elephant looked no more dangerous than a cow. I thought then and I think now that his attack of "must" was already passing off; in which case he would merely wander harmlessly about until the mahout came back and caught him. Moreover, I did not in the least want to shoot him. I decided that I would watch him for a little while to make sure that he did not turn savage again, and then go home.

But at that moment I glanced round at the crowd that had followed me. It was an immense crowd, two thousand at the least and growing every minute. It blocked the road for a long distance on either side. I looked at the sea of yellow faces above the <u>garish</u> clothes—faces all happy and excited over this bit of fun, all certain that the elephant was going to be shot. They were watching me as they would watch a conjurer about to perform a trick. They did not like me, but with the magical rifle in my hands I was momentarily worth watching. And suddenly I realized that I should have to shoot the elephant after all. The people expected it of me and I had got to do it; I could feel their two thousand wills pressing me forward, irresistibly. And it was at this moment, as I stood there with the rifle in my hands, that I first grasped the hollowness, the <u>futility</u> of the white man's dominion in the East. Here was I,

the white man with his gun, standing in front of the unarmed native crowd—seemingly the leading actor of the piece; but in reality I was only an absurd puppet pushed to and fro by the will of those yellow faces behind. I perceived in this moment that when the white man turns tyrant it is his own freedom that he destroys. He becomes a sort of hollow, posing dummy, the conventionalized figure of a sahib.[12] For it is the condition of his rule that he shall spend his life in trying to impress the "natives," and so in every crisis he has got to do what the "natives" expect of him. He wears a mask, and his face grows to fit it. I had got to shoot the elephant. I had committed myself to doing it when I sent for the rifle. A sahib has got to act like a sahib; he has got to appear <u>resolute</u>, to know his own mind and do definite things. To come all that way, rifle in hand, with two thousand people marching at my heels, and then to rail feebly away, having done nothing—no, that was impossible. The crowd would laugh at me. And my whole life, every white man's life in the East, was one long struggle not to be laughed at.

Suddenly I realized that I should have to shoot the elephant after all.

But I did not want to shoot the elephant. I watched him beating his bunch of grass against his knees, with that preoccupied grandmotherly air that elephants have. It seemed to me that it would be murder to shoot him. At that age I was not squeamish about killing animals, but I had never shot an elephant and never wanted to. (Somehow it always seems

12. **sahib.** Indian word for *gentleman*

gar • ish (ger´ ish) *adj.,* offensively or distressingly bright
fu • til • i • ty (fyü ti´ lə tē) *n.,* state or quality of being completely ineffective
res • o • lute (re´ zə lüt') *adj.,* marked by firm determination

eral, he isn't frightened. The sole thought in my mind was that if anything went wrong those two thousand Burmans would see me pursued, caught, trampled on and reduced to a grinning corpse like that Indian up the hill. And if that happened it was quite probable that some of them would laugh. That would never do. There was only one alternative. I shoved the cartridges into the magazine and lay down on the road to get a better aim.

The crowd grew very still, and a deep, low, happy sigh, as of people who see the theatre curtain go up at last, breathed from innumerable throats. They were going to have their bit of fun after all. The rifle was a beautiful German thing with cross-hair sights. I did not then know that in shooting an elephant one would shoot to cut an imaginary bar running from ear-hole to ear-hole. I ought, therefore, as the elephant was sideways on, to have aimed straight at his ear-hole; actually I aimed several inches in front of this, thinking the brain would be further forward.

When I pulled the trigger I did not hear the bang or feel the kick—one never does when a shot goes home—but I heard the devilish roar of glee that went up from the crowd. In that instant, in too short a time, one would have thought, even for the bullet to get there, a mysterious, terrible change had come over the elephant. He neither stirred nor fell, but every line of his body had altered. He looked suddenly stricken, shrunken, immensely old, as though the frightful impact of the bullet had paralyzed him without knocking him down. At last, after what seemed a long time—it might have been five seconds, I dare say—he sagged flabbily to his knees. His mouth slobbered. An enormous

worse to kill a large animal.) Besides, there was the beast's owner to be considered. Alive, the elephant was worth at least a hundred pounds; dead, he would only be worth the value of his tusks, five pounds, possibly. But I had got to act quickly. I turned to some experienced-looking Burmans who had been there when we arrived, and asked them how the elephant had been behaving. They all said the same thing: he took no notice of you if you left him alone, but he might charge if you went too close to him.

It was perfectly clear to me what I ought to do. I ought to walk up to within, say, twenty-five yards of the elephant and test his behavior. If he charged, I could shoot; if he took no notice of me, it would be safe to leave him until the mahout came back. But also I know that I was going to do no such thing. I was a poor shot with a rifle and the ground was soft mud into which one would sink at every step. If the elephant charged and I missed him, I should have about as much chance as a toad under a steam-roller. But even then I was not thinking particularly of my own skin, only the watchful yellow faces behind. For at that moment, with the crowd watching me, I was not afraid in the ordinary sense, as I would have been if I had been alone. A white man mustn't be frightened in front of "natives"; and so, in gen-

senility seemed to have settled upon him. One could have imagined him thousands of years old. I fired again into the same spot. At the second shot he did not collapse but climbed with desperate slowness to his feet and stood weakly upright, with legs sagging and head drooping. I fired a third time. That was the shot that did for him. You could see the agony of it jolt his whole body and knock the last remnant of strength from his legs. But in falling he seemed from a moment to rise, for as his hind legs collapsed beneath him he seemed to tower upward like a huge rock toppling, his trunk reaching skywards like a tree. He trumpeted, for the first and only time. And then down he came, his belly towards me, with a crash that seemed to shake the ground even where I lay.

> *I heard the devilish roar of glee that went up from the crowd.*

I got up. The Burmans were already racing past me across the mud. It was obvious that the elephant would never rise again, but he was not dead. He was breathing very rhythmically with long rattling gasps, his great mound of a side painfully rising and falling. His mouth was wide open—I could see far down into caverns of pale pink throat. I waited a long time for him to die, but his breathing did not weaken. Finally I fired my two remaining shots into the spot where I thought his heart must be. The thick blood welled out of him like red velvet, but still he did not die. His body did not even jerk when the shots hit him, the tortured breathing continued without a pause. He was dying, very slowly and in great agony, but in some world remote from me where not even a bullet could damage him further. I felt that I had got to put an end to that dreadful noise. It seemed dreadful to see the great beast lying there, powerless to move and yet powerless to die, and not even to be able to finish him. I sent back for my small rifle and poured shot after shot into his heart and down his throat. They seemed to make no impression. The tortured gasps continued as steadily as the ticking of a clock.

In the end I could not stand it any longer and went away. I heard later that it took him half an hour to die. Burmans were bringing dahs[13] and baskets even before I left, and I was told they had stripped his body almost to the bones by the afternoon.

Afterwards, of course, there were endless discussions about the shooting of the elephant. The owner was furious, but he was only an Indian and could do nothing. Besides, legally I had done the right thing, for a mad elephant has to be killed, like a mad dog, if its owner fails to control it. Among the Europeans opinion was divided. The older men said I was right, the younger men said it was a damn shame to shoot an elephant for killing a coolie, because an elephant was worth more than any damn Coringhee coolie. And afterwards I was very glad that the coolie had been killed; it put me legally in the right and it gave me a sufficient pretext for shooting the elephant. I often wondered whether any of the others grasped that I had done it solely to avoid looking a fool. ❖

---

13. **dahs.** Butcher knives

> **se • nil • i • ty** (si nil′ lə tē) *n.*, physical and mental infirmity of old age
> **pre • text** (prē′ tekst') *n.*, appearance assumed in order to disguise the truth

MIRRORS & WINDOWS

At the end of the selection, Orwell writes, "I had done it solely to avoid looking a fool." Why do people do things that go against their better judgment or beliefs?

Refer to Text ▶ ▶ ▶ ▶ ▶ **Reason with Text**

1a. What steps does Orwell take as soon as he sees the dead man?	**1b.** How do his actions set in motion a chain of events that leads to shooting an elephant?	**Understand** Find meaning
2a. Why does Orwell feel he had to shoot the elephant?	**2b.** How might he have acted if the people following him were fellow British citizens?	**Apply** Use information
3a. Describe how Orwell feels about his job and the practice of imperialism in general.	**3b.** How do these feelings conflict with his feelings about the Burmese people?	**Analyze** Take things apart
4a. According to Orwell, why do the Burmese people want him to shoot the elephant?	**4b.** Evaluate Orwell's decision to shoot the elephant. Does he do the right thing? Why or why not?	**Evaluate** Make judgments
5a. In the end, how does Orwell justify shooting the elephant?	**5b.** Explain how Orwell's actions in the situation exemplify "the hollowness, the futility of the white man's dominion in the East."	**Create** Bring ideas together

Analyze Literature

Thesis and Irony
Identify Orwell's thesis in "Shooting an Elephant." List the evidence provided to support it. Does the essay express the thesis consistently? Analyze the effectiveness of Orwell's exploration of the controlling idea.

Exaggeration, or overstatement, is one of several devices that authors use to achieve irony. Find examples of overstatement in Orwell's essay and explain the effect that these statements have on the tone of the essay.

Extend the Text

Writing Options
Creative Writing Imagine that you are Orwell. Write up a one-page official police report of the elephant shooting incident for your superiors in the imperial police. Think about the audience for this report, and pay attention to your tone and word choice.

Persuasive Writing Use the library or Internet resources to research the practice of imperialism, in both the past and present. Write the introductory paragraph of a personal essay expressing your opinion on the issue of imperialism. Concentrate on seizing your audience's attention in the introduction and stating a clear thesis. Share your paragraph with your class.

Media Literacy
Create a Pamphlet Imagine that you work for the Myanmar (formerly Burma) Tourism Promotion Board. Using library or Internet resources, research the history of British involvement in the region. How and when did Great Britain become involved in Burma, and what conflicts arose during Britain's rule there? What roles did religious and cultural differences play in these conflicts? How did British rule come to an end, and how is Myanmar ruled today? Create an informational pamphlet about the country's past and present for visiting tourists. Try to create a logo, or symbol, for your pamphlet. Brainstorm logos and their meanings from your contemporary environment (such as fast-food chains, clothing brands, etc.) to give you ideas.

Critical Literacy
Debate a Topic Conduct a debate on the following statement: Imperialism has been a force for economic growth and positive change in the world. You will need to form two teams: one will argue the pro, or supporting, case, and one will argue the con, or refuting, case. Review Orwell's essay for examples to support your argument.

 Go to **www.mirrorsandwindows.com** for more.

VOCABULARY & SPELLING
GREEK AND LATIN WORDS

Understand the Concept

In the essay "Shooting an Elephant," the narrator uses two expressions that do not sound like they come from the English language:

> With one part of my mind I thought of the British Raj as an unbreakable tyranny, as something clamped down, *in saecula saeculorum*, upon the will of prostrate peoples. . . . I took my rifle, an old .44 Winchester and much too small to kill an elephant, but I thought the noise might be useful *in terrorem*.

As indicated in the footnotes in the selection, these italicized terms both come from the Latin language. In fact, you may recognize and even use some common Latin phrases in everyday English. For instance, the term *status quo* means "the existing state of affairs."

What you may not recognize is that many English words are based on words or word parts from Latin and its predecessor, ancient Greek. For instance, the word *tyranny* in the first excerpt from "Shooting an Elephant" comes from the Greek word *tyrannos,* a term for a person who seized power and became the absolute ruler of a Greek city-state. The vocabulary word *prostrate* comes from the Latin prefix *pro-* ("before") and the verb *sternere* ("to spread out, throw down").

Knowing common Greek and Latin word parts can help you determine the meanings of unfamiliar words you encounter in reading materials and on tests. Familiarize yourself with these common Greek and Latin word parts:

Word Part	Meaning	Example
bene-, bon-	good	benefit
circum-	around	circumstance
eu-	well; good	euphoria
locut-, loqu-	to speak	ventriloquist
luc-, lumin-	light; to shine	illuminate
mal-	bad	malady
path-, pathy-	emotion; suffering	sympathy
ver-, veri-	true	verdict

Apply the Skill

Exercise A

As you read each sentence, determine the meaning of the underlined word. Use the preceding list of Greek and Latin words and context clues to help you. Also check the meaning of each word in the dictionary.

1. I have a hard time listening to his circumlocution. He uses a dozen words to say what could be said in one or two.
2. I cannot think of anything that may help elucidate her strange behavior.
3. His pathetic grades resulted in his being expelled from the academy.
4. If her malediction had come true, you would not have scored that goal.
5. The phrase "kicked the bucket" hardly seems a proper euphemism for *death.*

Exercise B

Greek and Latin are not the only sources of English words. Many words are based on affixes and roots from French, German, Spanish, Italian, Arabic, and other languages. With a partner, use an etymology dictionary (print or electronic) to find five words in different subject areas that originated from languages *other than* Greek and Latin. Identify prefixes, suffixes, and roots, and write down the definition and origin of each word part as well as the definition of the word itself.

SPELLING PRACTICE

Greek and Latin Words
Knowing Greek and Latin words and word parts will help you understand and spell many unfamiliar words. For example, if you know that the prefix *geo-* means "earth," you will better understand the words *geothermal* and *geode,* even if you are not sure exactly what they mean. Identify the Greek and Latin word parts in these words from "Shooting an Elephant."

agony	municipal	sufficient
crisis	oppressor	supplant
despotic	paralyzed	theoretically
furious	perspective	tyranny
imaginary	population	unendurable
irresistibly		

Dylan Thomas

"The land of my fathers. My fathers can have it."

Dylan Thomas (1914–1953) grew up in the industrial city of Swansea, Wales, where his father taught English at the local grammar school. Thomas's talent as a poet emerged at a young age; his first poem was published in the school magazine when he was eleven. He left school at age sixteen and worked briefly as a reporter for the *South Wales Evening Post.* During this time, his poetry was published in several periodicals and began to receive greater exposure.

In 1934, Thomas moved to London to pursue his dream of writing. That year, when he was only twenty years old, Thomas's first volume of verse, *Eighteen Poems,* was published. He quickly gained fame for his emotional, Romantic style and traditional themes—a departure from contemporaries such as T. S. Eliot and W. H. Auden.

Over the years, Thomas produced several more volumes of poetry, as well as prose works. His prose memoir *A Child's Christmas in Wales* is a popular classic. Throughout the 1930s and 1940s, Thomas also pursued a career in journalism and radio broadcasting, working for the British Broadcasting Corporation (BBC).

In 1950, Thomas traveled to the United States, where he began a series of public lectures and readings of his poetry. His rich, Welsh-accented voice captivated audiences and made him quite popular, even among people who ordinarily did not appreciate poetry. While his verse often makes great demands on the reader or listener, most people respond to its passion and to its vivid, charged language, reminiscent of the King James Bible and of Welsh preaching.

While in New York on another tour in 1953, Thomas first performed his most famous work, a radio drama called *Under Milk Wood,* which was later adapted for the stage. Thomas gained international fame during these tours, not only for his writing but also for his public performances. He died at the age of thirty-nine while he was on his fourth speaking tour of the United States.

Noted Works

Twenty-Five Poems (1936)

The World I Breathe (1939)

In Country Sleep and Other Poems (1952)

A Child's Christmas in Wales (1954)

Under Milk Wood (1954)

Do Not Go Gentle Into That Good Night
Fern Hill

A Villanelle and a Lyric Poem by Dylan Thomas

Build Background

Literary Context Dylan Thomas's poems are rich with imagery and music. Reading his first works, critics thought of him as a wild Romantic. In one review of his poetry from 1950, he is described as "a personal poet, not a political or social one." Indeed, Thomas's common themes of nostalgia, life, death, and lost innocence contrasted greatly with the social and intellectual concerns of his contemporaries, including T. S. Eliot and W. H. Auden.

But while Thomas dealt with the themes of everyday life, he was a serious craftsman. **"Do Not Go Gentle Into That Good Night"** shows his technical mastery of imagery, sound, metrics, and tone. The poem is an example of the complex French verse form known as the *villanelle,* a nineteen-line poem that usually has a pastoral theme. Thomas, however, goes beyond the complexity of the villanelle form by also making each line have ten syllables. Thomas wrote the poem in 1951 about the approaching death of his father, who had been ill for many years and with whom he had a close relationship. While many of Thomas's poems employ Christian imagery, this one does not, perhaps because his father was an atheist. Instead, the poem seems to draw spiritual strength from nature.

"Fern Hill" was written in 1945 while Thomas was living in the countryside of Wales. The poem first appeared in a volume called *Deaths and Entrances,* published in 1946, a collection of poems that greatly increased Thomas's popularity. In "Fern Hill," Thomas reminisces about his childhood perspective of the idyllic atmosphere at his aunt and uncle's dairy farm, where he spent his summers as a boy. Steeped in religion as a youth, Thomas's language and imagery in "Fern Hill" draw in part from biblical literature. His use of sensory language and details helps paint a vivid picture of his memory.

Thomas's desk at his house in Dyfed, Wales.

Reader's Context

How do you feel about death and youth? How has your attitude toward each changed as you have gotten older?

Analyze Literature

Villanelle and Sensory Details

A **villanelle** is a complex nineteen-line French verse form. The rhyme scheme is *aba aba aba aba aba abaa.* The first line is repeated as lines 6, 12, and 18. The third line is repeated as lines 9, 15, and 19. The first and third lines appear as a rhymed couplet at the end of the poem.

Sensory details are words and phrases that describe how things look, sound, smell, taste, or feel.

Set Purpose

Thomas's "Do Not Go Gentle Into That Good Night" may well be the finest example of a villanelle ever produced. While you read it, look for the characteristic structural elements. Identify the two lines that are repeated throughout the poem. As you read "Fern Hill," consider how Thomas uses sensory details to create a specific atmosphere. In particular, look for his use of sensory details to create a sense of innocence and freshness.

Do Not Go Gentle Into That Good Night

by Dylan Thomas

Do not go gentle into that good night,
Old age should burn and rave at close of day;
Rage, rage against the dying of the light.

Though wise men at their end know dark is right,
5 Because their words had forked no lightning they
Do not go gentle into that good night.

Good men, the last wave by, crying how bright
Their frail deeds might have danced in a green bay,
Rage, rage against the dying of the light.

10 Wild men who caught and sang the sun in flight,
And learn, too late, they grieved it on its way,
Do not go gentle into that good night.

Grave men, near death, who see with blinding sight
Blind eyes could blaze like meteors and be gay,
15 Rage, rage against the dying of the light.

And you, my father, there on the sad height,
Curse, bless, me now with your fierce tears, I pray.
Do not go gentle into that good night.
Rage, rage against the dying of the light. ❖

MIRRORS & WINDOWS

Thomas writes that when a person dies, he or she should "not go gentle into that good night." How should a person face death?

Fern Hill

by Dylan Thomas

[handwritten annotations:]
theme
- Unity of all life -
- workings of biology
rhythmic pattern
- Lyric poem
Positive - transforms dark
- an original poet of great power + beauty

Now as I was young and easy under the apple boughs
About the lilting house and happy as the grass was green, *→ adj. a free flowing/bouncy rhythm Feeling when going to a certain house poetic image*
    The night above the dingle starry, →
        Time let me hail and climb
5   Golden in the heydays of his eyes, *time is a looming presence*
And honored among wagons I was prince of the apple towns
And once below a time I lordly had the trees and leaves *everyday is a newborn experience (for a child)*
        Trail with daisies and barley
    Down the rivers of the windfall light. *→ fruits that fall on ground from wind, but used here as if light is a windfall*

10 And as I was green and carefree, famous among the barns
About the happy yard and singing as the farm was home, *Joy of childhood*
    In the sun that is young once only,
        Time let me play and be
        Golden in the mercy of his means,
15 And green and golden I was huntsman and herdsman, the calves
Sang to my horn, the foxes on the hills barked clear and cold,
        And the sabbath rang slowly
    In the pebbles of the holy streams. *> purity/beauty of nature, water is a purifying agent/developer of life*

green + golden → new, nature, fresh, unripe fruit (youth/unexperienced) universally symbolic springness

Day + Night imagery

All the sun long it was running, it was lovely, the hay
20 Fields high as the house, the tunes from the chimneys, it was air
    And playing, lovely and watery
      And fire green as grass.
    And nightly under the simple stars
As I rode to sleep the owls were bearing the farm away,
25 All the moon long I heard, blessed among stables, the nightjars[1]
    Flying with the ricks,[2] and the horses
      Flashing into the dark.

And then to awake, and the farm, like a wanderer white
With the dew, come back, the cock on his shoulder; it was all

Creation imagery

30   Shining, it was Adam and maiden, ›*evokes Eden*
      The sky gathered again
    And the sun grew round that very day.

biblical + science imagery

So it must have been after the birth of the simple light
In the first, spinning place, the spellbound horses walking warm
35   Out of the whinnying green stable
      On to the fields of praise.

And honored among foxes and pheasants by the gay house
Under the new made clouds and happy as the heart was long,
    In the sun born over and over,
40   I ran my heedless ways,
    My wishes raced through the house-high hay
And nothing I cared, at my sky blue trades, that time allows
In all his tuneful turning so few and such morning songs
    Before the children green and golden
45   Follow him out of grace,

loft – top floor of barn

Nothing I cared, in the lamb white days, that time would take me
Up to the swallow thronged loft by the shadow of my hand,
    In the moon that is always rising,
      Nor that riding to sleep
50   I should hear him fly with the high fields

movement towards darkness + hiding

eventually we lose the childhood heedlessness
- start to feel time

And wake to the farm forever fled from the childless land.
Oh as I was young and easy in the mercy of his means,
    Time held me green and dying *we are mortal beings*
    Though I sang in my chains like the sea. ❖

still there, but seen differently – can never really go back to this

but our imagination can take us far in our constraints (limitations)
young in process of dying

1. **nightjars.** Nocturnal birds that feed on large insects
2. **ricks.** Stacks of hay

MIRRORS & WINDOWS

What person, place, or event from your childhood do you remember fondly?
What types of experiences make people aware of the passing of time?

Refer to Text ▶ ▶ ▶ ▶ ▶   Reason with Text

1a. Identify the terms used to describe death in stanza 1 of "Do Not Go Gentle Into That Good Night."

1b. What attitude does the speaker believe people should adopt when near death?

Understand
Find meaning

2a. What words does the speaker use to describe himself as a child in "Fern Hill"?

2b. Would the child in "Fern Hill" have the same attitude about death as each type of man in "Do Not Go Gentle Into That Good Night"? Why or why not?

Apply
Use information

3a. In "Do Not Go Gentle Into That Good Night," what do the "wise men" know when they are close to death?

3b. How does this knowledge compare or contrast with the knowledge of other types of men?

Analyze
Take things apart

4a. What words at the end of "Fern Hill" illustrate the speaker's change in mood? Describe this mood.

4b. Do you agree with the speaker's views about childhood at the end of the poem? Why or why not?

Evaluate
Make judgments

5a. How does Thomas classify the different stages of life?

5b. Explain what both poems suggest about his attitude toward these different stages.

Create
Bring ideas together

Analyze Literature

Villanelle and Sensory Details

Review the structure of "Do Not Go Gentle Into That Good Night." Identify what makes it a villanelle. Explain the significance of the lines Thomas repeats throughout the poem.

What sensory details does Thomas use to create a sense of innocence and freshness in "Fern Hill"? How do the details change in the second part of the poem? How does this illustrate the change in the speaker's mood?

Extend the Text

Writing Options

Creative Writing Write a villanelle about a childhood memory. Review the structure noted under Analyze Literature on page 1123. Follow the length, rhyme scheme, and line repetitions. Try to use sensory details to paint a descriptive picture. Share your villanelle with your class.

Persuasive Writing Thomas wrote "Do Not Go Gentle Into That Good Night" to tell his father how to approach death. Write a personal statement about how people should approach life. Imagine that you will share your statement with a younger relative.

Collaborative Learning

Create an Anthology Work with several classmates to create an anthology of well-known villanelles. Each stu-
dent should choose one villanelle by a poet whose work is in the public domain (no longer protected by copyright). Decide how you will organize your anthology: Will it be organized thematically or by author? Find or create art to illustrate your anthology.

Lifelong Learning

Research Cultural Views of Death Work in small groups to research views of death and dying in different past and present-day cultures. For example, you might research why the ancient Egyptians created elaborate tombs filled with everyday necessities or how the concept of a wake developed. Compile your research into a short report, and present your findings to the rest of the class.

 Go to **www.mirrorsandwindows.com** for more.

The Hand That Signed the Paper

A Lyric Poem by Dylan Thomas

Build Background

Historical Context **"The Hand That Signed the Paper,"** written in 1933 when Thomas was just nineteen years old, is his most political poem. He generally did not draw inspiration from current events. However, at the time, Europe was moving toward World War II and fascism was taking root in Italy, Germany, and Spain.

The term *fascism* was coined by Italian dictator Benito Mussolini in 1919. It represents a political philosophy that puts the nation (and often a specific race) above the individual and establishes an autocratic government that controls every aspect of social and economic life. When capitalized, Fascism refers specifically to the Italian movement. However, other regimes of the time, such as those of Adolf Hitler in Germany and Francisco Franco in Spain, also were considered fascist in nature.

In the case of Italy and Germany, Mussolini and Hitler were able to gain dictatorial powers amid the economic hardships following World War I, when citizens were looking for changes in government that would end their troubles. In Spain, demands for social and political change broke out in civil war in 1936 and brought Franco to power.

Literary Context Many literary critics agree that "The Hand That Signed the Paper" is a criticism of authoritarianism in general. The poem evokes a sense of tyranny on a biblical scale, with references to locusts and famine. It also recalls rulers throughout history who have "taxed the breath" out of their people, and it compares a hand that "rules pity" to the hand of God—a hand that "rules heaven." The poem seems to attack all forms of power that are arbitrary and unfeeling—that make political decisions without considering the consequences they will have for ordinary citizens.

The structure of the poem is simple: four quatrains that each follow the basic rhyme scheme of *abab*. The uncomplicated formula of the stanzas seems to emphasize that the fundamental nature of power is also simple: Power is unfeeling.

Reader's Context Think of authority figures in your own life. How have these people exercised their power as leaders?

See the Author Focus on page 1122 for biographical information about Dylan Thomas.

Analyze Literature

Personification and Synecdoche

Personification is a figure of speech in which an animal, thing, force of nature, or idea is described as if it were human or is given human characteristics.

Synecdoche is a figure of speech in which the name of part of something is used in place of the name of the whole or vice versa. For example, in the command "All hands on deck!" hands is a synecdoche in which a part (hands) is used to refer to a whole (sailors).

Set Purpose

Dylan Thomas's poetry is noted for its passion and use of charged, vivid language. As you read "The Hand That Signed the Paper," pay close attention to how Thomas uses language to craft the poem. Identify where he uses personification, and consider what effect it has on your understanding of the poem. Also look for examples of synecdoche. Consider for what purpose Thomas uses this figure of speech.

Preview Vocabulary

sovereign, 1129
dominion, 1129

The Hand That Signed the Paper

by Dylan Thomas

The hand that signed the paper felled a city;
Five <u>sovereign</u> fingers taxed the breath,
Doubled the globe of dead and halved a country;
These five kings did a king to death.

5 The mighty hand leads to a sloping shoulder,
The finger joints are cramped with chalk;
A goose's quill has put an end to murder
That put an end to talk.

The hand that signed the treaty bred a fever,
10 And famine grew, and locusts came;
Great is the hand that holds <u>dominion</u> over
Man by a scribbled name.

The five kings count the dead but do not soften
The crusted wound nor pat the brow;
15 A hand rules pity as a hand rules heaven;
Hands have no tears to flow. ❖

sov • er • eign (sä´ vərn) *adj.*, possessed of supreme power
do • min • ion (də mi´ nyən) *n.*, supreme authority

Dylan Thomas, 1940. Rupert Shephard.
Private collection. (See detail on page 1128.)

MIRRORS & WINDOWS

In the poem, the speaker states, "Hands have no tears to flow." Do you agree with this statement? Can people truly act without feeling?

Not Waving but Drowning
A Lyric Poem by Stevie Smith

Build Background

Literary Context Stevie Smith writes in a conversational style, examining topics of life, death, and loneliness in a wry, unsentimental way. Unlike most of her contemporaries, Smith did not attend a university or participate in any literary group. Instead, she developed her voice on her own, forming a unique mix of nursery rhyme playfulness and somber seriousness. One literary critic remarked that Smith writes in three voices: little girl, lonely and cynical woman, and skeptical philosopher.

Smith's most famous poem, **"Not Waving but Drowning,"** is also the title of a collection of poems and drawings published in 1957. The poem was written in 1953, and its dark humor reflects the poet's melancholy perspective.

Reader's Context What do many people find appealing about dark humor, which satirizes and pokes fun at serious topics such as death and disease? What do others find offensive about it?

Meet the Author

Stevie Smith (1902–1971), whose real name was Florence Margaret Smith, was born in Yorkshire, England. When she was a young child, Smith, her mother, and two aunts moved to the London suburb of Palmers Green. Following the death of her mother when she was sixteen, Smith lived with her aunts for most of the rest of her life.

In 1923, Smith took a job as a secretary at Newnes, a magazine publisher in London, and worked there for thirty years. She first gained recognition for her writing in 1936, when she published her first book, *Novel on Yellow Paper*. Her first volume of poetry, *A Good Time Was Had by All*, appeared in 1937, complete with her own sketches, or doodles—a common feature in her books. Two more novels, both quite autobiographical, and several more volumes of poetry followed.

In the 1960s, after publication of her poetry collection *Not Waving but Drowning*, Smith gained a younger audience. Her originality and strong feminist outlook made her a popular figure in London, where she read and chanted her poems on stage and on radio. She was awarded the Gold Medal for Poetry in 1969 by Queen Elizabeth II.

After Smith's death from a brain tumor in 1971, a play and a movie were produced about her career.

Analyze Literature

Tone and Figurative Language
Tone is the emotional attitude toward the reader or toward the subject implied by a literary work.

Figurative language is writing or speech meant to be understood imaginatively instead of literally. Types of figurative language, or *figures of speech,* include hyperbole, metaphor, personification, simile, and understatement. (See the Literary Terms Handbook for definitions of these terms.)

Set Purpose

Smith was noted for creating a distinctive voice in her poems. In each poem, she created her voice through distinctive choices in tone and language. As you read "Not Waving but Drowning," determine its tone. Is it ironic, serious, playful, sarcastic, or sincere? Also look for examples of figurative language in the poem. Consider what Smith wants you to interpret figuratively and what she wants you to interpret literally. What effect does Smith's use of figurative language have on the tone of the poem?

Not Waving but Drowning

by Stevie Smith

Nobody heard him, the dead man,
But still he lay moaning:
I was much further out than you thought
And not waving but drowning.

5 Poor chap, he always loved larking[1]
And now he's dead
It must have been too cold for him his heart gave way,
They said.

Oh, no no no, it was too cold always
10 (Still the dead one lay moaning)
I was much too far out all my life
And not waving but drowning. ❖

---

1. **larking.** Kidding around; having fun

MIRRORS & WINDOWS

When have you felt isolated and helpless? How did you overcome these feelings?
What advice would you give to the drowning man?

That's All

by Harold Pinter

Floral Talks, 2005. Qin Weng.
Private collection. (See detail on page 1135.)

Mrs. A.   I always put the kettle on about that time.

Mrs. B.   Yes. (*Pause.*)

Mrs. A.   Then she comes round.

Mrs. B.   Yes. (*Pause.*)

Mrs. A.   Only on Thursdays.

Mrs. B.   Yes. (*Pause.*)

Mrs. A.   On Wednesdays I used to put it on. When she used to come round. Then she changed it to Thursdays.

Mrs. B.   Oh yes.

Mrs. A.   After she moved. When she used to live round the corner, then she always came in on Wednesdays, but then when she moved she used to come down to the butcher's on Thursdays. She couldn't find a butcher up there.

Mrs. B.   No.

Mrs. A.   Anyway, she decided she'd stick to her own butcher. Well, I thought, if she can't find a butcher, that's the best thing.

Mrs. B.   Yes. (*Pause.*)

Mrs. A.   So she started to come down on Thursdays. I didn't know she was coming down on Thursdays until one day I met her in the butcher.

Mrs. B.   Oh yes.

Mrs. A. It wasn't my day for the butcher. I don't go to the butcher on Thursday.

Mrs. B. No, I know. (*Pause.*)

Mrs. A. I go on Friday.

Mrs. B. Yes. (*Pause.*)

Mrs. A. That's where I see you.

Mrs. B. Yes. (*Pause.*)

Mrs. A. You're always in there on Fridays.

Mrs. B. Oh yes. (*Pause.*)

Mrs. A. But I happened to go in for a bit of meat, it turned out to be a Thursday. I wasn't going in for my usual weekly on Friday. I just slipped in, the day before.

Mrs. B. Yes.

Mrs. A. That was the first time I found out she couldn't find a butcher up there, so she decided to come back here, once a week, to her own butcher.

Mrs. B. Yes.

Mrs. A. She came on Thursday so she'd be able to get meat for the weekend. Lasted her till Monday, then from Monday to Thursday they'd have fish. She can always buy cold meat, if they want a change.

Mrs. B. Oh yes. (*Pause.*)

Mrs. A. So I told her to come in when she came down after she'd been to the butcher's and I'd put a kettle on. So she did. (*Pause.*)

Mrs. B. Yes. (*Pause.*)

Mrs. A. It was funny because she always used to come in Wednesdays. (*Pause.*) Still, it made a break. (*Long pause.*)

Mrs. B. She doesn't come in no more, does she? (*Pause.*)

Mrs. A. She comes in. She doesn't come in so much, but she comes in. (*Pause.*)

Mrs. B. I thought she didn't come in. (*Pause.*)

Mrs. A. She comes in. (*Pause.*) She just doesn't come in so much. That's all. ❖

Describe a conversation with someone in which you did not really communicate. What factors contributed to the lack of communication?

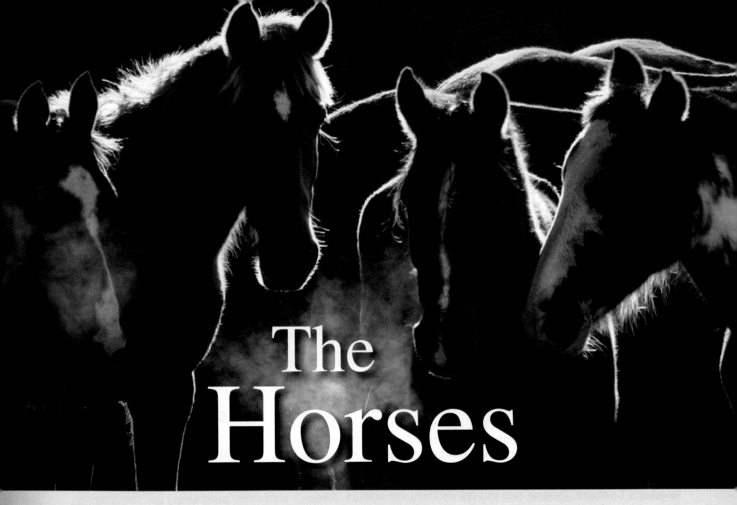

The Horses

by Ted Hughes

I climbed through woods in the hour-before-dawn dark.
Evil air, a frost-making stillness,

Not a leaf, not a bird—
A world cast in frost. I came out above the wood

5 Where my breath left <u>tortuous</u> statues in the iron light.
But the valleys were draining the darkness

Till the moorline—blackening <u>dregs</u> of the brightening gray—
Halved the sky ahead. And I saw the horses:

Huge in the dense gray—ten together—
10 Megalith-still.[1] They breathed, making no move,

---

1. **Megalith-still.** As large, quiet, and unmoving as a massive prehistoric stone monument; suggests nature's ancient beginnings

> **tor • tu • ous** (tôrch´ rəs) *adj.*, twisting; oddly shaped
> **dregs** (dregz) *n.*, last remaining parts

With draped manes and tilted hind-hooves,
Making no sound.

I passed: not one snorted or jerked its head.
Gray silent fragments

15 Of a gray silent world.

I listened in emptiness on the moor-ridge.
The curlew's tear[2] turned its edge on the silence.

Slowly detail leafed from the darkness. Then the sun
Orange, red, red erupted

20 Silently, and splitting to its core tore and flung cloud,
Shook the <u>gulf</u> open, showed blue,

And the big planets hanging—
I turned

Stumbling in the fever of a dream, down towards
25 The dark woods, from the <u>kindling</u> tops.

And came to the horses.
                         There, still they stood,
But now steaming and glistening under the flow of light,

Their draped stone manes, their tilted hind-hooves
30 Stirring under a thaw while all around them

The frost showed its fires. But still they made no sound.
Not one snorted or stamped,

Their hung heads patient as the horizons,
High over valleys, in the red leveling rays—

35 In din of the crowded streets, going among the years, the faces,
May I still meet my memory in so lonely a place

Between the streams and the red clouds, hearing curlews,
Hearing the horizons endure. ❖

---

2. **curlew's tear.** *Curlew*—long-legged wading bird; *tear* (ter)—quick movement

---

gulf (gulf) *n.*, wide gap
kin • dling (kin[d]´ liŋ) *adj.*, referring to wood that catches fire quickly

---

How has commercial development, suburban expansion, or another human activity changed a natural environment you visit or have heard about?

Follower

by Seamus Heaney

Tolstoy Ploughing in the Field, 1882. Ilya Repin. Tretyakov Gallery, Moscow, Russia. (See detail on page 1143.)

My father worked with a horse plow,
His shoulders globed like a full sail strung
Between the shafts[1] and the furrow.[2]
The horses strained at his clicking tongue.

5 An expert. He would set the wing
And fit the bright steel-pointed sock.
The sod rolled over without breaking.
At the headrig, with a single pluck

Of reins, the sweating team turned round
10 And back into the land. His eye
Narrowed and angled at the ground,
Mapping the furrow exactly.

I stumbled in his hobnailed wake,
Fell sometimes on the polished sod;
15 Sometimes he rode me on his back
Dipping and rising to his plod.

I wanted to grow up and plow,
To close one eye, stiffen my arm.
All I ever did was follow
20 In his broad shadow round the farm.

I was a nuisance, tripping, falling,
Yapping always. But today
It is my father who keeps stumbling
Behind me, and will not go away. ❖

---

1. **shafts.** Long, slender arms of a plow
2. **furrow.** Groove made in the ground by a plow

MIRRORS & WINDOWS

The speaker says that he "wanted to grow up and plough" just like his father. Did you ever want to grow up to be or do something just like a parent or relative? What was it and why did you feel that way?

Digging

by Seamus Heaney

Between my finger and my thumb
The squat pen rests; snug as a gun.
Under my window a clean rasping sound
When the spade sinks into gravelly ground:
5   My father, digging. I look down

Till his straining rump among the flowerbeds
Bends low, comes up twenty years away
Stooping in rhythm through potato drills[1]
Where he was digging.

10   The coarse boot nestled on the lug,[2] the shaft
Against the inside knee was levered firmly.
He rooted out tall tops, buried the bright edge deep
To scatter new potatoes that we picked
Loving their cool hardness in our hands.

15   By God, the old man could handle a spade,
Just like his old man.
My grandfather could cut more turf[3] in a day
Than any other man on Toner's bog.

Once I carried him milk in a bottle
20   Corked sloppily with paper. He straightened up
To drink it, then fell to right away
Nicking and slicing neatly, heaving sods
Over his shoulder, going down and down
For the good turf. Digging.

25   The cold smell of potato mold, the squelch and slap
Of soggy peat, the curt cuts of an edge
Through living roots awaken in my head.
But I've no spade to follow men like them.

Between my finger and my thumb
30   The squat pen rests.
I'll dig with it. ❖

---

1. **potato drills.** Small grooves in which potato seeds are planted
2. **the lug.** Top of the blade of a spade
3. **turf.** Slabs of peat used as heating fuel in Ireland

MIRRORS & WINDOWS

The speaker notes that his father "could handle a spade, / Just like his old man." What talents or occupations have been passed down from generation to generation in your family?

Refer to Text ▶ ▶ ▶ ▶ ▶ **Reason with Text**

1a. In "Digging," what are the speaker's father and grandfather doing?	**1b.** How does the speaker feel about his father's and grandfather's work? Cite specific line numbers, words, phrases, and images in the poem to support your answer.	**Understand** Find meaning
2a. Identify the father's physical condition at the beginning of "Follower." What is his condition at the end?	**2b.** Show how the son's relationship with his father shifts at the end of the poem.	**Apply** Use information
3a. What tool does the speaker use in "Digging"?	**3b.** Compare the tool the speaker uses with that of the tools used by his father and grandfather. How does the speaker use his tool to "dig" like his father and grandfather?	**Analyze** Take things apart
4a. In "Follower," how does the speaker feel about his father at the end of the poem?	**4b.** Evaluate the speaker's attitude toward his father. Is he justified in feeling this way? Why or why not?	**Evaluate** Make judgments
5a. List specific words the speaker uses in each poem to describe his father or grandfather.	**5b.** Explain how the speaker in each poem honors and dishonors his ancestors.	**Create** Bring ideas together

Analyze Literature

Flashback and Speaker

Locate the flashback in each poem. Explain how Heaney indicates the change in time. What necessary information does the flashback provide? How would your understanding of the poem be different if you did not have this information?

Describe the speaker in each poem. How are the speakers similar and different? What attitude toward the past does each speaker have?

Extend the Text

Writing Options

Creative Writing Imagine that you are the speaker in "Follower" and that your father has just died. Write a eulogy for your father that reveals the details of his life along with your feelings about him.

Expository Writing Assuming the speaker of "Follower" and "Digging" is the same person, write a one-paragraph analysis of his relationship with his father. Use details from both poems to support your ideas. Exchange analyses with a partner, and discuss how your views are similar or different.

Lifelong Learning

Conduct an Informational Interview The speaker in "Follower" decided he wanted to plow when he grew up because he saw his father do it. For most people, however, selecting a career requires more investigation. Arrange an interview with someone in a profession that interests you. Prepare by writing several questions to ask about the education, skills, and tasks involved in doing the job. Document the results in a one-page summary.

Media Literacy

Conduct a Television Interview With a partner, create a television interview segment on Seamus Heaney. Decide which role each of you will play: The interviewer should write out a series of questions to ask, and Heaney should prepare responses to the questions. Perform your segment for the class, either live or as a recording.

 Go to **www.mirrorsandwindows.com** for more.

A Shocking Accident

A Short Story by Graham Greene

Build Background

Literary Context Graham Greene can be distinguished from many of his contemporaries by his focus
on human emotions and actions, a recurring theme
in many of his works. In **"A Shocking Accident,"**
Greene writes about a young man coming to terms
with the death of his father. While much of the story
deals with the protagonist's inner struggle, Greene also manages to inject an
element of humor into the tragedy. The story first appeared in *May We Borrow
Your Husband?* a collection of comedic short stories published in 1967.

Reader's Context Recall a time you heard about a tragedy or shocking
event. How did you react to this news?

Meet the Author

Graham Greene (1904–1991) was born as Henry
Graham Greene in Berkhamsted, Hertfordshire, England,
where his father was the headmaster of Berkhamsted
School. Greene attended the school as a child but became
increasingly unhappy there. At age fifteen, he left school
and was hospitalized for six months, during which he
received counseling. He eventually returned to Berkhamsted, graduated, and went on to attend Balliol College at
Oxford University.

In 1926, Greene fell in love with a young woman named Vivien Dayrell-
Browning and converted to Catholicism, partly due to her influence. In time, his
Catholic faith became an important influence on his writing.

After working as an editor at the *Nottingham Journal,* Greene took a
job as subeditor for the *London Times.* He worked there until his first novel,
The Man Within, was published in 1929. Greene began to gain recognition
in 1932 with publication of the thriller *Stamboul Train,* one of his first works
to be made into a film. In 1938, he wrote *Brighton Rock,* his first book about
religious concerns. His novels of the 1940s and 1950s are among his most
famous, including *The Power and the Glory* (1940), *The Heart of the Matter*
(1948), and *The End of the Affair* (1951).

Greene was one of the most widely read British novelists of the twentieth
century. While much of his popularity can be attributed to his thrillers, he also
captured the public with his storytelling abilities, especially his use of fast-
paced dialogue. Toward the end of his life, Greene lived in Vevey, Switzerland,
where he died on April 3, 1991.

Analyze Literature

**Rising Action
and Resolution**
Rising action is the part of
the plot, or series of events in
a story, in which the central
conflict of the story is developed
and intensified.

The **resolution,** or denouement
(dā nü mä´), is the point in the
plot at which the central conflict
is ended or resolved.

Set Purpose

In his short stories and novels,
Greene develops a variety of
masterful plots. As you read "A
Shocking Accident," trace how
he develops the plot, and pay
particular attention to where
the rising action occurs. Identify
what events constitute the rising
action. Also locate where in the
story the resolution occurs. How
is the major conflict resolved?
Determine if the rising action
prepares the reader for the resolution of the story.

Preview Vocabulary

apprehension, 1149
convulsion, 1149
callousness, 1149
commiseration, 1150
discourse, 1150
obscure, 1150
intrinsically, 1151
brevity, 1151
appease, 1152

A Shocking Accident

by Graham Greene

'Your father has had an accident.'

1

Jerome was called into his housemaster's room in the break between the second and the third class on Thursday morning. He had no fear of trouble, for he was a warden—the name that the proprietor and headmaster of a rather expensive preparatory school had chosen to give to approved, reliable boys in the lower forms (from a warden one became a guardian and finally before leaving, it was hoped for Marlborough or Rugby, a crusader). The housemaster, Mr Wordsworth, sat behind his desk with an appearance of perplexity and <u>apprehension</u>. Jerome had the odd impression when he entered that he was a cause of fear.

'Sit down, Jerome,' Mr Wordsworth said. 'All going well with the trigonometry?'

'Yes, sir.'

'I've had a telephone call, Jerome. From your aunt. I'm afraid I have bad news for you.'

'Yes, sir?'

'Your father has had an accident.'

'Oh.'

Mr Wordsworth looked at him with some surprise. 'A serious accident.'

'Yes, sir?'

Jerome worshipped his father: the verb is exact. As a man re-creates God, so Jerome re-created his father—from a restless widowed author into a mysterious adventurer who traveled in far places—Nice, Beirut, Majorca, even the Canaries. The time had arrived about his eighth birthday when Jerome believed that his father either 'ran guns' or was a member of the British Secret Service. Now it occurred to him that his father might have been wounded in 'a hail of machine-gun bullets'.

Mr Wordsworth played with the ruler on his desk. He seemed at a loss how to continue. He said, 'You know your father was in Naples?'

'Yes, sir.'

'Your aunt heard from the hospital today.'

'Oh.'

Mr Wordsworth said with desperation, 'It was a street accident.'

'Yes, sir?' It seemed quite likely to Jerome that they would call it a street accident. The police of course had fired first; his father would not take human life except as a last resort.

'I'm afraid your father was very seriously hurt indeed.'

'Oh.'

'In fact, Jerome, he died yesterday. Quite without pain.'

'Did they shoot him through the heart?'

'I beg your pardon. What did you say, Jerome?'

'Did they shoot him through the heart?'

'Nobody shot him, Jerome. A pig fell on him.' An inexplicable <u>convulsion</u> took place in the nerves of Mr Wordsworth's face; it really looked for a moment as though he were going to laugh. He closed his eyes, composed his features and said rapidly as though it were necessary to expel the story as quickly as possible, 'Your father was walking along a street in Naples when a pig fell on him. A shocking accident. Apparently in the poorer quarters of Naples they keep pigs on their balconies. This one was on the fifth floor. It had grown too fat. The balcony broke. The pig fell on your father.'

Mr Wordsworth left his desk rapidly and went to the window, turning his back on Jerome. He shook a little with emotion.

Jerome said, 'What happened to the pig?'

2

This was not <u>callousness</u> on the part of Jerome, as it was interpreted by Mr Wordsworth to his colleagues (he even discussed with them whether, perhaps, Jerome was yet fitted to be a warden). Jerome was only attempting to visualize the strange scene to get the details right. Nor was Jerome a boy who cried; he was a boy who brooded, and it never occurred to him at this preparatory school that

---

ap • pre • hen • sion (a' pri hen[t]´ shən) *n.*, suspicion or fear

con • vul • sion (kən vul´ shən) *n.*, involuntary contraction of the muscles

cal • lous • ness (ka´ ləs nes) *n.*, lack of emotion

the circumstances of his father's death were comic—they were still part of the mystery of life. It was later, in his first term at his public school, when he told the story to his best friend, that he began to realize how it affected others. Naturally after that disclosure he was known, rather unreasonably, as Pig.

Unfortunately his aunt had no sense of humour. There was an enlarged snapshot of his father on the piano; a large sad man in an unsuitable dark suit posed in Capri with an umbrella (to guard him against sunstroke), the Faraglione rocks[1] forming the background. By the age of sixteen Jerome was well aware that the portrait looked more like the author of *Sunshine and Shade* and *Rambles in the Balearics* than an agent of the Secret Service. All the same he loved the memory of his father: he still possessed an album filled with picture-postcards (the stamps had been soaked off long ago for his other collection), and it pained him when his aunt embarked with strangers on the story of his father's death.

'A shocking accident,' she would begin, and the stranger would compose his or her features into the correct shape for interest and commiseration. Both reactions, of course, were false, but it was terrible for Jerome to see how suddenly, midway in her rambling discourse, the interest would become genuine. 'I can't think how such things can be allowed in a civilized country,' his aunt would say. 'I suppose one has to regard Italy as civilized. One is prepared for all kinds of things abroad, of course, and my brother was a great traveller. He always carried a water-filter with him. It was far less expensive, you know, than buying all those bottles of mineral water. My brother always said that his filter paid for his dinner wine. You can see from that what a careful man he was, but who could possibly have expected when he was walking along the Via Dottore Manuele Panucci on his way to the Hydrographic[2] Museum that a pig would fall on him?' That was the moment when the interest became genuine.

Jerome's father had not been a very distinguished writer, but the time always seems to come, after an author's death, when somebody thinks it worth his while to write a letter to the *Times Literary Supplement* announcing the preparation of a biography and asking to see any letters or documents or receive any anecdotes from friends of the dead man. Most of the biographies, of course, never appear—one wonders whether the whole thing may not be an obscure form of blackmail and whether many a potential writer of a biography or thesis finds the means in this way to finish his education at Kansas or Nottingham. Jerome, however, as a chartered accountant,[3] lived far from the literary world. He did not realize how small the menace really was, or that the danger period for someone of his father's obscurity had long passed. Sometimes he rehearsed the method of recounting his father's death so as to reduce the comic element to its smallest dimensions—it would be of no use to refuse information, for in that case the biographer would undoubtedly visit his aunt who was living to a great old age with no sign of flagging.[4]

> Sometimes he rehearsed the method of recounting his father's death so as to reduce the comic element to its smallest dimensions.

It seemed to Jerome that there were two possible methods—the first led gently up to the

---

1. **Faraglione rocks.** Three large rocks sticking out of the Mediterranean Sea just off the coast of Capri Island
2. **Hydrographic.** Having to do with the features and charting of bodies of water
3. **chartered accountant.** Member of England's Institute of Chartered Accountants
4. **flagging.** Becoming frail or weak

com • mis • er • a • tion (kə mi' zə rā' shən) *n.*, feeling of sympathy
dis • course (dis' kôrs') *n.*, verbal interchange of ideas
ob • scure (äb skyùr') *adj.*, relatively unknown

masterly attempt to make an <u>intrinsically</u> interesting subject boring.

The other method Jerome rehearsed had the virtue of <u>brevity</u>.

'My father was killed by a pig.'

'Really? In India?'

'No, in Italy.'

'How interesting. I never realized there was pig-sticking[5] in Italy. Was your father keen on polo?'

In course of time, neither too early nor too late, rather as though, in his capacity as a chartered accountant, Jerome had studied the statistics and taken the average, he became engaged to be married: to a pleasant fresh-faced girl of twenty-five whose father was a doctor in Pinner. Her name was Sally, her favourite author was still Hugh Walpole,[6] and she had adored babies ever since she had been given a doll at the age of five which moved its eyes and made water. Their relationship was contented rather than exciting, as became the love-affair of a chartered accountant; it would never have done if it had interfered with the figures.

One thought worried Jerome, however. Now that within a year he might himself become a father, his love for the dead man increased; he realized what affection had gone into the picture-postcards. He felt a longing to protect his memory, and uncertain whether this quiet love of his would survive if Sally were so insensitive as to laugh when she heard the story of his father's death. Inevitably she would hear it when Jerome brought her to din-

accident, so that by the time it was described the listener was so well prepared that the death came really as an anti-climax. The chief danger of laughter in such a story was always surprise. When he rehearsed this method Jerome began boringly enough.

'You know Naples and those high tenement buildings? Somebody once told me that the Neapolitan always feels at home in New York just as the man from Turin feels at home in London because the river runs in much the same way in both cities. Where was I? Oh, yes. Naples, of course. You'd be surprised in the poorer quarters what things they keep on the balconies of those sky-scraping tenements—not washing, you know, or bedding, but things like livestock, chickens or even pigs. Of course the pigs get no exercise whatever and fatten all the quicker.' He could imagine how his hearer's eyes would have glazed by this time. 'I've no idea, have you, how heavy a pig can be, but these old buildings are all badly in need of repair. A balcony on the fifth floor gave way under one of those pigs. It struck the third floor balcony on its way down and sort of ricochetted into the street. My father was on the way to the Hydrographic Museum when the pig hit him. Coming from that height and that angle it broke his neck.' This was really a

---

5. **pig-sticking.** Sport in colonial India in which a person spears a wild boar while on horseback
6. **Hugh Walpole (1884–1941).** Popular and prolific English novelist

---

in • trin • si • cal • ly (in trin´ zi k[ə] lē) *adv.,* by natural character or ability
brev • i • ty (bre´ və tē) *n.,* shortness of duration

ner with his aunt. Several times he tried to tell her himself, as she was naturally anxious to know all she could that concerned him.

'You were very small when you father died?'

'Just nine.'

'Poor little boy,' she said.

'I was at school. They broke the news to me.'

'Did you take it very hard?'

'I can't remember.'

'You never told me how it happened.'

'It was very sudden. A street accident.'

'You'll never drive fast, will you, Jemmy?' (She had begun to call him 'Jemmy'.) It was too late then to try the second method—the one he thought of as the pig-sticking one.

They were going to marry quietly in a registry-office and have their honeymoon at Torquay.[7] He avoided taking her to see his aunt until a week before the wedding, but then the night came, and he could not have told himself whether his apprehension was more for his father's memory or the security of his own love.

> The night came, and he could not have told himself whether his apprehension was more for his father's memory or the security of his own love.

The moment came all too soon. 'Is that Jemmy's father?' Sally asked, picking up the portrait of the man with the umbrella.

'Yes dear. How did you guess?'

'He has Jemmy's eyes and brow, hasn't he?'

'Has Jerome lent you his books?'

'No.'

'I will give you a set for your wedding. He wrote so tenderly about his travels. My own favourite is *Nooks and Crannies*. He would have had a great future. It made that shocking accident all the worse.'

'Yes?'

Jerome longed to leave the room and not see that loved face crinkle with irresistible amusement.

'I had so many letters from his readers after the pig fell on him.' She had never been so abrupt before.

And then the miracle happened. Sally did not laugh. Sally sat with open eyes of horror while his aunt told her the story, and at the end, 'How horrible,' Sally said. 'It makes you think, doesn't it? Happening like that. Out of a clear sky.'

Jerome's heart sang with joy. It was as though she had <u>appeased</u> his fear for ever. In the taxi going home he kissed her with more passion than he had ever shown and she returned it. There were babies in her pale blue pupils, babies that rolled their eyes and made water.

'A week today,' Jerome said, and she squeezed his hand. 'Penny for your thoughts, my darling.'

'I was wondering,' Sally said, 'what happened to the poor pig?'

'They almost certainly had it for dinner,' Jerome said happily and kissed the dear child again. ❖

---

7. **Torquay.** Seaside resort town on the southwest coast of England

ap • pease (ə pēz´) *v.*, calm; subdue

MIRRORS **&** **W**INDOWS   Think of a time you were afraid to learn how someone you cared about would react after learning one of your deepest secrets. How did you feel after you saw his or her reaction?

Refer to Text ▶ ▶ ▶ ▶ ▶ Reason with Text

1a. Name the profession of Jerome's father.	**1b.** Why does the young Jerome "re-create" his father?	**Understand** Find meaning
2a. How do most people react when they hear the story of the father's death? How does Sally react?	**2b.** Predict how the story might have ended if Sally had had the same reaction as other people. Cite specific examples from the story to support your answer.	**Apply** Use information
3a. How does Jerome's aunt deal with the father's death?	**3b.** Compare and contrast the feelings that Jerome and his aunt have about the event.	**Analyze** Take things apart
4a. Describe the two methods Jerome develops to tell people about his father's death.	**4b.** Determine how Jerome feels about his father. What evidence in the text supports your answer?	**Evaluate** Make judgments
5a. How does Jerome feel about Sally after she reacts to the news of his father's death?	**5b.** Why does Jerome feel this way? Describe the change that has come over him.	**Create** Bring ideas together

Analyze Literature

Rising Action and Resolution

Describe the rising action of the story. How does the subplot of Jerome's relationship with his father contribute to the rising action of the story?

Where does the resolution of the story occur? How is the major conflict resolved? Do the events outlined in the rising action help prepare you for the resolution? Why or why not?

Extend the Text

Writing Options

Creative Writing Imagine that you are Jerome as a young man. What effect has your father's death had on you? Write a one-page journal entry explaining how you feel about your father's death and how it is affecting your life.

Persuasive Writing Write a one-page critical analysis of "A Shocking Accident" that answers this question: Is Greene effective in his use of rising action to advance the plot to the moment of crisis? Use examples from the story to support your analysis, and share your analysis with a classmate.

Media Literacy

Analyze a Film Adaptation Find a copy of the 1982 short film *A Shocking Accident*. As you watch the film, note the similarities and differences between the film and the short story. Look for differences in plot, setting, and

characterization. Evaluate whether one version illustrates something better than the other. Create a short presentation in which you point out these differences to your class. Use clips from the movie and readings from the story to support your analysis.

Lifelong Learning

Research Psychoanalysis As a teenager, Greene was sent to London to undergo psychoanalysis, the approach to counseling pioneered by Sigmund Freud. Use the library and the Internet to research information on psychoanalysis and Freud's theories. Share your information with your classmates, and discuss how these theories may have influenced Greene's writing, especially in the story "A Shocking Accident."

 Go to **www.mirrorsandwindows.com** for more.

1. Greene writes, "The housemaster, Mr Wordsworth, sat behind his desk with an appearance of perplexity and apprehension. Jerome had the odd impression when he entered that he was a cause of fear." Which of the following words is a synonym for *apprehension?*
   A. appearance
   B. perplexity
   C. impression
   D. cause
   E. fear

2. Near the beginning of the story, Mr Wordsworth, the housemaster, tells Jerome the bad news about his father. How does Jerome respond?
   A. He cannot keep from laughing.
   B. He is calm but curious about the details of his father's death.
   C. He says he does not believe Mr Wordsworth.
   D. He cries uncontrollably.
   E. He leaves the room without saying a word.

3. What does the following sentence mean: "Jerome worshipped his father: the verb is exact"?
   A. Jerome had never met his father.
   B. Jerome truly worshipped his father.
   C. Jerome was exactly like his father.
   D. Jerome greatly admired his father.
   E. Jerome wished his father was different.

4. In the phrase "perhaps, Jerome was yet fitted to be a warden," what does the word *fitted* mean?
   A. suitable
   B. supplied
   C. dressed like
   D. the same size as
   E. attacked violently

5. Upon hearing about his father's accident, why does Jerome ask "What happened to the pig?"
   A. He does not care about his father.
   B. He wants to change the subject.
   C. He wants to understand all the details of the accident.
   D. He does not realize the pig has killed his father.
   E. He wants Mr Wordsworth to think he does not like his father.

6. Greene writes, "[T]he stranger would compose his or her features into the correct shape for interest and commiseration." Which of the following best restates this sentence?
   A. The listener would try to look both interested and sorry.
   B. The stranger would write an article about the accident.
   C. The person was sympathetic to the shocking story.
   D. The visitor thought about what would be the correct way to react.
   E. The individual who heard the story was attractive and in good shape.

7. Greene describes Jerome's aunt as "living to a great old age with no sign of flagging." What does the word *flagging* mean?
   A. being patriotic
   B. telling the truth
   C. becoming feeble
   D. changing how she showed her emotions
   E. understanding differences between countries

8. Jerome imagines how a listener would react to the story of his father's death if he gently led up to the accident so it came as an anticlimax. He thinks that the listener's "eyes would have glazed" midway through the story because the listener would
   A. expect to be shocked.
   B. be excited to hear the ending.
   C. find the story unbelievable.
   D. be bored by all the unimportant details.
   E. be angry about what happened to the father.

9. **Constructed Response:** Describe Jerome and his fiancée. Given what you know about these two characters, are they well suited for each other? Why or why not? Use details from the story to support your argument.

10. **Constructed Response:** Discuss Jerome's feelings for and attitude toward his father. Are they fairly typical for a nine-year-old child, or is Jerome odd in this respect? Cite examples from the text to support your argument.

Understand the Concept

When writing an essay or research paper, you should use information from other sources to lend credibility to your ideas. Knowing how to include this information correctly is essential to writing a paper that avoids **plagiarism,** which is using others' information without crediting them.

One way to incorporate information from other sources is to use **quotations,** repeating the exact words and punctuation from another source. To select quotations, look for statements that are particularly well expressed and that are made by recognized authorities on the topic. (See the Grammar & Style workshop about summarizing and paraphrasing on page 1222.)

Be sure to distinguish the quoted text from your own writing. For quotations that will run fewer than three printed lines in your paper, enclose the text within quotation marks. For a longer quotation, set off the text by indenting it five letter spaces from the left margin and adding blank line spaces above and below the block. Indenting the passage indicates it is being quoted, so quotation marks are not needed.

Finally, identify the source of each quote in the sentence in which it appears or that introduces it. This is particularly important if you are using quotes from more than one source. In a research paper, cite the author and page number, as well. (See the Grammar & Style workshop about documentation on page 1223. Or use Bartlett's *Familiar Quotations* or the Internet as a reference.)

Note the language and punctuation used to introduce the quotations in these short and long examples:

EXAMPLES

Short quotation In "A Shocking Accident," young Jerome's romantic view of his father's career becomes clear when he asks about his death, "Did they shoot him through the heart?"

Long quotation In "A Shocking Accident," Jerome reduces the comic impact of his father's death by explaining it in a bland manner:

> I've no idea, have you, how heavy a pig can be, but these old buildings are all badly in need of repair. A balcony on the fifth floor gave way under one of those pigs. It struck the third floor balcony on its way down and sort of richochetted into the street. My father was on the way to the Hydrographic Museum when the pig hit him. Coming from that height and that angle it broke his neck.

If only a fragment of a quotation is used, embed it in your own sentence and start it with a lowercase letter:

EXAMPLE

Fragment quoted Jerome's engagement to Sally is described as "contented rather than exciting."

Apply the Skill

Improve the Use of Quotations

Rewrite each of the following sentences to correctly use the quoted text, which is underlined. Consider the capitalization and use of punctuation (commas and quotation marks) in quoting either a fragment or an entire sentence, as indicated.

1. **Sentence quoted** In "A Shocking Accident," the narrator explains, as a man re-creates God, so Jerome re-created his father—from a restless widowed author into a mysterious adventurer.
2. **Fragment quoted** Sally is described as having babies in her pale blue pupils, babies that rolled their eyes and made water.
3. **Fragment quoted** Jerome learned not to refuse information to biographers, for in that case the biographer would undoubtedly visit his aunt who was living to a great old age with no sign of flagging.
4. **Sentence quoted** Upon his engagement, Jerome has a concern. The narrator states, he felt a longing to protect his [father's] memory, and uncertain whether this quiet love of his would survive if Sally were so insensitive as to laugh when she heard the story of his father's death.
5. **Fragment quoted** When he takes Sally to see his aunt a week before the wedding, Jerome could not have told himself whether his apprehension was more for his father's memory or the security of his own love.

Use Quotations in Your Writing

When you have gathered your sources for an essay or paper, write down or highlight phrases and sentences worthy of quoting. Remember to introduce the source, give page numbers if necessary, and use quotation marks and other punctuation appropriately. Integrate each quotation within your own writing by setting the context for it and explaining it, if needed.

from

Balzac and the Little Chinese Seamstress

by Dai Sijie

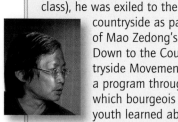

Dai Sijie (b. 1954) was born to a middle-class family in Communist China. As a member of the bourgeoisie (middle class), he was exiled to the countryside as part of Mao Zedong's Down to the Countryside Movement, a program through which bourgeois youth learned about agriculture from the peasants.

Sijie eventually was able to return home to complete his education and left China for France in 1984. There, he developed an interest in film and became a director, creating three critically acclaimed films. He then turned to writing. His first novel, *Balzac and the Little Chinese Seamstress,* published in 2000, became an immediate best seller and was made into a film in 2002.

Set during Mao's Cultural Revolution, the semiautobiographical novel tells the story of two middle-class boys who are sent to the countryside for "re-education" in the ways of the peasants. There, they meet and befriend the beautiful daughter of the local tailor.

Outside, it was raining. Not the usual fine drizzle, as it happened, but a heavy downpour drumming on the tiles overhead. No doubt this exacerbated Luo's gloom: it felt as if we were doomed to spend our entire lives being re-educated. Ordinarily the offspring of average parents, whether workers or revolutionary intellectuals, could rest assured that, provided they stayed out of trouble, they would be reunited with their families after a mere two years of re-education. That was the official Party[1] line. But for the sons and daughters of families classed as enemies of the people, the chances of returning home were infinitesimal:[2] three in a thousand. Statistically speaking, Luo and I were no-hopers. We were left with the dismal prospect of growing old and bald in the house on stilts, and of dying there too, after which our bodies would be wrapped in the white shrouds typical of the region. There was plenty of cause for dejection and insomnia.

That night I played a piece by Mozart, some Brahms and finally a Beethoven sonata, but even that failed to raise my friend's spirits.

"Try something else," he said.

---

1. **Party.** Communist Party of China
2. **infinitesimal.** Immeasurably or incalculably small

violin concertos.[4] But Luo couldn't play the violin, I reflected, and he wasn't much good at basketball or football either. In fact he didn't possess a single skill that might help him to become one of the three in a thousand. He couldn't even dream of it.

The only thing Luo was really good at was telling stories. A pleasing talent to be sure, but a marginal[5] one, with little future in it. Modern man has moved beyond the age of the Thousand-and-One-Nights,[6] and modern societies everywhere, whether socialist or capitalist, have done away with the old storytellers—more's the pity.

> *Modern man has moved beyond the age of the Thousand-and-One-Nights, and modern societies everywhere . . . have done away with the old storytellers—more's the pity.*

The only man in the world who truly appreciated his gift, to the point of rewarding him generously, was the headman[7] of our village, the last of the lordly devotees of narrative eloquence.[8]

"Any ideas?"

"Something a bit more cheerful."

I thought hard, running through my scant musical repertoire, but came up with nothing.

Luo started humming a revolutionary tune.

"How does that strike you?" he asked.

"Charming."

I launched into an accompaniment on my violin. It was a Tibetan song, which the Chinese had reworded so as to turn it into a glorification of Chairman Mao.[3] But the adaptation of the lyrics had not done too much damage: the song was still uplifting. With mounting excitement Luo scrambled to his feet and started jumping up and down on his bed, to the steady patter of the rain dripping down through the broken tiles.

"Three in a thousand," flashed across my mind. I had a three in a thousand chance, and our melancholy smoker here, currently disguised as a dancer, stood even less of a chance. Some day, perhaps, once I was an accomplished violinist, some modest local or regional propaganda committee—in the district of Yong Jing, for instance—might open their doors to me, and might even hire me to perform Red

---

3. **Chairman Mao.** Mao Zedong, Chairman of the Communist Party of China from 1949 to 1976
4. **Red violin concertos.** Music approved by the Communist Party
5. **marginal.** Limited in extent, significance, or stature
6. **Thousand-and-One-Nights.** Persian epic in which the heroine, Scheherazade, keeps from being executed by telling the king suspenseful stories over a period of 1,001 nights
7. **headman.** Chief of a community
8. **eloquence.** Quality of forceful or persuasive expressiveness

Phoenix mountain was so remote from civilisation that most of the inhabitants had never had the opportunity of seeing a film, let alone visit a cinema. There had been a few occasions when Luo and I entertained the headman with stories of films we had seen, and he was eager to hear more. One day, having found out when the next month's screening was due at Yong Jing, he decided to send Luo and me to watch it. We got two days off for the journey to town and two for the return, and we were supposed to see the show on the evening of our arrival. Back home in the village we were to relate the film from beginning to end to the headman and everyone else, and to make our story last exactly as long as the screen version.

We welcomed the challenge, and to be on the safe side we sat through two screenings in succession. The basketball court of the town's high school had been converted into a make-shift open-air cinema. The local girls were gorgeous, but we forced ourselves to concentrate on the screen, paying close attention to the dialogue, to the actors' costumes and gestures, to the setting of every scene, even to the music.

On our return to the village we put on an "oral cinema show" such as had never been seen before. Every single villager was crammed into the clearing in front of our house on stilts. The headman sat in the middle of the front row, holding his long bamboo pipe in one hand and our "phoenix of the earth" in the other, to time the duration of our performance.

I was overcome by stage fright and was reduced to a mechanical recitation of the setting of each scene. But here Luo's genius for

*He was sparing with his descriptions,
but acted the part of each character
in turn, adjusting his tone of voice
and gestures accordingly.*

storytelling came into its own. He was sparing with his descriptions, but acted the part of each character in turn, adjusting his tone of voice and gestures accordingly. He took complete control of the narrative, keeping up the suspense, asking the listeners questions, making them respond and correcting their answers. By the time we, or rather he, reached the end of the story, in the allotted time, our audience was ecstatic.

"Next month," the village headman announced with an imperious[9] smile, "I shall send you to another film. You will be paid the same as if you had worked in the fields."

At first we thought it would just be a welcome change; not for a moment did we imagine that our lives, particularly Luo's, were about to be completely shaken up.

T he princess of Phoenix mountain wore pale pink canvas shoes, which were both sturdy and supple and through which you could see her flexing her toes as she worked the treadle[10] of her sewing machine. There was nothing out of the ordinary about the cheap, homemade shoes, and yet, in a place where nearly everyone went barefoot, they caught the eye, seeming delicate and sophisticated. The fine shape of her feet and ankles was set off by white nylon socks.

A long pigtail three or four centimetres wide fell from the nape of her neck down to the small of her back, where the end was tied with a brand-new red silk ribbon.

When she leaned over her sewing machine, the shiny metal base mirrored the collar of her white blouse, her oval face and the sparkle in her eyes—without doubt the loveliest pair of eyes in the district of Yong Jing, if not the entire region.

A steep valley divided her village from ours. Her father, the only tailor on the mountain, was often absent from their home, which was old and spacious and served as both shop and dwelling. His tailoring was much in demand. Whenever a family needed new clothes they would first go all the way to Yong Jing to buy lengths of cloth, after which they would visit the tailor to discuss styles, prices and a convenient date for him to come and make the garments. On the appointed day an escort party would call for him at dawn, with

---

9. **imperious.** Commanding, dominant
10. **treadle.** Foot lever used to power a machine

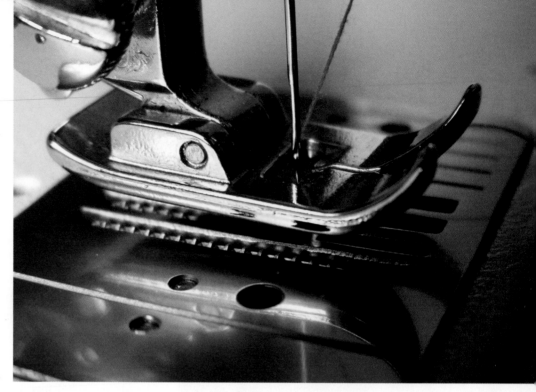

several strong men to take turns carrying the sewing machine on their backs.

The tailor owned two sewing machines. The first, which he took with him from one village to the next, was old: the brand and name of the manufacturer were no longer legible. The second was new, *Made in Shanghai,* and he left it at home for his daughter, "the Little Seamstress." He never took his daughter with him on his trips, and this decision, prudent[11] but pitiless, caused great distress to all the young bachelors aspiring to win her favour.

The tailor lived like a king. Wherever he went there would be scenes of excitement to rival a country festival. The home of his client, filled with the whirr of his sewing machine, would become the hub of village life, giving the host family the opportunity to display their wealth. He would be served the choicest food, and sometimes, if the year was drawing to a close and preparations for the New Year celebrations were under way, a pig might even be slaughtered. He would often spend a week or two in a village, lodging with each of his diverse clients in succession.

Luo and I first met the tailor when we went to visit Four-Eyes, a friend from the old days who had been sent to another village. It was raining, and we had to walk carefully along the steep, slippery path shrouded in milky fog. Despite our caution we found ourselves on all fours in the mud several times. Suddenly, as we rounded a corner, we saw coming towards us a procession in single file, accompanying a sedan chair[12] in which a middle-aged man

was enthroned. Following behind this regal conveyance[13] was a porter with a sewing machine strapped to his back. The man bent to address his bearers, and seemed to be enquiring about us.

He was of slight build, thin, wrinkled, but brimming with energy. His sedan was lashed to two sturdy bamboo shafts, which rested on the shoulders of two bearers, one in front and one behind. We could hear the chair and the shafts creaking to the rhythm of the bearers' slow, heavy tread.

When we were about to pass the sedan, the tailor leaned over to me, so close that I could feel his breath: "Wy-o-lin!" he bellowed, in an imitation of the English word.

His voice was like a clap of thunder and made me jump, at which he roared with laughter. He was the very image of a capricious[14] overlord.[15]

---

11. **prudent.** Marked by wisdom
12. **sedan chair.** One-person windowed cabin carried on wooden rails by porters
13. **conveyance.** Means of transport
14. **capricious.** Impulsive; unpredictable
15. **overlord.** Person who has supreme power or authority

"Do you realise that here, on this mountain, our tailor is the most widely travelled man of all?" one of the bearers asked.

"In my youth I even went as far as Ya An, which is two hundred kilometres away from Yong Jing," the great traveller declared before we had a chance to reply. "When I was young my master had a musical instrument just like yours up on his wall, to impress his clients."

Then he fell silent, and the procession set off again.

Just before he disappeared from view, he turned and shouted once more: "Wy-o-lin!"

His bearers and the ten peasants escorting him slowly raised their heads and let out a long drawn-out cry, so deformed that it sounded more like an anguished wail than an English word.

"Wy-o-lin!"

Like a pack of mischievous boys they fell about laughing. Then they bowed their heads and went on their way. Very soon the procession was swallowed up by the fog.

Some weeks later we ventured into the courtyard of his house, where a large black dog stared at us but did not bark. We entered the shop. The old man being away on one of his tours, we were greeted by his daughter, the Little Seamstress. We asked her to lengthen Luo's trousers by five centimetres; even his poor diet, insomnia, and constant worrying about the future had not stopped him from growing.

Introducing himself to the Little Seamstress, Luo told her about our encounter with her father in the fog and the rain, and he couldn't resist imitating and exaggerating the old man's funny English accent. She hooted with laughter. Luo was a born impersonator.

When she laughed I noticed an untamed quality about her eyes, which reminded me of the wild girls on our side of the mountain. Her eyes had the gleam of uncut gems, of unpolished metal, which was heightened by the long lashes and the delicate slant of the lids.

"You mustn't mind him," she said. "He's just an overgrown child."

Her eyes had the gleam of uncut gems, of unpolished metal, which was heightened by the long lashes and the delicate slant of the lids.

Her face clouded suddenly, and she lowered her eyes. She scratched the base of her sewing machine with a fingertip.

"My mother died far too young. Ever since her passing he has done exactly as he pleases."

She had a glowing complexion and her features were fine, almost noble. Her face possessed an impressive, sensual beauty, which aroused in us an irresistible desire to stay and watch her work the treadle of her *Made in Shanghai*.

The room served as shop, workplace and dining room all at once. The floorboards were grimy and streaked with yellow-and-black gobs of dried spittle left by clients. You could tell they were not washed down daily. There were hangers with finished garments suspended on a string across the middle of the room. The corners were piled high with bolts of material and folded clothes, which were under siege from an army of ants. The place lacked any sense of order or aesthetics, and exuded an atmosphere of complete informality.

I was surprised to see a book lying on a table, since the mountain people were mostly illiterate; it was an eternity since I had touched the pages of a book. I went to look at it at once, but was disappointed: it was an industrial catalogue of textile dyes.

"Can you read?" I asked.

"Not much," she answered, unabashed,[16] "But you needn't think I'm a fool, because I enjoy talking to people who can read and write—the young people from the city, for instance. Didn't you notice that my dog didn't bark when you came in? He knows my tastes."

---

16. **unabashed.** Undisguised; unapologetic

She didn't seem to want us to leave just yet. She rose from her stool, lit the iron stove in the centre of the room, set a saucepan on the burner and filled it with water. Luo, who followed her every move with his eyes, asked: "Are you intending to offer us tea or boiling water?"

"It'll be the latter."

This was a sign that she had taken a liking to us. On this mountain an invitation to take a drink of water meant that your host would crack some eggs over the boiling pan and add sugar to make a soup.

"Did you know, Little Seamstress," Luo said, "that you and I have something in common?"

"Us two?"

"Yes, you want to bet?"

"What shall we bet?"

"Whatever you like. I'm quite sure I can prove to you that there's something we share."

She reflected briefly.

"If I lose, I'll lengthen your trousers for free."

"Fine," said Luo, "Now take off your left shoe and sock."

After a moment's hesitation the Little Seamstress's curiosity got the better of her. Her foot, more timid than she but no less sensual for that, gradually revealed itself. A small foot, tanned, translucent, veined with blue, with toenails that gleamed.

Luo planted his bony, mud-encrusted foot alongside hers, and it was true, there was a resemblance: their second toes were longer than the others. ❖

What would you do if you were placed in a bleak, dismal situation? How would you keep up your spirits? What would help you survive?

Refer and Reason

1. Describe the boys' encounter with the tailor. What can you infer about the tailor's personality? What other information in the selection further supports your characterization?

2. What specific details does the narrator use to describe the re-education camp and the tailor's house? How does each description create a particular mood, or atmosphere, in which the action is set?

3. State the narrator's opinion of Luo's storytelling talent. What is the headman's opinion? Contrast the narrator's opinion with that of the headman, and propose two reasons that could account for this difference. What does the difference of opinion between these two men suggest about the value of storytelling?

Writing Options

1. Imagine that you are the narrator. Write a letter to your family about your experiences at the re-education camp. What type of work are you doing? What are your living conditions like? How does your situation make you feel?

2. Write a short paragraph in which you compare and contrast the Little Seamstress and her father. Use evidence from the excerpt to support your comparisons.

 Go to **www.mirrorsandwindows.com** for more.

Home Is So Sad

by Philip Larkin

Philip Larkin (1922–1985) was born in Coventry, England, where his father was city treasurer. After completing a degree in English at Oxford University, he found work in a library and studied to become a professional librarian.

By this time, Larkin's poetry had been published in various periodicals, but it was not until the publication in 1955 of his third book, *The Less Deceived,* that he gained his reputation as a leading figure in twentieth-century poetry. He followed this success with *The Whitsun Weddings* in 1964 and subsequently was awarded the Queen's Gold Medal for Poetry.

Larkin's works often are about everyday experiences and reflect the universal themes of mortality, love, and human solitude. **"Home Is So Sad"** is typical of Larkin's style: simple and straightforward with a conversational flow. His poetry often is compared with that of Thomas Hardy, whom Larkin greatly admired.

Home is so sad. It stays as it was left,
Shaped to the comfort of the last to go
As if to win them back. Instead, bereft[1]
Of anyone to please, it withers so,
5 Having no heart to put aside the theft

And turn again to what it started as,
A joyous shot at how things ought to be,
Long fallen wide. You can see how it was:
Look at the pictures and the cutlery.
10 The music in the piano stool. That vase. ❖

---

1. **bereft.** Lacking or deprived of something

MIRRORS & WINDOWS

Larkin mentions several items in the empty home: pictures, cutlery, music in a piano stool, and a vase. What items best characterize your home? What do they reveal about the people who live there?

Refer and Reason

1. Identify the human emotions displayed by the home. How does Larkin use personification to help create the mood of the poem?

2. The home "started as" what? Infer what the poem says about youthful dreams and the realities of life.

3. In what situation is the home at the end of the poem? Explain how the life of the home can be considered a metaphor for the life of a person.

Writing Options

1. In the style of Philip Larkin, write a poem that contrasts the theme in "Home Is So Sad." Consider what images you can use to create an entirely different mood.

2. Write an essay in which you compare and contrast the writing style of Larkin in "Home Is So Sad" with that of Dylan Thomas in "The Hand That Signed the Paper." Use details from the two poems to illustrates their similarities and differences.

Go to **www.mirrorsandwindows.com** for more.

THE MOMENT

by Margaret Atwood

Margaret Atwood (b. 1939) grew up in Ottawa and Toronto in Ontario, Canada, and she often spent summers in the Canadian wilderness in northern Quebec. She earned a bachelor's degree from the University of Toronto and a master's degree from Radcliffe College in 1962.

Atwood's first book of poetry, *The Circle Game,* won a Governor General's Award in 1966, and she has won many awards since. Often short and terse, Atwood's poetry is written in everyday language and filled with sharp or witty observations.

Atwood also is well known for her intense, ironic, and sometimes disturbing stories, such as *The Handmaid's Tale* (1985) and *The Blind Assassin* (2000). Her writing probes varied subjects, including male-female relationships, the Canadian pioneer spirit, the influence of myth, and international human rights.

"The Moment" first was published in Atwood's 1995 poetry collection *Morning in the Burned House.* It reflects on the relationship between humans and nature.

The moment when, after many years
of hard work and a long voyage
you stand in the centre of your room,
house, half-acre, square mile, island, country,
5 knowing at last how you got there,
and say, I own this,

is the same moment when the trees unloose
their soft arms from around you,
the birds take back their language,
10 the cliffs fissure[1] and collapse,
the air moves back from you like a wave
and you can't breathe.

No, they whisper. You own nothing.
You were a visitor, time after time
15 climbing the hill, planting the flag, proclaiming.
We never belonged to you.
You never found us.
It was always the other way round. ❖

---

1. **fissure.** Crack, divide

MIRRORS & WINDOWS

At the beginning of the poem, the speaker confidently declares, "I own this." Do most people want to own things? What does ownership do for someone's sense of achievement or worth?

B. Wordsworth

A Short Story by V. S. Naipaul

Build Background

Literary Context **"B. Wordsworth"** takes place in Port-of-Spain, the capital of Trinidad, where author V. S. Naipaul lived as a child. Like most of Naipaul's works, the story addresses themes of cultural confusion and alienation, feelings the author felt all too often as an Indian in the West Indies and as a West Indian in England. The story was published in *Miguel Street* (1959), a collection of stories in which a young narrator relates his experiences growing up in the West Indies.

Historical Context Trinidad, now part of the independent country Trinidad and Tobago, was a British colony from 1802 to 1962. From 1845 to 1917, workers from India, including Naipaul's grandfather, emigrated to the island and served as indentured servants on sugar plantations. (An *indentured servant* was enlisted to work for another person for a specified period of time, usually in return for payment of travel expenses and living expenses.) As members of a diverse population ruled by a colonial power, Trinidadians during this time were greatly concerned with names and cultural identity.

Reader's Context When have you felt like an outsider? What was the situation? Who else was there? How did you respond to the situation?

Meet the Author

V. S. Naipaul (b. 1932), who was born in Trinidad, was raised Hindu but absorbed elements of British culture in school. He inherited his talent for writing from his father, who was a Trinidadian journalist.

Naipaul won a scholarship to Oxford University in 1950 and decided against the wishes of his family, to remain in England. Alone in a new country, the young writer began to write stories that drew on his life in Trinidad. His first novel, *The Mystic Masseur,* was published in 1957 and then followed by two more books in 1958 and 1959. Not until the publication of *Mr. Biswas* in 1961, however, did Naipaul gain worldwide recognition. Modeled after the life of his father, the novel tells the story of an Indian searching for his independence and identity in colonial Trinidad.

Naipaul has since published twenty-one works of fiction, nonfiction, and essays. Although he sometimes has been criticized for portraying people from developing nations in an unsympathetic manner, he has won several literary awards and recognition. In 2001, he was awarded the Nobel Prize for literature for "having united perceptive narrative and incorruptible scrutiny in works that compel us to see the presence of suppressed histories."

Analyze Literature

Point of View and Dialect **Point of view** is the vantage point, or perspective, from which a narrator tells a story. In *first-person* point of view, the story is told by someone who participates in or witnesses the action. In *third-person* point of view, the narrator usually stands outside the action and observes.

A **dialect** is a version of language spoken by the people of a particular place, time, or social group. A *regional dialect* is one spoken in a particular place. A *social dialect* is one spoken by members of a particular social group or class.

Set Purpose

A writer's choice of point of view has a significant impact on the reader's understanding of the story. As you read, consider from what point of view "B. Wordsworth" is told. Also pay close attention to Naipaul's use of dialect. Determine which characters speak in a dialect and how the use of dialect helps create the personalities of the main characters.

Preview Vocabulary

patronize, 1172
distill, 1172

B. Wordsworth

by V. S. Naipaul

"You're a poet, too, you know."

Three beggars called punctually every day at the hospitable houses in Miguel Street. At about ten an Indian came in his dhoti[1] and white jacket, and we poured a tin of rice into the sack he carried on his back. At twelve an old woman smoking a clay pipe came and she got a cent. At two a blind man led by a boy called for his penny.

Sometimes we had a rogue. One day a man called and said he was hungry. We gave him a meal. He asked for a cigarette and wouldn't go until we had lit it for him. That man never came again.

The strangest caller came one afternoon at about four o'clock. I had come back from school and was in my home-clothes. The man said to me, "Sonny, may I come inside your yard?"

He was a small man and he was tidily dressed. He wore a hat, a white shirt and black trousers.

I asked, "What you want?"

He said, "I want to watch your bees."

---

1. **dhoti.** Loincloth worn by many Hindu men

"What your name, mister?"

"B. Wordsworth."

"B for Bill?"

"Black. Black Wordsworth. White Wordsworth[4] was my brother. We share one heart. I can watch a small flower like the morning glory and cry."

I said, "Why you does cry?"

"Why, boy? Why? You will know when you grow up. You're a poet, too, you know. And when you're a poet you can cry for everything."

I couldn't laugh.

He said, "You like your mother?"

"When she not beating me."

He pulled out a printed sheet from his hip-pocket and said, "On this paper is the greatest poem about mothers and I'm going to sell it to you at a bargain price. For four cents."

I went inside and I said, "Ma, you want to buy a poetry for four cents?"

My mother said, "Tell that blasted man I haul his tail away from my yard, you hear."

I said to B. Wordsworth, "My mother say she ain't have four cents."

B. Wordsworth said, "It is the poet's tragedy."

And he put the paper back in his pocket. He didn't seem to mind.

I said, "Is a funny way to go round selling poetry like that. Only calypsonians[5] do that sort of thing. A lot of people does buy?"

He said, "No one has yet bought a single copy."

"But why you does keep on going round, then?"

He said, "In this way I watch many things, and I always hope to meet poets."

I said, "You really think I is a poet?"

"You're as good as me," he said.

We had four small gru-gru palm trees[2] and they were full of uninvited bees.

I ran up the steps and shouted, "Ma, it have a man outside here. He say he want to watch the bees."

My mother came out, looked at the man and asked in an unfriendly way, "What you want?"

The man said, "I want to watch your bees."

His English was so good, it didn't sound natural, and I could see my mother was worried.

She said to me, "Stay here and watch him while he watch the bees."

The man said, "Thank you, Madam. You have done a good deed today."

He spoke very slowly and very correctly as though every word was costing him money.

We watched the bees, this man and I, for about an hour, squatting near the palm trees.

The man said, "I like watching bees. Sonny, do you like watching bees?"

I said, "I ain't have the time."

He shook his head sadly. He said, "That's what I do, I just watch. I can watch ants for days. Have you ever watched ants? And scorpions, and centipedes, and congorees[3]—have you watched those?"

I shook my head.

I said, "What you does do, mister?"

He got up and said, "I am a poet."

I said, "A good poet?"

He said, "The greatest in the world."

---

2. **gru-gru palm trees.** West Indian palms with spiny trunks

3. **congorees.** Large, scaleless eels found in the waters of the West Indies

4. **White Wordsworth.** William Wordsworth (1770–1850), English Romantic poet

5. **calypsonians.** West Indian folk musicians who sing syncopated, improvised songs (calypso music)

And when B. Wordsworth left, I prayed I would see him again.

About a week later, coming back from school one afternoon, I met him at the corner of Miguel Street.

He said, "I have been waiting for you for a long time."

I said, "You sell any poetry yet?"

He shook his head.

He said, "In my yard I have the best mango tree in Port-of-Spain. And now the mangoes are ripe and red and very sweet and juicy. I have waited here for you to tell you this and to invite you to come and eat some of my mangoes."

He lived in Alberto Street in a one-roomed hut placed right in the centre of the lot. The yard seemed all green. There was a big mango tree. There was a coconut tree and there was a plum tree. The place looked wild, as though it wasn't in the city at all. You couldn't see all the big concrete houses in the street.

He was right. The mangoes were sweet and juicy. I ate about six, and the yellow mango juice ran down my arms to my elbows and down my mouth to my chin and my shirt was stained.

My mother said when I got home, "Where you was? You think you is a man now and could go all over the place? Go cut a whip for me."

She beat me rather badly, and I ran out of the house swearing that I would never come back. I went to B. Wordsworth's house. I was so angry, my nose was bleeding.

B. Wordsworth said, "Stop crying, and we will go for a walk."

I stopped crying, but I was breathing short. We went for a walk. We walked down St. Clair Avenue to the Savannah and we walked to the race-course.

B. Wordsworth said, "Now, let us lie on the grass and look up at the sky, and I want you to think how far those stars are from us."

I did as he told me, and I saw what he meant. I felt like nothing, and at the same time I had never felt so big and great in all my life. I forgot all my anger and all my tears and all the blows.

I felt like nothing, and at the same time I had never felt so big and great in all my life.

When I said I was better, he began telling me the names of the stars, and I particularly remembered the constellation of Orion the Hunter,[6] though I don't really know why. I can spot Orion even today, but I have forgotten the rest.

Then a light was flashed in our faces, and we saw a policeman. We got up from the grass.

The policeman said, "What you doing here?"

B. Wordsworth said, "I have been asking myself the same question for forty years."

We became friends, B. Wordsworth and I. He told me, "You must never tell anybody about me and about the mango tree and the coconut tree and the plum tree. You must keep that a secret. If you tell anybody, I will know, because I am a poet."

I gave him my word and I kept it.

I liked his little room. It had no more furniture than George's front room,[7] but it looked cleaner and healthier. But it also looked lonely.

One day I asked him, "Mister Wordsworth, why you does keep all this bush in your yard? Ain't it does make the place damp?"

He said, "Listen, and I will tell you a story. Once upon a time a boy and girl met each other and they fell in love. They loved each other so much they got married. They were both poets. He loved words. She loved grass and flowers and trees. They lived happily in a single room, and then one day, the girl poet

---

6. **Orion the Hunter.** Constellation named after a giant hunter in Greek myth who is accidentally killed by Artemis, the Greek goddess of hunting

7. **George's front room.** George is a character in another story in *Miguel Street.*

View of Port-of-Spain, Trinidad and Tobago.

said to the boy poet, 'We are going to have another poet in the family.' But this poet was never born, because the girl died, and the young poet died with her, inside her. And the girl's husband was very sad, and he said he would never touch a thing in the girl's garden. And so the garden remained, and grew high and wild."

I looked at B. Wordsworth, and as he told me this lovely story, he seemed to grow older. I understood his story.

We went for long walks together. We went to the Botanical Gardens and the Rock Gardens. We climbed Chancellor Hill in the late afternoon and watched the darkness fall on Port-of-Spain, and watched the lights go on in the city and on the ships in the harbor.

He did everything as though he were doing it for the first time in his life. He did everything as though he were doing some church rite.

He would say to me, "Now, how about having some ice cream?"

And when I said, yes, he would grow very serious and say, "Now, which café shall we patronize?" As though it were a very important thing. He would think for some time about it, and finally say, "I think I will go and negotiate the purchase with that shop."

The world became a most exciting place.

One day, when I was in his yard, he said to me, "I have a great secret which I am now going to tell you."

I said, "It really secret?"

"At the moment, yes."

I looked at him, and he looked at me. He said, "This is just between you and me, remember. I am writing a poem."

"Oh." I was disappointed.

He said, "But this is a different sort of poem. This is the greatest poem in the world."

I whistled.

He said, "I have been working on it for more than five years now. I will finish it in about twenty-two years from now, that is, if I keep on writing at the present rate."

"You does write a lot, then?"

He said, "Not any more. I just write one line a month. But I make sure it is a good line."

I asked, "What was last month's good line?"

He looked up at the sky, and said, *"The past is deep."*

I said, "It is a beautiful line."

B. Wordsworth said, "I hope to distill the experiences of a whole month into that single line of poetry. So, in twenty-two years, I shall have written a poem that will sing to all humanity."

I was filled with wonder.

"I just write one line a month. But I make sure it is a good line."

Our walks continued. We walked along the sea-wall at Docksite one day, and I said, "Mr. Wordsworth, if I drop this pin in the water, you think it will float?"

He said, "This is a strange world. Drop your pin, and let us see what will happen."

pa • tron • ize (pā′ trə nīz′) *v.*, do business with; support
dis • till (di stil′) *v.*, obtain or extract the essence of

The pin sank.

I said, "How is the poem this month?"

But he never told me any other line. He merely said, "Oh, it comes, you know. It comes."

Or we would sit on the sea-wall and watch the liners come into the harbor.

But of the greatest poem in the world I heard no more.

I felt he was growing older.

"How you does live, Mr. Wordsworth?" I asked him one day.

He said, "You mean how I get money?"

When I nodded, he laughed in a crooked way.

He said, "I sing calypsoes in the calypso season."

"And that last you the rest of the year?"

"It is enough."

"But you will be the richest man in the world when you write the greatest poem?"

He didn't reply.

One day when I went to see him in his little house, I found him lying on his little bed. He looked so old and so weak, that I found myself wanting to cry.

He said, "The poem is not going well."

He wasn't looking at me. He was looking through the window at the coconut tree, and he was speaking as though I wasn't there. He said, "When I was twenty I felt the power within myself." Then, almost in front of my eyes, I could see his face growing older and more tired. He said, "But that—that was a long time ago."

And then—I felt so keenly, it was as though I had been slapped by my mother. I could see it clearly on his face. It was there for everyone to see. Death on the shrinking face.

He looked at me, and saw my tears and sat up.

He said, "Come." I went and sat on his knees.

He looked into my eyes, and he said, "Oh, you can see it, too. I always knew you had the poet's eye."

He didn't even look sad, and that made me burst out crying loudly.

He pulled me to his thin chest, and said, "Do you want me to tell you a funny story?" and he smiled encouragingly at me.

But I couldn't reply.

He said, "When I have finished this story, I want you to promise that you will go away and never come back to see me. Do you promise?"

I nodded.

He said, "Good. Well, listen. That story I told you about the boy poet and the girl poet, do you remember that? That wasn't true. It was something I just made up. All this talk about poetry and the greatest poem in the world, that wasn't true, either. Isn't that the funniest thing you have heard?"

But his voice broke.

I left the house, and ran home crying, like a poet, for everything I saw.

I walked along Alberto Street a year later, but I could find no sign of the poet's house. It hadn't vanished, just like that. It had been pulled down, and a big, two-storied building had taken its place. The mango tree and the plum tree and the coconut tree had all been cut down, and there was brick and concrete everywhere.

It was just as though B. Wordsworth had never existed. ❖

B. Wordsworth tells the narrator, "You're a poet, too, you know." How can someone become a poet? What is unique about a poet's outlook on life?

Telephone Conversation

by Wole Soyinka

The price seemed reasonable, location
Indifferent. The landlady swore she lived
Off premises. Nothing remained
But self-confession. "Madam," I warned,
5   "I hate a wasted journey—I am African."
Silence. Silence transmission of
Pressurized good-breeding. Voice, when it came,
Lipstick coated, long gold-rolled
Cigarette-holder pipped. Caught I was, foully.

10　"HOW DARK?" . . . I had not misheard . . . "ARE YOU LIGHT
　　OR VERY DARK?" Button B. Button A.[1] Stench
　　Of <u>rancid</u> breath of public hide-and-speak.
　　Red booth. Red pillar-box.[2] Red double-tiered
　　Omnibus[3] squelching tar. It *was* real! Shamed
15　By ill-mannered silence, surrender
　　Pushed dumbfoundedment to beg simpflication.
　　Considerate she was, varying the emphasis—

　　"ARE YOU DARK? OR VERY LIGHT?" Revelation came.
　　"You mean—like plain or milk chocolate?"
20　Her <u>assent</u> was clinical, crushing in its light
　　Impersonality. Rapidly, wavelength adjusted,
　　I chose. "West African sepia[4]"—and as an afterthought,
　　"Down in my passport." Silence for spectroscopic
　　Flight of fancy,[5] till truthfulness clanged her accent
25　Hard on the mouthpiece. "WHAT'S THAT?" <u>conceding</u>,
　　"DON'T KNOW WHAT THAT IS." "Like brunette."

　　"THAT'S DARK, ISN'T IT?" "Not altogether.
　　Facially, I am brunette, but madam, you should see
　　The rest of me. Palm of my hand, soles of my feet
30　Are a peroxide blonde. Friction, caused—
　　Foolishly, madam—by sitting down, has turned
　　My bottom raven black—One moment madam!"—sensing
　　Her receiver rearing on the thunderclap
　　About my ears—"Madam," I pleaded, "wouldn't you rather
35　See for yourself?" ❖

---

1. **Button B. Button A.** In a pay telephone booth of the time, the caller could press
   one of two buttons after inserting money. Button A would put the call through to
   the recipient; Button B would disconnect the call and return the caller's money.
2. **pillar-box.** British term for *mailbox*
3. **double-tiered Omnibus.** Double-decker bus
4. **sepia.** Brownish-gray color similar to the tint of old photographs
5. **spectroscopic . . . fancy.** A spectroscope is a tool that allows scientists to examine the range of colors in white light. This phrase indicates that the woman is
   silently thinking of all the colors she knows.

> **ran • cid** (ran[t]´ səd) *adj.*, having a bad smell or taste
> **as • sent** (ə sent´) *n.*, acknowledgment; agreement
> **con • cede** (kən sēd´) *v.*, acknowledge grudgingly or hesitantly

MIRRORS & WINDOWS

At the end of the poem, the speaker says, "Madam, . . . wouldn't you rather / See for yourself?" Why do people often make assumptions about individuals based on stereotypes? How is this unfair and potentially harmful to the individual?

Refer to Text ▶ ▶ ▶ ▶ ▶   Reason with Text

1a. What "self-confession" does the speaker make to the landlady at the beginning of "Telephone Conversation"?	**1b.** Why does he make this confession?	**Understand** Find meaning
2a. In "Midsummer XXIII," of what does the "stampeding hiss and scurry" of the leaves remind the speaker?	**2b.** How does this imagery help create the mood of the poem?	**Apply** Use information
3a. For what reason is the speaker in "Midsummer XXIII" in England?	**3b.** Compare and contrast the two speakers' encounters with prejudice.	**Analyze** Take things apart
4a. What does the landlady in "Telephone Conversation" want to know about the speaker? Describe her reaction to his answer.	**4b.** Argue whether this situation is an effective way to reveal prejudice. Use evidence from the poem to support your opinion.	**Evaluate** Make judgments
5a. How does "Telephone Conversation" end? How does "Midsummer XXIII" end?	**5b.** Explain what impression of England is created by each poem. Cite specific examples from each poem to support your answer.	**Create** Bring ideas together

Compare Literature

Purpose and Theme

Define the writer's purpose in each poem. Does either writer have more than one purpose? How effective is each writer in achieving his purpose?

Draw inferences as to the theme, or author's message, of each poem. How do the themes compare and contrast? How does each theme help support the writer's purpose? Support your answers by providing textual evidence that you used for your reasoning.

Extend the Text

Writing Options

Creative Writing Imagine that you are a member of the local housing discrimination authority and have received a complaint about the landlady from the speaker in "Telephone Conversation." Write a business letter to the landlady outlining the complaint and explaining what will happen to her rental permit if she continues to discriminate against prospective black tenants.

Expository Writing Write a comparison and contrast essay that discusses the purpose of each poem. Evaluate whether each poet is successful in achieving his purpose; use details from the poem to support your analysis.

Lifelong Learning

Present an Oral Report Use library and Internet resources to research the causes and effects of the Brixton riot in 1981. Prepare an oral report in which you outline the causes and explain one of the effects in greater detail. For instance, how did the riot affect public policy in Great Britain? How did it affect race relations?

Critical Literacy

Present an Oral Interpretation With two classmates, prepare a reading of "Telephone Conversation." Choose one member to read the dialogue of the landlady, one to read the dialogue of the tenant, and one to read the general lines of the speaker. Together, practice reading the poem out loud, using your voices and facial expressions to convey the thoughts and feelings of the different characters. Perform the reading for the class.

 Go to **www.mirrorsandwindows.com** for more.

1. In line 5 of "Telephone Conversation," why does the narrator say, "I hate a wasted journey—I am African"?
   A. He likes to tell about his heritage.
   B. He avoids traveling whenever possible.
   C. Historically, Africans have had to make many journeys in their lives.
   D. He wants to see if the landlady is prejudiced and unwilling to rent to him.
   E. Past experiences make him angry and sarcastic when dealing with rich people.

2. In line 12 of "Telephone Conversation," what is likely Soyinka's main purpose for using the term *hide-and-speak?*
   A. to force the reader to guess what is happening
   B. to emphasize the line by using strong imagery
   C. to make it clear that the speaker is not really prejudiced
   D. to make the poem seem more poetic by including assonance
   E. to compare what is being described with the children's game hide-and-seek

3. In line 22 of "Telephone Conversation," to what does the phrase "West African sepia" refer?
   A. a place
   B. a color
   C. a person
   D. a type of milk
   E. a kind of photograph

4. In lines 1–2 and 7–9 of "Telephone Conversation," what literary technique does Soyinka use?
   A. metaphors
   B. personification
   C. inversion of words
   D. omission of articles
   E. part-of-speech changes

5. In "Midsummer XXIII," Walcott uses all of the following *except*
   A. allusions.
   B. strong verbs.
   C. sensory images.
   D. references to race.
   E. nonstandard English.

6. Which of the following seems a likely reason for Walcott's choice of the title "Midsummer XXIII"?
   A. to tell when the scenes in the poem happened
   B. to explain that the poem is about a favorite time of the year
   C. to make the reader think of Shakespeare's *A Midsummer Night's Dream*
   D. to relate to the second line, "midsummer's leaves race to extinction like the roar"
   E. to emphasize that the events occurred in England, where the term *midsummer* is used

7. In "Midsummer XXIII," the phrase "like the roar of a Brixton riot" is an example of
   A. a simile.
   B. a stanza.
   C. a metaphor.
   D. an ironic tone.
   E. an iambic foot.

8. "Telephone Conversation" and "Midsummer XXIII" have all of the following in common *except* for
   A. subject matter.
   B. point of view.
   C. general setting.
   D. use of literary allusions.
   E. use of strong, almost violent images.

9. **Constructed Response:** Discuss Walcott's diction, or word choice, in "Midsummer XXIII." Does he use words that you would expect? What do many of his words have in common? Use examples from the poem to support your analysis.

10. **Constructed Response:** Analyze Soyinka's frequent references to color in "Telephone Conversation." Look for patterns among these references, and organize them into several sets. Do the sets have different purposes? Again, use details from the selection to support your analysis.

The Short Story Defined

The **short story** is a short fictional narrative. Like a novel, a short story must contain a well-developed plot, authentic characters, and a theme. However, a short story has a more narrow focus, introducing only a few important characters and resolving the conflict, if at all, in relatively few pages. Short story authors must quickly establish a setting and develop a particular mood. Like a poem, the short story requires economy of language. It also must have the momentum to carry readers along to its conclusion.

"Words have weight, sound, and appearance; it is only by considering these that you can write a sentence that is good to look at and good to listen to."

—SOMERSET MAUGHAM, MODERN NOVELIST
AND SHORT STORY WRITER

Elements of the Short Story

As you read the short stories in this unit, notice how the author creates a setting and mood, establishes a point of view, breathes life into characters, develops the action, and suggests one or more themes.

Setting and Mood

The **setting** is the time and place of the unfolding action and includes the details used to create a sense of a particular time and place. This might be a school compound in a Nigerian village at the start of the school term or a London cafe garden at tea time. The historical period of the story also is significant. For example, Chinua Achebe's "Dead Man's Path" is set in 1949, when Nigeria still was under British colonial rule. This setting helps establish the conflict between traditional African beliefs and modern European perspectives.

The details that create the setting also set a **mood,** or atmosphere, which is the emotion created in the reader. The relationship between setting and mood is highlighted in a passage from Anita Desai's "Games at Twilight," when the young boy named Ravi closes himself in a shed during a game of hide-and-seek and realizes "It was dark, spooky in the shed." The musty smell of dust and animal droppings is unpleasant and suggests death and decay. The low roof and lack of light are oppressive. These details establish a mood of uneasiness.

Narrative Voice and Point of View

The **narrator** is the character or speaker who tells a story. **Point of view** is the perspective from which the story is told. As a character in the story, a *first-person narrator* is limited by what he or she can observe directly about other characters and situations. Such a narrator is subjective in point of view and may or may not be reliable. For example, the young narrator of V. S. Naipaul's "B. Wordsworth" has limited life experience and knowledge about his antagonist. In determining how reliable the narrator's information is, readers must evaluate the narrator's ability to assess situations.

A *third-person narrator* can be either limited in point of view or omniscient (all knowing). The narrator with a *limited* point of view does not possess all the information needed to understand a situation. For example, the narrator of "Dead Man's Path" seems to support Obi's view that the traditional beliefs of the native villagers are clouded by superstition and ignorance. The identification of the narrator with Obi is a clue that the point of view is limited. The third-person *omniscient* narrator knows everything about the characters and the plot, as in Doris Lessing's "No Witchcraft for Sale."

Characterization

Characterization is the act of creating or describing a character. Using *direct characterization,* the writer tells what a character is like. Using *indirect characterization,* the writer shows what characters say, do, or think; shows what other characters say or think about them; and describes the physical features, dress, and personality of characters. For example, in "No Witchcraft for Sale," the Farquars are directly charac-

terized as being religious. Their piety also is suggested using indirect characterization when Mrs. Farquar tells Gideon, "God chose you as an instrument for His goodness."

Dialogue, or conversation, is Lessing's primary device for creating characters in the short story "Sparrows." The middle-aged parents of a young woman feeling her way toward independence have an exchange that illuminates a great deal about each of them:

> She was counting to ten before she spoke. "That's why she wants to leave and get a place of her own."
>
> "At our expense."
>
> "The money's only sitting in the bank."
>
> "But suppose we wanted it for something. Repairs to the house . . . the car's getting old . . ."
>
> She sighed, not meaning to. "I said, if you feel like that about it, then don't. . . ."
>
> "I don't see we've any choice. . . ."

The wife is generous and willing to take risks; the husband is stingy and fearful about the future. The brief dialogue clearly characterizes the couple and suggests how they have related to one another over the years.

Plot and Conflict

A **plot** is the series of events related to the central **conflict,** or struggle. Typically, the plot introduces the conflict, develops it, and resolves it.

The first element of plot, the **exposition,** provides background information about the characters, setting, or conflict and usually appears at the beginning of the story. The exposition helps readers understand what is to follow. The **rising action** sets up the conflict or problem that the protagonist (main character) must resolve. The **climax** of the plot is the high point of interest or suspense. It is the turning point of the action, during which the character takes a critical step or reaches an understanding of the problem. The **falling action** consists of all the events that follow the climax. The **resolution** is the point at which the central conflict is ended, or resolved.

Theme

A **theme** is a central message or perception about life that is revealed through a literary work. A *stated theme* is presented directly, whereas an *implied theme* must be inferred.

In "No Witchcraft for Sale," Gideon implies a central theme of racism when he says, "Ah, missus, these are both children, and one will grow up to be a baas [master], and one will be a servant." Often, a work of literature has several major themes.

HOW TO READ

A Short Story

Identify the point of view. In deciding who will tell the story, the author determines how much and what kind of information to give readers. Identify the point of view, and determine how the narrator's perspective may be limited or biased.

Trace the sequence of events. In a short story, the plot must be established and developed quickly. Pay attention to the exposition at the start of the story to ensure you understand crucial background information. Then identify the central conflict and trace its development to the climax. Predict how the conflict might be resolved.

Identify the theme. To identify the theme, consider what is suggested by how the conflict is resolved. Also consider the outcome of the story for the various characters, especially the protagonist.

Games at Twilight

A Short Story by Anita Desai

Build Background

Literary Context Anita Desai's fiction focuses on her native land of India. She is noted for her rich use of visual imagery and details. Although she portrays bustling urban life, she focuses on characters who are outsiders—who feel lost among or alienated from the crowd. Desai often depicts modern family life as chaotic and sometimes as violent. She once noted, "A lot of people tell me my books are extremely pessimistic and extremely dark, but I would prefer to think of them as facing the truth, not having illusions."

"Games at Twilight," the title story from Desai's first collection of short stories, centers on the character of Ravi, a young boy from a large, wealthy Indian family. The plot is about a simple game of hide-and-seek that changes the way Ravi looks at himself, his family, and his place in the world.

Reader's Context Recall a time when you felt left out, forgotten, or disillusioned by something. What happened to make you feel this way? How did you feel and what did you do about the situation?

Meet the Author

Anita Desai (b. 1937) was born in Mussoorie, India, a popular resort area for residents of Delhi. Her father was Bengali, a native of the northeastern region of India, and her mother was German. Three languages were spoken in Desai's home: German, English, and Hindi.

Desai attended a school run by British missionaries, so she learned to read and write in English before mastering Hindi. Desai also chose English as her "literary language" and displayed an interest in writing at a very early age, contributing to a children's magazine before she was ten. After graduating from the University of Delhi in 1957, she married Ashvin Desai the following year and had four children, one of whom is the award-winning novelist Kiran Desai.

Desai's first novel, *Cry the Peacock,* was published in 1963. Her other well-known and prize-winning works include *Fire on the Mountain* (1977), *Clear Light of Day* (1980), *In Custody* (1984), and *Fasting, Feasting* (1999). Her short stories have appeared in numerous magazines, as well as in the collection *Games at Twilight and Other Stories* (1978). Desai has taught creative writing at Mount Holyoke College and Smith College in the United States and is a Fellow of the Royal Society of Literature, the American Academy of Arts and Letters, and Girton College, Cambridge. She currently resides in the United States.

Analyze Literature

Setting and Archetype

The **setting** of a literary work is the time and place in which it occurs, together with all the details used to create a sense of a particular time and place.

An **archetype** is a type of character, image, theme, symbol, plot, or other element that has appeared in the literature of the world from ancient times until today. The story of a quest or journey, in which someone experiences adventure and danger and becomes wiser, is an example of an archetype.

Set Purpose

Desai's "Game at Twilight" provides vivid settings that help emphasize a particular mood at different instances throughout the story. While you read, record the different places Desai describes. What information does she reveal about each location? Consider how Desai's description of the setting helps create a particular mood. Also identify an archetype that appears in the story.

Preview Vocabulary

maniacal, 1185
stridently, 1186
intervene, 1186
jubilation, 1186
superciliously, 1187
defunct, 1187
temerity, 1188
lugubrious, 1190
funereal, 1190
ignominy, 1190

Games at Twilight

by Anita Desai

What fun if they were all found and caught—he alone left unconquered!

It was still too hot to play outdoors. They had had their tea, they had been washed and had their hair brushed, and after the long day of confinement in the house that was not cool but at least a protection from the sun, the children strained to get out. Their faces were red and bloated with the effort, but their mother would not open the door; everything was still curtained and shuttered in a way that stifled the children, made them feel that their lungs were stuffed with cotton wool and their noses with dust and if they didn't burst out into the light and see the sun and feel the air, they would choke.

"Please, Ma, please," they begged. "We'll play in the veranda and porch—we won't go a step out of the porch."

"You will, I know you will, and then—"

"No—we won't, we won't," they wailed so horrendously that she actually let down the bolt of the front door, so that they burst out like seeds from a crackling, overripe pod into the veranda with such wild, <u>maniacal</u> yells that she retreated to her bath and the shower of

> **ma • ni • a • cal** (mə nī´ ə kəl) *adj.*, characterized by intense excitement or frenzy

The children, too, felt released. They too began tumbling, shoving, pushing against each other, frantic to start. Start what? Start their business. The business of the children's day which is—play.

"Let's play hide-and-seek."

"Who'll be It?"

"You be It."

"Why should I? You be—"

"You're the eldest—"

"That doesn't mean—"

The shoves became harder. Some kicked out. The motherly Mira <u>intervened</u>. She pulled the boys roughly apart. There was a tearing sound of cloth, but it was lost in the heavy panting and angry grumbling, and no one paid attention to the small sleeve hanging loosely off a shoulder.

"Make a circle, make a circle!" she shouted, firmly pulling and pushing till a kind of vague circle was formed. "Now clap!" she roared, and clapping, they all chanted in melancholy unison "Dip, dip, dip—my blue ship—" and every now and then one or the other saw he was safe by the way his hands fell at the crucial moment—palm on palm, or back of hand on palm—and dropped out of the circle with a yell and a jump of relief and <u>jubilation</u>.

Raghu was It. He started to protest, to cry, "You cheated—Mira cheated—Anu cheated—" but it was too late; the others had all already streaked away. There was no one to hear when he called out, "Only in the veranda—the porch—Ma said—Ma *said* to stay in the porch!" No one had stopped to listen; all he saw was

talcum powder and the fresh sari[1] that were to help her face the summer evening.

They faced the afternoon. It was too hot. Too bright. The white walls of the veranda glared <u>stridently</u> in the sun. The bougainvillea[2] hung about it, purple and magenta, in livid[3] balloons. The garden outside was like a tray made of beaten brass, flattened out on the red gravel and the stony soil in all shades of metal—aluminum, tin, copper and brass. No life stirred at this arid time of day—the birds still drooped, like dead fruit, in the papery tents of the trees; some squirrels lay limp on the wet earth under the garden tap. The outdoor dog lay stretched as if dead on the veranda mat, his paws and ears and tail all reaching out like dying travellers in search of water. He rolled his eyes at the children— two white marbles rolling in the purple sockets, begging for sympathy—and attempted to lift his tail in a wag but could not. It only twitched and lay still.

Then, perhaps roused by the shrieks of the children, a band of parrots suddenly fell out of the eucalyptus tree, tumbled frantically in the still, sizzling air, then sorted themselves out into battle formation and streaked away across the white sky.

---

1. **sari.** Garment worn by Hindu women, consisting of a long piece of cloth that is draped across one shoulder and forms an ankle-length skirt
2. **bougainvillea.** Flowering tropical vines
3. **livid.** Brightly discolored, as by a bruise

---

stri • dent • ly (strī′ d'nt) *adv.,* in a harsh, insistent manner
in • ter • vene (in′ tər vēn′) *v.,* become involved in; mediate
ju • bi • la • tion (jü′ bə lā′ shən) *n.,* expression of great joy

their brown legs flashing through the dusty shrubs, scrambling up brick walls, leaping over compost heaps[4] and hedges; and then the porch stood empty in the purple shade of the bougain-villea and the garden was as empty as before; even the limp squirrels had whisked away, leaving everything gleaming, brassy and bare.

Only small Manu suddenly reappeared, as if he had dropped out of an invisible cloud or from a bird's claws, and stood for a moment in the center of the yellow lawn, chewing his finger and near to tears as he heard Raghu shouting, with his head pressed against the veranda wall, "Eighty-three, eighty-five, eighty-nine, ninety . . ." and then made off in a panic, half of him wanting to fly north, the other half counseling south. Raghu turned just in time to see the flash of his white shorts and the uncertain skittering of his red sandals and charged after him with such a blood-curdling yell that Manu stumbled over the hose pipe, fell into its rubber coils and lay there weeping, "I won't be It—you have to find them all—all—All!"

"I know I have to, idiot," Raghu said, superciliously kicking him with his toe. "You're dead," he said with satisfaction, licking the beads of perspiration off his upper lip, and then stalked off in search of worthier prey, whistling spiritedly so that the hiders should hear and tremble.

R avi heard the whistling and picked his nose in a panic, trying to find comfort by burrowing the finger deep—deep into that soft tunnel. He felt himself too exposed, sitting on an upturned flower pot behind the garage. Where could he burrow? He could run around the garage if he heard Raghu come—around and around and around—but he hadn't much faith in his short legs when matched against Raghu's long, hefty, hairy footballer legs.[5] Ravi had a frightening glimpse of them as Raghu combed the hedge of crotons and hibiscus,[6] trampling delicate ferns underfoot as he did so. Ravi looked about him desperately, swallowing a small ball of snot in his fear.

The garage was locked with a great, heavy lock to which the driver had the key in his room, hanging from a nail on the wall under his work shirt. Ravi had peeped in and seen him still sprawling on his string cot in his vest and striped underpants, the hair on his chest and the hair in his nose shaking with the vibrations of his phlegm-obstructed snores. Ravi had wished he were tall enough, big enough to reach the key on the nail, but it was impossible, beyond his reach for years to come. He had sidled away and sat dejectedly on the flower pot. That at least was cut to his own size.

But next to the garage was another shed with a big green door. Also locked. No one even knew who had the key to the lock. That shed wasn't opened more than once a year, when Ma turned out all the old broken bits of furniture and rolls of matting and leaking buckets, and the white ant hills were broken and swept away and Flit sprayed into the spider webs and rat holes so that the whole operation was like the looting of a poor, ruined and conquered city. The green leaves of the door sagged. They were nearly off their rusty hinges. The hinges were large and made a small gap between the door and the walls—only just large enough for rats, dogs and, possibly, Ravi to slip through.

Ravi had never cared to enter such a dark and depressing mortuary[7] of defunct household goods seething with such unspeakable and alarming animal life, but, as Raghu's whistling grew angrier and sharper and his crashing

---

4. **compost heaps.** Mixtures of decaying plant matter that are used as fertilizer
5. **footballer legs.** Legs like those of a soccer player
6. **crotons and hibiscus.** Crotons are tropical shrubs with ornamental, leathery leaves; hibiscus are plants and shrubs with large, colorful flowers.
7. **mortuary.** Place where dead bodies are kept before burial or cremation

---

su • per • cil • ious • ly (sü′ pər si′ lē əs lē) *adv.*, in a cool and haughty manner
de • funct (di fəŋkt′) *adj.*, no longer existing or functioning

and storming in the hedge wilder, Ravi suddenly slipped off the flower pot and through the crack and was gone. He chuckled aloud with astonishment at his own <u>temerity</u> so that Raghu came out of the hedge, stood silent with his hands on his hips, listening, and finally shouted, "I heard you! I'm coming! Got you—" and came charging round the garage only to find the upturned flower pot, the yellow dust, the crawling of white ants in a mud hill against the closed shed door—nothing. Snarling, he bent to pick up a stick and went off, whacking it against the garage and shed walls as if to beat out his prey.

He chuckled aloud with astonishment at his own temerity.

Ravi shook, then shivered with delight, with self-congratulation. Also with fear. It was dark, spooky in the shed. It had a muffled smell, as of graves. Ravi had once got locked into the linen cupboard and sat there weeping for half an hour before he was rescued. But at least that had been a familiar place and even smelt pleasantly of starch, laundry and, reassuringly, his mother. But the shed smelt of rats, ant hills, dust and spider webs. Also of less definable, less recognizable horrors. And it was dark. Except for the white-hot cracks along the door, there was no light. The roof was very low. Although Ravi was small, he felt as if he could reach up and touch it with his fingertips. But he didn't stretch. He hunched himself into a ball so as not to bump into anything, touch or feel anything. What might there not be to touch him and feel him as he stood there, trying to see in the dark? Something cold or slimy—like a snake. Snakes! He leapt up as Raghu whacked the wall with his stick—

then quickly realizing what it was, felt almost relieved to hear Raghu, hear his stick. It made him feel protected.

But Raghu soon moved away. There wasn't a sound once his footsteps had gone around the garage and disappeared. Ravi stood frozen inside the shed. Then he shivered all over. Something had tickled the back of his neck. It took him a while to pick up the courage to lift his hand and explore. It was an insect—perhaps a spider—exploring him. He squashed it and wondered how many more creatures were watching him, waiting to reach out and touch him, the stranger.

There was nothing now. After standing in that position—his hand still on his neck, feeling the wet splodge of the squashed spider gradually dry—for minutes, hours, his legs began to tremble with the effort, the inaction. By now he could see enough in the dark to make out the large, solid shapes of old wardrobes, broken buckets and bedsteads piled on top of each other around him. He recognized an old bathtub—patches of enamel glimmered at him, and at last he lowered himself onto its edge.

He contemplated slipping out of the shed and into the fray. He wondered if it would not be better to be captured by Raghu and returned to the milling crowd as long as he could be in the sun, the light, the free spaces of the garden and the familiarity of his brothers, sisters and cousins. It would be evening soon. Their games would become legitimate. The parents would sit out on the lawn on cane basket chairs and watch them as they tore around the garden or gathered in knots to share a loot of mulberries or black, teeth-splitting *jamun*[8] from the garden trees. The gardener would fix the hose pipe to the water tap, and water would fall lavishly through the air to the ground, soaking the dry, yellow grass and the red gravel and arousing the sweet, the intoxicating, scent of water on dry earth—that loveliest scent in the world.

---

8. *jamun.* Type of plum

te • mer • i • ty (tə mer′ ə tē) *n.,* foolish or rash boldness

Ravi sniffed for a whiff of it. He half rose from the bathtub, then heard the despairing scream of one of the girls as Raghu bore down upon her. There was the sound of a crash and of rolling about in the bushes, the shrubs, then screams and accusing sobs of "I touched the den—" "You did not—" "I did—" "You liar, you did not," and then a fading away and silence again.

Ravi sat back on the harsh edge of the tub, deciding to hold out a bit longer. What fun if they were all found and caught—he alone left unconquered! He had never known that sensation. Nothing more wonderful had ever happened to him than being taken out by an uncle and bought a whole slab of chocolate all to himself, or being flung into the soda man's pony cart and driven up to the gate by the friendly driver with the red beard and pointed ears. To defeat Raghu—that hirsute,[9] hoarse-voiced football champion—and to be the winner in a circle of older, bigger, luckier children—that would be thrilling beyond imagination. He hugged his knees together and smiled to himself almost shyly at the thought of so much victory, such laurels.

There he sat smiling, knocking his heels against the bathtub, now and then getting up and going to the door to put his ear to the broad crack and listening for sounds of the game, the pursuer and the pursued, and then returning to his seat with the dogged determination of the true winner, a breaker of records, a champion.

It grew darker in the shed as the light at the door grew softer, fuzzier, turned to a kind of crumbling yellow pollen that turned to yellow fur, blue fur, gray fur. Evening. Twilight. The sound of water gushing, falling. The scent of earth receiving water, slaking[10] its thirst in great gulps and releasing that green scent of freshness, coolness. Through the crack Ravi saw the long purple shadows of the shed and the garage lying still across the yard. Beyond that, the white walls of the house. The bougainvillea had lost its lividity, hung in dark

bundles that quaked and twittered and seethed with masses of homing sparrows. The lawn was shut off from his view. Could he hear the children's voices? It seemed to him that he could. It seemed to him that he could hear them chanting, singing, laughing. But what about the game? What had happened? Could it be over? How could it when he was still not found?

It then occurred to him that he could have slipped out long ago, dashed across the yard to the veranda and touched the "den." It was necessary to do that to win. He had forgotten. He had only remembered the part of hiding and trying to elude the seeker. He had done that so successfully, his success had occupied him so wholly, that he had quite forgotten that success had to be clinched by that final dash to victory and the ringing cry of "Den!"

With a whimper he burst through the crack, fell on his knees, got up and stumbled on stiff, benumbed legs across the shadowy yard, crying heartily by the time he reached the veranda so that when he flung himself at the white pillar and bawled, "Den! Den! Den!" his voice broke with rage and pity at the disgrace of it all, and he felt himself flooded with tears and misery.

Out on the lawn, the children stopped chanting. They all turned to stare at him in amazement. Their faces were pale and triangular in the dusk. The trees and bushes around them stood inky and sepulchral,[11] spilling long shadows across them. They stared, wondering at his reappearance, his passion, his wild animal howling. Their mother rose from her basket chair and came toward him, worried, annoyed, saying, "Stop it, stop it, Ravi. Don't be a baby. Have you hurt yourself?" Seeing him attended to, the children went back to clasping their hands and chanting, "The grass is green, the rose is red. . . ."

But Ravi would not let them. He tore himself out of his mother's grasp and pounded across the lawn into their midst, charging at

---

9. **hirsute.** Hairy and shaggy
10. **slaking.** Satisfying
11. **sepulchral.** Dismal, gloomy; suggestive of the grave or burial

them with his head lowered so that they scattered in surprise. "I won, I won, I won," he bawled, shaking his head so that the big tears flew. "Raghu didn't find me. I won, I won—"

It took them a minute to grasp what he was saying, even who he was. They had quite forgotten him. Raghu had found all the others long ago. There had been a fight about who was to be It next. It had been so fierce that their mother had emerged from her bath and made them change to another game. Then they had played another and another. Broken mulberries from the tree and eaten them. Helped the driver wash the car when their father returned from work. Helped the gardener water the beds till he roared at them and swore he would complain to their parents. The parents had come out, taken up their positions on the cane chairs. They had begun to play again, sing and chant. All this time no one had remembered Ravi. Having disappeared from the scene, he had disappeared from their minds. Clean.

"Don't be a fool," Raghu said roughly, pushing him aside, and even Mira said, "Stop howling, Ravi. If you want to play, you can stand at the end of the line," and she put him there very firmly.

The game proceeded. Two pairs of arms reached up and met in an arc. The children trooped under it again and again in a <u>lugubrious</u> circle, ducking their heads and intoning

"The grass is green,
The rose is red;
Remember me
When I am dead, dead, dead, dead . . ."

And the arc of thin arms trembled in the twilight, and the heads were bowed so sadly, and their feet tramped to that melancholy refrain so mournfully, so helplessly,

that Ravi could not bear it. He would not follow them: he would not be included in this <u>funereal</u> game. He had wanted victory and triumph—not a funeral. But he had been forgotten, left out and he would not join them now. The <u>ignominy</u> of being forgotten—how could he face it? He felt his heart go heavy and ache inside him unbearably. He lay down full length on the damp grass, crushing his face into it, no longer crying, silenced by a terrible sense of his insignificance. ❖

---

lu • gu • bri • ous (lù gü´ brē əs) *adj.,* exaggeratedly mournful
fu • ne • re • al (fyün´ rəl) *adj.,* befitting or suggesting a funeral
ig • no • mi • ny (ig´ nə mi' nē) *n.,* deep personal humiliation and disgrace

---

MIRRORS & WINDOWS

At the end of the story, Ravi has come to a new understanding about the world. When have you had an experience that significantly changed the way you interacted with the world?

Refer to Text ▶ ▶ ▶ ▶ ▶	Reason with Text	
1a. Describe what the children are doing at the beginning of the story.	**1b.** What does the children's interaction suggest about their relationships?	**Understand** Find meaning
2a. What is Ravi's impression of Raghu?	**2b.** Suggest how Ravi might have acted differently during the game of hide and seek if he had had a different impression of Raghu.	**Apply** Use information
3a. Why does Ravi hide in the shed?	**3b.** How do his actions during the game differ from those of Manu? What does this say about each boy's character?	**Analyze** Take things apart
4a. How does Ravi's family respond to his sudden reappearance at the end of the story?	**4b.** Determine whether they understand what he is feeling. Why or why not?	**Evaluate** Make judgments
5a. How does Ravi feel at the end of the story? What sudden realization does he have?	**5b.** Predict how this realization might affect him in the future.	**Create** Bring ideas together

Analyze Literature

Setting and Archetype

Choose one of the places vividly described by Desai. What information is revealed in the description of the setting? How does this description help create a particular mood? How does the setting description affect your understanding of the story?

What archetype appears in this story? Does it have to do with character, image, theme, symbol, or plot?

Extend the Text

Writing Options

Creative Writing Think of an experience from your childhood that changed your understanding of something significant in your life or the world in general. Write a one-page memoir that tells about the experience and your reflections on it. Imagine that you will share this memoir with young children you are mentoring.

Expository Writing Choose a novel or memoir that includes the same archetype as "Games at Twilight"—for example, the novel *Kite Runner*, by Khaled Hosseini. Write an essay in which you compare and contrast the presentation of the archetype in the two works. Explain how similarities and differences in the treatment of this element affect the narration. Cite examples from both texts to support your inferences and conclusions.

Media Literacy

Create a Catalog of Children's Games Many of the games played by the children in the story can be traced to a specific point in history. For instance, the game Ring Around the Rosy originated as a dance to ward off death and disease during the Black Plague. With a group of students, brainstorm a list of games you played as children. Research each game to find out more about its origin and rules. Then create a catalog of these games to share with a children's after-school program.

Critical Literacy

Interpret Imagery Think about the mood created by Desai's use of imagery in the story. Create a visual depiction of this imagery through some form of artwork: a drawing, painting, sculpture, computer-generated image, or collage. Title your artwork and write a paragraph explaining how it represents the mood in the story. Display your artwork and explanation in the classroom.

 Go to **www.mirrorsandwindows.com** for more.

The Train from Rhodesia

A Short Story by Nadine Gordimer

Build Background

Historical Context First published in 1952 in the short story collection *The Soft Voice of the Serpent,* **"The Train from Rhodesia"** takes place in South Africa. Rhodesia was a British colony that eventually became the Republic of Zimbabwe. The story is set during the era of apartheid, which became law in South Africa in 1948.

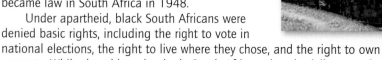

Under apartheid, black South Africans were denied basic rights, including the right to vote in national elections, the right to live where they chose, and the right to own property. While the white minority in South Africa enjoyed privileges and power, the black majority lived in poverty. The inequality and injustice of apartheid is a theme in much of Gordimer's writing.

Reader's Context When have you been ashamed or angered by the way someone you were close to treated another person? How did you respond?

Meet the Author

Nadine Gordimer (b. 1923) was born in Springs, a mining town near Johannesburg, South Africa. Her father was a Jewish watchmaker from Lithuania, and her mother was an English native.

Gordimer attended a Catholic convent school until age eleven, when her mother, believing her to be sickly, decided to educate her at home. Gordimer began writing at this time and had her first story published when she was only fifteen. She spent a year at Witwaterstrand University in Johannesburg before deciding to devote her life to writing.

An ardent opponent of apartheid, Gordimer began using her talent as a way of protesting its injustice. Her first novel, *The Lying Days* (1953), was based largely on her own life and experience. From there, she went on to write about a number of controversial issues of the time. For instance, the novel *Occasion for Loving* (1963) focuses on an interracial relationship, and *The Late Bourgeois* (1974) deals with the relationship between master and servant in South African life. The novel *Burger's Daughter* (1979), based on the life of Bram Fischer, Nelson Mandela's attorney who was sentenced to life in prison, was banned by the South African government.

Gordimer was awarded the Nobel Prize in 1991 for writing "with intense immediacy about the extremely complicated personal and social relationships in her environment."

Analyze Literature

Conflict and Climax

A **conflict** is a struggle between two forces in a literary work. A plot introduces a conflict, develops it, and eventually resolves it. In an *external conflict,* the main character struggles against an outside force such as another character, society or social norms, or fate. In an *internal conflict,* the main character struggles against some element within himself or herself.

The **climax** is the high point of interest and suspense in a literary work. The term also describes the turning point in the plot.

Set Purpose

Gordimer's fiction often focuses on the conflicts created by the complicated social and personal relationships of people in South Africa. As you read, look for the main conflict. Consider who is involved in it and whether it as an internal or external conflict. Also look for the climax of the plot. List the events that lead up to and that directly follow the climax. Determine the connection between the conflict and climax.

Preview Vocabulary

impressionistic, 1194
elongated, 1194
valance, 1195
segmented, 1196
splay, 1196
wryly, 1197
impotence, 1197
atrophy, 1198

The Train from Rhodesia

by Nadine Gordimer

> The heat of shame mounted through her legs and body and sounded in her ears like the sound of sand pouring.

The train came out of the red horizon and bore down toward them over the single straight track.

The stationmaster came out of his little brick station with its pointed chalet roof, feeling the creases in his serge[1] uniform in his legs as well. A stir of preparedness rippled through the squatting native vendors waiting in the dust: the face of a carved wooden animal, eternally surprised, stuck out of a sack. The stationmaster's barefoot children wandered over. From the gray mud huts with the untidy heads that stood within a decorated mud wall, chickens, and dogs with their skin stretched like parchment over their bones, followed the piccanins[2] down to the track. The flushed and perspiring west cast a reflection, faint, without heat, upon the station, upon the tin shed marked "Goods," upon the walled kraal,[3] upon the gray tin house of the stationmaster and upon the sand, that lapped all around, from sky to sky, cast little rhythmical cups of shadow, so that the sand became the sea, and closed over the children's black feet softly and without imprint.

The stationmaster's wife sat behind the mesh of her veranda. Above her head the hunk of a sheep's carcass moved slightly, dangling in a current of air.

They waited.

The train called out, along the sky; but there was no answer; and the cry hung on: I'm coming . . . I'm coming . . .

The engine flared out now, big, whisking a dwindling body behind it; the track flared out to let it in.

---

1. **serge.** Twill cloth
2. **piccanins.** Native children
3. **kraal.** Fenced-in area for livestock

fantasy held toward the faces on the train. Buck, startled and stiff, staring with round black and white eyes. More lions, standing erect, grappling[6] with strange, thin, <u>elongated</u> warriors who clutched spears and showed no fear in their slits of eyes. How much, they asked from the train, how much?

Give me penny, said the little ones with nothing to sell. The dogs went and sat, quite still, under the dining car, where the train breathed out the smell of meat cooking with onion.

A man passed beneath the arch of reaching arms meeting gray-black and white in the exchange of money for the staring wooden eyes, the stiff wooden legs sticking up in the air; went along under the voices and the bargaining, interrogating the wheels. Past the dogs; glancing up at the dining car where he could stare at the faces, behind glass, drinking beer, two by two on either side of a uniform railway vase with its pale dead flower. Right to the end, to the guard's van, where the stationmaster's children had just collected their mother's two loaves of bread; to the engine itself, where the stationmaster and the driver stood talking against the steaming complaint of the resting beast.

Creaking, jerking, jostling, gasping, the train filled the station.

Here, let me see that one—the young woman curved her body further out of the corridor window. Missus? smiled the old boy, looking at the creatures he held in his hand. From a piece of string on his gray finger hung a tiny woven basket; he lifted it, questioning. No, no, she urged, leaning down toward him, across the height of the train, toward the man in the piece of old rug; that one, that one, her hand commanded. It was a lion, carved out of soft dry wood that looked like spongecake; heraldic,[4] black and, white, with <u>impressionistic</u> detail burnt in. The old man held it up to her still smiling, not from the heart, but at the customer. Between its Vandyke teeth,[5] in the mouth opened in an endless roar too terrible to be heard, it had a black tongue. Look, said the young husband, if you don't mind! And round the neck of the thing, a piece of fur (rat? rabbit? meerkat?); a real mane, majestic, telling you somehow that the artist had delight in the lion.

All up and down the length of the train in the dust the artists sprang, walking bent, like performing animals, the better to exhibit the

---

4. **heraldic.** Resembling something found on a coat of arms
5. **Vandyke teeth.** Teeth that taper to a point
6. **grappling.** Wrestling

> **im • pres • sion • is • tic** (im pre' shə nis´ tic) *adj.,* characterized by a limited or subjective use of detail; not fully realistic
> **elon • gat • ed** (ē lôn´ gā təd) *adj.,* extended or lengthened

The man called out to them, something loud and joking. They turned to laugh, in a twirl of steam. The two children careered[7] over the sand, clutching the bread, and burst through the iron gate and up the path through the garden in which nothing grew.

Passengers drew themselves in at the corridor windows and turned into compartments to fetch money, to call someone to look. Those sitting inside looked up: suddenly different, caged faces, boxed in, cut off, after the contact of outside. There was an orange a piccanin would like. . . . What about that chocolate? It wasn't very nice. . . .

A young girl had collected a handful of the hard kind, that no one liked, out of the chocolate box, and was throwing them to the dogs, over at the dining car. But the hens darted in, and swallowed the chocolates, incredibly quick and accurate, before they had even dropped in the dust, and the dogs, a little bewildered, looked up with their brown eyes, not expecting anything.

—No, leave it, said the girl, don't take it. . . .

Too expensive, too much, she shook her head and raised her voice to the old boy, giving up the lion. He held it up where she had handed it to him. No, she said, shaking her head. *Three-and-six?*[8] insisted her husband, loudly. Yes baas![9] laughed the boy. Three-and-six?—the young man was incredulous. Oh leave it—she said. The young man stopped. Don't you want it? he said, keeping his face closed to the boy. No, never mind, she said, leave it. The old native kept his head on one side, looking at them sideways, holding the lion. Three-and-six, he murmured, as old people repeat things to themselves.

The young woman drew her head in. She went into the coupé[10] and sat down. Out of the window, on the other side, there was nothing; sand and bush; a thorn tree. Back through the open doorway, past the figure of her husband in the corridor, there was the station, the voices, wooden animals waving, running feet. Her eye followed the funny little <u>valance</u>

of scrolled wood that outlined the chalet roof of the station; she thought of the lion and smiled. That bit of fur round the neck. But the wooden buck, the hippos, the elephants, the baskets that already bulked out of their brown paper under the seat and on the luggage rack! How will they look at home? Where will you put them? What will they mean away from the places you found them? Away from the unreality of the last few weeks? The man outside. But he is not part of the unreality; he is for good now. Odd . . . somewhere there was an idea that he, that living with him, was part of the holiday, the strange places.

> Somewhere there was an idea that he, that living with him, was part of the holiday, the strange places.

Outside, a bell rang. The stationmaster was leaning against the end of the train, green flag rolled in readiness. A few men who had got down to stretch their legs sprang on to the train, clinging to the observation platforms, or perhaps merely standing on the iron step, holding the rail; but on the train, safe from the one dusty platform, the one tin house, the empty sand.

There was a grunt. The train jerked. Through the glass the beer drinkers looked out, as if they could not see beyond it. Behind the flyscreen, the stationmaster's wife sat facing back at them beneath the darkening hunk of meat.

---

7. **careered.** Moved at top speed
8. **Three-and-six.** Three shillings and sixpence
9. **baas.** "Master" in the Afrikaans language
10. **coupé.** Half-compartment at the end of a train car, with only one row of seats

va • lance (vaʹ lən[t]s) *n.,* canopy or drapery hung along an edge

Apartheid South Africa

Since the 1600s, South Africa has been inhabited by British and Dutch colonists (called *Boers* or *Afrikaners*). At various times, they have clashed with each other, most notably during the Boer War, which spanned from 1899 to 1902. After Great Britain granted South Africa independence in 1910, the Afrikaner and British populations agreed to share power. They formed the Union of South Africa, which had two British provinces (Cape of Good Hope and Natal) and two Afrikaner provinces (Orange Free State and Transvaal).

In the 1940s, the Afrikaner National Party gained a strong political majority and established a system of *apartheid,* or racial separation, to maintain white control of the economy and social system. The party also began enacting a series of segregation laws, which required all South African citizens to carry documentation that classified them as white, colored (of multiethnic ancestry), Indian, or black. In addition, apartheid laws prohibited nonwhite citizens from visiting white neighborhoods, using white public facilities, and having close relationships with white citizens. Furthermore, the laws declared that black neighborhoods were independent homelands, which meant blacks could not leave their localities without a permit.

The most disruptive apartheid policy was implemented in the 1960s and 1970s, when the government forced more than three million black South Africans to relocate. In many cases, blacks lived on valuable land that the government wanted to take over for mining or agriculture. In other cases, blacks were removed to urban areas so white suburbs could be built on the more desirable outlying land.

Nonviolent organizers such as Nelson Mandela and other members of the African National Congress publicly denounced apartheid laws, despite being threatened and imprisoned. Mandela, who was jailed for twenty-seven years, emerged as the leader of the resistance movement and refused to compromise his position to win freedom. In the late 1980s, a consortium of nations that included the United States instituted trade sanctions against South Africa, hoping to force the country into abandoning its system of apartheid. That finally happened in 1994, when the South African government became a democracy.

FOR USE BY WHITE PERSONS

THESE PUBLIC PREMISES AND THE AMENITIES THEREOF HAVE BEEN RESERVED FOR THE EXCLUSIVE USE OF WHITE PERSONS.

By Order Provincial Secretary

VIR GEBRUIK DEUR BLANKES

HIERDIE OPENBARE PERSEEL EN DIE GERIEWE DAARVAN IS VIR DIE UITSLUITLIKE GEBRUIK VAN BLANKES AANGEWYS.

Op Las Provinsiale Sekretaris

MANDELA

There was a shout. The flag drooped out. Joints not yet coordinated, the <u>segmented</u> body of the train heaved and bumped back against itself. It began to move; slowly the scrolled chalet moved past it, the yells of the natives, running alongside, jetted up into the air, fell back at different levels. Staring wooden faces waved drunkenly, there, then gone, questioning for the last time at the windows. Here, one-and-six baas!—As one automatically opens a hand to catch a thrown ball, a man fumbled wildly down his pocket, brought up the shilling and sixpence and threw them out; the old native, gasping, his skinny toes <u>splaying</u> the sand, flung the lion.

The piccanins were waving, the dogs stood, tails uncertain, watching the train go: past the mud huts, where a woman turned to look, up from the smoke of the fire, her hand pausing on her hip.

The stationmaster went slowly in under the chalet.

The old native stood, breath blowing out the skin between his ribs, feet tense, balanced in the sand, smiling and shaking his head. In

---

seg • ment • ed (seg´ men təd) *adj.,* divided into sections
splay (splā) *v.,* cause to spread out

his opened palm, held in the attitude of receiving, was the retrieved shilling and sixpence.

The blind end of the train was being pulled helplessly out of the station.

The young man swung in from the corridor, breathless. He was shaking his head with laughter and triumph. Here! he said. And waggled the lion at her. One-and-six!

What? she said.

He laughed. I was arguing with him for fun, bargaining—when the train had pulled out already, he came tearing after. . . . One-and-six baas! So there's your lion.

She was holding it away from her, the head with the open jaws, the pointed teeth, the black tongue, the wonderful ruff of fur facing her. She was looking at it with an expression of not seeing, of seeing something different. Her face was drawn up, <u>wryly</u>, like the face of a discomforted child. Her mouth lifted nervously at the corner. Very slowly, cautious, she lifted her finger and touched the mane, where it was joined to the wood.

But how could you, she said. He was shocked by the dismay of her face.

Good heavens, he said, what's the matter?

> **If you wanted it, why didn't you pay for it? Why didn't you take it decently, when he offered it?**

If you wanted the thing, she said, her voice rising and breaking with the shrill <u>impotence</u> of anger, why didn't you buy it in the first place? If you wanted it, why didn't you pay for it? Why didn't you take it decently, when he offered it? Why did you have to wait for him to run after the train with it, and give him one-and-six? One-and-six!

---

wry • ly (rī´ lē) *adv.,* in a bent or twisted shape or condition
im • po • tence (im´ pə tən[t]s) *n.,* state of being helpless or powerless

What does it mean to study *society?* Society is both the larger group and the individuals who comprise it. Such a group is not fixed but rather in constant flux.

This also is true of the works of art in which a society is reflected. As seen through the sociological lens, a literary text is part of a cultural process. It cannot be seen apart from the values and rules that govern the society at large. However, just as the social structure keeps changing, so do the expectations or attitudes of authors and readers. **Sociological criticism** considers how a work of art both mirrors and influences society.

> *"The creative act is not pure. History evidences it. Sociology extracts it. The writer loses Eden, writes to be read, and comes to realize that he is answerable."*
>
> —NADINE GORDIMER

Overview of Sociological Criticism

A sociological reading of literature proposes to discover the mindset and behavior of the individuals and groups a text portrays. At the same time, such a reading recognizes the power of the text to reshape social expectations.

Sociological literary criticism overlaps with political criticism in some ways (see Unit 5, pages 538–539). Both study a text for what it reveals about economic and social class. Sociological criticism is less rigid than political criticism, however, and looks at a text from a variety of perspectives: Who is the writer? Who is the audience for this text? How does the work reflect on the society it depicts? What is the writer's political and social agenda?

Sociological criticism is most pertinent when literature asks profound questions about the society it portrays. The very act of raising such issues can be seen as a form of political and social action.

Application of Sociological Criticism

Some works lend themselves particularly well to sociological analysis. Consider Nadine Gordimer's "The Train from Rhodesia," which is about a brief but telling interaction between privileged whites and poor black Rhodesians. As you study this short story, notice the following elements.

Setting and Mood

The story's setting, a railway station in the South African countryside, establishes the dominant mood of "The Train from Rhodesia." Notice the descriptive details that create a vivid sense of a place and a people unavoidably affected by the incursions of the Europeans:

> The train came out of the red horizon and bore down toward them over the single straight track.
>
> The stationmaster came out of his little brick station with its pointed chalet roof, feeling the creases in his serge uniform in his legs as well. A stir of preparedness rippled through the squatting native vendors waiting in the dust: the face of a carved wooden animal, eternally surprised, stuck out of a sack. The stationmaster's barefoot children wandered over. From the gray mud huts with the untidy heads that stood within a decorated mud wall, chickens, and dogs with their skin stretched like parchment over their bones, followed the piccanins down to the track.

❑ **Analyze** Consider how Gordimer juxtaposes "the little brick station" with the "gray mud huts" of the local people. Which of these seems out of place in the landscape? What does the comparative affluence of the train station suggest about the relationship of race, social class, and wealth in this rural area of South Africa?

Tone

As a white South African born in the 1920s, Gordimer grew up under the system of apartheid, with its oppressive racial and class distinctions. As the daughter of Jewish immigrants, her own identity as an outsider sharpened her perceptions of the social hierarchy.

impulse toward her cook; and at the end of the month she raised his wages. He had been with her now for several years; he was one of the few natives who had his wife and children in the compound and never wanted to go home to his kraal,[1] which was some hundreds of miles away. Sometimes a small piccanin[2] who had been born the same time as Teddy, could be seen peering from the edge of the bush, staring in awe at the little white boy with his miraculous fair hair and Northern blue eyes. The two children would gaze at each other with a wide, interested gaze, and once Teddy put out his hand curiously to touch the black child's cheeks and hair.

Gideon, who was watching, shook his head wonderingly, and said: "Ah, missus, these are both children, and one will grow up to be a baas,[3] and one will be a servant"; and Mrs. Farquar smiled and said sadly, "Yes, Gideon, I was thinking the same." She sighed. "It is God's will," said Gideon, who was a mission boy.[4] The Farquars were very religious people; and this shared feeling about God bound servant and masters even closer together.

> ## "Ah, missus, these are both children, and one will grow up to be a baas, and one will be a servant."

Teddy was about six years old when he was given a scooter, and discovered the intoxications of speed. All day he would fly around the homestead, in and out of flowerbeds, scattering squawking chickens and irritated dogs, finishing with a wide dizzying arc into the kitchen door. There he would cry: "Gideon, look at me!" And Gideon would laugh and say: "Very clever, Little Yellow Head." Gideon's youngest son, who was now a herdsboy, came especially up from the compound to see the scooter. He was afraid to come near it, but Teddy showed

off in front of him. "Piccanin," shouted Teddy, "get out of my way!" And he raced in circles around the black child until he was frightened, and fled back to the bush.

"Why did you frighten him?" asked Gideon, gravely <u>reproachful</u>.

Teddy said defiantly: "He's only a black boy," and laughed. Then, when Gideon turned away from him without speaking, his face fell. Very soon he slipped into the house and found an orange and brought it to Gideon, saying: "This is for you." He could not bring himself to say he was sorry; but he could not bear to lose Gideon's affection either. Gideon took the orange unwillingly and sighed. "Soon you will be going away to school, Little Yellow Head," he said wonderingly, "and then you will be grown up." He shook his head gently and said, "And that is how our lives go." He seemed to be putting a distance between himself and Teddy, not because of resentment, but in the way a person accepts something <u>inevitable</u>. The baby had lain in his arms and smiled up into his face: The tiny boy had swung from his shoulders and played with him by the hour. Now Gideon would not let his flesh touch the flesh of the white child. He was kind, but there was a grave formality in his voice that made Teddy pout and sulk away. Also, it made him into a man: With Gideon he was polite, and carried himself formally, and if he came into the kitchen to ask for something, it was in the way a white man uses toward a servant, expecting to be obeyed.

But on the day that Teddy came staggering into the kitchen with his fists to his eyes, shrieking with pain, Gideon dropped the pot full of hot soup that he was holding, rushed

---

1. **kraal.** South African native village
2. **piccanin.** Native child
3. **baas.** "Master" in the Afrikaans language
4. **mission boy.** Boy educated by Christian missionaries

re • proach • ful (ri prōch´ fəl) *adj.,* disapproving
in • ev • i • ta • ble (i ne´ və tə bəl) *adj.,* incapable of being avoided

Cecil Rhodes

Rhodesia was named for British entrepreneur Cecil Rhodes (1853–1902), who played an integral role in Great Britain's imperial presence in southern Africa. Rhodes began his legacy when he moved in 1871 to a frontier town named Kimberley, where he helped found the De Beers Mining Company. The area's abundant diamond deposits soon made Rhodes one of the wealthiest men in the world. He also became involved in local politics. By 1890, he had assumed almost complete authority over British rule in southern Africa. Upon his death, Rhodes gave most of his fortune to charity. A large percentage was used to establish the Rhodes Scholarships, which each year fund more than ninety outstanding students from many countries to pursue their studies at the University of Oxford in England.

Although Rhodes was a popular figure among British settlers in Africa, his modern legacy is controversial. He exploited many native Africans in his quest for wealth, and his aggressive diamond mining created a number of persistent social and environmental problems.

---

to the child, and forced aside his fingers. "A snake!" he exclaimed. Teddy had been on his scooter, and had come to a rest with his foot on the side of a big tub of plants. A tree snake, hanging by its tail from the roof, had spat full into his eyes. Mrs. Farquar came running when she heard the commotion. "He'll go blind," she sobbed, holding Teddy close against her. "Gideon, he'll go blind!" Already the eyes, with perhaps half an hour's sight left in them, were swollen up to the size of fists: Teddy's small white face was distorted by great purple oozing protuberances.[5] Gideon said: "Wait a minute, missus, I'll get some medicine." He ran off into the bush.

Mrs. Farquar lifted the child into the house and bathed his eyes with permanganate.[6] She had scarcely heard Gideon's words; but when she saw that her remedies had no effect at all, and remembered how she had seen natives with no sight in their eyes, because of the spitting of a snake, she began to look for the return of her cook, remembering what she heard of the <u>efficacy</u> of native herbs. She stood by the window, holding the terrified, sobbing little boy in her arms, and peered helplessly into the bush. It was not more than a few minutes before she saw Gideon come bounding back, and in his hand he held a plant.

"Do not be afraid, missus," said Gideon, "this will cure Little Yellow Head's eyes." He stripped the leaves from the plant, leaving a small white fleshy root. Without even washing it, he put the root in his mouth, chewed it vigorously, and then held the spittle there while he took the child forcibly from Mrs. Farquar. He gripped Teddy down between his knees, and pressed the balls of his thumbs into the swollen eyes, so that the child screamed and Mrs. Farquar cried out in protest: "Gideon, Gideon!" But Gideon took no notice. He knelt over the writhing child, pushing back the puffy lids till chinks of eyeball showed, and then he spat hard, again and again, into first one eye, and then the other. He finally lifted Teddy gently into his mother's arms, and said: "His eyes will get better." But Mrs. Farquar was weeping with terror, and she could hardly thank him: It was impossible to believe that Teddy

---

5. **protuberances.** Bulges, swellings
6. **permanganate.** Dark purple salt used as a disinfectant

ef · fi · ca · cy (ef´ fi kə sē) *n.,* ability to produce an effect

could keep his sight. In a couple of hours the swellings were gone: The eyes were inflamed and tender but Teddy could see. Mr. and Mrs. Farquar went to Gideon in the kitchen and thanked him over and over again. They felt helpless because of their gratitude: It seemed they could do nothing to express it. They gave Gideon presents for his wife and children, and a big increase in wages, but these things could not pay for Teddy's now completely cured eyes. Mrs. Farquar said: "Gideon, God chose you as an instrument for His goodness," and Gideon said: "Yes, missus, God is very good."

They felt helpless because of their gratitude: It seemed they could do nothing to express it.

Now, when such a thing happens on a farm, it cannot be long before everyone hears of it. Mr. and Mrs. Farquar told their neighbors and the story was discussed from one end of the district to the other. The bush is full of secrets. No one can live in Africa, or at least on the veld,[7] without learning very soon that there is an ancient wisdom of leaf and soil and season— and, too, perhaps most important of all, of the darker tracts of the human mind—which is the black man's heritage. Up and down the district people were telling anecdotes, reminding each other of things that had happened to them.

"But I saw it myself, I tell you. It was a puff-adder bite. The kaffir's[8] arm was swollen to the elbow, like a great shiny black bladder. He was groggy after a half a minute. He was dying. Then suddenly a kaffir walked out of the bush with his hands full of green stuff. He smeared something on the place, and the next day my boy was back at work, and all you could see was two small punctures in the skin."

This was the kind of tale they told. And, as always, with a certain amount of exaspera-

tion, because while all of them knew that in the bush of Africa are waiting valuable drugs locked in bark, in simple-looking leaves, in roots, it was impossible to ever get the truth about them from the natives themselves.

The story eventually reached town; and perhaps it was at a sundowner party,[9] or some such function, that a doctor, who happened to be there, challenged it. "Nonsense," he said. "These things get exaggerated in the telling. We are always checking up on this kind of story, and we draw a blank every time."

Anyway, one morning there arrived a strange car at the homestead, and out stepped one of the workers from the laboratory in town, with cases full of test tubes and chemicals.

Mr. and Mrs. Farquar were flustered and pleased and flattered. They asked the scientist to lunch, and they told the story all over again, for the hundredth time. Little Teddy was there too, his blue eyes sparkling with health, to prove the truth of it. The scientist explained how humanity might benefit if this new drug could be offered for sale; and the Farquars were even more pleased: They were kind, simple people, who liked to think of something good coming about because of them. But when the scientist began talking of the money that might result, their manner showed discomfort. Their feelings over the miracle (that was how they thought of it) were so strong and deep and religious, that it was distasteful to them to think of money. The scientist, seeing their faces, went back to his first point, which was the advancement of humanity. He was perhaps a trifle perfunctory: It was not the first time he had come salting the tail of a fabulous bush secret.[10]

---

7. **veld.** Grassland
8. **kaffir.** Derogatory term for a black African
9. **sundowner party.** British colloquial term for "cocktail party"
10. **salting . . . bush secret.** Trying without success to learn about a native cure

---

ex • as • per • a • tion (ig zas′ pə rā′ shən) *n.,* state of being irritated or annoyed
per • func • to • ry (pər fuŋ[k]′ t[ə] rē) *adj.,* lacking interest or enthusiasm

Eventually, when the meal was over, the Farquars called Gideon into their living room and explained to him that his baas, here, was a Big Doctor from the Big City, and he had come all that way to see Gideon. At this Gideon seemed afraid; he did not understand; and Mrs. Farquar explained quickly that it was because of the wonderful thing he had done with Teddy's eyes that the Big Baas had come.

Gideon looked from Mrs. Farquar to Mr. Farquar, and then at the little boy, who was showing great importance because of the occasion. At last he said grudgingly: "The Big Baas want to know what medicine I used?" He spoke <u>incredulously</u>, as if he could not believe his old friends could so betray him. Mr. Farquar began explaining how a useful medicine could be made out of the root, and how it could be put on sale, and how thousands of people, black and white, up and down the continent of Africa, could be saved by the medicine when that spitting snake filled their eyes with poison. Gideon listened, his eyes bent on the ground, the skin of his forehead puckering in discomfort. When Mr. Farquar had finished he did not reply. The scientist, who all this time had been leaning back in a big chair, sipping his coffee and smiling with a skeptical good humor, chipped in and explained all over again, in different words, about the making of drugs and the process of science. Also, he offered Gideon a present.

There was silence after this further explanation, and then Gideon remarked indifferently that he could not remember the root. His face was sullen and hostile, even when he looked at the Farquars, whom he usually treated like old friends. They were beginning to feel annoyed; and this feeling <u>annulled</u> the guilt that had been sprung into life by Gideon's accusing manner. They were beginning to feel that he was unreasonable. But it was at that moment that they all realized that he would never give in. The magical drug would remain where it was, unknown and useless except for the tiny scattering of Africans who had the knowl-

edge, natives who might be digging a ditch for the municipality in ragged shirt and a pair of patched shorts, but who were still born to healing, hereditary healers, being the nephews or sons of the old witch doctors whose ugly masks and bits of bone and all the uncouth properties of magic were the outward signs of real power and wisdom.

The Farquars might tread on that plant fifty times a day as they passed from house to garden, from cow kraal to mealie[11] field, but they would never know it.

But they went on persuading and arguing, with all the force of their exasperation; and Gideon continued to say that he could not remember, or that there was no such root, or that it was the wrong season of the year, or that it wasn't the root itself, but the spit from his mouth that had cured Teddy's eyes. He said all these things one after another, and seemed not to care they were contradictory. He was rude and stubborn. The Farquars could hardly recognize their gentle, lovable old servant in this ignorant, <u>perversely</u> obstinate African, standing there in front of them with lowered eyes, his hands twitching his cook's apron, repeating over and over whichever one of the stupid refusals that first entered his head.

And suddenly he appeared to give in. He lifted his head, gave a long, blank angry look at the circle of whites, who seemed to him like a circle of yelping dogs pressing around him, and said: "I will show you the root."

They walked single file away from the homestead down a kaffir path. It was a blazing December afternoon, with the sky full of hot rain clouds. Everything was hot: The sun was like a bronze tray whirling overhead, there was a heat shimmer over the fields, the

---

11. **mealie.** Corn

in • cred • u • lous • ly (in['] kreˊ jə ləs lē) *adv.*, with skepticism or disbelief
an • nul (ə nulˊ) *v.*, cancel
per • verse • ly (pur['] vursˊ lē) *adv.*, in a contrary or disagreeable manner

soil was scorching underfoot, the dusty wind blew gritty and thick and warm in their faces. It was a terrible day, fit only for reclining on a veranda with iced drinks, which is where they would normally have been at that hour.

From time to time, remembering that on the day of the snake it had taken ten minutes to find the root, someone asked: "Is it much further, Gideon?" And Gideon would answer over his shoulder, with angry politeness: "I'm looking for the root, baas." And indeed, he would frequently bend sideways and trail his hand among the grasses with a gesture that was insulting in its perfunctoriness. He walked with them through the bush along unknown paths for two hours, in that melting destroying heat, so that the sweat trickled coldly down them and their heads ached. They were all quite silent: the Farquars because they were angry, the scientist because he was being proved right again; there was no such plant. His was a tactful silence.

At last, six miles from the house, Gideon suddenly decided that they had had enough; or perhaps his anger evaporated at that moment. He picked up, without an attempt at looking anything but casual, a handful of blue flowers from the grass, flowers that had been growing plentifully all down the paths they had come.

He handed them to the scientist without looking at him, and marched off by himself on the way home, leaving them to follow him if they chose.

When they got back to the house, the scientist went to the kitchen to thank Gideon: He was being very polite, even though there was an amused look in his eyes. Gideon was not there. Throwing the flowers casually into the back of his car, the <u>eminent</u> visitor departed on his way back to his laboratory.

Gideon was back in the kitchen in time to prepare dinner, but he was sulking. He spoke to Mr. Farquar like an unwilling servant. It was days before they liked each other again.

The Farquars made inquiries about the root from their laborers. Sometimes they were answered with distrustful stares. Sometimes the natives said: "We do not know. We have never heard of the root." One, the cattle boy, who had been with them a long time, and had grown to trust them a little, said: "Ask your boy in the kitchen. Now, there's a doctor for you. He's the son of a famous medicine man who used to be in these parts, and there's nothing he cannot cure." Then he added politely: "Of course, he's not as good as the white man's doctor, we know that, but he's good for us."

After some time, when the soreness had gone from between the Farquars and Gideon, they began to joke: "When are you going to show us the snake root, Gideon?" And he would laugh and shake his head, saying a little uncomfortably: "But I did show you, missus, have you forgotten?"

Much later, Teddy, as a schoolboy, would come home into the kitchen and say: "You old rascal, Gideon! Do you remember that time you tricked us all by making us walk miles all over the veld for nothing? It was so far my father had to carry me!"

And Gideon would double up with polite laughter. After much laughing, he would suddenly straighten himself up, wipe his old eyes, and look sadly at Teddy, who was grinning mischievously at him across the kitchen: "Ah, Little Yellow Head, how you have grown! Soon you will be grown up with a farm of your own. . . ." ❖

em • i • nent (eʹ mə nənt) *adj.,* important; of high standing

IRRORS & WINDOWS

Think of someone from another culture whom you know or have seen in the media. What about this person's culture do you not understand? What about your culture may he or she not understand?

Refer to Text ▶ ▶ ▶ ▶ ▶ Reason with Text

1a. Describe Teddy and Gideon's relationship at the beginning of the story.

1b. Explain why Gideon begins to distance himself from Teddy.

Understand
Find meaning

2a. What does Gideon do to help Teddy after he is bitten by the snake?

2b. On a symbolic level, what ignorance or oversight might Teddy's blindness represent?

Apply
Use information

3a. How do the Farquars feel about sharing the secret root with the scientist? How does Gideon feel about it?

3b. Analyze why Gideon and the Farquars react so differently.

Analyze
Take things apart

4a. What does Gideon do when asked to show the root to the scientist?

4b. Is he justified in his behavior and his actions? Why or why not?

Evaluate
Make judgments

5a. What does the scientist offer Gideon to get him to show the root?

5b. In the Bible, Gideon leads his people to victory but refuses to become king, saying God is the only king. Why might Lessing have named her character after this biblical hero?

Create
Bring ideas together

Analyze Literature

Characterization and Motivation
Which characterization technique does Lessing use to create the character of Gideon? What does this technique lead you to discover about Gideon's character? What characterization techniques does Lessing use to develop other characters? How does this affect your response to them?

Examine the motivation of Gideon, the Farquars, and the scientist with regard to the root. Why do the Farquars and the scientist want to find it? Why does Gideon not want them to find it?

Extend the Text

Writing Options
Creative Writing In the story, news of Teddy's miraculous recovery from the snakebite spreads quickly throughout the community. Imagine that you are a reporter for the local paper. Write a news report in which you tell about the event. Include quotations from the people involved that are true to their characterization.

Expository Writing Write a one-paragraph analysis of the Farquars' motivation for wanting to know about the secret root. Using evidence from the story, explore possible primary and secondary reasons for their motivation. Share your analysis with your teacher and your class.

Critical Literacy
Perform Reader's Theater With your classmates, develop a script version of "No Witchcraft for Sale."

Divide the narrator's lines between several classmates, and turn the dialogue into lines for each character. Choose performers for each role, and perform your script for the rest of the class. You can use minimal costumes, set, and props; the main objective is to share the literature with your audience.

Lifelong Learning
Research Folk Medicine and Traditional Cures Conduct research on folk medicine and other traditional cures from a specific culture, such as a Native American tribe or indigenous Australian people. Give some examples of the group's practices, and provide evidence of their effectiveness. Prepare an oral report of your research and present it to your class.

 Go to **www.mirrorsandwindows.com** for more.

Sparrows

A Short Story by Doris Lessing

Build Background

Literary Context In addition to Africa, London serves as the setting for many of Doris Lessing's novels and short stories. London has been the author's adopted home since 1949, and she loves the city for "its variety, its populations from every-where in the world, its transitoriness, the way it connects the life of animals and birds in the parks to streets so old they have forgotten they ever had anything to do with nature."

London serves as a backdrop in a collection of fiction and nonfiction called *The Real Thing: Stories and Sketches* (1992), a work in which Lessing allows the reader to eavesdrop on a variety of strangers as they go about their mundane, daily existence. In the process, readers gain a glimpse of life from the varying perspectives of the people portrayed. For instance, in **"Sparrows,"** the second story in the collection, several vignettes unfold in an outdoor café, as various patrons arrive. Lessing paints a richly detailed scene with vivid descriptions and characterizations.

The last to arrive on the scene, a middle-aged couple, argue about their twenty-one-year-old daughter while watching a baby sparrow make its first attempt at independence. The sparrow takes on symbolic significance, mir-roring the daughter's desire for independence as a young adult. The reaction of each parent to the plight of the sparrow mirrors the way each responds to

the daughter. Their reac-tions as husband and wife also represent the ability of each individual to see beyond himself or herself.

Reader's Context When have you ever disagreed with someone close to you over something that was difficult to resolve?

See the Author Focus on page 1202 for biographi-cal information about Doris Lessing.

Analyze Literature

Symbol and Dialogue

A **symbol** is anything that stands for or represents both itself and something else. A *con-ventional symbol* has traditional, widely recognized associations, such as doves for peace. A *per-sonal* or *idiosyncratic symbol* assumes its secondary meaning because of the special way the author uses it.

Dialogue is conversation be-tween two or more people or characters. Dialogue may further develop other literary elements, such as setting and character.

Set Purpose

In the short story "Sparrows," Lessing develops both her char-acters and plot through the use of dialogue and symbols. As you read, look for a symbol in "Spar-rows," and consider what it might represent. Is it a conventional symbol or a personal symbol? Also consider how Lessing uses dialogue to develop the café set-ting and provide the reader with insight into the attitudes and beliefs of the characters.

Preview Vocabulary

indolence, 1213
frugal, 1213
ominous, 1213
emphatically, 1213
lithe, 1213
austere, 1214
expostulate, 1214
serenely, 1215
admonish, 1215
voracious, 1217

Sparrows

by Doris Lessing

"It's grown-up and it
expects its parents to feed it."

Twenty minutes after the rain stopped, the first visitors came into the café garden. They were two elderly women and a smiling Labrador, very much at home, for they went straight to a certain table at the back, and the dog took his place on the grassy strip there without a command. The women tipped up-right the chairs that had been slanted forward on to the table because of the rain. One hooked an umbrella on a chair-back and sat, bring-ing out packages of food from a holdall.[1] The

---

1. **holdall.** Traveling case or bag

other went into the café building and emerged with one little coffeepot and two cups. Assuring each other that one pot was plenty for two, they ate sandwiches with a contemplative detached air that disdained guilt.

All over the northern reaches of London people were saying, 'The rain's stopped: let's go up to the Heath.'[2] Already they wandered along the path where you can look down at the Kenwood lake, settled themselves on benches in case the sun did come out, and descended the stairs on the way to the café indoors. But where was the sun? It was sulking behind banks of black cloud, sliding for minutes at a time to their edges from where it stained trees and grass a promising sultry yellow, but then withdrew.

Some teenagers emerged from the building balancing trays loaded with fizzy drinks, coffee, cake. They pushed two tables together and sat sprawling. Elegant, dramatic clothes, profuse and many coloured hair, created a festive occasion. Their discontented indolence—their style—caused the two frugal observers to raise eyebrows and murmur, 'Some people don't know when they're lucky, do they, dear?'

A tall, pale, straw-haired youth like a ballet dancer appeared at the kitchen door. He was all yawns and sleep, but he was adjusting a blue and white striped apron, and this transformed him into the picture of a willing waiter. He surveyed his scene of operations, pondering whether to straighten the chairs around tables that had pools of rainwater on them, or even to wipe the tables. But he cocked an eye at the ominous sky and decided not to bother.

The two ladies were throwing bits of sandwich to sparrows that gathered around their feet, crowded the backs of chairs and even ventured on their table. At the end of the garden, not too emphatically displayed, a board said, PUBLIC HEALTH NOTICE. IN THE INTERESTS OF HYGIENE PLEASE DO NOT FEED THE BIRDS. The waiter shrugged and disappeared.

Three people appeared from inside, almost obscured by the heaped trays they bore, but when these were set down, three Japanese were revealed, a young couple in smart black silk jumpsuits, and the mother of one of them. She too was overdressed for this place in black 'designer' clothes, jewellery, the lot. They pulled a table near the one they had chosen to sit at in the middle of the scene, to hold all that they carried and what was on the tray brought to them by another waiter. This buffet not being enough, a second table was brought close and covered with food. They were about to eat full English breakfasts, wedges of cream cake, scones and butter and jam, several other kinds of cake, plates of salad and chicken, and, as well, coffee, Coca-Cola, fruit juice.

The waiter who was from somewhere around the Mediterranean, a dark, lithe, handsome youth, surveyed this repast with admiring incredulity.[3] 'Japanese? Good appetite!' He lingered, raised his brows in private exclamation, and went off. The sparrows, having exhausted the amenities of the two pensioners,[4] arrived in a flock to examine new possibilities. The Japanese mother let out cries of angry indignation, stuffing her highly made-up face ugly with bad temper and greed, with one hand, while she swatted ineffectively with the other at the sparrows as if they were flies.

The teenagers clearly felt they were being forced to examine all this from much too close so they gracefully rose and removed themselves to several tables away. They did not bother to take all their food and left crisps[5] and peanuts

---

2. **Heath.** Hampstead Heath, a public open space in northern London
3. **incredulity.** Disbelief
4. **pensioners.** People who live off sums of money paid by the government
5. **crisps.** British word for potato chips

---

in • do • lence (in´ də lən[t]s) *n.*, inclination to laziness
fru • gal (frü´ gəl) *adj.*, characterized by economy in the use of resources
om • i • nous (ä´ mə nəs) *adj.*, having a menacing or threatening aspect
em • phat • i • cal • ly (im faˊ ti k[ə] lē) *adv.*, with special emphasis or attention
lithe (līth) *adj.*, characterized by easy flexibility or grace

all over their deserted table. The sparrows fell on this bounty, arriving from trees, roof—everywhere. The Japanese matron loudly commented on this, but her children ignored her, eating as if they had been deprived of food for weeks.

The two elderly ladies watched this scene. They did not seem able to take their eyes off it. Their disapproval of the teenagers had been ritual, even indulgent, but this—their expressions said—was something else! One of them put down a hand that trembled, and stroked the big dog's head.

 The two elderly ladies watched this scene. They did not seem able to take their eyes off it.

'There you are, good dog,' she said in an unhappy voice. A sparrow arrived too close to the Japanese matron and she let out a shout. Still another waiter arrived at the kitchen door and examined the scene like a general. A short, stocky, competent youth, his hair brushed straight up, everything about him neat and clean, he was obviously destined to be running his own firm or at least a department within, at the most, five years. He strode forcefully about, scattering clouds of sparrows by flinging out his arms energetically as if he were doing exercises. He smiled with a nod at the Japanese and went back into the kitchen. The sparrows returned.

A middle-aged couple shining with health and sun-tan lotion arrived, each holding one <u>austere</u> cup of coffee. They had evidently just come back from a holiday in the blissful sun, and could afford to smile now at where it hid behind a bank of black that covered half the sky. They put their cups on either side of a small lake of rainwater on their table, and sat on the edge of their chairs in a way that told everybody they were about to demolish the distances of the Heath at a dedicated trot.

The middle-aged couple that arrived now couldn't be more unlike them. They walked cautiously up the steps and came forward, watching how they set down their well-cleaned shoes. Each carried a tray with tea and a single scone and butter. They chose a table at the back, near the little grassy strip.

Behind them was the tall brick wall with its mysterious, always-closed door, like the Secret Garden. The woman sat stirring her tea, while she smiled at the Labrador, then at the banks of bushes and trees on the right, all shades of heavy, lush green, then at the tops of the trees that showed over the palisade[6] on the left, finally looking straight ahead with approval at the long shapely building, a wing of Kenwood House,[7] once a coach house and servants' quarters, that was now rapidly filling with people having breakfast, tea and lunch. The open upper windows hinted at the satisfactorily interesting lives going on inside, and on the long, low, roof, birds of all kinds, but mostly sparrows and pigeons, carried on their no less interesting affairs. She regarded with particular appreciation the sparrows who crowded a tree just behind them, watching for what might befall them next. Her husband was already leaning forward to consume his scone in the fussy, urgent way of a man who would always attend to whatever was in front of him, finish it, and then wonder why he had been in such a hurry.

A sparrow dropped from the tree and sat on the back of the tilted-forward chair next to the woman. She carefully pushed some crumbs towards it.

'Hilda, what are you doing!' <u>expostulated</u> her husband in a low, urgent, peevish[8] voice.

---

6. **palisade.** Fence of tall metal stakes used to keep people out of an area
7. **Kenwood House.** Large English manor house that now serves as a public attraction
8. **peevish.** Fretful; whining and unreasonably stubborn

> **aus • tere** (ô stir´) *adj.*, giving little or no pleasure
> **ex • pos • tu • late** (ik späs´ chə lāt´) *v.*, speak with the purpose of dissuading or reprimanding

'It's not allowed, is it?' And he craned his neck around to assure himself the Public Health Notice was still safely there.

'Oh well, but that's just silly,' said she serenely, smiling at the sparrow. He glared at her, a piece of scone halfway to his mouth, with the frustrated look of one who did not feel in control of anything. Then, as the sparrow fluttered cheekily towards his hand and the scone, he stuffed it in, swallowed it, and said, 'They'd steal the food out of your mouth.'

Hilda gently set the tilted chair upright, and then the one next to it. At once sparrows descended to sit on their backs. She put a crumb quite close to her and sat waiting. A seasoned sparrow, one of many summers, a lean hunting bird, grey blotched with chocolate and black, darted in, snatched it, and flew off to the roof of the coach house, with two others in pursuit.

On the back of the chair nearest to her three sparrows sat watching, side by side.

'Look, Alfred,' she said, 'they are babies: look, they've still got a bit of their gape[9] left.'

The corners of their beaks were yellow. All three were neat and fresh. New-minted. Their greyish-brown feathers glistened. The man was staring at them with a look of apprehension too strong for the occasion.

From a distance this man seemed younger than he was, a sprightly middle age, being cleaned and brushed and tidy, but from close you could see fresh crumbs on his cardigan, and a new tea stain on his tie. He had a greyish, drained look. His wife was a large full-fleshed woman who sat up straight there beside him, everything about her showing she was in command, her hands kept and capable, hair neatly waved, clothes just so. If she was not much younger than he was, then that was what she seemed.

She laid some crumbs close to the three birds and the boldest hesitated, darted in, and flew off with one. The second fought with himself, took off from the chair-back, but halfway to the crumb, his goal, panic overtook him, and with a swirl and a flutter of wings he turned in mid-air and returned to the chair-back.

'Go on, be a brave bird,' she admonished it. Again the hesitant take-off, the mid-air swerve and whirl of wings when for a few seconds it hovered, then retreated. At last this sparrow managed to overcome its fear and resist the need to turn back halfway, and he reached the crumb and showed he would have a successful future because he picked up several, very fast, and flew off somewhere with a full beak to enjoy them.

The remaining sparrow sat on there, alone. He was very new, this little one, with remnants of baby fluff showing here and there. The yellow corners of his beak were bright. He had been sitting watching his fellow ex-fledglings[10] with the calm, round-eyed, detached look of a baby in a pram.

'Come on, you do it too,' she said. But the little bird sat on there, watching, not involved at all.

Then a new bird arrived on the table among the crumbs, and pecked as fast as it could. It was an older bird, its feathers no longer fresh and young. And now the little sparrow hopped on to the table, crouched, fluffed out its feathers so that it became a soft ball, and opened its beak.

---

9. **gape.** Open mouth of a baby bird
10. **fledglings.** Baby birds that have just learned to fly

se • rene • ly (sə rēn´ lē) *adv.*, calmly and with repose
ad • mon • ish (ad mä´ nish) *v.*, give advice or encouragement; express disapproval in a gentle manner

'What's the matter with it?' demanded the man, as if in a panic. 'It's sick.'

'No, no,' soothed his wife. 'Watch.'

The older bird at once responded to the smaller bird's crouching and fluffing by stuffing crumbs into its gape. This went on, the baby demanding, as if still in its nest, and the parent pushing in crumbs. But then a brigand sparrow came swooping in. The parent sparrow pecked it and the two quarrelling birds flew off together to the roof. The little sparrow, abandoned, stopped cowering and spreading its feathers. It closed its beak, returned to the chair-back and resumed its bland baby pose.

'But it's grown-up,' said the man, full of resentment. 'It's grown-up and it expects its parents to feed it.'

'It was probably still a baby in its nest yesterday,' she said. 'This is probably its first day out in the wicked world.'

'Why isn't it feeding itself, then? If the parents have pushed it out, then it should be supporting itself.'

She turned her head to give him a wary glance, removed this diagnostic inspection as if she feared his reaction to it, and sat with a bit of scone in her hand, watching the throng of sparrows who were looting the now empty plates and platters of the Japanese trio. The Japanese matron was grumbling loudly about the birds. Her children pacified her, and waved to the indolent waiter with the shock of straw hair, who came across at his leisure, piled up trays, and went off with them, depriving the sparrows of their buffet. They whirled up into the air and the baby sparrow went with them.

The little garden café was filling with people. The sun was again close to the edge of the clouds, and one half of the sky was bright blue. The athletic couple went striding efficiently away. The young male Japanese went back into the building. Surely he wasn't prepared to tackle even more food? The two elderly ladies sat on, though a waiter had removed their coffeepot and the two empty plates.

Plum Blossoms and Sparrows, c. 1660–1700. Zhou Xianji.

The dog lay with its chin on the grass and watched a sparrow hopping about within inches of him.

The baby sparrow returned by itself to sit on the chair-back.

'Look, it's back,' she said, full of tenderness. 'It's the baby.'

'How do you know it's the same one?'

'Can't you see it is?'

'They all look alike to me.'

She said nothing, but began her game of carefully pushing crumbs nearer and nearer to it, so that it would be tempted but not frightened.

'I suppose it's waiting for its father to come and feed it,' came the grumble which her alert but cautious pose said she had expected.

'Or perhaps even its mother,' she said, dry, ironic—but regretted this note as soon as the words were out, for he erupted loudly, 'Sitting there, just waiting for us to . . .'

She said carefully, 'Look, Father, I said this morning, if you don't want to do it, then you don't have to.'

'You'd never let me forget it then, would you!'

She said nothing, but leaned gently to push a crumb closer to the bird.

'And then if I didn't I suppose she'd be back home, expecting us to wait on her, buying her food . . .'

She was counting ten before she spoke. 'That's why she wants to leave and get a place of her own.'

'At our expense.'

'The money's only sitting in the bank.'

'But suppose we wanted it for something. Repairs to the house . . . the car's getting old . . .'

She sighed, not meaning to. 'I said, if you feel like that about it, then don't. But it's only £10,000. That's not much to put down to begin on getting independent. It's a very good deal, you said that yourself. She'll own a bit of something, even if it is only a share of the place.'

'I don't see we've any choice. Either we have her at home feeding her and all her friends and Uncle Tom Cobbleigh and all,[11] or we have to pay to get her out.'

'She's twenty-one,' said the mother, suddenly exhausted with anger, her voice low and tight. 'It's time we did something for her.'

He heard, and was going to retreat, but said first, 'It's the legal age, isn't it? She's an adult, not a baby.'

She did not reply.

Out came the Japanese young man with yet another tray. More cakes piled with cream and jam, more coffee. As soon as he had set these down before his wife (girlfriend? sister?) and his (her?) mother, the three of them bent over and began eating as if in an eating contest.

'They aren't short of what it needs,' he grumbled.

That peevish old voice: it was the edge of senility. Soon she would be his nurse. She was probably thinking something like this while she smiled, smiled, at the bird.

'Come on,' she whispered, 'it's not difficult.'

And then . . . the baby hopped down on to the table with its round eyes fixed on her, clumsily took up a crumb, swallowed it.

'Very likely that's the first time it has ever done that for itself,' she whispered, and her eyes were full of tears. 'The little thing . . .'

The small sparrow was pecking in an experimental way. Then it got the hang of it, and soon became as <u>voracious</u> as its elders as she pushed crumbs towards it. Then it had cleaned up the table top and was off—an adult.

'Marvellous,' she said. 'Wonderful. Probably even this morning it was still in its nest and now . . .' And she laughed, with tears in her eyes.

He was looking at her. For the first time since they had sat down there he was outside his selfish prison and really seeing her.

But he was seeing her not as she was now, but at some time in the past. A memory . . .

'It's a nice little bird,' he said, and when she heard that voice from the past, not a semi-senile whine, she turned and smiled full at him.

'Oh it's so wonderful,' she said, vibrating with pleasure. 'I love this place. I love . . .' And indeed the sun had come out, filling the green garden with summer, making people's faces shine and smile. ❖

---

11. **Uncle Tom Cobbleigh and all.** British idiomatic expression that is used to refer to a ridiculously long list of people. The expression comes from a British folk song called "Widecombe Fair."

vo • ra • cious (vô rā′ shəs) *adj.*, having a huge appetite

MIRRORS & WINDOWS

How would you describe a healthy relationship between an adult child and his or her parents? How would you describe your relationship with your parents?

Primary Source Connection

Doris Lessing does not enjoy making personal appearances or giving interviews to promote her books. She once told her publisher that instead of going on a fourteen-week worldwide tour, "it would be far more useful for everyone if I stayed at home, writing another book." This rare **interview with Nigel Forde** was broadcast on BBC Radio on May 1, 1992. As you read the transcript, think about how Lessing's childhood experiences may have influenced her writing.

Nigel Forde (b. 1944) was born in Leeds, England, and began his career as a theater actor in York, where he has remained ever since. As a radio broadcaster, he has contributed to many BBC programs, especially Radio 4's *Bookshelf.* He is an award-winning poet and screenplay writer. Of his eight published books, four are collections of poetry.

Reporting from the Terrain of the Mind

by Nigel Forde

Forde: How was growing up in Rhodesia important to you?

Lessing: From my point of view the most important thing was the space. You know, there was practically nobody around, and I used to spend hours by myself in the bush. My mother was a very remarkable woman, very tough, very brave. I remember seeing her holding my father's 1914–18 army revolver at the head of a cobra which had emerged from the flowerbed. She was such a brave woman and so resourceful. All of that was, of course, wasted on a much too small arena for all the talent she had.

Forde: Did you think of it as a harsh life? I mean, it was more harsh, much more conducive[1] to independence than a childhood in Britain, for instance.

Lessing: Yes, that was the great benefit of it, because not only as a child did I have more

independence but as a girl I did things that no girl of that time would have done in Britain, or in Europe. We had a kind of freedom and independence which now I marvel at—that I was so lucky to have had it.

Forde: You were sent away to school. Was that a happy time for you?

Lessing: It was awful. It was a convent school in Salisbury, and it was a horrible place, and I was desperately and miserably homesick. I look back at it now as the worst time in my life. Most of these women were peasant girls from Germany who'd become nuns because of the economic conditions in Europe. I've never forgotten one night. I was very young, seven or eight, and in the sickroom where so often I was. A young nun, who I then thought of as

---

1. **conducive.** Favorable; in support of

an old woman but she was probably eighteen, was weeping and weeping and weeping out of miserable homesickness for Germany, and, of course, she would never go back. How could one blame these girls? They were ignorant, uneducated peasant girls, very cruel, not meaning to be, and it was very, very bad for me. The whole thing was terrible.

Forde: So it was one of the pressures of your childhood?

Lessing: Yes, it was. It was very bad. . . . People become writers because they've had a very pressured childhood, and that doesn't necessarily mean a bad childhood. I don't think an unhappy childhood makes a writer; I think a child who has been forced to become conscious of what's going on very early often becomes a writer.

Forde: Have you used that part of your childhood creatively? I mean, is that something you close off from yourself now, or is it something you've actually been able to explore?

Lessing: I don't think I've directly used it, but I think it's contributed to a certain dark view of life which I now try to examine.

Forde: I understand that you came to London in 1949 with the manuscript of *The Grass Is Singing.*

Lessing: I didn't know it was impossible to live on what you earned by writing, which everyone said it was. I just didn't have very much money. Nowadays there's a very real difference between writers—our lot and this lot. This lot care passionately about money, as far as I can make out, and success, I think, much too soon. I think they should get on with what they're doing and let the success look after itself.

Forde: Is that easy for you to say now, because you had terrific success with that first book, didn't you?

Lessing: Yes, I did. I had very good reviews, and I had enough money to keep me going for a bit, but I certainly was extremely short of money, quite often. I remember walking in Kensington and weeping—I'm not a crier, you know—weeping because I literally did not have one penny. A man stopped me in the street and asked, "What are you crying about?" I said, "I haven't got any money." He said, "That's all right, because you'll have some next week, won't you?" I thought, He's quite right. ❖

Review Questions

1. What does Lessing state was the most important thing about growing up in Rhodesia? According to Lessing, how would her childhood have been different if she had grown up in Britain? Infer how her childhood experiences affected her as a person and as a writer.

2. Summarize Lessing's comments about her experience at the convent school in Salisbury. What influence did this experience have on her writing?

3. According to Lessing, why do people become writers? Do you agree with her reasoning? Why or why not?

TEXT ^{TO} TEXT CONNECTION

In the interview, Lessing remarks that "a child who has been forced to become conscious of what's going on very early often becomes a writer." How does Lessing's writing show this consciousness? Explain, illustrating with examples from "No Witchcraft for Sale" and "Sparrows."

Refer to Text ▸ ▸ ▸ ▸ ▸ **Reason with Text**

1a. List the different groups of people sitting at the café.	**1b.** Based on the narrator's description, how would you characterize the members of each group?	**Understand** Find meaning
2a. What does the baby sparrow accomplish by the end of the story?	**2b.** Predict what will happen to Hilda's daughter. Cite evidence from the story to support your answer.	**Apply** Use information
3a. How do Hilda and her husband each react to the sparrows?	**3b.** Explain how their reactions are consistent with their roles as parents.	**Analyze** Take things apart
4a. Why does the husband resent the baby sparrow? Why does he resent his daughter?	**4b.** Argue who has the right idea about the daughter: the husband or Hilda. Explain your reasoning.	**Evaluate** Make judgments
5a. Why do the two elderly ladies seem to disapprove of the teenagers? How does the Japanese family interact?	**5b.** How do the other patrons at the café provide examples and counter-examples of the argument debated by Hilda and her husband?	**Create** Bring ideas together

Analyze Literature

Symbol and Dialogue
What is the primary symbol in "Sparrows"? How does it serve as a symbol? What does it represent? Is it a conventional or a personal symbol?

How does the conversation of the married couple further develop the setting of the story? Examine their dialogue. What does their conversation reveal about the characters' attitudes and beliefs?

Extend the Text

Writing Options
Creative Writing Imagine that you are the waiter at the café in "Sparrows." Retell the events of the story from the waiter's point of view, as if he is describing his workday to a wife or friend.

Descriptive Writing Write a one-paragraph character sketch of one of the people at the café. What can you tell about the character from his or her words or actions? What can you tell from the narrator's observations? Develop as complete a picture as possible using details from the story.

Critical Literacy
Debate the Topic How much help should parents give to their adult children? At what point should they allow grown children to fend for themselves? Discuss the topic with your classmates. Decide on several different positions you could take, and form groups to represent the various views. Each group should begin with an opening statement that explains its position and then support the position with evidence. After each opening statement has been presented, the other groups should provide evidence to refute the opposition.

Collaborative Learning
Take Part in a Role-Play In a small group, role-play a possible conversation between the different groups of characters at the café. For example, what might the elderly ladies say to the teenagers? Use what you know about the character you choose to portray to influence your words and actions. Perform your role-play for the rest of the class.

 Go to **www.mirrorsandwindows.com** for more.

1. In "No Witchcraft for Sale," what is the connotation of Teddy's nickname, "Little Yellow Head"?
   A. It has no connotation; it simply describes his appearance.
   B. It is positive, meaning that he is good natured.
   C. It is awe inspiring because of how different Teddy's hair is from that of the indigenous people.
   D. It is negative, similar to calling someone "yellow bellied."
   E. It is derogatory, meaning that the boy is small for his age and odd looking.

2. In "No Witchcraft for Sale," why does Gideon begin to distance himself from Teddy?
   A. He becomes angry with Teddy because of his cruelty.
   B. He is worried that he likes Teddy more than his own son.
   C. He knows that being close to Teddy may limit the child's future success.
   D. He senses that Teddy will die soon and wants to lessen his future sorrow.
   E. He begins to accept that Teddy and he cannot be close because of their differences in racial and social status.

3. In "No Witchcraft for Sale," what does the word *efficacy* mean in the phrase "the efficacy of native herbs"?
   A. power
   B. magic
   C. closeness
   D. efficiency
   E. abundance

4. In "No Witchcraft for Sale," Lessing writes, "No one can live in Africa, . . . without learning very soon that there is an ancient wisdom of leaf and soil and season—and, too, perhaps most important of all, of the darker tracts of the human mind—which is the black man's heritage." Knowledge about which of the following is *not* alluded to in this sentence?
   A. prejudice
   B. native plants
   C. evil and greed
   D. farming or gardening
   E. human goodness

5. In "Sparrows," Lessing's description of the sun as "sulking" is an example of
   A. tone.
   B. irony.
   C. personification.
   D. point of view.
   E. plot development.

6. In "Sparrows," Lessing writes, "The sparrows, having exhausted the amenities of the two pensioners, arrived in a flock to examine new possibilities." Which of the following best restates this description of the sparrows?
   A. The sparrows were chased off by two waiters and returned to their nest.
   B. The sparrows became tired and went to their flock to rest while waiting out new options.
   C. The sparrows waited patiently for the next group of people to start feeding them.
   D. After the two elderly ladies stopped feeding them, the sparrows went to other patrons to get food.
   E. When there was nothing left for them to do there, the sparrows flew away in search of excitement.

7. In "Sparrows," the young sparrow can be viewed as a symbol of who or what?
   A. the other baby sparrows, who are afraid to approach the people at the café
   B. the daughter of Hilda, the woman who tries to get the sparrow to eat the crumbs
   C. the "tall, pale, straw-haired youth like a ballet dancer," who works as a waiter
   D. the two discontented teenagers, who are described as not knowing how lucky they are
   E. the sparrow that "showed he would have a successful future because he picked up several [crumbs]"

8. **Constructed Response:** Analyze Lessing's use of sensory details in describing the setting, characters, and events in "Sparrows." Discuss to what senses the details appeal and how they lend to your understanding of the story. Use details from the story to support your analysis.

9. **Constructed Response:** Based on what you know about Lessing's childhood, discuss how her experiences likely are reflected in "No Witchcraft for Sale."

Understand the Concept

In addition to using quotations to support your own ideas in an essay or report, you also can incorporate information from other sources by summarizing and paraphrasing. Developing these research skills will help you write a paper that demonstrates its validity by citing other sources and that also avoids **plagiarism,** which is using others' information without crediting them.

Summarizing involves identifying the main point of a story, essay, or article. When you summarize, you condense the information, stating the general idea in your own words but leaving out the details. For instance, Doris Lessing's short story "Sparrows" can be summarized as follows:

> **EXAMPLE**
>
> In "Sparrows," Lessing shows the reader a café garden and its various patrons before focusing on a middle-aged couple. It becomes clear that the man and wife's reactions to the baby sparrow at their table parallels their reactions to the situation with their daughter, who has asked for help in getting a place of her own.

When you **paraphrase** information, you essentially translate it, restating the text in your own words but maintaining the level of detail in the original. Consider this paraphrase of the description of the middle-aged man's wife from Lessing's story:

> **EXAMPLES**
> **Original sentence** His wife was a large full-fleshed woman who sat up straight there beside him, everything about her showing she was in command, her hands kept and capable, hair neatly waved, clothes just so.
>
> **Paraphrase** His wife was a large woman of erect bearing. The details of her tidy appearance conveyed the sense that it was she who was in command.

Notice that in the paraphrase, words are substituted and phrases are rearranged and simplified. The ideas being conveyed and the general level of detail are the same as in the original, however.

Summarizing is appropriate for incorporating information from sources that provide general or background information. Paraphrasing is appropriate for incorporating detailed information, such as facts and descriptions. Paraphrasing generally is preferable to quoting because you record the information in your own words. Doing so makes it easier to incorporate the information with the rest of your writing.

Whether you quote, paraphrase, or summarize information, you must document the original source of that information. (See the workshop on documentation on the following page.)

Apply the Skill

Use Summary

Write a two- or three-sentence summary of the other story by Lessing in this unit, "No Witchcraft for Sale." Then exchange papers with a classmate to check that you have not missed the main ideas or included too many details.

Use Paraphrase

Paraphrase each of the following sentences from "No Witchcraft for Sale." Again, exchange work with a classmate to get feedback on your accuracy.

1. "She had scarcely heard Gideon's words; but when she saw that her remedies had no effect at all, and remembered how she had seen natives with no sight in their eyes, because of the spitting of the snake, she began to look for the return of her cook, remembering what she heard of the efficacy of native herbs."
2. "He knelt over the writhing child, pushing back the puffy lids till chinks of eyeball showed, and then he spat hard, again and again, into first one eye, and then the other."
3. "No one can live in Africa, or at least on the veld, without learning very soon that there is an ancient wisdom of leaf and soil and season . . . which is the black man's heritage."
4. "Their feelings over the miracle (that was how they thought of it) were so strong and deep and religious, that it was distasteful to them to think of money."
5. "They were beginning to feel annoyed; and this feeling annulled the guilt that had been sprung into life by Gideon's accusing manner."

Understand the Concept

Many subject areas have their own systems of **documentation,** or citing sources. In English, the system is that of the Modern Language Association (MLA). MLA style has two components: (1) abbreviated citations of sources within the text of the paper and (2) a full listing of sources at the end of the paper.

To cite sources within the text, use **parenthetical citation,** in which a brief form of the source is provided in parentheses. Provide the author's last name and the page or pages that contain the information you are using. If you mention the author's name in your text, cite only the page or pages in parentheses.

To avoid plagiarism, cite sources for all the information you use from others' work. Follow these examples for citing information you quote, paraphrase, or summarize in your paper:

EXAMPLES

Quotation "I don't think an unhappy childhood makes a writer; I think a child who has been forced to become conscious of what's going on very early often becomes a writer" (Lessing 1219).

Paraphrase In the interview with Nigel Forde, Doris Lessing makes a distinction between a bad childhood and a childhood that leads people to become aware of life around them (1219).

Summary In the interview with Nigel Forde, Doris Lessing discusses the aspects of her childhood that helped shaped her as a writer (1218-19).

The second component of MLA documentation is the **bibliography,** or list of sources. Called *Works Cited,* this list should include all the sources you cite in your paper arranged in alphabetical order. Here are some examples of the information provided for common types of sources:

Book

Author name. *Title.* Place of Publication: Publisher, Year. Medium (print, film, web).
Smith, John. *The Science Behind Global Warming.* New York: Hutton House, 2007. Print.

Article in scholarly journal

Author name. "Title of Article." *Journal* Volume number (Year): Pages. Medium.
Jones, Markesa. "Alternative Fuel Advancements." *Science Studies* 26 (2006): 1012-43. Print.

Article in magazine

Author name. "Title." *Magazine* Date: Pages. Medium.
Singh, Rajiv. "Reducing Your Carbon Footprint." *Young Scientist* 22 April 2007: 34-41. Print.

Website

Website name. Editor name (if available). Date of publication or last update. Name of sponsoring organization. Medium. Date accessed site <URL>.
GreenGuardian.com. 10 January 2007. Solid Waste Management Coordinating Board. Web. 27 May 2007 <http://www.greenguardian.com>.

See the *Language Arts Handbook,* section 5.6, page 1276 for additional examples of types of sources. A complete Works Cited list appears on page 1237.

Apply the Skill

Identify and Use Correct Parenthetical Citation

For each of the following sentences, decide whether the parenthetical citation is correct. Rewrite in correct form the sentences that contain citation errors.

1. Lessing states, "This lot care passionately about money, as far as I can make out, and success, I think, much too soon" (Forde 1219).
2. Lessing's childhood in Rhodesia allowed her more freedom and independence than other girls in Europe at the time (Forde 1218).
3. The nuns in Lessing's convent school were "ignorant, uneducated peasant girls, very cruel, not meaning to be" (1219).
4. Lessing believes that writers starting out should just keep writing and not worry about the success (Forde, p. 1219).
5. In the interview with Nigel Forde, Lessing explains that her childhood provided a different way to look at life, which she occasionally draws upon in her work (1218-1219).

Create a Works Cited List

On a subject of your choosing, find one of each kind of source mentioned and write a Works Cited entry for it. Then compile the sources in a single Works Cited list.

DEAD MEN'S PATH

by Chinua Achebe

Nigerian **Chinua Achebe** (b. 1930) was born to a Christian family in the Ibo ancestral village of Ogidi. He attended the Government College at Umuahia, one of the best schools in West Africa. After graduating from the University of Ibadan, Achebe taught for a short time before joining the staff of the Nigerian Broadcasting Corporation in Lagos. He became a professor of English at the University of Nigeria.

Achebe says his duty as an African writer is "to help my society regain belief in itself and put away the complexes of the years of denigration and self-abasement" resulting from British colonialism. His early novels portray cultural clashes between traditional tribal life and British missionaries and government. His later novels address corruption and other aspects of postcolonial African life.

"Dead Men's Path" was published in 1972 in the short story collection *Girls at War*. In this story, Achebe portrays the cultural conflicts between new British ideas and old African customs.

Michael Obi's hopes were fulfilled much earlier than he had expected. He was appointed headmaster of Ndume Central School in January 1949. It had always been an unprogressive school, so the Mission authorities decided to send a young and energetic man to run it. Obi accepted this responsibility with enthusiasm. He had many wonderful ideas and this was an opportunity to put them into practice. He had had sound secondary school education which designated him a "pivotal[1] teacher" in the official records and set him apart from the other headmasters in the mission field. He was outspoken in his condemnation of the narrow views of these older and often less-educated ones.

"We shall make a good job of it, shan't we?" he asked his young wife when they first heard the joyful news of his promotion.

"We shall do our best," she replied. "We shall have such beautiful gardens and everything will be just *modern* and delightful . . ." In their two years of married life she had become completely infected by his passion for "modern methods" and his denigration[2] of "these old and superannuated[3] people in the teaching field who would be better employed as traders in the Onitsha[4] market." She began to see herself already as the admired wife of the young headmaster, the queen of the school.

---

1. **pivotal.** On which something depends
2. **denigration.** Belittling
3. **superannuated.** Old fashioned, outdated
4. **Onitsha.** Commercial center in Nigeria

Nancy was downcast. For a few minutes she became skeptical about the new school; but it was only for a few minutes. Her little personal misfortune could not blind her to her husband's happy prospects. She looked at him as he sat folded up in a chair. He was stoop-shouldered and looked frail. But he sometimes surprised people with sudden bursts of physical energy. In his present posture, however, all his bodily strength seemed to have retired behind his deep-set eyes, giving them an extraordinary power of penetration. He was twenty-six, but looked thirty or more. On the whole, he was not unhandsome.

"A penny for your thoughts, Mike," said Nancy after a while, imitating the woman's magazine she read.

"I was thinking what a grand opportunity we've got at last to show these people how a school should be run."

Ndume School was backward in every sense of the word. Mr. Obi put his whole life into the work, and his wife hers too. He had two aims. A high standard of teaching was insisted upon, and the school compound was to be turned into a place of beauty. Nancy's dream-gardens came to life with the coming of the rains, and blossomed. Beautiful hibiscus and allamanda hedges in brilliant red and yellow marked out the carefully tended school compound from the rank[5] neighborhood bushes.

The wives of the other teachers would envy her position. She would set the fashion in everything . . . Then, suddenly, it occurred to her that there might not be other wives. Wavering between hope and fear, she asked her husband, looking anxiously at him.

"All our colleagues are young and unmarried," he said with enthusiasm which for once she did not share. "Which is a good thing," he continued.

"Why?"

"Why? They will give all their time and energy to the school."

> # NDUME SCHOOL WAS BACKWARD IN EVERY SENSE OF THE WORD.

---

5. **rank.** Offensive

"THIS PATH WAS HERE BEFORE YOU WERE BORN AND BEFORE YOUR FATHER WAS BORN. THE WHOLE LIFE OF THIS VILLAGE DEPENDS ON IT."

One evening as Obi was admiring his work he was scandalized to see an old woman from the village hobble right across the compound, through a marigold flower bed and the hedges. On going up there he found faint signs of an almost disused path from the village across the school compound to the bush on the other side.

"It amazes me," said Obi to one of his teachers who had been three years in the school, "that you people allowed the villagers to make use of this footpath. It is simply incredible." He shook his head.

"The path," said the teacher apologetically, "appears to be very important to them. Although it is hardly used, it connects the village shrine with their place of burial."

"And what has that got to do with the school?" asked the headmaster.

"Well, I don't know," replied the other with a shrug of the shoulders. "But I remember there was a big row some time ago when we attempted to close it."

"That was some time ago. But it will not be used now," said Obi as he walked away. "What will the Government Education Officer think of this when he comes to inspect the school next week? The villagers might, for all I know, decide to use the schoolroom for a pagan ritual during the inspection."

Heavy sticks were planted closely across the path at the two places where it entered and left the school premises. These were further strengthened with barbed wire.

Three days later the village priest of *Ani* called on the headmaster. He was an old man and walked with a slight stoop. He carried a stout walking stick which he usually tapped on the floor, by way of emphasis, each time he made a new point in his argument.

"I have heard," he said after the usual exchange of cordialities, "that our ancestral footpath has recently been closed . . ."

"Yes," replied Mr. Obi. "We cannot allow people to make a highway of our school compound."

"Look, here, my son," said the priest bringing down his walking stick, "this path was here before you were born and before your father was born. The whole life of this village depends on it. Our dead relatives depart by it and our ancestors visit us by it. But most important, it is the path of children coming in to be born . . ."

Mr. Obi listened with a satisfied smile on his face.

"The whole purpose of our school," he said finally, "is to eradicate just such beliefs as that. Dead men do not require footpaths. The whole idea is just fantastic. Our duty is to teach your children to laugh at such ideas."

"What you say may be true," replied the priest, "but we follow the practices of our fathers. If you reopen the path we shall have nothing to quarrel about. What I always say is: let the hawk perch and let the eagle perch." He rose to go.

"I am sorry," said the young headmaster. "But the school compound cannot be a thoroughfare. It is against our regulations. I would suggest your constructing another path, skirting our premises. We can even get our boys to help in building it. I don't suppose the ancestors will find the little detour too burdensome."

While you are reading a poem, play, story, or novel, you probably react to the characters, and you may even identify with one of them. You also may respond to the work *critically,* or analytically. Taking a critical look does not necessarily mean emphasizing faults in the work. Rather, you consider whether or how such literary elements as characterization, conflict, setting, and suspense combine to create a well-written, thoughtful work.

Preparing an oral analysis of a literary selection gives you the opportunity to share your experience of the work. Most likely, you have written book reviews and analyses of short stories, poems, and essays. Using an oral presentation as the format for exploring a work of literature is similar to writing a review of the work.

1. Select a Short Story to Analyze
You might select a short story you have read and enjoyed, or you might select one that you have not yet read, such as a work by a writer you like. Ask your teacher, librarian, or classmates to recommend a suitable story. Read through the short story once to familiarize yourself with the plot and characters. Then read it a second time and focus on specific elements of it.

2. Read the Short Story from an Analytical Perspective
As you read the story the second time, keep in mind your purpose: to prepare and deliver an analysis of the work. While you read, you may find it useful to jot down important points to include in your presentation. For instance, is the narrative believable, or does the plot rely primarily on coincidence? What sort of change, if any, does the main character experience during the story? How does the character's self-awareness relate to the theme of the work? Look for other literary elements, such as conflict and climax, that are fundamental to most literary works. As you explore these features, you should develop an understanding and an appreciation of the story that will enrich your presentation.

3. Formulate a Thesis and Supporting Details
After you finish reading the story, go over your notes carefully to develop the thesis, or main idea, that will serve as the foundation of your presentation. Then look for specific details in the story that support the thesis.

4. Prepare Notes
After you have determined your thesis and gathered the necessary supporting details, organize your notes into *prompts,* or *cues,* for your oral presentation. Write down the key words and phrases, including brief supporting details, to document the main points of your analysis. Go over the notes carefully to be sure they are clear and complete. Make sure to include an attention-getting introduction, key transitions, and a strong conclusion.

Avoid writing out your presentation and then reading it word for word. Doing so makes it difficult to maintain eye contact and to use your voice and gestures effectively. Your delivery will be much more effective if you speak using notes.

5. Practice Your Presentation
As with any oral presentation, practice is key. Using the notes you prepared for the delivery, rehearse the speech, speaking clearly to an imaginary audience (or ask a friend or family member to provide feedback). Observing the presentation in a mirror can also be helpful. If possible, audiotape or videotape the presentation.

SPEAKING & LISTENING RUBRIC

Your preparation and delivery will be evaluated on these elements:

Content
- ❏ You select a suitable short story.
- ❏ Your analysis indicates that you have read the story from a critical perspective.
- ❏ The observations you make are supported by details from the story.

Delivery & Presentation
- ❏ You handle the notes (on cards or on paper) efficiently, using them as prompts rather than reading your story analysis word for word. You cover all the important ideas in your notes.
- ❏ You speak clearly enough for your listeners to follow your presentation, and you maintain eye contact with audience members.

In this unit, you have read selections about people struggling to resolve conflicts in their lives. In some selections, the characters have struggled to address a personal conflict, and in others, the conflict has involved a group of people. Struggles involving cultural expectations and traditions and humanity trying to dominate nature are seen throughout the stories and poems in this unit.

In this assignment, you will write a research paper stating an argument about a contemporary issue that creates conflict. You should defend your argument using information gathered from research and document your sources using Modern Language Association (MLA) format. Your research paper should be written in standard, formal English.

The fact that you are making an argument and supporting it with evidence makes the research paper a form of persuasive writing. In this sense, a research paper is different from an informational report, which presents information about a topic but does not take a stand on it.

Assignment Plan, write, and revise a research paper that describes a contemporary conflict and presents an argument about it.

Purpose To convince readers of your viewpoint

Audience Someone who disagrees with your viewpoint or has no opinion on the topic

WRITING RUBRIC

A successful research paper has these qualities:

- ❑ an introduction that generates interest and provides a context for the topic
- ❑ a thesis statement that clearly expresses the writer's argument about the issue
- ❑ a body that supports the thesis with detailed evidence gathered from research
- ❑ a conclusion that restates the thesis and makes a recommendation or call to action

❶ Prewrite

Select Your Topic

The general topic of your research paper, a contemporary conflict, already has been decided for you. That likely will be the case for many of the research papers you write in high school and college. Whatever the general topic, you should narrow it further by identifying a more specific and thus manageable topic about which to research and write.

Consider several contemporary conflicts and the arguments surrounding them. Look through newspapers and magazines for ideas. Pay attention to discussions of domestic and world issues on television and radio programs. Do some key-word searches online. Talk to your friends and discuss trends, laws, and policies that affect you. Consider your own experience, if relevant. Narrow your focus to a specific contemporary conflict.

What Great Writers Do

Your purpose in writing a research paper is not to solve a problem. Rather, it is to become informed about a topic and make an argument that you can defend to others. As Friedrich Dürrenmatt, twentieth-century Swiss author and dramatist, noted, "A writer doesn't solve problems. He allows them to emerge."

Gather Information

Begin your research by gathering background information on your topic. Although you already may have some knowledge about the conflict, look for information from a variety of sources. Familiarizing yourself with the full range of perspectives on your topic will help you cover it completely and address opposing views when you write your paper.

Proceed from gathering general background to gathering increasingly specific information about your topic. Move from general sources, such as encyclopedias and popular magazines, to books and journals that focus more specifically on your topic. This should be a natural progression as you learn increasingly more about your topic.

What Great Writers Do

Writers from Mark Twain to H. G. Wells have commented on the misuse of statistical information. One common error is to use statistics out of context, presenting only the numbers that support the argument and ignoring inconsistent or contradictory information. Doing so makes it possible to prove almost any point with statistics. As stated by contemporary journalist Gregg Easterbrook, "Torture numbers, and they'll confess to anything."

Another common error is to use statistics that are from unreliable sources or based on questionable methods of research. Early twentieth-century Supreme Court Justice Louis D. Brandeis offered this example of the misuse of averages: "A man may have six meals one day and none the next, making an average of three meals per day, but that is not a good way to live."

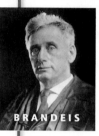

BRANDEIS

As you begin research, develop a system for recording notes and tracking sources. Possible note-taking systems include writing information in a research notebook, entering it into your computer, and recording it on note cards. Whatever system you use, make sure it is flexible enough to allow you to access and organize the information later. Experienced researchers record information in small amounts on single pages in a notebook or computer file or on individual note cards.

Also keep track of the sources you consult in your research. Use the time-tested method of preparing a **working bibliography,** in which you record all the information needed to prepare the bibliography entry for each source. That information usually includes the author's first and last names, the title of the work, the details of its publication, and the page numbers. Record the information for each source on a separate note card (see example at right), or keep a running list of sources in a notebook or computer file. You will use the information from your working bibliography later in preparing the final Works Cited list for your paper.

Many writers find it helpful to include several other details in the working bibliography. For instance, numbering the sources will help you keep track of what information came from which source (see example below). Assign a number to each new source you review, and then add that number to all the cards or pages of notes you take from that source. Another useful detail to record for each print source is where you found it—for instance, your school or local library. For a book from a library collection, include the call number, which identifies where the book is stored. Taking the time to record these details while you conduct research can save you valuable time later should you need to follow up on source information.

It is critical to put this note-taking/source-tracking system in place at the start of your research. Otherwise, you may waste considerable time later when you try to organize your information and write your paper. It is difficult, if not impossible, to retrace your steps and find missing source information.

> 1
>
> Larkey, Matilda
> Cutting Costs: The Environmental Impact
> of Lumber Practices
> New York: St. Ada's Press, 1997
> School library   QC992.3.L57

Write Your Thesis Statement

You may have a good idea of the argument you plan to make when you start doing research. If not, gathering background information should help you develop a tentative argument. Use that argument to guide the direction you follow in your research. As noted earlier, your research should gather increasingly specific information from professional sources. The more focused your research becomes, the more focused and definitive your argument will become.

As you near completion of your research, fine-tune your argument by writing a **thesis statement.** Your thesis should be a sentence stating the specific argument you plan to prove in your research paper. That means you must be able to support the thesis using the information you gathered in your research. As you work on your thesis statement, evaluate your notes and do additional research to fill in any gaps in your support material.

One student, Evan, began research with the idea of examining the impact of pollution on the environment. After background research, he shifted his focus to concentrate on the effects of human activity on global warming. After conducting further research about humanity's impact on the environment, Evan wrote this thesis statement:

> Given humans' contribution to global warming, they must take action now to slow the rate of change or be forced to adapt to a vastly different world.

Organize Your Ideas

With your thesis in mind, organize the information you have gathered by creating an outline. This will serve as the blueprint or master plan for writing the draft of your research paper.

Begin by making a simple list of possible main points for your paper. Review your notes to look for recurring ideas or patterns in the information. Try to identify three to five key ideas that can be supported by your research. For instance, Evan realized he had gathered a lot of information about how changing weather may affect human populations. He also had a lot of notes about how human activity has contributed to global warming. By reviewing his notes further, he came up with several more general ideas. He recorded his ideas in the list shown at the top of the next column.

Next, review the ideas you have listed against your thesis statement. Determine whether each idea can be offered as evidence or proof of the thesis, and eliminate any ideas that cannot. In reviewing the points on his list, Evan determined that discussing the effects of global warming on natural ecosystems was somewhat unrelated to his thesis, so he crossed it off the list. He also decided that his point about pollution contributing to the number of cases of asthma was off target and eliminated it from his list.

Finally, construct a **formal outline** of the body of your research paper. Follow the format shown at right, which includes four levels of information. Each of the main ideas you identified should label a major

TOPIC: Global warming

THESIS: Given humans' contribution to global warming, they must take action now to slow the rate of change or be forced to adapt to a vastly different world.

2 Changing weather and climate will have a significant impact on human life worldwide

~~Global warming disrupts natural ecosystems, leading to some species' extinction~~

1 Humans are primarily responsible for the conditions that create global warming

3 International efforts are being made to address the causes and effects of global warming

~~Pollution contributes to numerous health conditions, such as asthma~~

division of the outline, as indicated with a roman numeral. Develop each main idea by adding subpoints, which are illustrated with examples and then specific details, as shown in the sample below.

Remember the rule for outlining that "If you have an A, you must have a B." The logic underlying this rule is that it is impossible to divide something into just one subpart. Add subpoints to your outline only if you can create two or more under any given point.

Review your notes carefully to match the information with points in your outline. Again, make sure you can support every point you plan to make. Look for gaps in your notes and fill them in by doing additional research.

I. First main idea
  A. First subpoint
  B. Second subpoint
    1. First example
    2. Second example
      a. First detail
      b. Second detail

② Draft

Write your paper by following this three-part framework: Introduction, Body, and Conclusion.

> **Introduction** Draw readers in by creating interest and providing context; then present your thesis statement.
>
> **Body** Write at least one paragraph supporting each main idea of your argument.
>
> **Conclusion** Restate your thesis and provide closure, perhaps issuing a call to action or recommendation.

Draft Your Introduction

The introduction to a research paper should draw readers in by introducing the topic with an interesting quote, shocking fact, or revealing anecdote. The introduction also should put the topic in a context to which readers can relate. Providing context gives readers a reason for wanting to know more. Finally, the introduction should include a thesis statement that presents the main argument to be made in the paper.

Draft Your Body

Devote at least one body paragraph to each main idea you offer in support of your argument. State that main idea in the topic sentence of the paragraph, and then explain it using the subpoints, examples, and details you recorded on your outline. Follow your outline as closely as possible as you draft your paper; make notes about any topics or points you may need to check on or expand.

Use the information you gathered in note taking accurately and with purpose. Avoid committing **plagiarism,** which is using others' information without crediting them. Follow these general guidelines for quoting, summarizing, and paraphrasing:

- **Quoting** involves repeating the exact words and punctuation from the original source. In selecting quotations to use in your paper, look for statements that are particularly well expressed and are made by recognized authorities on your topic.

- **Paraphrasing** is essentially translating information, restating the text in your own words but maintaining the level of detail in the original. Paraphrasing is appropriate for incorporating details into your paper, such as facts and descriptions. Paraphrasing generally is preferable to quoting because you record the information in your own words. Doing so makes it easier to incorporate the information into your paper.

- **Summarizing** involves stating the main idea of a source. When you summarize, you condense the information, presenting the main idea in your own words but leaving out the details. Summarizing is appropriate for incorporating information from sources that provide general or background information.

As you write your draft, be sure to include the sources of the information you use within the body of the paper. To avoid plagiarism, you should cite sources

---

What Great Writers Do

Many writers make the mistake of using too many quotations in their work. Doing so makes it difficult to achieve a strong, consistent written style because the work is, in fact, a mixture of many people's writing. Overusing quotations may also imply that the writer is unable to state his or her own ideas and so repeats the ideas of others. Follow the advice of Transcendentalist writer Ralph Waldo Emerson, who wrote, "Stay at home in your mind. Don't recite other people's opinions. . . . Tell me what you know."

EMERSON

Use quotations with purpose, choosing expressions that are clever, eloquent, or simply well put. Use quotations to support your own ideas, not replace them. The originator of the essay, French Renaissance writer Michel de Montaigne, stated, "I quote others only in order the better to express myself."

for all the information you use from others' work, whether quoted, paraphrased, or summarized. Follow the **documentation** style of the Modern Language Association (MLA).

To cite sources within the text, use **parenthetical citation,** in which you add an abbreviated source reference in parentheses following the information from the source. Provide the author's last name and the page or pages that contain the information you are using. If you mention the author's name in your text, cite only the page or pages in parentheses.

Draft Your Conclusion

Finally, draft the conclusion for your research paper. A good conclusion should do two things: (1) restate the thesis and (2) wrap up the discussion, often by providing a recommendation or call to action.

Draft Your Works Cited Page

The final page of your research paper should provide a list of all the sources cited within it. Called *Works Cited,* this list should present the sources in alphabetical order. Refer to the *Language Arts Handbook,* section 5.6, page 1276. Also see the *MLA Handbook for Writers of Research Papers* for additional examples of types of sources as well as complete Works Cited lists.

❸ Revise

Evaluate Your Draft

Evaluate your own research paper, or exchange papers with a classmate and evaluate each other's work. Think carefully about what parts of the paper are sound and what parts can be improved.

Start by looking at the content and organization. Review the draft against the outline from which it was written. Make sure the body paragraphs work together to prove the thesis statement. Each main idea should be supported with subpoints, examples, and details, and information from researched sources should be documented. Review the Grammar & Style workshops in this unit to confirm the correct use of quotations, paraphrases, and summaries and to ensure the documentation style is correct.

Also review the introduction and conclusion to ensure you start and end the paper well. In a longer

---

> **REVISION CHECKLIST**
>
> **Content & Organization**
> - ❏ Does the introduction draw readers in and provide a context for the topic?
> - ❏ Does the thesis statement present a clear argument?
> - ❏ Does each paragraph in the body state a main idea that connects to the thesis?
> - ❏ Is the main idea in each body paragraph developed with supporting information?
> - ❏ Is all information from researched sources properly documented using MLA format?
> - ❏ Does the conclusion restate the main argument of the paper and bring it to a close by making a recommendation or call to action?
>
> **Grammar & Style**
> - ❏ Do you use quotations accurately and in appropriate instances? (see page 1155)
> - ❏ Do you paraphrase and summarize information correctly and in appropriate instances? (see page 1222)
> - ❏ Do you follow correct MLA style in your intext source citations and Works Cited list? (see page 1223)

---

work such as a research paper, your introduction and conclusion may be somewhat more detailed and thus longer than in a shorter work, such as an essay.

Use the Revision Checklist above to help you evaluate the draft. Make notes directly on the paper about changes to be made.

Revise for Content, Organization, and Style

Evan read over the draft of his research paper and found a number of things to improve:

● **Introduction:** To draw readers into his essay, Evan added a short paragraph that briefly described the effects of air pollution on students' lives. Doing so helped connect readers with the topic by providing an example to which they could easily relate. In the second paragraph, Evan added a definition of global warming to ensure readers would understand the topic before reading more about it.

- **Body:** After reviewing the body of his paper against his outline, Evan decided to break up some long paragraphs. He created two paragraphs for several of his main ideas, breaking out the subpoints (the A's and B's in his outline). Evan also added the credentials for several of the people he quoted—for example, noting that Richard Anthes is an expert on meteorology. Doing so highlighted these people's expertise and indicated why they were being quoted.

- **Conclusion:** Evan felt his paper ended too abruptly, without offering any solution or recommendation for change. He added information about the need to take global warming seriously and to act immediately to avoid disaster. He also decided to link his conclusion with his opening paragraph by mentioning the students walking home from school.

Read over the comments you or your partner made on your draft. Make appropriate changes as you revise your research paper.

Proofread for Errors

The purpose of proofreading is to check for remaining errors. Use proofreader's symbols to mark any errors you find. To complete the assignment, print out a final draft and read it aloud before turning it in. Doing so will allow you to catch any remaining errors.

Read Evan's final draft on the next several pages. Note how he worked through the three stages of the writing process: Prewrite, Draft, and Revise.

A Note About the Student Model

The sample shown on pages 1236–1237 is intended to illustrate the basic elements of a research paper but in a condensed or abbreviated manner. The sample is considerably shorter than most research papers. See the bracketed notations within the body of the paper that indicate where additional examples and details normally would be provided.

In writing your own research paper, be sure to meet the length requirement identified by your instructor. Also be aware of any requirements for including a specific number or certain types of sources in your Works Cited list.

Writing Follow-Up

Publish and Present

- Explore your classmates' different viewpoints on the many contemporary issues that generate conflict. Hold debates on the topics students have written about in their research papers. Try to reach some consensus on what should be done to resolve current problems or prevent future ones.
- Submit your research paper to an online forum that discusses contemporary conflicts.

Reflect

- How have your feelings toward certain conflicts changed since completing your research paper? Explain your answer.
- What other proposals, programs, or services will help people or countries avoid these conflicts in the future?

STUDENT MODEL

"It's the End of the World As We Know It":
The Effects of Global Warming
by Evan Thomas

Walking home after a boring day at school, a stream of students watch the never-ending line of cars drive by—loud, fast, old, and smelly. The clouds of exhaust the cars produce quietly fill the students' throats. Most try to ignore it and move on, but some start to cough and others hold their breath. The cars keep coming, and there is no escaping the fumes.

Sadly, this is how the world responds to pollution: by ignoring or tolerating it. However, the consequences of pollution are many and varied. One of the most threatening consequences is global warming, the phenomenon of global climatic change caused by human activities that create increased amounts of greenhouse gasses, such as carbon dioxide, in the earth's atmosphere (Anthes). Global warming has already had disastrous effects on the world's climate and weather. Given humans' contribution to global warming, they must take action now to slow the rate of change or be forced to adapt to a vastly different world.

Recent evidence proves that humans are primarily responsible for global warming. Journalist Mark Lynas, who has written extensively on the impact of global warming, notes that the carbon dioxide level in the earth's atmosphere is the highest it has ever been and that the 1990s was the warmest decade in the twentieth century (60). This increase in the level of carbon dioxide is directly related to human activities.

For instance, deforestation in some regions of the world has reduced the number of trees that gather carbon dioxide from the air and use it to produce oxygen (Larkey 149). [**Add examples and details**]

Changes in the climate and weather will have dramatic effects on humans worldwide. When the temperature of the entire planet increases by even a few degrees, huge changes result. According to meteorological expert Richard Anthes, extreme weather events such as droughts, heat waves, floods, severe storms, and hurricanes are becoming more frequent and more severe (Anthes).

In the 1960s, only sixteen major weather-related disasters were reported, but in the 1990s, over seventy were reported (Lynas 61). [**Add examples and details**]

The most dramatic effects of global warming on humans will be seen in the world's coastal cities. An increase in global temperatures will lead to glacial meltdown, causing the world's sea levels to rise and putting as many as 200 million people underwater. Studies suggest that if the West Antarctic Ice Sheet were to fall, the earth's oceans would rise six meters. To give some perspective, if the oceans rose just one meter, one-third of the planet's cropland would be flooded (Lynas 62). [**Add examples and details**]

In response to these dire predictions, international efforts are being made to reduce global warming. The most significant effort to date has

How does the first paragraph draw readers into the paper?

What context is provided for the topic? Why will readers want to know more?

What is the thesis statement?

What is the main idea of this paragraph? What support information is paraphrased and documented?

What is the main idea of this paragraph? Does it relate clearly to the thesis statement?

What examples and details might be provided about the research mentioned?

been the Kyoto Protocol, an international agreement reached in December 1997 and put in force in February 2005. This agreement puts binding limits on more than 120 countries, including all the world's most industrial countries, to reduce carbon dioxide emissions to 5.2% below 1990 levels (United Nations). [**Add examples and details**]

In March 2001, U.S. President George W. Bush pulled out of the Kyoto Protocol, claiming that "it would harm the U.S. economy" (Anthes). As an alternative, Bush has called for voluntary efforts to reduce greenhouse gases. Climate experts have described Bush's recommendations as "unsatisfying" (Anthes). [**Add examples and details**]

The International Panel on Climate Change's 2001 report recommends both engineering measures to prevent the problems resulting in increased temperatures and agricultural changes to save southern and coastal farmlands ("Climate Change 2001"). [**Add examples and details**]

Despite warnings of the life-changing consequences of global warming, many people worldwide fail to take the issue seriously. In some countries, including the United States, the topic has been politicized and the science underlying it has sometimes been ignored. Increased attention must be focused on the topic to convince everyone that global warming is real and will have disastrous results if not brought under control.

People must take action to protect the world and all who live in it. The students who walk home after a boring day at school deserve to be able to continue living in the "world as we know it" without having to hold their breath!

> How does the first sentence of this paragraph provide a transition to a new main idea? Evaluate the use of quotations here.

> Where is the thesis restated?

> What recommendation or call to action is made?

Works Cited

Anthes, Richard A. "Global Warming." *Grolier Multimedia Encyclopedia.* 2004. Scholastic Library Publishing. Web. 11 Nov. 2007 <http://www.gme.grolier.com/article?assetid=0121375>.

"Climate Change 2001: Impacts, Adaptation and Vulnerability." 31 Dec. 2001. International Panel on Climate Change. Web. 18 Nov. 2007 <http://www.grida.no/climate/ipcc_tar/htm#183>.

"Global Warming Impacts: Global Warming Is Already Affecting People and Nature." World Wildlife Fund. Web. 15 Nov. 2007 <http://www.panda.org/about_wwf/what_we_do/climate_change/index.cfm>.

Larkey, Matilda. *Cutting Costs: The Environmental Impact of Lumber Practices.* New York: St. Ada's Press, 1997. Print.

Lynas, Mark. "Storm Warning: Effects of Global Warming on Weather." *Geographical* July 2000: 60-64. Print.

United Nations. "Kyoto Protocol." United Nations Framework Convention for Climate Change (UNFCCC). Web. 12 Nov. 2007 <http://unfccc.int/kyoto_protocol/items/2830.php>.

> In what order are the sources arranged?

> What types of sources are included in this list?

Reading Skills

Analyze Characterization

Characterization is the act of creating or describing a **character:** an individual who takes part in the action of a literary work. Writers create characters using direct and indirect techniques.

Using *direct characterization,* the writer *tells* what characters are like. For instance, the writer may describe what physical features, dress, and personality characters display. Using *indirect characterization,* the writer *shows* what characters are like and allows readers to judge them. The writer does this by showing what characters say, do, or think and what other characters say or think about them.

When trying to get a sense of a character, consider the details the writer provides about him or her: for instance, age, clothing, looks, marital status, education, way of speaking and diction, skills, occupation, cultural background, interests, beliefs, and life goals. Not all of these necessarily will be revealed, and some may be more important than others. Consider what the author wants you to know about a character.

Also consider the character's importance in the story. The main character, or **protagonist,** is the most important figure in the work and is in conflict with the **antagonist.** Characters can also be classified in other ways. *Major characters* play significant roles in a work, and *minor characters* play lesser roles. A *flat character* shows only one quality, or character trait. A *round character* shows the multiple character traits of a real person. A *static character* does not change during the course of the action, whereas a *dynamic character* does change.

TEST-TAKING TIP

In the critical-reading section of the test, know what you should be focusing on before you start reading the passage. This means scanning the questions about the passage first. Then underline or make short notes about the relevant information.

Practice

Directions: Read the following passage from Alice Munro's short story "Red Dress—1946." The questions that come after it will ask you to analyze characterization.

My mother was making me a dress. All through the month of November I would come from school and find her in the kitchen, surrounded by cut-up red velvet and
5 scraps of tissue-paper pattern. She worked at an old treadle machine pushed up against the window to get the light, and also to let her look out, past the stubble fields and bare vegetable garden, to see who went by on the
10 road. There was seldom anybody to see.

The red velvet material was hard to work with, it pulled, and the style my mother had chosen was not easy either. She was not really a good sewer. She liked to
15 make things; that is different. Whenever she could she tried to skip basting and pressing and she took no pride in the fine points of tailoring, the finishing of buttonholes and the overcasting of seams as, for instance, my
20 aunt and my grandmother did. Unlike them she started off with an inspiration, a brave and dazzling idea; from that moment on, her pleasure ran downhill. In the first place she could never find a pattern to suit her. It was
25 no wonder; there were no patterns made to match the ideas that blossomed in her head. She had made me, at various times when I was younger, a flowered organdie dress with a high Victorian neckline edged in scratchy
30 lace, with a poke bonnet to match; a Scottish plaid outfit with a velvet jacket and tam; an embroidered peasant blouse worn with a full red skirt and black laced bodice.

I had worn these clothes with docility, even
35 pleasure, in the days when I was unaware
of the world's opinion. Now, grown wiser,
I wished for dresses like those my friend
Lonnie had, bought at Beale's store.
    I had to try it on. Sometimes Lonnie
40 came home from school with me and she
would sit on the couch watching. I was
embarrassed by the way my mother crept
around me, her knees creaking, her breath
coming heavily. She muttered to herself.
45 Around the house she wore no corset or

stockings, she wore wedge-heeled shoes
and ankle socks; her legs were marked with
lumps of blue-green veins. I thought her
squatting position shameless, even obscene;
50 I tried to keep talking to Lonnie so that her
attention would be taken away from my
mother as much as possible. Lonnie wore
the composed, polite, appreciative expression that was her disguise in the presence of
55 grownups. She laughed at them and was a
ferocious mimic, and they never knew.

Multiple Choice

1. In this excerpt, the character of the mother
   is revealed primarily through what character-
   ization technique?
   A. direct: the details the author provides in
       describing the mother
   B. indirect: the daughter's description of the
       mother
   C. indirect: the mother's interaction with
       others
   D. indirect: the friend's description of the
       mother
   E. indirect: dialogue between the daughter
       and mother

2. What is the narrator's biggest fear?
   A. getting sick
   B. being embarrassed by her mother
   C. not fitting in
   D. making a mistake
   E. failing to succeed

3. What is revealed by the fact that the mother
   continues to make clothes for her daughter?
   A. They are poor and cannot afford to buy
       ready-made clothes.
   B. The mother is thoughtful, and the
       daughter is thoughtless.
   C. Both the mother and daughter are
       thoughtless.

   D. The mother likes to sew, and the daugh-
       ter likes to have a lot of clothes.
   E. The mother either does not know or
       does not care how her daughter feels
       about the clothes.

4. In this excerpt, the character of the daughter
   is revealed primarily through what
   technique?
   A. direct: the details the author provides in
       describing the daughter
   B. direct: what the daughter says and does
   C. indirect: what the daughter says and
       does
   D. indirect: the friend's description of the
       daughter
   E. indirect: dialogue between the daughter
       and mother

Constructed Response

5. Argue whether the daughter in Munro's "Red
   Dress—1946" is a flat or round character.
   Use details from the excerpt to support your
   opinion.

Writing Skills

Prepare for the Test

Take advantage of any resources available to help you practice and prepare for the test. For most standardized tests, you can find a variety of study guides and Internet sites. Such resources usually provide test-taking tips specific to a particular test. They also provide information about scoring, such as whether credit is deducted for a wrong answer, and they contain samples of the types of questions from various sections of the test.

Although these resources may be useful, nothing can take the place of having seen sample prompts and writing similar essays. From this type of practice, you will learn how to function in a timed situation and how to pace yourself. When the actual test situation occurs, following the steps in writing an essay will seem natural to you and you will be accustomed to the time you should spend on each section. With enough practice, you will develop a built-in clock of sorts, so you will not need to check a clock so often.

Think of all the things about taking a test that make you feel anxious. Then think about ways to eliminate or reduce each source of stress. When you feel prepared, you will feel more in charge and less stressed. You will then be better able to stay focused and put forth your best effort.

TEST-TAKING TIP

While it is important to monitor the time during a test, frequent clock checking will make you anxious. During the writing portion of a test, plan on dividing the time allotted among the three stages of the writing process: prewrite, draft, and revise. Devote most of your time to planning and writing your response, but give yourself enough time at the end of the session to read and revise your work. Following this three-stage process will help you manage your time effectively.

Practice

Timed Writing: 25 minutes

Think carefully about the issue presented in the following excerpt and assignment.

The average life expectancy is increasing steadily. Given ongoing advances in the fields of science and medicine, it seems likely that many of the main causes of death will be eliminated in the near future. This raises the issue of whether increased longevity is indeed desirable.

Assignment: Would the world be a better place if most people lived to be 100 years old or more? Plan and write an essay in which you develop your perspective on this issue. Support your perspective with reasoning and examples taken from your reading, studies, experience, or observations.

Revising and Editing Skills

As part of the Writing section, some standardized tests ask you to improve sentences. The items in this section focus on your ability to recognize and write clear, effective, and precise sentences.

Practice

Directions: In each of the following items, all or part of a sentence has been underlined. For each sentence, decide whether to revise the underlined part and choose the best of the five answer options provided. If the original phrasing is better than any of the alternatives offered, select A. If not, choose one of the other options.

Multiple Choice

1. The literary movement <u>Romanticism, often being confused</u> with the general use of the word *romantic,* occurred in the seventeenth and eighteenth centuries.
   A. Romanticism, often being confused
   B. Romanticism, which is often confused
   C. Romanticism, since often being easy to confuse
   D. Romanticism, having often been confused
   E. Romanticism, if one often confuses it

2. <u>Ever since turning</u> sixteen, Jessica has been anxious to get her driver's license.
   A. Ever since turning
   B. From the time she first turned
   C. Ever since she has turned
   D. Ever since she was
   E. Since turning

3. Tyrone likes to watch old <u>movies, of which *Casablanca* is</u> his favorite.
   A. movies, of which *Casablanca* is
   B. movies, and *Casablanca* being
   C. movies; *Casablanca* is
   D. movies, among which *Casablanca* is
   E. movies, regarding *Casablanca*

4. Not only were we stranded in the <u>woods, we also had</u> no way of getting help.
   A. woods, we also had
   B. woods, we had
   C. woods, but we also had
   D. woods; we had
   E. woods, but we had

Language Arts Handbook

1 Reading Strategies & Skills

1.1 The Reading Process

The reading process begins before you actually start to read. All readers use a reading process, even if they don't think about it. By becoming aware of this process, you can become a more effective reader. The reading process can be broken down into three stages: before reading, during reading, and after reading.

BEFORE READING | DURING READING | AFTER READING

BUILD BACKGROUND

- Think about the **context** you as a reader bring to the selection based on your knowledge and experiences. What do you know about the topic? What do you want to know?

SET PURPOSE

- **Preview** the text to set a purpose for reading.

Skim the first few paragraphs and glance through the selection to figure out what it's about and who the main characters are. What can you learn from the art or photos?

USE READING SKILLS

- Apply **reading skills** such as determining the author's purpose, analyzing text structure, and previewing new vocabulary.

BEFORE READING | DURING READING | AFTER READING

USE READING STRATEGIES

- **Ask questions** about things that seem unusual or interesting, like why a character might have behaved in an unexpected way.
- **Visualize** by forming pictures in your mind to help you see the characters or actions.
- **Make predictions** about what's going to happen next. As you read, gather more clues that will either confirm or change your predictions.
- **Make inferences,** or educated guesses, about what is not stated directly. Things may be implied or hinted at, or they may be left out altogether.

- **Clarify** your understanding of what you read by rereading any difficult parts.

ANALYZE LITERATURE

- Determine what **literary elements** stand out as you read the selection. Ask whether the characters are engaging and lifelike. Determine if there is a strong central conflict or theme.

MAKE CONNECTIONS

- Notice where there are **connections** between the story and your life or the world beyond the story. Be aware of feelings or thoughts you have while reading the story.

BEFORE READING | DURING READING | AFTER READING

REFER TO TEXT

- Think about the facts. **Remember details** like characters' names, locations or settings, and any other things that you can recall.
- Determine the **sequence of events** or the order in which things happened.
- **Reread** the story to pick up any details you may have missed the first time around.
- Try to **summarize** the story in a sentence or two based on the events.

REASON WITH TEXT

- **Analyze** the text by breaking down information into smaller pieces and figuring out how those pieces fit into the story as a whole. Your knowledge of literary tools can help you analyze the author's technique.
- **Evaluate** the text. **Synthesize** and **draw conclusions** by bringing together what you have read and using it to make a decision or form an opinion. Decide if you agree with the author's views.

Framework for Reading

BEFORE READING

ASK YOURSELF

- ❏ What's my purpose for reading this?
- ❏ What is this going to be about?
- ❏ How is this information organized?
- ❏ What do I already know about the topic?
- ❏ How can I apply this information to my life?

DURING READING

ASK YOURSELF

- ❏ What is the best way to accomplish my purpose for reading?
- ❏ What do I want or need to find out while I'm reading?
- ❏ What is the essential information presented here?
- ❏ What is the importance of what I am reading?
- ❏ Do I understand what I just read?
- ❏ What can I do to make the meaning more clear?

AFTER READING

ASK YOURSELF

- ❏ What did I learn from what I have read?
- ❏ What is still confusing?
- ❏ What do I need to remember from my reading?
- ❏ What effect did this text have on me?
- ❏ What else do I want to know about this topic?

1.2 Using Reading Strategies

Reading actively means thinking about what you are reading as you read it. A **reading strategy,** or plan, helps you read actively and get more from your reading. The following strategies can be applied at each stage of the reading process: before, during, and after reading.

Reading Strategies

- Build Background
- Set Purpose
- Ask Questions
- Visualize
- Make Predictions
- Make Inferences
- Clarify
- Make Connections

1.3 Using Reading Skills

Using the following skills as you read helps you to become an independent, thoughtful, and active reader who can accomplish tasks evaluated on tests, particularly standardized tests.

Reading Skills

- Identify Author's Purpose and Approach
- Skim and Scan
- Find the Main Idea
- Determine Importance of Details
- Understand Literary Elements
- Meaning of Words
- Use Context Clues
- Take Notes
- Analyze Text Organization
- Identify Sequence of Events
- Compare and Contrast
- Evaluate Cause and Effect
- Classify and Reorganize Information
- Distinguish Fact from Opinion
- Identify Multiple Levels of Meaning
- Interpret Visual Aids
- Monitor Comprehension
- Summarize
- Draw Conclusions

2 Vocabulary & Spelling

2.1 Using Context Clues

You can often figure out the meaning of an unfamiliar word by using context clues. Context clues, or hints you gather from the words and sentences around the unfamiliar word, prevent you from having to look up every unknown word in the dictionary. The types of context clues include comparison, contrast, restatement, examples, and cause and effect.

2.2 Word Parts

Many words are formed by adding prefixes and suffixes to main word parts called base words (if they can stand alone) or word roots (if they can't). A prefix is a letter or group of letters added to the beginning of a word to change its meaning. A suffix is a letter or group of letters added to the end of a word to change its meaning.

Word Part	Definition	Example
base word	main word part that can stand alone	form
word root	main word part that can't stand alone	struc
prefix	letter or group of letters added to the beginning of the word	pre—
suffix	letter or group of letters added to the end of the word	—tion

Refer to the Vocabulary & Spelling Workshop, Word Parts, on page 85 for more instruction.

2.3 Using a Dictionary

When you can't figure out a word using the strategies already described, or when the word is important to the meaning of the text and you want to make sure you have it right, use a dictionary. There are many parts to a dictionary entry. Study the following sample. Then read the explanations of each part of an entry below.

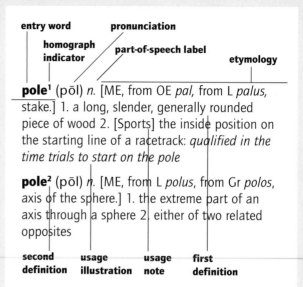

The **pronunciation** is given immediately after the entry word. The dictionary's table of contents will tell you where you can find a complete key to pronunciation symbols. In some dictionaries, a simplified pronunciation key is provided at the bottom of each page.

An abbreviation of the **part of speech** usually follows the pronunciation. This label tells how the word can be used. If a word can be used as more than one part of speech, a separate entry is provided for each part of speech.

An **etymology** is the history of the word. In the first entry, the word *pole* can be traced back through Middle English (ME) and Old English (OE) to the Latin (L) word *palus*, which means "stake." In the second entry, the word *pole* can be traced back through Middle English to the Latin word *polus*, which comes from the Greek (Gr) word *polos*, meaning "axis of the sphere."

Sometimes the entry will include a list of **synonyms**, or words that have the same or very similar meanings. The entry may also include a **usage illustration**, which is an example of how the word is used in context.

2.4 Understanding Multiple Meanings

Each definition in the entry gives a different meaning of the word. When a word has more than one meaning, the different definitions are numbered. The first definition in an entry is the most common meaning of the word, but you will have to choose the meaning that fits the context in which you have found the word. Try substituting each definition for the word until you find the one that makes the most sense. If you come across a word that doesn't seem to make sense in context, consider whether that word might have another, lesser known meaning. Can the word be used as more than one part of speech, for example, as either a noun or a verb? Does it have a broader meaning than the one that comes to your mind? For example, a line from *The Odyssey* reads "he gave me seven shining talents." The most common meaning of *talent* is "special skill or ability," but that doesn't fit here. Consulting the footnote at the bottom of the page, you would discover that the word *talent* can also refer to a type of old coin.

Keep in mind that some words not only have multiple meanings but also different pronunciations. Words that are spelled the same but are pronounced differently are called **homographs.**

2.5 Spelling

SPELLING RULES

Always check your writing for spelling errors, and try to recognize the words that give you more trouble than others. Use a dictionary when you find you have misspelled a word. Keep a list in a notebook of words that are difficult for you to spell. Write the words several times until you have memorized the correct spelling. Break down the word into syllables and carefully pronounce each individual syllable.

Some spelling problems occur when adding prefixes or suffixes to words or when making nouns plural. Other spelling problems occur when words follow certain patterns, such as those containing *ie/ei*. The following spelling rules can help you spell many words correctly.

SPELLING PATTERNS

The ie/ei Spelling Pattern

A word spelled with the letters *i* and *e* and has a long *e* sound is usually spelled *ie* except after the letter *c*.

EXAMPLES

belief	conceive
piece	receive
field	deceit

EXCEPTIONS

leisure	either

Use *ei* when the sound is not long *e*.

EXAMPLES

forfeit	surfeit	foreign	height

EXCEPTIONS

science	mischief	sieve

If the vowel combination has a long *a* sound (as in *eight*), always spell it with *ei*.

EXAMPLES

weight	vein	reign

When two vowels are pronounced separately in a word, spell them in the order of their pronunciation.

EXAMPLES

siesta	patio	diode	transient

The "Seed" Sound Pattern

The "seed" ending sound has three spellings: *–sede,* *–ceed,* and *–cede*.

EXAMPLES

Only one word ends in *–sede: supersede*

Three words end in *–ceed: proceed, succeed, exceed*

All other words end in *–cede: accede, concede, recede, precede, secede*

Silent Letters

Some spelling problems result from letters written but not heard when a word is spoken. Becoming familiar with the patterns in letter combinations containing silent letters will help you identify other words that fit the patterns.

- Silent *b* usually occurs with *m*.

EXAMPLES

| dumb | bomb | climb | lamb |

- Silent *b* also appears in *debt* and *doubt*.

- Silent *c* often appears with *s*.

EXAMPLES

| scissors | scent | scenic | science |

- Silent *g* often appears with *n*.

EXAMPLES

| design | resign | gnome | foreign |

- Silent *gh* often appears at the end of a word, either alone or in combination with *t (–ght)*.

EXAMPLES

| fright | freight | sought | wrought |

- Silent *h* appears at the beginning of some words.

EXAMPLES

| hourly | heir | honestly | honor |

- Silent *h* also appears in a few other words, as in *rhythm* and *ghost*.

- Silent *k* occurs with *n*.

EXAMPLES

| knack | knight | knot | kneecap |
| knapsack | | | |

- Silent *n* occurs with *m* at the end of some words.

EXAMPLES

| condemn | solemn | column | autumn |

- Silent *p* occurs with *s* at the beginning of some words.

EXAMPLES

| psyche | psychosis | psaltery | psoriasis |

- Silent *s* occurs with *l* in some words.

EXAMPLES

| island | islet | aisle |

- Silent *t* occurs with *s* in a few words.

EXAMPLES

| listen | hasten | nestle |

- Silent *w* occurs at the beginnings of some words.

EXAMPLES

| wreak | wrong | wraith | wrapper |

- Silent *w* also occurs with *s* in a few words, such as *sword* and *answer*.

Letter Combinations

Some letter combinations have a different pronunciation when combined and can cause spelling problems.

- The letters *ph* produce the *f* sound.

EXAMPLES

| sphinx | photograph | alphanumeric |
| phosphate | | |

- The letters *gh* produce the *f* sound usually at the end of a word. (Otherwise, they are silent.)

EXAMPLES

| cough | enough | neigh | weigh |

- The letter combination *tch* sounds the same as *ch*.

EXAMPLES

| sketch | pitch | snitch | hatch |
| such | hunch | grouch | torch |

If the letters *c* and *g* have soft sounds (of *s* and *j*), they will usually be followed by *e, i,* or *y*.

EXAMPLES

cyclone	giant
circle	gyroscope
cent	region
regent	outrageous

If the letters *c* and *g* have hard sounds (of *k* and *g*), they will usually be followed by *a, o,* or *u*.

EXAMPLES

candid	gasket
congeal	engorge
convey	garland
conjugate	argument
cunning	gun

Numerals

Spell out numbers of *one hundred* or less and all numbers rounded to hundreds. Larger round numbers such as *seven thousand* or *three million* should also be spelled out.

Joe Morgan hit more than **twenty** home runs and stole at least **thirty** bases in the same season **four** times in his career.

Joe DiMaggio was the first baseball player to receive an annual salary of more than **a hundred thousand** dollars.

Use a hyphen to separate compound numbers from twenty-one through ninety-nine.

forty-two birds
seventy-four candles
one hundred soldiers
sixty thousand dollars

Use a hyphen in a fraction used as a modifier, but not in a fraction used as a noun.

The glass is **two-fifths full** of water.

After an hour, I had mowed **three fourths** of the backyard.

Use Arabic numerals for numbers greater than one hundred that are not rounded numbers.

Our company sent out **493,745** mailings in just **145** days this year.

My uncle boasted that he has read **1,323** books thus far in his life.

If a number appears at the beginning of a sentence, spell it out or rewrite the sentence.

incorrect
356 years ago, my ancestors moved to North America.
correct
Three hundred fifty-six years ago, my ancestors moved to North America.
correct
My ancestors moved to North America **356** years ago.

Use words to write the time unless you are writing the exact time (including the abbreviation AM or PM). When the word *o'clock* is used for time of day, express the number in words.

Our meeting will start at **a quarter after ten.**

At **eight-thirty,** the show will begin.

I was born at **5:22 PM** on a Monday.

You have until **three o'clock** to finish the proposal.

Use numerals to express dates, street numbers, room numbers, apartment numbers, telephone numbers, page numbers, exact amounts of money, scores, and percentages. Spell out the word *percent.* Round dollar or cent amounts of only a few words may be expressed in words.

May 27, 1962
(402) 555-1725
5219 Perret Street
pages 49–73
seventy cents
three hundred dollars
Apartment 655
38 percent
$1.6 billion (or $1,600,000,000)
$2,634

When you write a date, do not add *–st, –nd,* or *–th.*

incorrect
August 17th, 1968   November 5th
correct
August 17, 1968   November 5 or the
                            fifth of November

COMMON SPELLING ERRORS

Pronunciation is not always a reliable guide for spelling because words are not always spelled the way they are pronounced. However, by paying attention to both letters that spell sounds and letters that are silent, you can improve some aspects of your spelling. Always check a dictionary for the correct pronunciations and spellings of words that are new to your experience.

Extra Syllables

Sometimes people misspell a word because they include an extra syllable. For example, *arthritis* is easily misspelled if it is pronounced *artheritis,* with four syllables instead of three. Pay close attention to the number of syllables in these words.

two syllables

foundry   carriage   lonely

three syllables

privilege   boundary   separate

Omitted Sounds

Sometimes people misspell a word because they do not sound one or more letters when pronouncing the word. Be sure to include the underlined letters of these words even if you don't pronounce them.

barbarous   candidate   drowned

gratitude   governor   grocery

literature   sophomore   quantity

mischievous

Homophones

Words that have the same pronunciation but different spellings and meanings are called **homophones.** An incorrect choice can be confusing to your readers. Knowing the spelling and meaning of these groups of words will improve your spelling.

allowed/aloud   compliment/complement

sole/soul   alter/altar

hear/here   some/sum

ascent/assent   lead/led

threw/through   bear/bare

night/knight   wait/weight

brake/break   pair/pear

weak/week   buy/bye/by

peace/piece   who's/whose

capital/capitol   plain/plane

coarse/course   site/sight/cite

Commonly Confused Words

Some other groups of words are not homophones, but they are similar enough in sound and spelling to create confusion. Knowing the spelling and meaning of these groups of words will also improve your spelling.

access/excess   farther/further

nauseous/nauseated   accept/except

formally/formerly   passed/past

alternate/alternative literal/literally

principle/principal   desert/dessert

loose/lose   stationary/stationery

3 Grammar & Style

3.1 The Sentence

THE SENTENCE

In the English language, the sentence is the basic unit of meaning. A **sentence** is a group of words that expresses a complete thought. Every sentence has two basic parts: a subject and a predicate. The **subject** tells whom or what the sentence is about. The **predicate** tells information about the subject.

EXAMPLE

sentence
The experienced detective **[subject]** |
asked the suspect several questions **[predicate].**

FUNCTIONS OF SENTENCES

There are four different kinds of sentences: *declarative, interrogative, imperative,* and *exclamatory.* Each kind of sentence has a different purpose. You can vary the tone and mood of your writing by using the four different sentence types.

- A **declarative sentence** makes a statement. It ends with a period.

EXAMPLE
Samantha is in the backyard trying to repair the lawnmower.

- An **interrogative sentence** asks a question. It ends with a question mark.

EXAMPLE
Will she be joining you for supper later tonight?

- An **imperative sentence** gives an order or makes a request. It ends with a period or an exclamation point. An imperative sentence has an understood subject, most often *you.*

EXAMPLES
(You) Please take a glass of lemonade to her.
(You) Don't touch that sharp blade!

- An **exclamatory sentence** expresses strong feeling. It ends with an exclamation point.

EXAMPLE
Samantha is a wizard at fixing lawnmowers!

SIMPLE AND COMPLETE SUBJECTS AND PREDICATES

In a sentence, the **simple subject** is the key word or words in the subject. The simple subject is usually a noun or a pronoun and does not include any modifiers. The **complete subject** includes the simple subject and all the words that modify it.

The **simple predicate** is the key verb or verb phrase that tells what the subject does, has, or is. The **complete predicate** includes the verb and all the words that modify it.

In the following sentence, a vertical line separates the complete subject and complete predicate. The simple subject is underlined once. The simple predicate is underlined twice.

EXAMPLE
Bright orange <u>tongues</u> of flame **[complete subject]** |
<u>danced</u> erratically in the center of the clearing **[complete predicate].**

Sometimes, the simple subject is also the complete subject, and the simple predicate or verb is also the complete predicate.

EXAMPLE
<u>Falcons</u> | <u>swooped</u>.

To find the simple subject and simple predicate in a sentence, first break the sentence into its two basic parts: complete subject and complete predicate. Then, identify the simple predicate by asking yourself, "What is the action of this sentence?" Finally, identify the simple subject by asking yourself, "Who or what is performing the action?" In the following sentences, the complete predicate is in parentheses. The simple predicate, or verb, appears in boldface.

EXAMPLES
one-word verb
Your friend on the track team (**runs** swiftly.)
two-word verb
Your friend on the track team (**will run** swiftly in this race.)
three-word verb
All season long, your friend on the track team (**has been running** swiftly.)

four-word verb
If he hadn't twisted his ankle last week, your friend on the track team (**would have been running** swiftly today.)

COMPOUND SUBJECTS AND PREDICATES

A sentence may have more than one subject or predicate. A **compound subject** has two or more simple subjects that have the same predicate. The subjects are joined by the conjunction *and, or,* or *but.*

A **compound predicate** has two or more simple predicates, or verbs, that share the same subject. The verbs are connected by the conjunction *and, or,* or *but.*

EXAMPLES

compound subject
Pamela and Else | read their books in the library.
compound predicate
Four maniacal crows | watched and waited while I washed the car.

The conjunctions *either* and *or* and *neither* and *nor* can also join compound subjects or predicates.

EXAMPLES

compound subject
Either Peter *or* Paul | sings the national anthem before each game.
Neither yesterday *nor* today | seemed like a good time to start the project.
compound predicate
Her dogs | *either* heard *or* smelled the intruder in the basement.
The police inspector | *neither* visited *nor* called last night.

A sentence may also have a compound subject and a compound predicate.

EXAMPLE

compound subject and compound predicate
Mandy and Eric | grilled the hamburgers and made the coleslaw.

SENTENCE STRUCTURES

A **simple sentence** consists of one independent clause and no subordinate clauses. It may have a compound subject and a compound predicate. It may also have any number of phrases. A simple sentence is sometimes called an independent clause because it can stand by itself.

EXAMPLES

Three bears emerged from the forest.

They spotted the campers and the hikers and decided to pay a visit.

The three bears enjoyed eating the campers' fish, sandwiches, and candy bars.

A **compound sentence** consists of two sentences joined by a semicolon or by a coordinating conjunction and a comma. Each part of the compound sentence has its own subject and verb. The most common coordinating conjunctions are *and, or, nor, for, but, so,* and *yet.*

EXAMPLES

Feeding bears is dangerous and unwise, **for** it creates larger problems in the long run.

Our zoo is home to two panda bears; they were originally captured in Asia.

A **complex sentence** consists of one independent clause and one or more subordinate clauses. The subordinate clauses in the examples below are underlined.

EXAMPLES

When you finish your report, remember to print it out on paper that contains 25 percent cotton fiber.

Jim will water the lawn after he returns home from the baseball game.

If you combine a compound sentence and a complex sentence, you form a **compound-complex sentence.** This kind of sentence must have two or more independent clauses and at least one subordinate clause. In the following examples, the subordinate clauses are underlined.

EXAMPLES

Rabbits, which like to nibble on the flowers, often visit my garden early in the morning, or they wait until early evening when the dog is inside the house.

Larry enthusiastically leaps out of bed each morning after his alarm clock rings, yet he often feels sleepy in the afternoon.

The Parts of Speech

IDENTIFYING THE PARTS OF SPEECH

Each word in a sentence performs a basic function or task. Words perform four basic tasks: they name, modify, express action or state of being, or link.

There are eight different parts of speech. Each part of speech is defined in the following chart.

Part of Speech	Definition	Example
noun	A **noun** names a person, place, thing, or idea.	**Apples, oranges,** and **potato chips** were the only **items** on the **list.**
pronoun	A **pronoun** is used in place of a noun.	Fanny whispered to **her** friend as **they** waited for **their** new teacher.
verb	A **verb** expresses action or a state of being.	Playful fox cubs **tumbled** out of the den and **chased** one another across the field.
adjective	An **adjective** modifies a noun or pronoun. The most common adjectives are the articles *a, an,* and *the.*	**Tattered** curtains hung in the **dark** windows of the **gray, sagging** house.
adverb	An **adverb** modifies a verb, an adjective, or another adverb.	**Sharply** turning to the left, the bicyclist **nearly** caused an accident.
preposition	A **preposition** shows the relationship between its object—a noun or a pronoun—and another word in a sentence. Common prepositions include *after, around, at, behind, beside, off, through, until, upon,* and *with.*	**During** winter, we often sit **by** the fireplace **in** the evening.
conjunction	A **conjunction** joins words or groups of words. Common conjunctions are *and, but, for, nor, or, so,* and *yet.*	**Neither** Grant **nor** Felix felt tired after two miles, **so** they ran another mile.
interjection	An **interjection** is a word used to express emotion. Common interjections are *oh, ah, well, hey,* and *wow.*	**Wow!** Did you see the dive he took from the high jump?

3.3 Nouns

NOUNS

A **noun** is a part of speech that names a person, place, idea, or thing. In this unit, you'll learn about the different kinds of nouns and what they name.

Types of Nouns	Definition	Example
common noun	names a person, place, idea, or thing	mother, garage, plan, flower
proper noun	names a specific person, place, or thing; begins with capital letter	John Adams, New York City, Monroe Doctrine
concrete noun	names a thing that can be touched, seen, heard, smelled, or tasted	ruler, mirror, giggle, garbage, banana
abstract noun	names an idea, a theory, a concept, or a feeling	approval, philosophy, faith, communism
singular noun	names one person, place, idea, or thing	governor, tree, thought, shoe
plural noun	names more than one thing	governors, trees, thoughts, shoes
possessive noun	shows ownership or possession of things or qualities	Jan's, Mrs. Wilson's, women's, intern's
compound noun	made up of two or more words	staircase, picnic table, brother-in-law
collective noun	names group	organization, platoon, team

3.4 Pronouns

PRONOUNS

A **pronoun** is used in place of a noun. Sometimes a pronoun refers to a specific person or thing.

Pronouns can help your writing flow more smoothly. Without pronouns, your writing can sound awkward and repetitive.

The most commonly used pronouns are *personal pronouns, reflexive and intensive pronouns, demonstrative pronouns, indefinite pronouns, interrogative pronouns,* and *relative pronouns.*

Types of Pronouns	Definition	Examples
personal pronoun	used in place of the name of a person or thing	I, me, we, us, he, she, it, him, her, you, they, them
indefinite pronoun	points out a person, place, or thing, but not a specific or definite one	one, someone, anything, other, all, few, nobody
reflexive pronoun	refers back to a noun previously used; adds —self and —selves to other pronoun forms	myself, herself, yourself, themselves, ourselves
intensive pronoun	emphasizes a noun or a pronoun	me myself, he himself, you yourself, they themselves, we ourselves
interrogative pronoun	asks a question	who, whose, whom, what, which
demonstrative pronoun	points out a specific person, place, idea, or thing	this, these, that, those
relative pronoun	introduces an adjective clause	that, which, who, whose, whom
singular pronoun	used in place of the name of one person or thing	I, me, you, he, she, it, him, her
plural pronoun	used in place of more than one person or thing	we, us, you, they, them
possessive pronoun	shows ownership or possession	mine, yours, his, hers, ours, theirs

PRONOUNS AND ANTECEDENTS

The word that a pronoun stands for is called its **antecedent.** The antecedent clarifies the meaning of the pronoun. The pronoun may appear in the same sentence as its antecedent or in a following sentence.

EXAMPLES

number

singular   **Robert Frost** wrote many poems. "Stopping by Woods on a Snowy Evening" is perhaps **his** most well-known poem.

plural   The visiting **poets** were asked if **they** would give a reading on Saturday night.

gender

masculine   **Robert Frost** was born in California, but **he** was raised in Massachusetts and New Hampshire.

feminine   **Toni Morrison** begins **her** writing day before dawn.

neutral   The **poem** is titled "Birches," and **it** is one of my favorites.

PRONOUN CASES

Personal pronouns take on different forms—called *cases*—depending on how they are used in sentences. Personal pronouns can be used as subjects, direct objects, indirect objects, and objects of prepositions. In the English language, there are three case forms for personal pronouns: *nominative, objective,* and *possessive.* The following chart organizes personal pronouns by case, number, and person.

Personal Pronouns

	Nominative Case	Objective Case	Possessive Case
Singular			
first person	I	me	my, mine
second person	you	you	your, yours
third person	he, she, it	him, her, it	his, her, hers, its
Plural			
first person	we	us	our, ours
second person	you	you	your, yours
third person	they	them	their, theirs

Indefinite Pronouns

An **indefinite pronoun** points out a person, place, or thing, but not a particular or definite one. The indefinite pronouns are listed below.

Singular	Plural	Singular or Plural
another	both	all
anybody	few	any
anyone	many	more
anything	others	most
each	several	none
each other		some
either		
everybody		
everyone		
everything		
much		
neither		
nobody		
no one		
nothing		
one		
one another		
somebody		
someone		
something		

3.5 Verbs

VERBS — PREDICATES

Every sentence can be divided into two parts: the **subject** and the **predicate.** The following sentence is divided between the complete subject and the complete predicate.

EXAMPLE

The tardy **student** | **raced** through the maze of hallways to class.

The subject of a sentence names whom or what the sentence is about. The predicate tells what the subject does, is, or has. A **verb** is the predicate without any complements, linkers, or modifiers. In other words, the verb is the simple predicate.

Verbs are the **expressers** of the English language. Verbs are used to express action or a state of being. They tell whether the action is completed, continuing, or will happen in the future. Verbs also express all kinds of conditions for the action. Verbs in the English language can be from one to four words long. When a main verb is preceded by one or more helping verbs, it is called a **verb phrase.**

EXAMPLES

Lauren **volunteers** at the food pantry.

Lauren **is volunteering** at the food pantry.

Lauren **has been volunteering** at the food pantry.

Lauren **might have been volunteering** at the food pantry.

The following chart lists the different types of verbs and their functions, along with examples of how they are used.

Type of Verb	Definition	Examples
action verb	names an action	howl, wobble, skitter, flutter, fly
helping verb	helps a main verb express action or a state of being	My dogs will howl when a siren sounds. A butterfly has been fluttering above the daisies.
linking verb	connects a noun with another noun, pronoun, or adjective that describes or identifies it; the most common linking verbs are formed from the verb *to be*	The butterfly is a monarch. It seems to float in the breeze.
transitive verb	has a direct object	The scientist remembered the secret code.
intransitive verb	does not have a direct object	My brother snores.
irregular verb	has a different past tense form and spelling	forget/forgot think/thought write/wrote

VERB TENSES

The Simple Tenses

Verbs have different forms, called **tenses,** which are used to tell the time in which an action takes place. The **simple tenses** of the verb are **present, past,** and **future.**

The **present tense** tells that an action happens now—in present time.

present tense singular
The short-order cook **flips** pancakes on the grill.

present tense plural
The short-order cooks **flip** pancakes on the grill.

The **past tense** tells that an action happened in the past—prior to the present time. The past tense of a regular verb is formed by adding *−d* or *−ed* to the present verb form.

EXAMPLES

past tense singular
The short-order cook **flipped** pancakes on the grill.

past tense plural
The short-order cooks **flipped** pancakes on the grill.

The **future tense** tells that an action will happen in the future. The future tense is formed by adding the word *will* or *shall* before the present verb form.

EXAMPLES

future tense singular
The short order cook **will (shall) flip** pancakes on the grill.

future tense plural
The short-order cooks **will (shall) flip** pancakes on the grill.

The Perfect Tenses

The **perfect tenses** of verbs also express present, past, and future time, but they show that the action continued and was completed over a period of time or that the action will be completed in the present or future. The perfect tense is formed by using *has, have,* or *had* with the past participle.

EXAMPLES

present perfect singular
Vincent **has watered** the garden. The garden **has been watered** by Vincent.

present perfect plural
Vincent and Lena **have watered** the garden. (have or has + past participle)

past perfect singular
Vincent **had watered** the garden yesterday. The garden **had been watered** yesterday by Vincent.

past perfect plural
Vincent and Lena **had watered** the garden yesterday. (had + past participle)

future perfect singular
Vincent **will have watered** the garden by now.

future perfect plural
Vincent and Lena **will have watered** the garden by now. (will have or shall have + past participle)

THE PROGRESSIVE AND EMPHATIC VERB FORMS

Each of the six tenses has another form called the progressive form. The **progressive form** of a verb is used to express continuing action or state of being. The progressive form is made of the appropriate tense of the verb *be* and the present participle of a verb.

EXAMPLES

present progressive
I **am singing.** He **is singing.** They **are singing.**

past progressive
I **was singing.** They **were singing.**

future progressive
I **will (shall) be singing.**

present perfect progressive
He **has been singing.** They **have been singing.**

past perfect progressive
I **had been singing.**

future perfect progressive
I **will (shall) have been singing.**

The **emphatic form** of a verb is used to express emphasis. Only the present and past tenses have the emphatic form.

EXAMPLES

present emphatic
I **do try** to be punctual.
It **does matter** to me.

past emphatic
I **did clean** my room.

3.6 Complements

COMPLEMENTS FOR ACTION VERBS

A sentence must have a subject and a verb to communicate its basic meaning. In the following sentences, the subject and verb express the total concept. There is no receiver of the verb's action.

EXAMPLES

The girls shopped.

Sandra seldom shouts.

The thunder boomed.

Many sentences that include action verbs, however, need an additional word or group of words to complete the meaning.

EXAMPLES

The musicians tuned.

The musicians tuned their instruments.

The group of words *The musicians tuned* contains a subject *(musicians)* and a verb *(tuned)*. Although the group of words may be considered a sentence, it does not express a complete thought. The word *instruments* completes the meaning expressed by the verb *tuned*. Therefore, *instruments* is called a **complement** or a completing word. The *completers* for action verbs are **direct objects** and **indirect objects.**

Direct Objects

A **direct object** receives the action in the sentence. It usually answers the question *what?* or *whom?* To find the direct object, find the action verb in the sentence. Then ask *what?* or *whom?* about the verb.

EXAMPLES

Sam **drove Jilly** to her mother's house. (*Drove* is the action verb. Whom did Sam drive? *Jilly* is the direct object.)

The coach **blew** her **whistle**. (*Blew* is the action verb. What did the coach blow? *Whistle* is the direct object.)

Remember to use object pronouns for a direct object.

singular me, you, him, her, it
plural us, you, them

EXAMPLES

Adam invited **us** to the party.

My dog follows **me** everywhere.

Indirect Objects

Sometimes the direct object is received by someone or something. This receiver is called the **indirect object.** It comes before the direct object and tells *to whom* the action is directed or *for whom* the action is performed. Only verbs that have direct objects can have indirect objects.

EXAMPLE

Lorelei **gave** the **teacher** her project. (*Gave* is the action verb. *Project* is the direct object because it tells what Lorelei gave. *Teacher* is an indirect object. It tells to whom Lorelei gave her project.)

To identify the indirect object: (1) Look for a noun or a pronoun that precedes the direct object. (2) Determine whether the word you think is a direct object seems to be the understood object of the preposition *to* or *for.*

COMPLEMENTS FOR LINKING VERBS

A **linking verb** connects a subject with a noun, a pronoun, or an adjective that describes it or identifies it. Linking verbs do not express action. Instead, they express state of being and need a noun, a pronoun or an adjective to complete the sentence meaning.

In each of the following sentences, the subject and verb would not be complete without the words that follow them.

EXAMPLES

Franklin D. Roosevelt **was** a popular president.

He **seemed** trustworthy and reliable.

Most linking verbs are forms of the verb *to be,* including *am, are, is, was,* and *been.* Other words that can be used as linking verbs include *appear, feel, grow, smell, taste, seem, sound, look, stay, feel, remain,* and *become.* When *to be* verbs are part of an action verb, they are helpers.

PREDICATE NOUNS AND PREDICATE PRONOUNS

A **predicate noun** is a noun that completes a sentence that uses a form of the verb *to be*. Similarly, a **predicate pronoun** is a pronoun that completes a sentence that uses a form of the verb *to be*. In fact, the relationship between the subject and the predicate noun or pronoun is so close that the sentence usually suggests an equation. Such sentences can often be reordered without changing the meaning.

EXAMPLES

predicate noun
Jacinta was the first girl to play on the boys' baseball team. (Jacinta = girl)

The first girl to play on the boys' baseball team was Jacinta. (girl = Jacinta)

predicate pronoun
The friend who took me bowling was you. (friend = you)

You were the friend who took me bowling. (You = friend)

To find a predicate noun or pronoun, ask the same question you would ask to find a direct object.

EXAMPLES

My aunt is a great **chef.** (My aunt is a what? *Chef* is the predicate noun that renames or identifies *aunt,* the subject of the sentence.)

The first contestant will probably be **you.** (The first contestant will be who? *You* is the predicate pronoun that renames or identifies contestant, the subject of the sentence.)

The ticket taker at the booth was **she.** (Think: She was the ticket taker at the booth.)

The leaders of the hike were Sara and **he.** (Think: Sara and he were the leaders of the hike.)

PREDICATE ADJECTIVES

A **predicate adjective** completes a sentence by modifying, or describing, the subject of a sentence. To find a predicate adjective, ask the same question you would ask to find a direct object.

EXAMPLE

Your directions were **precise.** (Your directions were what? *Precise* is the predicate adjective that describes *directions,* the subject of the sentence.)

3.7 Modifiers

ADJECTIVES AND ADVERBS

Adjectives and adverbs—two kinds of **modifiers**—add meaning to nouns, adjectives, verbs, and adverbs. An **adjective** modifies a noun or a pronoun. An **adverb** modifies a verb, an adjective, or another adverb.

EXAMPLES

adjective
The **yellow** roses have rambled up the **wooden** trellis onto the roof.
(*Yellow* modifies the noun *roses; wooden* modifies the noun *trellis.*)

adverb
The roses are **too** thorny to be trimmed.
(*Too* modifies the adjective *thorny.*)

The roses have grown **very** slowly, but they bloom **profusely** every spring.
(*Very* modifies the adverb *slowly; profusely* modifies the verb *bloom.*)

To determine whether a modifier is an adjective or an adverb, you can follow these steps.
1. Look at the word that is modified.
2. Ask yourself, "Is this modified word a noun or a pronoun?" If the answer is yes, the modifier is an adjective. If the answer is no, the modifier is an adverb.

In the following example, the word *balloonist* is modified by the word *daring.* The word *balloonist* is a noun, so the word *daring* is an adjective.

EXAMPLE

The **daring balloonist** traveled around the world.

In the next example, the word *landed* is modified by the word *safely.* The word *landed* is a verb; therefore, the word *safely* is an adverb.

EXAMPLE

After surviving a storm at sea, the balloonist **landed safely** in Australia.

3.8 Prepositions and Conjunctions

PREPOSITIONS AND CONJUNCTIONS

Prepositions and conjunctions are the linkers of the English language. They are used to join words and phrases to the rest of a sentence. They also show the relationships between ideas. Prepositions and conjunctions help writers vary their sentences by connecting sentence parts in different ways.

A **preposition** is used to show how its object, a noun or a pronoun, is related to other words in the sentence. Some commonly used prepositions include *above, after, against, among, around, at, behind, beneath, beside, between, down, for, from, in, on, off, toward, through, to, until, upon,* and *with.*

EXAMPLES

A bright beacon led them safely **to** the shore.

He placed the book **beside** the bed.

A **conjunction** is a word used to link related words, groups of words, or sentences. Like a preposition, a conjunction shows the relationship between the words it links. Some of the most commonly used conjunctions are *and, but, for, nor, or, yet, so, if, after, because, before, although, unless, while,* and *when.* Some conjunctions are used in pairs, such as *both/and, neither/nor,* and *not only/but also.*

EXAMPLES

We went out for dinner **and** a movie on Saturday night.

They played poorly **because** they did not warm up before the game.

Neither I **nor** my brother inherited our mother's red hair.

Certain words can function as either conjunctions or prepositions. There are two important differences between a word used as a preposition and one used as a conjunction.

1. A preposition is always followed by an *object,* but a conjunction is not.

EXAMPLES

preposition
You may have a turn **after** your sister. (The noun *sister* is the object of the preposition *after.*)

conjunction
After you arrived, we had a wonderful time. (*After* is not followed by an object. It introduces a group of words, or clause, that depends on the rest of the sentence for meaning.)

2. A preposition introduces a prepositional phrase that connects parts of a sentence. A conjunction connects words or groups of words (clauses containing a subject and verb).

EXAMPLES

preposition
I never eat breakfast **before** exercising. (*Before* introduces the prepositional phrase *before exercising.*)

conjunction
Put on sunscreen **before** the swim meet begins. (*Before* introduces a clause, that is, a subject and verb, that modifies *put,* telling when to put on the sunscreen.)

3.9 Interjections

An **interjection** is a part of speech that expresses feeling, such as surprise, joy, relief, urgency, pain, or anger. Common interjections include *ah, aha, alas, bravo, dear me, goodness, great, ha, help, hey, hooray, hush, indeed, mercy, of course, oh, oops, ouch, phooey, really, say, see, ugh,* and *whew.*

EXAMPLES

Hey, that's not fair!

Goodness, you don't need to get so upset.

Hush! You'll wake the baby.

Why, of course! Please do join us for dinner.

Interjections actually indicate different degrees of emotion. They may express intense or sudden emotion, as in *Wow! That was unexpected.* Notice that the strong expression of emotion stands alone in the sentence and is followed by an exclamation point. Interjections can also express mild emotion, as in *Well, that is the best we could do.* In this sentence, the interjection is part of the sentence and is set off only with a comma. Even when interjections are part of a sentence, they do not relate grammatically to the rest of the sentence.

3.10 Phrases

A **phrase** is a group of words used as a single part of speech. A phrase lacks a subject, a verb, or both; therefore, it cannot be a sentence. There are three common kinds of phrases: prepositional phrases, verbal phrases, and appositive phrases.

PREPOSITIONAL PHRASES

A **prepositional phrase** consists of a preposition, its object, and any modifiers of that object. A prepositional phrase adds information to a sentence by relating its object to another word in the sentence. It may function as an adjective or an adverb.

EXAMPLES

adjectives

Sue planned a party **with music and dancing.** (The prepositional phrase *with music and dancing* tells what kind of party Sue planned. The phrase is used as an adjective, modifying the noun *party.*)

She found the CDs and tapes in a box **under her bed.** (The prepositional phrase *under her bed* tells in which box Sue found the CDs and tapes. The phrase is used as an adjective, modifying the object of the prepositional phrase *in a box.*)

adverbs

Albert struggled **into his jacket.** (The prepositional phrase *into his jacket* tells how Albert struggled. The phrase is used as an adverb, modifying the verb *struggled.*)

My friend is generous **with her time.** (The prepositional phrase *with her time* tells how the friend is generous. The phrase is used as an adverb, modifying the adjective *generous.*)

Use prepositional phrases to create sentence variety. When every sentence in a paragraph starts with its subject, the rhythm of the sentences becomes boring. Revise your sentences, where it is appropriate, to start some with prepositional phrases.

EXAMPLE

Chad stacked sandbags **for nearly eight hours.**

For nearly eight hours, Chad stacked sandbags.

3.11 Common Usage Problems

INCORRECT USE OF APOSTROPHES

Use an apostrophe to replace letters that have been left out in a contraction.

EXAMPLES

that's = that is
aren't = are not
we'll = we will

Use an apostrophe to show possession.

Singular Nouns

Use an apostrophe and an *s* (*'s*) to form the possessive of a singular noun, even if it ends in *s, x,* or *z.*

EXAMPLES

storm's damage
Chris's guitar
Max's spoon
jazz's history

Plural Nouns

Use an apostrophe and an *s* (*'s*) to form the possessive of a plural noun that does not end in *s.*

EXAMPLES

geese's flight
women's conference

Use an apostrophe alone to form the possessive of a plural noun that ends in *s.*

EXAMPLES

dolphins' migration
wheels' hubcaps

Do not add an apostrophe or *'s* to possessive personal pronouns: *mine, yours, his, hers, its, ours,* or *theirs.* They already show ownership.

EXAMPLES

His homework is finished; **mine** is not done yet.

The red house on the corner is **theirs.**

DOUBLE NEGATIVES

A **double negative** is the use of two negative words together when only one is needed. Correct double negatives by removing one of the negative words or by replacing one of the negative words with a positive word.

EXAMPLES

double negative
They can't hardly afford the plane tickets.

corrected sentence
They can hardly afford the plane tickets.
They can't afford the plane tickets.

double negative
Cassidy hasn't never read *The Call of the Wild.*

corrected sentence
Cassidy hasn't ever read *The Call of the Wild.*
Cassidy has never read *The Call of the Wild.*

DANGLING AND MISPLACED MODIFIERS

Place modifying phrases and clauses as close as possible to the words they modify; otherwise, your sentences may be unclear or unintentionally humorous.

A **dangling modifier** has nothing to modify because the word it would logically modify is not present in the sentence. In the following sentence, the modifying phrase has no logical object. The sentence says that a spider was reading.

EXAMPLE

Reading in his rocking chair, a spider was spotted on the wall.

You can eliminate dangling modifiers by rewriting the sentence so that an appropriate word is provided for the modifier to modify. You can also expand a dangling phrase into a full subordinate clause.

EXAMPLES

Reading in his rocking chair, he spotted a spider on the wall.

While Frank was reading in his rocking chair, he spotted a spider on the wall.

A **misplaced modifier** is located too far from the word it should modify.

EXAMPLE

Jennifer arrived home after the two-week training session on Friday.

You can revise a misplaced modifier by moving it closer to the word it modifies.

EXAMPLES

Jennifer arrived home on Friday after the two-week training session.

On Friday, Jennifer arrived home after the two-week training session.

SPLIT INFINITIVES

An infinitive, the base verb combined with *to*, should not be split under most circumstances. Infinitives such as *to save, to teach,* and *to hold* should not be interrupted by adverbs or other sentence components.

EXAMPLES

nonstandard
I began to seriously think about becoming a vegetarian.

standard
I began to think seriously about becoming a vegetarian.

In some cases, a modifier sounds awkward if it does not split the infinitive. In these situations, it may be best to reword the sentence to eliminate splitting the infinitive. In certain cases, you may want to use a split infinitive to clarify the meaning of the sentence.

3.12 Punctuation

Punctuation Reference Chart

Punctuation	Function	Examples
End Marks	tell the reader where a sentence ends and show the purpose of the sentence; periods are also used for abbreviations.	Our next-door neighbor is Mrs**.** Ryan**.**
Periods	with **declarative** sentences	The weather forecast predicts rain tonight**.**
	with **abbreviations**	
	personal names	**N.** Scott Momaday, **W. W.** Jacobs, Ursula **K.** Le Guin
	titles	**Mr.** Bruce Webber, **Mrs.** Harriet Cline, **Ms.** Steinem, **Dr.** Duvall, **Sen.** Hillary Clinton, **Gov.** George Pataki, **Capt.** Horatio Hornblower, **Prof.** Klaus
	business names	Tip Top Roofing **Co.**, Green **Bros.** Landscaping, Gigantic **Corp.**
	addresses	Oak **Dr.**, Grand **Blvd.**, Main **St.**, Kennedy **Pkwy.**, Prudential **Bldg.**
	geographical terms	Kensington, **Conn.**, San Francisco, **Calif.**, Canberra, **Aus.**
	time	2 **hrs.** 15 **min., Thurs.** morning, **Jan.** 20, 21st **cent.**
	units of measurement	3 **tbsp.** olive oil 1/2 **c.** peanut butter 8 **oz.** milk 5 **ft.** 4 **in.** 20 **lbs.**
	exceptions: metric measurements, state names in postal addresses, or directional elements	**metric measurements** cc, ml, km, g, L **state postal codes** MN, WI, IA, NE, CA, NY **compass points** N, NW, S, SE
Question Marks	with **interrogative** sentences	May I have another serving of spaghetti**?**
Exclamation Points	with **exclamatory** sentences	Hey, be careful**!**
Commas	to separate words or groups of words within a sentence; to tell the reader to pause at certain spots in the sentence	Casey was confident he could hit a home run**,** but he struck out.
	to separate items in a series	The magician's costume included a **silk scarf, black satin hat,** and **magic wand.**
	to combine sentences using *and, but, or, nor, yet, so,* or *for*	An infestation of beetles threatened the summer squash and zucchini crops**, yet** the sturdy plants thrived. I'll apply an organic insecticide**, or** I'll ignore the garden pest problem.
	after an introductory word, phrase, or clause	**Surprisingly,** fashions from the 1970s are making a come-back. **Frayed and tight-fitting,** denim bellbottoms remain a fashion hit.

Punctuation	Function	Examples
	to set off words or phrases that interrupt sentences	Harpers Ferry, **a town in northeastern West Virginia,** was the site of John Brown's raid in 1859. The violent raid**, however,** frightened people in the North and South. **An abolitionist leader,** Brown was captured during the raid and later executed.
	between two or more adjectives that modify the same noun and that could be joined by *and*	A **warm,** [and] **spicy** aroma enticed us to enter the kitchen. Steaming bowls of chili satisfied the **tired,** [and] **hungry** travelers.
	to set off names used in direct address	**Olivia,** the zinnias and daisies need to be watered. Please remember to turn off the back porch light**, John.**
	to separate parts of a date	The United States Stock Exchange collapsed on October **28, 1929.** The stock market crash in October 1929 precipitated a severe economic crisis.
	to separate items in addresses	Gabriel García Márquez was born in **Aracataca, Colombia.** My brother will be moving to **1960 Jasmine Avenue, Liberty, Missouri 64068.**
Semicolons	to join two closely related sentences	It was a beautiful summer morning**;** we took advantage of it by going on a picnic.
	to join the independent clauses of a compound sentence if no coordinating conjunction is used	Marjory Stoneman Douglas was a pioneer conservationist. She formed a vigorous grassroots campaign to protect and restore the Everglades. Marjory Stoneman Douglas was a pioneer conservationist**;** she formed a vigorous grassroots campaign to protect and restore the Everglades.
	between independent clauses joined by a conjunction if either clause contains commas	Douglas was a writer, editor, publisher, and tireless advocate for the protection of the Everglades**;** and President Clinton awarded her the Medal of Freedom in 1993 for her work.
	between items in a series if the items contain commas	Members of Friends of the Everglades **wrote petitions; contacted local groups, political organizations, and governmental agencies; and gathered public support** for the restoration of the Everglades.
	between independent clauses joined by a conjunctive adverb or a transitional phrase	**conjunctive adverb** Starting in 1948, the Central and Southern Florida Project ditched and drained the Everglades**; consequently,** the four million acre wetland was reduced by half. **transitional phrase** Douglas knew that restoration of the Everglades would be a daunting task**; in other words,** she knew that it would take the combined efforts of local, state, and federal groups working in unison.
Colons	to mean "note what follows"	Make sure you have all your paperwork in order**:** passport, visa, and tickets.
	to introduce a list of items	*The Tragedy of Romeo and Juliet* explores **these dominant themes:** civil strife, revenge, love, and fate. The main characters in the play are **as follows:** Romeo, Juliet, Paris, Mercutio, Tybalt, and Friar Lawrence. The role of Juliet has been played by **the following actresses:** Norma Shearer, Susan Shentall, and Olivia Hussey.

Punctuation	Function	Examples
	to introduce a long or formal statement or a quotation	Shakespeare's prologue to *Romeo and Juliet* begins with **these memorable lines:** Two households, both alike in dignity, In fair Verona, where we lay our scene, From ancient grudge break to new mutiny, Where civil blood makes civil hands unclean. John Dryden made **the following remark about Shakespeare:** "He was the man who of all modern, and perhaps ancient poets, had the largest and most comprehensive soul." Nearly everyone recognizes **this line by Shakespeare:** "All the world's a stage."
	between two independent clauses when the second clause explains or summarizes the first clause	Shakespeare deserves the greatest of praise: his work has influenced and inspired millions of people over the centuries. For Romeo and Juliet, their love is star-crossed: If they tell their feuding parents of their love, they will be forbidden from seeing each other. On the other hand, by keeping their love secret, they follow a path that leads, tragically, to their deaths.
	between numbers that tell hours and minutes, after the greeting in a business letter, and between chapter and verse of religious works	Our English class meets Tuesdays and Thursdays from **9:00** AM to **10:00** AM Dear Juliet: Please meet me on the balcony at midnight. Ecclesiastes **3:1—8**
	not after a verb, between a preposition and its object(s), or after *because* or *as*	**after a verb** **incorrect** Three of Shakespeare's most famous plays are: *Romeo and Juliet, Macbeth,* and *Hamlet.* **correct** These are three of Shakespeare's most famous plays: *Romeo and Juliet, Macbeth,* and *Hamlet.* **between a preposition and its object(s)** **incorrect** I have seen performances of Shakespeare's plays in: London, New York, and Chicago. **correct** I have seen performances of Shakespeare's plays in the following cities: London, New York, and Chicago. **after *because* or *as*** **incorrect** Shakespeare was a great playwright because: he had an extraordinary skill in depicting human nature and the universal struggles all people experience. **correct** Shakespeare was a great playwright because he had an extraordinary skill in depicting human nature and the universal struggles all people experience.
Ellipsis Points	to show that material from a quotation or a quoted passage has been left out	"Doing something does not require discipline...it creates its own discipline."
	if material is left out at the beginning of a sentence or passage	...The very thought of hard work makes me queasy.
	if material is left out in the middle of a sentence	The very thought...makes me queasy.
	if material is left out at the end of a sentence	It's hard work, doing something with your life....I'd rather die in peace. Here we are, all equal and alike and none of us much to write home about....

Punctuation	Function	Examples
Apostrophes	to form the possessive case of a singular or plural noun	the **window's** ledge, **Carlos's** father, **jazz's** beginnings, **wolves'** howls, twenty-five **cents'** worth, **countries'** treaties, **students'** textbooks
	to show joint or separate ownership	**Zack and Josh's** experiment, **Lisa and Randall's** cabin, **Sarah's** and **Jason's** schedules, **Steve's** and **John's** trumpets
	to form the possessive of an indefinite pronoun	**anyone's** guess, **each other's** notes, **everybody's** dream
	to form a contraction to show where letters, words, or numerals have been omitted	**I'm** = I am **you're** = you are **she's** = she is **o'clock** = of the clock **they're** = they are
	to form the possessive of only the last word in a compound noun, such as the name of an organization or a business	brother-in-**law's** sense of humor; Teller, Teller, and **Teller's** law firm; Volunteer Nursing **Association's** office
	to form the possessive of an acronym	**NASA's** flight plan, **NATO's** alliances, **UNICEF's** contributions
	to form the plural of letters, numerals, and words referred to as words	two **A's**, **ABC's**, three **7's**, twelve **yes's**
	to show the missing numbers in a date	drought of **'02**, class of **'06**
Underlining and Italics	with titles of books, plays, long poems, periodicals, works of art, movies, radio and television series, videos, computer games, comic strips, and long musical works and recordings	**books:** *To Kill a Mockingbird, Silent Spring, Black Elk Speaks* **plays:** *The Tragedy of Romeo and Juliet, The Monsters Are Due on Maple Street* **long poems:** *Metamorphoses, The Odyssey* **periodicals:** *Sports Illustrated, Wall Street Journal, The Old Farmer's Almanac* **works of art:** *The Acrobat, In the Sky, The Teacup* **movies:** *Il Postino, North by Northwest, Cast Away* **radio/television series:** *Fresh Air, West Wing, Friends, Animal Planet* **videos:** *Yoga for Strength, Cooking with Julia, Wizard of Oz* **computer games:** *Empire Earth, Age of Wonders II* **comic strips:** *Zits, Foxtrot, Overboard* **long musical works/recordings:** *Requiem, Death and the Maiden, La Traviata*
	with the names of trains, ships, aircraft, and spacecraft	**trains:** *Sunset Limited* **ships:** *Titanic* **aircraft:** *Air Force One* **spacecraft:** *Apollo 13*
	with words, letters, symbols, and numerals referred to as such	The word *filigree* has a Latin root. People in western New York pronounce the letter *a* with a harsh, flat sound. The children learned that the symbol *+* is used in addition. Your phone number ends with four *7*'s.
	to set off foreign words or phrases that are not common in English	Did you know the word *amor* means "love"? The first Italian words I learned were *ciao* and *pronto*.
	to place emphasis on a word	Why is the soup *blue*? You're not going to borrow *my* car.

Punctuation	Function	Examples
Quotation Marks	at the beginning and end of a direct quotation	"Do you want to ride together to the concert?" asked Margaret. "Don't wait for me," sighed Lillian. "I'm running late as usual."
	to enclose the titles of short works such as short stories, poems, articles, essays, parts of books and periodicals, songs, and episodes of TV series	**short stories:** "Gwilan's Harp," "Everyday Use" **poems:** "Hanging Fire," "Mirror" **articles:** "Where Stars Are Born," "Ghost of Everest" **essays:** "Thinking Like a Mountain," "It's Not Talent; It's Just Work" **parts of books:** "The Obligation to Endure," "Best Sky Sights of the Next Century" **songs:** "At the Fair," "Johnny's Garden" **episodes of TV series:** "The Black Vera Wang," "Isaac and Ishmael"
	to set off slang, technical terms, unusual expressions, invented words, and dictionary definitions	We nicknamed our dog **"Monkey"** because he moves quickly and loves to play tricks. My mother says that **"groovy"** and **"cool"** were the slang words of her generation. Did you know that the word *incident* means **"a definite, distinct occurrence"**?
Hyphens	to make a compound word or compound expression	**compound nouns:** great-grandfather Schaefer, great-uncle Tom **compound adjectives used before a noun:** best-known novel, down-to-earth actor, real-life adventure **compound numbers:** ninety-nine years, twenty-five cents **spelled-out fractions:** one-half inch, three-fourths cup
	to divide an already hyphenated word at the hyphen	Finally, after much coaxing, our **great-grandfather** told his stories.
	to divide a word only between syllables	**incorrect:** After hiking in the woods, the novice ca-mpers became tired and hungry. **correct:** After hiking in the woods, the novice **camp-ers** became tired and hungry.
	with the prefixes *all-, ex-, great-, half-* and *self-,* and with all prefixes before a proper noun or proper adjective	**all-**purpose, **ex-**husband, **pre-**Industrial age, **great-**grandparent, **half-**baked, **self-**expression
	with the suffixes *-free, -elect,* and *-style*	fragrance-**free** detergent, mayor-**elect** Kingston, Southern-**style** hospitality
Dashes	to show a sudden break or change in thought	"I say it did," replied the other. "There was no thought about it; I had just—What's the matter?"
	to mean *namely, that is,* or *in other words*	Our puppy knows only two commands—*sit* and *stay.* The hotel rates were surprisingly reasonable—less than a hundred dollars—for a double room.
Parentheses and Brackets	around material added to a sentence but not considered of major importance	Toni Cade Bambara (1939–1995) grew up in Harlem and Brooklyn, New York. The Taj Mahal (a majestic site!) is one man's tribute of love to his departed, beloved wife. More grocery stores are stocking natural food ingredients (for example, whole grains, soy products, and dried fruits).

Punctuation	Function	Examples
	to punctuate a parenthetical sentence contained within another sentence.	When the quilt is dry (it shouldn't take long), please fold it and put it in the linen closet. The piping-hot funnel cakes (they were covered with powdered sugar!) just melted in our mouths. The vitamin tablets (aren't you supposed to take one every morning?) provide high doses of vitamins A and E.
	to enclose words or phrases that interrupt the sentence and are not considered essential to meaning.	They took pasta salad and fruit (how could we have forgotten dessert?) to the summer concert.
	to enclose information that explains or clarifies a detail in quoted material	A literary critic praised the author's new book, "She [Martha Grimes] never fails to delight her devoted fans with witty dialogue, elegant prose, and a cast of characters we'd like to consider our friends." Another literary critic wrote, "[Martha] Grimes is the queen of the mystery genre."

4.1 The Writing Process

All writers—whether they are beginning writers, famous published writers, or somewhere in between—go through a process that leads to a complete piece of writing. The specifics of each writer's process may be unique, but for every writer, writing is a series of steps or stages.

The Writing Process

Stage	Tasks
1. Prewriting	Plan your writing: choose a topic, audience, purpose, and form; gather ideas; arrange them logically.
2. Drafting	Get your ideas down on paper.
3. Revising	Evaluate, or judge, the writing piece and suggest ways to improve it. Judging your own writing is called self-evaluation. Judging a classmate's writing is called peer evaluation.
	Work to improve the content, organization, and expression of your ideas.
	Proofread your writing for errors in spelling, grammar, capitalization, and punctuation. Correct these errors, make a final copy of your paper, and proofread it again.
Writing Follow-Up: Publish and Present	Share your work with an audience.
Reflect	Think through the writing process to determine what you learned as a writer, what you accomplished, and what you would like to strengthen the next time you write.

1 PREWRITE

In the prewriting stage of the writing process, you decide on a purpose, audience, topic, and form. You also begin to discover your voice and gather and organize ideas.

Prewriting Plan

Set Your Purpose	A **purpose,** or aim, is the goal that you want your writing to accomplish.
Identify Your Audience	An **audience** is the person or group of people intended to read what you write.
Find Your Voice	**Voice** is the quality of a work that tells you that one person wrote it.
Select Your Topic	A **topic** is simply something to write about. For example, you might write about a sports hero or about a cultural event in your community.
Select a Writing Form	A **form** is a kind of writing. For example, you might write a paragraph, an essay, a short story, a poem, or a news article.

Purpose and Mode of Writing

When you choose your mode and form of writing, think about what purpose or aim you are trying to accomplish. Your purpose for writing might be to inform, to tell a story, to describe something, or to convince others to see your viewpoint. Your writing might have more than one purpose. For example, a piece of writing might inform your readers about an important event while persuading them to respond in a specific way.

Mode of Writing	Purpose	Form
expository	to inform	news article, research report
narrative	to express thoughts or ideas, or to tell a story	personal account, memoir, short story
descriptive	to portray a person, place, object, or event	travel brochure, personal profile, poem
persuasive	to convince people to accept a position and respond in some way	editorial, petition, political speech

Gather Ideas

After you have identified your purpose, audience, topic, and form, the next step in the prewriting stage is to gather ideas. There are many ways to gather ideas for writing.

- **Brainstorm** When you **brainstorm,** you think of as many ideas as you can, as quickly as you can, without stopping to evaluate or criticize them. Anything goes—no idea should be rejected in the brainstorming stage.

- **Freewrite. Freewriting** is simply taking a pencil and paper and writing whatever comes into your mind. Try to write for several minutes without stopping and without worrying about spelling, grammar, usage, or mechanics.

- **Question** Ask the **reporting questions** *who, what, where, when, why,* and *how* about your topic. This questioning strategy is especially useful for gathering information about an event or for planning a story.
- **Create a Graphic Organizer** A good way to gather information is to create a **graphic organizer,** such as a Cluster Chart, Venn Diagram, Sensory Details Chart, Time Line, Story Map, or Pro-and-Con Chart. For examples, see the Language Arts Handbook, section 1, Reading Strategies and Skills, page 1029.

Write Your Thesis Statement

One way to start organizing your writing, especially if you are writing an informative or persuasive essay, is to identify the main idea of what you want to say. Present this idea in the form of a sentence or two called a thesis statement. A **thesis statement** is simply a sentence that presents the main idea or the position you will take in your essay.

Example thesis for a persuasive essay

The development at Rice Creek Farm should be stopped because it will destroy one of the best natural areas near the city.

Example thesis for an informative essay

Wilma Rudolph was an athlete who succeeded in the elite sport of tennis before the world was willing to recognize her.

Methods of Organization

The ideas in your writing should be ordered and linked in a logical and easily understandable way. You can organize your writing in the following ways:

Methods of Organization	
Chronological Order	Events are given in the order they occur.
Order of Importance	Details are given in order of importance or familiarity.
Comparison-and-Contrast Order	Similarities and differences of two things are listed.
Cause-and-Effect Order	One or more causes are presented followed by one or more effects.

To link your ideas, use connective words and phrases. In informational or persuasive writing, *for example, as a result, finally, therefore,* and *in fact* are common

connectives. In narrative and descriptive writing, words like *first, then, suddenly, above, beyond, in the distance,* and *there* are common connectives. In comparison-contrast organization, common phrases include *similarly, on the other hand,* and *in contrast.* In cause-and-effect organization, linkers include *one cause, another effect, as a result, consequently, finally,* and *therefore.*

Create an Outline
An **outline** is an excellent framework for highlighting main ideas and supporting details. To create a rough outline, simply list your main ideas in some logical order. Under each main idea, list the supporting details set off by dashes.

EXAMPLE

What Is Drama?
Definition of Drama
—Tells a story
—Uses actors to play characters
—Uses a stage, properties, lights, costumes, makeup, and special effects
Types of Drama
—Tragedy
    —Definition: A play in which the main character meets a negative fate
    —Examples: *Antigone, Romeo and Juliet, Death of a Salesman*
—Comedy
    —Definition: A play in which the main character meets a positive fate
    —Examples: *A Midsummer Night's Dream, Cyrano de Bergerac, The Odd Couple*

2 DRAFT

After you have gathered your information and organized it, the next step in writing is to produce a draft. A **draft** is simply an early attempt at writing a paper. Different writers approach drafting in different ways. Some prefer to work slowly and carefully, perfecting each part as they go. Others prefer to write a discovery draft, getting all their ideas down on paper in rough form and then going back over those ideas to shape and focus them. When writing a discovery draft, you do not focus on spelling, grammar, usage, and mechanics. You can take care of those details during revision.

Draft Your Introduction

The purpose of an introduction is to capture your reader's attention and establish what you want to say. An effective introduction can start with a quotation, a question, an anecdote, an intriguing fact, or a description that hooks the reader to keep reading. An effective introduction can open with a quotation, question, anecdote, fact, or description.

EXAMPLES

"That's one small step for man, one giant leap for mankind." With these words, Neil Armstrong signaled his success as the first man to set foot on the moon...

What would it be like if all the birds in the world suddenly stopped their singing?

Draft Your Body

When writing the body of an essay, refer to your outline. Each heading in your outline will become the main idea of one of your paragraphs. To move smoothly from one idea to another, use transitional words or phrases. As you draft, include evidence from documented sources to support the ideas that you present. This evidence can be paraphrased, summarized, or quoted directly. For information on proper documentation, see the Language Arts Handbook 5.6, Documenting Sources.

Draft Your Conclusion

In the conclusion, bring together the main ideas you included in the body of your essay and create a sense of closure to the issue you raised in your thesis. There is no single right way to conclude a piece of writing. Possibilities include:

- Making a generalization
- Restating the thesis and major supporting ideas in different words
- Summarizing the points made in the rest of the essay
- Drawing a lesson or moral
- Calling on the reader to adopt a view or take an action
- Expanding on your thesis or main idea by connecting it to the reader's own interests
- Linking your thesis to a larger issue or concern

3 REVISE

Evaluate Your Draft

Self- and Peer Evaluation When you evaluate something, you examine it carefully to find its strengths and weaknesses. Evaluating your own writing is called **self-evaluation. A peer evalua-**

tion is an evaluation of a piece of writing done by classmates, or peers. The following tips can help you to become a helpful peer reader, to learn to give and receive criticism, and to improve your writing.

Tips for evaluating writing
- **Check for content** Is the content, including the main idea, clear? Have any important details been left out? Do unimportant or unrelated details confuse the main point? Are the main idea and supporting details clearly connected to one another?
- **Check for organization** Are the ideas in the written work presented in a logical order?
- **Check the style and language** Is the language appropriately formal or informal? Is the tone appropriate for the audience and purpose? Have any key or unfamiliar terms been defined?

Tips for delivering helpful criticism
- **Be focused** Concentrate on content, organization, and style. At this point, do not focus on proofreading matters such as spelling and punctuation; they can be corrected during the proofreading stage.
- **Be positive** Respect the writer's feelings and genuine writing efforts. Tell the writer what you like about his or her work. Answer the writer's questions in a positive manner, tactfully presenting any changes you are suggesting.
- **Be specific** Give the writer concrete ideas for improving his or her work.

Tips for benefiting from helpful criticism
- **Tell your peer evaluator your specific concerns and questions.** If you are unsure whether you've clearly presented an idea, ask the evaluator how he or she might restate the idea.
- **Ask questions to clarify comments that your evaluator makes.** When you ask for clarification, you make sure you understand your evaluator's comments.
- **Accept your evaluator's comments graciously.** Criticism can be helpful, but you don't have to use any or all of the suggestions.

Revise for Content, Organization, and Style

After identifying weaknesses in a draft through self-evaluation and peer evaluation, the next step is to revise the draft. Here are four basic ways to improve meaning and content:

- **Adding or Expanding** Sometimes writing can be improved by adding details, examples, or transitions to connect ideas. Often a single added adjective, for example, can make a piece of writing clearer or more vivid.

  draft Wind whistled through the park.

  revised The **bone-chilling** wind whistled through the park.

- **Cutting or Condensing** Often writing can be improved by cutting unnecessary or unrelated material.

  draft Will was firmly determined to find the structure of the DNA molecule.

  revised Will was determined to find the structure of the DNA molecule.

- **Replacing** Sometimes weak writing can be made stronger through more concrete, more vivid, or more precise details.

  draft Several things had been bothering Tanya.

  revised Several personal problems had been bothering Tanya.

- **Moving** Often you can improve the organization of your writing by moving part of it so that related ideas appear near one another.

After you've revised the draft, ask yourself a series of questions. Think of these questions as your "revision checklist."

REVISION CHECKLIST

Content

❏ Does the writing achieve its purpose?

❏ Are the main ideas clearly stated and supported by details?

Organization

❏ Are the ideas arranged in a sensible order?

❏ Are the ideas connected to one another within paragraphs and between paragraphs?

Style

❏ Is the language appropriate to the audience and purpose?

❏ Is the mood appropriate to the purpose of the writing?

Proofread for Errors

When you proofread your writing, you read it through to look for errors and to mark corrections. When you mark corrections, use the standard proofreading symbols as shown in the following chart.

Proofreader's Symbols

Symbol and Example	Meaning of Symbol
The very first time	Delete (cut) this material.
dog's life	Insert (add) something that is missing.
George	Replace this letter or word.
All the horses king's	Move this word to where the arrow points.
french toast	Capitalize this letter.
the vice-President	Lowercase this letter.
housse	Take out this letter and close up space.
book keeper	Close up space.
gerbil	Change the order of these letters.
end. "Watch out," she yelled.	Begin a new paragraph.
Love conquers all	Put a period here.
Welcome friends.	Put a comma here.
Get the stopwatch	Put a space here.
Dear Madam	Put a colon here.
She walked he rode.	Put a semicolon here.
name brand products	Put a hyphen here.
cats meow	Put an apostrophe here.
cat's cradle stet	Let it stand. (Leave as it is.)

After you have revised your draft, make a clean copy of it and proofread it for errors in spelling, grammar, and punctuation. Use the following proofreading checklist.

Proofreading Checklist

Spelling

- ❏ Are all words, including names, spelled correctly?

Grammar

- ❏ Does each verb agree with its subject?
- ❏ Are verb tenses consistent and correct?
- ❏ Are irregular verbs formed correctly?
- ❏ Are there any sentence fragments or run-ons?
- ❏ Have double negatives been avoided?
- ❏ Have frequently confused words, such as affect and effect, been used correctly?

Punctuation

- ❏ Does every sentence end with an end mark?
- ❏ Are commas used correctly?
- ❏ Do all proper nouns and proper adjectives begin with capital letters?

Prepare Your Final Manuscript

After proofreading your draft, you will prepare your final manuscript. Follow the guidelines given by your teacher or the guidelines provided here. After preparing a final manuscript according to these guidelines, proofread it one last time for errors.

Guidelines for Final Manuscript Preparation

- Keyboard your manuscript using a typewriter or word processor, or write it neatly using blue or black ink.
- Double-space your writing.
- Use one side of the paper.
- Leave one-inch margins on all sides of the text.
- Indent the first line of each paragraph.
- Make a cover sheet listing the title of the work, your name, the date, and the class.
- In the upper right-hand corner of the first page, put your name, class, and date. On every page after the first, include the page number in the heading, as follows:

EXAMPLE

Sharon Turner
English 9
March 25, 2009
p. 2

WRITING FOLLOW-UP

Publish and Present

Some writing is done just for oneself—journal writing, for example. Most writing, however, is meant to be shared with others. Here are several ways in which you can publish your writing or present it to others:

- Submit your work to a local publication, such as a school literary magazine, school newspaper, or community newspaper.
- Submit your work to a regional or national publication.
- Enter your work in a contest.
- Read your work aloud to classmates, friends, or family members.
- Collaborate with other students to prepare a publication—a brochure, online literary magazine, anthology, or newspaper.
- Prepare a poster or bulletin board, perhaps in collaboration with other students, to display your writing.
- Make your own book by typing or word processing the pages and binding them together.
- Hold an oral reading of student writing as a class or school-wide project.
- Share your writing with other students in a small writers' group.

Reflect

After you've completed your writing, think through the writing process to determine what you learned as a writer, what you learned about your topic, how the writing process worked or didn't work for you, and what skills you would like to strengthen.

Reflection can be done on a self-evaluation form, in small-group discussion, or simply in silent reflection. By keeping a journal, however, you'll be able to keep track of your writing experience and pinpoint ways to make the writing process work better for you. Here are some questions to ask as you reflect on the writing process and yourself as a writer:

- Which part of the writing process did I enjoy most and least? Why? Which part of the writing process was most difficult? least difficult? Why?

- What would I change about my approach to the writing process next time?
- What have I learned in writing about this topic?
- What have I learned by using this form?
- How have I developed as a writer while writing this piece?
- What strengths have I discovered in my work?
- What aspects of my writing do I want to strengthen? How can I strengthen them?

4.2 Modes and Purposes of Writing

Types of writing generally fall within four main classifications or modes: expository, narrative, descriptive, and persuasive. Each of these modes has a specific purpose. See the Mode of Writing Chart on page 1267.

Expository Writing

The purpose of **expository writing** is to inform, to present or explain an idea or a process. News articles and research reports are examples of informative expository writing. One function of expository writing is to define, since a definition explains what something is. Another function of expository writing is to analyze and interpret. For example, a book review is writing that analyzes and interprets a piece of literature to inform an audience about its worth. Similarly, a movie review evaluates and judges for its viewing audience how well a movie accomplishes its purpose.

Narrative Writing

Narrative writing tells a story or relates a series of events. It can be used to entertain, to make a point, or to introduce a topic. Narrating an event involves the dimension of action over time.

Narratives are often used in essays, reports, and other nonfiction forms because stories are entertaining and fun to read. Just as important, they are a good way to make a point. Biographies, autobiographies, and family histories are also forms of narrative writing.

Descriptive Writing

The purpose of **descriptive writing** is to entertain, enrich, and enlighten by using a form such as fiction or poetry to share a perspective. Descriptive writing is used to describe something, to set a scene, to create a mood, to appeal to the reader's senses. Descriptive writing is often creative and uses visual and other sensual details, emotional responses, and imagery. Poems, short stories, and plays are examples of descriptive writing.

Persuasive Writing

The purpose of **persuasive writing** is to persuade readers or listeners to respond in some way, such as to agree with a position, change a view on an issue, reach an agreement, or perform an action. Examples of persuasive writing are editorials, petitions, political speeches, and essays.

5 Research & Documentation

5.1 Critical Thinking Skills

In literature and informational texts, some things are stated as facts *(literal)* and other things are inferred or implied by the author *(inferential)*. We use **critical thinking skills** to fully understand and interpret what we read. There are six basic levels of understanding, or *cognitive domains,* which are listed below: The categories can be thought of as degrees of difficulty. That is, the first one must be mastered before the next one can take place. We apply these skills as we read a text.

Levels of Critical Thinking		
Refer to Text	**Remember**	**Recall facts:** Retrieve information presented in the text
Reason with Text	**Understand**	**Find meaning:** Interpret and explain ideas or concepts
	Apply	**Use information:** Utilize knowledge in another situation
	Analyze	**Take things apart:** Break down details to explore interpretations and relationships
	Evaluate	**Make judgments:** Justify a decision or course of action
	Create	**Bring ideas together:** Synthesize understanding to generate new ideas, products, or ways of viewing things

The paired **Refer to Text/Reason with Text** questions following the selections in this textbook are broken down into *literal* questions that refer directly to the facts in the text (Refer to Text) followed by inferential questions that ask you to apply higher levels of thinking to interpret the text (Reason with Text).

5.2 Research Skills

Learning is a lifelong process, one that extends far beyond school. Both in school and on your own, it is important to remember that your learning and growth are up to you. One good way to become an independent lifelong learner is to master research skills. Research is the process of gathering ideas and information. One of the best resources for research is the library.

How Library Materials Are Organized

Each book in a library is assigned a unique number, called a call number. The call number is printed on the spine (edge) of each book. The numbers serve to classify books as well as to help the library keep track of them. Libraries commonly use one of two systems for classifying books. Most school and public libraries use the Dewey Decimal System.

Dewey Decimal System	
Call Numbers	**Subjects**
000–099	Reference and General Works
100–199	Philosophy, Psychology
200–299	Religion
300–399	Social Studies
400–499	Language
500–599	Science, Mathematics
600–699	Technology
700–799	Arts
800–899	Literature
900–999	History, Geography, Biography[1]

1. Biographies (920s) are arranged alphabetically by the name of the person whose life is treated in each biography.

Most college libraries use the Library of Congress Classification System or the LC system, shown on the following page.

Library of Congress System

Call Numbers	Subjects
A	Reference and General Works
B–BJ	Philosophy, Psychology
BK–BX	Religion
C–DF	History
G	Geography, Autobiography, Recreation
H	Social Sciences
J	Political Science
K	Law
L	Education
M	Music
N	Fine Arts
P	Language, Literature
Q	Science, Mathematics
R	Medicine
S	Agriculture
T	Technology
U	Military Science
V	Naval Science
Z	Bibliography, Library Science

Internet Libraries It is also possible to visit the Internet Public library online at **http://www.ipl. org/.** The Internet Public Library is the first public library online of the Internet. This site provides library services to the Internet community by finding, evaluating, selecting, organizing, describing, and creating quality information resources; teaches what librarians have to contribute in a digital environment; and promotes the importance of libraries.

Computerized Catalogs Many libraries today use computerized catalogs. Systems differ from library to library, but most involve using a computer terminal to search through the library's collection. You can usually search by author, title, subject, or key word.

Using Reference Works

Most libraries have an assortment of reference works in which knowledge is collected and organized so that you can find it easily. Usually, reference works cannot be checked out of the library. Reference works that that may assist you in your research include dictionaries, thesauruses, almanacs, yearbooks, atlases, and encyclopedias.

Primary and Secondary Sources

Primary sources are the original unedited materials created by someone directly involved in an event or speaking directly for a group. They may include first-hand documents such as diaries, interviews, works of fiction, artwork, court records, research reports, speeches, letters, surveys, and so on.

Secondary sources offer commentary or analysis of events, ideas, or primary sources. They are often written significantly later and may provide historical context or attempt to describe or explain primary sources. Examples of secondary sources include dictionaries, encyclopedias, textbooks, and books and articles that interpret or review original works.

	Primary Source	Secondary Source
Art	Painting	Article critiquing the artist's technique
History	Prisoner's diary	Book about World War II internment camps
Literature	Poem	Literary criticism on a particular form of poetry
Science	Research report	Analysis of results

5.3 Internet Research

The Internet is an enormous collection of computer networks that can open a whole new world of information. With just a couple of keystrokes, you can access libraries, government agencies, high schools and universities, nonprofit and educational organizations, museums, user groups, and individuals around the world.

Keep in mind that the Internet is not regulated and everything you read online may not be verified or accurate. Confirm facts from the Internet against another source. In addition, to become a good judge of Internet materials, do the following:

• **Consider the domain name of the resource.** Be sure to check out the sites you use to see if they are commercial (.com or .firm), educational (.edu), governmental (.gov), or organizational (.org or .net). Ask yourself questions like these: What bias might a commercial site have that would influence its presentation of information? Is the site sponsored by a special-interest group that slants or spins information to its advantage?

Key to Internet Domains

.com	commercial entity
.edu	educational institution
.firm	business entity
.gov	government agency or department
.org or .net	organization

- **Consider the author's qualifications.** Regardless of the source, ask these questions: Is the author named? What expertise does he or she have? Can I locate other online information about this person? Evaluate the quality of information.

- **How accurate is the information?** Does it appear to be reliable and without errors? Is the information given without bias?

- **Check the date posted.** Is the information timely? When was the site last updated?

Search Tools

A number of popular and free search engines allow you to find topics of interest. Keep in mind that each service uses slightly different methods of searching, so you may get different results using the same key words.

All the Web	http://www.alltheweb.com
AltaVista	http://www.altavista.com
Go	http://www.go.com
Yahoo	http://www.yahoo.com
Excite	http://www.excite.com
HotBot	http://www.hotbot.com
WebCrawler	http://www.webcrawler.com
Google	http://www.google.com

Search Tips

- To make searching easier, less time consuming, and more directed, narrow your subject to a key word or a group of key words. These key words are your search terms. Key search connectors, or Boolean commands, can help you limit or expand the scope of your topic.

AND (or +) narrows a search by retrieving documents that include both terms—for example: Ulysses Grant AND Vicksburg.

OR broadens a search by retrieving documents that include any of the terms—for example: Ulysses Grant OR Vicksburg OR Civil War.

NOT narrows a search by excluding documents containing certain words—for example: Ulysses Grant NOT Civil War.

- If applicable, limit your search by specifying a geographical area by using the word *near*—for example, golf courses near Boulder, Colorado.

- When entering a group of key words, present them in order, from the most important to the least important key word.

- If the terms of your search are not leading you to the information you need, try using synonyms. For example, if you were looking for information about how to care for your garden, you might use these terms: *compost, pest control,* and *watering.*

- Avoid opening the link to every page in your results list. Search engines typically present pages in descending order of relevancy or importance. The most useful pages will be located at the top of the list. However, skimming the text of lower order sites may give you ideas for other key words.

- If you're not getting the desired results, check your input. Common search mistakes include misspelling search terms and mistyping URLs. Remember that URLs must be typed exactly as they appear, using the exact capital or lowercase letters, spacing, and punctuation.

For information on citing Internet sources, see the Language Arts Handbook 5.6, Documenting Sources.

5.4 Media Literacy

The term **media,** in most applications, is used as a plural of *medium,* which means a channel or system of communication, information, or entertainment. *Mass media* refers specifically to means of communication, such as newspapers, radio, or television, which are designed to reach the mass of the people. *Journalism* is the gathering, evaluating, and disseminating, through various media, of news and facts of current interest. Originally, journalism encompassed only such printed matter as newspapers and periodicals. Today, however, it includes other media used to distribute news, such as radio, television, documentary or news-reel films, the Internet, and computer news services. The media use words, images, graphics, and sounds to present content about issues and events. The way those elements are combined affects the meaning that is communicated. Like the authors of other literary works, the creators manipulate the elements, as well as the formality and tone of their presentation, to suit their audience and purpose. Depending on the type of media, you might expect to find varying degrees of bias, or personal opinions and prejudices. For example, reporters generally avoid bias, attempting to present the facts so that readers or viewers can make up their own mind about an issue. Editorialists, on the other hand, make their living writing highly opinionated (biased) articles designed to charge the audience with emotion and sway them to one side of an issue.

5.5 Evaluating Sources

To conduct your research efficiently, you need to evaluate your sources and set priorities among them. Ideally, a source will be:

- **Unbiased.** When an author has a personal stake in what people think about a subject, he or she may withhold or distort information. Investigate the author's background to see if she or he is liable to be biased. Using loaded language and overlooking obvious counterarguments are signs of author bias.
- **Authoritative.** An authoritative source is reliable and trustworthy. An author's reputation, especially among others who conduct research in the same field, is a sign of authority. Likewise, periodicals and publishers acquire reputations for responsible or poor editing and research.
- **Timely.** Information about many subjects changes rapidly. An astronomy text published last year may already be out of date. In other fields—for instance, algebra—older texts may be perfectly adequate. Consult with your teacher and your librarian to decide how current your sources must be.
- **Available.** Borrowing through interlibrary loan, tracing a book that is missing, or recalling a book that has been checked out to another person takes time. Make sure to allow enough time for these materials.
- **Appropriate for your level.** Find sources that present useful information that you can understand. Materials written for "young people" may be too simple to be helpful. Books written for experts may presume knowledge that you do not have. Struggling with a difficult text is often worth the effort, but if you do so, monitor your time and stay on schedule.

5.6 Documenting Sources

As you use your research in your writing, you must document your sources of information.
- Credit the sources of all ideas and facts that you use.
- Credit original ideas or facts that are expressed in text, tables, charts, and other graphic information.
- Credit all artistic property, including works of literature, song lyrics, and ideas.

Keeping a Research Journal A research journal is a notebook, electronic file, or other means to track the information you find as you conduct research. A research journal can include the following:
- A list of questions you want to research. (Such questions can be an excellent source of writing topics.)

EXAMPLES

How did the Vietnam Veterans Memorial come to be? Why is it one of the most visited memorials in America?

Where can I find more artwork by Faith Ringgold?

Why was Transcendentalism such an important literary movement in America but not in Europe?

As you conduct your research, rely on your research journal as a place to take notes on the sources you find and your evaluation of them. Keeping a research journal can be an invaluable way to track your research and to take notes.

Avoiding Plagiarizing Plagiarism is taking someone else's words or thoughts and presenting them as your own. Plagiarism is a very serious problem and has been the downfall of many students and professionals. Whenever you use someone else's writing to help you with a paper or a speech, you must be careful either to **paraphrase,** put the ideas in your own words; **summarize** the main ideas; or to use **quotation marks.** In any case, you must document your sources and give credit to the person whose ideas you are using. As you do research, make sure to include paraphrases, summaries, and direct quotations in your notes.

Citing Sources

The following chart shows the correct form for citing different types of bibliography entries, following the *Modern Language Association (MLA) Handbook for Writers of Research Papers*. Note that all citations should include the medium of the publication, such as *print*, *film*, or *web*.

MLA Forms for Works Cited	
Book	Douglass, Frederick. *Escape from Slavery: The Boyhood of Frederick Douglass in His Own Words.* New York: Alfred A. Knopf, 1994. Print.
Magazine article	Reston, James, Jr. "Orion: Where Stars Are Born." *National Geographic* Dec. 1995: 90-101. Print.
Encyclopedia entry	"Lewis and Clark Expedition." *Encyclopedia Americana.* Jackson, Donald. 1995 ed. Print.
Interview	Campbell, Silas. Personal interview. 6 Feb. 2007.
Film	*The Big Heat.* Dir. Fritz Lang. Perf. Glenn Ford and Gloria Grahame. Screenplay by Sidney Boehm. Columbia, 1953. Film.

Citing Internet Sources

To document your Internet sources, use your research journal to record each site you visit (See the Language Arts Handbook, 5.3 Internet Research, page 1002) or make bibliography cards as you search. An Internet source entry should include the following general pieces of information:

- Name of the author, if available, last name first, followed by a period.
- Title of the source, document, file, or page in quotation marks, followed by a period.
- If available, the information about the print publication, followed by a period.
- Name of the database or online source, in italics, and followed by a period.
- The date the website was last updated, followed by a period.
- The name of the institution or organization associated with the website, followed by a period.
- Medium of publication (Web).
- Date the source was accessed (day, month, year).

- Provide an electronic address, URL, only when needed to locate the source or if required by your instructor. Enclose the URL in angle brackets (< >), followed by a period. Avoid showing network and e-mail addresses as underlined hyperlinks. Note that when line length forces you to break a Web address, always break it after a slash mark.

The *Modern Language Association Handbook for Writers of Research Papers* acknowledges that all source tracking information on the Internet may not be obtainable. Therefore, the manual recommends that if you cannot find some of this information, cite what is available.

EXAMPLE INTERNET CITATIONS

Armstrong, Mark. "That's 'Sir' Mick Jagger to You." E! Online. 17 June 2002. E! Online, Inc. Web. 17 June 2009 <http://www.eonline.com/News/Items/0,1,10110,00.html>.

For sites with no name of the database or online source:
Chachich, Mike. "Letters from Japan Vol 1" 30 Mar. 1994. Web. 17 June 2009 <http://www.chachich.com/cgi-bin/catlfj?1>.

For sites with no author:
"The Science Behind the Sod." *MSU News Bulletin.* 13 June 2002. Michigan State University. Web. 17 June 2009 <http://www.newsbulletin.msu.edu/june13/sod.html>.

For an e-mail message:
Daniel Akaka (senator@akaka.senate.gov). "Oceanic Exploration Grant." E-mail to Joseph Biden (senator@biden.senate.gov). 17 June 2003.

Parenthetical Documentation

Parenthetical documentation is currently the most widely used form of documentation. To use this method to document the source of a quotation or an idea, you place a brief note identifying the source in parentheses immediately after the borrowed material. This type of note is called a parenthetical citation, and the act of placing such a note is called citing a source.

The first part of a parenthetical citation refers the reader to a source in your List of Works Cited or Works Consulted. For the reader's ease in finding the source in your bibliography, you must cite the work according to how it is listed in the bibliography.

EXAMPLE PARENTHETICAL CITATIONS

For works listed by title, use an abbreviated title.

Sample bibliographic entry
"History." *Encyclopedia Britannica: Macropædia.* 1992 ed. Print.

Sample citation
Historians go through three stages in textual criticism ("History" 615).

For works listed by author or editor, use the author's or editor's last name.

Sample bibliographic entry
Brown, Dee. *Bury My Heart at Wounded Knee: An Indian History of the American West.* New York: Holt, 1970. Print.

Sample citation
"Big Eyes Schurz agreed to the arrest" (Brown 364).

When the listed name or title is stated in the text, cite only the page number.

Brown states that Big Eyes Schurz agreed to it (364).

For works of multiple volumes, use a colon after the volume number.

Sample bibliographic entry
Pepys, Samuel. *The Diary of Samuel Pepys.* Eds. Robert Latham and William Matthews. 10 vols. Berkeley: University of California Press, 1972. Print.

Sample citation
On the last day of 1665, Pepys took the occasion of the new year to reflect, but not to celebrate (6: 341-2).

For works quoted in secondary sources, use the abbreviation "qtd. in."

Sample citation
According to R. Bentley, "reason and the facts outweigh a hundred manuscripts" (qtd. in "History" 615).

For classic works that are available in various editions, give the page number from the edition you are using, followed by a semicolon; then identify the section of the work to help people with other editions find the reference.

Footnotes and Endnotes

In addition to parenthetical documentation, foot-noting and endnoting are two other accepted methods.

Footnotes Instead of putting citations in parentheses within the text, you can place them at the bottom or foot of the page; hence the term *footnote*. In this system, a number or symbol is placed in the text where the parenthetical citation would otherwise be, and a matching number or symbol at the bottom of the page identifies the citation. This textbook, for example, uses numbered footnotes in its literature selections to define obscure words and to provide background information.

Endnotes Many books use endnotes instead of foot-notes. Endnotes are like footnotes in that a number or symbol is placed within the text, but the matching citations are compiled at the end of the book, chapter, or article rather than at the foot of the page. Footnote and endnote entries begin with the author's (or editor's) name in its usual order (first name, then last) and include publication information and a page reference.

EXAMPLE FOOTNOTE OR ENDNOTE CITATIONS

Book with one author
[1]Jean Paul-Sartre, *Being and Nothingness* (New York: The Citadel Press, 1966) 149-51. Print.

Book with one editor and no single author
[2]Shannon Ravenel, ed., *New Stories from the South: The Year's Best, 1992* (Chapel Hill, NC: Algonquin Books, 1992) 305. Print.

Magazine article
[3]Andrew Gore, "Road Test: The Apple Powerbook," *MacUser,* Dec. 1996: 72. Print.

6.1 Workplace and Consumer Documents

Applied English is English in the world of work or business, or *practical* English. Entering a new school, writing a professional letter, applying for a job, reading an instructional manual—these are but a few of the many situations you may encounter that involve **workplace and consumer documents.** You can apply English skills to many real-world situations, using your reading, writing, speaking, and listening abilities to help you be successful in any field or occupation you choose to pursue.

6.2 Writing a Step-by-Step Procedure

A **step-by-step procedure** is a how-to or process piece that uses directions to teach someone something new. Written procedures include textual information and sometimes graphics. Spoken procedures can be given as oral demonstrations. They can include textual and graphic information and other props. Examples of step-by-step procedures include an oral demonstration of how to saddle a horse; instructions on how to treat a sprained ankle; a video showing how to do the perfect lay-up in basketball; and an interactive Internet site allowing the user to design and send a bouquet of flowers.

Guidelines for Writing a Step-by-Step Procedure

- Demonstrate the steps. If you are showing how to make something, create several different samples to show each step of the procedure. For example, if you are showing how to make a wooden basket, you might want to display the raw materials, the started basket, the basket halfway finished, and then the finished product.
- Be prepared. The best way to prevent problems is to anticipate and plan for them. Rehearse an oral demonstration several times. If you are preparing the procedure in written form, go through your directions as if you knew nothing about the process. Anticipate what it would be like to learn this procedure for the first time. See if you can follow your own directions, or have a friend work through the procedure and offer suggestions for improvement.

- Acknowledge mistakes. If you are sharing a procedure "live" as an oral demonstration and you can't talk around or correct a mistake, tell your audience what has gone wrong, and why. If you handle the situation in a calm, direct way, the audience may also learn from your mistake.
- Know your topic. The better you know it, the better you will be able to teach others.

6.3 Writing a Business Letter

A **business letter** is usually addressed to someone you do not know personally. Therefore, a formal tone is appropriate for such a letter. Following appropriate form is especially important when writing business letters. If you follow the correct form and avoid errors in spelling, grammar, usage, and mechanics, your letter will sound professional and make a good impression. Above the salutation, a business letter should contain the name and title of the person to whom you are writing and the name and address of that person's company or organization (see the model on the following page).

One common form for a business letter is the block form. In the **block form,** each part of the letter begins at the left margin. The parts are separated by line spaces.

Begin the salutation with the word *Dear,* followed by the courtesy or professional title used in the inside address, such as Ms., Mr., or Dr., and a colon. If you are not writing to a specific person, you may use a general salutation such as *Dear Sir or Madam.*

In the body of your letter, use a polite, formal tone and standard English. Make your points clearly, in as few words as possible.

End with a standard closing such as *Sincerely, Yours truly,* or *Respectfully yours.* Capitalize only the first word of the closing. Type your full name below the closing, leaving three or four blank lines for your signature. Sign your name below the closing in blue or black ink (never in red or green). Proofread your letter before you send it. Poor spelling, grammar, or punctuation can ruin an otherwise well-written business letter.

Guidelines for Writing a Business Letter

- Outline your main points before you begin.
- Word process your letter, if at all possible. Type or print it on clean 8 1/2" x 11" white or off-white paper. Use only one side of the paper.
- Use the block form or another standard business letter form.
- Single space, leaving a blank line between each part, including paragraphs.
- Use a standard salutation and a standard closing.
- Stick to the subject. State your main idea clearly at the beginning of the letter. Keep the letter brief and informative.

- Check your spelling, grammar, usage, and punctuation carefully.

6.4 Application Letter

One of the most frequently used types of business letters is an **application letter,** which you would write to apply to a school or for a job. In an application letter, it is important to emphasize your knowledge about the business and the skills that you can bring to the position. The following is an example of a letter written to the owner of a dive shop to apply for a summer job.

EXAMPLE APPLICATION LETTER

498 Blue Key Rd.
Charleston, SC 02716

May 3, 2008

Mr. Davy Jones, Owner
Deep Sea Divers, Inc.
73 Ocean St.
Charleston, SC 02716

Dear Mr. Jones:

Please consider me for a position as a part-time clerk in your store for the coming summer. I understand that in the summer your business increases considerably and that you might need a conscientious, hardworking clerk. I can offer you considerable knowledge of snorkeling and diving equipment and experience working in a retail shop.

I will be available for work three days per week between June 1 and August 12. I am enclosing a résumé and references. Please contact me if you wish to set up an interview.

Sincerely,

Jorge Alvarez
Jorge Alvarez

Writing a Résumé

A **résumé** is a summary of a job applicant's career objectives, previous employment experience, and education. Its purpose is to help the applicant obtain the job he or she seeks. A résumé should be accompanied by a cover letter to the employer (see 6.4 Application Letter). Many helpful books and articles are available in libraries and bookstores on writing a résumé. Here are some guidelines.

Guidelines for Writing a Résumé

- Keep your information brief—to one page if possible. The goal of the résumé is to give a potential employer a quick snapshot of your skills and abilities.

- Include all vital contact information—name, address, phone number, and e-mail address, if applicable—at the top of the page.
- Use headings to summarize information regarding job or career objective, education, work experience, skills, extracurricular activities, awards (if applicable), and references. Note that work experience should be listed starting with your most recent job and working backward.
- Key or type your résumé on white or off-white paper. Proofread it carefully for any errors; all facts must be accurate as well. Make it as neat as possible.
- You may list references, or simply state that they are available on request.

EXAMPLE RÉSUMÉ

Pat Mizos
5555 Elm Street
Anytown, NY 20111
(212) 555-5555

Objective:
To gain employment working in a summer camp program for children

Education:
Orchard High School, 2008 graduate

Major area of study: College preparatory, with concentration in science and physical education classes

Grade point average: 3.5 (B+)

Work Experience:

| Summer 2007 | Summer youth counselor, Anytown Parks and Recreation Department |
| Summer 2006 | Dishwasher, The Lobster Shack, Anytown, NY |

Skills:
Intermediate level Spanish (3 years in high school)
Beginning level American Sign Language (1 semester at Anytown Vocational School)
Certified in CPR

Extracurricular Activities:
Swim team, tennis team, youth hot-line crisis volunteer

References:
Available on request.

6.6 Writing a Memo

In businesses, schools, and other organizations, employees, students, and others often communicate by means of *memoranda,* or **memos.** For example, the director of a school drama club might write a memo to the editor of the student newspaper announcing tryouts for a new play. Some memos will be more informal than others. If you know the person to whom you are writing well or if the memo has only a social function such as announcing a party, the tone can be fairly informal. Most memos, however, have a fairly formal tone. A memo begins with a header. Often this header contains the word *memorandum* (the singular form of memoranda) and the following words and abbreviations:

TO:
FR: (from)
DT: (date)
RE: (regarding)
cc: (copy)

In the following example, Jack Hart, the president of the drama club at Wheaton High School, wishes to have the upcoming tryouts for his club's production of *Oklahoma!* announced in the school newspaper. He decides to write a memo to the editor of the paper, Lisa Lowry.

EXAMPLE MEMORANDUM

MEMORANDUM
TO: Lisa Lowry
FR: Jack Hart
RE: Tryouts for the spring production of *Oklahoma!*
DT: February 12, 2008
cc: Ms. Wise

Please include the following announcement in the upcoming issue of the *Wheaton Crier:* Tryouts for the Wheaton Drama Club's spring production of *Oklahoma!* will be held on Friday, February 26, at 6:00 p.m. in the Wheaton High School Auditorium. Students interested in performing in this musical should come to the auditorium at that time prepared to deliver a monologue less than two minutes long and to sing one song from the musical. Copies of the music and lyrics can be obtained from the sponsor of the Wheaton Drama Club, Ms. Wise. For additional information, please contact Ms. Wise or any member of the Drama Club.

Thank you.

6.7 Writing a Proposal

A **proposal** outlines a project that a person wants to complete. It presents a summary of an idea, the reasons why the idea is important, and an outline of how the project would be carried out. Because the proposal audience is people who can help carry out the proposal, a proposal is both informative and persuasive.

EXAMPLES

- You want funding for an art project that would benefit your community.

- Your student council proposes a clothing drive for disaster relief.

- You and a group of your friends want to help organize a summer program for teens your age.

Proposal: To host a Community Arts Day at the park behind Jordan High School that would allow high school artists to try new art forms and to exhibit their works.

Rationale: The art students at Jordan High School have shown there is a lot of talent here worth sharing. A Community Arts Day would let everyone interested get involved, and build school and community pride. Art students could lead others through simple art projects, and people could learn new things. At the end, the art could be displayed in an art fair at the community park. Artwork and refreshments could be sold, with all proceeds going to the Jordan High School Art Scholarship.

Schedule/Preparation Outline

Present proposal to School Pride Committee	April 1
Meet with art students to organize event	April 6-15
Contact area businesses for donations	April 6-15
Advertise event and sell tickets	April 16-25
Have practice day to make sure art activities work	April 20
Hold Community Arts Day	April 26

BUDGET

Expenses

Posters, mailings, tickets	$30
Art supplies	$200
Refreshments	$75

Note: Expenses will be less if we ask area businesses to help sponsor event.

Total estimated expenses	$305

Income

Ticket sales (Estimated 150 tickets sold @ $3 each)	$450
Refreshment sales	$100
Earnings from art sold at exhibit	$200
Total estimated income	$750
Net proceeds	$445

Note: All proceeds will be donated to the Jordan High School Art Scholarship Fund.

Guidelines for Writing a Proposal

- Keep the tone positive, courteous, and respectful.
- State your proposal and rationale briefly and clearly.
- Give your audience all necessary information. A proposal with specific details makes it clear what you want approved, and why your audience—often a committee or someone in authority—should approve it.
- Use standard, formal English.
- Format your proposal with headings, lists, and schedules to make your proposed project easy to understand and approve.

6.8 Writing a Press Release

A **press release** is an informative piece intended for publication in local news media. A press release is usually written to promote an upcoming event or to inform the community of a recent event that promotes, or strengthens, an individual or organization.

EXAMPLES

- a brief notice from the choir director telling the community of the upcoming spring concert

- an informative piece by the district public information officer announcing that your school's art instructor has been named the state Teacher of the Year

Guidelines for Writing a Press Release

- Know your purpose. What do you want your audience to know from reading your piece?
- Use the 5 *Ws* and an *H*—*who, what, where, why, when,* and *how*—questioning strategy to convey the important information at the beginning of your story.
- Keep the press release brief. Local media are more likely to publish or broadcast your piece if it is short and to the point.
- Include contact information such as your name, phone number, and times you can be reached. Make this information available to the media representative or, if applicable, to the reading public.
- Type your press release using conventional manuscript form. Make sure the text is double-spaced and that you leave margins of at least an inch on all sides of the page.
- At the beginning of the press release, key the day's date and the date the information is to be released. (You can type "For immediate release" or designate the date you would like the press release to be printed in the newspaper.)
- At the end of the press release, key the word "END."
- Check a previous newspaper for deadline information or call the newspaper office to make sure you get your material there on time. Address the press release to the editor.

6.9 Writing a Public Service Announcement

A **public service announcement,** or **PSA,** is a brief, informative article intended to be helpful to the community. PSAs are written by nonprofit organizations and concerned citizens for print in local newspapers, for broadcast by television and radio stations, and for publication on the Internet.

EXAMPLES

- an article by the American Cancer Society outlining early warning signs of cancer

- an announcement promoting Safety Week

- an informative piece telling coastal residents what to do during a hurricane

Guidelines for Writing a Public Service Announcement

- Know your purpose. What do you want your audience to know from reading or hearing your piece?
- State your information as objectively as possible.
- As with most informative writing, use the 5 *Ws* and an *H*—*who, what, where, why, when,* and *how*—questioning strategy to get your important information at the beginning of your story.
- Keep your announcement brief. Local media are more likely to publish or broadcast your piece if it is short and to the point.
- Include contact information in case the media representative has any questions. You might also include contact information in the PSA itself.
- Key or type your PSA in conventional manuscript form. Make sure the text is double-spaced and that you leave margins of at least an inch on all sides of the page.
- At the end of the PSA, key "END" to designate the end of the announcement.
- Be aware of print and broadcast deadlines and make sure your material is sent on time.

7.1 Verbal and Nonverbal Communication

Human beings use both verbal and nonverbal communication to convey meaning and exchange ideas. When a person expresses meaning through words, he or she is using verbal communication. When a person expresses meaning without using words, for example by standing up straight or shaking his or her head, he or she is using nonverbal communication. When we speak to another person, we usually think that the meaning of what we say comes chiefly from the words we use. However, as much as sixty percent of the meaning of a message may be communicated nonverbally.

Elements of Verbal Communication

Element	Description	Guidelines for Speakers
Volume	Loudness or softness	Vary your volume, but make sure that you can be heard.
Melody, Pitch	Highness or lowness	Vary your pitch. Avoid speaking in a monotone (at a single pitch).
Pace	Speed	Vary the speed of your delivery to suit what you are saying.
Tone	Emotional quality	Suit your tone to your message, and vary it appropriately as you speak.
Enunciation	Clearness with which words are spoken	When speaking before a group, pronounce your words more precisely than you would in ordinary conversation.

Elements of Nonverbal Communication

Element	Description	Guidelines for Speakers
Eye contact	Looking audience members in the eye	Make eye contact regularly with people in your audience. Try to include all audience members.
Facial expression	Using your face to show your emotions	Use expressions to emphasize your message—raised eyebrows for a question, pursed lips for concentration, eyebrows lowered for anger, and so on.
Gesture	Meaningful motions of the arms and hands	Use gestures to emphasize points. Be careful, however, not to overuse gestures. Too many can be distracting.
Posture	Position of the body	Keep your spine straight and head high, but avoid appearing stiff. Stand with your arms and legs slightly open, except when adopting other postures to express particular emotions.
Proximity	Distance from audience	Keep the right amount of distance between yourself and the audience. You should be a comfortable distance away, but not so far away that the audience cannot hear you.

7.2 Listening Skills

Learning to listen well is essential not only for success in personal life but also for success in school and, later, on the job. It is estimated that high school and college students spend over half their waking time listening to others, yet most people are rather poor listeners.

Active Versus Passive Listening

Active listening requires skill and concentration. The mind of a good listener is focused on what a speaker is trying to communicate. In other words, an effective listener is an active listener. Ineffective listeners view listening as a passive activity, something that simply "happens" without any effort on their part. **Passive listening** is nothing more than hearing sounds. This type of listening can cause misunderstanding and miscommunication.

ADAPTING LISTENING SKILLS

Just as different situations require different types of listening, different tasks or goals may also require different listening strategies and skills.

- **Listening for comprehension** means listening for information or ideas communicated by other people. For example, you are listening for comprehension when you try to understand directions to a friend's house or your teacher's explanation of how to conduct a classroom debate.

- **Listening critically** means listening to a message in order to comprehend and evaluate it. When listening for comprehension, you usually assume that the information presented is true. Critical listening, on the other hand, includes **comprehending and judging** the arguments and appeals in a message in order to decide whether to accept or reject them. Critical listening is most useful when you encounter a persuasive message such as a sales pitch, advertisement, campaign speech, or news editorial.

- **Listening to learn vocabulary** involves a very different kind of listening because the focus is on learning new words and how to use them properly. For instance, you have a conversation with someone who has a more advanced vocabulary and use this as an opportunity to learn new words. The key to listening in order to learn vocabulary is to **pay attention to how words are used in context.** Sometimes it is possible to figure out what an unfamiliar word means based simply on how the word is used in a sentence.

- **Listening for appreciation** means listening purely for enjoyment or entertainment. You might listen appreciatively to a singer, a comedian, a storyteller, an acting company, or a humorous speaker. Appreciation is a very individual matter and there are no rules about how to appreciate something. However, as with all forms of listening, listening for appreciation requires attention and concentration.

7.3 Collaborative Learning and Communication

Collaboration is the act of working with one or more other people to achieve a goal. Many common learning situations involve collaboration.

- Participating in a small-group discussion
- Doing a small-group project
- Tutoring another student or being tutored
- Doing peer evaluation

Guidelines for Group Discussion

- **Listen actively.** Maintain eye contact with the speakers. Make notes on what they say. Mentally translate what they say into your own words. Think

critically about whether you agree or disagree with each speaker, and why.

- **Be polite.** Wait for your turn to speak. Do not interrupt others. If your discussion has a group leader, ask to be recognized before speaking by raising your hand.

- **Participate in the discussion.** At appropriate times, make your own comments or ask questions of other speakers.

- **Stick to the discussion topic.** Do not introduce unrelated or irrelevant ideas.

- **Assign roles.** For a formal dicussion, choose a group leader to guide the discussion and a secretary to record the minutes (the main ideas and proposals made by group members). Also draw up an agenda before the discussion, listing items to be discussed.

Guidelines for Projects

- **Choose a group leader** to conduct the meetings of your project group.

- **Set a goal** for the group. This goal should be some specific outcome or set of outcomes that you want to bring about.

- **Make a list of tasks** that need to be performed.

- **Make a schedule** for completing the tasks, including dates and times for completion of each task.

- **Make an assignment sheet.** Assign certain tasks to particular group members. Be fair in distributing the work to be done.

- **Set times for future meetings.** You might want to schedule meetings to evaluate your progress toward your goal as well as meetings to actually carry out specific tasks.

- **Meet to evaluate** your overall success when the project is completed. Also look at the individual contributions of each group member.

7.4 Asking and Answering Questions

There are many situations in which you will find it useful to ask questions of a speaker, or in which you will be asked questions about a presentation. Often a formal speech or presentation will be followed by a question-and-answer period. Keep the following guidelines in mind when asking or answering questions.

Guidelines for Asking and Answering Questions

- **Wait to be recognized.** In most cases, it is appropriate to raise your hand if you have a question and to wait for the speaker or moderator to call on you.
- **Make questions clear and direct.** The longer your question, the less chance a speaker will understand it. Make your questions short and to the point.
- **Do not debate or argue.** If you disagree with a speaker, the question-and-answer period is not the time to hash out an argument. Ask to speak with the speaker privately after the presentation is over, or agree on a later time and place to meet.
- **Do not take others' time.** Be courteous to other audience members and allow them time to ask questions. If you have a follow-up question, ask the speaker if you may proceed with your follow up.
- **Do not give a speech.** Sometimes audience members are more interested in expressing their own opinion than in asking the speaker a question. Do not give in to the temptation to present a speech of your own.
- **Come prepared for a question-and-answer period.** Although you can never predict the exact questions that people will ask you, you can anticipate many questions that are likely to be asked. Rehearse aloud your answers to the most difficult questions.
- **Be patient.** It may take some time for audience members to formulate questions in response to your speech. Give the audience a moment to do so. Don't run back to your seat the minute your speech is over, or if there is an awkward pause after you invite questions.
- **Be direct and succinct.** Be sure to answer the question directly as it has been asked, and to provide a short but clear answer.

7.5 Conducting an Interview

In an interview, you meet with someone and ask him or her questions. Interviewing experts is an excellent way to gain information about a particular topic. For example, if you are interested in writing about the art of making pottery, you might interview an art teacher, a professional potter, or the owner of a ceramics shop.

When planning an interview, you should do some background research on your subject and think carefully about questions you would like to ask. Write out a list of questions, including some about the person's background as well as about your topic. Other questions might occur to you as the interview proceeds, but it is best to be prepared. For guidelines on being a good listener, see Language Arts Handbook 7.2, Listening Skills, page 1111. Guidelines for interviewing appear on the following page:

Guidelines for Conducting an Interview

- **Set up a time in advance.** Don't just try to work questions into a regular conversation. Set aside time to meet in a quiet place where both you and the person you are interviewing can focus on the interview.
- **Explain the purpose** of the interview. Be sure the person you are interviewing knows what you want to find out and why you need to know it. This will help him or her to answer your questions in a way that is more useful and helpful to you.
- **Ask mostly open-ended questions.** These are questions that allow the person you are interviewing to express a personal point of view. They cannot be answered with a simple "yes" or "no" nor a brief statement of fact. The following are all examples of open-ended questions:

  "Why did you become a professional potter?"
  "What is the most challenging thing about owning your own ceramics shop?"
  "What advice would you give to a beginning potter?"

  One of the most valuable questions to ask at the end of the interview is, "What would you like to add that I haven't asked about?" This can provide some of the most interesting or vital information of all.
- **Tape-record the interview** (if possible). Then you can review the interview at your leisure. Be sure to ask the person you are interviewing whether or not you can tape-record the session. If the person refuses, accept his or her decision.
- **Take notes** during the interview, whether or not you are also tape-recording it. Write down the main points and some key words to help you remember details. Record the person's most important statements word for word.
- **Clarify spelling and get permission** for quotations. Be sure to get the correct spelling of the person's name and to ask permission to quote his or her statements.

- **End the interview on time.** Do not extend the interview beyond the time limits of your appointment. The person you are interviewing has been courteous enough to give you his or her time. Return this courtesy by ending the interview on time, thanking the person for his or her help, and leaving.
- **Write up the results** of the interview as soon as possible after you conduct it. Over time, what seemed like a very clear note may become unclear or confusing. If you are unclear of something important that the person said, contact him or her and ask for clarification.
- Send a thank-you note to the person you interviewed as a follow-up.

7.6 Public Speaking

The fear of speaking in public, although quite common and quite strong in some people, can be overcome by preparing a speech thoroughly and practicing positive thinking and relaxation. Learning how to give a speech is a valuable skill, one that you most likely will find much opportunity to use in the future.

The nature of a speech, whether formal or informal, is usually determined by the situation or context in which it is presented. **Formal speeches** usually call for a greater degree of preparation, might require special attire such as a suit or dress, and are often presented to larger groups who attend specifically to hear the presentation. A formal speech situation might exist when presenting an assigned speech to classmates, giving a presentation to a community group or organization, or presenting a speech at an awards ceremony. **Informal speeches** are more casual and might include telling a story among friends, giving a pep talk to your team at halftime, or presenting a toast at the dinner table.

Types of Speeches

The following are four common types of speeches:
- **Extemporaneous:** a speech in which the speaker refers to notes occasionally and that has a specific purpose and message. An example would be a speech given at a city council meeting.
- **Informative:** a speech used to share new and useful information with the audience. Informative speeches are based on fact, not opinion. Examples would include a speech on how to do something or a speech about an event.

- **Persuasive:** a speech used to convince the audience to side with an opinion and adopt a plan. The speaker tries to persuade the audience to believe something, do something, or change their behavior. Persuasive speeches use facts and research to support, analyze, and sell an opinion and plan. Martin Luther King's famous "I Have a Dream" speech and Nelson Mandela's "Glory and Hope" speech are examples of persuasive speeches.
- **Commemorative:** a speech that honors an individual for outstanding accomplishments and exemplary character. Examples are speeches honoring historical figures, leaders, and athletes.

Guidelines for Giving a Speech

A speech should always include a beginning, a middle, and an end. The **beginning,** or introduction, of your speech should spark the audience's interest, present your central idea, and briefly preview your main points. The **middle,** or body, of your speech should expand upon each of your main points in order to support the central idea. The **end,** or conclusion, of your speech should be memorable and should give your audience a sense of completion. The parts of your speech should be connected by *transitions* — words or phrases that show the relationships between the ideas.

- **Be sincere and enthusiastic.** Feel what you are speaking about. Apathy is infectious and will quickly spread to your audience.
- **Maintain good but relaxed posture.** Don't slouch or lean. It's fine to move around a bit; it releases normal nervous tension. Keep your hands free to gesture naturally instead of holding on to note cards, props, or the podium.
- **Speak slowly.** Oral communication is more difficult than written language and visual images for audiences to process and understand. Practice pausing. Don't be afraid of silence. Focus on communicating with the audience. By looking for feedback from the audience, you will be able to pace yourself appropriately.
- **Maintain genuine eye contact.** Treat the audience as individuals, not as a mass of people. Look at individual faces.
- **Speak in a genuine, relaxed, conversational tone.** Don't act or stiffen up. Just be yourself.
- **Communicate.** Focus on conveying your message, not "getting through" the speech. Focus on communicating with the audience, not speaking at or to it.

- **Use strategic pauses.** Pause briefly before proceeding to the next major point, before direct quotations, and to allow important or more complex bits of information to sink in.
- **Remain confident and composed.** Remember that listeners are generally "for you" while you are speaking, and signs of nervousness are usually undetectable. To overcome initial nervousness, take two or three deep breaths as you are stepping up to speak.

7.7 Oral Interpretation

Oral interpretation is the process of presenting a dramatic reading of a literary work or group of works. The presentation should be sufficiently dramatic to convey to the audience a sense of the particular qualities of the work. Here are the steps you need to follow to prepare and present an oral interpretation:

Guidelines for Oral Interpretation

1. **Choose a cutting,** which may be a single piece; a selection from a single piece; or several short, related pieces on a single topic or theme.
2. **Write** the introduction and any necessary transitions. The introduction should mention the name of each piece, the author, and, if appropriate, the translator. It should also present the overall topic or theme of the interpretation. Transitions should introduce and connect the parts of the interpretation.
3. **Rehearse,** using appropriate variations in volume, pitch, pace, stress, tone, gestures, facial expressions, and body language. If your cutting contains different voices (a narrator's voice and characters' voices, for example), distinguish them. Try to make your verbal and nonverbal expression mirror what the piece is saying. However, avoid movement— that's for drama. Practice in front of an audience or mirror, or use a video camera or tape recorder.
4. **Present** your oral interpretation. Before actually presenting your interpretation, relax and adopt a confident attitude. If you begin to feel stage fright, try to concentrate on the work you are presenting and the audience, not on yourself.

Interpreting Poetry

Here are some additional considerations as you prepare to interpret a poem. The way you prepare your interpretation of a poem will depend on whether the poem you have chosen is a lyric poem, a narrative poem, or a dramatic poem.

- A **lyric poem** has a single speaker who reports his or her own emotions.
- A **narrative poem** tells a story. Usually a narrative poem has lines belonging to the narrator, or person who is telling the story. The narrator may or may not take part in the action.
- A **dramatic poem** contains characters who speak. A dramatic poem may be lyrical, in which characters simply report emotions, or narrative, which tells a story. A dramatic monologue presents a single speaker at a moment of crisis or self-revelation and may be either lyrical or narrative.

Before attempting to dramatize any poem, read through the poem carefully several times. Make sure that you understand it well. To check your understanding, try to paraphrase the poem, or restate its ideas, line by line, in your own words.

7.8 Telling a Story

A story or narrative is a series of events linked together in some meaningful fashion. We use narratives constantly in our daily lives: to make a journal entry, to tell a joke, to report a news story, to recount a historical event, to record a laboratory experiment, and so on. When creating a narrative, consider all of the following elements:

Guidelines for Storytelling

- **Decide on your purpose.** Every story has a point or purpose. It may be simply to entertain or to share a personal experience, but it may have a moral or lesson.
- **Select a focus.** The focus for your narrative will depend largely on your purpose in telling it.
- **Choose your point of view.** The storyteller or narrator determines the point of view from which the story will be told. You can choose to speak in the *first person,* either as a direct participant in the events or as an observer (real or imagined) who witnessed the events firsthand, or in the *third person* voice to achieve greater objectivity.
- **Determine sequence of events.** The sequence of events refers to the order in which they are presented. Although it might seem obvious that stories should "begin at the beginning," this is not always the best approach. Some narratives begin with the turning point of the story to create

a sense of drama and to capture the listeners' interest. Others begin at the end of the story and present the events leading up to this point in hindsight. Wherever you choose to begin the story, your narrative should present events in a logical fashion and establish a clear sense of direction for your listeners.

- **Determine duration of events.** Duration refers to how long something lasts. Everyone has experienced an event that seemed to last for hours, when in reality it only took minutes to occur. A good storyteller can likewise manipulate the duration of events in order to affect the way listeners experience them.
- **Select details carefully.** Make them consistent with your focus and make sure they are necessary to your purpose. A well-constructed story should flow smoothly, and should not get bogged down by irrelevant or unnecessary detail. Details can also establish the tone and style of the story and affect how listeners react to the events being described.
- **Choose characters.** All stories include characters who need to be developed so that they become real for listeners. Try to provide your listeners with vivid, concrete descriptions of the mental and physical qualities of important characters in the story. Remember that listeners need to understand and relate to the characters in order to appreciate their behavior.
- **Create dialogue.** Although it is possible to tell a story in which the characters do not speak directly, conversation and dialogue help to add life to a story. As with detail, dialogue should be used carefully. It is important that dialogue sound authentic, relate to the main action of the story, and advance the narrative.

7.9 **Participating in a Debate**

A debate is a contest in which two people or groups of people defend opposite sides of a proposition in an attempt to convince a judge or an audience to agree with their views. Propositions are statements of fact, value, or policy that usually begin with the word "resolved." The following are examples of typical propositions for debate:

RESOLVED   That lie detector tests are inaccurate. (proposition of fact)

RESOLVED   That imagination is more important than knowledge. (proposition of value)

RESOLVED   That Congress should prohibit the sale of handguns to private citizens. (proposition of policy)

The two sides in a debate are usually called the affirmative and the negative. The affirmative takes the "pro" side of the debate and argues in favor of the proposition, whereas the negative takes the "con" side and argues against the proposition. Using a single proposition to focus the debate ensures that the two sides argue or clash over a common topic. This allows the participants in the debate to develop their logic and ability to argue their positions persuasively.

Guidelines for Participating in a Debate

- **Be prepared.** In a debate, it will never be possible to anticipate all the arguments your opponent might make. However, by conducting careful and thorough research on both sides of the issue, you should be able to prepare for the most likely arguments you will encounter. You can prepare briefs or notes on particular issues in advance of the debate to save yourself preparation time during the debate.
- **Be organized.** Because a debate involves several speeches that concern the same basic arguments or issues, it is important that you remain organized during the debate. When attacking or refuting an opponent's argument, or when advancing or defending your own argument, be sure to follow a logical organizational pattern to avoid confusing the audience or the other team.
- **Take notes** by turning a long sheet of paper sideways. Draw one column for each speaker, taking notes on each speech going down one column, and recording notes about a particular argument or issue across the page as it is discussed in each successive speech.
- **Be audience-centered.** In arguing with your opponent, it is easy to forget the goal of the debate: to persuade your audience that your side of the issue is correct.
- **Prepare in advance** for the most likely arguments your opponents, will raise. Use time sparingly to organize your materials and think of responses to unanticipated arguments. Save time for the end of the debate, during rebuttal speeches, when it will be more valuable.

7.10 Preparing a Multimedia Presentation

Whether you use a simple overhead projector and transparencies or a PowerPoint presentation that involves graphics, video, and sound, multimedia technology can add an important visual element to a presentation. Consider the following guidelines to create a multimedia presentation:

Guidelines for a Multimedia Presentation

- **Use effective audiovisuals** that enhance understanding. The multimedia elements should add to the verbal elements, not distract from them. Be sure the content of the presentation is understandable, and that the amount of information—both verbal and visual—will not overwhelm audience members.

- **Make sure the presentation is clearly audible and visible.** Video clips or graphics may appear blurry on a projection screen or may not be visible to audience members in the back or on the sides of the room. Audio clips may sound muffled or may echo in a larger room or a room with different acoustics. When creating a multimedia presentation, be sure the presentation can be easily seen and heard from all parts of the room.

- **Become familiar with the equipment.** Well before the presentation, be sure you know how to operate the equipment you will need, that you know how to troubleshoot if the equipment malfunctions, and that the equipment you will use during the presentation is the same as that which you practiced with.

- **Check the room** to be sure it can accommodate your needs. Once you know where you will make your presentation, be sure the necessary electrical outlets and extension cords are available, that lights can be dimmed or turned off as needed, that the room can accommodate the equipment you will use, and so on.

- **Rehearse with the equipment.** Make sure that you can operate the equipment while speaking at the same time. Be sure that the multimedia elements are coordinated with other parts of your presentation. If you will need to turn the lights off in the room, make sure you can operate the equipment in the dark and can still see your note cards.

8 Test-Taking Skills

8.1 Preparing for Tests

Tests are a common part of school life. You take tests in your classes to show what you have learned in each class. In addition, you might have to take one or more standardized tests each year. Standardized tests measure your skills against local, state, or national standards and may determine whether you graduate, what kind of job you can get, or which college you can attend. Learning test-taking strategies will help you succeed on the tests you are required to take.

The following guidelines will help you to prepare for and take tests on the material you have covered in class.

Preparing for a Test
- **Know what will be covered on the test.** If you have questions about what will be covered, ask your teacher.
- **Make a study plan** to allow yourself time to go over the material. Avoid last-minute cramming.
- **Review the subject matter.** Use the graphic organizers and notes you made as you read as well as notes you took in class. Review any study questions given by your teacher.
- **Make lists** of important names, dates, definitions, or events. Ask a friend or family member to quiz you on them.
- **Try to predict questions** that may be on the test. Make sure you can answer them.
- **Get plenty of sleep** the night before the test. Eat a nutritious breakfast on the morning of the test.

Taking a Test
- **Survey the test** to see how long it is and what types of questions are included.
- **Read all directions and questions carefully.** Make sure you know exactly what to do.
- **Plan your time.** Answer easy questions first. Allow extra time for complicated questions. If a question seems too difficult, skip it and go back to it later. Work quickly, but do not rush.
- **Save time for review.** Once you have finished, look back over the test. Double-check your answers, but do not change answers too readily. Your first responses are often correct.

8.2 Strategies for Taking Standardized Tests

Standardized tests are given to large groups of students in a school district, a state, or a country. Statewide tests measure how well students are meeting the learning standards the state has set. Other tests, such as the SAT (Scholastic Aptitude Test) or ACT (American College Test), are used to help determine admission to colleges and universities. Others must be taken to enter certain careers. These tests are designed to measure overall ability or skills acquired so far. Learning how to take standardized tests will help you to achieve your goals.

You can get better at answering standardized test questions by practicing the types of questions that will be on the test. Use the Test Practice Workshop questions in this book and other sample questions your teacher gives you to practice. Think aloud with a partner or small group about how you would answer each question. Notice how other students tackle the questions and learn from what they do.

In addition, remember these points:
- **Rule out some choices** when you are not sure of the answer. Then guess from the remaining possibilities.
- **Skip questions that seem too difficult** and go back to them later. Be aware, however, that most tests allow you to go back only within a section.
- **Follow instructions exactly.** The test monitor will read instructions to you, and instructions may also be printed in your test booklet. Make sure you know what to do.

8.3 Answering Objective Questions

An **objective question** has a single correct answer. The following chart describes the kinds of questions you may see on objective tests. It also gives you strategies for tackling each kind of question.

Description	Guidelines
True/False You are given a statement and asked to tell whether the statement is true or false.	• If any part of a statement is false, then the statement is false. • Words like *all, always, never,* and *every* often appear in false statements. • Words like *some, usually, often,* and *most* often appear in true statements. • If you do not know the answer, guess. You have a 50/50 chance of being right.
Matching You are asked to match items in one column with items in another column.	• Check the directions. See if each item is used only once. Also check to see if some are not used at all. • Read all items before starting. • Match those items you know first. • Cross out items as you match them.
Short Answer You are asked to answer the question with a word, phrase, or sentence.	• Read the directions to find out if you are required to answer in complete sentences. • Use correct spelling, grammar, punctuation, and capitalization. • If you cannot think of the answer, move on. Something in another question might remind you of the answer.

8.4 Answering Multiple-Choice Questions

On many standardized tests, questions are multiple choice and have a single correct answer. The guidelines below will help you answer these kinds of questions effectively.

- **Read each question carefully.** Pay special attention to any words that are bolded, italicized, written in all capital letters, or otherwise emphasized.
- **Read all choices** before selecting an answer.
- **Eliminate** any answers that do not make sense, that disagree with what you remember from reading a passage, or that seem too extreme. Also, if two answers have exactly the same meaning, you can eliminate both.
- **Beware of distractors.** These are incorrect answers that look attractive because they are partially correct. They might contain a common misunderstanding, or they might apply the right information in the wrong way. Distractors are based on common mistakes students make.
- **Fill in circles completely** on your answer sheet when you have selected your answer.

8.5 Answering Reading Comprehension Questions

Reading comprehension questions ask you to read a passage and answer questions about it. These questions measure how well you perform the essential reading skills. Many of the Reading Assessment questions that follow each literature selection in this book are reading comprehension questions. Use them to help you learn how to answer these types of questions correctly. Work through each question with a partner using a "think aloud." Say out loud how you are figuring out the answer. Talk about how you can eliminate incorrect answers and determine the correct choice. You may want to make notes as you eliminate answers. By practicing this thinking process with a partner, you will be more prepared to use it silently when you have to take a standardized test.

The following steps will help you answer the reading comprehension questions on standardized tests.

- **Preview the passage and questions** and predict what the text will be about.
- **Use the reading strategies** you have learned to read the passage. Mark the text and make notes in the margins.
- **Reread the first question carefully.** Make sure you know exactly what it is asking.
- **Read the answers.** If you are sure of the answer, select it and move on. If not, go on to the next step.
- **Scan the passage** to look for key words related to the question. When you find a key word, slow down and read carefully.
- **Answer the question** and go on to the next one. Answer each question in this way.

8.6 Answering Synonym and Antonym Questions

Synonym or antonym questions give you a word and ask you to select the word that has the same meaning (for a synonym) or the opposite meaning (for an antonym). You must select the best answer even if none is exactly correct. For this type of question, you should consider all the choices to see which is best. Always notice whether you are looking for a synonym or an antonym. You will usually find both among the answers.

8.7 Answering Sentence Completion Questions

Sentence completion questions present you with a sentence that has one or two words missing. You must select the word or pair of words that best completes the sentence. The key to questions with two words missing is to make sure that both parts of the answer you have selected work well in the sentence.

8.8 Answering Constructed-Response Questions

In addition to multiple-choice questions, many standardized tests include **constructed-response questions** that require you to write essay answers in the test booklet. Constructed-response questions might ask you to identify key ideas or examples from the text by writing a sentence about each. In other cases, you will be asked to write a paragraph in response to a question about the selection and to use specific details from the passage to support your answer.

Other constructed-response questions ask you to apply information or ideas from a text in a new way. Another question might ask you to use information from the text in a particular imaginary situation. As you answer these questions, remember that you are being evaluated based on your understanding of the text. Although these questions may offer opportunities to be creative, you should still include ideas, details, and examples from the passage you have just read.

The following tips will help you answer constructed-response questions effectively:

- **Skim the questions first.** Predict what the passage will be about.
- **Use reading strategies** as you read. Underline information that relates to the questions and make notes. After you have finished reading, you can decide which of the details you have gathered to use in your answers.
- **List the most important points** to include in each answer. Use the margins of your test booklet or a piece of scrap paper.
- **Number the points** you have listed to show the order in which they should be included.
- **Draft your answer to fit** in the space provided. Include as much detail as possible in the space you have.
- **Revise and proofread** your answers as you have time.

8.9 Answering Essay Questions

An essay question asks you to write an answer that shows what you know about a particular subject. A simplified writing process like the one below will help you tackle questions like this.

1. Analyze the Question

Essay questions contain clues about what is expected of you. Sometimes you will find key words that will help you determine exactly what is being asked. See the chart below for some typical key words and their meanings.

Key Words for Essay Questions	
analyze; identify	break into parts, and describe the parts and how they are related
compare	tell how two or more subjects are similar; in some cases, also mention how they are different
contrast	tell how two or more subjects are different from each other
describe	give enough facts about or qualities of a subject to make it clear to someone who is unfamiliar with it
discuss	provide an overview and analysis; use details for support
evaluate; argue	judge an idea or concept, telling whether you think it is good or bad, or whether you agree or disagree with it
explain	make a subject clearer, providing supporting details and examples
interpret	tell the meaning and importance of an event or concept
justify	explain or give reasons for decisions; be persuasive
prove	provide factual evidence or reasons for a statement
summarize	state only the main points of an event, concept, or debate

2. Plan Your Answer

As soon as the essay prompt is clear to you, collect and organize your thoughts about it. First, gather ideas using whatever method is most comfortable for you. If you don't immediately have ideas, try freewriting for five minutes. When you **freewrite,** you write whatever comes into your head without letting your hand stop moving. You might also gather ideas in a cluster chart like the one on the following page. Then, organize the ideas you came up with. A simple outline or chart can help.

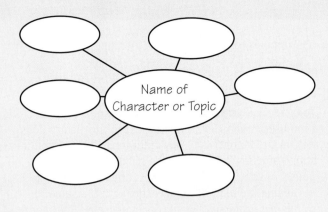

3. Write Your Answer

Start with a clear thesis statement in your opening paragraph. Your **thesis statement** is a single sentence that sums up your answer to the essay question. Then follow your organizational plan to provide support for your thesis. Devote one paragraph to each major point of support for your thesis. Use plenty of details as evidence for each point. Write quickly and keep moving. Don't spend too much time on any single paragraph, but try to make your answer as complete as possible. End your essay with a concluding sentence that sums up your major points.

4. Revise Your Answer

Make sure you have answered all parts of the question and included everything you were asked to include. Check to see that you have supplied enough details to support your thesis. Check for errors in grammar, spelling, punctuation, and paragraph breaks. Make corrections to your answer.

ACT. *See* Drama.

ALLEGORY. An **allegory** is a work in which characters, events, or settings symbolize, or represent, something else. In a *naive allegory,* of the kind found in *Everyman* (Unit 2) and in *The Pilgrim's Progress* (Unit 5), characters, objects, places, and actions are personifications of abstractions such as Good Deeds, Beauty, Vanity, and the journey to the Celestial Kingdom. *See* Extended Metaphor.

ALLITERATION. **Alliteration** is the repetition of initial consonant sounds in consecutive or slightly separated words. Although alliteration usually refers to sounds at the beginnings of words, it can also be used to refer to sounds within words. The following line from Thomas Gray's "Elegy Written in a Country Churchyard" contains three examples of alliteration: the repetition of the *pl* sound in *plowman* and *plods*; of the *h* sound in *homeward* and *his;* and of the *w* sound in *weary* and *way* (Unit 5).

ALLUSION. An **allusion** is a reference to a well-known person, event, object, or work from history or literature. W. H. Auden's poem "Musée des Beaux Arts" alludes to a painting of the fall of Icarus by Pieter Brueghel (Unit 8).

AMBIGUITY. An **ambiguity** is a statement that has a double meaning or a meaning that cannot be clearly resolved. The word *cleave* can mean either "to cling" or "to cut apart." Many figures of speech, including metaphors, similes, personifications, and symbols, are examples of intentional ambiguity—in which the true meaning is deliberately obscured. The apparitions' statement to Macbeth that "no man of woman born" can harm him is an example (Unit 4, Act IV of *Macbeth*). The words seem to suggest that no man can harm Macbeth, for the reader would assume that all men are "of woman born." However, the statement actually is a reference to Macduff, who was "from his mother's womb untimely ripped"—delivered by caesarean section rather than conventionally born.

AMPLIFICATION. *See* Elaboration.

ANALOGY. An **analogy** is a comparison of two things that are alike in some ways but otherwise quite different. Often, an analogy explains or describes something unfamiliar by comparing it to something more familiar.

ANAPEST. *See* Meter.

ANECDOTE. An **anecdote** is a usually short account of an interesting, amusing, or biographical incident. Anecdotes sometimes are used in nonfiction writing as examples to help support an idea or opinion. James Boswell's famous biography of Samuel Johnson contains memorable anecdotes (Unit 5). *See* Exemplum.

ANGLO-SAXON VERSE. **Anglo-Saxon verse** is the poetic form used in most Old English poetry. This poetry does not rhyme. It consists of lines that typically have four strong stresses, or beats. In the middle of the line is a pause, or caesura. Often, the first three stressed words in the line are alliterative, or begin with the same sound. An example of Anglo-Saxon verse is "Cædmon's Hymn" (Unit 1).

ANTAGONIST. An **antagonist** is a character or force in a literary work that is in conflict with a main character, or protagonist. *See* Character.

ANTIHERO. An **antihero** is a central character who lacks all the qualities traditionally associated with heroes. An antihero may be lacking in beauty, courage, grace, intelligence, or moral scruples. Antiheroes are common figures in modern fiction and drama.

ANTITHESIS. **Antithesis** is a rhetorical technique in which words, phrases, or ideas are strongly contrasted, often by means of a repetition of grammatical structure.

APHORISM. An **aphorism** is a short saying that makes an often witty observation about life. Examples of aphorisms include Alfred, Lord Tennyson's "Better to have loved and lost / Than never to have loved at all" and William Shakespeare's "All the world's a stage." An aphorism that gains currency and is passed from generation to generation is called a *proverb* or *adage.*

APOSTROPHE. **Apostrophe,** which is common in poetry and speeches, is a method by which a speaker turns from the audience as a whole to address a single person or thing. John Milton uses apostrophe at the beginning of *Paradise Lost* when he addresses the Holy Spirit, calling on it to be his Muse (Unit 5).

ARCHETYPE. An **archetype** is a type of character, image, theme, symbol, plot, or other element that has appeared in the literature of the world from ancient times until today. For example, the story of a quest or journey, in which someone sets, experiences adventure and danger, and becomes wiser, may be considered archetypal. Anita Desai's "Games at Twilight" is an example of a story containing an archetype (Unit 9).

ARGUMENT. An **argument** is a form of persuasion that makes a case to an audience for accepting or rejecting a proposition or course of action. *See* Persuasion.

ARTHURIAN ROMANCE. Arthurian romances tell of the adventures of King Arthur and his Knights of the Round Table. Magical events and characters that combine fantasy and reality are common in these stories. *See* Romance.

ASIDE. An **aside** is a statement made by a character in a play, intended to be heard by the audience but not by other characters on the stage.

ASSONANCE. Assonance is the repetition of vowel sounds in stressed syllables that end with different consonant sounds.

ATMOSPHERE. *See* Mood.

AUTOBIOGRAPHY. An **autobiography** is the story of a person's life written by that person. *The Book of Margery Kempe,* written by a medieval woman, may well be the first autobiography in the English language (Unit 2). *See* Memoir.

BALLAD. A **ballad** is a poem that tells a story and is written in four- to six-line stanzas, usually meant to be sung. Most ballads have regular rhythms and rhyme schemes and feature a refrain, or repetition of lines. *Folk ballads,* passed by word of mouth from generation to generation, have enjoyed enormous popularity from the Middle Ages to the present. Examples include "Sir Patrick Spens" and "Bonny Barbara Allan" (Unit 2). *Literary ballads,* written in imitation of folk ballads, also have been popular. A famous example is Samuel Taylor Coleridge's "The Rime of the Ancient Mariner" (Unit 6) (Understanding Literary Forms, Unit 2).

BIOGRAPHICAL-HISTORICAL CRITICISM. Biographical-historical criticism is a theory of literary criticism that examines the writer's life and look for ways in which his or her work is tied to the historical period and culture in which it was created. Much of the writing of William Shakespeare can be examined from this literary perspective (Understanding Literary Criticism, Unit 3).

BIOGRAPHY. A **biography** is the story of a person's life told by someone other than that person. Perhaps the most famous English biography is James Boswell's *Life of Samuel Johnson, LL.D.* (Unit 5).

BLANK VERSE. Blank verse is unrhymed poetry written in iambic pentameter. John Milton wrote the epic *Paradise Lost* in blank verse, which was unusual at the time for works outside drama (Unit 5). In doing so, he set a precedent that eighteenth-century poets would follow. *See* Meter.

CAESURA (si zyür´ ə). A **caesura** is a major pause in a line of poetry, as in the following line from William Shakespeare's *A Midsummer Night's Dream:* "I know a bank || where the wild thyme blows."

CANTO. A **canto,** from the Latin for "song," is a section or part of a long poem, such as *Beowulf* (Unit 1).

CARPE DIEM. Carpe diem, a Latin term, means "seize the day." The *carpe diem* theme, urging readers to enjoy themselves while they have the opportunity, was common in English Renaissance poetry. One of the most famous expressions of this theme in English occurs in this stanza by Robert Herrick: "Gather ye rosebuds while ye may, / Old Time is still a-flying; / And this same flower that smiles today, / Tomorrow will be dying" (Unit 5).

CATALOG. A **catalog** is a list of people or things. In the sonnet "How do I love thee?" Elizabeth Barrett Browning enumerates her feelings toward Robert Browning (Unit 7).

CHARACTER. A **character** is an individual that takes part in the action of a literary work. A character is usually a person but also may be a personified plant, animal, object, or imaginary creature. The main character, or *protagonist,* is the most important character in the work and is in conflict with the *antagonist.* Characters also can be classified in other ways. *Major characters* play significant roles in a work, and *minor characters* play lesser roles. A *flat character* shows only one quality, or character trait. A *round character* shows the multiple character traits of a real person. A *static character* does not change during the course of the action, whereas a *dynamic character* is does change. *See* Characterization *and* Motivation.

CHARACTERIZATION. Characterization is the act of creating or describing a character. Writers create characters using three major techniques: showing what characters say, do, or think; showing what other characters say or think about them; and describing what physical features, dress, and personality the characters display. The first two methods are examples of *indirect characterization,* in which the writer *shows* what a character is like and allows the reader to judge the character. The third technique is considered *direct characterization,* in which the writer *tells* what the character is like. "The Prologue" to Geoffrey Chaucer's *The Canterbury Tales* contains striking examples of characterization (Unit 2). *See* Character.

CHIVALRY. Chivalry was the code of conduct of the medieval knight. According to the code of chivalry, a knight was to be a loyal servant to his lord or lady and an exemplar of bravery, courage, courtesy, honesty, faith, and gentleness. Medieval romance literature, such as *Sir Gawain and the Green Knight,* typically presents a series of tests (trials or quests) of these knightly virtues (Unit 2). *See* Romance.

CHORUS. In drama, a **chorus** is a group of actors who speak directly to the audience between scenes, commenting on the action of the play. Christopher Marlowe's *The Tragical History of Doctor Faustus* includes a chorus (Unit 4).

CHRONOLOGICAL ORDER. **Chronological order** is the arrangement of details in order of their occurrence. It is the primary method of organization used in narrative writing and also is common in nonfiction writing that describes processes, events, and cause-and-effect relationships.

CLASSICISM. **Classicism** is a collection of ideas about literature and art derived from the study of works by the ancient Greeks and Romans. Definitions of what constitutes the Classical style differ, but most agree that it encompasses beauty, reason, restraint, self-control, simplicity, tradition, and unity. Classicism is most often contrasted with Romanticism and Realism. *See* Romanticism *and* Realism.

CLICHÉ. A **cliché** is an overused or unoriginal expression such as "quiet as a mouse" or "couch potato." Most clichés originate as vivid, colorful expressions but soon lose their appeal because of overuse.

CLIMAX. The **climax** is the high point of interest and suspense in a literary work. The term also is sometimes used to describe the turning point of the action in a story or play—the point at which the rising action ends and the falling action begins. *See* Plot.

COMEDY. A **comedy** is any lighthearted or humorous literary work with a happy ending, especially a drama. Comedy is often contrasted with *tragedy,* in which the hero meets an unhappy fate. Comedies typically show characters with human limitations, faults, and misunderstandings. The action in a comedy usually progresses from initial order to a humorous misunderstanding or confusion and back to order again. Standard elements of comedy include mistaken identities, word play, satire, and exaggerated characters and events. *See* Drama *and* Tragedy.

COMIC RELIEF. **Comic relief** is a technique used to relieve the seriousness or emotional intensity of a literary work by introducing a humorous character or situation. A well-known example is the appearance of the drunken porter in Act II, Scene iii of *Macbeth,* right after the murder of Duncan (Unit 4).

CONCEIT. A **conceit** is an elaborate or unusual comparison of two things. During the Renaissance Era, the conceit was a common element of poetry. The comparison between courtship and a deer hunt in Sir Thomas Wyatt's "Whoso list to hunt" and between the legs of a compass and love in John Donne's "A Valediction: Forbidding Mourning" are examples (Unit 3).

CONFLICT. A **conflict,** or *crisis,* is a struggle between two forces in a literary work. A plot introduces a conflict, develops it, and eventually resolves it. There are two types of conflict. In an *external conflict*, the main character struggles against another character, against the forces of nature, against society or social norms, or against fate. In an *internal conflict*, the main character struggles against some element within himself or herself. In William Shakespeare's *The Tragedy of Macbeth,* the character Macbeth experiences external conflicts with Banquo and Macduff, and he experiences an internal conflict between his ambition and his guilt (Unit 4). *See* Plot.

CONNOTATION. The **connotation** of a word is the set of ideas or emotional associations it suggests, in addition to its actual meaning. For example, the word *economical* has a positive connotation, whereas the word *cheap* has a negative connotation, even though both words refer to low cost. See Samuel Johnson's *A Dictionary of the English Language* for examples of both connotation and denotation (Unit 5). *See* Denotation.

CONSONANCE. **Consonance** is the repetition of consonant sounds at the ends of words or accented syllables, as in *wind* and *sound*. The final lines of Percy Bysshe Shelley's "Ode to the West Wind" provide an example: "The trumpet of a prophecy! O Wind / If Winter comes, can Spring be far behind?" (Unit 7).

COUPLET. A **couplet** is two lines of verse that rhyme. A *closed couplet* is a pair of rhyming lines that present a complete statement. A pair of rhyming iambic pentameter lines also is known as a *heroic couplet*. These lines from William Shakespeare's *Romeo and Juliet* provide an example: "For never was a story of more woe / Than this of Juliet and her Romeo."

COURTLY LOVE. **Courtly love** is a code of romantic love celebrated in songs and romances of the Medieval Period in France and England. According to this code, the man knows himself to be truly in love if he is overcome by transforming emotion. This emotion, felt for an idealized woman, may lead him to depths of despair or to heights of gentleness, courtesy, and heroism to prove his worth to his lady fair. *See* Romance.

CRISIS. *See* Conflict.

DACTYL. *See* Meter.

DENOTATION. The **denotation** of a word is its dictionary meaning without any emotional associations. For example, the words *dirt* and *soil* have the same denotation. However, *dirt* has a negative connotation of uncleanliness, whereas *soil* does not. *See* Connotation.

DÉNOUEMENT. *See* Plot.

DESCRIPTION. A **description** is a picture in words. *Descriptive writing* is used to portray a character, object, or scene. Descriptions include *sensory details:* words and phrases that describe how things look, sound, smell, taste, or feel.

DIALECT. A **dialect** is a version of a language spoken by the people of a particular place, time, or social group. A *regional dialect* is one spoken in a particular place. A *social dialect* is one spoken by members of a particular social group or class. Writers often use dialect to give their works a realistic flavor, as does Robert Burns in "To a Mouse" (Unit 6).

DIALOGUE. **Dialogue** is conversation between two or more people or characters. Dramas are made up of dialogue and stage directions. Fictional works are made up of dialogue, narration, and description. When dialogue is included in fiction or nonfiction, the speaker's words are usually enclosed in quotation marks. Fanny Burney has included striking exchanges of dialogue in her diary (Unit 5).

DIARY. A **diary** is a record of a person's activities, experiences, thoughts, and feelings, with entries made daily or periodically. Perhaps the most famous of all English diaries is that kept by Samuel Pepys (Understanding Literary Forms, Unit 5). *See* Journal.

DICTION. **Diction,** when applied to writing, refers to the author's choice of words. Much of a writer's style is determined by his or her diction, the types of words that he or she chooses. *See* Style.

DRAMA. A **drama** is a story told through characters played by actors. Dramas are divided into segments called *acts.* The script of a drama is made up of dialogue spoken by the characters and stage directions. Because it is meant to be performed before an audience, drama features elements such as lighting, costumes, makeup, properties, set pieces, music, sound effects, and the movements and expressions of actors. Two major types of drama are comedy and tragedy. William Shakespeare's *The Tragedy of Macbeth* is a famous example of the latter (Understanding Literary Forms, Unit 4). *See* Comedy; Dialogue; Stage Directions; *and* Tragedy.

DRAMATIC IRONY. *See* Irony.

DRAMATIC MONOLOGUE. A **dramatic monologue** is a poem written in the form of a speech of a single character to an imaginary audience. Robert Browning, who some literary scholars say created the form, popularized it in such poems as "My Last Duchess" (Unit 7). *See* Soliloquy.

DRAMATIC POEM. A **dramatic poem** relies heavily on dramatic elements such as *monologue* (speech by a single character) and *dialogue* (conversation involving two or more characters). Often, dramatic poems tell stories. Types of dramatic poetry include the dramatic monologue and the soliloquy. *See* Dialogue; Dramatic Monologue; *and* Soliloquy.

ELABORATION. **Elaboration,** or amplification, is a writing technique in which a subject is introduced and then expanded on by means of repetition with slight changes, the addition of details, or similar devices.

ELEGY. An **elegy** is a poem of mourning, usually about someone who has died. Thomas Gray's "Elegy Written in a Country Churchyard" (Unit 5) and Tennyson's *In Memoriam* (Unit 7) are famous examples.

ELIZABETHAN SONNET. *See* Sonnet.

END RHYME. *See* Rhyme.

END-STOPPED LINE. An **end-stopped line** is a line of verse in which both the sense and the grammar are complete at the end of the line. The opposite of an end-stopped line is known as *enjambment.* Excessive use of end-stopped lines gives verse an unnatural, halting quality. *See* Enjambment.

ENJAMBMENT. **Enjambment** is the act of continuing a statement beyond the end of a line**.** In contrast, an *end-stopped* line is a line of verse in which both the sense and the grammar are complete at the end of the line. Christopher Marlowe's "The Passionate Shepherd to His Love" contains both enjambment and end-stopped lines (Unit 3).

ENLIGHTENMENT. The Enlightenment was an eighteenth-century philosophical movement characterized by belief in reason, the scientific method, and the perfectibility of people and society. Thinkers of the Enlightenment Era, or Age of Reason, believed that the universe was governed by discoverable, rational principles. By extension, they believed that people could, through the application of reason, discover truths relating to the conduct of life or of society. Leading British thinkers of the Enlightenment included Alexander Pope and Jonathan Swift. *See* Neoclassicism.

EPIC. An **epic** is a long story, often told in verse, involving heroes and gods. Grand in length and scope, an epic provides a portrait of an entire culture—the legends, beliefs, values, laws, arts, and ways of life of a people. Famous epic poems include Homer's *The Odyssey* and *The Iliad*, Virgil's *Aeneid*, Dante's *The Divine Comedy*, the anonymous Old English *Beowulf* (Unit 1) and John Milton's *Paradise Lost* (Unit 5) (Understanding Literary Forms, Unit 1).

EPIGRAM. An **epigram** is a short, often witty saying. Alexander Pope is famous for many such sayings, including "To err is human, to forgive divine" (Unit 5).

EPIPHANY. An **epiphany** is a moment of sudden insight in which the essence or nature of a person, thing, or situation is revealed. The use of the term in this sense was introduced by James Joyce (Unit 8).

EPITAPH. An **epitaph** is an inscription or verse written to be used on a tomb or to commemorate someone who has died. The epitaph on the grave of William Butler Yeats, written by the poet himself, reads, "Cast a cold eye on life, on death. Horseman, pass by!" (Unit 8).

EPITHET. An **epithet** is a characteristic word or phrase used alongside the name of a person, place, or thing. *Spring, the season of new beginnings,* is an example. Some epithets are so familiar that they can be used in place of a name. Mary Wollstonecraft makes use of epithet in *A Vindication of the Rights of Woman* (Unit 6).

ESSAY. An **essay** is a short nonfiction work that presents a single main idea, or *thesis,* about a particular topic. There are three general types of essays, each defined by its purpose. An *expository,* or *informative, essay* explores a topic with the goal of informing or enlightening the reader. A *persuasive essay* aims to persuade the reader to accept a certain point of view. A *personal essay* explores a topic related to the life or interests of the writer. Personal essays are characterized by an intimate and informal style or tone. Major modern British essayists include Virginia Woolf (Unit 8) and George Orwell (Unit 9) (Understanding Literary Forms, Unit 8).

EXEMPLUM. An **exemplum** is a brief story or anecdote told to teach a moral lesson. Common in the Middle Ages, exempla often were inserted into homilies, or the sermons included as part of the Catholic mass.

EXPLICATION. An **explication** analyzes the meanings and relationships of the words, images, and literary techniques used in a literary work. The word *explicate* comes from the Latin for "unfold." Anniina Jokinen explicates a poem by John Donne in "A Quick and Rough Explication of Donne's 'Holy Sonnet 10: Death, Be Not Proud'" (Unit 3).

EXPOSITION. In a plot, the **exposition** provides background information, often about the characters, setting, or conflict. *See* Expository Writing *and* Plot.

EXPOSITORY WRITING. **Expository writing** is the type of writing that aims to inform or explain. An essay that explores a topic with the goal of informing or enlightening readers is considered expository. *See* Essay.

EXTENDED METAPHOR. An **extended metaphor** is a point-by-point presentation of one thing as though it were another. The description is meant as an implied comparison, inviting the reader to associate the thing

being described with something that is quite different from it. Thomas Wyatt's poem "Whoso list to hunt" is an example (Unit 3). In it, a woman is described as a deer, the pursuit of the woman as poaching, and the woman's mate as Caesar, the owner of the property on which the poaching might be done.

FABLE. A **fable** is a brief story, often with animal characters, told to express a moral. Famous fables include those of Aesop and Jean de La Fontaine. Fables are part of the oral tradition of many cultures.

FALLING ACTION. *See* Plot.

FANTASY. A **fantasy** is a literary work that contains highly unrealistic elements. Fantasy often is contrasted with science fiction, in which the unreal elements are given a scientific or pseudoscientific basis.

FARCE. A **farce** is a type of comedy that depends heavily on so-called low humor and improbable, exaggerated, extreme situations and characters.

FEET. *See* Meter.

FEMINIST-GENDER CRITICISM. **Feminist-gender criticism** is a theory of literary criticism that examines the text as both the product and the mirror of gender politics. This theory has supported and emerged concurrently with the movement to welcome the works of multicultural and multiethnic writers into the literary canon. Much of the writing of Virginia Woolf can be examined from this literary perspective (Understanding Literary Criticism, Unit 8).

FICTION. A work of **fiction** tells an invented or imaginary story. The primary forms of fiction are the novel and short story (Understanding Literary Forms, Units 7 and 9, respectively). *See* Novel *and* Short Story.

FIGURATIVE LANGUAGE. **Figurative language** is writing or speech meant to be understood imaginatively instead of literally. Many writers, especially poets, use figurative language to help readers see things in new ways. Types of figurative language, or **figures of speech,** include *hyperbole, metaphor, personification, simile,* and *understatement. See each of these terms.*

FIGURES OF SPEECH. *See* Figurative Language.

FLASHBACK. A **flashback** interrupts the chronological sequence of a literary work and presents an event that occurred earlier. Writers use flashbacks most often to provide background information about characters or situations. Elizabeth Bowen's short story "The Demon Lover" contains flashbacks (Unit 8).

FOIL. A **foil** is a character whose traits contrast with and therefore highlight the traits of another character. In Act I of William Shakespeare's *The Tragedy of Macbeth,* Banquo is presented as a foil for the title character (Unit 4).

FOLK BALLAD. *See* Ballad.

FOLK TALE. A **folk tale** is a brief story passed by word of mouth from generation to generation. Folk tales are part of the oral tradition of many cultures. In Geoffrey Chaucer's *The Canterbury Tales,* "The Pardoner's Tale" is a retelling of a folk tale (Unit 2).

FOLKLORE. **Folklore** is a body of beliefs, customs, rituals, traditions, songs, verses, or stories passed orally from one generation to another. Folk tales, fables, fairy tales, tall tales, nursery rhymes, proverbs, legends, myths, parables, riddles, charms, spells, and ballads are all common kinds of folklore.

FOOT. *See* Meter.

FORESHADOWING. **Foreshadowing** is the technique of hinting at events that will occur later in a story. In William Shakespeare's *The Tragedy of Macbeth,* the witches' statement that "Fair is foul" and "foul is fair" foreshadows later events, including Macbeth's confounding of illusion and reality and the several incidents that the witches predict (Unit 4).

FRAME TALE. A **frame tale** is a story that provides a means for telling another story or group of stories. Geoffrey Chaucer's *The Canterbury Tales* is perhaps the most famous frame tale in British literature (Unit 2).

FREE VERSE. **Free verse** is poetry that does not use regular rhyme, meter, or stanza division. Free verse may contain irregular line breaks and sentence fragments and tends to mimic the rhythms of ordinary speech. T. S. Eliot's "Preludes" is written in free verse (Unit 8). Much contemporary poetry is written in free verse.

GENRE. A **genre** (zhän' rə) is one of the types or categories into which literary works are divided. Major genres of literature include fiction, nonfiction, poetry, and drama. *See* Drama; Fiction; Nonfiction; *and* Poetry.

GOTHIC FICTION. **Gothic fiction** is a style of fiction characterized by the use of medieval settings, a murky atmosphere of horror and gloom, and grotesque, mysterious, or violent incidents. Essential to Gothic fiction is a setting that evokes strong feelings of foreboding or anticipation. Mary Wollstonecraft Godwin Shelley's *Frankenstein* is a well-known example of this form (Unit 6).

HAIKU (hi kü´). A **haiku** is a traditional Japanese three-line poem containing five syllables in the first line, seven in the second, and five again in the third. The syllable pattern often is lost when a haiku is translated into English. A haiku presents a single vivid image, often of nature or the seasons, intended to evoke in the reader a specific emotional or spiritual response. Matsuo Bashō's *The Narrow Road to the Deep North and Other Travel Sketches,* a collection of haiku written in 1694, has become one of the classics of world literature.

HEROIC COUPLET. *See* Couplet.

HYPERBOLE. A **hyperbole** (hī pür´ bə lē') is a deliberate exaggeration made for effect. Robert Herrick uses hyperbole in his poem "To the Virgins, to Make Much of Time" (Unit 5).

IAMB. An **iamb** is a poetic foot containing one weakly stressed syllable followed by one strongly stressed syllable, as in the words *afraid* and *release.* A line of poetry made up of iambs is said to be *iambic. See* Iambic Pentameter *and* Meter.

IAMBIC PENTAMETER. **Iambic pentameter** is a type of meter in which a line of poetry has five iambic feet, each comprising one unstressed syllable followed by one stressed syllable, as in the word *insist. See* Meter.

IMAGERY. **Imagery** is the figurative or descriptive language used to create word pictures, or images. In the Bible, Psalm 23, "The Lord is my shepherd," is notable for its vivid imagery (Unit 3). *See* Description *and* Figurative Language.

INCREMENTAL REPETITION. **Incremental repetition** is the repetition of lines with slight changes a the poem. The anonymous ballad "Bonny Barbara Allan" contains incremental repetition (Unit 2).

IN MEDIAS RES. *In medias res,* Latin for "in the middle of the action," refers to the technique of beginning a story in the middle and using flashbacks to fill in the events that happened before the story begins.

INTERNAL MONOLOGUE. An **internal monologue** presents the private sensations, thoughts, and emotions of a character. The reader is allowed to step inside the character's mind and overhear his or her thoughts. Which characters' internal states can be revealed in a work of fiction depends on the point of view from which the work is told. *See* Point of View.

IRONY. **Irony** is the difference between appearance and reality. There are three types of irony: *dramatic irony,* in which something is known by the reader or audience but unknown to the characters; *verbal irony,* in which a writer or character says one thing but means another; and *irony of situation,* in which an event occurs that violates the expectations of the characters, the reader, or the audience. Irony is a feature, for example, in "The Prologue" from Geoffrey Chaucer's *The Canterbury Tales* (Unit 2).

JOURNAL. A **journal,** like a diary, is a day-to-day or periodic record of a person's activities, experiences, thoughts, and feelings. In contrast to a diary, a

and Joseph Addison (see Unit 5). *See* Classicism *and* Romanticism.

NONFICTION. Nonfiction is prose writing about real events. Essays, autobiographies, biographies, and news articles are all types of nonfiction. *See* Prose.

NOVEL. A **novel** is a long work of fiction. Often, a novel has an involved plot, many characters, and numerous settings. Among the most noted British novelists are Victorian writers Charles Dickens, Thomas Hardy, and Charlotte Brontë (Understanding Literary Forms, Unit 7).

OBJECTIVE CORRELATIVE. An **objective correlative** is a group of images that together create a particular emotion in the reader. The term was coined by poet and critic T. S. Eliot. *See* Image.

OCTAVE. An **octave** is an eight-line stanza of poetry. A Petrarchan sonnet begins with an octave. *See* Meter *and* Sonnet.

ODE. An **ode** is a lyric poem on a serious theme, usually with varying line lengths and complex stanzas. John Keats's "Ode on a Grecian Urn" is an example (Unit 6).

OFF RHYME. *See* Rhyme.

OMNISCIENT POINT OF VIEW. *See* Narrator *and* Point of View.

ONOMATOPOEIA. Onomatopoeia (än' ō mat' ō pē´ ə) is the use of words or phrases that imitate the sounds of the entities to which they refer. Examples include *buzz, click,* and *pop.*

ORAL TRADITION. The **oral tradition** is the passing of a work, idea, or custom by word of mouth from generation to generation. Common works found in the oral traditions of peoples around the world include folk tales, fables, fairy tales, tall tales, nursery rhymes, proverbs, legends, myths, parables, riddles, charms, spells, and ballads. The anonymous ballads in Unit 2 are from the oral tradition. *See* Folk Tale *and* Myth.

OTTAVA RIMA. Ottava rima is a stanza form made up of eight iambic pentameter lines rhyming *abababcc*. *See* Rhyme.

OXYMORON. An **oxymoron** is a statement that contradicts itself. Words such as *bittersweet* and *pianoforte* (literally, "soft-loud") are oxymorons. John Milton uses an oxymoron in Book I of *Paradise Lost* when he describes the flames of Hell as giving no light but rather being "darkness visible" (Unit 5). *See* Paradox.

PARABLE. A **parable** is a brief story told to teach a moral lesson. The most famous parables are those told by Jesus in the Bible, such as "The Prodigal Son" (Unit 3).

PARADOX. A **paradox** is a seemingly contradictory statement, idea, or event that may actually be true.

William Wordsworth's statement that "the child is father to the man" is an example of a paradox that can be resolved, on analysis, into a coherent, noncontradictory idea. An example of an unresolvable paradox is the statement "This sentence is a lie." If the sentence is true, then it is false; if it is false, then it is true. John Donne's "A Valediction: Forbidding Mourning" contains a paradox (Unit 3). *See* Irony *and* Oxymoron.

PARALLELISM. Parallelism is a rhetorical device in which a writer emphasizes the equal value or weight of two or more ideas by expressing them in the same grammatical form. William Blake uses parallelism in these lines from "The Lamb": "And I made a rural pen, ∕ And I stain'd the water clear, ∕ And I wrote my happy songs ∕ Every child may joy to hear" (Unit 6).

PARODY. A **parody** is a literary work that closely imitates the style of another work for humorous purposes. Parodies often exaggerate elements of the original work to create a comic effect.

PASTORAL. A **pastoral** poem or other literary work depicts the lives of shepherds or rural life in general and often draws a comparison between the innocence and serenity of the country and the misery and corruption of the city. Examples of pastoral poems include Christopher Marlowe's "The Passionate Shepherd to His Love" (Unit 3) and William Blake's "The Lamb" (Unit 6).

PERSONIFICATION. Personification is a type of figurative language in which an animal, thing, force of nature, or idea is described as if it were human or given human characteristics. The speaker of Percy Bysshe Shelley's "Ode to the West Wind" uses personification when he addresses the wind as "thou breath of Autumn's being" (Unit 6).

PERSUASION. Persuasion, or *persuasive writing*, is intended to change or influence the way a reader thinks or feels about a particular issue or idea. Winston Churchill's wartime speech of May 19, 1940, is persuasive in purpose (Unit 8).

PETRARCHAN SONNET. *See* Sonnet.

PLOT. A **plot** is the series of events related to a central conflict, or struggle. A plot typically introduces a conflict, develops it, and eventually resolves it. A plot often contains the following elements, although it may not include all of them and they may not appear in precisely this order:

- The *exposition,* or introduction, sets the tone or mood, introduces the characters and setting, and provides necessary background information.

- In the *rising action,* the conflict is developed and intensified.
- The *climax,* or *crisis,* is the high point of interest or suspense.
- The *falling action* consists of all the events that follow the climax.
- The *resolution,* or *dénouement* (dā' nü män´), is the point at which the central conflict is ended, or resolved.

See Conflict; Exposition; *and* Resolution.

POETRY. Poetry, a major genre of literature, is characterized by imaginative language that is carefully chosen and arranged to communicate experiences, thoughts, and emotions. Poetry differs from prose in that it compresses meaning into fewer words and often uses meter, rhyme, and imagery. Poetry usually is arranged in lines and stanzas, as opposed to sentences and paragraphs, and can be more free in the ordering of words and use of punctuation (Understanding Literary Forms, Unit 1). Major types of poetry include narrative, dramatic, and lyric (Understanding Literary Forms, Unit 6). Specific forms include the epic, ballad, and sonnet (see Understanding Literary Forms, Units 1, 2, and 3, respectively). *See these topics.*

POINT OF VIEW. The **point of view** is the vantage point, or perspective, from which a story is told — in other words, who is telling the story. In *first-person point of view,* the story is told by someone who participates in or witnesses the action; this person, called the *narrator,* uses words such as *I* and *we* in telling the story. In *third-person point of view,* the narrator usually stands outside the action and observes; the narrator uses words such as *he, she, it,* and *they.* In a *limited point of view,* the thoughts of only the narrator or a single character are revealed. In an *omniscient point of view,* the thoughts of all the characters are revealed. *See* Narrator.

POLITICAL CRITICISM. Political criticism is a theory of literary criticism that suggests a work cannot be viewed clearly unless it is placed in its cultural context; the critic then studies the relationship of the text to social and economic class. The ideology of the author and the historical position of the literary work are given far more importance than, say, the structure or form of the work (Understanding Literary Criticism, Unit 5).

PRIMARY SOURCE. A **primary source** is direct evidence, or proof that comes straight from the individual or individuals involved in an event or activity. Primary sources include official documents as well as firsthand accounts such as diaries, letters, photographs, and paintings produced by participants or witnesses. For example, William Shakespeare found the outline of his story of Macbeth in Ralph Holinshed's *Chronicles of England, Scotland, and Ireland* (Unit 4). *See* Source.

PROSE. Prose is the broad term used to describe all writing that is not drama or poetry, including fiction and nonfiction. Types of prose include novels, short stories, essays, and news stories. Most biographies, autobiographies, and letters are written in prose. *See* Drama; Fiction; Nonfiction; and Poetry.

PROTAGONIST. The **protagonist** is the main character of a literary work. *See* Antagonist *and* Character.

PROVERB. A **proverb,** or adage, is a traditional saying, such as "You can lead a horse to water, but you can't make it drink" and the title of William Shakespeare's play *All's Well That Ends Well.*

PUN. A **pun** is a play on words, one that wittily exploits a double meaning. The porter scene in William Shakespeare's *The Tragedy of Macbeth* contains a pun based on an Elizabethan usage, in which *goose* referred both to a type of fowl and to a tailor's pressing iron (Unit 4). The porter pretends to be at Hell's gate, opening it to let in a tailor guilty of theft: "Who's there? Faith, here's an English tailor come hither for stealing out of a French hose. Come in, tailor. Here you may roast your goose."

PURPOSE. A writer's **purpose** is his or her aim, or goal. A writer usually has one or more of the following purposes: to inform or explain (*expository writing*); to portray a person, place, object, or event (*descriptive writing*); to convince people to accept a position and respond in some way (*persuasive writing*); and to tell a story (*narrative writing*).

QUATRAIN. A **quatrain** is a stanza of poetry containing four lines. *See* Stanza.

READER-RESPONSE CRITICISM. Reader-response criticism is a theory of literary criticism that suggests the reader creates the meaning of a text by reading and responding to it. As the reader delves into a literary work, he or she is engaged in a creative process that takes in the text and extends its significance in countless directions (Understanding Literary Criticism, Unit 6).

REALISM. Realism is the philosophy that works of art should be accurately portray reality. The theory that the purpose of art is to imitate life is at least as old as Aristotle. The eighteenth-century development of the novel, with its attention to details of character, setting, and social life, represents a step toward Realism. However, the term *Realism* is generally applied to literature of the late nineteenth century, created in reaction to Romanticism and emphasizing details of ordinary life. *See* Romanticism.

REFRAIN. A **refrain** is a line or group of lines repeated in a poem or song. Many ballads contain refrains.

RENAISSANCE. The **Renaissance** was the period from the fourteenth century to the early seventeenth century, when Europe was emerging from the medieval into the modern world. The term *Renaissance,* from the Latin for "rebirth," refers to the renewal of interest in Greek and Latin scholarship and literature. The Renaissance was characterized by a decline in both feudalism and the church's authority, heightened nationalism, the increased influence of universities and cities, and expanding opportunities for individual achievement and freedom.

REPETITION. **Repetition** is a writer's intentional reuse of a sound, word, phrase, or sentence. Writers often use repetition, which is a rhetorical device, to emphasize ideas or, especially in poetry, to create a musical effect. Examples of works that feature repetition include John Suckling's song "Why so pale and wan" (Unit 5) and Elizabeth Barrett Browning's sonnet "How do I love thee?" (Unit 7). *See* Rhetorical Device.

RESOLUTION. The **resolution,** or *dénouement* (dā' nü män´), is the point at which the central conflict of the plot is ended, or resolved. *See* Plot.

RHETORICAL DEVICE. A **rhetorical device** is a technique used by a speaker or writer to achieve a particular effect, especially to persuade or influence. Common rhetorical devices include parallelism, repetition, and rhetorical questions. Winston Churchill's speech of May 19, 1940, incorporates rhetorical devices to rouse the British people's patriotism and readiness to sacrifice (Unit 8). *See* Parallelism; Repetition; *and* Rhetorical Question.

RHETORICAL QUESTION. A **rhetorical question** is one asked for effect but not meant to be answered because the answer is clear from the context. In her essay collection *A Room of One's Own,* Virginia Woolf engages the reader's attention by posing rhetorical questions (Unit 8).

RHYME. **Rhyme** is the repetition of sounds at the ends of words. Types of rhyme include the following:

end rhyme, the use of rhyming words at the ends of lines

internal rhyme, the use of rhyming words within lines

exact rhyme, in which the rhyming words end with the same sound or sounds, as in *moon* and *June*

slant rhyme, in which the rhyming sounds are similar but not identical, as in *rave* and *rove*

sight rhyme, in which the words are spelled similarly but pronounced differently, as in *lost* and *ghost*

RHYME SCHEME. A **rhyme scheme** is a pattern of end rhymes, or rhymes at the ends of lines of verse. The rhyme scheme of a poem is designated by letters, with matching letters signifying matching sounds. *See* Rhyme.

RHYTHM. **Rhythm** is the pattern of beats or stresses in a line of verse or prose. Rhythm can be regular or irregular. A regular rhythmic pattern in a poem is called a *meter. See* Meter.

RISING ACTION. *See* Plot.

ROMANCE. **Romance** is a term referring to four types of literature: (1) medieval stories about the adventures and loves of knights; (2) novels and other fiction involving exotic locales and extraordinary or mysterious events and characters; (3) nonrealistic fiction in general; and, (4) in popular modern usage, love stories of all kinds. Some of the most famous British romances are stories, in prose or poetry, of heroic exploits, such as those featuring King Arthur and the Knights of the Round Table (Unit 2).

ROMANTICISM. **Romanticism** was a literary and artistic movement of the eighteenth and nineteenth centuries that placed value on emotion or imagination over reason, the individual over society, nature and wildness over human works, the country over the city, common people over the ruling class, and freedom over control or authority. Major writers of the Romantic Era include William Blake, William Wordsworth, Samuel Taylor Coleridge, Percy Bysshe Shelley, Mary Shelley, and George Gordon, Lord Byron (Unit 6).

SATIRE. **Satire** is humorous writing or speech intended to point out human errors, falsehoods, foibles, or failings. It is written for the purpose of reforming human behavior or human institutions. One of the most famous satires is Jonathan Swift's "A Modest Proposal," which criticizes political and social institutions (Unit 5).

SCANSION. **Scansion** is the art of analyzing poetry to determine its meter. *See* Meter.

SCOP. A **scop,** or gleeman, was Anglo-Saxon poet or minstrel. The scop composed verse orally and recited it to the accompaniment of a harp.

SENSORY DETAILS. **Sensory details** are words and phrases that describe how things look, sound, smell, taste, or feel. The use of sensory details is a key quality of descriptive writing. Percy Bysshe Shelley's "To a Skylark" is notable for its sensory details (Unit 6). *See* Description.

SESTET. A **sestet** is a stanza with six lines, such as the second part of a Petrarchan, or Italian, sonnet. *See* Meter *and* Sonnet.

SETTING. The **setting** of a literary work is the time and place in which it occurs, together with all the details used to create a sense of a particular time and place. Writers create setting by various means. In drama, the setting often is revealed by the stage set and the costumes, although it may be revealed through what the characters say about their environs. In fiction, setting is most often revealed by means of description of elements such as landscape, scenery, buildings, furniture, clothing, the weather, and the season. Setting also can be revealed by how characters talk and behave.

SHAKESPEAREAN SONNET. *See* Sonnet.

SHORT STORY. A **short story** is brief work of fiction. A short story is carefully crafted to develop a plot, characters, setting, mood, and theme, all within relatively few pages. Contemporary short story writers include Graham Greene, V. S. Naipaul, Anita Desai, Nadine Gordimer, and Doris Lessing (Understanding Literary Forms, Unit 9). *See* Fiction *and* Genre.

SIMILE. A **simile** is a comparison of two seemingly unlike things using the word *like* or *as.* Christina Rossetti's poem "A Birthday" begins with three similes: "My heart is like a singing bird," "My heart is like an apple tree," and "My heart is like a rainbow shell" (Unit 7).

SOCIOLOGICAL CRITICISM. **Sociological criticism** is a theory of literary criticism that suggests a literary text cannot be seen apart from the values and rules that govern the society at large. However, just as the social structure keeps changing and evolving, so do the expectations or attitudes of authors and readers (Understanding Literary Criticism, Unit 9).

SOLILOQUY. A **soliloquy** is a speech delivered by a lone character that reveals his or her thoughts and feelings. In William Shakespeare's *The Tragedy of Macbeth*, Macbeth's "Tomorrow and tomorrow and tomorrow" speech (Act V, Scene v) is an example of a soliloquy (Unit 4).

SONNET. A **sonnet** is a fourteen-line poem, usually in iambic pentameter, that follows one of a number of different rhyme schemes. The *English, Elizabethan,* or *Shakespearean* sonnet is divided into four parts: three quatrains and a final couplet. The rhyme scheme of such a sonnet is *abab cdcd efef gg.* The sonnets by Shakespeare in Unit 3 are examples. The *Italian,* or *Petrarchan,* sonnet is divided into two parts: an octave and a sestet. The rhyme scheme of the octave is *abbaabba.* The rhyme scheme of the sestet can be *cdecde, cdcdcd,* or *cdedce.* Sir Thomas Wyatt's "Whoso list to hunt" (Unit 3) is an example of the Petrarchan sonnet (Understanding Literary Forms, Unit 3). *See* Rhyme Scheme *and* Stanza.

SONNET SEQUENCE. A **sonnet sequence** is a group of related sonnets. Famous sonnet sequences in British literature include those of William Shakespeare and Edmund Spenser's *Amoretti* (Unit 3). *See* Sonnet.

SOURCE. A **source** is evidence of an event, idea, or development. *See* Primary Source.

SPEAKER. The **speaker** is the character who speaks in, or narrates, a poem — the voice assumed by the writer. The speaker and the writer of a poem are not necessarily the same person. The speaker of Robert Browning's "My Last Duchess," for example, is an Italian duke of the Renaissance Era (Unit 7). *See* Narrator.

SPECTACLE. In drama, **spectacle** refers to all the elements presented to the senses of the audience, including the lights, setting, costumes, make-up, music, sound effects, and actors' movements. *See* Drama.

SPEECH. A **speech** is a public communication or expression of thought in spoken words. The purpose of a speech is often to inform an audience about a given subject or to persuade them to a particular point of view. The speeches of Queen Elizabeth I (Unit 3) and Winston Churchill (Unit 8) are famous historical addresses.

SPONDEE. *See* Meter.

SPRUNG RHYTHM. **Sprung rhythm** is the term coined by Gerard Manley Hopkins to describe the unique metrical forms of his verse. Hopkins used a foot consisting of a single stressed syllable and feet containing a stressed syllable followed by one, two, or three weakly stressed syllables. One consequence of his use of sprung rhythm was the frequent occurrence of several stressed syllables in a row, as in this line from "Pied Beauty": "Summer ends now; now, barbarous in / beauty, the stoks [sheaves] arise" (Unit 7).

STAGE DIRECTIONS. **Stage directions** are notes included in a play, in addition to the dialogue, for the purpose of describing how something should be performed on stage. Stage directions describe setting, lighting, music, sound effects, entrances and exits, properties, and the movements of characters. These directions usually are printed in italics and enclosed in brackets or parentheses.

STANZA. A **stanza** is a group of lines in a poem. The following are common types of stanzas:

two-line stanza	couplet
three-line stanza	triplet or tercet
four-line stanza	quatrain
five-line stanza	quintain
six-line stanza	sestet
seven-line stanza	heptastich
eight-line stanza	octave

STREAM-OF-CONSCIOUSNESS WRITING. Stream-of-consciousness writing attempts to present the flow of feelings, thoughts, and impressions within the minds of characters. Modern British masters of stream-of-consciousness writing include Virginia Woolf and James Joyce (Unit 8).

STYLE. Style refers to the manner in which something is said or written. A writer's style is characterized by elements such as word choice (or *diction*), sentence structure and length, and other recurring features that distinguish his or her work from that of another. One way to think of a writer's style is as his or her written personality.

SUSPENSE. Suspense is a feeling of expectation, anxiousness, or curiosity created by questions raised in the mind of a reader or viewer. The high point of interest and suspense in a literary work is called the *climax*. *See* Climax.

SYMBOL. A **symbol** is anything that stands for or represents both itself and something else. Writers use two types of symbols. A *conventional symbol* is one with traditional, widely recognized associations. Such symbols include doves for peace; the color green for jealousy; winter, evening, or night for old age; wind for change or inspiration. A *personal,* or *idiosyncratic, symbol* is one that assumes its secondary meaning because of the special way the writer uses it. In Matthew Arnold's poem "Dover Beach," the sea represents elements of the human condition (Unit 7).

SYNESTHESIA. Synesthesia (sin′ əs thē′ zhē ə) is a figure of speech that combines, in a single expression, images related to two or more senses. William Blake's "The Lamb" contains synesthesia (Unit 6).

SYNECDOCHE. A **synecdoche** (sə nek′ də kē′) is a figure of speech in which the name of part of something is used in place of the name of the whole or vice versa. Addressing a representative of the country of France as *France* is synecdoche in which a whole (the nation) refers to a part (one citizen). "The Hand That Signed the Paper," by Dylan Thomas, contains synecdoche (Unit 9). *See* Metonymy.

TERZA RIMA. Terza rima is a three-line stanza form in which successive stanzas have the rhyme scheme *abas, bcb, cdc, ded,* and so on. Percy Bysshe Shelley's "Ozymandias" is written in terza rima (Unit 6).

THEME. A **theme** is a central message or perception about life revealed through a literary work. A *stated theme* is presented directly, whereas an *implied theme* must be inferred. Most works of fiction do not have a stated theme but rather several implied themes. A

universal theme is a message about life than can be understood by people of most cultures.

THESIS. A **thesis** is a main idea presented and supported in a work of nonfiction. *See* Nonfiction.

TONE. Tone is the emotional attitude toward the reader or toward the subject implied by a literary work. Tone may be revealed by such elements as word choice (*diction*), sentence structure, and use of imagery. Examples tone include familiar, ironic, playful, sarcastic, serious, and sincere. In William Shakespeare's Sonnet 29, "When, in disgrace with Fortune and men's eyes," the tone moves from despair to exultation (Unit 3).

TRAGEDY. A **tragedy** is a work of literature, particularly a drama, that tells the story of the fall of a person of high status. It celebrates the courage and dignity of a *tragic hero,* or the main character in a tragedy, in the face of inevitable doom. Sometimes that doom is made inevitable by a *tragic flaw,* or personal weakness that brings about a fall, in the hero. In William Shakespeare's *The Tragedy of Macbeth,* ambition is the tragic flaw that destroys the hero (Unit 4). Today, the term *tragedy* is used more loosely to refer to any work that has a sad ending. *See* Comedy *and* Drama.

TROCHEE. *See* Meter.

UNDERSTATEMENT. An **understatement** is an expression in which something of importance is emphasized by being spoken of as though it were not important, as in "He's sort of dead, I think."

VERNACULAR. The **vernacular** is the speech of the common people. During the Middle Ages, writing throughout Europe was mostly in Latin, the language of the church. Only gradually, during the late Middle Ages and the Renaissance, did the vernacular languages of Europe replace Latin for scholarly purposes. The term *vernacular* often is used loosely today to refer to dialogue or to writing in general that uses colloquial, dialectical, or slang expressions. *See* Dialogue.

VILLANELLE. A **villanelle** is a complex and intricate nineteen-line form of French verse. The rhyme scheme is *aba aba aba aba abaa.* Line 1 is repeated as lines 6, 12, and 18. Line 3 is repeated as lines 9, 15, and 19. Line 1 and 3 appear as a rhymed couplet at the end of the poem. Dylan Thomas's "Do Not Go Gentle Into That Good Night" is a villanelle (Unit 9).

VOICE. Voice comprises the writer's use of language to reflect his or her unique personality and attitude toward the topic, form, and audience. A writer expresses his or her voice through tone, word choice, and sentence structure.

Glossary of Vocabulary Words

A

abate (ə bāt´) *v.*, end; lessen; reduce in intensity

ab • hor • rence (əb hôr´ ən[t]s) *n.*, loathing

ab • jure (ab jür´) *v.*, renounce; give up

abom • i • na • bly (ə bä´ mə nə blē) *adv.*, disagreeably; terribly

ab • so • lu • tion (ab sə lü´ shən) *n.*, forgiveness, especially following confession

ac • crue (ə krü´) *v.*, accumulate or increase periodically

acute • ness (ə kyüt´ nəs) *n.*, state of high awareness

adieu (ə dyü´) *adj.*, goodbye in French

ad • mon • ish (ad män´ ish) *v.*, give warning or advice; show disapproval

ad • ver • sary (ad´ və[r] ser' ē) *n.*, enemy

ad • ver • si • ty (ad vʉr´ sə tē) *n.*, misfortune, trouble

af • fec • ta • tion (a' fek tā´ shən) *n.*, artificial behavior designed to impress others

agape (ə gāp´) *adv.*, open wide

agen • cy (ā´ jən[t] sē) *n.*, force or power

ague (ā´ gyü[']) *n.*, fever and chills

aim • less (ām´ ləs) *adj.*, without purpose or intention

alac • ri • ty (ə la´ krə tē) *n.*, eagerness

al • ter (ôl´ tər) *v.*, change

am • ble (am´ bəl) *v.*, move with a smooth, easy gait

ami • a • bil • i • ty (ā´ mē ə bi´ lə tē) *n.*, friendliness; pleasantness

an • ar • chy (a´ när' kē) *n.*, lack of order, law, or government

an • ni • hi • late (ə nī´ ə lāt') *v.*, destroy; eliminate

an • nul (ə nul´) *v.*, cancel

anoint (ə noint´) *v.*, apply oil as a sacred rite; choose as if by divine election

ap • pease (ə pēz´) *v.*, calm; subdue

ap • pre • hen • sion (a' pri hen[t]´ shən) *n.*, suspicion or fear

ar • bi • trate (är´ bə trāt) *v.*, settle a dispute

ar • dent (är´ d'nt) *adj.*, intensely enthusiastic or devoted; zealous

ar • du • ous (är´ jə wəs) *adj.*, extremely difficult

ar • ti • fice (är´ tə fəs) *n.*, crafted skill; often used to suggest a deception or insincere action

as • cend (ə send´) *v.*, go or move upward

as • per • i • ty (ä sper´ ə tē) *n.*, harshness

as • pire (ə spīr´) *v.*, seek to achieve lofty goals

as • sent (ə sent´) *n.*, acknowledgment; agreement

asun • der (ə sun´ dər) *adv.*, apart; separate

at • ro • phy (a´ trə fē) *v.*, weaken or decline

aug • ment (ôg´ ment') *v.*, add to; supplement

aus • tere (ô stir´) *adj.*, giving little or no pleasure

avail (ə vāl´) *v.*, be of use; help

B

baf • fle (ba´ fəl) *v.*, puzzle or confuse

bale • ful (bāl´ fəl) *adj.*, sorrowful; wretched

beau • te • ous (byü´ tē əs) *adj.*, beautiful

be • guile (bē gīl´) *v.*, engage the interest of; fascinate or captivate

be • lie (bē lī´) *v.*, misrepresent

blas • pheme (blas´ fēm' *or* blas fēm´) *v.*, show contempt or irreverence for something sacred

blight (blīt) *v.*, destroy; prevent growth

blithe (blī<u>th</u>) *adj.*, cheerful; carefree; happy

bolt (bōlt) *v.*, swallow (food) hurriedly; gulp down

breach (brēch) *n.*, break in an accustomed friendly relationship

brev • i • ty (bre´ və tē) *n.*, shortness of duration

brim • ming (brim´ iŋ) *adj.*, full; almost overflowing

brood (brüd) *n.*, offspring or a family of offspring of animals

C

ca • coph • o • ny (ka kä´ fə nē) *n.*, harsh and inharmonious sound

ca • lam • i • tous (kə la´ mə təs) *adj.*, accompanied by misery and loss

cal • lous • ness (ka´ ləs nes) *n.*, lack of emotion

ca • price (kə prēs´) *n.*, whim

ca • reen (kə rir´) *v.*, move at full speed

cav • ern (ka´ vərn *or* ka´ vrən) *n.*, cave

cer • ti • tude (sʉr´ tə tüd') *n.*, absolute sureness

cha • grin (shə grin´) *n.*, distress resulting from humiliation, disappointment, or failure

chasm (ka´ z'm) *n.*, deep crack or cleft in the earth

chaste (chāst) *adj.*, celibate; innocent; pure in thought and act

chas • tise (chas['] tīz´) *v.*, scold or condemn sharply

chide (chīd) *v.*, scold

cir • cum • scribe (sʉr´ k'm skrīb') v., constrict; enclose

cit • a • del (si´ tə deľ') n., fortress; safe place

clam• or • ous (klam´ rəs *or* kla´ mər əs) *adj.*, noisy and chaotic

com • mend (kə mend´) v., praise or recommend

com • mis • er • a • tion (kə mi' zə rā´ shən) *n.*, feeling of sympathy

com • pul • sion (kəm pul´ shən) n., coercion, driving force

con • cede (kən sēd´) v., acknowledge grudgingly or hesitantly

con • cil • i • ate (kən si´ lē āt') v., win over

con • cord (kän´ kôrď') n., agreement; harmony

con • fer • ence (kän´ fər ənts) n., conversation, discussion

con • found • ed (kən foun´ dəd) *adj.*, confused

con • sti • tute (kän[t]´ stə tüt') v., form or compose

con • temp • tu • ous (kən tem[p]´ chə wəs) *adj.*, disapproving; disrespectful; expressing disgust

con • trive (kən trīv´) v., scheme

con • vul • sion (kən vul´ shən) n., involuntary contraction of the muscles

copse (käps) n., thicket of small trees or bushes

cor • po • re • al (kôr pôr´ ē əl) *adj.*, of a bodily or physical nature

coun • te • nance (kaùn´ t'n ənts) n., appearance; facial features or expression

cov • et (ku´ vet) v., feel envious of or desire for something that belongs to someone else

cov • et • ous • ness (kə´ və təs nes) n., excessive desire for possessions, especially those belonging to others; greed

cow • er (kou´ ər) v., shrink and tremble, as from fear or cold

coy • ness (koi´ nəs) n., playful evasiveness; pretense of shyness or bashfulness

cyn • i • cal (si´ ni kəl) *adj.*, believing that people are insincere or selfish; sarcastic

---

D

dam • ask (da´ məsk) v., make a deep pink or rose

dap • pled (da´ pəld) *adj.*, marked with spots

daunt • less (dônt´ ləs) *adj.*, fearless

def • er • ence (de´ fə rən[t]s) n., respect for an elder or superior

de • funct (di fəŋkt´) *adj.*, no longer existing or functioning

deg • ra • da • tion (de' grə dā´ shən) n., process of being reduced to a lower social position or moral state

de • i • ty (dē´ ə tē) n., god

de • lu • sion (dē lü´ zhən) n., false belief held in spite of invalidating evidence; misconception; fantasy

des • o • late (de´ sə lət) *adj.*, barren, lifeless, or deserted

des • pot • ic (des pä´ tik) *adj.*, of, relating to, or characteristic of a tyrant

des • ti • tute (des´ tə tüt') *adj.*, lacking some necessary thing or quality

dex • ter • ous (dek´ st[ə] rəs) *adj.*, skillful

di • li • gence (di´ lə jənts) n., care

di • verge (dī vʉrj´) v., go in different ways; separate

di • ver • sion (dī vʉr´ zhən) n., entertaining type of distraction

di • vert (də vʉrt´) v., entertain; amuse

di • vin • i • ty (də vi´ nə tē) n., god or deity

dif • fu • sive (di fyü´ siv) *adj.*, tending to disperse

dil • i • gent • ly (di´ lə jənt lē) *adv.*, carefully; steadily; with great attention

din • gy (din´ jē) *adj.*, dirty and shabby

dirge (dʉrj) n., funeral song

dis • cern (di sʉrn´) v., recognize and understand; show good judgment

dis • course (dis´ kôrs) n., conversation; formal expression of thought

dis • dain (dis dān´) n., scorn

dis • pas • sion • ate (dis['] pa´ sh[ə] nət) *adj.*, unaffected by passion or emotion

dis • po • si • tion (dis pə zi´ shən) n., tendency; habit

dis • so • nance (di´ sə nən[t]s) n., disagreement or disharmony; also, clash of musical sounds

dis • till (di stil´) v., obtain or extract the essence of

dis • traught (di strôt´) *adj.*, anxious; worried

doff (däf) v., take off; remove

do • min • ion (də mi´ nyən) n., supreme authority

dreary (drēr´ ē) *adj.*, gloomy; cheerless

dregs (dregz) n., last remaining parts

drudge (druj) n., person who does tedious work

E

ear • nest (ər´ nəst) *adj.*, full of intense, serious feeling

ec • cle • si • as • ti • cal (i klē' sē as´ ti k'l) *adj.*, having to do with the church

ec • sta • sy (ek´ stə sē) *n.*, medical state in which the mind can focus only on one idea; also, a state of intense emotion

ec • stat • ic (ek sta´tik) *adj.*, thrilled; overjoyed

ef • fi • ca • cious (e fə kā´ shəs) *adj.*, effective, producing the desired result

ef • fi • ca • cy (e´ fi kə sē) *n.*, ability to produce an effect

ela • tion (i lā´ shən) *n.*, joy; excitement

elon • gat • ed (ē lôŋ´ gā təd) *adj.*, extended or lengthened

em • i • nent (e´ mə nənt) *adj.*, important; note-worthy; of high standing

emit (ē mit´) *v.*, send out or voice

em • phat • i • cal • ly (im fa´ ti k[ə] lē) *adv.*, with special emphasis or attention

em • u • la • tion (em' yə lā´ shən) *n.*, imitation

en • cum • ber (in kum´ bər) *v.*, burden or weigh down

en • deav • or (in de´ vər) *v.*, try; attempt to achieve through strong effort

en • sue (in sü´) *v.*, come after

en • tail (in tāl´) *v.*, pass on

en • tice (en tīs´) *v.*, tempt

en • treat (en trēt´) *v.*, beg

equiv • o • ca • tor (i kwi´ və kā' tər) *n.*, one who speaks ambiguously

es • ca • pade (es´ kə pād') *n.*, reckless adventure

es • teem (i stēm´) *v.*, think well of

ethe • re • al (i thir´ ē əl) *adj.*, not earthly; heavenly; celestial

ex • as • per • a • tion (ig zas' pə rā´ shən) *n.*, state of being irritated or annoyed

ex • hort (ig zôrt´) *v.*, warn; plead with

ex • hor • ta • tion (ek' sôr' tā´ shən) *n.*, strong urging

ex • pos • tu • late (ik späs´ chə lāt') *v.*, speak or discuss with the purpose of dissuading or repri-manding

ex • ult • ing (ig zul´ tiŋ) *adj.*, filled with joy; rejoicing

F

fam • ine (fa´ mən) *n.*, widespread shortage of food

fe • li • ci • ty (fi li´ sə tē) *n.*, happiness

fer • vent (fər´ vənt) *adj.*, characterized by strong feeling

fet • ter (fe´ tər) *v.*, bind using chains or shackles

fil • ial (fil´ yəl *or* fi´ lē əl) *adj.*, of, relating to, or befitting a son or daughter

fir • ma • ment (fur´ mə mənt) *n.*, sky

flecked (flekt) *adj.*, spotted or covered with spots

flout (flout) *v.*, show scorn or contempt for

for • lorn (fər lôrn´) *adj.*, sad; lonely

for • mi • da • ble (fôr´ mə də bəl) *adj.*, hard to overcome

fraught (frôt) *adj.*, accompanied by (used with the word *with*)

fru • gal (frü´ gəl) *adj.*, characterized by economy in the use of resources

fum • ble (fəm´ bəl) *v.*, handle clumsily

fu • ne • re • al (fyün´ rəl) *adj.*, befitting or sug-gesting a funeral

fu • til • i • ty (fyü ti´ lə tē) *n.*, state or quality of being completely ineffective

G

gall (gôl) *n.*, bitterness

gar • ish (ger´ ish) *adj.*, offensively or distressingly bright

gar • ru • lous (ger´ ə ləs) *adj.*, talkative

gaunt (gônt) *adj.*, haggard; emaciated

ge • nial (jēn´ nē əl) *adj.*, friendly and pleasant

ghast • ly (gast´ lē) *adj.*, horrible; ghostlike

glim • mer (gli´ mər) *v.*, shine or sparkle unsteadily

grav • en (grā´ vən) *adj.*, engraved

guf • faw (gu´ fô') *v.*, let out a short burst of laugh-ter

gulf (gulf) *n.*, wide gap

gut • ter (gu´ tər) *v.*, gurgle and sputter

H

hag • gard (ha´ gərd) *adj.*, worn, pale, and exhausted

hap • less (ha´ pləs) *adj.*, having no luck

har • bin • ger (här´ bən jər) *n.*, person or thing that comes before and hints at what is to follow

her • mi • tage (hər´ mə tij) *n.*, secluded resi-dence or private retreat

hoary (hôr´ ē) *adj.*, gray or white with age; extremely old

home • ly (hōm´ lē) *adj.*, simple; unpretentious

hov • el (hô´ vəl) *n.*, shed or hut

per • verse • ly (pʉr['] vʉrs´ lē) *adv.*, in a contrary or disagreeable manner

pes • ti • lence (pes´ tə lən[t]s) *n.*, virulent or infectious disease of epidemic proportions

pin • na • cle (pi´ ni kəl) *n.*, highest point of development or achievement

plain • tive (plān´ tiv) *adj.*, sorrowful; grieving

pli • a • bility (plī´ ə bil´ ə tē) *n.*, flexibility; state of being easily influenced

pli • able (plī´ ə bəl) *adj.*, yields easily to others

plight (plīt) *n.*, unfortunate situation

plight (plīt) *v.*, engage in

pos • ter • i • ty (pä ster´ ə tē) *n.*, succeeding generations

pre • cept (prē´ sept) *n.*, commandment or direction meant as a rule of action or conduct

prel • ate (pre´ lət) *n.*, high-ranking member of the clergy

pre • text (prē´ tekst') *n.*, appearance assumed in order to disguise the truth

pre • vail (pri vāl´) *v.*, be greater in influence or strength

pre • var • i • ca • tion (pri ver ə kā´ shən) *n.*, lie; falsehood

pro • di • gious (prə di´ jəs) *adj.*, amazing; huge; exceptionally large or numerous

pro • fuse (prō fyüs´) *adj.*, plentiful; freely flowing

pro • mis • cu • ous (prə mis´ kyə wəs) *adj.*, made up of assorted people or things; indiscriminate

prom • on • to • ry (prä´ mən tôr' ē) *n.*, peak of land that juts into water

pro • pound (prə paùnd´) *v.*, put forth for consideration

pro • pri • e • ty (prə prī´ ə tē) *n.*, quality of acting in a proper or socially correct manner

pro • sa • ic (prō zā´ ik) *adj.*, ordinary

pros • trate (prä´ strāt') *adj.*, completely overcome and lacking the will or power to rise; lying face down in submission

pro • trude (prō trüd´) *v.*, project; stick out from

prov • i • dence (prä´ və dənts) *n.*, benevolent guidance

pro • voke (prə vōk´) *v.*, stir up action or feeling

pru • dent (prü´ d'nt) *adj.*, discreet or careful

pry (prī) *v.*, look at closely or curiously

pue • rile (pyür´ əl) *adj.*, childish; immature

pun • gent (pun´ jənt) *adj.*, sharply painful

purge (pʉrj) *v.*, cleanse or rid of impurities and other undesirable elements

pur • vey • or (pʉr' vā´ ər) *n.*, one who supplies or provides

R

ra • di • ant (rā´ dē ənt) *adj.*, shining or glowing brightly

rai • ment (rā´ mənt) *n.*, clothing; garments

ran • cid (ran[t]´ səd) *adj.*, having a bad smell or taste

ran • cor (raŋ´ kər) *n.*, bitter, deep-seated ill will

rav • e • nous (ra´ və nəs) *adj.*, eager or greedy for satisfaction or pleasure

rec • om • pense (re´ kəm pen[t]s') *n.*, repayment; reward

re • course (rē´ kôrs') *n.*, turning to someone for help or protection

re • dress (ri dres´) *n.*, compensation for wrongdoing

rel • ish (rel´ ish) *v.*, enjoy; like

re • mon • strate (re´ mən strāt') *v.*, say in protest; object to

re • morse (ri môrs´) *n.*, pity; compassion

rend (rend) *v.*, rip apart

re • nown (ri noun´) *n.*, fame

re • pose (ri pōz´) *v.*, lie quietly; rest

re • proach • ful (ri prōch´ fəl) *adj.*, disapproving

re • proof (ri prüf´) *n.*, criticism

re • prove (ri prüv´) *v.*, correct; scold

re • pug • nant (ri pug´ nənt) *adj.*, repulsive; disgusting

re • qui • em (re´ kwē əm) *n.*, song for the dead

res • o • lute (re´ zə lüt') *adj.*, marked by firm determination

re • tal • i • ate (ri ta´ lē āt') *v.*, respond, especially with stronger force

re • vile (ri vīl´) *v.*, subject to verbal abuse

rev • er • ent • ly (rev´ rənt lē) *adv.*, with great respect or worship

righ • teous • ness (rī´ chəs nəs) *n.*, condition of being morally right or justifiable; being free from guilt or sin

ri • o • tous (rī´ ə təs) *adj.*, unrestrained; disorderly

ru • di • ment (rü´ də mənt) *n.*, basic principle or element

rue (rü) *n.*, sorrow; regret

S

san • guine (san´ gwən) *adj.*, ruddy, red; happy

sa • ti • e • ty (sə tī´ ə tē) *n.*, state of being full or satisfied

sat • i • rize (sa´ tə rīz') *v.*, attack or ridicule with satire

scorn (skôrn) *v.*, view with contempt

scru • ples (skrü´ pəlz) *n.*, doubts; qualms

scru • pu • los • i • ty (skrü pyə lä´ sə tē) *n.*, moral worry or concern

scru • pu • lous (skrü´ pyə ləs) *adj.*, extremely careful; possessing moral integrity; upright

se • clud • ed (si klüd´ əd) *adj.*, hidden from public view

sec • u • lar (se´ kyə lər) *adj.*, of the world; not sacred or religious

seg • ment • ed (seg´ men təd) *adj.*, divided into sections

self- • pos • sessed (self pə zesd´) *adj.*, in full control of one's feelings and actions

sem • blance (sem´ blən[t]s) *n.*, image; appearance

se • nil • i • ty (si ni´ lə tē) *n.*, physical and mental infirmity of old age

sep • ul • chre (se´ pəl kər) *n.*, burial vault or tomb

se • rene • ly (sə rēn´ lē) *adv.*, calmly and with repose; peacefully

si • new (sin´ yü[']) *n.*, tendon or nerve

sin • is • ter (si´ nəs tər) *adj.*, evil or ominous

sloth (slôth) *n.*, laziness

slouch (slouch) *v.*, reluctantly and slowly move forward

so • lic • it (sə li´ sət) *v.*, ask or seek pleadingly

so • lic • i • tous (sə li´ sə təs) *adj.*, showing concern

sor • did (sôr´ dəd) *adj.*, dirty; filthy; horrible; wretched; disgusting

sov • er • eign (sä´ və rən) *adj.*, above or superior to all others; greatest; supreme

spe • cious (spē´ shəs) *adj.*, seeming sound or logical while not really being so

splay (splā) *v.*, cause to spread out

spoils (spoi´ 'lz) *n.*, arms, money, or goods taken from a defeated foe

sprite (sprīt) *n.*, soul or ghost

spurn (spərn) *v.*, reject

squal • id (skwä´ ləd) *adj.*, dirty; marked by filthiness from neglect or poverty

stag • na • tion (stag nā´ shən) *n.*, state of no progress or development

stanch • less or (stänch´ ləs) *adj.*, unstoppable (modern form: *staunchless*)

stealth • i • ly (stel´ thə lē) *adv.*, slowly and secretly

stealthy (stel´ thē) *adj.*, furtive, sly

steep (stēp) *v.*, soak; immerse

stip • ple (sti´ pəl) *adj.*, fleck; speckle

stip • u • late (sti´ pyə lāt') *v.*, specify conditions of an agreement

stri • dent • ly (strī´ d'nt) *adv.*, in a harsh, insistent manner

strife (strīf) *n.*, contention; act of striving or vying

sub • lime (sə blīm´) *adj.*, majestic

suf • fice (sə fīs´) *v.*, satisfy

sul • len (su´ lən) *adj.*, gloomily or resentfully silent or repressed

su • per • cil • ious • ly (sü' pər si´ lē əs lē) *adv.*, in a cool and haughty manner

su • per • flu • i • ty (sü pər´ flü ə tē) *n.*, something unnecessary or extra

sup • plant (sə plant´) *v.*, take the place of and serve as a substitute for

sur • feit (sər´ fət) *n.*, overabundance

sur • ly (sər´ lē) *adj.*, rude; irritable

sur • mise (sər mīz´) *v.*, conclude; speculate

sur • mise (sər mīz´) *n.*, guessing; imagined action

swar • thy (swôr´ thē) *adj.*, having a dark color or complexion

T

taint (tānt) *v.*, infect

tar • ry (ter´ ē) *v.*, delay

te • dious (tē´ dē əs) *adj.*, boring; tiresome

teem (tēm) *v.*, bring forth

teem • ing (tē´ min) *adj.*, overflowing

te • mer • i • ty (tə mer´ ə tē) *n.*, foolish or rash boldness

tem • po • ral (tem´ pər 'l) *adj.*, lasting only for a time, limited; of this world, not spiritual

tor • tu • ous (tôrch´ rəs) *adj.*, twisting; oddly shaped

tran • quil (tran´ kwəl) *adj.*, peaceful; calm

trans • fixed (tran[t]s fiksed´) *adj.*, motionless; fixed in one position

trans • gress (tranz gres´) *v.*, violate a command or law

tra • vail (trə vāl´) *n.*, very hard work

treach • ery (treˊ chə rē) *n.*, treason

trem • u • lous (tremˊ yə ləs) *adj.*, trembling

trib • u • la • tion (tri' byü lāˊ shən) *n.*, deep sorrow, distress; suffering

trib • ute (triˊ byüt) *n.*, regular payment of money or goods made by one ruler or nation to another as acknowledgment of servitude, for protection from invasion, and so on

tri • fle (trīˊ fəl) *n.*, something of little value or importance

tu • mult (tüˊ mult') *n.*, loud commotion; agitation

tur • bid (tʉrˊ bəd) *adj.*, muddled

U

un • can • ny (un' kaˊ nē) *adj.*, seeming to have a supernatural or mysterious quality

un • de • filed (un də fīldˊ) *adj.*, unspoiled; honorable

un • pre • med • i • ta • ted (un prē medˊ ə tā' təd) *adj.*, unplanned; spontaneous

un • re • lent • ing (un' ri lenˊ tiŋ) *adj.*, not weakening in determination; firm

un • re • quit • ed (un' ri kwīˊ təd) *adj.*, not returned

un • scru • pu • lous (ən' skrüˊ pyə ləs) *adj.*, unprincipled

un • whole • some (un' hōlˊsəm) *adj.*, harmful to the physical or mental well-being

usurp (yʉ sərpˊ) *v.*, seize unlawfully, as a throne or other seat of power

usurp • er (yü sʉrˊ pər) *n.*, one who assumes power without right

V

va • cu • i • ty (va kyüˊ ə tē) *n.*, emptiness; absence of sense or meaning

va • grant (vāˊ grənt) *adj.*, nomadic; wandering

vain • ly (vānˊ lē) *adv.*, uselessly

va • lance (vaˊ lən[t]s) *n.*, canopy or drapery hung along an edge

vap • id (vaˊ pəd) *adj.*, lacking liveliness, zest, or interest

vast (vast) *adj.*, enormous; huge

vaunt (vônt) *n.*, a bragging statement; boast

ven • er • a • tion (ve' nə rāˊ shən) *n.*, respect or awe caused by a person's age, status, or accomplishments

ver • dant (verˊ d'nt) *adj.*, green

ver • dur • ous (verˊ jə rəs) *adj.*, green with thick plant growth

ver • i • ty (verˊ ə tē) *n.*, truthfulness

ver • nal (vʉrˊ n'l) *adj.*, having to do with spring

vex (veks) *v.*, agitate; irritate; bring trouble or distress

vin • di • cate (vinˊ də kātˊ) *v.*, justify or defend

vir • tu • ous (vərˊ chə wəs) *adj.*, morally excellent; righteous

vis • age (viˊ zij) *n.*, face

vi • va • cious (vī vāˊ shəs) *adj.*, filled with animation and spirit

vo • ra • cious (vô rāˊ shəs) *adj.*, having a huge appetite

W

wan (wän) *adj.*, pale, faint

wane (wān) *v.*, lose strength

wan • ton (wänˊ t'n) *adj.*, luxuriant

wary (werˊ ē) *adj.*, cautious; careful

whorled (wôrˊ 'ld) *adj.*, coiled

with • er (withˊ ər) *v.*, wilt and shrivel

wit • ty (wiˊ tē) *adj.*, imaginative; clever

wrought (rôt) *adj.*, worked

wry • ly (rīˊ lē) *adv.*, in a bent or twisted shape or condition

Y

yearn (yʉrn) *v.*, filled with longing

Z

ze • nith (zēˊ nəth) *n.*, highest point in the sky

Literary Acknowledgments

Gillon Aitken Associates Limited. "B. Wordsworth" by V. S. Naipaul from *Miguel Street* by V. S. Naipaul. Copyright © 1959 by V. S. Naipaul. Used by permission of Gillon Aitken Associates Limited.

Karen Asp. "Cardiac Arrest in Healthy, Young Athletes" by Karen Asp. Reprinted by permission of the author.

Vera Brittain Estate. Excerpt from *Testament of Experience* by Vera Brittain is included by permission of Mark Bostridge and Timothy Brittain-Catlin, Literary Executors of the Vera Brittain Estate, 1970.

Carcanet Press Limited. "War Poet" from *The Collected Poems of Sidney Keyes.* Edited with an Introductory Memoir and Notes by Michael Meyer, 1945. Used by permission of Carcanet Press Limited.

Columbia University Press. "Elizabeth I, Queen of England" published by Columbia Encyclopedia, Sixth edition 2001–05. Copyright © 2007 by Columbia University Press. Reprinted by permission of Columbia University Press.

Stephen Cook. "Simply Divine" by Stephen Cook, as appeared in *The Guardian,* April 27, 2002. Used by permission of the author.

Harlan Davidson Inc. Poem Sonnet 1 from *Petrarch, Selected Sonnets, Odes and Letters,* edited by Thomas G. Bergin (Crofts Classics Series) pp. 19, 40, 413. Copyright © 1966 by Harlan Davidson, Inc. Reprinted by permission.

Anita Desai. From *Games at Twilight and Other Stories* by Anita Desai. Copyright © 1978 by Anita Desai. Reproduced by permission of the author c/o Rogers, Coleridge & White Ltd., 20 Powis Mews, London W11 1JN.

Farrar, Straus and Giroux, LLC. "Digging" from *Opened Ground: Selected Poems 1966–1996* by Seamus Heaney. Copyright © 1998 by Seamus Heaney. Reprinted by permission of Farrar, Straus and Giroux, LLC. "Follower" from *Poems 1965–1975* by Seamus Heaney. Copyright © 1980 by Seamus Heaney. Reprinted by permission of Farrar, Straus and Giroux, LLC. "Home Is So Sad" from *Collected Poems* by Philip Larkin. Copyright © 1988, 2003 by the Estate of Philip Larkin. Reprinted by permission of Farrar, Straus and Giroux, LLC. "The Horses" from *Complete Poems* by Ted Hughes. Copyright © 2003 by The Estate of Ted Hughes. Reprinted by permission of Farrar, Straus, & Giroux LLC. Excerpt from "Midsummer XXIII" from *Collected Poems 1948–1984* by Derek Walcott. Copyright © 1986 by Derek Walcott. Reprinted by permission of Farrar, Straus and Giroux, LLC. Excerpt from "The Music of Poetry" from *On Poetry and Poets* by T. S. Eliot. Copyright © 1957 by T. S. Eliot. Copyright renewed © 1985 by Valerie Eliot. Reprinted by permission of Farrar, Straus and Giroux, LLC. "Words" from *The Complete Poems* by Keith Douglas. Copyright © 2000. Used by permission of Faber and Faber, Inc., an affiliate of Farrar, Straus and Giroux, LLC.

John Felstiner. "I Explain a Few Things" by Pablo Neruda, translated by John Felstiner. Reprinted by permission of the translator.

Ruth Folit. "Ten Steps to Keeping an On-Going Journal" by Ruth Folit from www.writedirections.com. Copyright © 2001–2007 Ruth Folit. All rights reserved in all media. Reprinted by permission of the author.

Grove/Atlantic, Inc. From "That's All" from *Complete Plays: Three* by Harold Pinter. Copyright © 1966 by H. Pinter Ltd. Used by permission of Grove/Atlantic, Inc.

Harcourt, Inc. "1823: To Julian Bell" from *The Letters of Virginia Woolf III* by Virginia Woolf. Reprinted by permission of Harcourt, Inc. Excerpts from *A Room of One's Own* by Virginia Woolf. Copyright 1929 by Harcourt, Inc. and renewed 1957 by Leonard Woolf, reprinted by permission of the publisher. "Shooting an Elephant" from *Shooting an Elephant and Other Essays* by George Orwell. Copyright 1950 by Sonia Brownell Orwell and renewed by 1978 by Sonia Pitt-Rivers, reprinted by permission of Harcourt, Inc. "The Hollow Men" and "Preludes" from *Collected Poems 1909–1962* by T. S. Eliot. Copyright 1936 by Harcourt, Inc. Copyright © 1964, 1963 by T. S. Eliot, reprinted by permission of the publisher.

HarperCollins Publishers. "Sparrows" from *The Real Thing* by Doris Lessing. Copyright © 1987 by Doris Lessing. Reprinted by permission of HarperCollins Publishers.

Houghton Mifflin Company. "The Head of Humbaba," from *Gilgamesh: A Verse Narrative* by Herbert Mason. Copyright © 1970 by Herbert Mason. Reprinted by permission of Houghton Mifflin Company. All rights reserved. "The Moment" from

John Middleton Murry. Used by permission of Alfred A. Knopf, a division of Random House, Inc.

Routledge/Taylor & Francis Group, LLC. Used with permission of Routledge/Taylor & Francis Group, LLC. "The Honeysuckle: Chevrefoil" by Marie de France from *The Writings of Medieval Women* translated by Marcelle Thiébaux, 1994. Permission conveyed through Copyright Clearance Center, Inc. "The Wife's Lament," Anonymous. Copyright © 1994 from *The Writings of Medieval Women* translated by Marcelle Thiébaux, Garland Library of Medieval Literature. Reproduced by permission of Routledge/Taylor & Francis Group, LLC.

Russell & Volkening, Inc. "Train from Rhodesia" from *Selected Stories* by Nadine Gordimer. Copyright © 1950 by Nadine Gordimer, renewed in 1978 by Nadine Gordimer. Reprinted by permission of Russell & Volkening as agents for the author.

Simon & Schuster Publishing. "No Witchcraft for Sale" Doris Lessing. Reprinted with permission of Simon & Schuster Adult Publishing Group from *African Stories* by Doris Lessing. Copyright © 1951, 1953, 1954, 1957, 1958, 1962, 1963, 1964, 1965, 1977, 1981 by Doris Lessing. "Sailing to Byzantium," "The Second Coming," reprinted with the permission of Scribner, an imprint of Simon & Schuster Adult Publishing Group, from *The Collected Works of W. B. Yeats, Volume I: The Poems, Revised,* edited by Richard J. Finneran. Copyright 1924 by The Macmillan Company. Copyright renewed © 1952 by Bertha Georgie Yeats.

Special Rider Music. Lyrics "A Hard Rain's A-Gonna Fall" by Bob Dylan. Copyright © 1963; renewed 1991 by Special Rider Music. Reprinted by permission of Special Rider Music.

The University of Chicago. Excerpts from "Sir Gawain and the Green Knight" from *Complete Works of the Gawain Poet,* translated by John Gardner, 1965. Used by permission of The University of Chicago Press.

Ed Victor Ltd. "What I Expected" from *Collected Poems 1928–1985* by Stephen Spender. Reprinted by permission of Ed Victor Ltd on behalf of the The Estate of Stephen Spender.

Yale University Press. "Riddle 1," "Riddle 2," "Riddle 14," "Riddle 15," "Riddle 47," "Riddle 57," and "The Seafarer" from *Poems and Prose from the Old English,* translated by Burton Raffel, 1998. Reprinted by permission of Yale University Press.

Art and Photo Credits

Cover
(top left) © Bettmann/CORBIS; (top right) © Marc Moritsch/National Geographic/Getty Images; (bottom left) Erich Lessing/Art Resource, NY; (bottom right) Photo by Asif Akbar; (spine) Erich Lessing/Art Resource, NY

Tables of Contents
viii (middle left) © Reed Kaestner/CORBIS; (bottom) Jamesgroup/www.stockxpert.com; **ix** (second from top) © Bridgeman Art Library, London/SuperStock; (bottom) Erich Lessing/Art Resource, NY; **x** (bottom) Detail of an animal head carving, from a sledge found with the Oseberg ship (wood), Viking, (9th century)/Viking Ship Museum, Oslo, Norway/ The Bridgeman Art Library; **xi** (top) © Ted Spiegel/ CORBIS; **xii** (bottom) Roy 18 D II f.148 Lydgate and the Canterbury Pilgrims Leaving Canterbury from the 'Troy Book and the Siege of Thebes' by John Lydgate (c. 1370–c. 1451) 1412–22 (vellum) (detail of 8063), English School, (15th century)/British Library, London, UK, © British Library Board. All Rights Reserved/ The Bridgeman Art Library; **xiii** (bottom) Chaucer, the Knight and the Squire from 'The Pardoner's Prologue' of 'The Canterbury Tales,' Mileham, Harry (1873–1957)/Private Collection/The Bridgeman Art Library; **xiv** (bottom) Library of Congress; **xv** (middle) The Granger Collection, New York; (bottom) © SuperStock, Inc./SuperStock; **xvi** (top) Library of Congress; (bottom) Photo by Jolanta Nietrzpiel; **xvii** (top) Photo by G & A Scholiers; **xviii** (bottom) © Stock Montage/SuperStock; **xix** (middle) The Granger Collection, New York; (bottom) © age fotostock/ SuperStock; **xx** (bottom) Photo by Colin Parsons; **xxi** (top) Photo by Dawn Allyn; (middle) The Granger Collection, New York; (bottom) © Roger Tidman/ CORBIS; **xxiii** (top) galdzer/www.stockxpert.com; **xxv** (top) The Granger Collection, New York; **xxvii** (top) © Colin Garratt; **xxx** Mariano Heluani/www.stockxpert. com

Unit 1

1 The Granger Collection, New York; **2** (top right) © Gianni Dagli Orti/CORBIS; **3** (top left) © Bettmann/ CORBIS; **4** (bottom left) © Christophe Boisvieux/ CORBIS; **10** (top) © Fine Art Photographic Library/ CORBIS; **11** © Fine Art Photographic Library/ CORBIS; **14** Inspiration of Caedmon (fl.670), Pocock, Lexden L. (1850–1919)/© Cheltenham Art Gallery & Museums, Gloucestershire, UK/The Bridgeman Art Library; **16** © Photodisc/SuperStock; **21** (top left) The Granger Collection, New York; (top right) The Granger Collection, New York; **22** (top left) Erich Lessing/Art Resource, NY; (top right) Erich Lessing/Art Resource, NY; **23** (top) Norrkoping Art Museum, Sweden; (bottom) Detail of an animal head carving, from a sledge found with the Oseberg ship (wood), Viking, (9th century)/Viking Ship Museum, Oslo, Norway/The Bridgeman Art Library; **25** Norrkoping Art Museum, Sweden; **33** Detail of an animal head carving, from a sledge found with the Oseberg ship (wood), Viking, (9th century)/Viking Ship Museum, Oslo, Norway/The Bridgeman Art Library; **39** © Stapleton Collection/ CORBIS; **41** © British Museum/Art Resource, NY; **45** Courtesy of Photofest; **49** © Viviane Moos/CORBIS; **52** Foto Marburg/Art Resource, NY; **56** © Erich Lessing/Art Resource, NY; **57** © Gianni Dagli Orti/ CORBIS; **60** Knudsens-Giraudon/Art Resource, NY; **61** © Ted Spiegel/CORBIS; **62** © Bettmann/CORBIS; **69** © Ted Spiegel/CORBIS; **73** © Bettmann/CORBIS; **74** The Board of Trinity College, Dublin; **76** Book cover *The Epic of Gilgamesh* translated by N. K. Sanders. Copyright © 1960, 1964, 1972 by N. K. Sanders. Reprinted by permission of Penguin Group (UK) Ltd; Book cover *Grendel* by John Gardner. Copyright © 1971 by John Grendel. Reprinted by permission of Random House, Inc.; Book cover *Beowulf, A New Verse Translation* by Seamus Heaney. Reprinted by permission of W. W. Norton and Company; "Book cover" copyright © 2006, from *A Needle in the Right Hand of God* by R. Howard Bloch. Used by permission of Random House, Inc.; Book cover *Sarum: The Novel of England* by Edward Rutherford. Copyright © 1987 by Edward Rutherford. Reprinted by permission of Random House, Inc.; Jacket book cover from *How the Irish Saved Civilization* by Thomas Cahill. Used by permission of Doubleday, a division of Random House, Inc.; **80** © Christopher Felver/CORBIS

Unit 2

90–91 © National Gallery Collection; By kind permission of the Trustees of the National Gallery, London/ CORBIS; **92** (middle left) Tony Bagget/www.stockxpert.com; (bottom left) © Smithsonian Institution/ CORBIS; **93** (middle right) HIP/Art Resource, NY; **95** (bottom left) © Department of the Environment, London, England/Bridgeman Art Library, London/ SuperStock; **96** (bottom right) King Henry VI of England at Towton, 1860 (oil on board), Dyce, William (1806-64)/© Guildhall Art Gallery, City of London/ The Bridgeman Art Library; **99** © Reed Kaestner/ CORBIS; **100** (top left) © Elio Ciol/CORBIS; (top

Glyn S. Burgess and Keith Busby, 1986, 1999; Book cover *Murder in the Cathedral* by T. S. Eliot, copyright © 1935 by Harcourt, Inc. and renewed 1963 by T. S. Eliot, reprinted by permission of the publisher; Book cover *Le Morte D' Arthur* by Sir Thomas Malory. Reprinted by permission of Penguin Group (UK) Ltd.; Book cover *The Book of Margery Kempe* translated and edited by Lynn Staley. Reprinted by permission of W. W. Norton & Company, Inc.; **223** Library of Congress

Unit 3

228–229 Erich Lessing/Art Resource, NY; **230** (middle left) Paul Cowan/www.stockxpert.com; (bottom right) Courtesy of NASA; **232** (bottom right) The Granger Collection, New York; **234** (bottom right) The Granger Collection, New York; **237** Victoria and Albert Museum, London/Art Resource, NY; **239** © National Maritime Museum, Greenwich, London; **247** (top left and middle) The Granger Collection, New York; (top right) Library of Congress; **248** (top) After the Hunt, c.1644, Dujardin, Karel (c.1622-78)/Michaelis Collection, Cape Town, South Africa/The Bridgeman Art Library; (middle and bottom left) The Granger Collection, New York; **249** After the Hunt, c.1644, Dujardin, Karel (c.1622-78)/Michaelis Collection, Cape Town, South Africa/The Bridgeman Art Library; **250** Unrequited Love (coloured print), Anonymous/O'Shea Gallery, London, UK/The Bridgeman Art Library; **253** © Stock Montage/SuperStock; **254** Lady with Book of Verse by Petrarch, c.1514 (oil on panel), Sarto, Andrea del (1486-1530)/Galleria degli Uffizi, Florence, Italy/The Bridgeman Art Library; **255** (top) © Fine Art Photographic Library/CORBIS; (bottom) © Bettmann/CORBIS; **256** © Fine Art Photographic Library/CORBIS; **260** (all) Library of Congress; **261–262** © The Irish Image Collection/CORBIS; **263** © Fine Art Photographic Library/SuperStock; **264** The Sonnet, 1839 (oil on panel), Mulready, William (1786–1863)/Victoria & Albert Museum, London, UK/The Bridgeman Art Library; **265** The Sonnet, 1839 (oil on panel), Mulready, William (1786–1863)/Victoria & Albert Museum, London, UK/ The Bridgeman Art Library; **267** Library of Congress; **269** (top) (detail) © Manchester City Art Gallery, England/A.K.G., Berlin/SuperStock; (middle left) The Granger Collection, New York; (bottom left) Library of Congress; **270** © Manchester City Art Gallery, England/A.K.G., Berlin/SuperStock; **271** © Fine Art Photographic Library/CORBIS; **274** (top) © Araldo de Luca/CORBIS; (bottom) The Granger Collection, New York; **275** © Araldo de Luca/CORBIS; **276** The Sick Child, c. 1820. Jean Augustin Franquelin. Private collection. (See detail on page 276)/© The Gallery Collection/CORBIS; **277** (left) Duke Ellington

(1899-1974) (b/w photo), American Photographer, (20th century)/Private Collection,/The Bridgeman Art Library; (right) © Hulton-Deutsch Collection/CORBIS; **278** The Gallery Collection/CORBIS; **280** © Fine Art Photographic Library/CORBIS; **281** © Fine Art Photographic Library/CORBIS; **282** (top) © SuperStock, Inc./SuperStock; **283** © SuperStock, Inc./SuperStock; **285** © State Hermitage Museum, St. Petersburg, Russia/SuperStock; **289** (top) © Gustavo Tomsich/CORBIS; **290** © Gustavo Tomsich/CORBIS; **291** Library of Congress; **294** (Left and Right) The Granger Collection, New York; **295** (bottom) Courtesy of NASA; **298** © Brooklyn Museum/CORBIS; **299** Library of Congress; **305** (top) © Alinari Archives/CORBIS; (middle left) © Bettmann/CORBIS; **306** © Alinari Archives/CORBIS; **308** The Granger Collection, New York; **309** Erich Lessing/Art Resource, NY; **312** The Granger Collection, New York; **318** Book cover *A Man for All Seasons* by Robert Bolt. Copyright © 1960, 1962. Used by permission of Random House, Inc.; Book cover *Queen of Scots: The True Life of Mary Stuart* by John Guy. Copyright © 2004 by John Guy. Reprinted by permission of Houghton Mifflin Company. All rights reserved; Book cover *Elizabeth I* by Anne Somerset. Copyright © 1991 by Anne Somerset. Reprinted by permission of Random House, Inc.; Book cover *Will in the World: How Shakespeare Became Shakespeare* by Stephen Greenblatt. Copyright © 2004 by Stephen Greenblatt. Reprinted by permission of W. W. Norton & Company, Inc.; Book cover *God's Secretaries: The Making of the King James Bible* by Adam Nicolson. Copyright © 2003 by Adam Nicolson. Reprinted by permission of HarperCollins Publishers.; Book cover *Renaissance Women Poets* edited by Danielle Clarke. Reprinted by permission of Penguin Group (USA) Inc. **322** © Bettmann/CORBIS

Unit 4

330–331 Banquet Scene from 'Macbeth,' 1840 (oil on canvas), Maclise, Daniel (1806–70)/© Guildhall Art Gallery, City of London/The Bridgeman Art Library; **332** (top left) Henk Jan Kwant; (top right) Photo by Sanja Gjenero; (bottom left) Library of Congress; **333** (bottom left) Mariano Heluani/www. stockxpert.com; (bottom right) WDesigns/www. stockxpert.com; **334** (top middle) Photo by Stephen J. Sullivan; (bottom) © Hulton Archive/Getty Image; **336** (bottom) © Adam Woolfitt/CORBIS; **338** (top right) Library of Congress; **340** (top) Erich Lessing/ Art Resource, NY; (middle left) Library of Congress; (bottom) © Andrew Fox/CORBIS/CORBIS; **342** Erich Lessing/Art Resource, NY; **345** © Robbie Jack/ CORBIS; **347** The Granger Collection, New York; **350** Victoria & Albert Museum, London/Art Resource,

NY; **361** (top) Victoria & Albert Museum, London/ Art Resource, NY; (bottom) Michael Quinton/Getty Images; **362** Victoria & Albert Museum, London/ Art Resource, NY; **365** © Creatas/SuperStock; **368** Victoria & Albert Museum, London/Art Resource, NY; **374** Photo by Dawn Allyn; **377** (top) Lady Macbeth approaching the murdered Duncan (ink and wash), Blake, William (1757–1827)/Private Collection, © Agnew's, London, UK/The Bridgeman Art Library; (bottom) Macbeth, Banquo and the Three Witches, illustration for a scene from 'Macbeth' by William Shakespeare (1564-1616) (woodcut) (b/w photo), English School, (17th century)/Private Collection,/The Bridgeman Art Library; **378** Lady Macbeth approaching the murdered Duncan (ink and wash), Blake, William (1757–1827)/Private Collection, © Agnew's, London, UK/The Bridgeman Art Library; **388** Tate Gallery, London/Art Resource, NY; **393** (bottom left) The Granger Collection, New York; **394** Stephen Johnson/Getty Images; **397** G & A Scholiers; **399** (top) © The Witches in Macbeth, c. 1841–42 (oil on canvas), Decamps, Alexandre Gabriel (1803–60)/© Wallace Collection, London, UK/The Bridgeman Art Library; (bottom) The Granger Collection, New York; **400** The Witches in Macbeth, c.1841–42 (oil on canvas), Decamps, Alexandre Gabriel (1803–60)/© Wallace Collection, London, UK/The Bridgeman Art Library; **401** © Hulton-Deutsch Collection/CORBIS; **408** © CORBIS; **416** Jolanta Nietrzpiel; **419** (top) Detail of The Death of Lady Macbeth (pen and ink on paper), Rossetti, Dante Charles Gabriel (1828–82)/© Ashmolean Museum, University of Oxford, UK/The Bridgeman Art Library; (bottom) © Bill_Cooper/ epa/CORBIS; **420** The Death of Lady Macbeth (pen and ink on paper), Rossetti, Dante Charles Gabriel (1828–82)/© Ashmolean Museum, University of Oxford, UK/The Bridgeman Art Library; **424** Library of Congress; **426** Photo by Sophia Lemon; **434** (top left) Photo by Rebecca Quam; (top middle left) Photo by Steven Church; (middle left) Photo by Michal Kralik; **438** Photo by Michal Kralik; **440** © Pixtal/SuperStock; **441** Gary Tamin; **442** (top) © Robert Huberman/SuperStock; (bottom) The Granger Collection, New York; **443** © Robert Huberman/ SuperStock; **451** © Zurbaran Galleria/SuperStock; **453** © Franklin McMahon/CORBIS; **455** © Christie's Images/SuperStock; **456** Nostell Priory, Wakefield, W. Yorkshire, England/SuperStock; **458** Book cover *Midsummer Night's Dream* by William Shakespeare ISBN: 978-1-8049-588-2. Copyright © 2005 Prestwick House. Reprinted by permission of Prestwick House Inc.; Book cover *Volpone or the Fox* by Ben Johnson Reprinted by permission of Yale University Press; Book cover *Shakespeare and Co.: Christopher Marlowe,*

Thomas Dekker, Ben Jonson, Thomas Middleton, John Fletcher and the Other Players in His Story by Stanley Wells. Reprinted by permission of Random House, Inc.; Book cover *Doctor Faustus* by Christopher Marlowe, edited by Sylvan Barnet, copyright © 1969 by Sylvan Barnet. Used by permission fo Dutton Signet, a division of Penguin Group (USA) Inc.; Book cover *Playing Shakespeare: An Actor's Guide* by John Barton. Used by permission of Anchor Books, a division of Random House, Inc.; Book cover *Shakespeare's Globe Rebuilt* edited by J. R. Mulryne and Margaret Shewring. Reprinted by permission of Cambridge University; **461** The Granger Collection, New York

Unit 5

466–467 Tate Gallery, London/Art Resource, NY; **468** (middle left) © National Portrait Gallery, London/SuperStock; **469** (bottom right) gleb/www. stockxpert.com; **470** (top right) Library of Congress; **471** (top left) Jamesgroup/www.stockxpert.com; (top middle) Stephen Coburn/www.stockxpert.com; (bottom) The Granger Collection, New York; **472** (top left) Library of Congress; (top middle right) Library of Congress; (top right) Library of Congress; (bottom) John Freeth and his Circle, 1792 (oil on canvas), Eckstein, John (fl.1787-1838)/© Birmingham Museums and Art Gallery; **473** HIP/Art Resource, NY; **474** (top) © Musee du Louvre, Paris/Lauros-Giraudon, Paris/SuperStock; (bottom) The Granger Collection, New York; **475** © Musee du Louvre, Paris/Lauros-Giraudon, Paris/SuperStock; **476** Rodolfo Clix; **477** (top) (bottom) The Granger Collection, New York; **478** © Pushkin Museum of Fine Arts, Moscow, Russia/ Giraudon, Paris/SuperStock (see detail on page 477); **481** The Wedding Present, 1874 (panel) by Ouderra, Pierre Jan van der (1841–1915) Private Collection/ Photo © Bonhams, London, UK/The Bridgeman Art Library Nationality/copyright status: Belgian/ out of copyright; **482** Mirko Delcaldo; **484** (top) Fine Art Photographic Library, London/Art Resource, NY; (middle left) © Hulton-Deutsch Collection/ CORBIS; (bottom left) The Granger Collection, New York; **485** Fine Art Photographic Library, London/ Art Resource, NY; **486** First Whisper (oil on canvas), Hook, James Clarke (1819–1907)/Private Collection, © Manya Igel Fine Arts, London, UK/ The Bridgeman Art Library; **488** Tracy Toh; **490** (bottom left) The Granger Collection, New York; (bottom right) © Stock Montage/SuperStock; **491** (bottom) © Herbert Kehrer/zefa/CORBIS; **493** Scala/Art Resource, NY; **494** Arjun Kartha; **495** The Granger Collection, New York; **496** The Granger Collection, New York; **498** The Granger Collection, New York; **499** The Granger Collection, New York; **501** Wellsley

College Library; **505** (top right) Alex Bramwell/www.stockxpert.com; **507** © Alinari Archives/CORBIS; **511** (bottom) The Granger Collection, New York; **516** "Plan of the Road from the City of Destruction to the Celestial City, engraved expressly for Williams's Elegant Edition of The Pilgrim's Progress,' 19th century (engraving), Private Collection/The Bridgeman Art Library; **519** © age fotostock/SuperStock; **521** (top) © age fotostock/SuperStock; (bottom) © National Portrait Gallery, London/SuperStock; **522** © age fotostock/SuperStock; **524** © Stock Montage/SuperStock; **526** Victoria & Albert Museum, London/Art Resource, NY; **530** Giraudon/Art Resource, NY; **532** © Stapleton Collection/CORBIS; **535** © Stock Montage/SuperStock; **539** © Bettmann/CORBIS; **540** © Stock Montage/SuperStock; **541** © Arte & Immagini srl/CORBIS; **544** © Bettmann/CORBIS; **546** (top) Fine Art Photographic Library, London/Art Resource, NY; (bottom) The Granger Collection, New York; **547** Fine Art Photographic Library, London/Art Resource, NY; **556** Henk L; **557** Oscar Murillo; **559** © Bettmann/CORBIS; **560** © The Metropolitan Museum of Art/Art Resource, NY; **562** © Michael Nicholson/CORBIS; **563** © Burstein Collection/CORBIS; **564** © Bettmann/CORBIS; **567** © National Gallery Collection; By kind permission of the Trustees of the National Gallery, London/CORBIS; **569** (top left) The Granger Collection, New York; (top middle) The Granger Collection, New York; (top right) The Granger Collection, New York; **570** (top) The Granger Collection, New York; (middle) © Hulton-Deutsch Collection/CORBIS; (bottom) © Pixtal/SuperStock; **571** The Granger Collection, New York; **573** © Bettmann/CORBIS; **575** © Michael Nicholson/CORBIS; **576** © Richard Baker/CORBIS; **579** © SuperStock, Inc./SuperStock; **582** The Granger Collection, New York; **587** © SuperStock, Inc./SuperStock; **589** (top) The Granger Collection; (bottom) The Granger Collection, New York; **590** The Granger Collection, New York; **592** © Historical Picture Archive/CORBIS; **594** sandralise/www.stockxpert.com; **595** (top) © Brooklyn Museum/CORBIS; (bottom) The Granger Collection, New York; **596** © Brooklyn Museum/CORBIS; **600** (top right) Photo by Sanja Gjenero; **605** (bottom) © Hulton-Deutsch Collection/CORBIS; **606** HIP/Art Resource, NY; **610** © Louie Psihoyos/CORBIS; **611** Piotr Bizior; **613** (top) © Fine Art Photographic Library/CORBIS; (bottom) The Granger Collection, New York; **614** © Fine Art Photographic Library/CORBIS; **620** (top) © age fotostock/SuperStock; (bottom) The Granger Collection, New York; **621** © age fotostock/SuperStock; **623** Indian Summer, 1891 (oil on canvas), Inness, George Jnr. (1853–1926)/Private Collection, Photo © Christie's Images/The Bridgeman Art Library; **625** © Brooklyn Museum/CORBIS; **628** Archive Photos; **629** Erich Lessing/Art Resource, NY; **630** Book cover *Waverly, or 'Tis Sixty Years Since* by Sir Walter Scott. Reprinted by permission of Penguin Group (UK) Ltd.; Book cover *Oroonoko: or, the Royal Slave* by Aphra Behn, edited with an introduction and notes by Janet Todd (Penguin Classics, 2003). Editorial matter copyright © Janet Todd, 2003. Reprinted by permission of Penguin Group, Inc.; Book cover *The History of Tom Jones, a Foundling* by Henry Fielding. Reprinted by permission of W. W. Norton Company, Inc.; Book cover *The Way of the World* by William Congreve. Reprinted by permission of A & C Black Publishers Ltd.; Book cover *Journals and Letters of Frances Burney* edited with an introduction and notes by Peter Sabor and lars E. Troide with the assistance of Stewart J. Cooke and Victoria Kortes-Papp (Penguin Books, 2001). This selection Copyright ©Peter Sabor and Lars E. Troide, 2001. Reprinted by permission of Penguin Group, Inc.; Book cover *The Life of Samuel Johnson* by James Boswell. Reprinted by permission of Penguin Classics/Penguin Group (USA), Inc.; **632** Getty Images

Unit 6

642–643 © Geoffrey Clements/CORBIS; **644** (middle right) Library of Congress **645** (top left) © SuperStock, Inc./SuperStock; (top right) Christopher Potter; (bottom left and right) The Granger Collection, New York; **646** (top middle left) Photo by Gary Scott; (top middle) Library of Congress; (top middle right) Photo by David Mora; **647** (top middle) Photo by Daniel Kirwilliam; (top middle right) © SuperStock, Inc./SuperStock; (top right) Photo by Karolina Przybysz; **648** (top left) The Granger Collection, New York; (top middle left) Christian Carollo Photography; (Top Middle) Library of Congress; (top right) The Granger Collection, New York; (bottom) © Stapleton Collection/CORBIS; **649** © Stapleton Collection/CORBIS; **650** (top left) © SuperStock, Inc./SuperStock; (top right) © Stock Montage/SuperStock; **651** (top) © Christie's Images/CORBIS; (bottom) Library of Congress; **652** © Christie's Images/CORBIS; **656** (bottom) © National Portrait Gallery, London/SuperStock; **657** © National Gallery Collection; By kind permission of the Trustees of the National Gallery, London/CORBIS; **658** © age fotostock/SuperStock; **659** Applicants for Admission to a Casual Ward, 1874 (oil on canvas), Fildes, Sir Samuel Luke (1844–1927)/Royal Holloway, University of London/The Bridgeman Art Library; **664** (top) Day Dream, 1880, Rossetti, Dante Charles Gabriel (1828–82)/Victoria & Albert Museum, London, UK/The Bridgeman Art Library; (bottom) The Granger Collection, New York; **665**

Day Dream, 1880, Rossetti, Dante Charles Gabriel (1828–82)/Victoria & Albert Museum, London, UK/ The Bridgeman Art Library; **666** © Peter Harholdt/ CORBIS; **668** © Peter Harholdt/CORBIS; **670** (bottom left) The Granger Collection, New York; (bottom right) The Granger Collection, New York; **671** (top) © Fine Art Photographic Library/CORBIS; **672** Guildhall Art Gallery, City of London; **673** © Fine Art Photographic Library/CORBIS; **674** Photo by Colin Parsons; **675** (top middle right) © Dorothy Burrows; Eye Ubiquitous/CORBIS; (top right) © Bob Krist/CORBIS; (bottom) Photo by Mark Taylor; **679** (bottom) © Frank Blackburn; Ecoscene/CORBIS; **680** Tintern Abbey, Watts, Frederick Waters (1800–62)/Private Collection, © Gavin Graham Gallery, London, UK/The Bridgeman Art Library; **682** Getty Images; **684** Photo by Joe Redfrn; **686** Vince Ed.; **687** (top) Landscape in the Guizhou province in southwestern China. © Keren Su/ CORBIS; (bottom) Library of Congress; **688–689** © Keren Su/CORBIS; **690** © National Palace Museum, Taiwan/ET Archive, London/SuperStock; **691** Head of an Old Man, Baldung Grien, Hans (1484/5-1545)/Galleria e Museo Estense, Modena, Italy/The Bridgeman Art Library; **693** The Granger Collection, New York; **699** The Granger Collection, New York; **704** The Granger Collection, New York; **712** Marco Michelini; **714** The Granger Collection, New York; **717** © Stapleton Collection/CORBIS; **718** (top) Portrait of Lady Caroline Lamb (1785–1828) c. 1827 (oil on canvas), Lawrence, Sir Thomas (1769–1830)/© Bristol City Museum and Art Gallery, UK/The Bridgeman Art Library; (bottom) © National Portrait Gallery, London/SuperStock; **719** Portrait of Lady Caroline Lamb (1785–1828) c. 1827 (oil on canvas), Lawrence, Sir Thomas (1769–1830)/© Bristol City Museum and Art Gallery, UK/The Bridgeman Art Library; **721**© Kunsthalle, Hamburg, Germany/Bridgeman Art Library, London/SuperStock; **722** © National Portrait Gallery, London, England/SuperStock; **723** Kamil Astapczyk; **724** © National Portrait Gallery, London/ SuperStock; **725** (top) © Mike McQueen/CORBIS; (bottom) The Granger Collection, New York; **726** © Mike McQueen/CORBIS; **731** (top) The Rising of the Skylark (oil on board) by Samuel Palmer (1805–81) © National Museum and Gallery of Wales, Cardiff/ The Bridgeman Art Library Nationality/copyright status: English/out of copyright; (bottom) © Roger Tidman/CORBIS; **732** The Rising of the Skylark (oil on board) by Samuel Palmer (1805-81) © National Museum and Gallery of Wales, Cardiff/The Bridgeman Art Library Nationality/copyright status: English/ out of copyright; **735** Hallstatter-See (oil on canvas) by Ferdinand Georg Waldmuller (1793–1865) ©Wien Museum Karlsplatz, Vienna, Austria/The Bridgeman

Art Library Nationality/copyright status: German/out of copyright; **737** Photo by Dawn Allyn; **740** (bottom left) The Granger Collection, New York; (bottom right) © Stock Montage/SuperStock; **741** (top) The Avenue of Chestnut Trees at La Celle-Saint-Cloud, 1867 (oil on canvas), Sisley, Alfred (1839–99)/© Southampton City Art Gallery, Hampshire, UK/The Bridgeman Art Library; (bottom) Corel; **742** The Avenue of Chestnut Trees at La Celle-Saint-Cloud, 1867 (oil on canvas), Sisley, Alfred (1839–99)/© Southampton City Art Gallery, Hampshire, UK/The Bridgeman Art Library; **744** © Roland Gerth/zefa/CORBIS; **746** © Gianni Dagli Orti/CORBIS; **748** © Richard Cummins/ CORBIS; **751** (top left) © Hulton-Deutsch Collection/ CORBIS; (top right) Barnard College Archives; **752** (top) The Granger Collection, New York; (bottom) © Araldo de Luca/CORBIS; **753** The Granger Collection, New York; **755** Photo by Sebastian Niedlich; **757** The Granger Collection, New York; **758** © age fotostock/SuperStock; **759** © National Portrait Gallery/ SuperStock; **760** Illustration from 'Frankenstein' by Mary Shelley (1797–1851) (engraving) (b/w photo), Holst, Theodor M. von (1810–44)/Private Collection/ The Bridgeman Art Library; **762** The Granger Collection, New York; **764** Book cover *The Mysteries of Udolpho* by Ann Radcliffe (1998). Copyright © by Oxford University Press 1966, 1970, 1998. Reprinted by permission of Oxford University Press; Book cover *Mary: The Wrongs of Woman* by Mary Wollstonecraft. Copyright © by Oxford University Press 1976, 2007. Reprinted by permission of Oxford University Press; Book cover *Napoleon* by Felix Markham. Copyright © 1963 by Felix Maurice Hippisley Markham. Reprinted by permission of Penguin Group (USA) Inc.; Book cover *Mary Shelley: Romance and Reality* by Emily W. Sunstein. Reprinted by permission of Little, Brown and Company an imprint of Hachette Book Group.; **766** The Granger Collection, New York

Unit 7

772–773 © Archivo Iconografico, S. A./CORBIS; **774** (top right) Library of Congress; (bottom left) Library of Congress; **775** (middle left) Stephen Coburn/www. stockxpert.com; **776** (top left) Photo by Sophie; (top middle left) © Christie's Images/SuperStock; (top middle) Greg Olsen; (top middle right) Library of Congress; (top right) Library of Congress; (bottom) The Granger Collection, New York; **777** (top left) Photo by Barbara Bar; (top middle left) Library of Congress; (top middle) The Granger Collection, New York; (top middle right) Christie's Images, London/Bridgeman Art Library, London/SuperStock; (top right) Library of Congress; **778** (top left) Library of Congress; (top middle left) Library of Congress; (top middle) Library of Congress;

Introduction and Appendix III © Margaret R. Higonnet, 1998. Notes, A History of the Text and Appendix II ©Tim Dolin, 1998. General Editor's Preface and Chronology © Patricia Ingham, 1996; Book cover *Queen Victoria: An Eminent Illustrated Biography* by Lytton Straachey. Reprinted by permission of Black Dog & Leventhal Publishers Inc.; Book cover *Dracula* by Bram Stoker ISBN: 978-1-58049-382-6. Copyright © 2005 Prestwick House. Reprinted by permission of Prestwick House Inc.; Book cover *Heart of Darkness* by Joseph Conrad ISBN: 978-1-58049-575-2. Copyright © 2005 Prestwick House. Reprinted by permission of Prestwick House Inc.; **917** © Christopher Felver/CORBIS; **919** Library of Congress

Unit 8

926–927 Art: © 2008 Artists Rights Society (ARS), New York/ADAGP, Paris/Photo: © Francis G. Mayer/CORBIS; **928** (bottom right) Library of Congress; **929** (middle left) Library of Congress; (bottom right) Library of Congress; **930** (all) Library of Congress; **931** (top banner) Library of Congress; (bottom) Scala/Art Resource, NY; **932** (top banner) Library of Congress; (bottom) © Bettmann/CORBIS; **933** Scala/Art Resource, NY; **934** (bottom) Library of Congress; **936** © Stapleton Collection/CORBIS; **938** (right) © Design Pics/CORBIS; **940** © Christie's Images/SuperStock; **944** The Abbey Theater in Dublin, Ireland. © Bettmann/CORBIS; **947** (bottom) © Hulton-Deutsch Collection/CORBIS; **949** (top middle left) The Granger Collection, New York; (top middle right) Library of Congress; **950** (all) Library of Congress; **952** (middle) The Granger Collection, New York; (bottom) The Granger Collection, New York **954** © Bettmann/CORBIS; **955** © Hulton-Deutsch Collection/CORBIS; **956** © Hulton-Deutsch Collection/CORBIS; **957** (top middle left) © Hulton-Deutsch Collection/CORBIS; (top middle right) Library of Congress; **958** © Hulton-Deutsch Collection/CORBIS; **962** © Bettmann/CORBIS **964** © Bettmann/CORBIS; **965** Art: © 2008 Estate of Pablo Picasso/Artists Rights Society (ARS), New York/Photo: © Museo Nacional Centro de Arte Reina Sofia, Madrid, Spain/SuperStock; **967** The Granger Collection, New York; **970** © Bettmann/CORBIS **973** © Burstein Collection/CORBIS **974** (left) © Alain Le Garsmeur/CORBIS; (right) The Granger Collection, New York; **975** (top) Mikhail Lavrenov/www.stockxpert.com; **976** Erich Lessing/Art Resource, NY; **978** © Pacific Stock/SuperStock; **979** © Harpur Garden Library/CORBIS; **980** © Harpur Garden Library/CORBIS; **981** © Massimo Listri/CORBIS; **982** © Massimo Listri/CORBIS; **984** © Richard Hamilton Smith/CORBIS; **988** (top) © Ashley Cooper/CORBIS; (middle) The Granger Collection, New York; (bottom) © Steffen Schmidt/epa/CORBIS; **989** © Ashley Cooper/CORBIS; **990** © Bettmann/CORBIS; **922** © Ashley Cooper/CORBIS; **933** © Ashley Cooper/CORBIS; **994** © Steffen Schmidt/epa/CORBIS; **997** (top left) © National Portrait Gallery, London/SuperStock; (top middle) © Bettmann/CORBIS; (top right) © Hulton-Deutsch Collection/CORBIS; **998** (left) Time & Life Pictures/Getty Images; (right) The Granger Collection, New York; **999** (top) Erich Lessing/Art Resource, NY; **1000** Erich Lessing/Art Resource, NY; **1005** (top left) © Hulton-Deutsch Collection/CORBIS; (top right) The Granger Collection, New York; **1006** © Hulton-Deutsch Collection/CORBIS; **1009** (top left) Daniel Radicevic/www.stockxpert.com; (top middle left) The Granger; Collection, New York; (middle left) The Granger Collection, New York; **1014** (all) The Granger Collection, New York; **1015** (bottom) © Bettmann/CORBIS; **1017** The Granger Collection, New York; **1019** (top) The Granger Collection, New York; (bottom) © CORBIS; **1020** The Granger Collection, New York; **1025** © CORBIS; **1026** (top) © National Geographic/SuperStock; (bottom) The Granger Collection, New York; **1027** © National Geographic/SuperStock; **1031** © Bettmann/CORBIS; **1033** © National Geographic/SuperStock; **1034** (top) © Alinari Archives/CORBIS; **1035** © Alinari Archives/CORBIS; **1036** © Bettmann/CORBIS; **1042** © Hulton-Deutsch Collection/CORBIS; **1046** The Granger Collection, New York; **1047** © Christie's Images/SuperStock; **1050** © Graham Salter/Lebrecht Music & Arts/CORBIS; **1052** © Michael Boys/CORBIS; **1057** Art © Estate of Aleksandr Dejneka/RAO, Moscow/VAGA, New York. Photo: Scala/Art Resource, NY; **1058** (top) © Bettmann/CORBIS; (bottom) Library of Congress; **1059** © Bettmann/CORBIS; **1062** © Hulton-Deutsch Collection/CORBIS; **1063** (top left) © Hulton-Deutsch Collection/CORBIS; **1065** © Bettmann/CORBIS; **1069** (top) © Hulton-Deutsch Collection/CORBIS; (bottom) © Bohemian Nomad Picturemakers/CORBIS; **1070** © Hulton-Deutsch Collection/CORBIS; **1074** (top) © The Gallery Collection/CORBIS; (bottom) The Granger Collection, New York; **1075** © The Gallery Collection/CORBIS; **1077** © James Leynse/CORBIS; **1079** Lim Yong Hian/www.stockxpert.com; **1081** (bottom) The Granger Collection, New York; **1084** (bottom) The Granger Collection, New York; **1092** Getty Images; **1093** © CORBIS; **1096** book cover of *The Somme* by Lyn Macdonald (Michael Joseph, 1983). Copyright Lyn Macdonald, 1983. Used by permission of Penguin Group (UK); book cover *Cathleen ni Houlihan* by William Butler Yeats and Lady Augusta Gregory.

Reprinted by permission of Kessinger Publishing, LLC; Book cover *A Portrait of the Artist as a Young Man* by James Joyce ISBN: 978-1-58049-574-5. Copyright © 2005 Prestwick House. Reprinted by permission of Prestwick House Inc; Book cover *James Joyce* by Edna O' Brien, copyright © 1999 by Edna O' Brien. Used by permission of Viking Penguin, a division of Penguin Group (USA) Inc; Book cover *Troublesome Young Men: The Rebels Who Brought Churchill to Power and Helped Save England* by Lynne Olson. Jacket cover copyright © 2007 by Aaron Artesso. Reprinted by permission of Farrar Straus & Giroux, LLC; Book cover *Mrs. Dalloway* by Vigrinia Woolf. © Hulton-Deutsch Collection/Getty Images; **1099** © JP Laffont/Sygma/CORBIS

Unit 9

1104–1105 © Contemporary African Art Collection Limited/CORBIS; **1106** (top right) © Karan Kapoor/CORBIS; (bottom right) Courtesy of NASA; **1107** (top left) © Colin McPherson/CORBIS; **1108** (top middle left) Library of Congress; (top middle) © Bettmann/CORBIS; (top middle right) Library of Congress; **1109** (top middle left) Courtesy of NASA; (top middle) © Bettmann/CORBIS; (top middle right) Library of Congress (bottom) © Bettmann/CORBIS; **1110** (top middle left) Photo European Parliament; (top middle) © TOUHIG SIO/CORBIS SYGMA; (top middle right) © Swim Ink 2, LLC/CORBIS; (top right) © Hulton-Deutsch Collection/CORBIS; (bottom) © Bettmann/CORBIS; **1111** © Chisholm Gallery, West Palm Beach, Florida/SuperStock; **1112** (top) Musee d'Orsay, Paris, France, Giraudon/The Bridgeman Art Library; (bottom) The Granger Collection, New York; **1113** Musee d'Orsay, Paris, France, Giraudon/The Bridgeman Art Library; **1114** The Shwe-zee-gon Pagoda in Myanmar. © age fotostock/SuperStock; **1116** Library of Congress; **1118** © Michele Burgess/SuperStock; **1120** © Michele Burgess/SuperStock; **1122** (bottom left) © Peter Andrews/CORBIS; (bottom right) The Granger Collection, New York; **1123** (bottom) © Bryan Pickering; Eye Ubiquitous/CORBIS; **1125** © Momatiuk-Eastcott/CORBIS; **1128** (top) The Granger Collection, New York; **1129** The Granger Collection, New York **1132** (bottom) © Hulton-Deutsch Collection/CORBIS; **1135** (top) © Artkey/CORBIS; (bottom) © Hulton-Deutsch Collection/CORBIS; **1136** © Artkey/CORBIS; **1139** (bottom) Getty Images; **1143** (top) Bildarchiv Preussischer Kulturbesitz/Art Resource, NY; (bottom) © Christopher Felver/CORBIS; **1144** Bildarchiv Preussischer Kulturbesitz/Art Resource, NY; **1145** © Farhad Parsa/zefa/CORBIS; **1147** (top) © owi/plainpicture/CORBIS; (bottom) © Bettmann/CORBIS; **1148** © owi/plain-picture/CORBIS; **1156** © FORESTIER YVES/CORBIS SYGMA; **1158–1159** © Keren Su/CORBIS; **1163** Getty Images; **1164** © Michel Arnaud/Beateworks/CORBIS; **1165** © Rune Hellestad/CORBIS; **1166** © Frank Lukasseck/CORBIS; **1167** © Christie's Images/CORBIS; **1168** (top) © Peter Guttman/CORBIS; (bottom) © Sophie Bassouls/CORBIS SYGMA; **1169** © Peter Guttman/CORBIS; **1170** Mango tree © Tony Arruza/CORBIS; **1172** © Atlantide Phototravel/CORBIS; **1175** (top) © Hulton-Deustch Collection/CORBIS; (middle) © Jacques Langevin/CORBIS SYGMA; (bottom) © Reuters/CORBIS; **1176** © Hulton-Deustch Collection/CORBIS; **1178** Steve Burton/Stringer; **1179** © Gérard Rancinan/Sygma/CORBIS; **1180** Steve Burton/Stringer; **1183** (top left) © Penny Tweedie/CORBIS; (top middle) © Bettmann/CORBIS; (top right) © Frank May/epa/CORBIS; **1184** (top) © Bloomimage/CORBIS; (bottom) © Colin McPherson/CORBIS; **1185** © Bloomimage/CORBIS; **1186** © Christophe Boisvieux/CORBIS; **1190** © C. Lyttle/zefa/CORBIS; **1192** (top) Colin Garratt; (bottom) © Reuters/CORBIS; **1193** Colin Garratt; **1194** © David Turnley/CORBIS; **1196** The Granger Collection, New York; **1197** © Pete Leonard/zefa/CORBIS; **1198** © Rob C. Nunnington/Gallo Images/CORBIS; **1199** © Rob C. Nunnington/Gallo Images/CORBIS; **1201** © EDELSTEIN JILLIAN/CORBIS SYGMA; **1202** © Christopher Felver/CORBIS; **1206** © Hulton-Deutsch Collection/CORBIS; **1211** (top) © Matthias Hiekel/dpa/CORBIS; (bottom) © Jeremy Horner/CORBIS; **1212** © Matthias Hiekel/dpa/CORBIS; **1215** © Joe McDonald/CORBIS; 1216 © Christie's Images/CORBIS; **1218** (top middle right) © Colin McPherson/CORBIS; **1224** © Ralph Orlowski/Reuters/CORBIS; **1225** © Martin Harvey/CORBIS; **1228** Book cover *Rebel Hearts: Journeys Within the IRA's Soul* by Kevin Toolis. Copyright © 1995 by Kevin Toolis. Reprinted by permission of St. Martin's Press; Book cover *The Birthday Party* by Harold Pinter. Copyright © 1991. Reprinted by permission of Faber & Faber; Book cover *Angela's Ashes* by Frank McCourt. Copyright © 1996 by Frank McCourt. Reprinted by permission of Simon & Schuster; Book cover *The Conservationist* by Nadine Gordimer, copyright © 1972, 1973, 1974 by Nadine Gordimer. Used by permission of Viking Penguin, a division of Penguin Group (USA) Inc.; Book cover *Fire on the Mountain* by Anita Desai. Copyright © 1977 by Anita Desai. Reprinted by permission of Random House, Inc.; Book cover *The Famished Road* by Ben Okri. Used by permission of Doubleday, a division of Random House, Inc.; **1231** © Bettmann/CORBIS; **1233** Library of Congress

Literary Analysis

allegory, 10, 17, 511, 518, 650

alliteration, 21–23, 54, 176, 201, 255, 258, 896, 900, 1139, 1142

allusion, 491, 494, 671, 677, 891, 895, 981, 986

anecdote, 613, 618

antagonist, 338, 793

antihero, 495

apostrophe, 495, 509, 741, 749

archaic language, 255

archetype, 873, 883, 1184, 1191

argument, 605, 611, 664, 668, 997, 999, 1011

Arthurian romance, 176, 201

aside, 339

assonance, 21

ballad, 100, 650

biographical-historical criticism, 266–267

blank verse, 495, 679, 686

caesura, 10, 17, 20

catalog, 788, 791

Cavalier poets, 473

character, 338, 725, 730, 793, 1034, 1045

characterization, 113, 133, 136, 155, 399, 416, 613, 618, 794, 803, 1182, 1203, 1210

chivalry, 176

chorus, 442, 448

climax, 377, 397, 792, 1034, 1045, 1183, 1192, 1199

collaborative learning
    board game, 518
    brainstorming, 310
    debate, 900
    dictionary, 712
    discussion group, 251, 557, 686, 755, 836
    dramatic monologue, 883
    fable, 730
    identify tone, 17
    informational list, 359
    interpretation of poem, 627
    oral interpretation, 110, 1025
    research project, 661, 980
    role-play, 813
    visual history, 749

comedy, 334, 337

comic relief, 361, 374

conceit, 295, 303

conflict, 340, 359, 1183, 1192, 1199.
    See also plot

connotation, 605, 611

couplet, 246, 546, 557

critical literacy
    anthology, 909
    artwork display, 1191
    classification of poetry, 272
    comic strip, 627
    critique, 278
    discussion group, 258, 737, 1130
    explication of poem, 488, 951
    poetry analysis, 836
    review, 1011
    rewrite, 310
    speech analysis, 359
    theater production, 603
    theme comparison, 448

denotation, 605, 611

description, 595, 603, 823, 831, 952, 960

dialect, 650–651, 655, 1168, 1174

dialogue, 20, 100, 339, 568, 595, 603, 934, 945, 1135, 1138, 1183, 1211, 1220

diaries/journals, 568–569

diction, 570, 587, 650, 1074, 1079

drama, 337–338

dramatic poem/monologue, 20, 780, 786

elegy, 20, 60, 69, 274, 620, 627, 885, 889

end rhyme, 20

end-stopped line, 269, 272

enjambment, 269, 272, 718, 723

epic, 20, 22, 495

epiphany, 988, 994

epithet, 664, 668

essay, 996–997

exemplar, 136

exposition, 337, 792, 823, 831, 1183.
    See also plot

expository essay, 996

falling action, 792, 1183. *See also* plot

feet, 21

feminist-gender criticism, 1004–1005

figurative language, 21, 1132, 1134

flashback, 1084, 1090, 1143, 1146

foil, 340, 359, 873, 883

foreshadowing, 1084, 1090

frame tale, 113, 211

free verse, 1019, 1025

gender criticism. *See* feminist-gender criticism

haiku, 519

hyperbole, 21–22, 305, 310, 361, 374, 484, 488, 731, 737

iambic pentameter, 246–247, 377

iambic tetrameter, 269

iambs, 247

imagery, 282, 288, 687, 712, 885, 889, 975, 980, 1139, 1142

internal rhyme, 20

irony, 113, 133, 136, 155, 338, 521, 535, 832, 836, 952, 960, 1112, 1120

journals/diaries, 568–569

kenning, 22

lifelong learning
    class presentation, 677
    displays, 594
    journal, 476
    oral interpretation, 278

lyric poem, 20, 650–651

Magical Realism, 1034

media literacy
    comic strip, 803
    film, 755
    film adaptation, 1153
    film portrayal analysis, 69
    illustration, 265
    review, 201, 730
    speech comparison, 244
    summary, 155

metaphor, 21–22, 261, 274, 278, 305, 310, 484, 488, 1069, 1072

Metaphysical poets, 281

meter, 21, 204, 209, 247, 274, 278, 651, 655

miracle plays, 334

mock epic, 546, 557

Modernism, 973

monologue, 20, 339, 568, 934, 945

mood, 60, 69, 100, 780, 786, 792, 947, 951

morality play, 162, 334

motif, 22, 54, 339, 377, 397

motivation, 495, 509, 1203, 1210

mystery plays, 334

narrative poems, 20

narrator, 570, 587, 793, 805, 813, 1182

Naturalism, 779

Neoclassicism, 473, 649

novel, 792–793

objective correlative, 1015, 1019, 1025

octave, 246, 491, 671

ode, 650

oral interpretation, 1180

paradox, 295, 303, 399, 416, 741, 749, 1081, 1083

parallelism, 238, 244, 656, 661, 997

Vocabulary & Spelling

Grammar & Style

Test Taking

Index of Humanities Topics

For Your Reading List